Sixth Edition

Personality Theories

Sixth Edition

Personality Theories
A Comparative Analysis

Salvatore R. Maddi
University of California, Irvine

WAVELAND

PRESS, INC.

Long Grove, Illinois

For information about this book, contact:
Waveland Press, Inc.
4180 IL Route 83, Suite 101
Long Grove, IL 60047-9580
(847) 634-0081
info@waveland.com
www.waveland.com

To Dr. Deborah M. Khoshaba,

my beloved wife

and treasured colleague

ABOUT THE AUTHOR

SALVATORE R. MADDI is currently professor in the Department of Psychology and Social Behavior at the School of Social Ecology at the University of California, Irvine. Before holding this position, Dr. Maddi was for many years professor in the Department of Behavioral Sciences at the University of Chicago. He received a B.A. and an M.A. from Brooklyn College in 1954 and 1956 and a Ph.D. in clinical psychology from Harvard University in 1960. The author of numerous books and articles, Dr. Maddi has been President of Divisions Ten (Psychology and the Arts) and One (General Psychology) of the American Psychological Association. He has also been a visiting professor at Harvard University, the Educational Testing Service, and the University of Rome, as well as a Fulbright Scholar in Brazil. In 1985, he founded the Hardiness Institute, Inc., a consulting company that offers various services concerning personal and organizational development and stress management. The American Psychological Association named him Master Lecturer for its annual convention in 1989. The University of California and HealthNet awarded him the title of Distinguished Wellness Lecturer for 1994.

PREFACE

In the mid-1960s, while struggling for tenure at the University of Chicago, I was cautioned by older colleagues not to spend so much time on a personality textbook, an endeavor that would certainly not gain me any prestige in the field of psychology. Though I worried that they were right, I felt the need to finish the project anyway. The first edition took four years to write. I wanted it to help not only students as a textbook but also my colleagues as a badly needed force toward organizing and focusing personality psychology. My model was the enduring treatises of my teachers Gordon W. Allport and David C. McClelland. Initially, I had several things that apparently needed to be said, and as I got further into the task, it took on a life of its own, as if there were a dialogue going on between me and my typewriter (I was not yet computerized), and I had to be up to answering the questions that emerged. Although my original publisher, The Dorsey Press, was infinitely supportive, I had no idea how what I produced would be received when it first appeared in 1968.

It is now 27 years and six editions later. Over the years, many undergraduates, graduate students, and colleagues, not only in psychology but also in education, social work, sociology, political science, business, and medicine, have gone out of their way to tell me of the book's value for them. Though they have made many of these comments face to face, even more comments have come in the mail from around the world, many from students thankful for a book that helps them think rather than merely memorize and uses an informal, first-person style. Regarding comments from peers, it is certainly gratifying when colleagues my age or older tell me how much they have learned from my book. If anything, it is even more gratifying when, as still keeps happening, I meet younger colleagues who tell me that reading my book in one of their undergraduate courses turned them on to becoming psychologists and has given them a sense of important direction for their efforts. And the influence of my book on subsequent personality texts is clear. When I see how useful and influential this book has been, the enormous time I have spent on it over the years seems so worthwhile to me. Perhaps my book has had something to do with the resurgence of interest in personality among academics, following the doldrums of the 1970s. I feel very fortunate and now encourage younger colleagues in similar efforts to organize and integrate their fields in ways that can help both fellow professionals and students.

More specifically, the success of this book has affirmed for me the utility of a comparative analysis of personality approaches. In this sixth edition, you will find the main features of that analysis still here: Once explicated, theories are compared and contrasted to illuminate the overall models of human behavior they express; then, rational and empirical efforts are made to resolve the issues separating these models. The overall aim of this analysis is to help people think through the most promising views of personality.

Despite the persistence of a comparative analytic approach, this edition includes many changes. There is a new chapter on my metatheory of personality and classification of models for personality theorizing, which pinpoints the necessary parts of a personality theory and the patterns of assumptions made in typical approaches to personality theorizing. In addition, I address several issues raised by other personologists concerning my metatheory. The chapters on personality research methods and on assessment and psychotherapy offered in the fifth edition remain, adding the concreteness of procedure and application to what was once a more abstract approach. I have also updated the theoretical and research sections. Notably, there are two new theories included, one of which is coauthored by a former student of mine. Overall, the sixth edition is a more complete and current comparison of personality approaches than the earlier versions were.

To render the book a more effective teaching tool, I have also made a major change in organization. Instead of the previous arrangement, which separated the core and peripheral aspects of theories into different chapters, with the developmental features fitting in here and there, each theory is now covered in one place. Also, the chapter on personality research methods now appears later, where it can serve as an introduction to research used in issue resolution rather than stick out like a sore thumb, as it did before. And the grouping of chapters into parts should also help the reader stay organized.

These days, teaching personality has moved away from theories and toward research findings. In various ways we are told that the comprehensive personality theories are too vague and interpretive—the leftovers of a previous, prescientific age in psychology. We are also told that the findings of personality research, however fragmentary and simplified they may be, provide the only sound basis for teaching. This trend has resulted in courses that emphasize seemingly unrelated topics overly defined by the research designs and assessment methods employed, with the whole person quite lost from view. This amounts to throwing the baby out with the bathwater. Indeed, comprehensive personality theories are still alive and well in psychotherapy and individual assessment, where one cannot operate without trying to understand the whole person. Happily, though the two new personality theories included in this edition emanate from research rather than practice, they nonetheless seem to attempt comprehensive, integrated explanations of lives. There are even signs that this book has had some influence on the development of these theories.

From its very beginning, *Personality Theories* was intended as an alternative to uncritical theoretical emphases on the one hand and fragmentary research emphases on the other. I still maintain that it is not only possible but also profitable to wed theory and research and that comparative analysis provides a ready mechanism for this. In this approach, research becomes relevant to theory and theory becomes rigorous and empirically sound. The person emerges clearly, and the requirements of science are served.

My book starts with comprehensive theories of personality not out of undue reverence for the past but because these seminal views would only be reinvented if they were to be discarded. I emphasize them less as individual bodies of thought to be preserved than as sources for models of personality. Although the three models that emerge may not be exhaustive, they are generic enough to have withstood the test of time. The issues separating these models provide an integrative structure for the notoriously fragmented personality field. And when efforts are mounted to resolve these issues by reason and research, a future of changing, ever-improving knowledge of personality is approached.

In some circles, previous editions of this book gained the reputation of being difficult for students to understand. This has certainly not been my intent. The organization of the book into clearly marked sections and subsections facilitates varied organizations and uses—some things can be emphasized and others omitted. Care is taken to indicate why material is included and placed where it is. Readers are encouraged to bring their own experience to bear in appreciating theoretical points. The overall thrust of approaches that lends organization to the parts is elaborated. Most important, readers receive a frame of reference that coordinates the parts of a personality theory, the models for human behavior, and relevant personality research.

Over the years I have talked with many undergraduate students who have used my book. Their message is that although the vocabulary and information to which they are exposed are demanding, they find themselves learning so much that it becomes exciting. Rather than engage in the dry task of memorizing facts, they master principles from which they can derive knowledge. Through the conversational style of the book, they feel in dialogue with me even if someone else is teaching the course. Many report that what they learned has stayed with them and informed their functioning even much later. That so many readers took the trouble to contact me is very gratifying.

Therefore, I encourage you not to turn away from this book, even though it may appear formidable. Give it a chance, as others have to their benefit. You should also know that the sixth edition has been simplified for style and vocabulary. I guess that on growing older, I cherish ease and directness of communication more than before.

Acknowledgments

As this sixth edition appears, I wish to thank Marianne Talflinger, who kept me working and was so helpful. I am very grateful to the reviewers of the manuscript for their insightful and helpful suggestions. They are: Harold D. Beard, Central Missouri State University; David C. Funder, University of California, Riverside; William Goggin, University of Southern Mississippi; James E. Marcia, Simon Fraser University; David Novak, Lansing Community College; Brian Stagner, Texas A & M University; and Patrick Vann, University of Colorado. I also owe a great debt to my students over the years for their enthusiasm and criticism, which have improved this book with each edition. Finally, I wish to express my profound appreciation and admiration to Dr. Deborah M. Khoshaba, my wife and colleague, for her discerning intellectual help and unflagging emotional support.

Salvatore R. Maddi

CONTENTS

PART ONE

INTRODUCTION

What will help you plunge into the fascinating though complex subject of personality? You will need to know which aspects of human behavior express personality. You will also need to know how to identify a personality theory by its various parts and how to classify it according to the basic models used to understand human behavior.

PERSONALITY AND PERSONOLOGY

The many books on personality fall into two main categories: benevolent eclecticism and partisan zealotry. A book written from the standpoint of *benevolent eclecticism* tends to include many theories of personality, with each given relatively equal attention. When the book is good, you are made to understand why the theorist felt compelled to make the stated assumptions. Theory follows theory neatly, with little concern for the possible incompatibilities organized between the two covers. An air of humility permeates the whole endeavor. The writer does not claim to be worthy of resolving the differences of opinion and assumption existing among the theorists, but justifies the presentation by saying that merely presenting the various theories demonstrates the richness of the field and that the existing differences of opinion are currently beyond anyone's power to resolve by reason or experiment. Sometimes you are even given the pious assurance that some day, in a glorious future of comprehensive knowledge, it will be clear which theory is best. At other times, the writer doubts that any particular theory will emerge victorious, as if theorizing were no more than a perpetual game engaged in primarily as a stimulant.

In this approach, it is assumed that all theorists are entitled to be heard and appreciated simply because they theorize. Sometimes in such books there is even a place—usually a final, short chapter—in which the writer gives a bit of attention to cataloging the similarities and differences among the various theories. But the aim is to ensure that the reader will grasp the essential meaning of each theory, not to provide springboards to further analysis. When empirical research is included in such books, it only illustrates individual theories; it does not bear on the crucial differences among them. Good examples of benevolent eclecticism are *Introduction to Theories of Personality* by Hall and Lindzey (1985) and *Personality: Theory, Assessment and Research* by Pervin (1970). Most books in which an editor brings together the writings of many authors also fall into this category.

The book written with *partisan zealotry* contrasts sharply with the previous approach. By intent, such books express one—and only one—approach to personality. From the assumptions of the approach, you can predict the topics considered, research presented, and conclusions reached. The writer sometimes adopts a polemical style aimed at persuading the reader that the writer's viewpoint is best, with other viewpoints either badly slighted or included only to be criticized. When such books are done well, they provide the reader with a vivid account of a theory. When done poorly, they are ludicrously one-sided, misinterpreting other theories or willfully insulating the reader against any possibility of recognizing another point of view. Some representative examples are *Personality: Dynamics and Development* by Sarnoff (1962), *Pattern and Growth in Personality* by Allport (1961), and *Personality: A Behavioral Analysis* by Lundin (1974).

It has become more common in recent years for personality textbooks to appear nontheoretical, emphasizing research and presenting conclusions in terms of facts rather than assumptions. In such books, comprehensive theories are abhorred on the grounds that they are subscientific or merely speculative. Most scientists agree, however, that one cannot do research without having some theory in mind. Therefore, it seems better to make one's theory explicit than to pretend that no theorizing has occurred.

Once one perceives the implicit theorizing in "nontheoretical" personality textbooks, they will usually fall into either the benevolent eclecticism or partisan zealotry camp. Those that show benevolent eclecticism may try to fit various research themes together with little concern for possible incompatibilities. Because these research themes are listed as "examples" of work being done, they need not be compared and contrasted. And partisan textbooks that avoid theoretical elaboration are no less zealous just because their underlying assumptions are implicit.

It is surprising that so many books on personality fall into one of these two categories, because there is another, obviously valuable possibility. This third type of book transcends the limitations of benevolent eclecticism and partisan zealotry while showing some similarity to each. From benevolent eclecticism, it borrows the breadth and balance necessary for considering many theories of personality; from partisan zealotry, it borrows the conviction that some theories are better than others. The first aim of this third kind of book, which I call *comparative analysis,* is to uncover the similarities and differences among many existing approaches to personality as a starting point for determining which type of approach is the most fruitful. Such comparison helps clarify the issues separating the various types of theorizing. Once these issues are posed, rational and empirical analyses can be conducted to determine which types of theorizing are best. In such a book, the writer includes research to help delineate the important issues separating the various approaches. Comparative analysis should be comprehensive, orderly, and evaluative in its search for improved understanding. This book is an example of this approach.

Several books that have appeared since this one was first offered in 1968 seem to have adopted a comparative analytic stance. An example is Liebert and Spiegier (1982). Such books usually consider several general approaches or categories of theorizing and also include research results, which are certainly characteristics of comparative analysis. They lack, however, a systematic method to compare and contrast approaches to bring out issues that are then resolved through research. Instead, such books have the more limited aim of giving examples of personality approaches and research. On close scrutiny, this approach tends more toward benevolent eclecticism than toward rigorous comparative analysis.

Benevolent eclecticism and partisan zealotry are useful orientations in the initial stage of the development of a field. People with partisan zeal ensure that the hard work of formulating, refining, selling, and defending particular viewpoints gets done. It is probably only through the loyalty and commitment of its supporters that a particular approach eventually gets a proper hearing. Benevolent eclectics, on the other hand, help keep people's minds open, leaving them free to accept or reject the zealots' arguments. In addition, benevolent eclecticism allows the difficult, heavily intuitive work of theory formulation to go forward without being prematurely hampered by hardheaded, cynical evaluation.

But once a number of coherent theories are available, neither benevolent eclecticism nor partisan zealotry will spur much further development of the field. The zealots will merely continue trusting in, advocating, and seeking rational and empirical demonstrations of their particular theories. The benevolent eclectics will stand aside and cast a blessing on all the bustling, partisan activity taking place. No one will try to determine the relative value of the various existing approaches. Succeeding generations will duplicate their predecessors, with slight increases in sophistication. But there will be no sweeping changes, no dramatic advances unless an attitude of comparative analysis develops.

With enough interest in systematic inquiry into the relative merits of different forms of theorizing, people in the field can conjoin their efforts rather than dissipate their energy in competitive, partisan disputes. This conjoining of efforts produces an intermediate stage in the development of the field, leading toward a determination of the really worthwhile theories. When, armed with truly trustworthy and effective theories, the field enters a fully mature stage of development, its knowledge will be applied in a way that significantly changes and improves the process of living.

It seems to me that the personality field is in an unnecessarily prolonged infancy. We have had a set of reasonably coherent theories for some time now. Occasionally a new one comes along, but it usually seems more of a rephrasing or elaboration of an earlier theory than a departure from it. More and more personality research gets done each year; yet, we have made little progress toward weeding out the empirically unworkable theories. This lack of progress is due partly to research that is partisan rather than directed squarely at the issues separating the various types of theorizing. Although researchers typically insist that the existing personality theories are irrelevant to their work, it is, of course, impossible to do personality research without being guided by a personality theory. The fragmentation of theory and research produced by supposedly atheoretical research currently presents a serious impediment to progress in the personality field. I fear that the retarded development of an attitude of comparative analysis has begun to produce stagnation. It is in the interest of helping to eradicate this problem that I write this book.

WHAT PERSONOLOGISTS DO ....

Privately, none of us seriously doubts that personality exists. Indeed, we routinely take our own and others' personalities into account in daily decisions and activities. But once we try to specify the nature of personality in some precise way, it seems to evaporate before our eyes, leaving us frustrated and uncertain. This has even happened to some psychologists, leading them to seriously contend that personality does not exist. Such a contention seems to me as unfounded as personality is elusive. We must expect the elucidation of personality to be difficult, for it is, after all, the most ubiquitous and human thing about us. We cannot gain much understanding of it by studying subhuman organisms, and our ability to accurately observe other humans is limited by the need to filter all observations through our own personalities. But personality is here to stay, so I suggest that we simply accept the difficulty of our task and plunge right in.

To understand what personality is, we could start by reviewing the available definitions; indeed, Allport (1937) did just this. But I think we would gain little by proceeding in this fashion, for there are myriad definitions, each quite detailed and complex. We would become lost in a maze of words that could make but little impact. I suggest instead that we look in a general way at what people in the personality field do. The implications of their activities will give us an overall, vivid idea of the nature of personality.

The statements I am about to make may not apply equally to the activities of every person in the personality field. Unless you grant me the leeway of searching for commonalities among most, but not necessarily all, of the workers in the field, we will get nowhere. After all, there are no statistics or explicit data we can use—indeed, it is difficult even to be sure just who is in the field and who is not. So we must approach our task in a rather general way.

Let me start by adopting a name for the kind of person I will be describing. Following Murray (1938), let us call him or her a *personologist:* an expert in the study and understanding of the consistent patterns of thoughts, feelings, and actions people demonstrate. Many psychologists and psychiatrists can indisputably be called personologists. Their work involves any or all of four activities: psychotherapy, assessment, research, and theorizing. *Psychotherapy* involves sensitively listening to and interacting with people in order to ameliorate their problems. In *assessment,* the personologist uses techniques such as personality or skills tests in order to pinpoint people's problems or capabilities, either for the people themselves or for someone else, such as a prospective employer. In psychotherapy and assessment, the personologist is interested mainly in clients' specific needs. In *research,* he or she is typically more concerned with general knowledge. The research may require people to perform certain tasks to determine similarities and differences in their behavior, both within themselves and with respect to one another. Personality *theorizing* both influences and is influenced by the experiences of psychotherapy, assessment, and research. With this brief introduction, let me focus more concretely on how the personologist habitually functions.

First, *the personologist tends to study groups of people or, if only a few ,individuals are studied, is concerned with how representative they are of people in general.* Occasionally, the personologist studies only one person for his or her own sake, as does the biographer, perhaps because the person is extraordinary (say, Abraham Lincoln), or the task of psychotherapy or assessment leads to a focus on one person. Nonetheless, he or she studies an individual to subsequently compare and contrast that person with others, because the personologist is interested in the *commonalities among persons.* Indeed, in research, a technical requirement is that the observed group represent people in general. The personologist approaches the task of understanding people with the systematic, orderly thoroughness of the scientist rather than the impressionistic anecdotalism of the fiction writer. The personologist, however, need not shun the imaginativeness of his or her humanist neighbor merely because of an insistence on systematic sampling.

Despite this deeply ingrained interest in commonalities, the personologist also *attempts to identify and classify differences among people.* There is no basic incompatibility between the search for commonalities and the search for differences, though individual personologists frequently show a preference for one or the other. Whereas the search for commonalities proceeds at an abstract, interpretive level, the quest for differences involves a concrete, face-value analysis of observable behavior. Personologists engaged in assessment are especially sensitive to individual differences, which are tapped, for instance, by the personality tests often taken on entrance to college or for job evaluation purposes. The personologist's overall aim is to classify styles of being, with the similarities and differences among the categories clearly specified. This interest parallels the chemist's concern with the periodic table of elements.

The personologist is not alone in identifying and classifying the similarities and differences that exist among people. Social and biological scientists study them as well, but they tend to be interested in those similarities and differences produced by pressures in the external environment or biological factors of the internal environment. Thus, a sociologist is concerned with such things as the similarities in voting behavior within a certain socioeconomic class or the differences in such behavior traceable to differences in socioeconomic class. Further, the sociologist may study the behavioral similarities of all people playing the social role of father and the differences between their behavior and that of persons not playing this role. In contrast, a neurophysiologist might be concerned with the similarities among people under the effects of a tranquilizer and the differences between them and people under the effects of alcohol. Of all the biological and social scientists interested in similarities and differences in people's behavior, *the personologist is unusual in not restricting interest to behavior easily traceable to the social and biological pressures of the moment.* This is not to say that the personologist is necessarily uninterested in behavior that reflects social or biological pressures. However, the personologist's interest is particularly piqued when it becomes apparent that not everyone in the same socioeconomic class votes the same way, that not all fathers act similarly in that role, and that there is a wide range of mentation in people under the effects of alcohol. In other words, one thing the personologist looks for is *evidence of differences among people when the biological and social pressures seem the same.* The personologist is also intrigued *when the same behavior is observed even though the biological and social pressures differ.* Still another way of saying all this is that the personologist is especially interested *in individuality.*

A philosopher or theologian might share the personologist's special interest in behavior not easily explained in social or biological terms but would tend to consider such behavior as spiritual, inspired by God, or expressive of free will. In contrast, the personologist attributes such behavior to the psychological characteristics and tendencies a person brings to an immediate situation. These characteristics and tendencies constitute *personality.* Though personality may well develop out of early family experiences, in itself, it becomes a cause of behavior. The personologist sees people's behavior as influenced not only by the momentary social and biological pressures but also by their personalities; that is, he or she thinks that exclusive emphasis on the former oversimplifies the understanding of living. Personality should be recognized as an integral part of behavioral processes, without recourse to any mysterious notions of the supernatural or free will. Among social and biological scientists, then, *the personologist believes most deeply in the complexity of life.*

But not just transitory similarities and differences among people intrigue the personologist.

The notion of personality as a structured entity that influences behavior implies an *emphasis on characteristics of behavior that show continuity in time.* If personality changes at all, it changes slowly. Therefore, if personality influences behavior, the direction and intensity of the influence ought to persist, producing behavior that is continuous and regular. If the sexual instinct is part of personality, for example, sexually relevant behavior—say, flirtation or dating—ought to be a stable aspect of people's lives. The personologist is interested not only in the repetition of certain behaviors but also in sequences of functionally related behaviors. This emphasis on recurrent behavior clearly is one reason why personologists like to study people through prolonged contacts such as psychotherapy. Repeated observation allows the personologist to see personality ever more completely and accurately. Even when only one observation is possible, he or she typically uses some test of personality that has been specially developed to detect just those aspects of the person's behavior most likely to persist. An important gauge of the adequacy of the test is its stability, or the likelihood that it will yield the same information about a person at many different points in time.

Actually, one can further pinpoint the kind of behavior studied by the personologist. Not interested in every aspect of the commonalities and differences in people's functioning that show continuity in time, *the personologist tends to restrict attention to behaviors that seem to have psychological importance.* Thus, they focus on thoughts, feelings, and actions, leaving to the biological scientist such continuous aspects of functioning as the acetylcholine cycle and blood pressure. The personologist is not even interested in such discrete phenomena as a muscle contraction or the time necessary for an eye to adjust to an increase of light, unless they are part of some larger unit of functioning with apparent psychological significance in the sense of some ready relationship to the major goals and directions of a person's life. Thus, the personologist is much more at home discussing such behaviors as studying for an examination or writing a love letter than with such behaviors as accurately discriminating between two tones or even increasing one's heart rate. Though personologists generally grant that the psychological functioning they study has a physiological substrate, they typically do not place primary importance on physiological study and explanations.

One definite implication of such emphasis on thoughts, feelings, and actions is that *subhuman organisms are not very useful to study.* It is simply too indirect and risky to try to understand jealousy, for example, by seeking to specify its precise, unique physiological substrate so that it can be studied in a subhuman organism that cannot say what it feels. The study of thoughts and feelings requires complex communication through a rich language. In this sense, the proper study of the human being is the human being.

Though other social scientists also concern themselves with thoughts, feelings, and actions rather than the more microscopic or fragmentary aspects of functioning, the personologist tends to study the same things more comprehensively. The economist is interested in economic behavior, the sociologist in behavior that affects or reflects the social system, and the political scientist in political behavior. In contrast, *the personologist is interested in all rather than only some of the psychological behavior that shows continuity in time.* It is often said that the personologist is concerned with the whole person, and this is reasonably accurate when qualified by the previously discussed restriction to psychological behaviors with continuity in time. The characteristics and tendencies called *personality* have comprehensive effects on thoughts, feelings, and actions. Hence, behavior must be studied widely. More than any other kind of social scientist or psychologist, personologists seek integrated knowledge of the human being. They are interested in the economic, social, and political behaviors emphasized by other social scientists. They are also interested in the processes of learning, perception, memory, development, and so forth, on which other kinds of psychologists focus. They aim to integrate all these bits of knowledge into an overall account of people's functioning.

Finally, a perusal of the theorizing and research that personologists conduct makes clear that *personologists are primarily interested in the adult human being.* Many believe that personality does not gel until some time after childhood and, hence, its effects appear clearly and consistently only after maturity. To be sure, personologists often explain present personality on the basis of learning experiences in early life. But they invariably use their investigation into early life experiences to understand adult functioning. Indeed, some personologists do not even elaborate on the developmental process, finding it sufficient to assume that it has taken place. By and large, the personologist is interested primarily in the fruit of development—a settled personality that exerts a pervasive influence on present and future behavior. Hence, the common subjects of observation, research, and psychotherapy tend to be adults.

Do personlitys change

WHAT PERSONALITY IS ....

At this point, you can understand a statement about the overall nature of personality that will be meaningful in terms of the kinds of things personologists do: *Personality is a stable set of tendencies and characteristics that determine those commonalities and differences in people's psychological behavior (thoughts, feelings, and actions) that have continuity in time and that may not be easily understood as the sole result of the social and biological pressures of the moment.*

The only part of this statement that may need elaboration is the reference to "tendencies and characteristics." *Tendencies* are the processes that determine directionality in thoughts, feelings, and actions; they serve goals or functions. *Characteristics* are static personality structures used to explain goals or requirements rather than the movement toward them. They are also used to explain thoughts, feelings, and actions that seem less directional than repetitive in nature. An example of a tendency might be the attempt to achieve perfection in living, whereas related characteristics would be the ideals, such as beauty or generosity, that define perfection. I will have much more to say about characteristics and tendencies later; for the moment, you need only a general sense of what they mean.

THE PERSONOLOGIST'S THREE KINDS OF KNOWLEDGE ....

Because psychology claims to be a science, one might think that all of the personologist's theoretical statements follow from research, which is either exploratory or confirmatory. Exploratory research involves *systematic observation* of behavior in a reasonably large group of subjects chosen to represent people in general, with the aim of stating hypotheses on the nature and purpose of the behavior. These hypotheses are then tested for their empirical truth or falsity in confirmatory research carefully designed for relevancy. Confirmed hypotheses represent *empirical knowledge,* which can be characterized as public, precise, and systematic.

Whatever claims to scientific validity the field may mount, personality theories are *not* based solely or even primarily on empirical knowledge. I find this neither surprising nor disadvantageous. It is not surprising, because the personality field is still in an early stage of development. When set alongside the richness and complexity of people and their lives, the empirical knowledge available to the personologist is scanty and sometimes limited by partisanship. Thus, it is little wonder that personality theories are not based completely on empirical knowledge. Far from being disadvantageous, the personologist's inclusion of statements not firmly based in research is potentially fruitful at this early stage in the field's development. This procedure permits theorists to consider the full complexity of the human being. Though theorists risk being wrong, they may also be right; when the empirical development of the field catches up, he or she will find out soon enough which is true.

To some, what I have said may sound heretical, but to me it hardly seems unusual. After all, theory in any field is virtually never restricted to statements based on empirical knowledge alone. Specifically, nonempirical statements represent those kinds of knowledge based on intuition or reason. To appreciate intuition, recall the times you have been seized by an inarticulate, private, and emotional, as well as vivid, immediate, and compelling, sense of the meaning of what is happening. The substance of these hunches constitutes *intuitive knowledge.* In contrast, there have been times when you have carefully and calmly thought through the meaning, parts, and implications of things and arrived at your conclusions through deduction from a set of assumptions. In this case you are dealing with *rational knowledge,* which is reflective, explicit, logical, analytical, and precise. Far from arbitrary and mysterious, intuitive and rational knowledge emanate from your own experience and the exercise of your own mind and may therefore contain useful clues to what is true.

Intuitive knowledge, operated on by reason, may become rational knowledge. Further, both intuitive and rational knowledge may merge with empirical knowledge when the appropriate research is done. But none of this changes the fact that at any time you may be functioning with a conglomerate of intuitive, rational, and empirical knowledge. So, too, a personologist's theories may embody such a mixture. To further justify intuitive and rational knowledge in a theory of personality, I can point to other respectable endeavors in which these kinds of knowledge are paramount and empiricism considered relatively unimportant. The artist in exercising imagination and the theologian in building faith both deal primarily with intuitive knowledge, with reason clearly the hallmark of the mathematician and the philosopher.

Each of the three modes of knowing can serve as a check on the others. Something that seems sensible to reason may so rankle the intuition as to suggest limitations in the rational assumptions being made. Something that seems clear empirically may turn contradictory when viewed rationally, which may alert us to an unrecognized and erroneous interpretation of data. An insistent intuitive idea may be less convincing when detailed analysis proves it illogical. In the early stages of a field such as personology, there is no royal road to truth; rather, there are three intertwining roads, all of which should be traversed to best assail the secrets of the terrain.

Whether or not you accept this attempt to justify the use of all three modes of knowing, you should recognize that personality theorists indeed use them. Inevitably, the initial stages of theory formulation are, as in any creative act, intuitive in nature. The theorist makes decisions about where to start and what assumptions to emphasize on grounds that are by no means exclusively rational or empirical. One has a hunch and follows it up. One feels comfortable with a particular view of life and so celebrates it in theory. Sometimes one realizes the intuitive bases of one's theorizing and sometimes not. To be sure, the intuitive early stage of theory construction gives way to a stage in which rationality rules. But this does not change the fact that the theorist begins with largely intuitive knowledge. Because of this, theories bear the stamp of intuition even when they have been developed to a respectable degree of rationality.

However intuitive the initial theorizing may have been, the personologist accepts the task of formulating explicit views in terms of a series of assumptions justified by common experience. From these assumptions, he or she will deduce the major theoretical propositions of the theory. Sometimes you will be asked to accept these propositions as necessary, inexorable conclusions following from the assumptions. Although personologists usually do not argue the unequivocal truth of their propositions in a way that indicates sole reliance on rationality, their obvious investment in their propositions and occasional disdain for empirical evidence suggest a strong commitment to reason.

Sometimes the personologist is more of an empiricist than this. Certainly he or she believes in the standard that nothing that cannot be supported by some kind of empirical evidence deserves inclusion in a theory of personality. In addition, many theorists actively formulate empirically testable hypotheses stemming from their assumptions. Some even conduct the empirical tests themselves rather than leave that task to others. But the personologist hardly insists on denying intuition and rejecting any assumptions supported only by reason. On the contrary, the personologist will tolerate intuitive and rational knowledge in theorizing while accepting the need to rely on empiricism whenever in doubt. Though this catholicity and lack of skepticism have not earned the personologist respect among psychologists, they have permitted conceptual vigor and a willingness to tackle complex problems.

In reading the chapters that follow, it will benefit you to remain alert to these three kinds of knowledge. Try to see their impact on each theory in terms of your own sense of intuition, reason, and empiricism. In this way, you will be not merely a passive bystander but someone developing his or her own views on what is valuable in the personality field. It is admittedly difficult to analyze a theory intuitively, for intuition is not really an evaluative process. The two best things you can do are to have a global intuitive reaction to a theory and to try to recognize when the theorist's formulations are primarily intuitive. Usually I will help you by suggesting, at the outset of a discussion of a theory, some basis in your own experience for intuitively understanding its essence. In addition, I will comment whenever a particular stance taken by a theorist is clearly and deeply intuitive or temperamental in character. Of course, much more detailed analysis of theory can be done rationally and empirically. As you can see from the chapter titles, the major analyses I will attempt involve reason and empiricism. In discussing rational analysis, I will try to alert you to the logical consistencies or inconsistencies in theories, the explicit or implicit status of their assumptions and propositions, and the conclusions that are presumed to require no empirical test. In discussing empirical analysis, I will try to evaluate theories on the basis of relevant research that permits some testing of predictions.

SELECTION OF THEORISTS FOR INCLUSION IN THIS BOOK ....

A book that attempts comparative analysis in the personality field is only as strong as the approaches it includes are comprehensive and representative. I have tried to keep this in mind in selecting theories for discussion, including not only theories popular in psychiatry (e.g., Freud, ego psychology) and psychology (e.g., Rogers, Murray) but theories not especially popular (e.g., Rank, Angyal). You will find theories postulated some time ago (e.g., Adler, Allport) and recently (e.g., Fiske & Maddi, Bakan). There are theories that stress the core (e.g., Rogers, Maslow) and others that emphasize the periphery (e.g., McClelland, Erikson). Some stress emotional phenomena (e.g., Freud, Rogers), while others focus on intellective phenomena (e.g., Kelly, existentialism). There are theories that emanate from the practice of psychotherapy (e.g., Adler, Jung) and those that reflect the academic and research pursuits of the university setting (e.g., White, Allport). I have included not only those that are reasonably comprehensive (e.g., Fromm, Freud) but those that are incomplete (e.g., White, Angyal). There are even positions that have ambiguous status as personality theories (e.g., behaviorism, social learning theory), though they are quite important in contemporary psychology. I have also tried to mention recent psychotherapies (e.g., transactional analysis, Gestalt therapy) in which the personality implications are incompletely developed.

If personologists quarrel with my choice of theories, it will likely involve the absence of Lewin, Sheldon, Sullivan, and Horney. I have omitted them because their thinking no longer seems to have great direct impact on the personality field. Few personologists would consider themselves followers of these theorists. In an older theory, this state of affairs signifies a decline in importance. But because Lewin—and, to some extent, the others—have influenced personologists whose own theories are currently more influential, it seemed sufficient to include just these later theories in the book. Finally, though I have excluded Horney, I have included many variants on the psychoanalytic theme.

Although I cannot claim to have included all theories of personality, I have covered quite a few and taken pains to ensure that my sampling accurately reflects the field. I have not excluded any that would dramatically change the conclusions reached throughout this book. Interestingly, I found all these theories to express only three basic models for personality theorizing. To be sure, each model has two versions and some variants. Nonetheless, the basic ways of theorizing about personality are apparently few.

COVERAGE OF THEORY, RESEARCH, ASSESSMENT, AND THERAPY ....

Among the four functions of the personologist, *theorizing* and doing *research* mainly produce new knowledge, whereas *assessment* and *psychotherapy* chiefly apply knowledge that is already available. As such, theorizing and research are intellective or speculative activities, while assessment and therapy are practical activities. By mentioning this difference, I do not mean to imply that one kind of activity is more or less important than another. Actually, the four activities form a meaningful whole. Theorizing has an integrative function because, whether explicit or implicit, it determines what and how research, assessment, and therapy get done. Research is important because it is especially suited, through the collection of systematic and relevant empirical observations, to testing the validity of existing theories and contributing new information that can shape further theorizing. Assessment and psychotherapy are important primarily because they serve the needs of people with disabled personalities. But assessment and psychotherapy also can help you evaluate theory and can contribute new observations that may influence future theorizing. The four functions are organically related to one another—indeed, some personologists engage in all of them. The most common orientation for a personologist is to engage in at least two functions; rarely will you find one isolated in a single function.

Although this book emphasizes personological theory and research, it by no means excludes assessment and therapy from consideration. As mentioned, the decision to emphasize theory stems from its integrative function. If one understands a personologist's theory, one has a ready basis for appreciating why and how he or she does research, assessment, and therapy. Therefore, an emphasis on theory is a sound introduction to personology. The corollary emphasis on research is important because the comparative analytical approach taken here requires considerable attention to the evaluation and testing of existing theory. Because of the importance of theorizing and research to the aims of this book, I will attempt to cover both areas of personology in depth.

I cannot claim the same breadth of coverage of assessment and therapy, which are complex, specialized activities that require more emphasis than possible in this book or a single personality course. There are many skills involved in assessment and therapy that take considerable time and effort to explicate, teach, and acquire. But in the chapters that follow, I discuss the theorizing behind the assessment and therapy practices deriving from the various theories of personality. I do this partly because all four functions of the personologist form an integral whole, partly to give a vivid sense of the similarities and differences among the various theories, and partly to provide a bridge to other books and courses on the practice of assessment and therapy.

The main discussion of assessment and therapy occurs after the explications of theory. In this way, you can get an organic sense of how the practical activities of the personologist issue from the intellective activities. The research sections are separate so you can focus on the evaluation of theories. Having research discussions follow theoretical ones is logical and will allow you to use this book in a flexible way that would be impossible if I presented the two together.

THE NATURE
AND MODELS
OF PERSONALITY
THEORIZING

The aim of this chapter is to prepare you to plunge into the content and structure of actual personality theories. Because personality theories are complex, you need to appreciate two things in advance, namely, the parts of a personality theory and the models of human behavior represented in personality theorizing. When trying to understand a personality theory, you will be helped enormously by identifying its parts and by pinpointing the model of human behavior it represents.

THE PARTS OF A
PERSONALITY THEORY . . . .

Typically, personologists write many papers and books on their positions. And the range of topics covered is truly staggering. How can you understand these numerous, complex writings without making a life's work of it? You need some benchmarks, some ways of recognizing what these theorists are getting at. One kind of benchmark is to have in mind the various parts of a personality theory and how these parts contribute to the overall goals of the theorizing. My own life's work of understanding personality theorizing has led me to abstract the parts of theory presented here. I hope that knowing the parts will help you, as much as it has me, to keep track of what each theorist is doing and how each compares with the others.

You know from Chapter 1 that personologists are very interested in identifying and understanding the ways in which people are similar to and different from one another in their overall patterns and directions of behavior. It is important to determine which of these similarities and differences are learned and which are inborn. The identification of learned differences and similarities among people involves the lifestyles they develop and express. I call this the *periphery of personality,* which emphasizes personality types. The identification of inherent, unlearned similarities and differences among people is the basis for theorizing about what I call the *core of personality,* which emphasizes the inborn characteristics and tendencies that define human nature and underlie all behavior.

The Core and Periphery of Personality

In considering the core of personality, one asks the question, What are the built-in attributes and directions of human beings? This core refers to whatever attributes people bring into the world with them that influence how they think, feel, and act. Core features can be the same in all people (e.g., a theorist might assume that all people have an inborn tendency to search for meaning in life) or can differentiate them (e.g., according to a theorist, one person may be born extroverted, and another, introverted). Whether they lead to similarities or differences among people, core features by definition do not change in the course of living but continue to exert an extensive, pervasive background influence on behavior. Thus, one would expect to see the influence of the personality core not in any particular, isolated aspect of behavior, but rather in the overall pattern of functioning as observed over long time periods.

By contrast, in considering the periphery of personality, one asks the question, What are the concrete, learned lifestyles that differentiate human beings from each other? One can much more readily observe personality types and the characteristics that form them than the core attributes that stand behind them. Of course, even in this peripheral emphasis, pattern and regularity matter, but the behaviors observed are much more concrete and tangible than are core features. And though peripheral theorizing emphasizes differentiating individuals, inevitably a typology is delineated in which all people sharing a type are considered similar to each other and different from those falling into other types.

Theories of personality typically include both core and peripheral statements. The core assumptions lead to a major statement about the overall directionality, purpose, and function of human life. This statement takes the form of postulating one or more *core tendencies,* which are directions all people innately share, such as the assumption that all behavior constitutes an attempt to actualize one's inherent potentialities. Core theorizing also includes *core characteristics,* or the personality structures implied in the core tendency. In the example of the actualizing core tendency given before, the core characteristics might include such inherent potentialities as sexuality, aggressiveness, or altruism.

The peripheral assumptions lead to a major statement about the concrete styles of life that differ from person to person. One way the theorist does this is by postulating a number of *peripheral characteristics,* the smallest, most homogeneous explanatory elements the theorist believes are possible, each of which relates to only some part of behavior. For example, the need for achievement is a peripheral characteristic referring only to competitive behavior in a context involving success or failure. Because this particular characteristic does not refer to loving, cooperative behaviors, or anything else, it can be used to explain only a range of observable behavior. Peripheral characteristics serve mainly to permit the understanding of observable differences among people. One can say that Alice has a need for achievement whereas Sterling has a trait of obstinacy. One can also say that Alice has a higher need for achievement than does Sterling. Theorists differ in the number of peripheral characteristics they postulate; the higher the number, the greater the concern shown for individual differences. Though many personologists use the term *trait* for peripheral characteristics, I avoid that because some theories of personality consider traits to be only one of a number of different kinds of peripheral characteristics.

The *type* is a more general concept also commonly employed in peripheral theorizing. Each type comprises a number of peripheral characteristics, organized into larger, less homogeneous units that relate to commonly encountered lifestyles. For example, if Sterling has not only a low need for achievement but also high needs for power and affiliation, he may be classified as a bureaucratic type and find his way into politics. In contrast, Alice, who has a high need for achievement and low needs for affiliation and power, may be an entrepreneurial type, preferring to work alone and in her own way.

Sometimes a personologist will offer a *typology,* or comprehensive classification of types. This is considered a complete statement of the different possible lifestyles. Typically, one or more types are designated as ideal ways of life, whereas the others are considered nonideal and believed to be either predispositions to psychopathology or actual kinds of it.

The Developmental Statement

The link between the core and periphery of personality is covered in the *developmental statement.* In personality theorizing, this statement explicates how the unlearned, inherent directions (core) get to find concrete, learned expressions in particular lifestyles (periphery). The question asked here is "How do the interactions with significant others (e.g., parents, siblings, friends, mentors) and social institutions (e.g., school, workplace, church, government) mold particular learned expressions (periphery) of inherent, unlearned directions (core)?" Typically, the theorist assumes that, at the beginning of life, the core tendency and characteristics are expressed by the developing person during interactions with other people and social institutions. The reactions of these other people and institutions to the developing person's actions yield the feedback (e.g., rewards, punishments, information) that leads to learning. The content of what is learned forms the peripheral characteristics and types. One's personality type is generally considered to be a function of the particular kind of family setting in which one grew up. The theorist assumes that the best developmental conditions lead to the ideal personality types, whereas less adequate conditions culminate in the nonideal personality types.

It may seem arbitrary to call one lifestyle ideal and others nonideal. Actually, this kind

of evaluation is common in life and no more arbitrary than anything else in personality theorizing. A type is considered ideal because it, among all possibilities, fully expresses the core tendency and characteristics. In other words, the personologist's basis for making an evaluation is internally consistent with the implications of personality theorizing; that is, the best lifestyle is the one that most fulfills the overall purpose of human life as articulated in the core theorizing.

Overview

The parts of a personality theory are depicted in Figure 2-1. As the circles get bigger, the units become more general, more fundamental to the core tendency. The dotted arrows indicate the several possible lines of development. The one that actually occurs depends on the kinds of experience the person encounters in the process of expressing his or her core tendency. I have filled in one arrow to show that personality theories typically specify an ideal course of development leading to an ideal peripheral personality (e.g., in the assumption of a core tendency to actualize inherent potentialities, ideal development may be considered to take place when parents foster and encourage the child, as this would likely culminate in a self-actualized peripheral personality).

Notice that the smallest circles in Figure 2-1 refer to the data the personologists wish to explain through their theorizing. As you know from Chapter 1, these data emphasize the thoughts, feelings, and actions regularly expressed by individuals that differentiate them from other individuals. Usually, personality theorists adopt categories that already exist in the culture as their relevant data terms. Thus, they will observe people being cooperative, competitive, diligent, relaxed, angry, tense, excited, thoughtful, or impulsive. But occasionally personologists invent data terms of their own that are more technical than what we find in ordinary observation. You will see how this works later when you examine specific theories.

As mentioned, personality theories arise from the personologist's activities of assessing people, helping them in psychotherapy, and doing research. Conversely, theories also influence these activities. First, those who assess personality must work with a particular typology and its component peripheral characteristics. The personality theory is useful here in that it permits them to pinpoint differences among persons—of the especially "Johnian" quality of John, as Allport used to say. Next, psychotherapists must decide on the basis of their view of human nature (core of personality) and the particular peripheral personality confronting them (Is it ideal or not?) what changes need to be implemented. Looked at in this way, psychotherapy is a special case of development (needed client change through interaction with the therapist), so the therapist's view of development is also involved. Finally, research in personality should also address, in precise fashion, the available theories. Thus, theory helps shape all the personologist's activities.

An Extended Example of Personality Theorizing

Suppose a theorist observed many instances in which adults as a group showed curiosity about each other, spent time giving as well as getting, worked side by side, went out of their way to support each other, and deferred to one another. Further, suppose the theorist also observed infants who, before much learning could have taken place, appeared to enjoy being near, touching, and hearing other humans. Together, these two kinds of observation might lead the theorist to assume that human beings possess an inborn altruism drive that is expressed in everything they do. Because it refers to something unlearned and pervasive, that drive would be a core assumption.

Let us say that this theorist also spends a lot of time observing the thoughts, feelings, and actions of particular people (say, Allison and

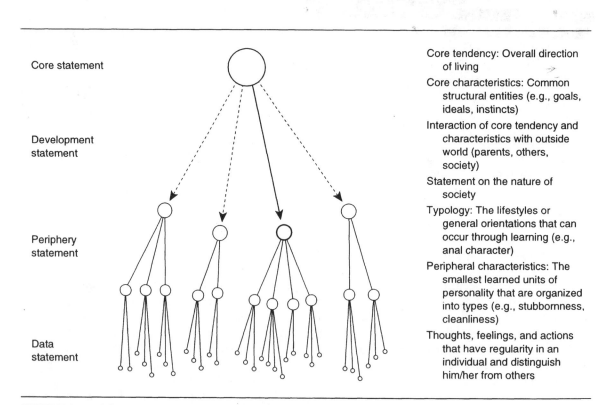

Core statement — Core tendency: Overall direction of living

Core characteristics: Common structural entities (e.g., goals, ideals, instincts)

Interaction of core tendency and characteristics with outside world (parents, others, society)

Statement on the nature of society

Development statement

Typology: The lifestyles or general orientations that can occur through learning (e.g., anal character)

Periphery statement — Peripheral characteristics: The smallest learned units of personality that are organized into types (e.g., stubbornness, cleanliness)

Data statement — Thoughts, feelings, and actions that have regularity in an individual and distinguish him/her from others

FIGURE 2-1   Schematic Representation of the Parts of a Personality Theory

Nathan) as they go through their daily lives. A mother and wife in a large family, Allison spends much of her time cooking, cleaning, talking, loving, disciplining, and sharing with this brood. In addition, she spends whatever spare time she has on socializing with friends and neighbors. She is rarely alone and much of the time gives to others. She does not enjoy being alone.

In contrast, Nathan has never married and lives alone, though he wishes he could find the right person on whom to lavish love. He has a hard time making small talk, and just never made many friends. He is a free-lance writer, specializing in political and social analysis. A real champion of the rights of the individual, he points out in his articles how social and political institutions and officials exploit the public rather than assist its members in living better. The rest of his writing is devoted to self-help books about how to grow in the ability to make loving commitments to others even if life brings one harrowing experiences. Nathan believes he helps others through his vocation even though he may never actually meet them.

Observations like these provoke the theorist to assume that two lifestyles that people can learn are extroversion (e.g., Allison's pattern) and introversion (e.g., Nathan's pattern). This is peripheral theorizing. Notice how useful it was to use names in this example of peripheral theorizing. That is because peripheral theorizing is about concrete lifestyles that differentiate one person from another, that are their psychological signatures, so to speak. In contrast, at the core level, with its emphasis on unlearned qualities, it is enough to talk about human beings in general.

To continue on our extended example, if the theorist is not provoked to make any more core assumptions, then he or she might assert that Allison and Nathan are both still expressing their inborn altruism drive, however different their learned, concrete lifestyles have become. Allison expresses altruism through continual nurturant contact with others. Although it may appear less obvious, Nathan also expresses altruism through writing that shows readers how to be closer to others and nurtured by the system. Thus, core and periphery of personality

are expressed at the same time in everyone's behavior.

Though the core never changes, the periphery is learned and is therefore the result of development. In formulating a position on development, the personality theorist might observe youngsters interacting with their parents. Of course, the theorist would expect all youngsters to express altruism at first, because that is their nature. Suppose the theorist observes that some parents respond positively, giving love, affection, attention, approval, and nurturance when their youngsters reach out to them. But suppose other parents are too busy, frustrated, reserved, or self-preoccupied to spend the time to respond affectionately. If you were the theorist, how would you think Allison's and Nathan's parents must have responded to them?

Most likely, Allison's parents gave as much love and attention, or more, than she did, whereas Nathan's parents were too preoccupied or busy to give this much. So, as she grew up, Allison would have learned to express altruism directly in an extroverted lifestyle. Nathan, on the other hand, would have learned to avoid direct contact with others, lest he be rejected. But his inborn altruism, needing to find some sort of expression, might have shown itself in the indirectly altruistic lifestyle of trying to help others without actually meeting or interacting with them, in this way minimizing the risk of rejection. If he was good at writing and got rewarded for it, then he might well have chosen it in an introverted lifestyle.

I hope this extended example has helped you understand the core, peripheral, and developmental aspects of personality theorizing and how they interact. Actually, the theorist could have gone even further, and concluded that extraversion (Allison's way) is the ideal, because it involves the most direct and complete expression of altruism. In contrast, introversion (Nathan's way) might seem too indirect and incomplete in its minimal interaction with others to be ideal. As an aspect of this conclusion, Allison's parents' response of attention and affection would be regarded as more developmentally ideal than Nathan's parents' more rejecting response.

Models of
Personality Theorizing ......

Because all three considerations—core, periphery, development—appear regularly in personality theories, such theories are complex, comprehensive, and holistic attempts to understand human behavior. And there are lots of personality theories identifiably different enough to qualify as worthy of our attention. To avoid becoming overwhelmed by all this complexity, you need to take the first step of comparative analysis (see Chapter 1), namely, to classify the individual theories into types or models. You gain much clarity once you grasp that however different from each other personality theories may appear at first, you can boil them down into a small, manageable set of models.

When I first began thinking about personality theories, I tended to classify them in a conventional fashion, such as whether they emphasize thought processes (cognitive), defenses or motivation (dynamic), or traits (habits), much as in Mischel (1981). But such classifications captured neither the overall meaning intended in these theories nor their holistic commitment to explaining behavior comprehensively. As you will soon appreciate, many aspects of dynamics and traits in theories classified as cognitive get lost in the shuffle. And comparable problems result for theories classified as dynamic, motivational, or trait. The conventional classification systems that permeate personality textbooks are just too partial and reductionistic to do justice to the comprehensive and holistic emphases of personality theories.

Accordingly, my task was to find a classification system that illuminated the core, peripheral, and developmental aspects of personality theories simultaneously. I made several attempts that turned out to be false starts, in the sense of omitting too many theories or just not seeming to grasp their essential elements. After all, there were no precedents for what I was trying to do in psychology except for the partial, reductionistic approaches I had already rejected as insufficient. Despite the frustrations, I kept at it until my efforts began to pay off. Feeling as if the sun

had broken through the clouds, I arrived at three broad, workable models of theorizing: conflict, fulfillment, and consistency. This chapter will present just the essence of the models. You will have to wait until later chapters to see if they illuminate personality theories as much for you as they did for me.

The Conflict Model

At the core level, the conflict model assumes that each person is inevitably caught in the clash between two great forces defined as continually acting, necessarily opposed, and unchangeable. In other words, a conflict theory assumes that the basic nature people bring into the world pushes them into conflict with each other or themselves and that this clash persists throughout life. For example, you are using conflict theorizing if you assume that people are born with not only an innate drive toward altruism but also an opposing drive toward selfishness. If you make this kind of assumption, then the rest of your theorizing about human behavior will reflect an unresolvable, basic conflict, because these two innate drives would lead in opposing behavioral directions. Though the conflict model is a truly tragic view of life, wherein you cannot fully get what you want, it has been quite popular in personality theorizing.

At the peripheral level, according to the conflict model, the best that can be accomplished in terms of lifestyle is compromise. The ideal lifestyle involves a dynamic balance of the two opposing forces, with both getting more or less equal expression. Sometimes a person seems altruistic and sometimes selfish, as in the case of the industrialist who makes a lot of money by ruthless competition with others, and then donates some of the profit to worthy social causes. Less ideal lifestyles involve a foredoomed attempt to deny the existence of one of the opposing forces while emphatically expressing the other. For example, people might deny the selfish part of themselves and be aware of and express only the altruistic part. However saintly they might seem, the inability to express their inborn selfishness will haunt them, maybe showing up as unexplainable tension or self-hatred, marking such a lifestyle as nonideal. Can you think of the problems that might show up in a lifestyle where the altruistic part of oneself was denied and only the selfish part expressed?

In terms of development, the conflict model also tends to emphasize compromise as ideal. Parents must be careful to neither reward nor punish too many of their developing child's behaviors, because youngsters need to learn to express all aspects of their inborn nature, however full of conflict they may be. If parents try to suppress some and augment other behaviors in their youngsters, to teach greater consistency or because some behavior seems unacceptable, they are encouraging nonideal development. For example, with the best of intentions, parents might punish every expression of selfishness in their child, while rewarding every expression of altruism. Unfortunately, their child will learn to deny selfishness. This suppression of an inborn, unchangeable drive might show up in mounting tension, anxiety, vague unhappiness, and an inability to find purpose in life. In contrast, parents who moderately reward and punish (and in that sense accept) all their youngster's behaviors (including the selfish expressions) serve as a more ideal developmental influence. They are encouraging an ideal lifestyle emphasizing compromise, in the sense of acceptance and expression of all inborn drives, despite their conflicting status. This lifestyle is the best that can be done with such a tragic nature, in that it minimizes tension, confusion, and self-criticality in the person.

THE PSYCHOSOCIAL VERSION. Personality theorists have used two versions of the conflict model, which differ in the degree to which society exerts an influence on human behavior. In each, conflict stems from the two *great forces* of the core tendencies. In the psychosocial version, one force lies within each individual, but the other force lies in groups or societies; that is, one force exerts requirements on individual behavior, whereas the other force exerts requirements on group functioning. For example, a theorist might assume that individual behavior shows the influence of the great force of selfishness, whereas group or social behavior is influenced by the altruistic great force. Because these great forces both express the core tendency, the individual and society would always be in an unresolvable conflict. In this kind of theorizing, the individualistic force emerges as antisocial, whereas the social force emerges as the definer of the common good.

At the peripheral level, psychosocial conflict theories have a telltale approach to the compromise that expresses ideal functioning. In particular, the ideal lifestyle involves the person in expressing both of the conflicting great forces, but without any recognition or awareness of the antisocial force. This lack of awareness is the result of defensiveness, a process of lying to oneself, implying that groups or societies are stronger than individuals. In the unbalanced conflict between the powerful society and the puny individual, the individual must give ground for a workable compromise to be found. But, because the core of personality cannot be changed and must be expressed (even if antisocial), the best that can be accomplished is for the person to conveniently lose awareness that some of his or her behavior is indeed antisocial.

As to development, psychosocial conflict theories postulate that it is best when the interaction between parents and children actually fosters that defensive lack of awareness of the antisocial behaviors that are being expressed! So, if we are all well socialized, we go around expressing what really amounts to selfishness without any of us noticing what is really going on. In psychosocial conflict theories, it is considered best that we not know the real truth about ourselves. Indeed, if complete consciousness of our antisocial side were to take place, it would be so overwhelming as to drive us crazy!

THE INTRAPSYCHIC VERSION. In the intrapsychic version of the conflict model, both great forces arise from within the person, regardless of whether he or she acts as an individual or as a member of society. Given, say, the core tendencies of altruism and selfishness, this time both tendencies would exert pressure for expression whether a person was alone or in the company of others. In the intrapsychic version, this person would be in just as much conflict as in the psychosocial version; however, rather than emphasizing the individual pitted against society, this approach presents one part of the individual pitted against another part.

In terms of peripheral theorizing, the ideal lifestyle would still express all conflicting core tendencies and would therefore represent some sort of compromise. But there would be no emphasis on the puny individual giving ground to a stronger social force. So, the intrapsychic version would emphasize defensiveness less in formulating the terms of the compromise. Ideal persons could actually be somewhat aware of their conflictful natures, even though they might suffer over their inconsistencies.

At the developmental level, intrapsychic conflict theories emphasize as ideal those interactions between parents and their children that foster an acceptance of the various conflicting aspects of human nature; however, it is quite a trick for theorists to formulate how an awareness of internal, unresolvable conflict might constitute the ideal. Intrapsychic conflict theories are as much the tragic mode as are psychosocial conflict theories.

The Fulfillment Model

In contrast to the conflict model, the fulfillment model assumes, at the core level, only one great force and locates it within the individual. Life is seen as the progressively greater expression of this force. Thus, if the force chosen is altruism, then the theory would explain the unfolding of human behavior through the life span as a progressively more complete, effective, sophisticated expression of this inborn tendency. In short, people would become more and more of what they were intended to be. By its nature, the fulfillment model is simpler and more heroic (i.e., you can become what you want) than the conflict model.

At the peripheral level, fulfillment theories idealize the lifestyle that constitutes this ever greater expression of the one great force. You accept and value who you are, and make every effort to express it in your daily living. In contrast, caused by the misguided influence of parents and society, nonideal lifestyles inhibit or cramp expressions of the great force. That is, you learn to devalue your strengths and try to inhibit their expression, preferring instead to fit in and do what others wish you to do.

Developmentally speaking, fulfillment theories see as ideal those interactions with parents that encourage in the children a sense of their inherent worth and a courageous willingness to follow their intuitions as to what to do and not do. The resulting ideal lifestyle includes much exploration and imagination, with little self-criticism and second-guessing. In contrast, nonideal development builds in the children lack of self-confidence, conformity to social norms, and an unwillingness to take chances.

As you can see, the kind of unavoidable, continuing conflict presented in the conflict model is considered far from ideal in the fulfillment model. In the latter approach, conflict always expresses nonideal development and lifestyle. If such conflict occurs between the individual and society, it reflects more about what is wrong with society than the individual, that is, the individual has been failed by society. Fulfillment theorists emerge as natural social critics. In contrast, conflict theorists, especially those of a psychosocial persuasion, regard society as exercising necessary control over antisocial individuals.

THE ACTUALIZATION VERSION. Like the conflict model, the fulfillment model has two versions. In the actualization version, the great force or core tendency involves becoming what one was meant to be. Living richly means actualizing the potentialities that people bring into the world with them at birth. The person is like an acorn growing into a mighty oak tree: Everything actually there in the tree is present as potential in the acorn.

In terms of development, actualization theorists emphasize unflagging parental appreciation and love of their children that encourage full expression in behavior of underlying potentialities, or the ideal lifestyle. Parents must be careful, however, not to impose their own potentialities, values, preferences, and fears on their children. After all, the acorn needs only earth, sunlight, and water to grow. If the earth is poor, or there is insufficient sunlight or water, growth is jeopardized.

At the peripheral level, the lifestyle learned is either a full expression of potentialities or some stunted version of that expression. The oak tree may be full sized or dwarfed, its leaves lush and green or withered and small, its shape upright or twisted to try to find the light. Needless to say, full expression of potentialities is the ideal lifestyle, whereas stunted expression is not. In trying to become what their parents want for them, the children fail to express their own potentialities fully.

For example, think of a child born with the potential for a big, strong, quick-reflexed body. If the parents appreciate and love their child for the physical prowess that comes naturally, they may well have an athlete on their hands. The highly physical lifestyle that ensues will be the ideal for this youngster. But, if the parents always wanted their child to be a doctor, they may discourage physical expressions in favor of more cerebral, scholarly activities. In trying to please the parents, the youngster may curtail natural physical expressions in favor of less-fulfilling mental activities. That youngster is on the way to a nonideal lifestyle.

People expressing the ideal lifestyle will be comfortable with themselves and generally well disposed toward others. They will not be incessantly questing after some elusive goal, being happy instead with whatever they are doing. Appreciative, loving, and understanding toward others, they will prefer interpersonal relations (e.g., friendships) to more abstract involvement with social institutions (e.g., being a politician). On the other hand, those with the nonideal lifestyle will feel frustrated and unfulfilled, all the while pursuing elusive goals and society's approbation, without much expression of themselves.

THE PERFECTION VERSION. In contrast to the actualization version, the perfection version of the fulfillment model does not emphasize

genetically determined potentialities so much as universal assumptions of what is fine, excellent, and meaningful in human life. The great force pressures people to strive toward these ideals of perfection regardless of whether that entails expressing their own genetic strengths or inferiorities. Perfection fulfillment theorists assume that finding a vivid sense of meaning in life is the highest goal, one to which we are all naturally drawn. Pursuing that goal of vivid meaning does not necessarily violate one's genetically inherited capabilities, but it might, as in the case of someone born with a selfish streak who struggles to be altruistic because this seems like a higher goal.

Perfection theorists characterize development as a struggle. You will remember that, for actualization theorists, development is an easy and natural expression of existing potentialities, as long as the youngster gets unconditional appreciation and love from parents. In contrast, for the perfection theorists, development is a continual process of self-improvement that is often painful because of the need to learn from one's failures. To be able to do this, the youngster needs the inner strength or courage to keep striving toward demanding ideals. This inner strength is the major goal of ideal development, and in order to foster it, parents need to be good role models and to encourage their children to keep trying until they succeed. When parents overprotect children by making things too easy for them or undermine them by fostering self-doubt, the road to ideal development is lost.

At the peripheral level, perfection theorists emphasize as ideal a lifestyle of individuality, wherein people make their own choices as they try to get ever closer to the overall goals that express them. Though they may encounter anxiety as they navigate uncharted waters, they will feel a lot of vitality and excitement as well, because whatever they accomplish will feel like their own doing. At their own choosing, their social relationships will be close and personal. Whatever they do will show a constructive, cooperative stance. They will tend to be involved in the fabric of society, expressing their desires and respecting those of others, always trying to improve themselves, others, and society at the same time.

Those with nonideal lifestyles will be more conventional, always seeking the approval of others. With little idea of what they want their life to be like, they will accept instead the norms and stereotypes of their society. They will be envious of others who appear to be getting ahead and likely to react with competitive, destructive behaviors. They too will be involved with society, but in the sense of desperately seeking its approval and recognition, rather than trying to improve it as they improve themselves.

The Consistency Model

At the core level, the consistency model places little emphasis on great forces, whether single or dual, in conflict or not. Rather, it emphasizes the formative influence of feedback from the external world on the individual. Whenever we approach interaction with the world, we do so with some expectation or norm. These expectations or norms may be inborn (e.g., fear of the dark) or learned (e.g., my mother always hugs me). Then, as we interact with the world, our experience either confirms or disconfirms these expectations or norms. If this feedback is consistent with what we expected, everything is fine. But if the feedback is inconsistent with our norms, this creates emotional discomfort (e.g., anxiety, anger) and the pressure to do something to alleviate the problem.

Life is understood as the extended attempt to maintain consistency, and one's learned lifestyle expresses this effort. What this means is that everything we do regularly enough to be considered part of our lifestyle was learned as the result of trying to minimize or resolve inconsistencies between our expectations or norms and our experiences. The best lifestyle minimizes experiential inconsistencies, whatever the patterns of habit it involves.

As you can surmise, consistency theories deemphasize content in their core and peripheral statements. They also deemphasize content in their developmental statements, with little explication of what parents need to do in concrete content terms. Rather, it is assumed that whatever parents can do to minimize inconsistencies is probably best. But there is also the bias that inconsistencies will probably occur in one or another area of living, and that the resulting behavior will influence emerging lifestyles. Thus, an overarching commitment to entrepreneurial activity or to gregarious interpersonal relationships will all be explainable, according to these theorists, in terms of the areas in which there was greatest or least inconsistency during development. Because of the deemphasis of potentialities, ideals, and the like, consistency theories downplay the distinction between ideal and nonideal lifestyles and developmental patterns, except to say that the overall goal of living is to minimize experiential inconsistencies.

Whereas the conflict assumed in conflict theories is continuous, unavoidable, set in content, and controllable but not eradicable, the inconsistency assumed in consistency theories is avoidable and varies in content. This is the main reason why consistency theories are not the same as conflict theories. In contrast to the fulfillment theories, consistency theories assume no predetermined capabilities or ideals as guides to living, calling instead for consistency, regardless of the expectations or norms with which interaction is approached. This is the main reason why consistency theories are not the same as fulfillment theories.

THE COGNITIVE DISSONANCE VERSION. The consistency model also has two versions. In the cognitive dissonance version, it is assumed that consistencies and inconsistencies invariably involve the thought processes. There may therefore be inconsistency between an expectation of what would happen and the perception of what actually happened.

In attempting to resolve inconsistencies, people need to alter either the expectation of what would happen or the perception of what happened. Altering the expectation is clearly an internal thought process (e.g., maybe I was wrong in expecting a present at the celebration). Altering the perception of what happened may be a thought process exclusively (e.g., maybe I just misunderstood, and the celebration was not about gift giving) or may involve a change in action that will permit different perceptions (e.g., if I give people a present, maybe they will give me one back, and then I won't be disappointed). As you can imagine, a wide range of lifestyles can result from attempting to minimize inconsistencies.

THE ACTIVATION VERSION. In contrast to the cognitive dissonance version, the activation version emphasizes consistency between the customary degree of bodily tension (called *activation*) and the degree of tension that actually exists. As bodily tension is assumed to be contributed to by all a person's thought processes, emotions, and actions, the activation version emerges as more complex and comprehensive than the cognitive dissonance version.

When customary and actual activation levels match, there is quiescence. But when inconsistency exists, there is pressure either to decrease or to increase actual activation in order to fit better with what is customary. Thoughts, emotions, and actions can be altered in this attempt

to reduce inconsistency by amplifying or diminishing activation. The learned lifestyles develop from one's habitual approaches to increasing or decreasing stimulation through particular patterns of thinking, emoting, and acting.

WHERE DO WE GO FROM HERE? ....

In presenting these three models and their versions, I have not tried to convince you of their meaningfulness and utility as tools for understanding human behavior. Rather, I have only introduced them to you as ways of approaching personality explanations. My hope is that having these models and versions in mind will help you in reading about and thinking over the personality theories that appear in Part Two of this book. When we have given these theories the detailed consideration they deserve, then we shall seriously evaluate in Part Three whether and how the three models and their versions contribute to understanding human personality.

Theories and Their Classification

Now that you have been introduced to the nature of the subject matter of the personality field, it is time to dive into the theories themselves. In the next six chapters, you will encounter many theories, complete and incomplete, practice-oriented and academic. Some will undoubtedly interest you more than others. As I present the content of these theories, I will struggle to classify them according to the three models of human behavior you have already encountered.

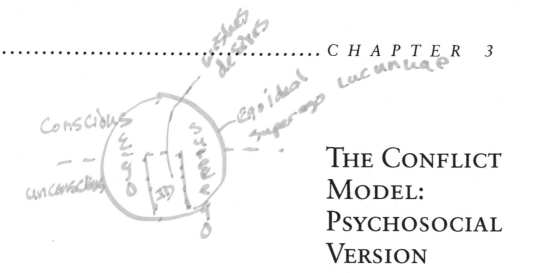

CHAPTER 3

THE CONFLICT MODEL: PSYCHOSOCIAL VERSION

By now the groundwork for a consideration of actual theories of personality has been laid. You now know that the personologist's theorizing stems from an interest in identifying and understanding the patterned ways in which people are similar to and different from one another. You have also seen that personologists will tend to make core, developmental, and peripheral statements and that, in the content of their theorizing, personologists generally express one of three models of human behavior and that each of these models has two versions. This chapter considers personality theories that express the *psychosocial version* of the *conflict model.*

You will recall that in the *conflict model,* it is assumed that people are continuously and inevitably caught in the clash between two great forces defined as continually acting, necessarily opposed, and unchangeable. According to this model, life must be a compromise, which at best involves a dynamic balance of the two forces and at worst a foredoomed attempt to deny the existence of one of them. In the *psychosocial*

version, one of the great forces is regarded as inherent in the individual and the other in groups or societies. The major example of this kind of theory is that of Freud, which I will discuss first, followed by the theories of Murray, Erikson, and other ego psychologists. Then I will go beyond ego psychology to the work of Kernberg and Kohut and the object-relations theorists. Similar to Freud, these other theorists back away somewhat from his notion that conflict is continual. For Murray and the others, a part of life remains free of conflict. While their theories drift away from the pure psychosocial conflict model, they remain sufficiently close to be considered a variant.

FREUD'S POSITION ....

Sigmund Freud (born in Moravia, 1856; died in London, 1939) looms as such a giant to both his advocates and his opponents that it is difficult to see him objectively even in our time.

Nonetheless, we must try. Freud was deeply committed to his work, family, friends, colleagues, and principles. From youth he showed the brilliant intelligence, tenacity, and independence that marked him for greatness and the resulting social rejection. A physician who strayed far from the orthodox medical emphasis on physical causes of disease, Freud promulgated views that seemed the devil's work to most of his colleagues. For most of his life, Freud was considered a fanatic obsessed with sex, and he was denied recognition by the medical community. In defense, Freud drew his circle of admirers even closer around him, insisting on their loyalty to his theoretical principles. Because Freud's views constituted a kind of intellectual indictment of his age, with its stuffy, sterile, Victorian values, it is not surprising that they were rejected even though they resulted directly from his observations of patients.

From the beginning, Freud and his inner circle emphasized the mental causation of certain maladies and set about developing a therapy for the mind rather than the body. Both on his own and through his group, Freud has exerted an immense influence on personology. So intense was the interaction between the members of the inner circle—mainly young, energetic, ambitious physicians—and their visionary though somewhat paternalistic leader, that sparks occasionally flew. Here and there a member of this extraordinary group would leave or be expelled. It is a tribute to Freud's intellectual impact on them that these outcasts typically went on to develop influential theories of their own that reflected their psychoanalytic parentage.

Freud's theoretical legacy is complex. He wrote a great deal, changed his mind often, and left many loose ends where he could not decide among theoretical alternatives. Further, he has been copiously interpreted by allies and enemies alike, as well as by revisionists interested primarily in using him as a respectable basis for their own thoughts. I have adopted a selective strategy that focuses on Freud himself and on his main ideas rather than on side statements and exploratory forays, however intriguing they may be.

Freud's Core Statement

Freud views the core tendency of living as the *tendency to maximize instinctual gratification while minimizing punishment and guilt.* You would do well to reflect for a moment on the commonsense meaning of this idea. Think of the last time you wanted to do something selfish and were worried about being hurt if you did or felt immoral for having had the wish in the first place. If your wish was strong enough, you could not resolve your conflict by simply saying to yourself that you would not carry it out. And if you resolved the conflict by acting on only the part of your wish that would not incur punishment from others or guilt from within, you had an intuitive, if homey, basis in personal experience for understanding what Freud meant.

Of course, Freud had in mind a more precise, formal concept of conflict than can be completely comprehended from looking at simple experiences of this type. As you will see later, some of Freud's ideas cannot be borne out by introspective analysis. In any event, when looked at from a formal, theoretical point of view, Freud's basic tendency of living includes a position on (1) the instincts, (2) the sources of punishment and guilt, and (3) the mechanism of defense whereby instincts are satisfied while punishment and guilt are avoided.

THE INSTINCTS. Freud postulates a number of instincts common to all human beings as an inherent, unchanging aspect of human nature. In my terminology, Freud's instincts are core characteristics of personality. Although he discusses three types of instinct, they all have the same general form, differing only in content. All instincts have a *source,* a type of *energy* or driving force, an *aim,* and an *object.*

Components of an Instinct. The source of an instinct is invariably rooted in the biological character of the organism—in the very process of metabolism itself. Freud (1925c) says:

> By the source of an instinct is meant the somatic process which occurs in an organ or part of the body and whose stimulus is represented in mental

life by an instinct. We do not know whether this process is regularly of a chemical nature or whether it may also correspond to the release of other, e.g., mechanical, forces. The study of the sources of instincts lies outside the scope of psychology. (p. 66)

Thus, the instinct is not the bodily process itself but the mental representation of it. Freud makes it clear that psychic manifestations, such as thoughts, wishes, and even emotions, express and depend on bodily activities and processes. This is why many personologists have dubbed Freud's theory *biological* rather than *psychological*. But while his emphasis is biological, Freud certainly considers the instincts influential through their grip on mental life.

What type of *energy* or *driving force* characterizes instincts? Having accepted that an instinct originates in the somatic and metabolic processes of organisms, we may inquire how the mind interprets this bodily message. Freud invariably considers the message to reflect a state of biological deprivation. The energy of an instinct is rooted in such bodily deprivation states as "dryness of the mucous membrane of the pharynx or an irritation of the mucous membrane of the stomach" (Freud, 1925c, p. 61). Thus, the source and energy of instincts originate within the organism itself. Freud can say "when a strong light falls on the eye, it is not an instinctual stimulus" (1925c, p. 61) because such stimulation is not achieved through internal processes intrinsic to the organism as a functioning biological system. By referring to such processes as dryness of mucous membranes, Freud establishes that the bodily messages to the mind are not only internal but that they also express the organism's biological requirements. An instinct is a sign that the organism lacks something it needs, that it is in a state of deprivation. Such states of deprivation are experienced as *tension*, or pressure. Freud (1925c) writes, "By the pressure . . . of an instinct we understand its motor factor, the amount of force or the measure of the demand for work which it represents. The characteristic of exercising pressure is common to all instincts; it is in fact their very essence" (p. 65).

Freud uses the distinction between stimulation entering the nervous system from the outside world and the internal stimulation of instincts to make another important point. In contrast to external stimulation, instinctual stimulation is constant. The amount of instinctual tension, pressure, or energy is above zero because such tension is a biological requirement of a functioning organism. An organism metabolizing normally will have such frequent need for food, water, and the like that parching or irritation of mucous membranes will almost always be taking place in one part of the body or another. Thus, Freud (1925) writes:

An instinct . . . never operates as a force giving a *momentary* impact but always as a constant one. Moreover, since it impinges not from without but from within the organism, no flight can avail against it. A better term for an instinctual stimulus is a "need." What does away with a need is a "satisfaction." This can be attained only by an appropriate . . . alteration of the internal source of stimulation. (p. 62)

The tension of deprivation states will always be with the person, which means that the instincts will always exert an influence on the person's living.

Thus far, you have seen that instincts have their source in bodily processes and are driven by the tension and pressure of biological deprivation. From this, you can guess what Freud considers the overall *aim* of instincts to be: "The aim . . . of an instinct is in every instance satisfaction, which can only be obtained by removing the state of stimulation at the source of the instinct" (1925c, p. 65). In other words, the aim of all instincts is to reduce the tension of biological deprivation. The ideal state, never reached because of the continuing nature of instinctual demands, is the bliss of quiescence, which is probably most closely approximated in deep sleep.

The final general attribute of the instinct is its *object,* by which Freud (1925c) means the thing or things, usually in the external world but possibly within the person, that satisfy or ease the tension of deprivation:

The object . . . of an instinct is the thing in regard

to which or through which the instinct is able to achieve its aim. It is what is most variable about an *instinct and is not originally connected with it,* but becomes assigned to it only in consequence of being peculiarly fitted to make satisfaction possible. (p. 65)

Typically, more than one thing or event can ease the tension of an instinct. One or another of these objects may become especially important, depending on one's particular learning experiences. Because they are implied in the instinct's definition, however, one can specify the range of potential satisfiers of a given instinct. For example, only edible things qualify as objects for the hunger need. When a person recognizes an object as an important satisfier, that process is called *cathexis,* defined as the investment of an object with instinctual energy.

You may be wondering what instincts have to do with mental life. Though basically biological, instincts have important psychic implications. Though the terminology for various attributes of instincts is not vividly mental, as long as one keeps in mind that Freud postulates that the body and the mind are closely interconnected, mental terms are appropriate. The psychic expression of the source and object of the instinct is a *wish.* A wish for food, for example, expresses the metabolic requirements for nutrients in psychological terms. The psychic or mental expression of the tension and aim of the instinct is *uncomfortable emotions.* According to Freud, wishes and associated emotions accurately express biological requirements through the close interconnection between the brain (the presumed physiological locus of wishes and emotions) and the soma and viscera (the presumed source of biological requirements), mediated by the autonomic or involuntary nervous system and the endocrine system. Recognize that Freud attributes a major and unchanging part of mental life, wishes and associated uncomfortable emotions, to the biological requirements of the organism. Recognize further that he gives this portion of mentation a huge role in determining a person's life.

Content of an Instinct. Now that you have a sense of the general form of the instinct as developed in psychoanalytic theory, you can profitably consider the content of the instincts postulated by Freud. There are three kinds of instinct present in each person, subsumed under the concept of the *id,* a summary term for all the instincts postulated by Freud. Id also means "it" in Latin, accurately conveying Freud's belief that instincts are experienced as foreign rather than as part of ourselves. In my terminology, the id is a core characteristic of personality, because the three groups of instincts arrayed within it were assumed by Freud to be common to everyone.

Throughout his career as a personologist, Freud argued for the existence of a group of instincts that function to preserve biological life. These *self-preservation* or *life instincts* (Freud, 1925c) include those for *food, water,* and *air.* Their source is in *anabolism,* or the aspect of metabolism that entails growth. The energy of these instincts comes from the discomfort and tension associated with irritated mucous membranes in the gastrointestinal and respiratory tracts. The instinctual aim is to reduce tension and discomfort by obtaining objects, such as food or water, that can ease the membrane irritation.

Although the life instincts are obviously basic, Freud gives them much less attention than he does the *sexual instinct,* also an integral part of his theorizing from the very beginning. This instinct originates in the metabolic process in those parts of the body differentiated for sexual reproduction in the broadest sense. This includes not only the genitalia per se but the secondary sexual areas, such as the breasts and the orifices (e.g., the mouth and anus) that can participate in sexual arousal. The energy of the sexual instinct, which Freud calls *libido,* comes from the sensitivity, irritation, or tension of these various organs when they are deprived of sexual expression. For Freud, the overall aim of the instinct is release of this tension through intercourse, orgasm, and ejaculation. And the most comprehensive object or goal for this instinct is intercourse with an attractive person of the opposite sex. Any other possible aims and objects, such as kissing; fondling of breasts, genitalia, and anus; stimulation of the mouth and anus through activities related to eating and eliminating; masturbation with orgasm; intercourse with an unattractive person; and homosexual relations are considered only partial by Freud and therefore capable of producing only partial gratification of the instinct.

According to Freud, when such partial aims and objects are more important to an adult than the comprehensive ones, the reason is developmental immaturity. The sexual instinct is considered to be much slower to mature than the other instincts. For a youngster, primary gratification through oral stimulation or masturbation is quite appropriate to the prepubescent developmental stage. But if an adult favors partial aims and objects, the explanation points toward faulty development and psychopathology.

Some critics object to Freud's notion of comprehensive and partial objects, in that it seems to designate human sexual processes only for procreation and not for pleasure. This is not a valid criticism, however, for Freud presents the function of the pleasurable "partial" sexual activities as setting the stage for vigorous intercourse and orgasm and contributing to one's overall sexual satisfaction. He means the sexual instinct to cover far more areas of the body and types of activities and pleasures than is associated with a "conventional" view of sex. It is only when one or another of the partial goals becomes primary for an adult that he would worry.

Freud's distinction between the sexual instinct and the previously mentioned life instincts seems to imply that the former does not have a survival function. But this is not entirely true. Although the sexual instinct does not insure the individual's survival by providing the impetus for obtaining needed nutrients and raw materials for metabolism (as do the life instincts), it does insure survival of the species by providing the impetus for procreation. And Freud certainly recognizes that survival of the species is ultimately important to the survival of individuals. Nonetheless, although the sexual instinct, like all instincts, is rooted in biological requirements, these requirements are not immediately relevant to the survival of the individual having the instinct. That the sexual instinct expresses a bio-

logical requirement can be shown by the painfully high levels of tension and discomfort that ensue from enforced sexual continence. But this requirement does not have a strong, obvious effect on individual survival; some people, such as priests and nuns, live in fairly complete sexual abstinence without taking any years off their lives (as far as anyone knows). It is true that once you define sexuality as broadly as Freud does, you can believe that even celibates can achieve some partial gratification of their sexual instinct, and it may be just this that permits them to survive. It is also true that Freud would expect the conditions of celibacy to lead to certain symptoms, however subtle, of psychological malady. In any case, the sexual instinct is rooted in biological requirements that do not affect the individual's immediate survival. After all, in the case of the life instincts, if you abstained from food or water for very long, there would be no need to search for subtle symptoms—you would die!

The disproportionate attention Freud gives to the sexual instinct certainly cannot be understood as a function of its greater importance for survival than needs for food, water, and the like. It has received so much attention because it seems to contribute much more to conflict than life instincts do. And in a theory such as Freud's, conflict forms and shapes the person's life. One reason why Freud sees the sexual instinct as the major source of conflict is that it matures so slowly and has so many parts that can be satisfied in so many ways. In contrast, the life instincts are simple, needing little maturation and capable of being satisfied in only a few ways. The sexual instinct can be more affected by what one learns in early life than can the life instincts. As you will see in the following section, Freud's views on society's reactions to expressions of the sexual instinct clearly explain why conflict arises from early influences.

During the latter part of his career, Freud began to be convinced that there is yet a third kind of instinct that functions as an antagonist to the life instincts. The aim of this *death instinct* is the biological death of the person. It is so extraordinary to assume that a basic tendency of the organism is to push toward death that consideration of Freud's reasons for doing this are clearly in order. Freud began theorizing about the death instinct when he was well along in his life. Not only could he note the physiological and psychological changes going on within him as he aged, he had also reached the age at which it is increasingly common to find those around us dying. Further, his own jaw cancer, though contained by treatment, must have brought the possibility of his death to the center of his attention during his last years. It is clear that Freud had a strong dread of death during this period (Bakan, 1966).

It is fashionable these days to consider death as rendering life meaningless in rational terms, because death, though one of the only absolute things in existence, is itself unpredictable. Ours is also a time in which even hard sciences, such as physics, are abandoning the attempt to attribute causes to every observable event. But in Freud's time, many scientists believed in a strong form of the deterministic hypothesis; in other words, they expected to be able to discover a cause for every event. Freud gave evidence very early in his career of the strength of his own belief in this when he took such phenomena as dreams and slips of the tongue to be important events with causes, a point of view then uncommon in medical circles. Such a strong believer in determinism would naturally take death to be a phenomenon with a rational, specifiable cause, especially when his or her own life circumstances conspired to render death personally salient.

In searching for a rational cause of death, Freud could not have been content with a purely physiological theory of the breakdown, fatigue, or rigidification of body systems, because he was too committed to assuming a psychological component to biological processes. Freud had to assume a psychological—indeed, motivational—cause of death that also reflected a profound biological truth so he could remain consistent with his previous theorizing.

Consistency and personal concern were not, of course, the only reasons for Freud's theory of the death instinct. This assumption provides a rational way of understanding death not only as

a natural concomitant of aging but as a result of decision making, as in murder and suicide. War can be understood as a mass expression of the death instinct. In this regard, it is not surprising that Freud's major interest in the death instinct developed after World War I. He explains even acts of aggression toward oneself and others as being partial or disguised expressions of the tendency toward death. Like the life instincts, the death instinct has its source in the biological process of metabolism. Even in the individual cell, along with the *anabolic processes,* which determine its birth and growth, are the *catabolic processes,* which determine its decay and eventual death.

Freud never develops the idea of the death instinct as completely as he does that of the life instincts. If the somatic source of the death instinct is catabolism, its aim is presumably the reduction of tension arising from the biological necessity of decay. It is not clear, however, that any such tension reduction really occurs. Nowhere does one find in Freud's theory detailed discussions of energy associated with the death instinct that would parallel libido theory. Further, while a few objects for the death instinct can be specified, Freud's writings lack comprehensive discussions of such matters. Finally, though the life and sexual instincts are embedded in a developmental theory, the notion of the death instinct is not.

As if there were not enough difficulties, an additional, logistical problem arises from Freud's assumption that the life instincts are actively opposed by a death instinct. To make the theory consistent, it is necessary to specify the precise nature of the relationship between the two antagonistic forces. Freud's rudimentary statements concerning the relationship are not theoretically satisfactory. He states that in the normal course of events, the life instincts are stronger than the death instinct, but late in life the tide turns. At any age, in some disordered personalities the death instinct can be more powerful than the life instinct. It is also possible for the death instinct to be stronger at certain times in a person's life, such as periods of sleep and self-condemnation. Here, Freud does no more than make observations and describe them in terms of the two notions of death and life instincts. His approach seems arbitrary and inconsistent. Such difficulties have led many psychologists to be particularly skeptical of the concept of the death instinct. According to them, everything that Freud can account for with the concept can also be explained as aggression resulting from frustration in the attempt to satisfy the life and sexual instincts, a position Freud himself would have agreed with until the latter part of his life. But to other intellectuals (e.g., Brown, 1959), the concept of the death instinct has been very intriguing.

In concluding this section on instincts, I would like to emphasize a crucial point that you must grasp fully if you are to understand Freud's position. The wishes and emotions of the id are deeply self-centered—indeed, selfish—in nature. They express the person's basic, unadulterated, biological nature. They have no social refinements. The id wants what it wants when it wants it, without regard for what other people may need, prefer, or insist on. Looked at as an individual, the human being is basically selfish and uncivilized, according to Freud. As you will see in the next section, this inherent selfishness makes conflict inevitable.

You should also recognize that the instincts, as they exist in the id, are hopelessly ineffective in the external world. What good does it do to have wishes and emotions expressing people's biological necessities unless they know how to reach what they want and have the capability to carry out that knowledge? Very little or no good, Freud answers. On the basis of the id alone, people would be able to satisfy instincts only through wish-fulfilling fantasy (called *primary process* thought), and fantasy would not help much when what you really need is bread. Luckily, infants ordinarily are tended by parents until the infants have learned to fend for themselves. They must learn which of the appropriate objects of their instincts are available in the environment, where those objects are likely to be, and what instrumental behaviors are likely to obtain them. In all this learning, infants must express selectivity, accuracy, memory, and self-

correction. In a word, they must act intelligently. In Freud's terms, the infant must develop an *ego* (the Latin word for *self*).

At birth, the infant's entire mind is composed of id wishes and emotions. But as experience accumulates, part of the mind differentiates from the id and becomes ego. In large measure, the ego is that part of the mind comprising the thinking and perceptual processes involved in recognition, remembrance, and action relevant to satisfying instincts (called *secondary process* thought). It is important to recognize that the ego functions to satisfy instincts in the external world. Furthermore, in bringing about satisfaction, the ego has the advantage of control over the voluntary nervous system and musculature. The ego and its component processes, because common to all people, should be considered core characteristics of personality along with the id and its components.

In this theorizing, Freud makes the mind a bridge from the metabolic requirements of the body to the intelligent actions and interactions with the world. The metabolic processes produce the wishes and discomforts of the id, and the ego comes into being to guide the intelligence and the muscles of the body in efficiently serving the metabolic processes. With the advent of the ego, the attempt to achieve biological necessities becomes not only selfish but effective. Freud calls this *pleasure principle functioning* to indicate both its selfish and its biologically satisfying quality. In early life, the human being engages solely in pleasure principle functioning. As you may have surmised, the part of Freud's core statement concerning maximization of instinctual gratification refers to pleasure principle functioning. But then society rears its head. . . .

THE SOURCES OF PUNISHMENT AND GUILT. The key to understanding Freud's view of the sources of punishment and guilt is his belief that the instincts are not simply self-centered but necessarily antagonistic to the principles of orderly, civilized living. The instincts aim only for the reduction of tension due to metabolic requirements. Such requirements are, after all, characteristic of solitary organisms. According to Freud, if all people were to act out their natural, uninhibited instinctual demands—that is, function at the level of pleasure principle alone—the world would be an unimaginably horrendous place. In grabbing what you want when you wanted it, you inevitably would encounter others who wanted the same thing at the same time or who would be disadvantaged by your gain. You would have to compete with them or vanquish their defense. You would fight violently, without regard for the restrained and orderly manners of civilization, and to the victor would go the spoils of instinctual gratification.

No one can be sure of victory always. But accepting that you may be unable to satisfy your instincts is anathema to the selfish id. Because people must live together, pleasure principle functioning leads to the risk of failure in obtaining precisely that which defines it. And, of course, a world in which people live as hermits is implausible. Actually, Freud's position makes such isolation impossible, for it would lead to frustration of at least one instinct—that for sex—which requires the social interaction of intercourse.

The best that aggregates of individuals, or societies, can do is aim for cooperation and order that maximizes gratification for all. This pressure toward the common good, which in Freud's terms means equalizing the possibilities of instinctual gratification for all society members, is the second great force, in my terminology. Social living requires rules and regulations for conduct that cut into pleasure principle functioning in the sense of uninhibited, unfettered pursuit of instinctual delights. But rules and regulations are the most effective measures for ensuring a predictable maximum of instinctual gratification for all. Freud assumes that the aims of the individual are selfish whereas those of society are for the common good. If people must function in groups, the apparently paradoxical development of civilized behavior in those who have no naturally generous, altruistic interest toward others is inevitable. Because Freud's theory presents individuals and society as having antagonistic aims, the one selfish and the other communal, I classify it as an example of the psychosocial conflict model.

From a position that takes selfish natural human characteristics as a starting point for understanding life, Freud derives the importance of civilization by simply accepting the fact that people must live in close interaction with one another. He expresses this view as a vivid parable in *Totem and Taboo* (1952), a story of the beginning of civilization. At the start, there are a father and mother and their many sons. True to the sexual instincts of the phallic stage of psychosexual development (to be discussed later), the sons wish to murder the father in order to sexually possess the mother. Being pleasure principle creatures, they actually carry out this instinctual wish. But once the father is out of the way, they find themselves thwarted in their selfish desires by the ensuing competition among themselves and thereby come to realize the futility of having committed murder. So the most direct route to instinctual gratification—pleasure principle functioning—turns out to be ineffective in the long run because all the sons unfortunately want the same goal. Finally, the sons band together and adopt a set of rules designed to avoid future difficulties by restricting the expression of instincts to those forms not damaging to the group as a whole. This, in the parable, is the beginning of civilization, with its emphasis on reverence toward the dead father (totem) and the taboo on incest, coupled with the institutionalization of marriage. Together, these taboos and sanctions ensure as much satisfaction of the sexual instinct for each member of society as is possible without inordinate risk of battle over and deprivation of sexual objects.

You are now in a position to consider the matters of punishment and guilt, which have their source in the communal requirements of society. When people transgress the rules of civilization, the society's representatives punish them. Young people are common transgressors, because they function at the level of the pleasure principle, not yet having learned the rules governing adult life. Acting in the role of societal representatives, parents are common punishers because they are around the youngsters the most. Such punishments as physical damage, psychological humiliation, and withdrawal of love are all effective, according to Freudians, because they increase tension in the organism. Even though the increase in tension is caused by an external action of punishment, its discomforting organismic effects are considered similar to those caused by instinctual deprivation. Tension is tension, which the person must try to decrease in some way. Because society is greater and more powerful than individuals, people curb instinctual expression so as to avoid punishment, especially when they are youngsters and relatively powerless.

Punishment thus comes from outside the person and expresses the requirements of communal living. Although it expresses the same requirements, guilt comes from within the person. To understand this, you must keep in mind that children grow up under the influence of their parents, who are in large part representatives of society with the assigned task of teaching children to accept the rules and regulations that will render them civilized adults. Certainly parents punish children for unbridled instinctual expression and, as a pattern of accumulated punishments emerges, children learn something of the nature of the rules. In addition, the parents supplement this dawning knowledge with verbal instruction. Over time, the combination of the two techniques leads children to internalize the rules. Once these exist in their memory, they can feel guilt. From then on, they can realize for themselves when some wish transgresses the common good and can feel morally culpable even if they do not act on it. A portion of the mind hitherto devoted to ego processes becomes differentiated, or set apart, for the purpose of representing the rules and regulations of society in terms of the abstract ideas of good/bad and right/wrong. Freud calls this set of ideas the *superego*. Because its presence and, to some extent, its contents are common to all people in the same society, it constitutes what I call a core characteristic of personality. As the internal counterpart of earlier punishments, guilt is assumed to have the same effect of raising organismic tension, which must then be reduced. Guilt, like the society it mirrors, is powerful enough to lead people to inhibit their instincts in an attempt to avoid punishment. Instincts can be expressed only insofar as guilt is kept to a minimum.

You now have all the elements for understanding Freud's core tendency of personality. People attempt to maximize instinctual gratification while minimizing punishment and guilt because that is the best way to decrease tension, given the basically antagonistic nature of the individual and society. With the accumulation of punishment and the development of the superego, the ego takes on its second major function. Recall that the first function of the ego is to provide the cognitive and behavioral structure for effective satisfaction of instincts in the external world. The second ego function is to translate instinctual demands into actions consistent with superego demands. The ego, therefore, is the architect of the core tendency, which Freud calls *reality principle functioning*. Reality principle functioning takes into account not only instinctual demands but also the equally inexorable—and, unfortunately, opposing—demands of society. In reality principle functioning, people choose only socially acceptable forms and routines of instinctual functioning. The young man will not sleep with his mother; instead, he will marry a young woman who is sexually attached to no one. Hungry people will not steal bread; rather, they will get jobs and earn the money to pay bakers for the time they have had to spend away from their own instinctual gratification.

Perhaps because of his early biological training in medicine, Freud always considered it important to determine where the energy or fuel for particular organismic functions came from. According to him, the instincts get their energy from their metabolic sources, and the ego and superego share the energy of the instincts. This is not really as strange as it might seem, for the ego and superego make possible maximum instinct gratification.

You are now in a position to reflect knowledgeably on why Freud emphasizes the sexual instinct much more than the life and death instincts. First, the death instinct is a concept from his later life, and he is so uncertain about it that its relative lack of emphasis seems understandable. Clearly, the sexual instinct receives the lion's share of attention because Freud believes it to be surrounded with much more psychosocial conflict than the life instincts. Although unbridled expression of the life instincts will conflict with societal requirements, these instincts are so obviously important that all societies provide institutionalized bases for satisfying them regularly and rapidly lest they become too strong. So, three meals a day, with one or two snacks thrown in, are common in our society, and water and other liquids are more or less continually available.

Because the life instincts are readily satisfied, they are not a chronic source of intense conflict. Not so with the sexual instinct. To be sure, we have the institution of marriage, which can provide the socially sanctioned basis for frequent sexual gratification. But what of the person who is not married or the child who has only rudimentary ways of repressing the sexual instinct? Society has no concrete way of planning for such people's sexual needs. They could indeed find sexual gratification, but generally not in a socially sanctioned and respectable way. When unmarried people had sex without "attachment," they were frowned on. When children masturbated, it was imagined that they would damage themselves through such "monstrous activity." Even though such attitudes have diminished since Freud's times, it is clear that Western society still provides less extensive and effective institutional means for the satisfaction of the sexual instinct than for the life instincts. This situation, according to Freud, surrounds the sexual instinct with conflict. Freud emphasizes the sexual instinct so much that he defines personality development in terms of it. His well-known oral, anal, phallic, latency, and genital stages are called *psychosexual* stages of development. And with the biological maturing of the

sexual instinct at puberty, the personality gels, changing little thenceforward.

DEFENSE. Freud's core theorizing involves not only a position on the nature of the instincts and the sources of punishment and guilt but also a position on the mechanism that maximizes instinct gratification while minimizing punishment and guilt, which is called *defense*. If you fully express your instincts in action, you will be punished by other people. If you fully recognize your instincts, you will experience guilt even without acting on them. The instincts are inexorable forces pushing for expression. This, the major conflict of life, is eased somewhat through the process of defense.

The way in which defenses are aroused is simple enough. Whenever an instinct becomes strong enough to be a potential source of conflict, an alarm reaction occurs in the form of anxiety, a diffuse, somewhat unspecific feeling of discomfort and impending disaster. This anxiety reaction, which represents the anticipation of punishment and guilt based on remembrance of past punishment and guilt, triggers the defensive process. Defense eases the conflict between the demands of instincts and society by striking a compromise between them. The defense limits personal awareness of the instinct, as well as its expression in action, to only that part or form of it acceptable to other people and to one's internalized standards. Hence, one's actions become acceptable both to society and to oneself, and one avoids punishment and guilt. For example, if a son's real instinctual wish is to possess his mother sexually, the defensive form of his wish may be the desire to stay close to her, nurture her, and keep her from harm. The defensive wish and actions are not only acceptable to others and to his own superego; they also permit partial instinctual gratification through closeness to the mother and keeping her for himself.

Defensive processes are aroused more frequently than you might think. To Freud's way of thinking, defense is ubiquitous because instincts (inherently antisocial) are never at zero intensity; hence, conflict between instinctual and societal aims (the basis for defense) never goes away. As all behavior is motivated by or infused with instincts, so *all* behavior, to a Freudian, is defensive!

This conclusion carries extraordinary implications. If all behavior is defensive, people are unaware of their true wishes, feelings, and aims, which are represented in the mind but inaccessible to awareness. The paradoxical ring of this position has incited many attacks on Freudian thinking (see Chapter 10). If all behavior is defensive, whatever mental content we are aware of is no more than epiphenomenal, or a pale shadow of the truth. Thus, though wishing to remain close to and nurture mother might very well be part of what one would feel if one really wanted to possess her sexually, one would never infer the presence of the latter wish from the former.

The defenses function to keep repressed desires out of consciousness more or less indefinitely. Thus, the truth about oneself is perhaps permanently inaccessible. To say that all behavior is defensive has much more alarming implications than does considering only some behavior defensive. If, as Freud charges, the truth about oneself is ordinarily unavailable, how can learning, or any real change in personality, take place? Leaving aside for a moment the possibility of change through psychoanalysis—the form of psychotherapy associated with the Freudian position—we should discard as useless some of our most cherished ideas about rationality as the basis for living and educating. If logical thinking and debate cannot even have the real truth to work with, how can such processes possibly produce any meaningful result? An eminent anti-Freudian personologist, Gordon W. Allport (1955), puts the problem this way:

Up to now the "behavioral sciences," including psychology, have not provided us with a picture of man capable of creating or living in a democracy. These sciences in large part have imitated the billiard ball model of physics, now of course outmoded. They have delivered into our hands a psychology of an organism pushed by drives and molded by environmental circumstance.... But

the theory of democracy requires also that man possess a measure of rationality, a portion of freedom, a generic conscience, propriate ideals, and unique value. We cannot defend the ballot box or liberal education, nor advocate free discussion and democratic institutions, unless man has the potential capacity to profit therefrom. (p. 100)

Because all behavior, according to Freud, is not only motivated but defensive, we are forced, in his frame of reference, to accept a view of humans as controlled by forces from within and pressures from without and, furthermore, as ignorant of that damning fact!

You may think that especially in this last phrase I am being unfair to Freud by making him seem overly pessimistic and deterministic. After all, does he not really mean that because we use defensive processes to ease conflict, we especially need to recognize that our conscious beliefs about ourselves are not necessarily the whole truth? If he does, there is really no incompatibility between the Socratic injunction to "know thyself" and the Freudian view. Isn't Freud merely emphasizing the importance of plumbing the full depths of our minds? One can see Freud's use of free association as proof that he believes one can circumvent the inhibition of consciousness produced by defense. However, although modern-day psychoanalytic thinkers have added to Freud's position as to make this "know thyself" interpretation plausible, I think it distorts what Freud himself meant.

Most people find this less-deterministic interpretation of Freud compelling because it presents humans as fallible but also perfectible, a position deeply rooted in Western thought and religion. But even if you think you know yourself rather well through introspection and experience, even if you think you have seen your own foibles, defensive operations, and bedrock instincts, Freud would not have accepted your self-knowledge as valid unless, perhaps, you had been in psychoanalysis for many years. He would have seen your beliefs concerning the nature of your defensive operations and real wishes as defensive in themselves! You cannot know the real truth about yourself simply because you have the pious goal of being honest and working hard at it.

You cannot get behind your own defenses because the defensive process itself lies outside awareness. If these defenses operated consciously, they would not be effective at all. You would know that you were constantly lying to yourself and the world. A consciously operating process of defense would not insulate you from guilt, though it could be successful in avoiding punishment. Indeed, we all employ techniques for hiding our conscious intent from others when we think they will find it unacceptable. While somewhat analogous to what Freud meant by defenses, these techniques fall short of the important meaning of defense—a way of lying to yourself as well as other people.

There are times when defenses break down and a glimpse of the real truth ensues. These occur when the person is in psychoanalysis or is severely debilitated through psychological or physical stress. The breakdown in defense is accompanied by acute guilt and anxiety—the feeling that life is about to end terribly—indeed, *should* end for someone so worthless. One cannot stay in such a state for very long and still maintain integrity and organization. If defenses are not reinstituted, madness or catastrophe will result regardless of whether the source of breakdown was debilitation or psychotherapy. I choose such strong words because Freud felt he was talking about matters of life and death. It is a tribute to the success of defensive processes that such starkness is rarely experienced fully.

If defenses, once breached, must be reinstated to avoid the catastrophic disintegration of personality, not even psychoanalysis can or should try to remove all the defenses. But then what did Freud mean when he characterized the goal of psychotherapy with the dramatic axiom, "Where id was there shall ego be" (1933, p. 112)? In trying to understand this statement, one must clearly understand the nature of id and ego. As you will recall, the id is the mental representation, in the form of wishes and feelings, of selfish instincts originating in somatic and metabolic processes. By themselves, instincts

are relatively ineffective in the world because they include knowledge of neither the instrumentalities governing the actions that ensure gratification, nor the necessity of avoiding open conflict with other people. The ego is largely the knowledge of such instrumentalities and techniques of conforming to the inescapable requirements of society. By guiding perception, memory, and judgment and their relation to the voluntary nervous system, the ego ensures a maximum of instinct gratification and a minimum of trouble. The most important part of the ego is the defenses. It is largely the defensive processes that permit effective operation of the only successful tendency of life—reality principle functioning.

Freud's statement "Where id was there shall ego be" is often interpreted to mean that in psychoanalysis, unconscious mentation is made conscious and defenses removed in favor of a more open basis for experiencing. However, this does not appear to be accurate. Though the id is largely unconscious, the ego is not largely conscious. Remember that the defenses, which are themselves unconscious, represent the lion's share of the ego, according to Freud. Furthermore, a large part of the id is unconscious only because of the action of the ego's defensive processes. So, the notion of replacing id with ego does not very likely mean making the unconscious conscious. The id has a permanent place in the Freudian psyche; he considered it a natural human endowment. What did he mean, then, by his famous statement, with all its figurativeness and fuzziness? As you may have guessed from my description of id and ego, I think Freud meant that pleasure principle *functioning,* so characteristic of the id in isolation and so ineffective in the world, must give way to reality principle functioning, if psychotherapy is to be judged successful. Reality principle functioning, you will remember, is what I have been calling Freud's core tendency of living.

Lacan, a contemporary French psychoanalyst, essentially agrees with my interpretation of Freud's famous statement (Mehlman, 1972). Reconsidering the original German *"Wo es war, soll ich werden,"* Lacan asserts that the translation could well have been "Where id (or it) was, there must ego (or I) arrive at." This definitely implies that the goal of psychotherapy is less to increase consciousness than to heighten instinctual gratification, brought about by rendering the ego an instrument of the id.

So far, I have focused on defensiveness as a general mechanism for striking a compromise between the demands of instincts and those of society. Actually, Freud's theory of personality details more kinds of defense than any other theory. His daughter Anna Freud (1946) lists such examples of defense as *repression, regression, reaction formation, denial, projection,* and *sublimation.* One crucial distinction among defenses is the degree to which they distort the underlying instincts. The more successful the psychosexual development has been, the more the person's functioning is characterized by defenses, such as sublimation, that minimally distort instinctual reality. Developmental failings, produced by fixations (or arrested growth), are defined partially by the existence of grossly distortive defenses, such as projection.

But even the highest form of functioning, bespeaking exemplary development, is characterized by defensiveness, because the true antisocial nature of the instincts must be hidden from oneself and the world. Freud (1938) takes this so far as to assert that well (not poorly) developed adults, in falling in love, unconsciously choose partners who resemble their opposite-sex parents. Expressing this love fulfills unconscious incestuous fantasies. This instinctual truth is hidden by that most sophisticated defensive operation, *sublimation.*

To maintain logical consistency, one must describe the goal of psychoanalysis as the replacement of defenses that heavily distort truth by defenses that more closely approximate it. But because there is no alternative to defensive behavior, there is always at least some distortion of truth and, hence, unconsciousness of some of the most basic things about oneself. Freud's theory of personality is probably the most pessimistic in existence.

A word more will enhance your understanding of the full dimensions of this pessimism. Freud discusses development in terms of the biological maturation of the sexual instinct and the mental state accompanying it. For the moment, it is enough to realize that the first three—and most crucial—stages of psychosexual development cover roughly the first 5 years of life. Then, a period of biological dormancy persists until the advent of puberty. Puberty opens the genital stage, which continues until death. The extraordinary discrepancy between the attention given the earliest childhood years and the rest of life indicates that for Freud nothing of real developmental importance happens after age five. The outlines of personality are essentially fixed by then, with the rest of life a repetition of the early patterns. To be sure, people become more complex with age, but nothing basic really changes.

Those familiar with Freud may contend that his pessimism characterizes mainly his earlier works. But there is also evidence of pessimism in the later works, in which the death instinct is formulated for the first time (Freud, 1922a) and the inevitability of defensiveness reasserted (e.g., Freud, 1922b). In the latter work, Freud suggests that World War I stripped away the comforting repression of the death instinct in which all humans were engaging. Had Freud been leaning toward a new-found optimism, he might have argued at this point that such a new level of consciousness would spur psychological development. Instead, he predicts that people's consciousness of their own viciousness will prove too much to bear, leading to a renewal of defensiveness. Some will revert to a primitive defense—projection—and imagine that there really are enemies out there, from whom they must protect themselves (through aggression, of course). Others will take a more sophisticated route by seeming to accept death as the outcome of aggression but rejecting it at a deeper level. Through rationalizations, such as the belief in an afterlife or the contention that we achieve immortality in our works and our children, the stark reality of the death instinct is blunted. One way or another, we defend ourselves against awareness of the instinctual truth because we cannot bear it.

Freud's Peripheral Statement

Freud assumes that all people have the same set of instincts concerning survival, sexuality, and death. Clearly this assumption involves the core of personality, for it is inconceivable, in his theory, that one person would have only survival and sex instincts but not the death instinct and another only the death instinct or only the sex instinct. All people are born with all three instincts, which exert a continual, general influence on all functioning. For Freud, then, the id or repository of the instincts is clearly part of the core of personality.

The parts of the personality called ego and superego should also be considered part of the core, though the reasons for this are not as obvious as in the case of the id. Although some psychoanalytic circles talk of people with more or less ego and superego, it nonetheless remains true that everyone must be seen as having an ego and a superego. The absence of ego is theoretically impossible, because the ego comes into being by virtue of the existence of the id and the consequent necessity of satisfying instincts through interaction with the world. Without an ego, there would be no chance of consistent gratification and therefore no chance of physical and psychological survival. Similarly, it is theoretically impossible to conceive of a person without a superego, because that part of personality is born out of the conflict between the person and the world, a conflict as inevitable as selfish instincts that cannot be gratified independently of other people and things. The requirements of society determine the superego—and, for Freud, individual life is inconceivable without the existence of society.

But to say that the ego and superego are core characteristics of personality along with the id is to mask an important difference between the first two and the last. In content, the id is the same for all people, but the ego and superego

are not. For Freud, the ego consists of defenses and their concrete expressions in traits or consistencies of everyday functioning; though all people are defensive, they are not defensive in the same way. Psychoanalysts have distinguished a number of different defenses and theorized about the developmental conditions determining their appearance in a particular person. In specifying the kinds of defenses that can be used, Freudians are making statements about the periphery of personality. This is even more obvious when they begin detailing the concrete habits that express the various defenses, as you will see in a moment. Each defense is learned and specific either to a particular person or to a part of a person's behavior. Similarly, though the superego is present in all people, its contents may vary according to the quirks of one's parents. Consequently, the taboos and sanctions of one person may differ somewhat from those of the next. The content of both ego and superego I call the periphery of personality, because it, in contrast to that of the id, is largely determined by the kinds of people and things one encounters in the external environment.

CHARACTER TYPES. Actually, the Freudian position on the periphery of personality is most vividly portrayed in the classification of character types, as Fenichel (1945) says:

> Character, as the habitual mode of bringing into harmony the tasks presented by internal demands and by the external world, is necessarily a function of the constant, organized, and integrating part of the personality which is the ego; indeed, ego was defined as that part of the organism that handles the communication between the instinctual demands and the external world. The question of character would thus be the question of when and how the ego acquires the qualities by which it habitually adjusts itself to the demands of instinctual drives and of the external world, and later also of the superego.... The term character stresses the habitual form of a given reaction, its relative constancy. (p. 467)

Later, Fenichel indicates that character is the content not only of the ego but of the superego:

The latest complication in the structure of the ego, the erection of the superego, is also decisive in forming the habitual patterns of character. What an individual considers good or bad is characteristic for him; likewise, whether or not he takes the commands of his conscience seriously, and whether he obeys his conscience or tries to rebel against it. (p. 468)

In these two quotes, it is clear that character is a learned pattern of fairly consistent ways of functioning, which varies somewhat from person to person. To undercut the abstract terminology Fenichel uses, I encourage you to recognize that character is the most obvious psychological thing or pattern about a person— what you would say if someone asked you to describe a friend.

Actually, one can be more concrete, even in the structure of psychoanalytic terminology. A character type is a group of traits that expresses (1) particular underlying defenses, (2) a particular underlying conflict, (3) a particular response on the part of others to an underlying conflict, or (4) any combination of these. A trait, it turns out, can be primarily a pattern of thought, feeling, or action or some combination of these. In my terms, traits are peripheral characteristics. Before I discuss the content of particular character types, note that the character type is learned and represents the results of the interaction between the child, who selfishly strives for instinctual gratification, and the society, in the form of parents, whose task is to uphold the common good. You will find that not only in this theory but in all others the periphery is the fruit of earlier attempts to express the core tendency in a particular social and cultural context.

Freud's View on Development

Because character types are the product of development, it is fitting that they bear the names of the various psychosexual stages, reflecting as they do the Freudian position on development. The major stages of psychosexual development are the *oral, anal, phallic, latency,* and *genital.* Each stage has a particular concrete form of sexual instinct and arouses a specific range of reactions from parents; that is, each stage is defined by a particular concrete version of the general conflict between the sexual instinct and society. Not surprisingly, each stage has its own typical defenses, since the various defenses are differentially effective against different forms of conflict. And, as you will see, each stage but one has a particular character type associated with it. The concrete forms of the sexual instinct associated with the various stages of psychosexual development are summarized in their names, with an anatomical location designated in each name but latency. The dubious status of the latency stage is reflected in the absence of an associated character type. Even conservative psychoanalytic thinkers are beginning to believe that the latency stage is not a true inherent aspect of the sexual instinct but a culturally determined period of developmental quiescence. Therefore, I will not discuss the latency period.

You may have noticed that the psychosexual stages refer exclusively to the sexual instinct. But what about the survival and death instincts? Are there developmental stages and character types associated with them as well? There are no developmental stages, and though some psychoanalysts have attempted to designate relevant character types, they are not widely accepted and are often fragmentary and confusing. Thus, it is not at all inappropriate to say that the Freudian theory of personality hinges on sexuality as the basic human nature.

The oral, anal, phallic, and genital stages of development roughly cover, respectively, the first year of life, the second year, the third through fifth years, and the years from puberty onward. Obviously one must go through the first three stages to reach the fourth. If the first three stages are successfully traversed, genitality is vigorous and full. But if any of the developmental experiences in one or more of the three pregenital stages is destructive, that stage or stages will exert a lingering effect on later behavior. To indicate this effect on the adult, each of the pregenital stages entails a particular form of childish sexual wish and impulse. To progress successfully through each stage, the child must receive from parents and the world enough gratification to not feel hopelessly deprived and frustrated but not so much that he or she wants to remain in that particular phase of immaturity. With either too much frustration or too much indulgence, the child develops a *fixation,* or becomes stuck, at that particular level of development. This means that in adulthood the person will show traits—thoughts, emotions, actions—characteristic of the particular conflict, defenses, and parental reactions defining that pregenital stage.

THE ORAL STAGE AND CHARACTER TYPE. Now you are in a position to examine the content of the various psychosexual stages of development. At the beginning we find the *oral stage,* in which the anatomical location of the sexual instinct is the mouth. According to Freud, the development of the nervous system proceeds from the brain downward and outward, ensuring that the mouth region will be the first body orifice to experience pleasure and pain. Of course, the survival instincts for food and water also ensure that the mouth will be an important region. But Freud emphasizes the mouth mostly as a tactually and gustatorily erotic area. In other words, the child is presumed to crave and enjoy stimulation of the mouth region through touch, taste, and use of muscle. The craving and enjoyment are early forms of what will finally become mature sexuality in the genital stage.

To understand the oral character type, you must recognize that the oral form of sexual instinct leads to actions and fantasies involved in *taking and receiving* and that the conflicts salient at the oral stage therefore are those precipitated by these selfish activities (Fenichel, 1945, pp. 488–492). Freudians consider taking and receiving as generalizations of the mouth activities during the first year of life. *Receiving* is the generalization of the earliest, passive (*oral incorporative*) situation: in the process of being fed and caressed, the mouth is pleasurably stimulated by people and things. *Taking* is the generalization of the slightly later, somewhat less passive (*oral aggressive*) situation, in which children contrive

to gain oral satisfaction through sucking, putting things in their mouths, chewing, biting, and even vocalizing.

There is, of course, an inevitable conflict between the child's unmitigated, selfish wish to receive and take and the parents' own needs and duties, which do not permit unlimited time and attention to their offspring. The best that can happen is that the parents will provide a modicum of instinctual satisfaction for their child. If they fall short of this modicum by severely punishing the child for his or her needs to receive and take or by simply not having enough nurturance within them to make any difference, the inevitable conflict will be greatly intensified, requiring the child to develop especially strong and pervasive defenses, the employment of which is tantamount to a fixation, or arresting of growth. Once such defenses are instituted, change and development are impaired. The parents can also exceed the modicum of oral gratification by trying to provide nurturance at the expense of their own needs and duties. This deviation from the ideal will also intensify the inevitable conflict, because the nurturance will be only superficially satisfying, carrying with it such resentment and having so many strings attached as to be counterfeit. Again, frustrated and in pain, the child will have to institute defenses of such intensity and pervasiveness as to constitute fixation.

Now that I have described how conflict is intensified, leading to oral fixation, the next theoretical step would be to compose an exhaustive list of defenses and traits that constitute the oral character. Unfortunately, however, psychoanalytic thinking is not that neat, although Abraham (1927a, 1927b) and Glover (1925, 1926, 1928) have made some beginnings. I interpret their remarks as indicating that some traits recurring frequently in the oral character are optimism/pessimism, gullibility/suspiciousness, manipulativeness/passivity, admiration/envy, and cockiness/self-belittlement.

It is common for Freudians to think in terms of traits having two opposing extremes—so-called *bipolar traits*—either pole of which indicates fixation. It is tempting to think that one pole of the dimension expresses the fixation due to overindulgence (e.g., optimism) and the other the fixation of deprivation (e.g., pessimism). However, it is difficult to determine how consistent such usage is with Freudian intent, because some Freudians suggest that people vacillate from one pole of a dimension to the other (e.g., now optimistic, now pessimistic). In any event, the bipolar traits refer fairly directly to attitudes, initiated in the course of interacting with parents, about whether the world is a satisfying or depriving place and whether one is capable of helping oneself achieve satisfaction. Optimism, pessimism, gullibility, suspiciousness, and admiration are unrealistic estimates of the likelihood of being nurtured by other people. Manipulativeness and passivity represent unconstructive tendencies to wrest satisfaction from the world or to lie back and wait until it falls into one's mouth. Cockiness indicates an unrealistically affluent sense of one's own resources, whereas envy and self-belittlement suggest quite the opposite. The unrealistic quality of all these extremes indicates their defensive nature.

Having described some traits of the oral character and having indicated their unrealistic nature, the next theoretical step would be to list the defenses typical of the oral stage that find expression in these traits. But, again, psychoanalytic thinking is not that neat, though a few beginnings have been made. The defenses most often mentioned as part of the oral character are *projection, denial,* and *introjection. Projection* is the process of being unaware of wishes, feelings, and impulses in oneself that might provoke punishment and guilt and simultaneously misperceiving other people as having these same wishes, feelings, and impulses. *Denial* is the simpler process of being unaware of the presence of things, people, or events in the external world that could arouse anxiety by either provoking selfish instincts or signaling impending punishment. *Introjection* is the process of incorporating another person—virtually becoming that person—to avoid either that person's threatening nature or the potential danger in one's own instincts. All three defenses are rather unsophisticated and quite debilitating in that they grossly distort reality. Denial is the main determinant of

optimism and pessimism, which involve attention to only some aspects of the world. Gullibility can also be attributed to denial. Although denial may affect it, suspicion is more clearly an expression of projection in that one attributes to others all those nasty, manipulative, and stingy tendencies that one fails to see in oneself. Manipulativeness and overgenerosity most likely express introjection, or the incorporation of overindulgent parents. One can explain the other traits as expressions of any of the three defenses.

THE ANAL STAGE AND CHARACTER TYPE. Happily, I can be more theoretically precise about the anal stage and character than the oral. The *anal stage* is marked by the shift in anatomical location of the sexual instinct from the mouth to the anal orifice. According to Freud, this shift is brought about by the joint impact of two things: (1) nervous system development to the point at which voluntary control of the anal sphincters is possible and (2) intensified parental attempts to encourage excretory continence in the child. For the first time, the child experiences the pleasurable and painful stimulation associated with eliminating and retaining feces and begins to experiment with manipulating this stimulation through conscious elimination and retention.

To apprehend the anal character type fully, you must recognize that the anal form of the sexual instinct includes actions and fantasies involved in *giving* and *withholding,* which are generalizations of the anal activities during the second year of life. *Giving (anal expulsiveness)* is the generalization of the voluntarily controlled voiding of the bowels. *Withholding (anal retentiveness)* is the generalization of the voluntary decision not to void the bowels. Both activities are inherently pleasurable but also bring children into inevitable conflict with their parents, who require that the giving and withholding be done according to schedule and propriety. Again the best that can happen is that the parents will permit a modicum of anal gratification while still upholding the socially important rules of hygiene. If the parents are too punitive and disgusted at the child's messing or, conversely, too indulgent for the child's own social and hygienic good and for their own proprieties, the conflict inevitably will intensify. Like oral overindulgence, anal overindulgence is counterfeit. With the intensification of conflict come the extreme and pervasive defenses that constitute fixation. This arresting of growth means that the adult personality will be anal in nature.

The traits and defenses of the anal character have been fairly precisely specified by both Freud (1925a, 1925b, 1925c, 1925d) and others (e.g., Abraham, 1927c; Fenichel, 1945, pp. 278–284; Glover, 1926). Among the traits are *stinginess/overgenerosity, constrictedness/expansiveness, stubbornness/acquiescence, orderliness/messiness, rigid punctuality/tardiness, meticulousness/dirtiness,* and *precision/vagueness.* These traits express—in thought process, interaction, and the general conduct of life—various concrete forms of the impulses to give and withhold and the conflicts surrounding them that characterize the anal stage. As in the oral character, these anal traits show an unrealistic orientation at both poles. Further, this unrealistic orientation points to the defensive nature of the traits.

The defenses considered characteristic of the anal stage and character type are *intellectualization, reaction formation, isolation,* and *undoing.* In *intellectualization,* one loses consciousness of the real, instinctual significance of wishes and actions and substitutes a false reason that is more socially acceptable but really amounts to mere rationalization. *Reaction formation* is the process of losing awareness of one's true wishes and impulses and substituting awareness of the directly opposite ones. In *isolation,* the connecting link normally present between the cognitive and affective components of wishes and impulses is severed, so that though a semblance of the true nature of the wishes and impulses remains in consciousness, they no longer seem the source of unpleasant emotions, such as anxiety. *Undoing* is a defense whereby certain thoughts and actions cancel out or atone for anxiety-provoking thoughts and actions.

Though it is impossible to explicate precisely and exhaustively just how these defenses give rise to the traits of the anal character, one can engage in some discussion along these lines. Reaction formation leads to the renunciation of such socially unacceptable qualities as messiness, tardiness, and stinginess and the assertion of oneself as quite the opposite: meticulously clean, painstakingly punctual, and incredibly generous. This defense leads to the "saintly" anal qualities. Through the intellectualization defense, these saintly qualities, plus such characteristics as precision and stubbornness, are strengthened in their status as part of the self. The reliance on isolation, as well as the other defenses, permits glaring examples of the opposite of the saintly qualities—for example, messiness and dirtiness—to be clearly shown in the person's behavior without discomfort or anxiety. Finally, the action of undoing is seen not only in such direct characteristics as orderliness, implying symmetry and organization, but indirectly in the sometimes rapid shift from one pole to the other of the various traits mentioned above. One can avoid intense discomfort at an act of messiness if one can quickly atone for it with an extraordinary act of orderliness.

I will close discussion of the anal character type with a striking description from the psychoanalytic literature:

A rough sketch . . . would depict him as highly opinionated and proud of his superior intelligence, avowed rationality, keen sense of reality, and "unswerving integrity." He may indeed be an honest man, but he may also turn out to be a sanctimonious hypocrite. He is the ultimate perfectionist. While very sensitive to his own hurt, he may, at the same time, be destructively critical, spiteful, vindictive and given to bitter irony and to bearing grudges in trivial matters. Or, on the contrary, he may be overcautious, bent on avoiding any possibility of conflict. His "common sense" militates against what he views as fancies of the imagination; he is a "man of facts," not of fancies. He smiles condescendingly at people who are fascinated by mysticism, including "the unconscious" and dreams, but let him undergo some psychoanalytic treatment of the classical type, and he will switch to attributing oracular significance to slips of the tongue or pen. As a "man of reason" he cannot admit even to himself that he is superstitious. His interest in fine arts is slight or pretended; his true admiration is reserved for mathematics, the exact sciences, technology, and the new world of electronic computing machines. In contrast to the expressional, so-called hysterical type, he rarely has artistic gifts and conspicuously lacks genuine charm and grace. His amatory interests are laden with ulterior motivations and pretense. (Rado, 1959, p. 326)

This lucid, if somewhat impressionistic, description makes it perfectly clear what a person with the kind of traits and defenses mentioned earlier would be likely to encounter. The extremes of behavior depicted and the pejorative language employed clearly indicate the presumed unconstructive, immature nature of the anal character.

THE PHALLIC STAGE AND CHARACTER. The *phallic stage* is the last of the so-called pregenital, or immature, stages of psychosexual development. This stage presumably is brought about by the shift in anatomical location of the sexual instinct from the anus to the genitalia, though how this can be explained in terms of nervous system development when the two regions are so close to each other remains one of the many obscurities in psychoanalytic thinking. Though the basis in physiological development for distinguishing an anal from a phallic stage is virtually absent, one can nonetheless consider a more general psychosocial basis for the distinction.

When children reach the third year of life, they begin to explore their bodies more systematically and are also more alert to the bodies of others. That the genitalia become a major source of pleasure and pain for the first time is an assumption based on the observed increase in self-manipulation, or masturbation, in the exploration and manipulation of the genitalia of other boys and girls, and in the initiation of fantasies that have a frankly heterosexual quality. Children talk of marrying the opposite-sex parent and displacing the same-sex parent. They talk of being a father or a mother. The phallic stage is the time of the well-known oedipal con-

flict, a concept of overwhelming importance in Freudian theory.

To understand the phallic character type, you must recognize that this final pregenital form of the sexual instinct involves *thoughts and actions concerning both the body as a frankly sexual thing and interaction between people as sexual in nature.* If the child's unabashed craving for genital stimulation and for genitalized contact with parents and others is severely frustrated out of the parents' own embarrassment, fears, and secret fantasies, the child will experience intense conflict. Children will also experience such conflict if their cravings seem to be overindulged, for the encouragement to replace the same-sex parent in the opposite-sex parent's affections inevitably runs afoul of the societal taboo against incest. Fixation is the result of both deprivation and overindulgence of craving for genital stimulation and genitalized relationships.

As in the case of the oral and anal stages, some conflict is inevitable in the phallic stage, even if the parents give a modicum of satisfaction to the child. The inevitability of conflict is seen in the fact that although children must obtain enough gratification of genital cravings to develop a sense of themselves as worthwhile sexual beings, they must also give up selfish interest in the opposite-sex parent as the object of their sexuality. As they give up interest in the opposite-sex parent, they begin to long to be adults (Freudians talk of this as a specialized part of the superego called the *ego-ideal*). But when the inevitable conflict is intensified by over- or underindulgence, children will experience anxiety in the form of concern not only that they will lose the affections of the opposite-sex parent but that the same-sex parent will retaliate for the competition by damaging the child's genitalia. Both the latter fear, so-called *castration anxiety,* and the former fear, so-called *separation anxiety,* play an extraordinarily important role in Freudian thinking. Freud meant them very literally, although it has been common among later psychoanalysts to generalize their meaning.

The traits and defensive patterns of the phallic character have been described in detail by Reich (1931, 1933) and others (e.g., Abraham,

1927d). Among the traits are *vanity/self-hatred, pride/humility, blind courage/timidity, brashness/ bashfulness, gregariousness/isolation, stylish- ness/plainness, flirtatiousness/avoidance of het- erosexuality, chastity/promiscuity,* and *gaiety/ sadness.* These traits are present in some degree in people with the phallic character and repre- sent either direct genital craving or its curtail- ment because of fear of separation or castration. Some of the poles, such as blind courage and promiscuity, represent acting on the cravings in the face of these fears. In general, the major defense underlying the phallic traits is *repres- sion,* or unawareness of one's own instinctual wishes and actions so as to avoid anxiety.

While the superficiality involved in the poles of some phallic traits may well be understand- able as the result of massive repression, it is quite difficult to imagine how the complex traits mentioned above could all result from that sin- gle defense mechanism. However, people in the phallic stage of development retain the defenses of the earlier stages through which they have already gone. Similarly, people in the anal stage have the defenses more typical of the oral stage available to them. You can easily understand how the traits of the phallic character come about if you consider them to express not only repression but also other defenses. Still, the con- tent of the phallic traits or, for that matter, the anal and oral traits is defined by the type of psy- chosexual conflict dominant during that stage of development.

Thus, a concrete description of people with a phallic character would go something like this. They are preoccupied with their own beauty and extraordinariness, needing constant recognition of such by others to feel comfortable. If they get this support and appreciation, they may well be delightful, interesting, provocative, spontaneous, and dramatic. If they are not greatly appreciated and sought after, they may slip into black thoughts of worthlessness, ugliness, and incom- petence, appearing to be a pale shadow of their former selves. In general, they seek the company of people of the opposite sex, enjoy enticing them and receiving their appreciation, but they shy away from vigorous, deep, committed sexual

relationships. In the male, the phallic character is either effeminate or masculine in an obvious and inflexible way. The phallic character in a female renders her an exaggeration of feminin- ity, either chaste or promiscuous, but, if the lat- ter, giving the impression of naiveté, childishness, and inner purity.

PREGENITAL CHARACTER TYPES ARE ONLY IMMATURE. Oral, anal, and phallic characters are not to be considered psychopathological (mentally ill), although they do represent imma- turity and carry the seeds of psychopathology. But for psychopathology to ensue, the person must encounter severe environmental stress that breaks down the pregenital character structure. Furthermore, the nature of the pregenital charac- ter determines the nature of the psychopatholog- ical state. For instance, the breakdown of the oral character frequently leads to schizophrenia, and the breakdown of the anal character leads to obsessive-compulsive neurosis. Breakdown of the phallic character often leads to hysteria in women and homosexuality or perversion in men.

THE FREUDIAN IDEAL, OR GENITAL CHARAC- TER. The *genital stage* and genital character represent the pinnacle of development and matu- rity, according to Freudians. Although the geni- tal stage is considered a true psychosexual stage, it is not easily distinguished from the others on the basis of anatomical location of the sexual instinct, the relevant location being the same as that of the phallic stage. But Freudians do point to the complete physical maturation of the sex- ual system such that orgasm, ejaculation, and pregnancy become possible. Indeed, orgasm is considered to be the hallmark of satisfaction. But only orgasm combined with the erotic plea- sures of the pregenital stages yields full adult expression of the sexual instinct. Although reach- ing the genital stage with no existing fixations at lower stages of development is the ideal condi- tion, according to Freudians, this does not mean that genital functioning is free of conflict and nondefensive in nature. The person must still subscribe to societal sanctions and taboos in expressing the sexual instinct. But the conflict in this case is minimal, managed by the most mature and least rigidifying of defensive processes, *sublimation.*

In sublimation, one changes the object of the sexual instinct to be more socially acceptable than the original or most obvious object but in no other way disrupts or blocks its expression. Of all the defenses, sublimation involves the least damming of the libido, or energy straining for expression. So instead of pursuing the opposite-sex parent, as youngsters are wont to do in the phallic stage, they pursue opposite-sex people outside the family and in so doing accept society's set of responsibilities and rules concerning heterosexual relationships. That all love is for Freud (1938) essentially "on the rebound" (the child having to give up its original attraction to the opposite-sex parent) demonstrates once again the compromise inherent in even the ideal personality.

Although sublimation is clearly the defense associated with the genital character, it is difficult to specify any list of relevant traits. This is because trait names of the genital character might sound too much like others already mentioned as pregenital to effectively convey what Freudians mean, which is that genital persons are fully potent and capable. They are fully socialized and adjusted yet do not suffer greatly from this. Courageous without the driven recklessness of the phallic character, they are satisfied with themselves without the overweening pride and vanity of the same. They love heterosexually without the alarming neediness and dependence of the oral character. Altruistic and generous without the cloying saintliness of the anal character, they work diligently and effectively without the compulsivity and competitiveness of the same. In short, they maximize instinctual gratification while minimizing punishment and guilt.

PREEMINENCE OF SEXUALITY. As I have said many times before, one cannot help but be struck by the extraordinary emphasis Freud gives to sexuality. Nowhere is this more apparent than in his treatment of the character types, or peripheral characteristics of personality. He sees even the obvious differences among people as determined by various facets of the sexual instinct and attendant conflicts. Freudian thinking has often been criticized for this single-minded sexual emphasis. Although the criticism seems cogent, we must recognize that they have been made in societies grossly different from that in which Freud worked at the turn of the 20th century. In his day, it was generally not conceded that sexuality plays an important, natural part in living. The sexual act was for reproduction, not pleasure, and partial expressions of sexuality and sexual interest before physiological adulthood were not regarded as natural at all.

Lest you doubt the picture I have painted, I will quote from an authoritative book entitled *Maiden, Wife, and Mother: How to Attain Health, Beauty, Happiness,* by Mary R. Melendy (1901), who was both an M.D. and a Ph.D. with seven or eight distinguished titles to her credit. In a chapter on being a good mother to boys, Melendy writes,

> Teach him that these [sexual] organs are given as a sacred trust, that in maturer years he may be the means of giving life to those who shall live forever.
>
> Impress upon him that if these organs are abused, or if they are put to any use besides that for which God made them—and He did not intend they should be used at all until man is fully grown—they will bring disease and ruin upon those who abuse and disobey those laws which God has made to govern them.
>
> If he has ever learned to handle his sexual organs, or to touch them in any way except to keep them clean, teach him not to do it again. If he does, he will not grow up happy, healthy, and strong.
>
> Teach him that when he handles or excites the sexual organs, all parts of the body suffer, because they are connected by nerves that run throughout the system. This is why it is called "self-abuse." The whole body is abused when this part of the body is handled or excited in any manner whatever.
>
> Teach them to shun all children who indulge in this loathsome habit, or all children who talk about these things. The sin is terrible, and is, in fact, worse than lying or stealing! For although these are wicked and will ruin their soul, yet this habit of self-abuse will ruin both soul and body.
>
> If the sexual organs are handled it brings too much blood to these parts, and this produces a

diseased condition; it also causes disease in other organs of the body, because they are left with a less amount of blood than they ought to have. The sexual organs, too, are very closely connected with the spine and the brain by means of the nerves, and if they are handled, or if you keep thinking about them, these nerves get excited and become exhausted, and this makes the back ache, the brain heavy and the whole body weak.

It lays the foundation for consumption, paralysis and heart disease. It weakens the memory, makes a boy careless, negligent and listless.

It even makes many lose their minds; others, when grown, commit suicide.

How often mothers see their little boys handling themselves, and let it pass, because they think the boys will outgrow the habit, and do not realize the strong hold it has upon them! I say to you, who love your boys—"Watch!"

Don't think it does no harm to your boy because he does not suffer now, for the effects of this vice come on so slowly that the victim is often very near death before you realize that he has done himself harm.

The boy with no knowledge of the consequences, and with no one to warn him, finds momentary pleasure in its practice, and so contracts a habit which grows on him, undermining his health, poisoning his mind, arresting his development, and laying the foundation for future misery.

Do not read this book and forget it, for it contains earnest and living truths. Do not let false modesty stand in your way, but from this time on keep this thought in mind—"the saving of your boy." Follow its teachings and you will bless God as long as you live. Read it to your neighbors, who, like yourself, have growing boys, and urge them, for the sake of humanity, to heed its advice.

Right here I want to relate a fact that came under my observation. In our immediate neighborhood lived an intelligent, good and sensible couple. They had a boy about five years of age who was growing fretful, pale and puny. After trying all other remedies to restore him to vigor of body and mind, they journeyed from place to place hoping to leave the offending cause behind.

I had often suggested to the mother that "self-abuse" might be the cause, but no, she would not have it so, and said, "You must be mistaken, as he has inherited no such tendencies nor has he been taught it by playmates—we have guarded him carefully."

Finally, however, she took up a medical book and made a study of it and, after much thought, said, "I cannot believe it, yet it describes Charlie's case exactly. I will watch."

To her surprise, she found notwithstanding all her convictions to the contrary, that Charles was a victim to this loathsome habit.

On going to his bed, after he had gone to sleep, she found his hands still upon the organ, just as they were when he fell asleep. She watched this carefully for a few days, then took him in her confidence and told him of the dreadful evil effects. Finding the habit so firmly fixed, she feared that telling him, at his age, what effect it would have upon his future would not eradicate the evil as soon as she hoped so, after studying the case for a time, she hit upon the following remedy. Although unscientific, literally speaking, it had the desired effect. Feeling that something must be done to stop, and stop at once, the awful habit, she said, "Did you know, Charles, that if you keep up this habit of 'self-abuse' that a brown spot will come on your abdomen, light brown at first, and grow darker each week until it eats a sore right into your system, and if it keeps on, will eventually kill you?"

After Charlie had gone to sleep, and finding his hands again on the sexual organs, to prove to him the truth of her argument, she took a bottle of "Iodine" and, with the cork, put on the abdomen a quantity sufficient to give it a light brown color, and about the size of a pea. Next night, in bathing him, she discovered the spot, and said, "Look! Already it has come!" The boy cried out in very fear, and promised not to repeat it again.

The next night the mother put on a second application which made the spot darker and a trifle sore. Charlie watched the spot as he would a reptile that was lurking about to do his deadly work—and the mother was never again obliged to use the "Iodine."

This harrowing excerpt is not untypical of the state of educated and sophisticated thought at the turn of the century. If Freud is right, how exacerbated would Charlie's oedipal conflict have been! And, of course, one can find accounts in the same book concerning the evils of "self-abuse" in girls: a moralistic, punitive attitude concerning bowel training and a depriving, rigidly regulated approach to early feeding. It was on this scene that Freud arrived to preach the naturalness of pregenital sexual cravings and actions and the evils of excessive punitiveness and deprivation on the part of parents. Perhaps it is no wonder that his theory is so preoccupied with sexuality when the period in which he lived had so denied eroticism. But our time and Freud's time differ. Having learned the lessons Freud taught, we accept and act constructively toward pregenital and genital sexuality. Thus, Freud's emphasis on sexuality seems almost irrelevant to the most important concerns of contemporary life.

Freud's emphasis on sexuality seems so extreme that many personologists have contended that he used sex as nothing more than a metaphor for pleasure seeking. However, this interpretation clearly ignores Freud's intent, for he is very explicit about his emphasis on sexuality per se. After all, he chooses to distinguish the sexual instinct from other pleasure-oriented instincts, and he names all the developmental stages *psychosexual,* not psychopleasurable. One can also point to his having disbarred certain psychoanalysts from his inner circle because they watered down the literal sexual message of his theory, thereby rendering it more palatable to nonbelievers (Jones, 1955). Substituting pleasure seeking for literal sexuality may make Freud's formulations seem more modern, but it does not illuminate his real intent.

MURRAY'S POSITION ....

Like Freud, Henry A. Murray (born in New York City, 1893; died in Cambridge, MA, in 1988) lived a rich, complex, cosmopolitan life. Based in New York society, and trained at Harvard, he began his career as a physician. Throughout his early professional years as a physiologist and surgeon, Murray demonstrated a profound interest in mental considerations by conducting serious psychological studies of his colleagues and patients. Eventually his psychological interests, fired by the psychoanalyst Jung, the study of philosophy, and his own intense life, took hold of him. Having decided on a serious commitment to *personology*—a word that he coined —Murray was appointed director of the Harvard

Psychological Clinic by Morton Prince. The years he gave to this role, which ended with the advent of World War II, constituted an extremely active, exciting, and productive period in the life of the clinic. Much as Freud had done, Murray gathered together an extraordinary group of young and capable psychologists, who worked in close collaboration on the development of a theory of personality. But the source of evidence for this theory was not as much psychotherapy with disturbed people as systematic research on the lives of the articulate, gifted undergraduates at Harvard University. The aspects of Murray's theory stemming from this source relate to the periphery of personality. This theorizing has had a tremendous impact on personology, both directly through Murray and his colleagues, many of whom are extraordinary figures in the field, and indirectly through its effect on the testing movement.

The core considerations in Murray's theory, however, are distinctly psychoanalytic. While Murray headed the Harvard Psychological Clinic, he was being trained as a psychoanalyst (by members of Freud's inner circle) and finally became a charter member of the Boston Psychoanalytic Society. His work as a psychotherapist for disturbed people expressed the side of him that was a committed Freudian.

As you may have surmised, Murray's position is frustratingly heterogeneous. Though rich and fertile, his thinking is also disturbingly eclectic, so much so that it is difficult to know whether to classify his view as a conflict position. In those statements about the core of personality most relevant to such classification, Murray greatly resembles Freud. But there is a great deal more to Murray, whose heterogeneous theorizing reflects the nature of his life. In the early days of World War II, Murray established and directed the first extensive, systematic assessment unit for the Office of Strategic Services. For his work he was awarded the Legion of Merit in 1946. Over the years, Murray made a strong commitment to the study of literature, ranking as an expert on the work of Herman Melville. And, far from restricting himself to the biological emphasis of Freudianism, Murray studied anthropology and sociology for their relevance to the understanding of human beings. (For additional information on Murray's life as it relates to his theorizing, see Maddi and Costa [1972]).

Murray's Core Statement

For Murray (1938), Freud's conceptualization of the core tendency of life will do quite well: *The person tries to maximize instinctual gratification while minimizing punishment and guilt.* Like Freud, Murray talks in terms of the core characteristics of id, ego, and superego. Murray too considers the id to be the part of personality that contributes energy and direction for behavior. In short, the id summarizes the person's motivation. In discussing motivation more precisely, Murray uses Freud's language of the life and sexual instincts and gives an important place to considerations of psychosexual development. The superego is for him, as for Freud, a cultural implant, learned through the punishment and approval of parents, that functions to inhibit the socially destructive expression of instincts. So, on the one hand, instincts are self-interested in nature; on the other, social living requires some relinquishment of complete instinctual gratification. Society protects itself by punishing antisocial actions. Because punishment is painful, individuals avoid antisocial actions and the resulting social punishment or superego-induced guilt, thus maximizing instinctual gratification. In carrying out this core tendency, the ego mediates between the poles of the conflict by using the voluntary nervous system and musculature in planning, ordering, and defensive processes. In all this, Murray and Freud are in close agreement: Conflict is inevitable, and life must therefore be, at best, a compromise that minimizes the conflict or at least makes it bearable. For this reason, I have called Murray a *conflict theorist*.

Even so, Freud and Murray, in conceptualizing the core of personality, show differences in emphasis. In Murray's approach, all these differences decrease the inevitability of conflict. Murray believes that while the id certainly contains the familiar selfish instincts, it also includes other motivational tendencies, such as the needs for love and achievement, that are less clearly inconsistent with social living. These basic motivational tendencies are inherent rather than secondary motivations derived from the selfish instincts, as they would be for Freud. So the notion of replacing id with ego is still not likely to mean making unconscious things become conscious. Clearly the needs for love and achievement are not inconsistent with civilized living—indeed, they promote it. For Murray, then, people in their most natural state are not temperamentally incapable of communal living. Hence, Murray's view of the id, compared with Freud's, has moved further from a conflict position.

Turning to the superego, you will find that here, too, Murray has elaborated on and eclecticized Freud's view. For Murray, the superego is not only the taboos and sanctions instilled by parents when a child is at a tender, cognitively uncritical age, but also a sophisticated set of principles and ideals for living based on considerable personal experience with many contexts. Even great literature contributes to superego development, according to Murray. The superego grows in individuality and sophistication throughout life rather than remaining, as Freud contends, the unshakable vestige of early trials and tribulations. In Murray's view, superego does not necessarily oppose id; as the id is not completely selfish, neither does the superego completely serve the needs of others. So, in his treatment of superego, Murray's modifications of Freud decrease the inevitability of conflict in living.

While conflict and its minimization remain essential to understanding the core of personality in Murray's theory, he does include functioning that is not defined in terms of conflict. He has also elaborated the idea of ego beyond what Freud had in mind. In classical Freud, the role of the ego is limited to carrying out the core tendency of maximizing instinctual gratification while minimizing punishment and guilt. Going beyond this, Murray elaborates ego functions that relate to the expression of socially acceptable id tendencies (Murray & Kluckhohn, 1956,

p. 26). Whereas Freud stresses defensive operations as the substance of the ego and as the primary basis for resolving conflicts, Murray stresses cognitive and behavioral procedures for planning and executing behaviors in the absence of conflict. These procedures include such things as *rational thought* and *accurate perception* (Maddi, 1963; Maddi & Costa, 1972). Murray even goes so far as to assume, somewhat implicitly, that the ego has an inborn basis separate from that of the id (Maddi, 1963, p. 194). He does this by attributing ego functioning in part to the nervous system's natural requirement for information.

These modifications of Freud's thinking have a number of general effects worthy of note. For one, consciousness—true, accurate representation of experience in awareness—is not only logically possible but also extremely important in Murray's position. Each person is some conglomerate of consciousness and unconsciousness, the former expressing conflict-free aspects of personality and the latter defensive resolutions of conflict. Another departure from Freud is that for Murray motivational tendencies do not necessarily aim for tension reduction. Murray contends that the absence of tension is less rewarding than the process of getting from higher to lower states of tension (Murray & Kluckhohn, 1956, pp. 36–37). People may actually increase their tension to heighten their pleasure when tension is subsequently decreased. Once again, Murray is unwilling to accept the most extreme form of classical Freudian thinking.

Murray's View on Development

When one focuses on his modifications of Freud, Murray looks like some of the theorists discussed in the chapters on the fulfillment model. But in his core theorizing, Murray is still basically a conflict theorist. His treatment of development also follows Freud's lead rather closely, with modifications that do not remove the emphasis on conflict. Murray (1938) identifies what he calls *complexes,* groups of traits and styles that result from fixations at one or another of the Freudian stages of development. To be

sure, Murray does add to Freud's developmental formulation. For example, Murray describes the *claustral complex,* a group of traits characteristic of the intrauterine stage of life. He also identifies a *urethral stage,* which falls between the oral and anal stages. In sum, Murray's view of complexes as the result of fixations in psychosexual development suggests that he is in the conflict camp.

Though Murray postulates an aspect of ego functioning that is independent of the id and therefore potentially free of conflict, conflict and its minimization still remain the most basic considerations. Given his views on development and core, it may be best to consider Murray's position as a variant on the pure conflict theory.

Murray's Peripheral Statement

THE NEED. Murray's major peripheral characteristic is the *need.* Needs are motivational in nature; that is, they are tendencies to move toward goals. Unlike the Freudian instincts, which are also motivational in nature, needs are largely learned, and they involve goals and actions more concrete and close to everyday life than instincts do. Given this concrete quality of goal definition, it should not surprise you to know that Murray postulates a large number of needs. Murray has in mind such needs as those for affiliation, achievement, power, succorance, and play. Even when Murray mentions the need for sex, it is clear that he is referring to the narrow meaning that most people would endorse, namely, the attempt to achieve the goal of intercourse. Indeed, Murray's concept of needs is functionally closer to the Freudian concept of trait than to that of instinct. Because different needs may be represented in different people, need analysis is useful in pinpointing individuality.

Since needs stand at the same level of personality analysis as the Freudian traits do, we might expect Murray to provide a scheme whereby needs are organized into psychologically meaningful patterns, such as the Freudian character types. Sure enough, Murray does talk of the oral, anal, phallic, and genital types I have already discussed, adding to these the claustral and urethral types (Murray, 1938). The *claustral type,* or, as Murray prefers to call it, claustral complex, stems from fixation during intrauterine life and refers to a set of characteristics amounting to amorphousness and extreme passivity. The *urethral type,* or urethral complex, which is also discussed by some theorists more closely associated with Freud, involves fixation during the time when urinating actively and passively is a great source of pleasure (between oral and anal stages) and refers to competitiveness, ambition, self-worship, and feelings of omnipotence. But nowhere in Murray's writings is it clear that he intends to use the six complexes or types as categories for subsuming or classifying the various needs he has delineated.

RELATIONSHIP OF CORE TO PERIPHERY. As you will recall, Murray, being basically a psychoanalytic thinker, also uses the concepts of id, ego, and superego. These three aspects of personality exist in each person and, hence, should be considered part of the core of personality. But, as you will also recall, Murray has changed the meaning of all three concepts from that favored by Freud. Even more than in Freud, the contents of superego and ego may differ from person to person and thus are, for Murray, peripheral aspects of personality. Also, in contrast to Freud, Murray finds the id to vary in content from person to person. Rather than one unchanging set of instincts, the id is the repository of any and all motivations, presumably even needs. Hence, the id's contents are also peripheral aspects of personality. But if the contents of id, ego, and superego are peripheral, what are the characteristics of the core? Core characteristics become, for Murray, very abstract and contentless. They are people's incessant motivation and their equally incessant attempts to reach their goals within the restrictions of the environment and of their own values and principles.

These conclusions suggest that Murray's needs might be considered the content characteristics of the id, whereas, you will recall, Freudian traits are considered content characteristics of the ego. But needs are not innate, according to

Murray, and hence do not fit neatly into the definition of the id. Needs are too motivational in character to be considered the content of the superego. This leaves the ego, but the fit is no better here, because Murray assumes the ego to be constituted of an elaborate set of functions (Murray & Kluckhohn, 1956, p. 26). These functions are really abilities in the perceptual, apperceptive, intellectual, and affective realms of experience. To complicate matters even further, although his emphasis seems to imply that the ego is a set of abilities rather than the specific, learned, habitual styles of coping that constitute needs, Murray does suggest in true psychoanalytic fashion that the general system of learned needs may well be part of the ego (Murray & Kluckhohn, 1956, p. 31).

Elsewhere I have discussed these complications and ambiguities at greater length than is possible here (Maddi, 1963). For present purposes, it is enough to recognize that the question of the nature of the relationship between core and peripheral characteristics of personality is an important consideration in understanding a theory fully and that Murray never achieved a clear statement of his view of this relationship. A reasonable lead, which does not seem inconsistent with his general intent, would be to consider learned needs as personality units formed out of the interaction between the core tendency (of maximizing instinctual gratification while minimizing punishment and guilt) and the specific environmental contexts encountered in living. The learned needs would then exist as a more changeable, less central, though more immediately expressed layer of personality than the core. In such a scheme, id, ego, and superego would differ from needs and indeed would play, along with environmental contexts, a causal role in the development of needs. Adopting such a scheme would also be useful to more traditional psychoanalytic thinking, for the subsuming of traits into the ego is a dubious theoretical step given the otherwise consistent emphasis on the ego as a set of abilities or functions. The emphasis on ego as a set of functions is actually as strong in psychoanalytic thinking as it is in Murray, even though Murray does not see all these functions as defensive. If Freudians adopted this suggestion, character types would be considered a peripheral layer of personality that is more immediately expressed and more changeable than is the core level.

CLASSIFICATION OF NEEDS. Murray's major contribution to personology has been his taxonomy of needs and his extensive and continuing attempts to collect systematic empirical evidence bearing on it. Because he is quite rare in his emphasis on the careful delineation and study of peripheral characteristics, it is worthwhile to dwell longer on the concept of need and its measurement. According to Murray (1938), the need is

> a construct (a convenient fiction or hypothetical concept) which stands for a force ... in the brain region, a force which organizes perception, apperception, intellection, conation and action in such a way as to transform in a certain direction an existing, unsatisfying situation. A need is sometimes provoked directly by internal processes of a certain kind ... but, more frequently (when in a state of readiness) by the occurrence of one of a few commonly effective [pressure]. (pp. 123–124)*

Needs affect functioning by producing perceptions, interpretations, feelings, and actions that are equivalent in meaning or purpose. To diagnose a particular need, one must observe equivalences of meaning in a person's (1) initiating or reacting inner state, (2) perception of the external situation, (3) imagined goal or aim, (4) directionality of concomitant movements and words, and (5) produced effect, if any (Murray, 1954, pp. 456–463). Take as an example the need for affiliation. First, the inner state may be those specific cognitive and affective conditions best described as loneliness, which may be either initiating in that it exists regardless of the actual environmental circumstances or reacting in that it must be aroused by affiliatively depriving circumstances. Second, whether or not the circumstances actually are depriving, the person must perceive them as such. Third, the person must have as an imaginary goal a state of close and warm interaction with people. Fourth, his or her plans, activities, and statements about what to do ought to show a consistent direction leading to closer contact with people. Fifth, any effects that follow from the actions must be consistent with the goals and aims. When all these things are present, one can be sure that the person has a need for affiliation. In general, Murray does not perceive needs as steady states: they are aroused by real or imagined deprivation. When aroused, they exist as tension leading to instrumental behavior, which, if successful, brings about the goal. Experience of the goal brings satiation and a reduction in tension. A necessary concomitant of choosing the need construct as the basic peripheral characteristic is an emphasis on the waxing and waning of directional behaviors.

Over the years, Murray experimented with a number of apparently overlapping classifications of types and qualities of needs. But unlike the Freudian character types, Murray's classificatory schemes do not tie groups of needs together into consistent and recognizable kinds of people. Instead, Murray tries to provide schemes for understanding the various kinds of possible needs. One of his classifications takes into account the degree to which the person's aim in activity is intrinsic or extrinsic to the form of that activity. This leads to the distinction between activity needs and effect needs. *Activity needs,* or tendencies to "engage in a certain kind of activity for its own sake" (Murray, 1954, p. 445), are subdivided into *process needs,* involving action, for the sheer pleasure to be derived from the exercise of available capabilities; and *mode needs,* which are satisfied by the excellence of activity rather than its mere occurrence (Murray, 1954, p. 446). Significantly, Murray is one of the few personologists to make a concrete attempt to conceptualize activity that occurs for its own sake. In contrast, *effect needs* are marked by attempts to bring about a particular desired effect or goal extrinsic to the activity undertaken, which serves a purely instrumental purpose (Murray & Kluckhohn, 1956, p. 15).

---

*From *Explorations in Personality* by Henry A. Murray, copyright 1938, renewed 1966 by Henry A. Murray. Used by permission of Oxford University Press, Inc.

Another classificatory attempt seems to emphasize the origin of the need and, hence, the particular direction of activity that it imposes. In this attempt, viscerogenic, mental, and sociorelational needs are distinguished (Murray, 1954, pp. 445–452; Murray & Kluckhohn, 1956, pp. 13–21). The well-known *viscerogenic* needs (e.g., need for food) stem from tissue requirements and have very specific, easily recognizable goals. The *mental* needs are usually overlooked; they stem from the fact that "the human mind is inherently a transforming, creating, and representing organ; its function is to make symbols for things, to combine and recombine these symbols incessantly, and communicate the most interesting of these combinations in a variety of languages, discursive (referential, scientific) and expressive (emotive, artistic)" (Murray & Kluckhohn, 1956, p. 16). As the viscera have certain requirements, so does the mind, and both sets of requirements stem from human nature. Mental needs do not have very specific goals. *Sociorelational* needs arise from the social nature of humans (Murray, 1959, pp. 45–57) and include

TABLE 3-1   List of Needs for Murray

NEED	DEFINITION
■ Abasement	To submit passively to external force. To accept injury, blame, criticism, punishment. To surrender. To become resigned to fate. To admit inferiority, error, wrongdoing, or defeat. To confess and atone. To blame, belittle, or mutilate the self. To seek and enjoy pain, punishment, illness, and misfortune.
■ Achievement	To accomplish something difficult. To master, manipulate, or organize physical objects, human beings, or ideas. To do this as rapidly and as independently as possible. To overcome obstacles and attain a high standard. To excel oneself. To rival and surpass others. To increase self-regard by the successful exercise of talent.
■ Affiliation	To draw near and enjoyably cooperate or reciprocate with an allied other (another who resembles the subject or who likes the subject). To please and win affection of a cathected object. To adhere and remain loyal to a friend.
■ Aggression	To overcome opposition forcefully. To fight. To revenge an injury. To attack, injure, or kill another. To oppose forcefully or punish another.
■ Autonomy	To get free, shake off restraint, break out of confinement. To resist coercion and restriction. To avoid or quit activities prescribed by domineering authorities. To be independent and free to act according to impulse. To be unattached, irresponsible. To defy convention.
■ Counteraction	To master or make up for a failure by restriving. To obliterate a humiliation by resumed action. To overcome weaknesses, to repress fear. To efface a dishonor by action. To search for obstacles and difficulties to overcome. To maintain self-respect and pride on a high level.
■ Defendance	To defend the self against assault, criticism, and blame. To conceal or justify a misdeed, failure, or humiliation. To vindicate the ego.
■ Deference	To admire and support a superior. To praise, honor, or eulogize. To yield eagerly to the influence of an allied other. To emulate an exemplar. To conform to custom.
■ Dominance	To control one's human environment. To influence or direct the behavior of others by suggestion, seduction, persuasion, or command. To dissuade, restrain, or prohibit.
■ Exhibition	To make an impression. To be seen and heard. To excite, amaze, fascinate, entertain, shock, intrigue, amuse, or entice others.

such specific dispositions as the need for roleship —the need "to become and to remain an accepted and respected, differentiated and integrated part of a congenial, functioning group, the collective purposes of which are congruent with the individual's ideas" (Murray, 1954, pp. 451–452). As described, the need for roleship seems to imply particular learning produced by the individual's experiences in keeping with the ever present background of his or her inherent sociorelational nature.

If you think that Murray's idea of the core of personality is simpler and more psychoanalytic in flavor than the view of human nature implied in his need classifications, you are right. Murray seems to transcend the narrow, sexually oriented conflict model precisely when he turns to describing and organizing people's needs at the level of their everyday behavior. However, he never actually comes to terms with the implications of his departure from the Freudian model. This has led to the rather chaotic quality of Murray's writings when looked at from the viewpoint of formal personality theory. Assuming, in

TABLE 3-1 (continued)

NEED	DEFINITION
■ Harm avoidance	To avoid pain, physical injury, illness, and death. To escape from a dangerous situation. To take precautionary measures.
■ Infavoidance	To avoid humiliation. To quit embarrassing situations or to avoid conditions which may lead to belittlement: the scorn, derision, or indifference of others. To refrain from action because of the fear of failure.
■ Nurturance	To give sympathy and gratify the needs of a helpless object; an infant or any object that is weak, disabled, tired, inexperienced, infirm, defeated, humiliated, lonely, dejected, sick, mentally confused. To assist an object in danger. To feed, help, support, console, protect, comfort, nurse, heal.
■ Order	To put things in order. To achieve cleanliness, arrangement, organization, balance, neatness, tidiness, and precision.
■ Play	To act for "fun" without further purpose. To like to laugh and make jokes. To seek enjoyable relaxation of stress. To participate in games, sports, dancing, drinking parties, cards.
■ Rejection	To separate oneself from a negatively cathected object. To exclude, abandon, expel, or remain indifferent to an inferior object. To snub or jilt an object.
■ Sentience	To seek and enjoy sensuous impressions.
■ Sex	To form and further an erotic relationship. To have sexual intercourse.
■ Succorance	To have one's needs gratified by the sympathetic aid of an allied object. To be nursed, supported, sustained, surrounded, protected, loved, advised, guided, indulged, forgiven, consoled. To remain close to a devoted protector. To always have a supporter.
■ Understanding	To ask or answer general questions. To be interested in theory. To speculate, formulate, analyze, and generalize.

describing sociorelational needs, that human nature is inherently gregarious contradicts the Freudian conflict model. Yet nowhere does Murray discuss this complication. His is a mind in transition, resulting in theoretical writings that seem fragmentary though provocative and intriguing. You will see a similar problem in the so-called ego psychologists.

Another discussion of need classification (Murray, 1954, pp. 445–452) includes two additional types of needs that presumably cut across the mental, viscerogenic, and sociorelational categories and seem to emphasize approach and avoidance tendencies. These are *creative* needs, which aim at the construction of new and useful thoughts and objects, and *negative* needs, which aim at the avoidance or termination of noxious conditions. Finally, Murray's earliest and most famous taxonomy (Murray, 1938, pp. 152–226) distinguishes mental, viscerogenic, and sociogenic effect needs on the basis of his most fine-grained consideration of goals. These needs appear in Table 3-1, along with the distinctions among certain qualities that they may possess. Needs can be proactive or reactive, diffuse or focal, latent or overt, conscious or unconscious (Murray, 1938, pp. 111–115; 1954, pp. 447–450).

I have gone into this degree of detail concerning these various schemes to point out that Murray's writings yield a bewildering array of overlapping classifications of needs. It is difficult to come by any one authoritative classification, and Murray has not addressed the relationships among the available schemes in sufficient detail to make his thinking clear. While his shifting distinctions and the resulting ambiguities probably represent the difficulty of conceptualizing human complexities, they also stem from the extreme heterogeneity of functioning subsumed by the need concept. As you must have noted before in the example of need for affiliation, each need can be manifested in many internal and external ways—and Murray wishes to consider a great number of needs. So, it is not surprising that they overlap. Also, reasoning from behavioral observations to a great number and variety of needs, as Murray has done, precipitates a large and heterogeneous mass of assumed organismic requirements. No wonder that finding a basis for clarifying needs that will keep them reasonably distinct in theory and in practice is difficult! Given the inherent heterogeneity of his need concept, Murray may be attempting a fineness of distinction too great for classificatory neatness and clarity.

Such overrefinement of a basically heterogeneous concept could make for considerable difficulty in using or applying need analysis. If so, this difficulty would present a great problem in verifying the theory, as peripheral concepts of personality are the ones that should relate most clearly, immediately, and obviously to the behavior that constitutes data. Murray (1938) pioneered a massive attempt to find empirical evidence for the existence of his long list of needs. This research project involved many personologists in the intensive observation and testing of 50 college students. Murray and his collaborators provided detailed operational descriptions for each need. Even so, one is not reassured by these descriptions, for there seems to be too much overlap among the needs, and it is very difficult to make fine distinctions among them. This difficulty is bound to be compounded in the typical research situation, in which the investigator finds available only some rather than all of the possible manifestations of needs. It is understandable, then, that in this major attempt to employ Murray's list of needs, it was necessary to reach the diagnosis of particular needs by majority vote of a group of skilled investigators after considerable debate concerning their observations. This hardly bespeaks objectivity, and I would implicate the inherent heterogeneity of the need concept as the main culprit.

RELATED AND INTEGRATIVE CONCEPTS. Perhaps because of the need heterogeneity problem, Murray moves toward substituting the *value-vector* concept for the need (1954, pp. 463–464). The *vector principle* refers to the nature of the directionality shown by behavior (e.g., rejection, acquisition, construction); the *value principle* refers to the ideals that are important to people (e.g., knowledge, beauty, authority). A value-vector matrix is compiled in diagnosing what each person believes is worthwhile and the particular ways in which he or she moves to make those beliefs actualities. At this stage in its use, the value-vector system seems to involve less heterogeneity and fewer organismic assumptions than the need system does. The values and vectors listed are simple and few enough to permit agreement among investigators on their identification.

Until the value-vector system is further developed, the need concept must be considered the major peripheral characteristic in Murray's theory. The need is by its nature something that waxes and wanes, that is strong during deprivation and weak under satiating conditions. Thus, the concept is best suited to the explanation of behavior that also increases and decreases rather than remaining steady. But much of the person's behavior is steady and repetitive. In attempting to account for such behavior, Murray has

recourse to the concept of *need-integrate,* which refers to the stable habits and attitudes that develop out of the previous expression of needs (Murray, 1938, pp. 109–110). In its implied stability, the need-integrate is more analogous to the trait concept used by other theorists than to the need concept. Unfortunately, Murray neither considers the possible content of major need-integrates nor elaborates on the concept in other ways that would alert one to its intended use.

Murray also details the various environmental events, called *press,* that can, by occurring in childhood, influence the strength with which needs develop (Murray, 1938, pp. 291–292). A list of these press is shown in Table 3-2. Once a need has been learned, press may trigger the need, which exists as a predisposition for certain actions. But the pressure referred to in the press concept can be either objectively real or only

TABLE 3-2   Press (p) Relevant in Childhood

1. p Family insupport	4. p Retention, withholding objects
a. Cultural discord	5. p Rejection, unconcern and scorn
b. Family discord	6. p Rival, competing contemporary
c. Capricious discipline	7. p Birth of sibling
d. Parental separation	8. p Aggression
e. Absence of parent: father, mother	*a.* Maltreatment by elder male, elder female
f. Parental illness: father, mother	*b.* Maltreatment by contemporaries
g. Death of parent: father, mother	*c.* Quarrelsome contemporaries
h. Inferior parent: father, mother	9. p Dominance, coercion, and prohibition
i. Dissimilar parent: father, mother	*a.* Discipline
j. Poverty	*b.* Religious training
k. Unsettled home	10. p Nurturance, indulgence
2. p Danger or misfortune	11. p Succorance, demands for tenderness
a. Physical insupport, height	12, p Deference, praise, recognition
b. Water	13. p Affiliation, friendships
c. Aloneness, darkness	14. p Sex
d. Inclement weather, lightning	*a.* Exposure
e. Fire	*b.* Seduction: homosexual, heterosexual
f. Accident	*c.* Parental intercourse
g. Animal	15. p Deception or betrayal
3. p Lack or loss	16. p Inferiority
a. Of nourishment	*a.* Physical
b. Of possessions	*b.* Social
c. Of variety	*c.* Intellectual

SOURCE: From *Explorations in Personality* by Henry A. Murray, copyright 1938, renewed 1966 by Henry A. Murray. Used by permission of Oxford University Press, Inc.

subjectively perceived. The subjectively experienced pressure is called *beta press* and is to be distinguished from the objective pressure, or *alpha press* (Murray 1938, pp. 115–123).

These considerations have led Murray to posit an interactional unit, the *thema*, or combination of a need and a press, as basic for the personologist. But Murray is unclear as to whether the press component of the thema refers to individuals' own perceptions of the situational forces acting on them or to objective forces themselves. If the beta (subjective) press is intended, this suggests a belief on Murray's part that the internal factors governing people's perception must be accepted if behavior is to be understood. But it may well be the alpha (objective) press that is intended, because, as the need and need-integrate concepts already include certain influences on perception, the beta press would seem to be superfluous as a component of the thema. If the alpha press is intended, Murray seems to be calling for analysis and clarification of the objective demand characteristics of situations that force the person's behavior.

However intriguing the concepts of value-vector, need-integrate, and press may be, they are so unelaborated as to lead me to conclude that theorists must simply accept the need concept as the one they can work with and await future theoretical developments. In closing, I should point out that Murray has also suggested how needs may be related to one another, including discussion of the *unity-thema* (Murray, 1938, pp. 604–605), a need-press combination that is very pervasive because it is formed in early life. He also offers the concepts of *prepotency* (Murray, 1938, p. 452), which refers to the degree to which a need takes precedence over others when it is aroused, and *subsidiation* (Murray, 1938, pp. 86–88), which indicates that less potent needs can actually become instrumental to the satisfaction of more potent ones. To indicate that any particular behavior may express a number of needs at the same time, Murray offers the notion of *fusion* (1938, p. 86). Clearly toying with hierarchical organization of needs, Murray really has done little more in this regard than point the way toward future theorizing.

EGO PSYCHOLOGY ....

Core Considerations

Murray is certainly one of the first theorists of general psychoanalytic persuasion to embrace the possibility that some part of functioning, however small, might not be concerned with conflict and its minimization. This possibility has found its most characteristic expression in the writings of Hartmann, Kris, and Loewenstein (1947), who developed the notion of a *conflict-free ego sphere*. They argue that some of the ego's functions are carried out with energy not derived from the id. In other words, the ego has some functions that do not serve instinct gratification and the avoidance of pain. The authors go so far as to assume that the ego does not emerge out of the inborn id at all; rather, both ego and id originate in inherited predispositions and have independent sources of development. The part of the ego that does not deal with conflict has its own inborn source of energy with which to carry out its functions. This conflict-free portion of the ego also has different objectives than the id's, including such functions (much like those Murray has stressed) as rational thought processes, accurate perceptual processes, and muscular coordination, which the person uses to accomplish intellectual and social objectives that are not psychosexual in nature. Some writers, such as Hendrick (1943), have even assumed the existence of ego instincts, such as *to master*. The source of the mastery instinct is in the environmental challenge to function effectively, and its aim is to reduce the tension resulting from this challenge. Though somewhat different from Murray's idea of the need for information, which influences ego functioning, the mastery instinct similarly provides a logical theoretical justification for assuming an inborn ego.

The innate bases of ego autonomy are called *primary*, to distinguish them from *secondary* bases, which are rooted in experience. In an authoritative statement, Rapaport (1958) says:

> We no longer assume that the ego arises from the id, but rather that the ego and the id both arise by differentiation from a common undifferentiated

matrix, in which the apparatuses that differentiate into the ego's means of orientation, or reality-testing, and of action, are already present. These, termed *apparatuses of primary autonomy,* serve drive gratification and enter conflict as independent ego factors. They are the memory apparatus, the motor apparatus, the perceptual apparatuses, and the threshold apparatuses (including the drive- and affect-discharge thresholds). They are evolutionary givens which, by virtue of their long history of selection and modification, have become the primary guarantees of the organism's "fitting in" with (adaptedness to) its environment. In other words, the primary guarantees of the ego's autonomy from the id seem to be the very apparatuses which guarantee the organism's adaptedness to the environment.

The *apparatuses of secondary autonomy* arise either from instinctual modes and vicissitudes, as these become "estranged" from their instinctual sources, or from defensive structures formed in the process of conflict-solution, as these undergo a "change of function" and become apparatuses serving adaptation. In other words, the apparatuses of secondary autonomy are not "innate" but arise from "experience." Thus this secondary guarantee of ego autonomy also involves reality relations. While it is obvious that without relationships to a real external environment we would be solipsistic beings, a long detour was necessary before we could see clearly that the autonomy of the ego from the id—our safeguard against solipsism—is guaranteed by these innate and acquired apparatuses which keep us attuned to our environment.*

The "change of function" by which initially instinctual and defensive considerations become autonomous remains a mystery. Rapaport somehow links the process with adaptation to the demands of external reality. From these ambiguities and the emphasis on the necessity of guarantees, it would seem that ego autonomy is precarious at best.

The brand of psychoanalytic thinking represented by Rapaport and Hartmann is called *ego psychology.* Many of those who profess it trace their intellectual lineage directly to Freud or members of his inner circle. To many personolo-gists, ego psychology seems to improve on Freud's cramped view of life in a way that preserves his basic insights. Ego psychologists are fond of pointing out that Freud must have held a rudimentary form of their position because he spoke of the life instincts as ego-preservative (Freud, 1925c). Be this as it may, Freud overwhelmingly emphasizes the ego as derived from the id and as striking the conflict-induced compromise of reality principle functioning. Anyone who finds ego psychology a worthwhile elaboration of Freud's thinking must face the implications of assuming an inborn ego and a conflict-free ego sphere. No mere extension of Freud, ego psychology represents a radical break with psychoanalytic tradition.

It is surely a radical change in psychoanalytic theory to decide that not all but only some behavior is defensive and that not all but only some behavior expresses selfish instincts. Fixations and psychosexual stages no longer adequately describe development. The decrease in the overwhelming importance of the early years as developmental stages is particularly notable in the work of ego psychologist Erikson (1950). I will detail his view of development later; for now, note that he describes eight developmental stages covering personality changes throughout the whole life span. As you know, Freud considered fewer developmental stages and saw personality as relatively well set by puberty. To this, ego psychology adds a belief in the human capacity to be rational and logical in reaching decisions and solving problems. As you will see in Chapter 5, further modifications of psychoanalytic theory toward decreasing the pervasiveness and significance of conflict and defense result in what I have come to call the *fulfillment model.* Ego psychology presents a view of humanity that is considerably more optimistic than that offered by Freud: It takes a step toward affirming the possibility of fulfillment in human life.

Certainly Murray and the ego psychologists have radically changed psychoanalytic thought. And even though the changes may render that

---

*Reprinted with permission from the *Bulletin of the Menninger Clinic,* Vol. 22, pp. 16–17, copyright 1958 by the Menninger Foundation.

body of thinking more satisfying to contemporary personologists, they undoubtedly cloud some of the most appealing aspects of the classical Freudian approach. When the ego comprised only the mechanisms of defense with which conflict could be reduced, the id was still the only inherent aspect of personality. And the id, of course, could be justified on biological grounds. The sexual instinct in particular was tied to physiological processes, and the psychosexual stages of development were thought to follow the organism's biological development. But can one attribute clearly biological bases of the drives or instincts to the conflict-free portion of the ego? Further, if one also considers Murray's modifications of the id, whereby motivations other than the survival, sex, and death instincts are considered inherent to the person, the id loses virtually all its original meaning. Murray's usage reflects only the wish to preserve the name id, for in his way of thinking id and motivation in its most general sense are one and the same. Thus one should take the modifications of Freudian theory by Murray and the ego psychologists seriously, because they constitute a shift in thinking and are more than just logical extensions of Freud's theories.

As you can imagine, I am reticent to abstract any definite statement of a core tendency from the ego psychology literature, which is heterogeneous enough to border on amorphousness. Since ego psychologists see themselves as basically in the Freudian camp, they can be considered to share Freud's core tendency; however, they also postulate some instincts that are not irrevocably opposed to society.

Erikson on Development and the Periphery of Personality

The ego psychologist's position on the periphery of personality, though similar to Freud's, deviates from it in the direction of seeing life as a series of developmental stages that continue into adulthood. The position of ego psychology is most clearly seen in the theorizing of Eric H. Erikson (born in Frankfurt am Main, Germany, 1902; died in Hamwich, MA, in 1994). Because of his advantage over other psychoanalytic thinkers of

being more explicit than they, his representative status among ego psychologists, and his attention to adulthood, I choose to devote considerable attention to Erikson.

Erikson delineates eight stages of human development, each with a particular pattern of traits, or peripheral characteristics, associated with fixation at that stage. The first four stages are closely related to the Freudian oral, anal, phallic, and latency periods, though Erikson clearly is more interested in their psychosocial significance than in their biological nature. This emphasis permits him to include the latency period as significant for adult functioning even though this period does not have a strong biological justification. Then, instead of one genital period extending from puberty to death, Erikson delineates four more developmental stages that bear no relationship whatever to biological considerations of sexual instinct and libido. In Erikson, the Freudian emphasis on biological sexuality has been almost completely lost except for those psychosexual conflicts surrounding feeling, eliminating, and such. Erikson's position is a peculiar, though intriguing, conglomerate of Freud and something much more like a fulfillment position.

According to Erikson, the first ("oral") developmental stage involves the bases for trust or mistrust. In this stage, in which children are more helpless than they will ever be again, other people must nurture, protect, and reassure them. If these needs are filled, children will look on the world and their participation in it with a generally trustful attitude; if severely deprived, they will be distrustful. In later years, their trusting or distrusting will make an extraordinary difference in the nature of their lives. By basic trust and distrust, Erikson implies a group of traits similar to a character type, though not detailed specifically. In this lack of detailing—characteristic of all the trait groups deriving from his eight stages—Erikson unfortunately falls short in his theorizing about the periphery of personality. Not knowing clearly what to look for to determine trust or distrust in a person's character, one cannot easily proceed from Erikson's statements to the concrete behavior of people. In any event, he does provide interesting descriptions of the overall emphasis of his position, such as the following:

> The firm establishment of enduring patterns for the solution of the nuclear conflict of basic trust versus basic mistrust in mere existence is the first task of the ego, and thus first of all a task for maternal care. But let it be said here that the amount of trust derived from earliest infantile experience does not seem to depend on absolute quantities of food or demonstrations of love, but rather on the quality of the maternal relationship. Mothers, I think, create a sense of trust in their children by that kind of administration which in its quality combines sensitive care of the baby's individual needs and a firm sense of personal trustworthiness within the trusted framework of their culture's life style. This forms the basis in the child for a sense of being "all right," of being oneself, and of becoming what other people trust one will become. . . . Parents must not only have certain ways of guiding by prohibition and permission; they must also be able to represent to the child a deep, an almost somatic conviction that there is a meaning to what they are doing. (Erikson, 1950, pp. 221–222)*

In this vivid description of the ways in which parents help the child to progress through the first stage successfully to develop trust or else fail the child by precipitating a fixation and subsequent distrust, Erikson makes it clear how far he has shifted from Freud's original emphasis in the direction of psychosocial rather than biological forces. This quote emphasizes a loving mother-child relationship that transcends the physical in its deep, human meaningfulness.

Like Freud's oral period, Erikson's first stage of development lasts for roughly the first year of life. Then comes the second stage, which coincides with Freud's anal stage of the second year of life. Although Erikson (1950) clearly intends this coincidence, saying "Anal muscular maturation sets the stage for experimentation with two simultaneous sets of social modalities: holding on and letting go," he emphasizes again the social rather than biological implications of the

stage (p. 222). According to Erikson, successful passage through this second stage leads to later traits showing autonomy, whereas fixation leads to later expressions of shame and doubt. In explaining how this comes about, Erikson (1950) starts by asserting that his is still basically a conflict position:

> As is the case with all of these modalities, their basic conflicts can lead in the end to either hostile or benign expectations and attitudes. Thus to hold on can become a destructive and cruel retaining or restraining, and it can become a pattern of care: to have and to hold. To let go, too, can turn into an inimical letting loose of destructive forces, or it can become a relaxed "to let pass" and "to let be." (p. 222)

For Erikson, the crucial development of this second stage is the psychosocial ability to make a choice for oneself. The child can choose to hold on or let go, the bowel movement being a particularly vivid example of this, but no longer the basic definitive characteristic of the stage. Continuing, Erikson (1950) says,

> If denied the gradual and well-guided experience of the autonomy of free choice . . . the child will turn against himself all his urge to discriminate and to manipulate. He will overmanipulate himself, he will develop a precocious conscience. Instead of taking possession of things in order to test them by purposeful repetition, he will become obsessed by his own repetitiveness. By such obsessiveness, of course, he then learns to repossess the environment and to gain power by stubborn and minute control, where he could not find large-scale mutual regulation. (p. 222)

Here we see the similarity in character traits attributed by Erikson and Freud to the second stage of development.

Erikson then clarifies why he thinks this second stage leaves the person with either autonomy or shame and doubt. If the social environment encourages children to stand on their own feet, and also protects them against meaningless and arbitrary experiences of shame and doubt resulting from excessive, unthinking punishment for

---

attempts to exercise their own decision-making powers, the seeds of later autonomy will be sown. But when children encounter a lot of punishment, which can easily happen at a time when their fledgling decision-making powers are unreliable, the seeds of later attitudes of shame and doubt will be sown. Erikson thinks that shame is rage, felt at being punished for trying to be autonomous, turned inward against the self— it is not the punishers who are wrong, it is I, because I am inept and unworthy. This sense of shame goes hand in hand with self-doubt. Instead of learning to rely on a gradually maturing decision-making prowess, severely punished children doubt their own ability to function competently and independently. As adults, they are constantly in doubt, scurrying to hide themselves lest they feel shamed by the scrutiny of others.

Erikson's third stage, much like the Freudian phallic stage, roughly covers the years from age 3 through 5. True to his psychosocial emphasis, Erikson sees successful outcome of this third stage in traits expressing initiative and responsibility and unsuccessful outcome in guilty functioning. As Erikson (1959) states, to the inventory of basic social modalities, this stage of infantile genitality adds

> that of "making," first in the sense of "being on the make." There is no simpler, stronger word to match the social modalities previously enumerated. The word suggests pleasure in attack and conquest. In the boy, the emphasis remains on the phallic-intrusive modes; in the girl it turns to modes of "catching" in more aggressive forms of snatching and "bitchy" possessiveness, or in the milder form of making oneself attractive and endearing. The danger of this stage is a sense of guilt over the goals contemplated and the acts initiated in one's exuberant enjoyment of new locomotor and mental power; acts of aggressive manipulation and coercion which go far beyond the executive capacity of organism and mind and therefore call for an energetic halt on one's contemplated initiative. (pp. 224-225)

As in Freud, the natural object of children's initiative is the opposite-sex parent, whom they wish to capture and possess. Children, of course, must inevitably fail. If the child's parents have

loved and helped him or her enough, however, the child will learn by the failure to "turn from an exclusive, pregenital attachment to his parents to the slow process of becoming a parent, a carrier of tradition" (Erikson, 1959, p. 225). The basis for adult initiative and responsibility will have been achieved. But if the failure is exaggerated by unnecessary punitiveness, the child will experience considerable resignation and guilt, experiences that will form the basis in later life for acquiescence, feelings of unworthiness, and even irresponsibility.

Next comes Erikson's view of the latency stage, eventful in development even though somewhat devoid of special biological significance. Erikson's (1950) own words are particularly worth quoting here:

> Before the child, psychologically already a rudimentary parent, can become a biological parent, he must begin to be a worker and potential provider. With the oncoming latency period, the normally advanced child forgets, or rather sublimates the necessity to "make" people by direct attack or to become papa and mama in a hurry; he now learns to win recognition by producing things. He has mastered the ambulatory field and the organ modes. He has experienced a sense of finality regarding the fact that there is no workable future within the womb of his family, and thus becomes ready to apply himself to given skills and tasks, which go far beyond the mere playful expression of his organ modes or the pleasure in the function of his limbs. He develops industry— i.e., he adjusts himself to the inorganic laws of the tool world. He can become an eager and absorbed unit of a productive situation. To bring a productive situation to completion is an aim which gradually supersedes the whims and wishes of his autonomous organism.
>
> His danger, at this stage, lies in a sense of inadequacy and inferiority. If he despairs of his tools and skills or of his status among his tool partners . . . he abandons hope for the ability to identify early with others who apply themselves to the same general section of the tool world. (pp. 226–227)

According to Erikson, the successful completion of the latency stage leads to the traits expressing industry, whereas unsuccessful completion leads to the traits expressing inferiority.

In this discussion of the four stages thus far, you have seen much that is similar to Freud, though with far more emphasis on the stages' psychosocial significance. But Erikson breaks up the period of adulthood into several segments and gives them the status of real developmental stages, which he could not do without dropping Freud's heavy emphasis on the organism's anatomy and physiology. Many people initially favorable to Freudian thinking have broken away from it because of the short shrift it gives to adulthood. Murray was among these, because in explaining the reasons for the course his career took, he said that he found Freud good as far as he went but that he did not go far enough to fulfill the allegory, to record "the heroic adult and his tragic end" (Murray, 1959, p. 13). But Murray does not go so far as to advance the story of adult development himself. In contrast Erickson, in reserving four of his eight stages for the years following puberty, certainly tries to improve on Freud.

For Erikson, each new stage inherits the legacy of past stages. Weak points in character contributed by earlier fixations will influence—indeed, jeopardize—successful development in the current stage. You should keep in mind this characteristic of Erikson's theorizing, evident in his description of the latency period quoted earlier, when you consider the four remaining stages.

The fifth stage is that in which identity or role diffusion occurs. Successful development leads to the bases of a clear adult identity, whereas unsuccessful development leads to a scattered, fragmentary, diffuse, shifting sense of who one is. In Erikson's (1950) words,

> With the establishment of a good relationship to the world of skills and tools, and with the advent of sexual maturity, childhood proper comes to an end. Youth begins. But in puberty and adolescence all sameness and continuities relied on earlier are questioned again because of a rapidity of body growth which equals that of early childhood and because of the entirely new addition of physical genital maturity. The growing . . . youths . . . are now primarily concerned with what they appear to be in the eyes of others compared with what they feel they are, and with the question of how to connect the roles and skills cultivated earlier with the occupational prototypes of the day.

> The integration now taking place in the form of ego identity is more than the sum of the childhood identifications. It is the accrued experience of the ego's ability to integrate these identifications with the vicissitudes of the libido, with the aptitudes developed out of endowment, and with the opportunities offered in social roles. The sense of ego identity, then, is the accrued confidence that the inner sameness and continuity are matched by the sameness and continuity of one's meaning for others, as evidenced in the tangible promise of a "career." (pp. 227–228)

According to Erikson, the task of settling on an identity is so hard and so fraught with anxiety that youngsters often overidentify, for protection, with the heroes of cliques and crowds to the point of apparent loss of identity. Much of youthful "falling in love" also can be understood in this fashion. Such overidentifying is to be expected, but if the task of finding an identity is too fraught with conflict because of a lack of proper environmental support and understanding, the youngster may remain in this condition. When he or she is older, this identity problem will show up as role diffusion, or an inability to maintain a clear sense of who one is and what one wants.

In the sixth stage, which begins certainly by the time adolescence ends, society expects the person to leave parents and other more protective societal institutions, such as school, and begin to function as a mature and able adult. According to Erikson, in order to reap the rewards available during this stage, people must direct their functioning toward intimacy. Any inevitable conflict in this stage, which is so undominated by parents and pleasure principle functioning, is brought about by the tremendous difficulty in achieving intimacy in complex, impersonal societies. With this stage and subsequent ones, Erikson has, like other ego psychologists, transcended the pure conflict model, for the inevitability of conflict based on societal complexity seems quite questionable. In any event, should people fail to achieve intimacy, they will slip into isolation. As before, people approach this sixth stage with the legacy of earlier development. The more successfully they have traversed earlier developmental stages, the greater the likelihood that they will achieve intimacy.

Erikson's idea of intimacy is an elaboration of Freud's sage remark that one aspect of normalcy is the ability to love. Erikson (1950) lists the concrete capabilities that this implies as "(1) mutuality of orgasm, (2) with a loved partner, (3) of the other sex, (4) with whom one is able and willing to regulate the cycles of work, procreation, and recreation, (5) so as to secure for the offspring, too, a satisfactory development" (pp. 230–231). As you can see, the characteristic of achieving intimacy would be very similar to what other psychoanalytic thinkers describe in the genital character type. But to have the chance to achieve intimacy, people must offer themselves freely in situations that require minimal self-protection, situations such as sexual union and close friendship. If previous development has been unsuccessful, people may be unwilling to risk the pain attendant on momentary failures in the search for intimacy. In that case, they will shrink into a deep sense of isolation and consequent self-absorption.

As adulthood progresses, the seventh stage of development opens. The particular focus of this stage is generativity versus stagnation. Interestingly, Erikson (1950) calls this a nuclear conflict, although it is still not clear that the conflict is inevitable (p. 231). Be that as it may, what Erikson (1950) means by generativity is

> primarily the interest in establishing and guiding the next generation or whatever in a given case may become the absorbing object of a parental kind of responsibility. Where this enrichment fails, a regression from generativity to an obsessive need for pseudo intimacy, punctuated by moments of mutual repulsion, takes place, often with a pervading sense ... of individual stagnation and interpersonal impoverishment. (p. 231)

Though generativity and stagnation are included in the intimacy or isolation of the sixth stage, Erikson singles out this seventh stage because he feels that questions of generativity or stagnation

gradually became more important as adulthood progresses.

Though the final stage of development is not clearly associated with any particular time in the life span, one may presume it to begin around middle age or perhaps a bit later. It is the stage in which persons achieve ego integrity, if they have developed successfully, and despair, if unsuccessfully. Once again the most direct way to Erikson's meanings is through his own words (1950):

> Only he who in some way has taken care of things and people and has adapted himself to the triumphs and disappointments adherent to being, by necessity, the originator of others and the generator of things and ideas—only he may gradually grow the fruit of these seven stages. I know no better word for it than ego integrity. Lacking a clear definition, I shall point to a few constituents of this stage of mind. It is the ego's accrued assurance of its proclivity for order and meaning. It is a post-narcissistic love of the human ego—not of the self—as an experience which conveys some world order and spiritual sense, no matter how dearly paid for. It is the acceptance of one's one and only life cycle as something that had to be and that, by necessity, permitted of no substitutions: it thus means a new, a different love of one's parents. ... Although aware of the relativity of all the various life cycles which have given meaning to human striving, the possessor of integrity is ready to defend the dignity of his own life style against all physical and economic threats. For he knows that an individual life is the accidental coincidence of but one life cycle with but one segment of history; and that for him all human integrity stands or falls with the one style of integrity of which he partakes. ... Before this final solution, death loses its sting.
>
> The lack or loss of this accrued ego integration is signified by fear of death; the one and only life cycle is not accepted as the ultimate of life. Despair expresses the feeling that the time is short, too short for the attempt to start another life and to try out alternate roads to integrity. Disgust hides despair. (pp. 231–232)

Although his precise meaning is perhaps a little obscured by the dramatic intent of his writing, Erikson does provide some basis for an understanding of the traits or peripheral characteristics of people with integrity or despair. In this final stage you can clearly see a definite shift in the person's concerns from what will happen in the future to what has already happened.

This closes the discussion of Erickson's eight stages of development. To have theorized about them is to have taken on a formidable task, as you must realize by now. Certainly Erikson's figurativeness and ambiguities must be regarded in the light of the enormity of the task. And actually, we can piece together a fairly clear typology of character. We have the person of integrity, who has such characteristics as an overall sense of what his or her life is about, who accepts that life, who does not fear death, and who is not typically in despair. These are all characteristics that could be measured, though Erikson comes nowhere near providing us with precise definitions of them. Such a person would also show the characteristics of successful development through the previous seven stages. The person who has failed to achieve integrity would show the characteristics of one or more developmental failures in the previous stages.

Continuing down the scale of development, we could say that the person who has achieved generativity shows a strong interest in public affairs, especially as they have influenced the future of the world, and a strong commitment to rearing children. If the person showed these kinds of characteristics but was too young for the stage of integrity versus despair, we would expect to find additional characteristics associated with successful development at earlier stages. But if the person was old enough for the eighth stage, he or she would show, in addition to generativity, either integrity or despair. If despair, we would expect, along with generativity, some attributes of developmental failure at earlier stages; if integrity, we would probably see only the attributes of earlier developmental success. To complete this scheme, if the person showed the opposite of generativity—stagnation—we would expect additional attributes signifying earlier developmental failures. When the person reached the age of the eighth stage of development, despair would be more likely than integrity.

It is probably not necessary for me to take this typology further. You can see by now that Erikson's position permits some reasonably clear statements to be made about the characteristics one can find in people as a result of their developmental past. Indeed, you should also be able to see that one can relate the various types of peripheral personality patterns to each other in the sense that one can predict—on knowing, say, that someone has achieved generativity—the nature of his or her future and past development. This is a sign that the various character types are integrated into Erikson's theory rather than simply representing descriptions of his observations of people. Though his position has an unfinished quality, with many loose ends, it is certainly a brave beginning.

THE OBJECT-RELATIONS POSITION ....

Psychoanalytic theory refers to people other than oneself as *objects*. This oddly impersonal usage is understandable in Freud, who regarded interpersonal relations in the early years as somewhat predetermined by instinctual demands and by the inevitable conflict between children and parents. Also, he regarded the interpersonal relations of adult years as transference phenomena, shadowy reflections of earlier unresolved conflicts. Originally, Freud believed that the only reason other people can become at all important is that instinctual energy—libido—is projected outward by a gratification-hungry id onto whoever can facilitate that gratification. This process is supposed to happen unconsciously, and any ensuing love or regard for objects amounts to a narcissism, or self-love, called *primary* or *basic* (Freud, 1927). Thus, although Freud talked a great deal about interpersonal relations, his theory rendered people other than oneself as surprisingly uninfluential except as stereotypic objects of one's instincts.

Object-relations theory grew as a corrective attempt to invest interpersonal relations with a more significant role in personality development. Its general message is that the value of others and the course and effect of interactions with them are not a programmed, automatic outcome of instinctual considerations. Personality can be shaped in many different directions, depending on the specifics of interpersonal encounters.

The early work on object relations was done by Klein (1948) and the founders of ego psychology, notably Hartmann. But this movement has never been a tightly unified enterprise. Modell (1975), for example, is the most conciliatory toward instinct theory, arguing that Freud (1927) had the kernels of object-relations theory in his views of *secondary narcissism,* a process whereby the ego identifies with the objects originally invested with value (cathected) by the id in order to be loved itself. Fairbairn (1954), on the other hand, calls for a radical break with Freud. Kernberg (1976), Mahler (1963), and Bowlby (1969) are somewhere in the middle.

Core Considerations

Nothing in object-relations theory is concrete and uncontroversial enough to serve as a core statement. But if there were, it would probably emphasize the *tendency to develop a self.* The self is regarded as a composite of units, each an image deriving from significant interpersonal relations. Some units concern *self-image* (what you think of and expect from yourself), others *object images* (what you think of and expect from other people), and still others *affect dispositions* (tendencies toward emotional states that reflect how you felt during interpersonal relations). For Kernberg (1976), the driving force behind interpersonal relations is still instinctual energy, or *libido,* and hence self-development occurs parallel to the character development based on psychosexual stages discussed by Freud. Thus, self units influence the content of ego and superego. But for Fairbairn (1954), instincts have receded into the background, because "libido is a function of the ego and the ego is fundamentally object seeking." Object-relations theory can still be classified as a variant on the psychosocial conflict model, because Kernberg's position is the most common of theorists of this stripe. But if Fairbairn's thinking were to prevail, one would be dealing with an outright fulfillment position.

Developmental Considerations

There is perhaps more agreement among these theorists on the developmental stages of the self than on core considerations (Mahler, 1963). The first stage is one of normal *autism,* a primary undifferentiated state covering the first few weeks of life. During this time, the infant is shut off from true interaction with others, relying instead on internal, almost hallucinatory wish fulfillments. If the infant's needs are nonetheless filled by its parents and development is hence ideal, autism gives way to a normal state of *symbiosis,* in which there is confusion of self and object in the child's mind because neither is perceived as independent of the other. Although the child is beginning to recognize others, he or she does not yet clearly discriminate them from the self. But slowly, the child comes to discriminate pleasurable and painful qualities of experience involving others. This symbiotic stage lasts 2 to 7 months, after which it gives way to a *differentiation* stage, in which self and object are separated with increasing clarity. During this time, children not only differentiate the various qualities of interaction with others in their lives, they also begin to recognize the differences between themselves and these others. As part of this process, children symbolize in their memories the characteristics of pleasurable (good) and painful (bad) interactions with others. What is best developmentally in this stage is for parents to offer supportive and pleasurable interaction, while at the same time not reacting with pained rejection or other punishment to signs of independence in their children. Under continuing ideal development, the differentiation stage shifts at about 2 years of age into an *integration* or *rapprochement* stage, in which the self- and object representations, perceived as independent, are fit into relationship with each other. This becomes the prototype for mature relationships, in which positive but also negative emotions can be expressed openly and there can be commitment that does not jeopardize personal identity. If all goes well, the child should enter the oedipal conflict with stable differentiated and integrated self- and object representations, all of which get consolidated, through dealing with that conflict, into the adult ego and superego.

The task of development is not only differentiation and integration but also the emergence of a sense of identity. In the earliest stage, infantile dependence (Fairbairn, 1954), the child vacillates between ways of thinking and being, expressing first one self unit and then another. This instability is characteristic of the phenomenon of *splitting* (Kernberg, 1976), a defensive attempt to deal with being overwhelmed by more potent adults by playing them off against each other. The next, or transitional, stage in identity development (Fairbairn, 1954), initially involves *introjection,* literal incorporation of objects into the mind. Later in development comes the less primitive process of *identification,* in which objects have influence but need not be "swallowed whole." Through the gradual increase in identifications, the stable differentiations and integrations that mark mature identity begin. They are fully developed in the final stage, mature dependency (Fairbairn, 1954), which involves lifelong interdependence between interacting people. It is unclear just how much reliance object-relations theorists wish to place on defensiveness in the developmental process. Splitting is clearly a defense, which, like all others, distorts reality. Introjection and identification are also considered defenses by Freudians, and the object-relations theorists do not clearly contradict this usage. Indeed, Kernberg (1976) suggests that, for development to be sound, the splitting defense characteristic of earliest mental life must be replaced by the more mature defense of repression. For all their emphasis on how interpersonal relations can influence persons in myriad ways, object-relations theorists are not quite ready to say that ideal functioning is devoid of defenses, suggesting that they are still best classified as psychosocial conflict theorists.

Considerations on the Periphery of Personality

The object-relations position does not as yet include a catalogue of types or styles of adult living. Ideal functioning, however, clearly involves deep and stable relations with others, tolerance of ambivalence toward loved objects, the capacity to tolerate guilt and separateness and to work through depression, an integrated self-concept, and correspondence between behavior patterns and self-concept (Kernberg, 1976). These positive attributes are most likely to occur when the interpersonal relations between children and their parents are characterized by love, support, and respect, without parental overindulgence. It is unclear to what degree mature self-identity is considered defensive, as various object-relations theorists stand on different sides of this question.

Object-relations theorists also specify pathologies of self development that qualify as nonideal personality types. Three levels of pathology in self-identity are discussed. At the lowest pathological level is a well-integrated but severe and punitive superego, a well-integrated ego, and overly inhibitory or phobic character defenses sometimes coupled with reaction formations. At this level, social adaptation is not severely impaired, so that fairly deep, stable relations with others can develop. Guilt and mourning are also possible. Much of what Freudians consider to be anal and phallic character types, plus their associated neuroses, would fit into this level of psychopathology.

The next level of self-identity pathology involves an even more punitive superego and a less integrated ego. Social adaptation is still fairly adequate, though the operation of more primitive defenses of an oral nature and a tendency toward splitting (emotional and behavioral instability) are present. In this category would fit what the Freudians regard as oral, passive-aggressive, and narcissistic character types.

The highest level of self-identity pathology involves considerable disintegration of ego and superego and socially maladaptive, ineffective behavior. Because superego integration is minimal, criminality and other forms of social deviance are common. Accompanying this is the relative inability to experience guilt. Reliance on the extremely primitive defense of splitting lends a chaotic, disintegrated quality to behavior. In Freudian terms, this level includes the borderline and frankly psychotic states.

BEYOND EGO PSYCHOLOGY: NARCISSISM AND TRANSACTIONAL ANALYSIS . . . . .

Two other theoretical developments within the psychoanalytic movement may go beyond even the transformations brought about by ego psychology: the *self-psychology* of Heinz Kohut (1971, 1977) and the *transactional analysis* of Eric Berne (1964). Originally psychoanalysts, both personologists assert that their positions mitigate the conflict emphasis of Freud without being incompatible with it. But they make very different assumptions from those of their great ancestor.

Core and Development in Kohut's Theorizing

It is difficult to specify a core tendency, or life purpose, for Kohut's position, because it has been devoted almost completely to conceptualizing psychopathological states. Nonetheless, the statements about pathology imply some ideas relevant to an understanding of human nature and ideal development. Kohut assumes that people are characterized from birth not only by the Freudian tendency to maximize instinctual gratification while minimizing punishment and guilt but also by the tendency to *enhance and order functioning through the experience of self.* The well-developed self has a consciously appreciated sense of who and what one is that lends meaning and direction to behavior.

Although not present at birth, the self begins to form in earliest childhood as the result of the expression of two core characteristics and parental reactions to them. The core characteristics, considered as basic as the Freudian instincts, are the *need to be mirrored* and the *need to idealize.* The first need refers to children's wishes to have their expressions and products recognized, approved of, and admired. The most important mirroring person in children's lives is their mother. Children also need to idealize and hence identify with others more

capable than themselves. The most important figure for idealization is the father. The mirroring and idealizing needs underlie later *ambitions* and *goals,* respectively.

When the mother mirrors her child, and the father permits himself to be idealized, the developmental condition necessary for vigorous selfhood is present. In this condition, a *nuclear* self will emerge, probably during the second year of life. This nuclear self is defined as *bipolar,* including archaic nuclear ambitions (deriving from having been mirrored) and archaic nuclear goals (deriving from having idealized). Kohut describes a "tension arc" between these two poles that stimulates the expression (and hence development) of the child's rudimentary skills and talents. In this fashion, a good beginning has been made toward a productive and creative maturity, characterized by a stable and secure sense of self that integrates and renders coherent the various facets of life experience.

But if the mother fails to mirror generously or the father removes himself as an object of idealization, the child's self-development will be damaged. The child may grow to adulthood feeling inadequate and apathetic. Also, talents and skills will be insufficiently developed. These immaturities are depicted as *narcissistic personality or behavior disorders.* Kohut believes that schizophrenia and borderline psychotic states also indicate faulty self-development.

Because Kohut's theorizing seems very far from Freud's, it raises the question of the relationship between the two. The psychosexual conflicts of traditional Freudian theory do take place, according to Kohut, but so does selfdevelopment. At the oral, anal, phallic, and latency stages of psychosexual development, a drama is enacted by expression of mirroring and idealizing needs and parental reactions to them. Kohut believes that at each stage the child must receive the optimal blend of sexual gratification and frustration if fixation and developmental problems are to be avoided. But this optimal blend must also include sufficient opportunities for mirroring and idealization, or development can also be jeopardized.

In most of his statements, Kohut appears to fit into ego psychology. He accepts the Freudian emphasis on inevitable conflicts between individual and society, child and parents, and id and superego. But he regards the equally important self-development as separate from the instincts and, if development has been good, potentially free of conflicts or defensive operations. Looked at this way, Kohut's position has something of the same internal implausibility of other ego psychologies: How can a person be at the same time in constant, inevitable conflict and conflict free?

Sometimes Kohut seems to resolve this difficulty by pushing Freudian assumptions even further into the background and moving still closer to a fulfillment (rather than conflict) mode of theorizing. For example, Kohut (1977) suggests that (1) the nuclear self is reasonably well formed *before* the supposedly all-important oedipal situation occurs; (2) the conflict and pain of the oedipal situation may be not inevitable but the result of having an insufficiently developed self with which to interact with parents; and (3) present-day society breeds disorders of the self more than the neuroses emphasized by Freud. However careful to credit Freud, Kohut may be leaving behind ego psychology and the conflict model.

Kohut on the Periphery of Personality

Kohut (1971) has offered a typology that deviates considerably from the Freudian view. To be sure, the definitions and descriptions are less precise than I would like, but they do give a flavor of things to come at this early stage of psychoanalytic self-theorizing.

The ideal type is the autonomous self, characterized by self-esteem and self-confidence. Because of this security, the person is not excessively dependent on others or a mere replica of the parents. Developmentally, the ideal situation is for the child to have its core needs—to be mirrored and to idealize—satisfied in interaction with the parents. It is less important how the parents resolve to interact than what they are—

in other words, they affect their child as models. If the parents are at peace with their own needs to shine and succeed, their child's exhibitionism will be accepted and responded to. Parental tranquility and pride of accomplishment will calm the child and encourage the development of his or her own goals. But true to his Freudian beginnings, Kohut believes that there must be some frustration, otherwise the child may become passive, complacent, and a mere shadow of his or her parents. He argues that even the best parents are sometimes too preoccupied to mirror and encourage idealization well but that these minor and transitory ruptures in the parent-child relationship will stimulate the child to develop a sense of self and strive for autonomy.

When the child does not have his or her mirroring and idealizing needs well satisfied, one or another of the nonideal personality types will result: narcissistic personality disorders or narcissistic behavior disorders. In Kohut's usage, *personality* refers to generalized attitudes, ways of thinking, or cognitive styles, whereas *behavior* refers to actions of a habitual nature. *Disorders* apparently include not only frankly psychopathological states but also states within the normal range that, though deviations from the ideal, are livable and common.

Grouped as narcissistic personality disorders are the understimulated self, the fragmented self, the overstimulated self, and the overburdened self. Individuals showing the understimulated self lack vitality, experience themselves as boring and apathetic, and express themselves that way to others. The understimulated self results from parents' prolonged lack of responsiveness toward their child. People who have been thus understimulated will do anything to create excitement to ward off the feeling of deadness that would otherwise overtake them. In childhood, such attempts to create excitement include head banging and compulsive masturbation. In adolescence, one observes daredevil activities. In adulthood, there is likely to be promiscuity and perversion in the sexual sphere and gambling, substance abuse, and hypersociability in the nonsexual sphere.

People with the fragmented self are extremely vulnerable to setbacks or reversals, responding with a sharp decrease in self-esteem, disorganization, and an anxious loss of a sense of continuity of the self in time and space. This fragmentation may even be observed in modes of dress and gait. Kohut describes this type as a result of the same deprivation of parental responsiveness to the child as in the case of the understimulated self. Perhaps he intends some shade of difference in the developmental formulation, for it would seem logical that fragmentation would stem from erratic parental responsiveness rather than a more general lack of response.

People with an overstimulated self are subject to being flooded by unrealistic fantasies of greatness that produce tension and anxiety; hence, they will try to avoid situations in which they could become the center of attention. They will often shy away from creative activities because they fear destruction by losing their sense of autonomy. According to Kohut, the developmental problem leading to the overstimulated self is excessive responsiveness of the parents through an overindulgence of the child's mirroring and idealizing needs. Thus, the child grows into adulthood with a grandiosity that is uncontrollable and frightening.

Similarly, the overburdened self involves perceptions of the external world as hostile and reactions to insignificant stimuli as attacks or frustrations. This attitude of irritability and suspicion flares up in response to specific slights and disappears quickly when the offense has passed. The developmental difficulty in this case is a frustration of the idealizing need more than of the mirroring need. In short, the child has not been provided with the opportunity to identify with the calmness of an apparently omnipotent parent, presumably because this parent is uncomfortable in the realm of accomplishment. Thus, the child has to do too much for himself or herself to set goals and grows into an easily overburdened adulthood.

While the narcissistic personality disorders, just mentioned, stress thought patterns that are only sometimes expressed clearly in action, the narcissistic behavior disorders, considered next, can be seen primarily in actions. They are the mirror-hungry personality, the ideal-hungry personality, and the alter-ego-hungry personality. The mirror-hungry personality is famished for admiration and appreciation, feeling an inner sense of worthlessness deriving from parental frustration of the need to be admired and appreciated. Consequently, the mirror-hungry personality leads people to display themselves incessantly. Such people generally flit from relationship to relationship and performance to performance, in an insatiable attempt to get attention.

Those with the ideal-hungry personality forever search for others whom they can admire for their prestige, power, beauty, intelligence, or moral stature. They feel worthwhile only as long as they can look up to someone because in childhood they were frustrated in the area of the idealizing need. As adults, their craving cannot really be satisfied, stemming as it does from early frustrations, and sooner or later each person they admire comes to appear less than perfect. So the search for someone to idealize continues.

People with the alter-ego-hungry personality can experience a sense of self as real and acceptable only when they relate to others who slavishly conform to their opinions, values, and ways. The developmental lack in this case is presumably due to the frustration of both mirroring and idealizing needs. Once again the void cannot be filled: the alter-ego-hungry person discovers that the other is not himself or herself and consequently feels estranged. This sort of person commonly engages in a restless search for one alter ego after another.

For Kohut, all the types discussed to this point fall within the normal range. They don't differ in degree of childhood frustration of self-needs (to be mirrored and to idealize)—all have had too much frustration of ideal self-development. Kohut considers their differences in content as the result of particular patterns of early frustration, though he does not clearly and precisely delineate these patterns. He does mention some types he regards as frankly pathological, suggesting that they result from self-need frustrations that are more intense and complete than those I have already discussed. Because these pathological types are beyond the scope of this book, I will only mention them: the merger-hungry personality (in whom other people literally function as the self-structure that is absent), the contact-shunning personality (who must avoid others because the need for them is so intense), and various borderline and schizophrenic states that Kohut suggests are better understood in terms of "self-psychology" than traditional psychoanalytic theorizing.

According to Kohut (1977), self disorders cannot be treated by traditional psychoanalytic therapy, in which the therapist alternates between being a "blank screen" and making telling interpretations. Such therapy is successful only when the client can project emotions felt for others onto the therapist in the process called transference. But people with self disorders cannot project emotions consistently because they are too personally preoccupied, even when they seem to be relating to others, and hence must be approached differently. They must be mirrored (appreciated, respected) and permitted to idealize the therapist (hence, the therapist must let himself or herself be known rather than remain shadowy) in the hope that by filling the void they experienced in childhood, sound self-development will be stimulated. Kohut's therapy seems a combination of the Rogerian emphasis on unconditional positive regard (mirroring) and the existential emphasis on providing the client with models (idealizing) (see Chapter 5). As such, a great break with psychoanalytic techniques has occurred.

Core Considerations in Berne's Theorizing

Eric Berne (1964), in formulating *transactional analysis,* a type of psychotherapy, may also be leaving ego psychology behind. A Freudian psychoanalyst by training, Berne begins by emphasizing what he calls *structural analysis,* which

assumes that in each person there are three ego (or mental) states: the Child, the Parent, and the Adult. The *Child* state involves an unsocialized appreciation and expression of physiological processes. The *Parent* state is an internalized representation of taboos and sanctions learned through interaction with one's parents. The *Adult* state emphasizes rational, unevaluative, problem-solving thought. Given all this, it is mystifying to find that Berne disavows the obvious parallel between his three ego states and the Freudian id, superego, and ego. He has two grounds for this disavowal. One is that Child, Adult, and Parent states are phenomenological, or readily apparent in personal experience, whereas id, ego, and superego are merely "theoretical constructs." Needless to say, Freudians would not agree with this portrayal of their approach as abstract. The second ground for disavowal is that transactional analysis supposedly makes little use of the concept of the unconscious. But Berne does speak of *exclusion,* which indicates the denial and inhibition of entire ego states, and *contamination,* or the intermixing of two ego states without awareness of what has happened. Exclusion is too close to repression or denial and unconsciousness to be entirely convincing. But because Berne deemphasizes this concept, transactional analysis appears to be much like other ego psychologies.

In the course of their psychotherapeutic work, Berne and his followers have moved further and further away from their Freudian roots. Although they still practice structural analysis of the Child, Adult, and Parent in people, much additional elaboration has taken place. At the core level, they assume that there are not only biological survival drives but also (even more important) psychological needs called *stroke hunger, structure hunger, excitement hunger, recognition hunger,* and *leadership hunger. Stroke hunger* basically involves a soothing sort of physical contact, though in adulthood many people get by with pale shadows of contact, such as simple attention. *Structure hunger* is evidenced when people invest their lives with meaning; it refers specifically to the activities selected to fill up the time. *Excitement hunger* is the wish not to be bored. *Recognition* and *leadership hunger* describe the person's basic need for social approval and influence, respectively. These drives and needs are core characteristics; that is, unlearned goals present in all human beings. Although Berne does not explicitly state a core tendency, he implies that *persons strive for socially satisfying and meaningful lives.* Something resembling the Freudian instincts and their gratification still exists, but it increasingly takes a back seat, with social and psychological matters gaining greater emphasis. Berne's discussions of these latter issues hardly assume necessary, inevitable conflict. As transactional analysis evolves, it becomes less of a conflict theory and more of a fulfillment theory.

Berne on the Periphery of Personality

The rest of Berne's position concerns the periphery of personality, or that which helps one understand individual differences. Out of the interaction with his or her parents and the broader society, the child develops a *life script,* or plan that organizes energies and directions. Associated with this is a *life position,* or set of learned assumptions people make about whether they and others with whom they interact are acceptable, or "OK." From this emphasis on whether "I'm OK and you're OK" develop other aspects of lifestyle useful in understanding characteristic patterns of interaction. These patterns are governed by the games that people play. These games involve *Gimmicks, Discounting,* and *Rackets,* all learned techniques with which people attempt to reach the goals of their life scripts. Although transactional analysis shares with the Freudian approach a propensity to ferret out the "basest" aspects of human nature—as you can perhaps tell from the concepts it employs—those same concepts show just how far the position has departed from its Freudian origin.

Although Berne's (1964) theorizing is concerned primarily with understanding constructive and destructive aspects of social interaction, types emerge in the explication of these many implicit and explicit assumptions about personality. Because the writings of transactional analysts represent a conglomerate of views, with no definitive personality typology, the best I can do is indicate some of the conceptual features presumably present in all types regardless of their content and give you some examples of particular types that have been delineated.

Early experience is important in that it leads to the development of a life script, or a plan (typically not conscious) that organizes energies and directions. As such, the life script qualifies as a personality type. It is learned not only out of direct interaction with parents but through other cultural influences (e.g., fairy tales, movie heroes). All life scripts include a life position, which comprises learned assumptions about the acceptability of self and others. There are four basic life positions: "I'm OK and you're OK," "I'm OK and you're not OK," "I'm not OK but you're OK," and "Neither you nor I are OK." The particular life position a person learns and the specific content contributed by the life script combine to make certain games likely for him or her.

Games are "a series of ulterior transactions leading progressively to a well-defined climax; a set of operations with a gimmick" (Berne, 1964). As such, a Gimmick is an unexpected twist. This interactional characteristic and others, such as Discounting (a procedure of persuading others that they are not OK) and Rackets (chronic emotions used manipulatively, such as anger or guilt), are learned techniques whereby people attempt to reach the goals of their life scripts. Both games and life scripts involve various configurations of the three ego states (Child, Adult, Parent) present in all people. Thus, one life script (and the games to which it leads) may have Parent predominating and Child suppressed, and so forth.

In transactional analysis, the life scripts, or personality types, merge with the games people play. For example, the Alcoholic is talked about both as a life script and as a part in a game. Similarly, the Rescuer and the Dummy, who are usually found playing the Alcoholic game along with the Alcoholic, are also life scripts. Other life scripts and associated games described include Debtor, Kick Me, Frigid Woman, Cavalier, Homely Sage, and Look How Hard I've Tried. Various suggestions have been made for classifying these life scripts, such as Get-On-With-It and Get-Nowhere-With-It scripts.

By and large, the scripts and games have the ring of obvious, recognizable foibles and in that sense need little further description here. In addition, there is just too much flux in transactional analysis to justify much more detailing. It should be noted, however, that Berne's therapy also constitutes a break with traditional psychoanalysis. The therapy is done in groups, both large or small, and takes the form of disclosure by the therapist through direct confrontation of the games engaged in by the group members. Then, of course, the group members also are free to comment on the manipulative attempts they employ on one another. In that it has some concern for understanding unconscious phenomena, transactional analysis somewhat resembles psychoanalysis. However, its techniques and goals are far more similar to those of Gestalt psychotherapy and other so-called confrontation approaches.

CONCLUDING REMARKS ....

You have come a long way in considering the psychosocial conflict approach to understanding human behavior. No doubt, the clearest and most complete expression of this approach is in the work of Freud. There you see the full effect of the underlying assumption of two antagonistic forces, one lodged in the individual and the other in society, on theorizing about core, developmental, and peripheral considerations. In this approach, the best one can accomplish in living is a compromise in which the truly selfish nature of the individual is lost from consciousness and behavior is adapted to what will gain satisfaction without bringing punishment and guilt with it.

To a greater or lesser degree, the other theorists covered in this chapter have deviated from a strong form of the psychosocial conflict position. Although all were initially highly influenced by Freud, they grew away from his extreme thinking. Consequently, their positions are a little hard to classify. There is still much of the psychosocial conflict position in their thinking, but there is also something of the fulfillment model (see Chapters 5 and 6).

THE CONFLICT MODEL: INTRAPSYCHIC VERSION

Thus far, I have discussed theories that exemplify the psychosocial type of conflict model, in which the inevitable conflict arises from two great forces, one of which has its source in the individual and the other in the group. The ideal lifestyle in this psychosocial conflict model expresses the necessity of compromise between the requirements of individuals and those of groups. Social aims are internalized at some point in a person's development, following which both great opposing forces are represented in the mind.

In contrast, the *intrapsychic version* of the conflict model starts by assuming the opposing forces that render conflict inevitable are inherent parts of the person. The conflict starts and remains within the psyche and does not depend on whether one lives for oneself alone or in the company of others. Although the theories considered in this chapter are clearly examples of the conflict model, some of their implications differ from those considered in the previous chapter. As you will see in more detail later, one important difference between the two conflict positions is that the intrapsychic type relies

much less heavily on the concept of defensiveness than the psychosocial type does.

Rank's personality theory is a clear and relatively simple expression of the intrapsychic conflict model. I will start with him, touch on the similar work of Angyal, Bakan, and Perls, then end with Jung, by all estimates the most complicated expression of intrapsychic conflict theorizing.

RANK'S POSITION ....

Otto Rank (born in Vienna, 1884; died in New York, 1939) started out as a member of Freud's inner circle and for many years was respected by that group as a brilliant nonmedical contributor to the psychoanalytic movement. Although he did practice psychotherapy, Rank spent much of his intellectual energy applying his view to understanding phenomena other than psychopathology. In addition to his own writing, Rank founded or edited three influential European journals on psychoanalysis. The fact that he was not a physician and that his training was in philosophy, psychology, history, and art was a welcomed stimulus to Freud and the other psychoanalysts.

But as Rank became increasingly invested in certain heretical ideas, his relations with the psychoanalytic circle were strained past the breaking point. Today the prevailing version of Rank's thinking seems very different from Freud's position, though there are unquestionable similarities in form. It is perhaps unfortunate for the psychoanalytic movement that Rank left the inner circle, for they lost his stimulating influence. As you review his theory, it will become clear that many of his thoughts have since flowered in personology.

Rank's Core Statement

The core tendency in Rank's (1929, 1945) theory is easily stated and clearly establishes his position as a pure expression of the intrapsychic conflict model. According to Rank, all functioning expresses the *tendency to minimize the fear of life while at the same time minimizing the fear of death*. To a Rankian, the terms *life* and *death* have a special meaning that you should understand before you attempt to relate this core tendency to your own experience. In this view, *life* is equivalent to the process of separation and individualization, whereas *death* is the opposite —union, fusion, and dependency. Thus, the core tendency concerns the opposing fears that one will be a unique (lonely) individual or, conversely, that one will be fused with (undifferentiated from) other people.

Many of you have experienced this opposition in deciding whether or not to leave home to go to college. When you thought you should leave home, you experienced, in the prospect of separating from people familiar and dear to you, the fear of life. When you thought you might stay at home, you experienced, in the prospect of failing to grow and develop further, the fear of death. To go away with no plan for continuing your relationship to those left behind would minimize your fear of death but intensify your fear of life. Conversely, to stay behind with no

plan for extending and broadening your personal development would minimize your fear of life but intensify your fear of death. You may have minimized both fears by deciding to go to a college close by so that you could continue to live at home or by leaving to go to school determined to write and visit home frequently.

According to Rank, life is essentially a series of situations in which you are called on either to achieve greater separation and individuality or, renouncing that possibility, to regress to the old and familiar. And from his statement of core tendency, it is clear that even the best solution in such situations will be a compromise, the two fears involved being unavoidably opposed. But as you shall see, there is much more than this to Rank's position.

NATURE AND BASES OF THE TWO FEARS. The two fears—of life and of death—are experienced as uncomfortable states of tension, much as in the anxiety concept of other conflict theorists. Rank prefers the term *fear* because it implies a definite object, whereas anxiety is a more diffuse state, although the two evoke similar effects in the body. The person's overall aim can be characterized as tension reduction. In this, Rank resembles the other conflict theorists; however, he differs when he discusses origins of the two fears.

Although he might agree with Freud that each person possesses certain biological instincts, such as those for food, water, and sex, Rank would not consider them of special importance for understanding personality, for they do not provide the intrinsic basis for conflict. Much more important is the inexorable tendency for living things to separate and individuate. The very act of launching into life, the act of birth, is a profound separation of the neonate from the mother's body. Rank (1929) believes that being born is a deeply traumatic experience because one must relinquish the warm, relatively constant environment of the womb, in which one's needs are automatically met, for the more variable, potentially harsher world outside, in which for the first time one experiences the discomfort of needs insufficiently and tardily served.

Early in his career, Rank considered the birth trauma the most significant event in life. Later on, though he still gave it a primary position, he came to consider it only the first in a long series of inevitable separation experiences. The separations are caused by biological, psychological, and social developments that define life. Typically, the second major separation occurs upon weaning, when the child must face the tragedy of relinquishing mother's fecund breast and the warm, protected place at her side. This separation is rapidly followed by the even greater decrease in contact with the mother precipitated by the maturation of locomotor processes. Other common separation experiences include going to school, seeing the friendships and attachments of an early age as meaningless and anachronistic, and leaving home to strike out on one's own. For Rank, to be alive is to be faced with a continual series of separations through which one becomes a unique psychological, social, and biological person. Living is a fearsome process because it inevitably entails separations, which simultaneously precipitate uncertainty as to what will happen, require one to assume greater and greater responsibility for oneself, and render one ever more alone and lonely.

If separation and individuation arouse so much fear, why not avoid them completely? According to Rank, to avoid them completely would be to repudiate life and could be accomplished only by killing oneself. But this is no solution at all. Individuation is an integral, normal part of being alive. The fact that life is an inevitable process of separation is also the basis of the fear of death. To avoid separation and individuation in any way, such as refusing to develop or merging mindlessly with other people and things, so blatantly violates the nature of life, according to Rank, that it engenders the fear of obliteration. Thus, the person is caught between two poles of a conflict inherent in being alive. Anything done to reduce the fear of living will increase the fear of dying, and vice versa. The only way to achieve a workable existence, therefore, is to strike a compromise that will balance, or hold to a minimum, both forces. In this

emphasis on compromise, one sees that Rank's is a true conflict theory even though it is intrapsychic rather than psychosocial.

The existentialists, as you will see in Chapter 6, take a position that appears similar to Rank's. In the existential view, life is also a continuous experience of choice between climbing the ladder of individuation, which involves separation, or refusing to do so. But, in contrast to Rank, the existentialists advocate achieving individuation, regardless of the toll. They do not endorse the compromise considered ideal by Rank, who stops short of damning the individual to social isolation.

THE WILL AS A FORCE IN LIFE. The other important core characteristic in Rank's theory is the *will,* which is somewhat logically analogous to Freud's ego in that it is the aspect of personality that has an overall organizing function and that integrates all separate experiences into a composite sense of total being. Both concepts refer to a necessary and unavoidable process of development. Children will inevitably develop an ego according to Freud, or a will according to Rank. Finally, both concepts are deeply implicated in the theorist's explanations of how the core tendency gets carried out. For Freud, the ego is a set of mainly unconscious defensive strategies for ensuring maximum instinctual gratification with minimum punishment and guilt. In contrast, Rank's concept of will refers to an organized sense of who and what you are that in its most vigorously developed form is not defensive and aids in minimizing the life and death fears. In further contrast to Freud's ego, Rank's will *consciously* implements the compromise solution to conflict.

Rank on Development

As you have seen, for Rank, birth disrupts the primitive unity of embryo and mother. From birth onward, many other separations occur between people and their environment, separations as inevitable as life itself. Through these enforced separations, people become more and more differentiated. The pressure toward unity can no longer take the primitive form of merging with the world but must involve complex and subtle integrations of the parts of the person and of the person with things and other people. As they grow in this sort of experience, children come to know their own selves as a totality. From this point onward, the active form of the self, or *will,* is a serious force in the shaping of life. Essentially, the will involves a sense of what one wants to accomplish and who one is in the context of the rest of the world.

The will has its beginning, according to Rank, as counterwill. As children come to learn that they can say no to adults and to their own impulses, they feel a sense of personal identity stemming from counterwill. Although immature, the expression of counterwill is an important accomplishment, as it presages, in normal development, the conscious, satisfying, active integration of person with world that for Rank constitutes maturity. Munroe (1955) provides an especially clear discussion of the counterwill:

> The counter-will, developed against the parents and later representatives of external forces, against the "other" or "others," is thus wholesomely rooted in the basic human striving toward life and individualization. By itself, however, it tends to destroy the union which is equally necessary to the human spirit. Assertion of the counter-will, therefore, tends to arouse feelings of "guilt." The profound distress implicit in the effort to be one's own self at the expense of the previous sense of union and support Rank calls ethical guilt. He contrasts this almost universal and potentially creative problem with moralistic guilt, which arises when one has committed an act disapproved by one's society or one's own socially developed code of behavior. Ethical guilt goes deeper. It may arise with any expression of the own will—and also with any compliance which, for the person, has involved an abrogation of such willing, even though correct from a moralistic standpoint. Ethical guilt, if I understand Rank aright, is his term for the tension between two poles of human experience—separation and union. . . .

Resolution of this guilt becomes, for Rank, the human ideal and the goal of psychotherapy. (pp. 585–586)*

Ethical guilt can be resolved only through the achievement of simultaneous differentiation and integration, or psychological growth, which is encouraged in the early years by a loving relationship between child and parent. This relationship must, of course, include in its definition children's need for succorance and support, even when they express counterwill against the parents. Ideally, the parents accept children's counterwill as a lovable part of their efforts to establish their own selves as independent beings. At the same time, the parents must assume responsibility for nurturing children and teaching them the realities of the external world. If children receive this kind of care, they will progress from the expression of counterwill to the expression of mature will, or selfhood.

Although the emergence of counterwill is a signal achievement—the beginning of a conscious integration of the person as a unit distinct from anything else—it has the effect of shattering that union between children and their parents which minimizes the fear of life. Rank theorizes that the expression of counterwill leads to *guilt* because such an isolating manifestation of will and the equally necessary pursuit of union are incompatible. Thus, the child may hit his or her mother and then feel guilty when the mother frowns. Rank believes that the highest form of living involves a more mature expression of will than that seen in counterwill with its attendant guilt over forced separation.

The isolation and separation forced by expression of counterwill can be overcome by parental love of children. As parents continue to support their children, counterwill soon begins to give way to a more mature expression of will. This mature will incorporates a sense of one's own separateness and uniqueness and the ties to things and other people. In the words of Munroe (1955),

---

*From *Schools of Psychoanalytic Thought,* by R. Munroe.

Ideally, the beloved and loving sexual partner supplies the full mutuality of relationship whereby their own will is accepted in and through the "other" and becomes a positive, constructive force. The own will does not arouse guilt because it is loved by the other. The mature person loves himself in the other, and the other in himself. Awareness of difference, of partialization, enriches the new sense of union. This union is not the effortless bliss of the womb, but a constantly renewed creation. (p. 584)

Clearly, the mature will provides the basis for successfully expressing the core tendency of minimizing fear of both life and death. The will eases fear of death by providing recognition of the separate parts of the person and of his or her difference from others. It eases fear of life by providing recognition of the organization of the parts of the person into a dynamic totality and by encouraging a sense of common cause with mutual respect for other people. Only when both functions of the will operate simultaneously are both fears minimized. Note that Rank does not explicitly rely on the concept of defense, even though his is a conflict theory that makes even the most successful life a compromise. Clearly, the most ideal, vigorous development of will has little defensiveness about it. The truth of one's real nature is not distorted because of its incompatibility with society. This position differs greatly from that of the pure psychosocial conflict theorists, to whom even the highest form of life is defensive. The intrapsychic version of the conflict model generally puts less emphasis on defensiveness than the psychosocial version does.

Rank's Peripheral Statement

Rank's position on the periphery of personality seems both lucid and simple, based as it is on the logical possibilities presented by his core-level assumptions. The key to understanding Rank's statement of personality types is the simple recognition that once you postulate one force leading toward individuation and another toward unity, three possibilities for stable patterns of functioning emerge. These patterns can express individuality to the exclusion of unity, unity to the exclusion of individuality, or a blend of the two.

The ideal personality type, according to Rank, is the *artist*. Rank does not use the term artist in its conventional meaning. Many painters, writers, and the like definitely would not be artists by his definition. The *artist* is the person who has accepted both the fear of life and the fear of death, both the inevitable pressure toward individuation and the unavoidable longing for union, and achieved an integration of the two. The artist's personal will expresses both differentiation and integration. Munroe (1955) gives something of the flavor of Rank's thinking on this type:

We have seen that this (psychological growth) requires an acceptance by the individual of his personal will as valuable—an acceptance begun in the counterwill. But this personal will cannot become truly constructive until it is accepted by another person. Until the person can feel that his own will is right (i.e., not guilty), until he can feel that it is accepted by "others," he cannot fully resolve the problem of separation with its counterpart of union. Rank's artist . . . does not stand alone on a pinnacle of individual worth. On the contrary "he who loseth his life shall find it." The act of separation is not enough, no matter how heroically accomplished. Neither is sacrifice of the self, whether it takes the form of heroic altruism and self-immolation or the unthinking compromise of the average man. These are the poles of experience, neither of which can fully express the human ideal. Rank's choice of the term artist for the human ideal is an attempt to convey a sense of creative integration as the highest goal of man. (pp. 585–586)

Rank has described what he means articulately enough to suggest some of the relevant peripheral characteristics. For example, the artist type certainly would include people who show a high degree of differentiation and integration in their thoughts, feelings, and actions. In addition, they would show intimacy with and commitment to other people without slavish loyalties or undue concern for social proprieties. In their work, they would be productive in innovative but also useful ways. In short, they would show many of the signs of transcendence associated with the ideal personality as characterized by the fulfillment model. But that Rank's position is still in the conflict tradition is indicated by his insistence that people cannot live ideally unless their way is acceptable to at least some other people.

One of the remaining two personality types is called the *neurotic person,* who expresses the tendency toward separation to the exclusion of the tendency toward union. Like artists, neurotics have committed themselves to the pain of separation from the herd but, unlike artists, have not achieved constructive integrations with the world. Instead of expressing mature will or selfhood, neurotics seem fixated at the level of counterwill. In other words, they act either against people or completely separately from them. Though their personalities show much differentiation, they are weak on integrating principles. Their sense of separateness is likely to be ridden by hostility and moralistic rather than ethical guilt, offering a clue to the developmental handicap that culminates in the neurotic type. The handicap comes from the child having been made to feel wrong and unworthy at the time when the negativism implied in counterwill was actually normal, with the result that the child overcompensated by strongly embracing counterwill as a defensive self-justification. In adulthood, neurotics continue to show counterwill as the only sign of their own selfhood. Again some of the peripheral characteristics embodying the neurotic personality type can be discerned: The neurotic would be hostile, negative, arrogant, isolationistic, critical of others, highly guilty, and so forth.

The final personality type is that of the *average person,* or someone who expresses the tendency toward union to the exclusion of the tendency toward individuation. Although the neurotic is, in Rank's mind, clearly inferior to the artist, the average person is inferior to both. Average persons are the most inferior because they have never seriously entertained the possibility of their own individuality. They act as if the right to individuality, guaranteed by the

trauma of birth, were not there at all. Munroe (1955) once again provides a vivid description of what Rank has in mind:

> Every child develops something of a counter-will through the ordinary pains and frustrations of post-uterine existence. Many children, however, soon find it possible to so identify their own will with that of their parents as to avoid much of the guilt of separation and the pain of developing their own will further. Adaptation to the will of the parents and later to the dictates of a wider society is the keynote of these characters. Where there is no effort toward individuation, there is also no conflict about conformance. The person's life may be hard or dull, but as long as the person takes its external conditions for granted, so long as they seem really part of himself, he is spared the inner distress of guilt. Rank does not refer here to people who consciously conform for the sake of expediency. The average man is the man who naturally conforms to his society because he has never thought of doing anything else. His relations with his society are reminiscent of the symbiotic relationships between person and environment which prevailed in the womb. They represent the first and easiest solution to the problem set by birth. This essentially adaptive individual has a relatively harmonious relationship to his society, but only because he has never truly differentiated his own will from the significant surroundings. He is the prey of social change as victim or executioner. His truths are illusory and his virtues may vanish overnight if the social configuration to which he belongs shifts its values. (p. 585)

The average person would be characterized by such peripheral characteristics as conformity, dependability, superficiality, suggestibility, and lack of dissatisfaction. The emphasis in this type is on adaptation. The developmental handicap involves an overwhelmingly negative response to the first expressions of counterwill that led the child to embrace for dear life the precise ways of her or his parents and the broader society.

This concludes my presentation of the personality types described by Rank. Intriguing and immediately identifiable in our own experience as they are, I urge you to realize that in Rank's position, you can describe only three kinds of people. This number cannot really be increased by considering mixed types, for the types offered largely exclude each other. One cannot be both artistic and average or even artistic and neurotic. You should carefully consider whether three personality types are enough to describe the full range of ways of life. I shall return to this point in Chapter 12.

Angyal and Bakan

Andras Angyal (1941, 1951, 1965) and David Bakan (1966, 1968, 1971) have independently developed positions very similar to each other's and Rank's. Although Angyal and Bakan do not cover all aspects of personality in their theorizing, they share with Rank many characteristics of intrapsychic conflict approach.

For Angyal, the core tendency is the *attempt to maximize both the expression of autonomy and the expression of homonomy* (surrender). Similarly, Bakan's core tendency is the *attempt to maximize both the expression of agency and the expression of communion*. The core characteristics of personality for Angyal are *autonomy* and *homonomy;* for Bakan they are *agency* and *communion*. All four concepts refer simultaneously to pressure on the person to function in a certain way or direction and to the stable aspects of personality that result from such functioning.

Autonomy and agency are similar in that they signify functioning that leads to separation from other people and from the physical environment and to separation of parts of oneself from each other. They also refer to the stable fruits of such functioning; namely, differentiation of personality and independence in relation to things and other people. Whereas the concept of autonomy tends to emphasize aloofness and the concept of agency manipulativeness, the differences between them are less important than the similarities. They also share a kinship with Rank's concept of the fear of death, leading as it does to separation and individuation.

Homonomy and communion are similar in that they emphasize functioning that leads toward relatedness with others and with the

physical environment, and both underlie the integration of the parts of oneself into a unified whole. They also signify the stable fruits of such functioning; namely, a network of intimate relationships (with lovers, children, friends), an embeddedness in social institutions larger than oneself (e.g., having a profession, religious affiliation, political commitment), and a sense of physical belonging (to a home, geographical area). While the concept of homonomy implies more passivity (surrender) than does the more instrumental communion, this difference is less important than the similarities. As you can see, these concepts cover ground similar to that of Rank's idea of the fear of life, leading as it does to union.

The simultaneous processes of differentiation and integration, considered by Angyal and Bakan to be the most constructive solution to the problem of the two opposing forces, is also emphasized by Rank. The process, called *psychological growth* by fulfillment theorists (for whom it is a common emphasis), seems terribly optimistic for the conflict model. Clearly, intrapsychic conflict theorists see the highest form of living as a process of development rather than the set, defensive state for which pure psychosocial conflict theorists argue. The process of simultaneous differentiation and integration smacks neither of reality distortion nor of screening some things out of consciousness. Indeed, so optimistic do Rank, Angyal, and Bakan seem concerning the most constructive form of living that one may well question whether it represents a compromise at all. But simultaneous differentiation and integration do represent a compromise—the best that can be arranged given the underlying background of two constant, intense, unchangeable forces pulling in opposite directions. The bedrock assumption of all conflict theories, be they intrapsychic or psychosocial, is that the person is a house forever divided.

Thus far, I have only discussed the highest form of living according to Bakan and Angyal. They also discuss less constructive ways of functioning, which constitute failures to establish compromises that balance the two opposing forces. Instead, a disproportionate or even overwhelming amount of one of the two forces is expressed. In describing the ways in which the person falls short of a workable compromise, Rank describes both the danger of renouncing union (neurosis) and the danger of renouncing separation (banality of adjustment), whereas Angyal and Bakan emphasize only the danger of denying union. Indeed, the entire range of psychological and physical maladies, from alienation to cancer, are traced by Bakan (1966, 1968) to the expression of agency unmitigated by the mellowing effects of communion.

GESTALT PSYCHOTHERAPY ......

Frederick Perls (1969a, 1969b, 1969c) developed a popular position called *Gestalt psychotherapy.* Primarily a therapy, this position nonetheless includes some assumptions about personality. Although these assumptions, hardly fixed, represent a complex amalgam of different theoretical emphases, the main thrust appears to fit the intrapsychic conflict model. The theorizing includes formulations similar in content to those of Rank, Angyal, and Bakan.

Perls's Core Statement

In Perls's complex position, the universe is seen as a continuous flow of energy and matter. Though part of this flow, the human is nevertheless uniquely predisposed to comprehend what is going on. In attempting to comprehend, the human breaks down the universal continuum into bits and pieces that are labeled and treated as separate entities. In this fashion are born the notions of different persons, things, events, times, places, parts of a person, and much else. By playing with these bits conceptually, the human finds relationships among them and, in that sense, discovers processes. A *process,* according to Perls, is two such bits and a happening. It is in the depiction of happenings that the basically intrapsychic nature of the theorizing is apparent.

A *happening* is the simultaneous attraction and repulsion, described as a "tendency-to-merge-with" and an "urge-to-remain-differentiated-from," that characterizes all relationships between bits. The term *gestalt* refers to the whole formed of two or more bits related by the dynamic tension of their inevitable opposition. Clearly, this is a conflict position.

What makes Gestalt psychotherapy an intrapsychic form of the conflict model is the origin in the human mind of not only the bits constituting comprehensible experience but their oppositional relationships. Relationships between bits do end (e.g., two friends may no longer see each other; the tension between going to work and relaxing at the beach may be resolved), which may suggest that the position does not really express the conflict model. However, as soon as the two bits cease to oppose each other in a relationship, each enters a relationship of opposition with other existing bits. The overriding fact of human existence is conflict fashioned out of human imaginativeness in the attempt to comprehend the universe.

THE CORE TENDENCY. Like Rank and the other intrapsychic conflict theorists, Perls believes that vigorous consciousness is possible. Though defenses and the resulting decreased levels of awareness can occur in people, these do not characterize the highest forms of development. In this belief, Perls clearly differs from Freud. He depicts vigorous awareness as that which flows between the two opposing bits. The opposition stimulates keen awareness, which leads to an understanding of the inevitability of conflict. In an adult, when awareness is minimal or takes the form of a sense of unity rather than opposition, there has been a disturbance of consciousness. Appreciation of opposition not only constitutes vigorous awareness; it paves the way for creativity as well. Although creativity involves changing meaning through altering relationships between bits, it does not imply conflict resolution but shifts in oppositions. Pulling these threads together, I can hazard a core tendency for Perls: *Humans strive to comprehend life by identifying bits of experience and construing them in relationships of simultaneous attraction and repulsion.*

It may seem odd that Perls emphasizes the perception of conflict as the main thrust of activity. But you should recognize just how pervasive he thinks this kind of perception is. For example, the sense of something external that we call "reality" is, for Perls, nothing more than the projection of human imaginativeness. The self, as contrasted but also involved with this external reality, is to be understood as an expression of the core tendency to construe bits of experience as simultaneously attracted and repulsed. Awareness is born out of contrast: the present with the past or future, oneself with others, good with bad. Without conflict, there is no understanding. And without a doubt, the conflict is intrapsychic.

THE CORE CHARACTERISTICS. As for core characteristics, Perls offers three phases, or modes of thinking: the social, the psychophysical, and the spiritual. Although they develop sequentially, they are also present as potentialities at birth and throughout adult life. These phases are abstract in meaning. Nevertheless, they involve the simultaneous attraction and revulsion of bits of experience.

Developmentally earliest, the *social phase* is so named because the child requires interaction with others for survival. During this phase, the child begins to develop an awareness of others as they fulfill and frustrate her or his physical needs and comfort.

Next comes the *psychophysical phase,* which encompasses most of life. Here, the person becomes self-aware, which sharpens the social awareness that has already been going on; indeed, most of the construing of bits and relationships takes place here. Also emerging during this phase is personality, which comprises the being, the self, and self-image. *Being* is the biological organism as construed by the mind. As such, being entails a greedy, growing composite of organically rooted processes and the resulting activity. The *self,* or awareness of one's dimensions and purposes as distinct from others and

from nature, emerges through experiences of conflict between being and the external world. The self is defined mainly in terms of one's interests and pleasures. *Self-image* reflects one's developing views of what one should want and be and results from incorporating the views of others. Being, self, and self-image, all figments of the person's imagination, are constantly in conflict.

Finally, some people develop beyond the psychophysical phase into a *spiritual phase,* characterized by an intuitive (rather than concretely sensory) apprehension of meanings beyond being, self, and self-image.

Perls on Development

Although the three phases, or modes of thinking, exist as potentialities at birth and throughout adult life, they do follow a developmental course involving interaction with others. The progressions from one phase to another and from being to self and self-image within the psychophysical stage are hastened by two types of reactions from others: acknowledgment and approbation. *Acknowledgment* is recognition by others of the person and his or her actions. It has a positive and approving implication, as in Kohut's mirroring. The child plays and calls to her or his parents, "Watch me!" Through acknowledgment by others, the person develops self-awareness and self-appreciation. But children learn the criticality involved in self-image through *approval* (and, presumably, disapproval) from others. Developmentally speaking, both acknowledgment and approval occur inevitably, consolidating the tendency to perceive bits of experiences as simultaneously attractive (acknowledgment) and repulsive (approval). In reacting to the child with acknowledgment and approval, the parents themselves participate in this ubiquitous cycle of attraction and repulsion.

Perls on the Periphery of Personality

Although Perls offers no typology, he does theorize about how the general flow and change of human behavior, which he regards as ideal, can be interrupted or fixed. This fixity constitutes something like character structure or personality types. You will recall that for Perls experience is the continual process of identifying bits of the ongoing flux and construing relationships of simultaneous attraction and repulsion among them. The conflict involved in this construing is resolved when the relationship among the bits ends, but it is immediately replaced by the conflict that occurs when these bits enter into relationship with other bits. The ideal person would be continually changing and thus indescribable in terms of personality types.

When the ongoing process of experience is interrupted, a *blister*, or fixed pattern of traits, is created. Although Perls does not provide much detail about blisters, some points are clear. Blisters express no more conflict than the uninterrupted process of experience does; rather, in a blister the conflict is static, or unchanging, because the relationship among bits continues instead of giving way to new relationships. It is clear that this fixity of conflict is somehow a function of external pressures, but there is little systematic discussion of such matters available. The final point you should keep in mind is that blisters form the symptoms to be dealt with in psychotherapy, in which Perls's aim is not to resolve conflict but is rather to restore the ebb and flow of conflicts. Psychotherapy almost always takes place in groups and involves confronting clients with interpretations that contrast what they say, do, or believe. The sense of contrast and conflict underlying the personality theory also permeates the psychotherapeutic technique.

JUNG'S POSITION ....

Carl Gustav Jung (born in Kessewil, on Lake Constance in Switzerland, 1875; died in Kusnacht, Switzerland, 1961) has provided a theory of such complexity and uniqueness as to be unlike anything else in the personality field. This does not imply its unequivocal soundness, however, for it is checkered with ambiguities and inconsistencies. Nonetheless, by any calculation Jung is a major figure in personology and an influential thinker of the 20th century. Perhaps because of the influence of his father, a clergyman, Jung first thought to study philosophy and archaeology. But supposedly a dream convinced him to study medicine and science.

His early interest in psychiatry was spurred by Eugen Bleuler and Pierre Janet. Jung was very impressed with Freud's first great book, *The Interpretation of Dreams* (1900), and by 1906 a regular correspondence had sprung up between them. Jung became a member of Freud's inner circle. Their mutual admiration was great, and Freud regarded Jung as his successor; indeed, Jung became the first president of the International Psychoanalytic Association in 1910. But soon after, the relationship between Freud and Jung became fraught with theoretical and personal disagreements, so that in 1917 Jung resigned his presidency of and membership in that organization. Freud and Jung never saw each other again, even though both wrote interpretations of their relationship and differences (e.g., Freud, 1922b, 1957; Jung, 1961). After the break, Jung went on to develop his own approach, which he called *analytic psychology*. Once again we have evidence of the excellence of Freud that attracted other strong, creative people—and once again evidence that such persons do not get along easily.

Jung's Core Statement

As its name suggests, Jung's approach retains much of its Freudian parentage. This is most apparent in its form, which emphasizes the importance of dreams as expressions of the unconscious and of the integration of biological and mental phenomena. But the differences between Freudian and Jungian theory are much more important than the similarities. Generally stated, the main differences entail, on Jung's part, a deemphasis of sexuality coupled with a greater emphasis on spirituality (in its mystical and religious senses) and focus on cultural universals in human experience rather than individual idiosyncrasies. These differences above all won Jung a small but devoted following and underlie a groundswell of current interest in his theorizing. Jung seems to speak of what he regards as a tendency toward spiritual bankruptcy by enabling us to feel grounded in the past and future of humankind rather than limited to our own insignificant life circumstances.

CORE TENDENCY. It is no simple matter to state Jung's core tendency in a few words. His is probably the most complex personality theory that exists. You will see how he tends to define terms uniquely, different from the common meanings established in much of the personological literature. You will also experience the inevitable indefiniteness associated with his mysticism. But one thing will emerge clearly: For Jung, life, behavior, and psyche reek with conflict. At great risk of oversimplification, I venture to say that the overall directionality in his theory is the *tendency toward attainment of selfhood*. It is less simple than you might think to arrive at some intuitive understanding of what Jung means here. For him, the *self* is definitely not a conscious sense of what one is or could be, as is commonly thought in personology. Instead, it is the totality of all the conflicting characteristics of personality. Perhaps the best way to grasp his meaning is to visualize the self as the hub of a wheel, with the spokes describing the force or tension of opposing personality characteristics. To attain selfhood is to have balanced all the conflicting polarities. Sometimes he sees selfhood as a conflict-free state, but more often as a balance among opposing forces (Jung, 1953b). In any event, complete selfhood is considered an ideal virtually impossible to attain.

CORE CHARACTERISTICS. Several core characteristics underlie Jung's theory and, as you shall see, tend to oppose one another. Of particular importance, the *ego* for Jung is the conscious mind directing the business of everyday living. It comprises complex combinations of conscious perceptions, thoughts, memories, and feelings, which lead to a sense of one's identity and continuity. In defining the ego as completely conscious, Jung deviates from Freud, for whom the ego is at least partly unconscious. The unconscious part, you will recall, is the defenses. Although Jung assumes defensiveness, he emphasizes it less than Freud does and does not localize its processes in the ego.

For Jung, unconscious processes are always in opposition to conscious ones. This opposition is inevitable and even helpful, you will see. For now, you need only note the distinction Jung makes between the personal unconscious and the collective unconscious.

The *personal unconscious* is very similar to what Freud meant by unconscious and preconscious material. It consists of experiences that were once conscious and either have been defensively forced out of awareness because of their threatening nature, as in Freud's unconscious, or merely no longer fall within the focus of attention, as in Freud's preconscious. For Jung, the preconscious material can become conscious by a shift in focus of attention, and the unconscious material can become conscious by a relaxation of defenses. He presents a true alternative to defensiveness, in which material defended against can once again gain accurate, complete consciousness. In contrast, Freud claims that our awareness never reflects more than a pale shadow of truth.

The *collective unconscious*, which reflects not individual experience but the accumulated experience of the human species, is Jung's most striking, unique, and controversial concept. According to Jung, all the events that have occurred over the eons of human history contribute to the life of each contemporary person in the form of a "species memory." People have suffered dilemmas, fought to the death, loved successfully and in vain, reared their young or abandoned them, found nutriments or starved, experienced the power of nature, and so forth since the beginning of time. Their fears, joys, triumphs, tragedies, beliefs, solutions—in short, the sum of knowledge they have gained—have not been lost. New generations of children are not blank slates who cannot know anything of importance unless they learn it themselves. Rather, the accumulated culture of humankind is lodged in the psyche at birth, in the form of a collective unconscious. In fact, Jung even implies that he believes prehuman and subhuman history to have made some contribution to the collective unconscious as well.

To be sure, this collective knowledge is unconscious—indeed, it cannot, in contrast to the experience constituting the personal unconscious, become conscious through redirection of attention or relaxation of defenses. Because the collective unconscious was never conscious in the history of an individual, it can never become so, no matter how hard people (or their therapists) may try. But the collective unconscious does have an enormous influence on behavior as well as an indirect effect on consciousness most clearly seen in such events as the déjà vu experience and the sense of the uncanny.

Jung probably arrived at his view of the collective unconscious out of a fascination with primitive mentality, art, and religion, to say nothing of dreams. He came to believe that the difference between primitive and modern mentality is not in degree of rationality but in the assumptions made about the nature of the world. Modern people assume that all events "have a natural and perceptible cause" (Jung, 1933a, p. 130), this being one of their principal dogmas. Jung contends that this assumption is *actually* borne out only about half the time but people shrug off this disturbing fact by references to "chance." But "Primitive man expects more of an explanation. What we call chance is to him arbitrary power," says Jung (1933a, p. 132), who does not find such thinking especially strange. He encourages people to see this primitive belief in the context out of which it emerged, at the same time indicating its hold on him with an engaging account of personal experience in the jungle (1933a):

> In the Kitoshi region south of Mount Elgo, I went for an excursion into the Kabras forest. There, in the thick grass, I nearly stepped on a puff-adder, and only managed to jump away in time. In the afternoon my companion returned from a hunt, deathly pale and trembling in every limb. He had almost been bitten by a seven-foot mamba which darted at his back from a termite hill. Without a doubt he would have been killed had he not been

able at the last moment to wound the animal with a shot. At nine o'clock that night our camp was attacked by a pack of ravenous hyenas which had surprised and mauled a man in his sleep the day before. In spite of the fire they swarmed into the hut of our cook who fled screaming over the stockade. Thenceforth there were no accidents throughout the whole of our journey. Such a day gave our Negroes food for thought. For us it was a simple-multiplication of accidents, but for them the inevitable fulfillment of an omen that had occurred upon the first day of our journey into the wilds. It so happened that we had fallen, car, bridge, and all, into a stream we were trying to cross. Our boys had exchanged glances on that occasion as if to say: "Well, that's a fine start." To cap the climax a tropical thunderstorm blew up and soaked us so thoroughly that I was prostrated with fever for several days. On the evening of the day when my friend had had such a narrow escape out hunting, I could not help saying to him as we white men sat looking at one another: "It seems to me as if trouble had begun still further back. Do you remember the dream you told me in Zurich just before we left?" At that time he had had a very impressive nightmare. He dreamed that he was hunting in Africa, and was suddenly attacked by a huge mamba, so that he woke up with a cry of terror. The dream had greatly disturbed him, and he now confessed to the thought that it had portended the death of one of us. He had of course assumed that I was to die, because we always hope it is the "other fellow." But it was he who later fell ill of a severe malarial fever that brought him to the edge of the grave.

> To read of such a conversation in a corner of the world where there are no snakes and no malaria-bearing mosquitoes means very little. One must imagine the velvety blue of a tropical night, the overhanging black masses of gigantic trees standing in a virgin forest, the mysterious voices of the nocturnal spaces, a lonely fire with loaded rifles stacked beside it, mosquito-nets, boiled swampwater to drink, and above all the conviction expressed by an old Afrikaner who knew what he was saying: "This isn't man's country—it's God's country." There man is not king; it is rather nature—the animals, plants, and microbes. Given the mood that goes with the place, one understands how it is that we found a dawning significance in things that anywhere else would provoke a smile. That is the world of unrestrained, capricious powers with

which primitive man has to deal day by day. The extraordinary event is no joke to him. He draws his own conclusions. "It is not a good place"—"The day is unfavorable"—and who knows what dangers he avoids by following such warnings.

Magic is the science of the jungle. (pp. 138–140)*

Jung is saying that in contexts not under human control, thoughts of evil omens, spirits, and bewitchment are universal psychic expressions, not just the illogical bent of primitive mentality. Modern people also become superstitious when confronting the real capriciousness of nature, from which they are usually protected.

Then Jung (1933a) goes on to ask himself whether this suspiciousness to which people are prone might be an accurate response to external, supernatural forces, be they gods or devils:

Shall we, for the moment at least, venture the hypothesis that the primitive belief in arbitrary powers is justified by the facts and not merely from a psychological point of view? The question is nothing less than this: does the psyche in general—that is, the spirit, or the unconscious—arise in us; or is the psyche, in the early stages of consciousness, actually outside us in the form of arbitrary powers with intentions of their own, and does it gradually come to take its place within us in the course of psychic development? (pp. 146–147)

Jung thus considers the real possibility of a supernatural order, however antithetical to science that may be. After considerable struggle however, he rejects a supernatural order in favor of the collective unconscious, which, though panindividual, need not imply anything different in kind from mentality.

Jung takes a step on the way to assuming a collective unconscious rather than a supernatural order when he decides that such phenomena as superstitiousness and sense of the uncanny are essentially elaborated projections. These phenomena occur in primitives somewhat more frequently than in moderns "because of the undifferentiated state of [the primitive's] mind and his consequent inability to criticize himself" (Jung, 1933a, pp. 142–143). Any proneness to

superstitious belief that moderns retain is due to accumulated memory of the past superstitious beliefs of the human species. While such beliefs are usually activated by some unpredictability or strangeness in the environment, their cause is nonetheless the collective unconscious.

In a sense, then, Jung contends that we are one with our ancestors. In us live the battles they fought, the fears they experienced, the loves they nurtured. The doctrine of inheritance of acquired characteristics seems to be what Jung had in mind, even though it is in ill repute these days. According to Jung (1933a),

Not only the religious teacher, but the pedagogue as well, assumes that it is possible to implant in the human psyche something that was not previously there. The power of suggestion and influence is a fact; even the most modern behaviorism expects far-reaching results from this quarter. The idea of a complicated building-up of the psyche is expressed in primitive form in many widespread beliefs—for instance, possession, the incarnation of ancestral spirits, the immigration of souls, and so forth. When someone sneezes, we still say: "God bless you," and mean by it: "I hope your new soul will do no harm." When in the course of our own development we grow out of many-sided contradictions and achieve a unified personality, we experience something like a complicated growing-together of the psyche. Since the human body is built up by inheritance out of a number of Mendelian units, it does not seem altogether out of the question that the human psyche is similarly put together. (p. 148)

But it is unclear whether Jung means the collective unconscious to be literally the accumulated specific experiences that our ancestors happen to have had or something less concrete. He does refer to recurring themes, problems, and preoccupations in the collective unconscious, suggesting that there is something universal about it that reflects the human condition more comprehensively than the mere specifics of actual experience. This quality of universality in the collective unconscious is most clearly seen in Jung's explanation of art and the artist (1933a).

---

*From *Modern Man in Search of a Soul*, by C. G. Jung. Copyright © 1933 by Harcourt Brace Jovanovich, Inc. Reprinted by permission of Harcourt Brace and Company.

He is critical of Freud here, on the basis of over-specificity:

> Freud thought that he had found a key in his procedure of deriving the work of art from the personal experiences of the artist. It is true that certain possibilities lay in this direction, for it is conceivable that a work of art, no less than a neurosis, might be traced back to those knots in psychic life that we call the complexes. . . . Freud takes the neurosis as a substitute for a direct means of gratification. He therefore regrets it as something inappropriate—a mistake, a dodge, an excuse, a voluntary blindness. . . . And a work of art is brought into questionable proximity with the neurosis when it is taken as something which can be analyzed in terms of the poet's repressions. . . . No objection can be raised if it is admitted that this approach amounts to nothing more than the elucidation of those personal determinants without which a work of art is unthinkable. But should the claim be made that such an analysis accounts for the work of art itself, then a categorical denial is called for. (pp. 167–168)

This statement makes two things clear. First, a work of art is not to be understood simply as expressive of what Jung calls the *personal unconscious*—those once-conscious experiences that have been defended against. Secondly, the collective unconscious, which also figures in the work of art, is probably not just the history of our ancestors' personal unconsciousness. The tone of universality that Jung intends (1933a) is clearly expressed in statements such as the following:

> What is essential in a work of art is that it should rise far above the realm of personal life and speak from the spirit and heart of the poet as man to the spirit and heart of mankind. The personal aspect is a limitation—and even a sin—in the realm of art. . . . The artist is not a person endowed with free will who seeks his own ends, but one who allows art to realize its purposes through him. As a human being he may have moods and a will and personal aims, but as an artist he is a "man" in a higher sense—he is "collective man"—one who carries and shapes the unconscious, psychic life of mankind. (p. 168)

What Jung means is that the work of art issues not from the artist's particular experiences or even talents but from the collective unconscious, to which he or she has become especially sensitive. In this sense, the collective unconscious must refer to the age-old considerations that form life, not merely the chronology of each individual ancestor's experiences.

As an aside, let me mention that Jung has an influence in a still-raging battle over the proper stance in art criticism. These days, many art critics adopt an approach that analyzes a work to clarify the particular facets of the artist's personality that have found expression. This somewhat Freudian school of criticism has gained considerable force. However, some traditionalists and a new wave of art critics both favor an approach that searches for the universality in each creation, regardless of the artist's personal life. These critics are, according to Jung, on the right track. I should also mention that many artists would favor Jung's view, having long resented what they perceive as an overconcretization and devaluation of their art by the Freudian emphasis on creativity as expressive of personal neurosis, or at least idiosyncrasy. To generalize beyond art, it seems clear that Jung gives more importance to the collective unconscious than to the personal unconscious. For him, though the personal unconscious is the stuff of neurosis, the collective unconscious permits a valuable identification with what is universal and eternal.

THE ARCHETYPES. Thus far, I have mentioned only general conceptions about the nature of the collective unconscious and some of the observations underlying Jung's assumption of it. It is now time to indicate the content of this highly complicated but intriguing concept. The content takes the form of *archetypes,* which are also, though less frequently, called *dominants, imagoes, primordial images,* and *mythological images* (Jung, 1953a). An *archetype* is a universal form of, or predisposition to, characteristic thoughts and feelings. Although the archetype is by nature unconscious and incapable of becoming conscious, it tends to create images or visions that correspond to aspects of conscious experience. Thus, the mother archetype in all of us produces a vague, intuitive image of a nurturant, loving, accepting force, which we then project onto our actual mothers. An archetype is an inherited, generic form or predisposition that determines in part how we perceive our experiences. From time immemorial people have experienced mothers, and their experiences have been homogeneous enough to have permanently emblazoned upon the psyche the essence of Mother. Our experience of actual mothers is, then, a conglomerate of the generic idea of mother and the particular characteristics our real mothers happen to have. These two sources of experience may or may not match well—indeed, it is unlikely that they will match completely, even in the best of circumstances, and hence conflict between archetypes (collective unconscious) and conscious experience (ego) is to be expected. There may well also be conflict between archetypes and the personal unconscious, since the latter is formed out of concrete and troublesome personal experience, while the former expresses essences.

But the matter is even more complicated than I have indicated. For Jung (1959b), the archetypes do not have content in any concrete sense but only form:

> Again and again I encounter the mistaken notion that an archetype is determined in regard to its content, in other words, that it is a kind of unconscious idea (if such an expression be permissible). It is necessary to point out once more that archetypes are not determined as regards their content, but only as regards their form and then only to a limited degree. A primordial image is determined as to its content only when it has become conscious and is therefore filled out with the material of conscious experience. Its form, however, as I have explained elsewhere, might perhaps be compared to the axial system of a crystal, which, as it were, preforms the crystalline structure in the mother liquid, although it has no material existence of its own. (p. 79)

Once you have grasped this emphasis on archetypes as forms or essences, you can understand why they can never become conscious: It is not that they are defended against; rather, they are only prototypes or possibilities. In addition, this definition in terms of forms makes it clearer why an archetype can, according to Jung,

express itself in such a wide range of content. Hence, the mother archetype can express itself in "the Church, university, city or country, heaven, earth, the worlds, the sea or any still waters, matter even, the underworld and the moon" (Jung, 1959a, p. 81). Of course, any actual human being can function as a symbol of an archetype. Thus, the president may be responded to as the archetypal hero, rather than as a particular person with a certain height and weight, fears and hopes. As you can imagine, it must be very difficult to determine when one is dealing with archetypal experience versus individual experience and, in the case of the former, which archetypes are involved. Jung offers no help beyond recognizing the difficulty and indicating the need for comprehensive, deeply intuitive observation done by people who are not only sensitive to what they hear and see but also steeped in the world's cultures and history.

Agreeing with Freud, Jung proposes that the most fertile ground for information about the unconscious in general is imaginative productions, such as works of art and dreams. Indeed, Jung seems to have invented the free-association test, in which the person is presented with various words to which he or she must respond with the first thought that comes to mind. But, as you have seen, Jung claims Freud overlooks the collective unconscious, focusing exclusively on the personal unconscious. The end result is overly concrete explanations. To illustrate this, Jung (1959a) criticizes Freud's interpretation of Leonardo da Vinci's painting of St. Anne and the Virgin with the Christ child. Freud concludes that the painting expresses Leonardo's wish to recapture the two mothers he had actually had (apparently he was born to one mother and wet-nursed by another). For Freud, the painting expresses repressed personal experiences only. Jung insists, however, that the theme of two mothers is very common in art, myth, and fantasy. Think, says Jung, of the myth of Heracles, born of a human mother and unwittingly adopted by the goddess Hera. Also, it is common for children to fantasize that their parents are not really their true ones. Relevant too is the widespread practice of providing godparents to supplement the blood parents. All this could not have been promulgated by persons who had actually experienced two mothers in childhood; rather, the theme of dual parentage is based, according to Jung, on something so universal as to alert us to the presence of an archetype. Leonardo was in the grips of this archetype, rather than playing out some strictly personal drama.

Another aspect of Freud's excessive concreteness, Jung says, is the use of biological rather than spiritual explanations for fantasies. Dreams provide Freud with the occasion to trace the vicissitudes of sex and death instincts, structured as biological imperatives. But, says Jung (1933a), it is nonsensical to assume that something concretely biological can be symbolically represented in fantasy:

> It is well known that the Freudian school operates with hard and fast sexual "symbols"; but these are just what I would call signs, for they are made to stand for sexuality, and this is supposed to be something definitive. As a matter of fact, Freud's concept of sexuality is thoroughly elastic, and so vague that it can be made to include almost anything. . . . Instead of taking the dogmatic stand that rests upon the illusion that we know something because we have a familiar word for it, I prefer to regard the symbol as the announcement of something unknown, hard to recognize and not to be fully determined. Take, for instance, the so-called phallic symbols, which are supposed to stand for the *membrum virile* and nothing more. . . . As was customary throughout antiquity, primitive people today make a free use of phallic symbols, yet it never occurs to them to confuse the phallus, as a ritualistic symbol, with the *actual* penis. They always take the phallus to mean the creative *mana,* the power of healing and fertility, "that which is unusually potent". . . . Its equivalents in mythology and in dreams are the bull, the ass, the pomegranate, the *yoni,* the he-goat, the lightning, the horse's hoof, the dance, the magical cohabitation in the furrow, and the menstrual fluid, to mention only a few of many. That which underlies all of these images—and sexuality itself —is an archetypal content that is hard to grasp, and that finds its best psychological expression in the primitive mana symbol. (pp. 21–22)

In sharp contradiction to Freud, Jung actually suggests that essences or archetypes lie at the heart of the unconscious and that even sexuality derives its importance from the archetype expressed in it. Jung simply does not believe that human biology (instincts, drives, metabolism) has much to do with psychic life and its hold on behavior.

This is not to say that sexuality and animal urges are unimportant for Jung; rather, he sees them as deriving not from biological imperatives but from an archetype, the *shadow,* that has evolved through time so far as to warrant being treated as a core characteristic of personality. The shadow consists of essentialistic forms of the animal instincts humans inherited from lower forms of life (Jung, 1959c). As such, it typifies the animal possibility of human nature. Jung's belief that the shadow underlies the sexual and death wishes thus suggests that by endorsing the Freudian view, one may actually be defining one's life along lines that are needlessly and excessively animalistic!

The shadow often expresses itself in socially unacceptable thoughts and behaviors, which may be either hidden from public view, remaining in the ego, or actually defended against, becoming part of the personal unconscious. The shadow is also responsible for the human conception of original sin and, when projected outward, becomes the devil or even some concrete enemy. But the shadow is not all bad, lending vitality and passion to life.

Several other archetypes have also evolved far enough to be considered core characteristics. Especially intriguing are the *anima* and the *animus* (Jung, 1953b, 1959b). These archetypes provide a basis for bisexuality. Of course, at the biological level, men and women secrete both male and female sex hormones, not just the one appropriate to their dominant sex. But even if this were not true, Jung would postulate an archetypal basis for bisexuality because he considers it to be so apparent once one adopts the purview of anthropology, history, and art rather than some narrower, culture-bound approach. Present in both biological sexes, the feminine archetype is *anima* and the masculine archetype, *animus.* These archetypes are based on the accumulated experience of man with woman and vice versa. Jung feels that the whole nature of each biological sex presupposes the other. The archetypes underlie the manifestation in each biological sex of characteristics of the other (e.g., sensitivity in a man, aggressiveness in a woman) and determine the attractiveness of the opposite biological sex. Through these archetypes, each biological sex can appreciate and understand the role of its opposite. But if in any concrete instance anima or animus is projected onto someone of the opposite sex without sufficient regard for his or her real character, misunderstandings and conflict will result. Perhaps a biological male will try to find his idealized image of a woman (anima) in an actual biological female he knows. If, after projecting his anima onto her, he realizes the inevitable discrepancies between ideals and actualities, he may suffer bitter disappointment and never know why. Once again you can see the ready potential for conflict between the archetypes of the collective unconscious and the actualities of experience.

Another important archetype is the *persona* (Jung, 1953b), which is basis for the mask that people adopt in response to the demands of social convention and tradition as well as their own archetypal needs. The purpose of the persona is to make a good impression both on others and on oneself. Presumably this archetype has developed out of the accumulated experience of human beings with the need to assume social roles to facilitate interaction. In fulfilling the persona archetype by developing a "public" personality, one can defend against unacceptable thoughts and feelings (thereby swelling the personal unconscious) or remain conscious of putting one's best foot forward (which involves the ego). The latter route leads to a sense of alienation from others, because one is conscious of tricking them; the former involves the alienation from self inherent in the personal unconscious.

Although other archetypes have been set forth, no definitive list is available. Jung and his associates have described the archetypes of the *old wise man, God, the child, the hero, magic, power, birth, rebirth,* and *death* in addition to those already covered. One more, that of *unity* (which underlies the *self*) is of great importance, and will be discussed later.

INTRAPSYCHIC CONFLICT AND SELFHOOD. There is little question that Jung's position exemplifies the conflict model. Polarization, the opposition of elements, is basic to understanding how his theory conceptualizes life. According to Jung, all that is human—indeed, everything in the universe—exists, changes, and thrives because of conflict and opposition. It is more difficult to determine whether his view is essentially psychosocial or intrapsychic. I will now examine his concepts further with a view toward settling this matter.

The existence of a personal unconscious certainly indicates that what appears to be psychosocial conflict exists. Some conscious thoughts and impulses are threatening and hence pushed out of awareness by defenses. As in Freud, the threat is punishment or guilt, those twin pains deriving originally from the individual's opposition to society. Though the unacceptable thoughts and impulses need not always be sexual or aggressive for Jung, the form of conflict is nonetheless Freudian.

There are two considerations, however, that cast doubt on the assertion that Jung's is a psychosocial form of conflict theory. First, it is not clear that the conflict between individual and social pressures is inevitable. Relying for most of his explanations on the collective unconscious, Jung makes very little of the personal unconscious. In addition, the ego represents true, accurate consciousness, not the half-truth of rationalization. A full-bodied psychosocial conflict theory cannot postulate a true, accurate consciousness, because the conflict between individual and society is inevitable and the individual —always the weaker—must engage in the distortion of defensiveness. Jung makes it clear that defenses can be relaxed and, therefore, the personal unconscious can become conscious. Because it is possible, in his view, to have a distortion-free consciousness, his theory is probably best not considered a psychosocial conflict theory.

The second reason against a psychosocial conflict classification is even more compelling. Recall that in Freud the individual's contribution to the psychosocial conflict is considered to be a biological selfishness as somatic and real as metabolism itself. In contrast, biology is incidental to Jung's view of conflict. It is vital to recognize that the shadow, or locus of animalistic thoughts and impulses, is an archetype, not a biological imperative. This essence of animalism is part of the collective unconscious, a mental phenomenon. Thoughts and impulses sufficiently selfish to clash with the common good are, therefore, recapitulations of past mental experience rather than biological imperatives. Even if one asserted that in the beginning—the first time in history that an individual clashed with others—a biological imperative was operating (and it is not certain that Jung would agree), this would not change the fact that all modern people inherit a mental (not biological) predisposition to think and act selfishly because their ancestors have done so.

In these subtle distinctions, I am trying to show that, for Jung, the only causation of any human importance is mental. Jung sometimes refers to mental life as *spirit* (1933a, pp. 171–195), in contrast to *matter,* which is everything else of a physical nature—animal, vegetable, or mineral. In extolling the nonbiological nature of mentality, Jung (1933a) says,

> But people who are not above the general level of consciousness have not yet discovered that it is ... presumptuous and fantastic for us to assume that matter produces spirit; that apes give rise to human beings; that from the harmonious interplay of the drives of hunger, love, and power Kant's Critique of Pure Reason should have arisen; that the brain-cells manufacture thoughts, and that all this could not possibly be other than it is. (p. 176)

What a far cry this is from Freud! And notice how the final phrase suggests that once you make mentality your primary explanatory principle, nothing is impossible anymore. The only limits of change are those of the imagination itself.

With such a psyche-centered view, one inevitably must come to question whether apparently causal considerations such as societal pressures (taboos and sanctions) are anything more than figments of the imagination. It seems quite clear that Jung (1933a) intends us to believe that since societal pressures must be perceived before they can be acknowledged as such, they have the status of psychic rather than social realities:

> Without a doubt psychic happenings constitute our only, immediate experience.... My sense impressions, for all that they force upon me a world of impenetrable objects occupying space, are psychic images, and these alone are my immediate experience, for they alone are the immediate objects of my consciousness.... All our knowledge is conditioned by the psyche which, because it alone is immediate, is superlatively real. Here there is a reality to which the psychologist can appeal—namely, psychic reality ... If I change my concept of reality in such a way as to admit that all psychic happenings are real—and no other use of the concept is valid—this puts an end to the conflict of matter and mind as contradictory explanatory principles. (pp. 189–190)

In the final sentence, Jung makes it perfectly clear that what may have appeared as a psychosocial conflict—the contradiction of mind by the "matter" of presumed social imperatives—is really no more than an intrapsychic conflict. If society seems opposed to the individual, it is because it is perceived that way, not because that opposition is its unchangeable real nature. If you have any remaining doubt, there is Jung's dramatic statement in which he indicates the prepotency of the psyche: "In that one moment in which I came to know, the world sprang into being; without that moment it would never have been." (Jung, 1959a, p. 96)

The basically intrapsychic nature of Jung's conflict theory is also apparent in the way he uses it to understand persons and phenomena. There is conflict between a person's conscious perception of his or her sexuality and the presence of both anima and animus; between persona, other archetypes, and consciousness—indeed, among any and all of the core characteristics postulated. Intrapsychic conflict is the basic fact of life. But conflict, though inevitable, is not merely painful, something to be defended against. On the contrary, the opposition of elements in the psyche provides energy, as you shall see in the next section, and stimulates growth. It is not surprising, therefore, to find Jung (1933a) extolling the unconscious:

> It is well known that the Freudian school presents the unconscious in a thoroughly depreciatory light,

just as also it looks on primitive man as little better than a wild beast. . . . Have the horrors of the World War really not opened our eyes? Are we still unable to see that man's conscious mind is even more devilish and perverse than the unconscious? . . . The unconscious is not a demonic monster, but a thing of nature that is perfectly neutral as far as moral sense, aesthetic sense and intellectual judgement go. It is dangerous only when our conscious attitude becomes hopelessly false. And this danger grows in the measure that we practice repressions. . . . That which my critic feared—I mean the overwhelming of consciousness by the unconscious—is most likely to occur when the unconscious is *excluded from life by repressions*, or is misunderstood and depreciated. (pp. 16–17)

To remain open to emanations from the collective unconscious is to stand on the shoulders of all who have gone before. And to permit the personal unconscious to become conscious again is to recapture the richness of one's particular past. In contrast to psychosocial conflict positions, intrapsychic ones see conflict as valuable and not to be defended against just because it is inevitable and painful.

Indeed, the ideal, according to Jung, is for people to concern themselves actively with unconscious as well as conscious experiences and to try to fit the two into a dynamic balance. The tension, pain, and difficulty involved are not to be avoided, for they are the stuff of life itself. Actually, Jung (1953b) postulates an archetype called the self in formalizing this ideal:

> If we picture the conscious mind with the ego as its centre, as being opposed to the unconscious, and if we now add to our mental picture the process of assimilating the unconscious, we can think of this assimilation as a kind of approximation of conscious and unconscious, where the centre of the total personality no longer coincides with the ego, but with a point midway between the conscious and unconscious. This would be the point of a new equilibrium, a new centering of the total personality, a virtual centre which, on account of its focal position between conscious and unconscious, ensures for the personality a new and more solid foundation. (p. 219)

Clearly, in pursuing selfhood, one does not eliminate conflict (the conscious and unconscious remain opposed) so much as set the two conflicting poles of personality into juxtaposition and communication. You will recall that, in contrast to common personological usage, Jung defines the self as a conglomerate of conscious and unconscious experience.

ENERGY CONCEPTS. You now have covered the core characteristics involved in the core tendency of attempting to attain selfhood. But Jung also postulates several energy principles intrinsic to this core tendency. The energy involved in the psychological activities of thinking, feeling, and acting is called *psychic energy* (Jung, 1960a). Its sources are presented ambiguously. Sometimes Jung states that it derives from the very conflict of the core characteristics already mentioned; sometimes, in more Freudian fashion, he considers it to be based on such biological processes as metabolism. In any event, the amount of psychic energy invested in thoughts, feelings, or actions as elements of personality is called the *value* of each element. Value is essentially a measure of element intensity and is related to Freud's notion of cathexis.

You are now in a position to appreciate Jung's two main energy principles, which are psychological versions of the first and second laws of thermodynamics. The *principle of equivalence* (Jung, 1960a) states that if the value of any element of personality increases or decreases, this shift will be compensated for by an opposite shift in another element. For example, if a person loses interest in someone or an activity, someone else or another activity will become more attractive. Applied to broader elements of personality, this principle indicates that if energy is removed from the ego, for example, it will be reinvested elsewhere, perhaps in the personal unconscious or the persona. The person who becomes concerned with internal experience does so at the expense of attention to external experience, and vice versa.

The *principle of entropy* (Jung, 1960a), in its psychological form, states that the distribution of energy in the psyche seeks an equilibrium, or balance. Thus, if two beliefs have unequal values or strengths, the general tendency will be for the stronger belief to become weaker and the weaker, stronger. Or, if the ego is stronger (more relied on in everyday life) than the shadow, the tendency over time will be for them to come closer together in value.

These two energy principles constitute the essential dynamic of the core tendency of seeking selfhood. Indeed, according to Jung, the ideal state is selfhood, in which the total energy is evenly distributed (the ultimate outcome of the two energy principles) throughout the various elements of personality. In that state, consciousness and unconsciousness have equal energy, as do particular thoughts, feelings, and actions. However, this state of balance is not conflict-free. That conflict still underlies psychic functioning even when selfhood is attained is shown by the emphasis on equilibrium. Though each element has the same value as the others, none has lost its identity, with their balance a dynamic one based on the tension of opposition.

In postulating the principles of equivalence and entropy, Jung emphasizes the psyche as a closed system, unaffected by input from external sources. It is only in such a system that decreases in the energy of one element would produce compensatory increases in the energy of another and there would be a general tendency toward a balance of energies. Nonetheless, Jung (1960a) does not believe that the psyche is a completely closed system. There are inputs of energy from somatic processes such as metabolism and from the outside world in such forms as punishment and encouragement. These external inputs are regular and inevitable enough to render it impossible, in Jung's view, for one ever to attain complete selfhood. Complete selfhood is, in this sense, an ideal to be striven for but never completed. Perhaps its unattainability is fortunate, because in physics, when perfect entropy is reached in a system, that system will run down and stop, there being no further possibility of the energy differentials that lead to movement. Perhaps there is a basis for rapport between Jung and the later Freud, for whom—paradoxically—the goal of all life is death.

In this discussion, I have considered three bases for interaction among elements of personality; namely, opposition, compensation, and dynamic balance. These are all consistent with the intrapsychic conflict model. But Jung (1960a) intimates a fourth: unity. On the face of it, this suggests an alternative to conflict in this system. Along these lines, Jung proposes a *transcendent function,* which works toward integrating personality elements into an overall whole. This transcendent function seems to be not another energy principle so much as a dynamic (rather than static) picture of the self, inclining the person toward a unification of the opposing trends within the personality. Though other forces, such as the defensiveness associated with the personal unconscious, may oppose the transcendent function, it will tend to work toward unification anyway. If nothing else, it will be expressed at the unconscious level in the desire for wholeness that Jung claims is seen in many dreams and myths.

But what sense of unity can a theory so steeped in intrapsychic conflict possibly have? The answer is a paradoxical or mystical sense. To appreciate Jung's ideas on unity, you must recognize his belief that opposites attract and that the opposite of every truth is also true. The metaphor he adopts for this paradoxical unity is the *mandala,* or *circle,* which appears in Sanskrit writings and in many religions. If opposing polarities, such as consciousness and unconsciousness, can be represented as a straight line, the ends of which race off in opposite directions, the mandala image transforms the straight line into a perfect circle. In this case, the ends simultaneously race apart and toward each other. In Jung's thinking, the mandala symbol is closely allied to the self and to the entropy principle.

The problem with the mandala metaphor is that it really does not aptly describe polarities and oppositions. One does not resolve the conflict inherent in a *defined* opposition by suddenly deciding to bend a straight line into a circle, because this only contradicts the defined opposition. Jung is working with a paradoxical sense of unity. Perhaps he even recognizes this, for he believes that the transcendent function cannot completely triumph, as selfhood cannot fully be attained.

Selfhood is not possible in the final analysis because the principle of entropy requires a closed system to culminate in equilibrium, but Jung adamantly believes that the psyche is not really a closed system. That Jung talks about unity at all rather than just compensation, opposition, and dynamic balance reflects the extraordinary complexity of his theorizing and his lack of concern for mere inconsistencies in his thinking. He may also have been holding out the possibility that the human will evolve, at some future time, into a being described better in fulfillment than in conflict terms. This evolutionary possibility is not inconsistent with his emphasis on the collective unconscious as the content of the human's past experiences. For the moment, however, we would do well to conclude that on balance Jung's views are of the intrapsychic conflict type.

Jung on Development

Once we turn to development, the optimism of Jung's position, in contrast to its Freudian ancestry, becomes apparent. Jung believes that individuals are constantly trying to grow and occasionally meet with some success in their efforts. The story of personality development hardly ends with childhood, as far as he is concerned. Indeed, as you have seen, for Jung the human species is also constantly evolving more differentiated and conscious forms of existence. In this regard, the collective unconscious provides a basis whereby all modern people stand on the shoulders of their predecessors and are therefore able to see a little further than their forebears could.

More specifically, Jung (1960b) believes that in the earliest years psychic energy is invested primarily in activities necessary for physical survival. Jung considers sexuality per se to start becoming important somewhere around the age of 5 (the time of Freud's oedipal conflict). Adolescence is basically an amplification of these early beginnings. Early adulthood involves employing these activities in more broad and complex commitments, such as in a vocation, a family, and a community. Although Jung does

not postulate hard and fast developmental stages, his position thus far is similar to Freud's.

The big contrast with Freud, however, occurs in Jung's conceptualization of the latter half of life. Subsequent personologists have taken up Jung's belief that a radical change takes place in people when they reach the late 30s and early 40s. Biological and social interests, activities, and orientations to the external, material world recede, to be replaced by an inward-turning spirituality. Wisdom and patience take the place of physical and mental assertiveness. The person becomes more religious, cultural, philosophical, and intuitive. In the ideal case, the strident emphasis on consciousness of the early years is tempered by an acceptance of unconscious experience (e.g., intuitions, mysteries) and an assimilation of it into everyday life. But if the transition is not well navigated, the result is spiritual bankruptcy and a hellish end of life. Jung (1933a) feels that people living now experience particular difficulty in making this transition, because traditional and religious values have deteriorated in the face of industrialization without being replaced by any other ideological justification for spirituality. In this, he agrees with existential psychology.

Jung uses many different concepts to articulate his views on development. He contrasts *causality* with *teleology* to lend philosophical sophistication to his optimism. According to the teleological viewpoint, human personality can be comprehended in terms of future goals. Causality, in contrast, explains the present in terms of the past. Jung felt both were necessary for complete understanding, and he criticized Freud for considering only causality. Similar in form is his distinction between *progression* and *regression*. Jung does not mean these as defenses in any strict sense; rather, he wants to emphasize the forward thrust of development as progression and the shrinking to a safe past as regression. Although both occur in any person's life, progression is more a sign of growth than regression is. In special instances, however, regression may involve a beneficial tapping of the well of the unconscious. Another, similar distinction concerns *sublimation* and *repression,* processes that, once again, are reminiscent of defenses but somehow less concrete and specific than in Freud. In sublimation, psychic energy is transferred from primitive, instinctual, undifferentiated processes to more cultural, spiritual, complex processes. For example, when energy is withdrawn from sexual activity and given to religious activity, sublimation is said to have occurred. But when the discharge of energy is blocked by some internal or external obstacle, repression takes place. The energy is then transferred to the personal unconscious, blocking development. Although his thinking is too complicated to recount here, note that Jung feels that the energy principles of equivalence and entropy underlie the processes of sublimation/repression and progression/regression.

Another way Jung discusses development is as psychological growth, or the progressive tendency toward differentiation and integration. The basis for differentiation is inherent in the conflicting nature of core characteristics. Integration expresses the self archetype and the transcendent function. The shift in adulthood from material to spiritual concerns is part and parcel of the tendency to attain selfhood and integration. Apparently Jung (1960c) is willing to carry his notions of spirituality to extremes quite uncommon in a scientist. He postulates the *principle of synchronicity,* intended to explain the contiguous or simultaneous occurrence of events that, though not causes of one another, indicate some commonality in the collective unconscious. With this principle, Jung intends to take seriously such disputed phenomena as telepathy and clairvoyance. For him, simultaneous events, such as thinking of a long-lost friend and having that friend arrive unexpectedly or awakening with the fear that someone has been hurt only to find out later that this has indeed occurred, express the principle of synchronicity. This principle does not cause the simultaneous events; instead, it indicates the multiple expressions of archetypes. An archetype can express itself in someone's thoughts (e.g., you remember a long-lost friend) and in the occurrence of an external event (e.g., the friend arrives unexpectedly).

With the addition of the principle of synchronicity, Jung has evolved the notion of collective unconscious into something very close to a universal force that does not even depend on the existence of individual psyches for expression. With this principle, he is at his most mystical.

It is extremely difficult to evaluate Jung's position. If the usual procedures of scientific, analytical thought were to be applied, the position could easily be faulted. For example, the principle of synchronicity is actually not an explanation at all but a description of an observed relationship. All Jung is saying is that two events occurring together do so because sometimes seemingly disparate events occur together. If he were to contend more—namely, that archetypes actively precipitate seemingly disparate though simultaneous events—archetypes would essentially constitute the very supernatural order Jung has also decried. Similarly, his assumption of a transcendent function seems to contradict the principles of equivalence and entropy and his other assumptions concerning the inevitability of conflict.

But I have the nagging feeling that, by tackling Jung's theory with the tools of logic, we are missing what there is of value in it. Let us conclude that the theory is full of logical inconsistencies and ambiguities but try nonetheless to capture its intent. In doing this, we will emerge with an emphasis on mind or spirit as the architect of life. Jung is much more humanistic than Freud and others who have given important roles to biological and social forces in the determination of behavior. In this regard, the collective unconscious and its archetypes can be considered the inherent structure of mind. This inherent structure, not the body or society, sets limits on human freedom of imagination and action. No doubt it is this extreme spirituality that underlies Jung's appeal.

Jung on the Periphery of Personality

Jung (1933b) offers an ingenious conceptualization of personality types that is in some ways consistent and in others inconsistent with the rest of his thinking. The main distinction he makes is between *introverted* and *extroverted* types:

> The two types are essentially different, presenting so striking a contrast, that their existence, even to the uninitiated in psychological matters, becomes an obvious fact, when once attention has been drawn to it. Who does not know those taciturn, impenetrable, often shy natures, who form such a vivid contrast to those other open, sociable, serene maybe, or at least friendly and accessible characters, who are on good terms with all the world, or, even when disagreeing with it, still hold a relation to it by which they and it are mutually affected. (p. 412)

At the observational level, extroverted people are concerned with the external world of things and people, whereas introverted people focus on the internal world of their own ruminations. This useful observational distinction has been adopted by many psychologists and laypersons.

Jung uses the distinction between introversion and extroversion not only in readily observed differences among people but in deeper elements of psychic life. You should note that everyone, according to Jung, is capable of being both introverted and extroverted. Even though these are opposite tendencies, this assumption is quite consistent with the intrapsychic conflict model—the personality is composed of intrinsically opposed elements. As the person grows to adulthood, one of the attitudes comes to be dominant so that observationally he or she is either introverted or extroverted. This assumption implies that an attitude becomes dominant through some process of learning, though Jung does not specify what it is; thus, because the introversion-extroversion distinction occurs through learning, I consider it part of the periphery rather than core of personality.

Once an attitude becomes dominant, the person seems to be somewhat ruled by it. This does not mean, however, that the opposing attitude has no effect at all. The nondominant attitude does not evaporate but becomes unconscious. As part of the personal unconscious, the nondominant attitude exerts a subtle effect, expressed in unexpected inconsistencies of behavior and vague longings to be other than what one seems.

Thus, people in whom introversion dominates will generally be ruminative, reflective, and concerned with their own inner worlds, but they nonetheless will experience a nagging wish to break out of their own minds into the world of action and interchange with others and will actually make occasional strange and unexpected forays into extroverted behavior. Another sign of the potency of repressed extroversion may be an introverted person finding overtly extroverted persons strangely attractive though different. Thus, when Jung speaks of an introverted person, he means someone in whom introversion is dominant and conscious and in whom extroversion is nondominant and unconscious but nonetheless present. For the extroverted person, the opposite is true.

In developing his typology, Jung (1933b) adds four additional distinctions he calls *functional modes*, which constitute general styles of experience: thinking, feeling, sensing, and intuiting. Thinking and feeling are grouped together as rational in that they involve value judgments. Evaluation in the *thinking mode* involves classifying separate ideas or observations under general concepts and organizing these concepts systematically to determine meaning. In the *feeling mode,* evaluation lies in determining whether an idea or observation is liked or disliked. However strange it may seem to consider feeling a *rational function* along with thinking, Jung does this because feeling, as he defines it, shares with thinking the capacity to order and organize experience. Feeling does this by enabling the person to determine preferences.

In contrast, sensing and intuiting do not lead to the establishment of order and involve no value judgments. Therefore, they are considered *irrational functions,* though Jung does not mean anything disparaging by this classification. In the *sensing mode,* one simply experiences the presence and qualities of things in an unevaluative, open way. The *intuiting mode* involves apprehending the essential characteristics of something in a manner that is immediately unreflective. Whereas sensing involves literal recognition, intuiting means grasping latent, underlying, or future possibilities.

As with introversion-extroversion, though everyone has the capability for thinking, feeling, sensing, and intuiting, typically one function becomes dominant through learning. According to Jung, the two rational functions oppose each other as do the two irrational functions. Thus, if one of the rational functions achieves dominance, the other is relegated to the personal unconscious, there to exert a subtle, underground influence on experiencing. Further, the two irrational functions are subordinated to the dominant rational function with the role of assisting it. For example, if thinking is dominant, feeling is unrecognized by the person, though it manifests itself in wishes and dreams, in occasional lapses into strong emotions, and in attraction to people in whom feeling is dominant. The functions of sensing and intuiting are conscious and active but serve the thinking function. The person might well accumulate a wide range of sensations to operate on them with thought processes, and his or her intuitions might serve to initiate more systematic thought. The same sort of relationship holds when one of the irrational functions achieves dominance. You should be able to puzzle through the other combinations, such as dominant sensing, with unconscious intuiting, served by thinking and feeling.

PSYCHOLOGICAL TYPES. Jung (1933b) combines the introversion-extroversion distinction with the thinking-feeling and sensing-intuiting distinctions in arriving at what he calls *psychological types.* The types are *introversive-rational, introversive-irrational, extroversive-rational,* and *extroversive-irrational.* Of course, each type involving rational functions is further subdivided according to whether thinking or feeling is dominant, and each type involving irrational functions is broken down into sensing or intuitive dominance. This makes a total of eight basic personality types.

Although Jung is explicit in his typology, he offers no systematic list of peripheral characteristics to go along with it. From his descriptions of the personality types, however, one can infer some notions as to concrete peripheral characteristics. Presumably, thinking introverts believe

theories and not facts are important, and they have a vague dread of the opposite sex. The latter occurs because sexual expression is in general both extroverted and concerned with feeling, and the thinking introvert has repressed these tendencies. The feeling introvert has a deep sense of God, freedom, immortality, and other values but can be mischievously cruel because not only extroversion but thinking has been repressed. Sensing introverts tend to be guided by what happens to them, with little operation of judgment, especially in regard to themselves. Finally, intuiting introverts discern possibilities and pursue them without regard for themselves and others but cannot understand why they are undervalued by others. The latter is true because of the repression of not only extroversion but also sensing, which produces people insensitive to what is going on around them.

Among the extroverted types, there is the thinking extrovert, whose ideas are banal and dull and for whom the end justifies the means. These characteristics are understandable in someone who represses introversive tendencies and, because of repressed feeling, lacks a sense of what is proper and worthwhile. The feeling extrovert displays extravagant though unbelievable feelings and, though enjoying excellent rapport with others, hurts them with tactlessness. The disadvantage of this type stems from the deemphasis on logical and problem-solving thought inherent in repression of thinking and introversion. In the sensing extrovert, one finds a thoroughly realistic person who nonetheless is rather slavishly bound to specifics and facts. This person never seems to get beyond the surface of things because of the repression of intuiting and introversion. Finally, the intuiting extrovert always seizes new things with enthusiasm but is apt to become involved with unsuitable persons of the opposite sex. Though capable of discerning possibilities, the intuiting extrovert, by having repressed sensing and introversion, is rendered somewhat unable to judge the results of his or her enthusiasms.

IDEAL AND NONIDEAL TYPES. In each personality type, there are strengths according to what is dominant and conscious and weaknesses from what is nondominant and repressed. None of these types can be considered ideal or even relatively better than the others, according to Jung. Instead, Jung considers the attainment of selfhood to be ideal. This process involves growing out of one's personality type, as it were, so that none of one's human capabilities is submerged and unconscious. In attaining selfhood, thinking introverts would have to become conscious of their feelings and extroversion and integrate these into their everyday lives. They would, at the point of success, have no personality type at all, having fulfilled all their capabilities. In selfhood, one attains a universal personality, in which the personal unconscious has shrunk to zero and life's actions are a joint function of the ego and the collective unconscious.

WHAT IS THE ROLE OF SOCIAL INTERACTION? Jung's statements on peripheral characteristics of personality are consistent with his core statements in that both express the intrapsychic model, as indicated earlier. But there is an inconsistency between core and periphery because of Jung's failure to tell us how the personality types develop out of interactions between core and society. Clearly, the types are learned. But it is not so clear how they develop as a function of experience. Certainly, to define the personality type in Jungian terms is to simultaneously make a statement about at least some of the content of the personal unconscious and ego. What is dominant in a type is represented in the ego as conscious experience, and what is nondominant appears in the personal unconscious as repressions. It is harder to know how the collective unconscious feeds into the personality types. One also misses reference to parent-child interactions in a manner that could help systematize ideas on the development of personality types.

Jung does say that personality types develop early in life and provide the major basis for behavior throughout young adulthood. But by one's early 40s, there has been a general shift in personality toward introspection and rumination. This is the time when the transition may be made

from a personality type to selfhood. If the transition is not made, general despair and hopelessness may attend later adulthood. To successfully make the transition, people must become more conscious of their personal unconscious and be attuned to the emanations into consciousness of the collective unconscious. What this will specifically mean is more or less determined by the personality type: thinking introverts will have to become sensitive to their feelings and extroversive tendencies, and so forth. In addition, one must accept and value the collective unconscious. This means, among other things, accepting experiences of the uncanny, of things beyond individual control. It also means identifying with humankind and all living things in an uncritical, appreciative way. This part of Jung's view of the ideal is not very different from Zen Buddhism. In psychotherapy, Jung has ingenious ways of aiding people in the transition from specific personality types to selfhood. These include spending time and effort at fantasy and imaginative activities, such as painting and daydreaming.

A FINAL WORD . . . .

By now, the particular quality of intrapsychic conflict theorizing is probably becoming clear to you. Because the inherent, unresolvable conflict present throughout life arises in the mind—in each of our minds—it is not so ideal to use defenses to dull awareness. The ideal lifestyle in intrapsychic theorizing is still a compromise, as you saw in Rank's artist type and Jung's foredoomed effort after selfhood. But, the more aware you are of the tragic conflict, the better you can fashion a life combining, somehow, the incompatibilities. Defenses, used to drop one of the incompatible forces out of consciousness, actually jeopardize an ideal lifestyle.

In contrast, what an ideal lifestyle is turns out quite differently in psychosocial conflict theorizing, with its emphasis on the antagonism between the individual and the society (of which the parents are representatives). Parents are stronger than the child and, hence, it is the individual who must give ground if an ideal lifestyle is to be fashioned. In that ideal lifestyle, defensiveness is valuable in order to curb actions that would incur society's punishment and blunt personal awareness that could arouse guilt.

The outcome of this difference is very clear in the specific patterns of thoughts, feelings, and actions considered ideal or nonideal by psychosocial and intrapsychic conflict theorists. The psychosocial theorists emphasize stability, responsibility, routine, and dependability as characteristic of the ideal lifestyle, and they conceptualize personal and interpersonal turmoil, as well as social unacceptability, as signs of nonideal lifestyles. Intrapsychic theorists, in contrast, emphasize a bittersweet awareness of inner and interpersonal turmoil as expressive of the ideal lifestyle; blandness, simplicity, and placidity, which mask underlying tensions, signify nonideal lifestyles. Despite these differences, both versions of conflict theorizing adopt a tragic view of the human condition in which there is no singular, triumphant way to live.

CHAPTER 5

THE FULFILLMENT MODEL: ACTUALIZATION VERSION

You have just considered some personality theories that conceptualize the core of personality as reflecting the ongoing conflict between two irrevocably opposed forces. In the conflict model, life is always seen as a compromise, the purpose of which is to minimize the conflict. But because the conflict is always potentially large and debilitating, the compromise has an uncertain quality.

The theories I will consider in the next two chapters conceptualize the core of personality quite differently. They typically assume only one basic force in the person. Therefore, life is considered not a compromise but the unfolding of the one force. I call the position exemplified by these theories the *fulfillment model*. There are two versions of the fulfillment model, the difference between them being the nature of the postulated force. If the force is the tendency to express to an ever greater degree the capabilities, potentialities, or talents based in one's genetic constitution, we are dealing with the *actualization version*. In the *perfection version*, the force is the tendency to strive for what will make life ideal or complete, perhaps even by compensating for functional or genetic weak spots. The actualization version is humanistic, whereas the perfection version is idealistic.

This chapter will deal with the actualization version. I will first discuss Rogers's theory and examine its basis in the work of Goldstein. Then I will turn to Maslow. Although similar in many important ways to Rogers, Maslow postulates not one but two forces within the person. The two forces, however, do not necessarily oppose each other, with one force much less important than the other. Though Maslow's theory clearly is an actualization version of the fulfillment model, its postulation of two different forces within the person prompts me to consider it a variant of that model. Finally, I will introduce you to a newer, more fragmentary personality theory. Espoused by Costa and McCrae, it comes out of the factor analytic research tradition of trait theory.

ROGERS'S POSITION ....

Carl R. Rogers (born near Chicago, 1902; died in La Jolla, California, 1987) differed from many psychotherapists in holding a Ph.D. rather than a medical degree and in his Protestant background. He apparently considered the strict religious background of his early life to be heavily restricting and burdensome. Early in life, Rogers was interested primarily in the biological and physical sciences. After graduation from college, however, his concerns shifted sufficiently to prompt him to enter the Union Theological Seminary in New York City. Perhaps this shift indicated an attempt to work through his feelings concerning his earlier background; the seminary he entered is well known for its liberality. Before long, Rogers transferred to Columbia University, where he was influenced by the humanistic philosophy of John Dewey and first encountered clinical psychology. In his initial clinical work, he was exposed to a strongly Freudian view, which even then was not convincing to him, because it denied the importance of people's conscious views of themselves. Rogers worked for several years at the Rochester Guidance Center and eventually became its director. Surrounded by colleagues of varied personological convictions and stimulated by the daily practice of psychotherapy, Rogers began to formulate his own position. The person whose work touched him most at this time was Otto Rank, who by then had broken with Freud.

On leaving his clinical post, Rogers entered university life, taking on the role of teacher and researcher. During his association with the Unversity of Chicago, he was elected president of the American Psychological Association (1946–1947). With his increasing attention to developing a theory of personality and psychotherapy—an inevitable effect of entering university life—Rogers became increasingly influenced by theorists who stressed the importance of one's self-view as a determinant of behavior, among them Goldstein, Maslow, Angyal, and Sullivan. Next came several years at the University of Wisconsin, where Rogers interacted with psychiatrists and worked with severely disturbed clients. Rogers continued his theorizing at the Center for Studies of the Person, an organization in La Jolla, California, dedicated to the investigation of not only interpersonal relations but broader social issues, such as war and peace.

Rogers's Core Statement

Although there are a number of theorists similar to Rogers, his position is the most comprehensive, developed, and psychological of its type. It is, therefore, a good introduction to the actualization version of the fulfillment model. Rogers (1959) is very clear about the core of personality. For him, the *core tendency of humans is to actualize their inherent potentialities.* This means that a pressure in people leads them in the direction of becoming whatever it is in their inherited nature to be. People find it difficult to appreciate this *actualizing tendency* on the intuitive ground of their own experience. Certainly we have all had the experience of wanting or feeling impelled to accomplish something. But these experiences are usually at a level too concrete to be directly relevant to the actualizing tendency as stated. We usually experience ourselves as wanting to get good grades, learn to dance well, or be imaginative, rather than as wanting to act in concert with our inherent nature. The relatively concrete experiences just mentioned may not be irrelevant, of course, since what the actualizing tendency will lead to in persons' functioning depends on the content of their inherent potentialities. For example, if being imaginative is an inherent potentiality, wanting to be imaginative will certainly qualify as one expression of the actualizing tendency. And in this search for some intuitive basis for understanding Rogers's position, you should not overlook the strong possibility that at least some people sometimes have personal experience of an urging to express themselves—somehow and in something—that is difficult to talk about because it is so formless and abstract. Perhaps such occasional experiences are direct representations of the actualizing tendency.

Keeping in mind the questions raised by trying to find a basis in your personal experience for understanding Rogers, you can better appreciate a more formal approach to his theory. Once one assumes an actualizing tendency as the basic directionality of the person, one raises consideration of (1) the content of the inherent potentialities, (2) the nature of the actualizing tendency itself, and (3) the manner in which the inherent potentialities and the actualizing tendency interact in the process of living.

THE INHERENT POTENTIALITIES OF HUMAN BEINGS. About the only statement Rogers makes concerning the nature of the inherent potentialities is aimed at differentiating his position from that of Freud. According to Rogers, all of the person's potentialities serve the maintenance and enhancement of life. Hence, one will not find anything such as a death instinct if Rogers is right. For Rogers, death occurs accidentally, as the end result of biological breakdown with no primarily psychological significance, or through a decision on the person's part, which is usually a sign of psychological maladjustment rather than something true to human nature. Actually, I am being much more explicit concerning the view of death in this theory than Rogers ever was, though I believe what I have said fits the spirit of his thinking.

But if we discount the concept of the death instinct, Freud and Rogers might seem less far apart. For instance, Freud would find congenial the notion that inherent potentialities (he would call them instincts) function to maintain and enhance life. There is a world of difference between the two theorists, however, which has to do with their views on the relationship of the person to society. Recall that for Freud the person emerges as selfish and competitive in the pursuit of life. He views society as necessarily in conflict with individuals, because the requirements of corporate living are antithetical to the most direct expression of instincts. In contrast, Rogers assumes that what is consistent with the maintenance and enhancement of individuals' lives is also consistent with the maintenance and

enhancement of the lives of the people around them. For Rogers, there is nothing in human nature that, if accurately and straightforwardly expressed, would obviate the possibility of community by being seriously destructive to other people. While Rogers does not assume that it is part of human nature to be communal, he does indicate that people, in their least corrupted form, will so appreciate themselves and be so vigorous in their living as to be capable of deep appreciation of others as well. Although people do not need community in some imperative way, their nature is such that if they are not maladjusted, they can delight in other people.

You may wonder at this point how Rogers would address the seemingly plausible reasons why Freud assumed human nature to be antithetical to social living. What about all the ways in which one person hurts another? Would not mutual destructiveness increase if society's rules and regulations were relaxed? Is it not merely pie in the sky to think people are pure deep down? Rogers would answer out of irrepressible optimism. He would point out that more countries are at peace than at war, that world wars are still more unusual than world peace, that societies with many complex laws and taboos do not have less crime than more lax societies, that the overwhelming majority of people abhor death as something foreign to them, and that infants show very little behavior indicating socially destructive tendencies. In other words, Rogers would not find Freud's reasons for believing the human to be selfish and potentially destructive compelling. To be sure, one can observe selfishness and destructiveness, but then one must interpret them, and decide what such observations really say about human nature. At one level, Rogers is saying that such observations are random enough to be best considered as expressions of distortions of true human nature rather than, as in Freud, direct expressions of that nature.

At another level, Rogers offers more positive reasons for his view on the constructive nature of the person. These reasons come from observations of people in social contexts ranging all the way from psychotherapy to international diplomacy. One observation is that misunderstandings and suspiciousness lead to antagonism and even competition among people. When the misunderstandings are spoken to directly, suspiciousness decreases and antagonistic, competitive behaviors give way to cooperation and appreciation. This is not to say that people will always agree among themselves; rather, it means that if there is no misunderstanding, the remaining disagreements will be honest and mutually respected. Another observation is that when people feel hopeless and unworthy, they will disregard others and treat them poorly. Conversely, when they begin to accept themselves, they will also gain appreciation and acceptance of others, not only of the ways others resemble them but—and probably more important—the ways they differ. These kinds of observations incline Rogers to believe that the person's true nature—her or his inherent potentialities—is consistent with the maintenance and enhancement not only of the person's own living but also of social living. It is only when the inherent potentialities suffer distorted expression because of maladjustment that behavior destructive to oneself and others is found.

The most important theoretical difference between Freud and Rogers these observations point out is the following. Rogers contends that behavior destructive to others always occurs along with behavior destructive to oneself. He also believes that if Freud were right, one would characteristically see behavior constructive to oneself taking place as the result of behavior destructive to others, at least when society is least vigilant. Rogers, however, finds little evidence of this.

Of course, the weakness in Rogers's observations is that they do not occur outside the regulatory function of society; hence, though reasonably compelling, they are not definitive. In attempting to find observations uncontaminated by social pressure, one could go to infants or subhuman organisms. Unfortunately, infants are not good sources of information because they are so undeveloped that one might erroneously decide they are basically selfish, confusing maturational primitivity with a true lack of interest in the welfare of others. Even at that, Rogers contends that little in children's behavior shows they are self-seeking at the expense of other people. But anyone awakened by the wail of youngsters in the middle of the night is justified, it seems to me, in not finding Rogers's contention completely convincing. While Rogers would surely agree that these children were preoccupied with their own needs at that point, he would ask whether the observation was really sufficient to justify the extreme conclusion that human nature is basically incompatible with community. In truth, the observation is insufficient.

This state of nondefinitive information prompts one to turn to the nonhuman animals. Rogers has indeed done this and, as you will see later, this is thoroughly appropriate logically, for the actualizing tendency is not restricted to humans or even nonhumans; rather, it applies to all living things, vegetable and animal. At one point, Rogers (1961, pp. 177–178) asks that we consider the lion, certainly a worthy and reasonably representative member of the animal world. Presumably the lion is unencumbered by societal restrictions in any Freudian sense. While this certainly can be disputed, I will accept it as true for now. The lion, it turns out, is rather benign, having intercourse mainly with its mate and only occasionally with other lions, caring for its young in a rather loving way until they are old enough to go out into the world, and killing only when hungry or in defense of self and family. Here there is neither gratuitous evil nor any evidence of self-interest that is truly incompatible with the interests of others. The similarity between the life of the lion and that of the human is not accidental, according to Rogers. If people expressed their natural potentialities, they would live a reasonably ordered, constructive, even moral life without needing to be held in check by society.

At this point, I must call a halt to this controversy over the compatibility of human nature with community, for it cannot be settled easily. Certainly, someone holding Freud's view could find in the animal world organisms that murder at random (rather than in self-defense), such as the wolverine or the weasel, or could focus on the severe limitation to the possibility of self-actualization inflicted by the lion on its prey. And so the argument goes. It will suffice for you to recognize that the fulfillment model exemplified by Rogers is a serious and worthy alternative to the psychosocial conflict model.

Having appreciated the view that the inherent potentialities function to maintain and enhance life, you are in a position to inquire further as to their precise content. Extraordinary as it is, however, Rogers is almost mute on this matter. About the most insight one can gain through careful reading of Rogers is that he is thinking in terms of some sort of genetic blueprint, to which substance is added as life progresses. But the precise outlines of the blueprint are a mystery. Does it have to do with such biological considerations as the size and tone of muscles, the excellence of brain structures and organization, and the rapidity of metabolic functioning? Or does it concern more psychological considerations, such as the need to master or be imaginative or gregarious? Rogers gives virtually no guidance. Another question that goes unanswered is whether and how people differ in their inherent potentialities. As you will see, when considering the peripheral level of personality in a theory of this type, one finds it useful to be able to postulate such individual differences. One gets the sense that Rogers agrees, but nowhere is he explicit enough to inspire certainty.

Surely it would be difficult to make a list of things that constitute a genetic blueprint from a personologist's point of view. This undoubtedly is part of the reason why Rogers is mute. But there must be a reason beyond this difficulty, for Rogers is an intelligent, perceptive person with no prior reticence to tackle difficult problems. I think that the basic reason for Rogers's muteness is that making a list of inherent attributes would violate his intuitive sense of human freedom. He so vividly sees life as changing, shifting, unfolding, unpredictable, and vibrant that to theorize about some set list of characteristics would amount to shackling something wild and free.

A word about the history of this theory will make this point more convincing. Rogers's first and abiding interest has been psychotherapy, helping people beset by problems of living to find the bases for a more adequate, meaningful existence. Early on, he broke away from orthodox theories and techniques of psychotherapy, such as the psychoanalytic approach, and for a period of time was known as an antitheoretical practitioner. He did not rush to develop a theory of psychotherapy, because he was so deeply enmeshed in helping people that he cared little whether he had conceptual clarity as long as what was happening was beneficial. And it seemed to be. After a time, when his therapeutic experience had accumulated, he began to develop a theory about how one could understand successful therapeutic outcomes.

His theory of personality grew out of his theory of psychotherapy. And here lies the crux of my point. In psychotherapy, it is very helpful—for client and therapist alike—to believe in a view of the organism as unlimited in what it can become. Typically, clients are terribly limited by self-destructive symptom patterns and have lost conviction about becoming anyone worthwhile. In such situations, the therapist must hold out a view of life extreme enough in its opposition to the client's view to serve as the needed corrective. Once the client believes this emphasis on freedom, he or she can draw tremendous strength from it that will help to mobilize the persistence and energy needed to change deeply entrenched and destructive life patterns. Rogers's emphasis on unlimited possibilities in life has been so valuable in psychotherapy that it is not surprising that he would retain it in his theory of personality.

But a theory of personality is not a theory of psychotherapy. In a theory of personality, you do not start with an already disordered person; rather, when you make statements about core tendencies and characteristics, you are talking about the true nature of humans. While we may admire Rogers's temperamental unwillingness to set limits to life's possibilities, we should also recognize that the model of personality theory he has adopted sets up the logical requirement of precision concerning the genetic blueprint, thereby making his position complete enough to be usable. Without doubt, by not including the substantive characteristics of the genetic blueprint, Rogers is doing what in Freud's position would amount to considering instincts to be important determinants of action without saying what they are. All the richness of understanding contributed by Freud's view that there are life, sexual, and death instincts would, of course, be lost.

It might seem that in view of the obvious difficulty of theorizing on the content of inherent potentialities, one is justified in inferring people's potentialities from their actual behavior. Certainly this inductive approach provides one important way to build theories. Though such a strategy is useful in theory construction, however, it is totally unacceptable except on this temporary basis. It behooves the theorist employing such a strategy to recognize it as simply an expedient that limits the theory's usefulness. Unless such a cautionary stance is adopted, the theorist will succumb to the fallacy of circular reasoning. In Rogers's case, the fallacy would go as follows. He would propose that inherent potentialities determine all behavior while advocating using any and all observed behavior to discover the inherent potentialities. The circularity in this position involves defining what is to do the explaining in terms of what is to be explained. With such an approach, the theorist can never be proven wrong—nor proven right. Acceptance of such a circular position can occur only on the basis of faith (a kind of intuitive knowledge). It is necessary to be able to define a person's inherent potentialities by some logical or empirical means independent of the behavior they explain. Only then will it be possible to determine the soundness of Rogers's position. Until then, the lack of specificity as to the content of inherent potentialities will remain a dangerously seductive elastic clause.

THE ACTUALIZING TENDENCY. I have already pointed out that the actualizing tendency is the organism's push to become what its inherent potentialities suit it to be, these potentialities

aiming toward the maintenance and enhancement of life. In taking a closer look at the actualizing tendency, the first thing to note is its organismic—actually, biological—rather than psychological nature. Rooted in the physiological processes of the entire body, it is a way of talking about the tendency of organic matter to develop and multiply. In this, the actualizing tendency is more like Freud's life and sexual instincts than his death instinct. But the actualizing tendency is much broader than the life and sex instincts per se. It certainly includes such things as food and water requirements, but only as a special case of the much more general characteristic of living matter to develop according to its function. So when a fetus develops from a fertilized egg, when muscle and skin tissue differentiate, when secondary sex characteristics appear, when hormonal instigation of an inflammatory reaction occurs in the case of bodily injury, we see the working of the actualizing tendency as fully as in the more obvious case of intentional actions. I say this because Rogers makes it quite clear that the actualizing tendency is characteristic of not just human beings and animals, but all living things. Waxing poetic, he makes this point clearly at the beginning of a paper (1963):

During a vacation weekend some months ago I was standing on a headland overlooking one of the rugged coves which dot the coastline of northern California. Several large rock outcroppings were at the mouth of the cove, and these received the full force of the great Pacific combers which, beating upon them, broke into mountains of spray before surging into the cliff-lined shore. As I watched the waves breaking over these large rocks in the distance, I noticed with surprise what appeared to be tiny palm trees on the rocks, no more than two or three feet high, taking the pounding of the breakers. Through my binoculars I saw that these were some type of seaweed, with a slender "trunk" topped off with a head of leaves. As one examined a specimen in the interval between the waves it seemed clear that this fragile, erect, top-heavy plant would be utterly crushed and broken by the next breaker. When the wave crunched down upon it, the trunk bent almost flat, the leaves were whipped into a straight line by the torrent of the water, yet the moment the wave had passed, here was the plant again, erect, tough, resilient. It seemed incredible that it was able to take this incessant pounding hour after hour, day after night, week after week, perhaps, for all I know, year after year, and all the time nourishing itself, extending its domain, reproducing itself; in short, maintaining and enhancing itself in this process which, in our shorthand, we call growth. Here in this palmlike seaweed was the tenacity of life, the forward thrust of life, the ability to push into an incredibly hostile environment and not only hold its own, but to adapt, develop, become itself. (pp.1–2)*

The actualizing tendency is the biological pressure to fulfill the genetic blueprint, whatever the difficulty created by the environment. This passage also indicates that the actualizing tendency does not aim at tension reduction as the core tendencies of conflict theorists do. The life and development of the seaweed, as described by Rogers, is not to be understood as the pursuit of comfort and quiescence. If the actualizing tendency is to be characterized in tension terms at all, it must involve tension increase rather than reduction. Certainly the expression of "tenacity of life" and "forward thrust of life" and such extraordinary phenomena as "to push into an incredibly hostile environment" would precipitate increased rather than decreased organismic tension. Satisfaction of the actualizing tendency is to be understood in terms of fulfillment of a grand design rather than in terms of ease and comfort. As you will see, all the fulfillment positions involve increasing tension, in sharp contrast to the conflict positions, all of which involve decreasing tension in one form or another.

While the actualizing tendency is common to all living matter, it is not surprising that some of its expressions in the human being, according to Rogers, would be unlikely to appear at the subhuman level. Like all living things, humans show the basic organismic or biological form of the actualizing tendency, the aim of which is to express the inherent potentialities. But humans

also show rather distinctly psychological forms of the actualizing tendency. The most important of these is the *tendency toward self-actualization* (Rogers, 1959, p. 196). This differs from the actualizing tendency in that it involves the self. For Rogers, the self is

> the organized, consistent conceptual gestalt composed of perceptions of the characteristics of the "I" or "me" and the perceptions of the relationships of the "I" or "me" to others and to various aspects of life, together with the values attached to these perceptions. It is a gestalt which is available to awareness though not necessarily in awareness. (p. 200)

Thus, the self-actualization tendency is the pressure to behave and develop—experience oneself—consistently with one's conscious view of what one is. As you will see later, Rogers's concept of self is similar to Rank's will.

The self-concept presumably is a peculiarly human manifestation. To understand how it comes into being, we must consider two additional offshoots of the actualizing tendency in the human being: the need for positive regard and the need for positive self-regard (Rogers, 1959, pp. 108–109). Both are considered secondary or learned needs, commonly developed in early infancy, that represent specialized expressions of the overall actualizing tendency. The *need for positive regard* refers to the person's satisfaction at receiving the approval of others and frustration at receiving disapproval. The *need for positive self-regard* is a more internalized version of this—in other words, it refers to personal satisfaction at approving and dissatisfaction at disapproving of oneself. Because people need positive regard, they are sensitive to, or can be affected by, the attitudes toward them of the significant people in their lives. In the process of gaining approval and disapproval from others, people develop a conscious sense of who they are, called a *self-concept*. Along with this, they develop a need for positive self-regard, which ensures that the tendency toward self-actualization will take

---

*From "Actualizing Tendency in Relation to Motives and to Consciousness," by C. R. Rogers in the *1963 Nebraska Symposium on Motivation*, edited by M. R. Jones. Copyright © 1963 by the University of Nebraska Press. Reprinted by permission.

the form of favoring behavior and development consistent with the self-concept. The person is unlikely to persist in functioning incompatibly with the self-concept because this would frustrate the need for positive self-regard.

I will now summarize using the terminology of this book. Rogers considers the core tendencies of personality to be (1) the inherent attempt of the organism to actualize or develop all its capacities in ways that will serve to maintain and enhance life and (2) the attempt to actualize the self-concept, which is a psychological manifestation of (1). The needs for positive regard and positive self-regard are secondary or learned offshoots of these core tendencies, explicating the motivational mechanism whereby the actualization of self-concept is attempted. The characteristics at the core of personality are (1) the inherent potentialities, which define the ways in which the actualizing tendency will be expressed, and (2) the self-concept, which defines the ways in which the self-actualizing tendency will be expressed. These tendencies and characteristics lie at the core of personality because they are common to all persons and have a pervasive influence on living.

Rogers on Development

How do we actualize our potentialities? To understand maximal fulfillment, one must recognize that though the inherent potentialities are genetically determined, the self-concept is socially determined. This makes it possible to imagine discrepancies between these two sets of core characteristics: one's sense of who and what one is may deviate from what one's organismic potentialities actually suit one to be. But for this kind of discrepancy to exist, people must be failed by society. Even so, although society often fails the person in this way, it does not *have* to do so. Society is not inevitably antagonistic to the individual, as Freud and the psychosocial conflict theorists assume it to be.

Rogers (1961, pp. 31–48) has a good deal to say about the nature of society's failure, which he calls *conditional positive regard.* What he means is the situation in which only some but

not all of our actions, thoughts, and feelings are approved of and supported by the significant people in our lives. Thus, as we each develop a self-concept, the fact that other people's opinions of us are important will lead us to see ourselves only in terms of those actions, thoughts, and feelings of ours that have received approval and support. Our self-concepts will be based on what Rogers calls *conditions of worth,* that is, standards for discerning what is valuable and what is not valuable about ourselves. Conditions of worth as a concept serve much the same logical function as the superego does in Freud's theory. Both concepts represent something implanted by society that serves as an ethical monitor of our functioning.

The existence of conditions of worth in the self-concept brings into operation a defensiveness similar to that postulated by Freud. Once we have conditions of worth, some of the thoughts, feelings, and actions in which we could well engage will make us feel unworthy or guilty; hence, a process of defense is set in motion. As in Freud, the defense is activated when the person receives some small cue, in the form of *anxiety,* that unworthy behavior is about to occur. Rogers details two general kinds of defenses: *denial* and *distortion,* thus falling short of Freud's elaborate list of defenses. Further discussion of these matters will be deferred until discussion of his peripheral statement.

Although Rogers and Freud have similar notions of how society affects ethical functioning and defensive operations, which shield the person from the pain of feeling unworthy and aid in bending behavior to moral standards, the two theorists also essentially disagree. For Freud, defensive operations lead to the most successful life, whereas for Rogers, they result in a crippling restriction on living. This difference follows from other differences in their positions. For Freud, the conflict between individual and society is inevitable because the individual is by nature unsuited for community, even though social living is obviously necessary to the broader matters of survival of the species and development of culture. In contrast, for Rogers, though there is often conflict between the individual and society—witness conditional positive regard as a reaction to expressions of inherent potentialities —the conflict is not at all inevitable. There is no necessary incompatibility between the individual and society, because there is nothing in the individual's genetic blueprint that obviates community. While for Freud the good life involves expression of your true nature only within the necessary limitations of other people's rights, for Rogers the good life involves nothing less than maximal expression of your true nature. Conditions of worth and defensive processes are considered crippling because they lead to a rejection of thoughts, feelings, or actions that truly express inherent potentialities, a state of rejection called *incongruence*. In other words, once conditions of worth and defenses exist, it is impossible to fully actualize your potentialities. You cannot become all that you could be. You will have lost out on part of your genetic birthright.

How can these dire consequences be avoided? You must be lucky enough to have experienced as a youngster *unconditional positive regard* from the significant people in your environment (Rogers, 1961, pp. 31–48). The main Rogerian developmental statement concerns the existence of this unconditional positive regard, which he defines as significant people valuing and respecting you as a person and, therefore, supporting and accepting your behavior even if they disagree with it. Rogers does not literally mean that every possible action must be approved regardless of the consequences to yourself and others. Obviously, a young child must be restrained if she or he tries to run into the path of a moving truck. But if the child is to experience a continuance of positive regard despite the restraint, it must be clear from the adult's way of restraining that no diminution of respect and general approval has occurred. If the child is beaten or told she or he is bad for wanting to run across the street, the child is not being positively regarded. If, in contrast, the child is simply held back and told in words appropriate to her or his age level that running across the street is dangerous, the child is still being respected as a human being. In conceptualizing unconditional positive regard, Rogers emphasizes an atmosphere of

valuing and loving more than an absence of all constraints. There are obviously a host of things that the child must learn about the world to effectively negotiate its complexities. But these things can be learned in an atmosphere fostering either self-acceptance or self-denial, and this makes all the difference for Rogers.

If you grow up in an atmosphere of unconditional positive regard, rather than conditional positive regard, you develop no conditions of worth and no defensiveness. Your self-concept is broader and deeper, including a much larger proportion of the thoughts, feelings, and actions that express your inherent potentialities. In addition, your self-concept is more flexible and changing, because new thoughts, feelings, and actions brought about by the continual unfolding of the actualizing tendency can be consciously appreciated (there being no defense) and incorporated into the self-concept (there being no limiting conditions of worth). The state in which the self-concept embraces more or less all your potentialities is called *congruence*, which signifies that the self-concept has not shriveled to only part of who you are and can be. The state of flexibility in which new experiences can occur and be consciously appreciated is called *openness to experience*, meaning that no watering down through defenses is taking place.

Thus, for Rogers, the way to actualize your potentialities in the fullest manner is to possess a self-concept that does not include conditions of worth and, therefore, precipitates no defenses. It follows from this that you will (1) respect and value all manifestations of yourself, (2) be conscious of virtually all there is to know about yourself, and (3) be flexible and open to new experience. In this way, the work of becoming what it is in your nature to be can go forward undisturbed. You will be what Rogers calls a fully functioning person. And, as indicated earlier, far from being self-interestedly antisocial, as you would expect in the Freudian view of a person without defenses, you will value, appreciate, enjoy, and approve of other people because you value, appreciate, enjoy, and approve of yourself.

ROGERS AND GOLDSTEIN. You can trace many of the concepts found in Rogers and other actualization theorists to the position of Kurt Goldstein (1963). A physiologist interested in how people adjust to brain damage, Goldstein offers less a theory of personality than a theory of the organism. Nonetheless, understanding Rogers will be easier for you if you note his similarity to and difference from Goldstein.

Like Rogers, Goldstein assumes that the core characteristics of personality are the inherent potentialities and the core tendency is the push toward realization in the actual living of these inherent potentialities. Furthermore, both theorists agree that the core tendency and characteristics ensure the maintenance and enhancement of life and are not in any necessary way incompatible with community. Although both theorists assume a basic push in the person toward realizing potentialities, Rogers calls this the actualizing tendency whereas Goldstein calls it the *self-actualizing tendency,* a term Rogers saves for the push to realize one's subjective sense of who one is. Goldstein accepts the biological nature of the push to realize one's potentialities and still calls it a self-actualizing tendency because he does not have a psychological sense of the concept of self. For Goldstein, the self is virtually the same as the organism. Nowhere in Goldstein's theory does recourse to the importance of a phenomenal self-concept appear.

This means that Goldstein gives no formal theoretical role to such matters as conditions of worth and attempts to become in actual behavior what you think you should be. He also gives no formal theoretical role to conflict due to expressions of the actualizing tendency threatening to, or actually falling outside of, the limits set by conditions of worth. Hence, he assigns no formal theoretical role to defense, at least as a mechanism for avoiding psychologically determined anxiety and guilt. There is also no role in Goldstein's thinking for offshoots of the basic push to actualize potentialities, which could be considered the need for positive regard and the need for positive self-regard. As you can see, Goldstein's theory is much simpler than that of Rogers. It also cannot explain as much. Strictly speaking, Goldstein cannot consider such phenomena as guilt, unconscious cognitions, and acting in terms of one's aspirations.

Goldstein generally stays away from the kinds of phenomena mentioned above. Only unconscious cognition receives any significant attention. Goldstein asserts that there is no such thing in Freud's sense. For the unconscious—cognitions in the mind actively barred from consciousness—Goldstein substitutes the view that cognitions not actually at the center of attention at the moment may remain in the mind in unsalient form. But whenever the situation the person faces warrants it, the unsalient cognitions can be called to the center of attention.

As is typical of all fulfillment theorists, Goldstein fails to see society as having requirements that not only must be served if civilization is to survive but also stand in opposition to human nature. For Goldstein, as for Rogers, the external environment serves two functions for the person. First, it provides contexts, even tasks, to be performed in the enactment of fulfillment. Second, the environment can interfere with normal, vigorous actualization of potentialities. Though Goldstein offers no complicated or detailed account of development through interaction with society and the physical world, what he does provide is consistent with the fulfillment position. The self-actualization tendency will lead to the fulfillment of the genetic blueprint unless normal social support and freedom from physical danger are lacking. Danger or actual damage to the person causes *catastrophic anxiety,* or the fear of coming to an end, being overwhelmed, or disintegrating. Catastrophic anxiety diverts self-actualization pressure from the vigorous pursuit of life enhancement to the equally valuable but more conservative pursuit of life maintenance. In this case, the person does not grow so much as survive. Although survival may sound less remarkable than growth, for Goldstein the one is as much an expression of the self-actualization tendency as the other. They differ only in environment: survival is the best that an injured organism can do, while growth occurs when no injury exists.

Note that Rogers's theory parallels Goldstein's at the more psychological level. In Rogers, functioning defensively because of conditions of worth amounts to the maintenance of life. For life to be enhanced rather than merely maintained, there must be freedom from defensiveness, freedom that is due to an absence of conditions of worth, which in Rogers are psychological entities analogous to physical injury in Goldstein. Another way of viewing this is that threat to the person from the outside takes more of a social form for Rogers than for Goldstein, though neither believes threat to be inevitable. As a physically damaged organism orients itself toward maintenance rather than life enhancement, so does the psychologically damaged organism, considered by Rogers, orient itself through the action of defensive processes.

Regarding inherent potentialities, both theorists agree on something like a genetic blueprint. Although neither Goldstein nor Rogers specifies the content of the blueprint, Goldstein does suggest a technique whereby one can diagnose the inherent potentialities from the behavior one observes. Goldstein believes that in a person's preferences and in what he or she does well, one can see specific evidence of the underlying genetic blueprint. You should recognize that this is merely the beginning of content specification, for as a theoretician you can say nothing about content that is general and prior to concrete observations. You must have a person in front of you to observe so that you can diagnose his or her preferences and competencies. Having done so, you can speculate about that person's inherent potentialities. Such speculation will not necessarily tell you anything valid about the next person's potentialities. Nonetheless, Goldstein's technique of diagnosis is a step forward in precision if it can be used in a manner that avoids complete circularity of reasoning. If you can assume that only some of any person's behavior will express his or her preferences and competencies, you can say that only those behaviors clarify the nature of potentialities. Behavior that does not express preferences and competencies is to be understood in some other way. Because Goldstein's position focuses on only some

behavior, it avoids the circularity inherent in saying that all behavior expresses potentialities and it is potentialities that produce behavior.

Rogers's Peripheral Statement

As I have implied, a good way to detect the parts of a personality theory that deal with peripheral characteristics is to try to spot the points at which statements about the differences among people occur. Rogers makes only one broad distinction among ways of living, leading to the separation of people into two general types. In core-level terminology, these types comprise (1) the people in whom the actualizing tendency is vigorously expressed, leading to the enhancement and enrichment of living, as opposed to (2) the people in whom the actualizing tendency is protectively and defensively expressed, leading to the mere maintenance of living. Someone falling into the first type would be called a *fully functioning person;* someone falling into the second would be considered *maladjusted* (Rogers, 1959). Presumably, Rogers does not really believe that all people fall neatly into one type or the other; rather, there are degrees to which people resemble one or the other extreme.

THE IDEAL LIFESTYLE. If Rogers went no further in his theorizing, all one could say about persons is that they are either fully functioning or maladjusted. Fortunately, Rogers elaborates on the meaning of this core-level distinction in peripheral-level terms. He delineates a set of peripheral characteristics pertaining to fully functioning people, thus giving this type the kind of specificity indispensable in actually describing people (Rogers, 1961, pp. 183-196). The first of these characteristics is *openness to experience,* intended to signify the polar opposite of *defensiveness.* According to Rogers (1961), in a person open to experience,

> every stimulus—whether originating within the organism or in the environment—would be freely relayed through the nervous system without being distorted by any defensive mechanism. There would be no need of the mechanism of "subception" whereby the organism is forewarned of any

experience threatening to the self. . . . Thus, one aspect of this process which I am naming "the good life" appears to be a movement away from the pole of defensiveness toward the pole of openness to experience. The individual is becoming more able to listen to himself, to experience what is going on within himself. He is more open to his feelings of fear and discouragement and pain. He is also more open to his feelings of courage and tenderness, and awe. He is free to live his feelings subjectively, as they exist in him, and also free to be aware of these feelings. (pp. 187–188)*

Actually, on studying this statement, you can see that openness to experience is probably a group of peripheral characteristics rather than only one. If you think in the most concrete terms of how you would expect people open to experience to be, you will recognize that a number of characteristics are involved. At the least, we can say that people open to experience would be *emotional,* showing both positive and negative affects, and *reflective,* showing a richness of information about themselves. These clearly are peripheral characteristics, because they would be used to describe only part of any person's behavior and to typify differences among people. Breaking down complex and heterogeneous concepts, such as openness to experience, into their components can only render peripheral-level theorizing more useful, for at the peripheral level we are, of course, concerned with understanding people on the most concrete levels.

Rogers's next characteristic of the fully functioning person, which he calls *existential living,* is even more clearly a set of interrelated characteristics. Existential living involves the nebulous quality of living fully at every moment. Subjectively, people experience each moment as new and different from the preceding one. In elaborating on this existential quality, Rogers (1961) says,

One way of expressing the fluidity which is present in such existential living is to say that the self and personality emerge from experience, rather than experience being translated or twisted to fit preconceived self-structure. It means that one becomes a participant in and observer of the ongoing process of organismic experience, rather than being in control of it.

Such living in the moment means an absence of rigidity, of tight organization, of the imposition of structure on experience. It means instead a maximum of adaptability, a discovery of structure in experience, a flowing, changing organization of self and personality. (pp. 188–189)

Among the peripheral characteristics discernible in Rogers's notion of existential living are *flexibility, adaptability, spontaneity,* and *inductive thinking.*

Another characteristic of the fully functioning person is what Rogers calls *organismic trusting.* Because the meaning of this concept is not immediately apparent, I will quote Rogers (1961):

The person who is fully open to his experience would have access to all of the available data in the situation, on which to base his behavior; the social demands, his own complex and possibly conflicting needs, his memories of similar situations, his perception of the uniqueness of this situation, etc., etc. The data would be very complex indeed. But he could permit his total organism, his consciousness participating, to consider each stimulus, need, and demand, its relative intensity and importance, and out of this complex weighing and balancing, discover that course of action which would come closest to satisfying all his needs in the situation. An analogy which might come close to a description would be to compare this person to a giant electronic computing machine. Since he is open to his experience, all of the data from his sense impressions, from his memory, from previous learning, from visceral and internal states is fed into the machine. The machine takes all of these multitudinous pulls and forces which are fed in as data, and quickly computes the course of action which would be the most economical vector of need satisfaction in this existential situation. This is the behavior of our hypothetical person.

The defects which in most of us make this process untrustworthy are the inclusion of information which does *not* belong to this present situation, or the exclusion of information which *does*. (p. 190)

Apparently Rogers has in mind the ability to let a decision come to one rather than trying to force it into existence and to trust the decision as a worthy format for action even if its bases are not completely, unassailably apparent. This characteristic amounts to trusting one's organism, of which, you will recognize, consciousness is only one part.

The two final characteristics are actually implied in those already discussed. The first is *experiential freedom*, the sense that one is free to choose among alternative courses of action. Rogers does not mean free will here in the traditional, philosophical sense, but rather that fully functioning persons *experience* themselves as choosing freely regardless of the fact that their actions may indeed be determined by their past experiences. The fully functioning person has the marvelous, exuberant feeling of personal power that comes with believing that anything is possible and that what happens really depends on him or her. The final characteristic is *creativity*, or the penchant for producing new and effective thoughts, actions, and things. You can see that if people have available to them all their organismic capabilities and experience and are also flexible, most likely, they will be consistent and useful producers.

Put all these qualities together and you have the fully functioning person—actualization theory's true gift to the human race. The composite picture is very rich:

> One last implication I should like to mention is that this process of living in the good life involves a wider range, a greater richness, than the constricted living in which most of us find ourselves. To be a part of this process means that one is involved in the frequently frightening and frequently satisfying experience of a more sensitive living, with greater range, greater variety, greater richness. It seems to me that clients who have moved significantly in therapy live more intimately with their feelings of pain, but also more vividly with their feelings of ecstasy; that anger is more clearly felt, but so also is love; that fear is an experience they know more deeply, but so is courage.

And the reason they can thus live fully in a wider range is that they have this underlying confidence in themselves as trustworthy instruments for encountering life.

> I believe it will have become evident why, for me, adjectives such as happy, contented, blissful, enjoyable, do not seem quite appropriate to any general description of this process I have called the good life, even though the person in this process would experience each one of these feelings at appropriate times. But the adjectives which seem more generally fitting are adjectives such as enriching, exciting, rewarding, challenging, meaningful. This process of the good life is not, I am convinced, a life for the faint-hearted. It involves the stretching and growing of becoming more and more of one's potentialities. (Rogers, 1961, pp. 195–196)

Rogers and psychosocial conflict thinkers, such as Freud, clearly present different ideas and values regarding what is ideal in living. The psychoanalytic ideal involves responsibility, capability, commitment, effectiveness, and adaptation to social "realities," whereas the Rogerian ideal stresses experiential richness, range of living, flexibility, spontaneity, immediacy, and change. These differences, which emerge clearly at the level of peripheral characteristics, are traceable primarily to the fact that psychoanalytic theory is a psychosocial conflict position and Rogerian theory a fulfillment position. The former emphasizes compromise and defense, while the latter focuses on expressing potentialities. That Rogers (1977) does not regard acceptance of social institutions and conventions as guides for adequate living is shown in his writings on the power of individuals to effect radical social reform.

THE NONIDEAL LIFESTYLE. Having covered the peripheral characteristics defining one of the two great Rogerian types, I will now discuss the other. The maladjusted type, which emphasizes maintaining rather than enhancing living, is nothing more than the opposite of the fully functioning personality. People in this maintaining mode are *defensive* rather than open to experience, *live according to a preconceived plan* rather than existentially, and *disregard their organism* rather than trust it. More or less as a consequence of these things, they feel *manipulated* rather than free and are *common* and *conforming* rather than creative. These characteristics of the maladjusted person all follow from the existence of *conditions of worth*, which, as mentioned earlier, are the kind of sanctions learned from significant others in the person's life. Because these others respected only some of the person's potentialities, he or she in turn was led to the same pattern of differential or partial self-acceptance and respect. Conditions of worth, like Freud's superego, form the basis for defense.

CONCLUDING COMMENT. However engaging and true to your own experience the two personality types presented here may be, I encourage you to recognize that they are only two. Also, there is no basis in Rogers's writing for considering various combinations of the set of peripheral characteristics that constitute fully functioning or maladjusted types. You have no formal theoretical justification for expecting, say, that one person might be high in openness to experience while being low in existential living, for being high in one implies for Rogers being high in the other. Although fairly concrete concerning the peripheral level of personality, Rogers nonetheless permits you to say only two kinds of things about people. This is particularly surprising because Rogers shows such humanistic emphasis on individuality, as in this passage:

> Perhaps it should be stressed that these generalizations regarding the direction of the [actualization] process in which [people] are engaged exist in a context of enormously diverse specific behaviors, with different meanings for different individuals. Thus, progress toward maturity for one means developing sufficient autonomy to divorce himself from an unsuitable marriage partner; in another it means living more constructively with the partner he has. For one student it means working hard to obtain better grades; for another it means a lessened compulsiveness and a willingness to accept poorer grades. So we must recognize that the generalizations about this process of change are abstractions drawn from a very complex diversified picture. (Rogers, 1963, p. 9)

This passage, in which Rogers discusses how clients come closer to the fully functioning life, sounds fine until you scrutinize it, whereupon it becomes apparent that *any* behavior—some act or its opposite—can express full functioning. As you saw before, such a position is too elastic for easy testing. One cannot determine whether it is true or false.

In my opinion, the difficulty stems from Rogers's obvious interest in a comprehensive understanding of living that inevitably means taking seriously such concrete behavior patterns as leaving or staying in a marriage, even though he gives only the formal theoretical apparatus with which to make a few general distinctions. You can trace the difficulty to Rogers's position being primarily a theory of psychotherapy and only secondarily a theory of personality. It is certainly appropriate for a theory of psychotherapy to concern itself with only two basic things— maladjustment and the fullest utilization of potentialities. But once you theorize about personality, you take on the task of understanding all there is about a person that has any regularity. This inevitably leads you to consider many specific differences among people—too many for proper understanding by a theory that recognizes only two personality types.

I do not for a moment deny that Rogerian theory can be developed so as to be more comprehensive, making it theoretically possible, for example, to understand why full functioning would take the form of leaving a marriage for one person and staying for another. I am simply saying that such development, though needed, has not as yet been accomplished. In contrast, Erikson's position permits many more distinctions among personality types than Rogers's does. My criticism of Rogers applies with only slightly less force to Rank, who postulates merely three personality types.

In concluding, I wish to point out that Rogers's theory, like the others, makes personality types and peripheral characteristics a function of the interaction between core tendencies and environmental encounters—in other words, development. For Rogers, if the core tendency of actualizing potentialities is met with unconditional positive regard from significant others, the person will show the peripheral characteristics of the fully functioning type. In contrast, if the core tendency is met with conditional positive regard, conditions of worth and the other signs of maladjustment will ensue. But unlike those found in Freud and Erikson, the Rogerian personality types do not refer to particular periods of life. Rogerian theory does not involve the idea of stages of development.

MASLOW'S POSITION ....

The second actualization position I will discuss is that of Abraham Maslow (born in New York City, 1908; died in La Jolla, California, 1970). Maslow received his Ph.D. in 1934. Throughout his career he concentrated on research, teaching, and writing. The observations he used in theorizing tended to stem from research on normal and creative people rather than from psychopathology and psychotherapy. An abiding concern of his was the betterment of society and the individual life. After serving at a number of universities, Maslow became chair of the Department of Psychology at Brandeis University in 1961 and was eventually elected president of the American Psychological Association. By the time of his death, he had emerged as a popular leader of humanistic trends in our society.

Maslow's Core Statement

Maslow developed his position slowly over many years and was responsive to and influenced by the work of like-minded personologists such as Allport and Rogers. The great influence Maslow's position has had is reason enough to study it. But there are other reasons as well why Maslow is important to consider here, despite his strong agreement with Rogers. First, on some very important matters he is more detailed and complete than Rogers. Second—paradoxically enough—his discursive, highly eclectic approach to theorizing and writing renders his position ambiguous at the same time that he is willing to tackle problems others have avoided.

Thus, there are both good and bad practices to be learned from Maslow by the student of personology. Third, Maslow's position qualifies as a variant of the fulfillment model. For Maslow, fulfillment is the most important, but not the only, directionality in the person.

THE CORE TENDENCIES OF PERSONALITY. Maslow (1962, 1967, 1968) agrees with Rogers and Goldstein about a core tendency to *push toward actualization of inherent potentialities.* Although Maslow seems to recognize the importance of the self-concept in much of his writing, he does not explicitly give it the significance and type of role that one finds in Rogers. For Maslow, actualization of inherent potentialities virtually ensures the development of a self-concept, and though he associates mental illness with faulty actualization, he does not attribute the cause of the faultiness to a restricting self-concept. Maslow lies somewhere between Rogers and Goldstein—to wit, Maslow names the push toward realizing one's potentialities the *self-actualizing tendency* and appears to emphasize the physiological organism at some times and the phenomenal self at others.

Now, what makes Maslow's theory a variant of the fulfillment model? Maslow (1955, 1962) recognizes another tendency, common to all persons and therefore part of the core of personality, that does not have the same connotations of fulfillment inherent in the actualizing tendency. Although he never quite puts it this way, this other tendency is the *push to satisfy needs ensuring physical and psychological survival (the survival tendency),* with the appropriate model of needing help rather than pursuing fulfillment.

The survival tendency appears prior to the actualization tendency in that a modicum of satisfaction of the former is necessary before the person can engage in vigorous expression of the latter. But this is not to say that the survival tendency is more important than the actualization tendency in any other way. The survival tendency can only maintain life; it cannot enhance it. Only the actualization tendency can lead to a rich and deeply meaningful life. Thus, although both survival and actualization tendencies are clearly part of the core of personality, the special importance Maslow gives to the latter makes his position a fulfillment theory, albeit a variant. His position is not in the conflict tradition, because he does not conceive of the survival and actualization tendencies as antagonistic. It is true that if the survival tendency does not achieve a measure of satisfaction, the actualization tendency will not be vigorously expressed. However, this is not the same as saying that one tendency inhibits or counteracts the other.

Maslow makes some lucid statements concerning the concrete nature of the actualizing tendency (1962):

> It is necessary to understand that capacities, organs, and organ systems press to function and express themselves and to be used and exercised, and that such use is satisfying and disuse irritating. . . . In the normal development of the normal child, it is now known that *most* of the time, if he is given a really free choice, he will choose what is good for his growth. This he does because it tastes good, feels good, gives pleasure or *delight.*

Maslow makes the concept of actualizing tendency more concrete and tangible by pinpointing its physiological sources and their psychological concomitants. The *physiological source* is the tendency of somatic components of the organism to function according to their design. The *psychological concomitant* is the person's tendency to make choices that are satisfying. When the person uses satisfaction as a guide, he or she will make choices consistent with the proper functioning of his or her somatic components, because using these components according to their design will cause satisfaction. Note the similarity between this position and the Freudian one in which bodily requirements (e.g., for food or sex) are represented in mental life in such a fashion that decisions and actions suit them. But once you consider the concrete content of organismic requirements, the similarity ends. Maslow's position clearly indicates that the person does not actualize potentialities out of any sense of destiny or any self-conscious desire to function well. Indeed, the person who truly actualizes potentialities experiences nothing grander than a general sense of well-being.

Actualization theorists tend to distrust self-conscious attempts to do well.

When we try to describe more fully the relationship of Maslow's two basic tendencies in the core of personality, we encounter ambiguities. The actualizing tendency is strong and vigorous only when the survival tendency has been satisfied. This relationship is certainly meant to hold developmentally—the major task of childhood is to satisfy the survival tendency, though once this is accomplished, the actualizing tendency increases in saliency—however, it can also be applied at any point in life. For example, a person who has achieved vigorous expression of the actualizing tendency might, through environmental circumstances, find survival threatened anew and revert temporarily or even chronically to expressions of the survival tendency. Interestingly, Machiavelli might have subscribed to a similar viewpoint, for he believed that refined, civilized, cultured persons can exist only in an environment devoid of personal threat and that, once threatened, they will be much meaner in appearance and easier to control. But Machiavelli also believed that this showed the greater importance of the survival tendency, whereas Maslow feels that the survival tendency is important only because it sets the stage for the actualizing tendency. Both beliefs are logically possible, and Maslow's choice exemplifies his irrepressible optimism.

Growth and Deprivation Motivation. Maslow's decision to cast the survival and actualizing tendencies in motivational terms has been popular with actualization theorists in general. According to Maslow (1955), the actualization tendency is growth motivation whereas the survival tendency is deprivation motivation. *Deprivation motivation* refers to urges to strive for goal states, the absence of which cause pain and discomfort. The aim of deprivation motivation is to decrease the organismic tension built up through deficit states that represent deviations from homeostatic balance (the self-regulating nature of the organism). Organismic survival requires nutritional substances; hence, when food has not been ingested for awhile, visceral organ activity produces a rising tension level, experienced psychologically as hunger, that precipitates instrumental actions designed to reach the goal state. In this case, the goal state is satiation, considered to be the normal, homeostatic state, characterized as tensionless. Note that it is the model subscribed to by Freud and the other conflict theorists.

In contrasting deprivation motivation and growth motivation, Maslow may have been taking a cue from Cannon (1929), who said that once the homeostatic needs are satisfied, the "priceless unessentials of life" can be sought. In any event, *growth motivation,* which Maslow claims has been inadequately recognized in the past, refers to urges to enrich living and to enlarge experience because to do so increases one's delight at being alive. Growth motivation involves not the repairing of deficits but rather the expansion of horizons. The goal states of growth motivation, if they exist at all, are very general in nature. Growth motivation does not start with sharp discomfort that must be eased, and its aim is not the reduction of tension, but its actual increase. Satisfaction has to do with realization of capabilities or ideals through a process whereby the organism becomes more complex, differentiated, and potent. This enlargement of the organism seems to require, if anything, that satisfaction go hand in hand with tension increase.

Unfortunately, growth motivation is a logically inconsistent idea. It assumes that there exists a kind of motivation that does not involve striving toward something that is lacking. But the motivation construct is such that in order to define a motive, you must specify a goal state that is to be achieved and the course of action instrumental to reaching it (Maddi & Costa, 1972; Peters, 1958). A motive without a specifiable goal state would not be a motive at all. And once you define a goal, you of necessity assume that the person having the motive is in a deprived state until he or she reaches it. In a logical sense, then, there is no way to define a motive that does not follow the deprivation model. Though Maslow reaches for a valuable distinction among kinds of tendencies, it is

poorly stated by the terms *deprivation motivation* and *growth motivation.*

By no means do I intend to suggest abandoning the concept of actualizing tendency; rather, I take issue with its status as a motive. In this regard, I have tried to convince you that if Maslow and the others wish to consider the actualizing tendency as a motive, it must conform to a deprivation model to be consistent with the logic of the motivation construct. The actualizing tendency as motive must refer to a goal state that is valued but not yet achieved (and that is where the deprivation comes in) and to the actions instrumental to its achievement. The actualizing tendency, however, need not be considered a motive simply because it exerts a causal influence on behavior. A theorist could decide to consider it an organismic tendency, much like metabolism or maturation, that does not engage the person's intelligence and decision-making capabilities. Since such a model does not imply purpose in a psychological sense (Peters, 1958), the language of motivation is irrelevant. Indeed, Maslow could easily give up the motivational model for the actualizing tendency, for he has said, "Maturity, or self-actualization, from the (motivational) point of view, means to transcend the deficiency needs. This state can be described then as meta-motivated, or unmotivated" (Maslow, 1962).

Although it would seem that Maslow recognizes the value of casting the actualizing tendency in nonmotivational terms, the disconcerting inconsistency and ambiguity of his writing are well exemplified by the fact that this quote directly follows the point in the article at which the idea of self-actualization as growth motivation has been developed! It is as if Maslow, in thinking of the intuitively apparent difference between a tendency to actualize one's capabilities and a tendency to satisfy one's survival needs, and in recognizing the inherently motivational nature of the latter, could not resist the symmetry produced by generalizing the motivational model to the actualizing tendency as well. Although such a generalization may have seemed elegant to him at first, the logical difficulties I have pointed out must have arisen to plague him, leading him to make contradictory statements in the same breath. In Chapter 11, I will show how one can consider core tendencies, such as that of actualizing one's potentialities, as forces that produce directionality in living without casting them in motivational terms.

THE CORE CHARACTERISTICS OF PERSONALITY. Now let us consider the core characteristics of personality that correspond to the two core tendencies. Regarding the tendency to satisfy physical and psychological survival needs, Maslow lists *physiological needs, safety needs, needs for belongingness and love,* and *esteem needs.* The first two are more physiological than psychological. But even the last two, though heavily psychological, relate more to survival, or the repairing of deficits, than to the fulfillment of one's potentialities. Notice the intent of producing a hierarchy. In other words, when the physiological needs are satisfied, the safety needs become salient and can be attended to; when the physiological and safety needs are both satisfied, the needs for belongingness and love become salient and can be attended to; and so forth.

Maslow also specifies the core characteristics relevant to the actualizing tendency. We should greet such specification with special interest, because we have already seen that most actualization positions suffer by not offering the content of inherent potentialities. Though Maslow includes such content, his presentation is confusing. I will try, however, to piece together the essence of his position concerning the inherent potentialities.

One relevant kind of information comes in Maslow's discussions of the hierarchy of needs. Maslow lists two additional needs that stand higher than those already discussed: the *need for self-actualization,* followed by the *need for cognitive understanding.* His manner of identifying these two needs in the hierarchy suggests not only that they are independent of each other but also that the need for cognitive understanding is an even higher expression of human nature than is self-actualization. But he cannot really mean this, because his position would then become

fraught with contradictions and incompletions. So, taking all he says into account, it seems to me most likely that these two needs refer to different aspects of the inherent potentialities that unfold from the action of the actualizing tendency. The need for cognitive understanding could be considered a psychological reflection of the inherent function of the nervous system, namely, the processing of information. A number of other theorists (e.g., Murray, Rogers, White, Allport) would also find such an assumption useful. This kind of view finds direct expression even in other Rogerians: Butler and Rice (1963) develop the notion that self-actualization occurs as a result of the nervous system's hunger for stimulation. But to return to the main theme, if the inherent potentialities referred to as "need for self-actualization" and "need for cognitive understanding" do indeed represent expressions of the actualizing tendency, the former must be inaccurately labeled, as can be seen by its redundancy. Let us delve further into Maslow's writing to see whether we can discover the proper label for this "need."

Of particular relevance are the statements he makes about human nature. At the outset, he emphasizes that people are both similar to and different from one another (Maslow, 1962). Then, in agreement with Rogers and Goldstein, he says, "This inner nature, as much as we know of it so far, is definitely not 'evil,' but is either what we adults in our culture call 'good,' or else it is neutral. The most accurate way to express this is to say that it is 'prior to good and evil.'" Furthermore,

> We have, each one of us, an essential inner nature which is intrinsic, given, "natural" and usually, very resistant to change. . . . I include in this inner nature instinctoid needs, capacities, talents, anatomical equipment, physiological balances, prenatal and natal injuries, and traumata to the neonatus. Whether defense and coping mechanisms, "style of life," and other characterological traits, all shaped in the first few years of life, should be included, is still a matter for discussion. I would say "yes" and proceed on the assumption that this raw material very quickly starts growing into a self as it meets the world outside and begins to have transactions with it. (Maslow, 1962)

You may experience an initial flush of enthusiasm at first reading this statement, but I ask you to reflect on it for a moment. I believe the statement teaches us little because it is too omnibus. As a specification of the inherent potentialities relevant to the actualizing tendency, it really offers no advantage over muteness. As a statement of all that is in human nature—that is, the inherent potentialities plus the deficiency needs —it might be helpful if we were told what things went in which of the two categories. Indeed, it is not clear that this is even the right track to follow, for Maslow includes such things as defenses and coping mechanisms. In his own terms, these things are not even clearly innate, rather than learned, and yet they occur in a statement of the human's "inner nature."

The other relevant statements in the same article are equally discursive and confusing. At one point, Maslow indicates that because humans have evolved away from strong instincts, it is hard for them to know and experience their inner nature. The same seems to be true for the theorist regarding the inherent potentialities! I conclude that Maslow's attempt to specify the content of these potentialities is, because of its omnibus and loose nature, no more useful than the absence of such statements on the part of other actualization theorists.

Maslow on Development

The developmental conditions under which fulfillment occurs are very similar for both Maslow and Rogers, although there are some superficial differences in terminology. According to Maslow, only satisfaction of the survival tendency is necessary to ensure that self-actualization will occur. While the existence of the survival tendency guarantees that people will seek the goal states prerequisite to self-actualization, whether they will be successful really hinges on the nature of their physical and social environment. This is true for young people because they are not developed enough to be independent of the assistance of others, as well as adults because if their environment lacks the basis for physical and psychological survival, no amount of effort

will result in success. But if the survival needs, both physical and psychological, are assuaged, the actualizing tendency and inherent potentialities will ensure the naturally unfolding process of fulfillment.

When you recognize that satisfaction of the deficiency needs requires that the person be loved, respected, and accepted, and also receive the stuff with which to assuage physiological want and be kept out of harm's way, it becomes clear that Maslow essentially agrees with Rogers. The difference between them is that the actualizing tendency incorporates both the maintenance and the enhancement of life for Rogers whereas it incorporates only enhancement for Maslow, with maintenance being the function of the survival tendency. As far as I can tell, however, this difference does not lead to much discrepancy in the views of individual and society that each theorist holds.

The two theorists also agree essentially on what the person achieving self-actualization would be like. Rogers speaks of the fully functioning person as characterized by congruence between sense of self and organismic qualities, openness to experience, love of self and others, and fairly continual change in living. Maslow uses slightly different words, such as *creative living, peak experiences, unselfish love,* and *unbiased understanding,* but, in point of fact, means very much the same things.

In closing this discussion of Maslow's developmental position, I call your attention to the general implications of the view that survival needs must be met before vigorous actualization of potentialities can occur. Clearly this means that the person must be nurtured, loved, and respected in order to amount to anything. As charmingly humanistic as this viewpoint is, I think it can be seriously criticized. There are countless examples of people who have been significantly creative despite early lives that included little nurturance, love, and respect. James Baldwin certainly offers an example of this. It is hard to imagine a developmental environment more destructive than his. Assailed on all fronts by psychological, social, and economic deprivation to the point of inhumanity, he still emerged as a productive and creative writer and critic. Furthermore, one implication of Maslow's position is that when survival needs are frustrated at any point in time—not simply in childhood—there ought to be a concomitant temporary decrease in vigorous self-actualization. But there are many contradictory examples to be found in the lives of great persons:

> We should keep in mind that John Bunyan began *Pilgrim's Progress* in the humiliating and rigidly regulated environment of a prison, and that Christ developed and preached his new ideas in a societal context that had become oppressively structured, to say nothing of the dangers he encountered. The blossoming of creativity during the Renaissance used to be attributed to the newly found wonder of leisure time, of time in which to contemplate and imagine. But it is now recognized that the Renaissance was an era of tremendous upheaval, chaos, and strife, in which flourished not only creativity, but also vice and intrigue of wondrous variety. Far from being free and permissive, it was an environment in which the artist and scientist had to scramble to get and keep the indulgence and protection of a patron, and hope that the patron would remain more powerful than his enemies for a while at least. And if further evidence were needed . . . I could turn to the concentration camp. Even in this environment so bent on psychological and physical destruction . . . some people could still think and observe creatively enough to develop the kernels of new philosophies of life, later to be written about in such books as *The Informed Heart* and *From Death Camp to Existentialism*. . . . And picture Galileo as he prayed on his knees by the side of the bed at night that he might gain God's aid in finding the inspiration for a creative idea to be converted into money to placate his creditors. Toulouse-Lautrec and many others were in rather constant physical pain as they expressed their creativity. I hardly need mention that Van Gogh created under the pressure of a fantastic assortment of torments. Finally, in *A Moveable Feast*, Hemingway specifically blames the atrophy of his creativity on his transition from a poor artist, who frequently went hungry and cold, to a pampered associate of the rich, for whom life had become easy and placid. (Maddi, 1965)

Is it really clear that when survival needs are unsatisfied, self-actualization will be curtailed?

Maslow might have responded to this criticism by saying that his position is accurate in general regardless of the fact that one can point to exceptions, as in the examples above. For most people, he might argue, the realization of potentialities requires the prior satisfaction of survival needs. Presumably there will always be a few people who are so extraordinary that their lives will be creative whether or not they are nurtured. Maslow might suggest that these people could have been even greater had their survival needs achieved more satisfaction. This is a plausible, but by no means devastating, retort to my criticism. I shall not attempt to solve the disagreement here; it is enough that you be aware of it.

Maslow's Periphery of Personality

Although Maslow names many peripheral characteristics in his discussion of personality, he is not at all systematic about delineating personality types. He names characteristics more for illustration than to provide a set, dependable scheme whereby one can identify and understand various lifestyles. In this, Maslow's writing is particularly deceptive, because it is so rich in vivid, illustrative references to courage, humor, spontaneity, and the like.

The only personality type that Maslow describes in the concrete terms necessary at the peripheral level of analysis is the psychologically mature or self-actualized person. In core terms, such people have fully actualized themselves through vigorous expression of potentialities, search for knowledge, and interest in beauty. Maslow (1955) informally collected information about a group of such people to better understand their peripheral characteristics. Among those he included in his group were Lincoln, Jefferson, Walt Whitman, Thoreau, Beethoven, Eleanor Roosevelt, and Einstein, as well as some of his own friends and acquaintances! The common features, or traits, of these people turn out to be (1) *realistic orientation*, (2) *acceptance* of self, others, and the natural world, (3) *spontaneity*, (4) *task orientation* rather than self-preoccupation, (5) *sense of privacy*, (6) *independence*, (7) vivid *appreciativeness*, (8) *spirituality* that is not necessarily religious in a formal sense, (9) sense of *identity with humankind,* (10) feelings of *intimacy* with a few loved ones, (11) *democratic values,* (12) recognition of *the difference between means and ends,* (13) *humor* that is philosophical rather than hostile, (14) *creativeness,* and (15) *nonconformism.* Although this list is long and heterogeneous enough to escape easy integration into an organized picture of personality, it certainly is consistent with Maslow's general emphasis and is similar in many respects to Rogers's description of the fully functioning person. We can certainly take these 15 characteristics as the starting point for delineating the mature personality type according to actualization theorists, even though a number of the designations would require additional elaboration and definition to be really useful in describing people.

Because he is preoccupied with fostering the growth of a humanistic psychology, Maslow presents little else that can pass as a personality type. But, if you recall his notion of hierarchy of needs, you will see that his position implies the possibility of fixation at some developmental point below full self-actualization, with the resultant logical capability of describing different immature personality types. Although Maslow himself does not explore these implications, one should note that there could be personality types oriented toward the satisfaction of (1) physiological needs, (2) safety needs, (3) needs for belongingness, and (4) needs for esteem. The potentiality for a typology of personality at the peripheral level of analysis is greater in Maslow than in Rogers, even though Maslow has done little to implement a concrete basis for understanding different ways of life.

THE FIVE-FACTOR POSITION ....

Considerable attention has been given by the present generation of psychologists to the *five-factor model* of personality. Based in *factor analytic research* (see Chapters 9, 11, and 12), these five factors were proposed earlier by Norman

(1963) but have achieved real popularity only within the last 20 years. Most psychologists interested in this model are content to explore it in research rather than elaborate its implications for personality theory. Academically based, they are not confronted on a daily basis with the clinician's applied task of understanding persons wholistically, the better to help them change in beneficial directions. The researchers Paul T. Costa, Jr., and Robert R. McCrae have attempted, however, to step out of that mold by exploring the implications of the five-factor model for personality theory. Although they still need to do a great amount of conceptualizing to have a bona fide personality theory, they have made enough of a start to be included here, on the assumption that we are seeing a new generation of personological thinking.

Costa and McCrae's Core Considerations

McCrae and Costa (1994) start from the assumption that there are five source traits represented in people, namely, *neuroticism* (anxiety, anger, depression), *extroversion* (warmth, gregariousness, assertiveness), *openness to experience* (fantasy, aesthetics, feelings), *agreeableness* (trust, straightforwardness, altruism), and *conscientiousness* (competence, order, dutifulness). From the emphasis on the term *trait* and the examples of the five traits, one might think that Costa and McCrae are referring to ways of behaving that are learned, and therefore best conceptualized in the periphery of personality. But these theorists feel that research justifies the view that these traits are inherited, and thus present despite shared cultural and familial influences. Further, despite their use of the trait concept, they make clear that they are viewing the *five factors* as basic, generic orientations which, if they change at all, do so through biological maturation rather than learning (Costa & McCrae, 1980; McCrae & Costa, 1994).

Clearly, Costa and McCrae are conceptualizing the five source *traits* as what I call *core characteristics.* Individual differences in people reflect the conditions of birth. And any change in the levels of traits during the life span is due to biological maturation rather than learning. Actually, the model used by McCrae and Costa is similar to Rogers's model of *inherent potentialities.*

What, then, qualifies as a core tendency in the five-factor approach? McCrae and Costa (1994) use the term *individuality,* but do not by that mean that people strive self-consciously for this quality. Rather, for a *core tendency,* they mean that each person *strives to express in behavior the thoughts, feelings, and actions that best reflect the pattern of neuroticism, extroversion, openness to experience, agreeableness, and conscientiousness that is inherent in them.* Costa and McCrae have thus gone one step further than Rogers by actually specifying *core characteristics.* But, whereas Rogers implies that the core characteristics are all positive, growth-oriented potentialities, McCrae and Costa include what appear to be negative characteristics (e.g., neuroticism) along with the positive.

Being aware of the classification scheme I have devised for this book, McCrae and Costa (1994) believe that their theory falls in the fulfillment category. On balance, I agree and find it closer to the *actualization fulfillment* than the *perfection fulfillment approach.* It is not a perfection approach, because there is no intimation that people try to rise above their inherent attributes, aiming at some ideal.

But think of what Costa and McCrae are telling us. Each of us is presumably set up constitutionally to express throughout our lives some higher or lower, but continuing, level of the concrete expressions of the five traits (anger, warmth, fantasy, etc.). Presumably, the levels of these five factors may be complementary in a given person (e.g., low neuroticism with high agreeableness, low openness to experience with low extroversion), but they may also be in conflict (e.g., high neuroticism with high agreeableness, high openness to experience with low extroversion). The internally-based possibility of conflict might suggest that the five-factor approach is really an intrapsychic conflict theory. But the conflict is not present in all of us—it may

or may not appear in each person's biological inheritance. On balance, therefore, McCrae and Costa's position fits best in the actualization fulfillment model.

Costa and McCrae on Development and the Periphery

McCrae and Costa (1994) certainly accept that expressing one's inherent five-factor pattern in interaction with the outside world leads to learned patterns of thoughts, feelings and actions that reflect both the inherent traits and the nature of the environment. But they have nothing further to say concerning just what the characteristics of others, the physical environment, or the interactions themselves may be that have this formative effect on what is learned. They find no guide in what research has shown and consider using more anecdotal observations too speculative.

Once again, McCrae and Costa (1994) seem to appreciate what is called for in a peripheral statement on personality, but fail to get very far. Indeed, one gets the impression that they have been backed into it by criticisms (e.g., Emmons, 1993; Helson, 1993; McAdams, 1992; Thorne, 1989) that the five-factor model is so abstract that it fails to provide a basis for understanding the specificity, complexity, directionality, and changeability of the concrete behaviors making up each of our lives.

Costa and McCrae appear to accept that particular "adaptations," "biographies," and "self-concepts" will develop, jointly reflecting the pattern of source traits and the specifics of interaction with the social and physical environment. *Adaptations* appear to be specific habits or activities expressing underlying source traits, such as extroverts joining social clubs and disagreeable people cultivating cynical attitudes. Such adaptations can change over time in response to biological maturation in source traits, changes in the environment (e.g., no social clubs in the town one has moved to), or "deliberate interventions" (e.g., attempts to change someone through putting them in jail or through psychotherapy).

It would seem that adaptations are what I call *concrete peripheral characteristics.* Biographies are "complex functions of all those characteristic adaptations that are evoked by the situation" (McCrae & Costa, 1994), rather like *types,* in the terminology of this book. In this regard, people have conscious goals, schedules, and plans that organize their thoughts, feelings, and actions over even long periods of time. In all this, people develop *self-concepts,* or cognitive-affective views of themselves that are accessible to consciousness. One function of the self-concept is to perceive information selectively in a manner consistent with one's source traits and lending a sense of personal coherence. In general, people also selectively construe and attempt to influence the social and physical environment in a conscious manner consistent with their pattern of source traits.

What McCrae and Costa lack is an explication of the content of the common types and peripheral characteristics we can expect to encounter in studying lives. Though they give examples here and there, they always fall back on the five source traits instead of conceptualizing particular combinations of these traits and the specific adaptations, biographies, and self-concepts that are learned through interaction with the environment. Thus, their incipient personality theory remains excessively abstract, too much a framework without descriptive flesh. How can we apply it to actual people in the attempt to understand them, let alone help them change in some desirable direction (if externally induced change is even possible)?

A final problem, which permeates all levels of this theory, is that there is no specification of an ideal personality type. Although Costa and McCrae shy away from specifying ideals, it might seem as if they could take another page from Rogers's book and conclude that the personality type that permits *fullest* expression of the individual pattern of the five source traits is the ideal. On further scrutiny, however, it is not clear that this approach makes sense in the five-factor model. After all, would it be ideal for someone to be strongly neurotic, or disagreeable,

or unconscientious, just because inheritance inclined in this direction? Further, would it be ideal to be completely agreeable or open to experience because that expressed inborn propensities? McCrae and Costa (1994) do imply some sort of stand on the question of ideal or at least acceptable behavior in suggesting that adaptations (concrete peripheral characteristics) might be "maladaptive," in the sense of "not being optimal with respect to cultural values or personal goals." This is an ambiguous statement. Because it is the underlying source trait patterns that influence both adaptations and personal goals, it is unlikely that the adaptations will do violence to the personal goals. That leaves us with cultural values as a way of determining whether individuals are maladapted, suggesting the kind of psychosocial conflict Rogers thought was possible but not inevitable. Perhaps this is indeed what McCrae and Costa (1994) mean, but they confuse one further by indicating that "individuals create societies and cultures that provide a range of options for expressing personality traits." It seems best at this point to raise these questions for theoretical development and wait for these theorists to delineate their thinking further as time goes on.

One possible route for McCrae and Costa in developing a peripheral statement in the spirit of their core statement is to reflect on the implications for personality types of combinations of high and low degrees of the five source factors. Because I make some suggestions along these lines in Chapter 12, I will be brief here. What will the typical adaptations, biographies, and self-concepts be of those, for example, high on neuroticism, extroversion, and conscientiousness, but low on openness to experience and agreeableness? And how will their work, family, and community patterns differ from people low on neuroticism and extroversion, but high on openness to experience, agreeableness, and conscientiousness? And what of the other possible combinations? Needless to say, it will help Costa and McCrae in this task to keep in mind whatever accumulated sense they may have of what people are like in everyday contexts.

CONCLUDING WORD ....

By now, I hope you appreciate the dramatic contrast between the actualization fulfillment model and the conflict model. About the only thing these models agree on is that what the person brings into the world in the form of inherent tendencies and characteristics is of major importance in the ensuing lifestyle. But here the agreement ends with a bang! Whereas the actualization fulfillment model structures core tendencies as personally and socially constructive forces in living, in the conflict model, the person is inherently bogged down in unresolvable incompatibilities. Even worse, according to the psychosocial form of the conflict model, the person is inherently selfish and socially destructive, needing to be curbed in this if any orderly social and personal life is to be possible.

Understandably, the actualization fulfillment approach is much more optimistic than the conflict approach. If only parents will unconditionally support the initiatives their offspring enter into through the natural tendency to express inherent potentialities, then the ensuing lifestyles will be truly heroic. We find terms for the assumed ideal lifestyle, such as Rogers's "fully functioning person" or Maslow's "self-actualized person." This contrasts sharply with Freud's psychosocial conflict emphasis on "civilization and its discontents," wherein the tragic requirement of compromise is apparent. Certainly, the intrapsychic version of the conflict model is less pessimistic, in emphasizing a higher possible level of awareness than its psychosocial counterpart; nonetheless, it does not approach the optimism of the actualization fulfillment model.

Is the high level of optimism you have encountered in Rogers and Maslow naive? Is the more tempered position of the conflict theorists more likely to be accurate? This and other related matters are important for you to consider as you read further.

CHAPTER 6

THE FULFILLMENT
MODEL:
PERFECTION
VERSION

In the actualization version of the fulfillment model, people are conceptualized as trying to become what their inherent potentialities actually suit them to be. If the person has genes pertaining to high intelligence, fulfillment will involve a life characterized by frequent intellectual endeavor. Fulfillment follows the course determined by something like a genetic blueprint.

The perfection version of the fulfillment model is quite different: Its fulfillment follows the course determined by ideals and values concerning the good life. These ideals and values need not mirror the person's inherent or genetically determined capabilities—indeed, perfection theorists frequently stress the person's attempt to overcome real or imagined inferiorities. Although both forms of the fulfillment model are in the heroic (rather than tragic) mode, the perfection version expresses idealism, whereas the actualization version expresses humanism.

The purest example of the perfection version comes from Alfred Adler, though Robert W.

White's writings are clearly in the same genre. Gordon Allport and Erich Fromm emerge as perfection theorists, with some tendencies toward the actualization position as well. Finally, existential psychology qualifies as a surprisingly valid example of the perfection version.

ADLER'S POSITION ....

Alfred Adler (born in Vienna, 1870; died in Scotland, 1937) received his M.D. in 1895 and practiced general medicine early in his career. Soon, however, he shifted to psychiatry and became a charter member of the Vienna Psychoanalytic Society. Ironically, as Adler came to serve as president of that august group, the ideas he was developing seemed so heretical that he was severely criticized and denounced, whereupon he resigned his office and membership. He then formed his own group, known as Individual Psychology, which became quite active. Following

World War I, in which he served as an army physician, Adler expressed his commitment to public service by establishing the first child guidance clinics in connection with the Viennese school system. In 1935 Adler came to the United States, where he taught at the Long Island College of Medicine and continued to be a prolific and forceful writer.

Adler's Core Statement

Although a clear thread of thought runs through Adler's writings, they also undergo considerable evolution. I shall therefore emphasize the last views Adler presents as I attempt to give some sense of how he got there as well.

The core tendency of personality for Adler can be simply stated: *the striving toward superiority or perfection* (Adler, 1927, 1930; Ansbacher & Ansbacher, 1956). Superficially, this core tendency seems similar to that of the actualization theorists, but it is actually quite different. To refer the actualizing tendency to your own intuitive experience, you would remember when you had a vivid sense of who and what you were and attempted to function consistently with that. But when you think of striving toward superiority or perfection, you inevitably are led to remember those times when you were dissatisfied with your talents or capabilities as you saw them and actively tried to transcend them to reach a higher level of functioning.

SOURCES OF STRIVING TOWARD PERFECTION. It would be well to start this section with a greater sense of Adler's thinking concerning his core tendency of personality. Although originally part of Freud's inner circle, Adler became convinced early in his professional life that aggressive urges are more important in life than sexual ones. He elaborated on this conviction by identifying as the basic drive in humans the famous will to power with its implications of competition and advantage. At this middle stage in his thinking, Adler clearly emphasized self-interest and Machiavellianism as the wellsprings of life. But as he grew older and attempted to find greater compatibility between his theoretical

view of humans and his personal commitment to public service, he shifted his core emphasis from power to superiority or perfection. The goal of striving toward perfection is not social distinction or a position of power; rather, it is the full realization of the ideal life. In describing the striving toward perfection, Adler (1930) says,

> I began to see clearly in every psychological phenomenon the striving for superiority. It runs parallel to physical growth and is an intrinsic necessity of life itself. It lies at the root of all solutions of life's problems and is manifested in the way in which we meet these problems. All our functions follow its direction. They strive for conquest, security, increase, either in the right or in the wrong direction. The impetus from minus to plus never ends. The urge from below to above never ceases. Whatever premises all our philosophers and psychologists dream of—self-preservation, pleasure principle, equalization—all these are but vague representations, attempts to express the great upward drive. (p. 398)

It may sound to you as if Adler means something very like the actualizing tendency, with its emphasis on inherent potentialities, but this is not the case. Adler draws the analogy to physical growth only to dramatize his belief in the inevitability and ubiquitousness of the tendency toward perfection. Achieving perfection is not a matter of expressing potentialities but of struggling for completion. One clearly sees Adler's emphasis in his concept of *fictional finalism,* which expresses the goal of the core tendency. *Finalism* refers merely to striving for an end or goal state. *Fictional* indicates that what the person is striving to reach is an ideal, or fiction. Ideals, however, are not potentialities rooted in the genetic blueprint. The most abstract and general ideal is that of perfection, which is the core characteristic associated with the core tendency. Later, in the section on peripheral personality, I shall discuss the more concrete fictional finalisms that develop as a function of the developmental courses outlined by Adlerians.

Another important aspect of the core tendency is Adler's presumption that all people strive toward increases rather than decreases of tension. Adler's references to attempting to be superior, to physical growth, and to a great upward drive that goes from minus to plus all strongly suggest increases in complexity, effort, and energy. Clearly Adler does not see the person as striving for peace, quiet, and tension reduction.

In this emphasis on increased tension, the perfection version of the fulfillment model is similar to the actualization version. But these two versions differ in an important way. In the actualization version, it is enough to be unencumbered by a destructive society. The core tendency will express itself spontaneously, because it is based on a genetic blueprint. In contrast, the perfection version requires that the person work hard to make a reality of what is only a vague possibility at birth. Striving for perfection will occur only if people have high ideals and discipline themselves accordingly. Witness Adler's (1964) words on the matter:

> The high degree of cooperation and social culture which man needs for his very existence demands spontaneous social effort, and the dominant purpose of education is to evoke it. Social feeling is not inborn; but it is an innate potentiality which has to be consciously developed. (p. 31)

Although he speaks here mainly of the striving that involves trying to perfect one's society as well, Adler gives the same emphasis to more individualistic efforts to better oneself.

THE CORE CHARACTERISTICS. At this point, I must pursue the content of the core tendency in much the same manner as I did with Rogers and Maslow. You will remember that Rogers assumes inherent potentialities to be the core characteristics of personality but never specifies their content. Maslow attempts such specification, but he is so scattered, amorphous, and confusing as to shed little light on the problem. Essentially, neither theorist gives us enough formal theoretical basis for determining what the assumed inherent potentialities are so that we can avoid the circular position of deciding that everything that people have already done must have stemmed from some potentiality of theirs. A position as circular as this cannot be put to empirical test and, hence,

cannot achieve the status of acceptable empirical knowledge. Content specification is no less important for Adler simply because his core characteristics are ideals, or fictional finalisms, rather than potentialities.

What, then, has Adler to say about the content of his core characteristics? First, he indicates that the striving toward perfection is innate and that it may manifest itself in myriad ways. From there, Adler offers a number of ideas concerning the precise sources of "the great upward drive." These ideas are *organ inferiority, feelings of inferiority,* and *compensation,* which in their most general forms should be considered core characteristics of personality. Early in his career, when Adler was still concerned with medicine, he developed the notion of organ inferiority as an explanation of the localization of illness in one part of the body rather than another. The notion is simply that the body breaks down at its weak spots, which are caused by peculiarities of either heredity or development (Adler, 1917). As Adler became more psychologically oriented, he developed the notion that people attempt to compensate for organ inferiorities and that this compensatory effort has important implications for their living. The compensatory effort can be directed at the organ inferiority itself—as in the case of Demosthenes, who stuttered as a child and became, through striving, one of the world's greatest orators—or at the strengthening of related though different organs, as in the case of the blind person who develops extraordinary auditory sensitivity.

As Adler's psychological sophistication deepened, he shifted emphasis from organ inferiority to *feelings of inferiority,* whether they arise from actual physical handicaps or from subjectively felt psychological and social disabilities. Such feelings arise from incompleteness or imperfection in any sphere of life (Adler, 1931). Indeed, an important and valuable sense of inferiority comes from the contemplation of complete perfection. Says Adler (1956), "In comparison with unattainable ideal perfection, the individual is continually filled by an inferiority feeling and motivated by it" (p. 23). For Adler, feelings of inferiority are the subjectively appreciated aspect of the striving for perfection. As such, feelings of inferiority are not only constructive forces in living, they provide a ready basis for diagnosing the lines along which the core tendency of personality will be expressed in any given person. Though Adler does not provide a complete catalogue of specific ways the striving toward perfection can manifest itself in all people, he offers a sign for identifying its specific manifestations that will always be consistent with his theoretical meaning. Identifying feelings of inferiority does not depend on achieved superiority. Indeed, such feelings normally precede attempts to achieve perfection and, hence, can be determined independently of the attempts and also used as predictors of them. Adler's formulation of the fulfillment position has avoided the circularity found in the actualization positions of Rogers and Maslow. In postulating a technique for diagnosing the content directions that the core tendency will take, Adler is very similar to Goldstein. I submit that Adler's emphasis on feelings of inferiority is as true to the perfection position as Goldstein's emphasis on preference is true to the actualization position.

Adler's emphasis on feelings of inferiority and Goldstein's on preferences dramatize the basic difference between the perfection and actualization versions of the fulfillment model. Actualization positions assume that the core tendency acts along the lines of real, usually innate organismic potentialities. If a person had a strong inclination toward wrestling, for example, actualization theories would assume wrestling to express some inherent potentialities, perhaps strong, resilient, and supple muscles. But Adler would not reach the same conclusion. For Adler, it is feelings of inferiority that would lead to strong inclinations toward wrestling. And feelings of inferiority might as easily stem from weak muscles as strong. Feelings of inferiority might also develop from having been beaten in wrestling or some other physical combat. Thus, for Adler, though the tendency to strive toward perfection is itself innate, the directions in which it leads

the person express idealizations of life. Indeed, the most likely directions are those in which inherent potentialities are meager. The aim of striving toward perfection carries the definite connotation of overcoming any limitations in potentialities that may exist in the person. To hazard an analogy from the game of bridge, actualization theorists tend to see fulfillment as the result of playing your long suit, whereas Adler tends to see fulfillment as the result of playing your short suit capably enough to make it as effective as your long suit.

So, in determining the lines along which the perfection tendency will find expression, the content of feelings of inferiority is of diagnostic importance. The other aspect of Adler's position on that which expresses the perfection tendency is his assumption that the person is both an individual and a social being. In the realm of individual living, people will strive for perfection of themselves; in the realm of group living, they will strive for the perfection of society. These individualistic and social expressions are simply different facets of the same tendency to strive for perfection. Agreeing with the actualization theorists, Adler sees the person and society as essentially compatible (Adler, 1939).

Interestingly, the assumption that fulfillment requires constructive social as well as individual functioning occurs late in Adler's thinking. In breaking with Freud, Adler shifted emphasis in the content of the core tendency from sexuality to aggressiveness. But during the early and middle portions of his career, Adler did not explicitly reject the Freudian model of the individual being inevitably in conflict with society. Adler's "will to power" clearly implied that social interaction was "dog-eat-dog" in character. Paradoxically enough, Adler held the private, extratheoretical belief that constructive social living is valuable and rewarding. Perhaps it was this belief that pried him loose over the years from the conflict aspects of the Freudian model —for certainly, in Adler's final position, both the individual and the social side of people are inherent, and there is no antagonism between them.

Adler's Developmental Statement

To understand Adler on development, you must start with his viewpoint on the periphery of personality, which is carried in his concept of *style of life* (Ansbacher, 1967; Ansbacher & Ansbacher, 1956). Your style of life (or type) is the pattern of interrelated peripheral characteristics that find regular expression in you and that determine your individuality. The rudiments of style of life are established by 5 years of age, and there is no basic change thereafter except from such special intervention as psychotherapy.

Adler clearly specifies the relationship between periphery and core of personality (Ansbacher & Ansbacher, 1956) when he indicates that a person's style of life is the concrete result of the course taken by the core tendency of striving for perfection in the context of existing and imagined inferiorities and the particular family situation involved. Real and imagined inferiorities stem primarily from organ weaknesses and the specifics of family constellation (Dreikurs, 1963). The idea of *organ weakness* is clear enough, I suppose, regardless of the ticklish problem of diagnosis. An organ weakness can be anything from overly small hands to a heart with leaky valves.

By *family constellation,* Adlerians generally mean the person's status with regard to his or her siblings. Adler (Ansbacher & Ansbacher, 1956) emphasizes the roles of oldest child, second child, youngest child, and only child. In brief, the oldest child must be "dethroned," that is, give up the position of undisputed attention and affection when another sibling is born. Because of this, the oldest child cannot escape some feelings of resentment and hatred toward siblings and parents. The second child is in a more advantageous position because he or she never receives undisputed attention and, hence, does not feel bereft at the birth of a younger sibling. The presence of an older sibling, or *pacemaker* (Ansbacher & Ansbacher, 1956, p. 379), is a challenge to develop rapidly. The youngest child has many pacemakers to goad development and never has the experience of losing attention to a "successor." Whereas the oldest

child reveres the past and views siblings with alarm and the second child accepts the realities of sharing attention, the youngest child can concentrate on catching up to elders, feeling secure in the affection lavished on her or him by everyone in the family. The other family constellation Adler discusses is that in which all siblings are of the same sex, in which case a special problem of sexual identity arises.

Birth order partially determines the network of inferiorities arising from the family constellation and complicated by the presence of real inferiorities with a basis in organ weaknesses. By the interaction of these inferiority feelings, a complex set of rivalries and alliances is formed. For example, an oldest child with strong intellectual capabilities may arouse rivalry in a younger child who might express it as direct intellectual competition or as avoidance of the intellectual domain in favor of areas less dominated by the older child. Or a youngest child, indulged in and helped by everyone else in the family, may respond to the pacemaking function of older siblings by excelling beyond them all (Ansbacher & Ansbacher, 1956, p. 381).

Thus, people's sense of their inferiorities and their means of circumventing or transcending them express the core tendency of striving for superiority. But there is more. The style of life will evolve not only from the content of real and imagined inferiorities but also from the manner in which they are transcended or circumvented. This manner of dealing with inferiorities will be greatly influenced by the family atmosphere, or general values, attitudes, and action patterns of family members, notably parents. If the parents establish an atmosphere of cooperation, mutual trust, respect, help, and understanding, the children will be encouraged to express their attempts to overcome inferiorities in a manner constructive for themselves and for others. In such an atmosphere, an oldest child, for example, will respond to being dethroned not with disobedience and criticality but with an attempt to nurture and develop the younger sibling. But if the family atmosphere is one of competition and distrust, neglect, or even pampering, the child will try to overcome inferiorities destructively

(Ansbacher & Ansbacher, 1956, pp. 369–375). Whether the child will be active or passive in these attempts will be influenced by whether the family atmosphere involves encouragement to give and initiate as well as to receive. Thus, two distinctions arise, out of which Adlerians have formulated a typology of style of life: *constructiveness-destructiveness* and *activeness-passiveness*.

This may sound as if family atmosphere provides a complete accounting of the constructiveness-destructiveness and activeness-passiveness of styles of life. Though this position indeed makes most sense in the framework of Adlerian thought, I must point out that some eminent Adlerians (e.g., Dreikurs, 1963) make this only part of the story, with the rest involving free will. According to them, people have free choice, uninfluenced by past experience, over the nature of their orientation toward inferiorities. Dreikurs (1963) says:

> This asserts the child's ability to decide what to do with an obstacle he encounters, although such a decision does not take place on the conscious level, for the child may not have developed more than a rudimentary verbal capacity when such a decision is required. Adler's contention of such freedom of choice was—and still is—incomprehensible to most students of psychology. They want to know what induces one child to give up, another to compensate, and still another to overcompensate. They cannot believe there is nothing that "makes" a child do it; that it is his own conclusion, his own response, his own evaluation of the situation which is influential. It is a creative act, which in itself is a phenomenon that our deterministically oriented contemporaries find difficult to comprehend. (p. 247)

If "creative acts" refer to something godlike, something that has no antecedents in past experience or personality itself, Dreikurs surely has left the scientific fold. But if "creative acts" can themselves be explained as the results of particular patterns of past experience, there is little problem except the confusion fostered by using words such as free will. I have assumed that Dreikurs really means this latter view and that his confusing terminology can be traced to a

zealous attempt to convince readers that the child indeed has a structure and a substance. I make this assumption on the basis of statements by Adler (1964), such as the following, that seem inconsistent with unmitigated free will:

> No soul develops in freedom. Each one is in mental, emotional and nutritional dependence upon his immediate environment on the earth and in the cosmos, yet so far independent that he must take up these relations seriously: he must answer them as the questions of life. (p. 36)

If Dreikurs means the freeing effect of an exercised consciousness, family atmosphere is the only concept necessary for explaining the means by which the child will strive for superiority.

In summary, although Adler views the periphery of personality as established through learning during the first few years of life, he does not, in contrast to Freud, distinguish personality types on the basis of developmental stages. Rather than stages, Adler uses family constellation, inferiorities, and family atmosphere as the bases of distinguishing types. This is consistent with Adler's holistic or global emphasis, in which the fine discrimination of the second year of life from the third or fourth would seem unfruitful. For Adler, such things as family atmosphere would be unlikely to change enough to allow one to attribute particular forms of adult personality to developments during brief periods of early childhood.

Adler on the Periphery of Personality

As you can surmise, four types of peripheral personality, or lifestyle, have been suggested by Adlerians: the *active-constructive, passive-constructive, active-destructive,* and *passive-destructive* styles. These styles, established in childhood, change little thereafter.

THE IDEAL LIFESTYLE. The constructive-destructive distinction refers mainly to the direction of social interest, while the active-passive distinction tends to concern the individual's strive for perfection. Actually, Adler

(1964) considers the *active-constructive style* as epitomizing the ideal of mental health:

> It is almost impossible to exaggerate the value of an increase in social feeling. The mind improves, for intelligence is a communal function. The feeling of worth and value is heightened, giving courage and an optimistic view, and there is a sense of acquiescence in the common advantages and drawbacks of our lot. The individual feels at home in life and feels his existence to be worthwhile just so far as he is useful to others and is overcoming common instead of private feelings of inferiority. Not only the ethical nature, but the right attitude in aesthetics, the best understanding of the beautiful and the ugly will always be founded upon the truest social feeling. (p. 79)

This passage emphasizes the importance of a cooperative connection with others and society, even so far as to define the healthiest form of inferiority feeling as that which links the person with the failings of all people. In the following passage, Adler (1964) emphasizes the active, or more individualistic, aspects of healthy living:

> Courage, an optimistic attitude, common sense, and feeling of being at home upon the crust of the earth, will enable [the healthy person] to face advantages and disadvantages with equal firmness. His goal of superiority will be identified with ideas of serving the human race and of overcoming its difficulties with his creative power. (pp. 47–48)

THE NONIDEAL LIFESTYLES. As you may have imagined, the *passive-destructive style* epitomizes psychopathology. To understand the intended emphasis, you must recognize that passivity need not involve inertia, or doing nothing. It can—and usually does—involve a concerted unwillingness to solve one's problems and assume one's responsibilities. Instead, other people are blamed:

> In the investigation of a neurotic style of life we must always suspect an opponent, and note who suffers most because of the patient's condition. Usually this is a member of the family, and sometimes a person of the other sex, though there are cases in which the illness is an attack upon society as a whole. There is always this element of concealed accusation in neurosis, the patient feeling as

though he were deprived of his right—i.e., of the center of attention—and wanting to fix the responsibility and blame upon someone. By such hidden vengeance and accusation, by excluding social activity whilst fighting against persons and rules, the problem-child and the neurotic find some relief from their dissatisfaction. (Adler, 1964, p. 81)

Of the remaining two styles, one could construe the *passive-constructive* as more healthy than the *active-destructive*, because the constructive-destructive dimension (having to do with social interest) is somewhat more important than activeness-passiveness in determining what is ideal. But here one meets an ambiguity, signaled by the absence of descriptions in the Adlerian literature of the passive-constructive style. Probably, Adlerians are uncertain about this style, because even the activeness-passiveness dimension is bound up with considerations of social interest, and constructiveness is not really thought of in passive terms.

For further clarification, we should focus more concretely on how these four (three?) styles are actually concretized in specific behavioral terms. Here there is not too much to go on, because concrete behaviors that express lifestyles are regarded by Adlerians as varying widely. Each of these styles comprises a set of goals or *finalisms* that are arbitrary and subjective and therefore considered fictional. Despite the striking term *fictional finalism,* it seems that here Adlerians are simply stressing the motivational character of the attributes that constitute styles of life.

Dreikurs (1963) has specified the fictional finalisms associated with the four lifestyles mentioned above. But it should be kept in mind that Dreikurs originally was attempting to explicate ways in which children could misbehave; hence, the lifestyles he details have little to do with constructiveness. But because he has attempted to generalize his position, one can consider its relevance to constructiveness without too much risk of distortion. The four goals he considers are (1) the attainment of attention and service, (2) the abrogation of power, (3) the achievement of revenge, and (4) the bid to be left alone. Actually, only the first kind of goal applies to the two constructive styles of life, which involve cooperation and respect for others as well as for self. Hence, considerations of power, revenge, and isolation are irrelevant. The hallmark of the active-constructive style of life is ambitiousness, or orientation toward success, whereas that of the passive-constructive style is charm, or receiving special attention for what one is rather than what one does. As implied above, all of Dreikurs's goals apply to the two destructive, or competitive and distrustful, styles. In the active-destructive style, the attention-getting goal takes the form of being a nuisance, whereas the power, revenge, and isolation goals take the forms of rebelliousness, viciousness, and denigration, respectively. The attention-getting, power, revenge, and isolation goals in the passive-destructive style take the concrete forms of laziness, stubbornness, passive aggression, and despair, respectively.

Let us consider how the organ inferiority of overly small hands might be dealt with in each of the four styles of life. The person with an active-constructive style of life might try to overcome smallness of hands in a direct, uncompromising, and socially useful fashion. Possessing musical talent and interest, this person might attempt to be a concert pianist in spite of small hands, relying on dexterity and practice to achieve excellence. The organ inferiority would be overcome by ambitiousness and success. In contrast, the passive-constructive person might beautify the small hands in some manner so that the very things that were inferior to begin with would now become the object of admiration. Superiority would have been achieved through charm. The active-destructive person might be a nuisance by nagging people to remember the handicap and seek power, revenge, and denigration by manipulating people with normal hands to feel guilty and irresponsible for being so well endowed and self-satisfied. Finally, the passive-destructive person might show laziness through not working because of the handicap and indicate stubbornness, passive aggression, and despair by refusing charity and other attempts to help.

Although my examples involve actual organ

inferiority, the same kind of thinking takes place in imagined, or psychologically determined, inferiorities. You will recall that it is the constructive-destructive distinction that carries the major implications for mental health and illness for Adlerians, with the two destructive orientations psychopathological, and the two constructive ones healthy. If the attempt to attain perfection occurs at the expense of others, it is pathological; if it proceeds in cooperation with others, it is healthy.

Though Dreikurs (1963) originally developed his typology for use with children and adolescents, it could readily be applied to adults as well. Another Adlerian attempt at a typology by Mosak (1971) is frankly concerned with adults. Unfortunately, Mosak devotes little attention to how the types he identifies fit into the Adlerian dimensions of constructiveness-destructiveness and activity-passivity. Mosak mentions (1) the getters, who exploit and manipulate life and others by actively or passively putting them into their service; (2) the drivers, whose overconscientiousness and dedication to their goals rarely permit them to rest; (3) the controllers, who wish either to control life or to ensure that it will not control them; (4) the good persons, who prefer to live by higher moral standards than their contemporaries; (5) the victims, who always lose; (6) the martyrs, who attain nobility through "dying" for causes or principles; (7) the babies, who find their place in life through charm, cuteness, and exploitation of others; and (8) the excitement seekers, who despise routine and revel in commotion. He also mentions several other types less easy to outline. You may have noticed that Mosak's typology casts styles in rather negative tones. Where he stands on ideal personality is therefore unclear.

Although Adlerian attempts at typology do not seem developed enough to be applied and studied objectively, a theoretical start certainly has been made. The goals discussed, especially by Dreikurs, are generally the kind one would expect given the overall emphasis of the Adlerian position on the painfulness of inferiority and the striving to overcome it. And certainly the attributes of everyday life considered by this theory are somewhat different from the well-known ones addressed by Freudians and Rogerians, and therefore especially interesting.

WHITE'S POSITION ....

Robert W. White (born 1904) received his Ph.D. in history and government in 1937. He initially taught in these fields but quickly shifted his interests to personology. White was part of the extraordinary group of psychologists gathered together by Murray at the Harvard Psychological Clinic. While teaching at Harvard, White began to formulate his views concerning psychopathology and personality, drawing his observations from the psychotherapeutic interaction and from research. From 1957 to 1962, he served as chair of the influential Department of Social Relations at Harvard.

White's Core Considerations

White's position is properly classed with Adler's because the differences between them are less important than the similarities. Although White's view constitutes the beginning of what could become a complete theory of personality, at the moment it is somewhat incomplete. White (1959) talks about the core tendency in two ways: as *the attempt to produce effects through one's actions (effectance motivation)* and *the attempt to achieve competence in one's functioning (competence motivation)*. The relationship between these two tendencies is not entirely clear. But most of White's writings (1959, 1960, 1963) suggest that one should consider effectance motivation as an early form of the developmentally later competence motivation. Effectance motivation can be seen in the young child who delights in the sound produced when she or he accidentally drops a rattle on the floor and quickly learns to drop it regularly. And what greater pleasure if the child can produce the additional effect of having an adult retrieve the rattle each time! White sees exploratory behavior and play as ways that young children can experience themselves as potent influences on the world.

Encouraging readers to take effectance motivation seriously, White (1960) cites evidence indicating that by the end of the first year of life, the typical child is playing 6 or more hours a day. This amount of time actually exceeds the working day of many adults—at a stage in the child's life usually considered as merely expressing oral forms of sexuality or of dependency!

On the ground of its generality, White (1959) concludes that effectance motivation must be at least as important as other tendencies that may exist in the child. It may even have a biological basis in the nervous system's requirement of stimulation and information. White suggests that the human nervous system must have developed, through natural selection, into a unit that continuously processes input from stimuli. If so, effectance motivation might well serve the basic biological purpose of keeping the nervous system supplied with a steady stream of such input. One definite accompaniment of such a view is the notion that White's core tendency, looked at in terms of biological energy, is best considered as serving increases rather than decreases in tension. In this, White agrees with other fulfillment theorists and opposes conflict theorists.

As the child grows, the mere attempt to affect the world shades naturally into the attempt to deal with life's tasks competently. The transition occurs when the expression of effectance motivation leads the child to become experienced and knowledgeable and to grow in actual competence as well as a sense of competence. The shift in core tendency from effectance to competence motivation is certainly functional, because the child receives an ever increasing number of tasks from society. Children must walk alone, feed and dress themselves, go to school, meet and interact with people outside the family, get good grades; young adults choose their life's work and pursue it, establish a family, and so forth. To achieve fulfillment in life, people must seek competence and experience some measure of success in this search.

White does not specifically detail the core characteristics associated with the tendency to strive toward competence. The fragmentary nature of his theory certainly makes unequivocal classification difficult. Nonetheless, I have little doubt that it is a perfection version of the fulfillment model. The tendencies toward competence and effectance are clearly innate. But this alone does not constitute an actualization position. Recall that Adler also assumes that the striving toward perfection is innate. It is also true that White sometimes implies that he would recognize certain inherent potentialities and that people might be assumed to differ in the nature of their endowment with such potentialities. I grant you that this begins to sound like an actualization position; however, White chooses to name the mature form of his core tendency in terms of competence. The denotations and connotations of *competence* are much more in line with a perfection than an actualization position. If you are driven to be competent, you will strive hardest when you perceive some evidence or possibility of incompetence, even though that incompetence might express some meager inherent potentiality. In striving for competence, you shall hardly do just what you prefer, because you have some conception of what it means to be competent. White's theory fits much more the idealistic mold of perfection positions than the humanistic mold of actualization positions.

White on Development and the Periphery

White offers no more than a sketch of the lines along which he might develop a position on the periphery of personality. These key concepts are *competence* versus *incompetence* and *sense of competence* versus *shame*. In the normal course of events, expression of the core tendency—the need to have an effect on the world—leads, through practice of capabilities, to actual competence as well as the subjective experience of a sense of competence. But if parents thwart and punish expressions of effectance motivation—the attempt to produce effects through one's actions—actual incompetence and the subjective experience of shame will result. White (1960) makes a neat distinction between shame and guilt: Shame is the experience of shortcoming or failure to reach a valued goal through lack of

ability; guilt implies touching or transgressing a moral boundary. Shame is connected to incompetence. In contrast, guilt does not imply that one is unable to do something; it signifies that one has done or is thinking of doing something within one's power that is forbidden. Guilt is connected to conscience, not competence. In any event, if White were to develop the implications of his position for the peripheral level of personality, he undoubtedly would offer a typology of people based on their specific competencies and incompetencies and on the contents of their shame and sense of competence.

PARTIAL ENDORSEMENT OF ERIKSON'S STAGES. Actually, the overall form such a classification would take may be inferred from White's (1960) great sympathy for Erikson's version of ego psychology. Erikson's view of the eight stages of the human, discussed in Chapter 3, is for White a very discerning developmental picture of the periphery of personality. But White disagrees with Erikson on the centrality of the psychosocial conflict model proposed by Freud. According to White, Erikson fails to recognize that most aspects of the character types and developmental stages he considers are better understood by a competence model than by a conflict model. Although Erikson certainly has, like other ego psychologists, championed a view of the ego as independent of the id rather than a mere extension of it, for White he is still too wedded to his early psychoanalytic beginnings.

To communicate his view, White (1960) provides an excellent discussion of the psychosexual stages of development in which he tries to show that the conflict model, though clearly relevant to some aspects of development, does not adequately explain most of the modes of functioning, or character traits, detailed by Erikson. Concerning the anal stage, White says,

> The bowel training model is wrong, I think, in two ways. First, it concerns a function that is governed by the autonomic nervous system, that never comes under direct voluntary control, and that does not carry the experience of initiative that goes with voluntary action. The child may be proud when he can meet parental expectations, but it will

be pride in meeting a somewhat mysterious demand by a somewhat mysterious process of habit formation, not the pride of mastering things directly by trial and by effort expended, as when one learns to throw or to bat a ball. Second, it is a situation in which cultural requirements inevitably prevail. Every child is bowel trained. This is a far greater victory for authority than generally prevails elsewhere; in other matters the child preserves more freedom to resist, plead, cajole, and force compromises on his surrounding adults. In short, the bowel training model all but eliminates the initiative and versatility on the child's part that is the essential aspect of any true autonomy. The best outcome of the bowel training problem is that the child will come to will the inevitable. (pp. 118–119)*

White thus points to what he considers a mismatch between Erikson's emphasis on autonomy as the result of successful completion of the anal stage and his choice, along with Freud, of bowel training as the major vehicle by which autonomy can be learned.

Similarly, White (1960) points out the difficulty in considering the oedipal conflict of the phallic stage the prototype of initiative:

And it seems to me that the Oedipal prototype falls short as a general model for the phallic stage in just the way toilet training failed for the anal stage. Once again Freud selected as his central image a hopeless situation, one where defeat for the child is inevitable. The child must learn to renounce the whole Oedipal wish, just as he must learn to renounce any thought of not being bowel trained. I submit the idea that if these were the true and determinative models it would be quite a problem to explain the survival of any sense of initiative. These models help us to understand why we have shame and guilt, but they do not give us much reason to suppose that we could emerge with autonomy and initiative. The competence model is not so harsh, though it certainly is not intended to gloss over the tragic features of childhood. (p. 125)

White follows through on his sense of the logical mismatch between Erikson's view of development and the Freudian conflict position by incorporating the genital stage into the general criticism presented above. According to Freudians, the sexual act—and, more specifically, the orgasm—is the prototype of maturity, or genitality. But while the orgasm is logically well suited to serve as the prototype for love in a general sense, it is not at all well suited for understanding work. Working and loving summarize most of what Erikson and other psychoanalytic thinkers typify as successful adult living. Love, like the orgasm, involves intense, sporadic, and impulsive emotions, thoughts, and actions. But working is quite the opposite in its emphasis on stability, persistence, and self-control. For White, the competence model is much more appropriate for understanding the many aspects of adult functioning that have to do with work and productivity than is the Freudian conflict position.

The thrust of White's remarks is that though the Freudian position is not exactly irrelevant to development, it is not nearly as central as many have supposed. White accepts Erikson's chronology and classification of character traits or types, but he finds them more naturally suited to a fulfillment rather than a conflict model and one that stresses effectance motivation and competence rather than sexuality per se. Although he cannot criticize orality as basically as he did the anal, phallic, and genital stages, White nonetheless has accumulated many observations of behavior during the first year that are not readily understood in oral terms:

Somehow the image has gotten into our minds that the infant's time [during the first year] is divided between eating and sleeping. Peter Wolff (1959) is now showing that this is not true even for newborn infants, who show distinct forerunners of what will later become playful exploratory activity. Gesell notes that at four weeks there is apt to be a waking time in the later afternoon during which visual experience begins to be accumulated. At 16 weeks this period may last for half an hour, and the times increase steadily up to one year, when Gesell's typical "behavior day" shows an hour of play before breakfast, two hours before lunch, an hour's carriage ride and another hour of social play during the afternoon, and perhaps still

*From "Competence and the Psychosexual Stages of Development," by R. W. White in the *1960 Nebraska Symposium on Motivation*, edited by M. R. Jones. Copyright © 1960 by the University of Nebraska Press. Reprinted by permission.

another hour before being put to bed. At the age of 12 months the child is already putting in a six-hour day of play, not to mention the overtime that occurs during meals and the bath. (White, 1960, pp. 110–111)

Clearly a lot of activity during the first year of life is difficult to understand as oral or even as a generalization from an oral prototype. And then, of course, White makes hay with the latency stage, which psychoanalysts have never pretended to be able to understand in terms of their sexual conflict position. White finds *latency* a complete misnomer, for the period is one of intense activity relative to social and work competence.

PARTIAL ENDORSEMENT OF CHARACTER TYPES. In criticizing the Freudian conflict position as an explanation of Eriksonian character types, White *implies a developmental theory of effectance motivation and a specific set of social consequences of this development.* During the first year of life, children do not act as an integrated unit, displaying instead rudimentary, discrete examples of effectance motivation. The rudimentary nature of children's capacities at this time is shown by the involvement of hands, mouths, and voices in the attempt to produce effects in the world and in the easy distractability that gives their attempts a playful, unimportant appearance. Actually, these attempts are very important, for by the end of their first year, children gain some of their basis for later competence in the inanimate and social worlds. According to White, the next developmental stage is marked by (1) the physical maturation that enables walking and other activities and (2) the cognitive maturation that enables a sense of self as an organized entity. In this stage, effectance motivation is expressed in a more concerted, organized, persistent way, building on the competencies gained during the first stage and expanding to include locomotion.

In the social domain, children experience themselves as much more of a force than before. Though the battle of the toilet is one result of this, it is only an example, rather than a prototype, *of a more general negativism to be understood as the beginning of assertiveness.*

Continuing, White suggests that what is called the phallic stage and initiated, according to psychoanalytic thinkers, by genital eroticism is really a stage of development marked by great increases in three spheres of competence: locomotion, language, and imagination. Locomotion reaches the point of being a serviceable tool rather than a difficult stunt. Language likewise reaches a state in which it can support wider understanding and social exchange. Imagination marks the first point at which children can maintain the fantasy of an imaginary companion. They also begin to cast themselves in adult roles. White believes that this growth in competence leads to intrinsic emotional and interpersonal crises that have little to do with sexuality:

> Perhaps the best way to make this clear is to imagine for the moment a child in the phallic stage *who is normal in every way except that no increase in genital sensitivity takes place.* This child would still make locomotor, linguistic, and imaginative progress, would become interested in being like adults, would make comparisons as to size, would be competitive and subject to defeats and humiliations, would be curious, ask endless questions and encounter rebuffs, would have had dreams and guilt feelings over imagined assertive or aggressive actions, would learn about sex roles, would struggle to understand his relation to other family members, and might very well ask about marrying one of the parents. All of these things arise inescapably from progress in the growth of competence. They all have important emotional consequences. In all these situations there is a chance to maintain and strengthen a sense of initiative; in all there is also a chance that the environment will act so as to impose a burden of guilt. (White, 1960, pp. 124–125)

According to White, by the time children have reached the latency period, they have progressed in competence and in organismic maturation to the point where they are no longer satisfied with exploration, play, and make-believe. In line with their interest in being adults, children need to feel useful and to be able to make things and deal with things significant in the adult world. And, of course, they go on to *the genital state, in which they really begin to* assume the roles and responsibilities of an adult.

In closing this section on White, I want you to recognize his endorsement of Eriksonian developmental stages and character types, as well as his spirited argument that these stages and types more naturally derive from a fulfillment model stressing effectance and competence than from a conflict model stressing sexuality and compromise. Although Adler and White have similar views of the core of personality, White has a more elaborate, differentiated view of the periphery of personality.

ALLPORT'S POSITION . . . .

Gordon W. Allport (born in Indiana, 1897; died in Cambridge, Massachusetts, 1967) received a Ph.D. in psychology in 1922. In addition to psychology, he studied philosophy and taught sociology, showing from the start the kinds of ethical and social concerns that would mark his personality theorizing. He was an extremely literate man, interested in what was going on in many fields neighboring his own. During a long and prolific career, Allport received many honors, including election to the presidency of the American Psychological Association and several other psychological organizations. In addition, for 12 years he was editor of the *Journal of Abnormal and Social Psychology.* Allport never practiced psychotherapy and did not see psychotherapeutic data as relevant to personality theorizing. He found observations of excellent, capable, and gifted people more pertinent.

Over the course of a long career, Allport wrote extensively on personality, social psychology, religion, and ethics. In all these fields, his views showed steady evolution. This evolutionary change, coupled with the diversity of his concerns, makes summarizing his views difficult. As with Freud, I will stress the most recent and most consistent statements Allport made.

Allport's Core Statement

Despite the strategy just mentioned, it is much more difficult than with Freud to formulate Allport's view of the core tendency of personality.

In the earliest expression of his position, Allport emphasizes traits and other peripheral characteristics of personality more than core considerations. But later he evolves concepts more naturally relevant to the understanding of basic, lifelong directions. Nonetheless, it is difficult to point to any specific core tendency. At times, Allport seems to assume an actualizing tendency, though he does not make such an assumption explicitly. And yet, he also seems to believe that competence motivation and similar notions are important. After much thought, I can firmly conclude that when Allport refers to such concepts as self-actualization and competence motivation, he gives them the status of examples of the kind of view of humans he has in mind. None of them is to be taken as the core tendency itself in any precise fashion. Allport's view of the core tendency is meant to be more general than these examples.

THE CORE TENDENCY. It seems to me that for Allport, the core tendency is *functioning in a manner expressive of the self.* He has a technical name for the self—*proprium;* hence, the core tendency may be called *propriate functioning* (Allport, 1955). Because he considers life a developmental process that the self (proprium) largely determines, Allport's view is properly regarded as a fulfillment position. As I will show later, although he incorporates elements of the actualization version, his theory is best considered an example of the perfection version. But first I should point out that there is an additional core tendency in Allport's system. As in Maslow, it is the *tendency to satisfy biological survival needs.* This tendency is clearly meant to be different from, though not incompatible with, propriate functioning. In addition, Allport definitely sees satisfying biological needs as less important in determining the value and meaning of life than is the heavily psychological propriate functioning.

Hence, Allport's theory is a variant of the fulfillment position in much the same way as is Maslow's actualization theory. Like all variants of the fulfillment position, Allport's theory assumes that one core tendency—propriate functioning—serves the highest development of the person, whereas the other core tendency—satisfaction of biological needs—merely ensures the person's physical survival. Indeed, Allport (1955) calls the tendency toward biological survival by the disparaging name, *opportunistic functioning*.

Just to start you thinking along Allport's lines, let me suggest a basis for intuitive understanding of propriate functioning. Recall the last time you wanted to do something or become some particular way because you felt it would express the most important things about yourself. Such ideals are an important part of the self, according to Allport. If the wish to reach the ideals was strong enough, you very likely also experienced ample energy and determination to work toward them. Such personally relevant striving is also part of the self for Allport. Finally, you may have been aware at the time of the deep way in which these ideals and striving came out of the most personal (and possibly unexpressed) sense of who and what you are. Such functioning impels the person toward the future, according to Allport, whereas opportunistic functioning is experienced as little more than the placation of internal biological forces tangential to the important things in life.

SPECIFIC PROPRIATE AND OPPORTUNISTIC FUNCTIONS. Since Allport (1955, 1961) says so little about the opportunistic functions, it will be easiest to consider them first. He is somewhat willing to accept whatever biological needs other psychologists and physiologists have uncovered, such as those for food, water, air, and the avoidance of pain. If he offers any definitive attribute of this class of needs, it is the aim to reduce physiological tension. Allport considers such functioning opportunistic because when release of tension and discomfort takes place, the actions aimed at removing the tension are not determined by such psychological considerations as values and principles. However useful such functioning may be in ensuring physical survival, it is opportunistic because, in Allport's view, it does not reflect psychological meaning (see Maddi, 1963; Maddi & Costa, 1972).

Allport's (1955, 1961) stance makes it abundantly clear that the important thing in life is propriate functioning. The *self* (or *proprium*) defines the lines along which life is meaningfully led, and the self has little to do with biological survival. One can die physically while one leads a meaningful life, as, for instance, religious martyrs do. The meaningfulness of life is a psychological consideration, and one cannot derive the psychological level of understanding from the biological one. In this regard, Allport is completely opposed to Freud and other instinct theorists. And, as you will have begun to see, his view of propriate functioning is not even as organismically or biologically based as the core tendency of actualization theorists is. Allport thus adheres to a perfection position.

As you can imagine, Allport has a great deal to say about the content of propriate functioning (core characteristics). Of all the theorists who consider the self important, Allport is distinguished in his detailed elaboration of just what that aspect of personality includes. Allport feels that such detailed specification is important not only because you can thereby be more sure of what he means but more specifically because the concept of self has been a source of so much misunderstanding and bitterness among psychologists. To many, the concept of self has seemed to be nothing more than a slightly dressed-up version of the old notion of soul, with its attendant implications of divine implantation and independence of the mortal laws governing organismic functioning. Allport's heroic attempt to specify precisely what comprises the self is not simply an effort to clarify, but also an expression of the view that this concept need not be mysterious or supernatural; rather, it is a collection of executive functions, clearly within the purview of psychology.

For Allport, the first step in specifying the content of self is to assume that it includes only those aspects of experience that seem essential, intimate, and of central importance to the person. Thus, his definition of self is phenomenological; that is, it follows what the individual personally believes is significant. The second step is to detail those functions of the self that are common to all sound adults. In perhaps a too extreme attempt to demystify the self, Allport

(1955, pp. 41–56) first considers the proprium to be a set of ongoing functions with no underlying structure. Later, however, he recognizes that function necessarily implies structure even though his emphasis is still on function (Allport, 1961, pp. 110–138). In any event, the functions of the proprium are *sense of body, self-identity, self-esteem, self-extension, rational coping, self-image,* and *propriate striving.*

You can easily demonstrate the pervasiveness and importance of your *sense of body,* even though it is usually automatic and outside the focus of attention, by performing an exercise suggested by Allport. Think of spitting saliva into a glass and then drinking it down. You are likely to feel revolted, even though you swallow the saliva in your mouth all the time. The saliva in your mouth is part of your sense of body, whereas the same saliva outside your body becomes a foreign thing. In less striking fashion, pain, injuries, and the like can make you aware of the sense of body constantly operating on the fringe of attention. Allport contends that bodily sense is a factor in the life decisions that one reaches, though in truth it is the most rudimentary of the propriate functions.

Whereas you have a sense of your body primarily through kinesthetic, proprioceptive, and tactual cues, the propriate function of *self-identity* is the set of ideas you use to define yourself. You may conceive yourself as a lawyer, a generous person, or a great lover, but whatever the set of ideas about yourself, the ones that self-identity comprises are those that are most central and important to you.

Self-esteem, another propriate function, is closely related to self-identity. Self-esteem defines the bases on which you feel worthwhile. These bases will be ideas of self, much like those that comprise self-identity, with the added feature of giving more precise guidelines for living. If you have a certain self-identity, you will try to function consistently with it. But functioning inconsistently with your self-identity will not necessarily produce pain. Once you begin to have ideas about yourself that are tied to your worthiness, however, you will have many fewer degrees of behavioral freedom.

By including *self-extension* in the propriate functions, Allport recognizes those things, people, and events that you define as central to your existence, even though they are outside your body. It is as though you extend your definition of self to include other aspects of the world. Thus, for a particular woman, her car, husband, daughter, and stamp collection may, for all intents and purposes, be parts of her self. This means that she sees them as really indistinguishable from herself, governed by the same laws and sharing the same fate. So a dent to the fender of her car is in some sense as painful as would be a disfigurement of her own face; her daughter's failing grade in school injures her own self-esteem; and her husband's unfaithfulness has the same effect as if she had betrayed her own principles.

By including *rational coping* as a propriate function, Allport indicates the importance to the person of thinking about and dealing with problems and tasks in a reasoned, logical way. Allport contends that people actually define themselves as rational beings and that this aspect of self-definition is very important to understanding the kinds of lives they lead. If you defined yourself as irrational, you would indeed be a very different and, for Allport, opportunistic person.

For Allport, the propriate functions, or core characteristics of personality, do not operate independently; rather, they mingle, producing a life that expresses *propriate functioning.* As you can tell from the core characteristics, propriate functioning involves the capacity to work hard for what you want, with what you want defined by a set of values and principles and by a less abstract, though pervasive, sense of who you are, all of this guided by a deep commitment to rationality. Thus, propriate functioning is *proactive, future oriented,* and *psychological.*

In calling propriate functioning *proactive,* Allport means to contrast it with *reactive* functioning, which to him is opportunistic. In distinguishing proactive behavior, Allport makes the point that psychology has a painfully ready tendency to deal with only behavior that is a response to environmental pressure (see Maddi,

1963; Maddi & Costa, 1972). Even the fact that behavior goes by the technical name of *response* for psychologists indicates that most believe life is a reaction to influences external to the person. For Allport, reactive behavior is the least important thing to understand about the functioning of sound adult human beings, for whom only that behavior which supports biological survival is reactive in nature. Such opportunistic functioning is determined by the organism's biological needs in conjunction with the features of the external environment that either frustrate or satisfy those needs. The person exercises little flexibility or individuality in opportunistic functioning.

In contrast, functioning in a manner that expresses the proprium, or self, is proactive because it influences the external environment rather than being influenced by it. When you express your own sense of who you are, your behavior shows choice, flexibility, and individuality—for, after all, your sense of self is not tied to simple, inexorable biological considerations that differ little from those of less complex animals. The proprium is developed from the rich store of psychological experience coming through imagination, judgment, social interaction, and familiarity with human culture and history. To label behavior caused by propriate aspirations and convictions *reactive* is to miss the extraordinary degree to which people can influence their own destinies.

In calling propriate functioning *future oriented,* Allport means to contrast it with opportunistic functioning in yet another way. Governed by unchanging biological needs, opportunistic functioning is therefore characterized by the development of habits. If you are hungry, you learn the most efficient ways to obtain food from your environment; then, every time you are hungry, you react in the way that proved efficient before. Opportunistic functioning is *past oriented* because it involves the operation of long-standing habits proven to ensure biological survival. Each time a biological need is aroused, the person must diminish tension to get back to a relatively painless state. According to Allport, propriate functioning is wholly different

from this. The goals of propriate functioning involve bringing about states that have no precise precedent in the person. For instance, aspirations can bring people to an existential state they have never experienced before, at least for themselves. The fact that propriate functioning relies so heavily on imagination as a guide to action means that it does not involve habitual functioning. In addition, propriate functioning is not an attempt to return to a past state of lack of tension. Indeed, it usually increases tension, because the proprium does not necessarily complement biological needs. So, a person driven by the propriate ambition to express something in a poem may work long into the night, caring little for the mounting tension of lack of food and physical fatigue. The point here is that propriate functioning is aimed at future, previously unexperienced states, in contrast to opportunistic functioning, which aims to reestablish the "good old days."

I need say little more concerning why Allport classifies propriate functioning as psychological in nature. The organism's biological givens underlie opportunistic functioning. In contrast, propriate functioning has much more to do with ideas, feelings, introspections, and other considerations more properly considered at the psychological rather than biological level of experience. This is not to say that there is no physiological substrate for mentation and emotion. But propriate functioning is not understood very well until one adopts the view that ideas and feelings are genuine and important determinants of behavior, which will very likely differ from determinants expressing biological survival. In this emphasis on the difference between the psychological and biological aspects of life, Allport comes close to being a conflict rather than fulfillment theorist. But I think his position is more appropriately considered a variant of the fulfillment position because opportunistic functioning can complement, as well as oppose, propriate functioning and because it is plays a negligible role in the life of the sound adult.

ALLPORT'S THEORETICAL PLACEMENT. You will remember that actualization theorists offered little about the content of people's inherent capabilities, and Adler did only slightly better in providing a diagnostic aid—feelings of inferiority—with which to identify the particular directions the push toward perfection takes in concrete instances. Allport goes still further with his specification of the content of the propriate functions. One may expect (if the theory is correct) to find a sense of body, self-identity, self-esteem, rational coping, self-extension, and propriate striving in all people. To be sure, these core characteristics may take somewhat different shapes in people as a function of differences in previous experience and even genetic constitution. Nonetheless, Allport has been much more explicit and precise concerning the directions life will take than other fulfillment theorists have.

Certainly, the kind of life—proactive, future oriented, or psychological—ensuing from expression of the propriate functions is much the same as that envisioned by other actualization and perfection theorists. These theorists also all emphasize the self and introspection as factors that determine life directions. But if we strain to discern the essential spirit of these theories, keeping in mind the possibility of error from insufficient precision of most of them, we arrive at certain differences in emphasis. Of the propriate functions, only the sense of body seems rooted in the organism's inherent nature. The other propriate functions bear little necessary relation to inherent potentialities. Add to this Allport's stress on aspirations (*self-image*) and working hard to reach them (*propriate striving*), and it becomes clear that his position is closer to those of the perfection theorists Adler and White than to the actualization theorists. Of course, Allport's position is diametrically opposed to Freud's. The propriate functions are noninstinctual, conscious, rational processes whereby life is led in an ever changing way that shows proaction, future orientation, and choice. In contrast, Freud sees unconscious, inexorable, unchanging, biological instincts as the only real determinants of life.

A final point needs to be made here. Fulfillment theorists usually stress individuality. Recall that the vagueness of content in the core characteristics seen in actualization theorists and the emphasis on free will in Adler are partly due to reticence to infringe on individual freedom. Of all fulfillment theorists, Allport has traditionally been the most ardent supporter of individuality. Indeed, he states early on (Allport, 1937) that because of each person's uniqueness, the concepts used to describe him or her cannot be used with anyone else. While he later adopts a less extreme version of this position (Allport, 1962), he still emphasizes individuality to an extraordinary degree, as you will see in the following section on the periphery.

Actually, Allport has been severely criticized by many other psychologists for having such an extreme notion of individuality that no generalizations from person to person seem possible. But with his notion of the proprium, Allport clearly takes a long step away from his previous position. What you should recognize is that the propriate functions appear in all persons and, therefore, define the commonality among them.

Allport on Development and the Periphery

Allport (1955) believes that at the beginning of life, the person is mainly a biological organism, with the psychological dimension of life developing gradually. Initially, then, human functioning is primarily opportunistic, with all the indications of reactivity and past orientation. Infants have little personality; their opportunistic behavior is determined by ongoing chemical processes and environmental pressures. At first, infants can express discomfort in only reflexive ways when strong viscerogenic drives exist, and they function solely to reduce tension. Infants are extremely dependent on others, particularly their mothers, for nurturance and affection.

THE IMPORTANCE OF NURTURANCE AND AFFECTION. For Allport (1955), what children's futures will be like depends substantially on whether or not they receive nurturance and affection. If so, the preconditions for the development of a gradually more differentiated and personally integrated personality are met. With enough security, the kernels of selfhood begin to develop near the end of the first year of life. The first signs of consciousness take the form of recognizable experience of the body (bodily sense). The second and third years see the beginnings of self-identity and then self-image. From ages 6 to 12, the rational coping qualities of the proprium become apparent. In adolescence, propriate striving increasingly appears. Although the various propriate functions begin their development at different ages, they all act interdependently by adulthood.

As the propriate functions are ever more richly and vigorously expressed, they lead to the development of a gradually increasing set of peripheral personality characteristics. Allport calls these peripheral characteristics *personal dispositions,* or concrete, readily expressed, and consistently observed traits such as gregariousness or honesty. I will consider personal dispositions a bit later; for now, recognize that as the proprium develops, undifferentiated, reactive, opportunistic behavior aimed at reducing tension caused by survival needs recedes in importance, being replaced by propriate functioning, which involves increased tension, is proactive, and leads to increasing subtlety and awareness.

IDEAL AND NONIDEAL LIFESTYLES. According to Allport (1961), the infant begins as a relatively undifferentiated organism, reacting more or less as a totality. As the proprium develops, the person becomes more and more differentiated through the accrual of personal dispositions. With still more experience and development, differentiated parts are continually integrated. In short, Allport sees development as the simultaneous increase in psychological differentiation and integration. He calls this *psychological growth* (see Maddi, 1963; Maddi & Costa, 1972). The differentiation is seen in the diversity of personal dispositions, a matter to be discussed later. The integration is seen in what Allport calls *psychological maturity,* the aspects of which suggest that it is the structural or stable result of the propriate functions' history of expression. The aspects of maturity are (1) specific, enduring

extensions of self, (2) dependable techniques (such as tolerance) for relating to others warmly, (3) stable emotional security or self-acceptance, (4) habits of realistic perception, (5) focus on problem solving, (6) established self-objectification in the form of insight and humor, and (7) a unifying philosophy of life, including a particular value orientation, differentiated religious sentiment, and personalized conscience. The more vigorous the expression of propriate functions, the greater the likelihood of developing all aspects of psychological maturity in adulthood. These aspects can serve an integrative function in the personality because, as you can see, they deal with general questions relating to the meaning and value of life—questions that concern every person. These characteristics of maturity permit the organization of the personal dispositions, which are, of course, much more concrete, orientations toward life. Clearly, for Allport (1955), psychological maturity is a state characterized by tension-increasing, perfection-oriented behavior that is not defensive. In these emphases, he is very much like the other fulfillment theorists.

You have just seen the course of development that unfolds when the infant's early dependency has been warmly met. But if succorance and affection are not readily available, the child may react with signs of insecurity, initially including aggression and being demanding, and later, jealousy and egotism. Vigorous development of propriate functioning will be jeopardized, the individual remaining relatively undifferentiated and deficient in the integrative characteristics of maturity. Tension reduction will remain an important aim. Such an adult will show evidence of defensiveness, with attendant lack of awareness of self. Allport would consider such a person mentally ill, though he is not interested enough in the matter to give it any further consideration.

In specifying the developmental course of propriate and opportunistic functions, Allport is once again more explicit and complete than other fulfillment theorists. And once again, he is closer in spirit to the perfection than the actualization theorists. The actualization theorists would probably be uneasy with Allport's strong emphasis on a stable structure of the self in the form of values, principles, and conscience, which serves an integrative function by ordering and rendering meaningful a person's more concrete experiences. In contrast, actualization theorists see the self-concept as a flexible entity, as continually changing, and as much less vividly conscious. To actualization theorists, Allport's view of psychological maturity might seem to stand in the way of real openness to experience.

ALLPORT AND MURRAY. Like Murray, Allport has given considerable attention to determining the best way to conceptualize peripheral characteristics. But reaching a rather different conclusion than Murray, Allport has chosen for his major peripheral characteristic something resembling a trait or grouping of habits. First, he calls his concept the *personal trait* (Allport, 1937) but later renames it the *personal disposition* (Allport, 1961), defined as "a generalized neuropsychic structure (peculiar to the individual), with the capacity to render many stimuli functionally equivalent, and to initiate and guide consistent (equivalent) forms of adaptive and stylistic behavior" (p. 273). I will compare the personal disposition to Murray's need concept, because Murray is the other personologist considered thus far who takes the concrete implications of his peripheral concepts seriously enough to offer careful definitions and detailed descriptions.

First, consider the presumed effects of personal dispositions on the person's functioning. Allport indicates that the personal disposition operates by producing equivalence in function and meaning among perceptions, interpretations, feelings, and actions not necessarily equivalent in the natural world. In discussing this influence, Allport (1961, p. 322) develops the following example (from the cold war). While Russians, college professors, liberals, peace organizations, and antisegregationists may seem different to many observers, to a person with the personal disposition *fear of communism,* all these stimulus configurations may be equivalent in their perceived "communist" properties. Such

a personal disposition would also engender response sequences that are equivalent in their function of reducing the perceived threat of communism. The person might advocate war with the Russians, be suspicious of teachers, vote for extreme right-wing candidates and policies, join the Ku Klux Klan, and so forth. Observing this person, we would identify stimulus and response equivalences through perceived meanings and related coping behaviors rather than any necessarily obvious similarities. Although similar to the personal disposition in some respects, the need concept (see Chapter 3) stresses to a greater degree the directional organization of behavior, with a sequence of acts that are instrumental to reaching a goal, followed by acts that involve consummation of the goal.

Another way of stating this difference between the personal disposition and the need concept is to say that the latter is more motivational than the former. For the need, the equivalences of functioning produced are closely tied to the goal the person is trying to achieve, to what one might call the "why" of behavior. Hence, need-produced behavior waxes and wanes according to whether the need is aroused or satisfied. In contrast, the personal disposition, like other trait concepts, is a steady, unvarying entity, exerting a continuous influence on functioning. There is little waxing and waning because, properly speaking, there is no goal to be striven for and reached. The personal disposition concept seems to give a larger place to the "what" and "how" of behavior than the need concept does. But you must take care not to conclude that Allport is uninterested in motivation. Actually, he considers all personal dispositions as having greater or less intention included within them (1961, p. 370), calling them dynamic and stylistic, respectively (pp. 222–223). All in all, dynamic personal dispositions are reminiscent of needs, whereas stylistic dispositions may be somewhat like Murray's need-integrates (see Chapter 3).

The next difference concerns the disposition of tension. The need functions according to some variety of the tension reduction principle, virtually by logical necessity, whereas most personal dispositions do not aim to reduce tension. This difference, however, does not indicate that Allport's concept must lack motivational significance, because for him motivation is, in its most important or propriate sense, somewhat synonymous with conscious intent rather than a tension state (Allport 1961, pp. 222–225).

THE PERSONAL DISPOSITION. Having seen some of the implications of the personal disposition concept, you can now turn to an emphasis of overwhelming importance for Allport. He believes that each personal disposition is unique to the person being studied. Actually, Allport (1961) includes in his peripheral theorizing the less important concept of *common trait* to account for the similarities that arise from a common human nature and a common culture (p. 349). But the common trait, though an admissible and useful concept, is for him an abstraction arrived at by generalizing across people, and hence it necessarily misses the actual dispositions of each person to some degree. The real personality is considered as emerging only when personal dispositions are assessed, requiring intensive study of a person's past, present, and anticipated future functioning through the use of such techniques as the case history and content analysis of personal documents (Allport, 1961, pp. 367–369; Allport, 1962). Allport (Allport & Odbert, 1936) has been unwilling to narrow the number of dispositions any further than the combinations that would be possible using the 18,000 or so common trait names in the English language.

Given the emphasis on uniqueness, it is not at all surprising that Allport nowhere offers any list of usual personal dispositions. The closest he comes to specifying the typical content of personal dispositions is to suggest two bases for classifying them. One classification (Allport, 1961, p. 365) involves the pervasiveness and consistency with which personal dispositions influence functioning. Distinctions are made among cardinal, central, and secondary dispositions. *Cardinal dispositions,* if they exist in a personality, will set the entire pattern of a person's

life. *Central dispositions,* possessed by virtually all people, are significant stabilizing features of functioning. *Secondary dispositions* produce relatively transient organization. The other classificatory principle is less clear and bears some resemblance to that just described. It refers to the degree to which a disposition lies at the core of a person's being (Allport, 1961, p. 264). Application of this principle leads to the distinction between the *genotypical* and *phenotypical disposition.* The latter, though it involves some regularity in responses, is less a reflection of the essential nature of personality than the former is. But Allport's discussion is sketchy, and it is not entirely clear what difference there is between genotypical and cardinal dispositions on the one hand and phenotypical and central dispositions on the other. You should also recognize that what little attempt Allport makes to organize or categorize personal dispositions is not for delineating types or styles of living, but for classifying.

Allport's absence of emphasis on types may also be due to his extreme position on uniqueness. If one person's personal dispositions can be entirely different from all others', how can you make lists of dispositions and organize them into types? By not offering lists of dispositions and a typology, Allport has certainly delivered a viewpoint on the periphery of personality that is very difficult to employ in any concrete way. About all Allport really gives us to go on is the notion that dispositions can be identified by whatever equivalences can be inferred from observation of the person. But this is hardly enough. Human functioning is sufficiently complex that without the benefit of more concrete guidelines, stimulus and response equivalences can be found at many different levels and in many different ways. Each investigator is thrown completely on his or her own artistry in each diagnosis of a disposition. An investigator cannot derive much assistance from others' diagnoses or even from his or her own prior diagnoses. And one certainly cannot predict, before observation, what any person's dispositions will be like. Nor can one be entirely sure that one is even using the personal disposition concept in the manner Allport intends.

But Allport, like Murray, must at least be given credit for having carefully delineated the nature, if not the content, of his peripheral characteristic and having attempted to describe the way it influences functioning. Such theoretical care concerning peripheral characteristics is valuable to personologists because it can lead to viewpoints so well developed and specified as to make their use and empirical testing really possible. Unfortunately, Allport's theoretical efforts have fallen short of this goal of usability and empirical testability because of his extreme emphasis on the uniqueness of personal dispositions. Certainly, then, we should carefully consider the reasons for his heavy emphasis in attempting to determine whether it is really necessary (see Chapter 11).

What remains for discussion here is the nature of the relationship between personal dispositions (the periphery of personality) and propriate functions (the core of personality). Allport has virtually never discussed this relationship directly, so I shall have to piece together what seem like relevant implications.

In his earliest relevant statement, Allport (1955, pp. 41–56) makes it quite clear that the proprium comprises general, pervasive functions or capabilities common to all humans and with little structure or fixed content. If so, personal dispositions clearly are not to be considered part of the proprium per se, representing as they do structural bases for lumping together certain stimuli and responses in a manner particular to one person alone. But later, Allport (1961, pp. 110–138) leaves one uncertain as to whether or not the proprium includes structural considerations. If it does, cardinal and genotypical dispositions, which are so general, might actually be included as part of the core of personality. But this is not likely to be Allport's true intent, for he also seems to suggest that personality structure is formed out of the interaction between propriate functions and environmental contexts.

A much more likely and useful position would be to consider that the propriate functions, which comprise the core tendencies and characteristics, are not themselves combinations of dispositions but the major forces precipitating and combining with the person's life experiences to form dispositions. For example, *propriate striving* would refer to the universal propensity for phenomenally important intentioning or, more simply, for working hard to reach goals that seem personally significant. Because of propriate striving, it would be possible to develop cardinal and central dispositions with dynamic properties. Cardinal—and, for that matter, even genotypical—dispositions would not, then, stand at the core of personality; rather, they would represent the most general and pervasive of a person's dispositions. No matter how general and pervasive, however, dispositions would be peripheral compared with propriate functions. In this manner, cardinal and genotypical dispositions could be put to their intended use of pinpointing individuality, because if considered part of the periphery, they would not have to be common to all persons.

A personality theory is a changing, growing thing, and it may well be that Allport was moving in the direction I have suggested. He was perhaps attempting to conceptualize components of personality that seem to be sets of personal dispositions that reflect the qualities of propriate functioning. Examples of this type of unit are his characteristics of maturity (see p. 141). If I see his movement accurately, Allport, in describing the characteristics of maturing, was breaking out of the trap of overemphasis on uniqueness. The result of doing so might have been a classification of personality types achieved along lines of content and reflecting the concrete ramifications in behavior of propriate functioning.

FUNCTIONAL AUTONOMY. Probably, early opportunistic striving provides the basis for what later becomes personal dispositions.

Allport suggests that the original opportunistic strivings are expressed in certain patterns of action that come into being because they are useful in satisfying these strivings. But once the person has matured a bit and been sufficiently nurtured and supported by other people, opportunistic goals recede in importance because they can be satisfied readily and their existence no longer causes anxiety. The instrumental action patterns do not necessarily atrophy, however, even though they are no longer needed. Some of the action patterns become *functionally autonomous* (Allport, 1961, p. 229) of their origins and continue to exist as personal dispositions. The action patterns that continue to exist in this fashion are probably those that are most consistent with the general propriate functions, which, you may recall, include such things as self-identity and self-extension.

By *functional autonomy,* Allport wishes to convey his belief that action patterns, including values, opinions, and goals, are not limited in importance simply because they may have begun by serving some biological need that is no longer central. But Allport often has been criticized for vagueness in delineating the concept of functional autonomy: How does it work? What are its implications? What is the organismic basis for such an idea? Allport does attempt to clarify and specify the concept somewhat, suggesting that propriate functional autonomy comes about because the presumed energy potential the person possesses exceeds that contributed by survival needs, and hence there is an ongoing tendency to use this excess by increasing competence and pressing toward a unification of life (Allport, 1961, pp. 249–253).

Allport's thinking on the specific mechanisms of functional autonomy remains somewhat vague, and thus provides a number of bases for controversy. He does not circumvent the repeated criticism that functional autonomy is more of an assertion than an explanation, although he does suggest that an extremely critical reception indicates an already closed mind to his concept, which, he says,

> is merely a way of stating that men's motives change and grow in the course of life, because it is the nature of man that they should do so. Only theorists wedded to a reactive, homeostatic, quasi-closed model of man find difficulty in agreeing. (1961, pp. 252–253).

FROMM'S POSITION ....

Erich Fromm (born in Frankfurt, Germany, 1900; died in New York City, 1980) studied psychology and sociology in his college years. He obtained a Ph.D. from the University of Heidelberg in 1922, after which he received training in psychoanalysis in Munich and Berlin. In 1933, he came to the United States as a lecturer at the Chicago Psychoanalytic Institute and subsequently entered private practice in New York City. Still later in his career, he taught at a number of universities and institutes in the United States, finally leaving to head the Mexican Psychoanalytic Institute in Mexico City. Fromm not only continued to write but also trained many students in his psychotherapeutic techniques and theorizing.

Fromm's intriguing viewpoint includes elements of the conflict model and of both the actualization and perfection versions of the fulfillment model. As you can see from his location in this chapter, I believe the perfection aspects of his position to be paramount.

Fromm's Core Statement

To begin, Fromm (1947) distinguishes between *animal nature* and *human nature.* Animal nature is roughly defined by the biochemical and psychological bases of and mechanisms for physical survival. While people certainly have an animal nature, they are the only organisms possessing human nature as well. This fact has, according to Fromm, rendered the human's animal nature his or her least important part. Even without knowing the specific content of human nature according to Fromm, you should recognize the similarity among Fromm, Allport, and Maslow. Fromm is especially close to Allport, for both deemphasize the importance of animal nature or opportunistic functioning in the human in favor of human nature or propriate functioning.

THE CORE TENDENCY. Indeed, the only really accurate rendition of a core tendency for Fromm would be *the attempt to fulfill one's human* *nature.* His theory may imply another core tendency concerning the satisfaction of one's animal nature, but nowhere does Fromm emphasize this. Even when persons shrink from vigorous expression of human nature, they are best characterized in Fromm's terms as avoiding humanness rather than embracing creatureness. Human beings can never really become creatures simply because they happen to possess biological survival needs. Because he emphasizes pursuing one's human nature, I have classed Fromm as a fulfillment theorist, even though he assumes an animal nature as well. It is not without uneasiness that I do this, for in at least one place in his writings (Fromm, 1947, p. 41), he specifically suggests that the antagonism between the person's human and animal natures provides the impetus to development and living—clearly a conflict statement. But this sort of statement rarely occurs in his writings, which generally stress the pursuit of humanness to an intense degree and barely acknowledge the person's animal nature.

To understand Fromm's position more fully and determine whether it is properly considered an actualization or perfection version of the fulfillment model, we must scrutinize the proposed content of human nature. Fortunately, Fromm has a good deal to say about what human nature entails and in this achieves a degree of theoretical precision equal to that of Allport and superior to that of the actualization theorists. Fromm (1947) starts by saying that organisms with a primarily animal nature are one with the natural world. There is no sharp separation among themselves, other organisms, and the environment around them. They do not experience separateness.

But human nature is unique, leading to extraordinary potentialities and problems. Perhaps the most basic characteristic of human nature is the ability to know oneself and the things that differ from one. Once an organism is endowed with such knowledge, it inevitably experiences separateness from nature and other organisms. Looked at positively, this separateness is freedom; looked at negatively, it is alienation (Fromm, 1941). The freedom and independence stemming from the person's human nature can lead to great heights of creative

accomplishment; however, fear of the loneliness and isolation involved in acting on human nature often leads people to forgo their birthright of freedom.

Though people can never function as if their nature were solely animal, they can approach this state by shrinking from the freedom that would come through acting vigorously on their human nature. This shrinking is not a straightforward expression of an animal nature; hence, it is never as satisfactory as the simple life of animals, and it is clearly inferior to the vigorous expression of humanness. Shrinking from freedom amounts to social conformity and what Allport calls reactive behavior on the individual level. It is a defensive way of life, though Fromm does not discuss defense systematically. In contrast, acting on one's human nature leads to productiveness and a nondefensive way of life. Fromm's emphasis on freedom, productiveness, individuality, and lack of defense as expressions of the highest form of living are thoroughly consistent with other fulfillment theories. Conflict theorists, such as Freud, also stress productiveness in the highest form of living. You may wonder, therefore, if Fromm really is making a fulfillment statement. He is, because he does not cast productiveness in the light of adjustment to society, as conflict theorists do. A productive person would be adjusted to society, according to Fromm (1955), only if the society were constructive or sane. If it were not, the productive person would choose to be maladjusted—only conformists, shrinking from their human nature, would adjust.

True to the fulfillment model, Fromm does not assume a basic antagonism between individual and society. He stresses that human nature will achieve expression in ways that are effective and possible given the existing societal and cultural climate. As in other fulfillment positions, Fromm believes that when human nature is pervertedly expressed (in the shrinking from freedom leading to conformity and reactivity), society is to blame. Authoritarian, dictatorial, monolithic, punitive societies increase the likelihood that their members will fall short of vigorous humanness. But society need not be coercive; hence, when it is, Fromm (1955) is quick to condemn it as pathological.

Fromm is often considered a social psychological theorist by psychoanalytic personologists. In a way, this is a mistake. Actually, Freud more than Fromm emphasizes society's importance by assuming it to be a force that cannot be avoided, transcended, or changed. Fromm, like all fulfillment theorists, gives primary importance to the full expression of the individual and cares little for adjustment to society. The only sense in which it is reasonable to consider Fromm a social psychological theorist is that he has been a consistent critic of past and contemporary societies, setting himself the task of clarifying how pathological societies pervert human nature. In this, he is similar to, though perhaps more systematic than, other fulfillment theorists.

THE CORE CHARACTERISTICS. Fromm has specified the content of human nature. The core characteristics associated with the core tendency are the needs for relatedness, transcendence, rootedness, identity, and frame of reference. The *need for relatedness* stems from the stark fact that the person, in becoming human, has been torn from the animal's primary union with nature. In place of this unthinking, simple merging with nature, the person must use reason and imagination to create relationships with nature and other people. The most satisfying relationships are based on productive love, which always implies mutuality, generosity, and respect. The *need for transcendence* is the motivational basis for proactive functioning, or the urge to become a productive individual rather than a mere creature. The *need for rootedness* is apparently very similar to the need for relatedness. Fromm says that it is part of human nature to seek roots in the world, and that the most satisfying roots are those based on a feeling of kinship with others. The person's *need for personal identity* is similar to the need for transcendence in that both lead toward individuality. In striving for an identity, the most satisfying procedure is to rely on one's talents and productive capabilities. Failing that, identity of a less satisfying sort can be achieved through identification with other people or ideas. Finally, there

is the *need for a frame of reference,* a stable and consistent way of perceiving and comprehending the world. Once one gets down to this level of concreteness concerning the content of human nature, the tension-increasing nature of its pursuit becomes apparent. Again Fromm emerges as a fulfillment theorist.

The similarities between Fromm's needs and Allport's propriate functions should not have escaped your attention. The need for transcendence is like propriate striving, the need for rootedness like self-extension, the need for personal identity like self-identity and self-esteem, and the need for a frame of reference like the rational coping out of which develops a philosophy of life. These similarities provide more evidence that inclines me to believe that Fromm's position is best considered a perfection rather than actualization theory. The person, according to Fromm, seems to strive toward an ideal conceptualization of the perfect life rather than merely express inherent capabilities in an unself-conscious fashion. To be sure, he defines perfection in terms of what human nature could be. But for any given person, perfection is not reached by passively expressing inherited strengths and weaknesses. This emphasis is clearly seen in Fromm's (1956) book *The Art of Loving,* which includes a set of exercises for becoming capable in loving. In contrast, actualization theorists usually believe that adequate loving and such obviously constructive things come quite naturally to the undefensive person. Fromm seems more a perfection theorist because he believes that conscious effort toward achieving an ideal is necessary for meaningful fulfillment.

Fromm on the Periphery of Personality

Fromm is one of the most sophisticated and perhaps the most complete of the personologists on the nature of the periphery of personality. His concrete peripheral characteristic is the *character trait,* and he describes orientations or *character types* that comprise sets of interrelated traits. Profoundly influenced by Freud, Fromm (1947) tends to compare and contrast his own view with that of the conflict theorist:

The theory presented . . . follows Freud's characterology in essential points: in the assumption that character traits underlie behavior and must be inferred from it; that they constitute forces which, though powerful, the person may be entirely unconscious of. It follows Freud also in the assumption that the fundamental entity in characters is not the single character trait but the total character organization from which a number of single character traits follow. These character traits are to be understood as a syndrome which results from a particular organization or, as I shall call it, orientation of character. (p. 57)*

You may recognize that not only Fromm and Freud but also Adler and Erikson rather explicitly agree on these assumptions. In addition, such personologists as White, Murray, and Allport would probably agree, though their emphasis on particular traits or needs rather than on types leads to some uncertainty. One note in the above quote sounds new to this discussion: the recognition of the difference between a character trait and the behavior it is used to explain. As I will argue in Chapter 11, it is important for personologists to recognize this, because doing so will lead them to focus on what the data are, after all, that they want to explain. Though any theorist should take this matter seriously, the personologist often does not. Fromm makes clear what must be true for all personologists; namely, that the peripheral characteristic of personality is an explanatory concept—something the theorist devises—rather than a mere description of observations.

NONPRODUCTIVE OR NONIDEAL ORIENTATIONS. Now to the content of Fromm's position on the periphery of personality. His character types are four *nonproductive orientations* and one *productive orientation*. In the nonproductive classification, there are the *receptive, exploitative, hoarding,* and *marketing orientations.* The person with a *receptive orientation*

feels "the source of all good" to be outside, and he believes that the only way to get what he wants—be it something material, be it affection, love, knowledge, pleasure—is to receive it from that outside source. In this orientation the problem of love is almost exclusively that of "being loved" and not that of loving. Such people tend to be indiscriminate in the choice of their love objects, because being loved by anybody is such an overwhelming experience for them that they "fall for" anybody who gives them love or what looks like love. . . . Their orientation is the same in the sphere of thinking: if intelligent, they make the best listeners, since their orientation is one of receiving, not of producing, ideas. . . . They show a particular kind of loyalty, at the bottom of which is the gratitude for the hand that feeds them and the fear of ever losing it. . . . It is difficult for them to say "no," and they are easily caught between conflicting loyalties and promises. . . .

They are dependent not only on authorities for knowledge and help but on people in general for any kind of support. . . . This receptive type has great fondness for food and drink. These persons tend to overcome anxiety and depression by eating and drinking. . . . By and large, the outlook of people in this receptive orientation is optimistic and friendly; they have a certain confidence in life and its gifts, but they become anxious and distraught when their "source of supply" is threatened. (Fromm, 1947, pp. 62–63)

Fromm has added to this vivid description a concrete list of the traits comprising the receptive orientation. These traits have a positive and a negative pole; that is, they sound more admirable at one pole than at the other. Fromm includes both poles because he feels that the more deeply your personality reflects the nonproductive, receptive type, the better the negative poles of the traits will describe your behavior. But if the receptive orientation is mitigated by some degree of a more productive orientation, the positive poles of the traits will be more accurate. I will return to this point after you have viewed all the orientations. For the moment, I shall focus on the list of traits, which follows (Fromm, 1947, p. 114):

---

*From *Man for Himself: An Inquiry into the Psychology of Ethics* by Erich Fromm, © 1947 by Erich Fromm. Reprinted by permission of Henry Holt and Company, LLC.

Receptive Orientation

Positive Aspect	Negative Aspect
Accepting	Passive, without initiative
Responsive	Opinionless, characterless
Devoted	Submissive
Modest	Without pride
Charming	Parasitical
Adaptable	Unprincipled
Socially adjusted	Servile, without self-confidence
Idealistic	Unrealistic
Sensitive	Cowardly
Polite	Spineless
Optimistic	Wishful thinking
Trusting	Gullible
Tender	Sentimental

You probably can imagine what Fromm means by the *exploitative orientation*. He describes it this way:

> The exploitative orientation, like the receptive, has as its basic premise the feeling that the source of all good is outside, that whatever one wants to get must be sought there, and that one cannot produce anything oneself. The difference between the two, however, is that the exploitative type does not expect to receive things from others as gifts, but to take them away from others by force or cunning. ... In the realm of love and affection these people tend to grab and steal. They feel attracted only to people whom they can take away from somebody else. ... We find the same attitude with regard to thinking and intellectual pursuits. Such people will tend not to produce ideas but to steal them. ... They use and exploit anybody and anything from whom or from which they can squeeze something. ... This orientation seems to be symbolized by the biting mouth which is often a prominent feature in such people. (pp. 64–65)

A list of character traits is also included for the exploitative orientation (Fromm, 1947, p. 115):

Exploitative Orientation

Positive Aspect	Negative Aspect
Active	Exploitative
Able to take initiative	Aggressive
Able to make claims	Egocentric
Proud	Conceited
Impulsive	Rash
Self-confident	Arrogant
Captivating	Seducing

The third nonproductive style of life is the *hoarding orientation*. Once again Fromm (1947) vividly describes this orientation:

> While the receptive and exploitative types are similar inasmuch as both expect to get things from the outside world, the hoarding orientation is essentially different. This orientation makes people have little faith in anything new they might get from the outside world; their security is based upon hoarding and saving, while spending is felt to be a threat. They have surrounded themselves, as it were, by a protective wall, and their main aim is to bring as much as possible into this fortified position and to let as little as possible out of it. Their miserliness refers to money and material things as well as to feelings and thoughts. Love is essentially a possession: they do not give love but try to get it by possessing the "beloved." ... Their sentimentality makes the past appear as golden; they hold on to it and indulge in the memories of bygone feelings and experiences. ... One can recognize these people too by facial expression and gestures. Theirs is the tight-lipped mouth; their gestures are characteristic of their withdrawal attitude. ... Another characteristic element in this attitude is pedantic orderliness. The hoarder will be orderly with things, thoughts, or feelings, but again, as with memory, his orderliness is sterile and rigid. ... His compulsive cleanliness is another expression of his need to undo contact with the outside world. (pp. 65–66)

The list of character traits comprising the hoarding orientation is as follows (Fromm, 1947, p. 115):

Hoarding Orientation

Positive Aspect	Negative Aspect
Practical	Unimaginative
Economical	Stingy
Careful	Suspicious
Reserved	Cold
Patient	Lethargic
Cautious	Anxious
Steadfast, tenacious	Stubborn
Imperturbable	Indolent
Composed under stress	Inert
Orderly	Pedantic
Methodical	Obsessional
Loyal	Possessive

It should not have escaped your attention that

the three orientations described thus far are similar in some ways to Freudian character types. Both the receptive and the exploitative orientations recall the oral character type. And indeed, if one follows some psychoanalytic thinkers, such as Abraham (1927a, 1927b), who distinguish between oral-incorporative and oral-aggressive character types, the fit becomes even closer. Oral-incorporativeness resembles the receptive orientation, and oral-aggressiveness seems like the exploitative orientation. In addition, the hoarding orientation is quite reminiscent of the anal character type.

These similarities should not surprise you, for Fromm started out as a psychoanalytic thinker, though he gradually developed a very different view. The existence in his theory of the first three orientations indicates that Fromm agreed with some Freudian statements concerning the periphery of personality. But, as you will see next, he includes some orientations that have no counterpart in psychoanalytic thinking. If you add to this the fact that Fromm is very different from Freud at the core level of personality, you will see that it is a mistake to consider Fromm a neo-Freudian. Even though he admits the value of some of Freud's statements concerning character types, Fromm explains their development on grounds that have nothing to do with psychosexuality, as you will soon see.

The final nonproductive style of life is the *marketing orientation,* and in delineating it, Fromm expresses much of his originality as a personality theorist. Fromm (1947) takes the modern marketplace as the model for this orientation, in which the person is nothing more than a commodity:

> The modern market is no longer a meeting place but a mechanism characterized by abstract and impersonal demand. One produces for this market, not for a known circle of customers; its verdict is based on laws of supply and demand; and it determines whether the commodity can be sold and at what price. . . . The character orientation which is rooted in the experience of oneself as a commodity and of one's value as exchange value I call the marketing orientation.
>
> In our time the marketing orientation has been

growing rapidly, together with the development of a new market that is a phenomenon of the last decades—the "personality market." . . . The principle of evaluation is the same on both the personality and the commodity market: on the one, personalities are offered for sale; on the other, commodities. Value in both cases is their exchange value, for which use value is a necessary but not a sufficient condition. . . . However, if we ask what the respective weight of skill and personality as a condition for success is, we find that only in exceptional cases is success predominantly the result of skill and of certain other human qualities like honesty, decency, and integrity. Although the proportion between skill and human qualities on the one hand and "personality" on the other hand as prerequisites for success varies, the "personality factor" always plays a decisive role. Success depends largely on how well a person sells himself on the market, how well he gets his personality across, how nice a "package" he is; whether he is "cheerful," "sound," "aggressive," "reliable," "ambitious"; furthermore what his family background is, what club he belongs to, and whether he knows the right people. . . . Like the handbag, one has to be in fashion on the personality market, and in order to be in fashion one has to know what kind of personality is most in demand. . . . Since modern man experiences himself both as the seller and as the commodity to be sold on the market, his self-esteem depends on conditions beyond his control. If he is "successful," he is valuable; if he is not, he is worthless. The degree of insecurity which results from this orientation can hardly be overestimated. If one feels that one's value is not constituted primarily by the human qualities one possesses, but by one's success on a competitive market with ever-changing conditions, one's self-esteem is bound to be shaky and in constant need of confirmation by others. Hence one is driven to strive relentlessly for success, and any setback is a severe threat to one's self-esteem; helplessness, insecurity, and inferiority feelings are the result. If the vicissitudes of the market are the judges of one's value, the sense of dignity and pride is destroyed. (pp. 68–72)

The marketing orientation underlies the problem of alienation that has been so vivid in the minds of contemporary social critics, sociologists, and personologists. This orientation is clearly different from anything Freud considered, and yet seems quite valid. The character traits comprising the marketing orientation are as follows (Fromm, 1947, p. 116):

Marketing Orientation

Positive Aspect	Negative Aspect
Purposeful	Opportunistic
Able to change	Inconsistent
Youthful	Childish
Forward-looking	Without a future or a past
Open-minded	Without principle and values
Social	Unable to be alone
Experimenting	Aimless
Undogmatic	Relativistic
Efficient	Overactive
Curious	Tactless
Intelligent	Intellectualistic
Adaptable	Undiscriminating
Tolerant	Indifferent
Witty	Silly
Generous	Wasteful

THE PRODUCTIVE OR IDEAL CHARACTER TYPE. Having discussed the four nonproductive orientations, I now come to what Fromm considers to be the ideal character type—the *productive orientation.* As you will see, the productive orientation bears similarity to the Freudian genital character, to the fully functioning or self-actualizing personalities of Rogers and Maslow, to the active-constructive style of life of the Adlerians, and to the mature personality according to Allport. Here, Fromm (1947) describes the productive orientation:

In discussing the productive character I venture beyond critical analysis and inquire into the nature of the fully developed character that is the aim of human development and simultaneously the ideal of humanistic ethics. . . . The "productive orientation" of personality refers to a fundamental attitude, a mode of relatedness in all realms of human experience. It covers mental, emotional, and sensory responses to others, to oneself, and to things. Productiveness is man's ability to use his powers and to realize the potentialities inherent in him. If we say he must use his powers we imply that he must be free and not dependent on someone who controls his powers. We imply, furthermore, that he is guided by reason, since he can make use of

his powers only if he knows what they are, how to use them, and what to use them for. Productiveness means that he experiences himself as the embodiment of his powers and as the "actor"; that he feels himself one with his powers and at the same time that they are not marked and alienated from him. . . . Productiveness is man's realization of the potentialities characteristic of him, the use of his powers. . . . How is man related to the world when he uses his powers productively? . . . The world outside oneself can be experienced in two ways: reproductively by perceiving actuality in the same fashion as a film makes a literal record of things photographed . . . and generatively by conceiving it, by enlivening and recreating this new material through the spontaneous activity of one's own mental and emotional powers. . . . Human existence is characterized by the fact that man is alone and separated from the world; not being able to stand the separation, he is impelled to seek for relatedness and oneness. There are many ways in which he can realize this need, but only one in which he, as a unique entity, remains intact; only one in which his own powers unfold in the very process of being related. It is the paradox of human existence that man must simultaneously seek for closeness and for independence; for oneness with others and at the same time for the preservation of his uniqueness and particularity. As we have shown, the answer to this paradox—and to the moral problem of man—is productiveness.

One can be productively related to the world by acting and by comprehending. Man produces things, and in the process of creation he exercises his powers over matter. Man comprehends the world, mentally and emotionally, through love and through reason. His power of reason enables him to penetrate through the surface and grasp the essence of his object by getting into active relation with it. His power of love enables him to break through the wall which separates him from another person and to comprehend him. Although love and reason are only two different forms of comprehending the world and although neither is possible without the other, they are expressions of different powers, that of emotion and that of thinking, and hence must be discussed separately. (pp. 83–97)

Fromm lists no set traits that compose the productive orientation. This is partly because he feels that the truly productive person would not be predictable enough to be pinned down to fixed traits. By productiveness, after all, he means not sticking to a job or acting in a repetitive way but something more like creativity and transcendence. But there are certainly some traits, such as imaginativeness, that one could list for the productive orientation, so unpredictability does not fully explain why Fromm chooses not to offer a list of traits. The rest of the explanation lies in the relationship he suggests between the productive and nonproductive orientations. According to Fromm, it is very unlikely that anyone would show a completely developed productive orientation. In this, Fromm is much like Rogers, who indicates that the fully functioning person is an ideal characterization of life, not actually achieved by anyone. What one normally finds, according to Fromm, is some combination of productive and nonproductive orientations. This is why Fromm bothered to include positive along with negative poles for the traits composing the nonproductive orientations. The more the productive orientation is combined with the nonproductive one, the more accurate the positive poles will be. Thus, the positive aspects of the traits listed under nonproductive orientations can be used to characterize the productive qualities of a person's style of life.

At this point, you can probably see how the productive orientation resembles the ideal peripheral personality of a number of other theorists. The emphasis on actualizing one's capabilities and being creative is similar to Rogers and Maslow. The emphasis on concrete productions and the orientation toward perfection are similar to White and Adler. The emphasis on reason and love is similar to Allport's discussion of psychological maturity. And, although the quotes I selected do not play it up, there is similarity to Freud in the fact that mature sexuality, in the sense of orgasm and progeny, are also considered productive. That Fromm's views are similar not only to other fulfillment theorists but to some conflict theorists reflects at the peripheral level the classificatory problem encountered at the core level. Although primarily a fulfillment theorist, Fromm incorporates elements of the conflict emphasis as well.

Fromm on Development

Before leaving Fromm, I should present his view of development, or the way in which the various orientations can come about through the interaction of core tendency and environments. As I indicated before, Fromm's view of development is very different from Freud's. First, the core tendency is different. For Fromm, a person's life is basically an attempt to realize human nature, which includes, you will remember, such needs as those for relatedness, transcendence, and identity. Psychosexuality plays a small part in all this. He also diverges from Freud in the nature of the particular parent-child interaction he considers important in understanding the resultant peripheral personality types. For Fromm, the three important types of interaction are *symbiotic relatedness, withdrawal-destructiveness,* and *love* (Fromm, 1947, pp. 107–108). In the symbiotic situation,

> the person is related to others but loses or never attains his independence; he avoids the danger of aloneness by becoming part of another person, either by being "swallowed" by that person or by "swallowing" him.

Being swallowed by parents, as it were, leads to the masochistic patterns of behavior culminating in the receptive orientation. This whole pattern is encouraged by parents who render the child dependent on them but in the specially violating way that entails laying oneself bare to be used by others in one's search for satisfaction. But if the reverse situation occurs—if the parents abnegate authority by catering to the child's every whim and encouraging him or her to use them— the resulting pattern will be more like sadism. This sadism in the child will culminate in the exploitative orientation, expressing as it does dependence on others in order to violate them.

The symbiotic relationship involves intimacy with the other person, though at the expense of freedom and integrity. In contrast, the withdrawal-destructiveness type of parent-child relationship is characterized by *distance.* According to Fromm (1947),

> In the phenomenon here described, withdrawal

becomes the main form of relatedness to others, a negative relatedness, as it were. Its emotional equivalent is the feeling of indifference toward others, often accompanied by a compensatory feeling of self-inflation. (pp. 109–110)

This withdrawal pattern, which will culminate in the marketing orientation, is encouraged by parents who are destructive toward the child. In other words, they will not simply frustrate the child's needs but will attempt to subjugate and destroy him or her. In the face of such an onslaught, the child will cope with the sense of powerlessness by retreating and becoming indifferent. On the other hand, if the parents are indifferent and withdrawn, the child may well develop the pattern of destructiveness, which, according to Fromm (1947, p. 110) is the active form of withdrawal. The resulting pattern of assertiveness will culminate in the hoarding orientation.

As you undoubtedly have anticipated, when the parent-child relationship is one of love—mutual respect, support, and appreciation—children will develop toward the productive orientation. Loved by their parents, children will love themselves and will have no reason not to love others.

Mainly as members of their culture do parents affect their children; hence, one may expect each of the various orientations to be prominent under a particular set of cultural conditions. Fromm feels that the receptive, exploitative, and hoarding orientations were especially characteristic of the 18th and 19th centuries, though they are by no means absent now. He dates their prominence thusly because they require a form of society in which one group has an institutionalized right to exploit another group. Because the exploited group has no power to change, or any idea of changing its situation, it will tend to look up to its masters as its providers—hence the receptive orientation. The societal model for the exploitative character goes back to piratical and feudal ancestors and goes forward to the robber barons of the 19th century, who exploited the continent's natural resources. "The hoarding orientation," according to Fromm (1947), "existed side by side with the exploitative orientation in

the eighteenth and nineteenth centuries. The hoarding type was conservative, less interested in ruthless acquisition than in methodical economic pursuits, based on sound principles and on the preservation of what had been acquired" (p. 81). Fromm associates the hoarding orientation with the Protestant ethic. But the marketing orientation has reached a position of predominance only in the 20th century, with its emphasis on the modern marketplace and its materialistic, superficial values. And, as you might expect, the societal model consistent with the productive orientation has not yet emerged on the world scene, according to Fromm. One can describe it, however, in terms of suiting human needs rather than economic needs. It would be a truly sane society (Fromm, 1955).

It is with some disquietude that I conclude this discussion of Fromm's position on development. Of the theorists already covered, he has offered by far the most explicit and complete description of traits and orientations. No one else has endeavored to actually list the traits that constitute the character types he wishes to consider. While it is true that Murray and Allport have more carefully delineated and defined their peripheral characteristics of need and personal disposition, Fromm surpasses them in organizing traits into types. One has the feeling that someone could easily provide precise definitions for the traits he employs. One should also be able to determine the empirical fruitfulness of Fromm's position, because he has gone a long way toward the theoretical formalism necessary for making a position really usable.

But for all this, I do not find myself particularly enlightened or convinced by his account of development. Sometimes he suggests that children will develop in manners opposite to the ways they have been treated by their parents. This is seen in the notion that parents who "swallow up" their offspring will produce children who ask the world to swallow them. But at other times, he suggests that children will develop in a manner similar to that of the parents or of the society that they represent. This seems implicit in such notions as that the existence in society of a downtrodden class was necessary as a model for the receptive orientation. But if you were a member of this downtrodden class, would you, according to Fromm, swallow up your children or encourage them to swallow you? Common sense suggests the latter, and yet knowledge that classes tend to perpetuate themselves indicates the former. Fromm himself seems unable to decide. I do not want to make too much of this criticism, as the difficulty may, after all, be resolved by a future theoretical effort. All in all, Fromm's position is an excellent example of peripheral theorizing, regardless of whether or not it turns out to be supported by empirical evidence.

EXISTENTIAL PSYCHOLOGY . . . . . .

The sharp increase of interest in existentialism in the 20th century has shown itself throughout a broad spectrum of society, including not only personologists and psychotherapists but other professionals, political activists, members of the clergy, students, and people on the street. This has happened even though the body of thought commonly labeled existentialism is extremely amorphous, shifting in emphases from country to country, continent to continent, and even theorist to theorist. It seems to me that much of existential thought really constitutes a set of attitudes for living, a manifesto more than a systematic theory of personality. On these grounds, existentialism could have been omitted from this book. But because of its unique and influential position, it deserves a place here.

I have selected those threads in existential thought most rigorous and relevant to personality theory. Thus, what follows concerns the theorizing not of any one person but of many. I shall refer little to the philosophical founders of existentialism, Kierkegaard and Heidegger, favoring instead those of their followers who have attempted to translate their thinking into statements about personality. Foremost among these are the Europeans Ludwig Binswanger (born in Kreuzlingen, Switzerland, 1881; died in Kreuzlingen, 1966), Medard Boss (born in St. Gallen,

Switzerland, 1903; has resided in Zurich for most of his life), and Victor Frankl (born in Vienna, 1905, where he still lives). Major figures who have worked in the United States are Rollo May (born in New York City, 1909, died in Tiburon, California, 1994), and Paul Tillich (born in Starzeddel, Kreis Guben, Prussia, 1886; died in Chicago, 1965). But it will also be necessary to refer to work by other existential psychologists.

Though Binswanger, Boss, and Frankl all knew Freud and were heavily influenced by his thinking early in their careers, Kierkegaard and Heidegger served as their primary intellectual influences. One can characterize Binswanger, Boss, and Frankl as having attempted to translate Heidegger's philosophical stance into a workable approach to psychotherapy. All were physicians; Binswanger served for many years as chief medical director (a post his father held before him) of the Bellevue Sanatorium in Kreuzlingen, Boss was professor in the University of Zurich medical school as well as director of the Institute of Daseinsanalytic Therapy, and Frankl has been a professor at the University of Vienna medical school and the director of the Neurological Polyclinic there.

Tillich was a theologian, an interpreter of Christianity in 20th century spiritual emptiness. He taught at such prominent schools as Harvard and the University of Chicago, creating an enormous effect on modern religious theory, to say nothing of psychology. May served as a training therapist at a distinguished center for psychotherapy, the William Alanson White Institute in New York City.

The Core of Existential Psychology

It is no easy feat to state the core tendency of existential psychology in a few words. Not only is there the difficulty of many different voices, all using slightly different words; there is also the complication that the words are often poetic, metaphoric, sometimes with polemical and emotional intent rather than intellectual precision. What is clear, however, is the emphasis on being genuine, honest, and true and on making decisions and shouldering responsibility for them.

THE CORE TENDENCY. All in all, an apt phrasing of the core tendency might be *to achieve authentic being.* The word *being* (or *existence,* or the German *Dasein*) is pregnant with meaning for the existentialist. It does not refer to some passive creatureliness, though it partially includes this. Instead, it signifies the special quality of existing that is characteristic of humans, a quality that heavily involves mentality, intelligence, and awareness. The adjective *authentic* connotes this and also indicates the emphasis of existential psychology on honesty. More often than not, according to existentialists, people shrink from authenticity because of the inherently frightening and demanding nature of life.

To gain a relevant but oversimplified intuition of achieving authentic being, search your memory for the times you understood and accepted yourself most, when you were aware of your vanities, sentimentalities, follies, and weaknesses, yet could somehow assert the importance of your life. You could anticipate with vigor your future experiences even though you could not entirely predict or control them, and this frightened you. As you will see, the main emphases of existential psychology are expressed in such experiences.

CORE CHARACTERISTICS. My attempt to render the existential viewpoint a systematic theory may violate existentialists' sensibilities as to what is important. They are steeped in the phenomenological approach, namely, the attempt to understand in no terms other than immediate, vividly appreciated, but unanalyzed sensory experience. In a sense, many existentialists consider what I have been calling *intuitive understanding* to be the only important psychological knowledge. A phenomenological approach logically implies that one person's reality differs from that of neighbors, for each person is likely to perceive things differently. Thus, the existentialist's aversion to formal, abstract theorizing is two-pronged. Abstraction is the antithesis of intuitive truth, and such truth varies from person to person.

This antitheoretical stance seems strongest among European existentialists. For example, Hall and Lindzey (1970) quote a personal communication from Boss:

> I can only hope that existential psychology will never develop into a theory in its modern meaning of the natural sciences. All that existential psychology can contribute to psychology is to teach the scientists to remain with the experienced and experienceable facts and phenomena, to let these phenomena tell the scientists their meaning and their references, and so do the encountered objects justice—in short, becoming more "objective" again. (p. 580)

Let me post a conundrum that may help here. Is that object I am sitting on a mass of relatively slow-moving atomic particles, a construction of shaped and polished woods having low brittleness and therefore able to carry weight, or a chair? Of course, it is all three, and any existentialist would agree. But in human terms, the existentialist would hasten to add, it is a chair, nothing else—except, perhaps, colors and textures readily perceived with the senses. To talk of atomic particles, and even of brittleness, is to theorize in the manner of the natural sciences.

Presumably Boss would accept theorizing in human terms. But once you have called a chair a chair, about all you can do without becoming abstract and analytical is to recognize that chairs may differ in shape and color. Boss and other European existentialists seem to accept a natural limitation on theorizing for it to remain true to the human experience of things. American existentialists are less sure, being somewhat more willing to theorize about antecedents to the phenomenal experience (e.g., What learning experiences condition perceptions?). However, the Europeans are not quite consistent, for their antitheoretical stance makes it impossible to define core characteristics of personality, but they themselves have gone furthest in formulating them. As you will see, although these core characteristics strictly adhere to phenomenological givens, they imply capabilities of the human organism. As such, a statement on human nature can be derived from them, which is necessarily abstract and essentialistic. Although the vivid appreciation of immediate sensory experience is all the more important because it is so often excluded from a role in everyday life, Boss seems to fight a losing battle by insisting that existentialism avoid formalization. Formalization does inevitably mean abstracting, but without it the transition from mere attitudes to working theories probably could not be made.

Being-in-the-world (Binswanger, 1963; Boss, 1963) is a basic core characteristic intended to emphasize the unity of person and environment. The person and his or her environment do not merely interact; rather, person and environment are essentially the same, because both are human creations, so interdependent as to be inseparable. Of course, the human body and the things in the environment have physical reality —shape, size, weight, but these physical properties are irrelevant to existentialists. When they speak of *being,* they emphasize the sum of intuitive sensory experiences, memories, fantasies, and anticipations. When they speak of *world,* they emphasize the environment people create for themselves by exercising the capacities that produce being and by expressing that being in action. Both being and world are intensely personal. *Being* is mentality considering one's individual self, and *world* is mentality considering one's surroundings.

To understand a person's existence, one must appreciate the ways being and world merge. In explicating being-in-the-world, May (1958) says:

> *World is the structure of meaningful relationships in which a person exists and in the design of which he participates.* Thus world includes the past events which condition my existence and all the vast variety of deterministic influences which operate upon me. But it is these *as I relate to them,* am aware of them, carry them with me, molding, inevitably forming, building them in every minute

of relating. For to be aware of one's world means at the same time to be designing it. (pp. 59–60)*

May's (1958) words concerning being complement those about world and also imply something about human nature:

> The full meaning of the term "human being" will be clearer if the reader will keep in mind that "being" is a participle, a verb form implying that someone is in the process of being something. It is unfortunate that, when used as a general noun in English, the term "being" connotes a static substance, and when used as a particular noun such as a being, it is usually assumed to refer to an entity, say, such as a soldier to be counted as a unit. Rather "being" should be understood, when used as a general noun, to mean *potentia,* the source of potentiality; "being" is the potentiality by which the acorn becomes the oak or each of us becomes what he truly is. And when used in a particular sense such as a human being, it always has the dynamic connotation of someone in process, the person being something. Perhaps, therefore, *becoming* connotes more accurately the meaning of the term in this country. We can understand another human being only as we see what he is moving toward, what he is becoming; and we can know ourselves only as we "project our *potentia* in action." The significant tense for human beings is thus the *future*—that is to say, the critical question is what I am pointing toward, becoming, what I will be in the immediate future.
>
> Thus, being in the human sense is not given once and for all. It does not unfold automatically as the oak tree does from the acorn. For an intrinsic and inseparable element in being human is self-consciousness. Man . . . is the particular being who has to be aware of himself, be responsible for himself, if he is to become himself. He also is that particular being who knows that at some future moment he will not be; he is the being who is always in a dialectical relation with non-being, death. And he not only knows he will sometime not be, but he can, in his own choices, slough off and forfeit his being. (pp. 41–42)

This passage clearly identifies self or being as a process rather than as some static, unchanging

---

*From *Existence: A New Dimension in Psychiatry and Psychology,* edited by R. May, E. Angel, and H. F. Ellenberger.

content and in that sense reminds one of the actualization fulfillment model epitomized by Rogers. But the crucial difference is that the process of becoming May describes is not natural in the sense of being easy or linking humans with less complex animals. Unlike Rogers, May could never offer as an example becoming a seaweed growing and flourishing though pounded incessantly by waves. Seaweed does not have mentality or self-consciousness and can therefore never choose. For May and other existentialists, being is so essentially a matter of choice that people can even choose against it by committing suicide— by precipitating nonbeing. When May and other existentialists refer to fulfilling one's potentialities, they mean something closer to the perfection fulfillment theories than to the actualization fulfillment position. Achieving one's potentialities involves, for May, a painful and continual process of soul searching and decision making in the face of doubt and loneliness. This is a matter more of striving to do the best one can than of indulging a genetic birthright, as you will further see.

BIOLOGICAL, SOCIAL, AND PERSONAL EXPERIENCING. But what are these potentialities that one expresses in authentic being? Like actualization fulfillment theorists, existentialists are far from clear on this matter. Such theorizing would probably be too abstract and essentialistic for their phenomenologically conditioned tastes. But there are some clues available. One is that these potentialities are expressed in a process rather than in something irrevocably fixed. The biggest clue, however, involves the distinctions made among three broad modes of being-in-the-world: *Umwelt, Mitwelt,* and *Eigenwelt* (Binswanger, 1963; Boss, 1963; Frankl, 1960; May, 1958). *Umwelt* (the world around you) connotes the biological and physical world. *Mitwelt* (the social world) refers to the world of persons, of one's fellow humans. *Eigenwelt* (own-world) refers to the internal dialogue of relationship to oneself. Note that all three modes assume the operation of mind—awareness. So the *Umwelt* is not some objective consideration

of the biological and physical characteristics determining a person's relationship to the surrounding world; rather, it concerns one's construing of the biological and physical tie between oneself and the world. So too with the *Mitwelt,* which refers to one's perceptions of and orientations toward one's interactions with others and with social institutions. It is hardly necessary to point out this operation of self-consciousness in the case of the *Eigenwelt,* for it cannot be defined at all unless it includes a consciousness that can consider itself an object.

It is best to interpret these three modes of being as general frames of reference. In any being-in-the-world, there will have to be some general orientation to biological, social, and personal experiences. But the precise nature of these three orientations can shift considerably and differ from person to person. Difficulties ensue from a narrower interpretation of the three modes, which ascribes to them some content considered necessary because of their biological, social, and personal nature. For example, Keen (1970) presents the three modes of being as being-in-the-world, being-for-others, and being-for-oneself. For him, being-in-the-world involves natural, unreflective experiencing; being-for-others adopts external, social criteria for functioning; and being-for-oneself involves self-conscious reflection on one's existence. Although these distinctions seem similar to those presented earlier, they are quite different in their emphases. Being-for-others has the negative connotation of someone who is subjugated to convention and that is not the defining characteristic of *Mitwelt.* Though one's *Mitwelt* may involve conventionality, it might also concern intimacy and even an unconventional social commitment. Also, for Keen there is an implied antagonism between being-in-the-world and being-for-oneself in that the former is easy and natural and the latter incessantly introspective. Small wonder that Keen seems to favor being-in-the-world as the mode of existence that leads to the good life. This, of course, leads to an inconsistency in spirit, for his being-for-oneself carries the major possibility for the considered, rational life so important to existentialists and is clearly more uniquely human than is his being-in-the-world. Yet, he considers the latter more advantageous.

BIOLOGICAL, SOCIAL, AND PSYCHOLOGICAL NEEDS. It is closer to the original meaning of Binswanger and Boss, who are primarily responsible for the three modes of being, to consider *Umwelt*, *Mitwelt*, and *Eigenwelt* as referring to biological, social, and personal experiencing, leaving aside for additional consideration what is good and bad about the person's commitment in each mode. From this position, one can discern a meaning for the human potentialities to which May refers. Following Frankl's (1960) lead, Maddi (1967, 1970) assumes that human nature comprises biological, social, and psychological needs. The biological needs include those for food, water, and air and refer to functions that must be expressed for the person to survive physically. The social needs include those for contact and communication, the frustration of which leads to intense loneliness and loss of sense of self. The psychological needs are those for symbolization (or classification), imagination, and judgment. Although the three sets of needs recall Maslow's biological, security, and cognitive-understanding (or self-actualization) needs, Maddi does not propose them as a hierarchy.

Of the three sets of needs, the psychological ones characterize the existential emphasis most. *Symbolizing* or classifying involves abstracting from the specifics of an experience that which is general enough to be compared with other experiences. When you symbolize, you end up with categories that you can use to recognize and order experiences. Because you cannot recognize an experience for which you have no category, then the more categories that exist in your cognitive mass, the greater the meaningfulness of experience for you. *Imagining* involves combining and recombining categories, memories, and ideas in a manner that does not require input from the external world. According to Maddi (1967, 1970), the aim of imagining is change, in the sense that the imagined state is invariably thought of as more interesting or advantageous than present actualities. With every change that

takes place (whether in thought or in action), the amount of information available increases. Thus, the more active the imagination, the greater the meaning, in the sense of amount of information. Finally, *judgment* involves evaluating experience in a manner that leads one to consider it either good or bad (moral judgment) or pleasant or unpleasant (preferential judgment). The values and preferences resulting from the judgmental process also increase meaning by giving one a personal basis for orienting oneself to experience.

What Maddi is saying is that the person needs to symbolize, imagine, and judge to feel satisfied and avoid frustration, because that is the nature of the human being. Maddi (1970) argues that psychological needs are core characteristics because symbolization, imagination, and judgment are universal. Once you recognize that words are symbols, it becomes apparent that thought and communication, if not perception as well, would be impossible without symbolization. That every society ever studied has a mythology suggests the universality of imagining on a grand scale. And Osgood (1962) indicates that the tendency to make evaluations is universal in all the societies and cultures he studied. An argument based on evolutionary theory supports this universality (Maddi, 1970). After all, the human mind is the ultimate wonder of evolution, winning for its owner a preeminent place among the creatures even though the human is physically puny and frail. The strength of that mind is that it can take in, order, evaluate, and anticipate vast amounts of information and hence act effectively. Once such a marvelous nervous system evolved, it could hardly lie fallow. It had to perform the operations for which it was designed. Some research (e.g., Riesen, 1961) indicates that neural structures must be used in infancy if they are to develop normally. The person needs to symbolize, imagine, and judge because that is what the central nervous system is designed to do. And since symbolizing, imagining, and judging all create meaning, it would seem that the search for meaning is an inherent, unlearned aspect of human nature.

Regarding the other two core characteristics,

the mere existence of biological and social needs does not differentiate the human from other animals. Biological needs reflect metabolic requirements and, in their most straightforward sense, leave little room for taste and subtlety. Cooked meat tastes better and is more digestible than raw meat, but in the absence of the wherewithal to cook, raw meat undoubtedly will be eaten. Although it may be much nicer and more hygienic to eliminate in a modern toilet, the pants will be fouled sooner than the biological organism will be damaged. Insofar as our biological needs do not differ from those of other animals, there is no basis in them for decorum, subtlety, and taste. Perhaps decorum, subtlety, and taste in deepened biological experiencing comes from other than biological needs.

Social needs also seem to exist in other animals, to judge from the prevalence in even relatively primitive species of a rudimentary social structure involving simple social roles. Social needs seem to be most straightforwardly met by engaging in these simple social roles through interactions with others. Talking with service personnel, colleagues, acquaintances, and friends, going to and having parties, dinners, and lunch meetings are ways to communicate and make contact. Even simply watching people go by or having them around as background fulfills social needs, as is attested to by the ubiquitous sidewalk cafe in Europe. All these things satisfy the social needs by increasing the number and variety of people interacted with.

But another way to meet these needs is to work in depth toward increasing the richness of a few intense relationships. This way involves intimacy and love, in that you come to feel that some other person or persons are very important to you and you to them. You do not wish to keep your mutual experience just on the surface but prefer to go progressively deeper, creating new levels of experience all the while. Perhaps intimacy and love in deepened social experiencing comes from other than social needs.

It is through vigorous expression of psychological needs that biological and social experiencing are deepened (Maddi, 1967, 1970). The more vigorous the expression of psychological

needs (symbolization, imagination, and judgment), the more will the *Umwelt* (biological experience) include taste and subtlety, the *Mitwelt* (social experience) intimacy and love, and the *Eigenwelt* (personal experience) complexity and individuality. This is because intense symbolization, imagination, and judgment will result in many categories with which to classify experience, many ideas about change, and many values and preferences. Also, the larger the number of these cognitions, the more unusual they will be. According to existentialists, this individuality is one criterion for an ideal personality (Binswanger, 1963; Boss, 1963; Frankl, 1960; Maddi, 1970; May, 1958). But you should note that uniqueness is characterized by individualism, not by stony isolation from people. Indeed, vigorous expression of psychological needs is considered encouragement toward intimacy and love rather than toward more superficial forms of socializing.

Assuming that human nature includes biological, social, and psychological needs, one naturally considers the ideal as the vigorous expression of all three. When this happens, there is a tendency for *Umwelt, Mitwelt,* and *Eigenwelt* to merge, producing a unitary whole. This unitary quality will be apparent not only at any given time but also in the manner in which present experience is tied to the past and the anticipated future. Spatial and temporal unity occur because the vigorous expression of symbolization, imagination, and judgment tends to order, interpret, and influence biological and social expressions. This unitary quality of being-in-the-world is another existentialist criterion for an ideal personality (Binswanger, 1963; Boss, 1963; Frankl, 1960; Keen, 1970; Maddi, 1970; May, 1958).

Vigorous expression of psychological needs lends humanness to the human being. Actually, a person cannot fail entirely to express psychological needs, because they are rooted in the very nature of the central nervous system. But this does not mean that everyone expresses them as vigorously as possible. Maddi (1967, 1970) believes that, through developmental failures, some people learn to make only rudimentary use of symbolization, imagination, and judgment.

These people have only a few categories for recognition, ideas about change, and values and preferences. In addition, the contents of these cognitions are common, stereotyped, and conventional. Such conforming people resemble less complex animals as much as humans possibly can; their *Eigenwelt* is simple and conventional, and their *Umwelt* and *Mitwelt* show a relative absence of taste, subtlety, intimacy, and love. In addition, their *Umwelt, Mitwelt,* and *Eigenwelt* are fragmented rather than unified. These people's sense of the present will not be tied to past or future. Though they may feel nagging dissatisfaction with their lives, they will be unable to pull themselves up by their mental bootstraps. Their personalities will be nonideal.

EXISTENTIAL DYNAMICS AS DECISION MAKING. The heart of the existential position is its view of directionality in living. The assumption that everything in life is a situation requiring decision or choice is basic to understanding what is concretely involved in the core tendency of striving for authentic being. Because they envisage no alternative to decision making, for existentialists, every moment in life expresses *intentionality* (Boss, 1963; Keen, 1970). Freud also believes that all behavior is motivated, but whereas to him motivation is largely unconscious, to existentialists it is largely conscious. Indeed, it is people's propensity for consciousness that requires them to formulate their lives as a series of decisions or choices. The human is by nature intelligent—a symbolizing, imagining, and judging organism—and therefore cannot avoid decisions, however much he or she might wish for some easier path.

Because there is no alternative to decision making, a person will live most fully by recognizing and accepting this fact. To properly recognize the necessity of continuous decision making, one must practice vigorous symbolization, imagination, and judgment, because this will ensure a complex and sophisticated cognitive mass. And rich expression of those psychological processes certainly helps one actually make decisions, for such expression underlies the ability to pose

problems, consider alternatives and possible outcomes, and enact plans. Life is a series of decisions whether or not one recognizes it. But life is best led by preparation for and commitment to the decisions that one must face.

EMOTIONS IN DECISION MAKING. In the decision-making process, emotions play an overshadowing role. A decision, whatever its content, always takes the form of posing one alternative that pushes the person into the future, the unknown, the unpredictable and another alternative that pulls the person into the past, the status quo, the familiar. While choosing the future is an attractive prospect because of the challenge and possibilities for growth it offers, it is uncharted and therefore provokes anxiety. And while choosing the past is an attractive prospect because it is comfortable and relaxing, it involves sacrificing the possibility of development and brings with it the *guilt* of missed opportunity. Existentialists speak of this anxiety and guilt as *ontological,* or an inevitable part of being (e.g., May, 1958). This formulation recalls Rank, who emphasizes the inherent opposition of fear of life and fear of death. But whereas intrapsychic conflict theorists advocate a compromise that minimizes both fears, existentialists do nothing of the kind. What is ideal for existentialists is to choose the future and accept ontological anxiety as an unfortunate concomitant of authentic being (Binswanger, 1963; Boss, 1963; Frankl, 1960; Kobasa & Maddi, 1977; May, 1958).

Of course, you cannot grow to adulthood without having shrunk from some chances to push forward. Thus, there will be in any person some accumulated ontological guilt. And like the anxiety, this guilt must be accepted, for it is a genuine expression of the life you have led. You cannot alleviate this guilt by resolving not to be so hard on yourself, because this would amount to a falsification of the reality of your life. Such a falsification would corrupt your being-in-the-world through the denial that by certain choices one has inevitably limited other opportunities. To falsify—to deny ontological guilt—is to forfeit attainment of authentic being (Kobasa & Maddi, 1977).

But merely accepting ontological guilt is not enough. You must also arrange to minimize it by choosing often to realize future possibilities, persisting in the face of ontological anxiety. Persisting does not mean denying the really frightening nature of moving toward the unknown. To deny ontological anxiety, all the while appearing to choose the future, is to make a pseudochoice and, by lying to yourself, to jeopardize attainment of authentic being (Binswanger, 1963; Boss, 1963; Frankl, 1960; May, 1958; Tillich, 1952). Indeed, much of what existentialists mean by the necessity of taking responsibility for your own life is just this: recognizing the hazards of choosing the future and choosing it nonetheless. To win the possibility of triumphing, you must recognize that through your own commitments you may end in tragedy (Kobasa & Maddi, 1977). This is not to say that you will triumph if you choose the future—you will win only the *possibility* of doing so. In the existentialists' emphasis on remaining aware of ontological anxiety and guilt and choosing to optimize the former and minimize the latter so one can realize one's possibilities, we see vividly why existential psychology is a perfection fulfillment rather than an intrapsychic conflict position. Although existentialism conceives of an inherent conflict between anxiety and guilt, it does not advocate a compromise designed to minimize both. It assumes that only through persisting in the face of anxiety can one win through a full realization of the potentialities for being.

Before considering the important question of how one can manage to persist in the face of ontological anxiety, we would do well to consider further the precise nature of this emotion. Tillich (1952) has identified three forms of ontological anxiety; namely, fear of human finitude, fear of the necessity of action in the absence of knowledge of outcomes, and fear of meaninglessness. The first presents the sheer terror of the fact, presumably known to humans alone, that they will die, perhaps when they least expect it. The second recognizes that though one tries to

make decisions toward achieving cherished goals, there is no guarantee of a successful outcome; as such, realizing that the decisions are one's own (and presumably could have been made differently had one only known) is very frightening. The third fear concerns the ultimate question of what existence is worth if one can shape it and has the responsibility to do so but may die or end up losing all one wanted. This contemplation raises the awful suspicion that life is meaningless—a very disconcerting experience indeed! To these fears, Bugental (1965) adds a fourth: the fear of isolation. This refers to the recognition, which comes with consciousness, that because you make your own decisions, you may be rejected by all and end up completely alone.

In the face of all this, how comforting it would seem to reject individuality and personal initiative in favor of convention and tradition! If you do not take chances, if you let others be your guide, if you agree at all costs, if you give up these foolish fantasies that life could be better than it is, if you stop trying to reflect on your experience in the vain attempt to understand, if you accept rather than judge—you will not have to face ontological anxiety. You can have a nice, solid, respectable, happy life. Right? Not at all, according to the existentialists. If you abnegate the birthright of individuality contained in the psychological needs, you will gain comfort only in the short run—if that. You will become conventional and banal, showing little taste and complexity and relating to others in only superficial ways. To remain conventional and keep alive the incredible lie you have perpetrated on yourself, you will have to avoid using your own wits (Keen, 1970). Worse still, yours will be an inauthentic being not only in the eyes of serious persons but in your own. You are, after all, a human being and cannot avoid self-scrutiny entirely, no matter how hard you try. Here and there a stray thought of beauty, a daydream of love, the observation of people who seem truly themselves, will haunt you. As life goes on and you feel the lie's inevitable effect of halting both development and enthusiasm for life, you will wonder why conventional success and approval do so little to lift your spirits. You will have fallen into the grips of severe ontological guilt. This is what provoked Thoreau to exclaim that "most men lead lives of quiet desperation" and Kierkegaard to warn of "the sickness unto death."

You cannot defend yourself successfully against the necessity of self-reliant decision making, according to the existentialists. If you try, all that will happen is that ontological anxiety and guilt, those natural concomitants of living, will get transformed into neurotic, inauthentic forms of themselves. *Neurotic anxiety,* which heavily involves shame, is the fear that you and others will know how frightened you are (Keen, 1970). Because you deny that ontological anxiety is a natural part of living, you try to hide it. But *neurotic guilt,* much more devastating, is the condemnation of one's entire being rather than of particular acts. There is some hope of rectifying particular acts but little of reclaiming a being comprehensively rejected (Keen, 1970; May, 1958). Suicide is, in the existentialist view, a frequent response to massive neurotic guilt.

Avoidance of decision making and growth causes dreadful psychopathology; ontological anxiety, honestly faced, is also gravely painful. How can the person hope to face it and have a satisfying life? An early existential answer (Kierkegaard, 1954) was *faith in God,* who made the human mind a godlike thing. This position contends that through the exercise of intelligence in decision making, one draws closer to a unity with God after death. For many modern-day existentialists, however, faith in God is not a convincing basis for persisting in the face of ontological anxiety. A particularly pessimistic position (Camus, 1955) considers a full appreciation of the *absurdity* of life (in which people search for meaning though there is none to be found) the only viable basis for living. More compelling, it seems to me, is the view that what people need is *courage* (Tillich, 1952), or a recognition of their true power and dignity among living things. In a sense, the courage to persist and ontological anxiety are two sides of the same coin. There is a sense of power in recognizing that it is precisely because

people are so beautifully intelligent—as to fashion life rather than be fashioned by it—that they can experience anxiety. Anxiety may seem a bearable burden in exchange for the power to create one's own meaning through symbolizing, imagining, judging, and the actions following therefrom.

This emphasis on ontological anxiety as a sign of freedom and power is why Tillich (1952) considers *doubt* to be the "god above God." Frankl (1960) gives powerful expression to the idea that ontological anxiety or doubt is actually a sign of ideal functioning:

> Challenging the meaning of life can . . . never be taken as a manifestation of morbidity or abnormality; it is rather the truest expression of the state of being human, the mark of the most human nature in man. For we can easily imagine highly developed animals or insects—say bees or ants—which in many aspects of their social organization are actually superior to man. But we can never imagine any such creature raising the question of the meaning of its own existence, and thus challenging that existence. It is reserved for man alone to find his very existence questionable, to experience the whole dubiousness of being. More than such faculties as power of speech, conceptual thinking, or walking erect, this factor of doubting the significance of his own existence is what sets man apart from animal. (p. 30)

Nothing so centrally part of human nature as ontological anxiety could ever be defined as psychopathological. And there is considerable dignity in confronting this anxiety, for to do so is to reach a high point of humanity. Only when you have clearly seen the abyss and jumped into it with no assurance of survival can you call yourself a human being. Then, if you survive, you shall be called a hero, for you will have created your own life.

FREEDOM AND NECESSITY. A theme running throughout existential theorizing is that through vigorous symbolization, imagination, and judgment one can achieve freedom. Through mental activity, one is supposed to create a world. Yet, there seem to be limits to this freedom, to judge from existentialists' frequent reference to the necessities or givens of life, which they call either *facticity* (Sartre, 1956) or the *ground* or *thrownness* of existence (Binswanger, 1958). Just what are necessity and possibility?

Perhaps as much as any personological position, existentialism respects necessities or givens. The major, unassailable given, after all, is that each person will die. Nonbeing is an inherent part of being. But there are other givens. If you are born a woman, dealing with menses and the childbearing function is a given. And there are particular social situations in which necessity abounds. Frankl (1960) is especially eloquent in this regard when he talks of being forcibly imprisoned in a concentration camp during World War II. Perhaps it will surprise you to find existential psychologists advocating acceptance of givens. For example, Binswanger (1958) says, "The more stubbornly the human being opposes his being-thrown into existence . . . the more strongly this thrownness gains in influence" (p. 340). The result of this is debilitating in that "a person does not stand autonomously in his world, that he blocks himself off from the ground of his existence, that he does not take his existence upon himself but trusts himself to alien powers, that he makes alien powers 'responsible' for his fate instead of himself" (Binswanger, 1963, p. 290). In other words, accepting the limits set on the possibilities of your existence by certain imposed biological and social forces enables you to be more authentic because you do not have to lie to yourself. The value of accepting givens is the same as accepting ontological anxiety and guilt as inherent aspects of living. It is only by remaining honest that one has any chance at all of pursuing those possibilities that are available. Accepting your inability to influence certain things makes you more aware of what you can influence, paradoxical though that may seem at first.

This is not to say that existential psychologists advocate passive acquiescence to social and biological forces. Actually, Frankl (1960) believes that those who could not survive the concentration camps succumbed either because they considered themselves completely and unalterably trapped or because they denied that they

were incarcerated at all. But those who survived did so through a frank acceptance that some portion of their existence was not under their control, coupled with a continual exploration, through symbolizing, imagining, and judging, of what freedom was left to them. The first value of this approach is that they discovered some freedom and therefore could retain some sense of human dignity. The second value is that as they set their wits to work constructively on the matter, they carved out more freedom than they initially imagined and than was available to others who did not. Recognize that their freedom was self-determined by their own courage to face straightforwardly a horrendous imposition on freedom in spite of the pain of such honesty. In other words, their persistence in being authentic in the face of suffering permitted them to use their wits to gain greater freedom. Thus, one accepts a necessity in order to more clearly explore the possibilities of freedom left. In this, one often discovers that the necessity is smaller and less important than initially thought.

But according to existentialists, there are very few *actual* necessities beyond some biological factors. Most of us never experience forced incarceration. Much more debilitating than failing to accept an actual necessity is construing things that are actually changeable as if they were necessities (Maddi, 1988, 1994). People unhappy in their jobs or their marriages may complain that they cannot make any changes. Perhaps they feel they could not get another job or that their responsibilities as husband or wife preclude dissolving the marriage. It would not be unusual in such a situation to hear an existential psychotherapist questioning whether there really are no other jobs and no other ways of fulfilling obligations. The people in this example have construed particular life commitments, which were freely made and can be freely changed, as necessities. This confusion of possibilities as necessities lies at the heart of psychopathology, according to existentialists (Binswanger, 1963; Boss, 1963; Keen, 1970; Maddi, 1987, 1994). Typically, when people draw this conclusion, they want to abdicate personal responsibility, blaming failures on a destructive society they can do nothing about. They want to roll over and die and be pitied for it. They lack the courage that would permit authentic being, choosing to lie to themselves and others instead.

Existential psychology is definitely a perfection fulfillment position. There is little sympathy in the existential position for the act of treating possibilities as necessities; people are considered to have the wherewithal to exercise greater freedom if they would only try. Some positions exemplifying the conflict model would be much more sympathetic to the failure to attempt some wanted goal, because the conflict model is built on compromise. For the existentialist, the guilt one feels from staying in a marriage against one's will is true or ontological guilt. An existential psychotherapist would not try to remove the guilt but rather amplify the experience of it to force the person to recognize the unnecessarily surrendered freedom. In contrast, a classical Freudian psychotherapist might try to help the person decrease guilt on the grounds that it was due only to an overly harsh superego blocking a workable compromise between necessary individual and social pressures. Similarly, an intrapsychic conflict therapist might find the cause of the person's guilt in an overbearing autonomy and encourage its diminution to pave the way for a compromise expressing more communion. Even an actualization fulfillment therapist might be skeptical that the guilt pointed toward a beneficial direction of movement on the grounds that feelings of well-being augur personal fulfillment. This therapist too might try to decrease the guilt.

You are now in a position to understand more fully what the existential psychologist means by *freedom*. It is not some mysterious free will, undetermined in any way by past experience, constituting something virtually supernatural and not to be understood. Rather, as Gendlin (1965–1966) makes clear, it is the process of using one's wits—symbolization, imagination, and judgment—to construct possibilities. In discussing freedom, Gendlin says,

> An oversimplified existentialism would have it that you can choose yourself to be any way you wish.

You simply leap out of your situation and your past. This would be a flat denial of all our sufferings and failing attempts to be a certain way just by wishing we were. That is not what existentialism means at all. But, then, what is choice and freedom? Sartre, discussing the example of a cafe waiter, points out that "cafe waiter" is, of course, only a role. The living man fills the role, rather than being defined by it. But, says Sartre, that does not mean that he can just simply choose to be a diplomat instead. There is "facticity," the situation and conditions about us which we cannot arbitrarily wave away. We must "surpass" situations in our interpreting them and acting in them; we cannot just choose them to be different. There is no such magic freedom as simply choosing ourselves to be other than what we are. Without difficult, sensitive steps, we do not become free of the constraints we are under.

The same may be said about a man's past, his upbringing, his learnings. The past is surpassed in the present, but this is no arbitrary anything-you-please. The same relationship between a given (facticity) and a movement (freedom, surpassing) holds here ... the given does not have in it what we later make of it; and yet, what we make of it is related to what was given, must follow from it in certain ways, and just some ways fit. How I can surpass my past is not logically or analytically deducible from it. Surpassing is living action; but not just any arbitrary action brings the felt response of authentic surpassing. It is hard to devise such a mode of action, and we often fail to do so.

What we construct through symbolization, imagination, and judgment is freedom in the sense that the result changes us and that we cannot predict it from a knowledge of our past. It represents a new frame of reference and format for action that we worked at creating, that we rendered consistent with our past, and that we can truly believe. We worked hard; we were not breathed on mysteriously by God. This achievement of freedom is properly called *transcendence*, and though its specific content in every case would be very difficult to predict in advance, the process of thought that renders it likely is predictably common in some people and uncommon in others. This is the story of development, which I will soon show you.

In his position on freedom, Gendlin (1965–1966) suggests that a full-blown sense of life is a series of decisions. As he makes clear, the alternatives in any decisional situation are as much posed by the person as they are given:

Another error committed when [the person's mental process of] explication is left out is to view choice as between already given alternatives. This is not existentialism but a bad misunderstanding of it. . . . Situations are all in terms of what we may do, not do, suffer, avoid, succeed in, or miss. A situation is never pure facticity. . . . The facticity of . . . posed alternatives is not to be accepted as though the binding facts I now see were ultimate; but neither can we simply wave away the facts. We don't always succeed in explicating new alternatives so well that we combine all we desire in one, while avoiding all that we wish to avoid. But free choice is not the choice between the two, bad, given alternatives. Free choice necessitates the creation of new alternatives which make stepping stones of what were obstacles. (pp. 135–136)

Thus, the involvement of symbolization, imagination, and judgment in the very posing of alternatives is also a part of transcendence, which turns what seems given into a possibility that can change.

Furthermore, although existentialists do take a position on *defensiveness*, they mean something quite different from the usual meaning of repressing from consciousness that which is socially unacceptable. The occasion for defensiveness, according to existentialists, is cowardice in the face of ontological anxiety (which is virtually the same as the inability to believe in one's own power of intelligence), resulting in the distortion constituted by neurotic anxiety and guilt and the confusion of possibilities with necessities. One has evaded the real cognitive work involved in achieving transcendence, as opposed to hiding one's antisocial tendencies from scrutiny, as in the Freudian explanation.

Existential Views on the Periphery of Personality

Although there are implications in existential thought that could lead to a position on periph-

eral personality, existentialists disagree on whether such theorizing is worthwhile. Binswanger (1963) and Boss (1963), at one extreme, say very little that is explicit, systematic, or formal about development, types, and peripheral characteristics. To be sure, their discussions of authentic as opposed to inauthentic being definitely imply two general styles of operating. But nowhere do they explicate these implications, probably believing, with the actualization fulfillment theorists, that to do so would be inconsistent with their overall emphasis on freedom. Less extreme is Keen (1970), who, though not offering a position on peripheral personality per se, does offer something on development in early life. At the other extreme, Kobasa and Maddi (1977) elaborate on two main personality types and several transitional types, all complete with a developmental history linking core to periphery (see also Maddi, 1967, 1970, 1994). What follows will be based largely on the writings of Keen, Kobasa (Ouellette), and Maddi, but you are cautioned to recognize that though they believe themselves to be working in the spirit of existentialism, there are others in that tradition who would disagree.

As you will recall, existential psychologists emphasize the difference between facing ontological anxiety and guilt squarely and lying to yourself. When you lie, you act as if life were not a series of decisions that you have the responsibility for making, relying instead on the erroneous belief that certain forces acting on you constitute necessities. But if you remain honest or authentic, you realize that these forces are actually only possibilities that you can choose to be affected by or to transcend. This process of creating your own life heavily involves the use of mental powers in what Gendlin (1965–1966) calls *the explication of experience* and Bugental (1976) *the search for identity*. The two main personality types Kobasa and Maddi (1977) propose state essentially the differences between authentic and inauthentic being as styles or habitual predispositions.

CONFORMISM AS THE NONIDEAL LIFESTYLE. The personality type that expresses inauthentic being comes about when people deny or defend against their psychological needs. Such people make minimal use of symbolization, imagination, and judgment, which means that their thoughts are few, undifferentiating, and stereotyped. They show the simplest, least subtle forms of biological and social needs because of the relative absence of psychological expression. Maddi (1970), who considers this personality type as showing biological and social reductionism, labels it *conformism* because of the self-definition (sense of identity) and the world view it entails. The conformist's *sense of identity* is as nothing more than a player of social roles and an embodiment of creature needs. What people are in addition to these two things finds little representation in the conformist's self-definition.

To focus on social reductionism for a moment, if your *Mitwelt* (construed social world) is such that you view yourself as nothing more than a player of social roles, you are, in effect, accepting the idea that the social system is a terribly potent force in living, with institutions and laws that transcend individuals and have lives of their own. This inclines you to the belief that the current content and form of the social system is its necessary and unchangeable nature and that individuals have no choice but to conform to its pressures. In the long run, conforming to social system pressures even comes to appear morally worthwhile. You develop the conviction that the social system as currently constituted protects everyone against chaos; therefore, we all ought to do our share to support its institutions, however restricting they may be. The way to give this support is to play adequately the social roles given to you as a responsible citizen.

There are parallel implications in biological reductionism. If your *Umwelt* (construed biological and physical world) is such that you view yourself as nothing more than an embodiment of creature needs, for you such needs as those for food and water are terribly important and real forces in living. Because physical survival seems of unquestionably paramount importance, you make the degree to which biological needs are satisfied the hallmark of adequate living. It becomes difficult to imagine justifying deprivation of these needs under any circumstances. Any alternative to direct, immediate, and constant expression of these needs—if an alternative could be construed as possible—would be unwise, because it would violate all that is important.

If your *Umwelt* and *Mitwelt* are characterized by biological and social reductionism, you must necessarily feel powerless in the face of social pressures from outside and biological pressures from inside. Creatureness and social roles seem like givens, like causal factors independent of your puny power to influence them. You will not experience life as a series of decisions willingly made. Indeed, you never seriously reject a social role or change it. You never think to question just how important physical survival is. Soon you will *become* your social roles and biological needs—there being no longer any act of consciousness worth speaking of to mark the fact that your identity is not the only one possible. You will have little reason to raise abstract questions about the nature of existence.

The generalization of your conformist identity into a *world view* potentiates your difficulties on a grand scale. This world view is based on pragmatism and materialism. The pragmatism comes primarily from viewing not only yourself but everyone else as having to play the assigned social roles. The only relevant question becomes how good the people are at enacting these roles. Materialism comes primarily from the belief that all people are no more than embodiments of biological needs. This leads to coveting not only the goods that are objects of the needs (e.g., clothes to make one attractive) but the processes instrumental to obtaining them (e.g., making money). The pursuit of material things is elevated to the status of a natural process.

Given this self-definition and world view, you can easily see how the conformist would often be in conflict. Social roles and creature needs will most likely lead in different, if not incompatible, directions. While social roles become institutionalized along the lines of what is socially acceptable, biological needs are defined in terms of biological urges, without regard for propriety. The only consciousness of self that conformists ever feel consistently has to do with their inability to satisfy both aspects of their identity with the same set of actions. They will try to assuage biological and social pressures at different times or in different places, keeping possible incompatibilities from the eyes of others and from their own direct awareness. Their being-in-the-world will be a fragmentary, disunified pastiche.

The conformist's relationships with others are contractual rather than intimate. If you and everyone else are considered bound by certain rules of social interaction and in need of certain material goods for satisfaction and survival, relationships will tend to be based on the economic grounds of who is getting what from whom, when, and for how much. Conformists will be willing neither to let an interaction go in whatever direction that develops nor to continue or terminate it on the basis of how interesting or stimulating it is. Instead, they will want it structured in advance and will have to know all along what it offers them in terms of social status or material advance. Once they get what they want, there will be no further reason for contact. Bonds of affection, loyalty, camaraderie, and love will tend not to develop in any meaningful sense. The conformist's relations will tend to be rather cold-blooded, even though the absence from them of intimacy and spontaneity will leave a nagging sense of loneliness and disappointment.

However unappetizing conformism seems, Maddi (1967, 1970, 1988, 1994) regards it not as frank psychopathology but as a predisposition to psychopathology. Too common and livable to be regarded as sickness, conformism nonetheless has its own characteristic sufferings and limitations. The main disadvantage of conformism, according to Maddi, is that it renders the person vulnerable to certain stresses that can precipitate existential sickness through disrupting being-in-the-world by disconfirming one's self-definition as a player of social roles and an embodiment of biological needs. The three such stresses Maddi (1967, 1970) lists are the threat of imminent death, major disruption of the social

order, and repeated confrontation with the limitations on deep and comprehensive experiencing produced by conformism. The first of these disconfirms self-definition by demonstrating human finitude to someone who has, in stressing the paramount importance of physical survival, forgotten that he or she will die. The second disconfirms the belief in society as absolute to someone who has assumed it cannot change. The third directly disconfirms the conformist's being-in-the-world, usually occasioned by the strenuous objections of someone who is suffering because of his or her superficiality. The sickness resulting from such disconfirmations is called *existential* because in all its forms it reveals a breakdown in the ability to consider life meaningful and worthwhile.

INDIVIDUALISM AS THE IDEAL LIFESTYLE. As you might expect, the personality type epitomizing authentic being is the opposite of conformism. In this ideal type, the vigorous expression of psychological needs along with biological and social needs leads to biological and social experiencing showing considerable taste, subtlety, intimacy, and love because of the humanizing, organizing effects of symbolization, imagination, and judgment. This personality type is called *individualism* because the vigorous expression of psychological needs involves an extensive and unusual set of ideas about self and world (Maddi, 1967, 1970, 1988, 1994; Kobasa & Maddi, 1977).

True to what has been said, as an individualist, you would define yourself (*sense of identity*) as a person with a mental life through which you can understand and influence your social and biological experience and urges. Although you recognize and accept social and biological pressures, you do not feel powerless in the face of them and experience considerable room to maneuver in the process of finding just the right life for yourself. You believe you are capable of choice and have freedom, though you are not so naive as to think that there are no constraints on you, no necessities. You question, however, whether things that seem constraints really are recalcitrant to influence.

Understandably, in your *world view,* you see society as the creation of people and as properly in their service. You believe humans to be unique among living things because their extraordinary mental powers make it possible for them to control their own fates. Certainly, as an individualist, you will be realistic enough to recognize that social systems are not always responsive to their publics and that people often act as if they believe themselves no different from apes. But you will consider such social systems and such people to be less than ideal, to have fallen short of what it is within human power to achieve. The value of this judgment is that it provides the individualist with a format for action. As an individualist, you may decide to withdraw from such inhuman societies and people. Alternatively, you may try to convince the people that they are wrong and influence the social system through political action.

This ideal personality type is called the *individualist* with no connotations of a steely aloofness or indifference to others. Individualists are so designated because their actions and thoughts are relatively uncommon and express psychological, rather than social or biological, needs. Actually, individualists relate to others more deeply than conformists do, substituting intimacy for contract. Their frequently changing and unfolding lives do not suggest lack of discipline or persistence. Do not be misled by the emphasis on subtlety, taste, intimacy, and love. More than anyone else, individualists will have standards, know what they want, and be willing and able to pursue their desires with rigor and self-reliance. They can even perform unpleasant tasks gracefully if these are definitely related to reaching their desired goals. And they will show the courage, born of a belief in their own power and dignity, to face ontological anxiety.

Certainly, individualists sound like fine people. But beyond this attractiveness, their value lies in not being vulnerable to stress. Neither the threat of imminent death nor large-scale disruption of the social order would disconfirm the self-definition of individualists. The accumulated sense of superficiality in living would simply not

occur and so would never be a problem. All in all, their being-in-the-world would be very hardy indeed (Maddi & Kobasa, 1984).

Like Rogers and Maslow, Maddi has postulated only two personality types, even though his general position emphasizes individuality so much that one would expect him to propose more types. Even though the individualist type embodies the emphasis on individuality (with its implication of heterogeneity in behavior), that the formal theorizing permits only two kinds of people to be distinguished is a drawback. Yet, one can probably distinguish several subtypes of individualist and conformist. Perhaps one route would be to subdivide the conformist type according to whether biological or social needs are paramount in expression. And perhaps the individualist type could be subdivided into those who are primarily symbolizers, imaginers, or judgers. This separation of mental styles recalls Jung's peripheral theorizing. Another drawback of Maddi's peripheral statement is that although types are proposed, there is no formal consideration of peripheral characteristics. Several are implied and perhaps could be more explicitly stated in the future.

Existential Views on Development

As is common among existential psychologists, Maddi (1967, 1970) is at first quite sketchy about development. Though existentialists generally assume that being-in-the-world is learned, they do not take one beyond this truism to a precise consideration of how a particular style, as opposed to some other, develops. Fortunately, Keen (1970) and Kobasa and Maddi (1977) have taken the plunge into developmental theorizing. Because it is the simpler of the two, Keen's account will be considered first.

Keen (1970) presents four developmental stages, which, though not tied to Maddi's personality types, are quite consistent with the general existential emphasis. The first stage is *fusion,* in which the distinction between subject and object has not been made by the child. The second stage is *separation,* which begins at the point during the first year when the child experiences himself or herself as different from the rest. In the third stage, *satellization,* "the child's experience of subjectness and objectness reverse themselves" (Keen, 1970, p. 41), and the child falls into orbit around the parents. Where the child had been the triumphant center of gravity in the separation stage, he or she must give ground to the superior judgment and power of adults, which amounts to emphasizing what Keen calls *being-for-others.* In return, the child gains considerable security. Here, Keen makes the point, reminiscent of the Freudian position on how parents can avoid instilling fixations, that to stimulate the child's being-in-the-world, it is useful to apply mild punishment. Though severe punishment renders the child unwilling to explore possibilities and lack of punishment does not allow possibilities to be recognized, mild punishment actually broadens the child's sense of alternatives and decreases acceptance of parentally endorsed options. The final stage then emerges as *similarity,* in which by age 7 or so the child is beginning to assess accurately the degree to which he or she and the others (parents, siblings, peers) are alike and different.

This, of course, is the sound developmental path, culminating in authentic being or an individualistic style. But the major developmental hazards are pressures that lead the child toward lying. Although Keen is clear about how lying to others and oneself jeopardizes authentic being, he is ambiguous about what brings this lying about. Presumably it is anything in parents and other significant adults that will interfere with the ideal developmental course. The most serious interference, according to Keen, is overly severe or insufficient punishment during the satellization stage such that the child never emerges from dependence on the wishes and beliefs of others.

EARLY DEVELOPMENT. In delineating how individuality or authenticity comes about, Kobasa and Maddi (1977) distinguish early and later development. In the former state, children are dependent on their parents and therefore quite

impressionable, whereas the latter state involves development by self-initiation. When conditions are ideal, what differentiates early from later development is the emergence in the early period of *courage,* or what Kobasa and Maddi call *hardiness* (Kobasa, 1979; Maddi, 1988, 1994; Maddi & Kobasa, 1984). If the conditions for development are faulty, hardiness will never be really learned and the self-initiation that marks later development will be jeopardized.

There are several ways in which parents can instill hardiness in their children. They can (1) expose children to rich and diverse experiences, (2) freely impose limits based on their own sense of what is meaningful in life, (3) love and respect their children as budding individuals, and (4) teach the value of vigorous symbolization, imagination, and judgment directly and by example. The role of the first activity is obvious: The greater their range of experience, the more likely children will symbolize, imagine, and judge richly and complexly, especially if parents communicate the importance of doing so, either as models or more didactically, even to the point of providing children with homey exercises. The imposition of limits (2) may appear out of place alongside the other seemingly more permissive techniques, but you should recognize that this emphasis is one reason why existential psychology is a perfection and not an actualization position. When the limits express the parents' sincere views on what makes life meaningful and worthwhile, when these do not therefore show spite or insecurity, and when they are applied with obvious love, they can be developmentally useful. Their usefulness is twofold: They provide an occasion to learn about *facticity* (unchangeable givens), and they encourage energetic use of symbolization, imagination, and judgment in the attempt to circumvent limits. All these developmental conditions need to be enacted with love and respect for children as immature persons struggling to become individuals. Not just any old love and respect will work; rather, such feelings must support children's decision-making initiatives. In other words, the parents must show their affection by truly helping their children to become independent of them. Kobasa and Maddi (1977; Maddi & Kobasa, 1984) suggest that the best way to do this is to structure situations so that children will be encouraged to reach always just beyond their grasp. In this way, the children will not be lulled into prolonged dependency. But it is also necessary to shield children from failure in tasks that are obviously too demanding.

To the degree that these various developmental conditions are met in the early years, children will develop the beginnings of courage. In this sense, *courage* refers to a willingness to make decisions for the future (the unknown) and take responsibility for the outcomes. Persons are aided in this by the secure belief that if outcomes are unsatisfactory, they can exercise symbolization, imagination, and judgment in corrective decision making. If you believe that your life is partly of your own making, you can accept reversals because you can change them as well. Once this sense of courage or hardiness emerges, early development comes to an end. Kobasa and Maddi do not specify an age for this but seem to presume a time during adolescence for most people, if later development occurs at all.

LATER DEVELOPMENT. Maddi and Kobasa postulate two developmental stages in later development that occur before authenticity is reached. First, the *aesthetic orientation* takes place as soon as the person emerges from the bosom of the family. In a wider world with a freshly developed sense of freedom and self-reliance, people with a good start usually become self-indulgent. They may use their decision-making powers for pleasure, reveling in the moment, exploiting others and the environment, and making no lasting commitments. This orientation is not merely passivity and dependency but the first (and therefore perhaps understandably misguided) attempt at independent functioning made by people whose early developmental experiences have been beneficial. The self-indulgence of aestheticism comes about because their early child-rearing experiences, though necessary and beneficial, have been

nonetheless strenuous. Because these children have had to strive and to assume responsibility, they become hedonistic at the first opportunity.

Although aesthetically oriented persons derive pleasure through hedonism for a while, sooner or later they experience failure. All parties end at some point, and their enjoyment does not outlive them. Relationships entered into with little commitment or discrimination also end quickly and are soon forgotten. What at first seemed like wonderful freedom becomes emptiness. Those whose early development has instilled courage or hardiness in them will finally learn from these failures. Painfully, such people realize that the trouble with self-centered aestheticism is that it involves living in the present only, as if the past and future were unimportant. Without commitment and planning, it is too easy to end up lonely and empty. The recognition dawns that aestheticism amounts to being controlled by others—whoever has the next party, the next person to fall in love with, some new political cause by which to be carried away. The aesthetic lifestyle that promised such independence is only a trap.

Having learned this, people in the grips of self-determined development proceed to the next phase—the *idealistic orientation*. Now they attempt to incorporate the future and the past into the present by making decisions as if current commitments and values have always been and always will be the same. When such people love, they love forever. When they engage in political behavior, it is with the undying belief that lofty principles can actually be embodied in particular people and events. In their zeal to correct their former errors, they fail to recognize that people, situations, and emotional commitments change and that the relationship between ideals and practical occurrences is problematic.

Because people with the idealistic orientation act as though they have complete control over events that in reality are too complex to be fully controlled by any individual, they inevitably encounter failure. A love vowed eternally ends all the more painfully because its end was unexpected. Event after event forces recognition that complex social phenomena involve shifting loyalties, vested interests, and even accidental factors beyond one's control. Once again, failures spur development.

With the deepening of insight of the limited control people have over events and others, the idealistic orientation comes to an end, and the period of *authentic being* begins. To the characteristics of individuality delineated by Maddi (1967, 1970), Kobasa and Maddi (1977) add a sense of the importance of integrating past, present, and future and an acceptance of the imperfect control that people have over events and others. It is not clear, once again, at what age the transition from idealism to authenticity takes place, undoubtedly because the rate of self-initiated development differs among people. Kobasa and Maddi, though, imply that this transition occurs no earlier than middle adulthood.

Clearly, those who have developed courage can learn from failure, because they are not so overwhelmed by it that they must shrink defensively from its implications. A sharp contrast is drawn with those whose developmental experiences have left them without courage or hardiness. To see what these debilitating experiences would be, you need only consider the opposite of the four parental stances mentioned earlier. When people do not develop hardiness, they remain in a prolonged period of early development, as it were. In other words, they remain dependent and passive as they advance in years. Though they may appear to have experiences of aestheticism and idealism, they cannot learn by failing, since failure is so debilitating that they never frankly confront it. They muddle through life, not engaged in any true developmental trajectory. As described earlier, they are conformists.

ELLIS'S POSITION ....

Albert Ellis (1962) has been developing a so-called rational-emotive psychotherapy since the 1950s that appears to fall within the perfection version of the fulfillment model. To date, this approach must be regarded as fragmentary in its formulations concerning personality, lacking a well developed and internally consistent core, developmental, and peripheral statement. But its current popularity prompts me to mention it here.

Ellis's Core Statement

Ellis appears to assume two core tendencies. One innate direction of people is *to think irrationally and harm themselves;* the other is *to gain understanding of their folly and train themselves to change their self-destructive ways.* Although this dual statement suggests a conflict position, because the core tendencies seem to contradict each other, it is actually a fulfillment statement, because the second tendency corrects the first. In other words, the ideal life does not involve a compromise between the two core tendencies but rather a counteraction of the first by the second; through discipline, one comes to live rationally despite one's initial proclivity toward irrationality. In the fulfillment mode, this is clearly an emphasis on perfection: One must rise above one's weaknesses to attain the good life.

Ellis on Development

The developmental statement in this theory is restricted to the assertion that interaction with parents and other adults typically intensifies the innate tendency of youngsters to be irrational and self-destructive. Thus, most people fail to learn to live rationally. When they do, rationality typically comes in adulthood or even later, and it necessitates considerable effort and even therapeutic help. This theory has little or no peripheral statement whereby one can understand persisting individual differences in any systematic way.

Basically a psychotherapy, Ellis's position most heavily emphasizes how the irrational and self-destructive tendency expresses itself. The process involves the irrational interpretation of events. Whenever an event is less than perfect for people, their tendency to be irrational and self-destructive leads them to exaggerate. For instance, a particular event is not merely unfortunate—it is *unbearable*. People are not merely unsatisfied with themselves—they are *worthless*. Then, shocked by their views of life as terrible and of themselves as incapable, they engage in yet another cycle of magical thinking from which they emerge as disgusting and in need of punishment. This cycle intensifies. The constructive core tendency tries to cut into all this irrationality. Through hard and consistent effort not to exaggerate, people can come to see events and themselves more realistically. According to Ellis, this entails perceiving negative events as unfortunate but bearable and oneself as having experienced a reversal but not being damaged in the ability to correct this in the future. With such insistence, obsessive spirals of self-destructive thought do not get under way.

RATIONAL-EMOTIVE PSYCHOTHERAPY. Rational-emotive psychotherapy attempts to strengthen the constructive, rational core tendency by direct assault on the irrational, destructive core tendency. In this confrontation therapy, the therapist battles the client's negative views of self and world through a combination of contradicting these views with evidence and insisting that the negative views be changed. There is no encouragement of transference, as in psychoanalytic therapies, nor is there the unconditional positive regard of actualization therapies. Ellis assumes that the client is wrong about how he or she has construed experience and needs to be shaken out of depression and self-pity with debate and exhortation. The therapy emphasizes the present and future rather than the past.

Ellis on the Periphery of Personality

There is really nothing to say here regarding rational-emotive therapy. It simply has no peripheral statement. Positions, such as Ellis's, that are primarily therapies and only secondarily personality theories deemphasize typologies. What is surprising is that any approach so concerned

with understanding human behavior could fail to provide an important part of the conceptual apparatus for doing so, whatever its main emphasis.

But rational-emotive therapy is a bona fide, if brutal, expression of the perfection fulfillment approach. Although it places much emphasis on self-destructiveness, it leaves no doubt that rationality and constructive living are possible and preferable. Like other perfection fulfillment positions, this one emphasizes how people attribute meaning to experience and thereby construct their worlds. For Ellis, this process is a much more important determinant of behavior than the genetic blueprints of the actualization theorists and the instincts of the psychoanalysts. Even the psychotherapeutic techniques offered by Ellis fit well into the perfection fulfillment approach, because they emphasize confrontation and the present. Although reminiscent of the existential approach, rational-emotive therapy deviates from this view in various ways. Perhaps the basic theoretical difference is that rational-emotive therapy assumes that there is indeed a true reality that will be seen the same way by all people who manage to be rational. In contrast, existential psychology proposes that each person constructs his or her own reality and that operating rationally does not amount to becoming the same as everyone else who does so. This difference shows up not only in various theoretical formulations in the theories but in the therapies as well. Although existential therapy is also a confrontation approach, it is better prepared to identify individual differences as rational and constructive. Perhaps this difference aids us in understanding why rational-emotive therapy has not yet developed a clear peripheral statement, as such statements emphasize individual differences.

A FINAL WORD . . . .

Both the actualization fulfillment and the perfection fulfillment positions agree that life best led involves a flowering of the human spirit, a thrust into the future, unencumbered by social or biological limitations. Whereas actualization fulfillment theorists regard this process of ideal living as relatively simple and straightforward, their perfection fulfillment counterparts posit a difficult struggle crowned by achievements but also involving failures. One must accept challenges and learn from them in order to achieve the ideal of maturity, say the perfection fulfillment theorists. For the actualization fulfillment thinkers, reaching the ideal is simpler, more direct, and less painful.

Although conflict between the person and the society (in the form of parents or others) can occur, according to actualization and perfection fulfillment theorists, this also need not happen. When it happens, some social failure is blamed. Because such conflict can be avoided and, if encountered, resolved, fulfillment positions are clearly different from conflict positions, the latter seeing conflict as inevitable and unresolvable.

THE CONSISTENCY
MODEL: COGNITIVE
DISSONANCE VERSION

In its version of the core tendency of personality, the consistency model emphasizes the importance of the information the person gets from interacting with the external world. The model assumes that people will develop personalities that increase the likelihood of their getting the kind of information that is best for them. The personality is determined much more by the feedback from interaction with the world than it is by the person's inherent attributes.

Compared with consistency theories, both fulfillment and conflict theories put much greater emphasis on an inherent nature as a component of personality that determines life's course. According to fulfillment theories, life is an unfolding of the person's inherent nature. And even when conflict theories stress society as an important force in living, they assume that personality is in large measure an expression of the person's inherent characteristics. For both fulfillment and conflict theories, personality is far more influenced by the attributes the person brings into the world than is the case for consistency positions.

Though consistency positions make some minimal assumptions about inherent human characteristics, they are much more concerned with the compatibility among aspects of the content of personality than with the nature of that content. For consistency theorists, such content is largely learned and represents the history of feedback resulting from interacting with the world. Certainly, feedback influences the content of personality along the lines of the assumed core tendencies of personality, and these core tendencies are inherent; however, one cannot specify what particular content will result. As you will see, the implications of this kind of position are very different from those of fulfillment and conflict positions.

Of the two basic versions of the consistency model, I will consider in this chapter what I call the *cognitive dissonance version*. In it, the important elements that determine consistency are *cognitions,* which may be thoughts, expectations, attitudes, opinions, or even perceptions. Discrepancies or consistencies among cognitive elements may occur either within or across these categories. That is, there may be agreement or disagreement between two thoughts, between a thought and a perception, and so forth. All cognitive dissonance versions of the consistency model assume that discrepancies among cognitive elements produce an emotional state that provides the energy and direction for behavior.

In the purest form of this position, exemplified by Kelly, both large and small discrepancies bring discomfort, anxiety, and tension. These emotional reactions in turn produce behavior aimed at reducing the discrepancy and ensuring that it will not recur. After exploring Kelly's position, I will examine its similarity to Festinger's. Then I will turn to cognitive-experiential self theory as expounded by Epstein. Finally, I will discuss McClelland, whose point of view is a variant on the cognitive dissonance version of the consistency model. For McClelland, only large discrepancies result in emotional discomfort and avoidance, whereas small discrepancies are actually thought to result in pleasurable emotion and attraction.

KELLY'S POSITION ....

George A. Kelly (born 1905; died 1967) received his Ph.D. in psychology from the University of Iowa after having studied both in the United States and England. He spent his career in university settings, where he combined teaching with student counseling. For a number of years he was director of the Psychological Clinic at Ohio State University, and he held a professorship at Brandeis University at the time of his death. Although Kelly did not publish as much as some other personologists, he influenced many students over the years, some of whom have remained avidly loyal to his views. These views have also aroused considerable attention, particularly in England, where philosophers and psychologists have joined in their praise and criticism. Typically Kelly is lauded for emphasizing how people create their own lives through construing experience (and are therefore free). He is criticized for not having recognized allies in existentialism and phenomenology, whose

stimulation could have led to greater specification of his theory.

Kelly's approach has a distinctly intellectual ring, therefore putting it somewhat at a disadvantage in a field long dominated by views of the person as emotional and instinctual. Actually, Kelly's position deserves a hearing precisely because it is so different from prevailing views, and because it is relatively complete and carefully wrought.

Kelly's Core Statement

The core tendency of personality, from Kelly's (1955) point of view, is easily stated: *the person's continual attempt to predict and control the events of experience.* Kelly bases his model for the person not on the biological organism or on the frame of reference of happiness and unhappiness but on the scientific pursuit of truth. Truth is not necessarily what pleases or satisfies our immediate desires and needs; rather, it is what convinces us of its inexorable reality. The scientific pursuit of truth is the empirical procedure of formulating hypotheses and testing them out in the tangible world. Depending on whether a hypothesis is supported by facts, the scientist retains it or discards it, regardless of its appeal. Kelly believes that people approach the task of living as scientists. The only important difference between real scientists and people in general is that scientists are more self-conscious and precise about the methods and procedures employed.

In arguing for the centrality of living the scientific model, Kelly (1955) asserts,

> It is customary to say *that the scientist's ultimate aim is to predict and control.* This is a summary statement that psychologists frequently like to quote in characterizing their own aspirations. Yet, curiously enough, psychologists rarely credit the human subjects in their experiments with having similar aspirations. It is as though the psychologist were saying to himself, "I, being a *psychologist,* and therefore a *scientist,* am performing this experiment in order to improve the prediction and control of certain human phenomena; but my subject, being merely a human organism, is obviously

propelled by inexorable drives welling up within him, or else he is in gluttonous pursuit of sustenance and shelter." (p. 5)

If both psychologists and their subjects are capable and intelligent humans, and since psychologists attempt to predict and control, why should not their subjects be making the same attempt? It is only naiveté that leads to any other conclusion.

Kelly could well bolster this logical argument with an empirical one. Psychologists who do personality research are very sensitive to the possibility that their measurements will be contaminated by the subject's wish to appear in a socially desirable and appropriate light. It seems that virtually any time a psychologist gives subjects a set of questions to answer about themselves, they will try to answer in ways that will make them look good or give the psychologist what is wanted. It is also clear that subjects are terribly interested in the measurement's purpose and in the outcome of their participation in the research. A personologist naive enough not to recognize that subjects are very interested in predicting what the experiment is about and controlling what is made of their performance will very likely fail in the research efforts. If the personologist apparently succeeds, it will only be by unintentionally using the subject's attempts to predict and control for her or his own ends. The most sophisticated approach to this problem of measurement is to construct tests that employ techniques for canceling out the effects of subjects' trying to determine the goals of the research and responding in a socially desirable manner (e.g., Edwards, 1957; Jackson & Messick, 1958).

If you have ever been a subject in a psychological experiment, you may intuitively understand Kelly's insistence on the importance of the attempt to predict and control one's experience. Perhaps you can remember wondering what was going to be done to you and what the point of the research was. Perhaps you asked questions or watched closely to try to find out what was going on. Failing this, perhaps you aimed to make a particular impact on the experiment rather than leave the matter undefined. You may

not have trusted the psychologist's account of why your participation was needed. All these possibilities exemplify the disrupting effect of uncertainty and the attempt to achieve certainty.

DEVELOPMENT OF CONSTRUCTS AND CONSTRUCT SYSTEMS. *Constructs* are interpretations of events arrived at through what amounts to a process of inductive reasoning. A *construct system* is essentially a theory of the world of experience or of subportions of it. According to Kelly, the person's first step in attempting to predict and control experience is to engage in the construing of events. Early in life, before much construing has taken place, experience is made up of a seemingly random and continuous flow of events. For Kelly, though events have an actual existence separate from the person, they do not achieve importance for understanding personality until the person construes them.

When you construe, you class certain events together with others that you consider similar and contrast them with others that you consider different. In the initial stages of construing, you begin to focus on certain general features of the random events flowing by until you recognize what you consider to be repetitions, or replications, of events. Because you have abstracted what for you is the essence of a particular event, you can identify a repetition of that event in the future. You have transcended the literal event and achieved abstract representation of its essence. It is only through such a process of generalization and abstraction that the events of your experience can become meaningful and orderly. Without active attempts to construe, you could not find the world a familiar place and form expectations about what will happen next. Kelly is very clear in his belief that since construing is an interpretive process, not a mere description of literal reality, different people do it differently.

Given the many possible ways of classifying events according to similarities and differences, all are plausible. Kelly, however, fails to explain why people construe along particular lines. To say that certain core characteristics of personality, or inherent capabilities, influence the direction of construing would not be in the spirit of the consistency model, which claims that environmental feedback mostly determines personality content. If Kelly dealt with the question of why different persons construe along different lines, he would probably do so in terms of their various histories of environmental experience. He would say that you construe either along the lines that have been taught to you by significant others or along those that are a natural outgrowth of your own world of experience. That Kelly has been reticent to develop his theory along these lines should be kept in mind, as we will encounter other reticences that we can interpret similarly.

THE CORE CHARACTERISTICS. The result of the process of construing is the construct. A core characteristic of personality, the *construct* is a dichotomous idea or abstraction, such as good-bad or chromatic-achromatic. Constructs are categories of thought that grow out of the interpretations we place on events and, as you will see in the next section, help us anticipate future events. In considering the construct to be dichotomous, Kelly believes that he is mirroring the nature of common thought. That is, to develop a construct at all, you must have noted a minimum of two events that seem similar to each other and different from a third. The process of perceiving similarity is deeply entwined with the process of perceiving difference. Whenever you claim that two things—say, wood and metal—are similar, perhaps in being hard, you also imply that they are different from soft things, such as water. The perception of things as hard requires that there also be things perceived as soft. In a more general sense, whatever we perceive contrasts with something other than itself. Thus, Kelly feels that constructs are inherently dichotomous. This is not changed for him by the fact that a person may seem to be using only one pole of a construct. If a person is, for example, talking only in terms of the goodness of people with no reference to badness, this merely means that the badness pole of the goodness-badness construct is implicit, not nonexistent. There are no unipolar constructs.

Here is an example of a construct and how it is formed. Imagine that you have no constructs in the area of heterosexual relationships. You do, however, have a basic tendency to predict and control the events of your experience. In the normal course of events, you will find yourself in the company of people of the opposite sex, and your urge to predict and control your experience will find expression in attempting to understand and interpret these encounters. You will look for similarities and differences in the encounters on which to base abstraction that will render the encounters meaningful and predictable.

Consider three encounters with people of the opposite sex. The first and third may leave you enthusiastic and joyous, while the second may threaten and disturb you. You could develop the idea, or construct, of *satisfying-dissatisfying* as a relevant dimension of heterosexual relationship. The first and third encounters may also involve people who are excitable, imaginative, inconsistent, and unusual and the second someone who is orderly, even-tempered, pragmatic, and acquiescent. On the basis of these observations, you could develop the construct of *creative-banal*. The first and second encounters might involve people who get good grades, have no trouble finishing papers, and make tangible contributions to other people's lives, whereas the third might involve a person who shuns evaluations, does not complete courses, and does nothing for other people. On the basis of these observations, you could formulate the construct of *productive-nonproductive* as yet another relevant dimension of heterosexual relationship. These are only a few of the many possible constructs that could be catalogued here.

In the course of experiencing events, a person will develop many constructs, because events are numerous and multifaceted enough to stimulate many separate interpretive conclusions. But rather than remaining separate, the many constructs a person develops tend to become organized into a hierarchical *construct system*. There are two kinds of relationships among constructs. First, "a construct may be superordinate to another because each pole of the subordinate construct forms a part of the context for the two poles of the superordinate" (Sechrest, 1963, p. 214). In my extended example, the construct *satisfying-dissatisfying* would be superordinate to the construct *creative-banal* if people who are creative are satisfying and people who are banal are dissatisfying and if things other than creativity and banality contribute to their satisfying or dissatisfying nature. In other words, creativity-banality is parallel but subordinate to satisfying-dissatisfying because of the lesser generality of the former construct.

To illustrate the second kind of subordinate relationship, I will have to extend my already extended example. But first, recall that the construct *productive-nonproductive* was formed on the basis of similarity between the first and second encounters, with the third being different. Regardless of whether that construct is more or less general than the other two, it remains independent of them and cannot be organized in the same hierarchy with them. Productivity-nonproductivity has nothing to do with whether the person will be considered creative or banal or whether interaction with him or her will be satisfying or dissatisfying. This is because productivity-nonproductivity is a construct that was formed on the basis of different groupings of events than the other two constructs. Observations such as this led Kelly to theorize that although constructs tend to be organized into systems, some constructs will be so independent of, or incompatible with, one another that they will exist either alone or as part of separate (and possibly competing) construct systems.

To illustrate this second type of hierarchical relationship, let me add a fourth encounter to the example and assume that the experience relates to the creative pole of the creative-banal construct. Thus, the first, third, and fourth encounters are with creative people, whereas the second is with a banal person. Assume further that characteristics of the first and fourth encounters suggest generosity, while the third encounter suggests stinginess and the second is neutral. The resulting construct, *generosity-stinginess,* has a hitherto undiscussed type of relationship with creative-banal. Regardless of which is the more general and, hence, higher in

the hierarchy, the entire generosity-stinginess construct fits into the creative pole of the creative-banal construct, because all the creative people in the example are either generous or stingy. It is meaningless to consider the generosity or stinginess of the banal people. Note that in both types of hierarchical relationship, the constructs to which a given construct is superordinate or subordinate is a matter of relative generality.

Kelly on Development

Kelly does not theorize about the lines along which construing will take place, even though he could do so within the framework of a consistency position by focusing on environmental determinants of construing. Kelly neither provides a list or typology of likely constructs nor describes the kinds of constructs one can expect to find in people with particular histories of environmental interaction. However, he does indicate an explicit, effective procedure for discerning the content of constructs that exist in any person whom you may confront. In other words, you can determine what a person's constructs contain once you are faced with him or her, even though as a theorist you could not have predicted them in advance. Thus, while Kelly's theory cannot be completely predictive— a puzzling fault in a position that takes the scientific model as the measure of the human—it is moderately usable in that you can at least describe people once you encounter them (Mischel, 1964; Holland, 1968). The procedure for determining a person's constructs, the *Role Repertory Test* or *Grid* (Kelly, 1955; Bannister & Mair, 1988), is thoroughly consistent with the theory. Briefly, it involves having people identify the significant people in their lives (e.g., mother, father, best high school teacher) and then judging their similarities and differences by considering them in all possible combinations of three. The judgment requires that two of the three people in each combination be specified as similar in some way and different from the third. Then, by analyzing and summarizing all these dichotomous judgments made by the people you are testing, you can determine the number and content of the constructs composing their systems. It is quite an ingenious test!

Although Kelly does not specify the likely content of constructs in people with particular histories, he does conceptualize some general attributes of constructs that help render his position concrete and usable. For example, he thinks it is important to know whether a construct is permeable and preemptive (Kelly, 1955, pp. 156–157). If a construct is *permeable,* hitherto unencountered events can be subsumed within it, whereas an impermeable construct can be used to understand only those events that went into its original formulation. A *preemptive* construct renders the events it subsumes unavailable for subsumption within other constructs. These characteristics of constructs seem related to how flexible and adaptable the person is likely to be.

THE USE OF CONSTRUCTS AND CONSTRUCT SYSTEMS. Thus far in examining how people attempt to predict and control the events of their experience, you have seen that they develop, through induction, constructs organized into one or more hierarchical construction systems. This is quite consistent with the model of the human as scientist, as is the use to which constructs and construct systems are put, according to Kelly. Once the scientist develops, through inductive reasoning, a theory concerning the significance of observed events, he or she will use that theory deductively to anticipate and influence future events. These deductive processes will lead to the formulation of hypotheses or predictions and to attempts to test them by manipulation of the environment.

The most ambiguous and fragmentary part of Kelly's position concerns how one uses constructs and construct systems in anticipation and action (Holland, 1968). To understand this, you must first recognize that events achieve significance for the person only when they are subsumed within constructs. Kelly says that the constructs and construct systems that you have right now will determine the importance of future events for you. Constructs are useful in

attempts to predict and control the future in that they give you a tangible basis for expecting the kinds of events that are likely to occur and for interpreting their meaning. For example, if you have the construct system mentioned earlier, you will look forward to a new heterosexual encounter with the expectation that it will be satisfying or dissatisfying, creative or banal, productive or nonproductive, and characterized by generosity or stinginess. You will not expect it to involve anything more or less in the way of possibilities. The higher a construct concerning heterosexual encounter is on the hierarchy, the more it will determine expectation. Thus, if satisfying-dissatisfying is the most general of these constructs, you will expect it to apply unequivocally to the imminent encounter, whereas you may be less certain of the applicability of a less general construct, such as productive-nonproductive.

So the first way in which construct systems are relevant to prediction and control is that they provide you with a set of expectations about future experience. But the only predictions you can make solely on the basis of a set of hierarchically organized constructs are very general: All you can say is that the forthcoming heterosexual encounter will be satisfying *or* dissatisfying, creative *or* banal, and so forth. You cannot expect it to be definitely one or the other. The decision as to which pole of the relevant construct to favor in forming expectations is terribly important if Kelly's theory is to permit precise understanding of people's attempts to predict and control.

When people favor one pole of a construct over the other in anticipating the future, they make what Kelly (1955, pp. 64–68) calls the *elaborative choice.* What determines this choice? It is not that one pole has turned out to be more accurate in the past, though such an actuarial basis is certainly plausible for Kelly's kind of theory. Instead, he says that "a person chooses for himself that alternative in a dichotomized construct through which he anticipates the greater possibility for extension and definition of his system" (Kelly, 1955, p. 64). This statement seems quite consistent with the core tendency of prediction and control. If your aim in life is prediction and control, you must strive to perfect the construct system on which the success of your aim depends. But there are really two strategies whereby one can succeed in predicting events. The first is to develop a construct system that works well for a given set of events and restrict yourself to experiencing just those events. The other is to develop a construct system so comprehensive and valid that no restriction of experiential possibilities is necessary, because virtually any event can be accurately anticipated.

Kelly recognizes both strategies in his notion of elaborative choice. The adventurous strategy is to favor the pole of the construct that is likely to expand the construct system. The conservative strategy is to favor the pole of the construct that is likely to lead to maintenance or protection of the construct system in its present form. The conservative choice leads to constricted certainty, whereas the adventurous choice leads to broadened understanding.

Although Kelly provides descriptive terminology for recognizing conservative and adventurous choices, he does not say why or when one kind of choice takes precedence over the other. This is a severe drawback in the position, because the elaborative choice determines the anticipations that so directly express the human's core tendency. In recognizing this drawback, Sechrest (1963), a student of Kelly, says,

> There is probably in the [elaborative choice] an implicit assumption of some alternating extension and consolidation of the construction system. When the person feels secure and capable of anticipating events correctly, he will make choices that offer possibilities of extending his system, even at the risk of being wrong, but then a period of consolidation will follow in which he will make choices that reduce exposure to error but are confirmative. (p. 221)

Although this is an ingenious extension of the theory, there is little direct evidence for it in Kelly's writings. For the present, you will have to make do with a theory that, while descriptively complete, falls short of explaining the use of conservative and adventurous choices in arriving at predictions.

This drawback needs to be seen alongside the other two mentioned earlier. Kelly fails to specify (1) the lines along which construing takes place, (2) the actual content of the ensuing constructs, and (3) the bases upon which constructs are used in adventurous or conservative ways. When theorists in the conflict and fulfillment traditions are confronted with the explanation of such directional behaviors, they tend to assume the determining influence of instincts, inherent potentialities, emotions, emotional conflicts, or motives. It is understandable that Kelly would not have recourse to such possibilities, as his is a consistency position that not only stresses the learned nature of personality but also is billed as being free of hedonic and motivational assumptions. What the person is trying to do, according to Kelly, is predict and control, not express some inner nature or set of needs or delight in pleasure. But his disavowal of fulfillment and conflict assumptions does not solve the problems just raised. He must find a basis for rendering his position more complete and predictive that is consistent with his kind of approach. But I am not sure Kelly would agree to the need for theoretical additions. His insistence on the individual's freedom of choice might make theorizing about life as a precisely determined thing an infringement of his idealistic stance. Recall that I also suggested this of Rogers, Adler, and Allport, all vociferous, uncompromising exponents of freedom of choice in living.

Thus far in the discussion of the use of constructs and construct systems, I have focused on anticipations or expectations rather than on actions. With regard to anticipation processes, you have seen that Kelly provides a partial basis for understanding how they result and what their content will be. They come about as a natural concomitant of the constructs that come to mind whenever one is faced with the possibility of certain kinds of events, and their content involves the favored poles of the relevant constructs. Kelly's position is only partial because we are not told why certain directions of construing are chosen instead of others or why and when particular poles will be favored.

Turning to the determination of action, I find that Kelly's position is even more sketchy and ambiguous than it is with regard to anticipation. In agreement with this criticism, Sechrest (1963) says,

> [The notion of elaborative choice] is the most directly related to the prediction of overt behavior, but, as will be seen, there are serious problems in moving from an individual's construct system to his behavior in any particular situation. . . . If [the elaborative choice] provides the essential link between the construction system and observable behavior, the nature of the link has not been precisely described. One gets the impression that the predictions to be made from the elaborative choice are not at all exact. (pp. 219–220)

In general, Kelly does not really discuss action, presumably subsuming it under anticipation broadly conceived (see Landfield, 1977; Mancuso, 1977; Sechrest, 1977). This indicates that insofar as one wanted to focus on action per se, one would imagine Kelly's position to be that action complements, or is an extension of, expectation. So if your constructs lead you to expect that a forthcoming heterosexual encounter will be creative, you presumably should act in a way consistent with that. But what this means more concretely remains a mystery in Kelly's position. We can speculate on what action complementary to anticipation might be and say, for example, that if you are expecting an interaction to be creative, you might act on it in terms of what creativity means to you. Perhaps you would be sensitive, free-associational, and unevaluative in the things you said and did in the interaction.

As you can imagine, if people act in a way complementary to their expectations and then succeed, this indicates that their construct system is valid. If your construct system leads to expecting a creative encounter, and you therefore act effectively in a creative manner, you are much more likely to conclude that you were right in your expectation than you would be had you acted in some other way. It is not at all clear, however, that the scientist model for the person leads to the view that action should complement expectation. When scientists have hypotheses, they set about testing them. Testing involves actions designed to show not only whether a hypothesis is true but—more important—whether it is false. Scientists essentially try to disprove their hypotheses, and only if they are unsuccessful in this will they accept the hypotheses as valid. Generalizing from the scientific model, one would expect Kelly to take the view that people would not act to complement their expectations but rather act to rigorously test them.

To be sure, this strategy of testing would require a rather cold-blooded attitude toward life, but such an attitude seems to be an integral part of Kelly's basic assumptions. If your aim in life is to anticipate experience accurately, you must spend all your time testing your expectations so that your construct system will closely conform to reality. Kelly's position suggests that actions are primarily hypothesis-testing in nature.

What would a hypothesis-testing action look like? Kelly gives no help whatsoever in this. But working in the spirit of his approach, we could take a stab at answering the question. If the construct you deem relevant to an imminent heterosexual encounter is *productive-nonproductive*, and you have made the elaborative choice to expect that the encounter will be productive rather than nonproductive, hypothesis-testing action would involve acting to keep the poles of productiveness and nonproductiveness in balance. In any event, hypothesis-testing action would not involve attempts to stimulate just productiveness or just nonproductiveness in the encounter. To encourage experience relevant to only one pole of the construct would be to jeopardize any possibility of determining whether the expectation based on elaborative choice was really accurate.

In trying to talk specifically about hypothesis-testing action, I exceed the formal theoretical apparatus provided by Kelly, who seems rather unconcerned about action as a category of human functioning separate from mentation. This is not a serious limitation for some personologists who believe in the purity of Kelly's approach, with its singular concern with anticipation as the core tendency. Seeing this purity as a drawback, however, Bruner (1956) asks if it is really true that the attempt to avoid the disruptive surprise associated with inaccurate prediction is the only force directing life. In specific criticism of the maintenance and expansion of the construct system as a whole as the only basis for decisions, Bruner says, "I rather suspect that when some people get angry or inspired or in love, they couldn't care less about their 'system as a whole.'" Later in the same book review, Bruner further criticizes Kelly's unwillingness to acknowledge that emotions have a determining influence on anticipation and actions:

> The book fails signally, I think, in dealing convincingly with the human passions. There was a strategy in Freud's choice of Moses or Michelangelo or Little Hans. If it is true that Freud was too often the victim of the dramatic instance, it is also true that with the same coin he paid his way to an understanding of the depths and heights of *la condition humaine*. By comparison, the young men and women of Professor Kelly's clinical examples are worried about their dates, their studies, and their conformity. If Freud's clinical world is a grotesque of fin de siècle Vienna, Kelly's is a gloss of the postadolescent peer group of Columbus, Ohio, who are indeed in the process of constructing their worlds. Which is more "real"? I have no idea. I wish Professor Kelly would treat more "most religious men in the most religious moments," or even just Nijinsky or Gabriel d'Annunzio.

Bruner suggests that even if many young college men and women can be well understood by assuming that they are trying to develop construct systems with which to successfully predict events, this is not necessarily true of everyone. Even if only a few people are more ruled by their passions than the Columbus college students— and certainly if many people are so ruled, or even highly influenced—Bruner's criticism needs to be taken seriously.

Kelly would probably argue that if one's constructs have emotional content (e.g., angry-happy, anxious-calm, joyous-sad), one's functioning will be governed by emotional considerations. Passionate persons are so because the constructs they have developed to deal with experience are of an emotional nature. And Kelly would see such persons as using these emotional constructs

in the attempt to anticipate experience accurately by an orderly application and elaboration of their construct systems. Bruner suspects, however, that people in the grips of passions may abandon their construct systems and their interest in accurately anticipating experience. The dispute between Kelly and Bruner is basic and not easily solved. Perhaps a step toward resolving it would involve a consideration of when emotions have a disruptive effect and when a mobilizing or organizing effect.

THE CHANGE OF CONSTRUCTS. Essentially, constructs change when they lead to anticipations that turn out to be inaccurate. You will recall that, for Kelly, the major task of life is to predict events accurately. Constructs are the bases on which anticipation and action occur. It follows from this that constructs are useful only when they permit accurate prediction of events. When they do not, constructs are changed and the new predictions are then tested. Thus, a person's construct system represents the results up to that time of a process of rational trial and error in the development of what amounts to a theory of the world of experience. It is the emphasis on congruence between this theory as a predictive system and the real world of events that makes Kelly's position a consistency theory.

When there is lack of consistency—in other words, when expectations are not confirmed by events—the person experiences *anxiety*. Kelly's (1955, p. 495) definition of anxiety as "the awareness that the events with which one is confronted lie outside the range of convenience of his construct system" is unusual in personology. In this definition, the content of expectations and events is really irrelevant to the arousal of anxiety. It is the lack of fit between expectations and events—inconsistency—that leads to the uncomfortable feeling we know as anxiety.

You should not imagine, as some serious students of construct theory have done (e.g., Sechrest, 1963), that Kelly sees anxiety as the result of only significant or large discrepancies between events and anticipations. Kelly (1955) clearly establishes that any and all inaccuracies of prediction, no matter how small or seemingly unimportant, precipitate anxiety:

> From the standpoint of the psychology of personal constructs, anxiety, per se, is not to be classified as either good or bad. It represents the awareness that one's construction system does not apply to the events at hand. It is, therefore, a preconsideration for making revisions. . . . Our definition of anxiety also covers the little confusions and puzzles of everyday living. The sum of a column of numbers does not check. Anxiety! We add it up again, it still does not check. More anxiety! We add it up another way. Good adjustment. Ah, there was our error! (pp. 498–499)

Statements such as this have led Bruner (1956) to characterize Kelly's core tendency as the avoidance of disruptive surprises. Clearly, Kelly offers a tension reduction view, with anxiety a tension state that one must minimize. Note that the anxiety of disconfirmation of expectations is the springboard for construct system change. Even if the anticipation expresses the adventurous form of the elaborative choice, anxiety will result as long as the ensuing events differ from those anticipated.

While Kelly's emphasis on the discomfort of unexpected events makes sense on the surface, consider its implications further. There is little in the theory that would help us gain understanding of boredom, which clearly is also a state of discomfort. How humdrum life would be if the goal involved in Kelly's core tendency of personality were actually achieved!

Oddly, Kelly does seem to recognize that complete anticipational accuracy—the aim of his core tendency—would involve unpleasant boredom. He suggests that people will like best those areas of experience complicated enough to yield small discrepancies between anticipations and occurrences but predictable enough not to cause whole construct systems to be called into question (Kelly, 1955, p. 735). Such areas of experience, he intimates, will stimulate adventurous rather than conservative choices. However sensible this position may seem from a descriptive point of view, it is hardly in the main thrust of a theory that so heavily emphasizes accuracy in

all one's anticipations—"the little confusions and puzzles of everyday living" as well as the large crises.

Construct system change is clearly based on the discrepancy between anticipation and occurrence. Anticipatory error leads to anxiety, which is uncomfortable enough to precipitate construct system change and, hence, to cause new anticipations to be tested for their accuracy. There are no immutable instincts, defenses, or unconscious determinants of functioning to interfere with the trial-and-error process whereby one tries to see the world accurately. The only aspects of the theory that could interfere with the straightforwardness of the trial-and-error process are guilt and hostility, and they stand out like sore thumbs amidst the rest. *Hostility,* according to Kelly (1955, p. 533), is the "continued effort to extort validational evidence in favor of a type of social prediction which has already been recognized as a failure." *Guilt* is defined as "the awareness of dislodgement of the self from one's core role structure" (Kelly, 1955, p. 533). These two concepts are unnatural to the theory not because it is particularly difficult to see the meaning intended but because there is no additional theoretical structure in which to embed them. They are swimming upstream, as it were, against the current formed by an otherwise consistent theoretical structure in which constructs are readily changed when they do not permit accurate anticipation. Nowhere in the theory aside from the notion of hostility is there any way of expecting that the person will maintain a construct in the face of evidence of its invalidity. And nowhere in the theory aside from the notion of guilt is there any particular emphasis on the self (which for Kelly is just another construct) as having a status somehow independent of the construct system. It is as if in these two notions Kelly were making concessions to other theories that adopt a model of living as an irrational and defensive process. Nonetheless, the concepts of hostility and self have captured the interest of some personologists (e.g., Bannister & Fransella, 1971) influenced by Kelly.

KELLY AND FESTINGER. Leon Festinger and a number of other social psychologists have developed a consistency position closely related to Kelly's. But as Festinger is concerned mainly with social psychological phenomena such as attitude change, his views will not be considered in any detail here. The basic principle of Festinger's (1958b) position is that *whenever cognitive dissonance exists, the person will employ procedures for reducing it.* This position, like Kelly's, takes *cognitions* to be the elements relevant to consistency. In Festinger's position, cognitions can be beliefs, attitudes, ideas, or perceptions. For example, a state of inconsistency or dissonance might exist when the idea of yourself as a fair person is confronted with the perception of yourself as acting in a discriminatory way. Though many dissonances involve the ethical domain, this need not be so. Indeed, any expectation that is disconfirmed by one's perception of events constitutes dissonance, regardless of whether the expectation and perception involve you, someone else, or the inanimate world. Kelly and Festinger agree that the consequence of dissonance or disconfirmed expectations is anxiety, or at least some generalized emotional discomfort and tension, which precipitates change aimed at avoiding that which caused the tension. But here the two theorists show an important difference in emphasis.

You will recall that Kelly emphasizes a rational procedure of trial and error in changing constructs so that they eventually provide an accurate basis for predicting events. In contrast, Festinger does not exclusively emphasize rationality and fitting cognition to real events. Instead, Festinger contends that the person will change one or the other of the cognitions involved in the dissonance, or the nature of the relationship between them, without regard for the niceties of the real world. According to Festinger, people are as likely to distort reality as not in their attempt to avoid dissonance. In this emphasis on the irrational, Festinger is much closer to Freud than to Kelly. For Freud, you will recall, defenses are procedures whereby reality is distorted so that anxiety over conflict will not be felt. The main difference between Freud and Festinger in this regard involves the content of conflict: For Freud, it is invariably sexual and moral, whereas Festinger casts his net more widely than this. Some other personologists, such as Rogers, who also use a notion of defense as a distortion of reality but do not especially restrict the content of underlying conflict, may therefore come even closer than Freud to Festinger.

An example may help dramatize the flavor of irrationality in Festinger's version of the consistency model. Suppose you believe that a man whom you respect and love very much is actually immortal—a god. This is one cognition. But suppose also that you see him die what is clearly a mortal's death on the cross. This second cognition is dissonant with the first and precipitates anxiety. The anxiety results not because you lost a loved one but because you are in turmoil as to what to believe. Therefore, to remove the anxiety, you have to decrease the dissonance. You may well do this by developing a third cognition that says that he did not really die but simply left earthly life. Armed with this belief, you even have the basis for rejoicing. And, to protect yourself from the possibility of anxiety in the future—for, after all, the perception of the death on the cross is rather vivid—you proselytize. If you can convince others of your new, dissonance-reducing belief, you can believe it more unequivocally yourself. Kelly would have agreed with this example up to the point of dissonance reduction, at which he would be more likely to predict, as the most realistic procedure, that you would change your belief that your friend was a god.

Festinger has developed his theory for the purpose of understanding attitude change rather than personality. It is understandable, therefore, that he offers little that could clarify core characteristics and peripheral aspects of personality. For this reason, it will suffice to record the substantial agreement in basic assumptions between Kelly and Festinger, that is, in both, boredom is not a significant human experience.

Kelly on the Periphery of Personality

Certainly, Kelly's basic unit is the *personal construct*. Personal constructs are organized into *construction systems,* which compose the personality. As you will recall, Kelly offers the general definition of the construct as a dichotomous idea or abstraction. He also gives some notion of the hierarchical way that constructs are organized into systems. Constructs lie at the core of personality, for they do not differentiate one person from another. To have a position on the periphery of personality, Kelly could have specified the content for sets of personal constructs defining the commonly encountered construction systems. Nowhere does he do this. Like Allport, Kelly is adamant on the uniqueness of people and the attendant uselessness of attempting to specify what they may be like in advance of actually encountering them. Each person is so different from the next, in Kelly's view, that the most a theorist can do is provide a consistent set of notions about the common units of personality and how they are organized. To presume that these units and organizations have typical content is to do violence to human uniqueness. Indeed, if Allport's specification of the contents of psychological maturity does indicate, as I have suggested, the first step in the development of a typology of character, he actually is less extreme than Kelly in his insistence on individuality.

The closest Kelly comes to a position on the periphery of personality can be seen in two aspects of his theorizing: (1) the specification of different types of constructs in terms of their logical and functional properties and (2) the specification of techniques for identifying the content of people's constructs once you have confronted them. As to the first point, Kelly presents such things as *permeable* and *preemptive constructs.* In addition, Kelly (1955, pp. 532–533) suggests that constructs can be *preverbal* (having no consistent word symbols to represent them), *comprehensive* (subsuming a wide variety of events), *incidental* (subsuming a narrow variety of events), *superordinate* (including other constructs as one of their elements), *subordinate* (being included as an element of other constructs), *tight* (leading to unvarying predictions), or *loose* (leading to varying predictions while maintaining their identity).

Further, Kelly (1955, p. 533) specifies what he calls *dimensions of transition,* which refer to change in constructs or their organization over time. Among these dimensions of transition are some familiar emotions, such as *anxiety* (the awareness that the events that confront one lie outside the predictive potentialities of one's construction system) and *aggressiveness* (the active elaboration of one's perceptual field). There are also some dimensions of transition that refer more to the successive use of different types of constructs than to emotional states. An example is the *creativity cycle,* in which one starts with loosened constructions and ends with tightened ones. In all this, Kelly clearly is trying to deal with a number of content considerations usually considered important by personologists. It is hard to avoid the feeling, however sympathetic one may be to Kelly's kind of theory, that these matters are given short shrift. Is creativity simply the process of starting with loose constructs, which lead to diverse predictions, and ending with tight constructs, which lead to specific predictions? Is anxiety nothing more than the awareness that you have encountered something you do not understand? Though spirited and ingenious, Kelly's theory tells only part of the story of personality, leaving the drama of peripheral characteristics undisclosed.

The other point at which Kelly comes closest to explicating the periphery is in his specification of the manner of assessing construct content. I have presented the *Role Repertory Test* as Kelly's most definitive manner of determining the content of the person's constructs. Not only will this test disclose content; it will also give information on how the various existing constructs are organized in the person's construction system. In addition to all this, Kelly (1955, pp. 452–485) also offers guidelines for assessment based on less definitive information than that available in the *Role Repertory Test.* Such information typically is found in interviews, but personal documents, such as diaries, can also be used in assessment. Interviews and personal documents can be useful if the personologist remains credulous and sensitive to what the person is actually saying. Kelly believes that through the adoption of credulity and perceptual literalness, the personologist can discover the constructs a person uses and the way in which they will influence perception of similarities and differences among events. But you can imagine how hard the identification of such regularities would be as soon as you deal with human experiences of any degree of complexity. Indeed, when Kelly (1955, pp. 319–359; 1962) tries to show how this kind of assessment actually gets done, you are left with a sense that the statements made about constructs are only among those that could be made rather than being definitive. In addition, it is hardly convincing that the statements about constructs permit insight into the essential features of the person's character or style of life. It is hard to avoid the conclusion that Kelly's position would be more meaningful if he offered some inklings as to typical character types.

EPSTEIN'S POSITION ....

Seymour Epstein, a professor of psychology at the University of Massachusetts at Amherst, is well known for his important role in defending personality in the last person-situation debate wherein social psychologists and behaviorists argued that behavior is completely under the control of environmental forces (see Chapter 14). He showed in research by the method of aggregation of observations that behavior has considerable regularity across situations. Epstein has for some years now been developing a cognitive-experiential self-theory that, though far from complete, is relevant here.

Epstein's Core Statement

Taking into account the enormous complexity of Epstein's personality theory, I would render his core tendency as *the attempt to construct a har-*

monious personal theory of reality through mutually compatible views of the self, the world, and how they interconnect (Epstein, 1984, 1994). In this, people operate by trial and error in an ongoing attempt to make their implicit theory of reality conform to their experiences. In this sense, Epstein's theory fits the consistency model, and its strong cognitive emphasis suggests the cognitive dissonance more than the activation version of that model.

In elaborating on the components of the implicit theory of reality that people develop, Epstein postulates a *hierarchical organization of schemata (constructs) and networks of schemata.* Presumably, constructs organized into self-theory, world-theory, and connecting propositions are *core characteristics* in this theory, because everyone has each, even though their specific content may vary from person to person as the conditions of learning vary. Highest in the hierarchy are the most general, abstract schemata (e.g., my self is worthy, people are untrustworthy, the world is predictable). Lowest in the hierarchy are the narrow, situation-specific schemata (e.g., Anne is a friendly person, I gravitate toward supportive people). Because of their more central role, schemata higher in the hierarchy can "destabilize the entire personality" when they are invalidated by experience (Epstein, 1994). In contrast, lower order schemata can be readily changed without jeopardizing personality stability. Although for Epstein, schemata do not appear to be dichotomous, his approach is similar to that of Kelly. Epstein does, however, make a distinction, not found in Kelly, between *descriptive schemata* (that express themselves in repetitive behaviors or habits) and *motivational schemata* (that express themselves in directional behaviors). This distinction is similar to that in Allport (see Chapter 6) between *stylistic* and *motivational dispositions* and in McClelland (later in this chapter) between *traits* and *motives.*

One major difference between Kelly and Epstein is the latter's postulation of three systems for processing information so that it can contribute to *schemata* and their *network.* The *rational-conceptual system* operates according to the rules of evidence and inference in deductive thought, and is thereby analytical and abstract. The *experiential-conceptual system* operates according to more intuitive, emotional, and hedonic principles, and is thereby concrete and holistic. This system is assumed to dominate the functioning of higher animals, and to have evolved over millions of years. It operates more rapidly, and requires less effort than the rational-conceptual system, which is historically a more recent development unique to humans. (These two systems are very similar to what I meant in Chapter 1 by *rational* and *intuitive knowledge*). Finally, the *primary-process system,* identified with Freud by Epstein (1994), "operates by loose association, symbolic representation, condensation, and displacement." Presumably, a schema might develop from one as opposed to the other of these three information processing systems. Thus, the experiential-conceptual system might yield the schema that job interviews are horribly threatening, whereas the rational-conceptual system might contribute the schema that the only way to get a good job is to go through job interviews. Whether, in your actions, you go to or avoid job interviews would be a function of just how emotionally upsetting the schema contributed by the experiential-conceptual system turned out to be.

Epstein does not elaborate on the role of the *primary-process system* for processing information, relegating it to those "Freudian" instances of unconscious functioning. As Freud relied on the operation of defenses in the effort to ease the inevitable, omnipresent conflict between the selfish person and society as guardian of the common good, this inclusion of unconscious functioning by Epstein might suggest that his theory is best classified under the psychosocial conflict model. But Epstein makes little of the primary-process system and relies so heavily on the other two that, on balance, it seems best to classify his approach as emphasizing cognitive consistency.

Nonetheless, as the example implies, there may well be intrapsychic conflict as a result of the dual operation of the rational-conceptual and experiential-conceptual systems. In the example, the schema from one system leads you toward

job interviews, while that from the other system leads you away from them. That Epstein's (1994) position is not best classified as expressing the *intrapsychic conflict model* is shown by his assumption that the ideal situation is when the rational-conceptual and experiential conceptual systems are "in harmony." Presumably, harmony occurs when the schemata contributed by the experiential-conceptual system fit well, and perhaps even coincide with, those contributed by the rational-conceptual system.

There is another major difference between Kelly and Epstein. For Kelly, whose approach is more purely cognitive, there is no pressure for the person to go in one direction or another in forming *constructs*. All that is important is the degree of consistency between what is expected and what happens. In contrast, Epstein (1994), drawing on the work of several other personality theorists, assumes that everyone comes into the world with four basic needs. These additional core characteristics are *the needs for pleasure, coherence of the conceptual system, relatedness,* and *self-esteem*. The first is so broadly defined that *it can be seen as consistent* with the already mentioned core tendency of constructing an implicit theory of reality. Presumably, the more articulate one's self-theories, world-theories, and connecting propositions become, the more pleasurable experience will be. The second need, for coherence of the conceptual system, basically reiterates the first as I have interpreted it. The need for relatedness, however, introduces further complexity and ambiguity. It is unclear what the relationship is between being driven to relate to others and the two needs already discussed, much less the previously stated emphasis on developing one's own theory of reality. Nor is it any clearer how the need to think well of oneself fits in. If relating to others is instrumental to, and thinking well of oneself is an outcome of, efforts to develop an implicit theory of reality, then there is at least some integration of these various tendencies. But, if interacting with others and feeling good about oneself are pleasurable in and of themselves, regardless of whether they further or follow from implicit reality theorizing, then

Epstein's theorizing is more reminiscent of the fulfillment than the consistency model.

It will take further theoretical development before we can see clearly just what this theory is saying. In implicit recognition that these four basic needs may not lead the person in compatible experiential directions, Epstein emphasizes the importance of harmony and coherence between the person's self-theory, world-theory, and their interaction. This may have to be achieved, according to Epstein, by compromise among expressions of the four basic needs. So the emphasis on cognitive consistency seems primary, hence, my current classification of this theory. What we are seeing is the beginnings of an extraordinarily complex position on personality, in which many of the questions concerning theoretical consistency and compatibility have not yet been answered.

Epstein on Development and the Periphery

Epstein does not appear to have the specifics of a position on development. Although he gives examples of how certain social and environmental pressures can influence how people might construe their experience with regard to the four basic needs, there is little systematic conceptualization available concerning either typical situations and interactions or critical periods in development.

Epstein does raise questions for future research about whether certain needs (e.g., need for relatedness) and information-processing modes (e.g., experiential-conceptual system) are stronger earlier in life, giving ground later to other needs (e.g., coherency of conceptual system) and information-processing modes (e.g., rational-conceptual system). But he does not take any definite conceptual stance on such questions at this time. For now, the most that can be said is that Epstein endorses reinforcement as a basis for learning, without being any more specific about the developmental implications of certain types of interaction between youngsters and their significant others.

Nor does Epstein have much to say about the common types of personality that emanate from particular developmental patterns. Once again, he uses examples of certain possible views on self, or world, but does not provide coherent overall patterns of subjective views of reality and the particular underlying needs that they express. There is, of course, the previously mentioned assumption that views of reality resulting from harmony within information-processing systems and need patterns are ideal. But there is little detailed explication of either this configuration or less harmonious ones. Consequently, there is nothing further that we can examine concerning Epstein's position on the periphery of personality.

McClelland's Position ......

David C. McClelland (born in New York City, 1917) received a Ph.D. in psychology from Yale University in 1941. The son of a Protestant minister who later became a college president, McClelland has spent his career teaching and researching personality in university settings. He showed his leadership capacity and interest in public servicee by serving as chair of the Department of Psychology at Wesleyan University and as deputy director of the Behavioral Sciences Division of the Ford Foundation. Later, he became head of the Center for Research in Personality and then chair of the Department of Social Relations at Harvard University. Deeply influenced by Murray and by the broad social science emphasis at Harvard, McClelland spent the early part of his career developing and testing his theory of personality and then began investigating its social applications in underdeveloped societies throughout the world. Then he investigated the physiological implications of various psychological motives.

McClelland's Core Statement

For McClelland, as for Kelly and Festinger, the consistency or discrepancy between expectations and events is basic to the understanding of behavior. But whereas Kelly and Festinger find all inconsistency to result in unpleasant feelings and avoidance, McClelland considers this outcome to occur only when the degree of inconsistency is large. For him, small discrepancies between expectations and events result in pleasant feelings and approach behavior.

THE CORE TENDENCY. McClelland's position, a variant of the consistency model, is that the core tendency of personality is *to minimize large discrepancies between expectation and occurrence while maximizing small discrepancies.*

In finding an intuitive basis for understanding McClelland's position, you would do well to think of times of uncertainty and times of boredom. In all our lives, there are times when our sheer inability to determine what will happen next and related inability to know clearly what is happening now threaten us and make us feel discomfort. Also, there are times when everything is so predictable and clear that we wish something unpredictable would happen. The fact that people sometimes want to increase predictability and sometimes decrease it was the starting point for McClelland's theorizing. As indicated in the core tendency, he believes that people crave small degrees of unpredictability and avoid large degrees of it. I can imagine that at least for some of you, the introspective evidence for this position is not readily available. Because of this, it will be useful now to go on to a more rational analysis of the position, returning later to a point of correspondence between reason and intuition.

THE CORE CHARACTERISTICS ASSOCIATED WITH THE CORE TENDENCY. For McClelland (McClelland, Atkinson, Clark, & Lowell, 1953), certain core characteristics are inherent and others learned. The innate core characteristics underlie the core tendency, but the learned ones do not. By virtue of being born, the person has the ability to experience pleasant feelings, or *positive affect,* and unpleasant feelings, or *negative affect.* McClelland is not concerned with distinctions between particular emotions, such as love and joy in the positive class or anger and fear in the negative class. Because the two broad classes suffice for his theoretical purposes, one gets the impression that he may even

assume, though he does not say so, that the innate apparatus for the experience of affect is simple and undifferentiated enough to permit only two affective states, which though amorphous and imprecise, clearly differ as to whether they are pleasant or unpleasant.

Another assumption, closely related to that of an innate basis for experiencing positive and negative affect, is that people find the latter affective state obnoxious enough to avoid and the former attractive enough to seek. There is nothing, however, in the innate tendency to avoid negative affect and seek positive affect to explain the particular techniques for avoiding and seeking that we may observe in a person. These techniques are a matter of learning and therefore a matter of the periphery.

Having assumed an innate basis for feeling positive and negative affect, McClelland tells us what it is that can trigger one reaction versus the other. As his core tendency indicates, he gives this role to the match between expectancies and occurrences. An *expectancy* is a cognitive unit, or thought, that refers to what you imagine will be the content and timing of events in the future. *Occurrences* are merely events or things that happen. Clearly the expectancy is similar to the construct of Kelly and the cognition of Festinger. As they do, McClelland recognizes events as real aspects of the world, though they must be appreciated by persons in order to have any significance for their living. Like Kelly and Festinger, McClelland assumes that expectancies are formed on the basis of past experience and that different people may well form different expectancies owing to peculiarities of their background. McClelland suggests that the mechanism whereby expectancies are learned is contiguity. In other words, if the events in a given set occur in the same sequence often enough, you will abstract from your experience the expectation that the same thing will happen in the future. So whenever you encounter the first of this series of events, you will have a definite idea of what is coming next. For McClelland, there need be no reward at the end of the series, such as the proverbial pot at the end of the rainbow, for you to learn the sequence. You learn it simply because it is there and is repeated in your experience a sufficient number of times. This idea of learning without reinforcement is similar in emphasis to Kelly, though for both theorists it is important to know whether an expectancy that is learned turns out to be accurate in order to understand when it is retained, discarded, or changed.

In this regard, you have seen that for Kelly any degree of inaccuracy of expectation leads to anxiety and pressure to discard and change the expectation. But for McClelland, only large discrepancies between expectation and occurrence have these consequences. In contrast, small discrepancies lead to positive affect and the retaining of the expectation. It is this emphasis that makes McClelland's approach a variant of the consistency model.

McClelland's emphasis on quantifying the match or mismatch between expectation and event, though intriguing, raises the question of the manner in which quantification is to be done, for a number of possibilities present themselves. McClelland himself is apparently undecided— even concerning the demarcation point between large and small discrepancies—undoubtedly out of a sense of the complexity of the problem. Perhaps the most obvious way of quantifying the agreement between expectation and occurrence would be to determine the number of elements of the expectation and of the corresponding event, then calculate the proportion of elements that agree. This technique, for all its ponderousness, would be useful for at least fairly complex expectancies. Expectancies referring to propositional speech provide good examples. The sentence "A rose is a rose is a rose" is striking because it is an occurrence discrepant from expectations concerning the sequence of words in understandable speech. In attempting to identify elements to quantify the degree of discrepancy, one might try parts of speech.

But here we encounter a vexing problem. Not all parts of speech are equally important— indeed, in almost all instances of naturally occurring sequences of events, some of the events will be more significant to the person than others.

Perhaps, then, another and more meaningful way to quantify the degree of discrepancy between expectancy and occurrence is to order elements of expectancy and occurrence by their importance. One could then say that the greater the importance of the event inaccurately predicted, the larger the discrepancy between expectancy and occurrence.

I am afraid this problem of quantification has not been overcome as yet. A theory that cannot tell you how to distinquish between small and large discrepancies when they supposedly have drastically different effects is severely handicapped in its ability to provide believable explanations of phenomena. But even so, it is not without utility, as I will show in Chapter 10. For the moment, I have tried to alert you to the value of attempts to develop the theory in such fashion that it can, at some future time, provide consistent, workable bases for quantification.

McClelland on Development

McClelland's theory differs in two important ways from the consistency positions already considered. I have already brought up the first— the emphasis on moderate rather than total anticipational accuracy as the ultimate goal of living. The second is the emphasis McClelland puts on action in addition to the more purely cognitive-affective considerations of consistency. These two emphases in McClelland's thinking are usually considered together in attempting to understand the way expression of the core tendency leads to personality development.

I have already indicated that positions such as Kelly's cannot logically consider boredom to be an important factor in life. McClelland has made moderate anticipational accuracy the ideal because of his belief that complete accuracy over any significant period of time would be too monotonous and boring for comfort. If you consider boredom to be an unpleasant state, you have an intuitive basis for understanding McClelland's position, however strange it may sound initially. In sum, McClelland's position grants a hardiness and vivacity to the person that is not really found in other cognitive consistency positions. For McClelland, as for other consistency theorists, the greater the discrepancy between expectation and occurrence, the more intense the organismic tension. But unlike the others, he does not support a simple tension reduction view. Instead, McClelland considers the moderate tension associated with moderate anticipational inaccuracy to be ideal. Not only too much but too little tension is avoided. This is the first consistency position we have encountered that explicitly takes this stance.

Of all the cognitive consistency positions, McClelland's is the most oriented toward explaining action. Kelly's theory considers actions as mere extensions of anticipations. While this is perhaps understandable in a position that stresses total accuracy of prediction as life's ultimate goal, there is still a critical problem created by the collapse of the distinction between anticipation and action, because then it no longer seems important to consider action strategies aimed at providing tests of anticipations.

The difference of opinion hinges on the fact that while Kelly makes the achievement of total accuracy the real aim of life, McClelland considers accuracy of anticipation as the basis for the development of personality characteristics that do not particularly serve accurate anticipation. For example, in Kelly's theory, constructs (which are the elements of personality) are formed, used, and changed for the single purpose of ensuring better and better prediction. In McClelland's theory, the expectation is only one element of personality. The other major element is the *motive* (McClelland, 1951). But though the nature and content of motives certainly reflect the person's history of anticipational accuracy and inaccuracy, the purpose of motives is not primarily to make correct predictions. Motives influence action toward specific goals, but they have little direct relationship to considerations of accuracy.

This point will become clearer if I explain how expression of the core tendency leads to the development of motives. Remember that the positive affect associated with moderate inaccuracy and the negative affect associated with

great inaccuracy lead, respectively, to approach and avoidance actions. When people have experienced a small discrepancy between expectation and occurrence, they bring themselves closer to the area of experience involved; if the discrepancy is large, they avoid it. Here I shall consider two common areas of experience: affiliation with people and achievement in work.

Suppose that a child's most frequent experience in the affiliative domain is to have her or his expectations greatly violated because of complex, inconsistent, and unpredictable parents. Assume that the child is young enough to be impressionable and unable to choose associates easily. The child's predominant affective tone in interpersonal relationships will be unpleasant. If this condition goes on for any length of time, the child will develop an enduring orientation (or motive) to avoid people. Every time the possibility of interaction arises, the memory of painful emotional consequences will also arise, leading the child to avoid others. But what you must see is that the goal of the motive is avoidance of interaction, not the achievement of total accuracy of prediction!

Now consider the area of work achievement. Suppose this youngster's most frequent experience in this area is that of having expectations violated only slightly by occurrences. The child's expectations will not be so greatly disconfirmed as to cause discouragement and not so completely accurate as to bring boredom and indifference. Instead, the youngster will come to regard working as a source of mild and pleasant surprises. This kind of accumulation of experience can be brought about by parents (McClelland et al., 1953, p. 62) who watch their children carefully enough to know when they have mastered some task they are working on and who are sensible enough to then give them another task that is a little harder but not beyond their capabilities. Under such conditions, the youngster will learn an enduring orientation (or motive) to strive for success (or achievement) in work. Again, the goal of the motive is to approach or seek work, not to try for total accuracy of prediction.

I should point out that if the parents in the affiliation example were more like the parents in the work example, a motive to approach interaction would have been learned. Similarly, if the parents in the work example were more like those in the affiliation example, a motive to avoid work would result. In every area of experience, an approach motive and an avoidance motive are possible, according to McClelland. I shall pursue this further in the next section, for motives are actually peripheral characteristics of personality in his thinking, because their main usefulness lies in explaining individual differences.

In closing this section, I should make it clear that the absence of reference to the concept of defense is not an oversight. Like Kelly, McClelland gives no role to this concept. Even avoidance actions and motives are not, strictly speaking, defensive in the sense of debarring mental content from awareness.

McClelland on the Periphery of Personality

Like Allport and Murray, McClelland concerns himself extensively with precise definition of peripheral characteristics. He does not just toss off concepts such as trait or style, leaving their real meanings to be discerned by others. His concern with the proper, clear definitions of the concrete units of personality that differentiate one person from another bespeaks his special emphasis on the periphery. Unlike the other theorists thus far considered, McClelland assumes not one but three kinds of peripheral characteristics: *motive, trait,* and *schemata.* Each characteristic has a separate definition, process of development, and type of effect on functioning.

MOTIVES. I shall first turn to a consideration of the motive concept, as it is the most important of the three in McClelland's thinking and follows most naturally from his conceptualization of the core of personality. McClelland (1951) defines a *motive* as "a strong affective association, characterized by an anticipatory goal reaction and based on past association of certain

cues with pleasure or pain" (p. 466). Surprisingly, the essence of this rather opaque statement is very straightforward. What McClelland means is that whenever some cue arouses in you the anticipation of some change in state that will increase either pleasure or pain, you have a motive. Anything from a ringing doorbell to a rapidly beating heart can serve as a cue as long as it constitutes a signal that some change in state is imminent. Stimuli become cues on the basis of past experience. The anticipated change in state also comes out of past experience and may have specific content, such as the expectation that you will be successful or that you will enter into close contact with other people. Finally, for the anticipated change in state to be a motive, it must be associated with the expectation of an increase in either positive or negative affect. To paraphrase, a motive is a state of mind aroused by some stimulus that signals an imminent change that will be either pleasant or unpleasant. McClelland assumes that people will act on their motives so as to bring about the anticipated pleasure or avoid the anticipated displeasure, as the case may be. When the anticipated change in state includes a positive affect, it is considered an *approach motive* in that the person tries to turn the anticipation into a reality. In contrast, the anticipated change in state that includes negative affect is an *avoidance motive* in that the person works to keep the anticipation from becoming a reality.

McClelland (1980, 1985; McClelland, Koestner, & Weinberger, 1989) also distinguishes between *operant* and *respondent forms of motivation.* Operant motives are implicit, internal, and personal, not a reaction to external, social expectations. They are, in essence, *approach motives.* Respondent motives are the opposite, namely, how we react in a socially appropriate way as to what our goals should be. In this sense, respondent motives are a subclass of schemata— goal-directed but explicit and socially elicited.

This division into two broad classes is the first step McClelland takes in specifying the content of people's motives. The second step is the endorsement of Murray's extensive list of needs for nurturance, compliance, and so forth. Of the needs on this list, McClelland has focused on three—the needs for achievement, affiliation, and power. In relating this list to the distinction between approach and avoidance motives, McClelland seems to postulate an approach and an avoidance version of each need. The avoidance version of the need for achievement is called *fear of failure,* which indicates reacting to a cue for a competitive situation by anticipating failure. The attendant negative affect leads to attempts to avoid the situation. In contrast, the approach version of the need for achievement involves reacting to a cue for a competitive situation by anticipating success and attendant positive affect and attempting to thrust oneself actively into the fray. Although McClelland's meaning is clear, he often slips into the confusing position of calling this approach version of the need for achievement nothing other than the need for achievement. It would be much less confusing to call it something like *hope for success,* as one of his associates does (Atkinson, 1957), and thereby preserve a verbal basis for distinguishing approach and avoidance versions of a common motivational characteristic. In any event, McClelland presumes that there are also approach and avoidance versions of other needs.

HOW MOTIVES AFFECT BEHAVIOR. There are two additional considerations regarding motives: their effect on behavior and their process of development. As to effects on behavior, McClelland presumes that the arousal of motives increases the amount and intensity of behavior. One can observe this effect not only in overt actions but also in thought processes (McClelland, 1951, p. 482). When there is a task to be addressed, increased motivation leads to increased work on the task. Another general effect of motives is the achievement of interrelatedness among diverse aspects of the person's behavior (McClelland, 1951, pp. 485–486). Motivation organizes responses and introduces trends into behavior, producing orientation and direction. According to McClelland, this capacity of the motive concept—to make sense out of varied responses—distinguishes it from other explanatory concepts of personality and makes it

particularly useful. The final effect of motivation is sensitization (McClelland, 1951, pp. 488–489). People in a state of motivation seem more sensitive to some kinds of environmental cues than to others. There seems to be a lowering of perceptual, if not sensory, thresholds to the specific kinds of stimulation relevant to the motive.

Although McClelland assumes that the effects of increase, interrelation, and sensitization of behavior take place in the case of both approach and avoidance motives, subtle differences mark these two motivation classes. Thus, though both approach and avoidance motives lead to increases in the amount of behavior, approach motives do so by augmenting effective, efficient behaviors, whereas avoidance motives do so by producing ineffective, obsessive behaviors. In imagination, for example, approach motives lead you to anticipate success and think about how best to plan for adequate task performance. In contrast, avoidance motives lead you to become obsessed with the obstacles to reaching the goal and dwell on magical thoughts of satisfaction. Although both kinds of motives can lead to behavioral interrelatedness, approach motives lead to organizations focused on effective instrumental actions and achievable goals, whereas avoidance motives produce organizations stressing passive expressions of need and frustration. Finally, in producing sensitization, approach motives would highlight cues associated with challenge and satisfaction, whereas avoidance motives would highlight cues associated with threat and dissatisfaction. So, approach and avoidance motives have similar general effects on behavior, with clear and distinct differences in behavioral effects at a more subtle level of analysis.

MORE ON HOW MOTIVES DEVELOP. In considering the process whereby McClelland believes motives develop, we can see the relationship between core and peripheral levels of personality in his theory. You will recall that the core tendency according to McClelland is the maximization of small discrepancies and the minimization of large discrepancies between expectation and occurrence. Small discrepancies result in positive affect and large discrepancies in negative affect. In McClelland's view, in a particular domain of living characterized by small discrepancies, people will come to learn an approach motive, whereas in a domain characterized by large discrepancies, they will learn an avoidance motive. If the domain yields little in the way of any discrepancy—if it is completely predictable—people will become indifferent to it altogether. You should begin to see clearly why McClelland defines motivation as he does. In simple terms, what McClelland means is that if you have enough pleasant emotional experiences in a certain area of functioning, then you will learn to expect pleasant experiences each time you approach a relevant situation involving that area. In contrast, if you have had sufficient unpleasant experiences in that area, you will learn to expect unpleasant experiences whenever some cue is present and, therefore, attempt to avoid the situation.

To dramatize McClelland's meaning, I will quote from his account of the development of the *achievement motive* (McClelland, et al., 1953):

> A concrete example involving the development of the achievement motive may help explain its implications in practice. Suppose a child is given a new toy car for Christmas to play with. Initially, unless he has had other toy cars, his expectations . . . as to what it will do are nonexistent, and he can derive little or no positive or negative affect from manipulating it until such expectations are developed. Gradually, if he plays with it (as he will be encouraged to by his parents in our culture), he will develop certain expectations of varying probabilities which will be confirmed or not confirmed. Unless the nonconfirmations are too many (which may happen if the toy is too complex), he should be able to build up reasonably certain expectations as to what it will do and confirm them. In short, he gets pleasure from playing with the car. But what happens then? Why doesn't he continue playing with it the rest of his life? The fact is, of course, that his expectations become certainties, confirmation becomes 100 per cent, and we say that he loses interest or gets bored with the car; he should

get bored or satiated, according to the theory, since the discrepancies from certainty are no longer sufficient to yield pleasure. However, pleasure can be reintroduced into the situation, as any parent knows, by buying a somewhat more complex car, by making the old car do somewhat different things, or perhaps by letting the old car alone for six months until the expectations about it have changed (e.g., decrease in probability). So, if a child is to continue to get pleasure from achievement situations like manipulating toy cars, he must continually work with more and more complex objects or situations permitting mastery, since, if he works long enough at any particular level of mastery, his expectations and their confirmation will become certain and he will get bored. (p. 62)*

Here McClelland clearly is talking about the approach version of the achievement motive. One would certainly expect that after this kind of early experience, each time the person recognized a cue indicating the existence of a mastery situation, he or she would experience a sense of challenge and anticipate that reaching mastery would lead to emotional satisfaction.

McClelland et al. (1953) also describe the development of an avoidance version of the achievement motive:

> In the second place, there are limits placed on the development of n achievement by the negative affect which results from too large discrepancies between expectations and events. Thus Johnny may develop expectations as to what a model airplane or a solved arithmetic problem looks like, but he may be unable to confirm these expectations at all, or only very partially. The result is negative affect, and cues associated with these activities may be expected to evoke avoidance motives. To develop an achievement approach motive, parents or circumstances must contrive to provide opportunities for mastery which, because they are just beyond the child's present knowledge, will provide continuing pleasure. If the opportunities are too limited, boredom should result and the child should develop no interest in achievement (and have a low n achievement score when he grows up). If the

---

*From *The Achievement Motive*, by D. C. McClelland, J. W. Atkinson, R. A. Clark, and E. L. Lowell. Copyright © 1953 by Appleton-Century-Crofts. Reprinted by permission of Prentice-Hall, Inc.

opportunities are well beyond his capabilities, negative affect should result and he may develop an avoidance motive as far as achievement is concerned. (p. 65)

After an early history of large discrepancies between expectation and experience in mastery situations, the person would learn an avoidance version of the achievement motive. This would mean that each time the person recognized a cue that a mastery situation existed, she or he would experience threat and anticipate failure.

The core tendency concerning the size of discrepancy and its relation to affective experience refers, of course, to any area of functioning, not only that concerning achievement. Therefore, people can learn approach or avoidance versions of many different motives, depending on the specific experiences they encounter in the world. As you can see from the last two quotes, in McClelland's theory parents serve the important role of influencing, if not determining, the degree of discrepancy characterizing the various areas of functioning, at least while the child is relatively dependent. McClelland indicates that most motives are learned in childhood, though he does not specify distinct periods in which children learn particular motives. There is little in his writing regarding stages of development— and indeed, the postulation of stages generally requires more emphasis on inherent attributes and capabilities than consistency theories present. Though McClelland et al. (1953, pp. 68–74) do detail the basis in development for different degrees of a motive, such detail is beyond my purpose here. Nonetheless, it should be clear by now that, of those considered so far, this theory offers the most detailed and precise account of peripheral characteristics.

In theorizing about the *power motive,* McClelland (1975) suggests that development is not complete once approach or avoidance goals have been established for an area through early experience. At least in the case of the power motive, there are four transformations; intake, autonomy, assertion, and generativity. The *intake* phase presumably covers the learning of the motive, as already discussed. The *autonomy*

phase encompasses the gradual independence of the motive from the conditions under which it was learned. In the *assertion* phase, an even more insistent attempt to reach the goals at any cost takes place. But in the *generativity* phase, feedback obtained in the course of acting from a motive results in a more socialized, less rapacious form of the motive that is consistent with the well-being of others and the social system. It is not clear whether this intriguing emphasis on changes in a motive after its establishment is intended to apply to motives other than that for power.

REVISING THE MOTIVE CONCEPT. Atkinson and Raynor (1975) have modified and extended McClelland's theorizing. First, they conceptualize motives as even more cognitive than originally proposed and incorporate expectancies (of what goes with what in the environment) and incentives (the value of outcomes) into the formulation whereby one attempts to predict behavior (Atkinson & Birch, 1970). Second, they present the motive construct as the explanation of changes in the ongoing stream of human action rather than the more mundane reference to single, concrete behaviors. This leads to a view of human action as a series of linked episodes perceived by the actor as extending into the future. Motivation for an immediate task depends on how one sees it as related to future events and opportunities. For example, studying in order to get a good grade on an exam reaches beyond the exam if one perceives it as a step toward passing the course, getting a job, and establishing a career. All the perceived future outcomes must be taken into account in assessing the motivation to study for the exam. Atkinson and Raynor provide complicated formulae for prediction attempts. This theoretical step moves McClelland's original formulation further in the direction of a comprehensive basis for understanding action and gives it an existential flavor through showing its impact on the decision-making process. Needless to say, the notion that motives explain behavioral changes rather than repetitions is retained.

THE HUNGER MOTIVE. Before turning from McClelland's motive concept to his views concerning the other two peripheral characteristics, I would like to introduce you to his unorthodox position concerning the biological drives, such as those for food and water:

> Now according to our theory, how could we explain the fact that the longer an animal is deprived of food the more motivated he appears to become? Since most psychologists have been accustomed to thinking of biological need states as the primary sources of motivation, this is a very important question for us to discuss. In the first place, it is clear that in terms of our theory food deprivation does not produce a motive the first time it occurs. The lack of food in a baby rat or a baby human being will doubtless result in diffuse bodily changes of various sorts, but these do not constitute a motive until they are paired with a subsequent change in affect. More specifically, if the organism is to survive, the cues subsequent to food deprivation must always be associated with eating, and eating results in two types of affective change— pleasurable taste sensations, and relief from internal visceral tensions. Thus internal (or external) cues resulting from food deprivation are associated very early and very regularly in all individuals with positive affective change, and thus they become capable of arousing the hunger *motive* with great dependability. (McClelland et al., 1953, pp. 81–84)

Though McClelland goes on to explain why the motive gets stronger as food deprivation increases, it will suffice to recognize that for him there are no motives at birth, even though there are physiological needs that can render the organism uncomfortable in a diffuse way. A motive involves a concrete, tangible set of goals and actions instrumental to reaching these goals. Hence, a motive must be learned on the basis of relevant experience. One can speak of motives in regard to physiological needs only when they have, through learning, come to be represented psychologically as anticipations, goals, and instrumentalities. This kind of learning is mediated for McClelland by affective experience, which is tied to discrepancies between expectations and experiences. For all these reasons, McClelland does not consider biological needs as the basic building block of personality.

TRAITS. The other two peripheral characteristics, traits and schemata, remain to be discussed. After presenting an extensive and excellent analysis of what other personologists have meant by the term *trait,* McClelland (1951) concludes that it should be defined as "the learned tendency of an individual to react as he has reacted more or less successfully in the past in similar situations when similarly motivated" (p. 216). In other words, when people are faced with what they perceive to be the same situation with the same variety and intensity of motivation that they have encountered in the past, they tend to perform the type of response that previously satisfied the demands of the situation and motivation.

By McClelland's definitions, a trait and a motive are actually very different. A motive is a set of anticipations that take the concrete form of goals, emotional involvement, and a commitment to whatever course of action is likely, given the nature of the existing situation, to lead to the fulfillment of those anticipations. Responses that express the need for achievement, for example, very likely will differ considerably over time, insofar as the situations in which this motive will be aroused may differ widely. A motive leads to consistency of intent but not necessarily of actual responses.

In contrast, a trait is no more than a collection of habits that have nothing of the goal-directedness of the motive. The trait of expansiveness, for example, leads you to act expansively every time a situation comes up that is similar to the ones in which you learned to be expansive. According to McClelland, a trait is learned because a certain style of functioning is rewarded consistently in a particular kind of situation. But this is not the same as saying that the trait has motivational properties. Perhaps people laughed and listened to you whenever you happened to be expansive in their presence, and so now you have the habit or trait of expansiveness in social situations. For McClelland, if your expansiveness has the status of a trait you will act this way in social situations because you are used to doing so and with no consciousness or intent. If, however, expansiveness had the status of a motive in you, or was part of an instrumental course of action leading to a goal, you might be expansive in a social situation because you intended to act that way rather than simply because it felt natural and familiar to you. A motive can often lead you to do unfamiliar, untried things, whereas a trait can never have this function.

In his definitions of motive and trait, McClelland celebrates a distinction so clear in human experience that it amazes me that virtually no other personologist has made it in any precise way. Generally speaking, those who rely on the concept of trait include in it both intentional and habitual behaviors, as do those who tend to rely only on the concept of need. According to McClelland, however, both concepts are needed because of clear differences between intentional and habitual functioning. The trait concept can explain response repetition, whereas the motive concept can explain sequentially arranged responses, in which each response is actually different. I think that Murray, in distinguishing needs and need-integrates, and Allport, in distinguishing dynamic and stylistic traits, were recognizing what McClelland makes explicit.

SCHEMATA. McClelland sees reason for yet another distinction, for which he employs the concept of *schema*. Though he offers no concise definition of the schema, he definitely means it to be a unit of cognition or mentation. Actually, it is a symbolization of past experience—it stands for the past experience and is inevitably a simplification (McClelland, 1951, p. 254). Words and language generally are good examples of schemata. But obviously McClelland means to emphasize not just any schemata that may exist but those that characterize the particular person one is trying to understand. For this, it would be much more important to know the person's effective vocabulary, for example, than it would be to know the full range of words available in the language.

Schemata recognized by McClelland (1951, pp. 239–282) include ideas, values, and social roles. Whereas one learns motives on the basis of the typical degree of discrepancy between expectations and occurrences, and traits on the basis of the acts that are consistently rewarded, one learns schemata through cultural assimilation. The particular peculiarities of parents and significant others strongly affect motive and trait learning. In contrast, such things as ideas, values, and social roles are usually determined by the nature of the culture in which the person exists. Ideas, values, and social roles often are communicated rather directly, in verbal terms, with the units of communication being social institutions—e. g., family, school, and church—rather than individuals per se. McClelland believes that schemata have a general, pervasive influence on the processes of perception, memory, and thinking. Obviously, the possibilities you can imagine, the observables salient enough for you to notice, the things you will remember, and even the thoughts you can have will be limited and influenced by the set of ideas, values, and social roles you have internalized.

INTERRELATIONSHIP OF MOTIVES, TRAITS, AND SCHEMATA. Although the identification of three distinct classes of peripheral characteristics may strike you as a breath of fresh air at this point, following all the fuzziness you have encountered in previously considered theories, it is probably not entirely clear that motives, traits, and schemata are all that different. Perhaps you will understand McClelland's meaning better if you consider the nature of the presumed relationship among these three entities, for related they surely must be.

You will recall that a motive's primary characteristic is intent; a motive is a directional force. In contrast, a trait is primarily a basis for habit, or performing as one performed before in a similar situation. Finally, a schema is primarily a cognitive unit referring to some aspect of the definitions shared by people in the same society. Though ideas, values, and roles often include prescriptions for action, the schema is not intentional in any strict sense.

Now I shall take a concrete example from the achievement domain and present some distinctions. Recall that a motive is defined as the arousal of an intention by a cue. The perception of aspects of the environment as cues to the presence of a success-failure situation requires the presence of achievement schemata in the form of ideas concerning achievement. But one could certainly have such achievement schemata without also possessing an achievement motive. If one had no such motive, one would be able to recognize the existence of an achievement situation and simply not participate in it. But if the achievement motive were also present, one would get involved in the sense of attempting to bring about success or avoid failure. So the trigger for the achievement motive is the achievement schemata. The content of these schemata can influence where and when the achievement motive is displayed, though the vigor and imaginativeness of attempts to reach success or avoid failure are clearly determined by the intensity of the motive itself. The eventual effectiveness of attempts to reach success or avoid failure is a function of achievement traits. Such traits are habits of persistence and are not, strictly speaking, a product of motive intensity or achievement schemata; they are separate entities. For example, though the trait of persistence could serve an achievement need, the trait could function quite separately from that need as well. We can generalize from this extended example to make the following preliminary statement: Schemata form the general frame of reference for living and determine the concrete possibilities available for each life; motives are the basis for personal rather than culturally shared intentions and determine the content and intensity of directional activity; traits form the style of a person's functioning and determine his or her habitual behaviors.

Before turning to the contents of these three kinds of characteristics, I would like to point out a problem concerning the relationship of the core and peripheral levels of personality in McClelland's theory. Because traits, schemata, and motives lie at the peripheral level of personality, they should all spring from the interaction of the core tendency with the external world. But the core tendency as described by McClelland is really relevant only to the development of motives. Traits and schemata seem to be formed in some way other than as the result of maximizing small discrepancies between expectations

and occurrences while minimizing large discrepancies. McClelland's statements about the learning of traits and schemata suggest other assumptions about the core of personality that go beyond the one already presented. Because he is not explicit about this, however, one can do little but live with the confusion resulting from the inconsistency between his core and peripheral statements. I will nonetheless consider the usefulness for understanding observable behavior of not only motives but also traits and schemata, even though the latter two concepts currently exist as disinherited from the core.

CONTENT OF MOTIVES, TRAITS, AND SCHEMATA. Having recognized this confusion, we can turn to the content of motives, traits, and schemata. For motives, McClelland adopts the list offered by Murray (1938), which includes the needs for achievement, affiliation, power, succorance, and change. There are 40 such needs, which are fairly concrete and mirror people's commonsense, everyday concerns. If you ask people what motivates them, they very likely will say that they want achievement, affiliation, power, and so forth. McClelland offers no particular list of traits, being inclined to accept whatever habits other psychologists may think are important. Finally, McClelland suggests two kinds of content for schemata. The first refers to ideas and values and constitutes an endorsement of the classification offered by Spranger (1928), which includes ideas and values concerning economic, aesthetic, social, political, religious, and purely theoretical realms of life. The second refers to social roles, and here McClelland endorses the classification offered by Linton (1945), which breaks down roles into those involving age, sex, family position, occupation, and reference-group membership. Different behavior is expected from people with different roles and ages. Fathers, sons, sisters, brothers, aunts, and cousins differ from one another, as do lawyers from laborers, Methodists from Muslims. McClelland analyzes the content of roles as culturally patterned sets of traits. Indeed, McClelland's (1951) definition of role is as "a cluster of traits (or pattern of behavior) which serves as the culturally normal or modal solution to recurrent, usually social problems peculiar to a particular status or position in society" (p. 293). Although roles are clusters of traits, the role characteristic is something that expresses a rather universalistic social problem and cultural solution. In contrast, traits that are not parts of roles are learned on the basis of experience peculiar to the family environment in which a person is reared, and they express no cultural or societal universal. Actually, it seems to me that roles must also include motives insofar as the regular and recurrent accomplishment of certain goals is necessary to maintain a culturally defined position. I will discuss this implication of the schema concept in Chapter 11.

One of the most striking things about the content McClelland gives motives, traits, and schemata is its eclecticism, exemplifying the point that consistency theories tend to be eclectic with regard to personality content. This tendency stems from minimal assumptions concerning the content and inevitability of inherent human attributes. As already indicated, McClelland includes two peripheral concepts—schemata and traits—not derived from the core tendency he offers. Similarly, we can see that the content attributed to the three peripheral characteristics does not stem from the overall fabric of his theory. Instead, McClelland has culled from the available psychological, anthropological, and sociological literature the lists that seem most complete and least tied to any particular theoretical assumptions. His theorizing about content is so eclectic that McClelland does not even consider whether the implications of the lists endorsed for schemata, traits, and motives are consistent. I mean to suggest not that they are inconsistent but that such consistency is not important to him.

Actually, McClelland's theory is, in terms of precision concerning peripheral characteristics, virtually a model for the personologist. Not only has he provided careful definitions of his three concepts—definitions that at least attempt to clarify the similarities and differences among them—but he has also offered guidelines for measuring their content. The technical way of

putting this is that McClelland has offered *operational definitions* to supplement his theoretical definitions. Operational definitions detail what operations you must perform in order to determine the existence and intensity of what you want to know about. An operational definition of body temperature, for example, is the mercury level on the calibrated scale of a thermometer. Of all the personologists considered thus far, McClelland and Murray stand alone in having attempted this tedious, difficult, and indispensable step in theorizing. Without operational definitions of peripheral characteristics, you, as the user of the theory, can never be sure whether what you are working with is what the theorist intended in his or her lofty, abstract writing.

I cannot hope to give a detailed accounting of the actual nature of the operational definitions here, but some examples should give you the flavor of what has been offered. Because a motive involves the intent to reach a currently absent goal, it is only reasonable that one not measure it under conditions in which the environment is so structured and familiar as to call up old, habitual ways of doing things or in which the socially proper things to do are so clear that only those ways of functioning will be elicited. The attempt to be socially appropriate is based on behavior determined by schemata, and habitual behavior is determined by traits. Motives refer more to very personal desires. It is therefore thoroughly understandable that McClelland would specify fantasy as the raw material in which to search for motives. To elicit fantasy in some sort of standardized way, he specifies a set of ambiguous pictures of people to be presented to subjects with instructions to compose stories about what has happened, is happening, and will happen. The pictures are ambiguous enough and the task sufficiently unusual that one may be reasonably sure that neither traits nor schemata will be major determinants of behavior. The stories are then scored for the presence or absence of motives.

Take as an example the need for achievement. The operational definition of this need is *competition with a standard of excellence,* with the approach form of it stressing hope for success and the avoidance form stressing fear of failure. So when scoring the approach form, one looks for aspects of the story indicating the concrete wish to succeed, anticipation of success, the overcoming of obstacles to success, and positive affect in connection with statements of competition with a standard of excellence. In contrast, when scoring the avoidance form, one looks for the concrete wish to avoid failure, worry about failure, specification of seemingly insurmountable obstacles to success, and negative affect in connection with statements of competition with a standard of excellence. McClelland et al. (1953) have formalized what I have said in terms of scoring rules for imaginative stories.

If one were interested not in the need for achievement but in schemata concerning achievement that might exist in the person, one would stress what the person says in describing himself or herself when the situation is publicly defined as relevant to achievement. McClelland suggests the operational format of a set of achievement-related questions that people answer as true or not true of themselves. McClelland is perfectly willing to have schemata measured by any standard questionnaire concerning values, such as the Allport-Vernon-Lindzey (1951) test called *A Study of Values*. This test attempts to measure Spranger's value orientations on the basis of true-false questions. You can by now predict what McClelland would specify as the operations with which to measure achievement traits. He would put people into familiar situations and observe the pervasiveness of such behaviors as persistence. He would not ask people whether they are persistent, or scrutinize their fantasy, but rather watch them perform in familiar, achievement-related situations, such as studying for tests.

Finally, you will recall that many personologists organize their proposed peripheral characteristics into personality types. Like Allport and Murray, McClelland has not gone far in this direction. The concrete traits, schemata,

and motives he specifies remain more or less separate from one another. He has told us how to measure them, so we could do just that and let their interrelationships emerge from our empirical work. But there certainly is little theoretical specification of probable interrelationships. This too is understandable in a consistency theorist, who would have little reason for predicting one organization of peripheral characteristics as more likely than another. About as far as McClelland (1961) has gone in specifying personality types is summarizing in theoretical terms the empirical fruits of a large-scale research attempt to determine the influence of achievement motives, and, to a lesser extent, achievement traits and schemata, on the behavior of people taken as individuals and as members of a society. I will discuss his research in Chapter 12.

A FINAL WORD . . . .

I hope you are grasping the full extent of the difference between the consistency model and the two models considered in previous chapters. The cognitive dissonance version of the consistency model emphasizes neither the conflict and defensiveness paramount in conflict theories nor the inexorable directionality and self-transcendence of fulfillment theories. In contrast, cognitive dissonance theories of personality limit core and developmental assumptions to those involved in general notions of learning somewhat detached from the specifics of inborn content and family interaction.

The major thrust of cognitive dissonance theories of personality concerns the behavior-shaping effects of anticipational accuracy and inaccuracy in the interaction between the person and the social and physical environment. In conceptualizing this concern, these theories are rather eclectic.

THE CONSISTENCY MODEL: ACTIVATION VERSION

The cognitive dissonance version of the consistency model considers the match or mismatch among cognitive elements, typically expectations and perceptions of events. In contrast, the activation version of the consistency model considers the match or mismatch between customary and actual levels of activation or tension. As in all consistency positions, content is relatively unimportant. The theory of Fiske and Maddi is virtually the only activation position that has elaborated its relevance for personality.

FISKE AND MADDI'S POSITION

Donald W. Fiske (born in Massachusetts, 1916), after an early education at Harvard, received his Ph.D. in psychology from the University of Michigan in 1948. At Harvard and in the Office of Strategic Services during World War II, Fiske came under the influence of Murray, Allport, and White. In a career of teaching and research in university settings, his major interests have

been measurement of personality variables and understanding the conditions under which human behavior shows variability.

Salvatore R. Maddi (born in New York City, 1933), received his Ph.D. in psychology from Harvard in 1960. At Harvard, he studied under Allport, Bakan, McClelland, Murray, and White. In a career involving teaching and research in the university setting and a clinical and consulting practice, Maddi has been predominantly interested in personality change, creativity, stress-related disorders, and the need for variety. His other theoretical commitment, to existential psychology, has already been covered in Chapter 6. Maddi's collaboration with Fiske began in 1960 and over the years produced the core and developmental statements described here. The peripheral statement, however, is Maddi's own.

Fiske and Maddi's Core Statement

Activation theory is a development in psychology that has arisen from several subfields of the discipline. Understandably enough, given the complexity of the personality field, it has been among the last and least affected by activation theorizing. But Fiske and Maddi (1961; Maddi & Propst, 1971) offer a version of activation theory that is not only more systematic and complete than most but also is quite relevant to personality. The cognitive dissonance version of consistency theory emphasizes the discrepancy or match between two cognitive elements, usually an expectation or belief on the one hand and a perception of some event on the other. In the activation theory offered by Fiske and Maddi, discrepancy is also the major determinant of behavior. However, the discrepancy is not between two cognitive elements but between the level of activation that people are accustomed to and the level of activation they actually have at a given moment. A discrepancy or gap between the customary and actual levels of activation always produces behavior that aims to reduce it. Therefore, Fiske and Maddi's position exemplifies the pure consistency model.

THE CORE TENDENCY. Let me plunge into a discussion of the position by stating its core tendency, which is that *persons will attempt to maintain the level of activation to which they are accustomed (i. e., that is characteristic of them).* To understand the meaning of this core tendency, recognize that *activation* refers to your level of excitement, or alertness, or energy. Try to remember times when what was going on excited you more or less than usual or required more or less alertness and energy than was customary. If you found the situation either too exciting or too dull and tried to do something about it, or found the alertness and energy demands too great or too slight and tried to do something about them, you have within yourself a basis for intuitive understanding of the core tendency offered by Fiske and Maddi.

THE CORE CHARACTERISTICS. According to Fiske and Maddi (1961, p. 14), activation is a neuropsychological concept, referring on the psychological side to the common core of meaning in such terms as alertness, attentiveness, tension, and subjective excitement and on the

neural side to the state of excitation in a postulated center of the brain. It is clear that on the psychological side, Fiske and Maddi are concerned with a general quality of organismic excitation similar to what many other theorists refer to as *tension.* Fiske and Maddi attempt to make this view more plausible by exploring its neural substrate. On the neural side, they suggest that the *reticular formation,* a large subcortical area of the brain, is the focus of activation. In this, they are following many precedents (e.g., Jasper, 1958; O'Leary & Coben, 1958; Samuels, 1959) and attempting to integrate psychological and physiological levels of theorizing.

Having offered a rough definition of activation, Fiske and Maddi turn to the determinants of this state of excitation. They postulate three dimensions and three sources of stimulation, subsuming all these activation-influencing characteristics under the term *impact.* The three dimensions of stimulation are intensity, meaningfulness, and variation. *Intensity,* defined in terms of physical energy, is an obvious attribute of stimulation. A loud noise is more intense than a soft noise. *Meaningfulness* requires more clarification. Generally speaking, any stimulus, to be recognized as such, has to have meaning. However, Fiske and Maddi use meaningfulness in a more restricted sense. They refer primarily to the significance of a stimulus for the experiencing organism. For example, the word *vase* has less meaningfulness for most people than do the words *fire* or *love.* In considering *variation,* Fiske and Maddi make a number of points. First, variation refers to a state in which the current stimulus differs from that which preceded it—differs in intensity, meaningfulness, or both. So, one aspect is *change.* Another aspect of variation is *novelty,* or the state in which the current stimulus is unusual—infrequent in the person's total experience—regardless of how much it differs from the stimulus immediately preceding it. The final aspect of variation is *unexpectedness,* or the state in which the current stimulus deviates from what the person has come to expect regardless of whether it constitutes a change or is unusual in an overall sense.

Talking about the dimensions of stimulation that can influence activation prompts a consideration of the sources of stimulation, if for no other reason than completeness. The three sources stipulated by Fiske and Maddi are exteroceptive, interoceptive, and cortical. *Exteroceptive stimulation* involves chemical, electrical, or mechanical excitation of those sense organs sensitive to events in the external world. In contrast, *interoceptive stimulation* refers to such excitation of those sense organs sensitive to events within the body. These two sources of stimulation are already well known and require no justification. But it is unusual to consider *cortical stimulation*. Most psychologists who consider physiological events in the cortex tend to see them as reflecting stimulation from other places in the body or from the outside world. What Fiske and Maddi are suggesting is that the cortex itself be considered one of the actual sources of stimulation, which is logically sound because they consider the brain's locus of activation to be the reticular formation, a subcortical center. That they are possibly on sound anatomical and physiological ground is suggested by the recent discovery that the cortex not only receives but sends nerve fibers to the reticular formation. Hebb (1955) has suggested that the fibers sent to the reticular formation by the cortex may constitute the physiological substrate for understanding "the immediate drive properties of cognitive processes."

Fiske and Maddi make activation level a direct function of impact. *Impact* is, in turn, some direct function of the moment-to-moment intensity, meaningfulness, and variation of stimulation from interoceptive, exteroceptive, and cortical sources. Activation, impact, and the dimensions and sources of impact, being common to all persons, are core characteristics of personality.

Thus far, the theorizing of Fiske and Maddi may seem too complex and removed from phenomena of psychological significance to be useful to the personologist. However, completeness in theorizing usually requires such complexity and often proves useful in fostering understanding. Perhaps you have noticed, for example, that

the discrepancy between expectation and occurrence stressed by McClelland and Kelly is represented as merely one aspect of variation by Fiske and Maddi. McClelland and Kelly make unexpectedness the basic determinant of tension or anxiety. Fiske and Maddi take this further in their broad definition of stimulus characteristics producing impact.

All this has concerned the *actual level of activation,* defined as the total impact of stimulation. In contrast, the *customary level of activation* refers to what feels normal or usual on the basis of accumulated past experience. Fiske and Maddi assume that the levels of activation a person experiences over the course of many days tend to be fairly similar. After all, the regularities and continuities of living should result in day-to-day similarities in the intensity, meaningfulness, and variation of stimulation from various sources. Over time, the person should come to experience a particular level of activation as normal or usual for a particular part of the day. These customary levels of activation can be roughly measured by averaging the actual activation curves for a person over many days. Such measurement was performed by Kleitman (1939), who found a regularity called the *cycle of existence,* with a single major rise and fall during the waking period. After waking, humans typically show an increasing degree of alertness, then a relatively long period with a gradual rise, then a gradual decline, a sharper decline toward drowsiness, and finally a return to the sleeping state. A number of physiological variables, such as heart rate and body temperature, follow the same course (Kleitman & Ramsaroop, 1948; Sidis, 1908). Fiske and Maddi assume that the cycle of existence is the customary curve of activation. Whatever differences in shape the customary level of activation may take from person to person, everyone possesses it. Thus, it is a core characteristic of personality.

MATCHES AND MISMATCHES. Once one has postulated an actual and a customary level of activation, it is almost natural to consider the match or mismatch between them to be important. And this is just what Fiske and Maddi do.

Their core tendency refers to the person's attempt to maintain actual activation at the level customary for that time of the day. If actual activation deviates from customary level, *impact-modifying behavior* is instituted. Two kinds of deviation are possible. When the actual activation level is above that which is customary, *impact-decreasing behavior* occurs; when the actual activation level is below that which is customary, *impact-increasing behavior* results. Note that impact-decreasing behavior must involve attempts to decrease the intensity, meaningfulness, or variation of stimulation from interoceptive, exteroceptive, or cortical sources and that impact-increasing behavior does the opposite.

Fiske and Maddi are classed as consistency theorists because they consider the overall directionality of living to be the search for a match between actual and customary levels of activation. In clarifying why people show the core tendency, Fiske and Maddi (1961) assume that the coincidence of actual and customary levels of activation is experienced as a state of well-being, whereas discrepancies between them lead to negative affect—the greater the discrepancy, the greater the affect. People attempt to reduce discrepancies between actual and customary levels of activation because they want to avoid the discomfort of negative affect. They experience success in this attempt as positive affect.

Fiske and Maddi's theory is a pure consistency position because the ideal state is a complete absence of discrepancy between actual and customary levels of activation. There is no notion, as in McClelland's variant position, that a small degree of discrepancy is a positive thing. Furthermore, Fiske and Maddi address the idea that positions such as Kelly's are limited because they do not give importance to avoidance of boredom. Fiske and Maddi theorize that the customary level of activation can be undershot as well as overshot by actual activation. When it is undershot, the person will actively seek out stimulation of greater variation, meaningfulness, and intensity. In part, this means he or she will seek out unexpected events. This property of Fiske and Maddi's position is associated with two others that deserve mention. First, those

theorists do not make tension reduction the aim of all functioning, as the other pure consistency theorists do. Fiske and Maddi agree with McClelland that some of the person's functioning aims to reduce tension or activation whereas some aims to increase it. Second, they assume that everyday, "normal" situations involve some variation (change, novelty, unexpectedness) as well as some intensity and meaningfulness. This assumption is implicit in the notion that the customary level of activation is high enough at all times during the day to be undershot by the actual level of activation. To Fiske and Maddi, the assumption in other pure consistency positions that an absence of unexpectedness is the ideal situation seems inconsistent with everyday life. Fiske and Maddi agree with McClelland that the human being would be bored in a situation of total certainty and predictability because its impact would be too low to produce activation that came up to customary levels.

Fiske and Maddi's theory is a good example of what is called a *homeostatic position*. In other words, whenever there is a deviation from some type of norm—in this case, the customary level of activation—there is an attempt, which gets stronger the greater the deviation, to return to the norm. In psychology, all tension reduction theories tend to be considered homeostatic. Thus, the theories of Freud, Angyal, Bakan, Rank, Kelly, and Festinger are considered homeostatic positions, although it strikes me that these theories use only half the homeostatic model, because the norm they assume is a minimum state. This means that the norm can be exceeded but not undershot, because it is a state of least excitation. Fiske and Maddi's theory seems, by comparison with the others, a true homeostatic position in that the norm is some quantity greater than minimum and less than maximum. Once a theory such as Fiske and Maddi's is established, the partial inapplicability to the other theories of the concept of homeostasis becomes apparent.

I think a summary might be useful here. The tendency of people to maintain the level of activation that is characteristic or customary for them is the core tendency of personality. The five core characteristics of personality associated with this tendency are actual level of activation, customary level of activation, discrepancy between the two, impact-increasing behavior, and impact-decreasing behavior. These concepts bear the same invariant relationships to one another in all people. To be sure, there are many sources of individual differences—customary levels of activation may vary, for example, and there may be many different strategies for increasing or decreasing impact—but these are matters of the periphery of personality.

Fiske and Maddi on Development

Fiske and Maddi do not consider the customary curve of activation to be present at birth; rather, it is probably formed out of experience. Certainly, they suggest the possibility that genetic considerations, presently not well understood, may predispose the person to a customary curve of activation having a particular shape and height. But the accumulated experience of particular levels of activation at specific times of the day is considered the major formative influence on this curve. Thus, the first important influence of the environment on the person is as the major determinant of the characteristic curve of activation. This determination takes place sometime during childhood, though Fiske and Maddi are quite vague on this. In a way, their vagueness is not surprising, for the consistency model gives little attention to the content of experience and of inherent nature. In Kelly and McClelland, only the fact of discrepancy between expectation and occurrence, not the content of the discrepancy, influences behavior. For Fiske and Maddi, only the impact of early stimulation, not its content, has a formative influence. Once you deemphasize the importance of stimulus content and of inherent nature, you have little logical impetus to develop elaborate theories of stages of development during which the content of a person's wishes and the content of reactions from significant others are important.

But Fiske and Maddi do believe that as experience accumulates, as the stimulation patterns of successive days recur, the characteristic curve of activation begins to solidify. Once set, this curve changes little under ordinary circumstances because of the nature of the effects on personality and the experience of the impetus to maintain activation at the characteristic level.

ANTICIPATIONAL AND CORRECTIONAL ATTEMPTS TO MAINTAIN CONSISTENCY. At this point, it is essential to distinguish between correction for discrepancies between actual and characteristic levels of activation that really occur and anticipatory attempts to ensure that such discrepancies will not occur (Maddi & Propst, 1971). I will discuss anticipatory functioning first, because it is basic to understanding why the characteristic curve of activation does not change once solidified. As experience accumulates, the person learns certain habitual ways of functioning that help preclude large discrepancies between actual and characteristic levels of activation. These ways of influencing the impact of present and future intensity, meaningfulness, and variation of stimulation from interoceptive, exteroceptive, and cortical sources form a large part of the peripheral personality. If peripheral personality is a successful expression of core tendency, the conditions under which the characteristic curve of activation would change are not encountered. The person's range of experience and activities is selected and maintained in order to yield degrees of impact at various times during the day that result in actual levels of activation that would match characteristic levels. If anything, the longer the person lives, the more deeply entrenched his or her characteristic curve of activation will be. Only if the person were forced to be in prolonged circumstances of unusual impact levels—for example, the battlefield—would he or she encounter conditions likely to shift the characteristic curve of activation.

It may seem to you that Fiske and Maddi, like Freud, consider personality to be essentially static after childhood, but this is not the case. Although they believe the customary curve of activation remains roughly the same under ordinary circumstances, behavior and personality processes expressing the anticipatory function of the core tendency must actually change in order for this curve to remain steady. This may seem paradoxical, but it is really very simple. One function of the anticipatory processes is to ensure that future levels of activation will not fall below characteristic ones. However, any stimulation, regardless of its initial effect, will lose impact as it is prolonged. We adapt to stimulation if it lasts a long time. A sound that initially seems loud becomes overlooked if it continues long enough. Something initially meaningful becomes ordinary as time goes on. Variation is especially short-lived, for any novel or unexpected stimulus loses so much impact after a while that it may become boring. A great deal of research testifies to the conclusion that the initial impact of stimulation decreases as its experience is prolonged (see Fiske & Maddi, 1961). What this means is that as people live longer and longer, they must continually shift their *anticipatory strategies* for ensuring that future levels of activation will not be too low for comfort. They must constantly broaden their range of activities and interests and become more and more subtle and differentiated in thought and feeling in order to increase the impact of future stimulation. A Jackson Pollack painting might have a low level of impact for you because it seems nothing more than a smear of colors, repetitive at best. But if you increase the subtlety of your cognitive and affective processes, you will be much more sensitive to the same painting when you see it later. Then it may have great impact, for you will perceive the many strands of paint built up layer upon layer and the subtle differences there. Whether or not you like Jackson Pollack, I think you can see what is meant by ever increasing cognitive and emotional differentiation as a basis for ensuring that activation will not fall too low in the future. To try to see the universe in a grain of sand is to make a cognitive, affective elaboration of experience to offset its natural tendency to lose impact when prolonged or reexperienced.

But to properly maintain characteristic activation, the person must also develop anticipatory strategies to ensure that future impact will not be higher than the characteristic level. This is especially necessary to balance off the possible,

though unintended, side effects of anticipatory attempts to keep activation from falling below the characteristic level. When you try to ensure this by becoming more cognitively, affectively, and actionally differentiated, you cannot precisely predict where your attempts will end. If you are forever intensifying your search for new and more meaningful and intense experiences, you increase the likelihood of precipitating a crisis in which your ability to keep what happens to you within manageable limits will be threatened. You might unwittingly precipitate a state of impact so great that it brings about an uncomfortably high level of activation. If this were to happen, according to the theory you would scramble to correct the high level of activation. But it is inefficient to wait until activation is already too high before acting, just as it is inefficient to rely on correction of levels of activation that are already too low.

Progressively greater cognitive, affective, and action-oriented differentiation is the anticipatory technique for maintaining activation, but what is the technique for keeping activation low enough? Maddi and Propst (1971) indicate that this strategy is the progressive increase in principles and techniques for integrating the elements of cognition, affect, and action that one has differentiated to ensure that activation will not be too low. The essence of integration is the organization of the differentiated elements into broad categories of function or significance. Integrative processes permit you to see how a given experience is similar in meaning and intensity to other experiences, regardless of how it may differ in terms of the more concrete analysis that expresses differentiation. There is no conflict between the processes of *differentiation* and *integration*. No matter how sensitive you become to the Jackson Pollack painting on the basis of differentiation processes, you can also exercise your integrative processes to place it in the overall scheme of his work, the work of contemporaries, and the history of art. Integrative processes function to ensure that activation levels experienced in the future will not be wildly high without compromising one's sensitivity to the need to avoid drastically low activation levels.

As you can tell, Fiske and Maddi offer a picture of personality in which continual change occurs through the life span, change in the service of ensuring a minimum of discrepancy between actual and customary levels of activation. The change involves progressively greater differentiation and integration, or what is also known as *psychological growth*. With varying emphasis, this notion appears in actualization and perfection versions of the fulfillment model. Though not characteristic of psychosocial conflict theories, it does play some role in intrapsychic conflict theories. Fiske and Maddi's position seems advantageous, because it explains psychological growth rather than simply assuming it.

Now you can understand the significance of *correctional strategies*. First, it is obvious that a correction for discrepancy between actual and characteristic levels of activation is necessary only when anticipatory processes have failed. For the adult, correctional attempts have the quality of emergency maneuvers (Maddi & Propst, 1971). Simply put, Maddi and Propst believe that *impact-decreasing behavior* operates to distort reality in the sense of screening out stimuli. *Impact-increasing behavior* equally distorts reality but does it by adding something that is not really there to the stimulation. These sensitizing and desensitizing aspects of correctional behavior come close to one aspect of the traditional meaning of defense. But one must be careful to recognize that Maddi and Propst do not mean to imply that the person actively debars from awareness those impulses and wishes that form a real but dangerous part of him or her. They merely assume a mechanism for exaggerating or underestimating the real impact of stimulation. In this, they come closer than any other consistency theorists to emphasizing a concept of defense.

In summary, Fiske and Maddi's position is a consistency theory that focuses on the discrepancy between actual and customary activation rather than on the accuracy of prediction. As worded, it is broad enough to subsume other consistency positions having this latter focus. Fiske and Maddi conceptualize behavior and personality as oriented partly toward tension reduction and partly toward tension increase. In this, their approach resembles McClelland's, though theirs is a pure rather than variant consistency position. Like other consistency theorists, Fiske and Maddi include an eclectic content in that their conceptualization of people and society includes little that is necessary and immutable. They believe that the essential features of the core of personality remain fixed but peripheral personality changes continually throughout life to satisfy the requirements of the core tendency. This continual change moves in the direction of simultaneous increases in differentiation and integration, or psychological growth.

Maddi on the Periphery of Personality

Elaborating on the core theorizing he and Fiske have offered, Maddi and his students have developed a view of the periphery of personality, including an emphasis on both peripheral characteristics and their organization into personality types. Although the activation view of the periphery of personality has an unfinished quality, it is a recent development within personology and has therefore profited from the earlier theoretical efforts of other personologists.

To understand the derivation of peripheral characteristics and personality types from the core aspects of activation theory, you must keep in mind three basic kinds of similarity and difference among people (Maddi & Propst, 1971). The first consideration is the shape of the characteristic curve of activation. Here the core statement of similarity among people is that they all have such a curve, which takes the general shape of Kleitman's cycle of existence, discussed earlier. You will recall that activation customarily rises sharply after waking, increases gradually to some point, declines gradually, and finally declines more rapidly as sleep approaches. But Maddi and Propst (1971) hold out the possibility of differences among people concerning the sharpness of rise and fall and the point during the day at which the shift from rising to falling takes place. Individual differences in the shape of the customary curve of activation may well help explain so-called night people and day people. Surely we have all encountered people who are most alert and effective early in the morning or late at night, with the middle of the day being somewhat indifferently placed between the two extremes. People who have an unusually high early morning or late night characteristic level of activation should, in comparison with the average person, show more intense, impact-increasing behavior in the early morning or late evening, respectively. Unfortunately, Maddi and Propst do not follow up on this intriguing suggestion. Made in passing, their suggestion represents one of the only references by personologists considered in this book to the possible importance of differences among people in the patterning of activities during a single day.

The second basic consideration of similarity and difference among people involves the average height of a person's characteristic curve of activation. The core statement is that everybody has a characteristic curve of activation that varies within a range of values between zero and an absolute maximum. But the statement of individual differences, leading to a position on the periphery of personality, is that the range of values covered by any person's activation curve need not be the same as that for another person. These differences can be pinpointed by comparing the averages of each person's range of characteristic activation values over the course of several days. This brings us to the basic distinction offered by Maddi and Propst (1971) in developing a typology of peripheral personality: the distinction between *high-activation* and *low-activation* types. At the most obvious level, this distinction refers to the assumption that the characteristic curve of activation is higher for some people than for others. But if you recall the earlier discussion of Fiske and Maddi's position on the personality core, you will recognize that this distinction must subsume many points of difference between these two kinds of people. High-activation people spend most of their time and effort *pursuing stimulus impact* to keep their actual activation levels from falling too low; low-activation people spend most of their time and effort *avoiding impact* to keep their actual activation level from getting too high.

To obtain a more concrete understanding of the peripheral personalities of these two kinds of people, we must consider the third basic kind of similarity and difference among people, which involves the anticipatory and correctional techniques used for maintaining actual activation at the characteristic level. At the core level, it is assumed that all people are similar in that they employ anticipational and correctional techniques for increasing or decreasing stimulus impact to minimize discrepancies between actual and customary levels of activation. But the theory also provides a basis for understanding individual differences in these anticipational and correctional techniques by explicating the many contributors to impact. You may recall that impact is considered a joint function of the intensity, meaningfulness, and variety of stimulation from interoceptive, cortical, and exteroceptive sources. Impact, of course, determines the actual activation level.

Maddi and Propst (1971) have outlined some of the implications of the definition of impact for differences among people in peripheral personality. First, a person may favor one of the three attributes of stimulation (i.e., intensity, meaningfulness, variety) in his or her anticipational and correctional strategies. The high- and low-activation personality types are each subdivided into three parts that reflect this distinction concerning preference for particular stimulus attributes. High-activation people who favor intensity, meaningfulness, or variety are considered as having an *approach motive* for intensity, meaningfulness, or variety, respectively. Low-activation people for whom intensity, meaningfulness, or variety is most salient are thought to have an *avoidance motive* for intensity, meaningfulness, or variety, respectively. The terms approach and avoidance motivation are used in much the same manner as in McClelland's position, with the approach motives often called needs and the avoidance motives fears.

AN ACTIVATION TYPOLOGY. At this point, it should be clear that Maddi and Propst offer a typology of peripheral personality that includes three high- and three low-activation types, with the three subdivisions of each major type bearing content resemblances. So, for example, *high-activation-need-for-meaningfulness persons* would spend most of their time and effort in instrumental behavior aimed at increasing the meaningfulness of their experience, with this concrete directionality having the overall function of keeping their actual activation levels from falling too low. Just the opposite would be true for *low-activation-fear-of-meaningfulness persons*. Orientations toward particular stimulus attributes are considered motivational because these attributes can actually augment or diminish impact. In the terminology of this book, the three approach and three avoidance motives represent peripheral characteristics.

To gain further understanding of the activation position on peripheral personality, you must be presented with additional distinctions. One has to do with the favored source of stimulation. Here Maddi, Propst, and Feldinger (1965) collapse the three distinctions offered by Fiske and Maddi (1961) into two—the *internal* and the *external*. As the distinction between cortical and interoceptive sources postulated by Fiske and Maddi undoubtedly will be quite hard to make in practice, the simplification suggested by Maddi et al. (1965) seems reasonable. In any event, they consider it important to know whether the person is oriented toward internal or external sources of stimulation. This distinction recognizes that one way of regulating impact is to look to sources of stimulation essentially outside the body (anything from thunderclaps or scenery to music or other people), and another way is to focus inside the body (anything from thoughts or daydreams to pains or dizziness). The former orientation is called the *external trait* and the latter the *internal trait*, with the term trait used in the manner of McClelland to emphasize habitual rather than motivational behavior. In finding internal or external stimulation salient, the person is not necessarily raising or lowering impact. The distinction being made is similar to Jung's regarding introversion-extroversion. Only when people begin to manipulate stimulation, be it external or internal, by pursuing or avoiding intensity,

meaningfulness, or variety, do they show the goal-directedness of motivation.

The external and internal traits are simply habits of emphasis and, of course, represent peripheral characteristics. The distinction of preferred source of stimulation must be made within each of the six personality types already mentioned, raising the overall number of kinds of people considered to 12.

As if this were not complicated enough, Maddi, Charlens, Maddi, and Smith (1962) offer yet another distinction that must be taken into account in understanding the activation position on peripheral personality: the distinction between the *active* and the *passive trait*, which recalls Allport's distinction between proactive and reactive functioning. People with the active trait have the habit of initiative, such that they influence the external and even internal stimulus environment, whereas people with the passive trait are habitually indolent, permitting themselves to be influenced by internal and external stimuli over which they have no subjective control. The activeness-passiveness distinction is especially important in understanding differences among people in the proportion of their time spent in *anticipational* as opposed to frankly *correctional* behaviors.

Active people will anticipate their activation requirements well, because they are self-reliant and initiating. We should expect to see in such people the fruits of anticipational functioning. As I will elaborate later, these fruits include such things as psychological differentiation and integration. In contrast, passive people will not anticipate their activation requirements well, and will therefore frequently have to correct for actual activation levels that have already become too high or fallen too low. There will be a "last-ditch-stand" quality to the passive person that Maddi and Propst (1971) suggest involves distorting reality. Although the activeness-passiveness distinction is not firmly attached to the rest of activation theory, Maddi, Charlens, Maddi, and Smith (1962) seem to consider it important, and hence you should too, recognizing that it represents an inconsistency in theorizing. I noted a similar inconsistency in McClelland's peripheral theorizing and give this one the same interpretation. Consistency theorists deemphasize core assumptions involving specified content to such a degree that they tend to be eclectic at the peripheral level. Nonetheless, the distinction as to activeness-passiveness must be made within each of the 12 personality types we already have, making a staggering total of 24 in all!

Lest you rush to criticize activation theory too harshly for postulating such a large number of personality types, let me make several points. First, some theorists, such as Allport and Kelly, apparently are willing to entertain an *unlimited* number of personality types, such is their emphasis on individuality. Furthermore, some theories, such as those of McClelland, Murray, and Erikson, may end up with quite a sizable number of personality types when their peripheral-level theorizing becomes complete and explicit enough for us to entertain a count. After all, Murray and McClelland have postulated a huge number of peripheral characteristics, and Erikson has only sketched out a typology, not bothering to consider the subtypes implicit in his theorizing. In this context, activation theory can at least say that only 24 types are likely given the nature and number of its core-level assumptions. And this brings me to a final point, which is that the actual number of types considered important by activation theorists may well dwindle as time goes on. After all, the theory has rarely been used in practice, and there has been little opportunity for the relevant empirical evidence to ride herd on the play of reason.

HIGH-ACTIVATION TYPES WITH THE ACTIVE TRAIT. Because my presentation of the activation typology has been very abstract, I would not be surprised if you found it lacking in vividness. Let me therefore try to describe the types a little more fully. In this description, you will also gain insight into the kinds of behavior the peripheral characteristics and typology are meant to explain. Most of the description that follows will indeed concern the kinds of observable phenomena that activation theorists feel it is important to explain.

High-activation persons with active and external traits will be "go-getters," seeking out challenges to meet in the physical and social environments. They will be energetic and voracious in all their appetites. Interested in a wide range of tangible events and things, they will be hard to keep up with. Although they will not be especially hampered by pressures toward conformity, they will tend to be insistent on facts, not fancies, and spend little time in rumination or daydreaming. They will be straightforward and not so much complex and subtle as extensively committed and enthusiastic. They will want to encounter people and things continually. If they also have a *high need for meaningfulness,* they will pursue causes and problems—as statespeople, businesspeople, or journalists rather than scholars. But if they have a *high need for intensity,* they may pursue action and tumult per se, as athletes, soldiers, or bon vivants. And if they have a *high need for variety,* they will show curiosity about causes and mechanisms governing people and things, as adventurers, explorers, or world travelers.

High-activation persons with active and internal traits will show little outward evidence of the pursuit of impact. Perhaps the most one would notice externally is a wealth of knowledge and similar fruits of an active orientation toward internal processes. These people will be thinkers and daydreamers, responding to the challenges posed by the limitations of mind and body with little regard for the affairs of the outside world. They will be subtle and complex, showing depth and considerable cognitive and emotional differentiation. They will not be especially social, though they may have some close, intimate friends. In general, they will not be interested in the obvious, surface manifestations of people and things. If they also have a *high need for meaningfulness,* they will lead the life of the mind, engaging in scholarly, ruminatory, philosophical pursuits. If instead they have a *high need for intensity,* they will pursue sensations and emotions, perhaps as poets and lovers. Should they have a *high need for variety,* however, they will strive for novelty and originality in some sort of creative or imaginative endeavor.

LOW-ACTIVATION TYPES WITH THE ACTIVE TRAIT. In sharp contrast are the personality types involving low activation. *Low-activation persons with active and external traits* will be the eternal conservationists, bent on heading off social and physical disorganization and conflict through negotiation, control, and integrative attempts. They will tend to be conformists and advocates of stability at any cost. Though reasonably energetic, they will tend to be simple in their tastes and involvements. If they also have a *high fear of meaningfulness,* they will express their organizational and integrational interest in a manner involving the simplification of problems and the avoidance of ambiguities. Should they have a *high fear of intensity* instead, they will tend to exert a dampening effect on vigorous, potentially disorganized external conditions, perhaps becoming efficiency experts. If they have a *high fear of variety,* they will seek to force routine on the environment, preferring the familiar and the predictable to the new.

Low-activation persons with active and internal traits will be somewhat different. They too will be conservationists, but with special emphasis on their own organisms. In other words, they will be advocates of the golden mean, taking care to avoid excesses and indulgences of any kind. They will avoid putting any kind of strain on themselves, be it a pleasant or unpleasant experience. Their personalities will be simple, uncomplex, devoid of inconsistencies—in short, integrated and dependable. If they have a *high fear of meaningfulness,* they will show a notable absence of detailed and diverse thoughts and daydreams, tending instead toward stable and recurring cognitive themes with the function of rendering any given experience similar to what has gone before. If they have a *high fear of intensity,* they will have an ascetic emphasis about them, naturally avoiding sensation for its own sake. And if they have a *high fear of variety,* they will force themselves to function consistently and stably, giving a picture of dependability and constancy devoid of flamboyance.

NOTES ON IDEAL AND NONIDEAL TYPES. Thus far, you have seen the personality types that include the *active trait.* As you can see, the various types differ, depending on considerations other than activeness. There is even the implication that the high-activation types are more extraordinary and interesting people than the low-activation types. Certainly the high-activation types are at least more vivid and describable. But high- and low-activation types do not mark the difference between the ideal and nonideal forms of living, which correspond more closely with the distinction between active and passive traits. All personality types involving the *active trait* are rich in *anticipational techniques.* This means that they provide a successful basis for selecting the kinds of experiences that will minimize discrepancies between actual and customary levels of activation. Because people falling into these types do not experience discrepancies often, they feel reasonably satisfied with their lives, experience little frustration and negative affect, and are, in truth, effective in their own ways. You may like the high-activation types better, considering them more interesting and important, but they are no different in their ability to fulfill their view of the good life than the low-activation types. In contrast, the personality types that include the passive trait are somewhat chronically frustrated and ineffective. It is these types that activation theorists consider nonideal.

TYPES WITH THE PASSIVE TRAIT. *High-activation persons with external and passive traits* will have the standards, attitudes, and goals of their counterparts with the active trait but will not have available to them the action habits with which to consistently bring about their own satisfaction. To be sure, they will profess an interest in challenges, show voracious appetites, and have a wide range of interests, but they will do little about them. They will have the same emphasis on concrete, tangible, external realities as their more action-oriented counterparts, but they will have few anticipational techniques for avoiding situations in which their actual levels of activation will be lower than is characteristic for them. About the only anticipational technique they will have is the passive one of preferring situations that have been associated with high impact in the past. But they will have no concrete way of bringing about these preferred situations, depending instead on their "natural" occurrence. They will be dilettantes or consumers rather than producers of impact. With regularity, they will be in the uncomfortable position of correcting for an actual level of activation that is already too low. The emergency nature of this position will contribute to their behavior its defensive or distortional quality (as mentioned earlier). Depending on whether they also have a *high need for meaningfulness, intensity,* or *variety,* the distortional corrections will take the form of artificially augmenting the meaning, intensity, or variety of what is happening in the environment. Something banal may be seen as pregnant with meaning, something simple as complex, and something monotonous as subtly new. Such distortions may sometimes involve paranoid suspiciousness toward other people and the imputation of human or even supernatural attributes to inanimate objects.

Next are the *high-activation persons with internal and passive traits.* These people too will profess many of the interests and activities expressed by their more action-oriented counterparts but without going after what they profess. Their personalities will not show the degree of differentiation and complexity one would expect from hearing them talk. Nor will they actually spend much time in true exploratory and imaginative thought. They will be bored, uninvolved, dissatisfied, and frequently faced with the emergency task of correcting for actual activation levels that have fallen too low. The particular way in which they distort the reality of their internal stimulation to bring about the correction will, as usual, be understandable in terms of whether *the need for meaningfulness, intensity, or variety* is strongest in them. Because the distortion involves internal more than external stimulation, the result of the process may even include such phenomena as hallucinations and delusions.

When people combine *low activation with external and passive traits,* they will sound like conservationists but somehow will be unable to protect themselves from high impact, because they cannot control and order their environment. In their simplicity and ineptitude, they frequently will be swamped by stimulation that leads to excessively high levels of activation. Rather than interact actively with the environment to bend it to their impact requirements, they will renounce it. Their best protection from the regular experience of excessive activation will be to shrink from the world, becoming hermits, tramps, or even schizophrenics. Of course, the quality of the withdrawal from the world will be influenced by whether it is *meaningfulness, intensity,* or *variety* that they especially fear.

Finally, we come to the personality type that includes *low activation with internal and passive traits.* Once again such people will appear to be much like their more active counterparts. They will advocate the golden mean and deplore excesses of any kind. Their personalities will indeed be simple and uncomplex. But they will not be especially effective in anticipating the imminent possibility of excessive impact and, hence, will find themselves faced with the need to reduce it fairly regularly. Being oriented toward internal sources of stimulation, they will tend to employ what are usually called the desensitizing or repressive defenses. In this fashion, they will render ineffective the organismic sources of impact. The particular defenses employed can be at least partially understood on the basis of whether the *fear of meaningfulness, intensity,* or *variety* is especially strong in them.

I hope this brief description has lent some vividness to the personality typology offered by activation theory. There is little more to say except to note that some developmental assumptions have been made in arriving at this typology. It has been assumed that the characteristic curve of activation becomes solidified in early life, after which it changes little. Also, some learned basis has been assumed for the activeness-passiveness and external-internal traits, as well as for the needs for or fears of meaningfulness, intensity, and variety. None of these assumptions are sufficiently detailed in developmental hypotheses by this as yet incomplete personality theory. Some rudimentary developmental statements concerning the characteristic curve of activation exist, and Maddi (1961b) has offered some suggestions concerning how high and low needs for variety may be learned, but nothing more is available.

CLOSING COMMENT ....

It seems clear now that activation theory differs somewhat in emphasis from most kinds of personality theory, although, of course, it is closest to other consistency theories. While activation theory can claim to address some phenomena (e.g., activity level, boredom) not emphasized elsewhere, it might well have difficulty explaining phenomena that are easy for other approaches. For example, it is not immediately apparent how activation theory would explain such universally accepted human events as guilt and self-condemnation.

Nonetheless, activation theory clearly lies in the consistency camp. As such, activation theory adds to the impression begun in Chapter 7 that consistency theories deemphasize content in various ways. At the core level, these theories merely consider the motivational import of matches or mismatches between content characteristics, without the teleological emphasis of conflict and fulfillment approaches; that is, what the person was meant to be or must become. At the developmental level, consistency theories deemphasize developmental stages that build on each other in favor of the simpler view that people learn from their interactions with others and the environment. At the peripheral level, consistency theories either elaborate types and concrete characteristics that express the effects of learning from matches and mismatches, rather than the necessary outcome of teleological assumptions concerning the core, or have little to say about the periphery at all.

The conflict and fulfillment models emerged as mutually exclusive. In other words, if the conflict model is correct, the fulfillment model must be incorrect, and vice versa. The consistency model, however, does not seem to have this kind of relationship to the other two. It is not necessarily true that if the conflict or fulfillment models are correct, the consistency model must be false. This suggests the possibility of intriguing combinations. For example, perhaps activation theory can gain a basis for explaining such phenomena as guilt and self-condemnation by combining with such fulfillment approaches as existential or Adlerian theory. For that matter, perhaps Rogerian fulfillment theory has something to gain in cognitive specificity by combining with Kelly's consistency approach.

PART THREE

ISSUES
AND THEIR
RESOLUTION

By now, we have covered a lot of ground concerning personality theories. We have finished the first step of *comparative analysis,* emerging with the *conflict, fulfillment,* and *consistency* models, each with two versions. It is time now for the second step of *comparative analysis;* that is, abstracting from the differences between the models the *issues* that permeate the personality field, and trying to resolve them. In truth, there are so many different positions regarding personality that the field appears fragmentary rather than

unified. But concerted effort toward
issue resolution on the part of
personologists would certainly have
the effect of integrating them. Issues
can be resolved by reason and empirical
effort. Although the former is hardly
irrelevant in a subject matter as
conceptual as personality, the latter
is bound to be more important in a
scientific endeavor like psychology.
Therefore, I first present the empirical
methods for generating data and results
that are most relevant in personology
to help you in the material on issue
resolution, which completes Part Three.
This material will differentiate between
approaches to resolving personality
issues relevant to theories of the core
and periphery.

METHODS IN PERSONALITY STUDY

Before I take you on this journey through issue resolution, I want you to consider the various ways that empirical information about personality can be obtained. As you will see, researchers use various formalized *methods of inquiry* to test personality theories in a systematic way. Application of these methods helps generate what I called *empirical knowledge* in Chapter 1. But these methods are not just the researcher's inventions; rather, we all use aspects of them informally and unselfconsciously in our everyday lives in trying to make sense out of our experience.

Because the inquiry methods I will cover are often used informally as well as formally, I will alert you to their basis in commonsense, everyday living. But I will also help you to see how they become the systematic procedures of the personality researcher. It is not my aim here to make you technically proficient in the researcher's use of these methods. Instead, I want to prepare you for critically understanding the theorizing and research you will be reading about in subsequent chapters.

COVARIATION — OR WHAT GOES WITH WHAT ......

An important task of the personologist is to determine which aspects of thoughts, feelings, and actions fit together and which do not. Do people who think critically of others also act competitively toward them? Do people who feel unhappy act shyly and think others dislike them? Human behavior is complicated, and the variety of combinations of human thoughts, feelings, and actions is mind-boggling. Systematic inquiry into these combinations has been by no means fully developed.

When we get to know someone, we intuitively try to figure out which of their characteristics go together. We express what we have learned through this process when we describe that person to ourselves or to others. Sarah dresses well, always seems to know what to say, keeps up not only with her studies but with current events; but she is always alone, and no one seems to feel close to her. Harry laughs too loudly, doesn't seem to listen to others, gets angry easily, gets good grades only if he likes the teacher; but he will sit up all night with a friend who is in trouble, and he dreams of being married and having lots of kids. By noting these things, we are observing correspondences, or *covariations,* and trying to see overall patterns.

Personality theorists start in much the same way. Their curiosity about people leads them to observe behavioral covariations in them. When the theorist considers which of these correspondences in behavior are common, the peripheral characteristics of the theory are born. These smallest aspects of personality that can be conceptualized refer to differences among people. Because the theorist tries to make his or her intuitions regarding behavior very explicit and systematic by formulating definitions and complete descriptions, the resulting peripheral characteristics may be termed *rational knowledge.* This peripheral statement in a personality theory is a more systematic version of what we all do out of common sense in trying to understand the people we meet.

Another important task of the personologist *concerns how covarying characteristics cluster* together to form *patterns.* The question of patterns is simply a more complex version of the question of *covariation.* Two characteristics may covary, or be related, at which point they begin to define a pattern, or cluster. Observing that people who are neat also tend to be punctual establishes covariation. When the observation extends not only to neatness and punctuality but also to stubbornness, a sense of justice, and a tendency to feel guilty, one is identifying a pattern in the clustering of several characteristics. Discerning a pattern is even more complex and difficult than establishing covariation.

Techniques for Measuring Covariation

RESEARCH METHOD: CORRELATION. To do research on the peripheral characteristics of personality theory, one must have some way of empirically evaluating which characteristics go together. This is done through statistical procedures that measure correlation.

We can calculate a correlation if we measure two or more peripheral characteristics in the same group of *subjects* (what people studied in research are called). The measurement must be *quantitative;* that is, it must produce numbers ordered by magnitude.

The quantification may be gross, as when we note the simple presence or absence of some characteristic. For example, we may have a test that tells us whether or not undergraduate subjects are neurotic. It may also indicate whether they have grown up in broken or intact homes. Because we have measured these two *dichotomous (either/or) characteristics* in the same group of subjects, we can formulate a contingency table, as illustrated in Table 9-1. It is called a *contingency table* because each of the four cells tells us something about how a subject's score on one characteristic is contingent upon or relates to the other characteristic.

The numbers in the cells are, of course, fictitious. But whatever numbers would actually result in such a study, you could calculate the likelihood that there was a meaningful empirical relationship between the two characteristics. The statistic commonly used with data of the sort shown in Table 9-1 is the *chi-square,* which gets larger as the difference between the cells in the table increases.

The numbers used in Table 9-1 show that the two pairs of diagonal cells differ appreciably. This pattern of results is called a *positive relationship,* indicating that the presence of one characteristic is associated with the presence of

TABLE 9-1   Contingency Table Relating Broken versus Intact Homes and Neurotic versus Normal Undergraduate Subjects: Positive Relationship

	BROKEN HOME	INTACT HOME
Neurotic undergraduates	20	5
Normal undergraduates	5	20

the other. In other words, neurotic subjects tend to come from broken homes. The reversed pattern of results, shown in Table 9-2, would be called a *negative relationship,* because the presence of one characteristic is contingent on the absence of the other. In other words, neurotic subjects come from homes in which there was no upheaval. In both tables, the calculated estimate of significance would be reported as *p* < .001. This means that the *probability (p)* of the observed pattern of results happening just by chance is less than 1 in 1000 times. We would be justified in thinking of this result as meaningful; because it would happen again and again, it must be real.

Frequently in personality research, one or both of the characteristics being studied are quantified at more subtle levels than just presence or absence. Suppose you could measure how much neuroticism subjects show rather than considering this an all-or-nothing phenomenon. If the other characteristic were still dichotomous, as in broken versus intact home, the statistic to be calculated would be called the *point biserial correlation.* You could still test the likelihood that the pattern of results obtained might have occurred merely by chance.

The most common situation in personality research occurs when both characteristics can be measured at several levels. Suppose your theory tells you that people who are stubborn also tend to be neat (as you saw in Chapter 3, Freud's theory actually says something like this). Suppose further that you use questionnaires in which

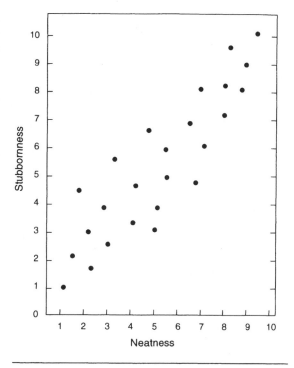

FIGURE 9-1   Contingency Table Relating Stubbornness and Neatness: Positive Relationship

people's answers to questions permit you to give them a numerical score of 0 to 10 on stubbornness and on neatness. Then you would be able to construct a contingency table with cells arranged 10 by 10. Figure 9-1 is an example of such a table; for convenience, points representing each subject's score on both characteristics at once take the place of cells.

The pattern of scores shown in Figure 9-1 seems to define a line sloping from the lower left to the upper right of the table. This is, once again, a *positive relationship* (the greater the stubbornness, the greater the neatness). The opposite pattern would reveal a *negative relationship* (the greater the stubbornness, the less the neatness). Whatever the pattern, the closer the points come to defining a line, the stronger the relationship is. Figure 9-2 shows what an absence of relationship would look like.

The statistic commonly used to test for the strength of relationship is the *Pearson product-*

TABLE 9-2   Contingency Table Relating Broken versus Intact Homes and Neurotic versus Normal Undergraduate Subjects: Negative Relationship

	BROKEN HOME	INTACT HOME
Neurotic undergraduates	5	20
Normal undergraduates	20	5

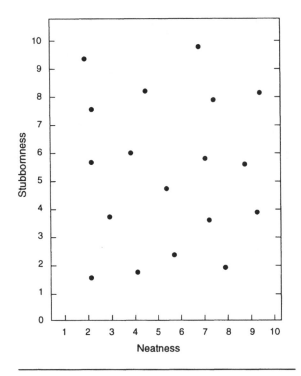

FIGURE 9-2   Contingency Table Relating
Stubbornness and Neatness: No Relationship

moment correlation. It can range from +1.00 (maximum positive relationship) through 0 to −1.00 (maximum negative relationship). Certain kinds of data require other statistics, such as the *rank order correlation* (used to determine whether a person's rank on one variable predicts his or her rank on the other). For all of these statistics, one can estimate the likelihood that the observed relationship occurred merely by chance.

By now, you can appreciate how correlational methods provide a powerful basis for evaluating the empirical accuracy and importance of rational or intuitive knowledge. If there is no empirical correlation between two characteristics, you may want to reconsider your pet notions and systematic theories. Even if there is a definite empirical relationship (i.e., it is not likely to have occurred by chance) but a weak one (e.g., +0.25, or −0.25), you may want to rethink them.

Correlational methods arise from the same

attempts to observe and understand human behavior that we engage in throughout our everyday lives and that personality theorists employ when they build their conceptualizations. The difference is that correlational methods transform these intuitive and rational modes of operation into the systematic, quantitative efforts we call *empirical.*

RESEARCH METHOD: FACTOR ANALYSIS. In addition to correlational methods, which relate individual characteristics, there is a statistical method for the empirical study of clusters of characteristics. Called *factor analysis,* it is based on a complex computation related to the simpler correlation already discussed. Factors can be extracted from the distribution of subjects' scores on the many characteristics.

The *factor analysis* procedure aims to identify the smallest number of factors needed to describe the ways in which several characteristics covary. The higher the correlations shared by some subgroup of characteristics under study, the greater the likelihood that it will define a factor. Factor analysis can also determine whether it is more accurate to describe the identified factors as correlated or uncorrelated. Because the analysis explores this question through geometric means, correlated factors are called *oblique* (i.e., the lines representing factors intersect at oblique angles). Uncorrelated factors are called *orthogonal* (i.e., the lines representing them intersect at right angles).

The major use of factor analysis in psychology has been to explore the covariation patterns among some group of characteristics that have been measured. Ideally, these characteristics have been selected for some specific theoretical reason, but in any case the factor analysis will identify the existing clusters.

Perhaps the most important use of factor analysis in personology is as an empirical check on some theoretical formulation about clustering. For example, in the Freudian view of the periphery of personality, the anal character type is neat, punctual, stubborn, and competitive, whereas the oral character type is suggestible, cooperative, passive, and dependent. If one could measure these eight characteristics on a sample of subjects, one could employ factor analysis to see whether there were two empirically identifiable factors and whether each was defined by the theoretically appropriate four characteristics.

I will discuss this use of factor analysis in more detail in Chapter 11. For the moment, it is enough for you to recognize that the *rational knowledge* arrived at by theorizing can be checked by the *empirical knowledge* emerging from factor analytic studies. Empirical factors correspond with the "types" in the peripheral statement of personality theories.

CAUSALITY—OR WHAT INFLUENCES WHAT ....

When a personality theorist proposes that neatness, punctuality, stubbornness, and competitiveness occur together and define the anal character type, there is little causal influence involved. It is not that neatness causes punctuality and so forth, nor that having an anal character type causes neatness; rather, having the characteristics of neatness and so on simply defines an anal character type. In personality theories, peripheral statements taken by themselves do not imply cause and effect.

Causal influence in personology usually arises when the developmental and core considerations interact to influence the peripheral considerations. Let me oversimplify to make an example: Freud theorizes that all youngsters express their sex instinct (core consideration), and if their parents respond too punitively during the oral or anal stages of maturation (developmental consideration), the emerging personality type (peripheral statement) will be oral or anal, respectively. Without the sex instinct there would be no character types. But you cannot understand how the types come about just from the core idea that we all have a sex instinct. The parental reactions in the various stages of development are an essential ingredient in causing the types. Separately, the sex instinct and the patterned, parental reactions are each "necessary

but not sufficient" conditions for the types. Together, the sex instinct and the parental reactions form the "necessary and sufficient" conditions for understanding the types.

Something similar to this *rational knowledge* occurs when, at a more intuitive level, we try to understand how people got to be the way they appear. Earlier we observed Sarah's and Harry's particular and different styles. When we wonder how Sarah came to be lonely and Harry to be quick to laugh or get angry, we are raising a causal question that implies core and developmental assumptions. These assumptions may not be psychoanalytic at all. We may think, for example, that Sarah must have been rewarded by her parents when she expressed her inborn needs for success, whereas Harry was probably rewarded by his parents when he expressed his inborn need for intimacy (the reward assumptions are developmental statements, and the inborn need assumptions are core statements). It is natural, once we have noticed patterns of behavioral covariation, to wonder how they came into being and to develop such assumptions. When personologists devise core and developmental formulations, they are doing more systematically (at a rational level of knowledge) what most of us do frequently at an intuitive level.

Techniques for Measuring Causality

RESEARCH METHOD: THE EXPERIMENT. The classic empirical procedure for testing causal theorizing is the *experiment*. As shown in Table 9-3, the experimental design calls for at least one group of subjects (called the *experimental group*), which is exposed to the supposed necessary and sufficient conditions (called the *treatment*) to produce the *effect* or result one is

TABLE 9-3 Experimental Design

GROUPS	TREATMENT	EXPECTED EFFECT
Experimental	Applied	Present
Control	Not applied	Absent

interested in understanding, and another group (called the *control group*) in which these conditions do not occur. It is important that the only difference between the groups concerns the supposed necessary and sufficient conditions. If the effect under study appears in the experimental group and not in the control group (or at least appears more strongly in the former than in the latter), it constitutes empirical evidence to support the causal theorizing.

The inference that it is the condition or *treatment* that caused the *effect* is supported by three crucial features of experiments. First, the effect must be seen (or seen most readily) only when the condition is present. Second, the condition or treatment must precede the effect. Finally, if it is apparent that the experimental and control groups differed in no respect other than the condition or treatment, it is reasonable to conclude that the condition caused the effect.

Imagine testing by experiment the Freudian causal theorizing mentioned in simplified form earlier. You might take infants shortly after birth and assign them at random to one of three groups—the oral experimental, anal experimental, and control groups. As the theory assumes that all persons have a sex drive (core statement), you need not worry about differences across groups in this attribute. Assignment of infants to groups *at random* means that each infant has the same probability as the others of being assigned to each group. You can achieve random assignment by some chance procedure, such as throwing dice, or you can use the tables of random numbers especially constructed for this purpose. Random assignment is important because it increases the likelihood that there will be no other differences (say in age or sex) between the groups except for the treatment.

To fulfill the experimental design, you would have the parents in the oral experimental group punish the sexual behaviors of their children during the first year of life (Freud's "oral stage") and the anal experimental group parents do so during the second year (Freud's "anal stage"). The parents in the control group would not punish the sexual behaviors of their youngsters in either the first or second years of life.

For Freud's theory of development to be supported empirically, the subjects in the oral experimental group would subsequently have to show predominance of the oral character type and the subjects in the anal experimental group predominance of the anal character type. The control group subjects must show predominance of neither character type. Needless to say, you would need some quantitative measurement of orality and anality with which to compare the three groups. The results obtained in this experiment can be evaluated by a statistical test called *analysis of variance,* which determines the probability that the difference among the averages occurred by chance. Another statistic called the *t-test* can be used to achieve the same purpose.

Note from this example that there can be more than one *experimental group* in an experiment, as well as more than one *control group.* What guides us in all this is the logic of the theoretical formulation being tested and the importance of ruling out alternative explanations of findings. Because Freud's formulation differentiates the causal conditions of oral and anal character types, it made sense to include two relevant experimental groups. Had it seemed cogent to us that perhaps orality and anality are produced not by parental punishment but by the very fact of having been reared by our natural parents, we might have added a second control group to check this alternative explanation. Such a control group would have involved youngsters reared by people other than their natural parents. If they showed less orality and anality than the other groups, this explanation would have been empirically supported.

I hope you have noticed the absurdity surrounding this extended example of an experiment! It is simply not practical to try to get parents to punish or not punish their children or have them reared by others just to satisfy research requirements. Even if it were feasible, it would be unethical to play with the lives of youngsters in this way. Although the experimental method is, on paper, a powerful technique for testing theoretical formulations, it is often not directly usable for personality theories. Of course, experiments that water down the causal formulations of personality theory are more feasible to do, but inference from their results is accordingly difficult and uncertain.

RESEARCH METHOD: THE NATURAL EXPERIMENT. Fortunately, there is a more feasible way to test causal formulations in personality theory. The *natural experiment* capitalizes on the fact that things often happen naturally that one would not intentionally make happen, for reasons of practicality and propriety. Careful study of these events can fulfill an experimental design that otherwise would be unfeasible.

To test the Freudian formulation with a *natural experiment,* you could work through hospital maternity wards to get information about the birth of infants. You could get their parents' permission to study (but not interfere with) family interaction patterns. By observing these patterns periodically during the first and second years of the youngsters' lives, you could judge which of them were punished during the first year, which during the second year, and which in neither year and assign them to the oral experimental, anal experimental, and control groups, respectively. You might even find some newborns given up for adoption if you wanted to fill out that second control group of those not raised by their natural parents. In this way, you would come very close to fulfilling the experimental design!

To go all the way, however, you would have to worry about whether these naturally constructed groups differed in any important ways besides punishment versus no punishment. For instance, if the control group contained more girls than the other two groups, the results, even if they appeared to support Freudian theory, might only reflect some unsuspected tendency of boys to develop more orality and anality than girls. This alternative explanation is plausible because, in this natural experiment, punishment/no punishment is *confounded* in this research design with maleness/femaleness, making it difficult to know which variable caused the result.

Fortunately, there is a statistical procedure that corrects confounding. It involves a quantitative way of deleting the effect of the confounding variable. Employing this procedure turns an analysis of variance into an *analysis of covariance* (which signifies that covarying or confounding variables have been statistically controlled).

The *natural experiment,* a powerful empirical technique in personology, is generally more useful than the contrived experiment. With appropriate attention paid to possible confounding factors, natural experiments are a valuable way to empirically test the causal formulations of personality theorizing.

To Summarize

Now you have had an introduction to the major methods of inquiry in personology. There are empirical techniques that are best for understanding covariation and patterning. Other techniques work best in cases of causal inference. Although these techniques are rather technical, they originate in the commonsense ways we all try to understand one another, whether intuitively as ordinary folk or rationally in systematic personality theorizing. But now it is time to change gears.

PERSONALITY DATA . . . .

Thus far, I have focused on how to analyze *personality data* by such means as correlations and factor analysis. In doing so, I have assumed the data to be analyzed. Now I shall consider how the data are generated in the first place. What do you measure when you want information about personality? One answer to this question concerns the sources of personality data and another the techniques of measurement.

Sources of Personality Data

There are three main sources of personality data: (1) the person's self-report, (2) the report about the person by those who know him or her, and (3) the judgment made about the person by an expert. The data obtained from these three sources may or may not agree. This does not mean that one source is more right or wrong than the others; rather, you must choose the data sources most appropriate to what you want to know.

If you want to know what people think about themselves, it is appropriate to obtain a *self-report*. If they say "I am intelligent," or "I'm capable of hard work," or even "I don't know who I am or what I want," you may learn something relevant. Notice that all these statements are interpretations the person makes about himself or herself. The conclusion "I am intelligent" is reached by ruling out possible alternatives such as "I am so persistent that I appear more intelligent than I really am" or "It is the stupidity of the others around me that makes me look more intelligent than I really am."

In contrast, if you want to know what others think of a person, it makes sense to ask them. Depending on your purpose, you might ask the person's friends, parents, lovers, or teachers, but you probably would not ask a complete stranger. If others say "John is a nasty, unpredictable, untrustworthy person" or "Mary is always so helpful and supportive," you learn something relevant to personality. Once again, these statements are interpretations or *judgments of others* made about the person. The same John described so unsympathetically by his associates might appear to himself merely frightened, overwhelmed, and desperately in need of friends. Who is right? Perhaps both sides! Clinical psychologists certainly know that it is not uncommon for frightened and desperate people to act in ways that are unpredictable and troublesome to others. This is the kind of pattern that led the sociologist Erving Goffman to define paranoia as acting so suspiciously as to force others to be unsupportive—a kind of self-fulfilling prophecy.

The final source of personality data is *expert judgment*. If you want to determine whether a person shows particular, concrete peripheral characteristics as explicated by a certain theory of personality, you might want a specialist in that theory to render a judgment. The raw material or observations for the judgment might be the very same ones the person and relevant others would scrutinize in reaching their interpretations. But the interpretation reached by the

expert presumably would be more sophisticated with regard to the personality theory. To a Freudian expert, John might appear to be an anal character type. Of course, if the expert is right, this does not mean that John and the others must be wrong. All could be right! Each interpretation is made from a different standpoint and for a different purpose.

Let us think through the implications of the three types of personality data. It might seem as if the basic source of data is expert judgment. After all, the expert makes relevant, sophisticated appraisals that refer explicitly to personality theories. But you should recognize that expert judgments are not made in a vacuum; they are based on observations, which often include self-reports or evaluations by others. Thus, all three sources of data are useful in personology.

Expert judgment may also be claimed as most basic because it is usually more explicit and less intuitive than self-report and judgments of others. We all reflect intuitively on ourselves and on others without strictly adhering to any full-fledged personality theory. In contrast, the expert is much more likely to organize observations specifically to explicate a particular theory of personality, using rational as opposed to intuitive knowledge (see Chapter 1).

To clarify the claim in favor of the experts, I shall return to the previous example of John, who feels frightened and desperate, whereas others see him as nasty and untrustworthy. The expert judgment that he is an anal character type is possible because Freudian theory assumes that ordinary people are not fully aware of what is really true about themselves and others. So the reports of John himself and of those around him are regarded as relevant but imperfect; they reveal their true meaning only through the interpretation of experts.

The limitation on this claim that expert judgment is the most basic source of data is the direct counterassumption made in some personality theories. The theory of Carl Rogers, for example, assumes that the expert can never know any person as well as that person knows himself or herself. The Rogerian expert would accept a person's self-report as the basic data on personality.

Each of the three sources of personality data can be useful. We need to be alert to our specific purposes and underlying theories in collecting personality data. These will help us decide which sources of data to emphasize.

Techniques for Measuring Generated Data

In attempting to grasp *personality measurement* techniques, one finds it helpful to distinguish those that generate the human behavior to be studied from those applied to human behaviors that take place naturally. Among the former techniques are the interview, the questionnaire, and the performance task.

RESEARCH METHOD: THE INTERVIEW. The *interview* is a verbal interaction in which a researcher obtains information, relevant to a specific research aim, in speaking with a subject. Usually the interaction is face to face; sometimes it may be conducted by other means, such as by telephone. Interview formats range from unstructured to structured.

In an *unstructured interview,* the researcher presents broad questions or topics (e.g., "How would you describe yourself?" or "What are your opinions about politics?"), and the subject is free to answer in any manner he or she wishes. Unstructured interview formats permit the researcher to follow whatever comes up in response to the broad questions and go wherever it may lead, as long as it is relevant to the research aim. In following up, the researcher may ask questions not part of the original set or contribute his or her own observations in a conversational manner.

In a *structured interview,* the researcher's questions are set in advance and are less global. Even follow-up is structured, because the additional questions, or *probes,* are specified in advance. Structured interviews try to get the same sort of information from every subject. A portion of a structured interview format appears in Table 9-4. As you can see, the researchers

devising such a sequence of questions have a clear initial idea of the kind of information they want from the subject.

Usually interviews are planned so that the most general, easiest, and least intimate questions come first. In Table 9-4, the strategy behind asking for factual details first is that they should be easiest and least threatening for subjects. Such questions help subjects get used to responding. Notice also that following the factual items, questions go from general to specific. The hope is that because subjects are relatively unconstrained at first, they will disclose what is really on their minds. The later questions are more specific to ensure that certain crucial information is obtained from all subjects in case they have not volunteered it already. As you can see, the most intimate questions appear last. It is assumed that by that time, subjects have become sufficiently familiar with being interviewed and trust the interviewer enough to divulge personal, potentially embarrassing information that they might otherwise withhold. Of course, this strategy does not always work.

RESEARCH METHOD: THE QUESTIONNAIRE. The *questionnaire* is a set of written questions or statements designed to elicit responses that yield information relevant to the research aim. Like interviews, questionnaires are *unstructured* or *structured*. Unlike interviews, with questionnaires, the researcher need not interact with the subject to obtain data. Hence, questionnaires can be administered to groups of subjects, sent through the mail, or put on computer diskettes. Generating data by questionnaire is less labor-intensive for the researcher. It can also preserve subjects' anonymity as they may not even have to identify themselves and may never actually be seen.

Unstructured questionnaires include broad questions that give the subject leeway in responding. Examples might include "List your best friends of this year and describe each of them in your own words" or "Describe yourself in your own words, indicating your most important attributes." In these unstructured questions, subjects can choose to write a lot or a little, and

TABLE 9-4   Part of a Structured Interview Format on Parental Attitudes Toward Teenagers

QUESTIONS	PROBES*
Section 1: Demographic Facts	
1. What is your name?	1. None
2. How old are you?	2. None
3. How many children do you have and what are their ages?	3. None
4. What is your current marital status?	4. How many times have you been married? Did your marriage(s) end in divorce or some other way?
Section 2: General Attitudes	
1. What do you think it's like being a teenager today?	1. Is it different from in your day? Is it easy? or hard?
2. What are the best and worst things about being a teenager today?	2. Can you think of any other things?
3. What would you do to help teenagers grow up well?	3. Anything else you can think of?
4. If you had a teenager, would you impose rules of conduct?	4. Would you let the teenager go his or her own way?
5. If so, what would those rules be? List them in order of importance.	5. Anything else you can think of?
Section 3: Personal Information	
1. How do you get along with your own teenagers?	1. Can you say more about what it's like when you are together?
2. Do you generally agree on what your teenager(s) should be doing or not doing?	2. Say more, please. Is there anything else you can remember?
3. Are you satisfied or frustrated with your teenager(s)?	3. Please say more.

*To be asked only if the question does not elicit the needed information.

TABLE 9-5   Part of a True-False Questionnaire on Parental Attitudes Toward Teenagers

QUESTION	RESPONSE (CIRCLE ONE)	
1. Teenagers tend not to understand their parents' problems.	T	F
2. Teenagers are very generous with their friends.	T	F
3. By the teenage years, youngsters are good company for their parents.	T	F
4. Cruelty characterizes the relationships of teenagers.	T	F
5. Teenagers drink too much.	T	F
6. Most teenagers do not use drugs.	T	F
7. Sometimes I can't understand how teenagers avoid disasters.	T	F
8. With a little help from their parents, teenagers get along just fine.	T	F
9. Teenagers try very hard to grow up.	T	F
10. I wish I were a teenager again.		

they may approach the questions in a variety of ways.

Structured questionnaires use less global questions and do not permit elaborate, open-ended responses from subjects. An example of part of a structured questionnaire appears in Table 9-5. Notice that in this case subjects respond only by indicating whether they agree or disagree with each item, which is called a *true-false* item. Another format for responding is the *rating-scale* item. The questions appearing in Table 9-5 would be transformed into rating-scale items if the subject were asked to pick the appropriate number, with 0, 1, 2, and 3 standing for "not at all true," "a little true," "somewhat true," and "completely true," respectively. Whatever the form of response required, structured questionnaires are calculated to yield the same quantification of magnitude in the answers to every question from every subject.

Two other common forms of questionnaire items are the forced-choice and the checklist. In the *forced-choice* format, questions or attitudinal statements are paired and the subject is asked which of the two seems more relevant or accurate. Examples of such item pairs are given in Table 9-6. Because each statement is paired with each of the other statements, one can rank the relative judged acceptability of each statement for all subjects.

The *checklist* typically includes simple statements or even single words that subjects check if relevant. Although checklist items are usually not themselves questions, they imply questions. You can see this in the items in Table 9-7, all of which can be transformed into questions by prefixing them with "Did you experience" and following them with "in the last year?"

Psychologists who develop questionnaires take great care to avoid *response biases* to which subjects may fall prey. An important bias is *image maintenance,* or the tendency of subjects to present themselves in a favorable (rather than accurate) light through their responses. To avoid this, questionnaire developers sometimes try to word items to hide their real intent or to make each choice appear equally favorable or even neutral. This is done so that the subject's score

---

TABLE 9-6   Part of a Forced-Choice Questionnaire on Beliefs Concerning Personal Control

---

Instructions: Circle the item number in each pair of items that best expresses your opinion.

1. If you try hard, you can usually reach your goals.
2. Those who get ahead are just lucky.

1. The best things in life come your way when you least expect them.
2. If you try hard, you can usually reach your goals.

1. Those who get ahead are just lucky.
2. Through learning, you can increase your competence.

1. If you try hard, you can usually reach your goals.
2. The best things in life come your way when you least expect them.

1. Through learning, you can increase your competence.
2. Those who get ahead are just lucky.

1. The best things in life come your way when you least expect them.
2. Through learning, you can increase your competence.

1. Through learning, you can increase your competence.
2. If you try hard, you can usually reach your goals.

1. Those who get ahead are just lucky.
2. The best things in life come your way when you least expect them.

TABLE 9-7   Part of a Checklist on Recent Life Events

Instructions: Please indicate whether the events listed in the left-hand column happened to you in the last year. Do this by putting a check mark in the second or third column if the event happened within 6 months or between 6 and 12 months of today's date, respectively. If the event happened in both 6-month periods, check both columns.

EVENTS	TIME FROM TODAY'S DATE	
	0–6 Months	6–12 Months
Death of a loved one		
You leave home for college		
Birth of a sibling		
Your parents divorce		
A parent remarries		
A serious financial reversal		
Personal bankruptcy		
You fail a course		
You fall in love		
A friend leaves town		

will reflect the hoped-for content rather than image maintenance. Other biases are *acquiescence* (the tendency to agree with statements) and *negativism* (the tendency to disagree with them). A way to minimize response biases is to word half the questionnaire items positively and half negatively. Questionnaire-item construction has become very technical; for now it is sufficient that you be aware of some of the major response biases that can interfere with obtaining sound research data.

INTERVIEWS VERSUS QUESTIONNAIRES. There are advantages and disadvantages to interviews and questionnaires. Going into some of these will help you understand the research you will be reading in later chapters. Basically, interviews have the advantage of giving subjects more freedom to express themselves, because they can respond in their own way to questions. In contrast, questionnaires require brief, unelaborated answers from subjects. Subjects feel more manipulated by questionnaires.

Freedom of response in interviews can also be a disadvantage. Using an interview, the researcher cannot be sure of obtaining comparable information from each subject. One subject may elaborate on a topic that another does not even address. This makes it difficult to arrive at a quantitative score for each subject on all the variables under study. In contrast, questionnaires aim at such quantification, which is one of their strengths.

You might, of course, wonder whether this quantification from questionnaires is valid, because subjects are somewhat forced into the mold shaped by the set of questions used and the lack of response elaboration permitted. For example, suppose I force you to answer only "yes" or "no" to the question "Do you have a lot of trouble studying?" You might end up saying "yes" even though you would have wanted to explain that although sometimes you are unable to study, at other times you have no trouble doing so. And it may all depend on whether or not you are in love with someone at the time. In an interview, you might have been able to express this complexity. But then the interviewer would have had to struggle with how to make your statement compare with that of another interviewee who did not mention such complexity. Did this other subject fail to elaborate out of a wish not to get into all that or because for him or her there is no complexity surrounding studying?

No doubt a major reason why questionnaires are used so much in personality research is their efficiency. One researcher can collect data on large groups of subjects, and these groups need not even meet (if the mail is used). Added to this efficiency factor is the ease of questionnaire quantification produced by subject responses that are unelaborated and comparable across the group studied. By comparison, interviews are labor intensive and often yield complex responses that are difficult to quantify and compare across subjects. But interviews yield richer, more complete, less manipulated or contrived expressions from subjects. This means that interviews are better used when the research aim is exploratory—that is, when the researcher is not sure which data are most important and needs to see only what subjects may or may not have to say about certain topics. Questionnaires are better used when the research aim is less exploratory than concerned with testing some settled hypotheses. This means that the researcher knows which data are important and is not concerned with extraneous things that subjects may say.

RESEARCH METHOD: THE PERFORMANCE TASK. In the *performance task,* the researcher has subjects perform an activity and judges their performance with regard to some research aim. You may think that both interviews and questionnaires should qualify as performance tasks; after all, answering questions qualifies as a task. But interviews and questionnaires differ in an important way from the performance task as defined here in that they require subjects to reflect on and judge their own behavior before giving a response. For example, if I ask you, "Are you too aggressive?" you must, to respond, remember past thoughts, feelings, and actions, then judge not only whether you express aggression but whether that aggression is too intense.

In contrast, a performance task might put you in a group of people with the instruction that everyone get to know one another. The researcher would observe what you say and do, reaching his or her own conclusion as to whether you are too aggressive. The most important feature of performance tasks is that the subject's response is not a self-evaluation but some relevant performance that the researcher will judge. Psychologists have been very ingenious in devising performance tasks that can elicit from subjects the kinds of thoughts, feelings, and actions that are relevant to research aims. Sometimes the performance tasks are highly staged; in the lost-letter technique, for example, a subject is led to find a stamped letter on the ground, and the research question is whether he or she will mail it or open it. Of course, the researcher is hidden somewhere watching the ensuing drama, forming judgments about the subject's honesty and social responsibility.

Sometimes performance tasks are less staged. In the extreme, for example, the researcher may merely follow the subject around during some period of daily activity. This relatively *unstructured approach* has the advantage of showing the whole range of the subject's actions. Like all unstructured techniques, however, the resulting observations may not be comparable with those of other subjects, and thus quantification may be difficult. Again, unstructured approaches are best when the research aim is exploratory. If the researcher is more sure of the observations needed to fulfill the research aim, *structured performance tasks* are preferable for ease of quantification and comparability across the group of subjects.

Whether structured or unstructured, performance tasks are important when the research aim is best served by expert judgment, as previously discussed. If, for example, your personality theory considers the real motives for actions to be unconscious (as in Freud's approach), you might be better off observing subjects' behavior in relevant tasks and forming your own judgments as to their motives than by asking them in interviews or questionnaires why they do things.

A particular form of performance task that has been important in personology is the *projective test,* in which ambiguous stimuli are presented to the subject, who must then determine the meaning of what is perceived. Because there are no right or wrong answers, the act of fantasy through which meaning is attributed involves a projection onto the stimuli of the subject's personality. The subject may or may not realize what he or she is revealing. What makes the projective test a performance task is that the researcher evaluates the subject's responses.

A famous example of a projective test is Murray's (1943) *Thematic Apperception Test (TAT).* It is composed of a set of ambiguous pictures of people about each of which the respondent is asked to compose a story with a beginning, middle, and end that indicates what is going on. You can imagine what a difference it would make in interpreting what a subject is like if the composed story were about hatching a murder plot as opposed to discussing an anticipated vacation! The requirement of composing entire stories makes it quite likely that subjects will reveal things they may not have intended to disclose or may not even have realized in themselves. Because they are thematic and, typically, interpersonal, the fantasies expressed on this test provide rich material with which the expert can interpret personality.

Another example of a projective test is the *Rorschach Test* (Rorschach, 1921), in which the subject is asked to imagine all the things each of ten inkblots might look like. Figure 9-3 shows the kind of inkblot that might be used. Once again, the responses "It's an avenging eagle swooping down on us sinners" and "It's a warm, fuzzy fur rug to snuggle into" provide very different personality implications. The procedures for scoring these test responses have become very complex and technical. There are not only several competing scoring systems but several forms of the test itself. However, there is no need to delve into these complexities here.

THE PSYCHOTHERAPY SESSION. Some contexts of data collection are complex combinations of interview, questionnaire, and performance task.

FIGURE 9-3   Inkblots

A good example is the *psychotherapy session*. It is contrived in the sense that it is not a naturally occurring relationship. Although it involves considerable intimacy (the client reveals innermost thoughts, feelings, and actions), the relationship is one-sided (the therapist does not reveal these things). It involves a contract for service (the client pays the therapist for services rendered), although an unusual one (the correspondence between service and pay is often intangible and complex). Further, this contrived situation we call "psychotherapy" typically includes aspects of the interview and the performance task and perhaps even questionnaires and other verbal tests. But it is not devised primarily for research aims. Instead, it serves treatment goals, which may sometimes jeopardize the needs of research.

I include the psychotherapy session as a research method because it is frequently used for collection of personality data. These data may include not only the therapist's expert judgments but also the client's self-reports and actions in performance tasks. These self-evaluations and actions may correspond with or contradict the expert judgments.

As described here, the psychotherapy session

may seem too complex to be useful as a measurement technique. Its major advantage, however, is that as sessions accumulate, the therapist (and perhaps the client) usually becomes increasingly sure of the evaluation. Clients typically reveal themselves in therapy because they want to facilitate the process of treatment and they want to come to trust their therapists. When researchers do one-time interview or questionnaire administrations, subjects may well withhold important information and present themselves in the best light. After all, subjects interviewed or given a questionnaire typically have no relationship with the researcher sufficient to build trust. So why should they reveal all without being sure of how it will be used?

Simple performance tasks might seem to circumvent this tendency toward image maintenance because they do not require the subject's self-evaluations. Even in performance tasks, however, no continuing relationship between the researcher and the subject usually occurs. Thus, subjects might be reticent to behave in a completely open fashion in many performance tasks, taking care to reveal only behaviors that will put them in a favorable light. So the researcher may not obtain all the observations needed to reach sound expert judgments. It would appear that the psychotherapy session, however complex, is worth struggling with in the attempt to reach meaningful empirical knowledge.

Reliability

As discussed in Chapter 1, personality refers to characteristics that have continuity over time and across situations. Thus, the measures we use to chart these characteristics must show them to be internally consistent and stable. Only then will we be sure that we have measured with *reliability.*

It is possible to determine the *internal consistency* of a questionnaire by looking at those several items considered conceptually relevant to each personality characteristic studied. For example, a measure of ego strength might include such questions as "Do you wake up in the morning full of energy to face the day?" "Are

you usually afraid to meet new people?" and "Do you often doubt the value of what you are doing?" In these, the highest score on ego strength would be responses of "Yes," "No," and "No," respectively. Other patterns are possible. You can study the internal consistency of such a set of questions by calculating the likelihood of a consistent pattern of answers in a sample of subjects. The most efficient statistic for doing this is *coefficient alpha.* The higher it is, the greater the consistency of the measure.

Stability of a measure is determined by repeating the measure one or more times on the same subjects under similar circumstances. The time between administrations of the measure is usually long enough so that subjects cannot merely remember and thus repeat what they said last time and not so long that one could legitimately expect subjects' personalities to have changed. For periods of, say, 2 weeks or a month, the higher the correlation between subjects' scores on both administrations, the greater the stability of the measure.

Techniques for Measuring Natural Data

Natural data are not generated by the researcher. They include anything people do in going through their days (and nights), much of which can be relevant to the broad research interests of personology. In empirical research, it is useful to have some record of natural data that one can return to again and again when measuring personality characteristics.

Written documents are a typical kind of record of natural data used by researchers. These can include anything from a record of business transactions to a diary. Needless to say, some written records are richer and more revealing than others and are therefore more highly valued in research. Other kinds of records can also be valuable. *Video-* or *audiotapes* of ongoing experiences are increasingly important resources in research.

Natural data may include statements about the subjects made by themselves or by others. Further, the documents may chronicle subjects' thoughts, feelings, and actions in a way that does not emphasize self-reflection. But, of course, none of these statements or chronicles have been made for research purposes. An additional important feature of natural data is that they are not necessarily restricted to present-day activities. The researcher can study subjects' remote pasts from any available documents.

RESEARCH METHOD: CONTENT ANALYSIS. The main procedure for turning documented natural data into measured personality characteristics is *content analysis*. In this approach, the researcher develops criteria for determining how the kind of natural data at hand can express the characteristic under study. For example, if the relevant characteristic is gregariousness and the data are a subject's diaries, the researcher can list, through the record of real and imagined events, all the ways the subject expresses interest in being with others. These can include not only concrete instances of meeting with others but also dreams of having been with them and waking-state feelings of loneliness (things that one might well find in diaries).

The researcher could be content with a global judgment of the degree of the subject's preoccupation with others or could push for more precise quantification. To do the latter, the researcher would need to specify what constitutes an *instance* of gregariousness. In a written record, an instance might be a verbal unit, such as a sentence or a paragraph. Or it might be some more functional unit (however long or short), such as the recording of an episode. Whatever the criterion of an instance, its specification is very important because it permits the researcher to count. The more instances of real or wished-for social interaction, the greater the gregariousness of the subject.

INTERSCORER AGREEMENT. Frequently, content analysis requires the researcher to interpret what he or she is observing. Sometimes the meaning seems clear. For example, the diary statement "I spent the whole evening wishing for a friend —or even just an acquaintance—to talk to or be with" clearly expresses gregariousness. But does the statement "I spent the whole evening feeling restless, as if something not entirely clear to me was missing" express gregariousness? Some researchers might think so, whereas others might not. Who would be right? It could be hard to determine, because researchers using the same scoring criteria may differ in opinion as to what they are perceiving.

The only safe procedure is to determine how much two or more scorers agree and not be satisfied until the agreement is high. It has become standard practice among researchers to demonstrate *interscorer* agreement whenever they use content analysis to generate personality data.

RESEARCH METHOD: PSYCHOBIOGRAPHY. Of late, a particular approach to content analysis has become popular in personology. It uses as many documents, past and present, as can be amassed and aims to understand the holistic pattern of an individual life. It is, therefore, aptly called *psychobiography* (Elms, 1994; Runyan, 1982). As the term indicates, this biography has a distinctly psychological slant (rather than political, for example). It also aims to be as systematic as possible; psychobiographers therefore analyze the content of many documents and interview the subject when possible. A sign of the growing popularity of psychobiography is that an entire issue of the *Journal of Personality* (1988, 56[1]) was devoted to it.

Usually, psychobiographies focus on people who are considered remarkable—eminent, famous, or talented—to discern the universal personality and social forces that produced them. In helping us understand these, the psychobiographer teaches us all about living.

One weakness of psychobiographies is that interscorer agreement on content analyses is almost never studied. The psychobiographer aims at providing a complex, in-depth understanding of an entire life. Because the data are numerous and often difficult to obtain—perhaps documents buried in archives or rushed interviews with the eminent, it is understandable (if unfortunate) that psychobiographers work alone.

To Summarize

In obtaining personality data, the researcher must decide whether to use existing materials or to generate data. We make similar decisions in our everyday efforts to understand one another: In learning about people, we can observe their natural comings and goings or we can ask them questions. Researchers try to make similar decisions in a conscious, systematic way. Their efforts have led to an extensive technology for generating and evaluating personality data. Now, before I shift from an appreciation of this technology to the personality theories, there is a final matter to ponder.

THE SUBJECTS STUDIED ....

Thus far, in considering personality research, I have focused on how personality data are generated and analyzed. A word should be added here on the choice of *subjects* to study. Perhaps it goes without saying that *human beings* are the natural subjects of personality research. But this may bear noting in a field—psychology—that often uses *lower animals* as subjects. To use lower animals in personality research is such an indirect approach to what personologists want to understand (patterns of thoughts, feelings, and actions) and presents such grave measurement problems (can we be sure of an animal's thoughts and feelings?) as to be virtually useless.

But which people should we study? Young or old, rich or poor, male or female, normal or psychotic, Christian or Jew? Certainly we should not fall into choosing a sample of subjects merely because they are available. A typical failing is that of using college sophomores as subjects because both they and the researchers tend to be at universities, even though the research aim is not limited to adolescents. However interesting they may be, college students are developmentally different from children, adults, and the aged, therefore making it difficult to generalize findings concerning them to other age groups.

Nor should psychotherapy clients be used as subjects without careful consideration. After all, people seek psychotherapy when they are in trouble, when they have failed to live satisfyingly. Is it appropriate, then, to generalize what is learned through psychotherapy sessions to people who have not sought such treatment? Once again you can see that in selecting subjects it is important to keep in mind a sense of their appropriateness to the research aims.

A FINAL WORD ....

In this consideration of how data are generated and analyzed, I have tried to accomplish several things. One is to show how the methods used to produce empirical tests of personality theories emanate from (though refine) the commonsense ways we all use to understand ourselves and others. Another is to express how using personality methods involves interrelated research decisions about whom to study, how to observe them, and how to analyze what is being observed so that empirical conclusions can be reached.

Chapters 10, 11, and 12 and, to some extent, 13 and 14 emphasize research. If you keep in mind what you have learned here as you read them, you may be helped to appreciate and evaluate the many avenues of personality research.

Rational
and Empirical
Analyses of Core
Considerations

The chapters of Part Two covered the theorizing of quite a few personologists. Yet, only three basic models for personality theorizing have emerged. These models characterize the person's inmost processes in terms of *conflict, fulfillment,* or *consistency*. Of course, some variants on the models exist, and each model has two discernible versions. Further, every personologist lends his or her own special emphases and verbal nuances. Nonetheless, it is very significant that there are so few ways of conceptualizing the overall directionality and universal features of life.

In Chapters 3 to 8, I focused on distinguishing among the various theories that exemplify each of the three models. In this chapter, I will emphasize some conclusions about the nature of the models and pinpoint some issues regarding the core of personality raised by the similarities and differences among the models, or conduct a *rational analysis*. Then, I will conduct an *empirical analysis* by discussing the results of systematic research that bear on the issues. This will

constitute a beginning for the arduous but necessary task of determining the strengths and weaknesses inherent in the three models.

Essential Features
of the Three Models . . . .

The Conflict Model

Everything essential to the *conflict model* can be understood once one grasps the idea that the person is inextricably caught up in the opposition of two great forces. In the *intrapsychic version* of the conflict position, exemplified by the theories of Rank, Angyal, and Bakan, great forces originate within the person. Although it may not be immediately apparent, Jung's position also stresses two great forces within the person: the individualistic, worldly, practical activities of the ego (or conscious mind) and the universal, communal, mysterious intuitions of the collective unconscious. In the *psychosocial version* of the conflict model, one of the forces is inherent in the person, the other in society. The theories of Freud, Murray, and the ego psychologists make this assumption. In all conflict theories, the person experiences conflict as an uncomfortable state of tension and anxiety. The overall aim of life, therefore, is to *reduce tension* and anxiety as much as possible by minimizing conflict.

In all versions of the conflict model, the *ideal* lifestyle is, at best, a compromise. This view is inevitable once one assumes an inherent and unavoidable conflict at the core of personality. The compromise cannot take the form of erasing one of the two great forces, for both forces are inherent and basic even if one of them does not originate in the person. Therefore, psychological sickness or maladjustment is usually defined by conflict theorists as the attempt to live as if only one of the two forces existed. Such an attempt must be considered a failure, if the logic of the conflict model is to be served. In Rank's theory, excessive placation of the death fear leads to neurotic isolation, whereas excessive placation of the life fear leads to "herd" conformity. In the theories of Freud and Murray, unmitigated expression of instinct, the force inherent in the person, is defined as psychopathy and leads in the direction of destruction of self and others, whereas unmitigated expression of the force inherent in society, in the form of superego, leads to the excessive, unrealistic, punitive guilt and defensiveness that create neurosis. Clearly, then, the attempt to live as if there were only one rather than two great forces is unworkable.

What will work is a *compromise* in which the person achieves a balance between the opposing forces. Thus, the concrete patterns of living must always express both forces at the same time for the life to be effective. While it is certainly possible within the limits of the conflict model to imagine a workable compromise in which one force will occasionally gain ascendancy over the other, these occurrences must be superimposed on an underlying dynamic balance between the forces. In Rank's terms, one must minimize both the fear of life and the fear of death. Jung dignifies the achieved balance between ego and the collective unconscious with the term *selfhood*. For Freud, Murray, and the ego psychologists, the highest purpose of life is to gain a maximum degree of instinct gratification with a minimum degree of punishment and guilt. Here too you can see a balancing of the two great forces, in the form of id and superego requirements. With a conflict model, the best that can be achieved in life is the compromise of balance.

But more must be said about the version of the conflict model that assumes one force to be inherent in the person and the other inherent in society. Because the forces must be opposed for conflict to ensue, this *psychosocial version* usually defines the person as an individual with selfish aims, and society as the repository of the corporate good. Because society is made up of intelligent beings, the individual's selfishness can be detected and severely punished, and he or she can be made to feel ashamed and guilty. This means that the social force has the power to detect and thwart the other, but not vice versa. Therefore, for one to achieve a compromise involving balance, the individualistic force must have some protection with which to offset the detecting and thwarting power of the societal force. If there were no such protection, the person would have to renounce human nature, which would obviate a compromise.

Thus, the logic of the *psychosocial version* of the conflict model readily leads to the concept of *defense* as a continuous, necessary process in successful living. This defensiveness offsets the special detecting and thwarting power of the societal force. To avoid the punishment and guilt they would suffer because of their selfish instincts, people institute defenses that have the dual purpose of shielding them from recognition of selfishness and of encouraging instinctual expression in ways that society sees as relatively innocuous. Freud's theory, of course, is the prime example of this kind of position. Recall that he even dubs unmitigated expression of instincts *pleasure principle functioning* and the attempt to maximize instinctual gratification while minimizing punishment and guilt *reality principle functioning*.

So, whenever you encounter a conflict position in which one force is inherent in the person and the other in society, you can expect, if the position is logically consistent, defense to preside in the achievement of a compromise of balance, which is the healthiest state. The distinction in such positions between mental health and mental illness is not made in terms of whether or not defenses exist, for there are always defenses. Instead, the distinction is made in terms of whether the defenses promote the effective compromise of balance or the ineffective denial of one of the two opposing forces.

Turning for comparison to the version of conflict theory that assumes both opposing forces to be inherent in the person, we do not find the emphasis on defense found in the psychosocial version. Because both forces originate in the person, there is no special problem of one force detecting and thwarting the other. Hence, there is no logical necessity for the more vulnerable force to be supplemented by some protective function. It does not surprise me that Rank, Angyal, and Bakan have not emphasized the concept of defense in their theorizing. In this context, Jung's emphasis on eliminating the personal unconscious and being as open as possible to the collective unconscious becomes understandable. In point of fact, the intrapsychic theories do not need a protective concept, and therefore their view of a compromise of balance does not emphasize defensiveness.

In the psychosocial position, involving as it does such emphasis on compromise and defense, the ideal or healthiest form of living is defined primarily in terms of the person's adjustment to the socially determined corporate good. Such a position inevitably involves defining the highest form of living in terms of dependability, considerateness, responsibility, generosity, morality, and conformity. Indeed, one finds this emphasis on what might be called "good citizenship" in the theories of Freud and the other psychosocial theorists. A little of this emphasis is also found in the intrapsychic theorists. That the *intrapsychic version* of the conflict model places less emphasis on adjustment to the pressures of society in its

definition of the ideal lifestyle is to be understood in terms of its relatively low reliance on the concept of defense coupled with its assumption that both opposing forces originate within the person.

Another concomitant of the conflict model's emphasis on compromise and defense is the view that the personality is rather set in its general outlines by the time childhood is over. The rest of life can be reasonably well characterized as a filling out and elaboration of the patterns established early in life. Whatever change in personality takes place during adulthood is more a matter of degree than of kind. And indeed, *stability of personality* is a more salient fact for conflict theorists than personality change is. Once again, what I have just said is more true for the psychosocial than the intrapsychic versions of the model, because the former more clearly emphasizes defense.

An additional word on the content of the two forces in conflict theories is in order. All versions of the conflict model tend to stress one force as *individualistic* and the other as *communal* regardless of whether or not both forces are seen as rising from the organism itself. Fear of death is a tendency toward independence and uniqueness, whereas fear of life is a tendency toward dependence and similarity with others. For Jung, the ego is a mainly individualistic thing whereas the collective unconscious is that which relates one to humankind. While there is perhaps no strict logical necessity that the two opposing forces of a conflict theory stress individualistic and communal content, they nonetheless do so.

The Fulfillment Model

To understand the *fulfillment model,* you must realize that it assumes only one great force in living rather than the two that conflict theories postulate. Although fulfillment positions sometimes conceptualize a way that the person can get into conflict, the state itself is not inevitable or basic. Hence, the fulfillment theories do not see life as a necessary compromise; rather, they see it as the unfolding of the one great force, with the most successful living involving the most vigorous expression of this force. In the fulfillment model, the more vigorous the expression of the force, the greater the experience of *tension*. However, tension is not intimately associated with anxiety, as it is in the conflict model. Although fulfillment positions do not assume that the person tries to increase tension per se, such increases are an integral part of expressing the great force and are not, therefore, avoided.

One version of the fulfillment model emphasizes the realization of one's inherent capabilities, as in Rogers's and Maslow's *actualization theories*. Adler, White, Allport, Fromm, and the existential psychologists define another version of the fulfillment model, which stresses the *perfection* of life through striving toward ideals. Rather than considering individually unique potentialities, as actualization theorists would, perfection theorists stress the capabilities of the human species. This can be seen in Fromm's emphasis on human nature and in Adler's and White's emphases on mastery and compensation for initial inferiorities.

Turning to a more concrete consideration of the content of the great force, one finds that fulfillment theorists agree on its heavily psychological nature. The great force is oriented less toward mere *survival* through use of capabilities than toward the *enhancement* of living, beyond survival, that can come through perfection or the expression of capabilities. Many fulfillment theorists, such as Maslow, Allport, Fromm, and the existentialists, actually separate the human's animal nature from its human nature. The pursuit of animal nature, which leads to survival, is relatively unimportant alongside the pursuit of human nature. Although the great force tends to be identified with human nature alone, there are exceptions among fulfillment theorists. Rogers is the only personologist in this group who makes little distinction between animal and human nature, preferring to consider the great force as underlying both enhancement and survival.

Although the great force of the fulfillment theorists tends to be individualistic in nature, it is not antisocial, as in the conflict theories.

Fulfillment theorists generally see no particular difference between successful *individual living* and successful *group living*. If people vigorously express the great force, their lives with themselves and with others will be rich, varied, and satisfying. Adler provides perhaps the most formal statement of this emphasis in specifying both mastery and social interest as facets of the core tendency of personality. As fulfillment theorists see no difference between the requirements of individual living and those of group living, they do not conceptualize any inevitability of conflict here.

But as existentialism makes especially clear, conventionality is not the most constructive social commitment. Probably because of this, conflict can arise between the person and the social context. Fulfillment theorists who have elaborated on this matter—notably Rogers, Maslow, Fromm, and existential psychologists—make it clear that such conflict is due to a society that has become inhuman and punitive. Only when society thwarts it can expression of the great force lead to conflict. Although fulfillment theorists are usually somewhat vague about how society can become inhuman and punitive, they do tend to stress, with Rogers, significant people in the person's life who are too crabbed to accept him or her completely and lovingly and suggest, with Fromm, the roots of such difficulties in the economic, political, and cultural milieu.

This kind of conflict, according to fulfillment theorists, jeopardizes vigorous expression of the great force, eventuating in an unnecessarily trivial, conforming, unsatisfying life. They define *mental illness* as the attempt to live as though the great force did not exist, so one can avoid conflict between it and society. As you can see, this inhibiting definition is similar in fulfillment and conflict theory. The difference, of course, is that in fulfillment theory there is only one great force that can be denied and hence, only one class of illness, whereas conflict theory conceptualizes two great forces that can be denied and thus two ways of becoming ill. Interestingly, some fulfillment theorists, in considering the conflict between the person and an inhuman social context, take up the concept of defense. This is most notably true of Rogers, but it appears in Maslow, Fromm, Allport, and existential psychology as well. In some ways, they use the concept of defense similarly to the way psychoanalytic theorists use it. In talking of a punitive, inhuman society, fulfillment theorists postulate an intelligent force bent on detecting and thwarting part or all of the great force. People can be punished and made to feel guilt. Therefore, they protect themselves by instituting defensive processes such that they (1) do not see the parts of the great force that would make them fear retribution and (2) channel expression of the great force along socially innocuous paths.

Although the concept of defense works in the same manner as and is similar in purpose to that in conflict theory, you must recognize a very important difference. For fulfillment theorists, conflict is not inevitable and the highest form of living is not a compromise. Thus, defense has a logical function in their thinking only if conflict actually develops. Even if conflict develops fairly often, fulfillment theorists have no reason to define defensiveness as part of the *ideal* lifestyle, or mental health. This is the major significance of the difference between fulfillment and conflict positions. It means that the fulfillment model defines the highest form of living in terms of *transcendence* of society rather than *conformity* to it. They emphasize imaginativeness, spontaneity, individuality, self-reliance, openness to experience, and an unflinching knowledge of the inmost recesses of oneself. This emphasis contrasts sharply with that of good citizenship found in the conflict theories.

When they consider the entire *life span*, fulfillment theorists think in terms of a fairly continual developmental process in which personality changes throughout childhood, adolescence, and adulthood. They usually claim that these changes indicate progressively greater differentiation and integration, or *psychological growth*, at least when conflict and defense do not interfere. This emphasis on *personality change* in the direction of growth is very understandable considering the fulfillment theorists' assumption of only one

great force that normally leads people to attempt to realize their capabilities or to perfect themselves. Continual personality change is as logically a part of fulfillment theory as is the conflict model's emphasis on *personality stability* following the childhood years.

The Consistency Model

To appreciate the meaning of the *consistency model,* you must recognize that it does not stress the importance of the specific *content of personality* and inherent forces; rather, it considers the importance of the *congruence,* compatibility, or fit among various aspects of personality or elements of content. In the *cognitive dissonance version* of the model, these elements of content are cognitive in nature. For Kelly, one such cognitive element is the construct, or hypothesis, and the other is the perception of actual occurrences. Similarly, McClelland presents one kind of element as the expectation and the other as the perception of events. Regardless of their differences, all these theories agree that one element deals primarily with ideas or expectations about what the world and one is like whereas the other primarily concerns observations or perceptions on what the world and one seems to actually be doing.

In contrast, the *activation version* of the consistency model, exemplified by Fiske and Maddi, concerns itself with the match between the level of excitation or tension customary for one and that which one actually experiences at some point in time. The activation version is nonetheless similar to the cognitive dissonance version in stressing past experience as a basis for coming to grips with what is happening now and in considering all content equally important.

In its pure form, the cognitive dissonance version of the consistency model is strictly a *tension-reduction* viewpoint. Its major message is that inconsistency or incompatibility between a given idea or expectancy and a certain observation is an intensely uncomfortable state of tension and anxiety—so uncomfortable that in the attempt to avoid incompatibilities and thereby reduce tension, the whole story of life is contained. For Kelly, the entire personality is either the result of attempts to avoid and resolve incompatibilities or the expression of unresolved incompatibilities.

McClelland's variant of the cognitive dissonance position, however, agrees with the purer theories only for large incompatibilities, but it considers small incompatibilities to be pleasant and therefore sought after. Though incompatibilities are still characterized as tension states, McClelland does not assume that all degrees of tension are unpleasant. He portrays the person as seeking small increments in tension but avoiding large increments.

Concerning tension, the activation version of the consistency model is more similar to McClelland than to Kelly. Though activation is characterized as tension, the person is not portrayed as uniformly minimizing tension. When the tension level is higher than customary it will be reduced, but when it is lower than customary it will be increased. The person finds tension of a too meager degree as unpleasant as tension of a too intense degree.

According to the consistency model, the only attributes of the person considered both inherent and important for understanding personality are (1) the bases for reacting emotionally to incompatibilities and (2) the broad techniques whereby unpleasant emotional experiences can be terminated. But the content of thoughts and perceptions are learned, as is the customary level of activation. Unlike conflict and fulfillment theories, consistency theories offer no definition of great forces in terms of concrete, immutable content. This eclecticism with regard to the likely content of personality is the major reason why consistency theories stress individual uniqueness and the periphery rather than core level of personality.

Because they do not stress conflict in which one of the two opposing forces has the power to detect and thwart the other, consistency theories have no need for the concept of defense. And lo and behold, they do not use it! In Kelly's view, when a construct fails to accurately predict an observed occurrence, the person modifies the construct to make it a better predictor. This process of modification is properly considered rational trial and error, not defense. McClelland believes that the person straightforwardly approaches those domains of experience that typically have yielded small degrees of unexpectedness and avoids those that typically have yielded great degrees of unexpectedness. Actually, McClelland and Kelly explicitly indicate that the concept of defense is unnecessary. This emphasis is even more extreme than in fulfillment theory, which, though it does not make defense constant, recognizes its importance under certain circumstances of living.

In contrast, Fiske and Maddi tend somewhat toward a notion of defensiveness. They refer to the person's attempts to correct for situations in which a discrepancy between actual and customary activation has already taken place. The person achieves such correction by manufacturing or denying stimulus impact according to whether the activation level needs to be raised or lowered. Such corrections distort the real impact of the stimulation. But Fiske and Maddi do not explicitly use the concept of defense and do not refer in their notion of correction to any inhibition of real parts of human nature to avoid conflict with society. All in all, it seems reasonable to conclude that the concept of defense is not very important in the consistency model.

In considering the person's entire *life span,* the consistency model, like the fulfillment model, portrays personality as changing fairly continuously. The emphasis on change seems understandable in a position that does not emphasize conflict, defense, or inherent personality characteristics with immutable content. *Personality change* should occur as a concomitant of the natural process of encountering different events in the world of experience. If there is any difference between the fulfillment and consistency models regarding the nature of personality change, it is that the former emphasizes patterned change in the form of ever increasing differentiation and integration, or *psychological growth,* more than the latter does. But this distinction comes very close to splitting hairs. After all, psychological growth is a notion implicit in Kelly's thinking and of explicit importance in the theorizing of Fiske and Maddi, who actually provide an explanation for it rather than merely assuming it as most of the fulfillment theorists do.

SOME ISSUES RAISED BY THE THREE MODELS ....

As you have seen, *conflict, fulfillment,* and *consistency models* differ in a number of ways, some abstract. Conflict theory, for example, assumes that the person and society basically aim at different things, while fulfillment theory assumes that the goals of the person and society are compatible. Such abstract differences raise issues that are difficult to resolve, certainly in terms of empirical evidence and even in terms of rational argumentation. From my point of view, the most fruitful inquiry that can be conducted with such abstract characteristics is that of determining whether each position has logical consistency. Thus, if a theory makes the assumption that the person and society are antagonistic, it is only logical to also assume that life is, at best, a compromise. To see life otherwise would be inconsistent with the assumption of inevitable conflict.

I tried to consider the internal logic of the three models and to determine, in some rudimentary way, how well certain theories exemplifying the models conform to that logic. This is a very difficult task, partly because the particular theories are sometimes incomplete and metaphorically stated. Nonetheless, it seems clear to me that most *conflict, fulfillment,* and *consistency theories* show reasonable logical consistency. But even more important, the essential features of these models, aside from any particular theories that fall within them, are quite consistent. These three models, then, emerge as serious descriptions of the *core of personality.*

But is there anything more we can do toward deciding which of the models, or their features, are most fruitful for understanding personality?

Certainly. Although further consideration of the abstract issues raised by their differences is not likely to be useful, it seems to me that there are some slightly more concrete issues deducible from these differences that may well bear further exploration here. The issues I will explore in this chapter refer to core rather than peripheral considerations, for these issues do not refer to individual differences but to shared attributes of people. Also, these core-related issues are concrete enough to render empirical research relevant. Hence, there is much to learn from addressing these issues. As you will see, some of them involve only differences between two of the models and others agreement of two of the models and disagreement with the third.

First Issue: Is the Concept of Defense Tenable?

Both conflict and fulfillment positions use the concept of defense, whereas consistency positions ordinarily do not consider the concept necessary. The concept of defense has also received considerable criticism from psychologists who are not personologists and from philosophers, mainly on the grounds that it seems too implausible. Therefore, this first issue is very important to this attempt to determine the most fruitful directions in which to theorize about human personality.

We should approach discussion of this issue by first ensuring agreement concerning the meaning of *defense.* According to all theorists who use the concept, a defense is a technique for avoiding the anxiety that would be aroused by recognizing that there existed in you some thought or action that would lead to punishment, guilt, or feelings of unworthiness, the bases of which lie in conflictual parent-child relationships. This conflict results either because the aims of the person and the society are inevitably incompatible or because these aims have become incompatible through society's failure. The defense is instituted virtually at the same time as the arousal of anxiety; therefore, little anxiety is actually experienced if the defense is effective.

Once instituted, the defense tends to persist because the underlying conflict also persists.

The successful defense avoids anxiety by distorting or denying to awareness the underlying conflict. It does so by blocking recognition of the thoughts or actions that would bring the person into difficulty with society or its internalized form in the conscience. This blocking of recognition is an active process, not merely the absence of awareness through inattention or habit. Indeed, the person would be unable to become aware of the thoughts or actions even if he or she tried or were pushed by others. The underlying conflict would have to be resolved or at least accepted before any awareness could occur.

As you can see, any theory of defense is complicated, including a conceptualization of both conflict and unconscious mental content. In addition, theorists who use the concept of defense generally recognize different kinds of defensive operations. The smallest number of defenses is found in Rogers's theory, which considers only out-and-out denial and distortion. The largest number is found in psychoanalytic thinking, which includes such examples as repression, projection, denial, reaction formation, intellectualization, undoing, and sublimation. In psychoanalytic theory, each of these defenses has a different effect on living, though all ward off anxiety by rendering conflicts unconscious.

FOUNDING CASE STUDIES. The development and popularity of *defense* came about through the observations of personologists interested prmarily in psychopathological states. By and large, these observations represent unsystematic empirical evidence in the form of certain insight-provoking cases. Summarizing them would help you sharpen your appreciation of the issue cocerning the tenability of *defense*. Many of the most compelling of these observations were made by Freud and his early collaborator (Breuer & Freud, 1936) in their study of women with *hysterical symptoms,* such as paralysis or anesthesia of the hands, blindness, incessant aches, inability to speak—most peculiar for people who seemed free of physical defects. Their

symptoms often made no sense from a physiological point of view. For example, an inability to feel in the hands—*glove anesthesia*—would be almost impossible to come by on the basis of injury to the nervous system (Freud, 1893). The nerve groupings in a hand make it much more likely to lose feeling in one side or the other than in the whole hand. Further, injury to the nerve tracts in the arm or shoulder would produce more widespread defects than in the hand alone. In addition, when both hands are rendered devoid of sensation, whatever strange injury that took place in one arm or shoulder would have also had to occur in the other—a most unlikely prospect! One could think that damage to the central nervous system was the cause, but again such damage would have more widespread effects than on the hands alone. As a further example of the physiological nonsense of hysterical symptoms, paralyses in these people were not associated with progressive deterioration of muscular tone even though the muscles were apparently unused. These weird phenomena inclined many physicians of that time to the belief that the apparent absence of physical injury was due not to their own limited diagnostic capability but to the nonphysical basis of the symptoms.

In an urgent attempt to learn more about this disorder, Freud and Breuer began hypnotizing their patients in the hope of overcoming the symptoms. Picture their amazement when it became apparent that hysterical symptoms are lost in the hypnotized state! Glove anesthesia, paralysis, blindness—all disappeared only to return soon after the hypnotic state ended, providing the definitive observation of the nonphysical basis of hysterical symptoms.

To learn more about what these hysterical women were like, Freud and Breuer began asking them questions and encouraging them to say whatever was in their minds. Two things were clearly established. First, these women were not particularly disturbed by their symptoms, however bizarre they were. One would think that such extreme symptoms in the absence of apparent cause would move anyone to anxiety. Instead, the women showed what the neurologist Charcot had already dubbed the sublime indifference of the hysteric. Second, the women understood and remembered less about themselves than people free of such symptoms did. Often, friends were more helpful in relating the patients' pasts than they themselves. In addition, the patients showed little curiosity about and awareness of what was happening to them and to the world around them. They were intellectually uncritical to an inordinate degree. But when pushed to remember specific events from childhood through the combined effects of saying whatever came into their heads and having their utterances interpreted by the physician, they often became extremely anxious. As these confrontations accumulated, the anxieties diminished—as well as the symptoms—all the while that it became progressively easier for them to remember past events.

These observations led Freud and Breuer to an explanation of hysteria stressing the concept of *defense.* For them, *hysteria* is clearly caused psychologically rather than physically. The immediate cause is a mechanism of defense—repression—that has the effect of blocking action and thought. Which actions and thoughts? Obviously ones that could provoke *anxiety.* What would they be? Obviously ones that would bring retaliation from society or make the person feel guilty. So the deeper cause is *conflict,* which, because of its ability to arouse anxiety, leads to defense. But because the actions and thoughts defended against are important and basic, they cannot be rendered nonexistent through defense, and they will hence surely find some sort of expression. The symptoms are their distorted expression of these, defended against thoughts and actions. From here, it was only a hop, skip, and jump to the identification of other defenses and conflicts as underlying other *psychopathological states.* The extraordinarily powerful model of defense was launched. Though later personologists interested in psychopathology have in some cases elaborated and in others simplified the theory of defense, they have left it essentially unchanged. Whenever that theory is used, it will invariably involve conflict, leading

to anxiety, responded to with defense, which takes the form of denying the conflict, to awareness so as to avoid the anxiety.

CONCEPTUAL CRITICISM. The tenability of defense is questioned most insistently by philosophers to whom the concept seems preposterous. If there is an active process whereby conflicts are held out of awareness, there must be some part of the person that can perceive reality and decide what the rest of the person shall and shall not be permitted to know. On the face of it, this idea of a person within a person seems nonsensical to critics of the concept of defense. In the following discussion, I shall consider a number of specific criticisms of attempts to demonstrate the action of defenses empirically. You should recognize that every one of these specific criticisms follows from the general stance that theorizing about persons within persons is foolish. Note that the person-within-a-person criticism refers not to the existence of different parts of the organism—a fact easy enough to accept—but to the attribution of characteristics of the whole organism, such as intelligence and choice, to the separate parts. So, the part of the organism that does the defending as well as the part affected by the defense is considered intelligent, perceptive, and capable of choice. This leads critics of the concept of defense to say that the notion amounts to merely talking about one organism as if it were two. But since it obviously is not two organisms, defense is a nonsensical concept, regardless of its dramatic appeal.

Clearly the organism is only one. Hence, if *defense* necessitated treatment of the organism as two, it would be untenable on *rational grounds.* But the question to be asked at this point is whether it would be possible to translate the extremely figurative language used by defense theorists into terms less implicative of persons within persons. Surely Freud did far too much talking about superegos "fighting" ids and egos "siding with" or "deceiving" one or the other. Such words properly characterize relations among people and, when used to describe relations among parts of the same person, are at best analogical and at worst illogical. It may be possible, however, to describe the relations among parts of personality in terms that capture the essential import of defense while avoiding nonsense. If so, this will amount to demonstrating the analogical status of current statements concerning defense by translating them into statements that describe the techniques whereby consciousness is denied in terms consistent with the known capabilities of organismic parts or systems.

But before any attempt at such translation is made, it must be clear that empirical evidence suggests that a rationally acceptable concept of defense is useful to invoke. Certainly the anecdotal observations I mentioned earlier are partial evidence—but only partial, because they have not been made systematically; that is, the psychotherapists making the observations did so only on people who came to them as patients and, by and large, did not require even that observations of defense be made on all or at least a large proportion of the subjects. Psychotherapists have been known to make conclusions based on striking observations of only one or two patients. However exciting these conclusions may be, they may not apply to people in general, even though it is typically assumed that they do. In addition, psychotherapists' conclusions are often too interpretive for disinterested psychological observers to accept. The bases on which the interpretations have been made are sometimes unstated, raising questions concerning the consistency and objectivity with which they have been applied. Such a state of affairs requires that there be a body of more rigorously systematic empirical observations before it is agreed that there is evidence suggesting the action of something like a defense.

REPRESSION AND REGRESSION. Fortunately, over the past 60 or so years a large number of research studies on the existence and operation of defenses have been done. Though I cannot cover them all here, I can refer you to a number of able reviews (Allport, 1955; Chabot, 1973; Erdelyi, 1974; Eriksen, 1963; Holmes, 1974; Hunt, 1975b; MacKinnon & Dukes, 1962;

Sears, 1944). Here I will discuss some of the more representative and instructive of these studies. Most often the research effort has been devoted to investigations of *repression* or *denial*, a type of defense relevant to all theories incorporating this concept. Some attention has also been given to *projection* and *regression*, methods of defense more specific to psychoanalytic theory.

The bulk of the studies reviewed in this chapter concern the general form of defensiveness that might be called *repression*. This process is important not only in psychoanalytic theory but also in many other positions. The studies concern defensiveness effects on perception and memory. Consideration of research on the specific, highly differentiated defenses associated most exclusively with Freud's position is deferred until Chapter 12.

But before turning to repression, I shall consider two studies on regression that suggest an important point about how and on whom studies of defensiveness should be done. The first study concerning regression is often cited but is not very useful. Mowrer (1940) used small numbers of rats in an experiment involving electric shock. One group of rats was permitted to learn by trial and error that the shock through the grilled floor on which they stood could be turned off by pressing a foot pedal. Another group was given shocks for an approximately equal amount of time but had no pedal to press. Eventually, the latter group learned to avoid shock by sitting up on their hind legs. Once this behavior was firmly instilled, a foot pedal was inserted and the rats were permitted to learn to use it in terminating the shock. From this point on, both groups were frustrated by receiving a shock whenever they pressed this foot pedal; in other words, when they tried to turn off the floor shock they got a shock from what had been the instrument of salvation! The rats that originally had learned to avoid shock by standing on their hind legs almost immediately "regressed" to that habit, while the other rats persisted in pushing the pedal.

What is wrong with this experiment as a demonstration of regression? The main problem is that it does not take into account the fact that regression is a notion inextricably embedded in a broader theoretical framework. For psychoanalysts, regression involves going from a latter stage of psychosexual development to an earlier one, in a partial or more complete sense, this movement being a function of fixation and frustration. By *fixation,* Freud means the overly strong attachment to a particular stage of psychosexual development; by *frustration,* he means the prevention of instinctual gratification in whatever stage the person is in. When frustration becomes strong, retreat to a previous, fixated psychosexual stage may take place. This is called regression. Now it is possible, I suppose, that rats undergo a rudimentary form of psychosexual development; at least, their mating behavior improves with practice. But even if this qualified the rat as an organism on which to test the concept of regression, standing up or pushing a pedal to avoid shock really does not bear sensibly on psychosexual development.

Although it may demonstrate that a newly learned habit may be relinquished, when no longer effective, for a previously learned one, this experiment has nothing to do with regression. One thing is clear: If defensiveness is to be studied in nonhuman organisms, they must at least have some form of psychosexual development, and the specific behaviors studied must be convincing analogues of the human behaviors on which psychoanalytic theory focuses (see Hunt, 1975b). Because these criteria are essentially unmet in animal studies, they thus far provide little for testing psychoanalytic notions of defense.

You might be thinking that if regression were divested of its psychoanalytic parentage, Mowrer's demonstration would be positive evidence. But even without considering psychosexual stages of development, the concept of defense requires some active process of debarring from consciousness for the sake of reducing anxiety. In regression, this debarring is effected when the person returns to some earlier state of being. If rats are to be proper organisms for study, they must have consciousness, for only then will debarring from consciousness constitute a useful procedure of defense. Many psychologists

might be willing to assume that rats or some of the more complex animals have consciousness. But even if consciousness analogous to what can be obtained in humans through self-report exists in animals, its methodological inaccessibility is a formidable barrier. Consciousness may or may not exist in an animal, and if it does it may or may not provide sensible analogies to the human conflict, guilt, and anxiety considered to be the springboards of defense. Even with an emancipated concept of regression, one can see that the study of subhuman organisms is so imprecise as to be of marginal use. The same is true for the study of other defenses, for all require an organism whose consciousness can be scrutinized.

Somewhat more convincing is a well-known study of *regression* by Barker, Dembo, and Lewin (1941). They used 30 preschool children as subjects, turning them loose in a free-play situation. All were above average in intelligence. The children were encouraged to play alone with some toys for a half hour. The next day they were brought back but this time played first with some much more desirable toys. After the first fifteen minutes, the investigator returned the children to the other end of the room without explanation and permitted them to play with the original, less attractive toys for a half hour. During this half hour, the desirable toys were in full view but unavailable. Barker et al. reasoned that if regression is a reality, the frustration involved in giving up the desirable toys would lead to more destructive play with the less desirable toys than the children had shown on the first day of play. The investigators tried to establish age norms for constructiveness of play to see whether any decrease in this characteristic could indeed be thought to represent becoming more childish. Their results clearly show that the expected destructiveness occurs.

This study incorporates one important element of the regression notion, namely, that it is a process of primitivization—of becoming more childish. But the study is not particularly relevant to the psychoanalytic notion of regression, because there was little concern with the specifics of psychosexual development. The results might be used, however, to support a concept of regression emancipated from psychoanalytic theory. The only fly in the ointment—which will crop up constantly in the following discussion—is that there is no way of knowing if the primitivization shown really occurred without conscious awareness, which would make it a bona fide expression of defense. After all, the subjects might have been well aware of their annoyance with the experimenter for showing them the desirable toys but not keeping them out of reach. This shortcoming might have been avoided, because the subjects were humans and not rats, and therefore could have been questioned.

You are now ready to traverse the terrain of repression research. Remember that the concept of defense contains the notion that something mental of an unpleasant nature is being denied awareness. It is important, therefore, to employ human subjects and attempt to determine whether the defensive process, though measurable by the experimenter, is really unavailable to the subject's awareness.

The defense mechanism of repression involves debarring from awareness any sensation, perception, thought, or action that would conflict with values and principles instilled in one by society and has the immediate function of avoiding the anxiety that would accompany awareness of the conflict. The meaning of *repression* in psychoanalytic theory is much the same as in other theories of defense, except that in psychoanalytic theory one can invariably trace the personal contribution to the conflict to the life, sexual, or death instincts. In considering research studies of repression, you will be working at the heart of the issue of the tenability of the concept of defense, because repression is ubiquitously recognized in theories of defense and is considered the basic defense even in psychoanalytic theory. Indeed, Freud first used the concept of repression before hitting on that of defense and switched his primary emphasis to the latter only when it became clear to him that there are additional, more elaborate techniques than repression for avoiding consciousness.

REPRESSION AND VIGILANCE STUDIES OF PERCEPTION. It is fortunate that repression comes so close to the heart of the concept of defense, for there have been many relevant studies. Indeed, such studies, dubbed the "new look" in perception, attracted intense interest in the 1950s and continued for about 20 years (Erdelyi, 1974). The tenability of defense waxed hot in the form of specific research controversies during this exciting time in personology. Studies of repression before the 1950s tended to involve memory of action more than perception and therefore were less striking than the "new look" work. I shall therefore turn to the more perceptual work before considering the memory work.

The notion that people can be especially defensive or especially vigilant in their perceptions, as a function of aspects of personality such as needs and values, was introduced in a series of articles by Bruner and Postman (1947a, 1947b) and Postman, Bruner, and McGinnies (1948). All these experiments use the *tachistoscope*, a device that presents visual stimuli for controllable and very brief lengths of time. Generally speaking, the tachistoscopic procedure involves presenting the stimulus for too short a time to permit recognition and then gradually increasing the duration of subsequent presentations. Subjects are to say what they think the stimulus is after each exposure, with the important data being the lengths of exposure that accompany correct perceptions. Stimuli that have different content or have been presented under varying conditions may have different exposure lengths associated with correct perception. The existence of a group of stimuli that required shorter or longer exposure times for correct perception than did the general run of stimuli led these investigators to invoke the notions of *perceptual vigilance* and *perceptual defense*.

Bruner and Postman (1947a) found that those stimuli associated with experimentally produced anxiety had shorter recognition times than did stimuli not associated with anxiety. In developing the notion of *perceptual vigilance*, these investigators suggest that stimuli of special importance to the person are enhanced in perception and recognized sooner. The other studies concern *perceptual defense.* In the first of these (Bruner & Postman, 1947b), a word-association task was initially administered. Subjects varied, of course, in the speed with which they could think of an associate to the words the experimenter presented. Then these words were presented to the subjects again, this time tachistoscopically. The researchers found that for some subjects, words that involved long association times—presumably indicating emotional disturbance—required much longer tachistoscopic exposures for recognition than did words with medium or short association times. They dubbed this lengthened recognition time *perceptual defense* and likened it to repression. But Bruner and Postman also found that in certain other subjects, words that required a long time for the initial association have lower tachistoscopic recognition time, again suggesting the relevance of perceptual vigilance.

The Postman et al. (1948) study supplements the other two in suggesting that values as well as anxiety and underlying emotional disturbance can affect perception. They chose words for tachistoscopic presentation that represented six broad value areas (e.g., religion, economics, aesthetics) and sought to determine beforehand their subjects' commitment to these areas through the use of a revelant standard psychological test. Sure enough, they found a relationship between the intensity of subjects' commitment to each value area and the speed with which they recognized tachistoscopically presented words relevant to those areas. Subjects with an intense commitment to theoretical values, for example, had faster recognition times for words from this value area and slower recognition times for words from value areas to which they had minimal commitment. The concepts of perceptual vigilance and perceptual defense are again used to explain the results.

Although these three studies have more or less bearing on the concept of repression, not until the subsequent study of McGinnies (1949) did the relevance of this kind of research became unquestionably clear. McGinnies selected a group of socially taboo words, such as *whore,*

bitch, belly, and *Kotex,* and a group of neutral, acceptable words for tachistoscopic presentation to college student subjects. While his subjects were trying to tell him what they saw in the tachistoscope, McGinnies was measuring their *galvanic skin response,* which is essentially an index of the electrical conductivity of the skin, which rises when sweating increases. Such increases in sweating generally indicate emotional arousal, such as anxiety.

McGinnies obtained striking results. Not only did the taboo words require longer tachistoscopic exposure for correct recognition, but subjects also showed increased sweating on the tachistoscopic exposures of the taboo words that were too brief to permit visual recognition. No comparable increase in sweating prior to conscious recognition occurred with neutral words. These findings are detailed in Table 10-1. The higher recognition time for taboo words was considered a manifestation of perceptual defense. The greater sweating accompanying prerecognition trials with taboo words was considered an indication not only of the active nature of defensive processes but of an unconscious detection or manifestation of anxiety elicited by the words.

Extraordinary as the results of this study may seem, they are just what you would expect from the action of the defense mechanisms of denial. If some percepts are to be debarred from consciousness, some part of the organism must be able to detect them and rule them out. The findings of increased sweating suggest that there is some kind of organismic response to taboo words and that this incipient emotional response is part of the process of denial. McGinnies's choice of taboo words was also appropriate, reflecting as they did psychosexual matters unsuitable for polite discussion and thought.

Lest we conclude prematurely that there is clear empirical evidence favoring the existence of the repressive defense, we should recognize that no sooner had McGinnies's results appeared than they were resoundingly attacked. The specific criticisms reflected the general belief that the concept of defense is untenable because it seems to require theorizing about a person

TABLE 10-1 Summary of the Raw Data and Statistical Tests for All Observers with Respect to Both Galvanic Skin Response and Thresholds of Recognition for Neutral and Critical Stimulus Words

| Observer | MEAN MICROAMMETER READINGS DURING PRERECOGNITION EXPOSURES | | MEAN THRESHOLDS OF RECOGNITION | |
	Neutral Words	Critical Words	Neutral Words	Critical Words
1	37.80	40.46	.055	.184
2	40.96	41.53	.044	.094
3	39.31	42.06	.054	.080
4	38.34	40.80	.103	.126
5	41.48	43.76	.040	.064
6	41.41	47.08	.070	.130
7	40.75	39.94	.057	.104
8	39.98	42.85	.063	.076
9	39.44	42.68	.059	.130
10	40.02	42.71	.049	.223
11	39.88	41.55	.046	.077
12	41.27	44.02	.057	.091
13	40.56	41.37	.033	.037
14	40.19	41.42	.034	.054
15	40.85	40.63	.046	.056
16	40.83	41.84	.036	.046
	Mean diff. = 1.98 $t = 5.10$ $P < .01$		Mean diff. = .045 $t = 3.96$ $P < .01$	

SOURCE: From "Emotionality and Perceptual Defense," by E. McGinnies, 1949, *Psychological Review, 56.*

within a person. Howes and Solomon (1950) voice two main objections. The first criticism is that subjects might well have known in a conscious way the content of the taboo words for some trials before they felt certain enough of their knowledge to voice it. After all, if you were in their position and saw what looked like *bitch,* you might not have wanted to risk saying that to an adult in authority—the experimenter —unless you were absolutely sure you were right. But maybe you started sweating as soon as you first thought the word was *bitch.* As you can see, this is a serious criticism. If it is true, all that is meant by the finding concerning longer tachistoscopic times for taboo words is that people decide which of their thoughts and perceptions to express so as to avoid unnecessary embarrassment. There is nothing here of defense in the sense of an unconsciously operating process

actively debarring certain perceptions from awareness.

The second criticism made by Howes and Solomon concerns the fact that the taboo and neutral words McGinnies used differ markedly in their familiarity, or frequency of past occurrence in subjects' experience. By consulting the listing of the frequency with which major words appear in written usage, prepared by Thorndike and Lorge (1944), Howes and Solomon determined that McGinnies's taboo words appear with much lower frequency than his neutral words. This led to the criticism that the different tachistoscopic lengths required for the perception of words was a function of the frequency with which those words had been experienced in the past rather than of any involvement with defensive operations. This criticism is general enough to apply to the three experiments described above as well as this one. These two psychologists really put their teeth into the criticism when they demonstrate in further studies (Howes & Solomon, 1951; Solomon & Howes, 1951) that tachistoscopic exposure lengths for word recognition could be predicted from the Thorndike-Lorge tables of word frequency.

Even though the frequency criticism has obvious cogency and some empirical support, there is the rankling thought that it is really not as devastating as it might seem at first. After all, if you are interested in the frequency with which people have experienced a word in the past, you must take into account not only external sources (e.g., books, speeches, other people) but also their own imaginations and thought processes. Once you recognize this fact, the engaging simplicity of the explanation Solomon and Howes put forth is largely lost. Not only does their frequency explanation become extraordinarily more complex, it is not clear that it is even testable anymore. What is a comprehensive measure of frequency of experience of a word in the past? Certainly the Thorndike-Lorge listings cannot be used, since they reflect rather formal, written usage for public consumption—the kind of usage found in magazines and newspapers. Especially concerning the experience of taboo words, you cannot possibly trust the Thorndike-Lorge word lists. Such lists certainly underestimate frequency of exposure to such words, especially when you take into account the person's own thoughts and fantasies alongside informal and private verbal interactions with others. So what could the relationship between Thorndike-Lorge word frequency and tachistoscopic recognition time found by Solomon and Howes (1951) and Howes and Solomon (1951) possibly mean?

Fortunately, psychologists such as Eriksen (1963) have scrutinized the data of these two studies and partially answered this question. It turns out that "practically all of the relationship can be traced to a difference between words having zero or very low frequencies in the Thorndike-Lorge counts and words having high frequency" (Eriksen, 1963, p. 40). For words in the frequency range of 10 to 3,000 occurrences per million in the above count, there is virtually no relationship between frequency of occurrence and tachistoscopic recognition time! This useful bit of information means that the frequency criticism of Solomon and Howes is cogent only when one works with words having especially high or low frequencies of occurrence in formal, public usage. This more accurate version of the criticism hardly destroys the findings of Bruner and Postman (1947a, 1947b), McGinnies (1949), and Postman et al. (1948). Following his analysis of the findings of Solomon and Howes (1951) and Howes and Solomon (1951), Eriksen (1963) concludes that "we may note that the empirical relationship between frequency of past occurrence and recognition threshold has been amply demonstrated, although the magnitude of this relationship has undoubtedly been considerably overestimated" (p. 44).

We can now return to the other criticism made by Solomon and Howes, namely, that the relatively long exposure times associated with taboo words reflect merely a conscious decision on the subjects' part not to risk embarrassment should they inaccurately identify the words as taboo ones. This criticism is completely sound from the viewpoint of reason when leveled at the McGinnies experiment but has considerably less relevance to the other experiments because they employed not taboo words but anxiety-provoking or value-related ones. It should not have been embarrassing for subjects to report such words, even if they turned out to be wrong. Nonetheless, it is the McGinnies experiment that comes closest to a demonstration of the defense mechanism of repression as it is normally used in theories of defense.

There is no logical counterargument to the Solomon and Howes criticism, but there is one empirical study that escapes the criticism while still bearing on repression. In this study, McCleary and Lazarus (1949) used nonsense syllables for stimuli in place of meaningful words. For half of the nonsense syllables, an unpleasant, anxiety-provoking effect was established by accompanying a series of one-second exposures of the syllable with an electric shock. Soon, even though the experimenters stopped using shock, the subjects were showing increased sweating, measured by the galvanic skin response, every time one of the syllables that had previously been shocked appeared. After this conditioning had been established, all the syllables, including the half that had not been associated with shock, were presented at tachistoscopic speeds ranging from extremely brief up to the approximate time required for accurate perception by most people. As in the McGinnies experiment, the galvanic skin response was recorded on each tachistoscopic trial, along with the subjects' verbal report of what they saw. In the tachistoscopic part of the experiment, no electric shock was used. As you can see, the experiment's design was the same as that of McGinnies except that nonsense syllables were used in place of taboo words, with some of the syllables rendered anxiety provoking by the pretachistoscopic pairing with electric shock. Clearly, it is unlikely that the shocked versus nonshocked nonsense syllables had differed in frequency in the subjects' past experience or that they were socially unacceptable and therefore the source of potential embarrassment. McCleary and Lazarus's study successfully avoids both criticisms made by Solomon and Howes.

We should, therefore, be especially interested in the results in order to consider the empirical tenability of the concept of defense. In the trials in which the subjects' verbal reports were wrong, McCleary and Lazarus (1949) found that sweating was greater for the previously shocked syllables than for those unaccompanied by shock. They conclude that "at tachistoscopic exposure speeds too rapid for conscious discrimination . . . the subject is still capable of responding in a discriminatory way." They suggest the term *subception* for this apparently autonomic form of perception. Clearly these results support the part of the theory of defense that involves the keen sensitivity of some aspect of the organism to potentially threatening perceptions that permits a person to guard against them. But this experiment does not show that the previously shocked syllables required longer tachistoscopic exposure times for accurate perception than did the nonshocked syllables—indeed, the opposite result

was obtained, something more consistent with the idea of perceptual vigilance than perceptual defense! Taken as a whole, this study only partially supports the repressive aspect of defense. Perhaps this state of affairs can be traced to what was lost in the process of developing a design that could circumvent the criticism of Solomon and Howes. While the shocked nonsense syllables undoubtedly were unpleasant stimuli, it is not at all clear—or likely—that they articulated in any deep way the kinds of intense underlying conflict that all defense theorists agree should provoke defenses. The McCleary and Lazarus study presents, as laboratory experiments frequently must, a pale shadow of life. Once this is appreciated, it may seem surprising that even the subception part of defensiveness could be demonstrated.

Another approach to circumventing the criticisms of Solomon and Howes is exemplified in a study by Cowen and Beier (1954). They retain taboo and neutral words as the stimuli, increasing the likelihood of engaging more deep-seated conflicts than could be done with the technique of McCleary and Lazarus. Instead of tachistoscopic presentation, these investigators achieved a similar effect by using blurred typewritten copies of the words arranged into booklets. The arrangement was such that successive pages went from very blurred to very clear for each word. The important datum was the number of pages that had to be turned before the word was correctly identified.

To avoid the criticism involving word familiarity, Cowen and Beier correlated number of pages turned for correct identification with the frequency of occurrence listed for the word by Thorndike and Lorge. They found the correlation to be zero for the words they used. To avoid the criticisms involving embarrassment at verbalizing taboo words, they had half the subjects report to an experimenter of the same sex and the other half to one of the opposite sex. In addition, all experimenters read the entire list of words to be used, including the taboo ones, to the subjects before the experiment began. Cowen and Beier claim that the combination of these two procedures should decrease the embarrassment factor to the point where it cannot be invoked in the explanation of findings. They also demonstrated that there were no important differences between the results obtained from experimenter-subject pairs of the same gender and those of opposite gender.

The main result of this study is that the taboo words indeed required more page turns for correct identification than did the neutral words. These results corroborate those of McGinnies in the context of a design that at least comes close to avoiding the criticisms of Solomon and Howes. Considering these results along with those of McCleary and Lazarus, whose study also avoids the criticisms, the empirical case for the existence of a repressive defense is reasonably sound. One could still say of the Cowen and Beier study that there was some remaining embarrassment, even though the experimenter had alerted subjects as to the nature of the words they would see, but this comes much closer to hairsplitting than it did in the McGinnies study.

Blum (1955) tried another approach to avoid the criticisms leveled at the initial perceptual defense studies. He used as stimulus materials pictures taken from his Blacky Test (Blum, 1949), which show a young dog in various interactions with two older dogs (its parents). As is described more fully in Chapter 11, the interactions were chosen to exemplify facets of parent-child relationships considered important in psychoanalytic theory. Blum presented a slide with 4 of these pictures tachistoscopically to subjects, who had to say which picture was in each of the four positions. All subjects knew the 11 Blacky pictures well but did not know that in reality the same 4 pictures were presented throughout the 48 trials (the pictures were rotated so that they appeared in each position the same number of times over the trials). After the experiment, all subjects said that they were unable to recognize any of the pictures and for them the experiment was a kind of guessing game.

On the basis of other information, it was determined that some subjects actually had conflicts relating to some of the pictures and no conflicts relating to others. Blum reasoned that there

should be fewer identifications of conflict-laden pictures than of nonconflictual pictures. But you should recognize that since subjects thought all 11 Blacky pictures would appear, though only 4 actually did, they might well have identified pictures that were not presented. Blum argues that there should be no difference in frequency of calling conflictual and nonconflictual pictures that were not presented, because the perceptual defense notion requires that a threatening stimulus actually occur. Otherwise, there is no special reason for defensiveness. The results were as expected. For actually presented pictures, the means on calling conflictual and nonconflictual pictures were 9.42 and 17.12, respectively; for pictures not presented, the mean calls were 15.20 and 16.69, respectively. It is especially interesting that among highly conflictual pictures, those not actually presented were called by subjects much more than were those presented.

Bootzin and Natsoulas (1965) performed a similar experiment that had some additional refinements and used a combination of threatening and nonthreatening stimuli on each trial. Suffice it to say that their results also justify the interpretation of a defensive process. While it is not entirely clear in this or Blum's study whether the defense takes place in the perceptual process itself or somewhere between perception and the subject's verbal response (see Natsoulas, 1965), there seems to be defensiveness of some kind.

Having concluded that there is at least some empirical support for the concept of repression, I shall now turn to the vexing problem posed by the findings that suggest perceptual vigilance. Thus far, you have observed in passing that some subjects seem to be particularly sensitive rather than insensitive to words that refer to their dominant values and to words and nonsense syllables that provoke anxiety. It is important to decide what meaning to attribute to perceptual vigilance, as it seems to exist alongside perceptual defense. But before pursuing the matter further, let me introduce you to an important related body of research concerning the effects of repression on memory rather than on perception.

REPRESSION AND VIGILANCE STUDIES OF MEMORY. Research interest in the effects of repression on memory actually predates concern with its effects on perception. Rosenzweig and Mason (1934) clearly did the first study in this tradition. As subjects, they used 40 children and gave each child the task of solving a series of jigsaw puzzles, with a prize for the child who did best. The experimenters had arranged things beforehand so that each child was permitted to finish half the tasks assigned to him or her but was interrupted in working on the other half. The interruptions were carried out in such a manner that the children thought they were failing at those tasks. After 45 minutes of puzzle solving followed by a free interval of one minute, subjects were asked to name the picture puzzles they remembered having worked on. Of the 40 children, 16 remembered more completed than "failed" tasks, 13 recalled fewer completed than "failed" tasks, 9 recalled an equal number of both, and 2 recalled no tasks. At best, only 16 of the 40 subjects could be thought of as remembering according to a theory of repression. Thirteen subjects seemed particularly sensitive to their failures, which should have been anxiety provoking.

These two groups offer phenomena analogous to perceptual defense and perceptual vigilance. The subjects especially good at recalling their failures should not be considered more accurate than those who could remember only their successes; rather, it is the 9 subjects who remembered an equal number of completed and failed tasks whose mental functioning was most accurate. The same holds true for subjects showing perceptual defense and vigilance, though the data are not as clear as in Rosenzweig and Mason. When people need more exposures to recognize some of a group of stimuli, they are being selectively insensitive and, therefore, inaccurate. When they need fewer exposures, they are being selectively sensitive, which is also a form of inaccuracy. Only people who are neither vigilant nor defensive have accurate perceptual processes. Although such people undoubtedly exist in the perception studies described earlier, they were not singled out for analysis in the way they were by Rosenzweig and Mason.

Thinking that the number of subjects showing repression could be increased, from 16 of 40, by arousing a sense of pride in accomplishment, Rosenzweig (1933, 1943) designed another experiment. He presented the same kind of puzzles to one group of adult subjects as an "intelligence test" and to another group in an informal manner emphasizing the test itself rather than individual performance. The first group should have had their pride aroused or self-esteem threatened, whereas the second group should not have. Then, as in the original study, each subject completed half the puzzles and "failed" the other half. Under the pride-arousing condition, 17 subjects remembered more finished tasks, 8 more unfinished tasks, and 5 an equal number. Under the less stressful condition, only 7 subjects remembered more finished tasks while 19 remembered more unfinished tasks and 4 showed no difference between the two. The findings clearly show that the greater the threat to self-esteem, the stronger the repressive tendencies. But it is still true that in this study some subjects seemed especially sensitive to their failures and some showed neither sensitivity nor insensitivity.

I should point out that it has been typical to criticize these studies for using the interrupted-task technique (e.g., Sears, 1950), because when there is no special threat to self-esteem and interruption is not structured by the experimenter as failure, the technique is widely known to lead to a preponderant tendency to recall the interrupted rather than the completed tasks (see Zeigarnik, 1927). The criticism states that it is unwise to try to demonstrate repression, requiring as it does the opposite recall, with such a procedure. From my point of view, this is not a sensible criticism. Special sensitivity to uncompleted tasks has never been convincingly explained and remains an intriguing phenomenon precisely because it suggests defensiveness in its inaccurate rendition of reality and is analogous to the phenomenon of perceptual vigilance.

In another study, MacKinnon and Dukes (1962) attempted to arouse guilt in their subjects, reasoning that this procedure would initiate defensive reactions. Each of the 93 subjects was left alone, though secretly observed by the experimenter through a one-way vision screen, to work on a series of tasks almost universally impossible to solve. The subjects were given a booklet containing the answers to all problems and told they could not look at the answers while working the problems. MacKinnon and Dukes argued that repression could be expected to occur only in subjects who violated the prohibition—43% of the group—and then, only if they felt guilty about their violations.

When subsequently asked to recall the problems they had worked on, violators (most of whom showed no signs of guilt) remembered most often the problems the solutions of which they had seen and least often those the solutions of which they had not. A small, atypical group of subjects, who had violated the prohibition and gave signs of guilt in behavior and verbal report, tended to recall problems the solutions of which they had looked up less well than they had other problems. These results are particularly interesting, because they suggest that one can expect a defensive reaction only when some conflict actually occurs for the person.

Several other studies have employed a different procedure to investigate the effects of repression on memory. Zeller (1950) first constructed experimental and control groups out of pretested subjects so that there were no group differences in number of trials necessary to learn a set of neutral verbal materials (nonsense syllables). Then the groups were given a psychomotor test rigged so that the control subjects would perform well and have an enjoyable experience while the experimental subjects would perform badly and feel threatened. Following this, all subjects had to relearn the originally neutral materials. It was interpreted as a sign of repression (instituted in the face of threat and generalizing to the associated verbal materials) that experimental subjects required more trials to relearn than the control subjects did. The final procedure involved explaining the rigging of success and failure on the psychomotor task to the experimental subjects and then retesting for speed of relearning. The effect of the debriefing should have been to remove the threat and, hence, the occasion for repression. Consistent with this, the experimental and control groups no longer differed in learning speed. This last finding suggests what Freud meant in "the return of the repressed": If that which has been repressed is still in the mind, it should be recoverable when defensiveness is no longer necessary. Zeller (1951) also demonstrated these effects when the behavior scrutinized for signs of repression is what they recall rather than number of trials to relearn. Several independent reports show similar findings (e.g., Flavell, 1955; Penn, 1964).

Predictably, criticisms have arisen from researchers convinced that an alternative explanation to that of repression is best. Aborn's (1953) findings suggest that when subjects in the kind of situation used by Zeller are given special instructions to attend to the material to be learned, there is no difference in performance between those who are threatened and those who are not. This simple instruction to remain alert should not have been effective if repression was indeed operating, because defenses are supposed to operate unconsciously. In a similar assault on the repression interpretation, D'Zurilla (1965) shows that in the kind of situation Zeller used, the threatened subjects reported thinking about the psychomotor task more than the nonthreatened subjects did. D'Zurilla argues that if the slower learning of the threatened subjects was indeed due to repression, they should have thought about the materials less, not more.

Holmes and Shallow (1969) have tried to provide direct evidence that an *interference* interpretation is at least as cogent as that involving repression. To a procedure similar to that of Zeller, they added a group that experienced interference (the task they were performing was interrupted at 30-second intervals by parts of a movie). As shown in Figure 10-1, both this group and the group threatened in the manner of Zeller's study recalled the materials previously learned less well than the control group, which was neither threatened nor interrupted. Following debriefing, there were no recall differences among the three groups. Holmes and Shallow believe that not only interruption but

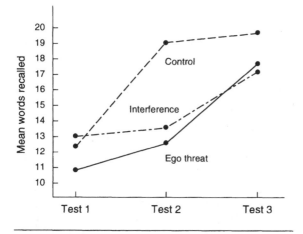

**FIGURE 10-1 Mean Number of Words Recalled
on Test 1, Before Experimental Manipulation;
Test 2, After Experimental Manipulation; and
Test 3, After Debriefing.**
SOURCE: From "Reduced Recall After Ego Threat:
Repression or Response Competition?" by D. S. Holmes
and J. R. Shallow, 1969, *Journal of Personality and Social
Psychology, 13.*

also threat is best interpreted as an interference
rather than a defensiveness phenomenon (see
Holmes, 1974). It is equally plausible, however,
that recall can be worsened in several ways,
including interference and repression. In a way,
it is surprising that results from experiments
such as these should at all support the defensiveness hypothesis, because the conditions of threat
are really not such extreme assaults on the person as those that have provoked personality theorists to their hypotheses about repression.

A flaw in the preceding studies concerning
recall and relearning is that only repression was
studied. Although repression is admittedly the
basic defense, there are others that might especially sensitize the person. Truax (1957) reports
an experiment of special importance because it
took this problem into account. Using a personality test, he selected subjects with a high or a
low tendency to repress, reasoning that only the
former would respond to threat by decreased
recall and slow relearning. Truax introduced
another procedural improvement in this research
tradition by associating threat with only some of

the stimulus materials to be learned and exposing all subjects to all stimuli. Thus, subjects
served as their own controls. His findings are
consistent with the defensiveness theory in that
subjects prone to repression indeed recalled and
relearned the threatening stimuli less well than
the nonthreatening stimuli. If anything, subjects
not prone to repression did better on threatening
than nonthreatening stimuli.

Although this study lends formidable support
for the existence of defensiveness, controversy
still abounds. Tudor and Holmes (1973) report
a similar study using recall for completed and
uncompleted tasks under stress and nonstress
conditions. They did not find that subjects
prone to repression recalled fewer incompletions
under stress, as one might expect. But their findings are severely complicated by differences in
the initial learning of completed and uncompleted tasks.

MORE-COMPREHENSIVE STUDIES. As is so
often the case in research, a number of ground-
breaking studies must be done for the methodological and substantive problems in an area to
become clear. Defensiveness is no exception. The
maturing of defensiveness research is clearly seen
in the work of personologists such as Eriksen
who join together emphases on perception and
memory in the context of a more sophisticated
version of defense theory than earlier investigators employed. Eriksen (1963) points out

that the clinical concept of repression is more
sophisticated than to assume that all people or
even a majority of people automatically repress
any sexual or aggressive ideation, or that all anxiety-arousing thoughts or feelings are repressed.
Instead, repression is a defense mechanism used
sometimes by some people to handle anxiety-
arousing thoughts or feelings whose anxiety-provoking nature is a function of the individual's own
unique past experience. Thus one would not
expect a great deal of communality among people
in terms of the kind of stimuli that should lead to
repression. Furthermore, theories of personality
dynamics also recognize that there are other types
of defense mechanisms. Repression is not the only
way individuals defend against ego-threatening
stimulation.

Intellectualization, reaction formation, and projection are defensive mechanisms that one might expect actually to lead to a sensitization for a stimulus related to the conflict. In the instance of reaction formation, the person manifesting this defense seems to be particularly alert to finding and stamping out the evil that he denies in himself. Similarly, in the case of projection, those manifesting this defense are considered to be hyper-alert to detecting the presence of the defended-against impulse in others. Intellectualization frequently leads to a considerable preoccupation with the subject matter of the unacceptable impulse.

These differences in defensive mechanisms would be expected to have different perceptual concomitants. In the case of repression or denial one might expect a tendency for the subject to manifest avoidance or higher duration thresholds for stimuli related to the sources of conflict. On the other hand, those manifesting defenses of intellectualization, reaction formation or projection might be expected to show a lower duration threshold for anxiety-related stimuli. (pp. 42–43)

There are two things of great importance in this passage. The first is that perceptual vigilance may reflect the sensitizing defenses, such as *reaction formation* and *intellectualization,* whereas perceptual defense reflects the desensitizing defenses, such as *repression* and *denial.* I would suggest, further, that the effects of sensitization and desensitization on memory, as the recall of failed or completed tasks, also reflect these two kinds of defensive process. The second important point is that research concerning the effects of defense on perception should include independent information on the kinds of defenses the subject generally tends to use, so that one can predict precisely what kinds of perceptual effects one will find. It seems to me that this point is well taken in the study of defensive effects on memory and other aspects of cognition.

Eriksen has done a number of studies guided by these criteria. In the first, he (Eriksen, 1951a) used hospitalized mental patients who were selected on the bases of their having conflicts in specified need areas and of their likelihood of manifesting desensitizing defensive operations. The degree of emotional disturbance in the need areas of

aggression, homosexuality, and succorance was assessed through use of a modified word-association technique. Disturbance scores on this test were then related to the subjects' tachistoscopic recognition times for pictures, some of which related to the three need areas and some of which did not. Patients whose word associations showed significant disturbance in a need area were found to require longer exposure intervals for recognition of the corresponding need-related pictures than for recognition of neutral pictures. The correlations describing this effect are shown in the first three rows of the final three columns in Table 10-2. In another, similar study, Eriksen (1951b) found that emotional stimuli did not necessarily lead to high tachistoscopic recognition times. Subjects who showed extensive, overtly aggressive behavior and who expressed aggressive content in composing stories about pictures were found to have lower recognition times for tachistoscopically presented pictures having aggressive content.

Lazarus, Eriksen, and Fonda (1951) pinpointed the meaning of the opposing trends found in these two studies. Psychiatric outpatients were used as subjects and classified on the basis of their therapeutic interviews and other clinical tests as either *sensitizers* or *repressers,* depending on whether they characteristically responded to anxiety in terms of *intellectualization* as a defense or tended to avoid and *deny* thoughts and ideas related to the conflicts. The results, as shown in Table 10-3, indicate that the sensitizers tended to give freely aggressive and sexual endings to a sentence-completion test whereas the repressers tended to block or distort into innocuous forms those sentence-completion items that normally would suggest either aggressive or sexual content. Further, when performance on the sentence-completion test was compared with auditory perception of hostile and sexual sentences heard against a background of noise, the sensitizers were superior to the repressers in recognizing the emotional content.

Eriksen (1952) also did a study relating the effects of repression on perception and on memory. He put a group of college undergraduates

TABLE 10-2   Intercorrelation of the Word Association and Perceptual Recognition Scores for the Three Need Areas*

Score		WORD ASSOCIATION			PERCEPTUAL RECOGNITION		
		Agg.	Suc.	Homo.	Agg.	Suc.	Homo.
Word association	Aggression	.636	.582		.417	.435	.216
	Succorance		.282		−.281	.611	.180
	Homosexuality				−.101	.264	.314
Perceptual recognition	Aggression					.352	.180
	Succorance						.060

*Eta is used as the measure of relationship. Evaluated via the *F* test, an *eta* of .415 is significant at the .95 level.
SOURCE: From "Perceptual Defense as a Function of Unacceptable Needs," by C. W. Eriksen, 1951, *Journal of Abnormal and Social Psychology, 46.*

through a series of tasks, half of which they were permitted to finish and half of which were interrupted, in much the manner of Rosenzweig's work. The tasks were structured as measures of intelligence and the interruptions as failures. As one would expect on the basis of Rosenzweig's work, the subjects showed wide differences in recall of completed or interrupted tasks. The two groups were then administered a word-association test, and in a subsequent testing session their tachistoscopic exposure times for correct recognition of long-, medium-, and short-association-time words were determined. As shown in Table 10-4, the subjects who recalled successfully completed tasks on the memory study showed higher tachistoscopic exposure times for correct recognition of long-association-time words, whereas subjects who recalled their failures on the memory study showed no significant relationship between recognition times and association times.

Once you get to a study that is this sophisticated, concerns itself with the related effects of a defensive process on more than one cognitive

TABLE 10-3   Comparison of Intellectualizers and Repressers on Perceptual Recognition and Sentence Completion Test

Auditory Perceptual Recognition	REPRESSERS (N = 12)		INTELLECTUALIZERS (N = 13)		
	Mean	S.D.	Mean	S.D.	t
Sex*	−.25	1.18	+1.60	1.48	3.32
Hostility*	−1.10	1.32	+.30	1.25	2.67
Neutral*	5.27	1.59	6.17	1.59	1.36
Sentence completion test					
Sex	6.20	1.39	9.10	4.52	2.02
Hostility	5.50	1.70	8.00	4.31	1.77

Note: For a one-tailed test, *t* values of 1.71 and 2.50 are significant at the .05 and the .01 levels, respectively.
*Using adjusted sense-perceived scores (that is, subtracting neutral score from score on critical materials— sex and hostility, respectively; if less critical material was correctly perceived than neutral, score would be minus).
SOURCE: From "Personality Dynamics in Auditory Perceptual Recognition," by R. H. Lazarus, C. W. Eriksen, and C. P. Fonda, 1951, *Journal of Personality, 19.*

function, and considers more than one kind of defensive process, the types of criticisms that seemed so weighty when leveled at the other perceptual studies virtually lose all significance. Though by now, numerous other studies like this one exist, I shall not review them all. I shall, however, consider two more research themes that exemplify the gradual broadening, deepening, and enrichment that has taken place in defensiveness research.

Regarding the first theme, Eriksen and his associates (Eriksen, 1954; Eriksen & Brown, 1956; Eriksen & Davids, 1955) successfully relate the difference between sensitizing and repressing to the difference between hysterical and psychasthenic tendencies as measured by a respected test of psychopathological tendencies, the *Minnesota Multiphasic Personality Inventory (MMPI)*. In current psychoanalytic conceptions of neurosis, the defense mechanism of repression is predominantly associated with hysteria, while that of intellectualization is considered characteristic of the obsessive-compulsive (psychasthenic) neurosis. Eriksen found that

subjects scoring high on the hysteria scale tended to recall successfully completed tasks on the memory test following task performance, whereas subjects scoring high on the psychasthenia scale tended to recall failed tasks. More recently, Cook (1985) reports that repressers showed more sweating (measured by electrical skin conductance) while giving a videotaped talk about themselves, even though they were conscious of less distress, than did sensitizers.

It is now common to measure a *repressive-defensive* style involving subjective report of low anxiety along with strong signs of image maintenance or responding in a socially desirable fashion (Weinberger, Schwartz, & Davidson, 1979). Such repressive-defensive subjects show greater physiological arousal in stressful tasks (Qualls, 1983) and have fewer memories of their activities (Davis & Schwartz, 1986) than do subjects low in image maintenance, whether they are high or low in reported anxiety. There is much support in this kind of research for the notion of defense.

Regarding the second research theme, Gur and Sackheim (1979; Sackheim & Gur, 1978,

TABLE 10-4   Correlations Between Association Times and Recognition Thresholds for the Success-Recall and Failure-Recall Groups Where Recognition Thresholds Have Been Corrected for Total Group Performance

Subjects	SUCCESS-RECALL		Subjects	FAILURE-RECALL	
	r	z		r	z
A	.49	.54	a	.02	.02
B	.46	.50	b	.11	.11
C	.24	.25	c	.05	.05
D	.29	.30	d	.21	.21
E	.43	.46	e	.04	.04
F	.30	.31	f	.00	.00
G	.29	.30	g	−.13	−.13
	.38			.04	

Mean z score:
Combined variance
   estimate: .012
                            $t = 5.73$ $P < .001$

Source: From "Defense Against Ego-Threat in Memory and Perception," by C. W. Eriksen, 1952, *Journal of Abnormal and Social Psychology, 47.*

1979) have meticulously investigated a particular kind of *self-deception;* namely, the misidentification of one's own voice when it is played back as one of a series of voices all reading the same passage. They argue that for such misidentification to qualify as true defensive self-deception, it must be shown that subjects (1) simultaneously hold two contradictory beliefs about which voice they are hearing, (2) are unaware or unconscious of one of the beliefs, and (3) have a motivational commitment to keep that belief unconscious.

In their ingenious and precise research, Gur and Sackheim found evidence for all three criteria of *self-deception.* First, in findings reminiscent of the "subception" mentioned earlier, they showed that subjects whose verbal report misidentified the voices to which they were listening showed in their sweating changes (galvanic skin response) that they discriminated their own voices from others at the physiological level. Thus, these subjects appeared to hold two contradictory beliefs at the same time. That they were unaware of one of these beliefs (second criterion) was shown by postexperimental interviews in which they gave no sign of realizing that they had misidentified voices and by a complex assessment of presence or absence of a well-known, telltale galvanic skin response change that normally occurs in response to the voice following one's own. It appears, therefore, that the subjects were not aware of having one of the contradictory beliefs. The final, or motivational, criterion was approached in two ways. In one study, it was shown that questionnaire respondents who indicated a tendency toward self-deception failed to correctly identify their own voices more often than those with high self-esteem did. In an attempt to demonstrate the causal status of motivational tendencies, Gur and Sackheim did another study in which they found that by increasing or decreasing subjects' self-esteem by making them think they had exceptional or poor intelligence, the researchers could increase or decrease the subjects' subsequent tendency to misidentify their own voices. Through a combination of these two studies, it seems plausible to conclude that the tendency to

misidentify voices is indeed defensive and not due just to inattention.

Too complicated to be presented in detail here, the Gur and Sackheim studies emerge as a model for defensiveness research, despite some controversy (Douglas & Gibbins, 1983; Sackheim & Gur, 1985; Gibbins & Douglas, 1985). Along with the work on repressive and sensitizing styles, these studies represent formidable evidence for the tenability of the concept of defense.

The studies cited demonstrate empirical support for the existence of human defensive reactions that extend across learning, perceptual, and memory processes. Other research in defensiveness adds little new to what I have already considered. To be sure, there seem to be at least two broad categories of defensiveness; namely, *desensitization* and *sensitization.* And certainly there are many loose ends, some of which will prove relevant to issues I will pose later. But with regard to the present issue of whether a concept of defense is tenable, we clearly must conclude that systematic empirical findings exist that support the concept. Happily enough, the systematic studies concur with the anecdotal clinical observations with which I began this discussion of the issue.

Now I shall summarize more precisely. The operation of defenses has been shown both when certain stimuli were rendered anxiety-provoking through experimental manipulation and when stimuli were chosen so as to be likely to engage common conflicts permeating the subjects' lives. The effects of sensitizing and desensitizing defenses have been shown on perception of stimuli exposed for brief periods of time and on memory of activities engaged in previously. Some of the studies show these two kinds of effect to occur together and in a manner consistent with the implications of various defenses for psychopathological tendencies.

PHYSIOLOGICAL MECHANISMS. Although we can now say with some authority that evidence supports the notion of defense as an explanatory concept, we are still left with the nagging criticism, underlying this whole issue, of the nonsensical nature of theorizing that assumes a person within a person. It is time to grapple with this criticism now that it is clear that rigorous scientific evidence recommends the concept of defense. As I suggested earlier, if one can find a basis on which the overly figurative language that surrounds the concept of defense can be translated into language that describes the known capabilities of single organisms, the person-within-a-person criticism will lose considerable force. I believe that recent physiological and cognitive experimentation and theorizing make this translation possible.

Much of what I will say follows the brilliant start made by Bruner (1957b) in his introduction of *gating*. To set the orientation from which the idea of gating emerges, Bruner quotes from the physiologist Adrian (1954), who was knighted for his excellence:

> The operations of the brain stem seem to be related to particular fields of sensory information which vary from moment to moment with the shifts of our attention. The signals from the sense organs must be treated differently when we attend to them and when we do not, and if we could decide how and where the divergencies arise, we should be nearer to understanding how the level of consciousness is reached. The question is whether the afferent messages that evoke sensations are allowed at all times to reach the cerebral cortex or are sometimes blocked at a lower level. Clearly we can reduce the inflow from the sense organs as we do by closing the eyes and relaxing the muscles when we wish to sleep and it is quite probable that the sensitivity of some of the sense organs can be directly influenced by the central nervous system. But even in deep sleep or coma there is no reason to believe that sensory messages no longer reach the central nervous system. At some stage therefore on their passage to consciousness the messages meet with barriers that are sometimes open and sometimes closed. Where are these barriers, in the cortex, the brain stem, or elsewhere? (pp. 238–239)

How far this statement goes beyond the old notion of the nervous system involving little more than stimulation of a sense organ, conduction of that stimulation to the sensory area of the cortex, translation into an action message in the motor cortex, and transmission from there to the muscles! Adrian is clearly positing central-nervous-system control of stimulation coming into the organism. Such control, dubbed *gating* by Bruner, would, if discovered, render the psychological concept of defense much more plausible. In this possible control lies the basis for translating the concept of defense into terms that will obviate the person-within-a-person criticism.

There is even some empirical evidence to support gating. Hernandez-Peon, Scherrer, and Jouvet (1956) did a physiological experiment on cats in which they recorded the electrical discharge, or *potential,* in the nerve cells just past the auditory sense organ, or the *cochlear nucleus,* on the way to the brain. They arranged their apparatus such that whenever they sounded a click in a cat's ear, they could determine the intensity and rate of electrical impulses in these nerves. After recording enough to determine the normal level of electrical activity as a response to the sounds, Hernandez-Peon et al. introduced three kinds of nonauditory distractors. While being exposed to the click, cats were shown two mice in a bell jar, were given fish odors to smell, or were shocked on the forepaw—that is, visual, olfactory, and somatic distractors were employed. Marvelous to tell, electrical activity in the nerves just central to the cochlear nucleus was markedly reduced under all three conditions over what it had been without the distractors. Presumably, messages being transmitted to the brain over one sensory channel can, through some central nervous system control, be inhibited from reaching the brain by some other competing sensory stimulation. Even without knowing more about this mysterious process, you can recognize that it clearly indicates the tenability of the concept of defense at the physiological level of analysis. The nervous system apparently can do what has seemed so nonsensical to many psychologists and philosophers.

Hernandez-Peon and his associates (1956) have offered evidence suggesting a physiological basis for *desensitizing defenses* at least in the auditory perceptual system. The work of other investigators (e.g., Galambos, Sheatz, & Vernier, 1956; Granit, 1955) suggests the generality of this phenomenon beyond the auditory modality and also gives evidence of a similar physiological mechanism for the *sensitizing defenses*. One of the clearest demonstrations of the latter—again in the auditory modality—occurs in Galambos et al. (1956). They utilized a recording procedure and experimental design similar to that of Hernandez-Peon et al., except that they made the click at the cat's ear a signal for subsequent shock. Once the cats had learned the click's signal value, the presentation of the click without the shock was enough to produce a greater burst of electrical activity than occurred in control animals for which the click did not function as a shock signal. It is as if the learning process tuned the auditory system to be more sensitive to clicks than normally.

In an ingenious study, Galambos (1956) provides more complete and precise evidence that the central nervous system tunes or detunes peripheral sensory systems. Arranging recording apparatus in a fashion similar to that in his previous study, Galambos also stimulated the superior olivary nucleus of his cats (the superior olivary nucleus is a major subcortical center of the brain for the auditory system). He found that whenever he stimulated this nucleus, the electrical activity occurring on the way from the cochlear nucleus to the brain in response to the clicks presented at the ear was markedly reduced. Thus, Galambos produced the effect, found by Hernandez-Peon et al., by stimulating a brain center directly rather than by providing stimulation in a nonauditory sensory modality. These results provide an important link in the chain demonstrating central-nervous-system control of peripheral sensitivity.

Although some of the research findings mentioned here have proven difficult to replicate, some additional research and theorizing have suggested the existence of a gating mechanism for pain (Clark & Hunt, 1971; Melzack & Wall, 1968), a sensation that has for so long resisted explanation. It is also compelling that effects in people have been found that may be macroscopic counterparts to physiological gating. For example, visual perception experiments show that subjects' pupils expand and contract in diameter partly as a function of their attitudes

and needs (Hess, 1958) and that these changes in pupil size may alter perceivers' sensitivity to external stimuli (Hutt & Anderson, 1967).

Though the kind of evidence provided by the studies in this section is clearly relevant to the effects of defenses on perception, it is not immediately relevant to other effects of defenses. Nevertheless, I encourage you to recognize that there are sensory systems other than the traditional, obvious ones having to do with stimulation reaching the organism from the outside world, such as sensory systems that alert the organism to its internal world (e.g., the kinesthetic and proprioceptive systems). It is certainly possible that such systems are also tuned by the central nervous system; if so, there is ample basis for more widespread effects of defense than on exteroceptive (external sensory) perception alone. Although evidence for interoceptive (internal sensory) tuning is absent at this point, I submit that the revolutionary step has already been taken in such work as Galambos and Hernandez-Peon and in the theorizing of Adrian, Bruner, and Melzack and Wall.

Perhaps one can compare exteroceptive and interoceptive sensory stimulation entering the central nervous system to a template or model of stimulation existing in the memory. This template or model could be affected by one's history of reward and punishment. When incoming stimulation and the template match well, no gating occurs. But when they do not match, the discrepancy may constitute the physiological concomitant of conflict and anxiety. The mismatch may instigate some control process that sensitizes or desensitizes some or all exteroceptive and interoceptive sensory modalities such that only the stimulation that matches the template would be permitted to pass on to the brain. Stimulation not permitted to pass on would then be unconscious, because it was literally not in the brain even though it existed at the level of the sense organs.

This position is consistent with the views on selective attention developing in the field of cognitive psychology. According to Erdelyi (1974), processing of stimulation by humans involves a great deal of central-nervous-system control of peripheral stimulation. He theorizes that stimulus input is first stored in the nervous system as raw, or uncoded, data. These raw data images fade rapidly, however, because they are too numerous for the storage capacities of the central nervous system. Therefore, they must be encoded, or reduced by a categorizing process (such as grouping by perceived similarities and differences), so that they can be retained for a longer period in short-term storage. This encoding process is controlled by the contents of long-term memory, such as the person's wishes, values, expectancies, and defensive requirements. According to Erdelyi, input stored as raw data is not yet conscious but can have such effects as arousing defensive operations. Only when input has entered short-term storage does it become conscious; note, however, that it will already have been transformed into something acceptable. Finally, input from short-term storage can undergo further alteration and become part of long-term memory, where it will, in turn, have a controlling effect on subsequent input. In the attempt to understand how people can use the enormous flood of stimulation they experience without becoming overwhelmed, cognitive psychologists have provided personologists with a view of mental life quite consistent with theories of defensiveness.

CONCLUSION. As you can see, the person-within-a-person criticism becomes less cogent in the face of such theorizing as that of Erdelyi (and the research that stands behind it). Now we can talk in more descriptive and less figurative terms of raw-data storage, short-term storage, and long-term memory and delineate how matches and mismatches among the contents of these units can trigger defenses and the transformation of stimulus input. It seems to me that all this renders the concept of defense more plausible than its critics would have admitted some years ago. For the moment, I am ready to conclude that it is tenable.

This conclusion has an obvious bearing on the three models of personality. Clearly the concept of defense is not a black mark against a model that includes or even relies on it. The empirical evidence showing the existence of sensitizing and desensitizing behaviors actually favors the models that specifically employ the concept of defense. On this basis, the conflict and fulfillment models, in all their versions, seem fruitful. The consistency model seems less so, for the concept of defense is not a logically integral part of it. However, in the activation version of the consistency model, Fiske and Maddi stress behavior that has the characteristics of the sensitizing and desensitizing processes supported by the research on defense.

Second Issue: Is All Behavior Defensive?

Having encountered empirical support for the belief that defensive behavior occurs, I shall now consider whether all or only some behavior is defensive in character. The pure form of the psychosocial conflict model would assume that all behavior is defensive whereas most other models assume this of only some behavior. Actually, the cognitive dissonance version of the consistency model gives no explicit role to defense. Most of the anecdotal and empirical evidence relevant to this issue has already been discussed in the previous section. Of particular importance is research permitting one to see whether there is behavior that does not distort reality in a context entailing pressure toward distortion.

Meager though the findings are, I have pointed out that each time a study was designed and analyzed such that it was possible to note not only desensitization and sensitization but normal or accurate sensitivity, some subjects fell into this last category. This result is most clear in the experiments on memory, and it has persisted through all experimental attempts to increase the likelihood of defense through pressuring subjects. Apparently some people do function nondefensively at least some of the time. It will do no good to say that this shows merely that the experiment was successful only for some people—that only some had their anxieties aroused and conflicts engaged. This very statement recognizes that some people function without defensiveness at least some of the time.

Although similar evidence from perceptual studies is harder to come by, some exists. For example, in their study of self-deception, Gur and Sackheim (1979) found that some subjects were always accurate (where inaccuracy signifies defensiveness) in the task of identifying their own voices and those of others presented in a series. But most perception investigators have not been particularly interested in the number of their subjects who perceived accurately—that is, not in an unsensitive or hypersensitive fashion— hence, they have not analyzed their data so as to make this information available. But a perusal of their findings clearly shows two things: There are marked differences in perceptual speed among the subjects in a typical study, and the average differences in time necessary for perception of critical as opposed to neutral words typically are quite small. These two kinds of results strongly suggest that the proportion of subjects perceiving accurately might well be sizable.

CONCLUSION. In my judgment, the evidence, though not extensive, suggests that some people do not appear to appreciably distort reality, even when pressured and threatened. Therefore, we have an empirical basis for favoring the position that some but not all behavior is defensive. This conclusion has far-reaching implications, particularly that the pure psychosocial conflict model is limited in usefulness for understanding personality. You will recall that this kind of model employs a concept of defense because it postulates an individual with essentially selfish concerns and a society with antithetical concerns and with the ability to ferret out and punish selfishness. In such theories, the concept of defense accounts for the whole orientation of a person's life, whereby he or she can avoid punishment and guilt while still protecting some small basis for self-satisfaction. The asserted ubiquitousness of defensiveness in this model is called into question by our empirical analysis. But the usefulness of the intrapsychic version of the conflict model is not challenged, for this version recognizes the existence of defensive behavior without assuming that all behavior is defensive. The same is true of the variant on the

psychosocial version of the conflict model exemplified by Murray and the ego psychologists. This position assumes an inherent basis for functioning without conflict and, therefore, without defense. On the basis of my conclusion concerning the second issue, Freud fares worst.

As you can see, the fulfillment model is completely supported by my conclusion, because the model conceptualizes conflict, anxiety, and defense as possible but not inevitable outcomes of living. In all versions and variants of this model, defense occurs but is not ubiquitous. As already suggested in the concluding discussion of the first issue, the cognitive dissonance version of the consistency model is called into question by the empirical evidence indicating the very existence of defensive behavior.

But the activation version of this model was considered tenable. The conclusion reached here reinforces this tenability, because the position does not make correctional (quasidefensive) behaviors ubiquitous; they occur only when anticipational behaviors have failed. Anticipational behaviors might well fail in laboratory situations, in which one cannot completely select one's experiences.

Third Issue: Is the Highest Form of Living Adaptive or Transcendent?

You will recall that according to the pure psychosocial version of the conflict model, the highest form of living involves adaptation to the imperatives of society. Clearly this position is related to the assumption of ubiquitous conflict between individual and society, with defensiveness being the individual's only protection. According to this position, maturity involves such traits as dependability, generosity, loyalty, respect for others and society, steady productivity, and evenness of mood. Immature behaviors involve impulsivity, rebelliousness, disrespect for others and social institutions, and general unpredictability. In sharp contrast, the fulfillment model considers repetitive, conforming, unimaginative behavior to be defensive and immature. This is consistent with the position's devaluation of social adjustment as a goal of life. *Transcendence* of social conventions (which are not considered imperatives) is virtually necessary for vigorous, mature living. Understandably enough, maturity is characterized by the fulfillment model as nondefensive and free of psychosocial conflict. Other versions and variants of the conflict model fall somewhere between the two extremes I have drawn. This issue does not concern the consistency model.

Although the third issue can be precisely pinpointed, it is not clear to me that it can really be settled by empirical analysis. Certainly we can well expect to find evidence in people of both adaptive and transcendent behaviors. Which type is better will inevitably be a matter of opinion. A conflict theorist can assert with cogency that someone showing good citizenship is an excellent person. A fulfillment theorist can wax equally eloquent on someone whose artistic inclination leads her or him to function outside of social conventions. For empirical analysis to resolve this issue in a definitive manner, conflict and fulfillment theorists would have to agree on the admirability of one discernible kind of person. Then a consideration of the behavioral traits of this kind of person might clarify whether she or he seems primarily adaptational or transcendent.

CREATIVITY STUDIES. Perhaps the closest we can come to such agreement is with the *creative person,* who is currently celebrated in our culture as having achieved a pinnacle of living. Creative people are lauded, envied, emulated, and supported by government grants. Both conflict and fulfillment theorists would consider them admirable people. We must be just a bit careful, however, for some people still harbor suspicion that the creative person is really unsavory, dangerous, and lazy. In addition, if we asked people to identify the creative members of their group, considerable disagreement very well might arise. Nonetheless, studying the behavioral traits of creative people is probably as close as we can come to an empirical basis for resolving the third issue.

Among the many studies of *creative people,* none is so carefully done and comprehensive as that of MacKinnon (1965; Hall & MacKinnon,

1969). MacKinnon asked eminent administrators and educators in architecture to nominate the most creative members of their profession. By pooling the information thus obtained, he selected a sample of architects who were generally agreed on as creative. Compared with a control group of randomly selected architects, the creative group included many more prizewinners and leaders. Although it is not entirely clear what *creativity* means in this study, it is not likely to be far from that of other psychologists, who have generally agreed that the creative act produces something both novel and significant and that the creative person is someone who produces creative acts consistently (Bruner, 1962a; Jackson & Messick, 1965; Taylor & Getzels, 1975).

MacKinnon's creative architects were compared with the control group on many tests of personality. One of the most overwhelmingly clear findings of this study is that the creative architects were more *transcendent* than the control group. They described themselves as being rather uninterested in socializing, unconcerned about their popularity with and acceptance by others, unusual and idiosyncratic in their habits and beliefs, and more concerned with quality than acceptability or quantity in their work. Although they considered themselves able to be intimate with friends, they cared little for social amenities. In addition, they did not seem overly concerned with their self-preoccupation and their disdain for the social system. Lest you doubt whether these self-descriptions bear any relationship to the way other people saw these creative architects, let me assure you that they do. On the basis of personal contact with them over a period of some days, MacKinnon's staff of psychologists found the creative architects to be much as they described themselves. The creative architects were less predictable, repetitive, and conforming but more imaginative, intense, and original than the control architects. Corroboration of the transcendent qualities mentioned thus far was also obtained from the creative architects' life histories. All in all, they did not adapt to social institutions so much as change them or else function outside them.

Albeit on a less comprehensive scale, many other studies of creativity support the findings just reviewed. For example, Cross, Cattell, and Butcher (1967) compared 63 visual artists and 28 craft students with a matched control group on scores derived from the 16 Personality Factor Questionnaire (devised by Cattell and Stice, 1957). Statistically significant differences in average scores were found on 12 of the 16 factors, with the craft students typically falling between the artists and the control subjects. Especially salient features of the artists' personalities were assertiveness (or dominance), self-sufficiency, personal integration, casualness, bohemian tendencies, and low superego strength. In addition to these transcendent qualities, they were high in suspiciousness, tension, emotional instability, and proneness to guilt. This hint of inconsistency was also found by Barron (1963), who summarizes 10 years of research as indicating the presence in artistically creative persons of spirituality and a belief in self-renewal but also the possibility of personal conflict. Helson and Crutchfield (1970) and Helson (1973a; 1973b; 1977) report that creative mathematicians and writers are more unconventional, assertive, and independent than their less creative counterparts.

Perhaps the intimation of difficulty in relating to others is a somewhat natural sequel of the transcendent orientation present in creative people. In this regard, Schaefer (1969), like so many other investigators, found creative adolescents (and, for that matter, adults) to show tolerance for ambiguity, impulsivity, craving for novelty, autonomy, and self-assertiveness. The theme of unconventionality is carried through by Getzels and Csikszentmihalyi (1976), who found their creative art students especially good at posing problems (rather than accepting problems as structured for them by others).

CONCLUSION. There is little point in chronicling the other studies on creativity (see Razik, 1965; Stein, 1968), for all essentially agree on the transcendent quality of the phenomenon. Even historical research into the lives of people remembered as having been greatly creative

(e.g., Maddi, 1965) testifies to the transcendent nature of their lives. There is a streak of what one could call selfishness in great people. Most of them have deeply believed in their own greatness. Even Freud, the arch conflict theorist, seems to have had such a belief (Jones, 1955). Studies of living people identified as creative also support this conclusion (e.g., Taylor, 1963). These various sources of evidence incline me to conclude that the highest form of functioning is transcendent rather than adaptive.

This conclusion clearly favors the fulfillment model over the conflict model in its psychosocial version. Not especially hurt by the findings are the intrapsychic versions of the conflict and consistency models. In classical Freudian thinking, which is the prototype of psychosocial conflict theory, there is no convincing explanation of creativity, which Freudians tend to see as somewhat akin to madness. In madness, the person is as close to lacking defenses as it is possible to be, according to classical psychoanalytic thinking. In this state, functioning is chaotic, destructive, and riddled with anxiety. Instincts are fairly directly expressed, to the detriment of the person and others in the surroundings. Creativity is considered less violent and psychopathological but on the same continuum. The creative act is accounted for as an instinctual expression over which the person has little control. Clearly this attempt to explain creativity is untenable in light of the findings of studies such as those reviewed here. Only with the advent of ego psychology could personologists who found themselves temperamentally in the psychoanalytic camp explain creativity in a manner that distinguished it from madness. But this explanation requires the addition to the psychosocial conflict model aspects of a fulfillment model. The result is really a new theory, as I pointed out in Chapter 3.

The ego psychologist's explanation of creativity involves *regression in the service of the ego* (Kris, 1952). In this context, regression, or the retreat to an earlier level of development, is not an unavoidable, unrecognized attempt to avoid anxiety. Instead, it is a consciously precipitated return to a more childish state in order to find inspiration by momentarily relinquishing the very socialization considered so valuable in everyday life. So, while regression in the service of the ego retains the reality-distorting element of defensiveness, there is nothing defensive about its conscious operation and subjection to self-control. This explanation of creativity comes as close to the fulfillment model as it can while retaining something of the conflict model; creativity is not properly considered defensive, even though it involves some relinquishment of social realities.

Very little systematic empirical evidence for or against this psychoanalytic view exists. In one relevant study, however, Gray (1969), aims at determining the relationship between a measure of regression in the service of the ego and a measure of creativity in a sample of 100 male undergraduates. Although he initially found a positive correlation between the two, the correlation was essentially removed by his correcting for the effects of sheer productivity of responses. This suggests that the presumed relationship between creativity and regression in the service of the ego is really a reflection of the more general variable of productivity.

Fourth Issue: Is Cognitive Dissonance Invariably Unpleasant and Avoided?

The pure cognitive dissonance version of the consistency model makes any degree and kind of discrepancy among expectancies, thoughts, and perceptions the source of emotional discomfort and attempts at avoidance. Though Kelly occasionally suggests that small discrepancies may be interesting as long as no construct is threatened with disconfirmation, this theory overwhelmingly values consistency. Even Kelly's dimensions of transition reflecting reactions to some sort of discrepancy are all negative emotions (e.g., anxiety, hostility). Obviously this position is very sensible. To perceive something different from what one thought or expected is to have been wrong—and who can rest easy with that? To think one way and perceive yourself as acting another way is to be dishonest, cowardly, or inept, none of which is acceptable. To harbor two discrepant

thoughts or beliefs at the same time is to be confused—and who wants that? The principle is the same whether the inconsistency is small or large, important or unimportant.

The issue of whether this position is accurate is raised from a number of sectors of psychology. Within the cognitive dissonance model itself, the variant position, exemplified by McClelland, contends that only large discrepancies are unpleasant and avoided whereas small discrepancies are actually pleasurable and sought after. Moreover, the activation version of the consistency model, exemplified by Fiske and Maddi, presents the view that cognitive dissonance, in the degree required for maintenance of customary levels of activation, will be pleasant and pursued. Disagreement with the pure cognitive dissonance version of the consistency model has been shown by an increasing number of psychologists who believe that variety has significant positive value for the organism.

In addition, the fulfillment model does not agree with the cognitive dissonance model in any proper sense. For fulfillment theorists, cognitive consistency would be actually unpleasant if it stood in the way of fulfillment. In this, fulfillment theorists would agree with Emerson (1940) in his crackling line from the essay on self-reliance, "A foolish consistency is the hobgoblin of little minds." In fulfillment theory, cognitive consistency usually means the person's conformity to an external, societal definition of life. Often, to be consistent is to give up fulfillment. The disagreement of fulfillment theorists would not depend on how large the cognitive dissonance was, as for McClelland and Fiske and Maddi, but on the content of the inconsistency.

Superficially, the conflict model would seem to agree rather closely with the cognitive dissonance version of the consistency model. After all, conflict is the incompatibility between two opposing forces. But you must keep in mind that in conflict theory it is not any discrepancy that is important but only discrepancies between the two forces considered to be basic to the person. So at the very least, conflict theory is much narrower than cognitive dissonance theory is. But the difference does not end here. You should also recognize that a conflict theorist could imagine a discrepancy that, because it involves no conflict between the two opposing forces, would not necessarily be considered unpleasant and to be avoided. It is only when discrepancy is synonymous with conflict that conflict theory would agree with cognitive dissonance theory. Thus, like fulfillment theory, conflict theory takes issue with cognitive dissonance theory only in certain matters of content.

COGNITIVE DISSONANCE REDUCTION STUDIES. You are now ready to see empirical evidence bearing on the issue. Surprisingly, Kelly's theory, the most comprehensive example of the pure cognitive dissonance version of the consistency model, has generated no systematic research to determine whether dissonance is invariably unpleasant and avoided. Happily, however, study upon study has come out of Festinger's position, which, though not a theory of personality, certainly agrees with Kelly's on the given issue. I shall now consider important and representative examples of this body of research, along with criticisms that have been raised. Following this, I will examine systematic research representing the opposing point of view—that of variety theory—along with relevant criticism. Finally, I will find some basis for resolving the issue.

Research attempting to demonstrate the avoidance of cognitive dissonance aroused considerable enthusiasm in the past. I think the reason for the enthusiasm is clear. Festinger and his various associates presented in a persuasive, impassioned, and committed way a scheme for understanding social and individual change that was both extraordinarily simple and comprehensive. In addition, they argued their position not in the arid arena of pure thought but in the rich, complex context of important life events. And when they did experiments, they focused on results that, though predicted by dissonance theory, would not have been predicted from more familiar and obvious frames of reference.

The following extended quote shows Festinger's (1958b) emphasis on significant life events. The episode described is from an observational piece of research:

Another intriguing example of the reduction of dissonance in a startling manner comes from a study I did together with Riecken and Schachter. . . . of a group of people who predicted that, on a given date, a catastrophic flood would overwhelm most of the world. This prediction of the catastrophic flood had been given to the people in direct communications from the gods and was an integral part of their religious beliefs. When the predicted date arrived and passed there was considerable dissonance established in these people. They continued to believe in their gods and in the validity of the communications from them, and at the same time they knew that the prediction of the flood had been wrong. We observed the movement as participants for approximately two months preceding and one month after this unequivocal disproof of part of their belief. The point of the study was, of course, to observe how they would react to the dissonance. Let me give you a few of the details of the disproof and how they reacted to it.

For some time it had been clear to the people in the group that those who were chosen were to be picked up by flying saucers before the cataclysm occurred. Some of the believers, these mainly college students, were advised to go home and wait individually for the flying saucer that would arrive for each of them. This was reasonable and plausible, since the date of the cataclysm happened to occur during an academic holiday. Most of the group, including the most central and most heavily committed members, gathered together in the home of the woman who received the message from the gods to wait together for the arrival of the saucer. For these latter, disproof of the prediction, in the form of evidence that the messages were not valid, began to occur four days before the predicted event was to take place. A message informed them that a saucer would land in the back yard of the house at 4:00 p.m. to pick up the members of the group. With coat in hand they waited, but no saucer came. A later message told them there had been a delay—the saucer would arrive at midnight. Midst absolute secrecy (the neighbors and press must not know) they waited outdoors on a cold and snowy night for over an hour, but still no saucer came. At about 3:00 a.m.

they gave up, interpreting the events of that night as a test, a drill, and a rehearsal for the real pickup which would still soon take place.

Tensely, they waited for the final orders to come through—for the messages which would tell them the time, place, and procedure for the actual pickup. Finally, on the day before the cataclysm was to strike, the messages came. At midnight a man would come to the door of the house and take them to the place where the flying saucer would be parked. More messages came that day, one after another, instructing them in the passwords that would be necessary in order to board the saucer, in preparatory procedures such as removal of metal from clothing, removal of personal identification, maintaining silence at certain times, and the like. The day was spent by the group in preparation and rehearsal of the necessary procedures and, when midnight came, the group sat waiting in readiness. But no knock came at the door, no one came to lead them to the flying saucer.

From midnight to five o'clock in the morning the group sat there struggling to understand what had happened, struggling to find some explanation that would enable them to recover somewhat from the shattering realization that they would not be picked up by a flying saucer and that consequently the flood itself would not occur as predicted. It is doubtful that anyone alone, without the support of the others, could have withstood the impact of this disproof of the prediction. Indeed, those members of the group who had gone to their homes to wait alone, alone in the sense that they did not have other believers with them, did not withstand it. Almost all of them became skeptics afterward. In other words, without easily obtainable social support to begin reducing the dissonance, the dissonance was sufficient to cause the belief to be discarded in spite of the commitment to it. But the members of the group who had gathered together in the home of the woman who received the messages could, and did, provide social support for one another. They kept reassuring one another of the validity of the messages and that some explanation would be found.

At fifteen minutes before five o'clock that morning an explanation was found that was at least temporarily satisfactory. A message arrived from God which, in effect, said that He had saved

the world and stayed the flood because of this group and the light and strength this group had spread throughout the world that night. The behavior of these people from that moment onwards presented a revealing contrast to their previous behavior. These people who had been disinterested in publicity and even avoided it, became avid publicity seekers. For four successive days, finding a new reason each day, they invited the press into the house, gave lengthy interviews, and attempted to attract the public to their ideas. The first day they called the newspapers and news services, informed them of the fact that the world had been saved and invited them to come and get interviews. The second day, a ban on having photographs taken was lifted, and the newspapers were once more called to inform them of the fact and to invite them to come to the house and take pictures. On the third day they once more called the press to inform them that on the next afternoon they would gather on their front lawn singing and that it was possible a space man would visit them at that time. What is more, the general public was specifically invited to come and watch. And on the fourth day, newspapermen and about two hundred people came to watch the group singing on their front lawn. There were almost no lengths to which these people would not go to attract publicity and potential believers in the validity of the messages. If, indeed, more and more converts could be found, more and more people who believed in the messages and the things the messages said, then the dissonance between their belief and the knowledge that the messages had not been correct could be reduced. (pp. 74–76)*

Dramatic as this episode is, it cannot be considered a completely convincing demonstration of the principle of cognitive dissonance reduction. There are just too many other possibly important factors. The situation, like most naturally occurring ones, involves so many overlapping factors that it only ambiguously demonstrates the sole importance of any one of them. Controlled and systematic laboratory research is needed to supplement naturalistic observation. Festinger (1958b) clearly agrees, for in the very next paragraph he says,

---

*Excerpts from *Assessment of Human Motives*, by Gardner Lindzey, copyright ©1958 by Holt, Rinehart, and Winston, reprinted by permission of the publisher.

These examples, while they do illustrate attempts to reduce dissonance in rather surprising directions, still leave much to be desired. One would also like to be able to show that such dissonance-reduction phenomena do occur under controlled laboratory conditions and that the magnitude of the effect does depend upon the magnitude of the dissonance which exists. (p. 76)

Festinger then goes on to describe an experiment (Festinger & Carlsmith, 1959) that aimed at such precise demonstration of the avoidance of inconsistency. Subjects were told they were participating in a study of measures of performance, whereas in reality they were made to do a boring, repetitive task for one hour. At the end of that time, the subjects were given a false explanation of the purpose of the experiment: that it concerned the effects of expectation on task performance. Some subjects were then asked if they would stay on and take the place of the research assistant for a few minutes, as he was away for the day. They would have to deceive the next incoming subject that the task to be performed—actually the same boring one the deceiving subject had just finished—was quite interesting and enjoyable. For supposedly taking the research assistant's place, subjects in one group were given $1 each and those in the other $20 each. Some subjects refused to be hired, but the others went along with the deception. A control group of subjects was not asked to take part in any deception.

At the end of the study, all subjects—deceiving and control—were seen by an interviewer, who supposedly was part of the psychology department's program of evaluating its members' experiments. During the interview, subjects were asked to rate the experiment along four dimensions. These ratings constitute the data of the study. Table 10-5 shows the averages based on them. Three dimensions showed no significant differences between the $1, $20, and control groups. But there were significant differences in ratings of enjoyment of the experiment, on a scale from −15 (dull), through 0 (neutral) to +15 (enjoyable). The control group rated the experiment as just a little on the dull side, the $1 group thought it was somewhat enjoyable, and the $20 group was neutral. The small difference between the control and $20 groups was not significant.

Festinger and Carlsmith find these results to support the hypothesis that people tend to reduce cognitive dissonance. They reason that whereas both the $1 and $20 groups had dissonance because of the inconsistency between their perception of the task as boring and their perception of themselves as publicly extolling its enjoyability, the dissonance is actually much less for the $20 group. This is because those subjects could at least tell themselves that they were being paid well to lie while the poor $1 subjects did not receive enough financial recompense for their deception. Therefore, it is understandable, according to the experimenters, that the $1 group actually reported most enjoyment of the task in retrospect, since this shift in their opinion of the task would constitute a reduction

TABLE 10-5   Average Ratings on Interview Questions for Each Condition

| | EXPERIMENTAL CONDITION | | |
Question on Interview	Control (N = 20)	One Dollar (N = 20)	Twenty Dollars (N = 20)
How enjoyable tasks were (rated from −5 to +5)	−.45	+1.35	−.05
How much they learned (rated from 0 to 10)	3.08	2.80	3.15
Scientific importance (rated from 0 to 10)	5.60	6.45	5.18
Participate in similar exp. (rated from −5 to +5)	−.62	+1.20	−.25

SOURCE: From "Cognitive Consequences of Forced Compliance," by L. Festinger and J. M. Carlsmith, 1959, *Journal of Abnormal and Social Psychology, 58.*

of dissonance. Note how ingenious this experiment really is. Common sense and reinforcement theory would predict that the $20 group, not the $1 group, would subsequently report the greatest enjoyment, because they got the most out of their participation but lied no more than the $1 group did. The results obtained are not only consistent with the resolution of inconsistency—they are quite surprising.

But even if one assumes that the results do mean what Festinger and Carlsmith conclude, there is no evidence to indicate that small inconsistencies lead to avoidance behavior. The difference between the control and $20 groups in rated enjoyment of the task does not exist from a statistical point of view. There is only evidence that large inconsistencies, as experienced by the $1 group, may lead to attempts to reduce them by concluding that the task must have been enjoyable. So, regarding the issue at hand, one should probably conclude no more than that there is evidence that large inconsistencies are unpleasant and avoided.

RESOUNDING CRITICISM. The criticism leveled at cognitive dissonance reduction experiments has been strong and compelling, raising doubt as to whether the results show anything at all about reactions to dissonance. Because the major critics of dissonance reduction research have been Chapanis and Chapanis (1964), I shall rely heavily on their analyses.

First of all, they wonder how successfully the experiment aroused dissonance at all. In this study, the experience of dissonance hinges on the repetitive task really being experienced as boring when being performed. And yet, the control group subjects, who did this task but were not asked to deceive subsequent subjects, rated it as only slightly boring, or close to neutral (see Table 10-5). Either the task was not really as monotonous as the experimenters thought or the general instructions initially given subjects about studying the effects of expectation on performance were sufficient to interest them in participating to the point where the monotonous nature of the task was not the single, or even most important, factor in their enjoyment. So

Chapanis and Chapanis (1964) conclude that the experiment does not permit one to check whether discrepant cognitions of any real magnitude were in fact produced.

An even more serious criticism involves the difference in plausibility between the $20 and $1 remuneration for acting as research assistants. At that time, $20 was a lot of money for an undergraduate, representing a whole day's pay. When offered for something that must have been less than 30 minutes' work, the money very well might have made students wary and alert to possible tricks. In fact, more than 16% of the original subjects in the $20 group had to be discarded because they voiced suspicions or refused to be hired! Under such circumstances, Chapanis and Chapanis conclude, it seems likely that those who were retained might have hedged or been evasive about their evaluation of the experiment because they were apprehensive about its nature and purpose. And, of course, the average enjoyment rating of neutral, representing as it does the middle point of a dimension running from unenjoyable to enjoyable, is a very ambiguous result in that it could well represent the canceling out of a number of opposing trends within the group. In any event, while the $1 remuneration seems plausible enough, the same cannot be said for the $20 one. Chapanis and Chapanis conclude correctly that it is therefore impossible to rule out explanations of the results that contradict Festinger and Carlsmith.

Rosenberg (1965) offers a cogent alternative explanation referring to a study that attempts to correct some of the pitfalls of a study very much like Festinger and Carlsmith's, except that it included four degrees of remuneration rather than two (Brehm & Cohen, 1962). In this study, Cohen predicted that the greater the remuneration, the smaller the dissonance reduction, where such reduction could be seen as a change in original attitude. The subjects were Yale undergraduates, and the study was conducted immediately following a campus riot that had been quelled by police. The experimenter, appearing at randomly chosen dormitory rooms, ascertained through inquiry that the subjects disapproved of the police actions. Then the subjects were asked to write an essay in support of the police actions, the justification being that the experimenter was interested in obtaining examples of arguments that could be supportive. The subjects were also told that they would receive a certain amount of pay for writing the essay against their own position; one group was offered 50¢, another $1, another $5, and another $10. After writing the essays, the subjects were asked to fill out a questionnaire concerning their real reactions to the police action on the following grounds:

> Now that you have looked at some of the reasons for the actions of the New Haven police, we would like to get some of your reactions to the issue: *you may possibly want to look at the situation in the light of this.* So, would you please fill out this questionnaire. (Brehm & Cohen, 1962)

A control group was given this final attitude questionnaire but was not required to write the essay and received no remuneration.

Cohen found that the $5 and $10 groups did not differ significantly from the control group in expressed attitude toward the New Haven police. But the subjects in the 50¢ group were less negative toward the police than the $1 subjects, who in turn were less negative than the $10 subjects. In addition, both the 50¢ and $1 groups significantly differed from the control group. As you can see, the results seem to bear out the original prediction rather well. But Rosenberg (1965) suggests the importance in explaining the results of evaluation apprehension and general annoyance toward the experimenter in following up the suspiciousness hypothesis of Chapanis and Chapanis. Rosenberg writes that he

> would suggest that in this study, as in others of similar design, the low-dissonance (high reward) subjects would be more likely to suspect that the experimenter had some unrevealed purpose. The gross discrepancy between spending a few minutes writing an essay and the large sum offered, the fact that this large sum had not yet been delivered by the time the subject was handed the attitude questionnaire, the fact that he was virtually invited to show that he had become more positive toward the New Haven police: all these could have served to engender suspicion and thus to arouse evaluation

apprehension and negative affect toward the experimenter. Either or both of these motivating states could probably be most efficiently reduced by the subject to show anything but fairly strong disapproval of the New Haven police; for the subject who had come to believe that his autonomy in the face of a monetary lure was being assessed, remaining "anti-police" would demonstrate that he had autonomy; for the subject who perceived an indirect and disingenuous attempt to change his attitude and felt some reactive anger, holding fast to his original attitude could appear to be a relevant way of frustrating the experimenter. Furthermore, with each step of increase in reward we could expect an increase in the proportion of subjects who had been brought to a motivating level of evaluation apprehension or affect arousal.

Rosenberg then performed his own experiment in an attempt to correct the problem he had found in previous studies. The general way to improve on previous designs would be to make the collection of information following the dissonance-engendering task as separate from the rest of the study as possible. Rosenberg accomplished this in two ways. First, he created a believable situation in which information on subjects' final attitudes was collected by experimenters other than those who had conducted the earlier part of the study. Second, subjects were paid for their performance before they progressed to the latter part of the study. The first method clearly improved on Cohen's procedure, in which the same person collected all data. It is true that Festinger and Carlsmith used different experimenters to administer the task and collect the enjoyment data, but their design allowed a suspicious subject to perceive a connection between the two. In contrast, Rosenberg developed an elaborate but believable rationale for the independence of the part of the experiment designed to arouse dissonance. The two parts were not only conducted by different people but involved different buildings and different institutional affiliations. Therefore, it is unlikely that either fear of evaluation or anger toward the experimenter could explain results such as Cohen's and Festinger and Carlsmith's as easily as dissonance reduction attempts could.

But with this improved design, Rosenberg obtained results directly opposed to those expected by dissonance theory. As shown by the averages (M) reported in Table 10-6, he found that the more money subjects got for writing essays discrepant with their views, the more their attitudes in the essays moved away from their original attitudes. This result is more obvious than that predicted by dissonance theory and throws the results of Festinger and Carlsmith and of Cohen into serious doubt.

The question concerning the studies just discussed is whether they demonstrate the effects of attempts to reduce dissonance or of the guardedness and resentment resulting from the subject's incredulity. There is another group of studies by the dissonance experimenters that have been criticized by Chapanis and Chapanis in a different though related manner. In one such study (Aronson & Mills, 1959), college women volunteered to participate in a series of group discussions on the psychology of sex. In a preparticipation interview, some of the women were told they would have to pass an embarrassment test to see if they were tough enough to stand the group discussion. Women in the severe-embarrassment group had to read out loud in the presence of the male experimenter

some vivid descriptions of sexual activity and a list of obscene sex words. Women in the mild-embarrassment group read some bland sexual material. All subjects were told they had successfully passed the embarrassment test. After this, each subject listened to a recording of a group discussion that they were told was a spontaneous discussion of the type they might be in, but in reality was carefully planned and staged by the experimenters as a dull and banal discussion of the sexual behavior of animals. Finally, the design called for a control group that did not take an embarrassment test, but only listened to the simulated group discussion. All groups then rated the tape-recorded discussion, its participants, and their own interest in future discussions. The results showed that the ratings of the severe-embarrassment group were, on the average, somewhat more favorable than those of the other two groups. Aronson and Mills believe these results show that the more painful the initiation, the more the subjects subsequently liked the group. In successfully passing the severe-embarrassment test, the females in that group had undergone a painful experience to gain the right to be part of the subsequent group discussions, which, however, turned out to be so dull that they must have

TABLE 10-6   Group Means and Differences Among Groups on Attitudes Toward the Rose Bowl Ban

Group	M	GROUP DIFFERENCES*			
		$.50	$1	$.50 and $1	$5
Control	1.45	$z = 1.97$, $p < .03$	$z = 1.80$, $p < .04$	$z = 2.31$, $p < .015$	$z = 3.93$, $p < .0001$
$.50	2.24		$z = .11$		$z = 1.77$, $p < .04$
$1	2.32				$z = 1.81$, $p < .04$
$.50 and $1	2.28				$z = 2.11$, $p < .02$
$5	3.24				

Note: Overall difference among groups as assessed by Kruskal-Wallis test: $H = 17.89$, $p < .001$.
*Tested by Mann-Whitney z, one-tailed.

SOURCE: From "When Dissonance Fails: On Eliminating Evaluation Apprehension from Attitude Measurement," by M. J. Rosenberg, 1965, *Journal of Personality and Social Psychology, 1*.

realized the initiation procedure was not worth it. This produced dissonance, which was reduced by reevaluating the group discussion as more interesting than it really was.

In criticizing this experiment and the conclusions reached, Chapanis and Chapanis (1964) say:

> All this may be so, but in order to accept the author's explanation we must be sure the girls really did hold these discrepant cognitions, and no others. We have to be sure, for instance, that they felt no relief when they found the group discussion banal instead of embarrassing, that success in passing a difficult test (the embarrassment test) did not alter their evaluation of the task, that the sexual material did not evoke any vicarious pleasure or expectation of pleasure in the future, and that the group discussion was so dull that the girls would have regretted participating. There is no way of checking directly on the first three conditions, although other experimental evidence suggests that their effect is not negligible. However, to check on the fourth factor we have the data from the control group showing that the group discussion was, in fact, more interesting than not (it received an average rating of 10 on a 0–15 scale). It is, therefore, difficult to believe that the girls regretted participating. To sum up, since the design of this experiment does not exclude the possibility that pleasurable cognitions were introduced by the sequence of events, and since, in addition, the existence of "painful" cognitions was not demonstrated, we cannot accept the author's interpretation without serious reservations.

These critics continue by suggesting that if there is anything to the notion that severity of initiation increased liking of the group, it lies in the feeling of successful accomplishment: "The more severe the test, the stronger is the pleasurable feeling of success in overcoming the obstacle. There is no need to postulate a drive due to dissonance if a *pleasure principle* can account for the results quite successfully." Chapanis and Chapanis point out that the problems with the Aronson and Mills study crop up in other dissonance studies as well.

The problem these critics pinpoint is called *confounding of variables.* In other words, the results could have been produced by either attempts to reduce dissonance or the behavioral effects of some sort of relief. The two variables overlap, or are confounded by the experimental design. Obviously, the principal aim of any experiment is to avoid such confounding. In natural situations, confounding often occurs, but the whole purpose of experimentation is to improve on nature in the sense of holding constant or neutralizing all possible factors save one. That one is made artificially stronger or weaker in the experimental group so that by comparing the effects in this group with the behavior of a control group, one can assess the causal influences of the single factor. What Chapanis and Chapanis are saying in all their criticisms is that the experiments performed by the dissonance investigators fail in one way or another because of the confounding of two or more factors.

This criticism, *confounding,* is leveled at even more studies in the dissonance tradition than presented thus far. In one dramatic instance, Chapanis and Chapanis discuss an experiment reported by Aronson (1961) that attempted to pit dissonance theory against reinforcement theory. *Reinforcement theory* says that stimuli associated with reward gain attractiveness, whereas *dissonance theory* indicates that stimuli not associated with reward may actually gain attractiveness if one has had to expend effort in attempting to attain them. What looks like an ingenious design with which to test this proposition Chapanis and Chapanis demolish by pointing out the confounding of effort expended and the rate at which reward is obtained. As a result, no unambiguous conclusions can be drawn as to the effect of effort on the attractiveness of stimuli worked for. Similar confounding of factors is pointed out in other studies as well.

To make matters worse, once the catalog of criticisms caused by faulty experimental design is exhausted, one finds a whole additional catalog of controversial treatments of data. Chapanis and Chapanis point out that dissonance research regularly discards subjects from the analysis of results after the way they performed is already known to the experimenter. This is a severe criticism, as such a procedure undermines the whole idea of scientific objectivity. As Chapanis and Chapanis point out, one can always find a rationalization for excluding subjects that leads to finding support for one's hypothesis. Hence, exclusion should always take place before the data have been scrutinized. Not only have there been frequent instances of violation of this rule; disinterested observers have often found the grounds given for exclusion of subjects unconvincing. Brehm and Cohen (1959), for example, indicate that "[subjects] who failed to choose the alternative initially marked as most liked, were excluded because they gave unreliable or invalid ratings." There is no further explanation of what the investigators might have meant! Using the study of Cohen, Brehm, and Fleming (1958) as an example, Chapanis and Chapanis point out how the reasons given for exclusion of subjects are often self-contradictory. In a study by Ehrlich, Guttman, Schonbach, and Mills (1957), one reason or another was given to justify excluding what amounted to 82% of the original sample! When such a large proportion of a sample is discarded, it is virtually impossible to know what the results really mean and certainly impossible to know to whom any conclusions reached could possibly apply. In other studies in which the proportion of subjects excluded was lower, the proportions excluded from different groups (e.g., high dissonance, low dissonance, control) often differed. Chapanis and Chapanis correctly conclude that some undetermined number of dissonance studies may be reporting as fact statistically significant differences among groups that are no more than artifacts due to exclusion of subjects.

Even worse than such exclusion of subjects is the kind of reallocation of subjects from one group to another found in the study by Raven and Fishbein (1961). These investigators took subjects who did not conform to their predictions and, instead of rejecting them—which would have been questionable enough—actually shifted them from the experimental group to the control group. As Chapanis and Chapanis (1964) conclude, "Rejection of cases is poor procedure, but reallocation of subjects from

experimental to control group, across the independent variable, violates the whole concept of controlled experimentation."

Continuing in their demolition of dissonance research, Chapanis and Chapanis (1964) point out that in some studies, the number of subjects who refused to participate, once they were informed that they would have to deceive others or write something they did not believe, was sufficiently large that not taking them into account in reaching conclusions led to misunderstandings. If people refuse to participate, they are actually showing themselves to be unexplainable on the grounds of dissonance theory; yet the conclusions reached offer no guidance as to what sector of the population the results of the studies apply. Following this, Chapanis and Chapanis close their review with a section on inadequate procedures for the statistical analysis of results, once again implicating many of the studies performed in the dissonance tradition.

What can we conclude about research billed as having demonstrated that cognitive dissonance is always unpleasant and avoided? Because investigators in this area have focused on showing how their predictions differ from those of more familiar, competitive theories, and because they have tried to apply their dissonance formulation to complex, important social events, they have developed experimental designs involving elaborate instructions and intricate relationships between subject and experimenter. Such complex designs almost always confound certain variables and require researchers to discard some subjects. But in dissonance research, so much confounding and discarding has occurred that one simply cannot know for sure if results clarify the effects of dissonance alone.

Now it may be that the problems of confounding and discarding could be corrected. Perhaps one could develop simpler, more believable designs that would better permit testing of dissonance theory. However, until such research is done, the case for dissonance as being always unpleasant and avoided has not been made. But the situation may be even worse than that. Chapanis and Chapanis (1964) seem to think that dissonance theory is such a whopping oversimplification that confounding of variables and exclusion of subjects are inevitable. The concluding statement of their review follows:

> The magical appeal of Festinger's theory arises from its extreme simplicity both in formulation and in application. But in our review we have seen that this simplicity was generally deceptive; in point of fact it often concealed a large number of confounded variables. Clearly much can be done to untangle this confounding of variables by careful experimental design. Nonetheless, there may still remain another problem more fundamental than this. In general, a cognitive dissonance interpretation of a social situation means that the relevant social factors can be condensed into two simple statements. To be sure, Festinger does not say formally that a dissonance theory interpretation works only for two discrepant statements; but it is precisely because in practice he does so limit it that the theory has had so much acceptance. Which brings us now to the crux of the matter: *is it really possible to reduce the essentials of a complex social situation to just two phrases?* Reluctantly we must say "no." To condense most complex social situations into two, and only two, simple dissonant statements represents so great a level of abstraction that the model no longer bears any reasonable resemblance to reality. Indeed the experimenter is left thereby with such emasculated predictors that he must perforce resort to a multiplicity of ad hoc hypotheses to account for unexpected findings. We see then that the most attractive feature of cognitive dissonance theory, its simplicity, is in actual fact a self-defeating limitation. (pp. 20–21)

Not even this, however, ended what apparently has been an extraordinary interest in and commitment to dissonance theory. Silverman (1964) rises to its defense by insisting that Chapanis and Chapanis have shown only that their alternative explanations of research findings in the area were possible, not persuasive. In addition, he asserts that the exclusion of subjects was done without knowledge of results and was therefore sound. But Silverman seems to be missing the point, which is made as soon as alternative explanations are plausible and when the exclusion of subjects is so rampant that it is difficult to know which population the results represent. When this kind of situation occurs, one can fairly say that the theory in question has not been proven. Although dissonance research continued to be done and believed in for many years, as attested to by the appearance of no less than a handbook (Abelson, Aronson et al., 1969) and several related studies (e.g., Cooper & Goethals, 1974; Cooper & Scalise, 1974), it was clearly dwindling.

But with virtually every accumulation of studies related to dissonance theory, another review of the literature appeared asserting the actual lack of support for the theory. Elms (1967) argues that although it is quite true that reinforcement (or incentive) theory and dissonance theory often provide opposite predictions of phenomena, the former seems more supported by research than the latter. He shows how some studies that initially appear to support dissonance theory actually support incentive theory; he also reports several studies that one can hardly construe except as supporting incentive theory. Among the latter are the studies of Janis and Gilmore (1965) and Elms and Janis (1965) concerning role playing. In both, student subjects were asked to role play counterattitudinally in return for either a high or a low monetary reward. Researchers led some subjects to believe that the sponsor of the role playing was a positively regarded organization and others to believe it was negatively regarded. Subjects received varying amounts of money as an incentive for role playing, and attitude measures were taken immediately following the experiment. Janis and Gilmore found that subjects who believed that the organization was positive showed significantly more positive attitudes about counterattitudinal role playing than did subjects who believed the organization was negative. Similarly, Elms and Janis found that in the positive-sponsorship situation, highly rewarded subjects showed greater positive attitude change than those receiving low reward and in the negative-sponsorship situation, low-reward subjects showed an insignificant trend toward more positive attitude change, compared with highly rewarded subjects. These studies, reminiscent of Rosenberg's (1965), are quite inconsistent with dissonance theory. In an attempt to contend that the Elms and Janis study was an unfair test of dissonance theory, Brehm (1965) omits reference to the positive-sponsorship situation, which provides, of course, the major refutation of the position.

As if dissonance theory were not beleaguered enough, Rhine (1967) raises serious problems about its ability to account for findings in the area of information selectivity. He asserts that failure to confirm hypotheses about information selectivity would be a serious blow to dissonance theory, for Festinger (1958b) has said, "When dissonance is present, in addition to trying to reduce it, *the person will actively avoid situations and information* which would likely increase the dissonance" (p. 3, italics mine). A main difficulty with available research on information selectivity, according to Rhine, is that it does not really apply to the test of dissonance hypotheses. The degree to which information is avoided or sought will be a U-shaped function of amount of dissonance by a complicated set of assumptions presented by Festinger (1957, p. 130). Any study that attempts to test predictions stemming from this U-shaped curve must include at least three levels of dissonance, preferably quite different in intensity. Yet, the available studies involve no more than two levels. In addition, proper empirical testing of the predictions requires researchers to separate seeking information from avoiding it. Once again Rhine (1967) demonstrates how available research has failed to permit such separation. He even suggests how this design limitation could be overcome with the proper control groups. In any event, Rhine concludes that the dissonance explanation of information selectivity has not been proven and even suggests the plausibility of an alternative explanation:

> Consider, for example, Adams' (1961) study of mothers who favored environment over heredity as an explanation of children's behavior. He found that mothers hearing a talk supporting heredity were more interested in getting further information about the heredity-environment issue than those

hearing a talk supporting their environment bias. This was interpreted by Adams to mean that dissonance leads to information seeking. If hearing the opposite side of the issue arouses more curiosity than hearing support for a view one already accepts, then the finding could be explained by curiosity instead of dissonance. Curiosity motivation is rarely, if ever, ruled out in selectivity research. If there is any problem from which curiosity should be considered a possible explanation, it is one in which information seeking is a critical dependent variable. Controlling curiosity is particularly imperative when instructions for determining seeking behavior often explicitly request ratings or rankings in terms of interest in the information.

And, of course, if curiosity might explain even some forms of information seeking, it becomes very difficult to contend that cognitive dissonance is invariably unpleasant and avoided.

Actually, when a position such as dissonance theory has attracted so many devoted researchers and generated so many studies but remains unproven, we can reasonably surmise that something is seriously wrong. Either the theory is so ambiguous as to be unprovable or it is more wrong than right, however much we try to stave off this conclusion with ingenious explanations and counterexplanations. It is beginning to seem as though empirical support for dissonance theory requires very delicately staged experimental situations and carefully primed subjects. At least, some studies done in naturalistic rather than contrived settings do not support the theory. For example, Petersen and Hergenhahn (1968) hypothesize that their elementary school subjects, when presented with evidence that they had done more poorly on an academic task than their self-images would tolerate, would consequently make some sort of effort to reduce this dissonance. But there was no difference in this regard between this group and a group whose members' academic performances matched their self-appraisals.

The research considered thus far focuses on presumed attempts to reduce dissonance. Also relevant to this issue would be the sheer demonstration that dissonance is invariably unpleasant (regardless of whether one then tries to reduce it). There is, however, remarkably little information concerning verbalizations or other direct measures of emotional response to dissonance. Kiesler and Pallak (1976), in their review of studies that aim to determine whether dissonance is "arousing," reach extremely tentative conclusions because the evidence they found was almost invariably indirect. The trouble with indirect evidence is that it must be interpreted a lot and, as we have seen, there has already been too much interpretation associated with dissonance research. Kiesler and Pallak do suggest that dissonance manipulations may arouse or motivate subjects, but they strongly hedge their conclusion. Even at that, however, there is no way of knowing whether "arousal" is an invariably unpleasant experience; after all, pleasant emotions are also "arousing." Once again we must conclude that the case for discrepancies between expectation and occurrence as invariably unpleasant and avoided simply has not been proven.

VARIETY RESEARCH. The next step in considering the issue would seem to be consideration of the body of data accumulated to demonstrate that *change, novelty,* and *complexity* of stimulation are desired and sought after. If these data are convincing, it can at least be said that cognitive dissonance cannot always be unpleasant and avoided. This is true because variety is almost necessarily dissonance, since such aspects of it as novelty and unexpectedness must be defined as a difference between some set of beliefs or expectancies on the one hand and some set of event perceptions on the other. *Variety* research essentially makes three points—that variety is (1) necessary for effective development and adult functioning, (2) sought after, and (3) pleasant, at least in moderate degrees. Fiske and Maddi (1961) have brought together research from various corners of psychology and physiology in support of these three points; therefore, the discussion that follows leans heavily on their formulations. But other psychologists (e.g., Berlyne, 1960; Duffy, 1963) have also provided able reviews of an extensive body of research.

The references to data obtained on nonhuman organisms in the following pages may strike you as inconsistent with my previous unwillingness to consider such data concerning defensiveness. Actually, there is no inconsistency. Animal data were ruled out of contention for the study of defensiveness largely because such study heavily concerns mentation, which is methodologically inaccessible in organisms below humans. But two of the three conclusions concerning variety need not rely primarily on the scrutiny of mentation. Nonhuman organisms can well be studied in determining whether variety is necessary for effective development and adult functioning and whether it is sought after, because these questions can be convincingly resolved by the observation of action and performance. Of course, it is much more difficult to determine whether variety is pleasant without verbal reports. Hence, you will see that the data I review with regard to this question are gleaned exclusively from research on people.

Development and Functioning. I will not spend much time on the conclusion that variety is necessary for effective development and adult functioning, because it is not as directly relevant to the issue at hand as are the other two points. Suffice it to say that the studies relevant to this conclusion generally proceed by reducing the variation and intensity of stimulation impinging on the organism and then observing the effects of doing so at either the physiological or the behavioral level. Whether the study concerns development or adult functioning depends on the subjects' ages. In studies of young monkeys deprived of variation and intensity of stimulation from infancy, Riesen (1961) has shown subsequent deficits at both the physiological level, in cellular abnormalities of the retina and optic nerve, and the behavioral level, in lack of physical coordination. At the human level, Ribble and Spitz (in Thompson & Schaefer, 1961) compare infants reared in orphanages with infants reared at home or in prison with their mothers. The children reared in the orphanage were retarded in walking, talking, smiling, and crawling and generally were more apathetic, unemotional, and subdued than the other infants were. In addition, the orphanage children were more susceptible to diseases and showed a higher death rate. Although Ribble and Spitz stress the ambiguous concept of "mothering" in attempting to explain their results, other psychologists, such as Yarrow (1961), argue cogently for the importance of a marked reduction in the intensity and variety of stimulation from what it would have been in a more usual environment. The studies of Ribble and Spitz were so imperfectly performed from a methodological point of view that I would not even mention them here except that they show such a striking parallel with Riesen's work on monkeys. Harlow and others (e.g., Griffin & Harlow, 1966; Harlow, Harlow, Dodsworth, & Arling, 1966) report results of carefully planned studies of monkeys that build on Riesen's work. Harlow found that rearing infant monkeys in the absence of intense and varying stimuli led to adults that were incapable of copulating, were afraid of other monkeys and living things, and appeared very disturbed emotionally. The monkeys did not seem able to learn to overcome these deficits. If more evidence of the generality of such effects were needed, there are similar studies involving other species (e.g., Konrad & Bagshaw, 1970; Lessac & Solomon, 1969). Apparently, beagles and cats have also showed behavioral deficits at adulthood after having been deprived of stimulation in childhood. There is strong evidence at the animal level, and suggestive evidence at the human level, that variety is necessary for normal development.

The research concerning the need for variety in order to function as a normal adult has been done largely under the well-known label of *sensory deprivation*. To make a long story short, a number of studies (see Fiske, 1961) suggest that markedly decreasing the variation and intensity of stimulation available to adult humans leads, in time, to a number of signs of disordered functioning, including the inability to concentrate, intense feelings of emotional discomfort, and bizarre mentation reminiscent of hallucinations and delusions. Some of the deficits persist for a short time after the sensory deprivation has been terminated. This is not to say that such strong

and disturbing results occur in all subjects or even in all studies done so far. Fuerst and Zubek (1968), for example, report mild or, in some instances, no impairment to their male subjects on cognitive tests administered following 3 days of either darkness and silence or unpatterned light and white noise. But the battery of tests was also administered prior to sensory isolation, and there was a relationship between pre- and postexperimental scores, suggesting that individual differences and the specifics of the experimental situation play as yet an only partially understood role in the effects of deprivation of stimulation. Nonetheless, these studies of adults, along with the already mentioned studies on infants, suggest that variety is necessary for normal development and functioning.

Variety Is Sought After. The second point variety research makes is that variety is sought after, rather than, as cognitive dissonance positions would predict, avoided. Many of the most important studies supporting this point have been done at the nonhuman level. Because there have been so many of these studies, I shall review a representative sample so you can grasp the import of this body of research, which essentially involves two kinds of experiments. One kind concerns habituation to a particular environment, followed by a change in or addition to it, and observation of the effects of doing so. A straightforward example is Berlyne's (1955) study in which rats were permitted to become familiar with a rectangular cage with a little alcove at one end. After familiarization had taken place, a series of objects were added to the environment by placing them in the alcove. The rats' reaction to the objects was what interested Berlyne. He found that the various objects produced exploratory behavior, such as sniffing, licking, and touching. These findings are typical for such studies; whenever you change or add to an already familiar environment, *exploratory behavior* increases. This conclusion applies at the human level also (Maddi, 1961b).

The second kind of study demonstrating that variety is sought after involves putting subjects in an environment that is arranged in a way that requires them to choose which part of it to experience; that is, they cannot experience it all at any one time. Subsequent to the first choice, the subject is put into the environment again and permitted to choose a part to experience next. Typical of such studies is that of Dennis (1939), who put rats into a maze shaped like the letter T. In running through the maze, the rats had to turn either right or left when they reached the bar of the T. In this study, as in many similar ones (see Dember, 1961), it was found that after choosing either the right or left arm of the T, the rats ran to the opposite arm when returned to the beginning of the maze. This phenomenon, called *spontaneous alternation,* suggests that variety is sought after, because on the second try, the subject chooses to experience that part of the environment not experienced on the first try. There is also ample evidence that spontaneous alternation also occurs at the human level (e.g., Schultz, 1964).

The major criticism leveled at this body of research concerns whether it really shows that variety is sought after or some other explanation of exploratory behavior and spontaneous alternation is more adequate. This general criticism takes a number of concrete forms. For example, spontaneous alternation has been attributed by some psychologists to such causes as satiation of the particular muscular movements made in turning one way rather than the other (reactive inhibition) and satiation of the stimuli in the part of the maze first seen (stimulus satiation). Both explanations present alternatives to the assertion that variety is an attractive stimulus.

Dember's (1956) ingenious experiment demonstrates conclusively that the variety explanation is better. Dember also used a T maze but modified it in two ways: He installed glass doors at the intersection of the stem and the arms of the T such that the rats could look into both arms but enter neither, and he painted one arm of the T black and the other white. Thus, on the first try in the maze, the rats saw both white and black portions that they could not actually enter. For the second try, the investigator made two changes: He removed the glass doors, making it possible to enter the arms of the T, and he

changed one of the arms from black to white, thereby rendering both arms the same color. Proponents of reactive inhibition, as an explanation of spontaneous alternation, would not expect any difference in the frequency with which the two arms were entered on this second try, because, since no arms were entered on the first try, there would have been no opportunity for the muscular movements involved in turning right or left to become satiated and therefore subsequently avoided. Similarly, proponents of stimulus satiation would not expect any difference in the frequency with which the two arms were entered, because on the second try both are the same color and, since that color was represented on the first try, there should be no difference in the satiating nature of the two arms. But proponents of the position that variety is sought after would clearly predict that on the second try rats would enter the arm whose color was changed from what it had been on the first try. In a resounding demonstration of the greater utility of one explanation over others, Dember found that 17 out of 20 rats entered the changed arm on the second try! This experiment was so incisively designed that in one fell swoop reactive inhibition and stimulus satiation were demolished as possible explanations of spontaneous alternation.

But there is another, alternative explanation of spontaneous alternation and exploratory behavior that Dember's experiment has not demolished. This explanation, offered by Berlyne (1957, 1960), holds that variety is certainly approached, not because it is pleasant, desired, or needed but because it increases conflict and uncertainty and thereby is unpleasant enough to instigate the attempt to gain greater familiarity with the source of the variety in hope of decreasing uncertainty and conflict. In exploring a new aspect of the environment, or in alternating spontaneously, the organism tries to obtain the information with which to render that which is novel old and familiar—and therefore unthreatening. Clearly this position would also have predicted entrance into the changed arm of the T in Dember's experiment and, hence, is a viable competitor to the position that variety is sought after because it is attractive and interesting. As long as Berlyne's position can explain these research results as well as the other position can, we cannot conclude that there is empirical support for the contention that variety is not always unpleasant and avoided.

Although Berlyne's position is ingenious, it is unlikely to be true, because it destroys the distinction between approaching a stimulus and avoiding it. If novelty were indeed threatening, Berlyne could as easily have predicted that it would be run from as that it would be pursued. Yet, running from and pursuing novelty are very different things, not convincingly understood as merely alternative ways of achieving the same end. On logical grounds, Berlyne's position seems weak.

Empirical research also suggests the faultiness of demolishing the distinction between approach and avoidance. Welker (1959) put rats into a large rectangular box that was well lit and included different kinds of objects. Off to one side of the rectangle was a small, dark, empty alcove. His rats darted about frantically until they found the alcove and then took shelter in it. After a while, they ventured forth from the alcove, with their movements in the larger rectangle now calmer and more deliberate. There is a clear distinction between the behavior in the large rectangle before entering the alcove and after leaving it. The early behavior seems like avoidance, while the latter seems like approach. If this distinction is important, we must take seriously the inability of a position such as Berlyne's to account for it. He would have to call both the early and the later behavior exploratory and explain them in the same fashion; namely, as attempts to decrease the conflict produced by novelty. In a later work, Berlyne (1967) seems to give up his earlier position, in part because of reports such as Welker's. In acknowledging that interest in novelty may occur because it is pleasing, Berlyne says,

> There has been much talk of the human craving for excitement and stimulation.... Experiments on exploratory behavior ... and play ... show that higher animals often find access to stimulation gratifying and that properties known to raise

arousal—such as novelty, surprisingness, complexity—may enhance the reward value of exteroceptive stimuli. (p. 29)

Then Berlyne actually goes on to marshal evidence against his former view of the aversive effects of variety through its enhancement of conflict! In conclusion, it seems clear that variety is sought after.

Variety Is Pleasant. Particularly relevant to the argument that variety is attractive are two studies by Maddi and Andrews (1966) that measure the degree to which variety is sought after by the novelty of stories subjects compose about pictures. They reason that because the pictures permitted a wide range of stories, people who produced novel stories were actually creating their own variety. That story novelty may well indicate seeking of variety and nothing else is suggested by the absence of relationship between it and such other general characteristics as intelligence; social class; productivity; the needs for achievement, affiliation, and power; and the tendency to respond in a socially desirable fashion (Maddi & Andrews, 1966; Maddi et al., 1965). Also included in the Maddi and Andrews studies are self-descriptions concerning the attractiveness of variety. These self-descriptions took the form of indicating whether one liked or disliked certain statements, such as "I move my furniture around frequently" and "I often vary my activities." These statements were organized into standard scales from a number of personality tests, such as the Need for Change Scale of the Activities Index (Stern, 1958). As you can see in Table 10-7, Maddi and Andrews found evidence in both studies that the greater the tendency to seek variety, the greater the preference for and attractiveness of variety.

Csikszentmihalyi (1975) has also reported an interlocking set of relevant studies. When questioned closely, his subjects reported liking best those situations in which their abilities were not entirely up to what was required by the task difficulty. Not only were such situations reported as most engrossing; direct observations of performance confirmed that subjects indeed became very involved in them, losing track of

TABLE 10-7   Product-Moment Correlations Between Novelty of Productions and Variables Reflecting Preferences for Variety

STUDIES	NOVELTY OF PRODUCTIONS	PROBABILITY BY ONE-TAILED TEST
Study I (N = 78)		
16 PF Factor H (Timid-adventurous)*	−.02	—
16 PF Factor I (Touch-sensitive)	.33	< .005
16 PF Factor Q (Conservative-experimenting)	.28	< .01
Study II (N = 56)		
AI *n* Change scale	.25	< .05
AI *n* Play scale	.18	—
AI Impulsivity scale	.27	< .025

*The terms listed are recommended by Cattel for identifying the poles of the factors. The list term
 is for the low end of the factor.

SOURCE: Adapted from "The Need for Variety in Fantasy and Self-Description," by S. R. Maddi
and S. Andrews, 1966, *Journal of Personality, 34.*

themselves and time. These situations must have involved perceived discrepancies, uncertainties, and novelty.

In the face of such results, one would find it difficult to maintain the view that people seek variety because of its discomforting and threatening nature. Apparently it is precisely those people who like variety most who expend effort to seek it. Also, people in general seem to regard situations involving novelty as the most engrossing and worthwhile.

Another study by Maddi (1961a) concerns the nature of the emotional reaction to different degrees of variety. Subjects were given a booklet and instructed to perform two tasks simultaneously. Whenever they received a signal, they were to write down a prediction as to whether the next page of the booklet would contain a number or the beginning of a sentence. After predicting, they turned the page, again received the signal to predict, again turned the page, and so forth. Thus, the first task was to predict what would take place. In the course of the experiment the subjects got fairly immediate feedback on the accuracy or inaccuracy of their predictions. The second task was to complete sentences. Whenever the page subjects turned to showed the beginning of a sentence, they were

supposed to finish the sentence in whatever manner they wished.

Subjects in the experimental group experienced a regular pattern of stimuli as follows. Each group of three successive pages of the booklet, starting from the first, showed the pattern of number, number, sentence beginning. This pattern recurred eight times without interruption. As you might expect, the average percentage of accuracy of the subjects' predictions increased from a low of 26 to a high of 95 during the eight pattern repetitions. The sentence completions made by the subjects at the end of each pattern were used as a measure of affective tone, or the degree to which the subjects were having pleasant or unpleasant feelings. Each sentence completion was scored on a 5-point scale according to whether it showed strongly positive affect (5), mildly positive affect (4), neutral affect (3), mildly negative affect (2), or strongly negative affect (1), and mean affect scores associated with each pattern repetition were computed.

As shown in Figure 10-2, Maddi found that in the experimental group affect was initially negative or unpleasant but, as the pattern was repeated, rose to a peak of positive or pleasant affect and then became negative once more. Interestingly, the greatest intensity of positive

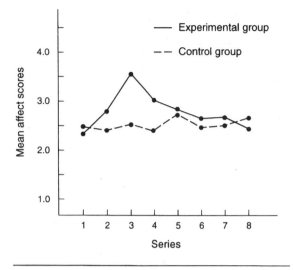

FIGURE 10-2   Mean Affect Scores As Function of Number of Series Experienced
SOURCE: Adapted from "Affective Tone During Environmental Regularity and Change," by S. R. Maddi, 1961, *Journal of Abnormal and Social Psychology, 62.*

affect occurred on the third pattern repetition, during which the subjects were inaccurate only 33% of the time. As inaccuracy of prediction decreased from 76% to 33% during the first three pattern repetitions, affective tone went from negative to positive. And while inaccuracy of prediction decreased from 33% to 6% during the last five pattern repetitions, affective tone went from positive to negative.

Think about these results. The percentage of inaccuracy provides a precise index of the degree to which a discrepancy exists between what is expected and what actually occurs. Therefore, if theorists who stress the unpleasant nature of unexpectedness and dissonance, such as Kelly and Festinger, were right, Maddi should have obtained results indicating that as the percentage of accuracy increased, negative affect gave way to positive affect. Berlyne would have expected the same thing, because inaccuracy in this case defines what is unexpected and therefore novel. However, Maddi's results show the peak of positive affect when prediction is still 33% inaccurate, with further decreases in inaccuracy associated with progressively greater negative

affect. These results favor the position that mild variety—call it unexpectedness, dissonance, or discrepancy—is a pleasant experience.

Maddi reports two other relevant findings from this study. The first finding involves the relationship between prediction and affect when the pattern of numbers and sentence beginnings was changed after the eight repetitions. Some subjects in the experimental group experienced a large change in pattern and others a small change, these effects being confirmed by the amount of increase in predictional inaccuracy. As shown in Figure 10-3, the subjects of the experimental group experiencing the small change showed a striking increase in positive affect even though they were actually becoming more inaccurate than they had been during the pattern repetitions. In contrast, the experimental group subjects experiencing the large change did not show a spurt in positive affect and, of course,

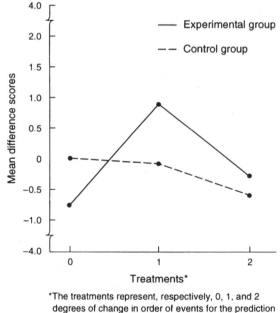

*The treatments represent, respectively, 0, 1, and 2 degrees of change in order of events for the prediction and no-prediction groups.

FIGURE 10-3   Mean Difference Scores Associated with Treatments 0, 1, and 2
SOURCE: Adapted from "Affective Tone During Environmental Regularity and Change," by S. R. Maddi, 1961, *Journal of Abnormal and Social Psychology, 62.*

were becoming greatly inaccurate. The final find-ing of this study concerns a control group, whose subjects also received numbers and words on the pages of the booklet but found them arranged in a random and therefore unpredictable order. Fig-ures 10-2 and 10-3 show results for this group that are entirely different from those already pre-sented. Affect for the control group generally was negative throughout the experiment.

Taking all of Maddi's results into account, the most comprehensive conclusion to draw is that small degrees of variety are pleasant and large degrees unpleasant. Given this and the various threads of discussion concerning the third issue, one can say that there is empirical support for the conclusion that cognitive dissonance is not invariably unpleasant and avoided. Furthermore, the evidence seems to be accumulating that mod-erate degrees of unexpectedness and novelty are approached and found pleasant, whereas larger and smaller degrees are unpleasant and avoided (e.g., Berlyne, 1960; Dorfman, 1965; Maddi, 1961c; Munsinger & Kessen, 1964; Vitz, 1966). In addition, some evidence (e.g., Maddi & Andrews, 1966) indicates that people may differ in the range of variety they consider pleasant. In light of all this, it is strange to find some psy-chologists still holding to the belief that variety is attractive in all degrees (e.g., Nunnally, 1971) or not at all (e.g., Zajonc, 1968). By now, there is enough known in variety research to suggest that Nunnally's conclusion is based on his hav-ing designed experiments that did not sample subjects' reactions over a wide enough range of variety to obtain avoidance as well as approach tendencies (see Maddi, 1971). But Zajonc's argu-ment is more elaborate and bears very directly on the issue under discussion here.

In his spirited monograph, Zajonc (1968) reviews many linguistic studies and reports sev-eral experiments done by him and his students to the effect that mere exposure to (familiarity with) stimuli increases their attractiveness. First he collected many correlational studies in which the judged value of words was found to covary with their frequency of usage. Impressive though this array of studies may seem, we must recog-nize that correlations do not permit us to infer

causality. Although Zajonc construes the studies as showing that the more a word is used, the more it takes on a positive emotional tone, he also could have concluded the opposite. Indeed, it makes more sense to consider the studies as showing that positively toned words get used most. Otherwise, one would be in the odd posi-tion of contending that even a word like *friendly* had a negative charge when first entering the language (because it was unfamiliar) and became positive only through use. At that point, the pre-fixed word *unfriendly* must have been devised in order to offset the positive drift due to increased familiarity. This is not a very plausible position on the creation of language, though Zajonc sub-scribes to it.

Perhaps the difficulty here is that Zajonc, in working toward a complete explanation of the affective charge of stimuli, uses only familiarity, just one of several important factors that can contribute to positive affective charge. After all, words have meaning in addition to familiarity. The positive affective charge of a word like *friendly* derives as much, if not more, from its agreeable meaning (in the form of connotations and remembrances of friendship) as from its fre-quency of occurrence. Zajonc does report some experiments, rather than correlational studies, using meaningful stimuli. As you might expect, he obtained much weaker, even inconsistent results when he tried experimentally to increase the positivity of meaningful stimuli by present-ing them often.

Most of Zajonc's reported experiments, how-ever, use meaningless stimuli (nonsense syllables, ideographs) that are presented at varying fre-quencies to subjects with the expectation that those presented most will be most attractive. In general, his results support this expectation. But other research suggests that Zajonc should have obtained a U-shaped curve, in which the stimuli presented with intermediate frequency would be most attractive and those presented less or more frequently less attractive. Perhaps the difficulty with Zajonc's procedure is similar to Nunnally's. Zajonc may not have employed a sufficiently large number of repetitions to render the initially meaningless stimuli monotonous and therefore unattractive. This is possible even though he did use up to 25 exposures of some stimuli. After all, in each experiment many meaningless stimuli were presented, all with different frequencies of occurrence and in an essentially unpredictable order. Amidst this uncertainty, 25 repetitions may have been just enough to render a stimulus moderately familiar and therefore positive in affective charge.

Finally, in an attempt to round out his position, Zajonc assumes that *exploratory behavior* results from conflict and negative affect over an unfamiliar stimulus, much like early Berlyne (1960). Most of the evidence he marshals for this view shows that unfamiliar stimuli increase reaction time and galvanic skin response. But these are certainly indirect measures of negative affective charge, the precise meaning of which is hard to determine. The most direct measures are verbal statements, but he reports such data in only one study done by a student of his (Harrison, 1967). In this study, one set of subjects was used to measure the intensity of exploratory behavior, and another to measure the preference value evoked by a set of stimuli. A substantial negative correlation was found between exploration and preference, but it is quite possible that this study ran afoul of individual differences. In Harrison's exploratory condition, the subjects who explored intensely might have expressed preference for the novel stimuli had they been asked; in the other condition, the subjects who disliked the stimuli might not have explored them. Such a state of affairs could have produced the obtained correlation for reasons opposite to those Zajonc assumed. The Maddi and Andrews (1966) study mentioned earlier is a better source of information on the relationship between exploration and preference, as both were measured on the same subjects.

Later research influenced by Zajonc has yielded results consistent with my remarks. Hill (1978) reviews this body of research as indicating that as exposure to stimuli is prolonged, preference initially increases, then decreases. Apparently the research tradition of "mere exposure" is merging with the earlier work of novelty theorists. The U-shaped curve of curiosity and preference is once again affirmed by Loewenstein (1994) in his review of this later literature.

CONCLUSION. The upshot of all this is to render the pure cognitive dissonance version of the consistency model rather untenable, insisting as it does that all degrees of inconsistency are unpleasant for and avoided by all people. The discussion, however, clearly favors the variant position represented by the theory of McClelland and the activation version of the consistency model. As I indicated before, this issue does not have trenchant implications for the question of whether conflict and fulfillment models are more or less tenable than consistency models. Conflict and fulfillment models sometimes agree with consistency models and sometimes do not, indicating that for the former, questions of consistency and inconsistency are not basic. More basic for them are considerations of the content involved in consistencies and inconsistencies.

Fifth Issue: Is All Behavior in the Service of Tension Reduction?

You will recall that the conflict model and the cognitive dissonance version of the consistency model consider the aim of all functioning to be reduction in tension. Thus, supporters of these models would answer the given question affirmatively. But supporters of all other models would give a flatly negative answer. If fulfillment theorists were at all willing to describe functioning in terms of tension, they would say that people aim toward tension increase in the major part of their living and only incidentally at tension decrease. Fiske and Maddi, exemplifying the activation version of the consistency model, assume that the person seeks both increases and decreases in tension, depending on specified circumstances. I shall pursue an empirical answer to this fifth issue, which clearly has powerful consequences for determining the most fruitful way to conceptualize personality.

Most of the research bearing directly on tension dispositions uses nonhuman subjects. Once again, though I considered empirical study of nonhuman organisms virtually useless in clarifying questions concerning the concept of defense, I do not feel similarly regarding the concept of tension. Tension, after all, seems to involve excitation of the nervous system and is rarely defined as a mental state. Clearly the concept of tension can be applied to human and nonhuman alike, without changing the meaning intended for it by the personologist. Therefore, it should not trouble us to rely heavily on empirical studies of animals in order to reach a conclusion concerning the fifth issue.

LEARNING STUDIES. The extensive literature on learning done in the tradition of behaviorism is clearly relevant. Many behaviorists have assumed that all behavior has the primary goal of reducing tension, and they have provided many empirical demonstrations of this point of view. According to the behaviorist, learning is the establishment of a bond between a particular stimulus and a particular response (S-R bond) such that the organism gives the response whenever the stimulus is presented to it. This learned link between stimulus and response becomes established when the response brings about a decrease in the level of tension existing in the organism. This decrease in tension is called a *reward* or *reinforcement*. Furthermore, if the stimulus is a T maze, seen by the rat from the vantage point of the starting box in the stem of the T, and if the rat has a high tension state produced by having been deprived of food for many hours, running down the stem of the maze and turning into the right-hand arm, which contains food that the rat then eats and thereby reduces the tension of hunger, constitutes *learning*. The next time the rat is put into the maze in a hungry state, it will turn right because the reward of having eaten, or having reduced tension there, will lead it to try the same behavior again. This type of result has been shown in hundreds of experiments (see Hilgard, 1956). A wide range of deprivation states have been used (e.g., food, water, and sexual deprivation), all with the same overall result: If the organism experiencing a high tension state can reduce that state by giving a particular response when faced with a certain

stimulus, it will learn to do that, whereas an organism lacking a high tension state (i.e., having all major needs satiated) will learn no such link between stimulus and response.

Although most of the studies have involved rats in a maze, a wide range of other organisms and stimulus contexts have been used. A number of studies even achieved the refinement of demonstrating that the speed and accuracy of learning rises with increases in tension level. Until some years ago, the literature on learning yielded the firm, secure conclusion that decreases in tension are so valuable to the organism that it will orient its behavior toward bringing them about. Certainly, these studies support the contention that all behavior is concerned with tension reduction.

Unassailable though the above body of findings has seemed, a few dissonant studies exist. Some of these studies concern what has come to be called *latent learning*. It was discovered (see Hilgard, 1956) that if rats were left in a maze for some period of time during which they were not in any particularly high tension state and had no opportunity to reduce tension states in any event, they would subsequently behave as if they had learned a good deal about the maze. When introduced into the maze on a later occasion with a high state of tension and the possibility of reducing that state by performing a particular response, they would learn that response more quickly than rats that had not received the earlier opportunity to explore the maze under tensionless conditions. Apparently, learning can take place without the occurrence of decrease in tension.

Another set of dissonant studies concerns *spontaneous alternation,* discussed under the fourth issue. These studies make perfectly clear that even had a rat filled with tension been able to reduce that tension by making a particular turn in a maze, it would quite likely turn the opposite way on the next trial (see Dember, 1961). Thus, the apparent tendency of an organism to give the response previously associated with tension reduction turns out to be an average tendency. In other words, over a set of trials, the organism will give the response associated with tension reduction more than any other response. But if you look at the sequence of responses given during the set of trials, you will also see a tendency to alternate responses, even though this means accepting that tension reduction will not occur as often as the situation makes possible. On the basis of such findings, it would seem that not all behavior serves tension reduction.

The final group of dissonant studies (e.g., Freeman, 1933, 1938, 1940; Yerkes & Dodson, 1908) challenges the conclusion that the greater the tension state, the more rapid and accurate the learning, when giving the learned response ensures a decrease in tension. These studies employed tasks or contexts for learning that were more difficult than the admittedly rudimentary T maze. The striking conclusion was reached that for complex learning tasks there is a level of tension beyond which learning becomes inaccurate and inefficient. In other words, moderate tension states lead to better learning than intense ones do when the task is complex. This is true even though learning involves giving the response that leads to tension reduction. It would seem that the neat relationship between amount of tension reduction and speed of learning described earlier is true only in rudimentary learning situations.

While these dissonant studies were still only a trickle, behaviorists tried to shore up their brave conclusion that tension reduction is necessary for learning. Latent learning was considered an anomaly, difficult to understand, and not even clearly something to be called *learning.* Surely, the behaviorist argued, one would not want to make any sweeping revisions in such a heavily supported conclusion on the basis of a mere handful of studies whose meaning everyone agreed was unclear. By calling the findings of these few studies *latent learning,* the behaviorist was able to put them in a category separate from the main body of learning studies and thereby forget about them. Concerning spontaneous alternation, the behaviorist hit on a formulation that rendered the findings consistent with the emphasis on tension reduction: Along with the usually considered biological survival needs, there is a need to explore, or manipulate. This

manipulo-exploratory need can, like the others, contribute to the organism's level of tension. Spontaneous alternation is, then, the best strategy for the rat to employ to bring about the greatest overall reduction of tension through satisfying not only the biological survival need heightened by experimental manipulation but also the need to explore. All things considered, one can still conclude that all learning occurs in the context of tension reduction. Finally, the behaviorist attempted to account for the findings of studies using complex learning tasks, by suggesting that the effect of very high tension states in such situations is to render the organism unable to search out all the relevant information with which to learn, so insistent is its search for the wherewithal for tension reduction. Fallible though an organism thus conceived is, it still can be presumed to orient *all* its behavior toward tension reduction.

LEARNING WITHOUT TENSION REDUCTION. Even with such ingenious and spirited interpretations of the dissonant studies, it soon became apparent that the behaviorist's position was inadequate. The dissonant studies went from a trickle to a torrent and, for a while, seemed to be done simply for the fun of demonstrating once again the inadequacy of the behaviorist's position. As the dissonant studies reached torrential proportions, the underlying unity of their meaning became apparent: Not all learning requires tension reduction, nor does all behavior serve tension reduction. In a brilliant speech voicing these conclusions, Harlow (1953) articulates what has become the modern view. He begins by giving rational arguments against the behaviorist's position:

There are logical reasons why a drive-reduction theory of learning, a theory which emphasizes the role of internal, physiological-state motivation, is entirely untenable, as a motivational theory of learning. The internal drives are cyclical and operate, certainly at any effective level of intensity, for only a brief fraction of any organism's waking life. The classical hunger drive physiologically defined ceases almost as soon as food—or nonfood—is ingested. This, as far as we know, is the only case in which a single swallow portends anything of importance. The temporal brevity of operation of the internal drive states obviously offers a minimal opportunity for conditioning and a maximal opportunity for extinction. The human being, at least in the continental United States, may go for days or even years without ever experiencing true hunger or thirst.

Harlow is suggesting that the situation of strong tension is not common enough in most people's lives to take it as the starting point for a motivational theory of learning. Not enough of the person's time is spent attempting to decrease high tension states. Much of the empirical evidence providing general support for these conclusions comes from Harlow's laboratory (Harlow, 1959; Harlow, Harlow, & Meyer, 1950), in which studies of *manipulatory behavior* in primates took place. These primates were intrigued by puzzles that they could manipulate and learned to solve them in the absence of biological drive reduction. Indeed, introducing food as a reward for solving a puzzle after the primate had solved it once actually increased the errors made in subsequent attempts. In another dramatic study, the major findings of which are shown in Figure 10-4, Butler and Alexander (1955) report that monkeys will learn to open the door to their opaque aluminum cage merely in order to gain the opportunity to gaze out on the activity in the laboratory and monkey colony. To judge from Figure 10-4, the monkeys hardly lost interest in observing the laboratory, though the activity may well have increased rather than decreased tension.

Summarizing these studies, Harlow (1953) says,

> Observations and experiments on monkeys convinced us that there was as much evidence to indicate that a strong drive inhibits learning as to indicate that it facilitates learning. It was the speaker's feeling that monkeys learned more efficiently if they were given food before testing, and as a result, the speaker routinely fed his subjects before every training session. The rhesus monkey is equipped with enormous cheek pouches, and consequently many subjects would begin the educational process with a rich store of incentives crammed into the buccal cavity. When the monkey made a correct response, it would add a raisin to

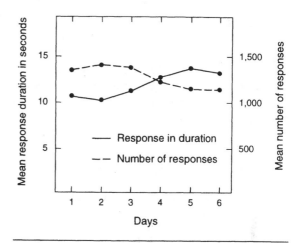

FIGURE 10-4   Mean Response Duration and Mean Number of Responses As a Function of Days
SOURCE: From "Daily Patterns of Visual Exploratory Behavior in the Monkey," by R. A. Butler and H. M. Alexander, 1955, *Journal of Comparative and Physiological Psychology, 48.*

the buccal storehouse and swallow a little previously munched food. Following an incorrect response, the monkey would also swallow a little stored food. Thus, both correct and incorrect responses invariably resulted in S-R theory drive reduction. It is obvious that under these conditions the monkey cannot learn, but the present speaker developed an understandable skepticism of this hypothesis when the monkeys stubbornly persisted in learning, learning rapidly, and learning problems of great complexity. Because food was continuously available in the monkey's mouth, an explanation in terms of differential fractional anticipatory goal responses did not appear attractive. It would seem that the Lord was simply unaware of drive-reduction learning theory when he created, or permitted the gradual evolution of the rhesus monkey.

Obviously Harlow does not mean that the rhesus monkey is a single exception to the law that learning is mediated by tension reduction. Indeed, he goes on in the speech to cite evidence similar to the above concerning other primates, including humans, and even rodents. One of the most striking studies mentioned is that of Sheffield and Roby (1950), in which learning in rats was shown without biological drive reduction. Hungry rats learned to choose the arm in a

T maze that led to water sweetened with saccharine, a nonnutritive substance, over the arm leading to plain water. The major results of this study are shown in Figure 10-5, which indicates that as days went by the rats made more choices leading to the saccharine solution; they ran faster and drank more. Harlow (1953) concludes:

> It may be stated unequivocally that, regardless of any relationship that may be found for other animals, there are no data indicating that intensity of drive state and the presumably correlated amount of drive reduction are positively related to learning efficiency in primates.
>
> In point of fact there is no reason to believe that the rodentological data will prove to differ significantly from those of monkey, chimpanzee, and man.

If such important behavior as that involved in learning is to some degree independent of tension reduction, we are justified in concluding that not all functioning is in its service.

Harlow actually goes further than this to suggest that some behavior in learning situations brings about increases rather than decreases in tension. Such increases, if not intended, are at least tolerated. Harlow (1953) cites some evidence for this from studies conducted in his laboratory and also includes one striking anecdote:

> Twenty years ago at the Gilas Park Zoo, in Madison, we observed an adult orangutan given two blocks of wood, one with a round hole, one with a square hole, and two plungers, one round and one square. Intellectual curiosity alone led it to work on these tasks often for many minutes at a time, and to solve the problem of inserting the round plunger in both sides. The orangutan never solved the problem of inserting the square peg into the round hole, but inasmuch as it passed away with perforated ulcers a month after the problem was presented, we can honestly say that it died trying. And in defense of this orangutan, let it be stated that it died working on more complex problems than are investigated by most present-day theorists.

The suggestion made here is that once you study learning tasks of sufficient complexity to resemble the actual life experiences of organisms (T mazes clearly fall short of this), you find evidence on every side of behavior that bears little

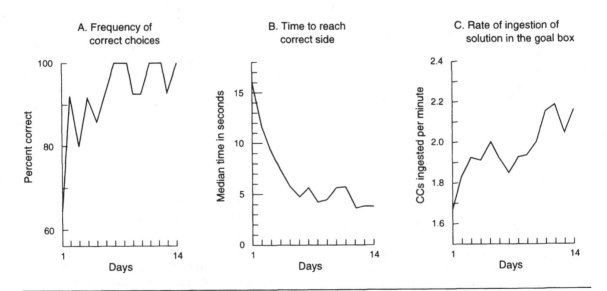

FIGURE 10-5   Acquisition in a T Maze with Saccharine Solution
(1.30 Grams per Liter) As Reward
SOURCE: From "Reward Value of a Non-Nutrient Sweet Taste," by F. D. Sheffield
and T. B. Roby, 1950, *Journal of Comparative and Physiological Psychology, 43.*

discernible relationship to any aim to reduce tension. Indeed, intriguing problems that spark the organism's curiosity may lead to persistent behavior that *raises* tension, even to dangerous levels. If you have ever become excited and stimulated at a party or by an intellectual task to such a degree that you stayed up long into the night and expended lots of energy, without the slightest thought for the next day, then you know what Harlow means. Some of the most interesting behaviors definitely seem to arouse rather than decrease tension.

TENSION-INCREASE STUDIES. In the years since Harlow made his speech, more systematic studies concerning the possibility of tension increase as an aim have been done. Most of these studies have already been mentioned in the discussion of the fourth issue. Perhaps the single most convincing body of work on the intent to increase tension is that involving *sensory deprivation* (see Fiske, 1961). These studies show that when you deprive people of the usual levels of sensory stimulation, they go to sleep (a sign of low tension level) but when they awaken experience great discomfort and an intense wish for stimulation. It is even possible that the hallucinatory mentation mentioned by investigators in this field is the organism's attempt to manufacture stimulation and tension.

Certainly research has clearly shown that the presentation of even the most banal stimulation (e.g., a recording of instructions) is greeted by subjects with enthusiasm and relief. Subjects will keep requesting such banal stimulation and, when all else fails, leave the experiment in intense discomfort. It is not hard to conclude from such evidence that some behavior serves tension increase. Also supporting this conclusion are the studies of Dember (1956) and Eisenberger, Myers, Sanders, and Shanab (1970) indicating that spontaneous alternation involves a positive interest in stimulus change, and Maddi and Andrews (1966), indicating that the people who most produce novelty are also the most interested in it. These studies are relevant because novelty and change undoubtedly increase tension.

These compelling findings have led some behaviorists to abandon their position. Consider Berlyne (1960), who you will recall initially developed an ingenious behavioristic argument in which one would explain tension-increase studies as special cases of the attempt to reduce tension, strange as that may sound. Berlyne postulates that in the absence of external stimulation the organism actually becomes very tense due to spontaneously occurring internal stimulation. Subsequent attempts to increase external stimulation should therefore be understood as attempts to decrease the overall level of tension. Presumably, external stimulation has some inhibiting effects on spontaneous internal stimulation.

You should recognize what an extraordinarily complicated explanation this is. Sometimes external stimulation is talked about as increasing tension, as when the laboratory rat is shocked and recoils in pain, and sometimes as decreasing tension, as when the sensorily deprived subject is permitted to hear the instructions. An explanation of this type stands or falls on the forcefulness of its treatment of whatever internal conditions are invoked to account for the two opposite effects of external stimulation. Even without this theoretical difficulty, the notion that external stimulation actually decreases overall tension cannot adequately cover all the data. It must be remembered that it is typical of subjects in sensory deprivation experiments to fall asleep and to remain groggy, lethargic, and unable to think even after awakening. None of this sounds like a high state of tension. And are the ulcers that killed Harlow's monkey to be understood as the result of tension decreases stemming from working on puzzles?

As you have seen, Berlyne (1967) subsequently modified his position to recognize tension increase as well as tension decrease as rewarding. Although he still believed that boredom may be a high tension state, he did admit to a lack of experimental evidence for this view and went on to define classes of reinforcers that function because they increase tension. The first is ecological stimuli, which presumably have been important for survival and adaptation and therefore are rewarding even though they increase tension. In this regard, Berlyne noted studies that have obtained introspective reports of pleasure accompanying painful sensations produced by pricks, pressures, and pinches. Another class of rewarding tension increasers are novel, complex, and surprising stimuli, called *collative properties* by Berlyne.

The research evidence here already has been covered in discussion of the fourth issue. Berlyne also notes that increases in tension seem to facilitate learning, particularly verbal. Some studies have shown that the higher the level of arousal during learning, the greater the probability of long-term recall, though the smaller the probability of short-term recall. In other studies, even immediate recall has been improved by the application of various arousal-raising treatments during learning, such as white noise, tones, induced muscular tension, and physical exercise. In trying to explain these findings, Berlyne (1967) says,

> We must therefore seek an alternative account of the effects of arousal on verbal learning. The one that emerges is . . . that verbal responses will be reinforced most effectively when arousal is at an intermediate level. Tests held some time after training—preferably 24 hours or more—give the surest measures of reinforcement. Immediate and short-term recall must depend on an interaction between the reinforcing effect of arousal and the effect of arousal on performance. We can expect these two effects to follow different inverted U-shaped functions. (p. 69)

Berlyne seems to be saying that moderate levels of arousal (or tension) are rewarding, whereas lower or higher levels are not. In some experimental settings it may seem as if only tension reduction is rewarding and in other settings just the opposite. In reality, the difficulty is that the settings "reveal only one portion of the nonmonotonic, 'U-shaped,' curve" (Berlyne, 1967, p. 69). In the years since Berlyne's statement, little has happened to provoke any change in conclusion. Apparently, agreement has been reached that tension increase is important to organisms, and empirical attention has settled on comparing the various theories to account for this phenomenon (see Eisenberger, 1972).

CONCLUSION. We can conclude that not all behavior is oriented toward tension reduction and that some behavior may even be directed at tension increase. This outcome of exploring the fifth issue tends to favor the fulfillment model and the activation version of the consistency model. Not so supported are the conflict model and the cognitive dissonance version of the consistency model.

Sixth Issue: Does Personality Show Radical Change After Childhood?

Consistency and fulfillment positions stand on one side of this issue and conflict positions stand, by and large, on the other. According to the pure psychosocial conflict model, there should be no radical change in personality once there is solidification of the defensive patterns established to avoid the anxiety that reflects underlying conflict. Because these patterns are considered set by the time childhood has passed, conflict positions would not expect adulthood, or even adolescence, to be a time of radical personality change. What I have just said does not apply as much to the intrapsychic version of the conflict model, because it emphasizes defense only in nonideal functioning. But absence of radical change after childhood is clearly assumed by pure psychosocial conflict theorists such as Freud. In this theory, it is even typical to name the patterns of peripheral characteristics, or personality types, in terms of the early childhood stages of psychosexual development. In considering adolescence and adulthood to reflect little more than the developmental stage of childhood, Freud vividly shows his emphasis on the essentially unchanging nature of adult personality. Any changes taking place beyond puberty are not basic or radical.

In contrast, fulfillment positions see personality as a rather continually changing thing, with no sharp difference in changeability between childhood, adolescence, and adulthood. This emphasis on fluidity is most apparent in Rogers and the other actualization theorists, who do not consider even the self-concept to be particularly stable. But the emphasis is also strong in some perfection theorists, such as the existential psychologists, who see life as a series of changes toward ever increasing individuality. Perfection theorists tend to emphasize personality change in the direction of psychological growth, or simultaneously increasing differentiation and integration. Consistency positions, having little recourse to a concept of defense, also assume rather continual change in personality. The cognitive dissonance version of the consistency model attributes to the person the frequent changes in personality that occur in the attempt to minimize the discrepancy between expectations and perceived occurrences. Finally, the activation version of this model emphasizes the concept of psychological growth.

You may have noticed that I stated the issue in such a way that what is of interest is the occurrence of *radical change* in personality. It was necessary to do this because no sensible theorist would dispute that certain unextraordinary changes at least in degree take place during adolescence and adulthood. If, say, a person with the kind of personality called *anal* by Freudians was stubborn in childhood and became a bit less or more so in adulthood, no one would consider this theoretically disconcerting. In a literal sense, change would have occurred, but no special difficulty for the conflict model would have been created thereby. Radical changes in personality are a different matter. If a person's personality type shifted from oral in childhood to phallic in adulthood, we would have a situation unexpected by Freudians. The only way Freudians could explain such a radical change in adulthood would be to postulate the intervention of an unusual and potent life context, such as psychotherapy or catastrophe. If radical change in personality can be shown in the absence of such extraordinary occurrences, the psychosocial conflict model will not have been confirmed. Thus, to pinpoint the issue such that it will really separate the various models, we must restrict ourselves to conditions or contexts that can be considered more natural and usual than participating in psychotherapy. These more natural conditions include such things as getting married, having children, going to college, changing jobs, and moving to a new location.

You should note that my depiction of the psychosocial conflict position is least accurate for ego psychology. The major ego psychologist, Erikson, does, after all, emphasize eight developmental ages stretching across the entire life span. And in his account, Levinson (1977) argues within a generally ego-psychological framework for such adulthood changes as the "mid-life crisis." But do not conclude that the Freudian emphasis on stability during adolescence and adulthood is a thing of the past. Litz (1979), an authoritative Freudian, wrote a book ostensibly about development throughout life that devotes barely 70 of 615 pages to adulthood years. Most of the book is about the first few years of life. Theorists influenced by psychosocial conflict thinking, be they ego psychologists or pure Freudians, tend to discount radical change following childhood.

LONGITUDINAL STUDIES. On the face of it, the study of personality change is most effectively done by testing the same group of people at the beginning and at the end of the period of time under consideration—the *longitudinal study* (see Chapter 9). Although this is the most appropriate kind of study, there are obvious difficulties associated with having to wait long periods of time to obtain data. After the initial testing, subjects may move to dozens of locations, no longer be willing to participate, or even die. Such difficulties have held down the number of longitudinal studies attempted. Fortunately, there are by now several such studies with reasonably careful data collection procedures, and they will be emphasized in what follows.

In earlier years, the difficulties inherent in longitudinal studies provoked investigators to rely instead on the *cross-sectional study*, in which a number of groups of subjects are compared, with each group differing in age. Groups are tested only once, and the differences among them are attributed to the effects of the span of years separating their ages. Obviously this kind of study has the advantage of taking very little time and effort compared with the longitudinal study. But the cross-sectional study is also more risky, because it must be assumed that the various groups had similar personalities when they were as young as those in the youngest group tested. Usually there is no way to check this assumption. But suppose the span of years separating the adolescent and adult groups is large, say, 30 years. In 30 years' time, it is rather likely that child-rearing practices would have changed enough to make it risky to assume similarity of childhood personality for all groups. And if the groups differed in personality during childhood, it may be no more than this fact that the investigator is observing and erroneously attributing to the effects of moving through adolescence. Because of these problems, I will not rely on cross-sectional studies, though they will be mentioned as suggestive.

Turning to relevant longitudinal studies, I shall present an instructive early effort by Tuddenham (1959). He interviewed 72 men and women first during their adolescence and again in their early or middle adulthood. The interview material was rated for 53 personality variables, some fairly descriptive and some inferential. Correlations between subjects' earlier and later scores generally were positive but quite low, the average being only .27 for men and .24 for women. These correlations are so low that one really could not effectively predict what a person would be like in young adulthood from his or her scores in early adolescence. But there are two problems in interpreting these findings as indicating personality change. Unfortunately, pairs of raters did not always agree strongly, and the pair of raters working on the interview data for the first testing was different from the pair working on the second testing. These two methodological problems could have produced the apparent lack of personality stability.

The college years offer a ready source of information about personality change following childhood. Although most such studies have been cross-sectional, a few have been longitudinal in design. Among these, the report by Freedman and Bereiter (1963) is notable not only for its carefulness but also because it extends even beyond the college years. Their subjects were women from the classes of 1954, 1955, and 1956 at Vassar College, numbering 78, 74, and

79, respectively. These subjects took the Vassar Attitude Inventory (VAI), the Minnesota Multiphasic Personality Inventory (MMPI), and the California Personality Inventory (CPI) as freshmen, again as seniors, and finally 3 to 4 years after graduation. The results offer evidence of systematic and important change during the college years, the nature of which other studies confirm (e.g., Sanford, 1962). On the VAI, the subjects seemed to have become, as seniors, less ethnocentric and authoritarian while expressing more impulses and rebellious independence. Changes in scores on the MMPI and CPI initially indicated a shift toward psychopathology and away from conventional adjustment. But 3 to 4 years after graduation, these general trends were more or less reversed. At the final testing, repression and suppression of impulses increased on the VAI, scores on the psychopathology scales of the MMPI decreased, and the CPI indicated a move toward conventional adjustment. Although the changes demonstrated in this study were not especially large, they are striking because they tended to reverse direction.

GENOTYPICAL STUDIES. All the studies mentioned thus far use *test-retest agreement* on the same measures as a procedure for determining the degree of personality stability or change. A few longitudinal studies, however, employ a more global, interpretive criterion of stability based on the determination of analogous rather than literally similar behaviors at the different ages considered. These studies work at a *genotypical* (underlying) level, whereas the others employ a *phenotypical* (obvious) level of analysis, to borrow a distinction from biology. Whether or not the genotypical approach is really more appropriate, you should recognize that it renders observation of change less likely because of the abstract, interpretive level at which observation takes place.

In one genotypical study, Anderson (1960) tested all school children in a Minnesota county from grades 4 to 12, and then retested them 5 to 7 years later, by which time some of them were in their 20s. He concludes that of the measures of intelligence and personality obtained at the first testing, only the former play an important role in predicting later adjustment. In spite of an approach unsuited to focusing on literal changes in behavior, Anderson reports that personality variables do not seem to be patterned by age.

In a major genotypical study, Kagan and Moss (1962) suggest the opposite conclusion. Twenty-one people were rated on a set of personality variables at four intervals during their childhoods and again during their 20s. Correlations were computed between certain childhood behaviors and their theoretically analogous adult behaviors. These results are presented in Figure 10-6, which also indicates the kinds of behaviors considered. Kagan and Moss (1962) conclude that

> Many of the behaviors exhibited by the child aged six to ten, and a few during the age period three to six, were moderately good predictors of theoretically related behaviors during early childhood. Passive withdrawal from stressful situations, dependency on family, ease-of-anger arousal, involvement in intellectual mastery, social interaction anxiety, sex-role identification, and pattern of sexual behavior in adulthood were each related to

reasonably analogous behavioral dispositions during the early school years. . . . These results offer strong support for the generalization that aspects of adult personality begin to take form during early childhood. (pp. 266–268)

Actually, this seems to me rather unconvincing as a conclusion based on the findings in Figure 10-6. Even with an approach weighted toward the discovery of *personality stability,* we find that five of the seven correlations shown for men and all seven for women are below .50. The average correlation is about .41 for men and .31 for women. To my mind, these findings show that there is more change than stability in personality, even when one adopts a genotypical approach!

Following their brave conclusions, Kagan and Moss (1962) make statements more consistent with the amount of change they observed. For example,

> Not all of the childhood reactions displayed long-term continuity. Compulsivity and irrational fears during childhood were not predictive of similar responses during adulthood. Moreover, task persistence and excessive irritability during the first three

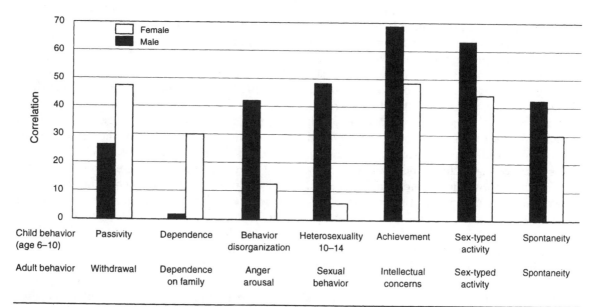

FIGURE 10-6   Summary of Relations Between Selected Child Behaviors (6 to 10 Years of Age) and Theoretically Similar Adult Behaviors
Source: From *Birth to Maturity: A Study in Psychological Development* by J. Kagan and H. A. Moss. Copyright © 1962 by John Wiley & Sons, Inc. Reprinted by permission.

years of life showed no relation to phenotypically similar behaviors during later childhood. (p. 269)

In another statement, Kagan and Moss (1962) give what seems to me the crux of the matter:

However, the degree of continuity of these response classes was intimately dependent upon its congruence with traditional standards for sex-role characteristics. The differential stability of passivity, dependency, aggression, and sexuality for males and females emphasizes the importance of cultural roles in determining both behavioral change and stability. (p. 268)

Indeed, with results showing more change than stability, it would seem wise to conclude that whatever stability exists from childhood to adulthood occurs along the lines of sex-role definitions important to culture. When some aspect of personality is not intimately connected with what is defined as a sex role, it may well change enough in adulthood to be virtually unpredictable from childhood personality.

In a study of large scope, Block (1971) collected follow-up data in adulthood from subjects who had been extensively tested by other investigators during childhood and adolescence. The variety of data available included interviews, teacher and peer reports, self-reports, and several structured personality tests. Genotypical data concerning stability or change in personality were derived from these protocols by ratings made by several psychologists. Mean correlations for the 171 subjects between junior high school and senior high school ages were .77 and .75 for male and female subjects, respectively. Between senior high school and adulthood, they were .56 and .54 for male and female subjects, respectively. But the range of correlations was so great as to indicate that a number of subjects had changed a good deal though some remained much the same. Block identified six female and five male types that differed not only in personality content but in degree of change from childhood to adulthood. Some of these types changed too much to be consistent with the contention that personality remains stable once the childhood years are past. Block's unusual approach of isolating types partly on the basis

of changeability has provided findings that clearly bear on the issue under discussion.

Also, Bachman, O'Malley, and Johnston (1978) have reported a *longitudinal study* using a sample of 16,000 subjects chosen to represent the U.S. population. The subjects were first tested when in high school and then followed for 8 years, during which the investigators examined the impact of such events as college, marriage, unemployment, childbearing, and military service on attitudes, self-esteem, aggression, and various behaviors. Bachman et al. conclude that these events had relatively little effect and that "the dominant picture that emerges from this research is not change but stability." Once again we are faced with a problem of interpretation. The test-retest correlations reported in this study rarely exceed the range of .40 to .50. Hence, one might choose to emphasize change over stability, as such correlations do not provide an adequate basis for predicting behavior over the 8-year period.

ADULTHOOD STUDIES. Regarding the latter half of life—middle adulthood to old age—we find very few longitudinal studies to go by. A report by Terman and Oden (1959) follows up on a group of gifted, extraordinary children studied years before who had since reached their 40s. Originally each child selected for study was in the top 1% of the population in intelligence quotient (IQ). The data on personality have not been systematically analyzed, but in general it appears that the superior child became the superior adult. Although there is evidence of stability here, one must be careful in generalizing from this study both because it deals with such an unusual group of people and because it is mainly concerned with intelligence rather than personality.

In another study, Kelly (1955) tested 300 engaged couples first when they were in their 20s and again when they were in their 40s. After correcting his correlations for attenuation, Kelly concludes that individual consistency was highest in the areas of values and vocational interests (correlations of approximately .50) and lowest with regard to self-ratings and other personality variables (correlations of approximately .30).

Kelly points out that "our findings indicate that significant changes in human personality may continue to occur during the years of adulthood." This conclusion is even more likely to be accurate, because the correlations of approximately .30 and .50 are only estimates of what would have been found had the measures employed been more adequate. Actually, Kelly's obtained correlations must have been lower than the figures mentioned here. In a more recent study, Haan and Dey (1974) present a picture of great change in their longitudinal study of personality in the period from adolescence to later adulthood. Their findings indicate that adulthood is a time of major reorganization in personality.

All in all, the studies reviewed to this point show so much evidence of change that many experts in human development (e.g., Neugarten, 1964; Stevenson, 1957) have concluded against stability during the adulthood years. For example, Neugarten (1964) says,

> Whether the studies are test-retest or antecedent-consequent in design . . . the general picture with regard to consistency of adult personality can be summarized by saying that measures taken at long time intervals tend to produce statistically reliable, but relatively low, correlations. . . . The indication is that while there is continuity of personality measurable by present techniques, the larger proportion of the variance in the measures used (in the final testing) remains unaccounted for. Making allowances for the fallibility of measures with regard to reliability, the implication is that there is at least as much change as there is stability.

But Costa and McCrae (1977, 1978) dispute this conclusion on the basis of factor analytic research. On a sample of male adults studied over a 10-year interval, they found that the genotypical variables of anxiety, extroversion-introversion, and neuroticism showed stability correlations ranging from .58 to .84. The individual questionnaire scales (from the 16 Personality Factor Questionnaire) on which these genotypical analyses were based showed lower stability correlations—from .44 to .63. In addition, Costa, McCrae, and Arenberg (1980) have reported another longitudinal study in which 460 males were tested three times over a 12-year period with the Guilford-Zimmerman Temperament Survey. Some of their results appear in Table 10-8, which shows strong evidence for stability over 12 years in the various traits measured. The stability is evident across young, middle, and old subsamples. This, and other recent work by Costa and McCrae (e.g., 1988, 1994) on their five-factor test (the NEO Personality Inventory), suggest that the adult years bring relative stability in some aspects of personality. But as the longitudinal studies mentioned earlier indicate, evidence seems to exist for personality change in the transition from childhood to adolescence and from adolescence to adulthood.

Recently, Helson (1993) has criticized the data analysis procedures used by Costa and McCrae as biasing the results toward stability. Specifically, she detects much evidence of change in their longitudinal data. In one source factor, neuroticism, and two of its facets, hostility and impulsivity, the sample of adults had lower scores when retested after 6 years. Further, the sample changed in several but opposite ways for various facets of the source traits, extroversion and openness to experience. That Costa and McCrae combined these opposite changes led to the appearance of no change on the source traits. Also, lower scores on a preliminary version of the traits of agreeableness and conscientiousness were found over a 3-year period. With all this evidence for change, Helson (1993) wonders why McCrae and Costa "dismissed all of the longitudinal findings on the grounds that none of them was consistently supported by cross-sectional analyses, cross-sequential analyses, and spouse-observer data." To reach their conclusion that personality is stable after age 30, McCrae and Costa (1991) had to invoke a half dozen factors treated as error variance to explain away what appeared to be change.

In her longitudinal study of women from average ages of 21 through 52, who completed several personality tests and questions about various life areas, Helson (1993) cites not only stability but also several kinds of change. First there is change associated with the entire sample. An example of this involves scores on the femininity/masculinity scale of the California

TABLE 10-8   Twelve-Year Retest Coefficients for Guilford-Zimmerman
Temperament Survey Scales in Different Age Groups

SCALES	TOTAL Age 20–76	YOUNG Age 20–44	MIDDLE Age 45–59	OLD Age 60–76
General activity	.77 (192)	.77 (60)	.83 (93)	.78 (39)
Restraint	.72 (193)	.61 (62)	.74 (94)	.76 (37)
Ascendance	.83 (194)	.85 (62)	.85 (95)	.77 (37)
Sociability	.74 (182)	.64 (62)*	.81 (88)	.66 (32)
Emotional stability	.70 (203)	.63 (68)	.76 (96)	.71 (39)
Objectivity	.69 (191)	.66 (64)	.76 (87)	.59 (40)
Friendliness	.74 (193)	.74 (64)†	.68 (88)‡	.87 (41)
Thoughtfulness	.73 (199)	.78 (64)	.71 (94)	.71 (41)
Personal relations	.68 (188)	.70 (62)	.64 (89)	.73 (37)
Masculinity	.72 (200)	.73 (66)	.71 (94)	.70 (40)
Mean stability	.73	.72	.75	.73

Note: Ns given in parentheses. All correlations significant at $p < .001$.
*Difference between Young and Middle significant at $p < .05$.
†Difference between Young and Old significant at $p < .05$.
‡Difference between Middle and Old significant at $p < .01$.
SOURCE: Adapted from "Enduring Dispositions in Adult Males," by P. T. Costa, Jr., R. R. McCrae,
and D. Arenberg, 1950, *Journal of Personality and Social Psychology, 38.*

Psychological Inventory, which show a pattern of curvilinear change, increasing from age 21 through age 27, but then decreasing from that point through age 52. Another kind of change is associated with different personality types. For example, a narcissistic subsample of women increased in effective functioning and confidence up to age 27, but then decreased in these factors while the rest of the sample continued to increase. The third kind of change involves role patterns. Women who had conformed to the "social clock" for their gender by having children had, by age 43, become less independent and dominant than the rest of the sample. All in all, there appears to be considerable evidence of personality change after the childhood years have passed if one looks carefully for it, rather than explaining it away as error variance.

A lively debate is under way, with whole issues of journals devoted to stability or change in personality (e.g., *Journal of Personality,* 1989, 57). A few studies (e.g., Carmichael & McGue, 1994; Caspi, Bem & Elder, 1989; Digman, 1989) support the view that general, underlying aspects of personality, such as childhood conscientiousness, shyness, and mother-offspring resemblance, continue to exert a recognizable influence in adolescence and adulthood. In contrast, other studies (e.g., Roberts & Donahue, 1994; Stokes, Mumford, & Owens, 1989) emphasize that although the more abstract, underlying aspects of personality are indeed there, at a concrete, behavioral level, there is a lot of variability in behavior at any given time and over time. A general consensus appears to be forming that although the more abstract, deep-seated aspects of personality (core characteristics and tendencies) show moderate stability over time, there is considerable variation at any given moment and change over time in the more concrete, social-interactional aspects of personality (peripheral characteristics and types). Unfortunately, these studies do not concern themselves much with the question of whether there is radical change in personality following the childhood years, and hence we must rely on earlier studies in attempting to resolve this issue. And, as indicated earlier, the earlier studies suggest that, in at least some people, radical personality change indeed occurs over the life span.

PSYCHOLOGICAL DIFFERENTIATION. Before I conclude this review, let me alert you to a body of research that, though relevant, is sometimes overlooked because it does not come out of the questionnaire tradition. I refer to the series of studies by Witkin and his associates (Witkin, Dyk, Faterson, Goodenough, & Karp, 1962; Witkin et al., 1954) on *psychological differentiation,* which they define as the "degree of articulation of experience of the world; degree of articulation of experience of self, reflected particularly in the nature of the body concept and extent of development of a sense of separate identity; and extent of development of specialized, structured controls and defenses" (Witkin et al., 1962, p. 16). The two things emphasized in this definition are the number of aspects or parts to the personality and the separateness of individuals from the world around them. These emphases square quite well with discussions of differentiation reviewed in previous chapters of this book. Witkin et al. (1962) also refer to *integration,* indicating its function in binding together and organizing the parts of personality discriminated from one another by differentiation. They present the intriguing view that integrative processes will determine the nature of the adjustment and degree of effectiveness that characterize the person, whereas differentiation bears little relationship to such matters; however, they conduct no research on integrative processes.

In measuring psychological differentiation, Witkin and his associates rely heavily on a number of ingenious tests that measure one's ability to be analytical in perceptual situations. Analytical perception ability is considered to indicate psychological differentiation, because it involves a separateness of self and body from the outside world and a sensitivity to the parts of things in general. In the Embedded Figures Test, the person is presented with a series of complex geometrical figures. The speed and accuracy with which he or she can detect previously seen simple figures that have been hidden within the complex ones is taken as a measure of psychological differentiation. To detect the embedded simple figure, the person must be able to analyze the complex figure into its component parts. The Rod and Frame Test presents the person with a rod surrounded by a square frame as the only visible things in a darkened room. The person is asked to adjust the rod to the upright position, which is complicated by the frame's tilt a certain number of degrees to either the left or the right. The average accuracy of rod adjustment to the upright position over a series of trials is taken as another measure of psychological differentiation. According to Witkin et al. (1962), accurate adjustment of the rod requires that the person disregard the cues provided by the surrounding frame and instead use kinesthetic and proprioceptive cues stemming from his or her body. Finally, in the Body Adjustment Test, the person sits in a seat placed within an experimental room. The experimenter can tilt both seat and room. The person must adjust his or her seated body to the upright position from a starting point at which the chair is tilted to either the right or the left and the room is tilted in the same or opposite direction. Once again the accuracy with which the body is adjusted to the upright position is taken as a measure of psychological differentiation because, to be successful, one must overlook visual cues from the external environment and rely on the awareness of kinesthetic and proprioceptive cues signaling the positioning of one's body. Scores on these three tests intercorrelate moderately and show adequate reliability (Witkin et al., 1962, p. 40).

Although these investigators have concentrated on their perceptual tests, they have also employed more cognitive measures involving people composing stories about vague pictures (Thematic Apperception Test), indicating what inkblots look like to them (Rorschach Test), and drawing pictures of themselves and others (Draw-A-Person Test). In all these tasks, the aim is to detect aspects of psychological differentiation such as articulateness of experience and articulateness of body image. A large body of empirical evidence (Witkin et al., 1954; Witkin et al., 1962) indicates that these nonperceptual measures correlate with the perceptual ones such that it is sensible to consider them all as mirroring some facet of psychological differentiation. Those of you familiar with Witkin et al.'s earlier (1954) emphasis on *field dependence-field independence* (the ability or inability to extricate oneself from the surrounding field forces) should note the fact that he (Witkin et al., 1962) shifted from these to psychological differentiation largely on the basis of the empirical association between the original perceptual measures and the cognitive ones just mentioned.

Having given you some background on Witkin's work, I can now describe the longitudinal studies relevant to determining what happens to the level of psychological differentiation during the life span. Witkin et al. (1962, pp. 374–377) report two studies of special relevance. One involved a group of 26 male and 27 female subjects, studied first at age 8 and again at age 13. The second group consisted of 30 male and 30 female subjects studied at ages 10, 14, and 17. With regard to the perceptual measures of psychological differentiation, the same trend was observed in both studies. In the words of the investigators, "The ability to determine the position of the body apart from the tilted room, to perceive the position of a rod independently of the tilted frame, to pick out a simple figure obscured by a complex design, tends to improve, on the whole, until about the age of 17" (Witkin et al., 1962, p. 374). Thereafter, the rate of increase in psychological differentiation decreases and, for female subjects, may actually reverse slightly in direction. A parallel finding was obtained concerning articulateness of body concept as measured in the figure drawings made by the subjects. Witkin et al. (1962) conclude, "Children who showed a relatively articulated body concept at 10 showed it 7 years later as well, even though the drawings at the two ages gave evidence of a general change toward more sophisticated representation of the human body" (p. 376). They also report (Witkin et al., 1962) other studies concerning the period from infancy to age 9 and the college years. The picture that emerges from all these studies is essentially the same: Psychological differentiation shows a rapid increase from infancy through about the middle of adolescence and a more gradual increase from that point on into young adulthood. In addition, the early differences among people in degree of psychological differentiation are maintained all the while everyone is increasing in that characteristic. Certainly there is clear evidence that differentiation continues to occur beyond the childhood years.

One last observation from these studies bears on the more general question of whether radical changes in personality occur following childhood. In connection with the attempt to study changes in body concept between the ages of 10 and 17, Witkin et al. (1962) had occasion to consider not only articulateness but content of figure drawings, concluding that there were:

1. Vast changes in kinds of interests . . . which resulted in marked differences in content of drawings by the same child.
2. Marked decrease in drawing features suggestive of disturbance or pathology.
3. Changes in main conflict areas. Thus, the large and varied changes that occur in this period of life are reflected in the drawings; some of the changes are in content aspects of personality, others refer to nature of integration, still others to extent of differentiation. (p. 376)

Witkin believes that along with the gradual increases in differentiation (and presumably integration, though he does not study that) there occur radical shifts in the content (including conflicts) of personality.

But there is one study (Schwartz & Carp, 1967) that suggests a peak in psychological differentiation (measured by both the Rod and Frame and Embedded Figures tests) at about age 25, and a gradual decline thereafter. If this finding holds up, we will be observing a phenomenon similar to that in the previously mentioned questionnaire studies. It may well be that personality changes from childhood through young adulthood but remains relatively stable from that point on.

CONCLUSION. The cross-sectional studies available generally favor the conclusion that radical change in personality takes place beyond the childhood years. As such, these studies agree with the longitudinal studies that consider the period from childhood to young adulthood and differ from those that cover the adulthood years. Again, because cross-sectional studies are less definitive than longitudinal ones, I will not elaborate on them here.

It is time to draw this consideration of the sixth issue to a close. There seems clear evidence for radical change in personality in the years immediately following childhood and some (though more equivocal) evidence for the ensuing years. In a recent review, Rutter (1984) concludes that the weight of evidence is against personality theories that posit an invariant set of developmental stages and a fixating effect of certain early experiences on later development. One intriguing notion that has gained force (e.g., Moll & Kuypers, 1977; Neugarten, 1980) is that while there may not be the regular stages (e.g., intimacy versus isolation, mid-life crisis) previously thought to punctuate adulthood and, hence, no correspondingly regular changes in behavior, there may be considerable individual variability as to how much change occurs and at what age it takes place.

All in all, the findings do not support the pure psychosocial version of the conflict model. But there is general support for the other models insofar as they would predict substantial personality change in the years from childhood to young adulthood. These models do tend to predict that change will continue throughout adulthood, however, and some recent findings suggest that this may not occur.

CONCLUDING REMARKS ....

We have come a long, long way in considering core-related issues and are finally in a position to put together what we have learned. In considering the first two issues posed in this chapter, we have an empirical basis for concluding that the concept of defense is tenable and that some, but not all, behavior is defensive. These conclusions support all bases for core-level theorizing except the pure psychosocial version of the conflict model, which assumes all behavior to be defensive. In pursuing the third issue, we reached the tentative conclusion that the highest form of functioning is transcendent rather than adaptive. This conclusion supports the fulfillment model, is contrary to the conflict model (at least in its psychosocial version), and fails to have any special significance for the consistency model. But we should give little weight to this conclusion, as it is no stronger than our assumption that fulfillment and conflict theorists alike would designate the creative person as the clearest embodiment of the highest form of functioning. Considering the fourth issue taught us that only large discrepancies from expectation (or dissonances) are unpleasant and avoided whereas small discrepancies are actually pleasant and sought after. This conclusion actively favors McClelland's and Fiske's and Maddi's forms of the consistency model but does not support Kelly's cognitive dissonance version of that model. The other models are not actively touched by this conclusion. We resolved the fifth issue by concluding that while some behavior aims at tension reduction, other behavior aims at tension increase. Favored are the activation and variant cognitive dissonance versions of the consistency model and the fulfillment model in general. Contradicted are the pure cognitive dissonance version of the consistency model and all forms of the conflict model except, perhaps, the variant of its psychosocial version. On investigating the sixth issue, it became apparent that there are radical shifts in the content of personality during the period from childhood to young adulthood. All in all, the fulfillment and consistency models are favored and the conflict model is not.

Merely by totaling the number of times a model has been supported or contradicted by our empirical analysis leads us to interesting and surprisingly clear overall conclusions. The only models that were never contradicted are both versions of the fulfillment model and the activation version of the consistency model. The only models that were never supported are the pure psychosocial versions of the conflict model and the pure cognitive dissonance version of the consistency model. The other models fall between these two extremes but are more frequently contradicted than supported.

It is interesting that the models most supported by our empirical analysis are also not at all logically incompatible. Although one could certainly adopt either version of the fulfillment model or the activation version of the consistency model, one could also combine them without being logically inconsistent. In combining them, one would be assuming both a tendency to actualize potentialities of perfect living and a tendency to minimize discrepancies between customary and actual levels of activation. That both assumptions could be harmoniously included in the same theory is suggested by their basic compatibility regarding defensiveness, tension reduction and increase, and personality change. Furthermore, I believe they stress different aspects of behavior and, hence, their combination might result in an even more comprehensive personality theory.

Lest you embrace these overall conclusions too completely, I must remind you that we have not yet considered the issues that arise from the statements at the peripheral level of personality made by the various models. Perhaps one of the models that falls between the extremes of support and disconfirmation with regard to core considerations will actually do a better job at the peripheral level than any other model. We must evaluate peripheral-level issues before attaining a comprehensive basis for judging the relative value of the models.

Rational Analysis of Peripheral Considerations

In the preceding chapter, we engaged in the rational and empirical analysis of issues raised by personality core considerations. It is now time to engage in similar analyses concerning the periphery of personality. As you will see, the issues arising from peripheral considerations involve individual differences more than the relatively universalistic issues raised by core considerations do. Because there is a lot to cover, this chapter will concern the rational, or more theoretical, analyses of what personologists consider to be people's concrete, learned lifestyles. This way, you can obtain an understanding of peripheral personality issues that will help you approach the empirical analyses in Chapter 12, the aim of which is to identify the kinds of peripheral assumptions that seem most fruitful in the light of available evidence.

The first section of this chapter will compare, contrast, and analyze the various kinds of peripheral characteristics that appear in peripheral theorizing. The next section will attempt a similar discussion of the conceptualizations of personality types. These two sections will not be organized by the three models of personality, because the formal issues arising from different peripheral conceptualizations are somewhat independent of the models involved. However, bear with these sections, even if they seem a bit disorganized, for they lead to several fairly definite conclusions. The final section of this chapter analyzes the content of peripheral statements by comparing and contrasting the particular theories as expressions of the three models.

The Various Kinds of Peripheral Characteristics ....

To begin this discussion, I shall first focus on the nature and function of peripheral characteristics in various theories. Despite the many differences in terminology and emphasis that we encounter in the peripheral theories, only three basic kinds of peripheral characteristics seem to emerge, which concern (1) goals and instrumental strategies; (2)

unself-conscious habits of performance; and (3) ideas, values, and principles of thought. Examples of the first, or motivational, unit are the *need* (Murray), *motive* (McClelland, Maddi), *dynamic disposition* (Allport), *fictional finalism* (Adler), and *defense* (Freud). If it seems strange to list defense with the others, recognize that defenses have the goal of avoiding anxiety and in this resemble avoidance motives. The major example of the kind of peripheral characteristic involving unself-conscious habits of performance is the *trait* as used by McClelland, Maddi, Adler, Fromm, and Freud. Also relevant, however, are the *need-integrate* (Murray) and *stylistic disposition* (Allport). Finally, the kind of peripheral characteristic emphasizing principles of thought is exemplified by the *schema* (McClelland), *personal construct* (Kelly), *sense of identity* (existential psychologists), and perhaps *condition of worth* (Rogers). Jung's functional *modes* also seem to emphasize thought, though they may be too broad for consideration as peripheral characteristics.

Interestingly enough, none of the three kinds of peripheral characteristics seems more pervasive in one of the models for personality theorizing than in the others. Some explicit form of motivational concept and an explicitly cognitive concept appear in examples of the conflict, fulfillment, and consistency models. The trait concept is the most popular, appearing in the theories that exemplify all three models. Actually, the trait concept is sometimes so broadly defined as to include a cognitive or motivational emphasis along with a focus on habit. One can hardly say, therefore, that the nature and function of the peripheral characteristics appearing in a theory follow in any precise way from the personality model they represent.

Probably the main factor in a theorist's decisions regarding the form and nature of the peripheral characteristics is a sense of what will explain the observed individual differences that seem important. After all, the models seem broad enough in their logical possibilities to permit all three kinds of peripheral characteristic. Though the models may well influence the kind of content emphasized at the periphery of

personality, I will discuss this possibility later. For the moment, I shall delve further into the tie between the kinds of peripheral characteristics a theorist employs and the behavioral phenomena she or he feels it is important to explain.

Motives and Traits

The most common distinction among kinds of peripheral characteristics is that between motivation and habit. Of the personologists, McClelland is the most insistent on this distinction, defining *motive* and *trait* as being mutually exclusive. Maddi is in complete agreement, having adopted McClelland's usage. Although Adler does not discuss the matter at any length, he must be in essential agreement, for he distinguishes sharply between the *fictional finalisms* (motives) and the *traits* that make up character. Murray, with his distinction between *needs* and *need-integrates,* and Allport, who distinguishes between *dynamic* and *stylistic dispositions,* show substantial similarity to McClelland. But they hardly agree with him completely, being unwilling to define motivational and habit concepts in a mutually exclusive fashion. Although it may not seem so at first, Freud also offers a basis for the distinction, in postulating not only *traits* but the more motivational *defenses* as components of character types. Clearly, he does not separate the two completely, as defenses are at a high level of generality and tend to subsume, or at least foster the learning of, traits.

To be sure, the remaining personologists who engage in peripheral theorizing to any degree do not offer an explicit basis for distinguishing between motives and traits. It is difficult, however, to determine whether this is so because the theorists actively consider drawing such a distinction a mistake or simply because they are relatively unconcerned about the precision and completeness of peripheral theorizing. Working in terms of the overall spirit of the theorizing, I would surmise that Erikson, Rank, and Fromm would not be against the distinction in principle. After all, that they rely on a broad, flexible definition of trait that seems to include motivation suggests they are not concerned with fine distinctions. It is more difficult to say how the few remaining personologists would react to the possibility of distinguishing between motives and traits. Only Rogers (1963) has formally opposed the distinction, asserting that the motive concept is unnecessary in what I call peripheral theorizing.

Taking all the positions into account, it seems clear that the distinction between motive and trait is important in the peripheral theorizing of at least half, if not a majority, of the personologists considered here. Those who most explicitly draw this distinction make it clear that they do so because they believe there are two different classes of behavior to be observed in people. So different do these classes of behavior seem that it appears natural and appropriate to explain them through different kinds of peripheral characteristics. You will recall from the discussion of McClelland's peripheral theorizing that the two classes of observed behavior are called *directional* and *repetitive*. I shall dwell further on the distinction between these classes to clarify the personologist's bases for employing the motive and trait concepts.

Repetitive behavior is very simple. Whenever a situation comes up that is similar to what you have experienced before, you will tend to repeat old behaviors automatically without having to make a decision about it. Indeed, you may well have no awareness of these old behaviors. Such habitual behavior is mechanical and does not express the intellect; you may not even notice yourself doing it. A great deal of behavior is of this sort. One person may have a particularly characteristic choice of words or voice pitch in social situations; another may have an especially aggressive way of driving a car; another may dress according to a certain color scheme; another may be expansive when confronted with people of the opposite sex. If you pointed out these behaviors to the people exhibiting them, they might well be surprised, perhaps even to the point of doubting the veracity of your observations. And if you asked them to decide their personal goals, they would not include expansiveness, particular choice of words, and so forth.

Goal-directed behavior is as different as it can be from the stylistic behavior just described. Obviously, in goal-directed behavior you have an explicit goal, something that you can put into words and you can work toward. The task of reaching the goal requires you to be ingenious in finding and performing just those instrumental acts that will bring you success in your environment. If you have the goal of feeding yourself because you are hungry and you are in the environment of a modern American home, the most successful instrumental acts will probably involve finding and searching the refrigerator and pantry. But if you have the same goal and find yourself in a forest, you will employ the instrumental acts of trying to find a stream where there might be fish to be caught, or of stalking land game, or of searching out edible vegetation. Which of these possibilities you carried out and in what order would likely be determined by the particular characteristics of the forest before you. Although the goal in the home and forest examples is the same, the directional behavior aimed at reaching the goal differs because it must be suited to the characteristics of the environment. If others pointed out to you what kinds of actions they observed you doing, you would hardly be surprised. Indeed, you would explain that you were doing those things to try to gain food in the particular circumstances you had encountered. The obviously different actions in the two examples are rendered functionally equivalent by the goal of getting food. Goal-directed behavior thus appears to be intelligent rather than mechanical in nature. What this means is that people pursuing goals must assess the nature of the environment and make decisions about the best strategy in a way that will enable them to change their minds if they encounter additional information. There is too much self-consciousness and decision making in this kind of behavior to consider it mechanical.

CONCLUSION. Although the distinction I am discussing seems clear, I can imagine some psychologists saying that it really cannot be drawn in practice, for behavior has a unitary quality.

From the standpoint of this holistic position, the distinction mentioned between goals and traits is false, however rational it may sound, because all aspects of behavior are so interdependent as to be inseparable. I do not find this argument convincing. If the holistic position objects to *any* separation of behaviors into classes, then it borders on an evasion of the psychologist's difficult but unavoidable task of deciding what he or she is supposed to explain. To say that all behavior is to be explained but not classify it into various categories is to structure the explanatory task in a way that must lead to failure. For personologists to avoid classification would be like physicists asserting that their task is to explain the universe without being willing to discuss the various physical entities that compose it.

But the holistic argument might be directed against the particular distinction between repetitive and directional behaviors rather than against all possible distinctions. To be sure, deciding whether one is observing repetitive or directional behavior is difficult in practice. But it pays to have an open mind and to explore the distinction further, especially because so many personologists seem to have adopted some form of it. How could we structure observation so as to enter into the spirit of the distinction? Certainly, if you permit yourself to do no more than observe the overt behavior of a person in some unspecified situation, it may well be unclear whether what you are observing is behavior that repeats old habits or behavior that is directed toward goals. But nobody advocating the distinction between repetitive and directional behaviors would be so naive. To distinguish between these two categories of behavior, you would first have to observe the person repeatedly over a wide range of situations. To discern repetitive behavior, you would look for recurrences that did not seem to be parts of sequences and that seemed tied to the repetition of situations. To discern directional behavior, you would look for discrete actions that seemed to bear a sequential relationship and that did not occur only in repetitive situations. The identification of sequences of action would be greatly facilitated by the person's verbal statements concerning his or her personal goals. Such statements certainly would be obtained by anyone wanting to distinguish between repetitive and directional behaviors. If you accept the importance of distinguishing repetitive and directional behaviors, it will seem natural and appropriate to explain the former with some sort of habit or trait concept and the latter with some type of motive concept.

To the Rescue of the Concept of Motivation

One definite implication of adopting some form of the motive and trait concepts in peripheral theorizing is that not all behavior is motivated! All behavior can be considered caused, for the trait is as much a cause of mechanical, repetitive behavior as the motive is of intellective, directional behavior. Nonetheless, a trait is not a motive. Some personologists, however, have difficulty accepting a theoretical formulation that suggests that not all behavior is motivated. Invariably, these personologists have attributed motivational significance to their postulated core tendencies. Certainly, if the core tendency is motivational, by virtue of the fact that it is considered to infuse all functioning, there can be no functioning without motivation. Some theorists who attribute motivational properties to their core tendency, such as Rogers and Maslow, do not make an explicit distinction between motive and trait at the peripheral level. Because they do not assume a nonmotivational entity at this level, there is no inconsistency between their core and peripheral theorizing. But other theorists who tend to attribute motivational significance to their core tendency, such as Freud, also fall into the logical dilemma of using the trait concept in discussing the periphery. Fortunately, I think there is a simple way out of this dilemma that does little or no violence to the real intent of the various personality theories and may at the same time render more clear and precise the nature of motivation.

Greater clarity and precision in the use of the motivation concept would certainly make it more intellectually appealing to many psychologists. We have reached the bewildering point at which some psychologist will call virtually any sort of behavior *motivated.* Birds flying, bees buzzing, women sweating, babies playing, monkeys solving problems, rats hoarding, cockroaches crawling, and men sleeping will all be described in a diverse array of motivational terms. So loosely is the concept used and so huge are the differences of opinion from psychologist to psychologist that it would not be surprising to find people turning away from motivational explanations altogether. A trend in that direction has taken hold, to judge from the fact that a number of eminent psychologists (e.g., Kelly, 1955; Skinner, 1950) can gather followings for approaches to understanding behavior that profess to exclude the motivation concept.

But because most personologists consider the motivation concept too valuable to abandon, it seems wise to work toward clarity and precision in its use. The distinction drawn between *motive* and *trait,* which involves restricting the relevance of the motivation concept to identifiably directional behaviors, seems a step toward clarity and precision. This view, apparently based on the intent of many personologists, is very close to that of Peters (1958), who concludes that the motivation concept is best suited to explaining behavior that involves the existence of a personal goal and strategies instrumental to achieving it. Kagan (1972) and Dember (1974) adopt similar views. Because anything that can properly be called a personal goal will be rather concrete and specific, it seems to me that the motivation concept is most appropriately applied at the peripheral level of personality, not at the core. A core tendency is simply too general and universalistic to achieve representation in the person's mind as a goal and attendant instrumental strategies.

ORGANISMIC REQUIREMENTS VERSUS PERSONAL MOTIVATIONS. There is a logical contradiction in assuming all behavior to be motivated at the same time that one of the concepts you employ at the peripheral level is essentially nonmotivational. The way out is to deny motivational significance to your core tendency. This path would encourage clarity and precision

in the use of the motivation concept. But before adopting this solution, we must consider what would be lost by divesting core tendencies of motivational significance. The main reason some personologists attribute motivational significance to core tendencies is the following: They wish to emphasize that these tendencies are meant to describe requirements of the organism and overall directionalities that are so basic as to be common to all people. I am prepared to grant that if core tendencies did not refer to these basic requirements and directionalities, they would not be fulfilling their intended theoretical purpose. The question is whether they can fulfill this purpose without being accorded motivational status. If we can find an affirmative answer to this question, we can resolve the given contradiction.

In pursuing the answer to the question, we should consider those core tendencies that do not seem heavily invested with motivational import. McClelland's theorizing offers a good example. According to him, it is common to all people to experience negative affect when the discrepancy between expectation and occurrence is large and positive affect when it is small. Negative affect leads to avoidance behavior and positive affect to approach behavior. As we would expect of any proper core statement, the positive and negative affects disclose certain organismic requirements and the approach and avoidance behaviors indicate directionality. But neither affect nor behavioral adjustment to it shows evidence of proaction or intellect. There is little choice, decision making, or flexibility (at least before considerable learning has occurred); rather, the approach and avoidance behaviors are automatic, almost reflexive organismic adjustments to comfort and discomfort. Such behavior is more like a tropism than anything else. Something happens and you are drawn to it, something else happens and you are repelled by it. There are no personal goals, instrumental strategies, choices, or manipulation of the environment and, hence, no motivational significance.

In McClelland's theorizing, the core tendency is the core tendency, not a motivation. Or, if you prefer another name, the core tendency could be referred to as a *drive,* once again distinguishing it from a *motive.* Actually, the distinction between drive and motive is often made in the psychological literature. A drive is more biological and/or mechanical and less self-conscious and/or intellective than a motive. Drive-induced behavior may lead to experiences through which motives are learned, but what is learned may bear little concrete relationship to the underlying drive. Thus, the drive to approach small and avoid large discrepancies between expectation and occurrence may lead to a strong achievement motive. But only when the concrete standards (goal) of excellence and competitive strategies for attaining them are present in the person's mind will McClelland talk in motivational terms.

Maddi's activation theorizing agrees in this respect with McClelland's. The core tendency to maintain activation at the characteristic level is not motivational, because it merely represents the organism's requirements and whatever automatic adjustments to them are available. Maddi attributes motivational significance only to the goal-oriented, intellective attempt to either increase or decrease the variety, meaningfulness, or intensity of stimulation. It is certainly true that in pursuing any of these motives, activation level may well change in the direction of the organism's requirements. But the person still does not directly intend to produce such activation changes.

From considering the theorizing of McClelland and Maddi, you have learned that it is possible to postulate a core tendency that expresses organismic requirements and overall directions without being motivational at the same time. To do this, you must couch your core tendency in terms of mechanical, reactive, driven behaviors existing prior to learning. Motives clearly emerge as learned units comprising goals and proactive, intellective behaviors that, though very likely consistent with the organismic requirements, do not express them directly. Now I shall try to apply these principles to other personality theories in order to determine what is gained and what is lost.

The principles fit Rogers's theory easily. He describes his *actualizing tendency* as the organism's natural, inherent requirement to develop along the lines of its potentialities. The process of actualization involves no conscious intent, awareness, or decision. Actualization goes on just because it is an expression of the organism's nature. Indeed, attempts to use the intellect and be proactive about the business of actualization usually misfire and are regarded with skepticism by Rogers. This is one of the clearest nonmotivational statements of core tendency in the personological literature.

In spite of this, Rogers often refers to the actualizing tendency as a motive. As you may recall from Chapter 5, Rogers imputes the actualizing tendency not only to humans and other animals but also to all other living things. I quoted Rogers's description of a giant seaweed actualizing itself all the while it is being buffeted by the surf. Poetically forceful as this example is, it makes it perfectly clear that Rogers cannot consider the actualizing tendency to be motivational and still be logically convincing. If the actualizing tendency is a motive, we would have to agree that seaweed assumes its size, shape, color, and other attributes because it intends to do so! This clearly cannot be. Seaweed becomes what it becomes because it is equipped with a genetic blueprint and is programmed to actualize it. No choice or manipulation of the environment is involved. What is operating are organismic requirements and drives, not motives. Similarly, when Rogers applies this same actualizing tendency to humans, it is not a motive.

My analysis does not doom Rogerians to forgo a concept of motivation. They could, if they so desired, develop a motivational concept at the peripheral level of personality that emphasizes learned goals and instrumental strategies. This peripheral motivation might even be structured as the development, through learning, of more psychological forms of the actualizing tendency. Perhaps the place where motivation inheres is Rogers's *need for positive regard* and *need for positive self-regard.* For that matter, even a concept such as *need for achievement* might be considered the concrete, peripheral result of expressing the actualizing tendency when an existing inherent potentiality happens to find best expression competitively and the environment supports competition. I cannot help but note that this kind of development of and emphasis on the peripheral level of personality would be welcome in Rogers's theory, which currently has very little to say in this regard. Unfortunately, Rogers (1963) has clearly stated a disbelief in the value of theorizing about specific motives in the manner of McClelland. This disbelief simply does not change the fact, however, that Rogers's imputation of motivational significance to the actualizing tendency itself seems rather poetical and inconsistent with the most precise use of the motivation concept.

Other personologists, such as Adler, Freud, Erikson, White, Fromm, and the existentialists, also tend to attribute motivational significance to their core tendencies, but they describe them in ways that indicate more proaction and intellect than Rogers does.

It may seem at first as if these theorists have adhered to the canons of clarity and precision concerning the motivation concept that I advocated earlier and still have found a way to apply it at the core level. If this is really true, we should simply accept that personologists can, with equal logical rigor, assume that all or only some behavior is motivated. But I for one still find it difficult to endorse attributing motivational characteristics to core tendencies, because organismic requirements are so general that they are unconvincing as personal goals. Let me express my meaning gradually by considering a few of the personologists just mentioned.

Adler, for example, sees the *tendency toward perfection* as underlying all functioning and as being motivational in nature. He does not impute this "great upward drive," as he puts it, to plants and animals, and he also describes it in terms that indicate the existence of personal goals and concern with appropriate instrumentalities. Out of a sense of inferiority, the person will develop a compensatory goal and then organize his or her energies and attention toward attaining it. All this certainly sounds like an admissible motivational explanation of directional, proactive behavior. But look more closely at the personal goal, which takes the form of what Adler calls a *fictional finalism*. A fictional finalism might be

the desire to be beautiful, charming, famous, respected, intelligent, or generous but not very likely the wish to be perfect. In other words, the actual goal a person has will be more specific, limited, and peculiar to him or her than the universalistic core tendency is. Motivation inheres in the fictional finalism and associated strategies of instrumental action. The overall core tendency toward perfection, while it provides an explanation of the directional commonality of all people, cannot properly be understood as a motive, for it is probably too ubiquitous to achieve direct representation in the mind as a personal goal. This kind of core tendency, though it applies more to organisms that can have personal goals than Rogers's does, is still better considered an organismic requirement than a motive. In Adler the motives are the learned fictional finalisms, which are understood, of course, at the peripheral level of personality.

As I indicated earlier, something that the organism requires can very well be called a *drive* and the learned attempt to satisfy that requirement a *motive*. So we can agree with Adler's designation of his core tendency as a drive if we are careful to recognize that drive and motive differ in their implications. In Adler, drive (tendency toward perfection) translates into motive (fictional finalism) through learning and development. It may sound to you as if I have done little more than change some words around and insist on a rigor of usage that borders on intellectual preciosity; however, I only wish to stress that once we accept that Adler's core tendency may be an organismic drive but not a motive and that motivation is a peripheral consideration, we can believe that not all behavior is motivated without giving up a belief in Adlerian theory. Indeed, we can even recognize, in addition to fictional finalisms, peripheral characteristics that are not motivational in nature without rationally damaging the theory. And certainly Adlerians seem to want to include in the style of life *traits,* such as charmingness, that explain repetitive behavior. Accepting my analysis means that you can avoid the problem that arises when you speak of traits in the periphery of personality and cast your core tendency in motivational terms; that is, the logical requirement that all behavior be motivated.

These conclusions can also be applied to the other personologists. Allport apparently does not consider his core tendency toward psychological maturity to be motivational, and that is a good thing. It is unlikely that this tendency would actually achieve representation in the mind as a personal goal. More likely, one would have much more concrete goals, such as becoming a good physician, parent, friend, or lover. These personal goals might well represent the results of the core tendency, but they are themselves peripheral manifestations and reasonable examples of what Allport might call *dynamic traits*. In Maslow's case, one can also say that the core tendency of self-actualization is unlikely to appear as a personal goal in people. Much more likely is the appearance of more concrete goals. Fromm's core tendency of attempting to express human nature is another case in point. Fromm does break down this general tendency into a number of parts, such as the need for rootedness. And it is more likely that these relatively concrete aspects of the core tendency would achieve mental representation as personal goals. But probably one must become even more concrete before the kinds of things that are commonly considered goals are encountered. So too with White's point of view. It is unlikely that people do all the things they do because they are imbued with the single motivation to be competent. All the things they do may well add up to a tendency toward competence in the theorist's mind, but this is a different thing. Similarly, the existentialist's emphasis on authentic being also is probably too broad and encompassing to be motivational, though the particular decisions that one faces in life could well be.

With regard to all these theories, it can be said that the core tendency is most clearly considered not a motive but an organismic requirement or even drive. This permits saving the motivation construct for the kind of concrete, goal-oriented behavior found at the periphery of personality. And this means that such theories could then easily incorporate the possibility that not all behavior is motivated.

I shall turn now to the psychoanalytic thinkers, Freud, Murray, and Erikson, whose shared position I can treat in much the same manner as I have the theorists already considered. The core tendency of maximizing instinctual gratification while minimizing punishment and guilt is probably at too high a level of generality to achieve concrete representation as goal states and attendant instrumentalities. Happily, however, psychoanalytic theory provides a built-in basis for more specificity concerning the locus of motivation. Let us consider the instinctive (*pleasure principle*) and defensive (*reality principle*) parts of the core tendency separately.

The *instincts* not only originate in and derive their energy from organismic requirements; they also have aims and objects. Indeed, the main psychic or mental manifestation of instincts lies in objects and the wish to obtain them. Psychoanalytic thinkers use the term *object* in much the same way one uses the term *goal* or *goal state*. Generally speaking, people learn to recognize and pursue those relevant objects available in their environment. This is not so different from saying that people learn personal goals and attendant instrumental strategies. Psychoanalytic thinkers would come most of the way toward adopting the motivational view considered in this section by using the term *motivation* to refer only to the objects and possibly the aims of the instincts, leaving their source and energy to be accounted for as organismic requirements and drives.

A matching concretization and restriction of imputed motivational significance would help clarify the defensive part of the core tendency. It is unlikely that the abstract, ubiquitous attempt to avoid all punishment and guilt registers in the mind as a personal goal. But it is very likely that people have specific avoidance goals that lead them to shun the very situations that express the specific objects and aims of their instincts. Such a goal might be to avoid, say, being hit by a parent, when the instinctual object and aim of stealing money is aroused. The specific defense instituted to realize the avoidance goal can, in my terminology, be considered an instrumental strategy. Interestingly, although

Freud considers the defenses as operating unconsciously, he describes them in the terminology of intellect and choice (Peters, 1958). All in all, specific avoidance goals and attendant defensive instrumentalities clearly can be considered motivational.

In this section I have tried to sketch how, with little loss in explanatory power, the various personality theories could be adjusted to permit a use of the motivation concept that is clear, precise, consistent, and reasonable. This use involves considering core tendencies and characteristics as representing organismic drives and requirements, saving the motivation concept to apply to the peripheral level, with its personal goals and instrumental strategies for reaching them. Of all the theories, only the psychoanalytic one appears to lose much of its original impact, which depends so much on the notion of unconscious motivation.

The Problem of the Unconscious

What does this new use of the motivation concept do to the unconscious contents of the mind? It must be clear that in stressing personal goals as the hallmark of motivation, I take the position that nothing that cannot easily register in a person's awareness as something he or she wants really has motivational significance. I seem to be embracing a *phenomenology, or consciousness, of motivation.* What the person professes wanting is what personologists would have to agree is wanted. This must disturb those of you who believe in unconscious motivation, for that position requires, by definition, that there be some goals that people work toward that they are also unaware of. You may recall, however, that in Chapter 10, I presented a strong empirical case for the existence of *defense* at least in some people and tried to translate defense theory into something more palatable to reason. Therefore, I must have some belief in the existence of unconscious processes. You could conclude that I am just being inconsistent in also taking the position described in the last few pages. Let me hasten to indicate that this is not the case.

In my position on motivation, it is necessary

that the personal goal have been conscious only at one time. If this condition is met, you can be sure that you are dealing with a genuine personal goal rather than some goal merely imputed to the individual by the personologist. But the personal goal, though conscious at first, need not stay that way. If it precipitates personal conflict (e.g., I really want to hug Mother, but if I do, Father will get angry and punish me), it may well be defended against and, hence, drop out of consciousness. My position can well accept the possibility that a personal goal that is defended against because it precipitates a personal conflict will continue to affect behavior though no longer conscious. The behavior thus affected will still show decision making and instrumental sequences of acts, though these might be a little less organized because there is no conscious appreciation of the pursued goal. What my position excludes is the possibility that what I call *organismic requirements* are unconscious motives. Recognize that this possibility is excluded only because I believe such organismic requirements to be too general, ubiquitous, and universal to ever achieve mental representation as personal goals, not because I do not believe in unconscious motivation. If something was never a personal goal, it can hardly be defended against.

Actually, I think my position is very close to Freud's real intent, granting the existence of some semantic differences and some confusions. Freud concerns himself mainly with unconscious motives that would, in his estimation, have been conscious except for the action of defenses. These unconscious motives seem close to what I am talking about. But Freud also makes occasional, and to my mind uneasy, reference to a part of the unconscious that had never been, and could never be, conscious. He thought this might be the collective unconscious emphasized by Jung. Freud was not always sure it really existed in the mind as, of course, the unconscious should in his view. I think I know what Freud was getting at. Might he not have been recognizing, however tentatively and imperfectly, that the most universal and general organismic requirements do not achieve mental representation as goals even though they exert a broad influence on behavior? In any event, I think my position on motivation does not do great violence to the notion of unconscious motivation in psychoanalytic thinking. And certainly it must do even less damage to other personality theories that use the concept of defense, for they are much less specific concerning the necessary content of conflicts than psychoanalytic theory is.

But you must recognize that even though acceptance of my position makes motivation a peripheral characteristic, therefore implying that not all behavior is motivated, it also leads to the notion that not all behavior has a component of unconscious motivation. One can consider as unconsciously motivated those behaviors stemming from a personal goal that has been forced from awareness by defenses. This conclusion accords nicely with the discussion of defensiveness in Chapter 10, which found that not all behavior is defensive. But accepting this conclusion will require a shift in thinking on the part of some people of psychoanalytic inclination who believe that all behavior is at least partially determined by unconscious motivation. Perhaps it will help to recognize that all behavior might well be influenced in a very general way by the organismic requirement of maximizing instinctual gratification while minimizing punishment and guilt, even though the precise explanation of the particular aspects of behavior you see now or at another time will be achieved primarily with peripheral constructs that will only sometimes involve unconscious motivation. Actually, what I am suggesting accords well with Freud's original intent in theorizing, which was to find an explanation for the oddities and paradoxes of behavior.

As Peters (1958) points out, Freud wanted to explain slips of the tongue, dreams, and hypnotic dissociation, which clearly colored his development of the notion of *unconscious motivation*. In other words, Freud developed the concept of unconscious motivation to explain those things that people did, or omitted doing, for which they had no adequate explanation themselves. These things were not accidental, as some theorists thought at the time, for the people to whom they

happened were displeased by their inability to understand, and the occurrences were so directional and predictable that they seemed motivated. Peters (1958) makes a very good point here. Had Freud been convinced by people's own explanations of these oddities of behavior, he would never have developed the notion of unconscious motivation. Peters generalizes, saying that only when the explanations people give for their behavior do not convince us should we look to the possibility of unconscious motivation. This is what Freud would have done and what we should do too.

Thus, imagine that you see a young man suddenly stop in the process of walking down the street, veer, and cross to the other side. If you ask him why he did this, and he says that he spied a tobacconist's shop on the other side of the street and went toward it because he needed tobacco, there is nothing to stop you from being convinced. The behavior was directional and appropriate to a personal goal that the person was aware of (i.e., to get tobacco). There is no call here to invoke unconscious motivation, for there is no oddity. But suppose everything else was the same save that the young man ran rather than walked across the street. If he gave the same explanation, you would still be left wondering why he ran. If there were no cars around, and if the store was not about to close, running would have been an oddity. If the man could tell you nothing more than that he wanted tobacco, you might well suspect that his actions were at least partly influenced by unconscious motivation.

It seems to me that my position on motivation has the advantage, in its consideration of unconscious motivation, of getting back to the kind of thing Freud had in mind. One should use unconscious motivation to explain behavior only when people's own accounts of goals are unconvincing. Using the concept this way is more rationally defensible than using it to explain all behavior. The latter approach seems understandable to me only if theorists have some investment in second-guessing people or in convincing them that theorists know people better than people know themselves, or in rendering people pessimistic and distrustful concerning themselves and others.

Jung's case is complicated by his assumption of both a *personal* and a *collective unconscious.* As with Freud, one can regard the personal unconscious, formed by the action of defenses, as a special case of motivation. But, according to the position I have been developing, the collective unconscious, having never been conscious at all, does not qualify as motivation. Do not be troubled by this, for it is not even clear that Jung meant the collective unconscious to be motivational in the precise sense of determining directional as opposed to repetitive behaviors. The collective unconscious emphasizes thought structures—typical ways of posing problems and seeking solutions—that are especially common for the human species. Only the derivatives of these essences or *archetypes* ever even become concrete enough to achieve or affect consciousness, according to Jung. It does not seem likely that he would have objected to considering the archetypes as expressing organismic requirements, saving the term *motivation* for the learned goals and aims that develop in people as the result of complex interactions between themselves and the environment.

Schemata

Thus far, I have taken the position that it is sensible for a peripheral theory of personality to include two explanatory constructs—*motive* and *trait*. In doing so, I have closely followed McClelland. But what of his *schema* concept? Is this also a useful ingredient in peripheral-level theorizing? You will recall that I advocated including both motive and trait concepts because they seemed useful in explaining two different categories of observable behavior—directional and repetitive. If we feel that classifying all behavior as either directional or repetitive is sufficiently comprehensive and differentiated, we will find little cause to advocate a schema concept. After all, what would it explain? But should we feel that this dual classification of behavior is so gross that it violates our sense of

what is happening in our own lives and those of the people around us, we will find additional classificatory categories helpful. Perhaps then the schema concept will seem a welcome explanatory device.

With this in mind, I shall examine the schema concept more closely. McClelland defines schemata as cognitive maps or units, primarily taking the concrete form of values and social roles. In addition, he feels that schemata represent a shared cultural, rather than personal, level of experience. What he had in mind was distinguishing between behavior that involves the pursuit of personal goals and behavior that involves the pursuit or upholding of societal goals—for, after all, what are values and social roles but mutually agreed-on standards of behavior in aggregations of people? McClelland is actually suggesting that the motive construct be used to explain behavior directed at attainment of personal goals and the schema concept to explain behavior directed at attaining or maintaining societal goals. When people act in order to be socially appropriate or moral, they are being determined by the sense of social roles and values they have incorporated from their culture. When they act in order to reach a goal that refers to their own advancement or satisfaction, they are being determined by their motives. And when they act in an automatic, unreflective manner, they are being determined by their traits.

What does this discussion of schemata imply for the classification of behavior as directional or repetitive? Essentially, schema-determined behavior is directional in nature, exhibiting the same qualities of intelligent functioning found in motivated behavior; namely, decision making and flexible tuning of instrumental actions to the characteristics of one's environment. Because, however, the goal worked toward will be determined by agreement among the members of the relevant society, and because the goal of a motive is not defined by consensus, nor does it necessarily regulate group behavior, a schema is not a motive.

Schema-determined behavior is also not repetitive in nature. To see this, take generosity as an example. People may act generously without intending to—in other words, in an automatic, repetitive way—or may consciously attempt to act generously. In the first instance, you would be observing the *trait* of generosity and in the second the *schema* of generosity. Someone actively trying to be generous could have the *motive* of generosity, but only in a culture that did not make generosity a value or a role. If you can recognize the possibility of analyzing behavior into two broad categories called repetitive and directional, with the directional category subdivided into that which is associated with personal goals and that with societal goals, you can conclude that it is useful to include in theories of the periphery of personality the concepts of trait, motive, and schema.

Theories of the periphery that employ only one concept, or even two, are not as likely to be clear, precise, and comprehensive as are those that employ more. This is especially true when the theory specifically restricts the consideration of behavioral categories to fewer than these three. So, when Kelly's consistency theory employs only cognitive explanatory constructs and construes behavior as if it were little more than mental activity, one may be left with a feeling of incompletion because not all that is important in behavior is considered. Actually, however, many theories of personality contain the rudiments of the triadic characterization of the periphery that I advocate. Psychoanalytic theories, such as those of Freud, Erikson, and Murray, propose not only an id but a superego, the content of which is essentially social goals. The process of satisfying id and placating superego could well lead the theorist to incorporate both motive and schema concepts at the peripheral level. And yet, interestingly enough, two out of three of these psychoanalytic theories employ only the concept of trait, which is the least predictable of the three from the core assumption of existence of id and superego! But in looking at the list of things these theorists call traits, it is easy to imagine reclassifying them as either traits, motives, or schemata. One may reclassify in other theories as well, notably those of Fromm, Maslow, and Rogers. Finally,

the universalistic social emphases of Adler and Jung suggest that their peripheral positions, if developed further, might find the schema concept useful. The existentialists may dissent, for though they emphasize cognition, they also stress the individualistic use of it.

THE PERIPHERAL CONCEPT OF TYPE ....

Until this point, I have concentrated on the peripheral characteristics, supposedly the indivisible, and therefore basic, building blocks of peripheral theories of personality. But by themselves they are too concrete to give much sense of the actual flavor of a person's life. They are the trees in the forest, and although a careful study of individual trees will yield much understanding of the nature of trees, it will not by itself clarify the overall dimensions of the forest to any great extent. Lest you lose the forest for the trees, I shall turn your attention to a more general kind of concept, which functions to subsume and group together the peripheral characteristics into meaningful patterns. An analogous concept in chemistry would be compounds, which represent the meaningful combination of elements into more complex units.

For Freud, Fromm, Maddi, Rank, and Jung, this more complex, organizational characteristic is character or *personality type*. Adler gets at the same thing when he offers the concept of *style of life*. So does Murray in his concept of *complex*, though he formally fails, for some mysterious reason, to subsume his more concrete concept, *need*, under this more general one. The other personologists do not really offer an organizational concept. In some cases—notably Rogers, Maslow, and existential psychology—the distinctions made among types of people are too few to require such a concept. These positions only distinguish between people who succeed and those who fail in vigorous expression of the core tendency. These theorists need do no more, therefore, than name these two kinds of people in terms of the content of their personalities. Thus, Rogers talks of the *fully functioning* and the *maladjusted person;* Maslow, though less terminologically consistent, has a similar emphasis; and Maddi considers *individualism* and *conformism.*

Other personologists, such as Allport and Kelly, so insist on the importance of individuality that they not only fail to offer type concepts but also avoid designating the possible contents of peripheral characteristics. These are related omissions, for organizing the peripheral characteristics into types must be done largely along lines of content; hence, to offer a type concept, the theorist must be committed to specifying the common content of personality. Allport, more than Kelly, provides a possible basis for theoretical development leading to a delineation of the content of peripheral traits in his nicely detailed propriate functions. Thus, one might explore the theoretical yield of considering some people as showing peripheral characteristics indicating a personality type that stresses rational coping, or propriate striving, etc.

Finally, there are personologists—notably McClelland—whose omission of a type concept is more difficult to understand. McClelland certainly specifies both the kind and the content of his peripheral characteristics and in so doing indicates a fine-grained interest in comprehensiveness. But he does very little in terms of organizing these peripheral characteristics into types. Perhaps this omission stems from his deep eclecticism concerning personality content. Because McClelland derives the content of his motive, trait, and schema concepts from the work of many different people, it is difficult to put it all together into meaningful patterns. And, of course, his core tendency is relatively contentless, so no help can be sought from that quarter.

It should be quite clear from this summary that the type concept provides no particular basis for distinguishing among conflict, fulfillment, and consistency positions. This is not surprising, because the kinds of peripheral characteristics are not specific to the three models, and types are combinations of these characteristics. It does not even seem that the omission of the type concept

is specific to one or two models, as this occurs in examples of all three.

You have encountered three reasons why personologists, in their peripheral-level theorizing, do not refer to coherent patterns of concrete characteristics for which the type concept is appropriate. The reason in McClelland's case is not a theoretical conviction obviating specification of types but rather a consequence of his eclecticism with regard to personality content. McClelland would never argue that the concept of personality type is unworthwhile. Indeed, his own work on personality factors leading to economic development (McClelland, 1961), in which he seems to be developing a type of personality involving achievement traits, motives, and schemata, indicates that he has nothing against the notion of types. He simply has little formal theoretical basis for postulating them.

The other two reasons for avoiding the type concept are backed by more ideological commitment. In one of these two cases (e.g., Rogers, Maslow, and existentialism), only two kinds of persons are considered important enough to specify in terms of content, rendering extensive elaboration of types superfluous. One cannot criticize a theorist for failing to be superfluous. But one can question whether considering only two kinds of people is complete. Such theorists seem to believe that the only important thing to know about people is whether or not they are actualizing themselves or becoming authentic. I hope that if this book has convinced you of anything, it is that such theorizing is not complete enough to do justice to the complexity of life.

The other ideologically bolstered reason for omission of the type concept is the general emphasis on individuality. I shall talk more about the problem of individuality in a moment; for now, you should realize the severe limitations on a theory imposed by its dedication to the proposition that each person is unique. You will have noticed that the theories of Allport and Kelly could not even be discussed in any detail in this chapter, so unspecific are they concerning the peripheral level of personality. The same extreme emphasis on individuality is found in some existential psychologists. These positions can only be used to understand data you already have in hand. They provide little or no basis for predicting what kinds of people you are likely to encounter. As such, they do not improve much on common sense.

The Problem of Individuality

Personologists differ in the degree to which they stress individuality. Those who tend to believe that people are similar enough to be understood adequately by grouping them into a small number of types include Freud, Rank, Adler, Fromm, Jung, and Maddi. Another group of personologists substantially agree with this position, though they have less to say about types. These personologists believe that a small set of dimensions or variables exist that one can profitably apply to all people to understand them. This group includes Erikson, White, and McClelland. In contrast to the personologists already mentioned, a third group holds a rather radical view of individuality. Regardless of whether or not their theories do justice to their beliefs, these personologists have a steadfast ideological commitment to the idea that people are more different from one another than similar. Included in this group are Rogers, Maslow, Allport, Kelly, and the existentialists.

It will be instructive to consider the point of view of the most ideologically committed and verbally forceful of the individualists, Gordon Allport. For him, "each person is an idiom unto himself, an apparent violation of the syntax of the species" (Allport, 1955, p. 22). In explicating this position, Allport focuses on the apparently limitless range of potential behavior available to the human by virtue of a big brain and a relative absence of instincts and ventures the opinion "that all of the animals of the world are psychologically less distinct from one another than one man is from other men" (p. 23). All this is strong medicine that could kill the patient —psychology—already feverishly struggling for general laws that psychologists believe would make its scientific status indisputable. To anyone engaged in this struggle, Allport's position must seem cruel heresy, and hence further consideration of it is in order.

Allport (1937, p. 4) argues that the major task of personology is to understand and predict the individual case rather than the contrived average case. Concepts and relationships aimed at predicting the average case are called *nomothetic*. A concept such as McClelland's need for achievement would be considered nomothetic by Allport because of the belief that many people can be given a score on need for achievement. According to Allport, it is only by distorting each person's behavior somewhat that the concept of need for achievement can be applied. The distortion invariably involves the disregarding of important qualitative differences among people in favor of describing them all in similar, average terms.

If nomothetic concepts and laws, derived from and applicable to the data on groups of people, completely predicted each individual case, there would be little purpose for Allport to champion the inviolability of individuality. In practice, however, perfect prediction and understanding using nomothetic concepts and laws are never achieved. Indeed, there is often a sizable minority of cases to which the nomothetic concept and general law do not seem to apply. For example, most people characterized as high in need for achievement will work harder than most people characterized as low. But some of the former will not work, whereas some of the latter will resemble beavers. This is not surprising to Allport (1961, pp. 332–356), who believes that nomothetic concepts are merely convenient fictions useful only insofar as they resemble the true personality of some people. If a moderate degree of understanding and predictive accuracy satisfies the investigator, Allport does not seriously oppose the nomothetic approach. But the paramount goal of the personologist requires a greater approximation to the truth.

In the attempt to achieve this goal, one must, according to Allport, develop concepts and laws that are derived from and applicable to the data of each individual case. At first he calls such theorizing *idiographic* (Allport, 1937, pp. 3–23) and seems to take such an extreme view that virtually no generalization across persons would be possible (Allport, 1942, p. 57). Organization of behaviors into classes is properly done only within, not across, people. Thus, if the need for achievement were used as an idiographic concept, it would refer to a class of behaviors in one person only and would not be used on anyone else.

Later, Allport (1961, pp. 257–361; 1962) substitutes the term *morphogenic* for *idiographic*, and seems to be formulating a position that is less extreme, permitting the use of concepts one can, in principle, apply across people. Though he still overwhelmingly emphasizes concepts and laws that reflect the individuality of the person studied, he at least considers it possible that those concepts and laws would apply to some other people as well. Allport makes a strong plea for freedom from the restricting nomothetic mold of other sciences, which he believes have not been confronted with uniqueness on a grand scale, and offers a number of suggestions for concrete morphogenic methods of study (Allport, 1962).

To the traditional view of science, Allport poses an alternative that he believes would lead to the highest level of prediction and control. Although in research one should certainly try the morphogenic approach, it raises a keen sense of futility when presented as a replacement for an approach that encourages generalization across persons. Must knowledge of individuals remain unrelated, odd bits of information? How can significant systematization of knowledge be achieved? It should be established with certainty that nomothetic methods have been adequately tested before they are discarded on the grounds that they typically leave some individual cases unexplained.

Whether or not other sciences have been faced with overwhelming individuality, they certainly recognize the necessity of deducing, from the general law and the particular situation involved, explanations and predictions that apply to the individual case. For this to be done well,

the general law must exhaustively specify the conditions under which it does and does not apply, and the investigator must have sufficient knowledge of the concrete situation to determine whether or not the law should be used. For example, the law contending that need for achievement leads to hard work might apply only under conditions of permissiveness and opportunity rather than authoritarianism or lack of resources. Furthermore, complex phenomena may well call for the application of more than one law; hence, the relationships among laws must be clearly specified. For example, in addition to the law relating need for achievement to hard work, there may be laws determining whether the person will approach or avoid permissive situations.

You would have to apply these latter laws to understand whether or not the person's need for achievement level was readily expressed in work intensity. Only with all this information could you evaluate the explanatory adequacy of nomothetic methods, and even then, particular general laws could turn out to be incorrectly formulated without this error constituting a demonstration of the inadequacy of the methods they represent. The degree of theoretical and methodological care and precision involved in the valid application of nomothetic methods often is not recognized as important or even attempted in psychology. Hence, the development of truly useful nomothetic concepts and laws may be stifled, and individuality may loom overly large as an explanatory problem.

It is by no means clear that any personologist who believes in individuality must reject the nomothetic approach in order to be true to this belief. To the contrary, the nomothetic approach is so natural to science that it seems straightforward to use it in the absence of evidence showing it to be inadequate. What the personologist believing in individuality should do is use the nomothetic approach in the manner most calculated to do justice to individuality.

Let me be more specific about what constitutes the nomothetic approach. Essentially it involves specifying not only the kinds of concepts at the peripheral level of personality but also their content. I emphasize specification of content in peripheral-level theorizing because it is so much more to the point than core-level specification of content is. The latter is nice to have, but it speaks to what is common to all people and therefore is not useful in understanding individuality. The specification of peripheral content, though, is crucial because it allows you to designate the classes of behavior in people that your theory will recognize. This means that even though you may recognize differences among people, you nonetheless expect to achieve an understanding of them with a standard, unchanging set of concepts. You are assuming that though individuality may exist, true uniqueness does not. The differences that exist among people are relative, not absolute.

Even with this assumption, you can use the nomothetic approach in a way that will facilitate the understanding of individual differences. This involves postulating as many different kinds of peripheral characteristics and types as seems practical and intuitively accurate. Clearly, the more peripheral characteristics you have and the more ways they can be combined to yield types, the more differences among people your theory will recognize. In other words, the nomothetic approach should be used complexly to permit an understanding of individuality.

In what I have said you should recognize a strong argument for the kind of theorizing about peripheral characteristics found in McClelland, who offers the most categories of concept (motive, trait, schema) and a good number of content distinctions (e.g., needs for achievement, affiliation, power, and so forth) within each category. Fromm's theory is another example of complex use of the nomothetic approach. While he offers only the trait concept for the base unit, he lists some 47 traits. And while he organizes these traits into only five types, he does indicate that there are many combinations or mixtures of types, at least some of which he specifies. Maddi's activation approach exemplifies the complex use of the nomothetic approach at the level of the type concept. He suggests 24 types of

peripheral personality. Beck (1953) provides spirited support for this position on the study of individuality.

Yet, the matter is far from settled. As Marceil (1977) makes clear in his review, there have been arguments presented on both the morphogenic and nomothetic sides. He advocates that one distinguish between forms of this controversy that apply to theories of personality and those that relate to methods of doing research. As to the latter, a good argument can be made for including both research dealing with single cases (or a very few cases studied in depth) and that dealing with aggregates. Though one learns different things from each kind of research, their results are not in principle incompatible.

THE CONTENT OF PERIPHERAL PERSONALITY......

Up to this point, I have emphasized the various kinds of concepts one finds in theorizing about the periphery of personality. In this section, I will shift emphasis to the content of this theorizing, giving no regard to the kind of concept in which this content is found. The content of peripheral personality offers a more vivid picture of what the theorist thinks characterizes life than considerations of the form of concepts does. One can certainly quibble about whether the theorist has expressed his or her views in the most elegant and precise form, but differences and similarities among peripheral-level theories show up primarily in matters of content. Furthermore, peripheral-level content is more useful in helping one understand the concrete ways adults lead their lives than core-level content is, the latter being unconcerned with particular types of people.

Although the three models for personality theorizing have not determined the kinds of peripheral concepts employed, they do have definite implications for the content emphasized. In pinpointing these implications, I have found it useful to use the distinction between the ideal and nonideal peripheral personalities.

The Conflict Model

You will recall that at the core level the essence of the conflict model is expressed in the inevitable opposition of two great forces. In the psychosocial form of this model, one of the forces expresses the person as an individual and the other as a member of society. Because society is more powerful than individuals, this version of the conflict model makes all behavior defensive. People will try to get what they want only if they can find a way of doing so that will be consistent with the corporate good, for fear of what would happen otherwise. One would expect such theories, at the peripheral level, to stress *ideal functioning* indicative of socialization (dependability, adaptation, adjustment to social pressures, attitudes and values consistent with and justifying the social order) and *nonideal functioning* indicative of social immaturity (irresponsibility, competitiveness, impulsivity, withdrawal, rebelliousness, conformity).

Sure enough, in the pure psychosocial conflict theory of Freud, we see much that conforms to the expectations stated above. The ideal or genital type is someone who can truly love and work. But remember that loving and working occur on the basis of a defensive process—sublimation—and hence even this highest form of living does not transcend societal regulations. One can even say that this theory defines *adults* as people who love on the rebound (having had to give up the original love object—the opposite-sexed parent) and *work* as a way of channeling antisocial instincts into acceptable behavior. Hence, the giving and receiving of love at biological, social, and psychological levels and the commitment to regular, productive enterprise will each involve stability, dependability, and adjustment to pressures. There will be generosity, responsibility, and predictability more than flamboyance and impulsivity—a picture of solidity in whatever one does. In contrast, the nonideal or pregenital types are bogged down in self-preoccupation with how, when, why, and whether to take and receive, give and withhold, and sexualize living. The task-oriented process

of straightforward, dependable, productive living is frequently interrupted by these signs of insecurity, self-preoccupation, selfishness, and rigidity. Pregenital people are too concerned with themselves to be good citizens. Freud's content emphases at the periphery consistently derive from his emphases at the core.

Two variants of the psychosocial conflict model, Murray and Erikson, generally show the expected peripheral content emphases in considering nonideal functioning. Murray endorses, with some elaboration, the pregenital types of Freud. So does Erikson, although he adds some nonideal emphases, such as identity-diffusion, social isolation, stagnation, and despair. But as you can see, these additions are quite in character with the psychosocial conflict model. With regard to the characteristics of ideal functioning, Murray and Erikson only partially express this model. In addition to the solid virtues designated by Freudians, Murray and Erikson consider the possibility of at least some degree of imaginativeness, originality, and changeability. These additional emphases, however, have not always seemed convincingly compatible with core assumptions. You will recall, for example, that White criticizes Erikson's view of ideal peripheral characteristics as too optimistic in their socially transcendent implications for a conflict model, with its inevitable subjugation of the individual to society. Further, I called to your attention in Chapter 3 the odd fact that Murray's peripheral theorizing, emphasizing needs and need-integrates, does not seem to fit, or be fitted by him, into the core characteristics of id, ego, and superego. Perhaps the most meaningful conclusion to reach is that the theories of Murray and Erikson are in transition away from the psychosocial conflict model.

Although the peripheral content emphases of Kohut and Berne are not particularly predictable from their classification under the psychosocial conflict model, neither is there any sense of incompatibility. The socially ineffective behaviors of people with narcissistic disorders or unfortunate life scripts clearly indicate that the ideal for these theorists emphasizes social adjustment. In a way, it is surprising that their peripheral theorizing is so compatible with Freud's, as they so clearly appear to be breaking away from his views.

In the intrapsychic version of the conflict model, all the inevitably opposed forces emanate from within the person. Because there is no assumption of a powerful society bent on detecting and thwarting the individual, ideal functioning does not emphasize defensiveness. This is not to say that the relationship between individuals and their society is irrelevant. It is always relevant, because one of the opposing forces leads in the direction of individuation and isolation, whereas the other leads in the direction of dependence and gregariousness. The best that you can achieve is a compromise in which you express both forces. Thus, at the peripheral level, ideal functioning should show a commitment to being an individual in some way that others can respect, and to associating yourself with people and ideas without hampering one's own growth. These adjustments will be made with flexibility and awareness, as there is little defensiveness. Nonideal functioning expresses the defensive negation of either the force toward individuality or the force toward union. The first alternative would stress rebelliousness and rejection of other people and the second anxious conformity. Both alternatives would involve inflexibility, because they are defensive. As you can perceive, nonideal functioning in both intrapsychic and psychosocial conflict theories is similar. Ideal functioning is a bit less steady and more flamboyant in the intrapsychic version. Actually, the intrapsychic version comes quite close to the variant of the psychosocial version.

Of the intrapsychic conflict theories, only those of Rank and Jung make an extensive statement concerning peripheral personality. The content emphases of Rank conform very well to expectation. The two nonideal types are the average person (emphasis on conformity, passivity, and dependence) and the neurotic (emphasis on rebelliousness and insistent alienation from people). The ideal type, or artist, transcends conventional society, but in a fashion that others can respect and therefore permits a relationship to them. Artists essentially are heroes. What they do is extraordinary, but they do not do it simply for themselves.

On the other hand, at first blush, Jung's position does not seem to conform so well to expectation. The ideal for him is to achieve selfhood, which involves developing a kind of universal personality, not individualistic so much as expressive of what is in us all. Consciousness is only one aspect of selfhood and must make way for acceptance and expression of the collective unconscious if the ideal is to be achieved. But in a way, Jung is agreeing with the other intrapsychic conflict theorists. After all, the ego, or seat of consciousness, is an individualistic force with which people navigate in the external world of events, affairs, and outcomes. They need to incorporate the collective unconscious into their daily lives for it to temper the individualistic ego with the accumulated, shared wisdom of humankind. Thus, in achieving selfhood, the person strikes a balance between individualistic and communal tendencies. The other personality types (e.g., introverted rational, extroverted irrational), in that they do not give an important role to the collective unconscious, can be interpreted as being too individualistic to be ideal. But one must admit that at the peripheral level Jung's position less clearly expresses the intrapsychic conflict model than Rank's does.

The Fulfillment Model

The fulfillment model postulates only one great force, thereby avoiding the assumption that conflict is inevitable. But the one force does express human individuality; hence, people may conflict with society. Though this happens only when they have been failed by society, the consequence for them is, nonetheless, nonideal functioning. Because society is stronger than the individual, nonideal functioning is defensive.

At the core level, the actualization version of the fulfillment model stresses the humanistic belief that the content of the great force is the person's inherent potentialities and the inexorable attempt to realize them. One need do nothing more to be ideal than give oneself over to one's genetic blueprint and follow it wherever it leads. The intentional, self-conscious actions one might wish to take will corrupt expression of the actualizing tendency. At the peripheral level, the actualization version of the fulfillment model should stress spontaneity, changeability, unselfconscious acceptance of self and others, simple confidence, sensitivity, imaginativeness, and impulsivity. In contrast, nonideal functioning should involve premeditation, an evaluative attitude, planning, anxious conformity, lack of confidence, and an overwhelming sense of obligation to a monolithic duty.

The peripheral statements of Rogers, the pure actualization theorist, conform almost exactly to these expectations. Fully functioning, or ideal, people will show openness to experience, existential living, organismic trusting, creativity, and congruence of their view of themselves and what their potentialities really suit them to be. In contrast, nonideal, or maladjusted, people will show strong preoccupation with how, when, why, and what they are or what they should do. These rigidifying concerns introduce a constraint in the direction of conformity and fixity that interferes with the more mature process of continually enlarging and experiencing one's capabilities. Maslow, the variant of the actualization version of the fulfillment model, shares these emphases with Rogers but adds certain ideological considerations to them. Ideal people, according to Maslow, also possess democratic and humanitarian values that presumably also guide their behavior. Nonideal persons possess authoritarian and materialistic values. In this emphasis on values, both ideal and nonideal, Maslow seems to approach the perfection version of the fulfillment model.

The perfection version presents little concern with inherent potentialities as a basis for individuality. Instead, there is a conception of what perfect life, or essential human nature, is like. It is this goal toward which the person is impelled, often regardless of real or imagined inferiorities.

At the peripheral level, perfection theorizing should emphasize evidence of transcendence over one's own limitations and those of society, guided always by ideals and principles superordinate to humans. In contrast, nonideal functioning should stress concern with mere biological survival and satisfaction, anxious conformity, and the avoidance of risk. As you can see, the content implications of the actualization and perfection versions of the fulfillment model are quite similar. The mild differences between the positions show the actualization version emphasizing intuitive functioning, sensitivity, spontaneity, and impulsivity and the perfection version emphasizing rational functioning and consistent striving toward goals that have little to do with either inherent potentialities or societal pressures. These differences all stem from the actualization emphasis on a genetic blueprint and the perfection emphasis on the best in living regardless of endowment.

Happily, the perfection theorists include much in their peripheral theorizing that matches what I have just said. In Allport's definition of *maturity* as the presence of a consistent philosophy of life, a religious sentiment, and a generic conscience, we see how ideals are expected to infuse ideal functioning. Nonideal functioning, for Allport, is opportunistic, erratic, impulsive, pleasure seeking, defensive, and conforming. One sees similar, though more rudimentary, implications in Adler, whose peripheral position is unfortunately not very elaborate. Taking his active-constructive and passive-constructive styles of life as the ideals, one emerges with a view that stresses ambition to reach certain goals and charmingness with regard to other people. Adlerians may intend in such emphases to imply transcendence of self and society in the service of ideals, but this will not be entirely certain until their peripheral theorizing is further clarified. White's emphasis on consistent, perfectionist striving and rationality can be seen in his adoption of Erikson's peripheral theorizing, with its concern at the ideal level with ego integrity, generativity, intimacy, and identity, and at the nonideal level, with its emphasis on despair, stagnation, isolation, and identity diffusion. It is interesting that White has explicitly borrowed Erikson's theorizing. Just as Erikson is a variant of the conflict model, moving toward the fulfillment model, White may also be an incipient fulfillment variant, with something of the conflict theorist in him. I say the latter because, in an important paper on competence and the psychosexual stages of development, White (1960) does accept that there is some value to the psychosocial conflict model, even though it must be supplemented by his fulfillment emphasis.

The key to understanding Fromm is his suggestion that ideal functioning be defined as the most constructive aspects of the nonproductive (nonideal) orientations. Generally speaking, from the receptive orientation, one would derive tolerance, acceptance, trust, and the ability to be dependent; from the exploitative orientation, initiative, impulsivity, and effectiveness in grappling with external pressures; from the hoarding orientation, conservation of resources, loyalty, and a sense of the value of things; and from the marketing orientation, adaptability, curiosity, changeability, and open-mindedness. Fromm includes both the spontaneity and openness of the actualization position and the striving and sense of industry of the perfection position. As I pointed out in Chapter 6, this combining of emphases also appears in his core statements. The opposites of the qualities just mentioned define nonideal functioning, which strongly emphasizes conformity, pleasure seeking, and concern with biological survival.

In existential psychology, ideal functioning is called individualism or authenticity and stresses the development of sufficient consciousness to permit proper understanding of the true nature of life as a series of decisions. With this understanding comes the ability to make decisions well, evaluate ontological anxiety against ontological guilt, and take responsibility for what one does. The emphasis here is on rationality, self-reliance, independence, and honesty. In nonideal functioning, or conformism, consciousness is not highly developed; one clings to the stereotypes and conventions of society in the vain attempt to avoid making decisions. Clearly, existential psychology expresses in its peripheral statements what we would expect of the perfection fulfillment model.

The Consistency Model

As the consistency model makes minimal content assumptions at the core level, there is little that can be formulated by way of expected content at the peripheral level. Any or no specification of peripheral content would be understandable. If content is specified, however, it should at least reflect the procedures whereby people can ensure maximal consistency.

Turning to the actual theories, we find that the pure cognitive dissonance theorist, Kelly, specifies no peripheral content. The variant of this position, McClelland, does specify content, but it is an eclectic, omnibus specification and, as such, does not deviate from what we would expect. The activation theorist, Maddi, specifies content in a less omnibus fashion than McClelland. Virtually all the content in Maddi's peripheral theorizing refers to specialized procedures for anticipating activation requirements or correcting discrepancies between actual and customary levels of activation. This is true for tendencies to approach or avoid intensity, meaningfulness, and variety of stimulation and for the development of differentiation and integration of functioning. The content emphases of the activation version of the consistency model do not appear as important considerations in the other models. The major basis in Maddi's thinking for differentiating ideal from nonideal functioning is the activeness-passiveness trait. At the same time, this trait is not strictly derivable from the core assumptions of the activation position but is similar in emphasis and implications to the bases for distinguishing ideal from nonideal that appear in the perfection version of the fulfillment model.

CONCLUDING WORD ....

In this chapter, I have tried to codify the explicit and implicit implications of peripheral-level theorizing. This is especially difficult because the influences on both the content and form of peripheral theorizing include not only the theoretical assumptions made at the core and developmental levels, but also the theorist's observations of everyday behavior in people. After all, peripheral theorizing is the closest of all the aspects of personality to concrete behaviors.

Despite the influential nature of behavioral observations, peripheral-level theorizing shows the definite effects of the core and developmental assumptions that have been made. Consequently, the emphases of this chapter prepare you for the empirically oriented peripheral issue resolution that follows. I hope the clarity reached en route concerning the various sorts of peripheral concepts and the difference between organismic requirements and motivation will be useful in what comes next.

EMPIRICAL ANALYSIS OF PERIPHERAL CONSIDERATIONS

In the end, any conceptualization is only as adequate as its empirical support. It would be of no use to have a theory that is beautiful from the standpoint of reason but does not account for the relevant facts or is contradicted by them. We should hasten, therefore, to consider the empirical studies that bear on peripheral theorizing. An analysis of empirical studies could yield evidence concerning which of the postulated peripheral characteristics really exist and how they actually organize themselves into larger units, or types. Empirical analysis could also indicate the amount of behavior (data) explained by each of the existing peripheral characteristics. Having all this information, it would be easy to decide on the relative fruitfulness of the various peripheral theories and the models they represent.

From what I have said, you can see that an empirical analysis could do great things. In the analysis I shall conduct, however, it will be possible only to reach more modest conclusions, many of them tentative at that. Although one can specify the kinds of studies that would permit the strong conclusions mentioned above, such ideal studies have not been done in the main. Nonetheless, I will outline studies that should be undertaken, organized in the form of a three-step strategy. If you comprehend this ideal strategy and the kinds of inferences it would permit, you will have no difficulty understanding why the actual studies I shall subsequently consider are relevant. And who knows—when you see the discrepancies between the conclusions you can and might reach, you may find yourself motivated to conduct studies that more closely approximate the ideal.

THE IDEAL STRATEGY . . . .

Step One: Measuring Concrete Peripheral Characteristics

In approaching an adequate empirical analysis of peripheral theorizing, the first step is to attempt to develop an empirical measure for each peripheral characteristic specified in the various theories under consideration. Arduous though this is, there is no way around it. An attempt must be made to measure all the traits mentioned by Freud, all the needs of Murray, and so forth down the list of personologists. Here and there on the list you will encounter some theorists, such as Allport and Kelly, who offer literally nothing on which to base a measurement attempt. Others, such as White, are so unspecific in describing personality types that it takes one much guesswork to decide which peripheral characteristics they consider important. Here is a striking demonstration of the drawback of lack of theoretical elaboration at the peripheral level. How are you supposed to measure something if you do not know what it is? Whoever attempts to carry out the first step of this ideal strategy will sigh with relief and gratitude on encountering a personologist who is explicit concerning the form and content of peripheral characteristics.

OPERATIONAL DEFINITIONS. In any event, in attempting to measure the various peripheral characteristics that have been postulated, you must be guided not by what you think a characteristic really means but by what the personologist under consideration thinks of it. Only in this way will the success or failure of the measurement attempt reflect the adequacy of the theorizing. We have little trouble being guided by the theorist's meaning when he or she has provided us with an operational definition of the postulated characteristic. An *operational definition* is a literal specification of what you must do in order to observe the entity under consideration. Unfortunately, only McClelland, Murray, and Maddi even try to provide operational definitions, with McClelland's being a little more useful because they are less ambiguous. And even McClelland offers complete operational definitions for only some motives.

To see the value of operational definitions, recall McClelland's discussion of motives. In Chapters 10 and 11, we saw that in a formal sense, a motive is a personal goal and the instrumental capability for pursuing it in a wide variety of situations. In discussing measurement operations, McClelland (1961) recognizes the

formal attributes of motives that distinguish them from traits and schemata. A motive involves a personal goal, and therefore the measurement operation must elicit mentation rather than merely actions. But not just any mentation will do. The goal to be measured is personal, not social, and hence one must favor measurement operations that will not suggest to people that their behavior will be judged by its social desirability. As soon as you start asking people questions about their goals or actions, you will likely get responses in terms of what is considered socially appropriate. Such questioning may be useful in the measurement of schemata, but it is misleading for measuring motives.

Taking the requirement of personal mentation into account, McClelland concludes that the best measurement operations involve eliciting fantasy from the person in the form of stories composed about pictures of fictitious people and then analyzing the content of the stories for evidence of personal goals and predispositions to instrumental behavior relevant to them. The meaning of the pictures should be ambiguous enough and the task of making up stories sufficiently unstructured to render it unlikely the person will respond with socially desirable rather than personal goals. Further, since the human content of the pictures arouses mentation concerning what the fictitious people are doing and may want, one is likely to get information about motives rather than traits, as the latter are so habitual as to be virtually unrepresented in the composition of stories. Some of you may recognize the task described here as Murray's (1943) famous Thematic Apperception Test. Although this technique was available prior to McClelland's attempt to measure motives, it is extremely well suited to his operationalization; Murray devised the test primarily for the measurement of his very similar need concept, though he never provided the compelling operational rationale available in McClelland's theorizing.

McClelland (1961) is almost as precise about how schemata are to be measured as he is about measuring motives. If you want to know about persons' social goals, defined by their values and sense of social roles, you might as well just ask them straightforwardly. It matters little whether they spruce up their answers because they think they will be evaluated by society, for it is just their sense of what society stands for that you want to measure. Questionnaires concerning the directionalities and goals in people's behavior tend to elicit schemata, as opposed to fantasies, or projective tasks, which tend to elicit motives. Finally, from a formal standpoint, traits are to be measured by creating familiar circumstances in which action is called for and then observing the regularities in people's functioning.

Though my summary of McClelland's operational attempts is necessarily brief, I want you to appreciate that no other personologists come close to his precision. Indeed, going beyond the formal attributes, McClelland even offers workable operational definitions for the content of the motives he has most strongly emphasized (achievement, affiliation, and power). For example, the operational definition for the achievement motive is *competition with a standard of excellence* (McClelland et al., 1953, pp. 110–112). Along with this overall definition, you are provided with a carefully devised scoring system with which to analyze fantasy for evidence of interest in competition with a standard of excellence (McClelland et al., 1953, pp. 107–138). With varying emphases and degrees of precision, Murray and Maddi provide measurement specifications similar to McClelland.

Once you leave McClelland, Murray, and Maddi, you are on your own in measuring the peripheral characteristics offered by personologists. The best you can find are vivid descriptions of the application of a characteristic to life events. If such descriptions are extensive enough, you can form an impression of what the theorist means that is sufficiently precise to help you decide on measurement operations. Once you have selected the appropriate measurement operations for the entire set of peripheral characteristics, you can proceed with the tedious but unavoidable and important job of determining whether their measurement is empirically adequate enough to convince you that they exist, or are real.

RELIABILITY. A peripheral characteristic is not considered to have empirical existence unless its measure has adequate *reliability*. As indicated in Chapter 9, there are two kinds of reliability: internal consistency and stability.

To appreciate *internal consistency,* you must keep in mind that a measure almost always has a number of parts. For example, if you are measuring need for achievement with a scoring system to be used on fantasy productions, the different categories in the scoring system will be the parts of the measure. If your measure is a questionnaire, each question will be a part of the measure. Internal consistency refers to the degree to which the parts of the measure, presumably put there for theoretical reasons, appear to go together at an empirical level of analysis. On a questionnaire, this will involve determining the likelihood that a person answering one of the questions will answer the others in a similar fashion. On a scoring system applied to fantasy, internal consistency will be expressed as the tendency to apply the various scoring categories in the same way to a given person's productions. If you demonstrate sufficient internal consistency, you will have found empirical support for the contention that your measure gets at some genuine entity. The entity is genuine in the sense that its postulated parts really do seem to hang together.

But exactly how internally consistent should a measure be before you conclude that it reflects something real? For some concepts, such as trait, you would expect a high degree of internal consistency because, theoretically, the range of behaviors that comprises it should be small and the behaviors very similar to one another. But a concept such as need or motive is inherently more heterogeneous, comprising not only goals but instrumental sequences of action, all of which wax and wane depending on whether the need has been satisfied or not. In short, even though peripheral characteristics are supposed to be the basic unit of peripheral personality, we should recognize that the degree of internal consistency required of such characteristics partially depends on their postulated status. Nonetheless, unless a measure has at least moderate internal consistency, it offers little empirical evidence of a genuine entity.

When you assess the *stability* of a measure, you are determining the likelihood that you will get the same result with it when you apply it to the same people on two or more similar occasions separated in time. Generally speaking, the more similar the results from the different testing sessions, the more justified you will be in claiming that your measure reflects some genuine entity. This is because peripheral characteristics are assumed to be reasonably stable over time. But exactly how stable should you require a measure to be? In theory, some peripheral characteristics, such as openness to experience (Rogers) and need for achievement (McClelland), should be less stable over time than some others, such as stinginess (Freud). If you are open to experience, you will literally be different from moment to moment, and your need for achievement should be high when it is frustrated but low when it is satisfied. So the degree of stability required as evidence of empirical existence is partially determined by how the theorist describes the nature of the characteristic assessed by the measure. As with internal consistency, however, there must be at least moderate stability before you have empirical grounds for considering the measure to reflect a genuine entity.

A measure must thus be made up of parts that are homogeneous and that work the same way more than once. If the attempt to measure a characteristic has been capably undertaken and internal consistency and/or stability is found to be lacking, you can be sure there is a heretofore unrecognized theoretical problem to blame. A common theoretical problem in such cases is the choice of peripheral characteristics that are less irreducible than they might have seemed (Fiske, 1963). If a peripheral characteristic can be subdivided further, when you attempt to measure it, you will find a lack of internal consistency because the measure incorporates disparate parts. If you build your theory of personality on peripheral characteristics that turn out to be inconsistent at the empirical level, you are building on shifting sands.

The failure of attempts to develop reliable measures can well make theorists return to the drawing board. They can revamp a peripheral characteristic in the hope of making it more homogeneous, or they can undertake a more sweeping reconsideration of all their peripheral-level theorizing. Clearly, knowing the reliability of measures of postulated peripheral characteristics can help you empirically evaluate the theories of personality they represent. You may find that one or another theory or model does a better job in this regard. If so, you will be justified in reaching the tentative conclusion that this theory or model for theorizing is more empirically genuine. The conclusion would be tentative, because assessment of the reliability of measures is only the first step in the ideal strategy for empirical analysis of peripheral-level theorizing.

Step Two: Interrelationships Among Measures

The completion of the first step in the empirical analysis of peripheral-level theorizing should leave you with measures of those peripheral characteristics that indeed lend themselves to reliable measurement. Some concrete peripheral characteristics postulated by certain theorists undoubtedly will have fallen by the wayside. In other words, they will not have met the empirical criterion of reliable measurement. Indeed, it is possible that most of some unfortunate personologist's peripheral theory will not have survived the first step in empirical analysis.

The second step begins with the surviving peripheral characteristics and concerns peripheral-level theorizing about types. You take all the reliable measures you have developed and determine the relationships among them. You do this by applying the measures to the same group of people and then analyzing the results with available statistical techniques for determining relationship. A useful technique for what I have in mind is *factor analysis* (see Chapter 9). This technique not only determines how strongly a number of measures are related to one another but also organizes those that are most closely interrelated into clusters, called *factors*.

Factor analysis is a very powerful and important technique in the empirical assessment of peripheral-level theorizing. Take Fromm's peripheral-level theorizing, for example. Assume all of the traits that he presents under the five character orientations have been reliably measured and that all the measures have been applied to the same group of people. One thing a factor analysis will tell us is whether these traits cluster together in the manner predicted by his theory. There should be clusters of trait measures (factors) corresponding to the receptive, exploitative, hoarding, marketing, and productive orientations. If there is nothing like this, we can say that there is no empirical support in the clustering of traits for Fromm's peripheral-level theorizing about types of people. Whatever the organization of traits happens to show does not conform to the theory. Alternatively, we could find that Fromm's theorizing is quite strongly supported by empirical evidence or even that it is only moderately supported.

Another important criterion of this second step is that all measures can be applied to all people studied. Hence, it becomes possible to determine the correlations and factor clusterings of the peripheral characteristics of not only one theory but of all theories under consideration. This is an ideal empirical procedure for determining the overlap among theories. We no longer have to rely on rationality alone to determine whether, for example, what Fromm talks about as the *hoarding orientation* is essentially what Freud means by the *anal character type*.

Step Three: Construct Validity of Peripheral Theorizing

The third and final step in the ideal strategy for the empirical analysis of peripheral theorizing concerns the *validity* of peripheral characteristics. Obviously these characteristics are meant to be used to explain something. It would be meaningless for them to explain nothing more than their own measures, for these measures are, after all, only the empirical form of the concept. It is important for you to grasp the idea that each peripheral characteristic has been theoretically developed so as to serve as the explanation for a particular set of human behaviors (other than the behavior involved in the measure itself). For

example, take McClelland's need for achievement and its measure involving fantasy behavior. In general, such a characteristic would be used to explain such entities—call them variables—as competitive social relationships, an interest in accumulating money, a strong commitment to work, an uneasiness with leisure time, and so forth. These variables can be said to be explained by the need for achievement. The higher a person scores on this need, the more pronounced should such variables be in his or her everyday life.

The hypothesized relationships between the need for achievement and these other variables can be tested empirically because a measure for this need exists that involves radically different behavior from that of the variables. If data obtained from a group of subjects showed that the fantasy measure correlates with other variables in a theoretically-predicted fashion, we would be in a position to conclude that the construct—need for achievement—had validity. To be extra careful, we would also want to demonstrate that the fantasy measure did not correlate with variables that bore no theoretical relationship to it.

What I have described comes very close to the assessment of *construct validity* as formulated by Cronbach and Meehl (1955). Though not the only kind of validity, it seems the most relevant to the empirical analysis of peripheral theorizing. Other forms of validity are more appropriate when the measure under consideration is intended to predict one variable to a very high degree (e.g., measure of high-school grades as a predictor of college success). In contrast, each peripheral characteristic of personality is usually conceptualized as influencing a reasonably wide selection of variables of human behavior. And the degree of influence is usually considered only moderate, as we can see from personologists' belief that to fully explain any one behavioral variable, a number of peripheral characteristics acting simultaneously must be invoked. This implies that we can consider a peripheral characteristic as valid if its measure shows moderate intercorrelation with a set of theoretically relevant variables (*convergent validation*) and an absence of intercorrelation with theoretically irrelevant variables (*discriminant validation*). For further discussion, see Campbell and Fiske (1959).

COMPREHENSIVE VALIDITY. Thus far, I have discussed the validation of only single characteristics. A further goal within the third step of this strategy is to determine whether the entire list of peripheral characteristics offered by a theorist really does account for all the variables of human behavior. Although each peripheral characteristic, taken by itself, is not intended to account for all behavior, the entire list offered really should do this job. Virtually all personologists say, in one way or another, that they accept the goal of explaining all behavior. So two criteria—namely, that each peripheral characteristic actually explains only the variables it was postulated to explain and that the entire set of characteristics offered comprehensively explain all variables—define the assessment of empirical validity.

To carry out this step, we need to know a good deal about the given variables of human behavior. After all, to arrive at data, we must categorize or define the "thingness" of experience. Here we encounter extraordinary difficulty. Of the personologists considered in this book, only Murray even touches the question of such *data categories*. He offers the data designations of proceedings and serials (see Maddi, 1963; Maddi & Costa, 1972). A *proceeding* is a psychologically meaningful unit of behavior, having a specifiable beginning and end and some duration in time. A proceeding might be having a conversation, solving a problem in your head, or writing a paper. Proceedings can be social or solitary, passive or action oriented, as long as they are meaningful to the person engaging in them. A *serial* is a number of proceedings organized in a sequential fashion, as in a marriage or a college career. Proceedings and serials, Murray argues, are to be explained by peripheral characteristics. Unfortunately, Murray gives us no help in deciding how to identify proceedings and serials. There is only the hint—in the insistence that they be meaningful to the person—that they are to be subjectively defined. In other words, people will virtually define them for themselves.

Generally speaking, the other personologists offer no more along the lines of *data categories* than the notion that a theory of personality ought to explain all behavior. This statement is so general as to be arid. All we are left with is the notion, mentioned in Chapter 1, that personologists tend to define behavior as having regularity across situations and continuity over time. If the person is competitive, or generous, or idealistic over a range of situations and time, the personologist is interested. As you can see, this position is even less concrete than Murray's. How in the world can we proceed with the third step?

Probably, the most feasible thing to do is read the descriptions and examples of life made by personologists when discussing the peripheral level of personality. In this reading, you should remain alert for indications of the variables considered relevant to particular peripheral characteristics and, in a more general vein, the full range of variables discussed. Even from the descriptions quoted in Part Two, you can get an idea of what I am suggesting. Recall, for example, the vivid description of the anal personality type by Rado (1959, p. 326) and Fromm's (1947, pp. 68–72) descriptions of marketing and other orientations, so replete with descriptions of behaviors different from those you would use as the actual measures of the relevant peripheral characteristics. In addition, the behaviors relevant to the need for achievement mentioned earlier in this chapter are straight from McClelland's descriptions. All the variables in the life descriptions offered by the personologists we are considering would constitute the behavior we have to work with in our empirical analysis. Perhaps it would be helpful to adopt, as a heuristic device to facilitate alert reading, the distinctions in Chapter 11 between repetitive behaviors and directional behaviors, each of which may have personal or social goals. These distinctions are implied in many personologists' writings.

With this large group of variables in hand, we could in principle proceed with the empirical analysis of validity. It would be best to have available the same group of people on whom the second step of our analysis was performed. We would have to determine how to best identify the existence and intensity of the variables constituting data in each person studied. Perhaps, for this purpose, each could be asked to give extensive descriptions of her or his own behavior; we could then scrutinize these descriptions. Even better, though more cumbersome, would be to observe these people over some period of time in many different situations and to use these observations as estimates of the variables' intensity. Or the two possibilities could be combined. Murray (1938) and his associates tried such a combination in their trail-blazing attempt to understand personality.

We could then combine in the same factor analysis not only behavioral variables but measures of peripheral characteristics. We would expect clusters composed of theoretically appropriate data variables and measures to emerge from the analysis. If, for example, the measure of need for achievement appeared in the same cluster with such variables as (1) competitive actions, (2) the sense of time as important, and (3) a commitment to hard work, we could conclude that there is convergent validational evidence for McClelland's theorizing. Further support would be the finding that the need-for-achievement measure did not appear in any other cluster, thus indicating discriminant validation. Although factor analysis usually is considered an exploratory technique, what I suggest amounts to using it deductively to test hypotheses concerning the relationship of certain peripheral characteristics to specific behaviors. Nor are we necessarily restricted to factor analysis, for that matter; there are now several forms of multivariate analysis that would serve. All that matters is that you grasp my logic.

Clearly, if a theorist's peripheral characteristics are to have empirical validity, they must show a relationship with the relevant variables. Also, if peripheral-level theorizing is to be considered complete by empirical standards, there should not be a large proportion of variables unrelated to the peripheral characteristics. This is so, incidentally, even if the unrelated behavior is not the kind referred to in the theorizing, because the personologists included here have committed themselves to explaining virtually all behavior. If they say that personality explains all behavior, without being more specific, they must account for all viable behavioral variables, even those they do not specifically mention in their descriptions.

A Word of Practicality

The strategy just described seems to me close to ideal for determining which of the postulated peripheral characteristics are homogeneous and stable enough to be considered genuine, for discerning the nature of their organization into types, and for specifying the validity of peripheral theorizing. Although the strategy offers a potentially great yield for personology, carrying out its procedures would be extraordinarily difficult and time consuming. Clearly, scoring and analyzing the data on the huge scale advocated could be done only with the help of giant computers and the financing of large foundations supporting basic research in psychology. One would also need the services of a large staff, which could count on the cooperation of many personologists in different locations and perhaps not directly involved in the work.

As to the results, with such large amounts of initial data, some of the factors obtained in the third, and perhaps even the second, step of the strategy will be virtually impossible to interpret in an intellectually satisfying manner. These uninterpretable factors would reflect such irrelevant things as common but theoretically unimportant procedures for measuring variables and even accidental similarities of data. To be sure, all large-scale research of personality is likely to uncover some results that are ambiguous or irrelevant to personality theorizing. If one avoids panicking, one can simply accept that some factors will be uninterpretable and still carry out the strategy reasonably effectively by requiring that those that are interpretable conform to what would be expected in one or another of the theories. Nonetheless, it must be noted that this ideal strategy would be difficult to carry out in a practical manner at this time because of its massiveness.

It will be valuable to keep this strategy in mind, however, so that it may serve as a goal toward which simpler, more feasible efforts can be pointed. For example, it may be more practical at this time to focus on single theories of peripheral personality rather than on all of them at once. But in focusing on a single theory, we could still employ the various steps in the strategy. Such a program of research would include only the variables and measures relevant to the particular theory in question, with the results clarifying which variables, peripheral characteristics, and types, if any, were not empirically viable. And if different groups of investigators were working on different theories, one could soon begin to gain an overall view of the most fruitful approaches to peripheral theorizing by comparing the results of these research projects. Even such approximations to the ideal strategy would be a big improvement over current research practice. As Carlson (1971) pinpoints ably in her review, broad (to say nothing of comprehensive) efforts to measure personality are virtually absent from the contemporary research literature.

Having discussed a proposed ideal strategy and a practical version of it, I would like to move on to procedures that are actually practiced in personology. As you may have surmised, the empirical evidence available on the basis of current practice falls short of the evidence required in the ideal strategy. Nonetheless, I shall turn to what is available in the hope of gaining some increased knowledge concerning the peripheral theories. Perhaps having considered an ideal strategy will alert you to the shortcomings of the work considered. But lest I arouse too much cynicism in you, let me point out that some of the work reviewed in the following pages is striking, dramatic, and important. Without it, the personality field would be far less vital.

FACTOR-ANALYTIC STUDIES ....

As you will recall, the third step in the ideal strategy calls for employing factor analysis in determining the intercorrelations among a large group of variables and measures of peripheral characteristics. The characteristics would be considered empirically validated only if their measures correlated with theoretically relevant variables. Although in this I am advocating a theory-testing use of factor analysis, it is generally used as a nontheoretical procedure for discovering the empirical clustering of any variables based on their intercorrelations. It is not at all necessary that measures of peripheral characteristics be included along with other variables. Indeed, such measures have almost never been included in the available factor-analytic studies relevant to personality. Typically the investigator obtains data on a group of variables, performs a factor analysis on them, and then attempts to interpret the meaning of the clusters or factors obtained. He or she only then concludes inductively that the factors expressed some particular peripheral characteristics described in the personological literature.

Going further, one could perform another factor analysis on the factors already obtained, resulting in a set of *second-order factors*. Those describe the way the original factors grouped themselves into larger units. One could then try to interpret how these larger units express particular personality types described in the personological literature.

I have just described what might constitute an inductive strategy for the empirical evaluation of peripheral theorizing. It is inductive mainly because no measures of peripheral characteristics are included; hence, you are not really testing hypotheses concerning the relationship of such characteristics to behavioral variables. The best you can do with the inductive use of factor analysis is arrive at clusterings of behavioral variables that suggest—but only suggest—the relevance of particular peripheral characteristics. This may sound acceptable, but once you include in the factor analysis a sufficient number of variables to do justice to even a small number of theories, you obtain factors so complex and ambiguous that the task of interpreting just which peripheral characteristics and types they express becomes extremely arduous. One of the most vulnerable points of inductive factor-analytic studies has been the almost inevitably intuitive, crude nature of the interpretation of factors.

The aura of empirical rigor and objectivity attending the inductive use of factor analysis is deceptive. Indeed, Block (1995a) argues persuasively that the inductive use of this procedure tells us little or nothing about personality structure and content, because it does not directly address theoretical considerations. In contrast, the deductive use of factor analysis advocated in the ideal strategy is designed to test hypotheses from personality theories rather than randomly explore human behaviors. Only when a factor includes both the measure of a peripheral characteristic and the major variables deemed expressive of it theoretically can that characteristic be considered empirically valid.

Most currently available factor analytic studies have been of the inductive type. Furthermore, virtually all these studies have fallen short of the ideal procedure in yet another way: They have not started with all the variables that crop up in the writings of all personologists. To be sure, it would be acceptable, in the interest of practicality, for a study to concern itself with all the variables in one theory alone; at least one could then say that the study comprehensively treated that theory. Fortunately, some available studies have approximated this goal. But sometimes one cannot specify a study's variables in an intellectually satisfying way (such as comprehensively treating a theory). The investigator, perhaps out of an atheoretical bias or theoretical naiveté, will include some heterogeneous array of variables and not be concerned with the implications of doing so. The outcome of such factor-analytic studies is of dubious value, for to consider the resulting evidence comprehensive or even representative with regard to life in general or some particular theory is erroneous and often seriously misleading. You get out of a factor analysis only what you put into it; therefore, it is never acceptable to be ignorant of the implications of the variables you have decided to consider. The set of variables considered should be comprehensive, or at least specifiable in a theoretically meaningful way. Another persistent difficulty with inductive factor-analytic studies is the restriction of data to subjects' self-report. Many concepts from personality theory cannot adequately be measured with only self-report, requiring instead expert judgment of the subjects' behavior (e.g., Block, 1995a). So, this is another way in which typical factor-analytic studies fall short of the ideal strategy.

Cattell, Guilford, Eysenck, and Others

Among factor analysts, the work of three people—Cattell, Guilford, and Eysenck—is especially pertinent to the empirical evaluation of peripheral theorizing. I will describe something of their procedures, leaving their results for later.

The factor analytic work of Raymond Cattell closely approximates the inductive procedure mentioned in the preceding section. Cattell has attempted to obtain comprehensive behavioral information so that his results will help reveal the most fruitful peripheral characteristics. Like many factor analysts, Cattell has been much concerned with building comprehensive, valid tests of personality. This task does not really differ from that of determining which peripheral characteristics one should represent in personality theory. In an effort to obtain behavioral observations comprehensively, Cattell (1946, 1957) began by assembling all personality-variable names from the dictionary (as compiled by Allport & Odbert, 1936) and from the psychological literature; then he reduced the list to 171 variable names by combining obvious synonyms. He next selected a sample of 100 adults from many walks of life. Associates of these people, who knew them well, were asked to rate them on these 171 variables. Intercorrelations and factor analyses of these ratings were followed by further ratings of 208 people on a shortened list of variables.

Factor analyses of the latter ratings led Cattell (1946, 1957) to identify what he describes as "the primary source traits of personality." Cattell and his associates then set out to build a personality test that would measure these source traits. The end result of considerable investigation was the *16 Personality Factor Questionnaire* (Cattell & Stice, 1957), made up of many items concerning life activities for which the respondent must indicate liking or disliking. Of the 16 factors, obtained through factor analyzing the answers to these items given by many people, 12 are similar to those obtained in the earlier work with ratings, while 4 appear only on the test.

In considering the findings most relevant to the task of empirical evaluation of peripheral theorizing, we should focus on the 16 factors of Cattell's test. We can consider each factor to reflect a peripheral characteristic. Cattell has also factor analyzed the 16 primary factors, or *source* traits, as he calls them, and derived from this analysis 7 second-order factors that link the first-order factors together. We can consider these 7 factors to reflect the organization of peripheral characteristics into types.

Before turning to the actual substance of Cattell's findings, I should briefly summarize the procedures of Guilford and Eysenck. In finding behavioral data on which to perform factor analyses, Guilford and his associates (Guilford, 1959; Guilford & Zimmerman, 1956) collected the items from a number of personality tests already in common use. These tests had, by and large, been constructed along rational, theoretical lines rather than by some empirical clustering procedure such as factor analysis. Guilford had a sample of people answer all the items from these tests, which mainly had them indicate whether or not they liked the various kinds of activities presented. The answers to items were then intercorrelated and factor analyzed. Through a long process of refining, pruning, and interpreting the resulting factors, a number of personality tests were constructed. The last of these, the most authoritative, is called the *Guilford-Zimmerman Temperament Survey* (Guilford, Zimmerman, & Guilford, 1976), which includes a large number of items to be endorsed as liked or disliked and yields 10 factors. These factors, like those in Cattell's test, can be considered to reflect peripheral characteristics. Three to four second-order factors are also identified.

Of the three factor analysts being considered, Eysenck samples the possible range of behavioral observations least widely. Although his work is therefore less valuable here than the others', it

can teach us something. In his first study (Eysenck, 1947), the sample was 700 neurotic soldiers. The behavioral data of the study includes some answers given by the soldiers to factual questions about themselves and also psychiatrists' ratings of the soldiers. The factor analysis was performed on only 39 information items. Eysenck finds two factors, or peripheral characteristics, as sufficient to describe the clustering of items. Subsequently, Eysenck (1947) added more subjects to this original sample in an attempt to determine whether these two factors still sufficiently described people. The final sample totaled roughly 10,000 normal and neurotic subjects, and the available information on them varied from responses on test items to behavior in performance situations. Eysenck reports that the same two factors found to describe the original 700 neurotic soldiers sufficiently describe the larger sample.

I find myself in a difficult position in evaluating the relevance of Eysenck's work to my present concerns. He has, in toto, included more kinds of behavioral observation in his studies than have the other two factor analysts, who have relied primarily on responses to test items. But, following the original study, Eysenck has used a procedure called *criterion analysis,* which is essentially deductive rather than inductive. In criterion analysis, because you have hypothesized what the important factors are, you plan your study to test that hypothesis. You select behavioral observations that you think will be theoretically relevant to the factors you consider important. You design your study to include criterion groups, which should possess discriminably different degrees of the hypothesized factors. The end result of this procedure is that you get information largely relevant to your hypotheses only rather than more general data. Since Eysenk's two factors were originally found to describe neurotic soldiers—a rather unusual group of people—all that the generalization of these results to other people may mean is that some evidence of these two factors can be found in people in general. It does not at all mean that these two factors are as basic in describing people in general as they might have been in describing neurotic soldiers. The conclusion that people in general can be adequately and comprehensively described by two factors alone may thus be quite spurious.

There has been an ongoing and lively debate among factor analysts as to whether the factors offered by the three psychologists under discussion are definitive. The intricacies of these contentions cannot be chronicled here. Suffice it to say that although none of the factor analytic schemes has gone uncriticized (e.g., Howarth, 1976; Howarth & Browne, 1971), there have also been defenses of them (e.g., Cattell, 1972; Eysenck, 1970, 1977; Guilford, 1975, 1977). Some investigators (e.g., French, 1973; Sells, Demaree, & Will, 1971) have attempted to compare the three factor schemes in the same research.

Of these attempts, the work of Coan (1974) is especially noteworthy, because he not only includes measures relevant to the factors of Cattell, Eysenck, and Guilford but tries to include measures reflecting various theoretical views of ideal personality. These latter measures are of such concepts as emotional adjustment, psychological differentiation and integration, experiential openness, personal control, and social activity. In addition, his measures are not only of self-report but of fantasy and performance ratings. Another important factor analytic study (Costa & McCrae, 1980) includes many of Coan's measures and others selected from the existing literature.

Actually, it is not surprising that such dispute surrounds the real first- and second-order factors. Relevant studies use different samplings of people and vary considerably in the content and form (e.g., self-report, fantasy, performance ratings) of measures included. Also, the number of measures encompass a broad range, as do the particular mathematical procedures for factor analysis. Given all this variation, it will be some time before analysts reach clarity and agreement concerning a definitive list of factors. Nonetheless, let us push on in our attempt to determine the implications of this body of research for the adequacy of peripheral theorizing. Needless to say, our conclusions will have to be tentative.

Number of Factors

The most obvious question regarding the relevance of factor analytic studies for peripheral-personality theorizing concerns the number of factors that emerge. The number of first-order factors should indicate how many peripheral characteristics one can fruitfully assume. The number of second-order factors should suggest the number of types that one might theorize about.

Much debate over how many first- and second-order factors exist has been generated. To some degree, this debate has been fueled by unfortunate differences from study to study in the number of measures included, the size of sample used, and the data-analysis decisions made. It is therefore difficult to arrive at any definite number of factors. After all, you get out of a factor analysis only some version of what you put in! There is, however, a range of first-order factors observed with some regularity, roughly 3 to 21. Eysenck, of course, is on the low end, but you will recall that his original work was done on a small number of psychopathological subjects. Although his 3 factors certainly can be uncovered in other larger and more representative samples, it is not clear that so few factors exhaustively describe the behavior of the subjects in these samples. Further, some investigators have argued that what Eysenck calls first-order factors are really second-order factors (e.g., Costa & McCrae, 1980).

Agreeing with Eysenck's low estimate are Peabody (1984), who derives 3 factors from influences concerning 120 traits, and Norman (1963), who estimates 5 factors from personality ratings made by peers. Despite the popularity of Norman's so-called "big five," other investigators continue to report more than this number of factors, even when working with such small databases as one personality test. For example, Costa, Zonderman, Williams, and McCrae (1985) find 9 factors (only one of which matches Norman's in content) on 1,576 subjects, and Johnson, Null, Butcher, and Johnson (1984) report fully 21 factors from their sample of 20,000 subjects! The clearest conclusion to be reached is that the number of first-order factors is probably more than 5 and maybe closer to 20. If we interpret Eysenck's factors as second order, putting his work alongside that of others already mentioned suggests that the number of second-order factors is about 3.

CONCLUSIONS ON PERIPHERAL CHARACTERISTICS. What are the implications of these conclusions for peripheral theorizing? Let me say tentatively that theories should include between 5 and 20 concrete peripheral characteristics and about 8 personality types. The number of personality types may sound odd, but consider that persons may be high or low on each of the three second-order factors. For example, if the second-order factors are introversion versus extroversion, anxiety versus calmness, and openness versus defensiveness, possible types would be introversive-anxious-open, introversive-calm-open, introversive-anxious-defensive, introversive-calm-defensive, extroversive-anxious-open, extroversive-calm-open, extroversive-anxious-defensive, and extroversive-calm-defensive. Moreover, these estimates are bound to be on the low side, because even the best factor-analytic studies do not sample types of behaviors or subjects comprehensively. As a case in point, Knapp (1976) utilizes only a few measures and nonetheless extracts 10 first-order factors. Consequently, we should be more willing to accept theorizing that exceeds the estimates rather than theorizing that falls short of them.

Among the theorists who are specific concerning the periphery, two—the conflict theorist, Erikson, and the fulfillment theorist, Adler—seem to suggest fewer than 10 characteristics. In Erikson's case this is not actually true, for, as you will recall, his eight developmental conflicts are probably intended as summaries of clustered peripheral characteristics. Those eight developmental conflicts would seem to correspond to second-order rather than first-order factors. Although Erikson has not therefore specified peripheral characteristics, it cannot be said that he has theorized about too few. Although one suspects a similar state of affairs for Adlerians, who probably would not really want to defend the position that there is only one peripheral characteristic associated with each lifestyle, they are, unfortunately, as unclear on this matter as Erikson.

Although the upper limit ventured for peripheral characteristics undoubtedly is an underestimation, you may wonder whether a more accurate figure would be great enough to justify the theorizing of Murray, McClelland, and Fromm, who have postulated a great many peripheral characteristics. Their lists suggest that at least some of the items are too synonymous to be considered separately. Given the relatively heterogeneous nature of Murray's need construct and the great number of needs postulated, there is bound to be some overlap among them at the empirical level. This difficulty will also be found in McClelland's position, because it adopts Murray's list of needs. And to convince yourself that Fromm has included some synonyms in his clusters of traits, simply go back to Chapter 6 and reread them.

CONCLUSIONS ON TYPES. Turning to types, you will recall that several theories consider only two types (Rogers, Maslow, existential psychology). Some others present four to six (Freud, Kohut, Rank, Adler, Fromm). This appears to be too few given the findings of factor analytic studies. It should be noted that at least existential psychology (see Kobasa & Maddi, 1977) is developing more types, but it has quite a distance to go. Among the theories reasonably specific concerning types, only activation theory specifies more than can be easily justified from factor analytic studies. Most likely, several of the types in this theory will fall by the wayside as more attempts to measure them are made.

Kind and Content of Factors

Factor analysts tend to label their factors traits, though on closer scrutiny it becomes clear that they do not mean this in the narrow sense of habitual behaviors alone. They use the term *trait* broadly enough for it to be synonymous with *peripheral characteristic*. When one looks at the content of their factors, it becomes apparent that distinctions could be made among habitual behaviors (or traits, in the narrow sense), cognitive behaviors (or such things as values), and motivational behaviors. Indeed, one factor analyst, Cattell (1950), even offers the distinction between dynamic and nondynamic traits, calling the former *ergs* and the latter *traits*. This is very close to McClelland's distinction between motive and trait. These distinctions will be discussed next, along with the factors' content.

Summarizing not only the first-order factors originally presented by Guilford and Cattell but also the results of other studies, we can arrive at a reasonably clear picture of the general content that we should take into account in peripheral theorizing. Costa and McCrae (1980) offer a well-documented and extensive list of first-order factors that is representative of the work of many other investigators: anxiety, hostility, depression, self-consciousness, impulsiveness, vulnerability, attachment, gregariousness, assertiveness, activity, excitement seeking, positive emotions, fantasy, esthetic sense, emotional variability, rigidity, theoretical orientation, and traditional values. People may score high or low on any of these factors. Thus, the name listed above for a factor needs to be thought of along with its opposite. For example, a person high on the first factor is anxious, but one low on the same factor is calm.

PERIPHERAL CHARACTERISTICS AND FIRST-ORDER FACTORS. The first matter for consideration is whether the grouping of peripheral characteristics into traits, motives, and schemata made by some theorists is supported by factor analytic studies. In truth, it is very difficult to say. In the list of factors, some (e.g., traditional values, self-consciousness) suggest schemata, with their emphasis on social-role playing and conscience. But it is unclear whether many of the others (e.g., gregariousness, assertiveness) are traits, in the sense of habitual and repetitive behaviors, or motives, in the sense of goal-directed behavioral change. It must be concluded that factor analytic studies do not at present shed much light on classification of peripheral characteristics.

How can we use results concerning first-order factors to evaluate the content emphases of peripheral theorizing? In approaching this question, you should keep in mind two points. One is that the list of factors may, as mentioned earlier, be an underestimation. Hence, if a factor on the list is not included in a theory, the theory may be criticized. But if the theory includes a factor not on the list, we cannot conclude that a theoretical error has been made. The other point is that considerable interpretation goes into designating the meaning of a factor by a label and verbal description. All in all, it is very difficult to find fault with a peripheral theory of personality as long as its factors come anywhere close to those on the factor list.

You will recall from Chapter 11 that conflict and fulfillment positions do not differ in the content of their peripheral-level theorizing. The difference between them lies in which content is considered ideal and which nonideal. The ideal in conflict theories stresses adjustment, dependability, and stability, whereas the ideal in fulfillment theories emphasizes the opposite: transcendence, voluntary commitment, and changeability.

The findings of factor analytic studies provide no empirical bases for favoring conflict over fulfillment positions. Factors have been found that refer to traditional values, gregariousness, and self-consciousness on the one hand and impulsivity, assertiveness, and excitement seeking on the other. People can be high or low on each of these. Little in the factor studies would lead us to interpret one or another factor as ideal or nonideal. Therefore, we must conclude that the adaptation-transcendence content of factor analytic studies shows the plausibility of both conflict and fulfillment models. The factors listed that concern social interaction (e.g., attachment, gregariousness) are also understandable from the standpoint of both models. In peripheral theorizing, the consistency model leads either to eclecticism of content or to content expressing the maintenance of consistency. It is difficult, therefore, to prove or disprove such theorizing on the basis of the factor list.

What emerges is that the three personality models are sufficiently comprehensive and the factor list sufficiently heterogeneous that it is really very difficult to determine the relative merits of the models in this particular empirical fashion. Factor analysis studies would have had to be done with the specific models of personality in mind for there to be much hope of concluding otherwise.

TYPES AND SECOND-ORDER FACTORS. Perhaps more can be learned by scrutinizing the content of second- or higher-order factors and the types conceptualized in peripheral statements. It would appear that there is broad consensus on the two most important second-order factors. This is especially true if you accept the interpretation of Eysenck's factors as second order and discount some of Cattell's highly disputed entries. The two higher-order factors are *introversion versus extroversion* (so called by Eysenck, Cattell, and Costa and McCrae, and called *social activity* by Guilford) and *emotional health versus neuroticism* (called *emotional health* by Guilford, *neuroticism* by Eysenck and by Costa and McCrae, and *anxiety* by Cattell). Other posited second-order factors either have achieved much less acceptance (e.g., Eysenck's psychoticism) or involve content that can be subsumed under the two already mentioned (e.g., Costa and McCrae's openness to experience, which includes content some investigators subsume under introversion-extroversion; and Guilford's social activity, which can be subsumed under extroversion). Thus, for purposes of considering content for peripheral theorizing, we lose little by focusing only on the two second-order factors that everyone seems to recognize.

To test high on emotional health, people must be composed, secure, trusting, adaptable, mature, stable, and self-sufficient. To be high on neuroticism, the other pole of the factor, people must be tense, anxious, insecure, suspicious, jealous, emotionally unstable, hostile, and vulnerable. To be high on extroversion involves warmth, sociability, enthusiasm, talkativeness, adventurousness, resourcefulness, friendliness, assertiveness, high activity level, and positive emotions. The introverted pattern involves aloofness, coldness,

shyness, conventionality, practicality, emphasis on thoughts, and low activity level.

These two second-order factors suggest four personality types. The first, *neuroticism-introversion,* applies to people who are tense, excitable, insecure, suspicious, jealous, emotional, unstable, lax, and unsure, as well as aloof, cold, glum, silent, timid, shy, Bohemian, unconcerned, and resourceful. The second type, *emotional health-introversion,* is phlegmatic, composed, confident, unshakable, trusting, adaptable, mature, calm, and self-sufficient in addition to being aloof, cold, glum, silent, timid, shy, Bohemian, unconcerned, and resourceful. The third type, *neuroticism-extroversion,* is tense, excitable, insecure, suspicious, jealous, emotional, unstable, lax, and unsure, as well as warm, sociable, enthusiastic, talkative, adventurous, thick-skinned, conventional, practical, imitative, and dependent. The final type, *emotional health-extroversion,* is phlegmatic, composed, confident, unshakable, trustful, adaptable, mature, calm, and self-sufficient, as well as warm, sociable, enthusiastic, talkative, adventurous, thick-skinned, conventional, practical, imitative, and dependent.

Do these personality types seem strikingly in line with any theory under consideration here? Some theories, such as those of Murray, Kelly, and McClelland, do not postulate personality types and thus need not be considered further. Others, such as those of Erikson, White, and Allport, are so nebulous concerning personality types that one cannot feasibly evaluate their positions with regard to the factorial information just presented. Among the remaining theories, those of Freud, Rogers, Maslow, and Fromm are not strikingly confirmed by the factorial evidence concerning personality types. Here and there, a bit of one of these theories seems to match one of the types presented above. So, for example, the emotional health-extroversion type seems somewhat similar to Freud's *genital character,* and there is some, albeit less, correspondence between the emotional health-introversion type and the *fully functioning person* of actualization theory. But neither Freud nor the actualization theorists have provided peripheral theorizing capable of rendering the other factorial types easily understandable.

The only peripheral theories that closely fit the types derived from factorial studies are those of Adler, Maddi, and, to some extent, Jung. It seems to me that the emotional health-extroversion and emotional health-introversion types bear much similarity to Adler's active-constructive and passive-constructive styles of life, respectively. Further, the emotional health-extroversion and neuroticism-introversion factorial combinations recall Adler's active-destructive and passive-destructive styles of life, respectively. It seems clear that high and low anxiety are much like high and low activation. Further, extroversion and introversion suggest the external and internal traits emphasized by Maddi. Although the emphasis on introversion-extroversion is quite accurate for Jung, it is not clear how low and high anxiety would fit his position. So once again one finds the empirical support tending toward the fulfillment model and the activation version of the consistency model.

In closing this section, I should mention that the factors, as uncombined into units to resemble personality types, obviously support the theorizing of McCrae and Costa about the core of personality (see Chapter 5). This is not surprising, because they built their theory on the results of their factor-analytic research. Because they offer no theorizing about peripheral types or characteristics, however, there is nothing further to discuss.

OTHER STUDIES OF PERIPHERAL PERSONALITY......

The studies just reviewed did not involve selection of the behavioral variables coinciding with those considered important by any one personality theory. In general, they included a broad, eclectic sampling of variables so that the factors emerging from the data analysis would not be biased in favor of one kind of theory over another. The virtue of inductive factor analytic studies, when they sample broadly, is that they help us determine the relative fruitfulness of different approaches to peripheral theorizing.

Some studies, however, restrict their concerns explicitly or implicitly to only one peripheral theory of personality. To be included here, such single-theory studies must focus primarily on the measurement of one or more peripheral characteristics or types and also be concerned with the assessment of construct validity for the entities measured. Less relevant here are those studies in which peripheral characteristics or types are used as explanatory concepts but not measured. In the main, I shall also exclude studies done on children, whose personalities may not be well formed. In addition, I shall emphasize only studies reasonably rigorous in their measurement attempts, systematic in their sampling of subjects, and undertaking appropriate data analyses. These restrictions are necessary for us to have any chance of obtaining a clear empirical analysis of peripheral considerations. Many studies in the literature are either so methodologically poor or so theoretically indirect and ambiguous as to be better left unchronicled here.

Even with the restrictions suggested, it must be said at the outset that the studies to be considered are of limited utility because they focus on one—and only one—peripheral theory of personality. Usually these single-theory studies have a partisan flavor; that is, they are performed by investigators who already believe the theory. Such partisanship often gives the theory the benefit of the doubt when findings can be interpreted in more than one way. All things considered, it would not be surprising to find some solid empirical evidence for each of the peripheral theories, given the fact that all these theories have been devised by especially sensitive, serious, and intelligent personologists.

Of major value in the empirical evaluation of peripheral considerations are studies that pit the various theories against one another by comparing their explanatory capabilities. But lacking enough carefully devised studies of this kind to make a difference, I shall have to make do with what exists. Do not be too ready to give the laurel wreath to a theory, even if it is the one you believe in, just because a few limited studies seem to lend it some empirical support. Look instead for a heavy accumulation of empirical support, many studies pointing in the same direction, and studies that truly impress you with their relevance to living.

You might be especially skeptical of a peripheral theory that cannot boast empirical support even from partisan research. But you should not conclude that a peripheral theory is unfruitful if it simply has never been the focus of research efforts. All in all, the best policy to adopt in reading the following pages is to be duly impressed when there is formidable empirical support for a peripheral theory while keeping an open mind concerning theories that lack such support unless research attempts in their behalf have been mounted but have failed.

I shall organize the following discussion in the simplest way—by individual theories. All the studies involve one or more of three basic ways of measuring peripheral characteristics and types. The first, *self-description,* involves presenting subjects with a set of questions or adjectives and explicitly instructing them to depict themselves in their responses (the approach most common in the factorial studies covered earlier). Which characteristic of the subjects the investigator hopes to glean from the responses need not be apparent, but the subjects must know that they are describing themselves in some way. The second measurement technique is the analysis of *fantasy.* Obtaining the fantasy productions involves providing subjects with an ambiguous, unstructured stimulus that they are to render clear and structured through an act of imagination. The presumption is that subjects' fantasy will disclose the characteristics of their personalities. The final measurement technique is the *rating of performance* or action. This technique involves the investigator in classifying and quantifying the subjects' behavior on some explicit and structured task. The task requires action and choice but depends little on fantasy. You may wish to refer to Chapter 9 for more details of measurement.

Freud's Position

To be considered especially pertinent to Freudian theory, research must involve measurement of some traits or defenses presumed to form the oral, anal, phallic, and genital character types. The subjects should usually be old enough to have attained at least puberty. By and large, the single traits included in the types are not so specific to Freudian theory alone that their study is definitive to someone interested in testing that theory. Understandably, we should prick up our ears only when a study includes clusters of traits that represent one or more types. Also of some interest are studies that, while focusing on only one trait, have singled out a trait that is fairly unique to the Freudian tradition (e.g., *castration anxiety*).

Having established these specifications, what comes immediately to mind are the studies concerning the *Blacky Test* (Blum, 1949). The stimuli in this test are 12 cartoons portraying the adventures of a male dog named Blacky, his mother, his father, and a sibling. The cartoons were carefully devised to pose familial situations reminiscent of the psychosexual themes and conflicts considered important in psychoanalytic theory. Subjects are asked to compose stories in response to the pictures, providing fantasy data. After doing so, they are asked to answer a series of multiple-choice and short-answer questions pertaining to the psychoanalytic theme or conflict presumably posed in the picture. Finally, subjects are asked whether they like or dislike each cartoon. The final two types of data resemble self-description.

Blum (1949) has offered a scoring procedure for these three sources of data, the result of which are scores reflecting the intensity of the subjects' disturbances on 13 dimensions. The content of these dimensions is shown in Table 12-1. You should realize that these dimensions do not actually reflect either the traits or the defenses listed in Chapter 3 under the various character types. Instead, some of the dimensions indicate the character types (or possibly subtypes) themselves (e.g., oral eroticism and anal

TABLE 12-1   Spontaneous Story Scoring Agreement

DIMENSION	OBTAINED PERCENT SCORING AGREEMENT	PERCENT EXPECTED BY CHANCE
Oral eroticism	100	56
Oral sadism	96	61
Anal expulsiveness	84	43*
Anal retentiveness	96	44*
Oedipal intensity	96	53
Masturbation guilt	84	50
Castration anxiety (males)	100	56
Penis envy (females)	76	53
Positive identification	100	79
Sibling rivalry	92	56
Guilt feelings	80	51
Positive ego ideal	100	92
Narcissistic love object	92	54
Anaclitic love object	100	85

	OBTAINED	EXPECTED BY CHANCE
Mean	92.6 ½	59.5 ½
Median	96.0 ½	55.0 ½
Range	76 ½–100 ½	43 ½–92 ½

*These two dimensions were scored on a four-point scale instead of a two-point scale. Hence, the chance expectancy of agreement is somewhat lower.

Source: From "A Study of the Psychoanalytic Theory of Psychosexual Development," by G. S. Blum, 1949, *Genetic Psychology Monograph*, 39.

retentiveness). Other dimensions seem to refer to general qualities that transcend any particular character type but probably indicate the overall degree of defensiveness and conflict (e.g., guilt feelings, sibling rivalry). In theoretical terms, it is certainly clear that the content of the dimensions is germane to Freud's position, though their precise status as peripheral characteristics, types, or conglomerates of these is unclear.

Consistent with this ambiguity is the global, intuitive scoring of these dimensions (in other words, there is no set scoring system that everyone can use). Nonetheless, even with intuitive scoring, Blum (1949) reports acceptable levels of agreement between himself and another psychologist working independently on the same protocols, indicating some objectivity. As can be seen from Table 12-1, the percentages of interscorer agreement on the various dimensions range from 76 to 100, with an average of 92.6. The scoring procedure mainly involves deciding whether a story shows a strong or weak emphasis on the dimension being considered. For example, Blum (1949) lists the following story, in response to a card showing Blacky nursing, as strong on oral eroticism:

Blacky has just discovered the delightful nectar that Mama can supply—it is an endless supply and she is enjoying it. She doesn't know where it comes from, but she doesn't care. Mama is pacific throughout it all—she doesn't particularly like this business of supplying milk, but she is resigned to it. It is a pretty day and they are both calm and happy.

In contrast, consider a story for the same card that is considered weak on oral eroticism (Blum, 1949):

Blacky, a male pup of a few weeks, is having his midday lunch. Mama is bored with the proceedings but as a mother with her maternal interests is letting Blacky have his lunch to Blacky's satisfaction.

In this story, there is none of the elaboration so indicative of lingering oral conflict seen in the first story.

Having encountered at least some evidence that well-trained investigators can agree on scoring the stories, I shall now turn to the question of whether the dimensions of the test have sufficient internal consistency and stability to be considered empirically genuine. Charen (1956) reports stability correlations for the 13 dimensions that range from a high of .52 through very low positive and even some negative values. The implication of low negative correlations is that people's responses changed almost completely from the first to the second testing. But one is justified in looking into the matter of reliability further, for Charen's study involves a period between testing of four months, which is long enough for one to expect certain real changes in personality not indicative of test inadequacy. The possibility of real personality change is heightened by the fact that in that four-month period the subjects were recovering from tuberculosis.

Granick and Scheflen (1958) have reported a study concerning stability, internal consistency, and interscorer agreement for the Blacky Test. Their results on interscorer agreement, which ranged on the 13 cards from 58% to 95% with an average of 77.5%, are poorer than those Blum obtained, but they are still somewhat acceptable. In considering stability and temporal consistency, these investigators adopted an unorthodox approach that is not really very relevant to the 13 dimensions as used. Fortunately, Berger and Everstine (1962) have studied stability in a more direct fashion. With an interval between testings of four weeks, they obtained stability correlations on 50 male college students for the 13 dimensions that ranged from .20 to .54, with an average of .44. The stability of the dimensions seems quite modest, especially for a theory that considers significant development and change to be largely over by the time puberty is reached. The difficulty, of course, may

lie in the test rather than the theory. After all, the dimensions do have the heterogeneity and ambiguity mentioned before. And, though an analysis of internal consistency could help determine whether this is the source of the difficulty, there do not seem to be extensive studies along these lines. I suggest pushing on to consider studies of validity, keeping in mind that these dimensions hardly represent the stable characteristics envisioned by psychoanalytic theory.

First we should consider two factor-analytic studies performed on the same set of data. The data were originally obtained by Blum (1949) by administering the Blacky Test to 119 male and 90 female college students. On the basis of scores obtained on these subjects, Blum computed the intercorrelations among the dimensions, separately for men and women, and felt that he had uncovered strong support for psychoanalytic theory. But instead of going over his results and conclusions, I will give attention to two factor-analytic studies done by other investigators on Blum's data, because the statistical procedures they employed are more sophisticated than his. Both studies tried to clarify the clustering of dimensions. If the dimensions really represent peripheral characteristics, such studies will yield evidence as to whether the psychoanalytic view on the subsuming of characteristics into types is accurate (think of the second step of the ideal strategy). But an air of ambiguity permeates the enterprise because of the difficulty in determining whether the dimensions are unitary enough to represent concrete peripheral characteristics. Nonetheless, let us push on.

The first factor-analytic study was done by Neuman and Salvatore (1958) and the second by Robinson and Hendrix (1966). Neuman and Salvatore obtained six factors for men that corresponded reasonably well to the oral, anal, phallic, latency, and genital characters. But the six factors they extracted for women seemed contradictory to psychoanalytic theory. They could not stretch their conclusions to grant any more than partial confirmation to the theory of character types. Working with the same data, Robinson and Hendrix applied a factor-analytic technique deemed more sophisticated and accurate than that employed in the earlier study. The factor matrices they obtained are reproduced for men in Table 12-2 and for women in Table 12-3. The 13 dimensions appear down the side of the table and the factors obtained across the top. The terms in parentheses under the factor numbers represent the interpretation that the investigators deemed best suited to the results appearing in the body of the table. The numbers in the body of the table are correlations and the higher they are (whether positive or negative), the more the dimension involved is a defining attribute of the factor.

Considering the results Robinson and Hendrix obtained for men, it would seem that the first factor represents orality because of the high positive contribution to the factor made by oral eroticism and oral sadism. The negative contribution made by anal retentiveness adds support to this interpretation, though the positive loading of oedipal intensity is, strictly speaking, a complication. The third factor is characterized by positive loadings for oral eroticism, anal expulsiveness

and castration anxiety. This seems to represent a developmental situation that in psychoanalytic terms would span from the oral through the phallic stages and, hence, can only roughly be considered to express the anal character. Fenichel (1945), however, points to the frequency with which castration anxiety is intermingled with anal-sadistic fears; thus, there is some justification for the interpretation offered by Robinson and Hendrix. The fifth factor is characterized by positive loadings for anal expulsiveness, masturbation guilt, and sibling rivalry. Except for anal expulsiveness, contributing dimensions accurately accord with the psychoanalytic view of the phallic stage. But once again even more consistent with the results would be some conglomerate of anal and phallic character types. The second factor includes a positive loading for positive identification and negative loadings for narcissistic love object and anal retentiveness. Robinson and Hendrix suggest that this represents something like a latency character type, because the latency period is supposed to be one

TABLE 12-2   Principal Component-Varimax Analysis of 13 Blacky Dimensions for 119 Males

	FACTORS						
DIMENSIONS	I (Oral)	II (Latent)	III (Anal)	IV (Genital)	V (Phallic)	VI (Guilt)	h^2
Oral eroticism	59†	10	50*	−22	−15	−10	71
Oral sadism	75†	01	05	−32	19	14	71
Anal expulsiveness	20	04	57*	−09	54*	−16	65
Anal retentiveness	−54*	−34	04	17	−32	00	54
Oedipal intensity	79†	−30	−12	24	−09	−06	74
Masturbation guilt	−10	08	−04	17	83†	−01	70
Castration anxiety	−15	−06	91†	08	04	14	88
Positive identification	09	30†	−03	14	−08	−04	68
Sibling rivalry	18	−22	11	−08	65†	09	54
Guilt feelings	04	−07	04	01	02	97†	95
Positive ego ideal	−17	−16	−30	87†	01	−08	91
Narcissistic love object	28	−83†	03	21	−01	06	80
Anaclitic love object	−02	08	21	86†	07	−09	79

*Significant at .05 level.
†Significant at .01 level.
SOURCE: From "The Blacky Test and Psychoanalytic Theory: Another Factor-Analytic Approach to Validity," by S. A. Robinson and V. L. Hendrix, 1966, *Journal of Projective Techniques and Personality Assessment, 30.*

in which the child is trying out identifications with various adults and social roles and relinquishing the selfish loves of the phallic period. The fourth factor is characterized by positive loadings for positive ideal (or personal aspirations and values) and anaclitic love object (choice of a love object resembling the person on whom the individual depended for comfort in infancy). If you had to call this factor anything, you might conclude, in light of the other factors, that it represents the genital period. But in all seriousness, it should be recognized that the two strong positive loadings are somewhat contradictory. Finally, the sixth factor for males seems clearly expressive of guilt feelings.

The results for women (Table 12-3) are somewhat similar to those for men. The fifth factor is clearly oral, with its positive loadings for oral eroticism and oral sadism and negative loadings for sibling rivalry and positive ego ideal. The first factor is defined positively by anal expulsiveness, sibling rivalry, and oedipal intensity but shows a negative loading for anal retentiveness.

If anything, this factor seems a conglomerate of anal and phallic periods, but even in such an interpretation the negative contribution of anal retentiveness is difficult to understand. But the second factor, defined by positive loading for penis envy and narcissistic love object, does conform reasonably well to the phallic character type in women. Interestingly, no factor was obtained for women that seemed relevant to the latency period. This finding seems consistent with many psychoanalysts' belief that the latency period is a cultural artifact. Finally, the fourth factor seems to express guilt feelings.

In the results reported by Robinson and Hendrix, more so than in those of Neuman and Salvatore, there is reason to believe that the theory of character types has some empirical viability. But a note of caution is necessary, because the dimensions are probably not the bedrock, irreducible, minimally interpretive, peripheral characteristics on which the theory of character types is built. Instead, the dimensions seem to be general, perhaps rather heterogeneous, conglomerates

TABLE 12-3 Principal Component-Varimax Analysis of 13 Blacky Dimensions for 90 Females

	FACTORS					
DIMENSIONS	I (Anal)	II (Phallic)	III (Genital)	IV (Guilt)	V (Oral)	h^2
Oral eroticism	42	05	00	31	57*	60
Oral sadism	−09	−21	−21	40	54*	54*
Anal expulsiveness	83†	04	−13	03	03	71
Anal retentiveness	−73†	31	−12	11	07	66
Oedipal intensity	71	06	04	07	04	51
Masturbation guilt	16	01	−17	90†	−13	88
Penis envy	−10	72†	13	14	08	57
Positive identification	−04	−09	−08	22	−83†	76
Sibling rivalry	46	12	32	13	−59*	69
Guilt feelings	17	−12	−47	−56*	−10	59
Positive ego ideal	−19	36	74†	−17	−09	74
Narcissistic love object	09	85†	−08	−11	−12	76
Anaclitic love object	26	−27	80†	−01	−10	79

*Significant at .05 level.
† Significant at .01 level.

SOURCE: From "The Blacky Test and Psychoanalytic Theory: Another Factor-Analytic Approach to Validity," by S. A. Robinson and V. L. Hendrix, 1966, *Journal of Projective Techniques and Personality Assessment, 30.*

requiring considerable interpretation in their scoring. The results of factor analyses can be predetermined by such interpretation. If the scoring of dimensions presupposes the truth of the theory of character types, the ensuing factor analysis may be doing little more than celebrating the scorer's acumen in putting his or her belief in the theory of character types into action. Were the dimensions of the Blacky Test less general and interpretive, one could well be impressed by results showing them as grouping themselves into types in a manner consistent with psychoanalytic theory.

I shall now turn from the factor-analytic studies to research investigating the construct validity of the thirteen dimensions of the Blacky Test. Blum and Hunt (1952) have reviewed much of the early work of this nature. I shall concentrate on studies that test psychoanalytic hypotheses concerning peripheral personality.

In one such study, Aronson (1953) focuses on the Freudian theory of paranoia. He administered the Blacky Test to 30 paranoid schizophrenics, 30 nonparanoid schizophrenics, and 30 normal control subjects. The three groups were comparable in age, intelligence, occupation, religion, and status as veterans. The basis for distinguishing paranoid schizophrenics from nonparanoid schizophrenics was the presence or absence of delusions (common in paranoid people).

In the psychoanalytic theory, paranoia and schizophrenia are considered breakdown products of the anal and oral character types, respectively. Consequently, Aronson hypothesized that the paranoid schizophrenics would show greater intensity of anal retentiveness, anal expulsiveness, oral sadism, and oral eroticism than would the normal subjects. Further, the paranoid schizophrenics would be stronger than the nonparanoid schizophrenics on only anal retentiveness and anal expulsiveness. The results support his hypotheses in all instances except anal expulsiveness, indicating considerable support for the Freudian position. But Aronson also found the paranoid group as showing greater evidence of masturbation guilt, conscious attempts at denial of strong underlying castration anxiety, a consistent tendency toward feminine identification, severe superego conflicts, and a preference for narcissistic types of love-object choice. Many of these differences could not have been precisely predicted from psychoanalytic peripheral theorizing.

A number of other studies (e.g., Blum & Kaufman, 1952) investigate scores on the Blacky Test of people with certain psychological disorders. In the main, these studies are less pertinent than Aronson's for illuminating the empirical validity of Freudian peripheral theorizing. Actually, the explicit intent of these studies is often to develop, rather than test, a psychoanalytic explanation of the disorder under consideration. Such studies assume the adequacy of the test and the validity of the theory, but actually clarify neither. In what is probably the most rigorous of these studies, Linder (see Blum & Hunt, 1952) administered the Blacky Test to 67 male sexual offenders and 67 male nonsexual offenders matched for age, race, IQ, education, socioeconomic and marital status, length of sentence, and previous convictions. Analysis of the data showed that the sexual offenders were significantly higher (more disturbed) on 9 of the 13 Blacky dimensions. Although this study may provide evidence that sexual offenders are disturbed people, it does not really clarify psychoanalytic peripheral theorizing.

In a radically different study, Swanson (1951) attempted to use the Blacky Test to test certain psychoanalytic predictions about the interpersonal behavior of groups of people. Scores on the Blacky dimensions were obtained on the 20 members of each of two training groups at the National Training Laboratory for Group Development at Bethel, Maine. The aim of the members of such groups is to get to know one another and themselves more deeply through their meetings. Swanson predicted that high scores on oral sadism, anal expulsiveness, oedipal intensity, sibling rivalry, or guilt feelings would raise the total amount of a person's actual participation in permissive groups such as those at the Training Laboratory. Swanson used the pattern of a person's scores on the Blacky dimensions just mentioned to reach an overall judgment concerning the likelihood of his or her participation in the group's interaction. These judgments were then correlated to several measures of actual participation. In general, the correlations obtained in both groups were sufficiently positive to indicate that Swanson's judgments had validity. It is quite difficult, however, to see how this study bears on the validity of psychoanalytic theory except in an indirect fashion.

Adelson and Redmond (1958) offer a very pertinent study concerning the anal character type. They obtained the Blacky Test scores on anal retentiveness and anal expulsiveness for 61 college women. The hypothesis was that anal-retentive subjects should have greater ability to recall verbal material than anal-expulsive subjects. The basis for this hypothesis is clear in the Freudian belief that fixation occurs later in the anal period for retentive than for expulsive subtypes. The later the anal fixation occurs, the greater the emphasis on "holding on" rather than "letting go." Of the 61 subjects, 32 were classified as expulsives, 18 as retentives, and 11 as neutral. Subjects read two prose passages, each containing several hundred words. One passage included sexual and aggressive themes, whereas the other was innocuous. Subjects were asked to reproduce the passages immediately after presentation and again 1 week later. As you can see from Table 12-4, the retentives showed greater recall under all conditions. In general,

neutral subjects scored midway between the other two groups. Adelson and Redmond also present evidence that these differences in verbal recall cannot be accounted for by differences in intellectual capacity. This very clear and rigorous study provides strong support for the construct validity of the psychoanalytic notion of anal-expulsive and anal-retentive subtypes of the anal character.

In another study, Kline (1968) attempts to determine the relationship between obsessional traits (which express extreme anality) and characteristics of toilet training (the conditions under which an anal fixation would have occurred). He uses the Blacky Test and four obsession scales to measure anality, attempting to correlate them with information about toilet training. Although his results are ambiguous and indicate the importance of sex differences, there is some small support for the hypothesis. Tribich and Messer (1974) put 107 male students in a group situation in which the task was to judge the magnitude of apparent movement of a light. Confederates of the experimenter, with the status of authority figures, were members of the group and tried to influence the students' judgments. Students with oral characters, as measured by the Blacky Test, were positively influenced by the "authorities," whereas those who were anal reacted against the attempted

TABLE 12-4   Differences Between Expulsives and Retentives in Verbal Recall
(Expulsives, $N = 32$; Retentives, $N = 18$)

TESTS	GROUP	M	SD	t	p
Innocuous passage—immediate recall	Expulsive	19.9	12.84	2.25	.05
	Retentive	28.3	12.08		
Innocuous passage—delayed recall	Expulsive	9.9	6.00	2.60	.02
	Retentive	15.1	8.66		
Disturbing passage—immediate recall*	Expulsive	21.6	9.59	2.68	.02
	Retentive	28.7	12.29		
Disturbing passage—delayed recall*	Expulsive	11.1	5.92	3.66	.001
	Retentive	19.3	8.94		

*The mean scores for the disturbing passages refer to thought units.

SOURCE: From "Personality Differences in the Capacity for Verbal Recall," by J. Adelson and J. Redmond, 1958, *Journal of Abnormal and Social Psychology, 57.*

influence. This result appears to be solid support for Freudian peripheral theorizing.

This sampling of studies using the Blacky Test will have to suffice. Annotated bibliographies for the test are available (Schaeffer, 1968; Taulbee & Stenmark, 1968), and there is even a form for women (Robinson, 1968).

There are, of course, studies pertinent to Freudian peripheral theorizing that have not employed the Blacky Test. Although I cannot hope to review them completely, I shall try to be representative. In presenting the studies, I shall cover the various character types in their presumed developmental order.

Sarnoff (1951) reports a study concerning the defense mechanism of identification (or introjection), which is a primitive technique for avoiding anxiety generally attributed to the oral stage of development. More specifically, he focuses on identification with the aggressor, a notion found nowhere else but in Freudian theory. This defense involves becoming more like the person who is hurting you so you can avoid the anxiety associated with the threat of pain and of your own destructive anger. Sarnoff reasoned that anti-Semitism among Jews was prima facie evidence of identification with the aggressor and constructed a questionnaire to assess it. Jews receiving a high score on this questionnaire "were regarded as having taken, toward their own Jewish group, the same anti-Semitic attitudes that are expressed by majority group bigots in our society" (Sarnoff, 1951).

On the basis of this questionnaire, 100 Jewish college students were divided into two groups of 45 high in anti-Semitism and 55 low in anti-Semitism. Several personality tests were also administered to these subjects to measure the personality differences between the two groups. The results, shown in Table 12-5, are offered by Sarnoff in support of hypotheses from Freudian theory. In the study, anti-Semitic Jews (highs) were likely to be insecure, chronically fearful people who had been severely rejected by their parents. They tended to dislike themselves through having experienced parental dislike. They also hated their parents. Being unable to accept themselves, these people seemed

compelled to search for devious means of increasing their adequacy and, at the same time, fulfilling the urge to reject themselves. In Sarnoff's (1951) words, "In becoming anti-Semitic, these Jews may be vicariously appropriating the power position of the majority-group chauvinists and simultaneously achieving a vehicle for perpetuating the negative images of themselves and their parents." Although this study provides some evidence for the validity of the concept of identification with the aggressor, it does not tie down this personality characteristic to the oral stage of development.

Another defense mechanism associated with the oral stage is projection, which involves attributing to others characteristics really your own so you can remain unconscious of their presence in you and therefore be free of anxiety. Remaining alert to this precise meaning will aid you in what follows, for projection often connotes simply expressing the characteristics of one's personality in external situations, especially if they are ambiguous. This general meaning, however, is not what Freud meant.

In one relevant and intriguing study, Sears (1936) obtained from nearly 100 college fraternity men character-trait ratings of themselves and one another. The traits rated were stinginess, obstinacy, disorderliness, and bashfulness. The degree of a given trait attributed to others by a subject was compared with the amount attributed to him by the others. No clear relationships were found. But when a rough measure of insight was taken into account, it was found that, provided insight was lacking, those men who possessed more than the average degree of a trait tended to attribute more than average degrees to others. In essence, this means that projection of these character traits appeared to be a function of lack of insight. This finding is not inconsistent with the concept of projection, which includes not only the attribution of one's own characteristics to others but the debarment from consciousness of those characteristics in oneself. The latter aspect of projection may have been tapped by Sears's insight measure.

Although the study provides no information as to whether the four traits involved were

TABLE 12-5   Differences Between the Number of Highs and Lows on Each of the Personality Variables

PERSONALITY VARIABLES	NUMBER OF HIGHS*	NUMBER OF LOWS*	p[†]
Death of mother, father, and parents-as-a-group	25	13	.01
Disparaging remarks about mother	19	11	.04
Disparaging remarks about father	12	6	.05
Derogatory remarks about home and home life	8	5	.13
Fear of parental disapproval	6	2	.05
Favorable comments about mother	16	32	.09
Favorable comments about father	5	11	.15
Favorable comments about home and home life	8	19	.08
Self-negation	15	6	.01
Fear of the future	5	1	.04
Fear of rejection by others	12	5	.03
Admission of psychic stress	21	13	.05
Self-derogatory remarks	20	21	.34
Self-assertion	0	4	.05
Absence of fears	2	7	.09
Favorable remarks about the self	5	11	.15
Passivity in response to aggression	20	12	.05
Suppression of desires to retaliate against aggression	3	0	.05
Turning hostility against the self	9	4	.05
Active retaliation in response to aggression	14	31	.06

*For the variables based on the Thematic Apperception Test, these differences represent a comparison between 43 Highs and 54 Lows. Three of the 100 TAT protocols were either lost or had to be omitted from the analysis because subjects did not adhere to the instructions. All of the other differences, those based on the Sentence Completion, involved 45 Highs and 55 Lows as previously stated.

[†] Since all of our specific predictions were made on an a priori basis, which took into account the direction of the differences, only one half of the probability curve is used in determining levels of significance. The level of significance of these predicted results was obtained by reducing by one half the probabilities reported to the conventional "t" tables since these tables use both halves of the probability curves.

SOURCE: From "Identification with the Aggressor: Some Personality Correlates of Anti-Semitism Among Jews," by I. Sarnoff, 1951, *Journal of Personality, 20.*

indeed undesirable to the subjects, it is fairly safe to assume that they were, because they are generally undesirable. In addition, the traits are relevant to the psychoanalytic notions concerning psychosexual stages of development (as you noted in Chapter 3, stinginess, obstinacy, and disorderliness are anal traits, while bashfulness is either oral or phallic). The chief difficulty with this study as evidence for projection is that Sears also found that subjects very low on a trait would attribute lowness to others if insight was lacking. But theoretically, being low on an undesirable trait should not lead to projection, because there is no personal basis for conflict with the superego and subsequent guilt and anxiety. This latter finding throws into serious question the interpretation of the prior finding as projection. Of course, one could say that, for some people, an absence of these traits is a potential source of guilt from particularly peculiar early life experiences and that both findings were obtained because these kinds of people existed in the sample alongside the more usual ones. But the study provides no information with which to check this possibility, and it seems rather farfetched anyway.

Actually, the methodology Sears used has come under considerable criticism (see Holmes,

1968), because the manner in which he measured "insight" essentially forced the negative correlation that he then interpreted as evidence of projection. The subject was considered as lacking insight if his peers rated him high on a trait but he placed himself below the rating he assigned to the group. That for an equal trait score so-called low-insight subjects attributed a greater amount of that trait to other people than did so-called high-insight subjects becomes a statistical artifact of method! The negative correlation Sears reports would have been found regardless of whether or not the subject was insightful. This is because an insightful subject (who, by Sears's definition, would have given himself a higher rating than his peers) would have had to see others as low on the trait.

Rokeach (1945) attempted to replicate Sears's findings, only to discover that the correlation supporting the hypothesis of projection occurred only when the data were analyzed in the erroneous manner described above. When the data were analyzed in a fashion that did not force the predicted relationship, it did not occur. Since then, the absence of relationship has been found by several investigators, such as Lemann (1952) and Wells and Goldstein (1964). In other studies (e.g., Murstein 1956; Page & Markowitz, 1955), what appeared as evidence for projection was thrown into considerable doubt by the existence of groups in whom the attribution of traits also occurred, but with the subjects' being conscious of it.

In an intriguing attempt to demonstrate projection, Wright (1940) carefully created conditions that would provoke guilt in his subjects. A pair of toys, one preferred and the other nonpreferred, were given to 8-year-old children. Then the children were asked to give away one of the two toys to a friend. Immediately after this, they were asked which toy they thought the friend would have given away. Control-group children were asked this question without first having been asked themselves to give away one of the toys. The number of times that the friend was considered generous (giving away the preferred toy) was much lower after the conflict situation,

in which the child was forced to give away a toy, than it was under the control condition. This indicates that stinginess is projected when one feels guilty about one's own stingy thoughts.

While this study certainly seems consistent with projection as a defense, it does not demonstrate that the attribution of stinginess occurred with no conscious relationship to the subjects' own stingy thoughts. If one's own stinginess were consciously appreciated, attributing stinginess to a friend would be generalization more than defensive projection. It appears that whenever a study in this area avoids being plagued by statistical artifacts, it only manages to demonstrate that "projection" may well take place with the subject's full awareness. This problem has led Holmes (1968) to contend that simple generalization explains the phenomenon better than projection does. Here and there, studies of projection (Adler, 1967; Andersen-Baum, 1994; Cramer, 1991; Katz, Sarnoff, & McClintock, 1956; Sarnoff & Katz, 1954) have been designed in such a way that it is difficult to determine whether subjects were aware of their presumed defense. Attempting to address this problem, Duberstein and Talbot (1992) focused on subjects who failed to show oral preoccupations in their imaginative productions, finding that they idealized one or both parents. It is difficult to determine in this study whether idealization is a nondefensive recognition of good parenting, or another defensive expression of oral fixations. If the latter, then why is there little oral imagery in the imaginative productions? In light of what has been said to this point, it is difficult to know what to make of these studies. Some (e.g., Baumeister, Stillwell, & Heatherton, 1994; Laursen & Collins, 1994) have contended that a social-relational, interpersonal explanation of the findings of such studies is as compelling as the more intrapsychic approach of Freud.

I shall now turn to research on traits rather than defenses associated with the oral character. A particular oral activity, smoking, is easily measured and has received considerable research attention. This research has sought mainly to determine the nature of general differences between smokers and nonsmokers. Matarazzo and Saslow (1960) conclude from a careful review of 44 such studies that despite much speculation about the relationship between early nursing experiences and smoking, no clear-cut pattern of personality peculiar to smokers has yet emerged from the literature. Although smokers seem to be more extroverted—which sounds plausible because smoking is an oral trait—they are also more anxious than nonsmokers. In a particularly extensive study, Schubert (1959a, 1959b) tested hypotheses derived from Freud and Fenichel concerning smoking as expressions of oral fixation, only to find that the smokers among his 1500 college students showed as much evidence of being arousal or activation seekers as of being oral in character. It seems fair to conclude that if striking empirical support for the concept of oral character is to be found, it should not be sought in the literature on smoking.

More supportive of Freud's position, a study by Masling, Weiss, and Rothschild (1968) tested the hypothesis that oral-dependent people need support and approval from others. Subjects were introduced to a type of conformity experiment, invented by Asch, in which a pseudosubject actually in the experimenter's employ insists on an apparently wrong judgment of some perceptual phenomenon, such as the length of a line. The true subject may or may not conform to the confederate's erroneous response. Masling et al. accumulated 23 male undergraduates who conformed and 21 who did not. On scrutinizing their performance on the Rorschach Test, a fantasy method of assessing personality (see Chapter 9), the researchers discovered that the conforming subjects tended to show evidence of an oral character type. Also promising is the work of Cooperman and Child (1969), who utilized 115 male undergraduates to determine the relationship between aesthetic preference and food preference. Certain hypotheses they derived from psychoanalytic theory were confirmed when 8 of the 12 oral personality variables they studied correlated significantly with the aesthetic preference score. Also, Masling, O'Neill, and Katkin (1982) report that subjects judged oral on a projective test responded to interaction with an emotionally cold interviewer with increased physiological arousal (skin conductance), whereas there was no such arousal for oral subjects interacting with a warm interviewer or for nonoral subjects regardless of interviewer warmth or coldness.

Of more developmental import is a meta-analysis of studies (Bornstein, 1992) showing that dependent or oral personalities (shown in such characteristics as suggestibility, conformity, and compliance) are the result of overprotective, authoritarian parenting. In a similar vein, Cramer (1987) reports that, as measured in imaginative productions, the defense of denial was used most by preschoolers, with projection peaking a bit later in childhood. These two primarily oral defenses gave ground steadily through adolescence to the defense of identification. These observed predominances of certain defenses in certain ages are consistent with Freudian theory. So too is the demonstration (Hibbard et al., 1994) that Cramer's method of scoring defenses in imaginative productions shows that hospitalized psychiatric patients used the primitive defenses of denial and projection more than college students did.

Turning to the anal character type, we encounter another study by Sarnoff (1960), who investigated the empirical validity of the reaction formation, a cornerstone of the Freudian position on the anal character. Sarnoff reasoned that warm, accepting, loving feelings toward others are anxiety provoking because they are socially unacceptable in our crass, market-oriented society. Therefore, when such warm feelings are aroused, people who tend to use reaction formation should show an increase in cynical, critical feelings toward others. To test this hypothesis, Sarnoff gave 81 male undergraduates one of two experimental manipulations. One of these manipulations, designed to arouse strong feelings of affection, involved listening to a live presentation of a portion of William Saroyan's play *Hello Out There*. The other manipulation involved listening to a taped version of the same thing and was supposed to arouse only mild feelings of affection. Before the presentations, all subjects filled out questionnaires yielding measures of cynicism and of reaction formation. Following the play, subjects again filled out the cynicism questionnaire.

The results showed, contrary to expectations, that regardless of the strength of the tendency to use reaction formation and of the degree of affection arousal, all subjects decreased in cynicism. The subjects who tended toward reaction formation decreased in cynicism the least, but this is very meager support for the hypothesis. This study can be attacked on a number of grounds, not the least of which is the theoretically unconvincing assumption that feelings of affection are disapproved of socially. In addition, the measurement of defensive tendencies through self-description in the form of answers to questions is not really in the spirit of Freudian thinking. After all, one is not supposed to be aware of one's defenses.

Nalven (1967) compared 30 subjects who relied on repression with 30 who relied on intellectualization (a defense mechanism often associated with the anal character type) to complete a task of some complexity requiring perceptual decisions. The measurement of repressive and intellectualizing defenses was accomplished using a sentence-completion test (which primarily taps fantasy). As one would expect from psychoanalytic theory, the intellectualizers could formulate more alternatives in the decision-making task than could the repressers. Although this study certainly supports Freud's position, an important basis for deciding that subjects were repressers was their sparsity of response on the sentence-completion test. The same sparsity was looked for in the perceptual-decision task. Thus, someone of a different theoretical persuasion could insist that no more has been demonstrated than a difference in productivity between the groups. To be convincing, studies of defense mechanisms must provide some basis in their design for believing that the mechanism under consideration has indeed been aroused. But putting the findings of this study together with those on sensitizing defenses (see Chapter 10) makes the existence of such mechanisms a reasonable surmise.

Of course, there is little, if anything, in any of this research that demonstrates sensitizing defenses to be strongly associated with the anal character.

Turning from defenses to the traits of the anal character, we encounter an interesting study by Pettit (1969) concerning attitudes toward time. He constructed a time scale of 40 items with which to ascertain the ways in which time has special meaning for a person and serves to organize her or his experience. This scale was administered to 91 undergraduates along with two questionnaire measures of anality and one of spontaneity. As one would expect from Freud's position, the preoccupation with time as an organizing principle correlated positively to the measures of anality and negatively to the measure of spontaneity. While it is likely that one feature of the anality measures is concerned with time, the correlations obtained seem too high to be explained away in this fashion.

Centers (1969) tested the hypothesis that people with an anal character type would express tough attitudes in regard to the mischievous behavior of teenagers and the dependence of social-welfare recipients. A sample of 562 adults answered his attitude questionnaire and two questionnaires devised to reflect anality. Modest support is reported for the hypothesis. In a similar study, Koutrelakos (1968) tested 100 males on the Authoritarianism (F) Scale and a questionnaire concerning perceptions of their attitudes toward their fathers. As will be discussed later, the Authoritarianism Scale is an instrument in general use that Freudians would interpret as indicating the severe conscience and aggressiveness of anality. As predicted, highly authoritarian subjects perceived their fathers as more authoritarian and more similar to their ideal person than did subjects low in authoritarianism. Although both these studies provide support for the Freudian position, it must be said that the measures employed may well overlap on methodological (but not theoretical) grounds. Hence, some amount of relationship found may be spurious. In addition, the measures are sufficiently general in content to be claimed as relevant to personality theories other than Freud's.

In a review, Pollak (1979) reaches several conclusions concerning studies of the anal character. He finds little evidence for the Freudian etiological hypothesis. But there does appear to be evidence in both factor-analytic and construct validity studies for the various traits of the anal character. Once again we see some, but not complete, support for the Freudian position.

There have been few studies of the clustering of traits constituting the phallic character. Those considered relevant concern repression and were reviewed in Chapter 10. As a whole they are rather convincing, even though some of them can be strongly criticized. Two recent studies will round out the general picture presented in Chapter 10. They involve comparing subjects considered high on repression as measured by the *Marlowe-Crowne Social Desirability Scale* or the *Repression-Sensitization Scale*. Weinberger and Davidson (1994) found that repressers (by comparison with subjects who just wanted consciously to present a good image) were highly defensive whether they were instructed to be expressive or restrained in performing a social task. In addition, the repressers were more physiologically aroused under both instructions, but denied that their heart-rate elevations were related to any emotional arousal. Baumeister & Cairns (1992) found that repressers were more likely to dismiss as false the threatening feedback given to them in private, all the while working harder to counter negative impressions of them they believed others had falsely developed.

Of the studies concerning single traits, the most uniquely relevant to Freudian theory are those of castration anxiety, castration wish, and penis envy, all matters that supposedly derive their importance in the adult personality from events during the phallic stage of development. Virtually all these studies have employed fantasy measures of the various castration and envy themes. This kind of measurement clearly is appropriate, because such themes supposedly are unconscious. Blum (1949) found significantly more responses to the Blacky Test indicative of castration anxiety among men than among women, a finding that obviously supports Freudian

thinking. Schwartz (1955, 1956) devised a method of scoring the Thematic Apperception Test for castration anxiety and found that male homosexuals displayed significantly more castration anxiety than other males. In addition, men obtained higher castration anxiety scores than women. In a self-descriptive approach to measurement, Sarnoff and Corwin (1959) used a multiple-choice questionnaire on castration anxiety to show that men with high-castration scores have a significantly greater increase in fear of death than low-castration males after being exposed to sexually arousing stimuli. This finding supports Freudian thinking in that the sexually arousing stimuli should lead to guilt and fear of punishment most often in those males who experienced fixation during the phallic stage as a result of harsh punishment of their sexual desires for their mothers. Castration anxiety presumably indicates the harshness of such punishment. Intriguing though this finding is, it has required considerable interpretation and assumptions to be construed as support for Freud's position.

Finally, Hall and Van de Castle (1965) looked for evidence of castration anxiety, castration wish, and penis envy in reported dreams. Their study is particularly careful. The scoring system for castration anxiety involved such themes as difficulty with the penis, the changing of a man into a woman, and threatened or actual damage to or loss of part of the body. The criteria for castration wish were the same except that the events occurred not for the dreamer but for another person in the dream. The scoring system for penis envy included the changing of a woman into a man, admiration of man's physical characteristics, and the acquisition of male objects. As scoring dreams for such characteristics involves some interpretation, it is important to demonstrate that the scoring systems result in adequate agreement among different investigators. Hall and Van de Castle (1965) report interscorer agreement of over 95% on each of the three scoring systems. The subjects were male and female college students, who reported their recent dreams as part of a class assignment. The results of this study show that there is more evidence of castration anxiety among men than women and that women show more penis envy and castration wish than men do. The findings of this and the other studies mentioned above are quite in line with Freudian thinking concerning the phallic character type; however, there is nothing that could testify to the accuracy of the Freudian viewpoint on development.

I am at a loss concerning research relevant to the genital character type. Freudians themselves do not seem to do such research, probably because this type represents an ideal to them. There are virtually no fully genital people according to Freudians. In addition, the peripheral characteristics of the genital character are hardly peculiar to Freudian theory; hence, research concerning them would not provide vivid support for or disconfirmation of the position. Personologists not of the Freudian persuasion, particularly actualization theorists, have conducted research bearing on the kinds of emphases to be found in descriptions of the genital character. But this research is more appropriately presented elsewhere in this review.

Before concluding this section, I should mention research themes involving the development of two paper-and-pencil tests of defensiveness. Both tests involve several defenses and, hence, imply several character types. One of the tests, the *Defense Mechanism Inventory,* was introduced by Gleser and Ihilevich (1969) in an attempt to measure the relative intensity of five major groups of defenses. The test is composed of 12 brief stories (two for each of the conflict areas of authority—independence, masculinity, femininity, competition, and situation), each followed by four questions regarding the person's actions, fantasies, thoughts, and feelings in the situations involved. Five responses exemplifying the five sets of defenses are provided for each question, and people select the one most and the one least representative of their reactions. The five sets of defenses are Turning Against Object (displacement and identification with the aggressor), Projection, Principalization (intellectualization and isolation), Turning Against Self (masochism and autosadism), and Reversal (denial, reaction formation, and repression).

Although Gleser and Ihilevich indulge in a confusing tendency to relabel well-known defenses with different names, their inventory appears at face value to have much bearing on Freudian theory.

Gleser and Ihilevich report internal consistency correlations that are comparable for men and women and range from .31 to .83. Even if the two lowest (and quite unacceptable) correlations are omitted, the range is still large—from .57 to .83. These unimpressive findings suggest that at least some of the defensiveness scores are too heterogeneous as presently measured to serve as convincing empirical existence. The test fares better with regard to stability over a 1-week interval, with correlations ranging from .85 to .93 and an average of .89.

As to validity, Gleser and Ihilevich report that psychologists were quite able to match stories with conflict areas and responses to questions with defense mechanisms. So the test appears to fit the accepted beliefs of experts concerning defensiveness. It was also found that subjects who relied mainly on global defenses (Turning Against Self and Reversal) were more field dependent (unable to break up the visual field into component parts) than subjects who relied on differentiated defenses (Turning Against Object and Projection). Disagreement among psychologists arose, however, concerning the interpretation of this last finding; furthermore, its relevance to Freudian thinking is far from clear.

Gleser and Sacks (1973) report a further validational attempt in which the Defense Mechanism Inventory was administered to 85 college students after they had been exposed to a conflict situation in which they were led to believe their scholastic ability had proven deficient. Included were several measures of the effects of this conflict on mood and estimates of self-worth. In general, subjects with a tendency to defend by Turning Against Self reacted to the conflict with self-depreciation, anxiety, and depression. In contrast, subjects with a tendency to defend by Reversal but not by Turning Against Others showed no decrease in self-worth or increase in anxiety and depression. But there were some gender differences in this study, and the results are far from conclusive. Clearly, the Defense Mechanism Inventory will require more reliability and validational evidence before we can unequivocally adopt it as strong evidence for Freudian thinking.

Another test of defenses is the *Repression-Sensitization Scale* introduced by Byrne (1961b) and later revised by Byrne, Barry, and Nelson (1963). Considerable research has been done with this scale, as indicated in several reviews (e.g., Byrne, 1964; Chabot, 1973). Originally devised as a paper-and-pencil test to measure the same dimension involved in perceptual defense and vigilance, the scale is best considered as incorporating several defenses at each of its two poles. The scale is constructed out of items from the Minnesota Multiphasic Personality Inventory, and it has proven acceptable with respect to internal consistency and stability. Finally, there is Cramer's (1990) manual for the assessment of defenses from the Thematic Apperception Test stories, and the supportive validational studies it has stimulated (e.g., Hibbard, et al., 1994).

Various studies (see Byrne, 1964; Chabot, 1973) have contributed construct-validational evidence that repressers differ from sensitizers in theoretically interesting ways in such areas of functioning as self-ideal discrepancy, physical illness, free-associative sex responses to double-entendre words, effects of task familiarity on stress responses, and various cognitive skills. But some nagging problems have also emerged. For example, the high correlation between the Repression-Sensitization Scale and Welsh's anxiety factor on the Minnesota Multiphasic Personality Inventory (.97 for men, .96 for women) as reported by Gleser and Ihilevich (1969) raises serious questions as to whether defenses or merely anxiety is being measured. In addition, Chabot (1973) has amassed evidence of a number of unresolved procedural and sampling problems surrounding the Repression-Sensitization Scale and alerts us to equivocal areas, such as gender differences, in which available findings are anything but clear. It would be difficult at this time to persuasively argue that this scale provides strong empirical validation for Freudian theorizing.

Silverman (1976) has summarized an interesting series of studies that have general significance for Freudian theory. These studies tend to employ the tachistoscopic method of exposing stimuli to subjects. When the subjects respond to sexual and aggressive stimuli with physiological signs of recognition (e.g., increased sweating) but cannot yet identify the stimuli verbally (the exposure times being very short), it is assumed that the stimuli are having an unconscious effect (this kind of interpretation was discussed in terms of the first issue in Chapter 10). A number of studies conducted by Silverman and others influenced by him have shown that stimuli having this presumed unconscious effect increase signs of depression and other symptoms in subjects more than do stimuli that cause no physiological reaction or that are accurately identified verbally. There is evidence here for the undermining effect of sexual and aggressive perceptions or thoughts that lie outside of awareness.

The studies I have covered tend to support Freudian theory in a general way, sometimes falling short of the comprehensiveness and incisiveness we should expect. Although the studies tend to offer suggestive results, they also suffer from inconsistent results or methodological shortcomings.

Murray's Position

Murray (1938) pioneered the modern emphasis on empirical measurement and validation of the characteristics present in a peripheral theory of personality. He and a capable staff of personologists collected huge amounts of data relating to his list of needs (e.g., for achievement, affiliation, power, nurturance, succorance, change) on a small group of male college students. Over 6 months or so, these investigators employed all methods of measurement—self-description, fantasy, and performance ratings—toward understanding the peripheral personalities of these young men.

To read the results of this extraordinary undertaking today is to invite a mixture of awe at the pioneering zeal of this group and a definite sense of the unsophisticated manner in which the business of measurement actually went forward. Instead of ensuring sufficient objectivity to permit a use of measurement techniques that would result in high agreement by different investigators working independently, Murray instituted a diagnostic council. In this council, debate would ensue as to what was actually being observed in a subject and a conclusion reached by majority vote. Though laudably democratic, this procedure is not very objective in the scientific sense of different people being able to observe the same thing independently. It is very difficult for me to be critical, however, because I sincerely believe that Murray's was the most constructive approach that could be taken at the time. The measurement of personality had not had sufficient time and use to achieve sophistication. Murray's procedures were brave beginnings, even if his findings cannot be taken as demonstrating the empirical existence and validity of his concepts. A gauge of his influence is that some of the techniques he and his colleagues invented, such as the Thematic Apperception Test (Murray, 1943), are still very much in use.

Another gauge of his influence is that his peripheral theory has had by far the greatest impact of any on those personologists whose main function is developing tests for assessing personality. Murray's list of needs has been a ready starting point for many investigators wanting to provide a comprehensive test of peripheral characteristics. Dramatic as this fact is, however, one must be careful not to conclude prematurely that Murray's theorizing is necessarily more accurate than other personologists'. The popularity of his needs is probably as much a function of their commonsense appeal and of Murray's care in trying to define them operationally as anything else. Before concluding anything, we must see how fruitful tests built on his needs are.

A popular test influenced by Murray's thinking is the *Activities Index* of Stern (1958). This test is composed of more than 300 items describing activities for which the person is supposed to indicate preference or dislike. Embedded in the test are 30 of Murray's needs, each measured by 10 of the items. Stern gathered the original items for the test on the basis of Murray's own descriptions of the needs. He used a number of procedures, including factor analysis, to pare down the items to only those relating to needs that highly intercorrelated. The items relevant to one need also had to be relatively separate from those relevant to other needs. The resulting need measures have adequate internal consistency and stability. It can therefore be said that most of the needs postulated by Murray in his peripheral theory of personality have some claim to empirical existence.

But this conclusion needs to be qualified in certain ways. First is the disconcerting fact that a number of the need measures correlate fairly highly with one another. This could call into question whether the postulated needs truly differ. The second qualification involves the fact that Stern's test uses only self-description in the form of answers to questions. Although Murray has advocated the use of self-description in measuring needs, he has also insisted that relevant fantasy and even performance be used to obtain the most accurate picture. Stern's decision to use only self-description reflects the test developer's bias that such information is more objective and quantifiable than fantasy. If McClelland is right in presuming that self-description elicits schemata more than motives, we would expect Stern's test to fail in that it reflects culturally appropriate images of people more than accurate descriptions of their true personal goals.

Indeed, the current testing literature is replete with evidence that self-description used as a method of obtaining information about traits and motives suffers from the effects of what have been called response styles (e.g., Jackson & Messick, 1958). The most pervasive response style seems to be the tendency on the part of the test taker to respond to the items in a socially desirable fashion (e.g., Edwards, 1957). There is no guarantee whatsoever that people taking Stern's test will respond in terms of their actual personal goals rather than the goals they think are proper and socially constructive to have.

Were the Activities Index the only empirical evidence of the tangible measurability of Murray's needs, we could not conclude strongly that they have empirical reality. But there are other tests based on his needs. Though these employ the self-description format, they aim to obviate the hazard of socially desirable responding. One such test is the *Edwards Personal Preference Schedule* (Edwards, 1963). Edwards started with 15 needs drawn from Murray's list and prepared sets of items, the content of which appeared to fit each need. At first he presented these items to a group of college students in the same form Stern used—namely, as descriptions of activities they were to indicate they liked or disliked. Being alert to the problem that people, when describing personal goals, tend to respond in a socially desirable fashion, Edwards also had other people judge each item for its social desirability. He found an extremely high correlation (.87) between the frequency with which the college students indicated preference for items and their judged social desirability. As a result of this disturbing finding, Edwards adopted the *forced-*

choice format, in which he presented items not singly but in pairs, taking care to ensure that each item in a pair was similar in judged social desirability. Then respondents were asked to choose which item in each pair they preferred. Need strength was estimated by totaling the number of times each item relevant to a need was chosen. The result presumably was free of the influence of social desirability. The resulting need scores were correlated with a separate scale, developed at another time, for the purpose of measuring the strength of people's tendency to respond in a socially desirable fashion. The correlation between the need scores and socially desirable responses was quite low, indicating the success of Edwards's procedure.

Table 12-6 shows that the fifteen need measures on this test have reasonable internal consistency (split-half correlations of from .60 to .87) and stability (test-retest correlations of from

TABLE 12-6   Coefficients of Internal Consistency and Stability for the PPS Variables

	INTERNAL CONSISTENCY*	STABILITY[†]		
VARIABLE	$r_{1/}$	$r_{1/}$	Mean	SD
1. Achievement	.74	.74	14.46	4.09
2. Deference	.60	.78	12.02	3.68
3. Order	.74	.87	11.31	4.45
4. Exhibition	.61	.74	14.43	3.67
5. Autonomy	.76	.83	13.62	4.48
6. Affiliation	.70	.77	15.40	4.09
7. Intraception	.79	.86	17.00	5.60
8. Succorance	.76	.78	12.09	4.59
9. Dominance	.81	.87	15.72	5.28
10. Abasement	.84	.88	14.10	4.96
11. Nurturance	.78	.79	14.04	4.78
12. Change	.79	.83	16.17	4.88
13. Endurance	.81	.86	12.52	5.11
14. Heterosexuality	.87	.85	15.08	5.66
15. Aggression	.84	.78	11.55	4.57
Consistency score				
N	1,509	89		

*Split-half, based on 14 items against 14 items, corrected.
[†] Test and retest with one-week interval. Means and standard deviations are for first testing.
SOURCE: From *Edwards Personal Preference Schedule,* by A. L. Edwards. Copyright © 1954, 1959 by The Psychological Corporation. All rights reserved. Reproduced by permission from the manual for the Edwards Personal Preference Schedule.

.74 to .88). Table 12-7 shows that the intercorrelations of the need measures are satisfactorily low, the highest being .46 and the lowest close to .00. Later studies (e.g., Waters, 1967) have reported varying stability and internal consistency estimates, but this is to be expected when samples and testing conditions vary. In particular, evidence has accumulated that the scale scores may vary with shifts in the instructions given subjects. This, of course, is to be expected and is a problem only if the variation is too large. But evidence in at least some studies (e.g., Weigel & Frazier, 1968) indicates some stability of scores despite instructional changes. It may be reasonably concluded, then, that there is empirical evidence in Edwards's test for the existence of many of Murray's peripheral characteristics, despite the occasional study (e.g., Piedmont, McCrae, & Costa, 1992) suggesting that the test's forced-choice format may be lowering its validity.

It would still be valuable, however, to attempt measurement of the needs by looking at the person's fantasy. I say this not simply because Murray thought fantasy an important means of measuring his needs, but because Edwards's procedure may not have completely avoided socially desirable responding. Anastasi (1961) raises the possibility that the social desirability of items changes when they are paired and cites research indicating precisely this. Edwards, however, did not recheck the social desirability scale values of his statements when presented in pairs. Later research suggests that the social desirability values do change under these conditions. Not only are there significant differences in social desirability scale values of paired items, but a correlation of .88 was found between the predetermined scale values of paired items and their frequency of endorsement. Also, studies on faking indicate that scores on the Edwards Personal Preference Schedule can be deliberately altered to create more favorable impressions, especially for specific purposes. The latter possibility, of course, exists in any forced-choice test in which items are equated in terms of general social norms only. On the whole, it appears that the social desirability variable was not as fully controlled

TABLE 12-7   Intercorrelations of the Variables Measured by the PPS (N = 1509)

VARIABLE	2 Def.	3 Ord.	4 Exh.	5 Aut.	6 Aff.	7 Int.	8 Suc.	9 Dom.	10 Aba.	11 Nur.	12 Chg.	13 End.	14 Het.	15 Agg.	Consistency Score
1. Achievement	−.17	−.05	.03	.14	−.33	−.09	−.14	.19	−.28	−.30	−.14	.07	.02	.09	.10
2. Deference		.26	−.22	−.30	.08	.10	−.09	−.22	.16	.05	−.09	.22	−.28	−.31	−.12
3. Order			−.21	−.15	−.16	−.06	−.08	−.16	.02	−.16	−.18	.33	−.16	−.16	−.06
4. Exhibition				.09	−.08	−.22	−.02	.11	−.18	−.17	.12	−.27	.12	.11	.00
5. Autonomy					−.33	−.10	−.21	.07	−.26	−.36	.15	−.13	.09	.29	.11
6. Affiliation						−.01	.09	−.12	.09	.46	.06	−.15	−.21	−.33	−.04
7. Intraception							−.16	−.12	−.01	.07	−.10	.03	−.19	−.20	.06
8. Succorance								−.22	.11	.16	−.18	−.31	.07	−.01	−.05
9. Dominance									−.34	−.20	−.11	.07	−.29	−.25	−.05
10. Abasement										.23	−.11	.07	−.21	−.33	.00
11. Nurturance											−.12	−.12	−.21	−.33	.00
12. Change												−.14	−.07	−.08	.00
13. Endurance													−.27	−.22	−.06
14. Heterosexuality														.15	.01
15. Aggression															.05

in the Edwards Personal Preference Schedule as had been anticipated. (p. 516)

We can conclude that the attempts of Stern and Edwards to develop tests of peripheral personality using Murray's list of needs, especially with the corrections for socially desirable responding, present empirical evidence that Murray's needs do indeed exist in people. This conclusion is supported by a similar test devised by Jackson (1974) to be less vulnerable to response biases than the others. Whether these measured entities have the status of needs is still unclear, not simply on the rational grounds suggested by McClelland and partially agreed to by Murray—that motivational entities are best measured in fantasy productions—but also on the empirical grounds of the pervasive influence on self-description of such response styles as socially desirable responding. From McClelland's point of view, it is understandable that tendencies toward socially desirable responding are aroused by the testing procedure that requires respondents to answer questions about what they are like. This procedure is, after all, best suited to the measurement of schemata. Therefore, no more precise conclusion is possible here than that there is empirical evidence for entities having the content specified by Murray, leaving open the matter of the kind of entities they may be.

Although the means of measuring them do not solidly conform to the spirit of Murray's theorizing, these entities still could be primarily motivational in nature. And in principle, one could garner additional information relevant to an empirical conclusion on this question of motivation through a vigorous attempt to determine the construct validity of the measures. Note that this is like the third step of the ideal strategy suggested earlier. But we have little to go on in assessing construct validity. The manuals describing the tests of Edwards, Stern, and Jackson report such meager investigation of validity as to be insufficient. Since their publication, however, these tests have been used extensively in research. But rarely has the research aimed at investigating the validity of the various measures; rather, their validity has been more or

less assumed, with the aim of the research banking on the adequate measurement of the range of needs specified in the test. Thus, it is difficult to validate the status of the various measures. Nonetheless, indirect evidence suggests the probable validity of some of the needs measured on the two tests. In a representative example of a study (Bernardin & Jessor, 1957) concerning the Edwards Personal Preference Schedule, people were put through three experimental task situations requiring the explicit demonstration of dependent or independent behavior. As shown in Table 12-8, Dependents (those scoring high on the need for deference and low on the need for autonomy) relied more on others for help and approval than did Independents (people low on the need for deference and high on the need for autonomy). No relationship was found, however, between these need measures and conformity to the opinions and demands of others. This study suggests that the measures of needs for deference and autonomy on Edwards's test are sufficiently free of the influence of schemata that we can interpret them as motivational.

Other studies have attempted to compare the need scores obtained on the Edwards Personal Preference Schedule with other tests of the same needs. To a sample of 132 male and female undergraduates, Poe (1969) administered an adjective checklist and both the standard form and a normative modification of the Edwards tests. Following the validational criteria formulated by Campbell and Fiske (1959), Poe attempted to determine whether scores for a particular need agreed more closely across tests than with scores on other needs within tests. This joint criterion of convergent and discriminant validation was satisfied to a minimal extent.

In a similar study, Megargee and Parker (1968) employed first one sample of 70 adolescent delinquents and then another of 86 female Peace Corps trainees. In comparing Edwards's questionnaire test with ratings made of Thematic Apperception Test stories, they found that the thematic apperception and questionnaire methods of measuring Murray's needs cannot be considered equivalent or parallel. They contend that

TABLE 12-8 Differences Between Dependents and Independents
in Both Suggestion and Corroboration Scores

	SUGGESTION SCORE		CORROBORATION SCORE	
	Independents	Dependents	Independents	Dependents
Mean	.95	3.50	1.45	10.90
SD	1.24	2.31	1.63	7.53
H value		12.42		22.98
p level		< .01		< .01

SOURCE: From "A Construct Validation of the Edwards Personal Preference Schedule with Respect to Dependency," by A. C. Bernardin and R. A. Jessor, 1957, *Journal of Consulting Psychology*, 21.

"investigators who study these variables using one of these tests as their operational definition should be cautious in generalizing the results to the construct as operationally defined by the other instrument." At first encounter, findings such as this may well produce skepticism as to the very existence of the needs Murray has postulated. And insofar as he accepts that they should be measurable not only in fantasy but in self-description questionnaires, this skepticism is justified. But, as I will detail later, in a position such as McClelland's, which posits a strong theoretical rationale for fantasy as the only appropriate basis for assessing needs, the findings just mentioned represent little challenge. I shall therefore consider once again in this chapter whether self-descriptive tests measure motivational entities.

Erikson's Position

Erikson's theorizing has stimulated a fair amount of research. Most of it, however, is not really relevant here, for either of two reasons. For one, you find research concentrating on childhood and adolescence; however, adulthood matters most here. For another, you will find studies that attempt to tie together a mass of findings by referring in some vague, post hoc fashion to Erikson's peripheral theorizing. This is a far cry from planning a study for the purpose of testing the empirical adequacy of his position. For a study to be valuable here, it would at least have to try to measure the subject's status with respect to the psychosocial stages of development and then apply this information to an understanding of his or her adult functioning. Such studies regarding Erikson are few.

Certainly the studies relevant to the Freudian position on peripheral personality are also appropriate here. To be sure, Erikson's theorizing is less biologically oriented, even for the childhood years. But the Freudian conceptualization of oral, anal, and phallic character types resembles the types covered by Erikson in the first three stages of human development. Erikson's position, then, receives the same general but somewhat unincisive support that I found for Freud's position. But Erikson's unique contribution to peripheral theorizing concerns adolescence and adulthood. Therefore, only with empirical support for these aspects of his position can we seriously demonstrate the fruitfulness of his position.

Of the few studies available, I shall review several that are particularly sound and relevant. The first, done by Peck and Havighurst (1960), has the advantage of comprehensiveness. It followed the character development of youngsters from ages 10 to 17. The traits or groups of traits studied showed consistent development during this period such that the youngsters tended to keep their rank order in the group. This suggests that whatever determined the rank order in the first place must have occurred sometime before 10 years of age. Fortunately, parental behavior that might have set the youngsters' traits had been examined three years before the beginning of the study. Meaningful relationships were obtained between themes of parental behavior and certain traits in the youngsters. Ego strength and moral stability in the youngsters were most closely related to mutual trust and consistency within the family. Superego strength was most highly related to parental consistency, and friendliness to familial trust and democracy. A pattern of hostility and guilt in the youngsters was highly related to parental behaviors displaying severe discipline, lack of trust, and lack of democracy. Apparently, if children receive trust, warmth, and love from their parents, and if they are permitted to make their own choices, they will appear more psychologically vigorous *and* affluent than if they experience the opposite parental attitudes. This study suggests the empirical validity of Erikson's idea that the first two stages of the person involve trust versus mistrust and autonomy versus shame and doubt.

In contrast to this broad, somewhat vague study with many loose ends, a study by Bronson (1959) concerns itself with the period of adolescence designated by Erikson as relevant to the development of firm identity versus role diffusion. Bronson attempted to determine whether a group of peripheral characteristics, referring at one pole to a firm sense of identity and at the other to identity diffusion, had actual empirical existence. Starting with a sensitive reading of Erikson's (1956) descriptions of identity and diffusion, Bronson decided on four such characteristics for measurement: (1) to be certain or uncertain that there is a relationship between one's past and current notions of oneself, (2) to show a low or high degree of internal tension or anxiety, (3) to be certain or uncertain about what one's dominant personal characteristics are, and (4) to have stable or fluctuating feelings about oneself. Bronson correctly hypothesized that significant positive intercorrelation among these bipolar characteristics would constitute support for Erikson's conceptualization of the fifth stage of development.

The subjects were 46 college students, mainly female. Bronson measured the first two characteristics through investigators' ratings of the subjects' behavior during a 20-minute interview. The investigators were three trained clinical psychologists, and the average of their ratings was used as the data. A self-descriptive procedure used to measure the final two characteristics was repeated after a 4-week interval to determine the fourth characteristic. As can be seen in Table 12-9, the correlations among the four measures ranged from .47 to .71, all highly significant from a statistical point of view. Apparently there are

TABLE 12-9   Correlations Among Measures Relating to Aspects of Identity Diffusion

	1 CONTINUITY WITH PAST	2 FREEDOM FROM ANXIETY	3 CERTAINTY OF SELF-CONCEPTION
1. Continuity with the past (interview rating)	—		
2. Freedom from anxiety (interview rating)	.59†	—	
3. Certainty of self-conception (semantic differential measure)	.71†	.47*	—
4. Temporal stability of self-rating (semantic differential measure)	.53*	.47*	.54†

Note: $N = 18$ for the correlations involving the interview measures; $N = 46$ for the remaining value.
*$p < .05$, two-tailed test.   †$p < .01$, two-tailed test.
Source: From "Identity Diffusion in Late Adolescents," by G. W. Bronson, 1959,
Journal of Abnormal and Social Psychology, 59.

some adolescents who are anxious, do not perceive a relationship between who they are now and who they were before, are not sure what their dominant attributes are, and change their minds about these matters as well. These people show identity diffusion. That some adolescents have a firm sense of identity is shown by the existence of a type with the opposite characteristics.

Other studies provide further support for Erikson's thinking on ego identity. Tobacyk (1981) reports that subjects with a stable identity show less mood variability than do subjects with ego diffusion. In a similar vein, Rappaport, Enrich, and Wilson (1985) found that subjects showing strong ego identity think more in terms of the future than do ego-diffuse subjects. Both findings definitely implicate Erikson's theorizing.

In another relevant study, Yufit (1969) attempted to determine whether the behavioral expressions of people classifiable as intimate relaters differed from those classifiable as isolates. You will recall that intimacy versus isolation is the sixth of Erikson's eight stages. A large battery of paper-and-pencil tests plus interviews were collected on 61 undergraduates, who were classified as intimates, isolates, or controls (i.e., neither one nor the other). Complex and sometimes intuitive scoring procedures were employed on interviews and other tests. Then the data were factor analyzed, with the emerging factors suggesting the value of classifying people as intimates and isolates.

In an unusual study employing fairly rigorous methods, Waterman, Buebel, and Waterman (1970) address Erikson's hypothesis that a positive outcome in any stage of development is rendered more likely by positive outcomes in earlier stages. In the first part of their study, Waterman et al. employed a questionnaire, the *Internal-External Locus of Control Scale* (James, 1957), concerning whether one believes the events of one's life are determined personally or by force of external circumstance, as an index of whether autonomy or shame and doubt had been the outcome of the second stage of development. They also used questionnaire methods to assess whether trust or distrust had taken place in the first stages. Their dependent variable

was outcome in the identity-versus-role-diffusion stage, which they also measured via questionnaire. As predicted, identity went along with internal locus of control (autonomy) and role diffusion with external locus of control (shame and doubt). But the hypothesized relationships linking identity with trust and role diffusion with distrust did not occur. In the second part of their study, these investigators employed a self-concept measure to test the predicted relationships. This procedure produced more consistent support for Erikson's view. In this part of the study, however, one source of data was employed to measure several characteristics, raising the possibility that the relationships were somewhat spurious reflections of overlap of method. In a similar vein, Tesch and Whitbourne (1982) report that young adults who show adequate ego identity (versus diffusion) are also likely to show intimacy (versus isolation).

Constantinople (1969) developed a 60-item self-rating scale called the *Inventory of Psychosocial Development*. This scale was based methodologically on a previous technique offered by Wessman and Ricks (1966) and theoretically on Erikson's stages. Constantinople reports a median stability correlation of .70 on 150 subjects with a 6-week interval between testings. Although its reliability is by no means overwhelming, it is sufficient to entertain the notion that this scale measures successful and unsuccessful development at the stages of trust versus mistrust, initiative versus guilty functioning, autonomy versus shame and doubt, industry versus inferiority, identity versus role diffusion, and intimacy versus isolation. Information concerning the validity of this scale is slowly developing. In a particularly relevant study, Reimanis (1974) reasoned that unsuccessful resolution of conflicts in psychosocial development should give rise to feelings of anomie, or social disorganization. To test this prediction, he administered both the Inventory of Psychosocial Development and a commonly used anomie scale to two samples (100 male veterans and 141 male and female students). Table 12-10 shows the resulting correlations. As expected, unsuccessful psychological development tends to be associated

TABLE 12-10 Correlations Between Anomie and the Inventory of Psychosocial Development

INVENTORY OF PSYCHOSOCIAL DEVELOPMENT ITEM	SROLE SCALE MEASUREMENT OF ANOMIE		
	Veterans Administration Members	College Males	College Females
Basic trust	−.17	−.17	−.28*
Mistrust	.31*	.21	.25*
Initiative	−.08	−.05	−.36*
Guilt	.31*	.40*	.25*
Autonomy	−.14	.26	−.14
Shame and doubt	.28*	.40*	.13
Industry	−.17	.06	−.36*
Inferiority	.16	.44*	.29*
Identification	−.10	−.14	−.35*
Role diffusion	.24	.43*	.22*
Intimacy	−.06	−.24	−.28*
Isolation	.42	.29*	.16

Note: Veterans Administration members, $N = 74$; college males, $N = 55$; college females, $N = 86$.
*$p < .05$.
SOURCE: Adapted from "Psychological Development, Anomie, and Mood," by G. Reimanis, 1974, *Journal of Personality and Social Psychology, 29.*

with anomie, whereas successful psychosocial development tends not to be. These findings are similar to those of Constantinople (1969), who found successful development to be associated with happiness.

Marcia (1966) has elaborated on Erikson's stage of ego identity versus role diffusion, which is certainly the most heavily emphasized period. According to Marcia, it is possible to distinguish no fewer than five orientations in Erikson's thinking about this period: identity achievement (people who have experienced the crisis and are committed to an occupation and an ideology), moratorium (people currently in the crisis with only vague commitments to occupation and ideology), foreclosure (people who, while committed to an occupation and ideology, seem to have experienced no crisis, their commitments being largely parentally determined), identity diffusion (people who may or may not have experienced the crisis, but who exhibit no commitment), and alienated achievement (people who have experienced the crisis and exhibit no commitment but have worked out an ideology condemning the

social system). Determination of a subject's identity status is made by rating his or her responses to a standardized interview according to rules provided by Marcia (1966). Interscorer agreement on ratings has hovered between 80% and 90% in several studies (e.g., Orlofsky, Marcia, & Lesser, 1973; Toder & Marcia, 1973). Apparently no internal consistency or stability information is available, so we cannot be sure that the statuses have solid empirical support.

Orlofsky et al. (1973) studied the relationship of the various identity statuses described above to measures of intimacy, isolation, social desirability, affiliation, and heterosexuality in an attempt to determine whether difficulties in identity would jeopardize later development. As expected from Erikson's theorizing, foreclosure and identity-diffusion subjects had the most superficial and stereotyped interpersonal relationships. Moratorium subjects were the most variable. And whereas identity-achievement subjects were characterized by social intimacy rather than isolation, it was actually the alienated achievement subjects who were most marked in this regard. Though the last finding is a bit surprising, the investigators reasoned that the capability of alienated-achievement subjects indicates that they have forgone the identity crisis in favor of the intimacy crisis. This is an intriguing notion, but not one readily derivable from Erikson's present theorizing.

Toder and Marcia (1973) studied the role of identity status in the response to conformity pressure by placing 64 female college students into a task situation in which confederates of the researchers would attempt to mislead the subjects in the judgments they were asked to make. Women with identity statuses regarded as stable (achievement and foreclosure) conformed to the pressure less than did those with unstable statuses (moratorium and diffusion). While not unequivocally supportive of Eriksonian thinking, this and the previous study represent a beginning that bears further attention.

In a psychobiographical study, Franz (1995) analyzed the work of a British female fiction writer, and found the greatest prevalence of self-identity themes when she was 20–21, and intimacy and generativity themes when she was 30–31. This is consistent with Erikson's ordering of the identity versus role diffusion, intimacy versus isolation, and generativity versus stagnation stages of development. Taking another implication of Erikson's theory, Tesch & Cameron (1987) show that only those persons who can manage being open to their experience go on to solid ego identity development. There are still other studies appearing (e.g., Berzonsky, 1992; Blasi & Milton, 1991; Novy, Frankiewicz, Francis, & Liberman, 1994; White, 1985) which have been stimulated by Eriksonian theory in a general way, but are not specifically relevant enough to constitute a test of that theory.

The studies I have reviewed suggest the fruitfulness of Erikson's peripheral theorizing. But more carefully planned work will have to be conducted before the position can be comprehensively evaluated from an empirical standpoint. I might mention that some investigators (e.g., Neugarten, 1964) especially concerned with the aging process believe Erikson's emphasis on such conflicts of maturity as ego integrity versus despair to be very helpful in ordering research findings dealing with the problems of old people. There are several studies charting the increase in depression as age advances (e.g., Grant, 1969; Lehr & Rudinger, 1969) and the possibility that a commitment to useful work may stem the tide (e.g., Rybak, Sadnavitch, & Mason, 1968). In general, however, these studies do not attempt to measure ego integrity versus despair so much as use it as an explanatory construct.

The Object-Relations Position

In its peripheral theorizing, the object-relations position tends to reinterpret and recombine the Freudian character types. As such, the preceding discussion of research is somewhat relevant here, too. But there are also studies sufficiently specific to the greater reliance in object-relations theorizing on early parent-child relationships to warrant mention here. For example, Renken, Egeland, Marvinney, Mangelsdorf, and Stroufe (1989) show that an early history of insecure parental attachment, hostile parental care, and stressful early life circumstances were all positive predictors of elementary-school aggressiveness or passive withdrawal. Taking a different approach, van Ijzendoorn (1995) did a meta-analysis of studies that used the *Adult Attachment Interview* in obtaining information from adult subjects about both their interactions with others and their early childhood interactions with their parents. Although it is difficult to determine the direction of causality with such an approach, the results show that those adults showing adequate attachment to others reported similarly adequate attachment to their parents. Classifying subjects into secure, avoidant, and anxious-ambivalent attachment styles, Mikulincer and Orbach (1995) found that the first of these groups reported moderate defensiveness and low anxiety and had easy access to negative memories, while the second of these groups reported just the opposite. The anxious-ambivalent group could not repress negative emotions and had easy access to negative memories but could not deal with them effectively. Studies such as these are generally consistent with Bowlby's notions of object relations, though some come closer to actually testing hypotheses than do others.

The primary emphasis of object-relations approaches is on psychopathology, however, and as such falls largely outside the scope of this discussion. There is, however, a body of promising research developing here. For example, Freedenfeld, Ornduff, and Kelsey (1995) scored the thematic apperception stories of a group of physically abused children on scales of social cognition and object relations; then they compared these scores to those of a group of mentally disturbed but not physically abused children of comparable age. Results show less adequate object relations for the abused group (e.g., less capacity for emotional investment in interpersonal relations and moral standards; less accurate, complex, and logical attributions of causality in understanding human interactions). Earlier, Ornduff, Freedenfeld, Kelsey, and Critelli (1994) reported, using similar measures, that the object relations of a group of sexually abused young women was similarly less adequate when compared to a group with emotional disorders and of similar age who had not experienced sexual abuse. Because child abuse is a cardinal sign of poor parental relationships, these studies generally support the object-relations position. Although less relevant to hypothesis testing, other studies (e.g., Rosenberg, Blatt, Oxman, McHugo, & Ford, 1994; Segal, Westen, Lohr, & Silk (1993) are appearing that provide methods in thematic apperception for evaluating the adequacy of object relations.

Kohut's and Berne's Positions

Because Kohut's and Berne's positions are sufficiently similar to those of object-relations theorists, the research covered in the preceding section lends some general support here. In addition, some studies particularly relevant to Kohut's position exist, though Berne's position appears to have generated little systematic research specific to it. Specifically, some researchers have taken up Kohut's emphasis on narcissistic personality and behavior disorders. For example, Buss and Chiodo (1991) have amassed a good deal of evidence in validating the *Narcissistic Personality Inventory,* showing that this disorder does seem to exist. In addition, Raskin, Novacek, and Hogan (1991) found, as expected, that narcissistic subjects pursued feelings of self-esteem by harboring images of grandiosity and pursuing social approval, much more than less narcissistic subjects did. Also, Raskin and Shaw (1988) report that narcissists used more personal pronouns in making a statement. In a particularly convincing study of three types of narcissism, Wink (1992) studied women from their college to midlife years. Results showed that hypersensitive narcissists declined in adequacy of career and family life from their 20s to age 43, whereas willful narcissists showed little change, and autonomous narcissists actually showed some positive personality growth. This study suggests the value of refining narcissism theory into subtypes. Needless to say, it is too early to tell how well careful research will support Kohut's overall position, but an interesting start has been made.

Rank's Position

Although Rank's peripheral personality types are clearly delineated, his theorizing has engendered scant research. This may be due to Rank's unpopularity with psychologists, who perform empirical research on a regular basis. Nonetheless, it is by no means true that Rank's position has been insufficiently pruned and developed to warrant the attempt at empirical analysis.

There is one large-scale research program that indirectly suggests the empirical promise of Rank's peripheral theorizing. MacKinnon (1965) conducted a complicated study of creativity in architects. Admittedly at a loss for a theory that would pull together his numerous findings in a coherent fashion, MacKinnon rediscovered Rank and found him very useful. MacKinnon felt that his creative architects displayed the acceptance of their own individuality coupled with the interest in and involvement with other people that Rank considered so characteristic of the type he called the artist. MacKinnon's ordinary architects seemed much like Rank's average persons, with their emphasis on conformity and mediocrity. Finally, MacKinnon even found an intermediate group of respected, productive, but not highly creative architects who resembled Rank's descriptions of the neurotic type, replete with a commitment to personal individuality without willingness to risk rejection.

Helson (1973a; 1973b) reports parallel studies focusing on the personalities of male and female creative writers. From interviews with the writers and various ratings of their works, she has abstracted, through cluster analysis, personality types reminiscent of Rank's artist, neurotic, and average person. The most creative of the writers tended to display the artist's temperament and lifestyle.

There are also a few studies that attempt to evaluate Bakan's constructs of agency and communion. Agency is sufficiently similar to the Rankian fear of death, and communion to the fear of life, that these studies are of interest here. In one of them, Brown and Marks (1969) administered a questionnaire concerning these two tendencies to 150 maladjusted subjects and 150 normal subjects, with the intent of determining whether unmitigated agency was higher in the former group, as Bakan would expect. The results provide some support for this expectation.

Carlson (1971a) studied sex differences in agency and communion in two ways. The first involved obtaining from 18 male and 23 female undergraduate subjects descriptions of seven remembered instances of intense emotion that they considered important. The instances were rated by judges as being agentic, communal, or mixed, and the interscorer agreement was a high 93%. As Bakan would expect, 60% of the men's responses were coded agentic as compared with only 40% of women's responses. Also, when each subject was classified as either agentic or communal on the basis of his or her responses, 10 of the 14 men emerged as agentic as compared with only 5 of the 20 women (this finding has statistical significance). It was also possible to determine whether "unmitigated agency" represents something undesirable (as Bakan contends) by determining whether agentic responses

tended to be unpleasant emotions (e.g., fear, anger) and communal responses pleasant emotions (e.g., joy, love). The results support this contention.

Carlson's second procedure was a bibliographic study in which she employed data already collected by others for other purposes. She looked at 100 studies in which differences between men and women could have been found, with a view toward determining whether such differences conformed to Bakan's general views on agency and communion. Although her results overwhelmingly support those views, they must be taken with a grain of salt, because it may be that the investigators who originally collected the data were already biased toward Bakan.

Very little rigorous research relevant to Rankian thought remains. Further, what has been reviewed tends either to end by recognizing the utility of Rank's conception of types rather than beginning by testing it or to involve another, though admittedly related, theorist. It is premature, therefore, to evaluate Rank's peripheral theorizing empirically, though there are some interesting leads to be followed.

Perls's Position

At this time, there is essentially no peripheral statement in Perls's theorizing. Needless to say, no research has been conducted with individual emphases of this position in mind, nor is it possible to construe research from other traditions as relevant.

Jung's Position

Believers in Jung's theory do not themselves seem to do much research. But others have performed intriguing studies. Notable among them is Stephenson's (1950) work, which considers not only extroversion versus introversion and the thinking, feeling, sensing, and intuiting modes but the consciousness versus unconsciousness of these characteristics. He considered the 16 combinations of these aspects of personality that would be of interest to Jung (e.g., conscious-thinking introvert, unconscious-intuitive extrovert) and set about finding descriptions of them in Jung's writings. He selected five descriptive sentences for each of the 16 combinations, which led to a pool of 20 descriptive sentences for each mode, 40 for each level of consciousness, and 40 each for introversion and extroversion. This approach is of special interest because it employs Jung's own words in measuring the peripheral considerations he is defining.

Armed with these descriptive sentences, how does one measure a subject's peripheral personality? Stephenson had each sentence written on a card and asked subjects to determine for each statement whether it applied to them (1) very definitely, (2) not at all, or (3) somewhere in between. The subject did this by sorting the cards into the three relevant piles. This technique came to be known as the *Q-sort*. When subjects are done, it is possible to determine, by counting the sorted cards, to what degree they are introverted, extroverted, conscious, thinking, and so forth. The Q-sort procedure is extremely flexible in that it is possible for subjects to describe not only themselves but others, if so instructed.

Stephenson chose for study Jung's contention that differences in personality type cause misunderstandings among people. For data, Stephenson described himself by a Q-sort and then had several judges supposedly familiar with him describe him by the same procedure. In addition, the judges described themselves. By Stephenson's own Q-sort, he was an extrovert. Five of the judges were introverts by their self-sort, and their Q-sort of him correlated with his own: .46, .45, .61, .59, and .61, for an average of .54. Two of the judges were extroverts, and their Q-sorts of him correlated with his own: .47 and .40, for an average of .44. Contrary to what Jung would have expected, the extroverts were certainly not superior to introverts in perceiving an extrovert. This conclusion is strengthened by evidence that the extroverted judges were drawing on their own personality characteristics to a much greater degree than the introverts in attempting to describe Stephenson. Correlations between judges' self-sorts and their sorts of Stephenson were, on the average, .23 for the introverts and .50 for the extroverts. Unfortunately, this study does not seem to have been followed up, and it employed a very small sample. Nonetheless, it does raise questions as to whether differing personality types misunderstand one another.

Actually, the introversion-extroversion dimension has led to considerable research, but with neither the procedure nor the hypothesis presented above. The work I shall now describe was inspired by Eysenck (1947), whose personality questionnaire, called first the *Maudsley* and now the *Eysenck Personality Inventory,* was devised to measure not only introversion-extroversion but neuroticism as well. Many of the studies relevant to the Jungian types were actually done by followers of Eysenck. In addition, Cattell (Cattell & Stice, 1957), in his *16 Personality Factor Questionnaire* (mentioned earlier), found evidence for a first-order factor of introversion-extroversion and a second-order factor that he thought came even closer to this Jungian concept. The studies I will review have, in the main, employed one or the other of these measures.

First, I shall consider works directed toward the adequacy of these measures. Marshall (1967), though he reports no new data of his own, cites existing evidence for the validity of Cattell's first- and second-order factors of introversion-extroversion as measures of Jung's distinction of the same name. Once this correspondence is established, the construct validation work on Cattell's factors is relevant to Jung's theory as well. On the average (Cattell, 1957), introversion is high among researchers, artists, and planning executives, as well as in creative workers in both art and science. In contrast, extroversion is high in mechanical occupations (e.g., engineers) and those requiring alertness (e.g., cooks, firefighters). Among teamsters, those high in introversion are accident-prone. Introversion is also slightly correlated with certain psychopathological symptoms, particularly depressive reactions. Finally, women are higher than men in introversion, though there is no change in the average value of this characteristic over the age range of 16 to 60 years. As you would expect, the second-order factor of introversion-extroversion operates similarly to the first-order factor.

Investigators have also explored the possible relationship between the introversion-extroversion scales offered by Cattell and by Eysenck. Crookes and Pearson (1970) compared scores on the two procedures obtained from 60 maladjusted subjects. Correlations between the separate measures of introversion-extroversion "are all very similar and quite substantial."

Several normative studies suggest that more needs to be known about the meaning of the questions and testing situations used for both these tests. For example, McQuaid (1967) reports on the basis of a sample of 1733 Scottish subjects compared with available U.S. norms for Cattell's measure that there is a definite trend toward greater extroversion among Americans. Salas (1967) and Skinner, Howarth, and Browne (1970) report that Eysenck's measure of introversion-extroversion can be shifted by instructional set. When subjects are asked to simulate a "nice personality," extroversion scores go up, with the opposite true when they are asked to fake being "bad." It is at present difficult to determine how much of a problem is involved.

Eysenck's measure does seem to have some validity in terms of subjects' self-description. Kramer (1969) administered the measure to 242 undergraduates who previously had rated themselves for (1) how extroverted they felt they really were, (2) how extroverted they felt they appeared to others, and (3) the ideal amount of extroversion one should have. The first two ratings correlated with Eysenck's measure of extroversion—.46 and .48, respectively. The 243 undergraduates used by Harrison and McLaughlin (1969) first took Eysenck's measure and then were read descriptions of the typical introvert and extrovert. Following this, they rated themselves on these two dimensions. Introversion-extroversion scores correlated .72 with the self-ratings of the same characteristics. It would seem that measures such as Eysenck's and, for that matter, Cattell's provide convenient ways of determining a person's level of introversion and extroversion.

The remaining studies to be discussed here concern the relationship between introversion-extroversion and various behaviors other than self-description. As Carrigan (1960) indicates, the body of research involved has produced ambiguous and even contradictory results. Some of this may be a function of the extreme generality of the theorizing behind introversion-extroversion. This generality has permitted investigators to work with particular corners of the theorizing that may not coincide with what other investigators are doing. But it also may be that other variables moderate the effect of introversion-extroversion such that its relationship to behavior is clear only when they are controlled. Wallach and Gahm (1960) introduced the use of moderator variables to good advantage, and their approach has been adopted by some investigators working with introversion-extroversion.

Taft (1967) attempted to determine the effects of introversion-extroversion on the expressive behavior involved in writing. He used 86 undergraduates, who took Eysenck's test and also gave a sample of handwriting. It was found that extroverts wrote in either a larger or a smaller hand than introverts but that to understand which it would be, one had to take a subject's anxiety or neuroticism level into account. Extroverts low in neuroticism wrote the largest letters and extroverts high in neuroticism the smallest. Geen (1984) permitted subjects to determine the level of background noise they would experience while performing a task. As expected, it was found that extroverts preferred more noise than introverts. When Graziano, Rahe, and Feldesman (1985) had their subjects play a competitive game, they found that introverts disliked the game but remembered their opponents' traits better than those of their teammates. This pattern was not found in extroverts. Heaton and Kruglanski (1991) found that, under time pressure to reach a conclusion about people, introverts reached decisions without waiting for additional information more than extroverts did. Further, Amirkhan, Risinger, and Swickert (1995) found extroversion to lead to coping with naturally occurring stressors by seeking social support. The management of one's own affairs appears to be better for thinking types than for intuiting or sensing types on the *Myers-Briggs Type Indicator,* a questionnaire specially devised to yield information on both Jung's introversion-extroversion dimension and the four modes of thought (Williams, Verble, Price, & Layne, 1995). Such results are generally consistent with Jungian thinking.

Some studies bear on the affiliative behavior of introverts and extroverts. On the basis of Jung's theorizing, Bieler (1966) hypothesized that extroverted persons should prefer paintings in which humans are present and introverts paintings without humans. When he employed Eysenck's test, he discovered that to make sense out of his data, he had to use anxiety or neuroticism level as a moderator variable. He found that extroverts low in neuroticism indeed preferred paintings including people and that introverts low in neuroticism preferred paintings devoid of people. But there was no difference between highly neurotic introverts and extroverts.

Shapiro and Alexander (1969) did a careful investigation following Bieler's lead. They chose as their measure of introversion-extroversion the Myers-Briggs-Type Indicator (Myers, 1962). The final sample was 130 undergraduates, all of whom not only took the Myers-Briggs Type Indicator but also were led to believe that they were to receive electric shocks. Anxiety was strongly aroused in those subjects who expected the shocks to be painful and only minimally aroused in others who were told that the shocks would be mild. They were also told that there would be a brief waiting period before the shocks, during which they could elect to either talk with other subjects or remain alone. Choosing to be with others was considered evidence of affiliative behavior. Several checks on the effectiveness of the procedure for arousing anxiety, carried out following the experiment, yielded positive results.

The principal results concerning the effects of introversion and extroversion on affiliative behavior moderated by anxiety appear in Table 12-11. As you can see, highly anxious extroverts showed the strongest affiliation tendencies, whereas highly anxious introverts showed the weakest. This difference was statistically significant. But

TABLE 12-11 Relation of Induced Anxiety and Extroversion-Introversion to Intensity of Affiliation for Males*

	I		E	
	Mean	N	Mean	N
High anxiety	−4.80	(25)	4.42	(21)
Low anxiety	3.36	(13)	1.18	(11)

Note: The higher the score, the higher the affiliation tendency. Isolation scores subtracted from affiliation scores for intensity. Means collapsed across birth order.
*Interaction: (Anxiety $\times$ EI)$F = 4.9$, $df = 1.62$; $p = .03$.
SOURCE: From "Extroversion-Introversion, Affiliation, and Anxiety," by K. J. Shapiro and I. E. Alexander, 1969, *Journal of Personality, 37.* Copyright © 1969 by Duke University Press. Reprinted by permission.

the difference between introverts and extroverts low in anxiety was not large enough to achieve significance. The last two studies taken together suggest that the potential differences between introverts and extroverts in affiliative behavior are actualized only in anxiety-producing circumstances or when neuroticism exists. Perhaps, then, neuroticism is a chronic state of anxiety.

Many other studies utilizing Eysenck's questionnaire have considered various aspects of affiliative behavior. For example, Brown and Hendrick (1971) found extroverts to be generally more popular because they were seen as more interesting, warm, and influential than introverts. This would seem to go along with findings that extroverts talk more and sooner in an interview situation than do introverts, but caution is necessary, since several studies have failed to replicate this finding (see Wilson, 1977). But the notion that extroverts are more socially oriented seems to persist. For example, Eysenck (1976) found extroverts reporting more sexual behavior and being more permissive in that regard than introverts. But results of many studies concerning whether extroverts are more suggestible than introverts have yielded conflicting results (see Wilson, 1977). What does appear clear, however, is that extroverts are more field dependent than introverts (Fine & Danforth,

1975); that is, extroverts are less able to discard the cues coming from background characteristics of the visual field in attempting to discern something in an independent fashion.

In a particularly interesting study, Duckworth (1975) tests the notion that introverts, being more sensitive in general, should be better able than extroverts to judge the feelings of others. He employed 36 married couples, split into experimental and control groups. The experimental group was subjected to emotionally provocative disagreements. Then both groups were asked to judge the vocally expressed feeling of their spouses. The introverts indeed judged more accurately, despite having been subjected to the disagreements, as long as they were also low in anxiety. When subjects were high in anxiety, there was no difference between introverts and extroverts.

Turning from manifestly social behaviors, we find evidence (Shaw & Sichel, 1971) that when driving, extroverts take more risks and have more accidents than introverts. In intellectual performance (Wankowski, 1973), introverts are superior in long-term memory tasks and get better grades, even though there is no difference in general intelligence between them and extroverts. But extroverts benefit more from "discovery learning" programs, which are informal, spontaneous, individualistic, and social compared with more traditional programs (Leith, 1974).

Before turning to other matters, I should mention a group of studies exploring the origins of introversion-extroversion. These studies employ one or more of the measuring instruments for introversion-extroversion already mentioned and focus either on parent-child relations or on heredity. The most consistent conclusion is that accepting, loving, positive parents frequently have extroverted children, whereas rejecting, cold, negative parents have introverted children (see Siegelman, 1968). Studies attempting to determine the relationship between birth order and introversion-extroversion differences have yielded contradictory results (see Siegelman, 1968). Finally, there seems clear evidence of hereditary differences in introversion-extroversion from studies of identical and fraternal twins, and these differences have been shown to persist over time (see Wilson, 1977). Because Jung's position concerning the origins of introversion-extroversion is not clear, it is difficult to determine what role these studies should have in evaluating his theory.

Carlson and Levy (1973) report an intriguing set of studies in which predictions concern the effect of Jungian personality types on memory, social perception, and social action. The Myers-Briggs Type Indicator was taken by all the female college students serving as subjects. As predicted, the results of the first study showed that introverted-thinking types performed best on a memory task involving impersonal stimuli (numbers), whereas extroverted-feeling types performed best when the stimuli were social and emotionally toned (faces with various expressions). The second study replicated the first, using a task that was comparable in structure for both types of subjects. The task in the third study was to interpret (rather than merely remember) emotions from facial expressions. A series of pictures of the same person, each showing a different emotional expression, were shown to subjects (the emotional expressions had previously been labeled with a high level of agreement among 100 judges). Results showed that intuitive-feeling types were significantly more accurate in interpreting emotional expressions than were sensing-thinking types, a finding predicted by Jung. In the final study, the predicted tendency for social service volunteers to be extroverted-intuitive types was confirmed by comparing the Myers-Briggs Type Indicator scores of such volunteers with a control group.

Also using the Myers-Briggs Type Indicator, Hanewitz (1978) collected personality profiles over four years on 1282 veterans and police recruits, 96 undergraduate social work students, 88 public-school teachers, and 946 dental students. For police recruits, the usual type was sensing-thinking, coupled most often with extroversion but also to some degree with introversion. The dental students showed the same picture. In contrast, teachers and social work students revealed much higher concentrations of intuition and feeling orientations. This study suggests that certain Jungian types are drawn differentially to professions. Helson (1982) reports similar findings with different methods. She analyzed the content of writings by literary critics and found evidence of all four of the Jungian modes of thinking.

Some years ago, research on psychological androgyny became popular. This combination of traditionally feminine and masculine characteristics can be found in people regardless of whether they are biologically female or male. You will recall that an expression in behavior of both the male and female archetypes in each of us is considered by Jung as consistent with the ideal of selfhood. Consequently, evidence that androgynous subjects perform best would support Jung's position. Despite androgyny as an ideal, Feingold's (1994) meta-analysis of relevant studies found that regardless of age, education, and nationality, boys/men tend to be more assertive and full of self-esteem, whereas girls/women are more nurturant, extroverted, trusting, and anxious. Similarly, Marsh, Antill, & Cunningham (1987) found that self-esteem was based more on masculinity than femininity for both genders.

Androgyny research is fraught with controversy. Championed by Bem (1974), androgyny has raised issues of both measurement and substance. As expected, Tunnell (1981) found that psychologically feminine women used more feminine and less masculine constructs on the *Role Repertory Test* than did psychologically androgynous women. Further, Shaw (1982) reports that androgynous women found life events less stressful than psychologically feminine women did. In addition, both androgynous men and women rated themselves as happier than nonandrogynous subjects did. In a related finding (Major, Carnevale, & Deaux, 1981), androgynous men and women were rated by peers as more adjusted and better liked than nonandrogynous subjects of both genders. Marsh and Richards (1989) report that the effect of participation in an Outward-Bound program was to increase not only masculinity but also femininity in both genders. Further, Hegelson (1994) has reviewed many studies showing that both masculinity and femininity are needed for the highest levels of well-being. And it appears that androgynous characteristics are the most attractive to both genders (Green & Kendrick, 1994). Such findings support the notion that being psychologically both masculine and feminine is developmentally advantageous.

But some studies have yielded more complex or ambiguous results. In a simulation study, for example, Senniker and Hendrick (1983) found that while androgynous women came to the aid of a "choking" confederate more quickly than did feminine women, so too did men whether they were psychologically androgynous, masculine, or feminine! Also, Heilbrun (1981) reports that androgynous men were higher in social cognition and lower in defensiveness than other men but that androgynous women showed the reverse pattern, compared with other women. In another study, Heilbrun (1984) found that although androgynous women showed greater social competence and less tolerance of ambiguity than other women, this pattern did not emerge with male subjects. To add further complexity, Harrington and Andersen (1981) found only slight support for androgyny as a predictor of creativity; male gender, regardless of psychological sexual orientation, was an equally good predictor. Taken together, these studies may be highlighting that androgyny is more of a developmental advantage for women than it is for men, a possibility not really consistent with Jungian thinking regarding selfhood.

Some studies even suggest that androgyny does not differ from masculinity or femininity per se (e.g., Lubinski, Tellegen, & Butcher, 1981, 1983). Consistent with this are the finding by Feather (1984) that no values distinguish androgynous men and women from others and the report of complex results concerning leadership in mixed-sex (by Porter, Geis, Cooper, & Newman, 1985). It is also possible that there is deficiency in the questionnaire measure of masculinity, femininity, and androgyny introduced by Bem and used by the researchers mentioned here. In this regard, Hall and Taylor (1985) offer several methodological suggestions important when the interaction of two dimensions (masculinity and femininity) are combined into a third, supposedly distinct dimension (androgyny). In any event, it presently is unclear how much support for the Jungian position on selfhood exists in the androgyny research.

The research discussed in this section provides some support for the Jungian emphasis on introversion-extroversion, which seems a seminal dimension for understanding human behavior. But the studies reported by Carlson and Levy and by Hanewitz are very important, because the aspect of Jung's peripheral theorizing most unique to him inheres in the combination of peripheral characteristics into types.

Before closing, I must mention the many studies yielding negative or conflicting results (see Wilson, 1977). Although there are too many to be mentioned here, one study by Domino (1976) is particularly telling. He obtained three dream reports from each of 62 male college students, which were rated on 15 personality dimensions by five judges. Interested in the Jungian prediction that dreams have a compensatory or contrast function, he correlated the personality scores obtained from the dreams with scores on the same dimensions as measured by self-report questionnaires of personality. The close correspondence he found between the dream and questionnaire scores is inconsistent with a compensation hypothesis.

Rogers's Position

Although Rogers's position on the periphery of personality is hardly elaborate, it does have some fairly definite empirical implications. To see this, recall that the fully functioning person has five groupings of peripheral characteristics, referred to as openness to experience (including emotionality and reflectiveness), existential living (including flexibility, adaptability, spontaneity, and inductive thinking), organismic trusting (including congruence between what you believe yourself to be and what you believe to be worthy), experiential freedom (a sense of free will and personal control over life), and creativity (an interest in producing new things). The groupings of peripheral characteristics comprised in the maladjusted personality are the opposite of

these, namely, defensiveness, living according to a preconceived plan, conditions of worth, feelings of being manipulated, and conformity. There are two ways in which empirical study could evaluate this theorizing. It could focus on whether or not the peripheral characteristics postulated for each personality type really show evidence of covariation. It could also focus on one or more of the postulated characteristics to determine whether they are associated with successful living if part of the fully functioning type or unsuccessful living if part of the maladjusted type.

Although there is much research that by its topic appears relevant to the second focus, little of it has been done with particular Rogerian emphases in mind. I cover that research that comes as close to his emphases as possible. Furthermore, some research mentioned elsewhere might also be construed as lending some general support to the Rogerian emphasis. This is true of many of the fulfillment positions.

In a study done to evaluate Rogerian theory directly, Pearson (1969, 1974) focuses on the existence and interrelationship of openness to experience and organismic valuing as peripheral characteristics. She conceives each characteristic as containing several parts. The parts or phases of openness to experience are (1) attention, or symbolizing the recognition of affective cues in a significant event; (2) reaction, or symbolizing the personal impact or significance of the event; and (3) exploration, or differentiating and symbolizing the personal impact or significance of the event. These phases were measured with paper-and-pencil performance tests (not questionnaires) and carefully developed for adequate reliability. The phases of organismic valuing are (1) information collection, relevant to eventual decision; (2) information appraisal; (3) decision making, or choosing from among formulated alternatives; and (4) decision implementation. These phases were measured by three paper-and-pencil tests, two of them performance tests and one a questionnaire on decision making. Once again these measures were carefully devised and showed adequate reliability. The scores obtained from 90 male and female undergraduates show that the various phases of each characteristic are reliable, indicating support for their existence. But contrary to what Rogerians would expect, openness to experience and organismic trusting scores did not intercorrelate. This rigorous study suggests that the various peripheral characteristics postulated by Rogers do not organize themselves neatly into his two personality types. This complication may even provide a basis for considering the existence of subtypes, thereby rendering his formal theorizing more complex and hence capable of dealing with individuality (see Chapter 5).

There have been other attempts to develop measures of openness to experience. Tittler (1974) offers a 38-item questionnaire, with the item content drawn from encounter and sensitivity group protocols. Scores on these items from 105 undergraduates were subjected to factor analysis. The result was nine openness-to-experience factors, four of which seemed to have construct validity in the sense of negative correlations with measures of dogmatism and conventionality.

In a similar approach, Coan (1972) administered theoretically relevant questionnaire items to 383 college students and factor analyzed the resulting scores. Sixteen factors resulted, many of which seemed reasonably valid on the basis of correlations between them and a battery of personality tests. In an attempt at cross-validation, Coan repeated this study on 219 college students, using a combination of original and fresh items. The result was an openness-to-experience instrument containing 83 items that yielded 7 factors corresponding very closely to the original 16. This instrument, called the *Experience Inventory,* contains scales concerning (1) aesthetic sensitivity, (2) openness to hypothetical ideas, (3) constructive utilization of fantasy, (4) openness to unconventional views of reality, (5) indulgence in fantasy, (6) unusual perceptions and associations, and (7) deliberate and systematic thought. Although it is too early to be at all sure that these measures are reliable and valid indicators of the Rogerian concept of openness to experience, their emergence signifies growing interest in this concept.

In a more general vein, Rogers contends that for the fully functioning person, the self-concept undergoes continual change and has distinct dimensions or parts whereas the self-concept of the maladjusted person is just the opposite. A few studies indicate that the self-concept does not undergo major changes (e.g., Block, 1962; Havener & Izard, 1962) but disagree as to whether self-consistency is a positive or negative indicator of effective adjustment. Concerning the possible dimensionality of the self-concept, Akeret (1959) provides evidence that it includes at least four major divisions, defined by academic, interpersonal, sexual, and emotional content. He finds that these four dimensions are not highly intercorrelated. In contrast, Sandvik and Diener (1993) found in their factor-analytic study only one unitary factor of subjective well-being in both self-report and other measures of their college student sample. The trouble with these studies is they do not bear on Rogers's contention that the self-concept is unitary only in the maladjusted person. Although the studies mentioned here have a ring of relevance to Rogers's theory, they actually are not very helpful in evaluating it.

The aspect of full functioning that has received extensive research attention is that of organismic trusting. According to Rogers, fully functioning people will have faith in their organisms, in the intuitive, even impulsive urges to action they experience, because they will not have developed the conditions of worth that could dictate which aspects of them are valuable and which are to be shunned. In contrast, maladjusted people live lives controlled so as to pass muster with their conditions of worth. The operational clue to understanding the research effort concerning these matters is that in organismic trusting there would be little difference between how people described themselves and what they wanted to be, whereas the difference between these two frames of reference would be great for people with conditions of worth.

Virtually all the studies I shall review concern the magnitude of the difference between descriptions of the perceived self and those of the ideal self. Moreover, the typical means of measuring this self-ideal discrepancy is to present subjects with a list of statements taken from actual verbalizations made by clients in Rogerian therapy and to ask them to sort these into a set number of categories ranging from very inaccurate to very accurate as descriptions of themselves. Then they are to sort the same group of statements into categories ranging from very inaccurate to very accurate as expressions of their ideals for themselves. As you may recognize, this is a variant on the Q-sort technique (Stephenson, 1953) described earlier, which yields information that can be factor analyzed to produce a quantitative index of the discrepancy between the perceived and ideal selves. This operationalization of organismic trusting and conditions of worth is very much in the spirit of Rogers's theory.

The first and most widely quoted study employing the self-ideal discrepancy measure is that of Butler and Haigh (1954). They measured self-ideal discrepancy in a group of patients both before and after therapy and also in a number of follow-ups. On average, the size of the discrepancy decreased over time. Matched control groups started out with a smaller discrepancy but the discrepancy did not decrease as time went by. The decrease in discrepancy shown by the patient group was considerable and, for the most part, involved a movement of the self-description toward the ideal description. These results are presented in detail in Tables 12-12 and 12-13.

It is not clear whether the findings support Rogers's viewpoint. Certainly, the closer the person is to fully functioning, the smaller the discrepancy between self and ideal should be. To be sure, psychotherapy should bring people nearer to full functioning. But statements of ideals are operational representations of conditions of worth; hence, one function of therapy should be to remove these aspects of maladjustment. Ideals would be considered beneficial from the standpoint of a perfection theory but not of an actualization theory. In this context, it is unfortunate for the Rogerian position that Butler and Haigh found the reduction in self-ideal discrepancy occurring as a function of therapy to be brought about primarily by a movement of self-description toward ideals. My interpretation of these results as somewhat inconsistent with Rogerian theory is bolstered by the report that the ideal descriptions tended to be fairly uniform, indicating a shared cultural context. Ideal descriptions seem the stuff of conditions of worth—that is, socially imposed beliefs as to what is important.

The difficulty I have mentioned has led to a modified Rogerian view concerning self-ideal discrepancy. Some Rogerians (see Shlien, 1962) have considered large discrepancies as representing poor adjustment and moderate discrepancies as reflecting full functioning. And extremely small discrepancies are suspected to be defensive statements made by maladjusted people (Chodorkoff, 1954a, 1954b). The thinking behind such statements is that a very large self-ideal discrepancy can come about only if the self-description is viciously critical, and a very small self-ideal discrepancy requires people to twist their views of themselves to conform to what is socially desirable. Perhaps both large and small discrepancies signify strong conditions of worth. In that case, only moderate self-ideal discrepancies would signify the absence of maladjustment.

Of direct importance to the empirical evaluation of this modified Rogerian viewpoint are studies determining the relationship between self-ideal discrepancy and general adjustment and happiness. Brophy (1959) collected from 81 female nurses self-reports of general satisfaction, vocational satisfaction, adjustment and values, and occupational and life roles. The results suggest that congruence between perceived and ideal selves is necessary for general happiness and for satisfaction in specific life areas. Turner and Vanderlippe (1958) obtained a broad range of information relating to effectiveness and satisfaction with life from 175 college students from whom they also had obtained self-ideal descriptions. The range of information included measures of general health, extracurricular participation, sociometric indexes, scholastic adjustment, and a test of temperament. Subjects with low self-ideal discrepancy needed fewer days in the hospital and fewer visits to the clinic. Further,

TABLE 12-12 Self-Ideal Correlations in the Client Group

CLIENT	PRE-COUNSELING r	POST-COUNSELING r	FOLLOW-UP r
Oak	.21	.69	.71
Babi	.05	.54	.45
Bacc	−.31	.04	−.19
Bame	.14	.61	.61
Bana	−.38	.36	.44
Barr	−.34	−.13	.02
Bayu	−.47	−.04	.42
Bebb	.06	.26	.21
Beda	.59	.80	.69
Beel	.28	.52	−.04
Beke	.27	.69	−.56
Bene	.38	.80	.78
Benz	−.30	−.40	.39
Beri	.33	.43	.64
Beso	.32	.41	.47
Bett	−.37	.39	.61
Bico	−.11	.51	.72
Bifu	−.12	−.17	−.26
Bime	−.33	.05	.00
Bina	−.30	.59	.71
Bink	−.08	.30	−.20
Bira	.26	−.08	−.16
Bixy	−.39	−.39	.05
Blen	.23	.33	−.36
Bajo	.16	.29	.47
Mean z	−.01	.36	.32
Corresponding r	−.01	.34	.31

SOURCE: From "Changes in the Relation Between Self-Concepts and Ideal-Concepts Consequent upon Client-Centered Counseling," by J. M. Butler and G. V. Haigh in *Psychotherapy and Personality Change*, edited by C. R. Rogers and R. F. Dymond. Copyright © 1954 by The University of Chicago Press. Reprinted by permission.

the lower the self-ideal discrepancy, the greater the tendency to be preferred as a companion. Finally, the results of the temperament test, shown in Table 12-14, indicate that people with low self-ideal discrepancy tend toward general activity, ascendance, sociability, emotional stability, and thoughtfulness. The authors conclude the following:

> The emergent composite picture of the college student high in self-ideal congruence (as contrasted with the student low in self-ideal congruence) is that of one who participates more in extracurricular activities, has a higher scholastic average, is given higher sociometric ratings by his fellow students, and receives higher adjustment ratings on ... certain traits.

Also relevant is the finding by Strauman and Higgins (1988) that self-ideal discrepancies predispose subjects to distinct syndromes of chronic emotional distress.

A similar picture is presented by Rosenberg (1962) in a study relating self-ideal discrepancy to the various scales of the *California Personality Inventory* (Gough, 1957/1987). This personality

TABLE 12-13   Self-Ideal Correlations in the Control Group

CLIENT	PRE-COUNSELING r	FOLLOW-UP r
Aban	.80	.50
Abor	.00	.30
Acro	.86	.89
Agaz	.75	.83
Akim	.84	.86
Akor	.48	−.03
Ajil	.49	.45
Afit	.73	.71
Abul	.58	.77
Adis	.42	.65
Abri	.35	.30
Abbe	.35	.36
Acme	.80	.65
Abco	.65	.76
Abet	−.01	.43
Adir	.30	.07
Mean z	.66	.68
Corresponding r	.58	.59

SOURCE: From "Changes in the Relation Between Self-Concepts and Ideal-Concepts Consequent upon Client-Centered Counseling," by J. M. Butler and G. V. Haigh in *Psychotherapy and Personality Change*, edited by C. R. Rogers and R. F. Dymond. Copyright © 1954 by The University of Chicago Press. Reprinted by permission.

test includes such variables as sociability, dominance, flexibility, and achievement. Rosenberg found that the greater the self-ideal discrepancy, the lower the score on 15 of the 18 variables of this personality test. What this means is that people with large self-ideal discrepancies usually are inept at the kinds of interests and capabilities relevant to successful living. A contribution to the emerging picture has been made by studies concerning the tendency to agree with statements regardless of their content. This acquiescent response style is most marked in people having a large self-ideal discrepancy (Murstein, 1961). Another study (Schulberg, 1961) suggests that acquiescent responding occurs in people who seem to be smiling on the outside while jeering on the inside. Hence, we can take Murstein's

(1961) findings as indicating yet another dimension of the ineptitude for living that accompanies a large self-ideal discrepancy. Similarly, Mahoney and Hartnett (1973) found that male and female subjects high on a self-actualization measure had much smaller self-ideal discrepancies than subjects low in self-actualization did. All in all, the modified Rogerian notion that both large and small self-ideal discrepancies would indicate maladjustment rather than full functioning seems to lack empirical support. More recently, there has been an upsurgence of theoretical and research interest in self-discrepancies (e.g., Higgins, 1987), though it is not specifically linked to Rogers's influence.

A final group of studies stems from another implication of organismic trusting. According to Rogers, if one has accepted oneself—that is, if the self-ideal discrepancy is small—one will also accept, respect, and value other people. As you will recall from Chapter 5, this expectation reflects the assumption made by actualization theorists that nothing in the basic nature of human beings is necessarily selfish and hostile. In this assumption, actualization theories differ

TABLE 12-14   Correlations Between Self-Ideal Congruence Expressed As Z Values and Traits Measured by the Guilford-Zimmerman Temperament Survey

TRAIT	CORRELATION WITH SELF-IDEAL CONGRUENCE
1. General activity	.50*
2. Restraint	−.10
3. Ascendance	.58*
4. Sociability	.36*
5. Emotional stability	.36*
6. Objectivity	−.03
7. Friendliness	−.16
8. Thoughtfulness	.41*
9. Personal relations	−.25
10. Masculinity	.10

*Significant at the .01 level.

SOURCE: From "Self-Ideal Congruence As an Index of Adjustment," by R. H. Turner and R. H. Vanderlippe, 1958, *Journal of Abnormal and Social Psychology*, 57.

greatly from psychosocial conflict theories. Suinn (1961) tested whether male high-school seniors who accepted themselves would show a generalized acceptance of their fathers and male teachers. On a set of adjectives, his subjects described their perceived and ideal selves, perceived and ideal fathers, and perceived and ideal male teachers. Suinn found that the smaller the self-ideal discrepancy, the smaller the father-ideal and teacher-ideal discrepancies. This supports the contention that if you accept yourself, you also accept other people.

Medinnus and Curtis (1963) studied the relationship between self-acceptance and child-acceptance in mothers. These 56 mothers filled out a questionnaire and a semantic differential scale, each of which yielded a measure of the degree to which self and ideal differed. There was also a semantic differential measure of the general degree to which their children were accepted by them. Medinnus and Curtis found that the two measures of self-acceptance intercorrelated, as you would expect, and that both of them were positively related to the measure of child-acceptance. So not only do male high-school students who accept themselves accept their fathers and male teachers; but also, mothers who accept themselves accept their children. Other studies also support the notion that acceptance of others occurs in the context of self-acceptance (e.g., Berger, 1953, 1955; Rosenman, 1955; Sheerer, 1949; Stock, 1949). Even though some of these studies are methodologically less relevant to the Rogerian frame of reference, they yield results similar to the previously described studies. The substantial evidence that people who accept themselves also accept others supports not only Rogerian theory but the theories of Maslow, Fromm, and existential psychology. Of course, it is possible that the tendency to respond in a socially desirable fashion may have contaminated the studies just considered, thereby weakening this conclusion.

Another Rogerian research theme involves the *Experiencing Scale,* developed by Gendlin and Tomlinson (1967). Experiencing is described as "the quality of an individual's experiencing of himself, the extent to which his ongoing, bodily, felt flow of experiencing is the basic datum of his awareness and communications about himself, and the extent to which this inner datum is integral to action and thought" (Klein, Mathieu, Gendlin, & Kiesler, 1969, p. 1). As you can see, the organismic trusting characteristic of full functioning is heavily involved here, as it is in the self-ideal discrepancy. Though the name might imply it, the Experiencing Scale is not a questionnaire filled out by the subject; rather, the subject verbalizes in some manner—usually in psychotherapy—about anything of interest or importance to him or her. Then the verbalizations are rated by the psychologist as to the degree of "experiencing." There are seven stages of experiencing, running from the lowest, in which subjects seem distant or remote from their feelings; through the middle range, in which subjects get their feelings into clearer perspective as their own and may even be able to focus on them as their inner reality; to the highest, in which feelings have been scrutinized and explored such that they become a trusted and reliable source of self-awareness. Klein et al. (1969) provide a scoring manual for the Experiencing Scale and report adequate interscorer reliabilities after practice.

Most of the research involving this scale has concerned clients' progress through psychotherapy and, as such, is not of great relevance here. Suffice it to say that clients who are judged by their Rogerian therapists as having improved during treatment have moved up the stages of experiencing (see Klein et al., 1969). There is also some evidence that the Experiencing Scale may be an adequate measure of organismic trusting, construed as a peripheral characteristic (as a predisposition that persists over time and stimulus situations). For example, it has been found (see Klein et al., 1969) that successful therapy clients start, continue, and end therapy at a higher level of experiencing than less successful clients do. Once you conclude that those who profit most from psychotherapy are those who needed it least to begin with, you are dealing with the kind of behavioral regularity that signifies the presence of a peripheral characteristic. In other studies amplifying this theme, neurotics showed higher levels of experiencing than did schizophrenics, who would, of course, be considered the sicker of the two groups (see Klein et al., 1969). Also, though not specifically directed at a test of some Rogerian hypothesis, the study of Gorney and Tobin (1969) shows that as people make the transition from adulthood to old age, their level of experiencing drops. The Experiencing Scale appears to be an intriguing tool with which to test Rogerian notions.

Another promising beginning at translating Rogerian theorizing into manageable empirical observations has been made by Wexler (1974), who reasoned that the self-actualizing process can be discerned in mental content as progressively greater differentiation and integration and in verbal style as a vivid, focused quality not unlike the higher levels of experiencing mentioned above. In considering verbal style, Wexler was influenced by the work of Rice and Wagstaff (1967). Using a sample of undergraduate men and women, Wexler demonstrates a positive correlation between degree of differentiation and integration and degree of focused voice style during the subjects' descriptions of emotional episodes. Further, both of these variables correlate positively with another purported test of full functioning. But as you will see later, additional studies lend general empirical support to Rogers's position, though these studies relate even more directly to other theories.

Finally, recent work on the effects of intrinsic and extrinsic motivation are relevant here, as Rogers theorizes that conditions of worth (extrinsic motivation) are a sign of maladjustment. Many studies have shown that extrinsic motivation actually decreases various indexes of performance. Quite supportive of the Rogerian position is Amabile's (1985) recent demonstration that the imposition of extrinsic motivation to perform actually decreases the creativity of poems composed by subjects.

Maslow's Position

Maslow's position is sufficiently similar in empirical implications to that of Rogers that anything supporting the latter also tends to support the former. There is, however, a cognitive emphasis in Maslow that is less explicit in Rogers. This is the emphasis on democratic values as part of the self-actualizing person as opposed to authoritarian and traditionalistic values in the nonactualizing person. While Rogers would probably agree, he does not stress such matters. But Allport, Fromm, and the existentialists clearly agree with Maslow. The body of personological research on the authoritarian personality (Adorno, Frenkel-Brunswik, Levinson, & Sanford, 1950), though planned independently, is especially relevant to Maslow's emphasis on this subject.

Adorno et al. developed a fascism, or *F scale*, for purposes of assessing the degree to which people have authoritarian values. As appropriate for studying values, the scale is derived from self-descriptions obtained through giving the subjects a list of relevant questions to answer. Examples of the items appearing on the F scale are "Obedience and respect for authority are the most important virtues children should learn" and "Familiarity breeds contempt," with "yes" answers considered authoritarian. The first version of the F scale had internal consistency of .74, but removal of some poor items increased reliability to .90.

Adorno et al. (1950) set about determining the kinds of behavior and attitudes that occur in people high and low on the F scale. Their large group of subjects included a majority of white, native, middle-class Americans functioning as university students, public-school teachers, public-health nurses, prison inmates, psychiatric patients, and labor union and other club members. The results reveal a fairly coherent group of correlates for the F scale. Persons high in fascistic values are also ethnocentric in the sense that they not only are opposed to other cultures but attribute correspondingly high importance to their own. They are hostile not only toward minority groups but toward everyone whose ways or values differ from their own. Further, they are hostile toward and contemptuous of anything that is weak. This was shown not only in the dislike of weakness but indirectly in the admiration and valuation of power and strength, as exemplified by money, masculinity, and age-status authority. Also, people high in fascistic values are essentially conformists, or moralists with absolute values. They are intolerant of ambiguity in parent-child, gender, teacher-child, and other social roles. Finally, they see the world as a dangerous place, full of chaos and unpredictability, with uncontrollable catastrophes imminent.

Also included in the study by Adorno et al. are interviews and unstructured tests of fantasy. By and large, the results obtained with these procedures corroborate the other findings, but the interviews and fantasy tests are seriously flawed methodologically (see Hyman & Sheatsley, 1954). To be sure, the F-scale findings have also been criticized, mainly on the grounds that the sample may not have fully represented the general population and that the test items may have been contaminated by response sets. Although these criticisms have some justification, attempts to explain away the attributes of the authoritarian personality have not been very convincing.

Since the appearance of the work of Adorno et al., a huge number of studies tracing the correlates of the fascism scale have been done. Many of these studies have complemented and extended the findings reported above. For example, in a study unusual for having been conducted in a "real-life" context involving performance rather than self-description, Vroom (1959) shows that among supervisors in a large delivery company, authoritarians were affected less positively by the opportunity to participate in company decisions than nonauthoritarians were. Presumably people high in fascistic values feel most comfortable in authoritarian work situations, even when they are not in power.

Of course, some studies using the F scale yield equivocal results. This situation may be due to a lack of purity in the fascism scale in that it measures not only authoritarian values but many unintended things (see Peabody, 1966). One such unintended factor may be the tendency to agree or disagree in answering questions regardless of their content. Another may be our old friend, socially desirable responding. To date, a great deal of effort has been expended in the attempt to rid the fascism scale of such contaminations

(Peabody, 1966; Byrne, 1977). Most recent studies use one or another of the newer scales, though the tendency toward conflicting results persists. I am not especially surprised by this state of affairs, as it has never been clear to me that an authoritarian value orientation can be accurately measured if the tendencies to acquiesce and to respond in socially desirable fashion are excluded. After all, the authoritarian person deeply believes in the importance of acquiescence and conformity. Perhaps we shall come closer to clarity by assuming that the authoritarian orientation can be expressed not only in fascistic values but also in acquiescent and conforming traits. Once we adopt this point of view, we are not likely to exclude acquiescent and conforming tendencies from a measure of authoritarianism.

The mass of authoritarianism research does permit some generalizations. Concerning the antecedents of authoritarianism, several studies have found that authoritarian parents tend to use autocratic child-rearing practices, whereas egalitarian parents are more democratic (e.g., Levinson & Huffman, 1955). Byrne (1965) studied the tie between parents' and children's personalities directly and found that the F scores of both the mother and the father are positively related to their son's, whereas only the mother's F score is so related to the daughter's. He also reports that if either parent is egalitarian, their child will also be egalitarian. These findings generally support the actualization theory's emphasis on unconditional positive regard as the important rearing practice for the encouragement of self-actualization.

Research has also accumulated on the behavioral expressions of authoritarianism. People high in authoritarianism favored American intervention in Vietnam (Iyzett, 1971), tend to endorse conservative political candidates (e.g., Leventhal, Jacobs, & Kudirka, 1964), and attend church more frequently (Byrne, 1977). Concerning thought processes, Kirscht and Dillehay (1967) conclude on the bases of several studies that authoritarian people show rigidity and are quick to attempt resolution of ambiguities. Elms and Milgram (1966) conducted an important experiment in which subjects were instructed to administer shocks to another subject of sufficient intensity to be painful and dangerous. In reality, the "victim" was a confederate of the investigators, and despite much screaming, no shocks actually took place. In the condition under which the victim was in another room and could not be seen, most subjects were willing to give what was presumed to be a shock. But when the condition called for being in the same room and even touching the victim, a number of subjects refused to participate. Elms and Milgram found that subjects willing to administer shocks when not confronted with the victim were more authoritarian than those who refused to participate when seated next to the victim. In general, it would appear that authoritarian subjects show some of the signs proposed by Maslow.

Lest we make a hasty conclusion, we should note the appearance of a theme in the research literature to the effect that not only highly authoritarian but highly egalitarian people show tendencies inconsistent with self-actualization. In studying attitudes of punitiveness toward victims, Epstein (1965) manipulated high and low socioeconomic status by varying the victims' dress, incomes, employment goals, and so forth. He found that while authoritarian subjects were punitive toward low-status victims, egalitarian subjects were punitive toward high-status victims. In an ingenious study, Mitchell (1973, May) described for the subjects a scenario involving a rock concert that gets out of hand. In one version, a citizen, variously described in positive or negative terms, is killed. In another a police officer, also presented negatively or positively, is killed. When the scenario involved a citizen, authoritarian subjects were more abusive toward the person when described negatively than when described positively. The negativity or positivity of the description made no difference to egalitarian subjects. But when the scenario involved a police officer, the findings were reversed: Egalitarian subjects were more punitive toward someone negatively described, whereas the description made no difference to authoritarian subjects. It would seem that the highly liberal, flexible, democratic subject, here called egalitarian, is in certain situations just as punitive, insensitive, and hasty as the authoritarian is in other situations. These findings are not really in keeping with Maslow's theorizing about the self-actualized person, whom he describes as possessing democratic values. But, of course, democratic values are only one peripheral characteristic of self-actualization. Studies that measure the type more comprehensively are needed.

In the hope of avoiding this problem of being authoritarian, which seems to characterize both high and low scores on the F scale, Rokeach (1960) has offered a *dogmatism scale*. Much research has been done attempting to show that low dogmatism scores indicate flexibility, openness, and emotional maturity. As part of this effort, various investigators have studied the relationship of dogmatism to political beliefs, with conflicting results. The upshot of this theme seems to be that the dogmatism scale is primarily a measure of underlying cognitive orientation and only slightly tinged with ideological or political beliefs (e.g., Granberg & Corrigan, 1972).

Many studies tracing the effects of dogmatism on various behaviors have been performed. Ehrlich (1955, 1961a, 1961b) compared the performance of 57 undergraduates enrolled in a sociology course on precourse and postcourse tests, separated by 10 weeks, and on a follow-up several months later. The higher the dogmatism scores, the poorer the performance on all three sociology tests, even when academic aptitude skills were controlled. Five years later, Ehrlich (1961b) obtained from many of the original subjects dogmatism scores, sociology test scores, and their reported grade-point averages on graduation. He obtained essentially the same results as before. But Costin's (1965) attempt to replicate Ehrlich's findings was unsuccessful. Baker (1964) performed a similar study of 56 student nurses, the measures of performance being the number of correct identifications of definitions for psychological concepts they were supposed to have learned. Oddly enough, he found that the higher the dogmatism scores, the better the performance. To make matters worse, Costin (1968), employing a design similar to that of his earlier work, obtained results indicating that dogmatism correlated positively with the students' retention of psychological misconceptions he had purposely given them but not with their acquisition of basic psychological principles, which also had been taught. The contradictory nature of these findings suggests the action of important variables that were not measured (Ehrlich & Lee, 1969).

These studies all occurred in classroom settings, where it was not possible to adequately control situations and experiences. Under more rigorous laboratory conditions, a more consistent picture of the effects of dogmatism on learning materializes. Adams and Vidulich (1962) compared the 18 highest and lowest dogmatism scorers in the number of errors made while learning two lists of 15 belief-congruent word pairs (e.g., ball-round) and 15 belief-incongruent word pairs (e.g., ball-square). As expected, the high-dogmatism subjects made more errors in retaining the belief-incongruent list. But they also, unexpectedly, made more errors in retaining the belief-congruent list. That there may still be some tendency among high-dogmatism subjects to learn well only belief-congruent or personally interesting materials is indicated in studies by Kleck and Wheaton (1967) and Pyron and Kafer (1967). Consistent with this, the research of Restle, Andrews, and Rokeach (1964) found that low-dogmatism subjects could solve a difficult problem more quickly than high-dogmatism subjects when the solution involved choosing an unusual alternative rather than a usual one. The implication that dogmatic persons do not learn well when operating in an unfamiliar situation or when the solution is novel is supported by further studies done by Rokeach, Swanson, and Denny (1960), Mikol (1960), Zagona and Zurcher (1965), and Jacoby (1967).

Not only are dogmatic people unable to learn effectively in conditions of novelty, they are also swayed in their judgments by the contradictory judgments of high-status people. Vidulich and Kaiman (1961) tested 30 high- and 30 low-dogmatism undergraduates in a situation requiring perceptual judgments (how far a spot of light had moved in a darkened room). All subjects were tested in the company of the experimenters' confederate, who tried to sway judgments. Sometimes the confederate was introduced as a college professor and sometimes as a high-school student. The results indicate a tendency for high-dogmatism subjects to acquiesce to high-status judgments. Support for this finding is found in research by Powell (1962) and Bettinhaus, Miller, and Steinfatt (1970), among others. The implications of conformity on the part of dogmatic people were authenticated by Zagona and Zurcher (1964) in observational evidence, gleaned over 4 months of contact, that in small groups dogmatic people are leader oriented, are unspontaneous, and prefer lectures to class discussion. Similarly, Gold, Ryckman, and Rodda (1973) found that dogmatic subjects exposed to information contradicting their attitudes in a group discussion changed their attitude toward the group position. That the conforming effect of dogmatism is not merely cognitive or attitudinal is suggested by Clark (1968), who investigated the relationship between dogmatism scores and the ability to discern a previously observed simple figure embedded in a more complex one (field dependence-independence). In his sample of 523 undergraduates, dogmatism was negatively correlated with this ability.

Of special relevance are studies charting the pattern of other personality characteristics that accompany dogmatism. Plant, Telford, and Thomas (1965) administered the California Psychological Inventory, a general test of personality, along with the dogmatism scale to their subjects and conclude that those high in dogmatism were also psychologically immature, impulsive, highly defensive, and stereotypic in their thinking. In contrast, subjects low in dogmatism were outgoing, enterprising, calm, mature, forceful, clear thinking, and responsible. Similarly, Hjelle and Lomastro (1971) found low-dogmatism subjects less accepting of traditional religious beliefs, more tolerant of ambiguities in their environment, and displaying fewer signs of emotional disturbance. Filling out the picture, Lee and Ehrlich (1971) found that dogmatic subjects held more negative and more contradictory beliefs about themselves and also had more negative attitudes toward others. Several studies (see Vacchiano, 1977) have attempted to demonstrate through performance tests that dogmatic subjects are more defensive than others, but the procedures are intricate and the interpretations elaborate. Nonetheless, evidence exists (e.g., Richek, Mayo, & Pirgean, 1970; Vacchiano, Strauss, & Schiffman, 1968) that subjects high in dogmatism are more maladjusted than those low in the sense of emotional instability, poor self-concept, and occupational impairment.

There is much more support for Maslow's peripheral theorizing in the dogmatism research than there is in the authoritarianism research. Unfortunately for Maslow's emphasis on democratic values as a peripheral characteristic, it would appear that the ideological, political flavor of the authoritarianism scale makes it theoretically closer to him as a measure than the dogmatism scale, with its emphasis on rigidity of thought processes regardless of content. In this there is a basis for theoretical revision. Actually, as it stands, the dogmatism research is more easily interpreted as support for Rogerian than Maslowian peripheral theorizing. Also, this research provides some general support for Allport, Fromm, and existential psychology.

At about the same time, a general questionnaire aimed at measuring the various facets of self-actualization was devised in strict adherence to Maslow's theorizing (Shostrom, 1965, 1966). Called the *Personal Orientation Inventory (POI)*, this test consists of 150 paired, opposing statements. In each instance, the subjects must choose one of the two as more relevant to them. The test is scored as two major scales—inner-directedness and time competence—and ten complementary scales—self-actualizing values, existentiality, feeling reactivity, spontaneity, self-regard, self-acceptance, nature of man, synergy, acceptance of aggression, and capacity for intimacy. An adequate degree of reliability is reported for the scales (Ilardi & May, 1968; Klavetter & Mogar, 1967; Shostrom, 1966).

Thus far, the POI displays considerable construct validity (see Fox, Knapp, & Michael, 1968; Guinan & Foulds, 1970; Shostrom, 1966). One facet of this validity concerns behavioral ratings made by trained personologists. Various POI scales correlate positively with the degree to which subjects are rated as self-actualizing (McClain, 1970; Shostrom, 1965). POI scales also correlate negatively with alcoholism (Zaccaria & Weir, 1967), felony (Fisher, 1968), and hospitalization for psychopathological symptoms (Fox et al., 1968). The relationship of the POI to other personality tests also has been studied. All POI scales correlate negatively with Eysenck's neuroticism score (Knapp, 1965). Also, the inner-directed scale of the POI correlates positively with the autonomy scale and negatively with the abasement scale of the Edwards Personal Preference Inventory (Grossack, Armstrong, & Lussieu, 1966). Positive correlations have also been found between POI scales and various tests of creativity (Braun & Asta, 1968; Damm, 1969). Finally, some studies have involved actual performance. The main scale scores of the POI are positively related to academic achievement (LeMay & Damm, 1968; Stewart, 1968). In addition, high scores on the POI are associated with teacher and therapist effectiveness (Dandes, 1966; Graff & Bradshaw, 1970). Also relevant is the finding that subjects scoring high in self-actualization seek novelty more than those scoring low (Schwartz & Gaines, 1974).

Several studies have investigated whether responses to the POI are seriously affected by the tendency to present oneself in a socially desirable light. Fisher and Silverstein (1969) and Foulds and Warehime (1971) found that instructions to fake responses in a favorable direction actually produced *lower* self-actualization scores in subjects. This is in striking contrast to other tests, which appear so vulnerable to subjects' putting their best feet forward. Also, it has been shown that the POI scales are actually negatively related to measures of the tendency to respond in a socially desirable direction (Warehime & Foulds, 1973) and of conformity behavior (Crosson & Schwendiman, 1972). Perhaps subjects who dissimulate on questionnaires do so in terms of cultural stereotypes of ideal behavior. If self-actualization differs from such stereotypes, it is understandable that encouragement to present oneself in a good light would have no or even adverse effects on POI scores.

In an attempt to determine just how resistant to faking the POI is, Warehime, Routh, and Foulds (1974) presented subjects with instructions concerning the content of the self-actualization concept. They reasoned that given this clue, subjects with a high tendency to respond in a socially desirable direction would be able to increase their self-actualization scores. Although they used 276 subjects, they could not demonstrate this effect. Only when they combined instruction about the self-actualization concept with practice in answering some of the actual items of the POI was there some tendency for subjects bent on appearing socially desirable to increase their self-actualization scores—and the tendency was very small at that. It seems likely that the POI is remarkably resistant to faking, which strengthens its claim to construct validity.

Lest you become too enthusiastic, I should point out the failures to establish the validity of this test (see Fox et al., 1968; Guinan & Foulds, 1970). In a particularly interesting finding difficult to reconcile with Maslow's thinking, de Grace (1974) demonstrated, using 30 subjects, that there is no difference in level of anxiety between high and low self-actualization scores on the POI. Nonetheless, the POI seems a promising lead in investigating broad patterns of functioning clearly associated with the positions of Maslow and Rogers.

Several studies stimulated by Maslow have not employed the POI. Leith (1972) obtained scores on three verbal creativity tests from 106 subjects immediately after they had been subjected to two kinds and degrees of stress that should have constituted a threat to needs at the lower end of Maslow's hierarchy. Oddly enough, stress seems to have increased the number and originality of responses. According to Maslow, the opposite should have taken place, because unsatisfied or frustrated lower needs should keep higher needs from being salient, and creativity is an expression of higher needs. Graham and Balloun (1973) attempted to show that in any pair of needs at different levels in Maslow's

hierarchy, satisfaction of the lower need should be greater than that of the higher need. Of the three scores derived from interviews testing this prediction, one produced the expected results, one did not, and the last yielded equivocal findings. Adding to this the scanty information that was provided concerning the interscorer agreement and the reliability of the ratings made from interviews, one might well conclude that there was not the support for Maslow's thinking that the researchers claimed. Finally, Ebersole (1973) interviewed students about their peak experiences, and found that in 55% of such instances, the subject regarded the experiences' effect on his or her life transitory. Although Ebersole regards this as supporting evidence for Maslow's position, it could easily be taken the opposite way. Furthermore, 55% is barely a majority.

Costa and McCrae's Position

There is considerable factor-analytic research documenting the five traits of neuroticism, extroversion, openness to experience, agreeableness, and conscientiousness (Costa & McCrae, 1992). These investigators not only have been able to derive the five factors from their own list of rating-scale items but have also recovered them in factor analyses of other personality tests. In addition, subsumed under each of these higher-order factors are several first-order factors. On the face of it, these findings would appear relevant to the periphery of personality, specifically, types (or lifestyles) and their component characteristics. Costa and McCrae appear to have taken something like the first two steps of the ideal strategy discussed earlier in this chapter, though they have proceeded less by deduction from a preexisting theory than inductively from data. Nor have they done much on the third step of the strategy. Nonetheless, they seem to believe that no other research is necessary to conclude that these five factors explain all significant behavior.

Several criticisms have emerged of the five-factor approach as a complete and adequate explanation of behavior (e.g., Block, 1995a, 1995b). To appreciate these criticisms, you should recognize that Costa and McCrae have tended to use as data only self-descriptions expressed in answers to questionnaire items (see Chapter 9) in arriving at their results. Less often, they have supplemented these data with descriptions of the subjects made on similar questionnaire items by others who know them. Agreeing with a point I made earlier in this chapter, McAdams (1992) argues that the sampling of behavior on which the factor analyses are based is too small to warrant the conclusion that the resulting five factors are ubiquitous and comprehensive indicators of significant elements of personality. He questions whether having subjects rate themselves on questions constructed by the researcher (or even supplementing this with ratings of them on the same questions by others) gets at the real stuff of personality. McCrae and Costa (1994) counter by insisting that these data suffice because their theoretical assumption is that people know themselves well enough to be aware of their status on the five factors, and can therefore tell you about it. This assumption is, of course, consistent with the actualization fulfillment model (remember Rogers's contention that people know themselves better than any even expert observer can).

Other criticisms arise from the same limitation raised by McAdams. Emmons (1993), for example, finds the five-factor model limited in its ability to recognize and explain the motivated nature of behavior. He offers a "personal striving concept" that helps explain subjective well-being, as well as the relationships of self-complexity to affective reactivity and daily life events to well-being. Also concerned with the contextual quality of individual lives, Thorne (1989) emphasizes "conditional patterns" such as, "My dominance shows when my competence is threatened" and "I talk the most when I am nervous." She thinks that full understanding of personality requires study and conceptualization of these conditional patterns whereby people live. It is not enough, she contends, to study and theorize about abstract traits alone. This criticism is echoed in the work of Buss and Craik (1983) on "personal project," and Cantor and Kihlstrom (1986) on "life tasks." Finally, Cantor (1990) insists that the five-traits (or any other trait)

approach covers only the "having" side of personality, not the "doing" side. Agreeing with all these criticisms, Block (1995a) adds that to maintain the appearance that their five factors and multiple facets fit together neatly, Costa and McCrae have had to change their factor-analytic assumptions in midstream. Further, Loevinger (1994) takes issue with the static rather than developmental view of personality inherent in the five-factor model.

These criticism would probably recede if Costa and McCrae would enter more completely into the task of personality theorizing, which is by its nature a comprehensive approach to understanding behavior (Maddi, 1993). One way of doing this is to conceptualize combinations of high or low scores on the five higher-order and associated first-order factors that would constitute bona fide personality types and their component peripheral characteristics. Then, the context-specific relationships between the type-clustered peripheral characteristics and concrete thoughts, feelings, and actions in various situations would have to be conceptualized and tested empirically. As this line of inquiry proceeded, we would be in a much better position to determine whether the claim of Costa and McCrae that their five-factor model explains all behavior is valid, and the flood of criticisms currently surrounding this contention might diminish.

At present, however, McCrae and Costa (1994) insist on conceptualizing the five traits as core characteristics, inherent rather than learned, and present in all people. Certainly, research findings suggest that something like these five factors are recoverable from self-descriptions and even other-descriptions. But the cogency of conceptualizing the five traits as core characteristics requires a full position on the periphery of personality, as well as research validating it. Until that happens, we cannot be sure how cogent the core theorizing of Costa and McCrae is.

Despite these serious problems, empirical work continues on the five-factor model. Indeed, an entire issue of the *Journal of Personality* (1992, *60*[2]) was devoted to this topic. In another context, Costa and McCrae (1995a) have tried to present their NEO Personality Inventory as encompassing broad factors (core characteristics) within which are nested more concrete facets or traits (peripheral characteristics). They have also reported construct validational correlations between the five factors and measures of psychological well-being (McCrae & Costa, 1991). Further, Piedmont (1993) shows that the five factors in Costa and McCrae's test correlated strongly with a test of burnout, even though that is usually thought to be a situationally induced stress reaction. Zuroff (1994) reports a complex picture of relationships between the five factors and two commonly used depression tests. Finally, Narayanan, Menon, and Levine (1995) contribute evidence that the NEO also yields interpretable results in a non-Western culture, though it also reveals some differences.

Adler's Position

Turning to the first perfection theorist, Adler, I am struck by the absence of research relevant to his peripheral theorizing in general. I believe the theorizing on lifestyles, fictional finalism, and traits is clear enough to have yielded meaningful research. Perhaps the Adlerian view simply has not been popular enough among psychologists for it to have captured their research attention. The one notable exception to what I have said regards birth order, which, as you will recall, is an important determinant of lifestyle according to Adler. Since Toman's (1959) elaboration of the Adlerian position on family constellation as a character and marriage determinant and Schachter's (1959) intriguing research on birth order and affiliative tendencies in female subjects, there has been a virtual flood of related studies. Here, you see another instance, to go along with Eysenck's stimulation of Jungian research and Rokeach's of Maslowian, of how a primarily research-oriented personologist can capture the imagination of others like him in the service of broader theoretical concerns. And you will see this again.

In his path-breaking study, Schachter (1959) observed that under stress, first-born college women tended to seek the company of others while later-born women tended to withdraw into themselves. As part of the same study, he also offers evidence that the general preference for affiliation and withdrawal on the part of first-born and laterborn children, respectively, who are under stress permitted understanding of such diverse behaviors as combat-flying effectiveness and alcoholism. With such dramatic findings, it is not surprising that researchers were attracted to the area. A general search for correlates of birth order began.

One consistent finding concerns attendance at college. Schachter (1963) concludes, on the basis of earlier studies, that eldest children are more likely to become eminent than later-born children. Many studies have shown that 50% to 65% of the student bodies in many colleges around the country, such as Columbia University (Schachter, 1963), Kansas State University (Danskin, 1964, September), Reed College (Altus, 1966), the University of Florida (Hall & Barger, 1964, May), were firstborn children. These percentages are larger than one would expect from the corresponding figures in the population at large (Schachter, 1963). This seems to be striking confirmation of Adler's contention that being born first precipitates ambition.

Although firstborn children more often go to college than others, there is inconsistent evidence that they do better there than later-born children. Campbell (1933) found no differences between these two groups in achievement. But Pierce (1959), Schachter (1963), and Falbo (1981) did find that firstborn children had higher grade-point averages. Although there is some evidence that these children have a higher need for achievement than later-born children (Sampson, 1965), it is known that this need is not a good predictor of grades (McClelland, 1961). In light of the general evidence that families place greater demands on firstborn children and expect them to reach greater heights (Bossard & Boll, 1955; Dittes, 1961; Rosen, 1961), it would seem that their going to college expresses ambition whether or not this produces excellent grades.

But the ambition suggested in firstborn children does not connote independence. Indeed, Sears (1950) and Schachter (1964) found that firstborn children are actually more dependent on others and more easily influenced than those born later. That later-born children are more accepted by their peers (Sells & Roff, 1963) suggests a more relaxed attitude in them. In this regard, Diamond and Munz (1967) found later-borns more able to break through social barriers by self-disclosure. But it does seem that when expected to undergo painful electric shock, firstborn women have a stronger desire than later-born women to await the experience in the company of others (Gerard & Rabbie, 1961; Schachter, 1959). Zucker, Manosevitz, and Langon (1968) have found evidence of the same effect in a naturally occurring catastrophe. This again suggests that the apparent ambition of firstborn children is sufficiently tinged with dependency to constitute a wish for approval rather than success in personal terms. Consistent with this interpretation are the results of Radloff (1961), who designed a study in which he was able to make some of his female subjects believe that their opinions varied with those of a large majority of their peers. Among firstborn women, those in presumed conflict with their peers expressed a stronger desire for further discussion than those in agreement with their peers did. This effect did not appear with later-born females. Similarly, Koenig (1969) found that firstborns gave consensual or group-related answers when asked to describe themselves. Other studies are consistent with these findings (e.g., Wrightsman, 1960), though it is possible that the picture for men is more complicated (Conners, 1963; Dember, 1964; Sampson, 1962).

There is also some intriguing information concerning birth order and psychopathology. Although the contention that firstborn children are more resistant to alcoholism than later-born children (Schachter, 1959) has not held up (Smart, 1963), later-borns do seem more prone to being "problem children" (Rosenow & Whyte, 1931) and are more apprehensive about dangerous situations (Longstreth, 1970). Actually, the highest proportion of delinquents seem to be middle children (Sletto, 1934). There is some rather inconclusive evidence that later-born children (at least girls) are more prone to schizophrenia than those born earlier (Schooler, 1961). Last-born children also seem to have lower social competence in general (Schooler, 1964). Although some studies find later-born children to be more creative (Staffieri, 1970), others report the opposite (Eisenman & Schussel, 1970). The picture simply is not yet clear.

Several studies have concerned the interaction and marriage patterns related to family constellation. Here again the evidence for Adler's position is inconsistent. Some studies (e.g., Mendelsohn, Linden, Gruen, & Curran, 1974; Birtchnell & Mayhew, 1977) find support for the theory in the relationship among sibling configuration, friendship formation, and mate selection. But there are also contradictory findings. For example, Hall (1965) reports that male only children have high divorce rates and female only children have low divorce rates. Further, Ickes and Turner (1983) found that having had an older, opposite-sex sibling makes it easier to interact with the opposite sex, a family constellation effect that contradicts Toman's hypothesis (and Adler's). It will take some careful sampling and measurement to sort out the confusing elements in this research area.

In one of the few studies planned to test a specific Adlerian hypothesis concerning family constellation, Croake and Hayden (1975) considered whether pairs of siblings show opposite traits. Contrary to Adlerian expectation, no such opposition was found in the responses of 90 college students and their siblings to the 16 Personality Factors Questionnaire.

Worthen and O'Connell (1969) provide one of the rare studies directly concerned with Adler's concept of social interest. Because they refer to this tendency's cooperative (rather than competitive) form, which can develop through learning, their study concerns Adler's peripheral statement. Constructive social interest was measured with a test of values formulated by the first author and humor appreciation with a test constructed by the second. A positive correlation was obtained between social interest and humor appreciation.

It remains to be seen how close to Adlerian constructs the measurement operations come.

Greever, Tseng, and Friedland (1973) developed a paper-and-pencil test called the *Social Interest Index* for determining the degree of positive social interest in four areas of life—work, friendship, love, and self-significance. On the basis of agreement among three prominent Adlerians, 32 items were selected, each of which was responded to by subjects on a 5-point scale of personal relevance. It was demonstrated that these items did not correlate with a scale of socially desirable responding. Internal consistency was .81, and stability over a 14-day period was .79.

TABLE 12-15   Correlations Between the Social Interest Index Score and 18 California Personality Inventory (CPI) Scores

CPI ATTRIBUTE	r[a]	r[b]	r[c]
Dominance	.27‡	.20†	.35‡
Capacity for status	.27‡	.25‡	.26†
Sociability	.27‡	.24‡	.27‡
Social presence	.07	.08	.08
Self-acceptance	.16†	.09	.20*
Sense of well-being	.36‡	.27‡	.36‡
Responsibility	.39‡	.29‡	.32‡
Socialization	.39‡	.31‡	.28‡
Self-control	.19†	.10	.26†
Tolerance	.26‡	.17*	.27‡
Good impression	.21‡	.14*	.35‡
Communality	.40‡	.37‡	.18*
Achievement via conformance	.35‡	.25‡	.35‡
Achievement via independence	.13*	.05	.14
Intellectual efficiency	.33‡	.24†	.30‡
Psychological mindedness	.09	−.02	.34‡
Flexibility	−.22‡	−.27‡	−.17*
Femininity	.29‡	.03	.08

[a]Total $N = 344$.
[b]Males $n = 189$.
[c]Females $n = 155$.
*$p < .05$.
†$p < .01$.
‡$p < .001$.

SOURCE: From "Development of the Social Interest Index," by K. B. Greever, M. S. Tseng, and B. U. Friedland, 1973, *Journal of Consulting and Clinical Psychology, 41.*

Having tested 228 male and female subjects, Greever et al. found that social interest scores were higher for women than men, increased with age and grade-point average, but were unrelated to socioeconomic level. With the possible exception of the finding concerning grade-point average, the results are consistent with Adlerian thought. The results of correlating the Social Interest Index with a standard, comprehensive test of personality, the California Personality Inventory, are shown in Table 12-15. A claim to construct validity is made because the Index shows correlates referring to communality, responsibility, socialization, sense of well-being, and achievement via conformance. This test seems worthy of additional empirical study.

White's Position

Because White's peripheral theorizing is the same as Erikson's, everything I have said concerning the ego psychologists is relevant here. There is surprisingly little research to go on, which renders us unable to assess the position from an empirical standpoint. In one study, Wherry and Waters (1968) attempted an objective measure of motivation by administering to 235 undergraduates a 150-item questionnaire about usual feelings involving individual, social, and accomplishment states. Through a factor analysis, they obtained factors best described as competence motivation and general satisfaction. Accordingly, they believed White's position to be supported. Also, Smith (1966) reports the results of a factor-analytic study of Peace Corps volunteers as indicating that an important difference among people is whether or not they have a basic attitude of self-confidence and self-reliance. This finding provides support for a number of fulfillment positions in addition to White's, just as certain results reviewed elsewhere can be construed as general support for them.

Goldfried and D'Zurilla (1969) have developed an inventory, the *Survey of Problematic Situations,* that attempts to determine the subject's level of competence. The Survey consists of a series of situations sampled from academic and social incidents provided by first-year college students, college staff, and faculty, and clinical folders. Responses to these situations were obtained from a group of first-year students and high-school seniors and then evaluated as inferior, average, or superior by teachers and counselors. These evaluations provided the scoring rules with which to assess competence. Although Goldfried and D'Zurilla have made an interesting beginning, there is simply too little information available about this inventory at this time to make any judgment about its empirical adequacy or its theoretical relevance to White's position.

Good and Good (1973) developed a test called the *Fear of Appearing Incompetent Scale*. Comprised of 36 true-false items, the reliability of this scale was tested on 355 undergraduate subjects, with a resulting internal consistency correlation of .89. It is possible that this scale will prove relevant to White's emphasis on sense of competence (Good and Good may be measuring its opposite), whereas Goldfried and D'Zurilla's inventory assesses actual competence.

White's (1959) paper on competence has stimulated research on intrinsic motivation, or the tendency to get involved in activities or work for which there is no tangible external reward. Most of this research has been done with either nonhuman organisms or children. The work on the former is not really relevant here, though it is interesting to find that even they seem to get involved in an activity for its own sake. Although I said earlier in this chapter that research involving children would not be emphasized, this is one place where such work is relevant. For White, affectance and competence motivation certainly appear early in human life.

Lepper, Greene, and Nisbett (1973) and Deci (1975) have accumulated evidence indicating that children initially involved in some activity will actually do it less following the introduction of external reinforcement. In the former case, children who chose to draw with felt-tip pens (over other activities) were reinforced by receiving a "Good Player" certificate and subsequently chose the activity less frequently than similar children not given the reinforcement. Deci's series of studies shows that tangible reinforcements, such as money, reduced initially preferred

activities. Negative reinforcements had the same effect. Further, Greene, Sternberg, and Lepper (1976) have shown that subjects rewarded for their most (rather than least) preferred activities decreased more in their subsequent willingness to choose the initially most preferred activity than did subjects who had been rewarded for their least preferred activity.

Lest you conclude that this research literature presents no disagreements, you should recognize that various explanations of supposedly intrinsic motivation have been offered (see de Charms & Muir, 1978), and all seem to have some empirical support. Much more needs to be known about this research area before one can draw firm conclusions. An interesting attempt in this direction is the work of Csikszentmihalyi (1975) which reports that when people were asked why they work on activities that do not promise external reward, they reported getting satisfaction out of the functioning if the task difficulty just exceeded their current capabilities. This finding is especially in keeping with the connotations of White's concept that there is a core tendency to achieve competency. Perhaps in intrinsically motivated activities persons are trying to increase their competence.

Allport's Position

It would be quite possible to pass over Allport with no attention, because he is so nonspecific on the periphery of personality. Nonetheless, he does offer some inkling of a peripheral viewpoint in stating his criteria of maturity. Research could be done, even at this rudimentary stage in his peripheral theorizing, to determine whether these criteria occur in people whose lives are successful, proactive, and propriate rather than unsatisfactory, reactive, and opportunistic. Although research has not explicitly addressed such matters, some findings in the literature are relevant. For example, the research on dogmatism and authoritarianism cited for Maslow is relevant, as well as the work on the self-concept reviewed in connection with Rogers. The studies on internal versus external locus of control, which I shall cover in the section on existential psychology, could also be considered as clarifying the existence and nature of proactive as opposed to reactive behavior, a distinction dear to Allport's heart.

Allport emphasizes the cardinal dispositions' general, overall effect on behavior more than the specific traits' more circumscribed effect. Some research has moved away from this emphasis and concerns itself with the specifics of acts (e.g., Buss & Craik, 1983). But there has also been a call for a return to Allport's broader emphasis (e.g., Funder, 1991) and, indeed, the accumulating research on the five-factor model is about general dispositions.

There are several specific content considerations unique to Allport that should be mentioned here. One concerns the sense of humor, incorporated into his criteria of maturity. Further, because for Allport maturity also implies having a philosophy of life and stable bases for social intimacy, the study by Worthen and O'Connell (1969) that I reviewed for Adler applies here. In any event, O'Connell (1960) has reported results suggesting that a sense of humor is indeed associated with successful living. Working with 332 college student subjects for whom self-ideal discrepancies were available, he found that those with small discrepancies appreciated humor more than those with large discrepancies. In addition, those with small discrepancies tended to appreciate nonsense wit, whereas those with large discrepancies tended to appreciate hostile wit. Further, Martin and Lefcourt (1983) have reported that subjects with a sense of humor show less mood disturbance in response to negative events than those without one.

A second consideration involves Allport's emphatic peripheral statement that there exist not only dynamic (motivational) traits but expressive (stylistic) traits, which may have even stimulated McClelland's distinction between motives and traits. Allport and Vernon (1933) did a pioneering study of performance (rather than self-description or fantasy) aimed at determining whether there is sufficient consistency to expressive movements to justify the belief in the importance of expressive traits. In one part of this large research program, a group of 25 subjects

was tested in three different sessions, each separated by about 4 weeks. During each session, the subjects responded to a large number of different tests providing measures of speed of reading and counting; speed of walking and strolling; length of stride; estimation of familiar sizes and distances; estimation of weights; strength of handshake; speed and pressure of finger, hand, and leg tapping; drawing squares, circles, and other figures; various handwriting measures; muscular tension; and so forth. In addition, observer ratings were obtained for various measures, such as voice intensity, speech fluency, amount of movement during natural speech, and neatness of appearance. First, Allport and Vernon assessed the stability of the various expressive measures over the three testing sessions. In general, these estimates of reliability were reasonably high and compared favorably with stability for self-descriptive measures of personality. It would seem that expressive characteristics have empirical existence. Next, Allport and Vernon examined the relationship among scores for the same tasks performed by different muscle groups, such as left and right side of the body, arms, and legs. Strikingly enough, they found about the same level of consistency as reported for the same muscle groups over time. This important finding suggests a general or central integrating factor that produces a consistent style no matter what peripheral manifestation is observed.

The final analysis attempted in this study was the intercorrelation of the major variables from all the tasks. Thirty-eight measures were intercorrelated by a form of cluster analysis roughly comparable to factor analysis. Three factors seemed to emerge, as indicated in Table 12-16. The first, the areal factor, included such variables as area of total writing, area of blackboard figures, area of foot squares, and length of self-rating checks. Motor expansiveness is what seems to have been involved here. The second factor, centrifugal-centripetal, seemed to involve introversion-extroversion, including such measures as overestimation of distance from body and underestimation of weights. The third factor, called the factor of emphasis, included such measures as voice intensity, movement during speech, writing

TABLE 12-16   Three Factors Based on Expressive Movements

Area group factor	
Area of total writing	.69
Total extent of figures	.67
Area of blackboard figures	.64
Slowness of drawing	.52
Area of foot squares	.48
Overestimation of angles	.45
Ratings on movement during idleness	.39
Length of self-rating checks	.38
Length of walking strides	.37
Centrifugal group factor	
Overestimation of distance from body with legs	.66
Overestimation of distance from body with hands	.55
Extent of cubes	.53
Underestimation (reverse of overestimation) of weights	.53
Verbal speed	.34
Underestimation of distances toward body with hands	.33
Ratings on speech fluency	.33
Group factor of emphasis	
Ratings on voice intensity	.71
Fewness of parallel lines	.65
Ratings on movement during speech	.53
Writing pressure	.52
Overestimation of weights	.46
Finger pressures on stylus	.45
Tapping pressure	.42
Underestimation of distances between hands	.42
Verbal slowness	.38
Ratings on forcefulness	.38
Overestimation of angles	.36
Pressure of resting hand	.32
Unoccupied space in drawing figures	.31

Source: Adapted from *Studies in Expressive Movement*, by G. W. Allport and P. E. Vernon. Copyright © 1933 by The Macmillan Company.

pressure, tapping pressure, and pressure of resting hand. In this kind of research lies the basis for determining the content of expressive traits that should be included in peripheral theorizing. Subsequent studies of expressive characteristics (e.g., Allport & Cantril, 1934; Estes, 1938; Huntley, 1940) are not very useful in this regard, having focused on the degree to which people can predict other features of persons' personalities from their expressive movements. These studies seem to make the assumption that the expressive movements are not themselves aspects of personality.

From time to time, studies emerge championing the idiographic (or morphogenic) approach so close to Allport's interests (see Chapter 6). Pervin's (1983) work is in this tradition of studying individuals rather than groups. Also, Lamiell, Foss, Larsen, and Hempel (1983) argue persuasively for the effectiveness of individual rather than aggregate data in understanding personality. Although the nomothetic counterarguments have been raised too (e.g., Paunonen & Jackson, 1986), rejoinders have also been made (e.g., Lamiell & Trievineiler., 1986).

A final topic important to Allport is body image, which is one facet of propriate functioning. Although it has been fueled more by eating-disorder concerns than Allport's theorizing, ongoing body-image research is nonetheless relevant here. There are body-image scales available, and data collected with them indicates the importance of separating perceptual from attitudinal features of how one's body is taken into account, and whether that is constructive or destructive to living (e.g., Cash & Pruzinsky, 1990; Cash & Szymanski, 1995; Jacobi & Cash, 1994; Thompson, 1990). Despite the possibility that Allport may have been one stimulus on these researchers, their findings really do not bear precisely on the adequacy of his theorizing.

Fromm's Position

As I have already indicated, the studies cited under the discussion of Rogers on the relationship between self-acceptance and acceptance of others also provide support for the emphasis in Fromm on the inextricably intermingled destiny of individuals and groups. In an even more general sense, other studies discussed in relation to fulfillment theorists lend indirect support for Fromm's position. Perhaps more relevant is a body of studies (Baumeister & Leary, 1995) indicating that people possess the fundamental desire for interpersonal attachments that Fromm meant in his core characteristic of need for relatedness.

None of this bears, however, on the receptive, exploitative, hoarding, marketing, and productive character types themselves. It is true that the first three types bear considerable similarity to the oral-incorporative, oral-aggressive, and anal types postulated by Freudians. Therefore, much of the research already discussed for Freud bears on Fromm's position as well. You will recall that there was some empirical support for the Freudian oral and anal types.

One large-scale field study (Fromm & Maccoby, 1970) bears directly on the hoarding, receptive, and exploitative character types. This is a naturalistic, anthropological study of a Mexican village, far from urban life. The researchers came to know and help the villagers over a period of years, studying them all the while. The portion of this large and interesting project most relevant here concerns a long, detailed questionnaire administered to the villagers in the hope of obtaining information about character types that could help the researchers understand day-to-day behavior and the social forces shaping it. Three questions are listed here as examples:

14. Describe your idea of a good mother. . . .

16. When you were a child, did you fear the anger of your father more, or that of your mother? . . .

47. Should women have the same rights as men? Why? (pp. 240–241)

Although these questions may appear easy to fake, Fromm and Maccoby knew their subjects well and had reason to believe they could be trusted.

The questionnaire was scored for 406 adult villagers, or 95% of the adult population. The scoring attempted to disclose which character types were present in a protocol and which was dominant. In attempting to accomplish this, the various traits Fromm (1947) lists under the types were used. The areas of concern were mode of assimilating experience, mode of relatedness,

sociopolitical relatedness, parental centeredness, and other behavioral traits. In addition to the supposedly nonideal character types, an attempt was made to score for productiveness directly. The scoring was inevitably somewhat global, and the scorers had to steep themselves in Fromm's position and the procedures involved. Nonetheless, reasonably adequate interscorer reliability was achieved for work of this kind (percentage of agreement ranged from 72 to 100). In addition, the Thematic Apperception and Rorschach Tests were employed in a subsidiary way, yielding some interesting agreements and disagreements with the primary measure (Fromm & Maccoby, 1970, pp. 271–191). Finally, the scored questionnaires were subjected to a factor analysis in order to determine whether the emerging factors conformed to character types. As you can see, this procedure conforms well to the first two steps of the ideal strategy discussed at the beginning of this chapter. Scores for traits relevant to Fromm's types were factor analyzed to see whether those types did in fact emerge. Of course, the scoring was rather interpretative, and the investigators can be presumed to have already believed in the value of the types. Nonetheless, emerging evidence for the position can be taken seriously.

The factors obtained include ones properly interpreted as receptive, exploitative, hoarding, and productive orientations. True to expectation, the last of these relates to the others such that one can speak of productive or nonproductive versions of them. Although an age factor accounted for the largest amount of the sample's behavior, productiveness-unproductiveness, exploitativeness-nonexploitativeness, and hoarding-receptivity followed in that order. In addition, there was a masculinity-femininity factor and one for mother-father centeredness. It is interesting to note that Fromm's marketing orientation did not seem to emerge. The investigators contend that this orientation was simply not present in this rather traditional, rural village. This is consistent with Fromm's position, which makes the marketing orientation a product of modern industrialization and urbanization.

In interpreting the results, the investigators

make some interesting and persuasive interpretations of how the existing orientations reflect long-standing cultural, social, and political realities of Mexican society. For example, the receptive orientation was found to be less often associated with productiveness than either the hoarding or exploitative orientations. Considering the authoritarian tradition of wealthy landowner and serfdom that has existed in Mexico for centuries, it is not surprising that villagers would be pushed into developing receptive orientations of an unproductive variety (they succumbed to excessive dependency on their masters). But the hoarding orientation is more likely to occur in a productive mode because it was also possible, given the sociopolitical situation, for a few villagers to own their own tiny plot of land, which would provide them with a slim but possible means of independence. That they had to hold onto this valuable parcel of land for dear life encouraged a hoarding form of productiveness. Finally, some with an exploitative orientation were able to achieve a productive mode because of the social changes taking place in Mexico, which were opening up the possibility for entrepreneurship among villagers who otherwise would be damned to poverty and dependence. My conclusion is that this comprehensive study, despite all its faults, provides general, if not the most precise, support for Fromm's position. Studies of its ilk should be mounted with regard to the other positions.

Understandably, no information has emerged concerning the marketing orientation. This is unfortunate, because it is the part of Fromm's peripheral theorizing most original to him. There is some available research, however, that bears on the phenomenon of alienation, central to the definition of the marketing personality. Unfortunately, work on alienation is often more polemical than scientifically rigorous. For example, Keniston (1966), studied 12 male college students intensively via repeated interviews, tests, and observations concerning their life situations and values. Unfortunately, Keniston does not see fit to include careful discussion of his procedures for selecting subjects, scoring their responses, and conducting statistical analyses of

the data. These omissions are consistent with Keniston's preference for intuitive, impressionistic portraits of people, used as examples to elucidate his theoretical views. In any event, Keniston contends that there is an alienated personality type, which includes such peripheral characteristics as a futile quest for positive values, possession of a pessimistic orientation, a distrust of commitment, and a disaffection for adulthood. His students emerge as people who know who they are not but have little conviction as to who they are. Although the general emphasis in Keniston's work is consistent with the marketing orientation, his research is not rigorous enough to have unequivocally demonstrated the empirical validity of Fromm's theorizing.

Indeed, Keniston (1966) thought he was providing a basis for understanding alienation in Freudian or at least ego psychology terms. He suggests that his alienated men had unresolved oedipal conflicts, stemming from their being mother's darling in the context of either literal absence of father or his extreme detachment from and unimportance in the home. As such, Keniston's research would not really support Fromm's position. But Keniston's Freudian explanation is very nebulous. It is not at all clear how the data bear him out in it. In this context, we can interpret the research conservatively to indicate the existence of a pattern of personality not unlike Fromm's marketing orientation. For that matter, these data are generally relevant to existential psychology as well.

Maccoby (1976) has researched male business executives, whom he studied in depth with interview techniques. Several types of personality were present among his subjects. One type, the "company man," is described in much the same terms as the marketing orientation. According to Maccoby, the company man is no longer making it big because businesses are becoming progressively bureaucratized and competition in the marketplace is diminishing. Thus, the company man is less able than before to get ahead by cleverly assessing what about himself will sell and expressing that above all. Although interesting, this study offers such impressionistic data and so many assumptions regarding trends in our society that it really does not constitute empirical support for Fromm's theorizing regarding the marketing orientation.

A few studies (e.g., Benson, 1966; Klein & Gould, 1969; Reimanis, 1966) concerning children in school situations indicate the existence of such characteristics as fatalism, meaninglessness, and powerlessness. Though these studies are rigorous enough in their measurement procedures and sampling, it is not clear what relationship their results bear to adult personality. After all, childhood being normally characterized by a sense of powerlessness does not necessarily augur an adult personality of the marketing type.

Existential Psychology

Although Kobasa's and Maddi's (Maddi, 1967, 1970; Kobasa & Maddi, 1977) peripheral theorizing might not be acceptable to those existential psychologists who prefer such an extreme position on individuality that no such theorizing is considered useful, I shall work with it nonetheless. The alternative would be to find very little research of any relevance to existentialism. In specifying the two main personality types as individualism and conformism, Kobasa and Maddi gear into a good deal of ongoing research in psychology. Some of this research might have been mentioned in other places, for it is certainly relevant to other theories. But it is perhaps most relevant here.

First is the burgeoning literature on whether people believe their lives to be controlled by them (internal locus of control) or by society and others (external locus of control). This research was pioneered by Julian Rotter (1954), who did not aim to provide any special support for existential psychology. Nonetheless, the findings are relevant here insofar as existentialists believe that people perceive themselves as having a mental life through which they can understand and influence their experiences and treat life as a series of decisions they must make responsibly (Kobasa & Maddi, 1977). This would clearly involve an internal locus of control. In addition, an external locus of control would bespeak the social reductionism of conformists, who perceive

their lives as being manipulated by social forces they cannot influence.

After several refinements, an *Internal versus External Locus of Control (I-E) Scale* was made available for general use (Rotter, Seeman, & Liverant, 1962). This scale consists of 23 items from which the following have been chosen:

I more strongly believe that:

6. a. Without the right breaks one cannot be an effective leader. [External]
   b. Capable people who fail to become leaders have not taken advantage of their opportunities. [Internal] . . .

9. a. I have often found that what is going to happen will happen. [External]
   b. Trusting to fate has not turned out as well for me as making a decision to take a definite course of action. [Internal] . . .

17. a. As far as world affairs are concerned, most of us are the victims of forces we can neither understand, nor control. [External]
    b. By taking an active part in political and social affairs, the people can control world events. [Internal]

Reliability for this scale seems quite adequate (Rotter, 1966). Several similar measures have also been developed (e.g., Bialer, 1961; Crandall, Katkovsky, & Crandall, 1965).

The first group of construct validation studies concerns the ramifications of belief in internal as opposed to external control of events on characteristics of primarily personal versus socially relevant behavior. Crandall et al. (1965) found that schoolboys high in internal control beliefs spent more time in intellectual free-play activities and scored higher on both reading and arithmetic achievement tests than those with external control beliefs. The more effective study habits and school performances of internally oriented persons is further supported by other studies (e.g., Findley & Cooper, 1983; Procink & Breem, 1974, 1975). Similarly, Seeman (1963) and Seeman and Evans (1962) found differential learning between internally and externally oriented people in two field settings. The latter investigators report that among hospitalized tuberculosis patients, those believing in external control had obtained less knowledge about their own conditions than those believing in internal control. This finding was not attributable to socioeconomic or hospital experience factors. Controlling for intelligence and the novelty of stimulus materials presented for learning, Seeman (1963) demonstrates that prison inmates scoring low in externality were high in retention of information presented to them concerning procedures relating to successfully achieving parole. Generalizing these findings to people at large, Pines and Julian (1972), Wolk and DuCette (1974), and several others have shown that internally oriented people gather more information in a range of situations and show more incidental learning than externally oriented people do. Maddi, Hoover, and Kobasa (1979), using a measure of powerlessness similar to that of the I-E Scale, report that subjects who believed they were powerless did not bother to explore an unfamiliar room in which they were asked to wait.

As you might expect, it has also been shown that subjects high in externality tend to be conformists whether conformity is measured by questionnaire (Odell, 1959) or performance (Crowne & Liverant, 1963). For example, Ryckman, Rodda, and Sherman (1972) exposed college students to influence from a high-prestige source depicted as having either relevant or irrelevant expertise. Externally oriented subjects changed opinion in the direction of the influence more often than internally oriented subjects, regardless of the relevance of expertise. This definite link between feeling externally controlled and conforming provides support for existential theorizing.

Consistent with the general picture of competence emerging from these studies are findings concerning risk taking. From a situation in which subjects were required to bet on the outcome of 30 trials of dice throwing, with the alternatives having objective probabilities, Liverant and Scodel (1960) report that the more the subjects believed in an internal locus of control, the more they could choose bets of intermediate probability and avoid low-probability bets. Similar results reported by Lefcourt (1965) also indicate that internally oriented subjects tended to regulate

their performances in terms of the realistic constraints contained in the probabilities. The only deviation from this conclusion concerns the observation made by Liverant and Scodel (1960) that internally oriented subjects never selected an extremely high or low probability bet.

In reflecting on the meaning of the risk-taking findings, one should consider Butterfield's (1964) study concerning anxiety, the results of which are presented in Table 12-17. Using questionnaire measures of anxiety, he found that the stronger the sense of external control, the greater the evidence that anxiety has a debilitating rather than facilitating effect on the person (see rows 5 and 6 of Table 12-17). Perhaps the seemingly unrealistic behavior of highly external people in risk-taking situations reflects the debilitating effects on them of anxiety about evaluation. In addition, row 4 of Table 12-17 indicates that the more external people are, the less constructive their reactions to frustration. Additional support for this position is provided by the studies of Platt and Eisenman (1968) and Feather (1967).

The general theme that internally and externally oriented people are sharply different in perception and performance is amplified by several recent studies. Using 98 male and female subjects, Alegre and Murray (1974) demonstrate that externally controlled people are more susceptible to verbal conditioning, which, of course, involves extrinsic reinforcements. That this may indeed reflect the generally greater experience of possibility or choice enjoyed by internally controlled people is suggested by Harvey and Barnes (1974), who presented their subjects with two options that differed in attractiveness, or were both attractive, or were both unattractive. Characteristically, internally controlled subjects experienced a greater sense of personal choice when the options were similar in attractiveness. Cherulnik and Citrin (1974) induced their 100 male and female subjects to express preferences for objects promised to them at a later time and then failed to make good on the promise. They found that internally controlled subjects increased in preference for the preferred and undelivered object when the reasons for its not being

TABLE 12-17   Intercorrelations of Measures

MEASURES	1	2	3	4	5	6	7	8	9	10	10	11	12	13
1. Locus of control														
Frustration reactions														
2. Intropunitive	184	—												
3. Extropunitive	149	135	—											
4. Constructive	−366*	623*	−042	—										
Anxiety reactions														
5. Debilitating	233	−081	267	−050	—									
6. Facilitating	−677*	−206	−139	488*	−766*	—								
Academic aspirations														
7. Range	398*	287	252	133	098	132	—							
8. Lowest grade	368*	044	722*	458*	199	123	027	—						
9. Actual grade	−073	063	−159	130	220	−035	−090	684*	—					
10. Satisfaction	246	−073	−019	−223	299*	−172	−475*	−415*	−075	—				
Fear of failure														
10. Satisfaction	246	−073	−019	−223	299*	−172	−475*	−415*	−075	—	—			
11. Satisfaction difference	064	093	020	−341	675*	−339*	010	−496*	187	888*	888*	—	—	
12. UE-LS	248	−033	149	−336*	014	126	218	−492*	124	277	277	−022		
13. (UE-LS) range	207	112	008	−342*	096	114	−419*	−463*	024	250	250	−020	093	—
Intelligence														
14. WAIS vocabulary	−174	210	037	601*	−429*	466*	091	−453*	387*	469*	469*	−367*	−055	042

*$p < .05$.

SOURCE: Adapted from "Locus of Control, Test Anxiety, Reactions to Frustration, and Achievement Attitudes," by E. C. Butterfield, 1964, *Journal of Personality, 32.* Copyright © 1964 by Duke University Press. Reprinted by permission.

delivered were made personally meaningful. In contrast, preference for the undelivered object increased for externally controlled subjects when the reason given was impersonal and arbitrary. It would seem that externally oriented persons feel more comfortable in arbitrary, uncontrollable conditions, whereas the opposite is true for internally oriented persons. Consistent with this are findings (e.g., Lefcourt, Hogg, Struthers, & Holmes, 1975; Sosis, 1974) indicating that internally oriented subjects tend to attribute success and failure in task performances to themselves and consider the driver of a car in an accident to be at fault. In contrast, the externally oriented see good or bad luck as responsible for both their own performances and others'. Internally oriented people appear to approximate the existential ideal in the sense that they regard life as a series of decisions that they can influence.

There are also interesting, if somewhat contradictory, findings concerning interpersonal behavior. Nowicki and Roundtree (1974) found internally controlled youngsters to be more popular with peers than those externally controlled. This does not stem from a lack of discernment on the part of the internally oriented, as suggested by Sherman (1973), who reports that when teamwork was important for success at a task, the internally oriented tended to select partners of equal ability whereas the externally oriented chose inferior partners. Further, Holmes and Jackson (1975) found the internally controlled to be less angry toward a person who gave both rewarding and punishing feedback to the subjects' responses on an interactive task than externally controlled people, who saw the communicator as less friendly and attractive than the internals did. All in all, it appears that internally controlled people are more task oriented and balanced in their social interactions and, perhaps for this reason, are more valued by others. Once again there is evidence to support existential theorizing concerning the authentic or individualistic type.

I shall now turn to some studies that compare various socially significant groupings of people as to the external or internal nature of their beliefs concerning control. In one of a series of studies on racial or ethnic groups, Battle and Rotter (1963) found that lower-class African Americans were significantly more external (measured by the *Children's Picture Test of Internal-External Control*) than lower-class Caucasians or middle-class African Americans and Caucasians. Using adult subjects, Lefcourt and Ladwig (1965, 1966) report higher rates of belief in external control among African-American prison inmates than among their Caucasian counterparts. In a third ethnic-group investigation, Graves (1961) adapted the I-E Scale for high-school students and found Caucasians to be more internal, followed by Hispanics and then American Indians. Concerning men enrolled in a Southern African-American college, Gore and Rotter (1963) found that subjects scoring the most internal (I-E Scale) signed statements expressing the greatest amount of interest in social action concerning civil rights. That these statements did not represent empty commitments is shown by Strickland (1965), who found that African-American activists had a stronger belief in their own power than did African Americans who did not take part in the civil rights movement. Pawlicki and Almquist (1973) found members of women's liberation groups to be more internal than college women who were not members. Similar results were obtained by Coleman et al. (1966) in their study of 645,000 pupils in grades 3, 6, 9, and 12 in 4000 American public schools. In summarizing this amazing study, they say,

> A pupil attitude factor, which appears to have a stronger relationship to achievement than do all the "school" factors together, is the extent to which an individual feels that he has some control over his own destiny. . . . The responses of pupils to questions in the survey show that minority pupils, except for Orientals, have far less conviction than whites that they can affect their own environments and futures. When they do, however, their achievement is higher than that of whites who lack that conviction. (p. 23)

In all of the ethnic studies, groups whose low social positions were due to either class or race tended to score higher in the external control direction. And to judge from the already reported attitudinal and action correlates of the belief in external control, it is easy to see why disadvantage because of class or race tends to perpetuate itself. Supporting the dire implication of the ethnic studies are the findings of Cromwell, Rosenthal, Shakow, and Kahn (1961) to the effect that schizophrenics have a stronger belief in external control (using three measures) than do normal people. If, as Maddi (1967, 1970) has contended, some proportion of people diagnosed as schizophrenic are actually suffering from existential sickness, this result lends some support to the contention that conformity is the premorbid state for this malaise.

A final group of studies concerns locus of control and health-related behaviors. Sampling this already vast body of literature, we find that the externally oriented are more likely than the internally oriented to experience debilitating rather than facilitating anxiety (e.g., Strassberg, 1973), to show more severe psychiatric symptoms, particularly schizophrenia (Lefcourt, 1976), to be more likely to contemplate suicide (e.g., Crepeau, 1978), and to suffer more from alcoholism (Naditch, 1975). Kobasa (1979) found powerlessness or externality to be one factor rendering business executives more likely to become physically or psychologically ill when confronted with highly stressful life circumstances. Needless to say, there are also some negative and equivocal findings in the literature (see Lefcourt, 1976; Strickland, 1978). But there is general support for the existential hypothesis that conformists are vulnerable to breakdown partially because they feel themselves to be victims of outside forces.

The investigators whose work I have summarized obviously want to reach the conclusion that internal control beliefs have a causal influence on actions. To be sure, this seems a sensible position, especially with regard to some of the studies, such as that of Coleman et al. (1966), in which beliefs concerning locus of control seem intimately related to school achievement. All the studies discussed, however, are correlational in nature, making conclusions of causality highly inferential. It could be, for example, that it is actual experiences of competence and effectiveness that incline one to believe in the internal control of rewards rather than the other way around.

In defense of their interpretation of belief as that which causes action, Rotter and his associates have marshaled experimental rather than correlational evidence. For example, Phares (1957) had two groups of subjects perform the same task of predicting a sequence of events. One group was told that success in the task depended on skill in deciphering the ordering of events; the other was told that success was due to chance, there being no rational ordering. Despite the fact that both groups received the same number and sequence of reinforcements, subjects with skill instructions changed expectancies more frequently and more in the direction of previous experience than subjects with chance instructions did. The differences in action between the two groups seems understandable on the basis of whether subjects did or did not believe that they could influence their own destinies. Analogous findings have been obtained concerning perceptual thresholds for nonsense syllables (Phares, 1962) and resistance to extinction (Holden & Rotter, 1962; James & Rotter, 1958; Rotter, Liverant, & Crowne, 1961). The evidence from these studies indicating that people who believe they can influence the occurrence of reward through their own skill act differently from people not having this belief certainly strengthens the inference concerning the direction of causality in the correlational studies (see Phares, 1976).

Before leaving the I-E Scale, I should point out that several studies have questioned its homogeneity. Collins (1974) administered the test to 300 college students and factor analyzed the scores. He found a common theme running

through the items, but he was also able to abstract four fairly distinct and unrelated factors. The factors seemed to distinguish the belief in the world as (1) a difficult place, (2) an unjust place, (3) a place governed by luck, or (4) a politically unresponsive place. Abramowitz (1973) separated the I-E Scale items into those of a political nature and those of a more personal nature. Utilizing 166 male and female subjects, he found that the political items correlated positively with membership in sociopolitical action groups, whereas the personal items did not. Through studies of this sort we may learn more about what admittedly is an intriguing test.

Turning from the I-E Scale, we find a gradually developing body of studies quite relevant to, and for the most part inspired by, existential theorizing. For example, Houston and Holmes (1974) exposed their subjects to conditions of threat involving temporal uncertainty. Some of the subjects were induced to avoid thinking about the threat by immersing themselves in distracting activities, while the other subjects were left to their own devices. Physiological measurement showed that the subjects who engaged in avoidance thinking actually experienced a greater stress reaction to the threat than did the other subjects. Through interviews, it was determined that the subjects who did not engage in avoidance activities spent the time thinking about the threat and reappraising it as less serious than originally believed. Insofar as a temporal uncertainty differs only slightly from ontological anxiety, this study provides support for the existential belief that accepting such anxiety rather than avoiding it is consistent with personal growth. Liem (1973) permitted some students in an undergraduate course to choose the type of recitation section they preferred, granting them considerable choice in the ongoing conduct of the section, and denied such choice to other students in the course. Subjects who were permitted choice performed better than the others on a course examination and gave higher ratings of satisfaction with their sections than did subjects not permitted choice. This is another demonstration of the value of control over one's own life for personal comfort and growth.

Some interest has developed in devising ways to measure the sense of meaninglessness that results from an accumulation of ontological guilt. Crumbaugh and Maholick (1964) and Crumbaugh (1968) have offered a questionnaire, called the *Purpose in Life Test,* aimed at assessing Frankl's concept of existential vacuum. Although their study of the reliability of the questionnaire is incomplete, they do report an estimate of internal consistency of .85 with 120 subjects. The construct validity of the instrument is also scant, but there is a correlation of .44 with the Depression Scale of the MMPI and another of .48 for men and .32 for women with a measure of anomie. Sharpe and Viney (1973) administered the Purpose in Life Test to 58 college students and interviewed them about their world views. Then three judges rated the interviews for indications of meaninglessness. Subjects showing existential vacuum on the Purpose in Life Test had world views that were negative, lacking in purpose, and devoid of transcendent goals. In one recent study, Soderstrom and Wright (1977) show that among 427 college student subjects, those who appeared on other questionnaires to be intrinsically motivated, religiously committed, and true believers had lower existential-vacuum scores on the Purpose in Life Test. Further, Paloutzian (1981) reports that following religious conversion, subjects showed higher Purpose in Life scores. Although this test is probably of value, much more care must be given to its development than has been offered thus far.

Another related test, called the *Existential Study,* was developed by Thorne (1973), Pishkin and Thorne (1973), and Thorne and Pishkin (1973). The 200-item questionnaire has been produced factor analytically to yield seven scales on self-status, self-actualization, existential morale, existential vacuum, humanistic identification, existence and destiny, and suicidal tendency. In one study, the test was administered to 193 felons, 89 alcoholics, 153 adherents to Ayn Rand's rational philosophy, 336 unwed mothers, 159 students, and 338 schizophrenics. The Rand followers were highest in existential morale, followed by students and felons. In contrast, alcoholics and unwed mothers appeared demoralized, and schizophrenics disintegrated. However interesting this test may be, you should recognize that (1) little information regarding internal consistency and stability is available, (2) little has been done to determine its construct validity, and (3) it has not been guided by a consistent and definite set of existential ideas (e.g., self-actualization is not really an existential concept).

Maddi, Kobasa, and Hoover (1979) have devised a 60-item questionnaire, called the *Alienation Test,* for assessing the powerlessness, adventurousness, nihilism, and vegetativeness aspects of meaninglessness that appear in existential theorizing. Each of these dimensions can be measured across relationships to work, persons, social institutions, family members, and self. The internal consistency of the dimensions and relationships ranges from .62 to .96, with an average of .86. Stability figures range from .54 to .87, with an average of .80. Relevant to discriminant validation are the findings that the Alienation Test is uncorrelated to intelligence or sex, though it does show a small and understandable relationship to socioeconomic class and age. A beginning on convergent validation has been made in that the scales of the Alienation Test show negative correlation of varying degree with a measure of creative attitudes toward living. Also, people scoring high on meaninglessness in interpersonal relationships and alienation from family spend more time watching TV and in solitary activities (Csikszentmihalyi, 1975). So apparently pervasive is the sense of powerlessness and vegetativeness that subjects high on these measures do not even bother to explore an unfamiliar room when left alone to wait for the experimenter (Maddi, Hoover, & Kobasa, 1982). Further, Kobasa (1979) has shown that business executives high in alienation from self, on vegetativeness, and on powerlessness are more likely to react to stressful life events with illness symptoms than are other executives. These findings indicate the general passivity and vulnerability involved in existential sickness as theorized by Maddi (1967, 1970). But an emerging difficulty with the Alienation Test is a rather high intercorrelation among the various dimensions, raising the possibility that there are in reality fewer usable scores than presumed.

There is also a large body of research on the regular tendency of some people to conform by trying to be socially desirable. This literature is clearly important for the existential position, though it is also relevant for Rogers, Maslow, and Allport. At the outset, however, I should address a ready criticism. Much of the research in which conformity is measured on some performance task suggests that conforming tendencies are specific to situations (e.g., Hollander & Willis, 1967). This could be taken as evidence that no conformist personality type exists. But such a conclusion seems premature, however mystifying the performance results may be. There is, after all, a considerable body of research suggesting that the tendency to conform indeed may be quite general. I refer to the research employing questionnaire measures of socially desirable responding and internal versus external locus of control.

Crowne and Marlowe (1960) have reported a concerted attempt at construct validation for their carefully developed *Social Desirability Scale* (M-C SDS). On the face of it, the tendency to respond in a socially desirable direction should express conformity and an emphasis on social-role playing. By and large, the empirical findings bear this out. In an extensive research program (Crowne & Marlowe, 1960), it was determined that people scoring high in socially desirable responding show greater attitude change after being induced to deliver an appeal for an attitude they did not originally endorse (thereby resolving cognitive dissonance), express higher need for affiliation, and terminate psychotherapy sooner (perhaps out of unwillingness to face themselves) than low scorers do. In addition, the higher the M-C SDS score, the greater the tendency to give common word associations and fewer, more concrete responses on the Thematic Apperception, Rorschach, and Sentence Completion Tests. In their fantasy productions, high M-C SDS scorers are especially rejecting of people but tend to underestimate the extent to which their friends really reject them. The highest threshold in a perceptual task requiring the recognition of obscene words belongs to these high social-desirability scorers.

There is also a group of findings concerning socially desirable responding and performance of simple laboratory tasks. Subjects high on the M-C SDS generally perform better on the pursuit rotor (Strickland & Jenkins, 1964) and perform more skillfully a motor steadiness task (Strickland, 1965) and other simple motor tasks (Willington & Strickland, 1965). Although the results may indicate superior motor ability in these subjects, it seems more likely to be the heightened attentiveness created by a wish to appear socially desirable. Consistent with this interpretation, one finding (Crowne & Marlowe, 1960) shows that subjects high in M-C SDS are less likely to rate a monotonous spool-packing task as dull.

In general, the picture emerging is that of a personality type characterized by intense interest in appearing attentive, consistent, competent, and acceptable in the context of conformity; superficial interest in but lack of deep commitment to others; and a general unwillingness to face these facts. The implications of defensiveness are supported by Conn and Crowne (1963), who found that high M-C SDS scorers selected euphoria as an alternative to the expression of anger in a manner suggestive of reaction formation. Similarly, Fishman (1965) found that subjects high in M-C SDS expressed less verbal aggression toward the experimenter when nonarbitrary frustration was imposed (whereas arbitrary frustration did not differentiate high from low M-C SDS scores). Apparently people high in socially desirable responding can express anger only when they can find justification (or rationalization) for it.

Any information concerning the relationship of M-C SDS to psychopathology should be of interest, as Maddi (1967, 1970) has contended that conformism is the premorbid state for existential sickness. Even though the M-C SDS was specifically designed to be independent of frank psychopathology, some research indicates that this is not so. Katkin (1964) reports the correlations between the M-C SDS and the MMPI scales commonly used to assess psychopathological trends. Eight of the 10 correlations reached significance but were negative, suggesting that conformity does not predispose one toward sickness. Further research is needed to determine whether Maddi's position requires reformulation. The additional research should involve measures of actual symptomatology rather than questionnaires such as the MMPI.

Although research on socially desirable responding continues to be done, the pace has slowed. Often these days this conforming tendency is studied not alone but along with other tendencies that may even be regarded as more important (see Strickland in Blass, 1977). Also, research on the self-monitoring tendency may fit alongside socially desirable responding. According to Snyder (1987), high self-monitors are very concerned with public appearances and the feedback they receive from others concerning their adequacy. Jones, Brenner, and Knight (1990) show that when subjects were compelled to perform a reprehensible task, those who succeeded thought better of themselves only if they were high self-monitors. Indeed, low self-monitors thought well of themselves only if they failed in the reprehensible task. Apparently, there is much support in this research theme of socially desirable responding and the self-monitoring tendency for existential psychology, Rogers, Maslow, Allport, and Fromm.

Before closing this section, I should mention Tyler's (1978) book integrating a wide range of research studies toward the end of understanding individuality. This is an especially interesting approach given the emphasis on the nonideal, conforming states in the work discussed thus far. Reviewing hundreds of studies, Tyler found considerable evidence of what she calls possibility-processing structures in people that underlie choice as a sign of individuality and creative living. This placing of the decision-making capabilities and the pursuit of possibility at the heart of the matter of individuality is, of course, quite consistent with existential theorizing. The emphasis Tyler identifies has continued since her book appeared, as shown in a review by Singer and Kolligian (1987). Intriguingly, Ullman (1987) shows that, in trying to express their true selves,

young adolescents emphasize revealing secrets whereas older (presumably more developmentally advanced) adolescents emphasize expressing their views and beliefs instead. Studying undergraduates (older adolescents and young adults), Johnson and Boyd (1995) found that, in identifying their authentic selves, subjects emphasized their concrete behavioral experiences whereas observers of them preferred to use more abstract trait terms. Presumably, as we grow up, we think of ourselves in complex, individualistic ways, even though others may oversimplify us. Support for this interpretation appears in the study of Schaller, Boyd, Yohannes, and O'Brien (1995), who found that, in describing others, subjects with a rigid intolerance of ambiguity were those most likely to engage in stereotypes. Thus, the kind of research interpreted by Tyler as highlighting individuality continues, lending general support to existential theorizing.

Though not available to Tyler, a previously mentioned study by Kobasa (1979) has initiated a relevant program of research bearing directly on existential psychology. This study introduces the personality style of hardiness, which, as indicated in Chapter 6, is considered a concrete manifestation of existential courage (see Maddi, 1988; Kobasa & Maddi, 1977). Hardiness involves three interrelated beliefs about self and world—namely, that (1) you can always find something in what you are doing that will make it interesting and worthwhile (commitment rather than alienation), (2) you can influence the events going on around you if you try (control rather than powerlessness), and (3) you can learn from frequent life changes in an ongoing growth process (challenge rather than threat). Kobasa (1979) reasoned that people showing hardiness (existential courage) should be able to resist the otherwise debilitating effects of stressful events because of their high level of awareness, their tendency toward future-oriented decisions, and the general individuality involved in this style. On the basis of questionnaire responses, Kobasa formed two groups of business executives, both high in stressful events, with one high and the other low in illness symptoms. As can be seen in Table 12-18, on various

TABLE 12-18   Differences Between High Stress/Low Illness* and High Stress/High Illness* Executives

VARIABLE	HIGH STRESS/ LOW ILLNESS		HIGH STRESS/ HIGH ILLNESS		*t* Value	Standardized Discriminant Function Coefficient
	(M)	(SD)	(M)	(SD)		
Control						
Nihilism	196.05	133.61	281.02	169.86	2.49‡	.73
External locus of control	5.92	4.10	7.90	4.61	2.03†	.22
Powerlessness	301.15	188.93	388.47	188.44	2.11†	—
Achievement	16.50	2.10	15.12	3.20	−1.20	—
Dominance	14.60	3.26	13.85	4.46	.86	—
Leadership	33.47	7.34	34.63	6.80	.73	.43
Commitment						
Alienation from self	102.35	117.24	219.15	185.77	3.36†	1.04
Alienation from work	181.67	122.04	223.73	175.09	1.22	.43
Alienation from friends	256.02	162.76	316.10	165.24	1.64	—
Alienation from family	158.47	139.02	198.72	144.33	1.27	—
Alienation from society	202.15	100.21	226.95	133.93	.94	—
Role consistency	29.22	6.42	29.50	6.44	.19	.30
Challenge						
Vegetativeness	155.50	140.24	216.27	160.94	1.98†	.99
Security	21.11	6.33	22.19	8.60	.34	.35
Cognitive structure	13.35	2.81	14.10	2.85	1.10	.21
Adventurousness	269.00	164.58	337.54	174.95	1.78†	—
Endurance	15.97	2.35	14.37	3.19	−.96	—
Interesting experiences	34.97	6.83	32.52	7.02	−.92	—
Perception of personal stress	3.00	1.21	3.83	1.73	2.46‡	.43

Note: For all variables, the higher the number, the greater the degree of the variable observed. Superior hardiness is indicated by higher scores on achievement, role consistency, endurance, and interesting experiences, and lower scores on nihilism, external locus, powerlessness, dominance, leadership, alienation (from self, work, social institutions, interpersonal relationships, and family), vegetativeness, security, cognitive structure, and adventurousness. A subject's scores on all areas of alienation, measured by the Alienation Test, have a possible range of 0 to 1,200. Vegetativeness, nihilism, powerlessness, and adventurousness scores, also from the Alienation Test, may range from 0 to 1,500. External locus has a low of 0 and an upper limit of 23. The scales taken from the Jackson test—achievement, dominance, cognitive structure, and endurance—have a minimum value of 0 and a maximum of 20. The California Life Goals scale—leadership, security, and interesting experiences—may range from 0 to 60. Role consistency has a low of 0 and a high of 40; perception of personal stress can range from 0 to 7.
*n = 40.
†$p < .05$.
‡$p < .01$.
SOURCE: From "Stressful Life Events, Personality, and Health: An Inquiry into Hardiness," by S. C. Kobasa, 1979, *Journal of Personality and Social Psychology, 37.*

personality questionnaires, the group low in illness symptoms showed greater evidence of all three aspects of hardiness than the group high in illness symptoms did.

To bolster the direction of causal inference from hardiness to illness, Kobasa, Maddi, and Kahn (1982) used a time lag design (in which hardiness and stressful event scores were obtained a year before illness scores) plus a statistical control for prior illness scores in their study of business managers. As hypothesized, the results show that hardiness buffers against illness most as stressful events mount. In explicating how hardiness buffers, subsequent research shows that subjects high in this personality style respond to stressful events with less physiological arousal (measured by skin conductance and blood pressure) and with greater efforts to make the events less stressful (Holahan & Moos, 1985; Hull & Schwartz, 1987; Kobasa, 1982; Maddi & Kobasa, 1984; Rhodewalt & Zone, 1989; Weibe & McCallum, 1986). In addition, recent studies show that hardiness expresses vigorous mental health (Maddi & Khoshaba, 1994) and leads to more effective performance (Maddi & Hess, 1992; Westman, 1990). For reviews of hardiness research, see Kobasa (1982), Maddi (1990), Blaney and Ganellen (1990), Funk (1992), and Orr and Westman (1990).

As to discriminant validity, it is also clear that personality hardiness is neither merely a mental reflection of a strong constitution (Kobasa, Maddi, & Courington, 1981) nor simply the glow that comes from physical exercise (Kobasa, Maddi, & Puccetti, 1982). In comparing the relative effectiveness of buffers in the stress-illness relationship, Kobasa, Maddi, Puccetti, and Zola (1986) found personality hardiness to be almost twice as powerful as either social support or physical exercise.

Although the hardiness research theme appears quite promising as support for existential psychology, Ganellen and Blaney (1984) found a buffering effect in their subjects for the commitment but not the challenge and control components of hardiness. Other investigators (Funk & Houston, 1987; Hull, Van Trueren, & Virnelli, 1987) have found that the challenge component of hardiness may not intercorrelate with the other two components. These findings raise the question as to whether hardiness is as unitary as proposed. Of course, the college students used as subjects in these studies may just be different psychologically than the business managers used in the studies by Maddi and his associates. In any event, more recent studies using an improved measure of hardiness (e.g., Bartone, 1989; Maddi, 1987; Maddi & Hess, 1992; Maddi &

Khoshaba, 1994) show the predicted interrelational pattern for commitment, control, and challenge components, regardless of whether the subjects are adolescents or adults. Further, a study by Jensen (1987) with quite different methods appears to support the existential notion that high levels of awareness are consistent with mental and physical health. It was found that among women with breast cancer, those who were most defensive (repressive or relying on escapist fantasies) showed greater spread of their illness. The implications of this finding are quite consistent with hardiness research.

Findings justifying the interpretation of hardiness as existential courage have continued to accumulate. In an unusually comprehensive and well-designed experiment, Weibe (1991) determined the hardiness levels of undergraduate subjects, then had them perform a difficult task on which they would be evaluated. The dependent variables were emotional arousal, behavioral effectiveness, and psychophysiological responsivity. Subjects high in hardiness showed greater frustration tolerance, evaluated the task as less threatening, and responded to it with more positive and less negative emotions than subjects low in hardiness did. All subjects showed increased heart rate during the task, but high hardiness men had lower elevations than low hardiness men. Hardiness did not influence heart rate in women. Results for women were different in the prospective study by Priel, Gonik, and Rabinowitz (1993) on a naturally occurring stressful circumstance—childbirth. Although the total hardiness score did not produce results, the component scores and their interaction did. Specifically, commitment and challenge, and also the interaction between challenge and control, predicted not only maternal appraisals of how difficult childbirth would be, but success in coping with labor and amount of analgesic intake as well. Women low in hardiness emerged as having an "anxious cognitive style." All the findings persisted when negative affectivity was controlled.

Other studies support the implication in these findings that hardiness protects against mental illness. For example, Maddi and Khoshaba (1994) report a pattern of negative relationships between hardiness and the "clinical" scales (e.g., depression, hysteria, paranoia, mania) of the MMPI-2, even with negative affectivity controlled. Also, negative relationships have been found between hardiness and various measures of anxiety and depression (Allred & Smith, 1989; Drory & Florian, 1991; Funk & Houston, 1987; Rhodewalt & Zone, 1989). Further, Shepperd and Kashani (1991) show direct effects of commitment and control, along with stress and gender, on psychological symptoms (these investigators used only the hardiness part scores, not the total). Finally, Florian, Milkulincer, and Taubman (1995) studied hardiness and coping among men and women undergoing Israeli combat training. Using path analysis to determine the direction of causality, they found that subjects high in commitment and control tended to appraise the training as less threatening, engage in more coping strategies, and seek more social support and, through these efforts, retained greater mental health at the end of the 4-month training period. Once again, these effects could not be explained away as negative affectivity. Although in this study and that of Shepperd and Kashani (1991), the challenge component was not predictive, it has been in other studies (e.g., Maddi & Khoshaba, 1994; Priel et al., 1993; Weibe, 1991); therefore, it would be premature to delete it from the measurement of hardiness. Meanwhile, evidence for the interpretation of hardiness as existential courage, with attendant implications for individuality, conformity, and mental health and illness, continues to accumulate.

In closing this section, let me mention a final theme in existential theorizing addressed by psychological research literature. In summarizing some research, Taylor and Brown (1988) argue that *positive illusions* (thinking that you and circumstances are better than is really true) promote well-being and mental health. This contention is quite inconsistent with existential thought, in which illusions, even positive ones, constitute what Sartre calls *self-deception*. Self-deception should disrupt constructive, full living, rather than enhance it. The supposed positive effect of illusions is also at variance with other

personological positions, such as ego psychology. In their critique, Colvin and Block (1994) identify several serious shortcomings in the interpretation of research engaged in by Taylor and Brown. In addition, Colvin, Block, and Funder (1995) report two longitudinal studies and one experiment, the findings of which show that subjects with positive illusions have poor social skills and are psychologically maladjusted. These findings support the existential view of positive illusions as self-deception.

Ellis's Position

Rational-emotive therapy is so devoid of peripheral theorizing that it is not even possible to determine how to construe any research as relevant.

Kelly's Position

Kelly, the consistency theorist, says virtually nothing substantive concerning the periphery of personality. Consequently, there is little we can do to determine the empirical validity of his position. Using Kelly's Role Constructs Repertory Test (see Chapter 7), Bieri (1961) has shown that people differ in the number of bipolar constructs they have available to them.

The notion of psychological complexity has been picked up by other investigators who do not necessarily use Kelly's test in measuring it. For example, Porter and Suedfeld (1981) report that the more complexity shown in the writings of literary figures, the less they were interested in war, but the more they supported social unrest. Also, Tetlock (1984) found that the ordering of members of the British House of Commons on complex views regarding political issues, from most complex to least, was moderate socialists, moderate conservatives, and extremes of both. However interesting these differences in psychological complexity or differentiation are, they do not really bear on the peripheral point of view that is explicitly Kelly's. They are potentially important, however, to any theory that conceptualizes degrees of differentiation in peripheral personality (e.g., Allport, existential psychology).

The same is true for studies showing that the constructs one holds influence the way one perceives and makes decisions. Studies such as those of Swann and Read (1981) and Leitner and Cado (1982) chronicle how perceptions of self and major values influence performance and stress levels. Also, Benesch and Page (1989) found that interpersonal congruence was predicted by self-construct system content. But such findings support Allport, Rogers, and existential psychology as much as they do Kelly.

In an intriguing study by Sechrest (1968), admittedly inductive rather than hypothesis testing, two samples of 57 and 67 nursing students filled out the Role Constructs Repertory Test and also took the MMPI and a sociometric instrument requiring them to specify how pleasant they thought each member of their group was. Sechrest determined that the personal constructs of intelligent-unintelligent, anxious-nonanxious, and friendly-unfriendly were among the most common in the group. He attempted, then, to determine whether the personal constructs one employs in some way express the realities of one's existence. This hypothesis is consistent with the general emphasis in Kelly's approach on a kind of rational trial and error in finding the best bases for navigating life. Sechrest also had available to him his subjects' linguistic ability scores on the *American Council of Education (ACE) Test* (an intelligence measure). He tried to evaluate scores on this against reliance on intelligence-unintelligence as a construct. From the MMPI, he extracted an anxiety score (the Psychasthenia Scale) to evaluate against reliance on the anxious-nonanxious construct. For similar purposes with regard to the friendly-unfriendly construct, he used the number of the subjects' sociometric nominations of other people as friendly. His results appear in Table 12-19.

As you can see, moderately intelligent subjects are more likely to use intelligence as a personal construct than highly intelligent ones are. Those subjects who employ anxious-nonanxious as a construct are likely to be either extremely high or extremely low on the MMPI measure of anxiety. But the findings concerning the low end of the scale on Sample 1 are washed out on Sample 2.

The safest conclusion is that highly anxious subjects use anxious-nonanxious as a construct. Similarly, subjects relying on friendly-unfriendly in their construct systems receive a large number of nominations as "most pleasant." This study provides evidence of correspondence between the way one construes the world and the way one behaves in it. It is not possible, however, to specify which comes first. Although the use of such presumably uninfluenceable variables as intelligence suggests that construals follow objective features of experience, this inference is not convincing with regard to anxiety and popularity.

The work of Adams-Webber (1970) on the discriminant validity of various forms of the Role Constructs Repertory Test does seem to have anticipated an increase in interest in this assessment technique. Fransella (in Bannister, 1970) has used this test to study construct change over the course of group psychotherapy, in which context the test seems to be a useful tool for quantifying directions that are perennially difficult to chart. Also, Bonarius (in Cole, 1976) has found Kelly's test a useful instrument for studying continuing interactions among people. And Mancuso (in Cole, 1976) shows that children in kindergarten and sixth grade perceive situations of coercion and rational explanation differently as measured by this test. Although interesting in their own right, these studies really do not test anything about Kelly's theory; rather, they show that his general approach and assessment device can be useful when quantification is difficult.

There should be a correspondence between Rosenberg's studies (in Cole, 1976) of the implicit "personality theories" that people carry around with them and Kelly's emphasis on personal construction of experience. Rosenberg indicates that the Role Constructs Repertory Test should be a useful instrument in getting at people's implicit notions. Using his own assessment devices, Rosenberg summarizes typical content categories observable in people. It would be quite valuable for psychologists of Kelly's persuasion to take this work seriously and use it as a basis for some peripheral theorizing. If that happened, Kelly's position might become truly predictive

TABLE 12-19   Relationships Between Employment of Certain Personal Constructs and Corresponding Personal Characteristics

PERSONAL CHARACTERISTIC MEASUREMENT INSTRUMENT	Score	PERSONAL CONSTRUCT			
		Sample 1 ($N = 57$)*		Sample 2 ($N = 67$)	
		Nonuse	Use	Nonuse	Use
		Intelligent-Unintelligent			
ACE Aptitude Test					
Linguistic ability score	70+	15	4	16	9
	60–69	6	11	8	14
	−59	12	9	10	10
	x^2	7.02; $p < .05$		3.57; $p < .20$	
		Anxious-Nonanxious			
MMPI					
Psychasthenia raw score	20+	2	13	2	12
	10–19	15	15	18	21
	−9	1	9	7	7
	x^2	8.66; $p < .02$		5.03; $p < .10$	
		Friendly-Unfriendly			
Nominating					
Number of nominations	10+	6	22	5	25
	−9	14	15	15	22
	x^2	4.52; $p < .05$		4.52; $p < .05$	

*For personal construct "anxious-nonanxious" $N = 55$ only.
SOURCE: From "Personal Constructs and Personal Characteristics," by L. Sechrest, 1968, *Journal of Individual Psychology, 24.* Copyright © 1968 by the University of Vermont. Reprinted by permission.

rather than merely descriptive of behavior (Mischel, 1964). Unfortunately, Kellian writings (e.g., Fransella, 1978) have not seemed to be going in this direction.

Epstein's Position

Because Epstein does little peripheral theorizing, not much exists to evaluate in terms of validity. But, research findings from a wide range of approaches are claimed by Epstein (1994) as general support for his cognitive-experiential self-theory. In particular, he assumes that the rational-conceptual system is well documented through studies of how people reach reflective,

logical conclusions through reflection on information they receive. For instance, you will recall those studies that led us to conclude, in Chapter 10, that although some behavior is distorted (and in that sense consistent with a theory of defense), the rest is accurate to experience.

Epstein (1994) summarizes various kinds of evidence to document the existence of an experiential-conceptual system, along with the more rational system. He sees the most concrete level of the experiential-conceptual system documented by the research on classical conditioning, which emphasizes how stimuli regularly paired with natural reinforcements (such as food) come to have learned reinforcement qualities for the subject. For example, if a tone is rung preceding the appearance of food, subjects will very soon begin to salivate when they experience only the tone. The tone will have become a conditioned stimulus through a process of associationistic learning. At a less concrete level, there is the research evidence on "heuristics," or cognitive shortcuts that people use frequently in decision-making contexts (Tversky & Kahneman, 1974). For example, subjects responding to vignettes typically report that the heroes become more upset following unfortunate but arbitrary outcomes preceded by acts of commission rather than omission, by near rather than far misses, and by freely chosen rather than constrained actions. The irrationality inherent in these subjects' responses suggests the existence of an experiential-conceptual system of information processing. There is by now much research supporting the existence of these irrational shortcuts in thinking (Fiske & Taylor, 1991).

Epstein (1994) and various associates have reported research to support his claim that irrational shortcuts in thinking are not merely failings of rationality, but rather evidence of the existence of a second, irrational way of thinking —namely, the experiential-conceptual system. First, they report that subjects are well aware that they and others operate by implicit inferential rules that differ from rational thought. For example, in circumstances similar to those used by Tversky and Kahneman, Epstein and his associates found that subjects were well aware that a "rational person" would not fall into the irrational shortcuts, even though they believed such shortcuts to be a reasonable way to proceed. Further, when the experimental conditions strongly favor the experiential-conceptual system, subjects will give in to it even more than usual. There is also evidence in Epstein's research that when multiple thoughts are solicited from subjects in response to the kinds of vignettes used by Tversky and Kahneman, the first two or three are experiential-conceptual (e.g;, emotional, irrational), but the later ones are rational-conceptual.

In an intriguing foray into individual differences (Epstein, 1994), results show that subjects who insist that their irrational shortcuts are indeed rational tend to have great faith in their intuition and to think in a more simplistic, undifferentiated way than others. Lest we regard these subjects as somehow inadequate, Epstein (1994) provokes us with the case history of a woman who is better able to understand her past through use of the experiential-conceptual than the rational-conceptual system.

However intriguing Epstein's (1994) research is, it does not play a decisive role in evaluating his personality theorizing because he has not elaborated a peripheral statement and because his core statement is so vast. It also includes so many assumptions that there are not currently sufficient findings to produce a very compelling case. Because core statements are so abstracted from the specific behaviors through which people lead their lives, personality theories need articulated peripheral statements that, because they are much more concrete, can be evaluated through research. Although Epstein (1994) has begun to raise theoretically relevant questions concerning development and individual differences, there are no current answers that we can scrutinize.

McClelland's Position

You will recall that fantasy techniques for measuring personality involve an ambiguous or incomplete stimulus and require people to structure or complete it by exercising their own imaginations, thus displaying their personalities. Although fantasy techniques may be difficult to interpret, they are more likely to circumvent response styles than self-descriptive techniques are. Because the investigator's aim is not apparent, the subject will not likely find some basis for being acquiescent or for responding in a socially desirable fashion. This is why McClelland has considered fantasy measures the most relevant to the motive construct, with its personal rather than societal goals.

At first, as covered in Chapters 7 and 11, McClelland contrasts his view of motives, which are expressed in fantasy, with values or schemata, which are expressed in self-description. More recently, he (McClelland, 1980, 1985; McClelland et al., 1989) has promoted the distinction between *operant* (implicit), and *respondent* (explicit) *motivation.* Operant motives are what he has been calling motives all along, and are to be measured in fantasy productions. Respondent motives are self-descriptions that are motivational (goal directed) in character, which one can measure in responses to such socially structured situations as questionnaires. The technique of eliciting operant motives in fantasy on which McClelland has relied is the Thematic Apperception Test (TAT) by Murray (1943), with its ambiguous pictures from which the subject must compose a story with a beginning, a middle, and an end. Various questionnaires have been used in determining respondent motives.

Several studies have demonstrated the utility of the distinction between operant and respondent motivation. For example, Koestner, Weinberger, and McClelland (1991) show that performance on a memory task with socially apparent right and wrong answers was best predicted by self-reported achievement motivation, whereas performance on an intrinsically challenging word-finding puzzle was more a function of achievement motivation expressed in fantasy. Berniat (1989) found that motive measures based on fantasy and those based on self-description were uncorrelated. Further, these measures predicted operant and respondent behaviors, respectively. Woike (1995) applied the operant-respondent motivation distinction to the experiences subjects remembered as most memorable. She found operant (or implicit) motivation related to memories of internal experiences, and respondent (or explicit) motivation related to more routine memories. In contrast, the study by Emmons and McAdams (1991) is not as supportive of the operant-respondent motivation distinction. They compared affiliation, achievement, dominance, and nurturance motives on the TAT and on a questionnaire, the *Personal Research Form,* and found considerable overlap rather than the expected independence. In addition, fantasy and questionnaire measures of motives correlated similarly with personal strivings. But this latter finding is equivocal with regard to McClelland's

position, because the personal strivings were generated by the subjects through self-description. A more relevant approach would have been to observe these strivings in performance situations. Finally, in two meta-analyses, Spangler (1992) found considerable support for the difference between operant and respondent motivation. On balance, evidence is accumulating in support of McClelland's distinction.

The first motive concentrated on was the need for achievement (McClelland et al., 1953). First, McClelland et al. devised a scoring system for thematic apperception that suited the definition of the need as goal-directed fantasy expressing competition with a standard of excellence. After reading a story composed by the subject, the investigator applies the first, or general, component of the scoring system. This component calls for an overall judgment as to whether the study includes imagery definitely relevant (scored 1), doubtfully relevant (scored 0), or definitively irrelevant (scored -1) to competition with a standard of excellence. If the story is scored as definitely relevant, the second (or specific) and third (or weighting) components of the scoring system are employed. The second component involves scoring for the presence (1) or absence (0) of each of the specific categories of goal-directed functioning. These categories are achievement wish, instrumental activity toward an achievement goal, block or obstacle to reaching the goal, goal anticipation, and associated goal affect. The third component involves giving an additional point to a story that is completely devoted to an achievement theme. All the stories the person composes are scored in this fashion, with the intensity of need for achievement indicated by the algebraic sum of the scores.

As you know from the ideal research strategy previously discussed, the first thing to consider is the reliability of this measure. Since fantasy measures require considerable judgment on the investigator's part, interscorer reliability is important. It has repeatedly been demonstrated (Atkinson, 1958; McClelland et al., 1953) that two experienced scorers working independently can obtain need-for-achievement scores from the same protocols that agree to the tune of correlations exceeding .90, or excellent interscorer reliability. The situation concerning the internal consistency and stability of the need-for-achievement measure is not nearly as satisfactory. Correlations range from .22 to .54 for stability (Haber & Alpert, 1958; Lowell, 1950) and are about .65 for internal consistency (Atkinson, 1950). Recognizing that one might conclude that there was no compelling empirical evidence for the need for achievement, McClelland (1958) has pointed out that validity is much more important than reliability, especially in a fantasy measure. After all, fantasy tests by their nature involve considerable measurement error, because the investigator cannot be sure in any particular instance whether he or she has properly understood the respondent's real meaning. McClelland recommends that we consider the internal consistency and stability results as indicating that the measure's reliability is somewhere above zero and proceed with due haste to an assessment of validity. Supporting this approach is the conceptualization of a motive as something that waxes and wanes, depending on its satisfaction. Because of this, we *should* expect no more than moderate reliability from a motive measure (McClelland, 1958).

A great many studies investigating the construct validity of the fantasy measure of the need for achievement have been done. One of these is experimental, whereas the others are correlational. The experimental study and most of the correlational studies concern the effects of high and low levels of the need for achievement on the behavior of individual people; the remainder of the correlational studies concern the effects of this need on economic growth. I shall first consider the studies concerning individuals.

An experiment by McClelland, Atkinson, and Clark (1949) launched the studies of individuals. Its main aim was to demonstrate that an investigator can arouse the *need for achievement* by theoretically relevant experimental manipulation. Two groups of male college students received a series of tasks to perform. In the experimental group, the tasks were introduced as tests of intelligence often used to select people of high administrative capacity for positions in Washington. These tests were described as tasks disclosing

a person's capacity to organize material, evaluate crucial situations quickly and accurately, and be a leader. In short, the instructions given to the experimental group were calculated to arouse a high level of need for achievement. In contrast, the control group was given the same task to perform but with neutral, relaxing instructions stressing that the investigator just wanted to try out some tests of uncertain utility. Following the brief but difficult tasks, the people in both groups were asked to compose stories about four ambiguous pictures showing human beings in work situations.

The important data of the study were these expressions of fantasy. There were striking and theoretically reasonable differences in the stories composed by the two groups. To make the differences vivid, I shall quote one story from each control group. Both stories are responses to a picture of a boy sitting at a desk with a book open in front of him. First, the control group story follows:

> A boy in a classroom who is daydreaming about something. He is recalling a previously experienced incident that struck his mind to be more appealing than being in the classroom. He is thinking about the experience and is now imagining himself in the situation. He hopes to be there. He will probably get called on by the instructor to recite and will be embarrassed.

Nothing in this story deals with achievement or with standards of excellence. Compare it with the experimental group story:

> The boy is taking an hour written. He and the others are high-school students. The test is about two-thirds over and he is doing his best to think it through. He was supposed to study for the test and did so. But because it is factual, there were items he saw but did not learn. He knows he has studied the answers he can't remember and is trying to summon up the images and related ideas to remind him of them. He may remember one or two, but he will miss most of the items he can't remember. He will try hard until five minutes is left, then give up, go back over his paper, and be disgusted for reading but not learning the answers.

Thinking in terms of the scoring system mentioned earlier, this story certainly qualifies as definitely relevant to competition with a standard of excellence under the first component. As to the second component of the scoring system, there is evidence for obstacle of a personal variety ("he saw but did not learn"), instrumental activity ("trying to summon up the images and related ideas to remind him of them"), goal anticipation ("he may remember one or two, but he will miss most of the items he can't remember"), and goal affect ("and be disgusted for reading but not learning the answers"). Clearly this story would also be weighted under the third component of the scoring system, because there is nothing but an achievement theme represented.

To be more precise about the results of this experiment, I should report two things. First, the average intensity of need for achievement, relying on total score attributed to each protocol through use of the entire scoring system, was significantly greater in the experimental group than in the control group. In addition, the scores for each specific category of goal-directed fantasy comprised in the second component of the scoring system were significantly greater in the experimental than in the control group. These results provide evidence of the validity of the fantasy measure of need for achievement.

But some of you may be wondering, since reading the second story, whether obstacles that are not surmounted, instrumental activity that is unsuccessful, and negative affect concerning the goal have a proper place in a measure of the need for achievement. Shouldn't such a measure include only fantasy positively oriented toward achievement? From the beginning, McClelland and his associates have contended that fantasy references to obstacles, instrumental activity, goal anticipation, and goal affect referring to competition with a standard of excellence are relevant regardless of the pessimism or optimism of their content, which may well define the avoidance and approach versions of the need, respectively. Indeed, some empirical support for this distinction between approach and avoidance versions of the need for achievement is to be found in this experiment. The experimental group was subdivided into two subgroups that experienced failure and success, respectively, on

performing the tasks following the achievement-arousing instructions. In the failure subgroup, pessimistic content in achievement-relevant fantasy was more common than it was in the latter subgroup. Furthermore, Atkinson (1960) has interpreted many findings of the performance of people high in test anxiety as indicating fear of failure rather than as suggesting the more positive need for achievement.

In the ensuing years, a great deal of correlational work has been done in an attempt to determine whether the fantasy measure of need for achievement predicts the sorts of actions and life patterns that one would expect. I cannot possibly review all the studies here, nor would that be necessary. It will suffice to summarize major findings toward establishing the significance of the need for achievement.

First, there is a group of findings suggesting the social and intellectual significance of high or low levels of the need for achievement. American men with a high need for achievement come more often from the middle class than from the lower or upper class. They have better memory than others for unfinished tasks in situations arranged so that everyone must complete an equal number of tasks but fail to do so. They are more apt to volunteer as subjects for psychological experiments, participate more in college and community activities, tend to choose experts over friends when asked whom they want as partners to work on difficult problems, and are more resistant to social pressure to conform (Atkinson, 1958; McClelland et al., 1953). Further, need for achievement at age 31 predicted earned income at age 41, and how subjects were parented (as self-reported) seemed to influence motive level in the expected ways (McClelland & Franz, 1992).

Of even more theoretical importance is a group of findings concerning how people high and low in need for achievement actually perform when confronted with a work situation. Lowell (see McClelland, 1961) presented people with a task requiring them to unscramble many scrambled words and recorded how many words a person unscrambled in each of five consecutive periods of 4 minutes each. As you can see in

Figure 12-1, people high and low in need for achievement started at about the same level of performance. But as time went on, those with high levels of the need did progressively better than those with low levels. The people high in need for achievement appeared to be sufficiently concerned about doing the task well to learn to do it better as they went along. But you should not assume that these people would have done better at just any kind of task. Indeed, with a routine, ordinary task, which one cannot learn to do better as one proceeds—crossing out the *S*'s in printed material, for example—there is no difference in the performance of people with high and low need for achievement. Similar results were obtained by French (1955) using a decoding task, presented under instructional conditions encouraging relaxation. Further, French had another group of people perform the decoding task under instructional conditions relevant to motives other than the need for achievement. The instructions indicated that those people who did the work the fastest would be allowed to leave the room, whereas the others would have

to continue working. Under these instructional conditions, the people low in need for achievement actually did a little better than the others, indicating that the possibility of getting out of work is what appealed to them the most.

All these results taken together suggest that high need for achievement will lead people to perform better when they perceive that they can display significant excellence through their attempts. If the task is routine or if finishing it sooner implies getting some nonachievement reward such as time off, subjects low in need for achievement (and presumably high in some other needs) will perform better.

That people high in need for achievement are challenged by situations in which they can display significant excellence is echoed in studies concerning risk taking. McClelland (1958) reports that people high in need for achievement will choose to take moderate risks in a ring-toss game permitting people to stand as close to the ring as they want, whereas those low in need for achievement will take either large or small risks. You can convince yourself of this by observing, in Figure 12-2, that the biggest differences between the curves for high- and low-need-for-achievement groups occurred in conjunction with moderate probability of success. McClelland suggests, ingeniously, that taking either large or small risks makes success or failure either ensured or a matter of chance rather than a reflection of your own skill and excellence. But in taking a moderate risk, you are trying to be successful in a context that properly tests your skill. It is the high-need-for-achievement person who would be challenged by such a possibility.

Later studies have used sophisticated methods of analysis in providing general support for McClelland's formulations regarding achievement motivation. For example, Cooper (1983) reports a network of interrelated variables indicating that need for achievement finds expression in choice of task difficulty, persistence and performance at the task, importance of success and failure, and subjects' estimates of task difficulty. Similarly, Slade and Rush (1991) found that in a vigilance task permitting choice of performance difficulty, subjects with a positive need

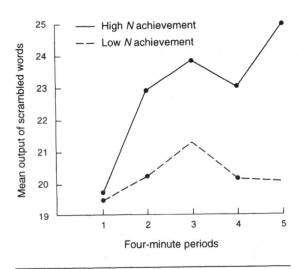

FIGURE 12-1   Mean Output of Scrambled Words per Four-Minute Period for Subject with High and Low N Achievement Scores

SOURCE: From *The Achieving Society*, by D. C. McClelland. Copyright © 1961 by Van Nostrand. Reprinted by permission.

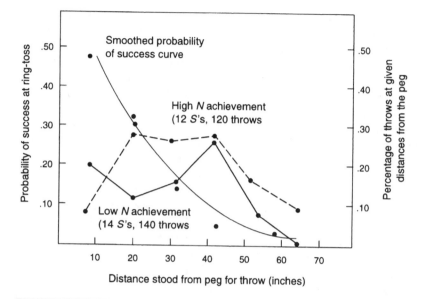

FIGURE 12-2 **Percentage of Throws Made by Five-Year-Olds with High and Low "Doodle" N Achievement at Different Distances from the Peg and Smoothed Curve of Probability of Success at Those Distances**

Note: 26 S's. 10 throws each. Plotted at midpoints of intervals of 11 inches beginning with closest distance stood (4"–14", 5"–15", etc.).

SOURCE: From "Risk Taking in Children with High and Low Need for Achievement," by D. C. McClelland in *Motives in Fantasy, Action, and Society,* edited by J. W. Atkinson. Copyright © 1958 by Van Nostrand. Reprinted by permission.

for achievement shifted to a harder level sooner than other subjects. Using causal modeling, Reuman, Alwin, and Veroff (1984) demonstrate that need for achievement predicts work satisfaction in adult men. Lest you think achievement motivation is uniformly good, there is Johnson's (1981) finding that it predicts cheating on an examination among college students.

It seems clear, then, that one can develop a fantasy measure of the peripheral characteristic of need for achievement that, though not distinguished regarding internal consistency and stability, operates in a theoretically meaningful fashion in both experiment and correlational study.

Having found a measure that has brought us this far, we can ask the more precise question of whether the measure has motivational status. One would expect three things of a measure with motivational status, in McClelland's terms: It would refer to striving toward a goal; it would

reflect at least momentary satiation when the goal is reached; and it would concern personal rather than societal goals. The first expectation is shown in the results already covered. Not only does the measure itself indicate striving toward a standard of excellence, but its work-relevant correlates do as well. The evidence concerning momentary satiation, though not extensive, is intriguing. To better understand the measure's reliability, Atkinson (1958) correlated the need-for-achievement score obtained on each story with that of every other story. The results indicate a kind of saw-toothed effect, in which writing a story high in need for achievement seems to satiate one momentarily, so that the next story is low in the need, while the story immediately following this will be high again, and so forth. This effect occurs in most people, regardless of their overall score on need for achievement. The effect is just what we would expect in a motive measure, and it helps us take a more sophisticated view of the low reliability that results from actually measuring a motive—which, after all, waxes and wanes. On the basis of such findings, measurement experts (e.g., Jackson & Paunonen, 1980; Reuman, 1982) are beginning to agree with McClelland that traditional reliability theory does not really apply to thematic apperception or fantasy measures.

The final requirement of a motive measure is that it tap personal rather than societal goals. There is evidence that the fantasy measure does just this. It seems clear that the fantasy measure of need for achievement is either unrelated or only slightly related to structured self-descriptive measures purporting to assess the same need (de Charms, Morrison, Reitman, & McClelland, 1955; Lindzey & Heineman, 1955; McClelland, 1958; McClelland et al., 1953). Whereas the fantasy measure is based on those thoughts unencumbered by societal restrictions, the structured self-description measures are based on the degree to which the person subscribes to universalistic achievement sentiments posed by other people. As such, the latter measures should tap achievement values or schemata more than motives, with the opposite being true of the fantasy measure. The absence or meager correlation between the two types of measure is therefore understandable. This interpretation is strengthened by the nature of the correlates obtained for the two kinds of measure. De Charms et al. (1955) found that whereas the fantasy measure was correlated to behaviors involving memory and performance, a structured self-description measure involving achievement values was not related to such behaviors but did relate to the tendency to be influenced by the opinions of experts in an ambiguous situation.

The fantasy measure seems to tap an achievement operant motive in McClelland's sense, and the structured self-description measure may well tap an achievement respondent motive or schema. This conclusion requires discussion of the position put forward by Campbell and Fiske (1959) that one must be able to measure a peripheral characteristic by more than one method to be sure that it exists. If the characteristic

shows up on only one measurement operation, there is too much risk that one is measuring no more than a peculiar attribute of that type of operation and nothing of substantive significance for personality. Although this seems like a sound position, the results we have just examined alert us to the need for greater precision. For example, to require that attempts to measure the need for achievement in fantasy and in structured self-description agree before concluding that the need really exists would directly contradict theoretical formulations of the nature of the need. The only form of Campbell and Fiske's position warranted here is that one might want to develop two fantasy measures of need for achievement to ensure that the current measure is not somehow an artifact of the thematic apperception task.

In general, attempts to measure peripheral characteristics with more than one method should be guided by theorizing concerning the nature of the characteristic. One should not require a characteristic to show generality across any arbitrary selected measurement operations. Thus, the negative findings in studies such as that of Gelbort and Winer (1985) are not really problematic for McClelland, because these investigators failed to use fantasy measures and therefore may not have been tapping operant motives at all.

Convincing as the thematic apperception studies are, there do exist some perplexing results as well (see Katz, 1967; Klinger, 1966). Notable among these is the role of achievement motivation in women. It has long been recognized that this motive measure is less than useful in understanding the actions of women, though this phenomenon has been poorly understood. But Horner (in Atkinson & Raynor, 1975) has proposed that the usual male-relevant achievement cues produce the avoidance motive of fear of success rather than the approach motive of need for achievement. This, she speculates, is because women do not really feel they can or should succeed in traditionally male activities. She provides evidence for this position from the imaginative productions of female college students asked to contemplate medical school application. Her findings, however, have been criticized on methodological grounds (e.g., Zuckerman & Wheeler, 1975) and have received little support in recent studies (e.g., Peplau, 1976). It is possible that only some women holding traditional sex-role stereotypes respond as Horner contends (Peplau, 1976).

I should also mention that some empirical support has emerged for the extension of McClelland's position formulated by Atkinson and Raynor (1975). From this extension, Raynor and Sorrentino (in Atkinson & Raynor, 1975) derived the surprising prediction that success-oriented people will work harder and perform better when steps in a long, contingent path are perceived as easy than when they are perceived as hard. They report two studies that tend to confirm this prediction. Also, several studies reported in Atkinson and Raynor (1975) chart how persistence and risk taking relate to achievement orientation differently in future-oriented contingent steps than in individual tasks. Additional studies are needed to determine the precise relationship between the original and this new formulation of achievement motivation.

I shall now turn to the correlational studies linking the need for achievement to economic development. These studies constitute the most exciting demonstration of the effects of personality on the social system that exist in the social science literature, however much one may criticize the fine points of method and interpretation. The theoretical impetus for considering the need for achievement as a determinant of economic development comes from the classical sociologist Max Weber (1930). In his view, the impact of Protestantism spurred industrialization and capitalism. As a sociologist, Weber sought causes for social system phenomena in the social system itself. As a social institution, Protestantism is not an attribute of individuals. Weber's explanation is therefore not bound to cover every person—indeed, the explanation does not even hold for all societies. Although the most prominent societies to become industrialized were predominantly Protestant, there were definite exceptions. Belgium, for example, had as vigorous an industrial revolution as any

northern European country, even though its principal religion was Catholicism. And renaissance Venice achieved a form of capitalism that was perhaps more pure and vigorous than any seen in modern times all the while it was Catholic.

Such observations lead the personologist to speculate that Weber was right insofar as his social system "cause" mirrored an underlying psychological or individual cause. An even more accurate version of the supposed cause than Protestantism might be protestantism, or the existence of a set of values in people stressing the importance of hard work, excellence, and self-reliance. These values generally overlap with Protestantism as a religious institution but need not always do so. According to McClelland, values such as these lead parents to create the kinds of developmental experiences for their children that lead to high levels of need for achievement in much the same manner as described in Chapter 7. If enough parents in a society bring up their children this way, there eventually will be many citizens who choose a way of life involving the challenge of competition with a standard of excellence. Following Weber, McClelland contends that this challenge is most vivid and salient in entrepreneurial activity, which is basic to economic development.

Within this general theoretical framework, three extraordinary studies have been performed. In the first of these, Berlew (1956) attempted to determine the relationship between the modal (or most frequent) level of need for achievement and economic growth in ancient Greece. Following accepted historical belief, Berlew considered three time periods for this society: the period of growth, from 900 B.C. to 475 B.C.; the period of climax, from 475 B.C. to 362 B.C.; and the period of decline, from 362 B.C. to 100 B.C. For each time period, he tried to measure both need for achievement and economic development. For the first, Berlew analyzed surviving literature in much the same way one would analyze thematic apperception stories. From each time period, he selected literature in the following categories: man and his gods, farm and estate management, public funeral celebrations, poetry, epigrams, and war speeches of encouragement. He selected these categories to sample literature that was more imaginative than realistic or descriptive and therefore expressed the writers' personal motives. Because these writers were all famous and excellent men, Berlew felt sure that in measuring their need-for-achievement levels he was obtaining a representative picture of the modal level of this need in the society at large. If these writers were so valued by their society, they must have mirrored it fairly accurately. Finally, the number of written lines in each category of literature and in each time period was the same in order to ensure that there was no bias in the measurement of need for achievement. In this manner, Berlew obtained average levels of the need associated with each of the three periods.

The measurement of economic development was more difficult to obtain. After considering and rejecting various possible measures, Berlew decided on an intriguing though somewhat indirect measure: vases. To understand the significance of this, you must remember that the economic life of the Greek city-states was organized around agriculture and overseas trade. Maritime commerce brought prosperity; Athens and its seaport, Piraeus, lay at the very center of Greek commerce. Greece traded surplus wine and olive oil for grain from Sicily, rugs from Persia, perfumes from Arabia, foodstuffs, basic metals, and other materials. Olive oil and wine were carried in large, earthenware jars, which remained in the cities of delivery after their contents had been consumed. These jars, many of which were made by potters in or near Athens, have been found in regions all around the Mediterranean, and many of them date back to at least the century in which they were produced and used. From the anthropological literature concerning the location of these vase remains, Berlew could calculate the area of Greek trade in millions of square miles. He contends that, especially for Greece, whose prosperity depended so much on commerce, extent of trade area is a plausible measure of economic development.

What were the results of this ground-breaking study? In the periods of growth, climax, and decline, the average levels of need for achievement were 4.74, 2.71, and 1.35, respectively, a

trend that is statistically significant. The levels of economic growth associated with these three time periods were 1.2, 3.4, and 1.9 million square miles, respectively. These dramatic results, depicted in Figure 12-3, led Berlew to conclude that the high level of need for achievement in the period of growth had the effect of spurring economic development, as shown by the sharp increase in trade area from this period to the period of climax. In addition, the decrease in level of need for achievement in the period of climax determined a decrease in economic growth, as shown by the sharp decrease in trade area from this period to the period of decline.

In truth, these results, however striking, can be criticized on many methodological grounds. Nonetheless, the results obtained and the conclusions formulated are upheld in equally striking fashion by two similar studies concerning different societies. One study (Cortes, 1960) concerns Spain in the late Middle Ages. Cortes identified the following periods: economic growth, A.D. 1200 to A.D. 1492; climax, A.D. 1492 to

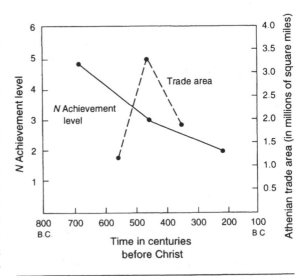

FIGURE 12-3   **Average *N* Achievement Level Plotted at Midpoints of Periods of Growth Climax, and Decline of Athenian Civilization As Reflected in the Extent of Its Trade Area**
SOURCE: From "The Achievement Motive and the Growth of Greek Civilization," by D. E. Berlew, 1956, unpublished bachelor's thesis, Wesleyan University, Middletown, CT.

A.D. 1610; and decline, A.D. 1610 to A.D. 1730. The measure of modal level of need for achievement was very similar to that of Berlew. Literary categories of fiction, verse, history, and legends were sampled with the same precautions used in the previous study. The measure of economic growth was shipping cleared from Spain for the New World in thousands of tons per year. Cortes found the level of need for achievement highest in the period of growth and lowest in the period of decline. Economic growth, in contrast, was highest in the period of climax and quite low in the other periods.

The final study indicating that modal level of need for achievement in a society will exert an influence on subsequent economic activity is that of Bradburn and Berlew (1961) concerning England from Tudor times to the Industrial Revolution. The investigators divided this span of time into 50-year segments. To measure need for achievement, they sampled the literary categories of drama, sea voyages, and street ballads, with the same precautions employed by Berlew. Their measure of economic development was gains in coal imports at the port of London above and beyond what would have been expected on the basis of past figures. This method of using gain estimates is a more sophisticated measure, economically speaking, than relying on gross amounts of coal imported. The results of the study are shown in Figure 12-4. The average level of need for achievement continued to be fairly stable from A.D. 1500 through A.D. 1600, then declined sharply to a low point at A.D. 1650, which was maintained through A.D. 1700, and then increased sharply from that time on to a high point in A.D. 1800. Strikingly enough, the measure of economic activity follows a very similar course, but 50 years later. This study improves on the previous two because it shows for the first time that level of need for achievement can go up as well as down and that economic activity will follow these vicissitudes fairly precisely.

Important as these three studies are, they are dwarfed by a similar study done by McClelland (1961). Taking the world as his frame of reference, McClelland decided on stories appearing

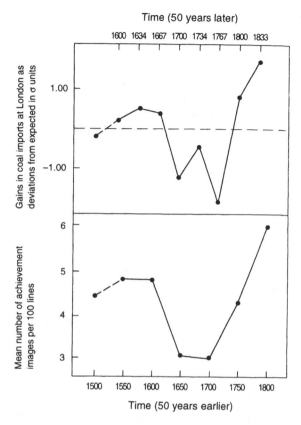

FIGURE 12-4   Averaged N Achievement Levels in English Literature (1550 A.D.–1800 A.D.) Compared with Rates of Gain in Coal Imports at London Fifty Years Later
SOURCE: From "Need for Achievement and English Industrial Growth," by N. M. Bradburn and D. E. Berlew, 1961, *Economic Development and Cultural Change, 10*. Copyright © 1961. Reprinted by permission of University of Chicago Press.

in children's readers. These stories are fictional and imaginative, sometimes even articulating the given society's mythology. As such, they are appropriate raw material for the measurement of need for achievement in their composers. But they also represent the level of need in the society, argues McClelland, because the society has decided to use them as instructional material for its children. Thus, the level of need for achievement obtained in children's readers can be considered modal for the society. McClelland was able, albeit with considerable difficulty, to obtain 21 stories from the children's readers used in each of 23 countries in 1925 and 21 stories used in each of 40 countries in 1950. The 23 countries in the 1925 sample also appeared in the 1950 sample. All the stories were translated into English and mixed together so that scorers could not guess where they came from. The original form of the need-for-achievement scoring system was employed (McClelland et al., 1953), with the usual high level of interscorer agreement and unusually high internal consistency. Estimates of internal consistency based on the split-half method corrected for length of test in the 1925 and 1950 samples was .75 and .80, respectively. This is more than adequate reliability for a fantasy measure. In addition, McClelland found virtually no relationship between level of need for achievement and story length.

Obtaining a measure of economic development that could be applied to so many countries at the same time was even more difficult than measuring the need for achievement. After much consideration and investigation, McClelland decided on two economic measures. The first one, offered by an economist (Clark, 1957) involves international units of income. Obviously, income is the best gauge of economic development, but money has different value in different societies. To overcome this difficulty, Clark advocates translation of each currency into international units of income, each unit representing the average quantity of goods exchangeable in the United States for $1.00 from 1925–1934. Although there are certain difficulties with this measure of national income, McClelland adopted it as one of the few that permitted comparisons across many nations. Because of the difficulties, however, he decided to include another economic measure as well: the amount of electricity produced in a given country. Conveniently enough, there is a worldwide standard unit for measurement of electricity. In justifying the theoretical utility of the kilowatt-hour as a measure of economic growth, McClelland (1961) says,

> We have argued that economic growth, in its most unambiguous sense, is growth in the production, service, and use of the most modern technology ("hardware") known to society at a given moment

in history. Certainly in our time the production and use of electricity in a country should be highly diagnostic of the level of its technology, since it is the form into which most of the energy is converted which runs our complex civilization. Though the sources of energy may be quite varied (water power, animal power, wind, coal, oil), electricity has become the form in which energy is most economically stored and transmitted. (pp. 85–96)

Armed with two reasonably adequate measures of economic growth, McClelland next faced the problem of determining whether or not a country made substantial gains in the period from 1925 to 1950. Some manner of determining the rate of growth seemed proper, for the absolute size of gains did not seem useful. The trouble with absolute size of gain is that it is highly correlated with the initial level of development. In other words, a society relatively high in kilowatt-hours per capita in 1925 would show more absolute gain from 1925 to 1950 than would a society relatively low in 1925. After considering many faulty methods of obtaining a measure of economic growth rate, McClelland settled on a procedure that involves predicting, from the regression line that best fits the overall relationship between initial level and gain, the amount of gain that can be considered normal. A gain exceeding or falling short of this amount is considered extraordinary. Unusually high or low economic gain is to be related to the level of need for achievement.

Let us pass over much of the interesting and complex results of this huge study to those findings most relevant to this discussion of the economic effects of need for achievement. As indicated in Table 12-20, McClelland (1961, p. 92) found that the higher the need for achievement level in a country in 1925, the greater its rate of economic growth from 1925 to 1950 as measured by both international units of income ($r = .25$) and kilowatt-hours of electricity per capita ($r = .53$). Strikingly, there was virtually no relationship between need-for-achievement level in 1950 and the measures of economic growth from 1925 to 1950. These results, obtained from a truly grand-scale study, lead to the same conclusion as that suggested by

TABLE 12-20 Correlations of Reader N Achievement Scores
with Deviations from Expected Economic Gains

N ACHIEVEMENT LEVEL BY YEAR	I.U./CAP 1925–50 N = 22	KW-HR./CAP 1929–50 N = 22	BOTH COMBINED N = 21
1925	.25	$.53, p < .01pd$	$.46, p < .02pd$
1950	−.10	.03	−.08

pd = predicted direction.
SOURCE: From *The Achieving Society*, by D. C. McClelland. Copyright © 1961 by Van Nostrand.
Reprinted by permission.

the three studies described previously. The level of need for achievement in a society is a clear influence on the subsequent rate of economic development. It is equally apparent that the influence does not work the other way around.

More than any other psychological studies, those inspired by McClelland render in tangible form the contribution of social system phenomena to the personologist's understanding. Neither economists nor other social scientists besides personologists would have seriously pursued in research the possibility that a motivational variable plays a causal role in economic growth. I assume that the far-reaching implications of McClelland's work for international economic and political policy are apparent. In terms of our more immediate concern in this chapter, it is clear that the need for achievement has motivational status and should be included in peripheral-level theorizing about personality.

McClelland's work with the need for achievement has stimulated similar studies of the needs for affiliation and power. These studies are not as extensive or convincing as those cited previously. Fantasy in the form of stories composed about pictures served as the raw material for measuring the needs for affiliation and power; scoring systems were patterned after the one for the need for achievement. The scoring or operational definition of the need for affiliation in thematic apperception involves evidence of concern with establishing, maintaining, or restoring a positive affective relationship with another person. This affective relationship is most adequately described by the word *friendship*. In

contrast, the scoring definition of the need for power stresses concern with control of the means of influencing a person, expressed in such ways as pleasure in situations of dominance and reference to dominance and persuasion. Although the interscorer agreement associated with both scoring systems is high (generally correlations of .85 to .90), their internal consistency appears to be even lower than that for need for achievement. Reliability estimates are in the neighborhood of only .43 and .32, corrected to full test length for the needs for affiliation and power, respectively (McClelland, 1961, pp. 161, 168). But if we were willing to rely on the validity studies of the need-for-achievement measures as a gauge of the acceptability of its underlying concept, why not do so for these two measures as well? You will see why shortly.

Heyns, Veroff, and Atkinson (1958) conducted an experiment to determine whether this scoring system measured a higher need for affiliation in a group of people in whom the need was aroused than in a group in which no arousal took place. The 31 college fraternity brothers in the arousal (experimental) group performed a sociometric task before composing stories about pictures of people. The sociometric task consisted of (1) ranking a given set of traits according to the degree to which possession of the trait would make a person likable, (2) describing themselves and the other group members in terms of these traits, and (3) choosing at least three people as the most desirable personal friends in the group. Heyns et al. felt that this task would arouse a high level of the need for affiliation. A control group of 36 college men was drawn from a psychology class without experiencing any arousal condition before composing stories about the same pictures used in the experimental group. The overall score for need for affiliation was considerably higher in the experimental group than in the control group, and the various subcategories of the scoring system also tended to distinguish the groups in this direction. So one can conclude that the measure of need for affiliation operates as it should experimentally and therefore has a claim to construct validity.

There are also a few correlational studies indicating that the measure of need for affiliation has empirical validity. Atkinson and Walker (1958) indicate that people high in need for affiliation tend to seek approval and to be especially sensitive to faces presented along with other stimuli in a perceptual task. This task involved having subjects decide which of four simultaneous stimuli, presented tachistoscopically (at speeds too short for complete perception) was a face. People high in the fantasy measure of need for affiliation picked out the face more accurately than people who were low. Consistent with this is the study by Hill (1991), which shows that subjects high in need for affiliation preferred interacting with people who had been described to them as warm and responsive. McClelland, Sturr, Knapp, and Wendt (1958) also report that people high in the need for affiliation are generally considered likely to succeed by their peers. That this reflects the strong interpersonal commitment these people have made is suggested by French's (1956) evidence that people high in the need for affiliation choose friends over experts to work with them on performance tasks, even though skill is important in completing the task that offers the greatest reward. In addition, Atkinson, Heyns, and Veroff (1954) found that people scoring high in need for affiliation were considered unpopular by their peers on a sociometric rating. This result has been confirmed in similar circumstances by Groesbeck (1958) and Byrne (1961a). De Charms (1957) found that those high in need for affiliation perform best with cooperative task instructions, but under competitive instructions they perform more poorly than those low in this need. Additional studies have been reviewed by Mehrabian and Ksionzky (1970).

There is now a variant on affiliation motivation called need for intimacy, introduced by McAdams and various associates. One study (McAdams & Powers, 1981) shows that intimacy motivation measured in thematic apperception is expressed in the themes and activities of subjects in a psychodrama task. Specifically, those high in the need for intimacy develop drama scenarios involving mutual delight in interaction, rich reciprocal dialogue among characters, and the surrender of manipulative control. Also, subjects high in intimacy motivation are seen by others involved in the psychodrama task as being especially sincere, likable, and natural. McAdams and Constantian (1983) extended this kind of construct validation approach to demonstrate that subjects high in the need for intimacy engage in more relevant social interactions than other subjects do. Further, McAdams and Bryant (1987) report in a nationwide sample that the need for intimacy is associated in women with greater happiness and gratification and in men with lack of strain and uncertainty.

There is also considerable research available on the fantasy measure of need for power. In developing the scoring system, Veroff (1958) tried to perform a natural experiment that would show the scoring system to be sensitive to a situation of high power motivation. This arousal situation involved people who were candidates for election as student leaders at their college. The candidates had to petition for their candidacy and, following this declaration, were given 1 month to campaign before the actual election. After 2 days of balloting, the candidates congregated at the polls to see what the ballot had decided. At least 2 hours elapsed after they had congregated before the results of the election were known. During this time, the candidates were asked to compose stories about pictures of people in the manner of previous studies. Veroff reasoned that whatever other motives would be aroused in these candidates, the need for power certainly would be high. The control group consisted of 34 college men from the same school who were asked merely to compose the stories as part of a psychology course. The average need-for-power score, based on the entire scoring system, was higher in the experimental group than in the control group. In addition, most of the subcategories of the scoring system discriminated between the two groups in the same direction. There are also two other measures of need for power available (Uleman, 1965; Winter, 1971), both derived from arousal experiments; the latter claims to emphasize the positive wish for power rather than the negative fear of powerlessness.

Construct validational research on the need for power is also available. McClelland, Davis, Kalin, and Wanner (1971) report, primarily from Winter's (1971) findings, that men with a high drive for personal power tend to drink and gamble more than others, to own prestige items (such as power cars and credit cards), and to confess to more aggressive impulses (such as wanting to walk out on a date and to yell at someone in a traffic jam). These seem to be ways of feeling big and important. Failing these, a tendency toward alcoholism may develop, which is interpreted as being powerful in one's fantasy without the usual requirement of consistent, effective social action. If the inclination of power motivation is tempered by a sense of social responsibility, it tends to express itself more in political and social commitments and actions (McClelland, 1975). Further, Fodor and Smith (1982) found that groups having a leader low in the need for power used more of the information available to them in trying to reach goals and developed more action proposals than groups with high-power leaders did. Regarding physiological reactions, Fodor (1984) reports that leaders high in need for power responded with more bodily arousal to group criticisms. Evidence tends to support the finding that the need for power leads people to manipulate and gain control over others.

There is also a research theme concerning the joint effects of the needs for affiliation and power. McAdams, Healy, and Krause (1984) report that subjects high in affiliation motivation showed much self-disclosure, listening, and social concern for friends, while those high in power motivation preferred large-group interactions and goal-oriented group activities. Further, McAdams (1982) shows that the experiences remembered by subjects high in the needs for intimacy or power were consistent with those motives. Accumulating evidence indicates that although both power- and affiliation-oriented people are interested in social activities, the types of people, interactions, and experiences they find rewarding are quite different. Concerning the joint effects of the needs for power and achievement, McClelland and Franz (1992) report that whereas the need for achievement at age 31 predicted earned income at age 41, the need for power predicted work accomplishment.

McClelland (1961) included measures of need for affiliation and need for power in his previously mentioned large-scale study of social system phenomena. Although his primary focus concerned the relationship between need for achievement and economic growth, he felt it valuable to include these other measures for two reasons. First, only the need for achievement, not other motives such as affiliation and power, should relate to economic development. If it could be shown that affiliation and power motivations bear little on economic growth, the case for the relevance of need for achievement would be all the stronger. Second, McClelland wanted to see what, other than economic development, these other two needs would affect at the social system level. In obtaining information concerning economic development, much other social system information was obtained as a matter of course and put to use in assessing the empirical value of the other motive measures.

The results concerning need for affiliation indicate that it bears a complex relationship to population growth, a matter that should not be too surprising. The need for affiliation is positively related to birthrate in 1950 ($r = +.41$) and negatively related to birthrate in 1925 ($r = -.41$). But why should high need for affiliation have led to having more children in 1950 and fewer children in 1925? McClelland's reasoning is complex and will only be summarized here.

Generally speaking, there seems to be evidence that before large-scale public-health measures, the birthrate was largely controlled by the death rate. But although the correlation between birthrate and death rate was high prior to 1950, by that time it had been significantly reduced by modern public-health measures. Perhaps the meaning of the positive relationship between need for affiliation and birthrate in 1950 is that people determine how many children to have by how many they want, without fear that many will die. But the negative relationship between need for affiliation and birthrate in 1925 is more difficult to understand. It will help to know that even though there is a general positive relationship between birthrate and death rate in 1925, there turns out to be a negative relationship between need for affiliation and death rate at that time. This negative relationship does not appear in 1950. These data taken together suggest that in the time before public health, the number of children who would survive depended more on how much care and attention their parents gave them than it does in contemporary times. McClelland (1961) concludes that in 1925,

> The parents with higher need for affiliation care more for their children, fewer of them die, and there is therefore less need for "excess" children to take the place of those who die off. In other words, those countries with a high [need for] affiliation have a lower infant mortality rate, and a lower birth rate. (p. 163)

Although one can hardly claim that this indirect but plausible and intriguing chain of reasoning really substantiates the validity of the need-for-affiliation measure, further research seems worthwhile.

The final matter of relevance from McClelland's study concerns both the need for affiliation and the need for power. It turns out (McClelland, 1961, p. 168) that a combination of high need for power and low need for affiliation is very closely associated with a nation's tendency to resort to totalitarian methods of governing its people. Strikingly enough, every one of the notorious police states (e.g., Germany, Japan, Spain, Russia, Argentina, Portugal, Republic of South Africa) in the sample showed this particular pattern of the two motives! I take this to mean that in countries whose residents are personally motivated to dominate others and avoid warm relationships with them, political forms will tend toward denial of equality and individual freedom.

McClelland (1971a) has prepared an especially useful discussion of the intertwining of needs for affiliation, achievement, and power in both personal and social behaviors. Notably, LeVine (1966) uses the percentage of achievement dreams in the Yoruba and other tribes in northern Nigeria as a basis for understanding the tribes' social patterns and interrelationships. Also, Donley and Winter (1965) have coded the inaugural addresses of American presidents from Theodore Roosevelt to Richard Nixon for the needs for achievement and power. The scores seem surprisingly accurate in predicting their administrative decisions. These results are schematically presented in Table 12-21.

What do these intriguing findings tell us about peripheral-level theorizing? Despite their poor reliabilities, the measures of need for affiliation and need for power are empirically consistent with theory in relating to both individual and social system phenomena. It would appear that peripheral-level theorizing ought to include these two needs along with need for achievement.

This conclusion is further strengthened by an important book on the need for power, in which Winter (1973) has amassed an enormous amount of empirical information concerning how this need, as measured in fantasy, influences personal and social action. It is impossible to recount these vast findings here, so an example or two will have to suffice.

Given the proposition that people high in need for power want to control the existing social system whereas those high in need for achievement want to change it, Winter and his associates predicted that, among student activists, members of the Black Power Movement would he high in n power but members of the New Left Movement would be high in n achievement. This prediction was confirmed with various student samples. These results are consistent

TABLE 12-21   Motive Characteristics of American Presidents and Associated Trends in Office

PRESIDENT	HIGH n ACHIEVEMENT	HIGH n POWER	ASSOCIATED TRENDS IN OFFICE
T. Roosevelt	6.2	8.3	Strong and active presidents, attempting to accomplish much, quite willing to use political influence and expand government to gain ends
F. Roosevelt	5.2	6.3	
Truman	4.1	7.3	
Kennedy	6.8	8.3	
Johnson	7.5	6.8	
	LOW n ACHIEVEMENT	HIGH n POWER	
Wilson	3.0	5.4	Stubborn desire to impose his will, even at cost of accomplishments [George & George, 1956]
	HIGH n ACHIEVEMENT	LOW n POWER	
Hoover	4.0	3.0	Stress on accomplishing more at less cost, smaller government involvement, willing to sacrifice political influence for goals of economy and efficiency
Nixon	8.5	5.1	
	LOW n ACHIEVEMENT	LOW n POWER	
Taft	.9	2.0	Relatively inactive, not trying to achieve major accomplishments or use the power potential [of the] office of the president
Harding	2.3	3.4	
Coolidge	1.7	3.1	
Eisenhower	2.8	4.1	

SOURCE: Adapted from "Measuring the Motives of Public Officials at a Distance: An Exploratory Study of American Presidents," by R. E. Donley and D. G. Winter. Reprinted from *Behavioral Science*, Volume 15, No. 3, 1970, by permission of James G. Miller, M.D., Ph.D., Editor.

with those concerning the average level of n power among people in various occupations. The highest average occurred in business management, followed by teaching, psychotherapy, and the religious vocations. Although these findings would not always be expected in terms of common assumptions, they are consistent with McClelland's peripheral theorizing.

McClelland (1978) has also been involved in attempts to alter motivation levels in groups of people in various underdeveloped countries. Important for such training efforts is an understanding of how motives develop during early life. McClelland and Pilon (1983) found that parents of children who went on to have high need for achievement used definite feeding schedules and severe toilet training approaches, whereas those whose children developed high need for power were permissive regarding sexual and aggressive activities.

Overall, there is no more striking evidence of the empirical fruitfulness of postulated peripheral characteristics than that offered by McClelland and his associates. But the great bulk of characteristics designated in his peripheral theorizing have not been touched. Further, the numerous characteristics are not organized into a few types that could be manageably studied empirically. The soundest conclusion is that while there is support for some of the theory, most of it has not been tested.

Maddi's Position

Most of the research directly relevant to Maddi's peripheral theorizing has concentrated on the need for variety and the traits of activeness-passiveness and internal-external orientation. In this research, Maddi and his associates follow McClelland in using thematic apperception as the raw material for measurement, because the need for variety is considered a motive. In addition, they conceptualize different forms of the need for variety according to the trait characteristics that occur with it, making a rich, multifaceted source of information such as fantasy potentially valuable. They turn to the analysis of thematic apperception with the idea that the need for variety will take active-internal, active-external, passive-internal, and passive-external forms. As you will recall from Chapter 8, these forms of the need for variety actually constitute four of the personality types supposedly characterized by high activation requirements.

Attempts to devise measures of these four motivational types have evolved over a number of studies. In the first of these, Maddi et al. (1962) selected the two types that would have the most obvious kind of expression in thematic apperception. Clearly, a person could compose stories about pictures of people that imbued them with a sense of boredom and dissatisfaction with the status quo, coupled with interest in the possibility that something more unusual might happen. But it would be equally possible for people simply to compose stories that are themselves novel and unusual, thereby producing their own variety. Scrutiny of some sample stories inclined Maddi et al. to conclude that the former orientation toward novelty is passive and external and the latter active and internal.

As such, Maddi et al. have defined two scoring systems to be studied for construct validity. The scoring system for the passive-external form of the need for variety is patterned after those pioneered by McClelland. Called *desire for novelty,* it refers to the extent to which stories reflect dissatisfaction with the status quo because of its boring nature and reflects an appreciation of externally caused, novel occurrences. The scoring

system has the same three components as that for the need for achievement and can be used by different scorers with a high level of agreement—correlations range from about .80 to about .90 (Maddi & Andrews, 1966; Maddi & Berne, 1964; Maddi et al., 1962; Maddi et al., 1965). Estimates of internal consistency range from .31 to .41 (Maddi & Andrews, 1966; Maddi et al., 1965), and an estimate of stability is .47 (Maddi & Andrews, 1966). These reliability results are better than those reported for the need-for-achievement measure.

Maddi et al. (1962) have also developed a scoring system for the active-internal form of the need for variety. Called *novelty of productions,* the scoring system concerns how unusual or novel the stories themselves are, regardless of how much goal-directed striving toward novelty is attributed to characters. The scoring system includes three aspects each of character treatment and plot treatment. The categories of plot treatment are unusual event, unusual interpretation (scored when a story is strange, humorous, or ironic), and unexpected ending (scored when the end of a story violates a definite expectation built up by the preceding narrative). The categories of character treatment are unusual role designation for characters actually pictured in the stories (such designations as "spy" and "diplomat"), unusual role designation for characters the subject introduces into the story, and uncommon naming. That the agreement in the use of this scoring system is high is shown by estimates of interscorer reliability ranging from .84 to .92 (Maddi & Andrews, 1966; Maddi et al., 1962; Maddi et al., 1965). Also high for fantasy measures are estimates of internal consistency of the scoring system, which have ranged from .63 to .80 (Maddi & Andrews, 1966; Maddi et al., 1965). The sole estimate of stability is adequate—.65 (Maddi & Andrews, 1966). It seems as if the tendency to infuse fantasy with a desire for novelty and the tendency to fantasize in unusual ways are distinct and homogeneous entities in people.

Maddi et al. (1962) performed an experiment to see whether the scoring systems would be sensitive to conditions that should arouse the need for variety. People in the aroused (experimental) group were made to be bored by being required to listen to a tedious recording of the physical characteristics of a town delivered in monotonous tones and with much repetition. Following this experience, the people composed stories about four pictures of people in the standard manner. There were two control groups. In one, the period of time prior to composing stories was taken up by whatever the people chose to do that could be accomplished in a classroom setting. In the other, a novel, unusual, and somewhat humorous recording was played prior to the composition task. Maddi et al. reasoned that in neither control group should there have been much arousal of the need for variety. The experimental treatment was expected to arouse not only the need for variety but the trait of passivity. The tendency to be passive should have been strong, because the subjects were asked to give their full attention to the recording. They could comply with these instructions only by relinquishing the many active procedures (e.g., tapping feet, daydreaming, walking out) whereby people avoid monotonous situations. Thus, people in the experimental group should have shown on the thematic apperception task an increase in passive expressions and a decrease in active expressions of the need for variety. The results of this experiment conformed to expectation: The aroused group showed a higher level of desire for novelty (passive-external) and a lower level of novelty of productions (active-internal) than either control group did. In addition, the control groups did not differ from each other in desire for novelty or novelty of productions. In the control groups, desire for novelty and novelty of productions were negatively correlated, and this relationship was even stronger in the aroused group. Maddi et al. conclude that their arousal condition had the joint effects of arousing the need for variety and stimulating the trait of passivity.

Although it certainly is reasonable to consider novelty of productions and desire for novelty as being active and passive measures, respectively, of the need for variety, there is at least one major alternative view that questions whether novelty

of productions is motivational at all. Certainly this measure does not include the obviously goal-directed fantasy characteristic of other motive measures. Perhaps novelty of productions is a stylistic expression of a flexible, original, creative turn of mind. Further, perhaps desire for novelty is the only real measure of the need for variety. If it is also true that vigorous expression of flexibility and originality require freedom from strong motivational states, the negative relationship between desire for novelty and novelty of productions and the effects on each of the experimental manipulation would be very understandable: When the need for variety, or any motive, is strong, flexibility and creativity will be low.

This alternative explanation recalls White's contention that the expression of effectance motivation in exploration of the world occurs only when the major survival needs have been satisfied. It also recalls Harlow's (1953) demonstration that the monkey's hunger drive interferes with its solving puzzles. Maddi and Berne (1964) did a correlational study to determine which of the two interpretations of the desire-for-novelty and novelty-of-productions measures was more accurate. From the thematic apperception tests of a group of people, they obtained scores not on only these two measures but on the needs for achievement, affiliation, and power. They reasoned that if the alternative explanation were accurate, there would be a negative correlation between novelty of productions and each of the motive measures, whereas if the interpretation of Maddi et al. were accurate, there would be a negative correlation only between novelty of productions and desire for novelty. The latter result was obtained, clearly supporting the position that novelty of productions and desire for novelty are alternative forms of the need for variety.

The next step for Maddi and his associates was a series of correlational studies (Maddi, 1968b; Maddi & Andrews, 1966; Maddi et al., 1965) aimed at determining the construct validity of the two posited measures of need for variety. Indeed, at this point a third measure was devised. Also involving analysis of thematic apperception, this measure, called *curiosity,* reflects the degree to which stories are infused with the asking of questions and the posing of problems with concomitant interest in obtaining additional, new information with which to resolve the perplexities. On rational grounds, it was presumed that this measure is an active expression of the need for variety, as is novelty of productions, but differs from the latter in that it reflects an external rather than internal trait. In other words, in the active pursuit of variety, novelty of productions involves favoring internal sources of stimulation whereas curiosity involves favoring external sources. The curiosity measure, like the other two, can be used with adequate agreement by different scorers (.83 to .90) and has sufficient reliability to justify further consideration (internal consistency = .50 to .68; stability = .39).

The correlational studies support the claim of the novelty-of-productions and desire-for-novelty measures to construct validity but suggest an alternative interpretation of the curiosity measure. Some of the findings of these studies are presented in Table 12-22. Working down the first column, you can see that the higher people are in novelty of productions, the less they will explore the objects in a room with which they are unfamiliar but the more they will examine their internal environment through introspection. A high degree of novelty of productions also predisposes people to complete fragmentary line drawings in a complex way and to be original in thinking up uses for common objects. The active, internal search for novelty indicated in these performance characteristics is also shown in self-description. People high in novelty of productions describe themselves as being interested in change, disjunctive thinking, and contemplative activities. In complementary fashion, they are

TABLE 12-22   Selected Correlates of Novelty of Productions, Curiosity, and Desire for Novelty

	FANTASY VARIABLES			
	Novelty of Productions	Curiosity	Desire for Novelty	Number of Ss
Performance variables				
Time spent exploring a room	$-.42^\dagger$	$.38^\dagger$	.11	62
Introspective productivity	$.27^*$	.06	$-.07$	62
Complexity of line-drawing completions	$.39^\dagger$	$-.05$	$-.20$	62
Original uses for common objects	$.42^\dagger$	$-.05$	$-.22$	42
Self-description variables				
n change	$.31^*$	$-.26$	$.44^*$	42
n order	$-.27$	$.42^\dagger$	.27	42
Conjunctivity-disjunctivity	$-.32^*$	$.36^*$	.11	42
Impulsivity	.21	$-.10$	$-.34^*$	42
Rigidity factor	$-.38^*$	$.38^*$	.20	42
n understanding	$-.02$	.25	$-.41^\dagger$	42
Reflectiveness	$.33^*$	$-.02$	$-.36^*$	42
Exteroception	$-.48^\dagger$	.27	.18	42
n sentience	.13	$-.01$	$-.43^\dagger$	42
Energy	.12	$-.03$	$-.50^\dagger$	42

*Significant at .05 level.
†Significant at .01 level.

Source: Adapted from "Three Expressions of the Need for Variety," by S. R. Maddi, B. Propst, and I. Feldinger, 1965, *Journal of Personality, 33;* "The Need for Variety in Fantasy and Self-Description," by S. R. Maddi and S. Andress, 1966, *Journal of Personality, 34;* and "The Seeking and Avoiding of Variety," by S. R. Maddi, 1968, unpublished manuscript, University of Chicago.

uninterested in order, in appearing rigid, and in the practical external world of affairs (exteroception). The performance correlates of the fantasy measure of novelty of productions suggest that it reflects behavior indicative of striving toward variety; its self-descriptive correlates clarify that variety is indeed a personal goal.

In contrast, the desire-for-novelty measure has shown no performance correlates to date, a fact that would cause alarm concerning its empirical validity were it not for the reasonable argument that something measuring passivity should not, after all, reflect such active tendencies as performance, which actually create novelty. People high in desire for novelty should appreciate novelty when they encounter it but not be active creators of it, being consumers rather than producers of novelty. Indeed, as shown in the third column of Table 12-22, people high in desire for novelty describe themselves as interested in change and offer insight into their passivity by also describing themselves as lacking initiative, interest in understanding, contemplativeness, sentience, energy, or anything else that might help them pursue novelty. You may ask, "What good is motivation that does not provide a format for action?" But that is another question, the answer to which may lead to the study of psychopathology. For the moment, we can safely conclude that there is empirical support for viewing desire for novelty as a passive form of the need for variety.

The original conceptualization of the fantasy measure of curiosity has not received empirical support. It is true that people high in curiosity actively explore the objects in an unfamiliar room. But that this finding should not be construed as indicating an active, external form of the need for variety is disclosed by the self-descriptions of people high in curiosity. As you can see in the second column of Table 12-22, these descriptions indicate an interest in order, conjunctivity of thought, and rigidity. Maddi and his associates seem to have inadvertently developed a measure of the active tendency to fear variety rather than revel in it! Once again we are alerted to the wisdom of McClelland's distinction between approach and avoidance

versions of each of the needs. People who score high in curiosity on fantasy measures seem to be concerned with variety because it is a threat to them and wish to avoid the threat by ordering their experience so as to minimize or at least dampen novelty and change.

Especially because the novelty-of-productions and curiosity measures deviate from the usual format stressing obviously goal-directed fantasy, Maddi and his associates planned a further demonstration of the motivational nature of these measures. With the motivation construct, you can manipulate people to learn something if it leads to satisfaction of motivation. The stronger the motive, the more you can manipulate them to learn. Thus, if novelty of productions and desire for novelty are really approach versions of the need for variety, people high in one or the other ought to learn something more thoroughly when rewarded by novelty than people low on these measures. Further, if curiosity really measures an avoidance version of the need for variety, people high in it ought to learn less well when rewarded by novelty than people low on that measure.

Feldinger and Maddi (1968) did an experiment to test these predictions. First they obtained thematic apperception stories from a large group of people and, by applying the scoring systems, isolated groups high and low on each of the three measures. All groups were given the learning task, which consisted of viewing cards presented one at a time. Each card contained two pairs of lines, one pair parallel and the other unparallel but symmetrical. The subjects were asked to choose one pair of lines from each card. For half the people in each group, choosing parallel lines led to viewing a line drawing of a usual object but choosing nonparallel lines led to viewing a line drawing of an unusual version of a usual object. The only difference in procedure for the people in the other half of each group was that choice of the nonparallel lines led to seeing the usual object whereas choice of the parallel lines produced the unusual object. There were 45 cards with parallel and nonparallel lines, and the measure of learning employed was the number of choices leading to viewing unusual or novel objects. For novelty of productions, the high group showed more choices that led to viewing novel objects than the low group did. There was a similar trend in the high- and low-desire-for-novelty groups. The people high in curiosity made fewer choices leading to novelty than the group low in curiosity did. These results, taken with those of the correlational studies, indicate that novelty of productions and desire for novelty represent approach versions of the need for variety and curiosity as an avoidance version.

The combination of high need for variety with active-internal or passive-external traits defines two of the high-activation types postulated by Maddi. Also, the combination of high fear of variety with active-external traits constitutes one of his low-activation types. Strictly speaking, in assessing the position's construct validity, one should determine whether the activation requirements of people high in novelty of productions, desire for novelty, or curiosity conform to the theoretical expectations.

A study by Thayer (1967) purports to have solved the problem of simple measurement of customary level of activation. He devised the *Activation-Deactivation Adjective Check List*, composed of adjectives relevant to activation that subjects select if descriptive of them. The self-descriptions of 221 male and female college students were factor analyzed, with four of the resulting factors clearly indicating activation. Thayer listed the factors and the adjectives loading highest on each as follows: general activation (lively, active, full of pep, energetic, peppy, vigorous, activated); high activation (clutched up, jittery, stirred up, fearful, intense); general deactivation (at rest, still, leisurely, quiescent, quiet, calm, placid); deactivation sleep (sleepy, tired, drowsy). According to Thayer, these factors roughly constitute four points on a hypothetical activation continuum running from sleep to anxious tension. Although complete reliability information is unavailable, estimates of stability were obtained for some of the adjectives and ranged from .57 to .87, with a median of .75.

Thayer attempted two kinds of validation of these factors as points on an activation continuum. The first involves other self-descriptions

and the second physiological recordings of autonomic nervous system activity. One of the validation attempts involving self-description was based on the conceptualization of the characteristic curve of activation as being low on awaking, rising to a peak near the middle of the day, and falling thereafter until sleep occurs (see Chapter 8). In one study (Thayer, 1967), subjects filled out the adjective checklist in the middle of the day and again in the evening. As expected, general-activation and high-activation scores went down, while general-deactivation and deactivation-sleep scores went up from one testing to the next. In a similar study (Thayer, 1967), subjects took the checklist four times, at roughly 9:00 A.M., 12:30 P.M., 5:00 P.M., and 11:00 P.M. As shown in Figure 12-5, general-activation and

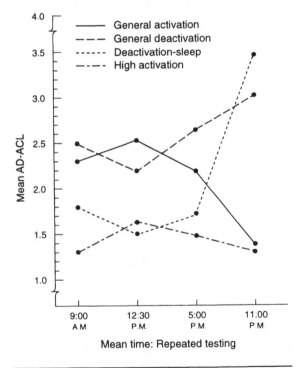

FIGURE 12-5   Mean Scores of Four AD-ACL Factors at Four Diurnal Periods
SOURCE: From "Measurement of Activation Through Self-Report," by R. E. Thayer, 1967, *Psychological Reports,* 20, 663–678 (Monogr. Suppl. 1-V20). Reprinted with permission of the author and publisher.

high-activation scores went from low to high to low again, while general-deactivation and deactivation-sleep scores did just the opposite. These findings provide striking evidence that the adjective checklist indeed measures characteristic level of activation and that the four factors do represent points on a continuum of characteristic activation.

Further support for this conclusion is found in studies involving physiological correlates of the adjective checklist. Thayer (1967) obtained recordings of heart rate and degree of sweating for a small number of undergraduates who had also filled out the adjective checklist. The four activation factors were correlated with heart rate and sweating measures taken singly and also combined into a composite indicator of autonomic activity. In the three separate studies he reports, the composite indicator of autonomic activity correlated with the four activation factors in a way indicating that the factors represent points on a continuum of activation. The heart-rate and sweating measures, taken singly, correlated less strongly and dependably with the activation factors but yielded no information contradictory to that already presented. All in all, Thayer's work seems to have demonstrated the reasonableness of theorizing about a customary level of activation and provides the opportunity to further evaluate the construct validity of Maddi's peripheral theorizing by determining whether the two approach and the avoidance orientations to variety really do have the expected activation characteristics. Despite effort to reconceptualize arousal, there seem solid grounds for making conclusions based on an inverted U-shaped curve (Anderson, 1990).

Costa (1970) attempted such a demonstration in a large-scale investigation of the interrelationships among measures of activation, need for variety, originality, and other cognitive abilities. He administered many tests to a group of 60 undergraduates and subjected the data to an elaborate procedure of analysis (not unlike factor analysis) permitting the test of hypotheses concerning interrelationships. His results indicate little support for Maddi's position in that

customary and actual levels of activation (measured by Thayer's adjective checklist) did not relate to thematic and questionnaire measures of personality types expressive of novelty orientation. But neither the novelty nor the cognitive measures intercorrelated among themselves in the same way as in previous studies, raising the question of whether the testing situation or subjects somehow contributed to the negative findings.

In another study, Maddi et al. (1982) seem to have found some supporting evidence for the notion that in understanding behavior, one must take into account not only the customary level of activation but also whether the person is internally or externally oriented. Customary level of activation was measured by means of Thayer's checklist and subjects were also given Eysenck's introversion-extroversion scale. In addition, subjects composed stories to ambiguous pictures, which were then scored for richness of imagination. Subjects also waited alone in an unfamiliar room sometime during their participation, with their activities observed and scored for evidence of exploratory behavior. It was hypothesized that external exploration (of the room) would be engaged in most by people with a combination of high customary activation and an external orientation (extroversion), whereas internal exploration (richness of imagination) would be done most by people with a combination of high customary activation and an internal orientation (introversion). That the results support this expectation suggests the value of further empirical efforts to test activation theorizing. Further, perusing the general implications of this position, Wolters (1976) interpretively reviewed much research in quest of a motivational component for creativity. He concludes that an active-internal form of the need for variety predisposes people toward creative functioning.

Further evidence of the value of assuming a characteristic level of activation with implications for under- and overactivation is suggested by Zuckerman, Persky, Miller, and Levin (1969). They measured anxiety and activation (adrenocortically), and they manipulated stimulation. Their 22 male subjects were tested first on two control (normal) days and then on one under-stimulation day and one overstimulation day. Understimulation consisted of confinement in darkness and silence; overstimulation consisted of an 8-hour, multichannel, multimedia pro-gram. The overstimulation condition resulted in greater autonomic and adrenocortical activity than the understimulation condition. In con-trast, the understimulation condition produced greater increases in anxiety, depression, and feel-ings of unreality. With both under- and over-stimulation, subjects showed greater activation adrenocortically than they had on the control (normal) days. To some degree, under- and over-stimulation seem to have comparable effects on the body. Carrol, Zuckerman, and Vogel (1982) report similar findings. In an intriguing approach, Lesnik-Oberstein and Cohen (1984) report a similar pattern of sensation seeking by couples.

There are by now several other measures of variety-seeking that involve questionnaires rather than fantasy techniques (e.g., Garlington & Shi-mota, 1964; Zuckerman, Kolin, Price, & Zoob, 1964). Because they are less relevant to Maddi's position than those already covered, I will not discuss them at length. In an attempt to provide normative data on three of these questionnaire measures, McCarroll, Mitchell, Carpenter, and Anderson (1967) found them to overlap con-siderably. Furthermore, Mehrabian and Russell (1973) regard these various questionnaires as agreeing sufficiently on underlying assumptions about activation level and sufficiently overlap-ping, without being comprehensive, to warrant an attempt to derive one overall measure from them. Through a careful process of excluding from this large pool items that were either un-related to the others or tainted with the tendency to respond in a socially desirable fashion, the investigators devised a final questionnaire of 40 items. This measure of arousal-seeking tendency has internal consistency of .87 and stability of .88 with a 7-week interval between testings. In-formation concerning construct validity shows that the test correlates negatively with anxiety and neuroticism measures and positively with measures of extroversion, affiliation, and prefer-ence for arousing situations. It is unclear at this

time whether this test measures activation per se or a conglomerate of novelty and intensity pref-erences, though subsequent empirical work should provide further clarification.

CONCLUDING REMARKS . . . .

We have reached the end of our empirical analy-sis. The time has come to integrate the conclu-sions reached in this chapter with those in Chapter 10 on the empirical validity of core con-siderations. I must admit that the studies per-formed under the aegis of the various theories are of limited value in the empirical analysis of peripheral considerations. There is danger of deciding that a theory is empirically sound for no better reason than that it is championed by personologists who are especially energetic and capable concerning empirical inquiry. At most, we should use the results of the essentially parti-san research just reviewed to supplement the other empirical conclusions reached in this chap-ter and in Chapter 10.

Recall that in Chapter 10 we found consider-able empirical support for both versions of the fulfillment model and the activation version of the consistency model. Nothing in this chapter changes that view. Both the factor analytic stud-ies and the more partisan studies that follow suggest empirical support for the peripheral the-orizing associated with these models. It is true that there is little research associated with some of the fulfillment theories, but this should not be held against them, for little research effort has been mounted. Further, the research listed under each theory has been arbitrary to some extent. Little personality research has been so specific to a particular theory that it applies to that theory alone. More frequently than not, theories belonging to the same class as the one under consideration are also supported by the findings.

The analysis of core considerations presented in Chapter 10 showed that the only ill-sup-ported models are the pure psychosocial version of the conflict model and the pure cognitive dis-sonance version of the consistency model. Although the review of factor-analytic studies conducted earlier in this chapter seems to support conflict as well as fulfillment models, it should be kept in mind that this may be due in part to the studies' generality and ambiguity. In addition, the partisan studies show spotty but intriguing support for Freudian peripheral theorizing. While the evidence in this chapter is not persuasive enough to change the conclusions drawn in Chapter 10, there is certainly a call for more frankly comparative analytic research.

A vexing problem, which I hope you have noticed, plagues a field dominated by research that concerns only small, isolated corners of particular theories. Though most theories seem to have reasonable empirical support, they generate a disquieting suspicion that they have not been tested at all. There is a great need for personology research that stems from a comparative analytic orientation. Such research, whether comprehensive or concerning a specific issue, will yield evidence of the relative fruitfulness of the theories involved. The problem of lack of comparative orientation is further aggravated when the research does not even follow precisely from any particular personality theory. Because this is true of much of the research reviewed in the latter part of this chapter, it has been difficult to reach definite conclusions concerning whether the theories are really supported empirically. This is not to say that the research is uninteresting or even methodologically unrigorous. But even had the research considered here as relevant to single theories been more partisan, as long as it remained precise in its relevance to its personality theory, definite conclusions might have been drawn. And think of what might have been accomplished with more comparative analytic studies!

PART FOUR

OTHER RELEVANT POSITIONS

There are two significant positions in psychology that have something to say about personality but do not fit neatly into the conflict, fulfillment, or consistency models. They are *behaviorism* and *social learning theory,* which was derived from behaviorism but now deviates from it. Should you think worse of the three models because behaviorism and social learning theory cannot be classified within them? Not necessarily. After all, behaviorism arose in part through the insistence on explaining behavior without reference to mentalistic concepts, and personality is the most mentalistic of all. Most behaviorists intend not to be classifiable as personality theorists. And, although they emphasize mentalistic or cognitive processes more than behaviorists do, social learning theorists also try to avoid sounding like personality theorists. It is therefore especially interesting that behaviorism and social learning theory end up having some personality implications that are almost classifiable under my three-model scheme.

THE BEHAVIORISTIC ALTERNATIVE

From the early days of this century to modern times, the movement known as *behaviorism* has exerted an enormous influence on psychology. But what behaviorism actually entails has been less apparent. Even a highly regarded behaviorist, Berlyne (1968), has been provoked to say,

> It is extremely difficult to say exactly what "behavior theory" is and to delineate its boundaries. Is it a branch of psychology, a school of psychology, a theoretical position, a methodological approach? It is certainly not quite any of these, and yet it is all of them to some extent. What is the relation of behavior theory to the rest of psychology? All sorts of answers to these questions have been put forward at one time or another. There are those who have felt that behavior theory is destined to assimilate more and more of psychology as time goes on, so that everything in psychology will eventually be marked with its stamp, and the sooner the better. Others, of course, have felt that behavior theory is a transitory aberration whose pernicious influence will soon be seen for what it is and annihilated. Some have maintained that all psychologists are behavior theorists, but that some realize it and some do not; the implication is that those who are aware of what they are doing will do it better. *

When ranking behaviorists themselves make such statements, behaviorism could justifiably be excluded from consideration here on the grounds that its form and content are not yet sufficiently clear. But such an exclusion would be unfortunate, because behaviorism, for all the confusion over what it really is, has penetrated every fiber of psychology today.

Actually, for all the ambiguity about the boundaries of behaviorism, its main thrust has been clear all along and has not changed. This thrust is *learning*—the increase or decrease in frequency of overt, easily discernible movements (called responses), when followed by stimuli that act as positive or negative reinforcers. Berlyne (1968) is quite definite about this emphasis of behaviorism on learning:

> The term "behavior theory" has been used fairly interchangeably with the term "learning theory." "Learning theory" seems to have come into use rather earlier, and some writers, notably Mowrer, have favored it. Hull and Spence have preferred to speak of "behavior theory." There have been some not very happy attempts to distinguish between the theory of learning and "behavior theory" as the

---

*From "Behavior Theory as Personality Theory," by D. E. Berlyne in *Handbook of Personality Theory and Research*, edited by E. F. Borgatta and W. W. Lambert. Copyright © 1968 by Rand McNally & Company. Reprinted by permission.

theory of performance, but, although, according to most theories, there are differences between the principles that determine the acquisition of habit-strength and those that determine the probability and vigor of responding, it is certainly impracticable to separate the two completely, let alone to assign them to two distinct bodies of theory. The term "behavior theory" is perhaps to be preferred, on the grounds that "learning theory" has come to encompass much more than a statement of the principles that govern learning. (p. 629)

We should expect a theory of learning to have ramifications for many areas of psychology. What does need careful scrutiny is the nature and extent of the impact of behaviorism on these areas. In the *personality* area, we should identify what is relevant and determine its similarities and differences to the other theories in this book. In this regard, we should consider whether behaviorism represents a frank alternative to personality theory as an explanation of behavior.

As I have said many times, a personality theory must include statements about a core, a periphery, and a developmental process linking the two. You will recall that the *core statement* concerns assumptions about what is unchangeable in human nature; the *peripheral statement* concerns the lifestyles that people can acquire; and the *developmental statement* shows how each peripheral style derives from the interaction of the core with the environment. As the developmental statement heavily involves learning, behaviorism should impact this aspect of personality theorizing, all the more so because many personality theorists merely assume some process of learning that can link the core and the periphery and fail to describe it.

Actually, one can say that behaviorism does just the opposite, namely, focuses on the process of learning with little emphasis on core and peripheral considerations. Behaviorists are loath to make pronouncements about unchangeable human nature and are almost equally unwilling to elaborate on lifestyles. For the behaviorist, to consider inherent human nature is to stray too far from tangible observations; to assume lifestyles is to overemphasize predispositions to behave that are not a function of the stimulus characteristics of situations.

I find that behaviorism is less concerned with personality than with other areas of psychology. Berlyne (1968) seems to agree when he says, "It can hardly be overlooked that problems of personality have figured much less prominently in the writings of the behavior theorists than in psychological literature as a whole" (p. 638). He does lay some responsibility for this on ambiguity as to what personality is and is not, but he recognizes that the primary factor is the differing emphases of behaviorism and personology. Whatever else it considers, personology must be concerned with individual differences. It studies individuals acting differently under the same stimulus conditions and acting similarly under several different stimulus conditions. Behaviorism understandably has little to say about such individual differences, because it has sought general laws stating invariant relationships between *stimuli* and *responses* (Berlyne, 1968). If the responses of two individuals differ, the most likely explanation, according to behaviorists, is that the stimuli that elicited or reinforced the responses also differed. And if an individual responds the same way twice, the most likely reason is that the stimulus situation also was the same. But to get a more differentiated view of behaviorism as it relates to personality, we shall have to go into greater detail.

MODERATE BEHAVIORISM . . . .

In understanding the behaviorist movement, one should recognize that it has not been wholly uniform. The moderate, as opposed to the radical, form of the position has been fashioned by psychologists such as Clark Hull (1943) and Kenneth Spence (1948). As you will see, *moderate behaviorism* is more willing to consider organismic factors (e.g., biological needs, habits) than radical behaviorism is. Hull's work at Yale University stimulated such similarly inclined associates as Dollard and Miller (1950). At Iowa State University, Spence's colleagues included Farber (1948) and Taylor (1953). These psychologists, along with many others (e.g., Berlyne, 1960; Brown, 1961) have continued over the years to produce a corpus of research and theorizing that represents a reasonably distinct form of behaviorism. It derives, in essence, from the pioneering work of Ivan P. Pavlov (1927).

In explaining learning, moderate behaviorism has focused on *stimulus-response, or S-R, bonds.* An S-R bond is formed when a specific stimulus regularly elicits a particular response from an organism. With an occasional exception, moderate behaviorists have contended that the strength of an S-R bond is increased when the occurrence of the response in question is followed by a *reward* and decreased when followed by *punishment.* In other words, the stimulus comes to elicit the response dependably because the response obtains for the organism something of positive value. To pinpoint just what this positive value is, moderate behaviorists have theorized about the nature of organisms. They have assumed the existence of *drives,* such as hunger, thirst, and sex, which have the status of biological imperatives in that they support physical survival. So, if an organism is thirsty, it can be taught to emit a particular response in the presence of a stimulus if response is regularly followed with something to drink. The organism will learn that the stimulus is a reliable sign that it can reduce its drive if it performs in a particular fashion.

THE CORE OF PERSONALITY. Although the main thrust of moderate behaviorism clearly is on learning, the various assumptions mentioned above can be considered as framing a position on the core and periphery of personality. The *core tendency* is the attempt to reduce the tension of biological drives. The drives having received most emphasis are hunger, thirst, sex, activity, curiosity, and pain. Since increments in each of these drives are experienced bodily as *tension,* one can speak of general drive, or the total amount of tension across all the aroused drives at any given time.

The *core characteristics* are the appropriate goals, or rewards, corresponding to the various drives. Food is the reward for the hunger drive

and the removal of food the punishment. The reward for thirst is liquid; for sex, sexual experience; and for activity, exercise. To discern the presumed reward for the curiosity drive, remember that all drives are uncomfortable tension states that must be reduced. Thus, the tension of curiosity (or uncertainty) is reduced by information (Berlyne, 1960). The pain drive is ambiguous. In one sense, it is nothing more than another way of stating the core tendency of tension reduction. In another, it is associated with the reward of safety. In any event, as in the example concerning removal of food, the opposite of the reward in the case of each drive is the punishment. All of the above drives are inherent and unlearned. For this reason, moderate behaviorists call them *primary drives* and their corresponding goals *primary rewards.*

THE PERIPHERY OF PERSONALITY. Moderate behaviorism also has something to say about the periphery of personality. After all, a strong S-R bond, or *habit* (Dollard & Miller, 1950), is in my terminology a concrete peripheral characteristic. The habit is learned on the basis of expression of the core tendency in the stimulus environment and is suited to the discussion of individual differences. Certainly two people encountering the same stimulus conditions and response contingencies for reward or punishment will learn identical habits. But if the learning histories of two people are different, their habits will differ even though their core drives are the same.

Once learned, habits persist for some time (this is called *resistance to extinction*) even if reward no longer follows the emission of the response. A man who had learned to be intimidating toward women because doing so frequently led to their having sexual intercourse with him would continue in his ways, at least for a while, even if gentility eventually became more valued. This is one way in which moderate behaviorism recognizes that a person's behavior sometimes imposes itself on the environment rather than being controlled by it. But if the reward for responding in a particular way continues to be absent, the habit eventually will be extinguished. The number of trials to extinction of an unrewarded habit is one measure of its strength.

From its inception, behaviorism has appealed to psychologists largely because it promises a simple, clear understanding of learning. The stimuli serving as signals for responses and the rewards or punishments contingent on the responses were all observable, concrete aspects of the external environment. Indeed, the aspect of behavior chosen for study—the *response*—was a movement rather than a thought or feeling and, therefore, also clear and observable directly. It is true that influential behaviorists, such as Hull, have recognized that such simple depictions of the learning process as the S-R bond should take into account certain complications concerning individual differences.

Hull has asserted that though individual and species differences exist, they need not jeopardize the search for general laws governing learning in all organisms. If such general laws are possible, individual differences can be considered no more important than something to be taken into account in the application of the laws to everyday life. For example, bridge designing is governed by general laws, even though the building of a particular bridge involves unique problems of application. So, Hull (1945) has searched for general laws by "assuming that the forms of the equations representing the behavioral laws of both individuals and species are identical, and that the differences between individuals and species will be found in the empirical constants which are essential components of such equations." In other words, researchers should cancel out, or neutralize, individual and species differences by adding to their equations those constants (which are, after all, arbitrary numbers) that will help make the data of learning seem identical across the individuals and species studied.

But if there are important individual and species differences in the nature of learning, researchers will fail to recognize them because their methods of study are not suited to identification of these differences. The only way you can have any sort of test of the validity of the assumption that there are general laws governing learning is to observe how easy or difficult it actually is to find and manipulate the constants that must be employed to yield general laws.

In this regard, the elegant emphasis on S-R bonds seems to be an oversimplification. Berlyne (1968) summarizes much research and theorizing as follows:

> Contemporary . . . behavior theorists make copious use of "intervening variables," as we have noted. These are essentially mathematical devices to make cumbersome relations between inputs (stimulus-variables) and outputs (response-variables) conceptually manageable. There must be some sort of correspondence, but not necessarily a one-to-one correspondence, between values of these variables and conditions within the organism that are not directly observable. Spence recognizes this and mentions two additional types of psychological laws, the one (O-R laws) identifying response variables as functions of "organic variables" (i.e., measurements of neuroanatomical or neurophysiological properties of the organism) and the other (S-O laws) identifying organic variables as functions of stimulus variables. Most psychological laws must surely be placed in a final category, containing what we may call "S-O-R laws," stating how response variables are determined jointly by stimulus and organic (i.e., intervening) variables. (p. 642)

Berlyne (1968) has said that it is necessary to include *organismic variables,* which are internal and therefore unobservable, in formulations of the stimulus control of behavior. He goes on to list four classes of organismic variables:

1. Transient intervening variables, the values of which change within a matter of minutes or hours (e.g., emotional state, motivational condition)
2. Age as a variable, which focuses on how stimulus-response relationships change over long periods of time
3. Variables the values of which can remain fixed over long periods of time (e.g., habits)
4. Constitutional or congenital predispositions to particular kinds of behavior

It seems to me that when one has devised a theory that fills out Berlyne's outline of what is needed, this theory will have considerable relevance to the understanding of individual differences, with personality as an important subject matter. The statement about learning as being inviolably constant will have so many exceptions and be shored up by so many intervening variables as to lose its position of centrality and elegant simplicity. Moderate behaviorism will then be closer to personality theory.

APPLICATIONS TO HUMANS. Actually, developments in the direction of personality theory have been taking place, mainly in the attempt to apply behaviorism to human beings, who are obviously so much more complex than lower animals. The initial emphasis on responses as tangible, directly observable movements, and stimuli as manipulatable aspects of the external environment has been considerably modified. Now behaviorists consider thoughts and feelings as responses along with movements. Behaviorists may even consider such internal, relatively unobservable states as thoughts and feelings as implicit or incipient movements, in an attempt to save the old emphasis on that which is tangible. Perhaps more striking is the declaration that internal events (e.g., thoughts, feelings, metabolic states) can be considered stimuli with potential for influencing responses. Recently, it has become common to see, inserted between the old S and R of the S-R bond, *s*'s and *r*'s that stand for the internal, unmeasured stimuli and responses that have been assumed.

In addition, the moderate behaviorist's position on drives has undergone considerable elaboration. It became too cumbersome and unconvincing to try to explain the myriad forms of human behavior as attempts to reduce the tension of a few biological drives, such as hunger and thirst, or gain rewards, such as food and water. So, the concepts of *secondary drive* and *secondary reward* were devised. In contrast to the primary drives and rewards, these are learned and changeable.

According to Berlyne (1968), "The principle of secondary reinforcement postulated that neutral stimuli accompanying primary rewards (i.e.,

conditions in which primary drives are reduced) would acquire a conditioned reward-value in their own right." (p. 664). Thus, if a person always ate food in a blue room, the color blue would come to have a pleasant, comforting effect on him or her even when encountered in a noneating context. Blue would have become a secondary reward.

A *secondary drive* is assumed to be evoked as "a consequence of conditioning by any stimulus (warning signal) that has habitually preceded or accompanied pain" (Berlyne, 1968, p. 664). So, if the person were locked in a blue room with no food available, the pain of mounting hunger would become associated with the color blue. Subsequently, on encountering blue in a context unrelated to food deprivation, the person would experience discomfort, or anxiety. If some stimulus such as blue is associated with an increase in primary drive, the stimulus becomes a secondary drive. To continue functioning as a secondary drive or reward, a stimulus such as blue must at least occasionally be paired once again with the primary drive or reinforcement from which it derived its power. Consistent with the notion of secondary (nonbiological) drives is Miller's (1959) assumption that any strong stimulus functions as a drive.

Because they are learned and changeable, secondary drives and rewards qualify as *peripheral characteristics* in the terminology of this book. Along with habits, they constitute the statement on peripheral personality that can be derived from moderate behaviorism. Secondary drives and rewards play a major role in the behaviorist's attempt to understand human behavior. Thus, such diverse goals as money, fame, and truth can be conceptualized as secondary rewards linked by past association with such primary rewards as food and water. Further, such uncomfortable states as anxiety and aggression can be considered secondary drives learned by association with primary drives. Since learning histories are likely to differ, secondary drives and rewards can show considerable variation from individual to individual. The same, of course, is true of habits.

Anxiety Research

Moderate behaviorism has produced an enormous amount of research. Most of it is experimental, focuses on learning, and employs nonhuman organisms as subjects. Despite the emphasis on learning, much of this research supports the assumption that biological needs exist and that tension reduction is rewarding. Thus, an organism deprived of food or water will learn an S-R bond ever more rapidly with ever more deprivation, at least when the learning task is relatively simple; however, when the learning task is relatively complex, there may actually be a level of drive too great to permit effective learning (e.g., Farber & Spence, 1953; Yerkes & Dodson, 1908). Although the bulk of the research has concerned the hunger and thirst drives, or the more general avoidance of pain, more recent work has also indicated that the postulated curiosity drive exists. Various organisms will perform work in order to obtain information (e.g., Berlyne, 1960) or to experience stimulus change (e.g., Dember, 1961). Although most of the research has employed nonhuman subjects, enough of it has been done with humans to suggest that one can safely conclude the existence of various biological drives in them as well.

Of course, the existence of such *drives* is hardly surprising. Furthermore, because relevant to a behaviorist theory of personality as core characteristics, drives would play an insignificant role in explaining those persisting individual differences that lie at the heart of the personological enterprise. Further, the putative core tendency of moderate behaviorism, which makes tension reduction the aim of all functioning, is not unassailably supported by research, as you saw in Chapter 10.

Another representative theme in behavioristic research concerns manifest anxiety. This research has focused exclusively on human beings and concerns itself with individual differences. The behavioristic conceptualization of anxiety, however, is ambiguous. In the main, anxiety has been viewed as an expression of general drive or tension. But it is also possible to consider anxiety a secondary drive, learned through association with primary drives. The latter formulation, though less common in the literature, would actually be more consistent with the focus on individual or group differences in the research and the implication carried in many measurement operations that it is truly anxiety and not just tension that is being studied.

In the 1950s and 1960s, a great deal of behavioristic research on anxiety was done, but the emphasis appears to have dwindled. Most of the studies employed the *Manifest Anxiety Scale,* a questionnaire devised by Taylor (1953), which includes such items as "I have very few headaches" and "I am very confident of myself." This test proved to have adequate reliability. Before long, several other anxiety scales became available (e.g., Sarason, 1958; Welsh, 1956). Endler, Hunt, and Rosenstein's (1962) was unusual in that it assesses the degree of subjective anxiety in a number of different situational contexts.

Several hypotheses following from the assumption that anxiety functions like a general drive were tested. This research has been ably reviewed by Spence and Spence (1966). One such hypothesis is that high anxiety should facilitate learning in simple tasks but disrupt it in complex ones. Although many studies support this contention, many do not. Another hypothesis is that anxiety should show a positive relationship to physiological indices of emotionality or tension. Although this expectation has been neither fully nor sophisticatedly researched, the available findings are generally negative. But most available studies do confirm the hypothesis that highly anxious people are more disrupted in their functioning by personal threat or stress than low-anxiety people are. It would not be surprising to find highly anxious people generally self-depreciatory and tending toward psychopathology—indeed, such evidence exists (e.g., Lauterbach, 1958; Trapp & Kausler, 1958). In general, there are more confirming than contradicting findings for the interpretation of anxiety as general drive. There is, of course, extensive modern literature on anxiety that I will not summarize because it is so far removed from the explicit attempt to test moderate behavioristic theorizing that it is not especially relevant here. Some of this research was considered in Chapter 12.

As you can tell, the Manifest Anxiety Scale and similar anxiety questionnaires have been employed in numerous studies that go beyond the specific predictions stemming from the concept of general drive alone. The correlation of anxiety scores with scores on other performances constitutes the makings of R-R (response-response) rather than S-R laws in the terminology of moderate behaviorism (Spence, 1948). In searching for *R-R laws,* the investigator tries to determine invariances in the relationship among responses without tying the responses in any rigorous way to antecedent stimuli. It is my impression that when moderate behaviorists become interested in human behavior per se, they tend to abandon strict emphasis on the stimulus control of behavior and focus instead on how the various facets of behavior go together. This seems appropriate given the enormous complexity of human as opposed to nonhuman behavior. Research themes such as that concerning manifest anxiety show an implicit distinction in moderate behaviorism between nonhuman and human behavior, even though in explicit, formal theorizing no such distinction is assumed.

Moderate Behaviorism and Psychoanalytic Theory

Several other kinds of research are considered part of the behavioristic movement; for example, the research stemming from the proposition that frustration breeds aggression. Although Berlyne (1968) classifies this research as concerned with aggression construed as a secondary drive, it is not clear from behavioristic theory just how this interpretation can be made. As in the case of manifest anxiety, one could as easily consider aggression to be primary, or unlearned drive, because the tie between frustration and aggression is thought to be invariant. Other investigators loosely in the behavioristic tradition (e.g., Berkowitz, 1974) have considered

aggression as a learned drive by detaching it from any necessary connection with frustration. In general, these investigations have focused on how experiences of success and failure in fighting lead to learned patterns of dominant and submissive behavior.

But aggression research is deviating even further from any pure behavioristic orientation. For example, Tedeschi, Smith, and Brown (1974) suggest the central importance of the concept of coercive power, with emphasis on the subject's attempt to influence. Investigators report evidence that intent must be taken into account along with various other personality variables (e.g., Nickel, 1974; Scarpetti, 1974). That some of these more personalistic emphases have been supported from within the behaviorist camp may be partially due to the long-standing affinity between behaviorism and psychoanalytic theory.

This affinity becomes even more apparent in research themes within the behaviorist movement that appear to bear an uncertain relationship to behavioristic thinking. An example is conflict, a subject that has provoked considerable study among moderate behaviorists (e.g., Berlyne, 1964; Brown & Farber, 1951; Miller, 1959). Although one might, by doing theoretical handstands, derive this interest in conflict from behavioristic thinking, it does not seem to follow from it naturally. I do not think behaviorists would have emphasized conflict so much if psychoanalytic theorizing had not had such an impact on them. I feel similarly about the study of defenses, which behaviorists have mounted with great energy (e.g., Farber, 1948; Miller & Dollard, 1941; Mowrer, 1940; Sears, 1943). In general, these studies have employed nonhuman subjects and focused on observable responses without regard to underlying mentation.

Indeed, the behaviorists who have done the most to elaborate on the position so as to account for individual differences in human behavior (e.g., Dollard & Miller, 1950) explicitly consider themselves to be dealing with the same range of phenomena important to Freud. In their view, Dollard and Miller focus on those aspects of Freud most amenable to operationalization and empirical test and, by dispensing with the rest, improve on psychoanalytic formulations. In the main, they have dispensed with Freud's mentalistic aspects and his theoretical statements about the necessarily incompatible nature of individuals and society. What they have emphasized instead are the most biological aspects of his thinking and tangible movements rather than thoughts.

In my estimation, though it seems to resemble psychoanalytic theory, behaviorism in reality is quite different from it. Although it is true, for example, that Freud would have endorsed the behaviorist's assumption of primary drives, such as hunger, thirst, and sex, he would not have agreed to define them as devoid of mentality and therefore similar to what is present in nonhuman animals. Freud has presented the instincts as wishes and attendant emotions, present in the mind, and, although derived from metabolism, not merely biological phenomena. In addition, he has considered the chief importance of instincts to be their incompatibility with the social requirements of maintaining the common good. From this assumption, as you know, comes Freud's emphasis on conflict and defense. But for him, conflict is not merely the presence of incompatible response tendencies. More important, conflict also involves a mental dilemma in which guilt and fear of punishment are inevitable participants. Defensiveness, for Freud, is a mental operation, denoting conscious and unconscious thoughts, only one small expression of which occurs in some actual movement or response.

On the basis of these differences in theoretical emphasis, Freud would have justifiably disagreed with the behaviorist's reliance on nonhuman subjects for experimentation. Further, he would not have accepted such experimental designs as that of Mowrer (1940), mentioned in Chapter 10, in which the measure of defensive behavior is the substitution of a weaker habit for a stronger one in the face of stress. The defense mechanism of regression, which Mowrer thought he was demonstrating, makes no sense in Freud's thinking unless it derives from his conceptualization of

psychosexual stages of development. It is clear neither that rats have psychosexual stages of development nor how, pushing a bar or rearing on their hind legs would articulate such stages in any important way.

Strictly speaking, research emphasis on conflict and defense proceeds mostly from Freudian-style theorizing, replete with the very assumptions that behaviorists have found objectionable. In addition, the frustration-leading-to-aggression hypothesis follows much more readily from Freud's thinking concerning the anal stage of psychosexual development than it does from moderate behaviorism. Even the study of manifest anxiety has, among behaviorists, involved more focus on mental content (e.g., socially desirable responses, experiences of low self-confidence, obsessive thinking) than they can easily justify. It is not enough for behaviorists to insist that they are studying what Freud believed important when the changes in psychoanalytic thinking that have been made radically alter its emphases.

I am drawn to the conclusion that the rudimentary theory of personality contained in moderate behaviorism is either a pseudo-conflict theory, with its assumptions about the inevitability of hidden but implicit conflict, or else a kind of fulfillment theory, in which the story of human behavior is to be understood as nothing more than the styles each person learns for reducing tension from drives. If the former, a fuller embracing of Freud's mentalistic and social assumptions would lead to research of greater relevance. If the latter, one probably would want to expend less research effort on such topics as conflict and defensiveness.

RADICAL BEHAVIORISM ....

Radical behaviorism derives from Watson (1924) more than from Pavlov and finds its contemporary expression in Skinner (1938, 1953, 1957) and those he has influenced (e.g., Krasner & Ullmann, 1965; Lundin, 1974; Verplanck, 1954).

Like moderate behaviorism, it focuses on the way in which stimuli control actions and considers the laws of learning, whereby this control takes place, as invariant across individuals and species. But what makes radical behaviorism radical is its unwillingness to make assumptions about the existence and importance of drives—primary or secondary—and its insistence that even the minimally mentalistic concept of habit is unnecessary for understanding. Apparently, in radical behaviorism there are not even the rudiments of a position on the core and periphery of personality. Yet, radical behaviorism claims to be able to predict, control, and understand all behavior. As such, it should represent a frank alternative to personality theorizing (and, for that matter, any kind of theorizing in psychology).

Radical behaviorists have championed many useful concepts and distinctions in understanding learning and in this have influenced all areas of psychology, including moderate behaviorism. Speaking for all radical behaviorists, Skinner asserts that the only appropriate criterion for scientific explanation is prediction and control. To accept an explanation merely because it seems to make sense or has coherence (i.e., appeals to intuitive and rational knowledge) is to be deluded. The extreme emphasis on prediction and control leads to a preoccupation with changing behavior. You must be able to change behavior in order to demonstrate the ability to control. Thus, the first break with personality theorizing is the radical behaviorist's lack of interest in behavior that remains the same over many different situations.

Operant and Respondent Conditioning

Radical behaviorists' distinctions concerning stimuli and responses are all aimed at providing a basis for understanding how responses change by increasing or decreasing in frequency. At the outset, you should recognize that for an event to be classified as a stimulus it must be observable and manipulable and for an event to be classified as a response it must be observable and quantifiable. There are two classes of response. In Frankel's (1971) words:

> When a response is regularly elicited by a stimulus as the result of the inherited characteristics of the organism, it is called an unconditioned respondent. If we were to change the diaper of an infant and accidentally stick him with a pin, he would probably start crying. Since the response of crying when pin-pricked is not the result of previous experience but the consequence of the inherited structure and capacities of the infant, it is an unconditioned respondent. When a previously neutral stimulus can elicit a response, it is called a conditioned respondent. The process whereby neutral stimuli function as conditioned eliciting stimuli is called respondent conditioning. Thus the sight of the pin may now cause the infant to cry. (p. 447)*

Respondent conditioning was heavily emphasized by Pavlov (1927) and forms much of the basis of moderate behaviorism. Because it was recognized early on, respondent conditioning is often called *classical*. Emotional behaviors often have respondent components; for example, a slap in the face may elicit crying from a child. The respondent components of our emotions (i.e., their unlearned tie to particular eliciting stimuli) may well underlie our feeling of helplessness about our moods (Frankel, 1971).

Much more important than respondent conditioning for radical behaviorism is operant conditioning. Although some of our behaviors are by nature reflexive, most of them are voluntary. These responses are called *operant* to emphasize that they "operate" on the environment and their shaping or control is achieved by operant conditioning. In Frankel's (1971) words,

> Opening a refrigerator is an operant response insofar as it is a function of subsequent stimuli (food). If the refrigerator were always empty we would not open refrigerator doors. The presence of the food increases the strength of the operant response.

---

*Excerpts from *Perspectives on Personality: A Comparative Approach*, Salvatore R. Maddi. Copyright © 1971 by Little, Brown and Company (Inc.). Reprinted by permission.

When a stimulus following an operant response increases the strength of the operant, it is called a reinforcing stimulus. The difference between a reinforcing stimulus and an eliciting stimulus is that the former always follows an operant response whereas the latter always precedes a respondent.

A reinforcer is said to be positive when the effect of the operant response is experimentally observed to "produce" the reinforcing stimulus. Food is therefore a positive reinforcer for opening refrigerator doors. In contrast, whenever the effect of an operant response is experimentally observed to "eliminate" a stimulus, that stimulus is called a negative reinforcer. Let us suppose that the infant is now six months old, and he has not forgotten that we stuck him with pins. If we discover that whenever we enter the room the infant turns to the wall, we might hypothesize that we were an aversive stimulus that negatively reinforced facing the wall. By regularly facing the wall in our presence, the child eliminates us from his visual field. (pp. 447–448)

Thus, the organism performs an *operant (or voluntary) response* in order to bring about a *positive reinforcing stimulus* or eliminate a *negatively reinforcing stimulus*. If the investigator wishes to increase the frequency of an operant response, he or she must wait until it occurs and then follow it with either the presence of a positive reinforcer or the absence of a negative reinforcer. An increase in the frequency of an operant response indicates that learning (operant conditioning) has taken place.

Radical behaviorists also distinguish between *unconditioned and conditioned reinforcers*. When it is not the organism's past training that has produced the ability of a reinforcer to increase the rate of an operant response, the stimulus is considered an unconditioned reinforcing stimulus. Examples are food and water, which are presumed to be intrinsically reinforcing. But we also seek stimuli that are not immediately relevant to food and drink. For example, adults work for money and students work for grades, though they are not born with needs for money or grades. A neutral stimulus (money or grades) may subsequently function as a conditioned reinforcer when it has been present during the occurrence of an unconditioned reinforcer. Unconditioned and conditioned reinforcers are similar to the primary and secondary rewards (or punishments) of moderate behaviorism.

Discriminative Stimuli

A final class of stimuli are those that supply information rather than elicit or reinforce responses. Information is provided by *discriminative stimuli,* which in large measure control our lives. In our society, some people's functions are advertised by their uniforms. In this case, the uniforms are discriminative stimuli. Frankel (1971) clarifies how the classifications radical behaviorists offer are used in understanding complex human behavior:

> A stimulus may function as a discriminative stimulus at one point in time and as a conditioned reinforcer at another. In the presence of our mother (a discriminative stimulus) we may ask (an operant response) for money (a conditioned reinforcer). With the money in our hand (a discriminative stimulus) we may go (an operant response) to the grocer (a discriminative stimulus) for candy (an unconditioned positive reinforcer). (p. 449)

You will note from this example that the discriminative stimulus must precede or accompany the operant response whereas the conditioned reinforcer always follows the operant response.

Stimulus and Response Generalization

You should also keep in mind that radical behaviorists (and their more moderate counterparts) emphasize *stimulus and response generalization*. A response associated with a particular discriminative stimulus may occur, through stimulus generalization, in the presence of some similar discriminative stimulus not involved in the original learning. Response generalization refers to the tendency of very frequent (strongly learned) responses to occur in the context of stimulus conditions other than those in which they were learned. The concepts of stimulus and response generalization carry a distinct possibility for personalistic exploration; some responses occur in stimulus circumstances other than those that were learned.

Schedules of Reinforcement and the Extinction Process

Radical behaviorists have been especially adept at determining the effects of different contingencies (or relationships) of reinforcement on the strength of a learned response. An operant response that is reinforced every time it is emitted is called a *continuous schedule of reinforcement*. But reinforcements are more often intermittent, especially outside the laboratory. *Intermittent reinforcement* can occur according to a ratio schedule, in which a relationship exists between the number of responses emitted and the number of reinforcements taking place (e.g., every third response is reinforced), or an interval schedule, in which reinforcement occurs after a certain period of time regardless of the number of responses that have occurred.

Many other reinforcement contingencies have been recognized. Suffice it to say that each reinforcement schedule has a different effect on the acquisition, maintenance, and weakening (extinction) of an operant response. Frankel (1971) gives evidence of this in an extended example close to everyday life:

A child asks his father for money to buy bubble gum. Whenever he makes this request, he is given the money for the gum. Suppose that in the course of two months the child has received money two hundred times. When reinforcement follows an operant every time, the schedule is one of continuous reinforcement. Imagine now that another child makes the same request for the same time period and the same number of times, but his father does not always grant the request. This is an intermittent schedule of reinforcement. Suppose the dentist subsequently tells both parents that their children must stop chewing bubble gum. The parents agree, and from that day on they refuse to grant the request of their children. In operant terms, a previously rewarded operant response (asking for bubble gum) will undergo extinction as a result of non-reinforcement. Extinction refers to the procedure of continuous non-reinforcement which results in a lowering of response rate. Both children on discovering that their requests were going to be refused (non-reinforced) would suddenly begin asking more frequently. At first non-reinforced

trials result in a rise in the frequency of the operant. This observation has been confirmed in hundreds of experiments. It is also not uncommon in our experience to find ourselves trying harder after frustration. However, as the non-reinforcement of the operant response continues over trials, the weakening of the response manifests itself in lower and lower rates of responding, until finally it returns to its initial level (prior to the first reinforcement), or disappears altogether. In our example, both children will gradually stop asking their parents for bubble gum. However, the child who has been reinforced on a continuous schedule will extinguish faster than the child who has been reinforced on an intermittent schedule. If we observe an individual seemingly struggling in vain, and we wonder how someone can work so hard when achieving so little reinforcement, we may speculate that a history of intermittent reinforcement for that individual effects the present drawn-out extinction process. Ironically, the very perseverance of an individual who has refused to give up and has inspired us with a sustained effort despite repeated failures may be at that moment undergoing extinction. (pp. 452-453)

Apparently, intermittent reinforcement schedules can produce response patterns difficult to unlearn even when no further reward is forthcoming. Here too is something relevant to personology: Some response patterns continue unchanged even if they do not lead to reinforcement.

There is little point in inquiring as to whether there is empirical support for the various tenets of radical behaviorism, as they are largely the result of painstaking and rigorous research. We encounter, of course, the same problem as in moderate behaviorism; namely, that organisms such as pigeons and rats are subjects much more often than humans are. As long as one is willing to assume that the laws of learning are universal, this emphasis on nonhuman species is no special limitation. But it arouses the skepticism of personologists, who are loath to make that assumption, even about learning. Some psychologists (e.g., Kohler, 1925; Tolman, 1948) believe that learning in humans takes place much more cognitively, through insight and the like, than behaviorism would ever admit. (See one criticism of behaviorism mounted on cognitive grounds in Chapter

14.) Nonetheless, it must be said that, within its own set of assumptions, radical behaviorism has achieved considerable empirical support.

The Absence of Core and Periphery in Radical Behaviorism

As indicated earlier, the moderate behaviorist's emphasis on primary and secondary drives and on habits can be construed as a rudimentary position on the core and periphery of personality. There is not even this much of a position on personality in radical behaviorism. According to Skinner, the organism should be treated as a "black box," which, though perhaps not empty, need not be explored in order for one to understand behavior. The responses constituting behavior are tangible and can be controlled by manipulating the external stimulus environment—and that is that. Of course, the emphasis of such a position would be on behavior modifications or learning. But radical behaviorists disapprove of their moderate counterparts for conceptualizations linking external stimuli to observable responses by way of internal stimuli and responses.

Do radical behaviorists really deny the existence of common, unchangeable aspects of human nature? No, but they will not speculate about them, and they consider them unimportant in behavior modification. Any enduring, relatively unmodifiable behavior that might stem from, say, a particular genetic constitution would not be of interest. Skinner (1957) puts it this way:

> Even when it can be shown that some aspect of behavior is due to season of birth, gross body type, or genetic constitution, the fact is of limited use. It may help us in predicting behavior, but it is of little value in an experimental analysis or in practical control because such a condition cannot be manipulated after the individual has been conceived. The most that can be said is that the knowledge of the genetic factor may enable us to make better use of our causes. If we know that an individual has certain inherent limitations, we may use our techniques to control more intelligently, but we cannot alter the genetic factor. (p. 371)

It should be recognized that in his single-minded emphasis on behavior modification, Skinner is disagreeing to some extent with the personologist over what is to be explained. The personologist would include as important data behavior that does not change.

But what of the drives that moderate behaviorists and virtually everyone else in psychology recognize as important influences on behavior? Here surely are inherent or core characteristics that can have a variable influence on behavior (e.g., one may be more active when hungry than when satiated). In general, radical behaviorists abhor concepts that refer to unobservable, internal states construed as causes of behavior. To radical behaviorists, what virtually every personologist does is thus regarded as unscientific. To theorize about unconscious motivation, defenses, life fear, will to power, achievement motivation, or even hunger drive is to deny the external stimuli that supposedly control the various behaviors.

Although the primary drives of the moderate behaviorist are less abhorrent because they are more believably biological than these other concepts, the radical behaviorist still does not consider them useful explanatory devices. For the radical behaviorist, one gains nothing of scientific value in "explaining" that people eat at one time and not at another by saying that they were hungry at first and not subsequently. One gains nothing because it is then necessary to determine the mechanism governing the waxing and waning of whatever it is that is called hunger. The tangible, observable, external stimulus situation that governs eating behavior turns out to be the number of hours since one has last eaten. To talk of a hunger drive is at best superfluous (if we know the external stimuli controlling the responses to be explained) and at worst misleading (by dulling our curiosity to find the external stimuli if we do not yet know them).

It is instructive to observe how radical behaviorists attempt to maintain this unwillingness to assume the existence of internal motivating states. All experimenters know that animals become more active when deprived of food or water and that an active animal is easier to train. So, radical behaviorists indeed deprive their subjects of food and water. But in describing their experimental procedure, they do not say that the animal was hungry or thirsty. At most they refer to the effects of deprivation on the body. A pigeon will be described as at "80 percent of its free-feeding weight." The more active the animal, the greater the likelihood that it will emit the desired operant response along with others. When the desired operant occurs, it can be reinforced with the same food or water that had been withheld before the beginning of the experimental task. Soon enough, the food or water reinforcement will increase the rate at which the operant is emitted, and learning will be said to have occurred. But once again the effectiveness of the food or water will not be discussed in terms of its drive-reducing properties as would be done in moderate behaviorism. For the radical behaviorist, a stimulus qualifies as a reinforcement if it increases the rate of an operant, and nothing else need or should be asked.

For me, the gymnastics that radical behaviorists must perform to avoid the mentalistic, personological implications of the learning process are, in the final analysis, unconvincing. One problem is the definition of reinforcement as the stimulus that increases or decreases the rate of emission of an operant response. But the reinforcement concept is also a major part of the explanation of learning. How do we know that *learning* has taken place? Because an operant response has changed in rate through the action of a reinforcement. How do we know that a stimulus has *reinforcing properties?* Because it can change the rate of an operant response. With all their rigor and concern for science, radical behaviorists have fallen into a serious circularity here. Moderate behaviorists have avoided this circularity by defining a reinforcing stimulus in terms of the drive or tension it reduces rather than of the change in response rate it may produce. With reinforcement defined in terms of tension-reducing capability, it becomes an empirical question whether a reward or punishment affects response rate. Hence, the use of reinforcement as an explanation of such rate changes is not circular in moderate behaviorism.

Of course, radical behaviorists do not think

they deny the existence of physiological processes that might be called drives; rather, they prefer to refer only to observable and manipulable things—hence the emphasis on body weight rather than hunger. But then why not tie the definition of reinforcement to such body states as weight rather than to the very data (operant rate) that reinforcement is supposed to explain? This is not done, because radical behaviorists insist that physiological processes such as drives affect not learning but only activity level. One reduces a subject's body weight only because the ensuing high activity level means that many operant responses are being emitted, so it is easier to focus on one of them for conditioning purposes. To define reinforcement in terms of bodily states would be to admit that they too affect learning.

But not only would it be more scientific to define reinforcements in terms other than what they are supposed to explain; it would also be thoroughly consistent with commonsense, or intuitive, knowledge. Radical behaviorists come perilously close to functionally decorticating themselves (Murray, 1959) in their concern for scientific purity. Are we really supposed to believe that the procedure of decreasing subjects' body weight by depriving them of food was hit on by empirical exploration alone and not assumed all along to increase activity level because of its effect on hunger? Are we really supposed to believe that food qualifies as a positive reinforcer merely because it has been observed to affect the rate of operant responding, with no tie to already known nutritional requirements of organisms? Why was food tried as a possible reinforcer in the first place? Do we not already know that it was tried because we all accept the fact that food-deprived subjects want food and will do almost anything to get it? And is not the substitution of rigorous-sounding terminology (e.g.,"80 percent of free-feeding body weight") for the commonsense terms that cover the same phenomena a sleight of hand intended to convey that some new, grand knowledge has been obtained?

I must admit, however, that some empirical knowledge derived from radical behaviorism is striking and useful. In particular, I would point to the research showing the differential effects of various schedules of reinforcement on the acquisition, maintenance, and especially extinction of operant responses. To explain human behavior, one finds considerable value in knowing that a response becomes extinct more slowly if learned with an intermittent schedule of reinforcement than if learned with a continuous one. I suspect even here, however, that the plan for the radical behaviorist's research comes from his or her intuitive knowledge, which heavily includes the very speculations concerning what is inside the black box that supposedly are inadmissible in psychological science. If so, the radical behaviorist is really doing nothing that different from the moderate behaviorist, who is, as indicated before, rather more willing to make assumptions constituting personality theory.

If it is true that intuition and common sense play a greater role in the radical behaviorist's enterprise than is admitted or should be expected from the noninferential terminology, one might expect to find little slips of the tongue, as it were, that belie the rigor. Frankel (1971) believes he has found evidence of one such slip in Skinner's explanation of superstitious behavior. As you know, it is common for personologists such as Freud (1960) to refer to such mentalistic considerations as repressed hostile feelings projected onto others when he explains superstitious (excessively fearful) behavior. Thus, one thinks of the world as dangerous because of one's own projected anger. Skinner, of course, will have none of this, preferring to search for the external manipulable stimulus conditions producing superstitious behavior.

In offering a laboratory demonstration of superstitious behavior, Skinner (1961) placed a pigeon maintained at 75% of its free-feeding body weight in an experimental chamber arranged so that food was presented every 5 seconds no matter what the pigeon was doing (fixed-interval reinforcement). In such a situation, if the "clock is arranged to present the food . . . at regular intervals with no reference whatsoever to the bird's behavior, operant conditioning usually takes place" (Skinner, 1961). Skinner (1961) goes on to describe the results of such conditioning:

One bird was conditioned to turn counterclockwise about the cage, making two or three turns between reinforcements. Another repeatedly thrust its head into one of the upper corners of the cage. A third developed a "tossing response," as if placing its head beneath an invisible bar and lifting it repeatedly.

These responses involved orientation to some aspect of the environment rather than mere execution of movements. Skinner interprets these findings as the development of superstitious behavior. Apparently, such superstitious behavior is very resistant to extinction. With learning taking place according to an interval of 15 seconds between presentations of food, one conditions an operant response that will then be emitted 10,000 times despite the absence of food (Skinner, 1961). In accounting for this superstitious behavior, Skinner does not have recourse to covert stimuli and responses such as impulses, emotions, repressions, or projection, relying instead on an analysis of the stimulus conditions under which an organism will behave as if its actions were effective in determining the reinforcing consequences.

What makes it possible to call this superstitious behavior is that Skinner and we know that the pigeon's responses are not really effective in bringing about the reinforcement, which occurs only after some time interval regardless of the responses being made. Frankel (1971) asks,

> How did Skinner know that the bird was superstitious? Presumably because Skinner was outside the pigeon's universe, and thus was able to know that the ritualistic behavior . . . was not instrumental in getting the pellet of food. But is it really possible to call one behavior superstitious and another behavior unsuperstitious within the framework of the operant model? (p. 455)

In elaborating on the challenge in the last sentence, Frankel (1971) presents an extended but apt parable:

> Let me make the point clearer through the use of a pigeon parable. Imagine that one of the pigeons, Max, begins to wonder whether it is necessary for him to walk in circles in order for the food to arrive. Max decides to perform an experiment and

walks to another section of the cage, only to discover that the food is delivered. Shall he conclude that the reinforcement is unrelated to his behavior? He might also conclude that there are two behaviors related to the delivery of food. Max may try another experimental excursion to another part of the cage and once again discover that a pellet of food is delivered. He then might conclude either that his behavior is unrelated to the delivery of food or that three behaviors are related to the food. Suppose Max now decides to see whether doing nothing leads to the same result. He discovers that again food is delivered and again he is faced with the dilemma of deciding whether the behavior of doing nothing is related to food delivery or whether food delivery is unrelated to behavior. Suppose Max had access to a philosopher pigeon, whom he asks for advice. He may say to the philosopher, "Food is a life and death matter and it comes at intervals so long as I am doing something. When I purposely do nothing it also comes. Must I worry about it or think about it at all?" The philosopher may reply, "The ways of the world are strange. Life is given and life is taken (reinforcement) both in the experimental chamber and back in the cage (present reinforcement and historical contingencies), and it is difficult for us to comprehend the ways of our Lord, B. F. Skinner. Sometimes he is benevolent in the experimental chamber and sometimes he is not. It is a question of deciding ultimates. If what we do is irrelevant to life and death, then it becomes a problem to decide what is relevant to behavior and if anything can be "relevant" in the context of a universe that remains ultimately beyond reach. The teachings of Skinner are clear about this—Man must assume control and behave as if his behavior is relevant to important goals. One of our prophets has developed a system whereby it would have been possible to kill many German men and women—because German men and women killed many Polish men and women. Thus the prophet, an American, developed a missile system carrying one of our own species to eventual destruction. The judgement of Skinner (1961, p. 426), as related in the book, is simply: "The ethical question of our right to convert a lower creature into an unwitting hero is a peacetime luxury." It is clear that Skinner is concerned with our species and more concerned with us than he appears to be with German men and women. So, in practical matters, one must assume there is a meaning, a reinforcement, to which our operants are directed.

Max may reply: "Philosopher, I take it you are not an atheist, but that you do believe that there is a God, called Skinner, though his ways are inscrutable." The philosopher answers, "Yes, I do believe." "Are you not merely superstitious?" asks Max. The philosopher replies: "You come to me with a problem and I provide you with a solution which implies that inscrutability need not eliminate meaningfulness—go about your daily affairs as if things mattered, as Skinner suggests." Max walks away from the philosopher and ponders the solution. He doesn't want to be superstitious. He doesn't want to live as if anything he does matters, if it does not, in fact, matter. Max then hits upon a clever idea. "If my behavior is irrelevant (no God—no Skinner) then I may as well commit suicide or do nothing. However, if my behavior is relevant, then I must commit myself accordingly. It is also true that life would be better if behavior mattered. Since I will never understand even if he 'is,' I will never know the solution to my problem. However, it makes sense to choose the alternative that would be better if true, and that alternative is to act as if my behavior were relevant to the consequences." Max then returns to his experimental chamber and continues his walking in circles.

Are we not all like Max insofar as we are inhabitants of a Skinner box? As inhabitants of a Skinner box, can any of us discover whether a given behavior is superstitious or non-superstitious? Skinner, the scientist, informs us that through the operation of contingencies of reinforcement our behavior is controlled. Skinner also informs us that the only relationship necessary to establish the effectiveness of a reinforcer is the "order and proximity of response and reinforcement." Such a formula does not allow for distinctions such as right and wrong, superstitious or non-superstitious, unless these refer to receiving reinforcement after a response. Clearly, the pigeons accomplish this. They do get reinforced; therefore, they are as correct as they can be within the confines of an operant conditioning paradigm. Since reinforcement will always take place when the organism is doing one thing or another, there is no way for it to decide the relevance of its behavior to reinforcement.

The best the organism can hope to accomplish is to discover that the reinforcement is delivered on a certain time schedule, but this would require that the organism leave his universe and consult with the controlling network outside of his universe. By definition, this is not possible. At best, one may

442   PART FOUR   *Other Relevant Positions*

infer, deduce, or extrapolate that there must be a universal clock (interval schedule of reinforcement), and indeed, such deductions, inferences, and extrapolations on the parts of priests, medicine men, and philosophers take place. This is what Skinner calls superstitious behavior. He seems to think that science is freed from such superstitions. If so it is also uninvolved in the nature of that "universal clock" that regulates the reinforcement schedule. In fact, scientists are as superstitious as anyone else. It is the scientist who has developed the extraordinary ritual of the scientific method in an effort to understand the nature of the universe, or, as in the case of our pigeons, the nature of Skinner.

The scientist is searching for meaning in the form of laws. But what proof is offered that a law has been discovered? For the behaviorist, the ultimate criterion as to whether we know anything is contingent on reinforcements. A law must be proven to have reinforcing consequences. To say we will discover other laws is to do nothing more than express the faith that we shall find behaviors that lead to reinforcing consequences. Of course, the Pope will also undoubtedly tell us that belief in Christ has reinforcing consequences, and further religiosity will lead to behaviors that lead to other reinforcements. We have already seen that "persevering" may become an interpretation of another person's behavior when he does not extinguish a response. If he is on an extinction schedule of nonreinforcement, then we would know whether such a response is right or wrong, but we can never know that unless we could get outside our universe. Thus, like our pigeons we require faith to believe that behavior is relevant to the universal clock.

When Skinner writes an essay concerning the ways in which the world operates and the ways in which it should operate, he is presuming to have an insight into the nature of that clock as a result of his scientific background. Skinner's statement (1961, p. 4) "Let us agree to start with, that health is better than sickness, wisdom better than ignorance, love better than hate, and productive energy better than neurotic sloth" ignores the implication of his own writings. It was Skinner who argued that one reinforcement is not better or worse than another. Reinforcements simply reinforce behavior. To say love is better than hate is to say nonsense, unless he adds that it is better to love X reinforcement than to hate Y reinforcement. This is absurd because loving or hating a

reinforcement is contingent upon a history of other reinforcements or present contingencies. Thus, to hate or love a reinforcement is to love or hate the law of gravity. Yet Skinner writes as though knowledge of reinforcement effects the law of reinforcement. (pp. 455–458)

Of course, Skinner is careful to put the term *superstitious* in quotes, on the grounds that he will not interpret behavior or make value judgments about it. Because of his own assumptions, he knows he cannot know anything more than what he observes. Actually, here and there (e.g., Skinner, 1961), he also uses drive names such as "hunger," again in quotes. But as Frankel (1971, p. 458) aptly charges, words such as *hunger* or *superstitious* are interpretations of behavior, not mere descriptions. And interpretations are miniature theories insofar as they purport to describe the "meaning" of what is seen. Although Skinner considers theory to be explanatory fiction at worst and irrelevant at best, he is in fact theorizing when he interprets movements as if he knew their meaning. That the interpretations make good common sense should not dull your recognition that he is theorizing nonetheless.

What Frankel has pinpointed is hardly unimportant. Consider another ramification of radical behaviorists' theorizing intuitively without admitting that doing so affects their actions and conclusions. Skinner has provided a powerful technology with which to change and control behavior; hence, it is not surprising to find his approach used in psychotherapy (e.g., Ayllon & Azrin, 1968; Goldiamond & Dyrud, 1967). But especially in something as crucial as psychotherapy, one must consider which behavior shall be changed and in which direction change shall be implemented. Skinner asserts again and again that his is merely a technology for behavior modification that is all the more scientific for carrying no value judgments within it. And when behavioristic psychotherapists discuss cases, they refer to the curing of stuttering, or autism, or some other abnormality the correction of which is such an unquestionable good that no value judgment seems to be involved.

When pressed further on just what changes

should and should not be made, behavioristic psychotherapists are likely to say that they bring about specifically those changes that the patient wants. The therapist is not so much a manipulator as a helper. But suppose that a patient came to the radical behaviorist's office asking for aid in becoming courageous enough to assassinate the President. What would the therapist say or do? He or she might turn the patient away, indicating lack of interest in or even opposition to such an aim. If therapists did this, they would be admitting that their behavior modification technology serves their theory as to what is good and bad, constructive and unconstructive. Alternatively, they might engage the patient in conversation, on the expressed or private presumption that the stated aim was not the real one. Perhaps the patient just wants to feel more effective or substantially change his or her life. In choosing this alternative, the radical behaviorists would be subjugating technology to a theory no less than they would be by turning the patient away. Only by helping the patient gain courage to murder would the therapists be true to their nonevaluative position. And yet, we all know they would not do that. Once again we see the operation of theory—rife with value judgments similar to those forming the corpus of personology—in the decisions, plans, and conclusions of the radical behaviorists.

The upshot of all this is that radical behaviorism as an alternative to personality theorizing is not as pure as it purports to be. There is the distinct possibility that insofar as it is relevant to the understanding of complex human behavior, it is so by virtue of implicit, intuitive theorizing similar to what takes place more explicitly in moderate behaviorism. To refer to "hunger" and to maintain subjects at some fraction of body weight at the same time that one chooses food as a reinforcer is to assume the existence of hunger as a primary drive and the effectiveness of the reinforcer as a tension reducer. To try to explain the resistance to extinction of "superstitious" behavior is to admit that there are learned traits or habits that affect behavior relatively directly even though the stimulus justification of such behavior in the

environment may not be particularly apparent. And, for that matter, to turn patients away or to become convinced that they do not know their own minds is to have a theory of psychopathology and mental health. If radical behaviorism indeed contains the intuitive seeds of a personality theory, the theory should be brought to flowering so that its strengths and weaknesses can be clearly judged in the marketplace of ideas.

If it still be insisted that radical behaviorism includes no theorizing with implications for core and peripheral statements on personality, the sorts of slips and therapeutic decisions discussed above should be ruthlessly weeded out. Radical behaviorists are describers and manipulators of physical movements and nothing more. If the radical behaviorist adhered strictly to this, Frankel's (1971) words would be well worth noting:

> One can wonder what Skinner's appeal would be if he described only movements and did not add theoretical projections. Would the reader have the patience to project his own interpretations upon the movements or would he read someone like Freud who at least makes systematic projections? Skinner and Freud are similar in that both have an ingenious ability to take a unit of behavior and establish its meaning. Freud interprets dreams. Skinner interprets movements. The undemonstrable conjectures of Freud are perhaps no worse than the meaningless movements of Skinner. (p. 459)

To say that all behavior is the result of learning and then say nothing about developmentally common themes as to what is learned is to make very little headway in understanding human life. To say that learning is dependent on reinforcers and give no basis for discovering or identifying reinforcers except as learning actually occurs is to damn us to a minute analysis of every event of human life that amounts to searching for a needle in a haystack. To insist that we need not speculate about the contents of that black box we call the organism is to force us to act as if those wonderfully simplifying and organizing inferences about the true nature of complex phenomena we wish to understand, which have produced rapid advances in every other science, are irrelevant in ours.

TOWARD A RAPPROCHEMENT....

Until recently, the debate between radical behaviorists and personologists was quite intense. But a spirit of reconciliation is developing now in which the personality theories becoming most influential are those that give weight to situations as one determinant of behavior, and behaviorism is acknowledging its implicit theorizing about human core and peripheral characteristics. For behaviorists, this shift is most apparent when attempts at psychotherapy are made. According to those "card-carrying" behaviorists, Hunt and Dyrud (1968),

> innate proclivities of man have an important bearing on behavioral modification. They can lie waiting as traps or can be employed as powerful allies. ... There is no reason why we cannot devise methods to play into man's ethology, to turn the apparent rigidities of innate tendencies to our advantage.... In a sense, the important part of the modification would consist of putting the individual into a position in which "nature would take its course," in a new and better direction. (pp. 149–150)

In another statement, Hunt (1975b) admits implicit theorizing among behaviorists far beyond core characteristics alone:

> Identification of the effective reinforcers for a particular person and his particular behavior can be quite difficult, requiring shrewd guesses based on personal experience and empathy, clinical knowledge and dynamic theory, plus a good green thumb for behavior-in-context.

It is understandable that in the act of finding reinforcers that will work for the client, the behavior therapist's implicit personality theory will be shown.

Hand in hand with the growing willingness to make implicit personality assumptions explicit is an increase in self-criticism among behaviorists. Where there used to be an optimistic, almost incautious attitude of invincibility, there is now a more sober appraisal of the whole approach. Hunt (1975b) provides a good example of this evaluative attitude. He identifies three related weaknesses in behaviorism as a

scientific approach and a psychotherapy that are beginning to gain wide discussion.

First is the problem of unexpected side effects. It is now apparent that schedules of reinforcement may have unintended but important and systematic effects on behavior other than the behavior the treatment or shaping targets. Examples are (1) aggression as a side effect of *aversive (or avoidance) conditioning* (e.g., Ulrich, Dulaney, Kucera, & Colasacco, 1972); (2) behavioral "contrast," in which changes in the reinforcement schedule in one segment of a session change behavior in another segment though the schedule there remains unchanged (e.g., Reynolds in Hunt, 1975b); and (3) "autoshaping," in which even pigeons seem to acquire an operant response (pecking) without there having been direct reinforcement of it (e.g., Jenkins, 1973).

The second or ethological weakness of radical behaviorism is its inadequate ability to deal with *species-specific behaviors*, especially the differences between lower organisms, certain nonhuman primates, and human beings. Specifically, it is the human's symbolization and active use of it to control his or her own and others' behavior that wreak havoc with attempts at *shaping behavior* (Hunt, 1975a). Not only therapists and experimenters can shape behavior, but so can clients and subjects! Related is the accumulating evidence (e.g., Medin, 1972) that even in monkeys "reward can function to decrease as well as increase the probability of choosing an object," thus casting doubt on positions based on an automatic strengthening function of reinforcement. There are also humorous examples of animal research in which strange "misbehavior" results from the shaping of responses that are not a natural part of the relevant organism's repertoire (e.g., Hinde & Stevenson-Hinde, 1973). At the human level, recent research on empathy and prosocial behavior has led many investigators (e.g., Feshbach, 1982; Hoffman, 1981b; Staub, 1978) to conclude that children are not the "blank screens" at birth that radical behaviorism would have us believe; rather, children appear ready early in life to behave altruistically.

The third weakness of radical behaviorism is

the difficulty in rigorously accounting for self-regulation of behavior. Just what this mysterious "self" is that can control its actions is a vexing problem for such a situational position as radical behaviorism (Hunt, 1975a). According to Hunt and Dyrud (1968), an entirely new set of assumptions may be necessary in order to understand human symbolization, replacing the earlier attempt to generalize from organisms with rudimentary mentation. Consistent with this clinical conclusion, experimental evidence shows that human adults do not seem to learn without an awareness of doing so. Dulany (1962, 1968), Spielberger (1962), and Bandura (1969) have convincingly demonstrated that for learning to occur in humans, they must be able to verbalize not only the relationship between the target response class and the reinforcement but their intentions to cooperate with the learning task. In situations in which this cooperative attitude is presumed not to exist, it has been shown (e.g., Calder & Staw, 1975a, 1975b) that extrinsic reinforcement (the usual kind recognized by behaviorists) does not add to, but rather interacts with, intrinsic reinforcement (the inherent value in the task), decreasing overall performance.

In his presidential address before the American Psychological Association, Bandura (1974) said,

> After individuals discern the instrumental relation between action and outcome, contingent rewards may produce accommodating or oppositional behavior depending on how they value the incentives, the influencers and the behavior itself, and how others respond. Thus reinforcement, as it has become better understood, has changed from a mechanical strengthener of conduct to an informative and motivating influence. . . . Theories that explain human behavior as the product of external rewards and punishments present a truncated image of man because people partly regulate their actions by self-produced consequences. (p. 860)

For Bandura, recent research developments of the sort we have been discussing have shifted the emphasis of behaviorism from the study of response learning to analyses of memory and cognition. The rest of his address theorizes about these mental functions. Other behaviorists have joined Bandura in this new emphasis (e.g.,

Boneau, 1974; Dember, 1974; Mischel, 1973b). Self-regulation research has been gathering force, documenting a cognitive influence on action that is way beyond anything accountable by radical behaviorism (e.g., Bandura, 1978; Kuhl & Beckman, 1985).

Holland (1978) reluctantly suggests that *behavior modification therapy* has deviated from its parent discipline, radical behaviorism. He observes that whereas behaviorism assumes behavior to be the result of contingencies and that lasting behavior change involves altering these contingencies, most behavior modification programs do no more than arrange special contingencies in a specific environment. Behavior modification therapy is itself the result of certain contingencies imposed on it by current social structure (e.g., weekly therapy on an outpatient basis). Lazarus (1977) notes that behavior modification therapy is no longer the rallying cry for rigorous intervention that it once was. He blames this change on accumulating evidence that cognitive mediation of human functioning is paramount and on radical behaviorism's inability to account for this. It is best, he counsels, to adopt a more comprehensive framework than radical behaviorism.

Volpe (1969), a leader of the behavior modification movement, nonetheless argues that this form of therapy has always considered actions, feelings, and thoughts, treating all of them as learned phenomena subject to the laws of radical behaviorism. In attempting to account for the current emphasis on thought processes as determinants of action, he argues that this conception is mistaken in failing to recognize work on internal, neuronal sources of reinforcement (e.g., Olds, 1975). Although the reinforcement contingencies for thoughts may be internal, they operate by the same laws as external reinforcers. But this very argument itself shows how far we have come from radical behaviorism, which insists on regarding the organism as a "black box." In his attempt to save the child, behavior modification therapy, Volpe may have sacrificed the parent, radical behaviorism. It certainly is clear that Skinner (1974) adopts a much more restrictive view of the nature of behaviorism.

The dissenting voices from within behaviorism are by no means restricted to behavior modification therapists. Hernstein (1977) concludes that "new data undermine traditional assumptions." He asserts that self-control and other phenomena require a conceptualization involving motivation, which requires looking into the black box. All the elements of a rapprochement are present. On their part, behaviorists can start developing more comprehensive approaches to human behavior, cognition, and choice. And personologists can freely avail themselves of the methodological and cognitive rigor of behaviorists.

CONCLUDING REMARKS ....

In considering the relative merits of personality theorizing and the behavioristic approach, one must recognize that to some extent they have been oriented toward different empirical phenomena. In terms of data, behaviorism emphasizes the learning process, or behaviors that change. In contrast, personology emphasizes behavior that remains the same or at least changes only slowly. The main concepts in behaviorism concerning stable behavior are stimulus and response generalization and resistance to extinction, but these concepts do not lie at the heart of behaviorism. Furthermore, personology emphasizes individual and species differences, whereas behaviorism attempts to hold these constant toward specifying that which is universal in the learning process. In a sense, it is the constants in learning formulae that most directly address the personologist's concerns, and these constants could hardly be construed as central in behaviorism.

Even so, although their emphasis lies elsewhere, behaviorists do accept some aspects of behavior as at least relatively stable. We may therefore find it worthwhile to consider how much their theorizing about behavioral stability resembles what the personologist does. You have seen that moderate behaviorism makes assumptions that can be construed as statements about the core and periphery of personality. Radical behaviorism, in contrast, attempts to explain behavior without recourse to such organismic variables as primary and secondary drives, tied definitionally to primary and secondary rewards. Nor does radical behaviorism use terms, such as habit, that refer to lifestyles. But it does seem extraordinarily difficult to keep the radical behaviorist's extreme purity separate from interpretations based on the contents of what is within the skin, or black box. If such purity were strictly adhered to, behaviorism might even be too cumbersome, too dependent on empirical study of each and every minute external stimulus and manipulatable movement to be of much practical use. While the risk of being wrong is certainly present once one theorizes about what is important, that risk is minimized if theorizing is done carefully enough to lead to hypothesis testing. Fortunately, even radical behaviorists now seem more willing to theorize explicitly.

What remains an unanswered question is just what kind of personality theorizing will go on in behaviorism. The persistent reference of moderate behaviorists to Freud and their choice of such research topics as conflict and defense suggest that they are using the conflict model. However, they exclude the dynamic aspects of Freudian theory so that defenses become habits learned as the result of certain reinforcement schedules rather than ego operations that render certain thoughts unconscious. The very things that make psychoanalytic formulations express the conflict model are disputed. And behaviorism has recently emphasized human choice, memory, and perception, topics that at least imply intention.

In the final analysis, it may be that behavioristic personality theorizing follows the fulfillment model, with life being understood as the general attempt to satisfy primary, biological drives through cognitive effort and intention. Understood in this way, behaviorism ceases to be a frank alternative to personology. Instead, it becomes an approach to understanding learning —which, in some of its statements, is not so different from the enterprise of personality theories covered in this book.

THE RISE OF SOCIAL
LEARNING THEORY

An emphasis called *social learning theory* has gained considerable popularity in psychology. Because of its implications for the study of *personality,* I shall consider it here. Initially an offshoot of moderate behaviorism, the social learning position seems to have emerged in response to the difficulty human behavior has posed to emphases on learning developed in laboratory experiments using rats and other lower organisms. Human beings are so complex that their behavior often seems different both in kind and in degree from that of other animals. Faced with this problem, some behaviorists have clung steadfastly to their simple *S-R,* associationist emphases, shoring up their theories with an additional assumption here and there and attempting wherever possible to translate apparent human complexity into the simple response repertoires of their rats and pigeons.

But other behaviorists have chosen instead to develop more complex theoretical approaches that, though retaining something of the flavor of behaviorism, provide understanding of human complexity without seeming to explain it away. *Social learning theory* has arisen from the work of this latter group of behaviorists. As the name

of this approach suggests, it emphasizes learning rather than inherent characteristics, and the social surroundings rather than internal dispositions as the determinant of behavior.

The main architects of social learning theory are Albert Bandura (1969), Richard Walters (Bandura & Walters, 1963), Julian B. Rotter (1964), Walter Mischel (1968, 1971), and, to some extent, Hans J. Eysenck (1957) and Joseph Wolpe (1958, 1969). Although there certainly are differences among their views, the substantial similarities have begun to define a consistent approach to understanding and influencing human behavior.

THE BREAK WITH
PSYCHOANALYTIC THOUGHT....

You will recall from Chapter 13 that moderate behaviorism has had a fascination with psychoanalytic theory. This has taken the form of trying to purge psychoanalytic theory of its most metaphysical features, such as the unconscious and defenses, by translating everything possible into the behavioristic concepts of habit and drive. Although one can fairly question whether what has emerged from this translation is still psychoanalytic theory, behaviorists nonetheless have been cheered that they could appear to retain the clinical insights of Freud without doing violence to their view of scientific rigor.

Social learning theorists, on the other hand, have explicitly detached themselves from psychoanalytic theory even though they are, if anything, more interested in abnormal or neurotic behavior than the general run of moderate behaviorists are. Social learning theory emphasizes cognition, or information processing, which implies thought that is rational and logical. Although Freud certainly emphasizes mental functioning, for him, unconscious wishes, impulses, and conflicts emerge as the major determinants of behavior. You cannot engage in vigorous rational trial and error if unconscious mental processes are paramount. You are left with rationalization or that which appears to be rational but really is not.

Social learning theorists emphasize a rational process of learning from experience:

> How does our theory compare with the psychoanalytic one? In the formation of neurotic symptoms, Freud emphasized the traumatic nature of the events leading up to the neurosis, as well as their roots in early childhood. . . . The Freudians' stress seems to be rather misplaced in allocating the origins of all neuroses to this period. It is possible that many neurotic symptoms find their origin in this period, but there is no reason at all to assume that neurotic symptoms cannot equally easily be generated at a later period, provided conditions are arranged so as to favor their emergence.
>
> The point, however, on which the theory here advocated breaks decisively with psychoanalytic thought . . . is in this. Freudian theory regards neurotic symptoms as adaptive mechanisms which are evidence of repression; they are "the visible upshot of unconscious causes." Learning theory does not postulate any such "unconscious" causes, but regards neurotic symptoms as simply learned habits; there is no neurosis underlying the symptoms, but merely the symptom itself. *Get rid of the symptom (skeletal and autonomic) and you have eliminated the neurosis.* (Eysenck & Rachman, 1965, pp. 9–10)

In attributing psychopathology to certain learned habits alone, social learning theorists are also

rejecting Freud's emphasis on the inherent conflict between instincts and society or superego. Where Dollard and Miller (see Chapter 13) retain an intuitive reliance on this conflict formulation, all the while trying to divest Freud of seemingly untestable metaphysics, the social learning theorists want to make their break complete.

But one must recognize that some social learning theorists, especially Eysenck and Wolpe, are very close to the moderate behaviorists. These social learning theorists recognize the existence and importance of the primary drives (see Chapter 13). They mainly emphasize the drive for avoidance of pain, and the anxiety they see as the heart of neurotic symptomatology is considered a secondary drive derived from this primary one. *Anxiety* is a conditioned reaction, brought about by the conjunction on one or more occasions of an initially neutral stimulus with a painful event. This emphasis on habits and secondary drives rather than on conflicts and defenses stems in part from research evidence.

Psychoanalysts commonly refer to Masserman's (1943) classical studies of "neurosis" in cats as justification for a conflict explanation of psychopathology. Masserman trained cats to receive food at a given location and later shocked them at that location. They developed what looked like intense anxiety reactions, which were explained in terms of conflict over whether to approach or avoid the location. Wolpe (1958) repeated Masserman's experiment but added another group of animals. This additional group was shocked in the experimental apparatus but had not had the prior approach training with food that the conflict group received. The "anxiety responses" observed were similar in both groups, suggesting that pain but not necessarily conflict is the essential ingredient in anxiety reactions.

If anxiety is simply a learned reaction, it should be removable, however persistent it has become, by some process of new learning that cancels out the old S-R bond. This statement underlies the psychotherapeutic efforts of the branch of social learning theory closest to moderate behaviorism. Wolpe (1958), for example, employs what he calls *systematic desensitization* therapy, in which people are encouraged to think of anxiety-provoking thoughts while relaxing. As soon as anxiety occurs, they are to think of something else. They try this over and over until they can contemplate the previously anxiety-arousing thoughts without this emotion. As you can see, this is very far from the psychoanalyst's encouragement to patients to freely associate and thereby rediscover suppressed experiences.

Systematic desensitization therapy and other behavioristic techniques of psychotherapy promise a simple and quick antidote for nagging symptoms that clients have seemed capable of talking about forever without any behavioral change. However, relevant case histories show that even direct attempts to remove symptoms with no concern for underlying problems are long, arduous, and not invariably successful. For example, Wolpe (Krasner & Ullman, 1965) reports the use of systematic desensitization therapy with a woman who suffered with an intense fear that she would be involved in a collision whenever she drove a car. Wolpe claims this phobia developed when she experienced a collision while her husband was driving. It took more than 60 sessions of concentrated, arduous desensitization to get this symptom to go away. At that, Wolpe considers his patient fortunate, indicating that sometimes fears simply cannot be treated effectively by this approach. An additional vexing problem with this case (and many others like it) is that despite Wolpe's insistence that it was systematic desensitization therapy that finally produced symptom remission, many psychoanalytically inclined readers will find many descriptions suggesting otherwise.

Near the end of his discussion, Wolpe mentions that as the woman was questioned further, it became clear that her fear was more generalized than it had originally appeared. In addition, the only two men besides her husband whom she had loved were her first fiancé, who died in an airplane crash just before they were to marry, and her father, who had died some time after that in the same year that she married her present love. It may be that behind what seemed a simple phobia deriving from an accident was the deeper fear of abandonment by beloved men. If one were so inclined, it would be easy to implicate the Freudian oedipal triangle (see Chapter 3) as an abandonment that she never fully resolved. Further, Wolpe's claim that systematic desensitization therapy must have produced symptom remission because no transference was permitted to develop is also less than convincing. The therapist even went riding in a car with the client at one point in his attempt to help her overcome her fear. Psychoanalysts would regard events of this sort as definitely courting transference.

It is probably too early to evaluate behavioristic psychotherapies fully and well. Suffice it to say that they are not the dramatic end to all our searching for methods to alleviate human suffering—if any psychotherapy ever could be. Further, the claim that they do not implicitly employ techniques derived from more dynamic, mentalistic theories of personality has not been proven. We can be sure, though, that psychotherapy research seeking to study outcome could profit from an explicit comparative analytic stance. I do not mean anything as simple as comparing proportions of cures across various psychotherapies, though this would certainly be useful. At some point in the near future, it will be necessary to determine whether therapists employing a particular technique use it and no other and, if they do, whether it leads to more or less symptom remission than other single techniques. We cannot rely for this determination on what the therapist says he or she did and did not do. There seems no alternative to detailed and painstaking observational studies of ongoing psychotherapy sessions.

In short, Wolpe's approach, with assumptions similar to Eysenck's, conceptualizes learning as S-R bonds cemented by reinforcement, with primary and secondary drives providing the motive force for activity. In this regard, the positions are similar to the older moderate behaviorism discussed in Chapter 13. The core tendency is still tension reduction, and the core characteristics are still the primary drives and rewards. The peripheral characteristics are habits and secondary drives and rewards.

COGNITION AS PARAMOUNT . . . .

It is common to regard Bandura, Rotter, and Mischel as moderate behaviorists. But with them the notion of social learning has reached a peak that virtually removes them from the behaviorist camp. To me this seems true for two reasons: (1) the assumption that learning can take place without the person emitting a response and receiving positive or negative reinforcement for it and (2) the paramount importance attributed to cognition (which is, after all, internal and not directly observable).

Turning first to Bandura (Bandura & Walters, 1963; Krasner & Ullmann, 1965), I find that he emphasizes what might be called *S-S (stimulus-stimulus) laws,* in contrast to the S-R laws of behaviorism. He believes that one need not actually emit a response in the presence of a stimulus cue, with a reinforcement following the response, for learning to take place. For him, persons can observe someone else behaving in a particular way in response to a given situation and learn just by seeing what happens to them. When the observers find themselves in such a situation, they will most likely behave in similar fashion. The person observed has served as a model for *imitative learning* on the part of the observers.

In this view, *modeling behavior* is the most common and important form of learning in humans. In making this point, Bandura (Krasner & Ullmann, 1965) argues that

> one does not employ trial-and-error or operant conditioning methods in training children to swim, adolescents to drive an automobile, or in getting adults to acquire vocational skills. Indeed, if training proceeded in this manner, very few persons would ever survive the process of socialization. It is evident from informal observation that the behavior of models is utilized extensively to accelerate the acquisition process, and to prevent one-trial extinction of the organism in situations where an error may produce fatal consequences.

Going further, Bandura (Krasner & Ullmann, 1965) contends that operant conditioning is not only a less common but also a less effective procedure for learning at the human level. He quips that if a child had no occasion to hear the phrase "successive approximations" or any other combination of unusual words, it is doubtful whether such a verbal response could ever be shaped by differential reinforcement of the child's random utterances. This frontal assault on radical behaviorism would probably produce the rejoinder that verbal behavior is not sufficiently universal across animal species to warrant granting it such importance. Anticipating this, Bandura (Krasner & Ullmann, 1965) concludes that such a position "simply highlights the inadvisability of relying too heavily on infrahuman organisms for establishing principles of human behavior." He is incredulous that we would actually be asked to believe that verbal communication in humans is unimportant merely because no researcher has ever succeeded in teaching a rat to talk in a recognizable language. Instead, we might well conclude that modeling procedures are superior to operant conditioning procedures in promoting learning. He suggests that one relegate the role of operant conditioning in humans to that of regulating performance of behavioral sequences once they already have been learned through modeling.

To get a vivid sense of Bandura's meaning, consider one of the many research studies (see Bandura & Walters, 1963; Mischel, 1968) supporting learning by imitation. Bandura (1965) had his child subjects watch a film about an adult who displayed novel aggressive responses, such as hitting and kicking a Bobo doll. The subjects were split into three groups based on the consequences of the adult's behavior. In one group the adult's aggression was punished, in another it was ignored, and in the third it was rewarded. When tested after the film, children who had observed aggression punished expressed less aggression in their behavior than did children who had observed it either ignored or rewarded. But in subsequent testing, when the children were offered attractive incentives to reproduce the adult's behavior, the differences among the groups vanished! Presumably all the subjects had learned the observed aggressive behavior. The effect of punishing the observed behavior seems to have been merely to inhibit its exhibition in the children. On this basis, it is argued that reward and punishment increase or decrease not what is learned but the likelihood that it will be expressed in performance.

Cognition (information processing, thought) must be very active and important, even in children, for people to learn by observing others and then decide whether to express what has been learned on the basis of presumed outcomes. Cognition definitely does not play such a major role in moderate behaviorism. In what sense, then, is the position of Bandura and his colleagues behaviorism at all? Their position does not consider rewards and punishments important to learning; it also emphasizes cognition as much as, if not more than, action. According to Mischel (1968), whose own position is quite similar, Bandura is a behaviorist because, though he emphasizes cognition, he does not assume elaborate motivations, impulses, conflicts, and the like to underlie the behavior being observed. Mischel and the others attempt to explain expectations and imitative (heavily cognitive) learning in terms of a relatively uninterpretive analysis of the observable stimulus conditions that are occurring. This new body of theory is, according to Mischel, truly a "social learning" position in that it attempts to explain thoughts and actions in terms of concrete social, functional realities. Mischel (1971) sees social learning theory as an alternative to other personological approaches, which seem to emphasize either traits (broad, cross-situational consistencies in behavior) or motivational states (which underlie many, apparently dissimilar behaviors).

In discriminating the social learning approach from positions emphasizing traits, Mischel (1971, p. 75) considers the case of a woman who seems hostile and fiercely independent some of the time but passive and dependent on other occasions. His position is that the woman is all these seemingly contradictory things, but each behavior is tied to the particular stimulus conditions that elicit it. This seems a reasonable position. Mischel contends, however, that trait theorists would have difficulty understanding the woman, because traits are general dispositions presumably finding expressions across a great many unspecified stimulus situations. But surely

it is a vague use of the trait concept that Mischel criticizes rather than any use one would want to defend. I grant that some personality theorists name traits and then leave them hanging there, as if there were no limits to their influence on behavior. But if this were not mere sloppiness why would theorists ever postulate more than one trait? They postulate many because they at least implicitly recognize that the sphere of influence of each is limited. Traits are, after all, used primarily in explaining individual differences. In personology, one certainly can point to a use of the trait concept rigorous enough to make it hard to distinguish from that which Mischel advocates. Allport (see Chapter 6), for example, considers personal dispositions as rendering a definite delimited range of stimuli and responses functionally equivalent. Also, McClelland (see Chapter 7) defines a motive as a predisposition that becomes active only in the presence of certain situational cues. Murray (see Chapter 3) shares this view, taking pains to implicate, both subjectively and objectively, perceived situational cues (alpha and beta presses) arousing the motive. It is my impression that when used carefully, the trait or motive concept comes very close to Mischel's emphasis.

This similarity becomes even more apparent when Mischel (1971) stresses that social learning theory is interested in "the functional relations between what [one] does and the psychological condition of [one's] life" (p. 77). Clearly he does not want to be restricted to a mindless listing of the links between particular cognitions and particular stimulus situations. He wishes to consider how these links go together into larger functional units relevant to the main enterprises of life.

How does this differ from Allport's intent, or, for that matter, from the intent of theorists who emphasize underlying motivations for observed behaviors? I certainly grant that many personality theorists have used the motivation concept loosely. But once again we must distinguish loose from rigorous usage, for only the latter is a proper target for Mischel if he is to demonstrate the inherent superiority of his position. In carving out the relevant domain of social learning theory, Mischel (1971) emphasizes "covert representation" (for learning unexpressed externally), the whole matter of "the individual's interpretation of events and experiences," and the occurrence of "mediation" (pp. 78–79). In discussing mediation, Mischel (1971) emphasizes the importance of the human as an active organism who "evaluates, judges, and regulates his own performance" and "in addition to being rewarded and punished by the external environment . . . [learns] to monitor and evaluate [his] own behavior and to reward and punish [himself], thus modifying [his] own behavior and influencing [his] environment" (p. 81). Is there any personality theorist who would find this emphasis different from his or her own? Hardly, unless it were those who so stress unconscious motivation that they would find the self-deterministic ring of Mischel's words objectionable. At this early stage in the development of social learning theory, opposing it to theories of unconscious motivation alone rather than to all motivational emphases would answer many of these objections.

Indeed, from the examples and cases he raises, Mischel mainly objects to psychoanalytic theory. A notable case in point concerns Pearson Brack, an American pilot during World War II, whose problem is discussed by two psychoanalysts, Grinker and Spiegel (1945, pp. 197–207). During a bombing mission, Brack's plane was severely damaged by flak, and he was rendered unconscious. The plane began to dive, and Brack barely regained consciousness in time to right it before it crashed. Seriously injured, Brack was hospitalized for a month. After this time, he seemed fully recovered and was returned to duty. But on his next two missions, he fainted when the plane reached about 10,000 feet, the elevation at which the original flak damage had occurred.

After intensive interviewing, the psychoanalytically oriented psychiatrist at the hospital concluded that Brack's fainting was connected to deep, unconscious anxieties rooted in his childhood experiences. The diagnosis involved basic immaturity, long-standing insecurity, and faulty identification with the father. The incident of nearly being shot out of the sky was perceived as

rather trivial except as it precipitated anxiety in an already insecure and immature person. In contrast, Mischel (1968) offers a social learning analysis of the case that emphasizes the severe emotional reaction that had been conditioned to altitude cues specific to 10,000 feet. According to Mischel, it explains sufficiently the fainting for one to recognize that the occurrence of any cues specific to the near fatal incident would be enough to bring back the emotional debilitation associated with that trauma.

It is my impression that virtually all fulfillment and consistency theorists would tend to agree with Mischel in his interpretation of the Brack case. This further underscores the fact that Mischel's main dispute regarding motivation is with the Freudians, who persist in postulating basically unconscious conflicts and purposes underlying behavior. But if what I am saying is so, Mischel could acknowledge that there indeed are personalistic approaches to the motivation construct that are much more compatible with his own.

The final social learning theorist I shall consider is Rotter (1954), who takes as his task an understanding of the probability that a particular act will occur, or what he calls the *behavior potential.* You will recall that in moderate behaviorism the probability of a response is determined by the strength of the habit or S-R bond. The more times in the past the response has followed a particular stimulus cue and been stamped in by a reinforcement, the greater the likelihood that the cue will elicit the response in the future. Radical behaviorism offers a similar formulation, except that it does not use the terminology of habit and explicitly recognizes that intermittent reinforcement may produce a higher response probability than invariant reinforcement.

The differences between these formulations and Rotter's pinpoint what is different about social learning theory. For Rotter (1954), *behavior potential is a function of both the expectancy that reinforcement will follow the behavior and the perceived value of the expected reinforcement.* First, the emphasis on expectancy and perceived value shows the strong cognitive commitment that Rotter has made. Expectancies and perceived values are internal, mental events and are given the role of jointly determining whether or not action will take place. Second, Rotter is dealing with a subjective rather than an objective basis for predicting behavior. One person's expectancy that reinforcement will follow a response may differ from another person's expectancy. Similarly, there may well be individual differences in the perceived value of any particular reinforcement. Consequently, what is being said is that if you wish to understand why humans behave or fail to, you must refer to their own individualized views of the world. Indeed, Rotter has a name for this—the *psychological situation* —which is clearly intended to be the person's general construction of the value and likelihood of the stimuli making up his or her environment.

True to his social learning assumptions, Rotter does not regard individual differences in reinforcement expectancy and value to stem merely from instincts or underlying motives; rather, he believes that such differences strongly reflect differences in previous experience. Having assumed this, Rotter could take a reasonably conservative stance that would come as close as possible to an objective position. He could say that the value one places on a reinforcement reflects what its actual utility has been in one's past. Thus, sports cars would have more reinforcement value for a man who has won the company of attractive women by owning such cars than for someone whose female associates regard fancy cars as ostentatious. Further, he could say that the expectancy of a reinforcement mirrors its actual frequency of occurrence in a person's past. Such an approach certainly would generate an ability to understand individual differences, for one could safely assume that the chances are great that past experiences would cause such objective differences among people.

Certainly Rotter recognizes these actuarial bases for differences in reinforcement value and expectancy in the present, but he goes even further. In a leap into subjectivism from which there is no return, he (Rotter, Chance, & Phares, 1972) asserts that "people's probability statements, and other behaviors relating to the probability of occurrence of an event, often differ systematically from their actuarial experience with the event in the past." He regards a variety of factors as influencing one's probability estimates away from objective occurrence. These factors include the way in which a situation is categorized, various patterning and sequential considerations, the uniqueness of events, the degree of generalization that occurs, and how the person perceives causality. These factors are not meant to be derived from the person's reinforcement history in any precise way; rather, they are best understood as cognitive commitments or decisions that interact with the objective frequency and utility of reinforcements to produce each person's particular reinforcement expectancies and values, or psychological situation. It is this psychological situation that determines the relative likelihood of the person taking various actions in the future.

In his reference to factors that influence cognition and perception away from actuarial experience, Rotter shows the influence of his longtime colleague, George A. Kelly (see Chapter 7). You should see by now why I think that the cognitive emphasis of these social learning theorists and Bandura is so extreme as to place them outside behaviorism. To try to somehow subsume not only the notion of observational learning but also that of subjective perceptions as determinants of reinforcement value and expectancy under behaviorism would destroy its original intent. When social learning theorists assert that they remain behaviorists nonetheless, it seems to me that what they really mean is that they still wish to be regarded as serious scientists. They are still concerned with the prediction and control of behavior, and they fervently believe that the cognitive concepts they employ are measurable and manipulable experimentally. In this, most personologists would agree with them. But that does not make any of them behaviorists.

If you are wondering whether the conclusion that social learning theory is beyond the limits of behaviorism really applies to Bandura, set your mind at rest. In his presidential address before the American Psychological Association, Bandura (1974) goes as far as Rotter.

Bandura first reasserts the preeminence of cognition by indicating that in his judgment, research has shown that there is no operant conditioning at all without both the subject's awareness of the contingencies existing between responses and reinforcements and his or her consent to being manipulated by the experimenter in this fashion.

Second, he regards self-regulation of one's own behavior through manipulation of the environment as the hallmark of human functioning. According to him, people progress toward maturity by gaining greater and greater control over their behavior through a combination of internal or self-reward and actual shaping of the external environment to make it more self-rewarding. Moreover, the procedure whereby certain events become more or less rewarding than others is essentially internal, even subjective in the sense that there may not be complete correspondence between reinforcement value and reinforcement histories.

Third, he claims that people learn largely through observing the reinforcement consequences of action without having to perform any act or experience any reinforcement themselves. Bandura does not intend this imitative learning to imply a slavish following of the literal behaviors that have been observed. If this were so, nothing new would ever happen. In attempting to explain how new behaviors can occur through imitative learning, Bandura considers how it is possible to learn by merely observing. The key is the human capacity to represent observed behaviors symbolically, not just literally. In other words, people can generalize from what they see to categories of behavior:

> From observing others, one forms an idea of how certain behavior is performed, and on later occasions the coded information serves as a guide for action. . . . Some of the limitations commonly ascribed to behavior theory are based on the mistaken belief that modeling can produce at best mimicry of specific acts. This view is disputed

by growing evidence that abstract modeling is a highly effective means of inducing rule-governed cognitive behavior. (Bandura, 1974)

Going further, he clearly recognizes that, in the process of abstracting from specific acts observed, the person uses internal "judgmental orientations, conceptual schemes, linguistic styles, information-processing strategies, as well as other forms of cognitive functioning." Thus, when Bandura calls himself a behaviorist, what he really means is that he is still a rigorous scientist.

THE IMPACT OF SOCIAL LEARNING RESEARCH . . . .

For some psychologists, the cognitive, internal, subjective emphasis of social learning theory will indeed brand it as no longer fully scientific. But Bandura, Mischel, Rotter, and others who share their beliefs consider themselves quite interested in and capable of articulating, measuring, manipulating, and predicting the cognitive variables and learning process they have assumed. Although in a purist sense a behaviorist might argue that there is no way to measure a thought or an idea because it is internal and intangible (remember that to a philosopher it would be spiritual, not material), a social learning theorist would insist that adequate measurement is possible through oral and written verbal report. This is the same assumption all personologists make. Were it not for the subject's verbalizations, be they spontaneous or in response to interview questions or paper-and-pencil tests, little by way of empirical study of personality would be possible. Thus, it would be hard for personologists to fault social learning theorists in their claim to being serious scientists.

Observational Learning

Moreover, if impact is any gauge of research soundness, the work of social learning theorists certainly has been important. Bandura and his colleagues have provided a body of research showing that observational learning takes place in humans, is more rapid than standard conditioning, and can lead to generalization beyond what is literally observed. The studies have often focused on aggressive behavior (e.g., Bandura & Walters, 1963). By choosing in this fashion, Bandura and his associates have brought their work close to present concerns in our society.

Their conclusion is clear: By merely observing, on TV or in the movies, *aggressive behavior* that is rewarded or at least not punished, a person can learn that it pays to be aggressive. This will happen even if the program or film contains only cartoon characters. Such findings raise an insistent question for a society beset by a steadily increasing rate of violence: When and under what circumstances is censorship of public communications appropriate? You may be appalled by the merest posing of the question of censorship. But recall that Plato, in *The Republic,* puts into Socrates' mouth the defense of censorship in order to preserve the ideal state and foster sound character in its members. And, after all, the work of Bandura and his associates does not lead to the conclusion that all portrayals of violence breed violence in the observer. When what is observed is aggression leading to punishment, aggressive behavior is learned but its performance is not likely.

Self-Control

Another important research theme that Bandura shares with Mischel concerns *self-control,* which marks one of the major differences between social learning theory and ordinary behaviorism. A general procedure has been devised for studying the person's criteria for self-reward. The usual subjects are schoolchildren, who are asked to work on a performance task that seems to require skill. In reality, their scores on the task are predetermined by the experimenter so that they will experience varying degrees of success or failure. They also have available to them a large supply of rewards (e.g., candy, cake, toys), and they are usually left alone, though secretly observed, during testing. But before testing, the children observe

adults performing the same or a similar task and rewarding themselves according to a high or low criterion of success. Often the adult models also verbalize rationales that are consistent with self-reward decisions.

Using such a procedure, Bandura and Kupers (1964) demonstrate that people can acquire patterns of self-reward by imitating models. Children who observed adult models rewarding and praising themselves after low scores on the performance test tended to do the same when they were subsequently tested. Children who observed self-reward and praise only after high scores followed that example. These findings are shown in Figure 14-1.

Because the children were alone when tested, they should not have experienced any direct social pressure influencing self-reward. That they did not deviate from the self-reward pattern they had previously observed is quite consistent with social learning theory. There are several

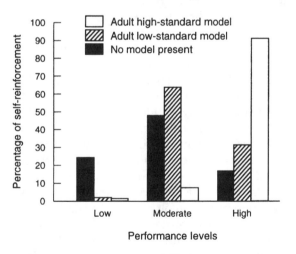

FIGURE 14-1   Self-Reinforcement at Each Performance Level by Control Children and Those Exposed to Adults Modeling High and Low Standards for Self-Reward
SOURCE: Adapted from "Transmission of Patterns of Self-Reinforcement Through Modeling," by A. Bandura and C. J. Kupers, 1964, *Journal of Abnormal and Social Psychology, 69.* Copyright © 1964 by the American Psychological Association. Reprinted by permission.

additional studies consistent with this one. As a whole, these studies have entailed a range of performance tasks, performance criteria, and model characteristics. The consistency of the findings lends some generality to the conclusion that self-reward patterns are strongly influenced by observed behavior in models.

Immediate or Delayed Gratification

A particularly interesting direction in self-control research involves the decision for immediate or delayed gratification. One can certainly argue that adequate adjustment to our society requires the ability to delay rewards. If, as social learning theorists contend, people are at least partially able to manipulate reinforcement contingencies in the environment rather than succumb, they must be able to delay reinforcement even though they could have it immediately. In research on this matter, subjects usually must choose among actual rewards that differ in time of occurrence and in value. Typically the choice of immediate reinforcement brings a smaller reward, whereas delaying reinforcement qualifies one for a larger reward. Again children are the common subjects, and again subjects observe an adult model making choices similar to those they will subsequently be asked to make.

In such a study, Bandura and Mischel (1965) preselected children such that their sample, and each treatment group, included both subjects who characteristically sought immediate though small rewards and others who sought delayed and large rewards. In one treatment group, children observed an adult model who made choices counter to their own self-reward patterns. For example, if the children were initially high in delay of gratification, the adult model chose immediate rewards, and children who preferred immediate gratification observed a model who chose the delayed rewards. Also, models always gave verbal rationales for their choices. In another treatment group, subjects again received information about a model performing counter to their pretest patterns, but this time in written form. Children in a control group had no exposure to or information about models.

The children's own choices to have immediate or delayed gratification were tested immediately after they had observed the model. Figure 14-2 shows clearly that the subjects' choices were strongly influenced toward the model's choices. The effects of the treatment persisted in a different social setting 1 month later. Further, they occurred even with the written responses rather than the "live" model. These findings are impressive, especially when you keep in mind that observing the model actually reversed a predilection that the child had brought to the experimental situation!

A fair amount of work attempting to pinpoint the mental state of subjects who are able to delay gratification has been done. The subjects must have the expectation or "trust" that the delayed reward will indeed be granted (e.g., Mischel, 1966). Also, to choose the delayed reward, the subjects must be able to spend the time preceding the reward either not thinking about anything in particular (Mischel & Ebbesen, 1970)

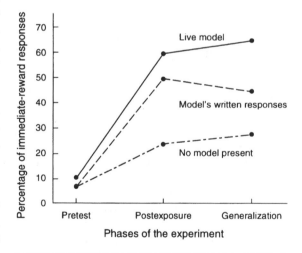

FIGURE 14-2   Mean Percentage of Immediate-Reward Responses by High-Delay Children on Each of Three Test Periods for Each of Three Experimental Conditions
SOURCE: Adapted from "Modification of Self-Imposed Delay of Reward Through Exposure to Live and Symbolic Models," by A. Bandura and W. Mischel, 1965, *Journal of Personality and Social Psychology*, 2. Copyright © 1965 by the American Psychological Association. Reprinted by permission.

or distracting themselves with other pleasant thoughts (Mischel, Ebbesen, & Roskoff, 1972).

Despite the many intriguing findings in this and other research themes involving imitative learning, an important question remains unanswered: To what extent is the learning and performance of adults influenced by observing models? After all, research to this point has almost invariably used children as subjects and adults as models. But adult subjects might be less impressionable in observing other adults or children as models.

Individual Differences Research

The concern with the mental state of subjects who delay gratification forms a natural transition to research that more squarely involves personality. This mainly correlational research focuses primarily on individual differences, clarifying the construct validity of a particular measure of a construct (see Chapter 9).

DELAYED VERSUS IMMEDIATE GRATIFICATION. There is research that treats the preference for delayed versus immediate gratification as a peripheral characteristic. Mischel (1958) has measured this in a simple way. After subjects had filled out a questionnaire, he displayed a large and a small piece of candy and indicated that he wished to give a piece to each of them but that he did not have enough of the larger ones just then to go around. The subjects were given their choice of getting the smaller piece immediately or the larger one a week later, when another shipment would arrive. Since this early study, the simple measure of immediacy or delay of gratification has been extended to include a variety of similar situations. The resulting test seems to have adequate internal consistency and stability (e.g., Mischel, 1961).

Considerable research correlating the measure of delayed versus immediate gratification with other behaviors has been done. People who prefer delayed rewards are high in achievement orientation, social responsibility, and resistance to temptation; they are older, are future oriented, tend live in a home with no father present, and

plan carefully for distant goals (see Klineberg, 1968; Mischel, 1966). Socioculturally, preference for delayed gratification tends to be found most often in the middle and upper classes and in industrialized societies (e.g., Mischel, 1958). There clearly is empirical overlap between delay versus immediate gratification and McClelland's need for achievement (see Chapters 7 and 12). The extent of this overlap remains to be determined. For the present, however, we can accept delay versus immediacy of gratification as a peripheral characteristic with sufficient empirical support to be taken seriously.

LOCUS OF CONTROL. Turning to Rotter's research, I discussed its most influential theme, internal versus external locus of control, in Chapter 12 under existential psychology. In this, Rotter is concerned with people's generalized and pervasive expectancy that they have control over and responsibility for what happens to them rather than feeling manipulated and controlled by external factors. Strictly speaking, this peripheral characteristic derives from the least explicit part of Rotter's theorizing. Generalized expectancies, such as those concerning locus of control, are not as concrete as the expectancies and values attributed to reinforcements; rather, generalized expectancies are what form the psychological situation, according to Rotter.

Considerable research correlating various questionnaire measures of locus of control with other variables has been done. But there is no point in repeating what we covered in Chapter 12. Suffice it to say that people with an internal locus of control at a personal level are more individualistic, assertive, interested in gaining knowledge, and willing to rely on their skill in risky situations than are people who believe they are externally controlled. At the societal level, people with an internal locus of control are more concerned with social problems and more activistic in attempting to solve them than are people who feel extremely controlled. You should also keep in mind that Rotter and his associates have done experimental studies in this area that bolster the claim that internal versus external locus of control has a causal influence on behavior.

Some evidence (e.g., Lao, 1970) has begun to suggest that the construct of internal versus external locus of control is not as unitary as initially thought. People who regard themselves as able to influence their own and their friends' lives do not necessarily believe they can influence events in the broader society, and vice versa. Parallel to this empirical complication is the theoretical likelihood of overlap between locus of control and McClelland's need for achievement. Similarly, the overlap between locus of control and the emphasis in existential psychology on the individualist's self-definition and world view is so great that Rotter's research is as relevant to that body of theory as it is to his own (see Chapter 12). Despite all these complications, the personologists' reaction to locus-of-control research has been enthusiastic. It seems to be an intuitively and rationally compelling peripheral characteristic.

SELF-CONCEPT AND SELF-EFFICACY. The emphasis on cognitive control seen in social learning theory has fueled a general reconsideration of the self-concept (see Markus & Wurf, 1987). In this, some studies have focused on the sources of information people use when they formulate self-representations. People appear to make conclusions about themselves from (1) direct attempts to evaluate their own actions (e.g., Trope, 1986), (2) communications from and comparisons with others (e.g., McGuire, 1984), and (3) inferences concerning their own physiological reactions (e.g., Bandura, 1977). Further, the generalizations people make from these sources appear to be influenced by their ability to process information cognitively (e.g., Harter, 1983).

A growing body of research concerns the processes whereby the self-concept is formed, changes, and influences behavior (e.g., Cantor & Kihlstrom, 1986; Carver & Scheier, 1981). As to regulation of action by the self-concept, Bandura (1977, 1986) and Kirsch (1985) have demonstrated an impressive range of effects. In emphasizing self-efficacy, Bandura (1977, 1986) refers to both a generalized perception of controllability over action and a specific perception of ability to execute a particular task. It appears that the self-efficacy concept is similar to that of internal locus of control.

Bandura (1986) identifies the four principal sources of perceived self-efficacy as *mastery experiences* (successes incline us to believe we will be successful), *modeling* (we judge our abilities partially through comparison with others), *social persuasion* (we sometimes believe what others tell us about ourselves), and *physiological state inferences* (we try to make sense out of our bodily events). These serve as the cornerstone for teaching self-efficacy to people in the hope of having a beneficial effect on their actions. Bandura (1986) reports that postcoronary recovery patients who perceived themselves (through training) as having greater physical efficacy complied more fully with prescribed exercise programs. Further, a wife's support of her postcoronary husband is more likely to lead to his curtailing efforts to become physically active if she regards his heart function as impaired than if she judges it to be robust (Taylor, Bandura, Ewart, Miller, & DeBusk, 1985). There is also some evidence (e.g., O'Leary, 1985) that enhancing a patient's self-efficacy increases the likelihood that needed changes in health habits, once made, will be maintained. Although such results are not surprising, they are consistent enough with social learning theory to recommend that position to us.

Perhaps more remarkable are the findings suggesting a link between perceived self-efficacy and physiological reactivity. For example, Bandura, Taylor, Williams, Mufford, and Barchas (1985) show that to understand elevated catecholamine secretions in the blood (usually interpreted as a stress reaction) one must compare task demands with level of perceived self-efficacy. Only discrepancies between demands and self-efficacy produce an elevated catecholamine secretion. Though dramatic, this result appears to support consistency theories (Chapter 7) as much as social learning theory. Nonetheless, the lively research surrounding the self-efficacy concept seems well worth following in the coming years.

There is further evidence that research on social learning theory is going in an applied direction. Topics to which this theoretical approach has been considered relevant are drug use (Sadave & Forsyth, 1977), Japanese socialization (Sukemune, Haruki, & Kashiwagi, 1977), witchcraft (Spanos, 1978), and moral development (Brody, 1978). But there is a problem with the last of these. According to Loevinger and Knoll (1983), research on empathy and prosocial behavior (e.g., Feshbach, 1982; Hoffman, 1981a; Staub, 1978) shows that there may be an inborn basis for altruistic behavior in children. This seems inconsistent with social learning theory's assertion that morality is learned. In a set of interrelated papers, some writers found social learning theory useful in understanding how children learn, but Berlin (1978) feels that it cannot adequately explain rule invariance in the face of capricious and informationally impoverished situations and the process whereby abstract rules are acquired. Although controversy always surrounds social learning theory, it continues to have a lively reception.

PERSONAL VERSUS SITUATIONAL DETERMINATION OF BEHAVIOR......................

For all Mischel's emphasis on self-control and a cognitively based ability to delay gratification, he has somewhat reluctantly played a major role in the recent controversy over whether it is personal dispositions or situational forces that determine behavior. The controversy seems to have begun with Mischel's (1968) attempt to demonstrate that there is scant empirical support for the view that traits and underlying motivational states control behavior. In this argument, he criticizes the view that traits and underlying motives exert a pervasive, even ubiquitous influence on behavior to the exclusion of situational forces. In the context of such a view, the modest reliability and validity correlations associated with nearly all measures of peripheral characteristics seem particularly damaging. If a person's score on the measure of a trait or motive varies over time, and if its relationship to

behavior is small, how can traits and motives be conceived as important in determining action? Moreover, Mischel has amassed evidence that situational factors seem to have a much larger role than traits or motives in controlling action.

As I have indicated earlier, this seemingly damning criticism must be examined more closely. For one thing, it takes as its starting point a version of trait theory that many personologists would call sloppy. There is ample precedent among personality theorists (e.g., Allport, McClelland, Murray, Fiske & Maddi) for a conceptualization of peripheral characteristics as potentialities that await situational cues for arousal. Only when these potentialities are aroused should one expect them to influence action. This more rigorous usage than that considered by Mischel is not only rationally more satisfying; it would also lead to the empirical prediction of only a moderate rather than a large relationship between measures of peripheral characteristics and the behavioral variables they are supposed to explain.

Similarly, as Mischel clearly would have to shoot down the best usage in order to demonstrate the inherent superiority of the view that it is the situation alone that controls behavior, what appeared at first to be a damning criticism of emotional states ends up being considerably blunted (see Maddi, 1979). As I indicated earlier, his criticism seems most cogent in the case of views, such as psychoanalysis, that emphasize the constant effect on action of underlying unconscious motivations. But Mischel has much less quarrel with fulfillment and consistency positions.

Mischel's critique has ignited many heated arguments. Defending the personological view, Alker (1972) argues that Mischel, in his zealous situationalism, overlooked several available studies crucial to the issue of whether the person or the situation determines action. These studies are important because they permit evaluation of the contribution to behavior of not only traits and situations but also the interaction between them. In perhaps the best known of these studies, Endler et al. (1962) constructed an *S-R Inventory* of anxiousness consisting of 11 anxiety-provoking situations and 14 modes of response indicating anxiety. Subjects indicated the intensity of each of their modes of response in each situation. Through their analysis of the data, Endler et al. initially conclude that the situation predicted behavior more than the mode of response did. But in reanalysis of the data, Endler and Hunt (1966) have revised their conclusion to the position that the interaction between mode of response and situation is by far the best predictor of behavior. This finding has been confirmed for the S-R Inventory in several subsequent studies (e.g., Endler & Hunt, 1969; Endler, 1973).

But the S-R Inventory is, after all, a questionnaire, which means that subjects merely describe how they would respond in various situations without actually being in them. Moos (1968, 1969, 1970) has improved on this by putting subjects in a range of situations and observing their reactions in addition to obtaining their self-descriptions. His results also show that the interaction between the person and the situation is a far better predictor of behavior than either the person or the situation alone.

Although Alker's citation of such studies seems persuasive, Bem (1972) identifies certain weak spots in Alker's position and insists that the situationists be given a chance since, he asserts, personology had failed. The general argument has subsided in the face of strong agreement on an *interactionist position.* Many believe that the controversy was a pseudo-issue in the first place (e.g., Bowers, 1973; Carlson, 1971b; Hogan, DeSoto, & Solano, 1977; Maddi, 1984; McClelland, 1981) in the sense that personality theories uniformly aim to predict behavioral regularity across situations and time rather than literal behavioral repetitions.

In what seems to be a definite settlement of the disagreements, Bowers (1973) has amassed no fewer than 11 studies of this sort demonstrating that behavior is largely a function of the interaction between personality and situation. Bowers also demonstrates the rational implausibility of asserting that either personality or situation provides the whole explanation of behavior. A broader perspective on the controversy and its end has been provided by Ekehammar (1974),

who reminds us of the various personologists and other psychologists who have called for an interactionist approach. Recently Mischel himself (1973b) has endorsed interactionism. And no less a figure than Cronbach (1975b) has reminded us that he called for the same thing years ago.

Just what is the nature of the interactionist solution? It rejects the idea that traits determine literal response repetition across situations regardless of their characteristics and demands. It also rejects the idea that the person is without structure and shifts behavior passively from one situation to the next. Instead, it focuses on the way people construe the situation and the effects of this construed or subjective environment on their behavior. It is assumed that there will be individual differences in response to what has been construed. There is sufficient enthusiasm for this new accord that the difficulties it creates for empirical study do not seem to be a deterrent.

The interactionist position is, of course, very similar to the emphases of several personologists, including Lewin, Angyal, Sullivan, Murray, Allport, McClelland, and the existentialists (see Maddi, 1979). True, some personologists (e.g., Freud, Jung), essentially regarding reality as an internal mental state, put more emphasis on personality and less on situation than is consistent with the interactionist stance. But they are in the minority, however influential they may have been in the past.

I do not mean to suggest that there has been no value in the person-situation controversy. It has alerted psychologists to the need for an articulate theory of situations. A start on this (see Ekehammar, 1974) distinguishes (1) an a priori definition of physical and social stimuli, (2) need concepts, (3) single reactions elicited by situations, and (4) perceptions of situations. Bem and Funder (1978) even speak of situations as having "personalities," by which they refer to the shared interpretations observers make.

The controversy has also pinpointed the need for personality theory to have a cognitive emphasis so that one can explain how the person construes the environment. This emphasis occurs not only in *prototype theory* (Cantor & Kihlstrom, 1986), an outgrowth of the social learning approach, but also in other cognitive approaches, such as *script theory* (Carlson & Carlson, 1984; Tompkins, 1979) and *schemata* (Helson, 1992; McAdams, 1985). Although these cognitive emphases are consistent with the social learning approach and many personality theories, they are at odds with moderate behaviorism, with its emphasis on mindless habits and automated responses.

Also, psychologists have begun to theorize specifically about the nature of the interaction between person and situation (e.g., Endler & Magnusson, 1976). Although these attempts have aroused reactions of hurt concerning the similar insights of earlier theorists presently overlooked (Krauskopf, 1978), the ferment seems constructive. Bandura (1978) has postulated reciprocal determinism, a process in which person and situation not only influence each other but cease to be independent entities because each ends by changing the other. In this theorizing he relies on a concept of self not unlike that found in Rogerian and existential positions.

Further, there seems to be renewed interest in theorizing more precisely about the nature of peripheral characteristics. In their return to the concept of *acts*, Buss and Craik (1983) rethink such matters as the conceptual distinctions (such as behavioral versus dispositional consistency in actions) needed to understand the person's contributions to stable individual differences in behavior. Though similar in some respects to the early work of Allport (Chapter 6) and Murray (Chapter 3), Buss and Craik are bringing fresh ideas to personology.

Similarly, Cantor and Kihlstrom (1986) suggest that the concept of prototypes carries the implications needed for a viable peripheral characteristic. Roughly, a *prototype* is more in the nature of a hypothetical construct held in the person's mind than of some precisely and operationally defined category. Thus, the person may not be able to enumerate before experience everything encompassed by this vague notion existing in his or her mind. But this idea may well serve as a basis for interpreting experience once it has happened. Through interpreted experiences, prototypes may also change. Cantor and Kihlstrom

believe that the peripheral characteristics personologists postulate have been vulnerable to situationist critiques because they have not been of the prototype sort. Supporting this is de Jong's (1988) study, which shows that the more prototype items that scales of motivation include, the stronger their validity is. But what, if not prototypes, are the traits of Fromm, the needs of Murray, and the personal dispositions of Allport? Although Cantor and Kihlstrom seem to exaggerate the novelty of their approach, I nonetheless find it heartening to see a rekindling of interest in peripheral theorizing.

Lingering Controversies

Although the person-situation controversy has largely ended in a general accord, there still lingers a splinter position of situationalism. Fiske (1974, 1978) is troubled not only by the low reliability of most personality trait measures but by the many and diverse disagreements in personologists' theorizing. Adopting the behaviorists' pessimism about theorizing, Fiske asserts that personologists can never reach agreement or measure reliably as long as they are focusing on personality constructs, because they probably do not really exist empirically. Disregarding the methodological and theoretical criticism of extreme situationism (and extreme personalism) presented by Bowers (1973) and Ekehammar (1974), Fiske advocates that personologists abandon theorizing and devote themselves instead to the observational study of small, and therefore objective, actions and their controlling stimuli. He cites his work with Duncan (Duncan & Fiske, 1977) as a model for personological research. From observations of people interacting, they have abstracted the nonverbal cues or rules signaling that someone is starting or ending speech. The study does not consider individual differences at length.

But if the interactionist accord mentioned earlier is correct, there really is no virtue in assuming an objective environment that affects all people similarly. Duncan and Fiske's work is as interpretive as anyone's. Though they have tried to deemphasize individual differences, one could undoubtedly scrutinize the relationship between their data and findings, noting which cues for initiating and ending speech they choose to observe, and thereby discover their own subjective construction of the environment. One could also discern individual differences among subjects in perception and action. Similarly, Fiske's (1974, 1978) proposed direction for personology expresses a behavioristic preference on his part rather than a necessary conclusion for anyone else. Indeed, one might as easily be moved to excitement by the disagreements among personality theorists, because they provide the occasion for comparative analytic research. Once the disagreements are taken seriously enough to be organized into precise issues of the sort attempted in Chapters 10–12, empirical and rational effort can well be expended in resolving them.

The sting is even being taken out of the argument that virtually all personality measures are too unreliable to signify empirical existence for the underlying construct. Rejoinders to the effect that the level of reliability desirable in a measure is a function of the theoretical nature of the underlying construct (e.g., Maddi, 1984; McClelland, 1981) have been supplemented by supportive extensions of classical reliability theory (e.g., Jackson & Paunonen, 1980). Very systematic psychometric proofs now show that high reliability is not necessary for a measure to show validity. Even if this were not so, Epstein (1984) has accumulated considerable evidence that the more observations one makes of a subject, the more reliable his or her behavior appears to be.

Another splinter position of lingering controversy is identified with D'Andrade (1974) and Shweder (1975), who also argue that behavior is indeed less reliable than personality theory construes it to be. They believe that all people engage in a systematic distortion whereby they imagine more regularity in behavior than there really is. The distortion, they claim, is based on similarity in word meanings rather than accurate observations of actions. But Block, Weiss, and Thorne (1979) have effectively counterargued that the structure of meaning in personality ratings must accurately reflect behavioral regularity

and pointed to several serious weaknesses in empirical data supporting the systematic distortion hypothesis. Shweder (1982) has counterattacked. Perhaps the most sensible position to take is that as the existing data support both positions equally well, there is no empirical basis for concluding counterintuitively that personality does not exist (Brown, 1986; Rohrer & Widiger, 1983).

PERSONALITY IMPLICATIONS OF SOCIAL LEARNING THEORY......

Social learning theorists clearly intend to have an impact on personality theory in addition to theories of learning. They recognize full well that the aim of personality theory is to specify those characteristics and tendencies of people that partially determine behavior. They also recognize that individual differences in perception, cognition, emotionality, and action form the main subject matter of personology. And they have indeed offered some theoretical statements toward a view on personality. Though these statements are not sufficiently extensive or developed to constitute a full personality theory, they do make a recognizable start.

Core Considerations

Certainly the statements social learning theorists make about learned dispositions, which qualify as peripheral considerations, suggest underlying assumptions about core considerations. But discerning these core conditions is not particularly easy. Mischel (1973b) is clearest in the recognition that core assumptions are necessary in personology. He suggests that *all people have an inherent tendency to construe the events of their experience and thereby give them meaning.* As a core tendency, this bears resemblance to that of Kelly (see Chapter 7), though with less emphasis on prediction and control of events. Further, Mischel's position is very reminiscent of the existentialists' emphasis on creating meaning through decisions (see Chapter 6).

A word of caution is necessary. Mischel's main interest lies in emphasizing individual differences in the ability to construe one's world. Because he presents these differences as inherent rather than learned, one can regard them as aspects of a core statement. Along with Rogers (see Chapter 5), Mischel has taken the unusual route of a core statement that refers to individual differences. In any event, Mischel nominates the kinds of cognitive capabilities and skills that appear on intelligence tests (e.g., memory, perception of similarities, discernment of differences, ability to abstract) as what he means. He suggests that much of what others have referred to as ego strength, maturity, and competence is really a reflection of inherent differences in the cognitive abilities whereby meaning is attributed to events.

There is little else in social learning theory concerning core considerations. Little or no direction is provided whereby one can understand why people construe one way or another. Rotter (1964) makes a passing reference to "unlearned or biologically based satisfactions of the organism" but says no more than that (p. 58). The rest of the personality emphasis in social learning theory lies at the peripheral level. That is, I suppose, understandable in a position derived from behaviorism and its preoccupation with the learning process.

Development

Whatever notion of personality development in social learning theory exists is simple enough. Endowed with a particular level of *cognitive capabilities,* you encounter the social world, which is comprised of *models* to observe and persons who will apply *positive and negative reinforcements.* The greater your cognitive capabilities, the more actively you will construe the events and people of your world, accept or resist the reinforcements applied to you, and engage in the self-control that mitigates the effects of those reinforcements.

Though the major form of learning is observational, with models playing an important role, learning does not necessarily mean a slavish repetition of just what is observed. Presumably, the more cognitive capabilities you have, the more you will generalize and transform what you observe into something more specific to you. Although there are no notions of developmental periods or stages in social learning theory, Bandura (1974) has indicated that the process of maturing involves progressively greater freedom from reinforcements imposed by others, accompanied by progressively greater self-control of reinforcements.

Peripheral Considerations

Most of what social learning theory has to say about personality involves learned orientations. There is general agreement that peripheral characteristics develop out of the interaction between people and their environment. But Rotter and Mischel disagree on how to conceptualize these learned characteristics.

According to Rotter (1964, pp. 58–60), development results in motives or needs, which vary from very specific to very general. A need has three essential components: (1) the set of behaviors, all directed toward the same goal, that together define the expression of the need, (2) expectancies that certain behaviors will lead to satisfactions or goals that are valued, and (3) value, or the degree to which a person prefers the goal state associated with a need. You will recognize the three components as the *behavior potential, reinforcement expectancy,* and *reinforcement value* considered earlier in this chapter.

To get a more complete sense of Rotter's approach, let us consider six very broad needs he offers as examples, listed in Table 14-1. According to Rotter, the needs for recognition-status, dominance, independence, protection-dependency, love and affection, and physical comfort are common among people, though learned. He believes that each of the six broad needs would have to be broken down into subneeds to approach the level of specificity necessary for predicting behavior. For example, the need for recognition-status could be regarded as including needs for certain social, occupational, and intellectual activities.

Mischel's (1973b) approach differs a great

deal from Rotter's. He considers any conceptualization that resembles the traditional approach concerning traits and needs unwise. He also will not consider definitions of personality variables that include content. Instead, he offers cognitive and response styles and strategies as peripheral characteristics. One set of these is *encoding strategies,* similar in emphasis to Kelly's personal constructs. According to Mischel, people do not passively absorb external stimulation; rather, they reflect on and transform stimulation, thereby rendering it more personally meaningful. These processes of transformation constitute how the information is coded, which in turn determines how it can be used then and in the future. Another set of peripheral characteristics

TABLE 14-1 List of Needs for Rotter

1. *Recognition-status:* The need to excel, to be considered competent, good or better than others in school, occupation, profession, athletics, social position, physical appeal, or play; that is, the need to obtain high position in a socially valued competitive scale.
2. *Dominance:* The need to control the actions of other people, including family and friends; to be in a position of power, to have others follow one's own ideas and desires.
3. *Independence:* The need to make one's own decisions, to rely on oneself, to develop the skill necessary to obtain satisfaction and reach goals without the help of others.
4. *Protection-dependency:* The need to have another person or persons prevent frustration, provide protection and security, and help obtain other desired goals.
5. *Love and affection:* The need for acceptance and liking by other people, to have their warm regard, interest, concern, and devotion.
6. *Physical comfort:* The need for physical satisfactions that have become associated with security and a state of well-being, the avoidance of pain, and the desire for bodily pleasures.

SOURCE: From *Clinical Psychology,* 2nd ed. (p. 60), by J. B. Rotter. Copyright © 1971. Reprinted by permission of Prentice-Hall, Inc., Englewood Cliffs, New Jersey.

offered by Mischel are expectancies concerning behavior outcome and stimulus outcome. *Behavior-outcome expectancies* concern the perceived consequences of action, whereas *stimulus-outcome expectancies* concern perceptions as to how the surrounding stimuli relate to one another (the S-S laws mentioned previously). Behavior-outcome and stimulus-outcome expectancies give the person a sense that the environment is familiar and predictable. Also at the peripheral level are what Mischel calls *subjective stimulus values.* This concept is very similar to Rotter's reinforcement value and is intended to refer to the varying degrees to which people find events satisfying or dissatisfying. The final set of peripheral characteristics are *self-regulatory systems and plans,* which essentially are contingency rules that guide the person's behavior in the absence of, or even despite, immediate external pressures and rewards. Such rules indicate to people their own sense of the kinds of behavior appropriate under particular conditions, the performance levels they will require of themselves, and the consequences of reaching or falling short of these standards.

As you can see from the discussion of self-regulatory systems, the five sets of peripheral characteristics interact complexly to determine behavior. To know what people will do, you must know how they have coded information (what their personal constructs are), what relationships among stimuli and consequences of their actions they expect, what value they place on various outcomes of their actions, and their plans for regulating their own behavior. As if this were not complicated enough, Mischel insists that it is foolhardy to try to specify the typical content of these characteristics. He feels that they will reflect in each person some combination of actual reinforcement history, observational learning, and the fruits of internal cognitive competencies and transformations.

Echoing Allport's morphogenic approach (see Chapter 6), Mischel contends that each person is indeed unique in the sense that the specific content of one's personality cannot be determined in advance of studying it, and that one's present peripheral characteristics cannot accurately be discerned from a simple analysis of one's past. Part of Mischel's objection to traditional trait and motive terms is, as Allport also contends, that they are too general to permit precise understanding or prediction of individual behavior. But in championing the morphogenic view, Allport gives us very little conceptual apparatus with which to know even how to scrutinize individuals to determine their peripheral personalities. Fortunately, Mischel gives us much more guidance by offering as concrete peripheral characteristics the five sets of cognitive styles and strategies. In a later development, Mischel and Shoda (1995) suggest that peripheral characteristics be viewed as "processing structures characterized by stable cognitive-affective organizations in the processing system that become activated when the individual encounters relevant situational features." This, incidentally, is their way of recognizing that although concrete behaviors may show considerable variability across situations and over time, there is some persisting, underlying structure to personality.

As you might imagine, Mischel does not provide anything remotely approaching a typology. He does not regard such general categories as having any empirical value. Perhaps Rotter (1964) is less extreme, offering the notion of *generalized expectancies,* which are more or less conglomerates of behavior potentials, reinforcement expectancies, and reinforcement values and together define the psychological situation as the person construes it. Internal versus external locus of control, as mentioned before, is an example of a generalized expectancy. But it is difficult to pursue this lead further, because Rotter was not sufficiently explicit concerning the relationship of generalized expectancies to other peripheral aspects of personality.

The work of Cantor and Kihlstrom (1986) on prototypes is properly understood as an extension of Mischel's thinking in the area of peripheral characteristics. They believe that prototypes are constructs, which people hold in their minds, that are not precisely defined. These prototypes are models used in the effort to understand and influence experience. Cantor and Kihlstrom believe that the trait concepts in more common use among personality theorists imply a greater precision than people can achieve as they go through their lives. As indicated earlier, although the prototype concept is consistent with social learning theory and has been the focus of some spirited research, it is similar to the peripheral characteristics of other personologists such as Allport, Murray, Fromm, McClelland, and Maddi.

CONCLUDING REMARKS ....

Although the social learning approach was born in the attempt to understand human learning and has been critical of certain aspects of personology, it does show the beginnings of a theory of personality. Though social learning theory is too young for extensive criticism to be constructive, we should at least briefly consider toward which model of personality theorizing the social learning position seems to be developing.

It seems apparent that little in the approach suggests the conflict model. Indeed, social learning theorists are ardent critics of the psychoanalytic approach to theorizing and psychotherapy. It is possible, however, that the consistency model best illuminates the social learning approach. After all, Mischel's approximation to a core tendency nominates cognitive capabilities somewhat like Kelly's approach. The expectations and plans the person forms do not follow any lines that are necessary in the sense of reflecting some inner nature. And the feedback obtained through interaction with the environment is regarded as important in changing one's expectations. Rotter's emphasis on needs is not inconsistent with this classification, because they are learned, not inherent.

But one point provokes me to at least mention the fulfillment model as possibly being relevant. Social learning theorists emphasize a very active use of cognitive processes. People do not just sit back passively and receive information and meaning from outside; rather, they actively develop encoding strategies, expectancies, reinforcement values, and plans. In this way, they exercise considerable self-control. This suggests the existence of an implicit assumption, perhaps of the sort made by existential psychology, to the effect that the core tendency is to search for meaning. Actually, Mischel (1973a) mentions existential psychology as compatible with his own approach. Bandura (1974, 1978) discusses freedom similarly, conceptualizing the person's struggle to escape externally imposed reinforcement and emerge into autonomous self-control.

When there is conflict between what the person wants and what others want, the person is in difficulty, according to Bandura. But this conflict is not inherent and can be surmounted through the person's gaining control of the reinforcement contingencies at play in his or her life.

It is probably best to regard the current personality theorizing in the social learning approach as expressing the consistency model. But I suspect that the theorizing is moving steadily toward the fulfillment model, away from Kelly and toward existential psychology.

PART FIVE

Applications, Conclusions, and the Future

Having come a long way in this book, you now have a sense of what personality and personology are; you have experienced many relevant theories that fit into the conflict, fulfillment, or consistency models; you have struggled to identify relevant issues and clarify them with available research; and you have also explored supposed alternatives to personology. Now it is time to bring this journey of inquiry to a close. I shall first detail the clinical and psychotherapeutic applications of the various positions and models in personology, because most personality theories have arisen from practice, and continue to have their major utility there. Next, I shall bring together the various strands of this book into a set of conclusions that evaluate personology today and point to its future. What do we know now? What are the fruitful directions for tomorrow? What does the personological perspective contribute to our lives?

PSYCHOTHERAPY
AND ASSESSMENT

By now you know a good deal about personality theories. You have experienced how they are put together out of various parts, each of which has a logic and a function. You have also seen how these theories influence research and are in turn influenced by it. In Chapter 1, I called all these things the *intellective functions* of personality theory to highlight that such theory involves the pursuit of new knowledge rather than the application of what is already known.

As you read, however, you also encountered many applications of personality theory, mainly in examples used in the hope of making these theories more tangible and vivid for you. It is now time to pull these examples (and others) into a more systematic expression of typical applications. It will not surprise you, after reading Chapter 1, that the major applications involve *psychotherapy* and *assessment*.

In this chapter, my aim is to alert you to the main features of psychotherapy and assessment according to the conflict, fulfillment, and consistency models on which we have focused. I will also include the behavioristic and social learning approaches. Although the comparison and contrast of approaches will certainly mark a comparative analytic inquiry, do not expect any marshaling of research evidence to resolve issues. The psychotherapy and assessment research literature is just too vast and complex to permit evaluation and review here. These research areas are rightly the subject matter of their own courses in the psychology curriculum. It will be enough in this course for you to appreciate the stark differences in psychotherapy and assessment practices that the three models for personality theorizing produce.

LOGICAL REQUIREMENTS OF PSYCHOTHERAPY AND ASSESSMENT...............

Before we examine the three models' emphases in psychotherapy and assessment, I shall clarify the logical requirements of these two practical activities. This will guide us in identifying the particular parts of a personality theory that are most relevant.

Aims of Assessment and Psychotherapy

The general aim of assessment is *to characterize a person in terms of how he or she differs from others.* This is true whether the assessment concerns only one aspect of behavior or the totality of characteristic thoughts, feelings, and actions. Theoretically, the peripheral statement of a personality theory is the most relevant aspect here. If you were a Freudian, it would not help you much in the assessment task to conclude that both Mary and John have a sex instinct, especially because you would believe all humans to be so endowed. But it would help to conclude that John expresses his sex instinct in the form of an oral character type and Mary as an anal character type.

Further, the assessment task commonly involves *an evaluation of the person assessed against some norm, usually a standard of maturity.* Thus, you might conclude that although Mary is developmentally more advanced than John (for Freud, the anal stage is later than the oral stage), neither has reached maturity (for Freud, the ideal is the genital character type). Even assessments that concern one peripheral characteristic (rather than the pattern-forming types) at least imply the desirability of being well supplied with or devoid of that characteristic. As you have come to know, personality theories conceptualize maturity by evaluating the peripheral types as to how fully they permit expression of the core tendency (or purpose of human life).

Turn your attention to psychotherapy and you will find the same thing. To be helpful, the therapist must have a sense of the client's personality and whether or not it is fully mature. If it is not, the therapist may decide that there is a good reason for psychotherapy and also will discern the developmental direction that the treatment should take. So you can see that psychotherapy too relies on the peripheral statement of a personality theory and its relationship with the core statement.

In its additional reliance on the developmental statement of a personality theory, psychotherapy differs somewhat from assessment.

The therapeutic task is to stimulate development from an immature personality type toward the ideal type as conceptualized in the theory. Indeed, you might view psychotherapy as a constructed microcosm of the developmental interactions thought to lead to the ideal type. Thus, the therapist may act toward clients the way their parents should have, such as giving freedom, advice, or support.

Finally, the various personality theories imply specific content of observations (data) that are most relevant to assessment and psychotherapy. Also, these theories often suggest the kinds of approaches that should work in obtaining the assessment data and doing the psychotherapy.

The Conflict Model

In both the psychosocial and intrapsychic versions of the conflict model, the most revealing data about personality are dreams, followed by waking-state fantasies (or daydreams). The least revealing observations are the person's more controlled, instrumental attempts to do things (reach goals, solve problems, shoulder responsibilities) in the social world.

This data orientation is thoroughly consistent with the emphasis on defensiveness inherent in the conflict model. In the psychosocial version, there is, of course, no alternative to defensiveness in dealing with the inevitable antagonism between antisocial instincts and society as the protector of the common good. In the intrapsychic version, the conflict is no less real or inevitable just because it arises from two aspects of the mind rather than from the individual and the society. In dreaming, people are as close to being undefended as they can tolerate. This is why, according to conflict theorists, dreams are sometimes so frightening. Daydreams can also be frightening, but they are usually less so because they involve a greater level of defensiveness, being products of the waking state. The psychosocial and intrapsychic versions of the conflict model differ in that the latter emphasizes defensiveness less, but this difference appears not to matter in the construal by both approaches of dreams and fantasies as the most revealing data.

THE ASSESSMENT TASK. It is not surprising that assessment tests common in conflict approaches are designed to stimulate the person's fantasies. Because the person is given wide latitude in concocting responses to the items of such assessment devices, it is assumed that private fantasies will be revealed. It is even expected that some of these fantasies will reveal unconscious thoughts and feelings. In this, the approach of the conflict model to assessment seems quite consistent with its theorizing.

An example of technique is Jung's *Word Association Test,* in which the tester presents various words, one at a time. The respondent is instructed to react to each word with the first word that comes to mind, regardless of its sense or propriety. In this rather unstructured approach, the tester is free to choose whatever stimulus words might elicit areas of fantasy of particular interest. The assumption is that the response "nasty" to the stimulus word "mother" reveals something quite different from the response "father." You can see how in such an approach respondents might reveal things they intended to keep private or may even have been unaware of themselves.

Murray's (1943) Thematic Apperception Test, discussed in Chapter 9, and the Rorschach Test (Rorschach, 1921) are also imagination-stimulating techniques. You will recall that the former is a set of ambiguous pictures about each of which the client is to compose a story; the latter is a set of 10 inkblots for the client to identify. Composing a story about people stealing nuclear secrets is a lot different from imagining a father and son having a friendly chat. Similarly, seeing an inkblot as a menacing gorilla is not at all like imagining a fuzzy teddy bear. Such assessment devices for stimulating fantasy tend to stem from conflict theorizing, with its emphasis on the compromise that involves people lying to others (not revealing private thoughts and feelings, to avoid punishment) and to themselves (not being aware of the full truth about themselves).

The major assessment tests that express conflict theorizing provide test responses that the tester must interpret in order to arrive at conclusions about personality. One should expect this

from a line of thinking that emphasizes unconscious processes as the basis of personality. For Freud, people cannot reveal underlying truths about themselves because their defenses are designed to drop these antisocial concerns from awareness lest they be too anxiety provoking or clamor too strongly for raw expression. For Jung, even if this *personal unconscious* is eliminated, there is still the *collective unconscious,* which cannot ever be squarely in awareness. Thus, in conflict approaches the tester needs, as raw material for interpretations, expressions of the respondent's imagination, for these expressions will likely reveal the underlying nature of personality.

Certainly questionnaires have been used as assessment tests in the conflict approach, but uncommonly. After all, questionnaires restrict the elaborateness of responses (often to "true" or "false" reactions to items) and tend to emphasize events in everyday life (rather than stimulating fantasy). For personality assessment, it is much more difficult to obtain revealing information in questionnaires than in relatively unstructured tests that provoke imagination.

THE PSYCHOTHERAPEUTIC TASK. In the relevant psychotherapies (usually called psychoanalysis, whether done by Freudians, ego psychologists, Rankians, or Jungians), clients are encouraged to recount their dreams. Also, they are instructed to relate anything and everything that comes into their minds without regard for coherency, orderliness, or propriety. For Freudians, this is the cardinal principle of free association, with which other conflict approaches agree. Clients are even encouraged to free associate to their dreams once they have recounted them.

Psychoanalytic therapies are so weighted toward dreams and fantasies that they have engendered various other techniques for supporting free association. The hope of stimulating imagination was one reason, for example, why Freud felt that the client should be lying down on a couch in a quiet, simple, darkened room while the therapist sat out of the client's view. These arrangements are not very common anymore, even in Freudian psychoanalysis. Jung and his followers have, from time to time, encouraged sensitivity to the collective unconscious by playing music and burning incense during therapy sessions, by reading poetry to clients or having them read or compose it themselves, and even by carefully using drugs that heighten the senses and induce fantasies.

Needless to say, psychoanalysis is more than just an opportunity for the client to exercise imagination. In all forms of this therapy, which so well expresses the conflict model, therapists feel free to interpret the meanings of their clients' fantasies and dreams once those meanings have clearly emerged. Typically the therapist discerns the meaning before the client does. Again this should not surprise you, because the therapist assumes that the true significance of what clients say will be unavailable to them (unconscious). It is considered good practice for the therapist to withhold an interpretation until enough evidence has accumulated for it to be reasonably convincing. Psychoanalysts like to insist that the client's reaction to the interpretation is an important source of new information with which to evaluate the accuracy of understanding. Certainly interpretations sometimes are refined, changed, or even abandoned by therapists, but not as any straightforward result of counterpersuasion on the client's part.

The therapist decides whether the interpretation is accurate; the client's response to it is, once again, more raw material for interpretation. If the client vigorously protests the inaccuracy of the interpretation, the therapist may well take that as a sign of its accuracy (considering the protest an expression of the very defenses that have protected the client against true self-knowledge). If the client readily accepts the interpretation, the therapist may conclude the same thing on the same grounds or decide that he or she has missed the real mark. The latter is likely because to be accurate, an interpretation must be threatening (a defensive unconsciousness must be assailed). And if the client responds to an interpretation with indifference, the therapist can interpret that too as a sign of accuracy or inaccuracy. The conflict assumptions that psychoanalysts make lead them to expect resistance

to any accurate interpretations. So clients who think they can enter into a merely interesting dialogue with their psychoanalysts have another think coming.

What I have said thus far applies reasonably well to all forms of therapy in the conflict tradition. Freudians, ego psychologists, Rankians, and Jungians certainly emphasize and adopt the various techniques differently. But they share the assumption that for development to be stimulated, the client must focus on dreams and fantasies and the therapist must convincingly express interpretations.

Among conflict therapies, however, Freudian psychoanalysis has a cardinal feature that distinguishes it from the rest; namely, the therapist is regarded as having the job of interpreting not only dreams and fantasies but also the transference, or the thoughts, feelings, and actions that the client experiences about the therapist. The therapist assumes that these thoughts, feelings, and actions are not accurate responses to the therapist's role in the therapy. For Freudians, that role is to be a shadowy stranger who stands prepared to help but is not to be known by the client. This is the other reason why Freud advocated that the therapist always sit out of the client's view. Although most Freudians no longer go to these lengths, they try very hard not to disclose themselves. Certainly they do not answer questions about themselves that clients may raise, nor do they engage in ordinary conversation, even about simple things like the weather. This insistence on remaining anonymous may sometimes lead in strange directions. If, for example, a therapist is 30 minutes late in seeing a client, no explanation may be given. In any explanation, there is too much risk that the client will learn something personal about the therapist or have reason to expect some normal, social relationship.

So the assumption the Freudian makes goes like this: If the client has no basis in knowledge of the therapist for strong thoughts, feelings, or actions toward him or her, these reactions must be defensively transferred from past relationships—hence, the term *transference*. Interpreting the transference is yet another way whereby the

Freudian assesses clients' personalities and attempts to persuade them about themselves, all in the hope of stimulating needed development.

You are now ready to appreciate a final characteristic of therapies expressing the conflict model: They concern themselves primarily (sometimes even exclusively) with the contents of the mind. In terms of technique, they have been called *talk therapies*. The talk may or may not get around to problems of action or inaction in the social world, such as whether one gets along with one's boss or is making a lot of money. Such practical problems can be resolved by psychoanalysis only because interpreting dreams and fantasies will have increased the maturity of personality. Psychoanalysts generally consider it an unnecessary waste of time to focus heavily on practical, everyday problems. What is important to them is the client's pervasive personality type, the limitations on overall outlook (or immaturity) it represents, how it all developed, and whether the outlook can be improved. If outlook is improved, they assume that at least the most important practical problems will solve themselves.

The therapist must be initially concerned with determining what is wrong with the client. In terms of content, the assessment task is to identify the client's personality type. As long as the type (or mixed type) identified falls short of the ideal or mature type, there is reason for psychotherapy. Grounds for psychotherapy also include psychopathological states, which are breakdowns in functioning produced by excessive stress operating on the weaknesses inherent in immaturity. In identifying psychopathology, most therapists endorse the classification of psychopathological states offered by the *Diagnostic and Statistical Manual of Mental Disorders,* fourth edition (1994), which includes such states as *major depression* and *obsessive-compulsive disorder.*

For Freud (see Chapter 3), the immature personality types are designated as oral, anal, and phallic, all of which deviate from the ideal, or genital, type. As the client free-associates, recounts, works on dreams, and responds to interpretations, the therapist forms conclusions about the person's personality type. In doing this, the therapist looks for traits and defenses that express receiving and taking (oral type), giving and withholding (anal type), or excessive and insufficient sexualization (phallic type). If one or another predominates in the client, the therapist looks for evidence of relevant fixations through the client's recounting of early life. The therapist knows that therapy is complete when predominance of oral, anal, or phallic modes gives way to a balanced combination of them such that the client is fully able to love and work.

For Freud, this process of increasing maturity does not mean that the client now knows the full, stark truth about his or her antisocial impulses. Because genitality is still a defensive state (relying on sublimation), maturity is more a matter of adjustment to and acceptance of social norms than of radical self-knowledge. Ego psychologists are, of course, less pessimistic than traditional Freudians about how possible and worthwhile radical self-knowledge may be.

Although the intrapsychic conflict theorists also emphasize dreams and free associations in therapy, the content they look for differs from that sought in the psychosocial conflict approach. For example, Rankian therapists would listen for evidence of being neurotic, which suppresses the fear of life (such a client would be alienated from others, institutions, and belief systems) or being average, which suppresses the fear of death (such a client would avoid changes, challenges, and critical thought). Having identified either immature style, the therapist would look for corroborating evidence in the client's report of early punitive reactions of parents toward negativistic behaviors signifying the emergence of self. Finally, through supportive and instructive interventions, the therapist would hope to stimulate the client to become more aware of both fears and to achieve a pattern of behavior that would balance them.

CONTENT EMPHASES. Also concerned with dreams and waking fantasy life, Jungians try to determine whether the client is introverted or extroverted and rational or irrational in thinking mode (see Chapter 4). Having identified the client's psychological type, the therapist would use the treatment techniques to stimulate the development of selfhood—the balance of ego and collective unconscious that transcends the psychological types in the direction of universality (maturity). For most Western clients, achieving this balance means becoming more sensitive to and receiving guidance from the collective unconscious (as shown in accepting intuitions, mysteries, and one's limited control over self and world). Here you can see a clear example of how conflict positions really do not adopt radical self-knowledge as the definition of maturity and the goal of therapy.

Though a conflict position, Jung's intrapsychic emphasis is very different from Freud's psychosocial emphasis. Nowhere is this more starkly shown than in therapeutic dream interpretation. As you may know, Freudians assume that dreams are almost always *wish fulfillments*. Even when your dream is so frightening that you wake up in a cold sweat, there is assumed to be some unconscious fantasy being fulfilled. If a client dreams of being attacked by people of the same sex, the unconscious wish may be for homosexual experience. So you can see that even dreams are usually defensive expressions for Freudians—the client is aware of being afraid but not of the unacceptable desire. The work of dream interpretation is to unravel the defensive expressions to better glimpse the underlying truths. In this process, the therapist assumes that some dream content may stand for itself, its opposite, a condensation of many related thoughts, or a symbolic expression of one concrete element. Thus, the therapist has many ways of tracing the dream back to its essential meaning, which invariably is something sexual or aggressive of an antisocial nature.

Freudian interpretation is incorporated as one element of Jung's approach to the meaning of dreams. But Jungian interpretation of the personal unconscious is not limited to underlying sexual or aggressive meanings. Jungians assume a larger range of antisocial unconscious thought. The main difference between the two approaches, however, lies in Jung's emphasis on dreams expressing the collective unconscious. Themes

from the collective unconscious are universalistic, shown either by their directly mythic or archetypal quality (e.g., hero figures, wise old men, or earth mothers), by their recurrence in a sequence of the client's dreams, or even sometimes by the strangely elevating effect of having dreamed.

Jungians assume that archetypal material appears in dreams because greater expression of the collective unconscious is needed than the client permits in waking life. It is not surprising, therefore, that Jungians use the principle of *symmetry* when interpreting dreams. Symmetry indicates the lines along which functioning must proceed for the balancing of ego by collective unconscious (selfhood or maturity) to be achieved. To illustrate, Jung (1933a) recounts a male client's frightening dream of killing his father. The fear was no defensive expression of father hatred, according to Jung; rather, the client loved and admired his father too much to be able to engage in the developmentally valuable struggle for independence. Jung assured the client that his dream was nothing more than a symbolic expression that it was time to grow up by drawing away from (not literally killing or having homosexual relations with) his father. The dream was necessary for symmetry because the client, in the waking, or ego, state, had so much affection for his father that it was jeopardizing his development.

Jungians also believe in the prophetic quality of dreams. It certainly is not new in the history of thought to believe that dreams foretell the future. But it is odd to include such an idea in a personality theory! Recall that we have encountered Jung's mysticism before (see Chapter 4). Actually, the emphasis on prophecy is not that strange given the focus on symmetry. If the male client in Jung's example understood the meaning of his dream, he might well have taken steps to detach himself from his father by tempering his affection. This developmental process often lies at the root of the criticisms and anger that adolescents generate toward their parents. Symbolically it constitutes a kind of "killing" of the parent and, in that sense, the dream is prophetic. But you should recognize that Jung very likely also means something more mystical related to the individual features of the collective unconscious. In any event, you now have some sense of the differences in dream interpretation between psychosocial and intrapsychic versions of the conflict model.

The Fulfillment Model

Fulfillment approaches do not regard dreams and fantasies as any more revealing of, or important in helping clients than any other thought processes and experiences are. Indeed, fulfillment positions are more likely to focus on problems of everyday working life, such as attempts at intimate relationships or difficulties at work or school, than on dreams and fantasies. These problems most clearly reveal personality style, according to fulfillment theorists. Dreams, while also potentially revealing, are considered more indirect and difficult to understand.

This data orientation is quite consistent with the general deemphasis on defensiveness seen in fulfillment positions. While it is true that defensiveness can happen, maturity is a state of true openness (see Chapters 5 and 6). This leads to taking what people are aware of in themselves literally as a guide to understanding them and not as an occasion for interpretation. Approaches that are literal in this sense have been called *phenomenological*.

THE PSYCHOTHERAPEUTIC TASK. In fulfillment therapies, clients are encouraged to talk about their problems. They are not instructed to free associate. On the contrary, they are supposed to recount ongoing interactions with others and social institutions, clarifying as much as possible their perceptions, feelings, frustrations, and anxieties. There is no emphasis on recounting dreams, unless these constitute special problems. These therapies are entirely concerned with what is going on here and now. Although past experiences are of some interest, there is no insistence that present problems can be understood only as reflections of past ones. Within the general fulfillment approach, several

telling differences in technique distinguish its two versions. The actualization fulfillment approach emphasizes accepting and supporting clients in whatever they experience and recount. In contrast, the perfection fulfillment approach is much more confrontational (though the confrontation is done in a caring manner).

In the actualization approach, the person-centered psychotherapy of Rogers is rather simple in technique. The client presents and discusses current problems, and the therapist gives unconditional positive regard (you will remember this from Chapter 5, as the way in which parents must react to their offspring in order to ensure ideal development). To do this, the therapist must reflect back to the client the emotional essence of what the person is saying. This is not done by merely repeating. The client's remark "Nothing ever happens, and I could scream" is not well reflected by the therapist who responds, "You feel that nothing ever happens, and you could scream." A helpful reflection that summarizes or identifies emotional essences in the client's statement might be "You're terribly bored and restless." Or, if a female client said, "We sit there all evening watching TV, barely talking to each other. It's not like it used to be, and I don't know why. He's a fine person, but nothing ever happens," a sensitive reflection might be "The romance seems gone—maybe you're not sure you love him anymore."

I gave the second example so that you can see how the reflective response can appear to interpret the client's statements. And yet, person-centered therapists insist that they, unlike the Freudians, do not interpret. What they mean is that they strive to identify essences without adding any frame of reference to the client's statement that is not already there. In contrast, an interpretation would shift attention away from the statement itself by trying to understand it in terms of unresolved past conflicts. Such an interpretation in response to the above female client's statement might be "Your relationships with men all seem to end up this way—notice how differently you feel when you have those wonderful visits with your father on weekends."

In contrast to such interpretations, reflections intensify rather than shift attention from what is being experienced in the here and now.

Perceptive reflections give clients the sense that they have really been heard and encourage them to go further in expressing themselves. Sometimes clients will respond to sensitive reflections in statements such as "That's exactly what I meant—I couldn't have put it so well." They feel stimulated and freed in a way that leads to additional emotional experiences in the area under discussion. This is why Rogerians feel that unconditional positive regard is the major technique of therapy—it leads clients to feel so understood and appreciated that they can drop their defenses and experience things more completely. Through being acceptable to another, they learn to temper their own conditions of worth and be more open to their organismic experience. In that way, they develop more fully (see Chapter 5).

An implication of giving unconditional positive regard is so basic to this approach that it deserves mention here: The person-centered therapist characteristically avoids giving advice. Clients often ask the therapist's opinion, especially as they come to feel understood and appreciated. "What should I do?", "I'm right, aren't I?", and "Will you help me?" are frequent client questions. These too are reflected by the therapist, who may say, "It's hard to be making these decisions alone" or "You wish there were some definite way to know." If the client's requests for help are insistent and show much suffering, the therapist may explain the reticence to offer advice, as in "I wish I could help you, so that the uncertainty wouldn't hurt so much, but I know that the best answers for you are the ones that you find for yourself." This is very consistent with the Rogerian assumption that people (including clients) know themselves better than anyone else (including therapists) ever can.

In the early days of Rogerian therapy, therapists did nothing more than has been discussed. Now, however, they are willing to share their own feelings with clients, especially if these feelings might be interfering with listening carefully. So

the therapist might say, "Today I feel as if I'm not helping you enough, and it's making it hard for me to listen to you fully" or "I'm really preoccupied with something in my life, and it made me miss what you were saying." You can see in such remarks, and in the general emphasis on reflection, that there is simply no basis in person-centered therapy for identifying transference in the client, much less interpreting it (Shlien, 1987). I hope you are seeing just how different psychotherapies can be!

This sense of difference can only be heightened as we turn to therapies that represent the perfection version of the fulfillment model. The major relevant approach is existential, which means a confrontational approach to current problems. Once again clients are encouraged to focus on their everyday problems rather than on dreams or fantasies. In listening and reacting, the existential therapist is guided by several content emphases that will be mentioned shortly. First, a word on existential techniques is in order.

Until recently, existential therapy borrowed techniques from other approaches, and its distinctiveness lay mainly in content. But techniques consistent with its perfection fulfillment stance have started emerging from this approach. *Paradoxical intention* (Frankl, 1985) arose from the recognition that we call something a psychological symptom specifically when we cannot control it. For example, a persistent fear or obsession may so fill one's mind that there is little chance of doing whatever else one feels is important. Extreme symptoms often require dramatic treatment. With paradoxical intention, the therapist encourages the client to intensify the symptoms even further rather than fight against them. This can have the effect of outmaneuvering the symptom so that it will recede and no longer appear troublesome.

Another existential technique is *focusing* (Gendlin, 1973). By going through a series of steps, clients temporarily push aside everyday conventional meanings and attend instead to the messages coming from their bodies in the hope of reaching some more personal, individualized meaning. The starting point for focusing may be quite general (e.g., contemplating what stands in the way of feeling well) or more specific (e.g., what it is about a particular problem that disrupts well-being). Whatever the starting point, clients are led to progressively greater awareness of bodily states (e.g., rumbling stomach, neck muscles tightened, lumps in the throat) for their potential clues to personal reactions.

The techniques of *situational reconstruction* and *compensatory self-improvement* are meant to be used along with focusing to provide a comprehensive basis for coping with stressful circumstances (Maddi, 1987). In situational reconstruction, clients are stimulated by the steps of the exercise to stretch their imagination in construing stressful circumstances. Through considering how the circumstances could be better and worse than they are, and pinpointing just what constitutes the problem, clients develop a perspective that facilitates effectively coping. In this sense, they feel more in control.

But not all stressful circumstances (such as serious physical illness) can be controlled. When attempts at control fail, the technique of compensatory self-improvement helps clients accept unchangeable "givens" without giving up on themselves. In this technique, the client regains momentum by identifying another problem that, though related to the given, appears changeable, then he or she works on changing that instead. Perhaps a male client's wife is diagnosed as having a severe breast cancer. Beyond obtaining medical care, there is little to be done. But compensatory effort can focus on the quality of their married life, and working along these lines will have a therapeutic effect.

In the existential techniques outlined here, you can see how different this approach is from person-centered counseling. Though dealing with the here and now, as does the person-centered approach, the existential techniques are more directive and confrontational. Their general aim is to increase clients' sense of control and individualized meaning. Notice, however, that they do not involve interpretation in the sense that the therapist imposes his or her sense of meaning on the client. All in all, the techniques are quite consistent with existential theorizing and the perfection version of the fulfillment model.

THE ASSESSMENT TASK. Rogerians spend little time and energy assessing whether and how clients are maladjusted (as indicated in Chapter 5, maladjustment is their view of the nonideal personality). Generally, clients' requests for therapy provide sufficient justification for giving it. Rogerians also assume that if they can give unconditional positive regard, clients will develop in the direction of greater maturity no matter what their problems. So there does not seem much point in assessing whether there exist conditions of worth, defensiveness, or the other characteristics of maladjustment.

Sometimes—usually for research purposes—Rogerians collect empirical data on clients' personality characteristics. The measurement devices they use tend to be of the self-report variety—either interviews or questionnaires (see Chapter 9), such as the Personal Orientation Inventory (Shostrom, 1965, 1966). Self-report measures are thoroughly consistent with the fulfillment position, which insists that people know themselves better than others can ever hope to.

The same is true of existential psychology. Its practitioners do not emphasize assessment as a precursor to therapy. And when they do assess—also usually for research purposes—they use interviews and questionnaires because they are convinced of the validity of self-report. But existential psychologists are more willing than Rogerians to evaluate clients' self-reports in order to reach conclusions regarding personality. In this, existential psychologists pay special attention to self-reports that reflect on clients' decision-making processes (future versus past oriented) and conventionality versus individuality (see Chapter 6). A recent example of the approach is the *Personal Views Survey III* (Maddi & Khoshaba, 1994), a measure of personality hardiness.

CONTENT EMPHASES. Little remains to be said regarding actualization fulfillment positions. Insofar as they consider content, person-centered psychologists are interested in whether clients express such characteristics of maladjustment as conditions of worth and defensiveness or of maturity as organismic trusting and openness to experience (see Chapter 5). As the former decrease and the latter increase, the therapist assumes the client is improving.

Existential psychologists, being more inclined to influence the direction of therapeutic interactions, concern themselves more than Rogerians with evaluating content. Summarizing many relevant themes, Yalom (1980) indicates that existential psychotherapy deals especially with responsibility, isolation, and death. These topics may be raised by either the client or the therapist, but they must be considered, because they underlie a sense of meaning in life. To experience a sense of freedom and vitality, people must assume responsibility for their own lives. This is exceedingly difficult to do, because we have indeed been shaped by our pasts. It is necessary to accept the effects of the past on our present functioning as a given but still recognize that because we know and understand that given, we can transcend it with future-oriented decision making.

Isolation is omnipresent because no matter how well we know another person, some things will always remain unknown. The key to overcoming a sense of isolation is accepting the limits on knowing others. This is analogous to achieving freedom by accepting that we are shaped by the past and making future-oriented decisions anyway. We need to attempt intimacy with others even though we cannot fully succeed.

As the ultimate given, death has a special place in existential therapy. We cannot live fully without accepting that death is beyond our control—it is both inevitable and unpredictable (Yalom, 1980). Once death has been truly accepted, life is enhanced, appearing more vivid and precious by comparison. Such acceptance requires trying to make the most of one's life despite its fragility and poignancy.

People who have hardiness or courage (Maddi, 1984) are considered as dealing with responsibility, isolation, and death more effectively than others. Therefore, a content emphasis in existential therapy is the building of hardiness through the various techniques mentioned.

The Consistency Model

As mentioned before (see Chapters 7 and 8), consistency theories deemphasize content in their core and peripheral personality statements. It is understandable, therefore, that they are quite eclectic concerning what is most revealing in thoughts, feelings, and actions. Fantasies, dreams, practical problems, and decisions all reveal personality equally, according to consistency theorists.

THE ASSESSMENT TASK. The cognitive dissonance version of the consistency model leads one to look for signs of the various constructs clients use and how these constructs are organized into construction systems (see Chapter 7). A particularly useful way of doing this involves the Role Repertory Test (Kelly, 1955). First, clients provide the names of people fulfilling certain roles (e.g., mother, father, siblings, lovers, major teachers, close friends) in their lives. Then, every possible combination of three of these names is presented in turn to the clients with the same instruction—namely, to say how two of the people are similar to and different from the third. As you can tell, this is a performance test (see Chapter 9) that involves sorting people (or roles) into categories. The names given to these categories define the client's categories. Thus, if a client said that "mother" and "father" were similar to each other and different from "major teacher" in being "family," "family-nonfamily" would be identified as a relevant bipolar construct. The more frequently a client uses a construct in going through all the combinations of three names (roles), the higher it is in his or her hierarchically organized construct system. Various other relationships of constructs to each other can also be determined through the Role Repertory Test.

As you can see, this test is very appropriate for the cognitive dissonance version of the consistency model. Clients reveal their constructs by performing a classificatory task. Clients will be very aware of some of the constructs thus revealed, but not so aware of those constructs difficult to articulate except for the requirements imposed by the task. When the Role Repertory Test cannot be given to clients, interviews can be used to glean information about constructs. In general descriptions that clients make of the people, activities, and things in their lives, the assessor tries to discern the content and frequency of constructs.

McClelland's variant on the cognitive dissonance approach and Maddi's activation approach both use a plurality of assessment strategies. Peripheral characteristics that are motivational (*motives* for McClelland and Maddi) typically are measured through such fantasy tasks as the Thematic Apperception Test, because motives are regarded as being private goals (see Chapter 11). Peripheral characteristics that involve habits (*traits* for McClelland and Maddi) have been measured through performance tasks designed to reveal repetitive responses or through questionnaires. Finally, McClelland's schema concept, which expresses societal norms, has been measured through self-report of values. As you can see, consistency theories consider a wide range of content and assessment approaches.

THE PSYCHOTHERAPEUTIC TASK. Of all the personality models, the consistency approach is the least developed regarding psychotherapy. Among consistency theorists, only Kelly has a relevant procedure, called *fixed role therapy* (Kelly, 1955). It begins with the therapist listening to the new client's problems. When the therapist believes he or she has understood how the client's constructs have led to the problems, a role is constructed for the client to play that is calculated to end the difficulty.

For example, a male client may complain of being lonely because he is too shy to date girls. Perhaps behind this is the superordinate construct "unworthy-worthy" and, parallel to it, the subordinate construct "male-female." Being a man, the client considers himself unworthy and women worthy. This makes it hard for him to approach women for dates and to interact with them as equals. With such a set of beliefs, it is not surprising that he is without female company and lonely. A possibly corrective role that

the therapist might construct for this client to play is that of an extroverted, assertive, worthy person. How such a person would act toward women would be carefully reviewed with the client. Then the client's assignment would be to enact this fixed role, even if it did not feel right and was painful. Each time the client returned for a session, he would report his experiences in enacting the role, and modifications to it might be made as needed. The general aim of this fixed role therapy would be to ease his loneliness at the same time that the relationship of the construct "worthy-unworthy" and "male-female" was shifted 90 degrees. This would mean that men and women would not invariably be considered unworthy and worthy, respectively. Once this was accomplished, a man (including himself) might be considered by the client either worthy or unworthy, presumably on other grounds. In the process of the interaction with women forced by the fixed role, the client might well have obtained signs of his worthiness. The problem that brought him into therapy would have been solved.

Despite its simplicity, I hope this example helps you grasp the essential features of fixed role therapy. Therapist and client interact in conversational style about the latter's experiences and constructs. The emphasis is on the present and the lines along which new experience can influence construction systems.

Although McClelland's variant on the cognitive dissonance approach does not have a psychotherapy in the sense of something with which to remediate behavior problems, it does offer a training program for people who want to increase such motives as the need for achievement, characterized by fantasies involving competition with a standard of excellence (see Chapter 7). McClelland's (1971b) notion of increasing the need for achievement involves simply teaching people to fantasize along these lines. A characteristic mechanism for doing this is for the person to read stories, which others have composed about pictures, that are high in the need for achievement and to take these stories as a model for his or her own fantasy efforts. These efforts are then evaluated by the trainer, who gives feedback and supervises the person in correcting stories to make them even more achievement oriented, if necessary. McClelland's assumption here is that learning to fantasize about achievement will lead one to act accordingly in the real world. A similar approach would be taken regarding other motives.

In both Kelly's and McClelland's approaches to intervention, we see a cardinal feature of the consistency position—namely, *feedback* as a basis for corrective effort. The therapist or trainer devises a task for the client to perform calculated to produce shifts in behavior in the desired direction. The feedback from all this is then used to fine-tune behavior even more. All in all, these approaches assume that desired change takes place by trial and error. In the intervention effort, there is little concern for the past, for dreams, for the unconscious, or for the client's discovering directions on his or her own. The approaches of Kelly and McClelland closely fulfill the thrust of the consistency model.

CONTENT EMPHASES. At first glance, the content aims of consistency approaches to assessment and therapy or intervention are clear. The content goal is defined by the client (e.g., to become less lonely or to increase in need for achievement) and accepted by the therapist (trainer). Assessment focuses on determining how the client's thought processes (e.g., constructs, fantasies) obstruct reaching his or her content goals. The intervention is planned in terms of where the client is and wants to be. In considering approaches, no criteria of maturity and immaturity arise. This general eclecticism with regard to content accurately expresses the consistency model.

Kelly's position, though, requires a bit more scrutiny before we move on. Let us return to the example of the young man who felt lonely. In Kelly's approach, he could not have felt lonely unless he had a relevant construct—say, "lonely-social"—and placed himself on the "lonely" pole of it. But if this were so, why, in Kelly's system, would the young man have had any problem at all? If his expectations about being lonely were confirmed by his experience, he would not have

cognitive dissonance and, hence, no problem that would lead him to seek therapy. You and I may feel that loneliness is painful, even if expected, but Kelly has no theoretical basis for regarding a confirmed construct as problematical.

Because Kelly (1955) considers it possible for a person to have two partial construction systems that are inconsistent with each other, we may have a theoretical way out of the dilemma just identified. Perhaps in one construction system the young man expects to be lonely and has this confirmed, but in the other construction system he expects to be loved and has this confirmed. In this case, the complaint he brought to psychotherapy about being lonely would have to be regarded as imprecise, to say the least. Perhaps the complaint should have been something like "Sometimes I'm lonely and sometimes I'm loved, and the difference is confusing." Although this may clarify our dilemma somewhat, Kelly's position certainly does seem difficult to pinpoint.

Behavioristic and Social Learning Approaches

There is much in behavioristic and social learning approaches that touches on what we have already encountered in the positions of Kelly, McClelland, and the existential psychologists. All these positions assume that change in thoughts, feelings, and actions takes place through guided trial and error.

Consistent with its deemphasis on personality, behaviorism has not developed an assessment approach. When measurement of such factors as general drive has been necessary in research, behaviorists have used experimental manipulations, such as shocks, or questionnaires concerning self-report of tension (see Chapter 13). In their therapeutic efforts, behaviorists have emphasized operant conditioning techniques, in which the therapist accepts the client's definition of the problem but recasts that problem in terms of a response that needs to be either increased or decreased in rate of occurrence (an example of the former might be studying for exams and of the latter, smoking). This *behavior modification therapy* involves altering the rate at which the target response is emitted in the relevant stimulus circumstance by carefully planned applications of reinforcements. Thus, if eating candy serves as a reinforcement for the client, he or she will be permitted to do that following desired studying or nonsmoking responses. Over time, the rate of studying or smoking will change. When the aim of the therapy is to decrease the client's fear responses, and the imagination of pleasant scenes is used as the reinforcement, the approach is called *systematic desensitization* (Volpe, 1969).

These approaches are quite consistent with behavioristic principles in their avoidance of elaborate theorizing (notice that the client determines what the problem is and, hence, what the desired direction of therapy will be), focus on actions or responses, and reliance on reinforcement as the mechanism of change. This approach is distinct from more personological positions on therapy. The distinction has dwindled, however, because of the increased role given by behavioristic therapists to their clients' cognitive processes. A good example of the shift in what is now called *cognitive behaviorism* is the new emphasis on self-control.

Behavioristic therapists have also begun to use a technique called *flooding* (Goldstein, 1973), which at first consideration seems similar to existential psychology's paradoxical intention. Typically, flooding has the client sitting with closed eyes, imagining and feeling, as the therapist paints word pictures of situations known to be anxiety provoking to the client. The client is "flooded" with negative emotions, hour after hour, until "reactive inhibition" takes place, and these emotions subside. Sometimes, subject to feasibility, flooding is conducted in vivo, that is, by immersing the client in anxiety-provoking situations (Wilson & O'Leary, 1980).

Certainly a client engaging in paradoxical intention will also experience negative emotions. But in paradoxical intention, the client is the one who tries to increase the symptom through willing and doing. In contrast, the flooding technique renders the client passive, and the reduction of anxiety is more likely to come from exhaustion than a renewed sense of personal control. Once again the similarity between cognitive behaviorism and existential approaches is more apparent than real.

Like behaviorism, the social learning approach has deemphasized personality and, hence, has spent little effort on an approach to assessment. When social learning psychologists need to measure subjects in research, they too tend to rely on either experimental manipulations or questionnaires (see Chapter 14). The social learning approach has only recently concerned itself with therapy, with the resulting emphasis on self-efficacy (Bandura, 1977, 1986). Here, the therapeutic approach builds on theorizing concerning the four principal sources of perceived self-efficacy; namely, mastery experiences (successes incline you to the belief that you will be successful), modeling (you judge your abilities partly through emulating others), social persuasion (you believe what others tell you about yourself), and physiological state inferences (you try to make sense out of what is going on in your body). The social learning therapist employs various combinations of these sources in an effort to convince clients that they can be efficacious. Typically, particular tasks or goals are adopted as the problems to be worked on.

At this stage in its development, social learning therapy is rather eclectic in technique. This is consistent with its greater concern with how learning takes place rather than what needs to be learned. It is not surprising, given its eclecticism, that self-efficacy therapy appears similar in part to a range of behavioristic and personological approaches.

CONCLUDING REMARKS ....

In this chapter, I have not considered every theory, because my aim was to give you a sense of how the various models conduct assessment and therapy. The theories covered well exemplify the general approaches. Some of the theories not considered are fairly mixed or eclectic at the practical level of therapy and assessment, even though they are more consistent at the level of theorizing about personality. This applies to the therapeutic approaches of Berne (1964), Kohut (1971, 1977), Perls (1969b), and Ellis (1962). At the level of technique, the therapies of Berne and Kohut resemble not only conflict but fulfillment approaches. In the case of Perls and Ellis, the resemblance is to existential, Kellian, and cognitive-behavioristic approaches. Perhaps the eclectic nature of the therapies associated with Berne, Kohut, Perls, and Ellis is a function of their relatively recent inception.

Throughout the chapter, I have presented assessment and psychotherapy as practical applications of personality theories. This is not to say, however, that the application does not also affect theory. As in any application, the practice of psychotherapy and assessment often provides vivid observations, unexpected successes, or abysmal failures that provoke the practitioner to revise or elaborate a theory. In a real sense, the processes whereby knowledge is developed and applied are intertwined.

This intertwining is one reason that I have not tried to evaluate here the relative effectiveness of psychotherapy and assessment as done through conflict, fulfillment, and consistency models. No sooner does some practical application reveal a theoretical shortcoming than that shortcoming is corrected. No sooner does some practical application achieve remarkable success than it is adopted by practitioners of other theoretical persuasions. In trying to help people through assessment and psychotherapy, the stakes are just too high for practitioners to worry about logical niceties such as whether their pet theories really lead to the particular practice they observe as being successful. Whatever works is adopted! I believe this is an important factor in the currently eclectic nature of the assessment and psychotherapeutic approaches of Berne, Kohut, Perls, and Ellis.

Ultimately, positions that have become eclectic through the headlong attempt to do an important, practical job well will be subject to a pruning period. External and internal scrutiny will, over time, render such positions more internally consistent in their assumptions. To my mind, this will involve becoming less eclectic in the sense

that all their explicit and implicit assumptions will move in the same core and peripheral directions. Any of these pruned positions may, of course, transcend the conflict, fulfillment, and consistency models of current relevance and express some new, clear, internally consistent model that you and I may not have imagined.

The other reason that I have not attempted an issue-resolving comparative analysis of psychotherapies and assessment approaches here is the complexity involved. Although much psychotherapy outcome and process research has been done in recent years, it is extremely difficult to reach convincing conclusions, because a host of methodological and theoretical problems exists.

Regarding psychotherapy, some approaches (e.g., psychoanalysis) require more time—years —than is practically possible in a research design, whereas others (e.g., person-centered counseling) can sometimes be completed in months. Also, when the researcher arbitrarily decides on a term of therapy for the study, that time line may be too short for some techniques to be effective. You can see how this could prejudice results.

Further, in comparing psychotherapeutic approaches, separating the effectiveness of a particular therapist from that of his or her technique is difficult, because therapists often do not consent to applying more than the one technique they favor. Even in the unlikely event that therapists would cooperate for the sake of research, they might not be effective with their nonpreferred, less practiced techniques. This would have a homogenizing effect on results even with a counterbalanced design in which all therapists participating would use all therapeutic techniques being evaluated comparatively.

Also, it is difficult (if not unethical) in a practical setting (in which clients need help) to institute the kind of control conditions really necessary for the evaluation of therapy effectiveness. To have some clients merely wait longer than others to get psychotherapy is sometimes unavoidable (if there are not enough therapists to handle demand anyway) and therefore ethically neutral, but it does not provide a sufficiently precise control (the best that one could conclude is that some therapy was more effective than the mere passage of time—and that is not saying much).

Furthermore, when comparing psychotherapeutic approaches, how does one decide what the best criteria of therapy outcome or process are? Sharp disagreements stem from the approaches themselves (e.g., psychoanalysis aims at changing underlying belief systems about self and world, whereas behaviorism attempts to change unwanted actions).

If these matters are not complicated enough, add to them the difficulty in determining which measurement operations work best in evaluating psychotherapy outcome and process. Shall we ask the client, the therapist, or some third party whether a session or an entire therapy was effective? Who decides when it is time to terminate? Even if using all three were practically feasible (and it would be very hard), the resulting complexities would be overwhelming, because each source of data would involve different criteria of effectiveness.

It is not surprising, given the problems mentioned (and others as well), that the empirical evidence regarding the relative effectiveness of therapeutic approaches is unclear. Eysenck (1952), after reviewing much research, has reached the pessimistic conclusion that psychotherapy is no more effective than the mere passage of time.

Although this view has receded with the advent of more sophisticated research, it is still echoed from time to time (e.g., Rachman, 1973). And conclusions concerning whether empirical evidence favors one psychotherapy or another seem to be waning, replaced by the identification of effective factors present across many psychotherapies (e.g., Bergin & Lambert, 1978). However interesting and useful this trend is, it does not further issue-resolution in comparative analysis very much.

The comparative analysis of assessment approaches is only slightly less complex than that concerning therapies. Battles have raged concerning whether projective or questionnaire, structured or unstructured techniques are more supported by research findings (e.g., Ciminero, Calhoun, & Adams, 1977; Waskow & Parloff, 1975). Behind these battles stand the differing theoretical views on personality contained in the conflict, fulfillment, and consistency models, to say nothing of behaviorism and social learning theory. There appear to be no easy resolutions to these disputes. Perhaps this chapter has given you enough of a flavor for the complexity of doing psychotherapy and assessment research to allow you to appreciate why I will not enter into a full-fledged, issue-resolving comparative analysis of these matters here.

FORMAL AND SUBSTANTIVE CHARACTERISTICS OF THE GOOD THEORY OF PERSONALITY

In the preceding chapters, I compared and contrasted theories, posed issues, and conducted rational and empirical analyses. My overall aim has been to identify the most promising bases for conceptualizing personality. In pursuit of this goal, I have made statements concerning the value of certain models of personality theorizing. Hopefully these statements will serve as a guide to the development of theories of personality that are more sophisticated and effective than those considered in this book. What remains to be done in this concluding chapter is to set forth in one place the implications of the preceding discussions for future personality theorizing. This amounts to considering the formal and substantive characteristics that the good theory of personality will have. What I say here will not always agree with current orthodoxy. If I do not convince you entirely, perhaps you will at least be provoked to rethink the nature of the task of personality theorizing.

FORMAL CHARACTERISTICS . . . . .

In this section, we will consider the form that a *good theory of personality* should take, delaying discussion of content. I shall discuss two things: the parts that properly compose a personality theory and the overall criteria of formal adequacy that a good theory should fulfill.

The Parts of a Personality Theory

It will come as no surprise to you that I believe the good theory of personality will include both *core and peripheral levels.* The first level will include one or more *core tendencies,* which emphasize inherent attributes of persons, whether viewed individually or as part of a social aggregate. The attributes will tend to be inherent in the sense that they are not learned but rather comprise part of the nature of the organism. Although *core characteristics* may be physiological in nature, it is not at all necessary that they be so. For example, perfection theorists consider ideals as inherent attributes of the person. From the formal point of view, core-level statements only need to refer to inherent, or unlearned characteristics. Although most personality theorists regard their core tendencies and characteristics to be common to all people, one can construct core statements referring to individual differences that are inherent rather than learned (Rogers's inherent potentialities are an example).

At the *peripheral level of theorizing,* theorists emphasize the easily discernible, learned regularities in functioning that distinguish one person from another. Theorizing at this level should include a minimum of two kinds of concept. First, the *peripheral characteristic* refers to those entities in people that cannot sensibly be subdivided further and that differ in intensity and content from person to person. From the formal point of view, the peripheral characteristic is the smallest, most homogeneous unit of personality. It should be quantitative in nature so one person can be said to have more or less of it than another. It is also necessary that more than one peripheral characteristic be assumed if the peripheral theorizing is to successfully celebrate the differences among people.

The second kind of concept necessary for good peripheral-level theorizing is the *type,* which indicates how the peripheral characteristics get organized into broader units, more nearly approximating the styles of living that people show. Here too theorists must include a minimum of two types if their peripheral theorizing is to permit understanding of differences among people. We have every reason to expect of the theorist a *typology,* or exhaustive listing, of the types of peripheral personality considered important, each type with its array of peripheral characteristics. With such a typology in hand, we can know clearly what the theorist considers an adequate description of the different lifestyles people can have.

Also necessary are *developmental statements* that express the nature of the relationship between the core tendencies and characteristics on the one hand and the peripheral characteristics on the other. Generally, it will be assumed that the core tendencies and characteristics are general enough to permit expression in a wide range of concrete forms. The actual forms of expression that become fixed are shaped by interaction with the external environment in the form of parents, culture, social and economic conditions, and so forth. Thus, the personality theorist will disclose his or her position on the relationship between core and peripheral considerations through assumptions concerning development.

Finally, the good theory of personality will include a *data language,* or set of conventions for observation, which indicates what is important to explain. Application of a data language yields a group of *behavioral variables* arrived at through minimal interpretation of observations—certainly less interpretation than is involved in peripheral characteristics. Because it involves minimal interpretation, a behavioral variable usually is considered descriptive rather than explanatory.

Thus far, I have been somewhat abstract about the parts of a personality theory, asserting their necessity rather than attempting to convince you of it. In the following paragraphs, I shall try to be more concrete about why each of these parts is valuable and exactly what explanatory capability would be lost without each one.

THAT WHICH IS TO BE EXPLAINED. The whole point of theory is to foster understanding of something hitherto not understood. Once the function of theory is stated this way, it becomes very clear that there must be some well-developed sense of the data or phenomena to be explained; that is, they must be clear enough in the theorists' minds for them to direct their theoretical efforts as if to solve a problem. Thus, the good theory of personality must include a clear statement of the data it is attempting to explain. In other areas of theorizing, this point is so obvious that it need not be articulated. But in the personality area, one tends to find an emphasis on developing a theory without data, which is left open for future discovery. This is perhaps understandable in that the personality field is so broad that one is hard-pressed to be very specific about the data to be considered. Everything rushes to mind whenever one attempts to determine just which behavioral observations need to be understood in terms of personality.

Unfortunately, the difficulty in specifying data does nothing to diminish the necessity of doing it—indeed, perhaps the opposite is true. In any event, theorizing about the nature of personality without keeping in mind just what you want to understand about human behavior is like building a boat without knowing what water is like. The organization of the things people do, feel, and think into specifiable, communicable, tangible behavioral variables requires a data language. Personologists have sadly failed in developing or adopting a data language, however basic to theorizing such a step is. Rather than criticize further, however, let me simply conclude that a good theory of personality will specify a language for describing human functioning in terms that indicate what the theory needs to explain. Whether the language has been invented by the theorist or adopted from more widespread usage is unimportant as long as what needs to be explained is clear.

Although personology does not yet have a consistently developed data language, there is some guidance to be found in numerous discussions in this book. An appropriate data language for the personologist will be heavily psychological rather than biological or sociological. It will describe complete human thoughts, feelings, and actions, especially recurrent ones. Furthermore, current rudimentary descriptions of data lead in this direction. So, in saying that a good theory of personality ought to specify a data language that is psychological in nature, I am at least not doing violence to the apparent intent of personologists.

PERIPHERAL CHARACTERISTICS AS EXPLANATIONS. The first level of explanation of the behavioral variables, the peripheral characteristic, is a postulated entity in the person that renders a number of behavioral variables understandable by indicating their similarity or functional equivalence. For example, the behavioral variables of competitiveness with work associates, moderate risk taking in situations with outcomes that can be influenced by skill, and greater involvement in complex rather than simple tasks might all be

explained as expressions of a particular peripheral characteristic—the need for achievement. Invoking the need for achievement would not amount to merely describing the behavioral variables; rather, it would entail interpreting or explaining them.

Some personologists who strongly emphasize core-level theorizing would dispute the explanatory value of peripheral characteristics, considering them no more than descriptive generalizations of behavioral variables. To convince yourself that peripheral characteristics are more than data descriptions, consider in the example how easy it would be to devise some characteristic other than the need for achievement to explain the observations. Ready alternatives include insecurity and dominance. Seeing the observations as expressing need for achievement rather than these alternatives indicates that what has been done is an interpretation or explanation, not a description.

The criticism that peripheral characteristics are descriptive rather than explanatory may imply a more valid criticism: The peripheral characteristic has no logical existence apart from the behaviors it is supposed to explain; hence, its adequacy as an explanation cannot be determined. Suppose, as in the previous example, the presence or absence of the need for achievement could be decided on only by inference from the presence or absence of the behaviors concerning risk taking and so forth. If this were so, the need-for-achievement characteristic would have no existence apart from the data it is used to explain. Another personologist could easily invoke an alternative characteristic, such as dominance, with equal persuasiveness. One could never determine which explanation was the better. The criticism being made here is not that the need for achievement would have no explanatory value but that the explanation offered would be inconclusive.

Fortunately, there is a simple way around this criticism. It involves offering an operational definition of each peripheral characteristic. An operational definition tells you how to measure the characteristic in terms that differ from the data it is meant to explain. In our example, once an operational definition of need for achievement is offered, it becomes possible to conduct an empirical test of the adequacy of explaining those particular behaviors with that particular characteristic. One would measure the strength of need for achievement in, say, fantasy and then determine the relationships between achievement fantasy and the relevant behavioral variables, which, of course, would be measured in a very different way. To render the explanatory power of peripheral characteristics more compelling, the good theory of personality must include operational definitions of its peripheral characteristics.

THE TYPE AS AN EXPLANATION. Though personality types are more general than peripheral characteristics, they are similar in other respects. The behavior explained by a type is a composite of the behavioral variables explained by each of the peripheral characteristics it subsumes. The typology explains differences among people that are more general and, in commonsense terms, more obvious than those explained by single peripheral characteristics.

Types need not include operational definitions, because types do no more than subsume a specified set of peripheral characteristics, each of which is already operationally defined. The general style and directionality of individual lives are best understood in terms of types and typology. This is true even though one can pinpoint a more restricted, less sweeping directionality at the level of peripheral characteristics, as Murray, McClelland, and Maddi do with their motive concepts.

THE CORE AND DEVELOPMENT AS EXPLANATORY. Core-level theorizing, you will recall, explains the attributes and directions found in all people by virtue of their common human nature. Such theorizing is necessary insofar as one thinks of humankind as a whole and contrasts it with other forms of life. In addition, the core tendency has the vital function of explicating the overall directionality of life. The concrete directions identified at the peripheral level must be derived from the overall directionality and are not themselves understandable without it.

The core tendency and characteristics function

at a level of theorizing further removed from the behavioral observations that prompt peripheral-level theorizing. As such, the core of personality only indirectly explains particular behaviors through its relationship to the periphery. There is no point, therefore, in attempting an operational definition of core tendencies and characteristics. Empirical validity of core-level theorizing is not to be assessed directly; rather, the process of empirically testing peripheral theorizing determines the adequacy of core theorizing by weight of evidence. In any theory only indirectly related to data, weight of evidence is the most sensible empirical standard. But the weight of evidence cannot be brought to bear on core-level theorizing unless it is carefully articulated with peripheral-level theorizing. This means that developmental statements relating core and periphery through the mediation of experience in the world are essential to a good theory of personality.

Because core theorizing refers to data only indirectly, one may question its explanatory value. Indeed, some personologists who prefer to stay very close to data would consider core-level theorizing not only dispensable but a waste of time and effort. But anyone who values considering people as sharing some inherent nature and direction will find it hard to agree. And anyone who wishes to explain human behavior in terms of an initial impetus to behave before any learning takes place could never agree. Core-level theorizing explicates the "prime mover" of behavior and clarifies the restrictions imposed on what is subsequently learned by the common characteristics of human nature. Any theory of personality that makes a claim to comprehensiveness must explain these matters and, therefore, requires a core statement.

In summary, each part of a theory of personality has a specific and important function. Without a *data language,* a theory cannot specify what it intends to explain. A theory in such a position is less an explanatory device than a world view, religion, or myth. *Peripheral characteristics* are necessary if one seriously believes there are many obvious, though concrete and small, differences among people. Without a *typology,* a theory is mute concerning larger patterns of difference among people. If a theory does not include a statement of *core tendencies and associated core characteristics*, the theorist cannot consider people as sharing some attributes by virtue of their common species, nor can the theorist consider how any functioning occurs in the absence of considerable learning. And the explication, through statements about *development*, of the process whereby core considerations come to be expressed in particular peripheral lifestyles, is essential for the core statements to be at all accessible to an empirical test of adequacy.

Obviously, complete personality theories do not spring full-blown from the theorist's mind. One part or another may well be developed before the rest. Theorists may want to—and should—express their views even before they can make an ideally comprehensive statement. Nonetheless, the ideal defines what the theorist should work toward. Failure to include any part of a personality theory leads to a particular, recognizable kind of drawback. Comprehensive understanding of personality requires all the parts.

Overall Criteria of Formal Adequacy

Even assuming that the good theory of personality will have all its parts, it must adhere to some overall principles of theorizing. These frequently mentioned principles are that a theory should be *important, operational, parsimonious, precise, empirically valid, and stimulating*. It is generally believed that a theory is adequate only if it can fulfill these formal criteria. I agree with some of the criteria more than others and will therefore discuss each separately. Much of what I am about to say has been implicit or even directly mentioned before. But it is high time to be explicit.

A THEORY SHOULD BE IMPORTANT. Although psychologists often evaluate theories on the basis of their triviality versus importance, this kind of evaluation is very difficult to justify. Mandler and Kessen (1959) make this point forcefully:

> Were there at hand a rigorous criterion for triviality, the psychological community could agree with confidence on the study of genuinely important issues, the ones that "really matter." Unfortunately

no such criterion of exclusion can be stated. The polemic use of terms such as "inconsequential," "limited," "far from reality," and so on, when applied to theories of behavior, misses the fact that science has no dead-end markers. We can look back into the past and see with relatively high acuity the junctures at which a line of theory went awry, but no satisfactory method can be proposed for making a similar judgment about contemporary systems of explanation. A responsible scientist may choose to work on whatever problems interest him but he is fooling himself if he claims to know that he is on a more direct route to some future truth than his colleagues. Franklin and Faraday were both asked "What good is it?" by curious and puzzled friends who were watching the demonstration of a new device. Franklin's famous reply "What good is a new-born child?" was a pointed recognition of our ignorance of future utilities, but Faraday expressed more accurately the disdain of the pure scientist for questions of applicability when he responded to Gladstone, "Why, sir, there is every probability that you will soon be able to tax it." ... Much the same answers can be made to attacks against psychological theories on grounds of triviality; their ultimate contribution to knowledge is determined by so many unknown considerations that it seems wisest to recognize that attacks of this order cannot be justified by reference to an unambiguous criterion. (pp. 253–254)

As a spirited argument for theoretical freedom, this statement is very effective. Yet you must consider just how far you would endorse it. Consider, in this regard, an equally spirited indictment of a theory Bruner makes on the grounds of triviality. The theory criticized is Spence's version of general behavior theory, which holds that the hallmark of all learning is the associative bonding of stimuli and responses that have been experienced as contiguous in time. This theory has been formulated mainly on the basis of experiments in which rats had to learn a particular route through a maze. Railing against this concretistic theory of learning, Bruner (1957a) says,

> Let me illustrate one source of my discouragement in attempting to evaluate this truly distinguished book. It is estimated that there are 10^{75} possible sentences in the English language 50 words in length, and that in the course of a year we hear perhaps 10^6 sentences altogether. If one learned the

sentences we uttered by a process that is Markovian [associationistic] in nature, eliminating alternatives according to the gradual build-up of excitatory strength, our lives would be far too short to master even the simple prattle of a child. And there is little doubt, moreover, that we would be able to indicate which sentences among the 10^{75} constructed by an algorithm were proper sentences and which were not, even though we have never encountered them. It is obvious that "verbal responses" are not what is "learned" but, rather, rules and principles of structuring that make it possible for us to generate sentences. The answer to such a point as this is by now familiar: You cannot criticize a thing for what it does not attempt to account for. But the ultimate end of such a defense is that the critic is then forced to celebrate behavior theory of this type as the applied psychology of CS-US linkages, T mazes, and straight runways. (p. 156)

Elsewhere in his review, Bruner (1957a) says in the same vein, "Donald Hebb recently remarked that if one made a set of microphotographs of Cambridge, inch by inch, very likely one would fail to discover the Charles River" (p. 156). In pointing out that Spence's theory will either have to answer his criticism or be celebrated as the applied psychology of mazes, Bruner is raising the question of triviality.

Bruner does not really dispute the fact that humans can learn in an associationistic fashion. What he disputes is that such learning is to be considered characteristic of how the human operates. He feels that it obviously cannot be, from his example of language learning. One does not need to do empirical research to recognize that Spence has trivialized human beings by failing to acknowledge their ability to learn principles, which they obviously show. It will not help Spence to say, with Mandler and Kessen, that one could hardly have known in advance of theorizing that people learn predominantly by principle rather than association, because Bruner, in his very example—which is rational rather than empirical—is saying that he and lots of other psychologists would have known in advance. This is why he is so disappointed in the book.

What brought about the trivialization of learning theory constituted by Spence's approach? Surely it was not a necessary concomitant of

adopting a laboratory paradigm for the investigation of learning. Indeed, the value of laboratory paradigms can be great if they truly represent simpler, more controllable forms of the naturalistic phenomenon under consideration. Through systematically varying one variable at a time while holding the others constant, a phenomenon such as learning can be analyzed more effectively in the laboratory than in a natural setting. But, for the promise of the laboratory to be realized, the paradigm chosen must represent, or at least be homologous with, the phenomenon as it occurs in a natural setting.

If humans learn primarily principles rather than associations, the T maze is not a suitable paradigm because it is too simple to lend itself to learning principles. Further, if rats learn primarily by association rather than principle, no matter how carefully they are studied, any application of the conclusions to human beings is likely to be an oversimplification. Whenever theorizing about some phenomenon is not directed toward understanding it as it naturally occurs—being directed instead at some laboratory paradigm supposedly similar but not truly representational—it runs a great risk of being trivial. The difficulty with Spence's approach is not that it relies on a laboratory paradigm but that it grappled insufficiently with the paradigm's suitability as a basis for generalizing to natural human learning.

In theorizing, one can minimize the risk of being trivial by relying on observations of nature in deciding what should constitute the major phenomena to be explained. If truly representative laboratory paradigms are available, observations from them can be relied on as well. But theorists need not be especially alarmed at finding their position unable to account for laboratory observations if their relationship to natural occurrences is unclear (e.g., hypnotic behavior, because hypnosis does not occur naturally). Reliance on naturalistic observation in theorizing is especially important for personologists, whose aim of understanding the whole human being can be so easily trivialized by oversimplification. After formulating the rudiments of their theory through reliance on such observations, they can, of course, design laboratory experiments to their hearts' delight to determine whether their theorizing is really sound. If they start with naturalistic observation, they are unlikely to be working on a trivial problem or designing laboratory experiments that are so oversimplified that they no longer represent the phenomenon under consideration.

Actually, most personality theorists would agree with much of what I have said. They certainly rely on naturalistic observation, as can be seen from the case histories and even appeals to common experience that are often provided as the bases for theorizing. The more formal and systematic ratings of subjects' behavior in various tasks, so effectively employed by such persologists as Murray (1938) and Cattell (1946), still resemble everyday functioning enough to be considered natural. Also close to nature are those personality tests that are least structured (e.g., Thematic Apperception Test), permitting persons to disclose themselves in their own way. Rarely do personologists rely heavily on laboratory forms of phenomena as a guide in theorizing.

But the danger with some personologists is that they use the psychotherapeutic interaction with much of the same alacrity that Spence exhibits with the T maze. After all, the psychotherapeutic situation is a highly specialized one, created to facilitate treatment, a contrived rather than natural situation. To my mind, it only partially represents naturally occurring interactions. When personologists devise a personality theory on the basis of psychotherapeutic observations alone, they run a large risk of being trivial in the depth and breadth of their understanding of life. You may recall that in Chapter 5, I suggested that the reason Rogers offers only two personality types—thereby simplifying life—is that his theory was developed almost exclusively on the basis of observation of clients' behavior. A theory of psychotherapy is one thing; a theory of personality is another.

A THEORY SHOULD BE OPERATIONAL. Simply put, the doctrine of *operationism* indicates that the meaning of a concept is determined by the measurement operations associated with it. This has been a very useful notion to scientists, because it forces them to be precise about what they mean lest someone else measure it in a way at variance with their intended meaning. Further, it alerts them to the implications of various measurement operations for influencing what they mean. But some overzealous psychologists have interpreted the doctrine of operationism in ways that to me do not seem at all advantageous.

One such interpretation of operationism is that concepts mean whatever we want them to mean—nothing more and nothing less. This seems a misuse of operationism, which was never meant to be a substitute for theorizing. When we use our measurement operations to define a concept rather than first defining the concept and then choosing the measurement operations most relevant for it, we assume that the concept is nothing more than an arbitrary symbol. This assumption is virtually always violated in psychology, which uses as concepts not mathematical symbols but words, which acquire fairly consistent meanings as conventions of usage for them develop. These conventions are not merely semantic; distinctions among words generally coincide with perceived differences among events in experience.

Denying this "real" meaning of a concept (see Mandler & Kessen, 1959, pp. 93–101) and defining it merely in terms of a set of measurement operations (e.g., intelligence is the score on the *Stanford-Binet Test*) would lead psychologists into even more blind alleys than it already does were it not for the fact that in reality we rarely give up the real meaning completely. It usually hovers on the fringe of consciousness all the while it is disavowed and exercises an intuitive influence on investigations. This intuitive influence is what probably keeps investigators from making too many mistakes even as they are foolishly saying that they know nothing of the meanings of their concepts except the steps they took in measuring them. They do not land in blind alleys unequivocally enough to force a reconsideration of the madness of capitulating, as theorists, to arbitrarily chosen measurement operations. After all, there are an infinite number of measurement operations, and if they have no theory to guide them in choosing among them, the choice will be arbitrarily made. Their undetected intuition leads to just enough reward to perpetuate the misguided belief in the value of remaking concepts in the image of their measurement operations!

Clearly, then, I believe that concept definition is a matter of theory and that only when definition has already been achieved does it make sense to select measurement operations. These may well provoke a reconsideration of the concept's meaning, but the contribution of measurement operations to the meaning of a concept is secondary to that made by the theorist using all the intuition and reason available to him or her. In the good theory of personality, therefore, the cart will not lead the horse; the measurement operations for concepts will follow from their theoretical definitions rather than actually constitute the definitions.

The other disadvantageous version of operationism is simply that all concepts, regardless of their logical function, must be operationalized to justify their inclusion in a theory. You already know that I disagree with this, because I have asserted that only peripheral characteristics need have operational definitions. I see little reason why a concept should have an operational definition if its primary function is not to explain data directly but to indicate the relationship and organization among concepts. To require that only operationalized concepts be included in theories might have the unfortunate effect of decreasing emphasis on core statements. In the good theory of personality, only peripheral characteristics are equipped with operational definitions.

Most personality theorists fall short of providing operationalizations of their peripheral characteristics. It is not likely, therefore, that they will fall prey to the two disadvantageous versions of operationism. These versions are common in other fields of psychology, however, and perhaps what I have said can help personality theorists defend themselves against critics. I hope I have also been convincing concerning the need for operational definitions of peripheral characteristics. In providing such definitions, the theorist has much to gain and nothing to lose.

A THEORY SHOULD BE PARSIMONIOUS. For a long time in psychology, it has been orthodox to believe in parsimony as a standard of adequacy in theorizing. What parsimony means is that given a set group of phenomena to be explained, the best explanation among them is the one that makes the fewest assumptions. Assumptions, for present purposes, are roughly equivalent to concepts and the interrelationships among them. The aim of parsimony is theoretical simplicity. Sensible and sound though it may seem, the principle of parsimony may be virtually impossible to apply in psychology. In order to do so, one would have to specify the domain of behavioral variables to be explained and the assumptions of all theories that claim to explain them. Specification of theoretical assumptions is difficult, because psychological theory generally is incomplete and based on implicit assumptions (Mandler & Kessen, 1959). Such implicitness is not consistent with an application of parsimony. Specification of the domain of behavioral variables cannot be done meaningfully because even similar personality theories show little agreement in the data they attempt to explain. As you know, some theories do not even specify the data to which they pertain.

Even if there were both more specification of relevant data and more agreement or overlap among the specifications, the current rates of increase in psychological data would not remain constant long enough to permit any meaningful assessment of parsimony. These conditions render the principle of parsimony virtually useless as a basis for evaluating alternative theories. After all, can anyone remember a personality theory being found unparsimonious not only by its opponents but by its adherents and disinterested persons? What this means is that the principle of parsimony has not been useful as a guide to theoretical fruitfulness in personality theories.

Indeed, even if parsimony could be used in assessing personality theories, I am not sure I would put much stock in it. Let us say that you could, at some point in time, specify some domain of data that theorists agreed was what they wanted to explain. Let us also say that you could make all the assumptions of the various theories explicit. Further, let us suppose that a theory emerged as the one that explained the facts with the fewest assumptions. Would you be willing, on the basis of this possibly transitory victory, to discard the unparsimonious theories? I would not, because the victory would tell us little about the ability of the parsimonious theory to continue providing good explanations of future data. Indeed, it is distinctly possible that a theory that looks parsimonious in explaining today's facts may actually be such an oversimplification in terms of explaining all human functioning as to be wholly inadequate to cope with tomorrow's facts.

Recognizing this, it does not seem important in theorizing to strive for simplicity for its own sake. Better to use all your intuition, reason, and empirical knowledge in striving for a theory that is as comprehensive concerning human functioning as you can make it. Happily, personality theorists seem to have done this, being rather indifferent to the parsimony of their formulations.

A THEORY SHOULD BE PRECISE. A criterion so obviously important that it requires little elaboration here is that a theory be as clear and *precise* as possible. In defining concepts and relating them to one another and to data, the theorist should avoid being implicit and using figurative, metaphorical, or analogical language. The trouble with implicit formulations is that they are not recognized and therefore exert an ambiguous, frequently inconsistent influence on the use of a theory. Figurative, metaphorical, and analogical formulations also create ambiguity and inconsistency. To make statements such as "The superego does battle with the id" or "The ego is the executive organ attempting to strike a compromise between the id and superego" is inconsistent with clarity and precision. As I pointed out in Chapter 10, such statements cannot be literally true, for doing battle and striking compromises are attributed to whole organisms whereas id, ego, and superego are intended to be only parts of organisms. To theorize in this loose fashion is to court misunderstanding.

At the earliest, most intuitive phase of theory formulation, metaphorical usage and some general implicitness may be inevitable and perhaps even stimulates imaginativeness. But the theorist nonetheless should strive toward precision and clarity in his or her formulations. All too often, personality theories remain characterized by implicitness and metaphorical usage long after their inception. Actually, were theories of personality more precise, my task of analysis in this book would be much simpler and my conclusions less equivocal.

There is a fairly simple way to determine if a theory is sufficiently precise. Try to use it for what it was intended. Apply it to observations of people and see if it helps you understand them better. Or try to generate predictions concerning the behavior of particular kinds of people whom you have not yet observed. Try to decide how, in the theory's terms, these predictions should be tested. If you encounter difficulty in using the theory this way, it will be because the theory is either incomplete (recall the parts of a personality theory previously listed as necessary) or imprecise. If all the necessary parts are present in some form, imprecision is the flaw. Often, a careful scrutiny of the theory will disclose where the imprecision lies. Remember that a precise theory can be used readily even by someone who has no special faith in it. Indeed, theories that can be applied only by people who believe in their truth usually lack some degree of precision, which can sometimes be overcome by zeal. But it would be better to use the zeal to decrease the implicitness and metaphorical qualities of the theory so that it can communicate to all potential users.

A THEORY SHOULD BE EMPIRICALLY VALID. In discussing the principles of theorizing, I have been considering rational rather than empirical standards of adequacy. Only after one demonstrates the rational adequacy of a theory does an assessment of empirical validity become relevant. The crucial evidence on empirical validity involves systematic empirical tests of the predictions made by the theory.

Explanations generated for data known before the explanation was formulated are interesting and useful, but they do not directly clarify the matter of empirical validity. Such explanations are called *post hoc,* to indicate that they do not involve putting yourself out on the limb of predicting the kind of data you will find before you have looked. In determining empirical validity, the empirical test of such predictions is much more important than the fineness of post hoc explanation. Given that theories of personality are complex and inevitably somewhat elastic, it is just too possible that post hoc explanations sound as good as they do because of some degree of unintentional twisting and stretching of the theory to square it with what you already know the data to be.

No such theoretical "body English" can operate in predictions, whose relevant data are not yet available. To test a prediction, one must determine whether the relevant data, obtained under strict scientific standards, are indeed as expected. If a theory's predictions are disconfirmed often enough, it will be thrown into serious doubt, regardless of its rational adequacy and the apparent adequacy of its post hoc explanations.

The assessment of empirical validity, though a basic method of evaluation, is premature until the theory is sufficiently developed so that one can unequivocally discern the kinds of data that are actually relevant and the precise manner in which the theory addresses itself to them. The rational standards already discussed mark such development; therefore, you need them before you can assess empirical validity. Before rational adequacy has been attained, empirical observations probably are more effectively used for theory construction and refinement rather than testing.

A THEORY SHOULD BE STIMULATING. It is often said that a theory justifies its existence if it provokes others to thought and investigation. Personologists might find a theory congenial and be motivated to enhance and support it; they might simply associate freely with it and be caught up in the novel ideas thus generated; they might react against it and be driven to demonstrate its inadequacies. It makes little difference which course is taken as long as it generates careful thought and research that otherwise might not occur. Clearly a theory need not meet any other criterion of adequacy, rational or empirical, in order to be considered worthwhile

by the standard of stimulation. And I certainly would agree that a theory that stimulates is a good thing.

But legitimate and important as stimulation is, a theory will not make a lasting, specific contribution to understanding in a scientific discipline such as personology unless it achieves rational adequacy and empirical validity. It is fruitless, however, to condemn personology because it has made little progress in producing such theories. The standards discussed here simply define goals to work toward. But personologists should not permit themselves to avoid the tedious and difficult work of rendering their theories more rationally and empirically adequate by satisfying themselves with the thought that their theories have been stimulating.

SUBSTANTIVE CHARACTERISTICS . . . .

The content, or substantive characteristics, of a theory determines the predictions it will make. If the predictions are supported by empirical research, it will be because the theory's substantive characteristics were wisely chosen. Therefore, in attempting to develop better theories of personality, one should take into account the substantive conclusions I have reached in analyzing the various positions included in this book. For vividness, I have organized substantive considerations into broad, somewhat interpretative units. I have also italicized the most important statements.

DEFENSIVENESS. One of the most salient substantive conclusions from Chapter 10 is that *defensiveness is a common, though not ubiquitous, occurrence in living.* There are likely to be differences among people in their degree of defensiveness and in the areas of living in which defensiveness occurs. The evidence suggests two general techniques of defense: *to repress,* by failing to remember or perceive, and *to be hypersensitive,* by remembering or perceiving only some especially problematic things. The stimuli shown to elicit defensiveness have been of an anxiety-provoking or socially taboo nature. All these findings suggest that *defensiveness occurs in the attempt to avoid anxiety that arises out of some conflict pitting the person and society against each other.* But such conflict is not an inevitable outcome of interaction between individuals and groups, for defensiveness is not ubiquitous.

CONSCIENCE AND COMMITMENT. Consistent with the view that the conflict involves the person and society are the conclusions from Chapter 12 to the effect that two common characteristics in which people show differences in intensity are *conscience* (a set of values bearing on the regulation of personal action) and *commitment to or endorsement of existing social institutions and role structures.* Apparently some people accept the importance of society and its restrictions more than others do. People differ in the degree to which they are *stable, predictable, and dependable;* these characteristics probably refer to the conformance of behavior to social responsibilities. At a more abstract level, Chapter 12 also testifies to the existence in people of *personal goals (motives)* as well as *social goals (schemata).* It is important to recognize that personal goals can have a wide range of content.

CONFORMITY VERSUS TRANSCENDENCE. Let us conclude that there can, but need not, be anxiety-inducing conflict between *personal and social goals.* Let us also conclude that this anxiety is often reduced by *defensiveness* aimed at convincing oneself and others of the social purity of one's intent. We are left with the insistent question of whether defensiveness is a good thing. The evidence summarized in the next paragraph suggests that whatever the possible short-term gains, defensiveness is disadvantageous to the individual and, in a general sense, even to the vigorous development of his or her society. Clearly, defensiveness implies conformity to what people around you do and believe. That people differ in the strength of such conforming tendencies when interacting with others is suggested by evidence in Chapter 12. Common bipolar characteristics emerging from factor-analytic research

are *gregariousness-aloofness, cooperativeness-competitiveness,* and *dominance-dependence.* The existence of *needs for power, achievement, and affiliation* is also well documented.

Knowing that it is possible to be conforming or individualistic, we can then ask what are the implications of these ways of being. In Chapter 10, you learned that people who transcend the roles and institutions of society and are individualistic rather than conforming in their interpersonal behavior are more likely to be creative in their work. Chapter 12 contributes evidence that people who conform by answering questions about themselves in a socially desirable fashion show less initiative and self-confidence and can be more easily influenced by others. In contrast, people who accept themselves and their individuality are involved in a broader range of activities, have a more positive impact on other people, and are especially able to accept them. A number of studies suggest that people who do not see themselves as controlling their own fates are less likely to show initiative and proaction in the service of not only their own goals but of social problems. *These kinds of findings suggest that transcendent persons are not only more capable of fulfilling their own personal goals but are more socially useful than those who conform.* Supporting this conclusion is the evidence that *a personal goal, the need for achievement, is an important factor in the socially crucial matter of economic development.*

GENERAL ENERGY OR ACTIVATION. Another group of findings prompt the substantive conclusion that activation and its adjustment are important attributes of the person. From the factor-analytic studies reviewed in Chapter 12, we find that an important characteristic in which people show differences is *general energy or activation.* Chapter 10 made it clear that *people decrease tension in some of their functioning and actually increase tension in the rest.* You will recall that *tension* and *activation* are virtually interchangeable terms.

Another aspect of the picture is the evidence in Chapter 10 that *people seek moderate degrees of variety while avoiding large degrees of it.* Additional evidence in Chapter 12 indicates that *there are individual differences in the strength of the motivation to seek or avoid variety.* It is not hard to believe that seeking and avoiding variety serves to increase or decrease activation, respectively. Other behaviors that possibly increase or decrease activation that Chapter 12 shows to be differentially represented in people are *stability-impulsivity* and *rigidity-flexibility.*

DIFFERENTIATION OR COMPLEXITY. Also apparent from Chapter 10, people differ in the degree to which their personalities show *differentiation,* or *complexity.* Moreover, *differentiation increases from birth at least until some time in early adulthood.* Further, *integrative processes may well increase as the years pass.* Because differentiation and integration are the two aspects of psychological growth, these findings impact that concept. Chapter 10 provides general evidence for *the occurrence of significant change in personality over the life span.*

The Aims of Comparative Analytic Research

The substantive considerations mentioned above provide a provocative basis for improving personality theorizing. However, because true comparative analytic research is still rare in personology, there remains some uncertainty about what is crucial substantively. One way in which research qualifies as comparative analysis is its intent to resolve an issue or issues separating two or more theories or models (Chapter 10 gives examples of such issues). Another kind of comparative analytic research aims to determine the relative ability of one or more theories or models to account for the dimensions of individual differences that are observed (see Chapter 12).

The methods employed may vary widely—from *experimental* to *correlational analysis,* from *naturalistic observation* to *structured tests,* from *longitudinal* to *cross-sectional approaches.* As long as the methods are appropriate to the problem, the main thing that qualifies a study as

comparative analysis is an explicit emphasis on assessing the relative merits of differing theories. A concerted effort to do so on the part of many researchers would simultaneously lead to a giant step forward in knowledge and give personology the boost in vitality it currently needs.

Ideally, comparative analysis deals with *models* or families of theories, because by doing so one gets the greatest return for the effort. But such a grand approach is not always feasible or practical. Comparative analysis can also deal fruitfully with small issues concerning two individual theories rather than broader models. It seems likely that most comparative analytic research that gets done in the near future will be of this sort.

Perhaps an example or two of what might be done will be helpful. One might address the issue concerning whether defensiveness facilitates or inhibits sound functioning (for example, Rogers would regard it as inhibiting and Freud as facilitating). Adopting an *experimental approach,* one might use the same threatening treatment on several experimental groups to arouse defensiveness and then have each group perform some relevant task. The threatening treatment would have to be theoretically appropriate to the arousal of defensiveness in both theories (e.g., constituting what Rogers would call *conditional positive regard* and Freud *psychosexual trauma*). The tasks performed by each group together would have to constitute a broad and reasonably representative cross-section of life's activities (e.g., problem-solving performance, creative endeavor, interpersonal functioning). It would also be useful to have a built-in way (e.g., posttest interviews) of determining whether (and in which subjects) defensiveness has actually occurred. Control groups for each experimental group would perform the same tasks without prior defensiveness arousal. The aim of the study would be to chart the actual effect of defensiveness on the various tasks. The results would show either a general inhibition (favoring Rogers) or facilitation (favoring Freud) of performance, or some more complex pattern of inhibition on some tasks and facilitation on others. The latter result would also be quite valuable in that it would constitute a basis for modification of both theories or for new theorizing.

Another example involves using *correlational methodology* in comparing the existential and Freudian views of guilt. Because the actual experience of guilt is similar (e.g., self-criticism, feelings of unworthiness, pessimism, depression, lack of energy, self-destructiveness) in the conceptualizations of both theories, a common measure of this state (probably *questionnaire* or *interview*) could be applied to a group of subjects. The subjects could also complete tests (probably other questionnaires or interviews) indexing the explanations of guilt that prevail in the two theories (for existential psychology, the chronic tendency to choose the past or status quo rather than the future or change; for Freud, an unresolved love for the opposite-sex parent and hatred for the same-sex parent and their representation in contemporary life). Then, by correlating the measure of guilt with the measures of ontological choice and psychosexual conflict, one could determine whether guilt is best explained by Freudian or existential psychology. Once again, even complex patterns of results (e.g., some subjects appear more "Freudian" and others more "existential") would be useful for theory modification or new theorizing.

The Psychology of Possibility

One of the most constant features unique to personality theory is the identification of *ideal lifestyles* and *developmental directions*. As you will recall from Chapter 1, this willingness to make value judgments about the good life is basic to statements and techniques in the area of psychotherapy, with its aim of changing destructive behavior to something better. Personologists are often criticized by their colleagues for making such value judgments, which frequently are seen as unscientific and appropriate, if at all, only in the nonempirical disciplines of philosophy and theology.

But it seems to me that personologists have a definite contribution to make to science through their concern with ideal functioning. Whereas most empirical psychologists are preoccupied with what is actual, with preponderance or majority, generalizing from this to the way things inevitably must be, personologists have the ability, because of their theoretical concerns, to explicate bases for human improvement. They carry the seeds of a psychology of *possibility* (Maddi, 1984).

All they need do is study people in a rigorous empirical fashion who approximate their theoretical ideal. By definition, few people achieve ideal functioning. But some approximate it and, by searching them out, one can accumulate a sample large enough for rigorous study. Then these supposedly ideal people can be compared, on many theoretically relevant dimensions of living, with a group of supposedly less-ideal people. Empirical information on how the ideal people live and how they got to be that way can then be translated into prescriptions for personal development, parental actions, and psychotherapy so that those who wish to follow suit will have some guidance. Indeed, one might even have a comparative analysis of conceptualizations of the ideal life! There is nothing at all unscientific about this—quite the contrary. And there is much for the human species to learn and become.

Concluding Remarks ....

I believe that the substantive considerations just summarized indicate the fruitfulness for personality theorizing of using some combination of the fulfillment model and the activation version of the consistency model. But it certainly is possible for someone to order the important substantive considerations in an even more powerful way by developing some other kind of personality theory. I will be satisfied if reading this book has rendered the task of personality theorizing more understandable, tangible, important, and engaging for you. As I mentioned in the preface, this book carries within it the seeds of its own demise, which will occur when a comparative analytic orientation takes such root as to lead to theories of personality more precise and powerful than any mentioned here. That will surely be a happy day! But the demise could also take the form of the promulgation of a more trenchant comparative analysis than I have been able to manage. If this book spurs others to better comparative analyses, then it will have fulfilled its purpose.

Theoretical Summaries

Freud's Theory (Conflict, Psychosocial) .....

Core of Personality

CORE TENDENCY. *To maximize instinctual gratification while minimizing punishment and guilt* (called the *reality principle*). This is a compromise necessitated by the inevitable conflict between the individual (whose instincts are selfish) and society (which aims at the common good). The reality principle involves *secondary process thinking,* characterized by formulating and testing strategies for maximizing instinctual gratification while minimizing punishment and guilt.

CORE CHARACTERISTICS

Id: Consists of the *instincts,* which are the original contents of the mind. All instincts have their *source* in the biological (metabolic) requirements of the organism and derive their energy from this source. The aim of all instincts is tension reduction (or satisfaction), which is achieved by obtaining objects appropriate to the source and aim. Instincts function according to the *pleasure principle,* or tendency to maximize instinctual gratification without regard for external reality. The pleasure principle involves *primary process thinking,* in which imagined objects give hallucinatory (and therefore only partial) satisfaction and tension reduction. All people possess life, death, and sexual instincts, the last being by far the most important.

Ego: With experience, a part of the person's mind becomes differentiated for the purpose of facilitating reality principle functioning through secondary process thinking. The major function of the ego is defensive in that it permits only the forms and parts of instincts unlikely to engender punishment and guilt to remain in consciousness. The reality principle is largely engineered by the defensive process, which is itself unconscious.

Superego: The part of the mind, differentiated from the ego, that contains the traditional *values* and *taboos* of society as interpreted for the child by its parents. The superego makes *guilt* possible, which is the internal version of *punishment.* The values and taboos set restrictions on the forms of instinctual gratification that one can seek. When some instinctual impulse threatens to produce punishment or guilt, *anxiety* occurs as a warning. Some form of *defensiveness* occurs to avoid the anxiety by removing the instinctual impulse from consciousness. Because conflict between id and either society or superego is inevitable, all behavior is defensive.

Development

PSYCHOSEXUAL STAGES

Oral (first year of life), in which the erogenous zone is the mouth and the primary activities are *receiving* (oral incorporative) and *taking* (oral aggressive). Feeding is the important area of conflict.

Anal (second year of life), in which the erogenous zone is the anus and the primary activities are *giving* (anal expulsive) and *withholding* (anal retentive). Bowel training is the important area of conflict.

Phallic (third through fifth year of life), in which the erogenous zone is the genitals and the primary activities involve *heterosexualizing interaction*. This is the time of the oedipus conflict, when the child vies with the same-sex parent for the affection of the opposite-sex parent. Especially important for the boy is *castration anxiety* and for the girl *penis envy*.

Latency (sixth year through puberty), in which the sexual instinct is dormant and the child is learning skills not directly related to sexuality.

Genital (puberty to death), characterized by mature sexuality that combines all that is learned in the pregenital stages and relies primarily on *intercourse* and *orgasm*. The person reaching genitality is fully able to *love* and *work*.

FIXATION. When the inevitable conflict encountered at each psychosexual stage is minimal, the stage is successfully traversed. But when the parents intensify the conflict by *depriving* or *indulging* the child unduly or inconsistently, growth is arrested through the occurrence of massive defensiveness aimed at avoiding anxiety through avoiding conflict. This arresting of growth is called *fixation*, and it signifies that the activities of the psychosexual stage involved will remain especially important to the person, even after he or she has achieved puberty.

Periphery of Personality

CHARACTER TYPES COMPOSED OF TRAITS AND DEFENSES. In adulthood, the types express the activities and conflicts of the various psychosexual stages of development and of the *defenses* common to those stages.

Oral character: Major defenses are *projection* (attributing to others an objectionable trait that one really possesses), *denial* (failing to perceive some threatening object or event in the external world), and *introjection* (incorporating other people in order to avoid threats posed by them or one's own instincts). Some typical traits are *optimism-pessimism, gullibility-suspiciousness, manipulativeness-passivity,* and *admiration-envy.*

Anal character: Major defenses are *intellectualization* (substituting a fictitious, socially acceptable reason for the genuine, instinctual reason behind one's behavior), *reaction formation* (substituting for one's own true wishes the directly opposite wishes), *isolation* (severing the connecting links normally present between the cognitive and emotional components of wishes so that something of their true nature can remain conscious without a concomitant sense of threat), and *undoing* (engaging in certain thoughts and actions so as to cancel out, or atone for, previous threatening thoughts or actions). Some typical traits are *stinginess-overgenerosity, stubbornness-acquiescence, orderliness-messiness,* and *precision-vagueness.*

Phallic character: Major defense is *repression* (the active debarring from consciousness of instinctual wishes and actions of a threatening nature). Some typical traits are *vanity-*

self-hatred, pride-humility, blind courage-timidity, stylishness-plainness, and *chastity-promiscuity.*

Genital character: Major defense is *sublimation* (changing the object of the sexual instinct to make it more socially acceptable than the original but in no other way blocking the instinct). Traits indicate full socialization, adjustment, and potency.

MURRAY'S THEORY (CONFLICT, PSYCHOSOCIAL) . . . . .

Core of Personality

CORE TENDENCY. Similar to Freud. Raises the possibility that not all functioning is determined by the attempt to avoid conflict between individual and society.

CORE CHARACTERISTICS

Id: Similar to Freud, but not all the instincts are selfish and socially deleterious in nature.

Ego: Similar to Freud, but with considerable elaboration of nondefensive processes whereby the socially acceptable instincts can be vigorously expressed. These processes include such cognitive and action-oriented procedures as *rational thought* and *accurate perception.*

Superego: Similar to Freud, but with proviso that the values and taboos it contains are not fixed in childhood. Following childhood, one's peers, events, and reading matter can influence the superego.

Development

PSYCHOSEXUAL STAGES. Similar to Freud, but with the addition of the following stages:

Claustral (intrauterine period of life), in which there is no clearly definable erogenous zone, but there is passive dependency on the mother.

Eurethral (between oral and anal stages), in which the urinary apparatus is the erogenous

zone and the primary activities involve urinary display.

FIXATION. Similar to Freud.

Periphery of Personality

COMPLEXES. Similar to Freud's character types, with the addition of two types corresponding to the two additional psychosexual stages:

Claustral complex: Major defense is *denial;* traits express *passivity* and *withdrawal.*

Eurethral complex: Major defenses resemble the anal character type; traits stress *competitiveness* or *acquiescence.*

NEEDS. A major contribution of uncertain relation to the rest of the theory is the concept of *need,* which is defined as an entity that organizes perception, apperception, intellection, conation, and action so as to transform in a certain direction an existing, unsatisfying situation. A list of 40 needs (e.g., achievement, power, affiliation, nurturance) is offered, along with several overlapping classifications of their functions and attributes. Needs are triggered by *press,* or environmental forces, real or perceived, that have arousing properties. Associated with the need concept is the *need-integrate,* or set of stable values and action patterns that are learned as a function of need expression.

ERIKSON'S THEORY (CONFLICT, PSYCHOSOCIAL) . . . . .

Core of Personality

CORE TENDENCY. Similar to Freud, but with a definite emphasis on some part of functioning that is not determined by the attempt to avoid conflict between individual and society.

CORE CHARACTERISTICS

Id: Similar to Freud.

Ego: Similar to Freud, but with considerable

elaboration of ego processes (such as rational thought and realistic perception) that are unrelated to the conflict between id and society. Ego is believed to be partially innate and to have a facsimile of its own instincts.

Superego: Similar to Freud.

Development

PSYCHOSEXUAL STAGES. Similar to Freud, but with biological sexuality deemphasized in favor of the psychosocial features of conflict between child and parents. Development is seen as a process extending throughout life, which is divided into either periods or stages. In all stages, the amount of conflict determines whether the positive or negative pole is learned. The greater the conflict, the more likely the negative pole.

Trust versus mistrust (similar to Freud's oral stage), in which the issue is whether the child can feel dependent on and comfortable with others.

Autonomy versus shame and doubt (similar to Freud's anal stage), in which the issue is whether the child can feel independent of others.

Initiative and responsibility versus guilty functioning (similar to Freud's phallic stage), in which the issue is whether the youngster can feel competent and be active.

Industry versus inferiority (similar to Freud's latency stage), in which the issue is whether the youngster can feel satisfied in working hard.

Identity versus role diffusion (puberty to the end of adolescence), in which conflict is produced by the socially imposed task of becoming an independent and effective adult and the difficulty for the adolescent of performing this task.

Intimacy versus isolation (young adulthood), in which conflict is produced by the socially imposed task of developing close and comprehensive relationships and the difficulty of doing so.

Generativity versus stagnation (middle adulthood), in which conflict is produced by the socially imposed task of forgoing one's own immediate concerns in favor of fostering children and others and the difficulty in doing this.

Ego integrity versus despair (middle adulthood through death), in which conflict is produced by the decrease in important social and biological roles as old age approaches and the difficulty in accepting this.

FIXATION. Similar to Freud in that conflict is intensified through excessive deprivation or indulgence.

Periphery of Personality

Erikson is not explicit but presumably assumes *character types* comprising combinations of the sets of *traits* related to the eight stages of development. As development continues throughout life, one must know not only a person's history of fixation but also his or her approximate age to access the individual's personality. For example, a person in late adulthood who had not experienced fixations would show ego integrity, generativity, intimacy, identity, industry, initiative, autonomy, and trust, whereas a person also without fixations but only in young adulthood probably would not yet show generativity and ego integrity. Whenever a fixation occurs, it is likely to jeopardize sound development in subsequent stages as well. Thus, a young adult who shows isolation rather than intimacy is likely also to exhibit at least one negative quality relevant to earlier stages.

OBJECT-RELATIONS THEORY (CONFLICT, PSYCHOSOCIAL).....

Core of Personality

CORE TENDENCY. *To develop a self.* This tendency, according to most object-relations theorists, is parallel to but independent of (and perhaps even more basic than) the Freudian core tendency.

CORE CHARACTERISTICS. The components of the self, namely,

Self-image, or what one thinks of and expects from oneself.

Object-images, or what one thinks of and expects from other people.

Affect-dispositions, or tendencies toward emotional states that reflect how one felt during formative interpersonal relations.

Development

STAGES OF SELF-DIFFERENTIATION AND INTEGRATION

Autism (first several months of life), in which there is little differentiation of self and objects (others). Characterized by the defense mechanism of *splitting,* or vacillation between the ways of being of self and others as a response to feeling overwhelmed.

Symbiosis (about 2 to 7 months of age), in which there is some differentiation of self and other but frequent confusion of the two. Characterized by the gradual diminution of splitting, if development is ideal, in favor of the defense of *introjection* (literal incorporation of objects into the mind). Self and object, though differentiated, remain an inseparable unit in the child's mind.

Differentiation (from 1 to 2 years of age), in which self and objects are clearly separate, are no longer confused, and have separate destinies. Characterized by the process of *identification,* usually regarded as a defense, in which objects have influence on the child through his or her imitation of them.

Integration (beyond 2 years of age), in which the self and object representations independently perceived are fit into relationship with each other. Although identification processes are still important, the self is sufficiently formed to constitute an *identity,* definite and unique. It is unclear whether this stage is defensive or nondefensive under ideal developmental conditions.

DEVELOPMENTAL IMPLICATIONS OF INTER-ACTIONS. Also unclear is the precise nature of interactions, between the child and others, as ideal and nonideal. Presumably something like the Freudian notion that there should not be too much frustration or indulgence operates for object-relations theorists.

Periphery of Personality

MATURE SELF-IDENTITY. Deep and stable relations with others, tolerance of ambivalence toward loved objects, capacity for tolerating guilt and separation, having an integrated self-concept, and correspondence between behavior patterns and self-concept.

PATHOLOGICAL STATES. Three levels of self-pathology are mentioned. Important are how disintegrated the self is, how punitive the superego is, and how much social relations and work are impaired. Many of the traditional neuroses and psychoses are subsumed under self-pathology.

KOHUT'S SELF-PSYCHOLOGY (CONFLICT, PSYCHOSOCIAL).....

Core of Personality

CORE TENDENCY. To *enhance and order functioning through the experience of self.* When it has developed well, the self is a consciously appreciated sense of who and what one is that lends meaning and direction to behavior.

CORE CHARACTERISTICS

Need to be mirrored, expressed in the child's wish to have its expressions and products recognized, approved of, and admired. The most important mirroring person in the child's life is the mother. Early mirroring experiences underlie *ambitions.*

Need to idealize, expressed in the child's admiration of and identification with others more powerful and developed than itself. The most important object of idealization in the child's life is the father. Early idealization experiences underlie *goals*.

Development

The *nuclear self* emerges during the second year of life if development is ideal. This nuclear self is defined as bipolar, including archaic nuclear ambition on the one hand and archaic nuclear goals on the other. The "tension arc" between these two poles stimulates the expression (and hence development) of the child's rudimentary skills and talents.

CONDITIONS FOR IDEAL DEVELOPMENT. The mother must mirror her child, and the father must permit himself to be idealized. When parents are too preoccupied, ungenerous, or unable to accept their own selves, the child's development will be jeopardized.

Periphery of Personality

AUTONOMOUS SELF. This ideal type is characterized by *self-esteem* and *self-confidence*. One is not dependent on others and has both *ambition*, in a general sense, and specific *goals*. *Talents* and *skills* are developed in the service of ambitions and goals.

NARCISSISTIC PERSONALITY DISORDERS. Involve thought processes more than action:

The *understimulated self* (resulting from lack of parental response) will do anything (e.g., promiscuity, perversion, gambling, drug and alcohol abuse, hypersociability) to create excitement and ward off feelings of deadness.

The *fragmented self* (resulting from lack of parental response) is extremely vulnerable to setbacks, responding with disorganization and a sharp decrease in self-esteem.

The *overstimulated self* (resulting from excessive parental response) shies away from creative and leadership activities for fear of being flooded by unrealistic fantasies of greatness.

The *overburdened self* (resulting primarily from frustrated idealizing need) perceives others as hostile, reacting with irritability and suspicion to minor events as frustrations or attacks.

NARCISSISTIC BEHAVIOR DISORDERS. Expressed primarily in action rather than in thought:

The *mirror-hungry personality* (resulting from failure to mirror parental response) is famished for admiration, leading to incessant displays in an insatiable attempt to get attention.

The *ideal-hungry personality* (resulting from lack of parental response) can experience self as real only when related to others who conform slavishly to the person, though full satiation of the hunger is never really achieved.

Other types mentioned are considered frankly pathological.

BERNE'S TRANSACTIONAL ANALYSIS (CONFLICT, PSYCHOSOCIAL) ....

Core of Personality

CORE TENDENCY. *To strive for a socially satisfying and meaningful life*. Something like the Freudian instincts and their gratifications are still there, but increasingly they form the background, with social and psychological matters gaining greater emphasis. There is little to suggest the assumption of necessary, inevitable conflict.

CORE CHARACTERISTICS. In addition to the usual biological survival drives (which are relatively unimportant), there are the following psychological needs:

Stroke hunger, for physical contact of a soothing sort.

Structure hunger, which refers specifically to how people invest their lives with meaning by deciding how to fill up their time.

Excitement hunger, which recognizes that people wish not to be bored.

Recognition hunger, for social approval and respect.

Leadership hunger, which shows people's need for influence and control.

EGO STATES. All people have within them the *Child* (dependent, biologically oriented, undisciplined views of life), the *Parent* (morally oriented, disciplined, authoritative views of life), and the *Adult* (unevaluative, realistic perceptions of life). The content of these three ego states is influenced by learning.

Development

No specific position is taken.

Periphery of Personality

At the moment there is no definitive statement on types, but there are some leads.

LIFE SCRIPT. A plan (typically not conscious) that organizes energies and direction. It develops through parental interaction and other cultural forces (e.g., fairy tales). All scripts include a *life position,* or learned assumptions about acceptability of self and others. The four basic life positions are "I'm OK and you're OK," "I'm OK but you're not OK," "I'm not OK but you're OK," and "Neither you nor I are OK."

GAMES. A series of social transactions with a well-defined climax or *gimmick.* The particular life position and script influences the games that are played. Examples of games are *Alcoholic, Debtor, Kick Me, Frigid Woman,* and *Look How Hard I've Tried.*

EGO STATES. Games and life scripts involve various configurations of the three ego states: Child, Parent, and Adult.

RANK'S THEORY (CONFLICT, INTRAPSYCHIC) .....

Core of Personality

CORE TENDENCY. *To minimize the fear of life while minimizing the fear of death.* Because these two fears are inherent and opposed, conflict is inevitable and compromise must be sought.

CORE CHARACTERISTICS

Fear of life, where *life* refers to the inevitable process of separation and individualization, starting with being born and continuing through being weaned, locomoting independently, leaving the home for school, and so forth.

Fear of death, where *death* refers to the inherent tendency toward union, fusion, and dependency.

The *will,* or organized sense of who and what one is that in its most vigorous form is not defensive and functions to establish a basis for minimizing the fears of both life and death.

Development

COUNTERWILL AND WILL. Soon after birth, the child begins to differentiate between self and others and develops a rudimentary form of the will. This is the *counterwill* and involves the child's learning that he or she can say no to the pressures of adults and to his or her own impulses. If this negativistic counterwill shatters the union between child and parents, the result will be *guilt* (a specialized expression of fear of life). But if union between child and parent is not shattered, counterwill will mature into will. No precise developmental stages are specified.

Periphery of Personality

PERSONALITY TYPES COMPOSED OF TRAITS

Artist: Expresses ideal development, in which

the fears of life and death are effectively minimized and will is strong. Characterized by high degree of *differentiation* and *integration* of thoughts, feelings, and actions; *intimacy* without slavish loyalties or concern for propriety; creation of products that are *unusual* but also *useful*.

Neurotic person: Expresses the tendency toward separation (fear of death) but has denied the tendency toward union (fear of life) and shows counterwill more than will. Such people have committed themselves to the pain of separation from the herd but have not, like the artist, also won through to constructive interactions with the world. They are *hostile, negativistic, arrogant, isolationistic, critical of others, guilty,* and so on. When developing counterwill, they were made to feel wrong and unworthy.

Average person: Expresses the tendency toward union (fear of life) but has denied the tendency toward separation (fear of death). Out of fear of life, such people never entertain the possibility of their own individuality. They are *conforming, dependable, superficial, suggestible,* and *self-satisfied.* The developmental handicap is an overwhelming negative response of parents to first expressions of counterwill.

ANGYAL'S THEORY (CONFLICT, INTRAPSYCHIC) .....

Core of Personality

CORE TENDENCY. *To maximize both the expression of autonomy and the expression of surrender.* Autonomy and surrender are inherent and opposing tendencies; thus, conflict is inevitable and compromise must be sought.

CORE CHARACTERISTICS. *Autonomy* refers to separation from others and the physical environment, with emphasis on independence and aloofness. *Surrender* refers to functioning that leads to merger or union with other people, ideals, or the inanimate environment, with emphasis on dependency. Expressing both characteristics leads to simultaneous differentiation and integration. Relevant to Angyal's theorizing about the interaction between the person and the environment is the concept of *biosphere,* which encompasses individuals and their worlds. The personality is one component of the biosphere. The *symbolic self* is the sum of the person's self-conceptions, but little specification of its content is available.

Development

No specific position is taken.

Periphery of Personality

Although the distinction is made between periphery and core, little specification of periphery is offered. Of possible relevance is the notion of *dimensions* (which may be somewhat like traits):

Vertical dimension: Refers at one pole to concrete, overt behavior and at the other to deep, underlying forces.

Progressive dimension: Comprises a series of surface actions, which are organized in such fashion as to bring the person nearer to a goal.

Transverse dimension: Involves the coordination of discrete actions into a larger, better integrated, and more effective behavior unit (e.g., the type).

BAKAN'S THEORY (CONFLICT, INTRAPSYCHIC) .....

Core of Personality

CORE TENDENCY. *To maximize the expression of both agency and communion.* Agency and communion are inherent, opposed tendencies; thus, conflict is inevitable and compromise must be sought.

CORE CHARACTERISTICS

Agency: Separation from others and the physical environment, with emphasis on manipulativeness.

Communion: Merging with or joining other people, ideas, or the inanimate environment, with emphasis on unity.

Development

No specific position is taken.

Periphery of Personality

No formal position is taken, although implicit emphasis is put on the importance of living according to the compromise involving expression of both agency and communion. The result is simultaneous differentiation and integration. When agency is expressed with communion denied, the result is psychological or physical illness.

PERLS'S GESTALT THERAPY (CONFLICT, INTRAPSYCHIC) . . . . .

Core of Personality

CORE TENDENCY. *To strive to comprehend life by identifying bits of experience and construing them in relationships of simultaneous attraction and repulsion.* Intrapsychic conflict is a characteristic of mental life in this theory.

CORE CHARACTERISTICS

Bits: Things, events, times, places, people, parts of a person, and so on. The person breaks up experience into *bits* in an attempt to comprehend what is going on.

Process: Two bits and a happening. A *happening* is the simultaneous attraction and repulsion that characterizes all relationships between bits. The whole involved in the process is sometimes called a *gestalt.*

Personality: Composed of *being* (the biological organism construed by the mind), *self* (awareness of one's dimensions and purposes as distinct from others and nature), and *self-image* (what one ought to want to be).

Development

THREE PHASES OR MODES OF THINKING

Social phase, developmentally earliest, is so named because the child requires interaction with others for survival. The child begins to develop an awareness of others as they aid and frustrate her or him.

Psychosocial phase, which encompasses most of life, involves awareness of self and resultant sharpening of social awareness. Most construing of bits and relationships takes place at this time, as does the emergence of personality.

Spiritual phase, or an intuitive apprehension of meanings beyond being, self, and self-image. Not everyone reaches this phase.

ACKNOWLEDGMENT AND APPROBATION. Progression from one phase to another is hastened by these reactions from others. *Acknowledgment* refers to recognition of the person and his or her actions by others. It implies acceptance with little criticality. *Approbation* is critical (positive or negative) response from others.

Periphery of Personality

No firm position is taken. In ideal development, the relationships between bits run their course and end, whereupon the bits enter into other relationships with other bits. Thus, new occasions of conflict are always being born, and the personality has fluidity. In the nonideal state, some particular relationship between some bits will become frozen, presumably through failures of acknowledgment or negative approbation. These frozen relationships are called *blisters,* which are as close to personality types as this position comes. The aim of psychotherapy is to remove blisters.

JUNG'S THEORY (CONFLICT, INTRAPSYCHIC) .....

Core of Personality

CORE TENDENCY. *To attain selfhood.* Selfhood represents a balance between the opposing forces of personality and includes both conscious and unconscious material. Energy concepts instrumental in achieving selfhood are the *principle of equivalence* (if the value of any aspect of personality increases or decreases, this shift will be compensated for by an opposite shift in another aspect) and the *principle of entropy* (the distribution of energy in the personality seeks an equilibrium, or balance). Of uncertain relationship to the rest is the *transcendent function,* which aims to integrate personality elements into a whole.

CORE CHARACTERISTICS

The *ego* (or conscious, individualistic mind), which is in conflict with the *personal unconscious* (formed of socially unacceptable mental content that was once conscious but has been forced out of awareness by defenses).

The *collective unconscious* (a communal, species memory, never achieving consciousness, representing the accumulated experiences of humankind and possibly even subhuman life). Composed of archetypes, or essences (universal forms) that predispose one toward characteristically human thoughts and feelings. Although these thoughts and feelings can become conscious, the underlying archetypes cannot. Major archetypes include the *shadow* (the animalistic possibilities of people), the *anima* (the feminine possibility in people), the *animus* (the masculine possibility in people), and the *persona* (the conventional mask adopted by people in the face of social pressures).

Development

There is little emphasis on stages, though a distinction is made between early life and later adulthood. In early life, sexuality and the individualistic concerns of the ego dominate. In later adulthood, there is a shift to spirituality and the universal emphases of the collective unconscious. Concepts employed in understanding development are

Causality (influence on behavior of the past) versus *teleology* (influence on behavior of the anticipated future).

Progression (forward thrust) versus *regression* (shrinking to a safe past).

Sublimation (energy transformed from primitive to cultural spiritual concerns) versus *repression* (defensive blocking of consciousness and energy).

Periphery of Personality

PERSONALITY TYPES COMPOSED OF ORIENTATIONS AND MODES

Introversive-rational: Oriented toward the inner world of experience (introversion). Emphasizes either the thinking or the feeling modes (both are considered rational in that they involve evaluation of experience). Subtypes are introversive-thinking and introversive-feeling.

Extroversive-rational: Oriented toward the outer world of experience (extroversion). Emphasizes either the thinking or the feeling modes, leading to subtypes extroversive-thinking and extroversive-feeling.

Introversive-irrational: Oriented toward the inner world of experience (introversion). Emphasizes either the sensing or the intuiting modes (both are considered irrational in that they passively record but do not evaluate experience). Subtypes are introversive-sensing and introversive-intuiting.

Extroversive-irrational: Oriented toward the outer world of experience (extroversion). Emphasizes either sensing or intuiting modes, leading to the subtypes extroversive-sensing and extroversive-intuiting.

Selfhood: The ideal peripheral personality. Involves a form of transcendence of the other personality types such that the introversion-extroversion and rational-irrational modes are balanced. Selfhood can be approached but never completely attained.

ROGERS'S THEORY (FULFILLMENT, ACTUALIZATION) ....

Core of Personality

CORE TENDENCY. *To actualize one's inherent potentialities.* This tendency serves to maintain and enhance living not only for the individual but also for the species. Because there is nothing in inherent potentialities that is unacceptable to society, conflict is not inevitable. The actualizing tendency, as stated, is common to all living things. In humans, the tendency takes the additional form of the *attempt to actualize the self.*

CORE CHARACTERISTICS. Important to the *self-actualization tendency* are the need for positive regard, the need for positive self-regard, and the self. Both needs are offshoots of the self-actualizing tendency. The *need for positive regard* (from other people) renders one influenceable by social approval and disapproval. The *need for positive self-regard* refers to the satisfaction involved in finding one's experience of oneself consistent with one's self-concept. The *self* refers to one's conscious sense of who and what one is.

Development

No developmental stages are specified. In general, the important consideration is whether the person receives *unconditional positive regard* (basic, complete acceptance and respect) or *conditional positive regard* (acceptance of some and rejection of other behaviors) from significant others. If unconditional positive regard is received, the self-concept (view of oneself) will reflect all that there is in the inherent potentialities; that is,

the self will be *congruent* with the potentialities. But if the person encounters conditional positive regard, he or she will develop *conditions of worth* (evaluative notions concerning which behaviors are worthy and which unworthy). The self-concept will have been socially determined and therefore will be *incongruent* with the inherent potentialities. To keep this incongruence from becoming conscious and, hence, the source of *anxiety* concerning unworthiness, *defenses* are instituted. Defensive functioning involves either *repression* or *distortion.*

Periphery of Personality

PERSONALITY TYPES COMPOSED OF TRAITS. For all his emphasis on individuality, Rogers specifies only the following two personality types. Subclassifications within each broad category might be possible if the contents of inherent potentialities were stated.

Fully functioning person (or ideal person): Has received unconditional positive regard. Hence, there are no conditions of worth, no defensiveness, and congruence between self and potentialities. Such people are characterized by *openness to experience* (emotional depth and reflectiveness), *existential living* (flexibility, adaptability, spontaneity, and inductive thinking), *organismic trusting* (intuitive living, self-reliance, confidence), *experiential freedom* (subjective sense of free will), and *creativity* (penchant for producing new and effective ideas and things).

Maladjusted person: Has received conditional positive regard. Therefore, there are *conditions of worth, incongruence* between self and *potentialities,* and *defensiveness.* Also, such people *live according to a preconceived plan* rather than existentially, *disregard their organism* rather than trust it, *feel manipulated* rather than free, and *feel common and conforming* rather than creative.

MASLOW'S THEORY (FULFILLMENT, ACTUALIZATION) ....

Core of Personality

CORE TENDENCIES. *The push toward actualization of inherent potentialities and the push to satisfy needs ensuring physical and psychological survival.* The actualizing tendency leads to the enhancement of life (called *growth motivation*), whereas the survival tendency merely ensures the maintenance of life (called *deprivation motivation*). Although these tendencies are hierarchically organized such that the survival tendency must be satisfied before the actualization tendency can be strongly expressed, they are not really in conflict with each other.

CORE CHARACTERISTICS. Associated with the survival tendency are *physiological needs* (food, water, etc.), *safety needs* (avoidance of pain), *needs for belongingness and love* (intimacy, gregariousness, identification), and *esteem needs* (approval of self and others). Each of these needs becomes important only when those preceding it are satisfied. When all the needs associated with survival are satisfied, those associated with actualization become salient. They are the *need for self-actualization* (emphasis on the person's special capabilities) and the *need for cognitive understanding* (emphasis on information and stimulation hunger).

Development

Not much specification, though what there is agrees with Rogers. If the survival tendency is not blocked by other people, the actualization tendency will be vigorously expressed. Blockage leads to defense.

Periphery of Personality

PERSONALITY TYPE COMPOSED OF TRAITS AND VALUES. The *self-actualized person* (has had satisfaction of the survival tendency) is characterized by *realistic orientation; acceptance* of self, others, and natural works; *spontaneity; task orientation* (rather than self-preoccupation); *sense of privacy; independence;* vivid *appreciativeness; spirituality* that is not necessarily religious in a formal sense; *sense of identity with mankind;* feelings of *intimacy* with a few loved ones; *democratic values;* recognition of the *difference between means and ends; humor* that is philosophical rather than hostile; *creativeness;* and *nonconformism.*

THE FIVE-FACTOR POSITION OF COSTA AND MCRAE (FULFILLMENT, ACTUALIZATION) ....

Core of Personality

CORE TENDENCY. *Striving to express in behavior the thoughts, feelings, and actions that best reflect one's inherent pattern on the five factors.* There may be differences among people in whether they are high or low on the five factors, or source traits. These differences are inherent, influence all of functioning, and change only in the sense of biological maturation (not learning).

CORE CHARACTERISTICS. The five factors, or source traits, present in varying degrees in all people are *neuroticism* (anxiety, anger, and depression), *extroversion* (warmth, gregariousness, and assertiveness), *openness to experience* (fantasy, aesthetics, and feelings), *agreeableness* (trust, straightforwardness, and altruism), and *conscientiousness* (competence, order, and dutifulness). These source traits are considered inherited and unaffected by cultural and familiar influences.

Development

Although this position accepts that expressing one's inherent five-factor pattern in interactions with the outside world leads to learned patterns of thoughts, feelings and actions, no specific position is taken on development. It is unclear what kinds of interactions and situational forces are important or formative, and no explicit position is taken on ideal development.

Periphery of Personality

It is assumed that *adaptations, biographies,* and *self-concepts* will develop as people interact with their environments. *Adaptations* appear to be specific habits or activities directly expressing source traits. *Biographies* are complex patterns of all the adaptations that are evoked by situations. And *self-concepts* are cognitive-affective views of oneself that are available to consciousness. Although biographies are a bit reminiscent of types, and adaptations of concrete characteristics, the five-factor model is not very clear or developed concerning the periphery of personality.

ADLER'S THEORY (FULFILLMENT, PERFECTION) ....

Core of Personality

CORE TENDENCY. *To strive toward superiority or perfection.* This tendency applies to functioning not only as an individual but also as a member of society. Hence, there is no necessary conflict between the person and society. An earlier form of the core tendency, the *will to power,* had more competitive implications.

CORE CHARACTERISTICS. The bases of the perfection tendency are *organ inferiorities* (actual physical weaknesses and incapacities), *feelings of inferiority* (psychic states of inferiority regardless of physical condition), and *compensation* (the attempt to overcome real or imagined inferiorities). The direction of the compensations can be seen by the nature of the inferiorities but also by the ideals of perfect living (which are called *fictional finalisms*). There is also the somewhat mysterious notion of *creative self,* which essentially expresses people's capability of exercising free will to transcend the forces acting on them.

Development

No stages are postulated. Instead, there is emphasis on family constellation and family atmosphere. *Family constellation* refers to the sociological facts of the family as they affect each member. Included are such matters as birth order of the child and presence or absence of the father. *Family atmosphere* refers more to the quality of emotional relationship among family members. Family constellation affects development by giving the child a particular set of problems (e.g., only child or oldest child) with which to cope. Family atmosphere influences whether the child is active or passive and constructive or destructive in striving toward perfection. Cooperative atmospheres of mutual trust and respect encourage constructiveness, whereas the opposite atmosphere encourages destructiveness. Family emphasis on personal initiative encourages activeness, while the opposite atmosphere encourages passiveness.

Periphery of Personality

STYLES OF LIFE COMPOSED OF FICTIONAL FINALISMS AND TRAITS

Active-constructive style: Includes the fictional finalism of *service* and the set of traits that can be summarized as *ambitiousness* or orientation toward success. This style may be the Adlerian ideal.

Passive-constructive style: Includes the fictional finalism of *attention getting* and the set of traits summarized as *charm,* or receiving special attention for what one is rather than for what one does. This style is also considered desirable.

Active-destructive style: Includes the fictional finalisms of abrogation of *power,* achievement of *revenge,* and the bid to be *left alone.* The traits include *being a nuisance, rebelliousness, viciousness,* and *degeneration.*

Passive-destructive style: Includes the fictional finalisms mentioned for the active-destructive style, as well as the traits of *laziness, stubbornness, passive aggression,* and *despair.*

WHITE'S THEORY (FULFILLMENT, PERFECTION) ....

Core of Personality

CORE TENDENCY. *To produce effects through one's actions (effectance motivation) and to achieve competence in one's functioning (competence motivation).* Probably effectance motivation occurs first and with maturation becomes competence motivation.

CORE CHARACTERISTICS. Associated with effectance motivation is the requirement of the nervous system for *information*, or stimulation. Associated with competence motivation is *actual competence* and *sense of competence,* though it is not yet clear what role in personality these characteristics play.

Development

Not specified, though White adopts some of the most psychosocial (least biological) features of Erikson's views on the eight developmental stages.

Periphery of Personality

Not specified extensively, but partially endorses Erikson's emphases on trust versus mistrust and so on.

ALLPORT'S THEORY (FULFILLMENT, PERFECTION) ....

Core of Personality

CORE TENDENCIES. *To function in a manner expressive of the self or proprium (propriate functioning) and to satisfy biological survival needs (opportunistic functioning).* The self is phenomenologically defined, and functioning in terms of it is considered more important, human, and extraordinary than functioning in terms of survival needs. There is little real conflict between the two tendencies. The survival tendency must be satisfied first, but once it is, the attempt to express the self becomes paramount.

CORE CHARACTERISTICS. Opportunistic functioning involves biological characteristics such as the *needs for food, water,* and *air.* Propriate functioning includes *sense of body, self-identity, self-esteem, self-extension, rational coping, self-image,* and *propriate striving.* Propriate functioning is *proactive* (influences the world), whereas opportunistic functioning is *reactive* (is influenced by the world).

Development

No specific stages are postulated. It is assumed that the organism is opportunistic at birth and that it requires nurturance and affection. If the biological needs are satisfied easily, propriate functioning will develop vigorously. The first signs of a sense of body begin to develop by the end of the first year. The second and third years see the beginnings of self-identity and then self-image. From 6 to 12, the rational coping qualities of the proprium become apparent. In adolescence, propriate striving is in increasing evidence. Although the various propriate functions begin their development at different times, they all act interdependently by the time adulthood is reached. All this presupposes nurturance and support of the child early in life. If this does not occur, propriate development will not be vigorous, and opportunistic functioning will continue to predominate in adulthood. The process of shifting from opportunistic to propriate functioning involves the principle of *functional autonomy,* which indicates that a behavior pattern originally instrumental to satisfaction of a biological need can persist as a fully independent aspect of living even after the biological need is no longer an important force.

Periphery of Personality

No typology is offered. The major peripheral characteristic is the *personal disposition,* which is a generalized neuropsychic structure (peculiar to the individual) with the capacity to render many stimuli functionally equivalent and to initiate and guide consistent (equivalent) forms of adaptive and stylistic behavior. Personal dispositions can be primarily *dynamic* (motivational) or *expressive* (stylistic). Personal dispositions are virtually unique to individuals, and are thus expressive of individuality. In studying personal dispositions, Allport advocates the *morphogenic* (idiographic) approach, in which laws applying to individuals rather than groups are sought. Of secondary importance is the concept of *common trait,* an abstraction that describes the average rather than individual case. To study common traits, one adopts a *nomothetic* approach, which seeks to arrive at laws by generalizing across people.

With Allport's strong emphasis on individuality, it is not surprising that little specification of content for personal dispositions is offered. The closest Allport comes to content specification is in his criteria of maturity: enduring *extensions of the self;* techniques for *warm relating to others* (such as tolerance); stable *emotional security* or self-acceptance; habits of *realistic perception;* focus on *problem solving;* established *self-objectification* in the form of *insight* and *humor;* and a *unifying philosophy of life,* including particular *value orientations,* differentiated *religious sentiment,* and a generic, *personalized conscience.* In stable aspects of behavior, these criteria of maturity seem to be the results of expressing the propriate functions.

FROMM'S THEORY (FULFILLMENT, PERFECTION)....

Core of Personality

CORE TENDENCY. *To express one's human nature.* A person's human nature differs radically from his or her animal nature. Yet the two are not really in conflict (1) because one's animal nature is the least important thing about one and (2) because one's animal nature is usually satisfied continuously.

CORE CHARACTERISTICS

Need for relatedness (to be in contact with people and physical nature).

Need for transcendence (to be separate from other people and things).

Need for rootedness (to have a sense of belongingness).

Need for identity (to know who and what one is).

Need for a frame of reference (to have a stable way of perceiving and comprehending the world).

Development

There are three types of relationship between parents and child: *symbiotic relatedness,* in which the people are related but never attain independence; *withdrawal-destructiveness,* in which there is a negative relatedness or distance and indifference; and *love,* in which there is mutual respect, support, and appreciation. Development is more a function of the type of relationship between child and parents than one of stages.

Periphery of Personality

ORIENTATIONS (OR TYPES) COMPOSED OF TRAITS

Receptive orientation: Stems from the masochistic patterns of behavior learned by the child who is the passive party in a symbiotic relationship with its parents. In this orientation, people feel the source of all good to be outside themselves and expect to receive things passively. Typical traits show *passivity, lack of character, submissiveness,* and *cowardliness.*

Exploitative orientation: Stems from the sadistic behavior patterns learned by the child who is the dominant party in a symbiotic relationship with the parents. In this orientation, people believe the source of all good to be outside themselves but do not expect to receive it so much as take it forcibly. Typical traits show *aggression, egocentrism, conceit, arrogance,* and *seductiveness.*

Hoarding orientation: Stems from the behavior pattern of destructiveness learned by the child who is reacting to parental withdrawal in the withdrawal-destructiveness type of relationship. In this orientation, there is little faith in anything new to be obtained from the outside world; security is based on hoarding and saving what one already has. Typical traits are *stinginess, unimaginativeness, suspiciousness, stubbornness,* and *possessiveness.*

Marketing orientation: Stems from the behavior pattern of withdrawal learned by the child who is reacting to parental destructiveness in the withdrawal-destructiveness type of relationship. In this orientation, the person experiences self as a commodity obeying the laws of supply and demand and has the values of the marketplace. Typical traits are *opportunism, inconsistency, aimlessness, lack of principle, relativism,* and *wastefulness.*

Productive orientation: Stems from the behavior patterns learned through a loving relationship with the parents. In this orientation, the person values self and others for what they are and experiences security and inner peace. Typical traits reflect the potentially useful aspects of the other orientations (e.g., *modesty, adaptability, trust, activeness, pride, confidence, practicality, patience, loyalty, flexibility, openmindedness,* and *experimenting spirit.* Clearly the productive orientation is Fromm's ideal.

EXISTENTIAL PSYCHOLOGY (FULFILLMENT, PERFECTION) ....

Core of Personality

CORE TENDENCY. *To achieve authentic being. Being* signifies the special quality of human mentality (called *intentionality*) that makes life a series of decisions, each involving an alternative that precipitates people into an unknown future and an alternative that pushes them back into a routine predictable past. Choosing the unknown future brings *ontological anxiety* (fear of the unknown), whereas choosing the safe status quo brings *ontological guilt* (sense of missed opportunity). Authenticity involves accepting this

painful state of affairs and finding the *courage* or *hardiness* to persist in the face of ontological anxiety and choose the future, thereby minimizing ontological guilt.

CORE CHARACTERISTICS. *Being-in-the-world* emphasizes the unity of person and environment, since, in this heavily phenomenological position, both are personally or subjectively defined. Being-in-the-world has three components: *Umwelt* (the construed biological and physical world), *Mitwelt* (the construed social world), and *Eigenwelt* (the internal dialogue of relationship to oneself). It is assumed that behind these three components lie the person's inherent biological, social, and psychological (symbolization, imagination, and judgment) needs.

Development

EARLY DEVELOPMENT. The period during which the child is dependent and requires parental guidance in order to develop *courage.* Ideally, parents (1) expose the child to a richness of experience, (2) freely impose limits expressing their own views, (3) love and respect the child as a budding individual, and (4) teach the value of vigorous symbolization, imagination, and judgment directly and by example. Experiencing these things, the child develops courage, or the willingness to consider what is *facticity* and what *possibility,* and the tendency to chose the *future* rather than the *past,* tolerating *ontological anxiety* (fear of unknown) rather than building up *ontological guilt* (sense of missed opportunity).

LATER DEVELOPMENT. Begins when courage has been developed (presumably sometime in adolescence, if conditions have been ideal). This period, which continues throughout life, involves self-initiated learning from failures. There are two transitional stages to go through before authenticity or individuality can be reached. The first is the *aesthetic phase,* which takes place as soon as the person leaves the family. It is characterized by living in the moment (without regard for past or future) and failing to form deep relationships. The loneliness and aimlessness of this orientation teaches the person her or his short-comings. Thus, the *idealistic phase* begins, characterized by undying commitments and uncompromising principles. Sooner or later the person recognizes, through failures, that commitments cannot be made forever and that the relationship between principles and any particular people or events is problematic. With this learning, the phase of authenticity or individuality begins.

NONIDEAL DEVELOPMENT. If the conditions for learning courage are not present during early development, later development never really takes place. In other words, the person is unable to discern facticity and possibility, does not choose the future, and shrinks from failure too often to learn anything from it.

Periphery of Personality

PERSONALITY TYPES EMPHASIZING SELF-DEFINITION AND WORLD VIEW

Authenticity or *individuality* (ideal type) involves defining oneself as having a mental life permitting comprehension and influence over one's own social and biological experiences. The world view is characterized by considering society the creation of people and properly in their service. The individualist's functioning has unity and shows originality and change. Biological and social experiencing show subtlety, taste, intimacy, and love. Doubt (or ontological anxiety) is experienced as a natural concomitant of creating one's own meaning and does not undermine the decision-making process. There is a minimum of ontological guilt, or sense of missed opportunity.

Conformism (nonideal type) is the expression in adulthood of not having learned courage in early development and, hence, being unable to learn from failures. The self-definition is nothing more than a player of social roles and an embodiment of biological needs. Expression of symbolization, imagination, and judgment is inhibited, leading to stereotyped, fragmentary functioning. Biological experiencing is isolated and undifferentiated, and social experiencing is contractual rather than intimate. The conformist feels worthless and insecure because of the buildup of ontological guilt through frequent choice of the past rather than the future. The relevant world view stresses materialism and pragmatism. This type represents a vulnerability to existential sickness, which tendency becomes an actuality when environmental stresses occur that are sufficient to disconfirm the conformist's self-definition and world view.

ELLIS'S RATIONAL-EMOTIVE THERAPY (FULFILLMENT, PERFECTION) . . . .

Core of Personality

CORE TENDENCIES. To *think irrationally and harm oneself and to gain understanding of one's folly, training oneself to change self-destructive ways.* This is not a conflict position, because the second tendency corrects the first. No compromise is advocated.

CORE CHARACTERISTICS. Various characteristics are implied, such as *self-pity* and *irrationality,* which express the personally destructive core tendency, and *patience* and *levelheadedness,* which express the constructive core tendency. However, very little systematic theorizing is available.

Development

Little systematic theorizing has been done. It is assumed that parents generally intensify the person's destructive, irrational tendencies.

Periphery of Personality

Little emphasis is given, the concern being mainly with psychotherapeutic considerations.

KELLY'S THEORY (CONSISTENCY, COGNITIVE DISSONANCE) . . . .

Core of Personality

CORE TENDENCY. *To predict and control the events one experiences.* The model adopted for understanding people is that of the scientist, construing events and subjecting the resulting constructs to testing, retaining those that are confirmed and rejecting or changing those that are disconfirmed.

CORE CHARACTERISTICS. *Constructs* are abstractions or generalizations from concrete experience. All constructs take the form of a dichotomy, with the two poles having opposite meanings (e.g., good-bad). Constructs are organized into *construction systems* on the basis of two hierarchical principles:

1. A construct may be superordinate to another, because each pole of the subordinate construct can form a part of the context for the two poles of the superordinate.

2. An entire construct may fit in one pole of another construct without relevance to the remaining pole.

In anticipating events, one selects the constructs that seem relevant and then chooses which poles of the relevant constructs to apply. Choosing the pole of the construct is called the *elaborative choice,* and it reflects deciding on the alternative through which one anticipates the greater possibility for extension and definition of one's construction system.

Although constructs that are disconfirmed by actual events are changed or discarded, Kelly is not explicit about the procedure for testing constructs. But he does indicate something of the emotional conditions surrounding construct disconfirmation and change:

Anxiety: The awareness that the events with which one is confronted lie outside the predictive capacity of one's construction system.

Hostility: The continued effort to extort validational evidence in favor of a social prediction that has already been recognized as a failure.

Guilt: The awareness of the self's dislodgement from one's core role structure.

Development

There is no consideration of development aside from the statements concerning the construing of events and the changing of disconfirmed constructs. The nature of significant relationships in childhood and adulthood is not considered important.

Periphery of Personality

There is no specification of typical constructs or organization of constructs into personal styles. Some differentiations concerning constructs are offered, however, that could be of use in understanding individual differences. Constructs differ in their degree of *permeability* (hitherto unencountered events can be subsumed within a construct that is permeable) and *preemptiveness* (a preemptive construct renders the events it subsumes unavailable for subsumption within other constructs). In addition, constructs can be *preverbal* (having no consistent word symbols to represent them), *comprehensive* (subsuming a wide variety of events), *incidental* (subsuming a narrow variety of events), *superordinate* (subsuming other constructs), *subordinate* (being included as an element of other constructs), and *loose* (leading to varying predictions while maintaining their identity).

EPSTEIN'S POSITION (CONSISTENCY, COGNITIVE DISSONANCE).................

Core of Personality

CORE TENDENCY. *The attempt to construct a harmonious personal theory of reality through mutually compatible views of the self, the world, and how they interconnect.* In this, people operate by trial and error in an ongoing attempt to make their implicit theory of reality conform to their experiences.

CORE CHARACTERISTICS. These fall into *content* and *process* classifications. As to content, everyone has a *self-theory,* a *world-theory,* and a theory about how they *interconnect.* Further, all people have inherent *needs for pleasure, coherence of the conceptual system, relatedness,* and *self-esteem.* As to process, there is a *rational-conceptual system,* an *experiential-conceptual system,* and a *primary-process system* for processing the information of experience. The rational-conceptual system operates according to logic and inference and is relatively slow, requiring deliberation. The experiential-conceptual system is more intuitive, emotional, and hedonic and operates very quickly. The primary-process system is unelaborated but likened to Freud's view of mental operations. Though not very clearly explicated, the overall goal is for the differences among the needs, information-processing systems, and resulting aspects of personal theories of reality to be organized harmoniously, through compromise if necessary.

Development

Although examples are given as to how certain social and environmental pressures can influence people to construe their experience, there is little systematic conceptualization concerning typical situations, interactions, or critical periods in development.

Periphery of Personality

Little is available about the typical types of personality that emanate from particular learning patterns. Once again, some examples are available, but no systematic theorizing has emerged.

McCLELLAND'S THEORY (CONSISTENCY, COGNITIVE DISSONANCE).................

Core of Personality

CORE TENDENCY. *To minimize large discrepancies between expectation and occurrence while maximizing small discrepancies between them.* People are perceived as craving small degrees of unpredictability to offset boredom and avoiding large degrees of unpredictability to avoid threat.

CORE CHARACTERISTICS. *Expectancies* are cognitive units, referring to what one believes will be the content and timing of events in the future. *Positive* (pleasurable) and *negative* (displeasurable) *affect* (emotion) are inherent reactions to small and large discrepancies between expectation and occurrence, respectively. Also on an inherent basis, positive affect leads to *approach,* whereas negative affect leads to *avoidance.*

Development

There is little emphasis on stages. Rather, the position states simply that if the parents arrange to make most of the child's experiences in a particular area of endeavor small rather than large discrepancies, the child will learn stable patterns of approach behavior for that area. If large discrepancies predominate, the child will learn stable patterns of avoidance behavior. If there is little discrepancy, the child will be indifferent to the area.

Periphery of Personality

No personality types are postulated. For peripheral characteristics, motives, traits, and schemata are offered.

A *motive* is a strong affective association characterized by an anticipatory goal reaction and based on past association of certain cues with positive or negative affect. In *approach motives,* people try to act so that their anticipations will indeed become a reality; in *avoidance motives,* people work to keep their anticipation from becoming a reality. Approach motives are the stable behavior patterns learned on the basis of a predominance of small discrepancies between expectation and occurrence. Avoidance motives result from large discrepancies between expectation and occurrence. McClelland adopts Murray's needs (e.g., achievement, affiliation, power), postulating an approach and an avoidance version of each one.

A *trait* is a learned tendency in people to react as they have reacted more or less successfully in the past in similar situations when similarly motivated. The trait, much like the *habit,* is not considered motivational because it leads to repetitive rather than goal-directed behavior. It is not clear how the trait is developed, and it almost certainly does not express the core tendency. No list of traits is offered.

A *schema* is a unit of cognition or mentation that symbolizes past experience. Three major classes of schemata are *ideas, values,* and *social roles.* For content, McClelland suggests that ideas and values primarily concern *economic, aesthetic, social, political, religious,* and purely *theoretical* realms. Social roles can be understood as involving *age, sex, family position, occupation,* and *reference-group membership.* The manner in which schemata are developed is not clearly specified, although they are considered to be cultural knowledge communicated socially. They also do not seem to express the core tendency.

Fiske and Maddi's Theory (Consistency, Activation) . . .

Core of Personality

CORE TENDENCY. *To maintain the level of activation to which one is accustomed (that is characteristic of one).* At any given moment, activation may be higher or lower than what is customary, leading to an avoidance of or search for additional activation.

CORE CHARACTERISTICS. Activation refers psychologically to excitement or tension and physiologically to the state of excitation in a postulated brain center. *Customary* or *characteristic activation* refers to the typical levels of activation a person experiences over the course of many days. The level of activation at any time is determined by the *impact of stimulation,* meaning the degree of *intensity, meaningfulness,* and *variety* of stimulation emanating from *internal* and *external sources.*

When the actual level of activation has fallen below what is customary, *impact-increasing behavior* occurs. When the actual level of activation is above what is customary, *impact-decreasing behavior* occurs.

Development

No specific developmental statements are made. However, it is assumed that early experience contributes to the development of a customary level of activation. Different customary levels of activation lead people to differ in the amount of activation they need. High-activation requirements lead to development of *needs* for stimulus *intensity, meaningfulness,* or *variety.* Low-activation requirements will lead to *fears* of stimulus *intensity, meaningfulness,* or *variety.* Further, it is assumed that some people learn to *anticipate* activation requirements well (through an *activeness trait*), whereas others frequently have to *correct* (through a *passiveness trait*) for discrepancies between actual and customary activation levels. The former show simultaneously increasing differentiation and integration of thoughts, feelings, and actions (future impact is increased by differentiation and decreased by integration). Also, it is assumed that some people learn to rely on external sources of stimulation and others on internal sources.

Periphery of Personality

PERSONALITY TYPES COMPOSED OF MOTIVES AND TRAITS

High-activation people with *active* and *external* traits will be "go-getters," seeking out challenges to meet in the physical and social environments. Such people will be energetic and voracious. If they also have a high *need for meaningfulness,* they will pursue causes and problems. But if they have a high *need for intensity,* they may pursue action and tumult per se. If they have a high *need for variety,* they will show curiosity, adventurousness, and impulsiveness.

High-activation people with *active* and *internal* traits will pursue impact through thinking, daydreaming, and responding to challenges posed by limitations of mind and body, with little regard for the tangible affairs of the external world. Such people will be subtle and complex. With a high *need for meaningfulness,* they will lead the life of the mind. With a high *need for intensity,* they will pursue sensations and emotions. With a high *need for variety,* they will strive for originality in creative endeavors.

Low-activation people with *active* and *external* traits will be external conservationists, bent on heading off social and physical disorganization and conflict by using negotiation and control. Such people will tend to be conformists and have simple tastes. If they also have a high *fear of meaningfulness,* they will try to oversimplify problems and avoid ambiguity. With a high *fear of intensity,* they will exert a dampening effect on vigorous, disorganized external events. If they have a high *fear of variety,* they will seek to force routine on the environment, preferring the familiar to the new.

Low-activation people with *active* and *internal* traits will be conservative with their own organisms by advocating the golden mean, taking care to avoid excesses and indulgences of any kind. Such people will be uncomplex and devoid of inconsistencies. With a high *fear of meaningfulness,* they will show absence of detailed or diverse thoughts and daydreams. With a high *fear of intensity,* they will have an especially ascetic aura. With a high *fear of variety,* they will force themselves to function consistently and stably, in a manner devoid of flamboyance.

Each of these personality types has a counterpart in which the passive rather than active trait occurs. All these passive personality types will seem similar to those with the active trait in stated aims, values, and interests. But on finer analysis, those with the passive trait will emerge as somewhat unable to practice what they preach. If high in activation requirements, they will be consumers rather than producers of impact. They will frequently be in the uncomfortable position of having to correct for activation levels that have become too low. If low in activation requirements, they will not actively and effectively manipulate the world or themselves to keep impact low. Instead, they will just try to renounce stimulation, ending frequently in the uncomfortable position of having to correct for actual activation levels that have become too high.

MODERATE BEHAVIORISM . . . .

Core of Personality

CORE TENDENCY. *To reduce tension or general drive. Tension* is defined as the somatic effect of drives.

CORE CHARACTERISTICS. The *primary drives* (e.g., hunger, thirst, sex, pain, avoidance, curiosity) are biological in nature, and their satisfaction is consistent with physical survival. *General drive* is the tension from all drives at any given time. Also relevant are the *primary reinforcements,* or the rewards and punishments corresponding to the primary drives (e.g., food, water, sexual experience, cessation of pain, information). Cognitive behaviorism now emphasizes memory and choice as human capabilities.

Development

No stages are specified. Development amounts to *learning,* defined as an increase in the probability of a response in the presence of a particular stimulus. This increase in probability occurs when the response is followed by a reinforcement. In effect, tension reduction can be brought about by performing the response. *Resistance to extinction,* a major measure of the strength of what is learned, refers to the number of times a learned response will occur when it has ceased to lead to reinforcement.

Periphery of Personality

For peripheral characteristics, there are habits, secondary drives, and secondary reinforcements.

A *habit* is a stable stimulus-response bond established through the regular occurrence of reinforcement. Through *stimulus generalization,* a learned response can occur in the presence of stimuli similar (but not identical) to the original stimulus. Through *response generalization,* responses similar (but not identical) to the original learned response can occur in the presence of the original stimulus.

A *secondary drive* (e.g., anxiety) occurs when the stimulus conditions that have been regularly associated with primary drive arousal take on arousing properties themselves.

A *secondary reinforcement* occurs when the stimulus conditions that have been regularly associated with primary reinforcement take on reinforcing properties.

Although secondary drives and reinforcements are learned, both can mediate further learning.

Radical Behaviorism . . . .

Core of Personality

CORE TENDENCY. None specified.

CORE CHARACTERISTICS. None specified.

Development

Operant conditioning refers to the process of bringing a voluntary (spontaneously occurring) response under stimulus control. Learning has taken place when a particular stimulus serves as a cue (*discriminative stimulus*) for the operant response. This learning is brought about by following the operant response with a *positive* or *negative reinforcement.* A *reinforcement* is defined as anything that can increase or decrease the rate of occurrence of an operant response.

Respondent conditioning refers to the occurrence of responses in the presence of stimuli when the responses are "natural" sequels to the stimuli (e.g., a response of blinking to the stimulus of a puff of air in the eye).

Schedules of reinforcement of various kinds have different effects on the rate of acquisition and extinction of a learned response. *Partial reinforcement* (reinforcements that occur intermittently) produces learned responses with greater resistance to extinction than *continuous reinforcement* does.

Periphery of Personality

No position taken. However, statements about a response's *resistance to extinction* and *stimulus* and *response generalization* have some relevance (see Moderate Behaviorism).

Social Learning Theory . . . . . .

Core of Personality

CORE TENDENCY. *Expressions of inherent individual differences in cognitive capabilities (e.g., memory, differentiation, generalization).* This approach is rare in that it considers certain cognitive differences among people to be unlearned and important for personality. These inherent differences underlie differences in amount and content of meaning.

Development

Observational learning is emphasized. Learning does not require the occurrence of either responses or reinforcements on the learner's part. It is enough to observe a model responding. In such observation, the person associates stimuli with one another *(S-S laws)*. Whether the observed model receives positive or negative reinforcement for responses will determine if and when the learner will perform what he or she has learned.

Operant conditioning is also believed to occur but is given little importance at the human level. People mature by gaining greater and greater autonomy from reinforcements applied by others and increasing their ability to apply reinforcements to themselves through a process of self-control that changes their environment.

Periphery of Personality

For peripheral characteristics there are *needs,* composed of reinforcement values, reinforcement expectancies, and behavior potentials. *Reinforcement value* refers to how satisfying the goal of the need is to the person. *Reinforcement*

expectancy refers to how likely he or she thinks the attainment of the goal is. *Behavior potential* summarizes the implications of the other two components for actual performance and specifies the set of actions that such performance would entail. Examples of broad sets of needs common in people are *recognition-status, dominance, independence, protection-dependency, love and affection,* and *physical comfort.*

Other peripheral characteristics offer strategies and styles rather than content. These include encoding strategies, behavior and stimulus outcome expectancies, stimulus values, and self-regulatory systems and plans. *Encoding strategies* emphasize the manner in which people transform and lend meaning to information and the resulting personal constructs. *Behavior and stimulus outcome expectancies* and *stimulus values* are similar to reinforcement expectancies and reinforcement values. *Self-regulatory systems and plans* involve settled procedures for controlling oneself and regulating one's environment and, as such, constitute combinations of the other strategies and styles. The emerging conception of peripheral characteristics in this tradition is the *prototype,* which structures the person's perceptions and actions around several exemplary expressions of content but leaves other possible expressions to be discovered through experience. As such, prototypes are similar to Kelly's *permeable constructs.*

Strictly speaking, no types are specified. But one theme in social learning theory does refer to broader peripheral characteristics, such as *generalized expectancies.* An example is people's view as to whether they are controlled externally or control themselves. Related to this is the notion of *self-efficacy,* which includes both generalized and task-specific views as to whether one can perform effectively.

GLOSSARY
OF TERMS

Activation-Deactivation Adjective Check List A checklist devised by Thayer to measure customary level of activation according to Fiske and Maddi. (See Chapter 12.)

activation version See *consistency model.*

Activities Index A questionnaire of 300 items, devised by William Stern, that yields scores on some of Murray's needs. (See Chapter 12.)

actualization version See *fulfillment model.*

adaptation Usually refers to adjusting to social and physical pressures rather than avoiding or changing them. (See Chapter 10 and *transcendence.*)

Adler's position See Appendix.

Alienation Test A 60-item questionnaire, devised by Maddi, Kobasa, and Hoover, that measures powerlessness, adventurousness, nihilism, and vegetativeness in the person's relationship to work, people, social institutions, family, and self. (See Chapter 12.)

Allport's position See Appendix.

Analysis of Variance (and Covariance) A statistical test to determine the significance of effects in such research studies as experiments, whether continued or natural. In analysis of covariance there is a statistical control for relevant factors that have not been controlled through the design of the study. This statistical control is frequently necessary in natural experiments because they are usually designed less rigorously than continued experiments. (See Chapter 9 and *experiment.*)

Angyal's position See Appendix.

assessment One of the practical applications of personology that involves determining through some sort of measurement (interview, questionnaire, performance test) the lifestyle or personality type of the person and evaluating his or her developmental maturity. Often done as a precursor to the other practical application of personology, psychotherapy. (See Chapters 1 and 15.)

Bakan's position See Appendix.

behavior modification therapy Originally the radical behavioristic means of therapy, which did not consider thought processes as being any different from actions. All behavior is regarded as controlled by stimulus cues and the principles of reinforcement. Therapy involves manipulating schedules of reinforcement so as to alter unwanted behaviors. By now, this approach is becoming more eclectic, and thought processes are emerging as the source of self-control, with implications that set it apart from other behaviors in some practitioners' minds. (See Chapter 13.)

benevolent eclecticism An attitude toward inquiry in which all points of view are accepted as plausible and there is little effort to pinpoint and evaluate differences among them. (See Chapter 1, *comparative analysis,* and *partisan zealotry.*)

Berne's position See Appendix.

Blacky Test A set of pictures, devised by Gerald S. Blum, that depict a young dog in various situations, mainly with its parents, having special significance in psychoanalytic theory. The subject composes stories about the pictures, thereby projecting his or her personality for the tester to observe. (See Chapters 10 and 12.)

Briggs-Myers Type Indicator A questionnaire, devised by Myers, to measure introversion-extroversion and the thinking, feeling, sensing, and intuiting modes of Jung. (See Chapter 12.)

California Personality Inventory (CPI) A questionnaire yielding scores on many peripheral characteristics covering mentally healthy functioning. (See Chapters 10 and 12.)

chi-square   A statistical test of significance for the data of frequency of occurrence of various categories of two or more characteristics. (See *contingency table*.)

client-centered or person-centered therapy   A Rogerian approach that involves the therapist in reflecting the client's verbalizations clearly enough that the client realizes that the therapist understands, cares, and approves. Through this empathic and unconditional positive regard, it is believed that the client will drop defenses and grow in confidence to be able to actualize inherent potentialities. (See Chapters 5 and 15 and Appendix.)

cognitive dissonance version   See *consistency model*.

cognitive-experiential self-theory   Epstein's position, see Appendix.

comparative analysis   An attitude toward inquiry in which similarities and differences are sought among the various viewpoints on a subject matter, with the aim of posing issues for resolution by thought and research. (See Chapter 1, *benevolent eclecticism*, and *partisan zealotry*.)

comprehensive understanding   Occurs when empirical, rational, and intuitive knowledge match. (See Chapter 1, *empirical knowledge, intuitive knowledge*, and *rational knowledge*.)

conflict model   A form of personality theorizing that postulates that the person is continuously in the grips of a clash between two great, opposing forces. Life is necessarily a compromise, which at best involves a balance of the two forces and at worst a foredoomed attempt to deny the existence of one of them. In the psychosocial version, the source of one great force is in the individual and of the other in society. In the intrapsychic version, both great forces arise from within the person. (See Chapters 2, 3, 4, 10, 11, and 12, *consistency model, fulfillment model*, and *personality theory*.)

consistency model   A form of personality theorizing that places little emphasis on great forces whether single or dual and in conflict or not. Instead, emphasis is on the formative influence of feedback from the external world. Life is to be understood as the extended attempt to maintain consistency. But consistencies and inconsistencies can have any content, themselves having been determined by prior experience. In the cognitive dissonance version, the relevant aspects of the person in which there may or may not be consistency are cognitive in nature. In the activation version, the degree to which bodily tension is consistent or inconsistent with what is customary is considered important. (See Chapters 2, 7, 8, 10, 11, and 12, *conflict model, fulfillment model*, and *personality theory*.)

content analysis   Application of a set of interpretive rules to performance so that the content of that performance can reveal personality characteristics. Content analysis is an integral part of the use of performance tasks such as projective tests. Because content analysis is interpretive, it is important to demonstrate that two or more raters can agree in the application of the interpretive rules. (See Chapter 9, *performance task*, and *projective test*.)

contingency table   When two (or more) characteristics are measured by determining the number of people falling into such categories as presence-absence, or low-medium-high, the resulting data can be recorded in a contingency table, the cells of which are defined jointly by the categories of the characteristics. The statistical significance of the emerging pattern is often evaluated by the chi-square test. (See Chapter 9 and *chi-square*.)

core characteristic   An unlearned, inherent structural entity of personality shared by all human beings. (See Chapters 1–8, 10, 14, and 15 and *core of personality*.)

core of personality   The unlearned, inherent aspects of human nature that all people share. Included are one or two core tendencies, which give the overall directionality or purpose of human life, and core characteristics, or structural entities, that the tendencies imply. (See Chapters 1–8, 10, 14, and 15, *core characteristic, core tendency*, and *personality theory*.)

core tendency   The unlearned, inherent, overall directions or purpose of life shared by all human beings. (See Chapters 1–8, 10, 14, and 15 and *core of personality*.)

correlation   A statistical measure of covariation. The product-moment correlation is computed when both characteristics are measured on a continuous numerical scale having more than two values (e.g., 0 to 3, or 1 to 10). When both characteristics are measured in a dichotomous fashion (e.g., 0 and 1 for absence-presence or low-high, respectively), then the contingency coefficient is computed to assess covariation. When one characteristic is measured continuously and the other dichotomously, the point-biserial correlation is computed. In the case where people are rank ordered with regard to the degree to which each of two characteristics are expressed in them relative to other persons, then rank-order correlation is computed. (See Chapter 9, *covariation, point-biserial correlation,* and *rank-order correlation.*)

correlational research Relatively naturalistic research in which information on the intensity of two or (usually) more aspects of behavior are obtained from all subjects with the intent to determine how the aspects are related. If many aspects are included, factor analysis can be used on the data to determine how the aspects cluster. Correlational research is especially relevant to identifying peripheral characteristics and types. (See Chapters 9, 10, 12, and 14, and *experimental research, peripheral characteristic,* and *type.*)

covariation The degree to which two characteristics (in the case of personality, they may be core or peripheral characteristics) vary interdependently. Increases in one characteristic involving increases in the other as well shows positive covariation. Negative covariation involves decreases in one characteristic for increases in the other. A typical statistical measure of covariation is the correlation. (See Chapter 9 and *correlation.*)

creativity In a person, the predisposition to produce ideas and things that are new and useful. In an idea or thing, the quality of novelty and utility. (See Chapter 10.)

criterion analysis A special case of factor analysis that is deductive (hypothesis testing) rather than inductive (exploratory). (See Chapter 12 and *factor analysis.*)

data language The designation of the form and content of thoughts, feelings, and actions (dependent variables) that are to be explained in personology. No such language has yet been generally adopted. (See Chapters 9, 11, 12, and 16.)

Defense Mechanism Inventory Devised by Gleser and Ihilevich, a test that requires subjects to respond to stories and yields scores on five sets of defenses (turning against object, projection, principalization, turning against self, and reversal). (See Chapter 12.)

defensiveness The tendency to distort reality in order to make what one is conscious of conform to what is socially acceptable. Theorists differ in their reliance on this concept, in what they think is defended against, and in the elaborateness and precision with which they conceptualize the techniques of defense. But all agree that the technique of defense must operate unconsciously. (See Chapters 2–8, 10–12, 15, and 16.)

development The interaction between expressions of the personality core and social and physical influences in the external world that culminates in the particular lifestyle or personality type that is learned. (See Chapters 1–8, 10, and 13–16, *core of personality, periphery of personality,* and *personality theory.*)

Dogmatism Scale A questionnaire, devised by Rokeach, for measuring inflexibility in thinking. (See Chapter 12.)

drive Often used synonymously with *need, motive,* or *motivation,* but connotes something more biological and mechanical, less self-conscious and intellective than the term *motive.* (See Chapter 11, *motivation, motive,* and *need.*)

Edwards Personal Preference Schedule A preference test, devised by Edwards, that uses the forced-choice format to obtain scores on several of Murray's needs. (See Chapter 12.)

ego psychology See Appendix (Erikson's Theory; Murray's Theory).

Ellis's position See Appendix.

empirical knowledge Hypotheses, derived carefully from theories, that have been confirmed in rigorous, systematic, and relevant research studies. This knowledge is public, precise, and systematic. (See Chapters 1 and 9, *intuitive knowledge,* and *rational knowledge.*)

Erikson's position See Appendix.

Existential Psychology See Appendix.

Existential Study A questionnaire, devised by Thorne, for measuring several dimensions of general relevance to the existential position, including self-status, self-actualization, existential morale, existential vacuum, humanistic identification, and existence and destiny. (See Chapter 12.)

existential therapy Although hardly a homogeneous movement, this approach involves the therapist stimulating, confronting, supporting, and urging the client to recognize decisions made in life and begin to choose the future, however fearful, rather than the past, however safe. The client is encouraged to symbolize, imagine, and judge vigorously in order to take responsibility for his or her life. A technique employed in severely uncontrollable symptoms is paradoxical intention, or the willful attempt to exaggerate a symptom in order to outmaneuver it. Other techniques include situational reconstruction, focusing, and compensatory self-improvement. (See Chapter 15 and Appendix.)

Experience Inventory A factor analytically developed

questionnaire, devised by Coan, for measuring various aspects of openness to experience, such as aesthetic sensitivity, openness to hypothetical ideas, constructive utilization of fantasy, unconventional ideas of reality, and unusual perceptions and associations. (See Chapter 12.)

experiment   A contrived procedure in which a characteristic or environmental factor is artificially increased or decreased in order to determine the effect of so doing on subsequent behavior. The magnitude and direction of the produced effect is evaluated by comparing the experimental (manipulated) group (of subjects) with one or more control groups. For rigor of method, the control group(s) must be similar in all respects to the experimental group except in the characteristic or factor manipulated. Sometimes experiments are impractical or unethical. In such cases, the natural experiment is useful, though rigorous. The natural experiment involves capitalizing on the natural (rather than continued) increase or decrease in the target characteristic or environmental factor, and compares the group to which this has happened to one or more control groups not having this experience. (See Chapter 9.)

experimental research   Research in which subjects in an experimental group are treated in a particular way to determine what the effect of the treatment will be. Subjects not receiving the treatment are used as a control group to ensure that the effect observed in the experimental group really did not result from the treatment. Experiments are best employed in the testing of hypotheses. (See Chapters 9, 10, 12, and 14 and *correlational research*.)

exploratory behavior   Behavior that brings the subject into contact with previously unfamiliar aspects of the environment. A special case of this is spontaneous alternation, in which an organism that chose one part of the environment (usually a maze) on the first trial chooses the other on the next trial. (See Chapter 10.)

extrinsic motivation   See *intrinsic versus extrinsic motivation.*

Eysenck (formerly Maudsley) Personality Inventory   A questionnaire, devised by Eysenck, for measuring neuroticism and introversion-extroversion. (See Chapter 12.)

factor analysis   A statistical procedure for determining the covariation among some number of characteristics larger than two. Employing a correlational approach, factor analysis results in the smallest number of clusters of characteristics (called factors)

that define the data. The researcher can force the factors to be unrelated to each other (orthogonal factors) or permit them to covary with each other (oblique factors). First-order factors are those that emerge from the covariation in the characteristics. Second-order factors are those that emerge from the covariation in the first-order factors (See Chapters 9 and 12, *characteristics, correlation,* and *covariation.*)

fantasy test   Frequently called a *projective test,* an unstructured technique for obtaining scores on some variable or variables often used in personality research. The subject is presented with ambiguous stimuli (usually pictures) and given the task of rendering them less ambiguous by identifying them or using them in a story. The test should be shown to have adequate interscorer agreement, reliability, and validity. Such a procedure can be regarded as an indirect test of performance. (See Chapters 9, 10, 12, 15, *performance test, personality research, projective test, questionnaire, reliability, unstructured test,* and *validity.*)

Fascism (F) Scale   A questionnaire, devised by Adorno and colleagues, for measuring fascistic attitudes and values. (See Chapter 12.)

Fear of Appearing Incompetent Scale   A 36-item questionnaire, devised by Good and Good, for measuring White's emphasis on sense of incompetence. (See Chapter 12.)

field dependence-independence   Individual differences, studied by Witkin and associates, in the degree to which a person can use gravitational rather than visual cues to orient the body or other objects in space. It is called psychological differentiation regarding the related phenomenon of discerning a simple figure embedded in a complex one. Typical tests are the Body Adjustment Test and the Embedded-Figures Test. (See Chapter 12.)

Fiske and Maddi's position   See Appendix.

Five-factor position of Costa and McCrae   See Appendix.

fixed role therapy   Introduced by Kelly (see Appendix), an approach that involves the therapist in planning a role for the client to play that will provide corrective or broadening experiences. The ensuing experiences are discussed in therapy as a basis for producing change in the client's constructs and construction system. (See Chapters 7 and 15.)

forced-choice format   A variant of the questionnaire in which each item is paired with one other item and the subject's task is to choose which in each pair he or she prefers or considers correct. The items can be ranked on the basis of number of choices. This test is regarded as less vulnerable to response sets than the ordinary questionnaire, but it should be shown to have reliability and validity. (See Chapters 9, 10, and 12, *personality research, questionnaire, reliability,* and *validity.*)

formal criteria of theoretical adequacy Criteria for evaluating theories that include the theories' importance, operationalization, parsimony, precision, stimulating nature, and empirical validity. (See Chapter 16, *importance of a theory, operational definition, parsimony,* and *precision of a theory.*)

Freud's position See Appendix.

Fromm's position See Appendix.

fulfillment model A form of personality theorizing that postulates that the person embodies one great force. Life involves a progressively greater expression of this force at best and inhibition of it at worst. Conflict between individual and society is possible (indeed, causes inhibition) but is not necessary, as it is in the conflict model. In the actualization version, the great force takes the form of a genetic blueprint of the person's special capabilities. In the perfection version, the great force constitutes ideals of what is fine, excellent, and meaningful. (See Chapters 2, 5, 6, 10, 11, and 12, *conflict model, consistency model,* and *personality theory.*)

gating A phenomenon, promulgated by Bruner, in which some central nervous system process "tunes" peripheral sense organs to receive or reject certain stimulation. Could be a physiological substratum of defensiveness. (See Chapter 10 and *defensiveness.*)

Gestalt psychotherapy Introduced by Perls, an approach that involves reestablishing the flow of experience that has been interrupted by some reversal or punishment. Often practiced in groups, it encourages the client to take all points of view in a situation in order to gain a comprehensive gestalt, or understanding. Contrasts among viewpoints are regarded as being rich in insight. (See Chapter 4 and Appendix.)

Guilford-Zimmerman Temperament Survey A questionnaire, devised by Guilford and Zimmerman, that yields 10 personality factors from a large pool of items. (See Chapter 12.)

habit See *trait.*

Hardiness Test A questionnaire, introduced by Kobasa and Maddi, for measuring a concrete expression of existential courage. After three revisions, this test appears to have adequate reliability and construct validity. (See Chapter 12.)

idiographic (or morphogenic) law A law that concerns the functioning of individuals rather than the average case. The term is emphasized by Allport. (See Chapter 6 and *individuality.*)

importance of a theory A formal criterion of a good theory. There is disagreement as to whether the importance of a theory can be determined except after the fact. One viewpoint is that to ensure its importance, a theory should take as its subject matter (data to be explained) that which can be observed naturally rather than behavior produced in the laboratory by experimental manipulation and hence contrived. (See Chapter 16.)

individual commonalities Similarities on one or more dimensions or variables among people in any group. Of special interest to personology are those commonalities that seem to reflect the inherent nature of people rather than the regularizing effect (or demand characteristics) of stimulus or social pressures. (See Chapters 1 and 2 and *individual differences.*)

individual differences Differences on one or more dimensions or variables among people in any group. Of special relevance for personology are differences that occur under what appear to be the same stimulus situations and differences that persist over time and across situations. (See Chapters 1 and 2 and *individual commonalities.*)

individuality The uniqueness of a person, usually considered as residing in the total pattern of the personality rather than in one aspect of it. This is an extreme case of individual differences, especially emphasized by theorists such as Allport, Kelly, Rogers, Maslow, ego psychologists, and existential psychologists. (See Chapter 1, Appendix, and *individual differences.*)

Internal-External Locus of Control (I-E) Scale A questionnaire, introduced by Rotter and refined by James, that measures whether subjects believe they are in control of their own fate or externally controlled. (See Chapter 12.)

interscorer reliability The degree to which two scorers analyzing the same ambiguous data agree. (See Chapters 9 and 12.)

interview A procedure, which can be relatively structured or unstructured, whereby information about the subject is obtained through a face-to-face question-and-answer session. Because it is more flexible than the questionnaire, this technique is useful when the investigator is exploring. Also, the option of patterning one's questions on the subject's responses to prior questions sometimes makes this technique more desirable than even performance and fantasy tests, which are more restrictive. (See Chapters 9, 10, and 12, *fantasy test, performance test, questionnaire, structured test,* and *unstructured test.*)

intrapsychic version   See *conflict model.*

intrinsic versus extrinsic motivation   Behavior engaged in for its own sake and interfered with by external reinforcement is considered intrinsically motivated. Curiosity, play, and exploratory behavior are examples of intrinsic motivation. Behavior engaged in to obtain external reinforcement is extrinsic motivation. All instrumental behaviors not engaged in for their own enjoyment are examples of extrinsic motivation. (See Chapter 12.)

intuitive knowledge   The relatively inarticulate, private, and emotional—though vivid, immediate, and compelling—sense of the meaning of things. (See Chapter 1, *empirical knowledge,* and *rational knowledge.*)

Inventory of Psychosocial Development   A questionnaire, developed by Constantinople, for measuring the salience of Erikson's stages of development. (See Chapter 12.)

Jung's position   See Appendix.

Kelly's position   See Appendix.

Kohut's position   See Appendix.

latent learning   The phenomenon whereby a subject seems to learn a maze (or other task) even when he or she receives no reinforcement for doing so. (See Chapter 10.)

lifestyle   See *type.*

Manifest Anxiety Scale (MAS)   A questionnaire, devised by Taylor and Spence, for measuring general drive in the framework of moderate behaviorism. (See Chapter 13.)

Marlowe-Crowne Social Desirability Scale (M-C SDS)   A questionnaire, devised by Marlowe and Crowne, for measuring the tendency to respond in a socially desirable fashion. (See Chapter 12.)

Maslow's position   See Appendix.

maze   Usually in the form of a T, a ubiquitous apparatus for studying learning in rats. In more complex, paper-and-pencil, or stylus form, mazes have also been used on human subjects. (See Chapter 10.)

McClelland's position   See Appendix.

Minnesota Multiphasic Personality Inventory (MMPI)   A questionnaire comprising many items to be answered "true" or "false" that provides several scores concerning psychopathological trends in personality. The scales from which the scores are derived have adequate reliability and have been validated by determining that they predict the assumed psychopathologies. (See Chapters 10 and 12.)

modeling behavior   Imitative or observational learning, in which what is learned is linkage among stimuli (S-S) rather than between stimuli and responses (S-R). Learning takes place without need for responses and reinforcements. (See Chapter 14.)

moderate behaviorism   See Appendix.

motivation   The pressure or energy to produce activity and the goal or direction that guides it. Some core tendencies are considered motivational even though they are probably too abstract to achieve mental representation as goals. Some theorists reserve the concept of motivation for peripheral characteristics.

motive   Usually refers to a kind of peripheral characteristic having motivational properties in that it produces behavior aimed at reaching a goal. (See Chapters 3–9, *motivation,* and *peripheral characteristic.*)

Murray's position   See Appendix.

narcissistic behavior disorders   In Kohut's position, personality types characterized by acting out lack of confidence and insufficient sense of self. (See Chapter 3 and Appendix.)

narcissistic personality disorders   In Kohut's position, personality types characterized by persistent thoughts of personal unworthiness and vulnerability to slights. (See Chapter 3 and Appendix.)

need   Often used synonymously with *drive, motive,* or *motivation.* Usage varies widely by theorist. (See Chapter 11, *drive, motivation,* and *motive.*)

NEO Personality Inventory   A self-rating questionnaire devised by Costa and McCrae to measure the five-factor model. (See Chapter 12.)

nomothetic law   A law that concerns the functioning of the average case rather than of any particular individual. The term is emphasized by Allport. (See Chapter 11.)

Object-Relations position   See Appendix.

operational definition   A precise, literal statement of which operations to perform in order to measure concepts and variables. In personology, such definitions are especially important for identifying peripheral characteristics. (See Chapters 9, 12, and 14 and *peripheral characteristic.*)

parsimony   The criterion (of a good theory) that, other things being equal, the best of several explanations of a phenomenon is the one that makes the fewest assumptions. This criterion is difficult to apply to personality theory and may stifle imagination. (See Chapter 16.)

partisan zealotry An attitude toward inquiry in which the viewpoint one already holds is regarded as true and championed energetically regardless of plausible contrary arguments and disagreements. (See Chapter 1, *benevolent eclecticism*, and *comparative analysis*.)

perceptual defense The phenomenon whereby subjects require longer tachistoscopic exposures of threatening than nonthreatening stimuli in order to recognize them. (See Chapter 10, *perceptual vigilance*, and *tachistoscope*.)

perceptual vigilance The phenomenon whereby subjects require shorter tachistoscopic exposures of threatening rather than nonthreatening stimuli in order to recognize them. (See Chapter 10, *perceptual defense*, and *tachistoscope*.)

perfection version See *fulfillment model*.

performance task A source of personality data in which the person performs some task, and the investigator or some specific group judges the performance in terms of the personality characteristics it reveals. In contrast to the interview and the questionnaire, performance tasks need not rely on the person's self-report. Hence, performance tasks may reveal to the investigator things that people do not understand or recognize in themselves. Psychotherapy sessions and projective tests are examples of performance tasks that have been useful in personality. (See Chapter 9, *interview, personality data, prective test, psychotherapy session*, and *questionnaire*.)

performance test A standardized technique, usually structured, for obtaining scores on some variable or variables that is sometimes used in personality research. The subjects reveal themselves by their effectiveness at and manner of performing the task rather than in describing themselves directly. The test should be shown to have reliability and validity. (See Chapters 9, 10, 12, and 15, *personality research, questionnaire, reliability, structured test*, and *validity*.)

peripheral characteristic The smallest, most homogeneous learned aspect of personality that a theorist believes can properly be conceptualized. Exerts an influence on thoughts, feelings, and/or actions such that they show continuity over time and across stimulus situations. (See Chapters 1–8, 11–12, and 14 and *periphery of personality*.)

periphery of personality The learned, relatively concrete aspects of personality that develop out of the interaction of the personality core and the external, mainly social world. Included in peripheral statements are the types of personality (or lifestyles) it is possible to develop and the peripheral characteristics (motives, traits, schemata) that the types comprise. (See Chapters 1–8, 11–12, 14, and 15, *personality theory*, and *type*.)

Perls's position See Appendix.

Personal Orientation Inventory (POI) A questionnaire, devised by Shostrom, for measuring various characteristics of actualization fulfillment theory—for example, Rogers and Maslow. (See Chapter 12).

personality A stable set of characteristics and tendencies that determine those commonalities and differences in the psychological behavior (thoughts, feelings, and actions) of people that have continuity over time and that may or may not be easily understood in terms of the social and biological pressures of the immediate situation alone. (See Chapter 1.)

personality change Theorists differ in their views as to the degree of personality change that occurs as a function of aging. According to some, little real change takes place after childhood, whereas others see change as continuous throughout life. Most believe that even radical change can take place through psychotherapy. (See Chapter 10.)

personality data Thoughts, feelings, and actions that show continuity over time and across various stimulus situations. (See Chapter 1, *data language*, and *personology*.)

personality research May be designed primarily to test hypotheses (deductive method) or to explore in order to generate hypotheses (inductive method). Naturalistic observation and correlational data analyses seem well suited to exploratory research, whereas experimental designs seem more appropriate for hypothesis testing. Research is particularly relevant to personality when, whether exploratory or hypothesis testing, it concerns thoughts, feelings, and actions that have continuity over time and across situations. Usually this continuity involves stable individual differences. Often, personality research also concerns many facets of each person's behavior rather than only one or two elements. (See Chapters 1, 9, 10, 12, and 14, *correlational research, experimental research, personality data*, and *personality theory*.)

personality theory A set of interconnected and logically consistent assumptions having the aim of explaining personality data (thoughts, feelings, and actions having continuity over time and across situations). Consists of a core statement (concerning the inherent nature that is unlearned and common to all), a peripheral statement (concerning the lifestyles that are learned and that differentiate people, and a developmental statement (explicating how expressions of the core lead, through interaction with the external, mainly social environment, to the periphery). (See Chapters 1, 10, 11, and 14, *core of personality, development, periphery of personality,* and *personality data.*)

personologist Someone who practices personology. (See Chapter 1 and *personology.*)

personology A field of psychology concerned with the holistic study of entire persons. The data for the field are thoughts, feelings, and actions that characterize a person over time and across situations; the explanations employed concern personality (a set of concepts that are within the skin rather than in the environment and may or may not have biological substrata). In addition to this theorizing function, personology includes the conducting of research (to test the theorizing), the practical application of knowledge in the form of assessment (the systematic identification of a person's personality), and psychotherapy (the systematic attempt to change personality to approach some theoretical ideal). (See Chapters 1, 15, and 16, *assessment, personality, personality data, personality research, personality theory,* and *psychotherapy.*)

point-biserial correlation A statistical measure of covariation (See *correlation* and *covariation*).

precision of a theory A formal criterion of a good theory. Effort should be made to avoid inconsistencies, loose ends, and metaphorical language. (See Chapter 16.)

product-movement correlation A statistical measure of covariation (see *correlation* and *covariation.*)

projective test A source of personality data of the performance-task sort in which the person is presented with ambiguous stimuli that must be identified or incorporated into a composed story. Because they require the use of imagination, projective tests are thought to reveal aspects of personality that people are unwilling to reveal or of which they are unaware. (See Chapters 9 and 10, *fantasy test,* and *performance task.*)

prototype A peripheral characteristic proposed by Mischel and Cantor that is defined by the person in terms of one or two definite expressions and other, more ambiguous examples. The prototype is gradually defined as the person's experience accumulates. Mischel and Cantor believe that prototypes differ from traits. (See Chapter 14 and *trait.*)

psychoanalysis A general body of theory in which fantasy, especially dreams, is believed to reveal

people most clearly. Because people are construed as distorting reality through defensiveness, fantasy comes closest to revealing the truth. As a therapy, psychoanalysis includes various techniques (e.g., free association) for stimulating waking fantasy and interprets these and nighttime dreams in terms of the transference of the client's pent-up emotions from past conflicts onto the therapist. The therapist analyzes the patient's free verbalizations, attempting thereby to get behind the defenses. Originally Freudian, psychoanalysis has been developed in various directions by ego psychologists, object-relations psychologists, and self analysts. (See these and Rank, Jung, Adler, and Fromm; see also Appendix.)

psychobiography A personologist's interpretation of the personality characteristics and their organization into a holistic pattern as revealed in a person's life history. Relevant to this task are written documents (e.g., diaries, speeches, scholarly works, and interviews) with the person and significant others. A psychobiography usually emphasizes the overall pattern of the person's life, the underlying causal factors, and the individuality that emerges. Usually, psychobiographies are done on historically important people (See Chapter 9.)

psychological growth Progressively greater differentiation and integration of experience, especially emphasized by Allport, Adler, Maslow, Fiske, Maddi, and existential psychology. (See Chapters 5–8.)

psychosocial version See *conflict theory.*

psychotherapy session As considered in this book, the psychotherapy session is a source of personality data, specifically, a performance task. In relating his or her problems to the therapist, the person reveals much about personality. (See Chapters 9 and 15 and *performance task.*)

questionnaire A source of personality data involving printed items to which the person responds. These items are usually questions, which, because they are printed, tend to be specific and delimited. Because of this, the questionnaire is usually considered a structured technique most useful when the data that are needed are known and richness of responses is not necessary. The questions used may be of the true-false (dichotomous) or rating-scale (continuous) sort. Sometimes, questions are paired, and the person is asked which member of each pair is most true or relevant (this is called the forced-choice format). Checklists are also used, in which the person checks which of a number of descriptive words are most true or relevant. Although questionnaires can be administered to large groups, this advantage is mitigated by the prevalence of response biases (tendencies to answer in particular ways because of the form rather than content of the questions, and to maintain a socially acceptable image). When questionnaires are used in assessing personality characteristics, it is important to minimize response biases and to demonstrate the reliability (internal consistency and stability) of the measurement. (See Chapter 9.)

radical behaviorism See Appendix.

rank-order correlation A statistical measure of covariation. (See *correlation* and *covariation*.)

Rank's position See Appendix.

rational-emotive therapy Introduced by Ellis, an approach that involves strenuous confrontations in which the therapist cajoles, exposes, and encourages the client to recognize destructive self-pity and wasteful repetition of ineffective functioning. (See Chapter 6 and Appendix.)

rational knowledge Conclusions deduced from a set of assumptions by the careful, reflective use of logic rather than arrived at by systematic observation. (See Chapter 1, *empirical knowledge,* and *intuitive knowledge.*)

reliability In measuring personality characteristics, one can show that the various presumed expressions of the characteristic covary (internal consistency) and that they show consistency over time (stability). Especially when one uses questionnaires, the internal consistency and stability of the measurement should be demonstrated. (See Chapter 9 and *questionnaire.*)

Repression-Sensitization Scale A questionnaire, devised by Byrne, for measuring the defensiveness shown in either too little or too much sensitivity to stimuli. (See Chapter 12.)

response set Subjects, particularly when taking questionnaires, respond in set ways, or response sets, that bear little relationship to the questions' content. Response sets include being socially desirable and being acquiescent. (See Chapters 9 and 12.)

Rogers's position See Appendix.

Role Constructs Repertory (REP) Test A categorizing performance test, devised by Kelly, that measures the subject's personal constructs and their organization into a construct system. (See Chapter 12.)

Rorschach Test A series of inkblots, devised by Rorschach, that the subject is asked to identify. In indicating what the blots resemble, the subject reveals her or his personality. (See Chapters 9, 10, and 15.)

schema Usually refers to a kind of peripheral characteristic mainly cognitive in nature and expressive of cultural or social influences. Examples are values and social roles. (See Chapters 5, 10, 12, and 14 and *peripheral characteristic.*)

self-analysis Practiced by Kohut and object-relations theorists, an approach that involves reflecting the client's statements and serving as a model for him or her to admire. Little confrontation or interpretation takes place. It is believed that in this way the patient's narcissistic needs will be filled and development can progress. (See Chapter 3 and Appendix.)

self-control An emphasis in social learning theory and behaviorism on the person's gaining control over the reinforcements influencing his or her behavior. This control is considered a sign of maturity. (See Chapters 13 and 14.)

Self-Ideal Q-Sort A test, devised by Stevenson, that employs a procedure for sorting statements into groups and that has been used to measure the discrepancy between self-concept and self-ideal in a Rogerian framework. Butler and Haigh devised this particular Q-sort. (See Chapter 12.)

sensory deprivation An experimental procedure whereby the amount of stimulation from external (and sometimes internal) sources is markedly decreased. Sleep and disordered thought frequently ensue. (See Chapter 10.)

sentence completion test A partially unstructured test in which the subject is provided with a series of sentence beginnings that he or she is to finish in some way. The test should be shown to have adequate interscorer agreement, reliability, and validity. (See Chapters 9, 10, and 12, *interscorer reliability, personality research, unstructured test,* and *validity.*)

Sixteen Personality Factor (16 PF) Questionnaire A questionnaire, devised by Cattell, yielding scores on 16 first-order and eight second-order factors. The factors result from numerous factor analyses of the items, and the test offers a comprehensive description of personality. (See Chapters 10 and 12.)

skin conductance (or galvanic skin response) A procedure for measuring increases in sweating (considered emotional arousal) by passing a mild electric current over the skin. Sweating increases skin conductivity. (See Chapters 10 and 12.)

Social Interest Index Devised by Greever, Tseng, and Friedland, a questionnaire that measures Adler's emphasis on constructive interest in other people and society. (See Chapter 12.)

social learning theory An offshoot of moderate behaviorism that stresses the importance of imitative or observational learning. Children especially frequently learn by observing a model, in which case, subsequent performance of what they learn depends on anticipated reinforcement contingencies. In its emphasis on cognition and deemphasis of reinforcement as necessary to learning, this position, as developed by Bandura, Walters, and Mischel, deviates significantly from moderate behaviorism. (See Chapter 14.)

S-R Inventory Devised by Endler, Hunt, and Rosenstein, a questionnaire that measures various types of anxiety response over a range of situations. (See Chapter 12.)

stages of development Stages demarcated by some theorists during which particular core functions mature and certain types of social experiences can have special impact on personality. (See Chapters 2–8, 10, and 12 and *development.*)

Strong Vocational Interest Blank A questionnaire, devised by Strong, often used to assess vocational interests. (See Chapter 10.)

structured test Often called objective, a type of test that presents the subject with a structured, organized, specific situation to which to respond. Structured tests are usually questionnaires, but they can also be performance tasks. Some techniques, such as the interview, can be either somewhat structured or unstructured. Structured tests have greater reliability than unstructured tests and are regarded by some theorists as especially valuable in assessing socially directed personality characteristics. (See Chapters 9, 10, 12, and 15, *interview, performance test, questionnaire, reliability, unstructured test,* and *validity.*)

subception A phenomenon in which a subject responds physiologically (e.g., by sweating) even when stimuli are presented tachistoscopically at exposure times too brief for conscious recognition. (See Chapter 10, *perceptual defense,* and *tachistoscope.*)

Survey of Problematic Situations A questionnaire, developed by Goldfriend and D'Zurilla, for measuring White's emphasis on actual competence. (See Chapter 12.)

systematic desensitization Wolpe's psychotherapy, in which the person is encouraged to relax while thinking of threatening material in the hope that it will become less threatening. (See Chapter 13.)

tachistoscope A device for presenting visual stimuli for controllable and very brief lengths of time. Has been used extensively in personality research to study how and whether there are differences among subjects and among types of stimuli in recognition time. (See Chapter 10, *perceptual defense,* and *perceptual vigilance.*)

tension reduction or increase Tension (sometimes called arousal or activation) is usually regarded as a state of bodily discomfort or pent-up energy. Many theorists believe tension reduction to be pleasurable and the major aim of life. Other theorists believe that increases in tension will be tolerated (even enjoyed) in order to achieve certain aims. (See Chapter 10.)

Thematic Apperception Test (TAT) A set of pictures, devised by Murray, showing people alone or in various relationships with one another. In composing stories for the pictures, the subject projects his or her personality for the tester to observe. (See Chapters 9, 10, 12, and 15).

trait Usually refers to kinds of peripheral characteristics producing habitual, routinized, unreflective behaviors having little or no apparent motivational significance. (See Chapters 2–8, 10–12, and 14, and *peripheral characteristic.*)

Transactional Analysis Introduced by Berne, an approach typically practiced in groups. Through scrutiny of group behavior, the therapist clarifies the destructive features of the client's life script and life position and the associated games that are played. (See Chapter 3 and Appendix.)

transcendence Usually refers to transforming or surmounting social and physical pressures rather than adjusting or acquiescing to them. (See Chapter 10 and *adaptation.*)

type A learned lifestyle composed of peripheral characteristics (motives, traits, schema) that exert an influence on thoughts, feelings, and actions. (See Chapters 1–8, 11–12, 14, and 15, and *periphery of personality.*)

typology A classification of types that is part of a statement of the periphery of personality. (See *type* and *periphery of personality.*)

unstructured test Often called *projective,* a type of test that presents the subject with an unstructured, ambiguous situation to which to respond. Unstructured tests usually engage the subject's fantasy, but they can also involve other aspects of performance. Some techniques, such as the interview, can be either somewhat structured or unstructured. Although unstructured tests have lower reliability than structured tests, many theorists regard them as more appropriate for assessing underlying defenses, conflicts, and unconscious material that may not be readily apparent in overt behavior. (See Chapters 9, 10, 12, and 15, *fantasy test, interview, performance test, personality research, reliability, structured test,* and *validity*.)

validity The degree to which a test or scale predicts the naturally occurring behavior it was intended to forecast. In personality research, construct validity is most relevant. In construct validity, there is no single naturally occurring behavior crucial in the validation of a scale; rather there are several, each linked to the scale (perhaps indirectly) by theory. The process for validating the scale is the same as that for validating its underlying constructs. (See Chapters 9, 12, and 14.)

White's position See Appendix.

Word Association Test A procedure for studying personality, devised by Jung, in which a series of words are presented to subjects one at a time, and they associate a word to each of them as quickly as they can. (See Chapter 12.)

REFERENCES

Abelson, R., Aronson, E., McGuire, W., Newcomb, T., Rosenberg, M., & Tannenbaum, P. (Eds.). (1969). *Theories of cognitive consistency: A sourcebook.* Chicago: Rand McNally.

Aborn, M. (1953). The influence of experimentally induced failure on the retention of material acquired through set and incidental learning. *Journal of Experimental Psychology, 45,* 225–231.

Abraham, K. (1927a). The first pregenital stage of the libido. In K. Abraham (Ed.), *Selected papers.* London: Institute for Psychoanalysis and Hogarth Press.

Abraham, K. (1927b). The influence of oral erotism on character formation. In K. Abraham (Ed.), *Selected papers.* London: Institute for Psychoanalysis and Hogarth Press.

Abraham, K. (1927c). Contributions to the theory of the anal character. In K. Abraham (Ed.), *Selected papers.* London: Institute for Psychoanalysis and Hogarth Press.

Abraham, K. (1927d). Character formation on the genital level of libido development. In K. Abraham (Ed.), *Selected papers.* London: Institute for Psychoanalysis and Hogarth Press.

Abramowitz, S. (1973). Internal-external control and sociopolitical activism: A test of the dimensionality of Rotter's internal-external scale. *Journal of Consulting and Clinical Psychology, 40,* 196–201.

Adams, H. E., & Vidulich, R. N. (1962). Dogmatism and belief congruence in paired-associate learning. *Psychological Reports, 10,* 90–94.

Adams, J. S. (1961). Reduction of cognitive dissonance by seeking consonant information. *Journal of Abnormal and Social Psychology, 62,* 74–78.

Adams-Webber, J. R. (1970). An analysis of the discriminant validity of several repertory grid indices. *British Journal of Psychology, 60*(1) 83–90.

Adelson, J., & Redmond, J. (1958). Personality differences in the capacity for verbal recall. *Journal of Abnormal and Social Psychology, 57,* 244–248.

Adler, A. (1917). *Study of organ inferiority and its physical compensation.* New York: Nervous and Mental Diseases Publishing Company.

Adler, A. (1927). *The practice and theory of individual psychology.* New York: Harcourt Brace Jovanovich.

Adler, A. (1930). Individual psychology. In C. Murchinson (Ed.), *Psychologies of 1930.* Worcester, MA: Clark University Press.

Adler, A. (1931). *What life should mean to you.* Boston: Little, Brown.

Adler, A. (1939). *Social interest.* New York: Putnam.

Adler, A. (1956). *The individual psychology of Alfred Adler.* New York: Basic Books.

Adler, A. (1964). *Problems of neurosis.* New York: Harper Torchbooks.

Adler, H. A. (1967). Cognitive controls and the Hoan-Kroeker model of ego functioning. *Journal of Abnormal and Social Psychology, 72,* 434–440.

Adorno, T. W., Frenkel-Brunswik, E., Levinson, D. J., & Sanford, R. N. (1950). *The authoritarian personality.* New York: Harper.

Adrian, E. D. (1954). The physiological basis of perception. In E. D. Adrian et al. (Eds.), *Brain mechanisms and consciousness.* Oxford, England: Blackwell.

Akeret, R. U. (1959). Interrelationships among various dimensions of the self-concept. *Journal of Counseling Psychology, 6,* 199–201.

Alegre, C., & Murray, E. (1974). Locus of control, behavioral intention, and verbal conditioning. *Journal of Personality, 42,* 668–681.

Alker, H. A. (1972). Is personality situationally specific or intrapsychically consistent? *Journal of Personality, 40,* 4–16.

Allport, F. H. (1955). *Theories of perception and the concept of structure.* New York: Wiley.

Allport, G. W. (1937). *A psychological interpretation.* New York: Holt.

Allport, G. W. (1942). *The use of personal documents in psychological research.* New York: Social Science Research Council.

Allport, G. W. (1955). *Becoming: Basic considerations for a psychology of personality.* New Haven, CT: Yale University Press.

Allport, G. W. (1961). *Pattern and growth in personality.* New York: Holt, Rinehart & Winston.

Allport, G. W. (1962). The general and the unique in psychological science. *Journal of Personality, 30,* 405–422.

Allport, G. W., & Cantril, H. (1934). Judging personality from voice. *Journal of Social Psychology, 5,* 37–55.

Allport, G. W., & Odbert, H. S. (1936). Trait names: A psychological study. *Psychological Monographs, 47*(211), pp. 1–171.

Allport, G. W., & Vernon, P. E. (1933). *Studies in expressive movement.* New York: Macmillan.

Allport, G. W., Vernon, P. E., & Lindzey, G. A. (1951). *A study of values* (2nd ed.). Boston: Houghton Mifflin.

Allred, K. D. & Smith, T. W. (1989). The hardy personality: Cognitive and physiological responses to evaluative threat. *Journal of Personality and Social Psychology, 56,* 257–266.

Altus, W. D. (1966). Birth order and its sequelae. *Science, 151,* 44–49.

Amabile, T. (1985). Motivation and creativity: Effects of motivational orientation on creative writers. *Journal of Personality and Social Psychology, 48,* 393–399.

American Psychiatric Association. (1994). *Diagnostic and statistical manual of mental disorders* (4th ed.). Washington, DC: Author.

Amirkhan, J. H., Risinger, R. T. & Swickert, R. J. (1995). Extraversion: A "hidden" personality factor in coping? *Journal of Personality, 63,* 190–212.

Anastasi, A. (1961). *Psychological testing* (2nd ed.). New York: Macmillan.

Andersen, S. M. & Baum, A. (1994). Transference in interpersonal relations: Inferences and affect based on significant-other representations. *Journal of Personality, 62,* 459–497.

Anderson, J. D. E. (1960). Prediction of adjustment over time. In I. Iscoe & H. A. Stevenson (Eds.), *Personality development in children.* Austin: University of Texas Press.

Anderson, K. J. (1990). Arousal and the inverted-U hypothesis: A critque of Neiss's "reconceptualizing arousal." *Psychological Bulletin, 107,* 96–100.

Angyal, A. (1941). *Foundations for a science of personality.* New York: Commonwealth Fund.

Angyal, A. (1951). A theoretical model for personality studies. *Journal of Personality, 20,* 131–142.

Angyal, A. (1965). *Neurosis and treatment: A holistic theory.* New York: Wiley.

Ansbacher, H. L. (1967). Life style: A historical and systematic review. *Journal of Individual Psychology, 23,* 191–231.

Ansbacher, H. L., & Ansbacher, R. (1956). *The individual psychology of Alfred Adler.* New York: Basic Books.

Aronson, E. (1961). The effect of effort on the attractiveness of rewarded and unrewarded stimuli. *Journal of Abnormal and Social Psychology, 63,* 375–380.

Aronson, E., & Mills, J. (1959). The effect of severity of initiation on liking for a group. *Journal of Abnormal and Social Psychology, 59,* 177–181.

Aronson, M. L. (1953). A study of the Freudian theory of paranoia by means of the Blacky Pictures. *Journal of Projective Techniques, 17,* 3–19.

Atkinson, J. W. (1950). *Studies in projective measurement of achievement motivation.* Unpublished manuscript, University of Michigan at Ann Arbor.

Atkinson, J. W. (1957) Motivational determinants of risk-taking behavior. *Psychological Review, 64,* 359–372.

Atkinson, J. W. (Ed.). (1958). *Motives in fantasy, action, and society,* Princeton, NJ: Van Nostrand.

Atkinson, J. W. (1960). Personality dynamics. In P. R. Farnsworth & Q. McNemar (Eds.), *Annual Review of Psychology.* Palo Alto, CA: Banta.

Atkinson, J. W., & Birch, D. (1970). *The dynamics of action.* New York: Wiley.

Atkinson, J. W., Heyns, R. W., & Veroff, J. (1954). The effect of experimental arousal of the affiliation motive on thematic apperception. *Journal of Abnormal and Social Psychology, 49,* 405–410.

Atkinson, J. W., & Raynor, J. Q. (1975). *Motivation and achievement.* Washington, DC: Winston.

Atkinson, J. W., & Walker, E. L. (1958). The affiliation motive and perceptual sensitivity to facts. In J. W. Atkinson (Ed.), *Motives in fantasy, action, and society.* Princeton, NJ: Van Nostrand.

Ayllon, T., & Azrin, N. (1968). *The token economy.* New York: Appleton-Century-Crofts.

Bachman, J. R., O'Malley, P. M., & Johnston, G. (1978). *Adolescence to adulthood: Change and stability in the lives of young men.* Ann Arbor, MI: Institute for Social Research.

Bakan, D. (1966). *The duality of human existence.* Chicago: Rand McNally.

Bakan, D. (1968). *Disease, pain, and sacrifice.* Chicago: University of Chicago Press.

Bakan, D. (1971). *Slaughter of the innocents.* San Francisco: Jossey-Bass.

Baker, S. R. (1964). A study of the relationship of dogmatism to the retention of psychological concepts: A research note. *Journal of Human Relations, 12,* 311–313.

Bandura, A. (1965). Vicarious processes: A case of no-trial learning. In L. Berkowitz (Ed.), *Advances in experimental social psychology* (Vol. 2). New York: Academic Press.

Bandura, A. (1966). Behavioral modifications through modeling procedures. In L. Krasner & I. P. Ullman (Eds.), *Research in behavior modification.* New York: Holt, Rinehart & Winston.

Bandura, A. (1969). *Principles of behavior modification.* New York: Holt, Rinehart & Winston.

Bandura, A. (1974). Behavior theory and the models of man. *American Psychologist, 29,* 859–869.

Bandura, A. (1977). Self-efficacy: Toward a unifying theory of behavioral change. *Psychological Review, 84,* 191–215.

Bandura, A. (1978). The self system in reciprocal determinism. *American Psychologist, 33,* 344–358.

Bandura, A. (1986). Self-efficacy mechanism in physiological activation and health-promoting behavior. In J. Madden, IV, S. Matthysse, & J. Barchas (Eds.), *Adaptation, learning and affect.* New York: Raven Press.

Bandura, A., & Kupers, C. J. (1964). Transmission of patterns of self-reinforcement through modeling. *Journal of Abnormal Social Psychology, 69,* 1–9.

Bandura, A., & Mischel, W. (1965). Modification of self-imposed delay of reward through exposure to live and symbolic models. *Journal of Personality and Social Psychology, 2,* 698–705.

Bandura, A., Taylor, C. B., Williams, S. L., Mufford, I. N., & Barchas, J. D. (1985). Catecholamine secretion as a function of perceived self-efficacy. *Journal of Consulting and Clinical Psychology, 53,* 406–414.

Bandura, A., & Walters, R. H. (1963). *Social learning and personality development.* New York: Holt, Rinehart & Winston.

Bannister, D. (Ed.). (1970). *Perspectives in personal construct theory.* New York: Academic Press.

Bannister, D., & Fransella, K. (1971). *Inquiring man.* Baltimore: Penguin.

Bannister, D., & Mair, J. M. M. (1988). *The evaluation of personal constructs.* London: Academic Press.

Barker, R., Dembo, T., & Lewin, L. (1941). Frustration and regression: An experiment with young children. *University of Iowa Studies of Child Welfare, 18*(1), 1–314.

Barron, F. (1963). *Creativity and psychological health.* Princeton, NJ: Van Nostrand.

Bartone, P. T. (1989). Predictors of stress-related illness in city bus drivers. *Journal of Occupational Medicine, 31,* 857–863.

Battle, E., & Rotter, J. B. (1963). Children's feelings of personal control as related to social class and ethnic group. *Journal of Personality, 31,* 482–490.

Baumeister, R. F. & Cairns, K. J. (1992). Repression and self-presentation: When audiences interfere with self-deceptive strategies. *Journal of Personality and Social Psychology, 62,* 851–862.

Baumeister, R. F. & Leary, M. R. (1995). The need to belong: Desire for interpersonal attachments as a fundamental human motivation. *Psychological Bulletin, 117,* 497–529.

Baumeister, R. F., Stillwell, A. M. & Heatherton, T. F. (1994). Guilt: An interpersonal approach. *Psychological Bulletin, 115,* 243–267.

Beck, S. (1953). The science of personality: Nomothetic or idiographic? *Psychological Review, 60,* 353–359.

Bem, D. J. (1972). Constructing cross-situational consistencies in behavior: Some thoughts on Alker's critique of Mischel. *Journal of Personality, 40,* 17–26.

Bem, D. J., & Funder, D. C. (1978). Predicting more of the people more of the time: Assessing the personality of situations. *Psychological Review, 85,* 485–501.

Bem, S. L. (1974). The measurement of psychological androgyny. *Journal of Consulting and Clinical Psychology, 42,* 155–162.

Benesch, K. F. & Page, M. M. (1989). Self-construct systems and interpersonal congruence. *Journal of Personality, 57,* 139–173.

Benson, J. K. (1966). *Alienation and academic achievement: An empirical study of the reactions of college students to academic success and failure.* Unpublished doctoral dissertation, University of Texas, Austin.

Berger, E. M. (1953). The relation between expressed acceptance of self and expressed acceptance of others. *Journal of Abnormal and Social Psychology, 47,* 778–782.

Berger, E. M. (1955). Relationships among acceptance of self, acceptance of others and MMPI scores. *Journal of Counseling Psychology, 2,* 279–284.

Berger, L., & Everstine, L. (1962). Test-retest reliability of the Blacky Pictures Test. *Journal of Projective Techniques, 26,* 225–226.

Bergin, A. E., & Lambert, M. J. (1978). The evaluation of therapeutic outcomes. In S. L. Garfield & A. E. Bergin (Eds.), *Handbook of psychotherapy and behavior change: An empirical analysis* (2nd ed.). New York: Wiley.

Berkowitz, L. (1974). Some determinants of impulsive aggression: Role of mediated associations with reinforcements for aggression. *Psychological Review, 81,* 165–176.

Berlew, D. E. (1956). *The achievement motive and the growth of Greek civilization.* Unpublished bachelor's thesis, Wesleyan University, Middletown, CT.

Berlin, H. (1978). An alternative to social learning theory. *Contemporary Educational Psychology, 3,* 27–31.

Berlyne, D. E. (1955). The arousal and satiation of perceptual curiosity in the rat. *Journal of Comparative and Physiological Psychology, 48,* 238–246.

Berlyne, D. E. (1957). Uncertainty and conflict: A point of contact between information-theory and behavior-theory concepts. *Psychological Review, 64,* 329–339.

Berlyne, D. E. (1960). *Conflict, arousal, and curiosity.* New York: McGraw-Hill.

Berlyne, D. E. (1964). Emotional aspects of learning. *Annual Review of Psychology, 15,* 115–142.

Berlyne, D. E. (1967). Arousal and reinforcement. *Nebraska Symposium on Motivation* (pp. 1–110). Lincoln: University of Nebraska Press.

Berlyne, D. E. (1968). Behavior theory as personality theory. In E. F. Borgatto & W. W. Lambert (Eds.), *Handbook of personality theory and research.* Chicago: Rand McNally.

Bernardin, A. C., & Jessor, R. A. (1957). A construct validation of the Edwards Personal Preference Schedule with respect to dependency. *Journal of Consulting Psychology, 21,* 63–67.

Berne, E. (1964). *Games people play.* New York: Grove Press.

Berniat, M. (1989). Motives and values to achieve: Different constructs with different goals. *Journal of Personality, 57,* 69–96.

Berzonsky, M. D. (1992). Identity style and coping strategies. *Journal of Personality, 60,* 771–788.

Bettinhaus, E., Miller, G., & Steinfatt, T. (1970). Source evaluation, syllogistic content, and judgments of logical validity by high and low dogmatic persons. *Journal of Personality and Social Psychology, 16,* 238–244.

Bialer, I. (1961). Conceptualization of success and failure in mentally retarded and normal children. *Journal of Personality, 29,* 303–320.

Bieler, S. H. (1966). *Some correlates of the Jungian typology: Personal style variables.* Unpublished master's thesis, Duke University, Durham, NC.

Bieri, J. (1961). Complexity-simplicity as a personality variable in cognitive and preferential behavior. In D. W. Fiske & S. R. Maddi (Eds.), *Functions of varied experience.* Homewood, IL: Dorsey Press.

Binswanger, L. (1958). The existential analysis school of thought. In R. May, E. Angel, & H. F. Ellenberger (Eds.), *Existence: A new dimension in psychiatry and psychology.* New York: Basic Books.

Binswanger, L. (1963). *Being-in-the-world: Selected papers of Ludwig Binswanger.* New York: Basic Books.

Birtchnell, J., & Mayhew, J. (1977). Toman's theory: Tested for mate selection and friendship formation. *Journal of Individual Psychology, 33,* 18–36.

Blaney, P. H., & Ganellen, R. J. (1990). Hardiness and social support. In I. G. Sarason, B. Sarason, & G. Pierce (Eds.), *Social support: An interactional view.* New York: Wiley.

Blasi, A., & Milton, K. (1991). The development of sense of self in adolescence. *Journal of Personality, 59,* 217–242.

Blass, T. (Ed.). (1977). *Personality variables in social behavior.* Hillsdale, NJ: Erlbaum.

Block, J. (1962). Some differences between the concepts of social desirability and adjustments. *Journal of Consulting Psychology, 26,* 527–530.

Block, J. (1971). *Lives through time.* Berkeley, CA: Bancroft.

Block, J. (1995a). A contrarian view of the Five-Factor approach to personality description. *Psychological Bulletin, 117,* 187–215.

Block, J. (1995b). Going beyond the five factors given: Rejoinder to Costa and McCrae (1995) and Goldberg and Saucier (1995). *Psychological Bulletin, 117,* 226–229.

Block, J., Weiss, D. S., & Thorne, A. (1979). How relevant is a semantic similarity interpretation of personality rating? *Journal of Personality and Social Psychology, 37,* 1055–1074.

Blum, G. S. (1949). A study of the psychoanalytic theory of psychosexual development. *Genetic Psychology Monograph, 39,* 3–99.

Blum, G. S. (1955). Perceptual defense revisited. *Journal of Abnormal and Social Psychology, 51,* 24–29.

Blum, G. S., & Hunt, H. F. (1952). The validity of the Blacky Pictures. *Psychological Bulletin, 49,* 238–250.

Blum, G. S., & Kaufman, J. B. (1952). Two patterns of personality dynamics in male ulcer patients, as suggested by responses to the Blacky Pictures. *Journal of Clinical Psychology, 8,* 273–278.

Boneau, C. A. (1974). Paradigm regained? Cognitive behaviorism restated. *American Psychologist, 29,* 297–309.

Bootzin, R. R., & Natsoulas, T. (1965). Evidence for perceptual defense uncontaminated by response bias. *Journal of Personality and Social Psychology, 1,* 461–468.

Bornstein, R. F. (1992). The dependent personality: Developmental, social, and clinical perspectives. *Psychological Bulletin, 112,* 3–23.

Boss, M. (1963). *Psychoanalysis and Daseinanalysis.* New York: Basic Books.

Bossard, J. H. S., & Boll, E. S. (1955). Personality roles in the large family. *Child Development, 26,* 71–78.

Bowers, K. S. (1973). Situationism in psychology: An analysis and a critique. *Psychological Review, 80,* 307–336.

Bowers, K. S. (1977). There's more to Iago than meets the eye: A clinical account of personal consistency. In D. Magnussen & N. S. Endler (Eds.), *Personality at the crossroads.* Hillsdale, NJ: Erlbaum.

Bowlby, J. (1969). *Attachment: Vol. 1. Attachment and loss.* New York: Basic Books.

Bradburn, N. M., & Berlew, D. E. (1961). Need for achievement and English industrial growth. *Economic Development and Cultural Change, 10,* 8–20.

Bradley, R. W. (1968). Birth order and school-related behavior: A heuristic review. *Psychological Bulletin, 70,* 45–51.

Braun, J., & Asta, P. (1968). Intercorrelations between the Personal Orientation Inventory and the Gordon Personal Inventory scores. *Psychological Reports, 23,* 1197–1198.

Brehm, J. W. (1965). Comments on Counter-norm attitudes induced by consonant versus dissonant conditions of role-playing. *Journal of Experimental Research in Personality, 1,* 61–64.

Brehm, J. W., & Cohen, A. R. (1959). Re-evaluation of choice alternatives as function of their number and qualitative similarity. *Journal of Abnormal and Social Psychology, 58,* 373–378.

Brehm, J. W., & Cohen, A. R. (1962). *Explorations in cognitive dissonance.* New York: Wiley.

Breuer, J., & Freud, S. (1895/1955). *Studies in hysteria.* Standard edition, *The Complete Works of Sigmund Freud* (Vol. 2). London: Hogarth.

Brody, G. H. (1978). A social learning explanation of moral development. *Contemporary Educational Psychology, 3,* 20–26.

Bronson, G. W. (1959). Identity diffusion in late adolescents. *Journal of Abnormal and Social Psychology, 59,* 414–417.

Brophy, A. L. (1959). Self, role, and satisfaction. *Genetic Psychology Monographs, 59,* 236–308.

Brown, D., & Marks, P. A. (1969). Bakan's bi-polar constructs: Agency and communion. *The Psychological Records, 19,* 465–478.

Brown, J. S., & Farber, I. E. (1951). Emotions conceptualized as intervening variables with suggestions toward a theory of frustration. *Psychological Bulletin, 38,* 465–495.

Brown, N. O. (1959). *Life against death.* Middletown, CT: Wesleyan University Press.

Brown, N. O. (1961). Apocalypse. [Phi Beta Kappa address.] *Harper's, 222,* 46–49.

Brown, R. (1986). *Social psychology: The second edition.* New York: Free Press.

Brown, S. R., & Hendrick, C. (1971). Introversion, extroversion and social perception. *British Journal of Social and Clinical Psychology, 10,* 313–319.

Bruner, J. S. (1956). You are your constructs. *Contemporary Psychology, 1,* 355–358.

Bruner, J. S. (1957a). Mechanism riding high. *Contemporary Psychology, 2,* 155–157.

Bruner, J. S. (1957b). Neural mechanisms in perception. *Psychological Review, 64,* 340–358.

Bruner, J. S. (1962a). The creative surprise. In H. E. Gruber, G. Terrell, & M. Wertheimer (Eds.), *Contemporary approaches to creative thinking.* New York: Atherton.

Bruner, J. S. (1962b). *On knowing: Essays for the left hand.* Cambridge, MA: Harvard University Press.

Bruner, J. S., & Postman, L. (1947a). Emotional selectivity in perception and reaction. *Journal of Personality, 16,* 69–77.

Bruner, J. S., & Postman, L. (1947b). Tension and tension-release as organizing factors in perception. *Journal of Personality, 15,* 300–308.

Bugental, J. F. T. (1965). *The search for authenticity.* New York: Holt, Rinehart & Winston.

Bugental, J. F. T. (1976). *The search for existential identity.* San Francisco: Jossey-Bass.

Buss, D. M., & Chiodo, L. M. (1991). Narcissistic acts in everyday life. *Journal of Personality, 59,* 179–216.

Buss, D. M., & Craik, K. H. (1983). The act frequency approach to personality. *Psychological Review, 90,* 105–26.

Butler, J. M., & Haigh, G. V. (1954). Changes in the relation between self-concepts and ideal-concepts consequent upon client-centered counseling. In C. R. Rogers & R. F. Dymond (Eds.), *Psychotherapy and personality change.* Chicago: University of Chicago Press.

Butler, J. M., & Rice, L. (1963). Adience, self-actualization, and drive theory. In J. M. Wepman & R. W. Heine (Eds.), *Concepts of personality.* Chicago: Aldine.

Butler, R. A., & Alexander, H. M. (1955). Daily patterns of visual exploratory behavior in the monkey. *Journal of Comparative and Physiological Psychology, 48,* 247–249.

Butterfield, E. C. (1964). Locus of control, test anxiety, reactions to frustration, and achievement attitudes. *Journal of Personality, 32,* 298–311.

Byrne, D. (1961a). Anxiety and the experimental arousal of affiliation need. *Journal of Abnormal and Social Psychology, 63,* 660–662.

Byrne, D. (1961b). The Repression-Sensitization Scale: Rationale, reliability, and validity. *Journal of Personality, 29,* 344–349.

Byrne, D. (1964). Repression-sensitization as a dimension of personality. In B. A. Maher (Ed.), *Progress in experimental personality research.* New York: Academic Press.

Byrne, D. (1965). Parental antecedents of authoritarianism. *Journal of Personality and Social Psychology, 1,* 369–373.

Byrne, D. (1977). Authoritarianism. In T. Blass (Ed.), *Personality variables in social behavior.* Hillsdale, NJ: Erlbaum.

Byrne, D., Barry, J., & Nelson, D. (1963). Relation of the revised Repression-Sensitization Scale to measures of self-description. *Psychological Reports, 13,* 323–334.

Calder, B. J., & Staw, B. M. (1975a). Interaction of intrinsic and extrinsic motivation: Some methodological notes. *Journal of Personality and Social Psychology, 31,* 76–80.

Calder, B. J., & Staw, B. M. (1975b). Self-perception of intrinsic and extrinsic motivation. *Journal of Personality and Social Psychology, 31,* 599–605.

Campbell, A. A. (1933). A study of the personality adjustments of only and intermediate children. *Journal of Genetic Psychology, 43,* 197–206.

Campell, A., Converse, P. E., Miller, W. E., & Stokes, D. E. (1960). *The American voter.* New York: Wiley.

Campbell, D. T., & Fiske, D. W. (1959). Convergent and discriminant validation by the multitrait-multimethod matrix. *Psychological Bulletin, 56,* 81–105.

Camus, A. (1955). *The myth of Sisyphus and other essays* (J. O'Brien, Trans.). New York: Knopf.

Cannon, W. B. (1929). *Bodily changes in pain, hunger, fear, and rage.* New York: Appleton.

Cantor, N. (1990). From thought to behavior: "Having" and "doing" in the study of personality and cognition. *American Psychologist, 45,* 735–750.

Cantor, N., & Kihlstrom, J. (1986). *Personality and social intelligence.* Englewood Cliffs, NJ: Prentice-Hall.

Cantor, N., Smith, E. E., French, R. D., & Mezzich, J. (1980). Psychiatric diagnosis as prototype categorization. *Journal of Abnormal Psychology, 89,* 181–193.

Carlson, L., & Carlson, R. (1984). Affect and psychological magnification: Derivations from Tomkins' script theory. *Journal of Personality, 52,* 36–45.

Carlson, R. (1971a). Sex differences in ego functioning: Exploratory studies of agency and communion. *Journal of Consulting and Clinical Psychology, 37,* 267–277.

Carlson, R. (1971b). Where is the person in personality research? *Psychological Bulletin, 75,* 203–219.

Carlson, R., & Levy, N. (1973). Studies of Jungian typology: 1. Memory, social perception and social action. *Journal of Personality, 41,* 559–576.

Carmichael, C. M. & McGue, M. (1994). Mother-offspring resemblance. *Journal of Personality, 62,* 2–20.

Carrigan, P. (1960). Extraversion-introversion as a dimension of personality: A reappraisal. *Psychological Bulletin, 57,* 329–360.

Carrol, E. N., Zuckerman, M., & Vogel, W. H. (1982). A test of the optimal level of arousal theory of sensation seeking. *Journal of Personality and Social Psychology, 42,* 572–575.

Carver, C. S., & Scheier, M. F. (1981). *Attention and self-regulation: A control theory approach to human behavior.* New York: Springer-Verlag.

Cash, T. F., & Pruzinsky, T. (1990). (Eds.). *Body images: Development, deviance, and change.* New York: Guilford.

Cash, T. F., & Szymanski, M.L. (1995). The development and validation of the Body-Image Ideals questionnaire. *Journal of Personality Assessment, 64,* 466–477.

Caspi, A., Bem, D. J., & Elder, G. H., Jr. (1989). Interactional and cumulative continuities over 30 years. *Journal of Personality, 57,* 375–406.

Cattell, R. B. (1946). *Description and measurement of personality.* New York: World Book.

Cattell, R. B. (1950). *Personality: A systematic, theoretical, and factual study.* New York: McGraw-Hill.

Cattell, R. B. (1957). *Personality and motivation structure and measurement.* New York: World Book.

Cattell, R. B. (1972). The 16 PF and basic personality structure: A reply to Eysenck. *Journal of Behavioral Science, 1,* 169–187.

Cattell, R. B., & Delhees, K. (1973). Seven missing normal personality factors in the questionnaire primaries. *Multivariate Behavior Research, 8,* 173–194.

Cattell, R. B., & Stice, G. F. (1957). *Sixteen Personality Factor Questionnaire* (rev. ed.). Champaign, IL: Institute for Personality & Abilities Testing.

Centers, R. (1969). The anal character and social severity in attitudes. *Journal of Projective Techniques & Personality Assessment, 33,* 501–506.

Cervone, D. (1991). The two disciplines of personality psychology. *Psychological Science, 2,* 371–377.

Chabot, J. A. (1973). Repression-sensitization: A critique of some neglected variables in the literature. *Psychological Bulletin, 80,* 122–129.

Chapanis, N. P., & Chapanis, A. (1964). Cognitive dissonance: Five years later. *Psychological Bulletin, 61,* 1–22.

Charen, S. (1956). Reliability of the Blacky Test. *Journal of Consulting Psychology, 20,* 16.

Cherulnik, P. D., & Citrin, M. M. (1974). Individual difference in psychological reactance: The interaction between locus of control and mode of elimination of freedom. *Journal of Personality and Social Psychology, 29,* 398–404.

Chodorkoff, B. (1954a). Adjustment and the discrepancy between perceived and ideal self. *Journal of Clinical Psychology, 10,* 266–268.

Chodorkoff, B. (1954b). Self-perception, perceptual defense, and adjustment. *Journal of Abnormal and Social Psychology, 49,* 508–512.

Ciminero, A. R., Calhoun, K. S., & Adams, H. E. (1977). *Handbook of behavioral assessment.* New York: Wiley.

Clark, C. (1957). *The conditions of economic progress* (3rd ed.). London: Macmillan.

Clark, S. L. (1968). Authoritarian attitudes and field dependence. *Psychological Reports, 22,* 309–310.

Clark, W. C., & Hunt, H. F. (1971). Pain. In J. A. Powney & R. C. Darling (Eds.), *Physiological basis of rehabilitation medicine.* Philadelphia: Saunders.

Coan, R. W. (1972). Measurable components of openness to experience. *Journal of Consulting and Clinical Psychology, 39,* 346.

Coan, R. W. (1974). *The optimal personality.* New York: Columbia University Press.

Cohen, A. R., Brehm, J. W., & Fleming, W. H. (1958). Attitude change and justification for compliance. *Journal of Abnormal and Social Psychology, 56,* 276–278.

Cole, J. K. (Ed.). (1976). *Nebraska symposium on motivation.* Lincoln: University of Nebraska Press.

Coleman, J. S., Campbell, E. Q., Hobson, C. J., McPartland, J., Mood, A. M., Weinfeld, F. D., & York, R. L. (1966). *Equality of educational opportunity.* (Superintendent of Documents, Catalog No. FS 5.238.38001). Washington, DC: U.S. Office of Education.

Collins, B. E. (1974). Four components of the Rotter Internal-External Scale: Belief in a difficult world, a just world, a predictable world, and a politically responsive world. *Journal of Personality and Social Psychology, 29,* 381–391.

Colvin, C. R., & Block, J. (1994). Do positive illusions foster mental health? An examination of the Taylor and Brown formulation. *Psychological Bulletin, 116,* 3–20.

Colvin, C. R., Block, J. & Funder, D.C. (1995). Overly positive self-evaluations and personality: Negative implications for mental health. *Journal of Personality and Social Psychology, 68,* 1152–1163.

Conant, J. B. (1947). *On understanding science.* New Haven, CT: Yale University Press.

Conley, J. J. (1984). Longitudinal consistency of adult personality: Self-reported psychological characteristics across 45 years. *Journal of Personality and Social Psychology, 42,* 1325–1333.

Conn, L. K., & Crowne, D. P. (1963). Instigation to aggression, emotional arousal and defensive emulation. *Journal of Personality, 32,* 163–179.

Conners, C. K. (1963). Birth order and needs for affiliation. *Journal of Personality, 31,* 408–416.

Constantinople, A. (1969). An Eriksonian measure of personality development in college students. *Developmental Psychology, 1,* 357–372.

Cook, J. R. (1985). Repression-sensitization and approach-avoidance as predictors of response to a laboratory stressor. *Journal of Personality and Social Psychology, 49,* 759–773.

Cook, P. (1958). Authoritarian or acquiescent: Some behavioral differences. *American Psychologist, 13,* 338.

Cooper, J., & Goethals, G. R. (1974). Unforeseen events and the elimination of cognitive dissonance.

Journal of Personality and Social Psychology, 29, 441–445.

Cooper, J., & Scalise, C. J. (1974). Dissonance produced by deviations from life styles: The interaction of Jungian typology and conformity. *Journal of Personality and Social Psychology, 29,* 556–571.

Cooper, W. H. (1983). An achievement motivation nomological network. *Journal of Personality and Social Psychology, 44,* 841–861.

Cooperman, M., & Child, I. L. (1969). Esthetic preference and active style. *Proceedings of the 77th Annual Convention of the American Psychological Association, 4,* 471–472.

Cortes, J. B. (1960). The achievement motive in the Spanish economy between the 13th and 18th centuries. *Economic Development and Cultural Change, 9,* 144–163.

Costa, P. T., Jr. (1970). *Multivariate analysis of the Maddi model of forms for variety.* Unpublished doctoral dissertation, University of Chicago.

Costa, P. T., Jr., & McCrae, R. R. (1976). Age differences in personality structure: A cluster analytic approach. *Journal of Gerontology, 31*(5), 564–570.

Costa, P. T., Jr., & McCrae, R. R. (1977). Psychiatric symptom dimensions in the Cornell Medical Index among normal and adult males. *Journal of Clinical Psychology, 33*(4), 941–946.

Costa, P. T., Jr., & McCrae, R. R. (1977–1978). Age differences in personality structure revisited: Studies in validity, stability, and change. *International Journal of Aging and Human Development, 8*(4), 261–275.

Costa, P. T., Jr., & McCrae, R. R. (1980). Still stable after all these years: Personality as a key to some issues in aging. In P. B. Baltes & O. G. Brim (Eds.), *Lifespan development and behavior* (Vol. 3, pp. 65–102). New York: Academic Press.

Costa, P. T., Jr., & McCrae, R. R. (1988). From catalog to classification: Murray's needs and the Five-Factor Model. *Journal of Personality and Social Psychology, 55,* 258–265.

Costa, P. T. Jr., & McCrae, R. R. (1992). *Revised NEO Personality Inventory (NEO-PI-R) and NEO Five Factor Inventory (NEO-FFI) professional manual.* Odessa, FL: Psychological Assessment Resources.

Costa, P. T., Jr., & McCrae, R. R. (1995a). Domains and facets: Heirarchical personality assessment using the revised NEO Personality Inventory. *Journal of Personality Assessment, 64,* 21–50.

Costa, P. T., Jr., & McCrae, R. R. (1995b). Solid grounds in the wetlands of personality: A reply to Block. *Psychological Bulletin, 117,* 216–220.

Costa, P. T., Jr., McCrae, R. R., & Arenberg, D. (1980). Enduring dispositions in adult males. *Journal of Personality and Social Psychology, 38,* 793–800.

Costa, P. T., Jr., Zonderman, A. B., Williams, R. B., Jr., & McCrae, R. R. (1985). Content and comprehensiveness in the MMPI: An item factor analysis in a normal adult sample. *Journal of Personality and Social Psychology, 48,* 925–933.

Costin, F. (1965). Dogmatism and learning: A follow-up of contradictory findings. *Journal of Educational Research, 59,* 186–188.

Costin, F. (1968). Dogmatism and the retention of psychological misconceptions. *Educational & Psychological Measurement, 28,* 529–534.

Cowen, E. L., & Beier, E. G. (1954). Threat expectancy, work frequencies, and perceptual prerecognition hypotheses. *Journal of Abnormal and Social Psychology, 14,* 469–477.

Cramer, P. (1987). The development of defense mechanisms. *Journal of Personality, 55,* 597–614.

Cramer, P. (1990). *The development of defense mechanisms: Theory, research, and assessment.* New York: Springer-Verlag.

Cramer, P. (1991). Anger and the use of defense mechanisms in college students. *Journal of Personality, 59,* 39–56.

Crandall, V. C., Katkovsky, W., & Crandall, V. J. (1965). Children's beliefs in their own control of reinforcement in intellectual-academic achievement situations. *Child Development, 36,* 91–109.

Crepeau, J. J. (1978). The effects of stressful life events and locus of control on suicidal ideation. Unpublished research, University of Massachusetts at Amherst.

Croake, J. W., & Hayden, D. J. (1975). Trait oppositeness in siblings: Test of Adlerian tenet. *Journal of Individual Psychology, 31,* 175–178.

Cromwell, R., Rosenthal, D., Shakow, D., & Kahn, T. (1961). Reaction time, locus of control, choice behavior and descriptions of parental behavior in schizophrenic and normal subjects. *Journal of Personality, 29,* 363–380.

Cronbach, L. J. (1975a). Beyond the two disciplines of scientific psychology. *American Psychologist, 30,* 116–127.

Cronbach, L. J. (1975b). The two disciplines of scientific psychology. *American Psychologist, 12,* 671–684.

Cronbach, L. J., & Meehl, P. E. (1955). Construct validity in psychological tests. *Psychological Bulletin, 52,* 281–302.

Crookes, T. G., & Pearson, P. R. (1970). The relationship between EPI scores and 16 PF second order factors in a clinical group. *British Journal of Social and Clinical Psychology, 9*, 189–190.

Cross, P. G., Cattell, R. B., & Butcher, H. J. (1967). The personality pattern of creative artists. *British Journal of Education Psychology, 37*, 292–299.

Crosson, S., & Schwendiman, G. (1972). *Self-actualization as a predictor of conformity behavior.* Unpublished manuscript, Marshall University, Huntington, WV.

Crowne, D. P., & Liverant, S. (1963). Conformity under varying conditions of personal commitment. *Journal of Abnormal and Social Psychology, 66*, 547–555.

Crowne, D. P., & Marlowe, D. (1960). A new scale of social desirability independent of psychopathology. *Journal of Consulting Psychology, 24*, 349–354.

Crumbaugh, J. C. (1968). Cross-validation of the Purpose in Life Test based on Frankl's concepts. *Journal of Individual Psychology, 24*, 74–81.

Crumbaugh, J. C., & Maholick, L. T. (1964). An experimental study in existentialism: The psychometric approach to Frankl's concept of noogenic neurosis. *Journal of Clinical Psychology, 20*, 200–207.

Csikszentmihalyi, M. (1975). *Beyond boredom and anxiety.* San Francisco: Jossey-Bass.

Damm, V. J. (1969). Overall measures of self actualization derived from the Personal Orientation Inventory. *Educational & Psychological Measurement, 29*, 977–981.

Dandes, H. M. (1966). Psychological health and teaching effectiveness. *Journal of Teaching Education, 17*, 301–306.

D'Andrade, R. G. (1974). Memory and the assessment of behavior. In T. Blalock (Ed.), *Social measurement.* Chicago: Aldine-Atherton.

Danskin, D. G. (1964, September). *An introduction to KSU students.* Unpublished report, Kansas State University, Student Counseling Center. Cited in J. B. Warren (1966), Birth order and social behavior, *Psychological Bulletin, 65*, 38–49.

Davis, A., & Dollard, J. (1940). *Children of bondage.* Washington, DC: American Council on Education.

Davis, P. J., & Schwartz, G. (1987). Repression and the inaccessibility of affective memories. *Journal of Personality and Social Psychology, 52*, 155–162.

de Charms, R. C. (1957). Affiliation motivation and productivity in small groups. *Journal of Abnormal Social Psychology, 55*, 222–226.

de Charms, R. C., Morrison, H. W., Reitman, W., & McClelland, D. C. (1955). Behavioral correlates of directly and indirectly measured achievement motivation. In D. C. McClelland (Ed.), *Studies in motivation.* New York: Appleton-Century-Crofts.

deCharms, R. C., & Muir, M. S. (1978). Motivation: Social approaches. In M. R. Rosenzweig & L. W. Porter (Eds.), *Annual Review of Psychology* (Vol. 29). Palo Alto, CA: Annual Reviews.

Deci, E. L. (1975). *Intrinsic motivation.* New York: Plenum.

de Grace, G. R. (1974). The compatibility of anxiety and actualization. *Journal of Clinical Psychology, 130*, 566–568.

de Jong, P. F. (1988). An application of the prototype scale construction strategy to the assessment of student motivation. *Journal of Personality, 56*, 487–508.

Dember, W. N. (1956). Response by the rat to environmental change. *Journal of Comparative and Physiological Psychology, 49*, 93–95.

Dember, W. N. (1961). Alternation behavior. In D. W. Fiske & S. R. Maddi (Eds.), *Functions of varied experience.* Homewood, IL: Dorsey Press.

Dember, W. N. (1964). Birth order and need affiliation. *Journal of Abnormal and Social Psychology, 68*, 555–557.

Dember, W. N. (1974). Motivation and the cognitive revolution. *American Psychologist, 29*, 161–168.

Dennis, W. (1939). Spontaneous alternation in rats as an indicator of persistence of stimulus effects. *Journal of Comparative Psychology, 28*, 305–312.

Diamond, R. E., & Munz, D. C. (1967). Ordinal position of birth and self-disclosure in high school students. *Psychological Reports, 21*, 829–833.

DiCaprio, N. S. (1974). *Personality theories: Guides to living.* Philadelphia: Saunders.

Digman, J. M. (1989). Five robust trait dimensions: Development, stability, and utility. *Journal of Personality, 57*, 260–269.

Dittes, J. E. (1961). Birth order and vulnerability to differences in acceptance. *American Psychologist, 16*, 358.

Dollard, J., & Miller, N. E. (1950). *Personality and psychotherapy: An analysis in terms of learning, thinking, and culture.* New York: McGraw-Hill.

Domino, G. (1976). Compensatory aspects of dreams: An empirical test of Jung's theory. *Journal of Personality and Social Psychology, 34*, 658–662.

Donley, R. E., & Winter, D. G. (1965). Measuring the motives of public officials at a distance: An exploratory study of American presidents. *Behavioral Science, 3*, 227–236.

Dorfman, D. D. (1965). Esthetic preference as a

function of pattern information. *Psychonomic Science, 3*, 85–86.

Douglas, W., & Gibbins, K. (1983). Inadequacy of voice recognition as a demonstration of self-deception. *Journal of Personality and Social Psychology, 44*, 589–592.

Dreikurs, R. (1963). Individual psychology: The Adlerian point of view. In J. M. Wepman & R. W. Heine (Eds.), *Concepts of personality*. Chicago: Aldine.

Drory, Y., & Florian, V. (1991). Long-term psychological adjustment to coronary heart disease. *Archives of Physical Medicine and Rehabilitation, 72*, 326–331.

Duberstein, P. R., & Talbot, N. L. (1992). Parental idealization and the absence of Rorschach oral imagery. *Journal of Personality Assessment, 59*, 50–58.

Duckworth, D. H. (1975). Personality, emotional state and perception of nonverbal communications. *Perceptual and Motor Skills, 40*, 325–326.

Duffy, E. (1963). *Activation and behavior*. New York: Wiley.

Dulany, D. E., Jr. (1962). The place of hypotheses and intentions: An analysis of verbal control in verbal conditioning. In C. W. Eriksen (Ed.), *Behavior and awareness*. Durham, NC: Duke University Press.

Dulany, D. E., Jr. (1968). Awareness, rules, and propositional control: A confrontation with S-R behavior theory. In T. R. Dixon & D. L. Horton (Eds.), *Verbal behavior and general behavior theory*. Englewood Cliffs, NJ: Prentice-Hall.

Duncan, S. D., Jr. (1972). Some signals and rules for taking speaking turns in conversations. *Journal of Personality and Social Psychology, 23*, 283–292.

Duncan, S. D., Jr., & Fiske, D. (1977). *Face to face interactions: Research methods and theory*. Hillsdale, NJ: Erlbaum.

D'Zurilla, T. (1965). Recall efficiency and mediating cognitive events in "experimental repression." *Journal of Personality and Social Psychology, 3*, 253–256.

Ebersole, P. (1973). Effects and classifications of peak experiences. *Psychological Reports, 40*, 22–28.

Edwards, A. L. (1957). *The social desirability variable in personality assessment and research*. New York: Dryden Press.

Edwards, A. L. (1963). *Edwards Personal Preference Schedule*. New York: Psychological Corporation.

Ehrlich, D., Guttman, I., Schonbach, P., & Mills, J. (1957). Postdecision exposure to relevant information. *Journal of Abnormal and Social Psychology, 54*, 98–102.

Ehrlich, H. J. (1955). *Dogmatism and intellectual change*. Unpublished master's thesis, Ohio State University, Columbus.

Ehrlich, H. J. (1961a). Dogmatism and learning. *Journal of Abnormal and Social Psychology, 62*, 148–149.

Ehrlich, H. J. (1961b). Dogmatism and learning: A five-year follow-up. *Psychological Reports, 9*, 283–286.

Ehrlich, H. J., & Lee, D. (1969). Dogmatism, learning and resistance to change: A review and a new paradigm. *Psychological Bulletin, 71*, 249–260.

Eisenberger, R. (1972). Explanation of rewards that do not reduce tissue needs. *Psychological Bulletin, 77*, 319–339.

Eisenberger, R., Myers, A. K., Sanders, R., & Shanab, M. (1970). Stimulus control of spontaneous alternation in the rat. *Journal of Comparative and Physiological Psychology, 70*, 136–140.

Eisenman, R., & Schussel, N. R. (1970). Creativity, birth order and preference for symmetry. *Journal of Consulting and Clinical Psychology, 34*, 275–280.

Ekehammar, B. (1974). Interactionism in personality from a historical perspective. *Psychological Bulletin, 81*, 1026–1048.

Elder, G. H., Jr. (1965). Family structure: The effects of size of family, sex composition and ordinal position on academic motivation and achievement. In B. A. Maher (Ed.), *Progress in experimental personality research*. New York: Academic Press.

Elliot, L. L. (1961). Effects of item construction and respondent aptitude on response acquiescence. *Educational & Psychological Measurement, 21*, 405–415.

Ellis, A. (1962). *Reason and Emotion in Psychotherapy*. New York: Lyle Stuart.

Elms, A. C. (1967). Role playing, incentive, and dissonance. *Psychological Bulletin, 68*, 132–148.

Elms, A. C. (1994). *Uncovering lives: An uneasy alliance of biography and psychology*. New York: University Press.

Elms, A. C., & Janis, I. L. (1965). Counter-norm attitudes induced by consonant versus dissonant conditions of role-playing. *Journal of Experimental Research in Personality, 1*, 50–60.

Elms, A. C., & Milgram, S. (1966). Personality characteristics associated with obedience and defiance toward authoritative command. *Journal of Experimental Research in Personality, 1*, 282–289.

Emerson, R. W. (1940). *The selected writings of Ralph Waldo Emerson*. (B. Atkinson, Ed.). New York: Modern Library.

Emmons, R. A. (1993). Current status of the motive concept. In K. H. Craik, R. Hogan, & R. N. Wolfe (Eds.), *Fifty years of personality psychology* (pp. 187–196). New York: Plenum.

Emmons, R. A., & McAdams, D. P. (1991). Personal strivings and motive dispositions: Exploring the links. *Personality and Social Psychology Bulletin, 17,* 648–654.

Endler, N. S. (1973). The person versus the situation —a pseudo issue? A response to Alker. *Journal of Personality, 41,* 287–303.

Endler, N. S., & Hunt, J. McV. (1966). Sources of behavioral variance as measured by the S-R Inventory of Anxiousness. *Psychological Bulletin, 65,* 338–346.

Endler, N. S., & Hunt, J. McV. (1969). Generalizability of contributions from sources of variance in the S-R inventories of anxiousness. *Journal of Personality, 37,* 1–24.

Endler, N. S., Hunt, J. McV., & Rosenstein, A. J. (1962). An S-R Inventory of anxiousness. *Psychological Monograph, 76*(536).

Endler, N. S., & Magnusson, D. (1976). Toward an interactional psychology of personality. *Psychological Bulletin, 83,* 956–974.

Epstein, R. (1965). Authoritarianism, displaced aggression, and social status of the target. *Journal of Personality and Social Psychology, 2,* 585–589.

Epstein, S. (1984). The stability of behavior across time and situations. In R. A. Zucker, J. Aronoff, & R. I. Rabin (Eds.), *Personality and the prediction of behavior.* New York: Academic Press.

Epstein, S. (1994). Implications of cognitive-experiential self-theory for new directions in personality and developmental psychology. In R. Parke, G. Tomlinson-Keasey, K. Widemen, & D. C. Funder (Eds.), *Studying lives through time: Approaches to personality and development.* Washington, DC: American Psychological Association.

Erdelyi, M. H. (1974). A new look at the new look: Perceptual defense and vigilance. *Psychological Review, 81,* 1–25.

Eriksen, C. W. (1951a). Perceptual defense as a function of unacceptable needs. *Journal of Abnormal and Social Psychology, 46,* 557–564.

Eriksen, C. W. (1951b). Some implications for TAT interpretation arising from need and perception experiments. *Journal of Personality, 19,* 283–288.

Eriksen, C. W. (1952). Defense against ego-threat in memory and perception. *Journal of Abnormal and Social Psychology, 47,* 430–435.

Eriksen, C. W. (1954). Psychological defenses and ego strength in the recall of completed and incompleted tasks. *Journal of Abnormal and Social Psychology, 49,* 45–50.

Eriksen, C. W. (1963). Perception and personality. In J. M. Wepman & R. W. Heine (Eds.), *Concepts of personality.* Chicago: Aldine.

Eriksen, C. W., & Brown, C. T. (1956). An experimental and theoretical analysis of perceptual defense. *Journal of Abnormal and Social Psychology, 52,* 224–230.

Eriksen, C. W., & Davids, A. (1955). The meaning and clinical validity of Taylor Anxiety Scale and the Hysteria-Psychasthenia Scales from the MMPI. *Journal of Abnormal Social Psychology, 50,* 135–137.

Erikson, E. H. (1950). *Childhood and society.* New York: Norton.

Erikson, E. H. (1956). The problem of ego identity. *Journal of the American Psychoanalytic Association, 4,* 56–121.

Erikson, E. H. (1959). *Identity and the life cycle.* (Psychological Issues Monograph No. 1, Vol. 1). New York: International Universities Press.

Estes, S. G. (1938). Judging personality from expressive behavior. *Journal of Abnormal and Social Psychology, 33,* 217–236.

Eysenck, H. J. (1947). *Dimensions of personality.* London: Routledge & Kegan Paul.

Eysenck, H. J. (1952). The effects of psychotherapy: An evaluation. *Journal of Consulting Psychology, 16,* 319–324.

Eysenck, H. J. (1957). *The dynamics of anxiety and hysteria: An experimental application of modern learning theory to psychiatry.* London: Routledge & Kegan Paul.

Eysenck, H. J. (1970). *The structure of human personality* (3rd ed.). London: Methuen.

Eysenck, H. J. (1976). *Sex and personality.* London: Open Books.

Eysenck, H. J. (1977). Personality and factor analysis: A reply to Guilford. *Psychological Bulletin, 84,* 405–411.

Eysenck, H. J., & Rachman, S. (1965). *The causes and cures of neuroses.* San Diego, CA: Knapp.

Fairbairn, W. R. D. (1954). *An object-relations theory of personality.* New York: Basic Books.

Falbo, T. (1981). Relationships between birth category, achievement, and interpersonal orientation. *Journal of Personality and Social Psychology, 41,* 121–131.

Farber, I. E. (1948). Response fixation under anxiety and non-anxiety conditions. *Journal of Experimental Psychology, 38,* 111–131.

Farber, I. E., & Spence, K. W. (1953). Complex learning and conditioning as a function of anxiety. *Journal of Experimental Psychology, 45*, 120–125.

Feather, N. T. (1967). Some personality correlates of external control. *Australian Journal of Psychology, 19*, 253–260.

Feather, N. T. (1984). Masculinity, femininity, psychological androgyny, and the structure of values. *Journal of Personality and Social Psychology, 47*, 604–620.

Feingold, A. (1994). Gender differences in personality: A meta-analysis. *Psychological Bulletin, 116*, 429–456.

Feldinger, I., & Maddi, S. R. (1968). *The motivational status of measures of the need for variety.* Unpublished manuscript, University of Chicago.

Fenichel, O. (1945). *The psychoanalytic theory of neurosis.* New York: Norton.

Feshbach, N. D. (1982). Sex differences in empathy and social behavior in children. In N. Eisenberg-Berg (Ed.), *The development of pro-social behavior* (pp. 315–338). New York: Academic Press.

Festinger, L. (1958a). The motivating effect of cognitive dissonance. In G. Lindzey (Ed.), *Assessment of human motives.* New York: Holt, Rinehart & Winston.

Festinger, L. (1958b). *A theory of cognitive dissonance.* Stanford, CA: Stanford University Press.

Festinger, L., & Carlsmith, J. M. (1959). Cognitive consequences of forced compliance. *Journal of Abnormal and Social Psychology, 58*, 203–210.

Findley, M. J., & Cooper, H. M. (1983). Locus of control and academic achievement: A literature review. *Journal of Personality and Social Psychology, 44*, 419–427.

Fine, B. J., & Danforth, A. V. (1975). Field-dependence, extroversion and perception of the vertical: Empirical and theoretical perspectives of the Rod and Frame Test. *Perceptual and Motor Skills, 40*, 683–693.

Fink, D. R., Jr. (1958). Negative evidence concerning the generality of rigidity. *Journal of Abnormal and Social Psychology, 57*, 252–254.

Fisher, G. (1968). Performance of psychopathic felons on a measure of self-actualization. *Educational & Psychological Measurement, 28*, 561–563.

Fisher, G., & Silverstein, A. G. (1969). Simulation of poor adjustment on a measure of self-actualization. *Journal of Clinical Psychology, 25*, 198–199.

Fishman, C. G. (1965). Need for approval and the expression of aggression under varying conditions of frustration. *Journal of Personality and Social Psychology, 2*, 809–816.

Fiske, D. W. (1961). Effects of monotonous and restricted stimulation. In D. W. Fiske & S. R. Maddi (Eds.), *Functions of varied experience.* Homewood, IL: Dorsey Press.

Fiske, D. W. (1963). Problems in measuring personality. In J. M. Wepman & R. W. Heine (Eds.), *Concepts of personality.* Chicago: Aldine.

Fiske, D. W. (1974). The limits for the conventional science of personality. *Journal of Personality, 42*, 1–11.

Fiske, D. W. (1978). *Strategies for research in personality: Observations vs. interpretation of behavior.* San Francisco: Jossey-Bass.

Fiske, D. W., & Maddi, S. R. (Eds.). (1961). *Functions of varied experience.* Homewood, IL: Dorsey Press.

Fiske, S. T., & Taylor, S. E. (1991). *Social cognition* (2nd. ed.). New York: Norton.

Flavell, J. (1955). Repression and the "return of the repressed." *Journal of Consulting Psychology, 19*, 441–443.

Florian, V., Milkulincer, M., & Taubman, O. (1995). Does hardiness contribute to mental health during a stressful real life situation? The roles of appraisal and coping. *Journal of Personality and Social Psychology, 68*, 687–695.

Fodor, E. M. (1984). The power motive and reactivity to power stresses. *Journal of Personality and Social Psychology, 47*, 853–959.

Fodor, E. M., & Smith, T. (1982). The power motive as an influence on group decision making. *Journal of Personality and Social Psychology, 42*, 178–185.

Foulds, M. L. (1969). Self-actualization and the communication of facilitative conditions during counseling. *Journal of Counseling Psychology, 16*, 132–136.

Foulds, M. L., & Warehime, R. G. (1971). Effects of a "fake good" response set on a measure of self-actualization. *Journal of Counseling Psychology, 18*, 279–280.

Fox, J., Knapp, R., & Michael, W. (1968). Assessment of self-actualization of psychiatric patients: Validity of the Personal Orientation Inventory. *Educational & Psychological Measurement, 28*, 565–569.

Frankel, M. (1971). Personality as a response: Behaviorism. In S. R. Maddi (Ed.), *Perspectives on personality.* Boston: Little, Brown.

Frankl, V. (1960). *The doctor and the soul.* New York: Knopf.

Frankl, V. (1992). The first published cases of

paradoxical intention. *International Forum for Psychotherapy, 15,* 2–6.

Fransella, F. (Ed.). (1978). *Personal constructs 1977.* New York: Academic Press.

Franz, C. E. (1995). A quantitative case study of longitudinal changes in identity, intimacy, and generativity. *Journal of Personality, 63,* 27–46.

Freedenfeld, R. N., Ornduff, S. R., & Kelsey, R. M. (1995). Object relations and physical abuse: A TAT analysis. *Journal of Personality, 64,* 552–568.

Freedman, M. B., & Bereiter, C. (1963). A longitudinal study of personality development in college alumnae. *Merrill-Palmer Quarterly, 9,* 295–302.

Freeman, G. L. (1933). The facilitative and inhibitive effects of muscular tension upon performance. *American Journal of Psychology, 45,* 17–52.

Freeman, G. L. (1938). The optimal muscular tension for various performances. *American Journal of Psychology, 51,* 146–150.

Freeman, G. L. (1940). The relationship between performance level and bodily activity level. *Journal of Experimental Psychology, 26,* 602–608.

French, E. G. (1955). Some characteristics of achievement motivation. *Journal of Experimental Psychology, 50,* 232–236.

French, E. G. (1956). Motivation as a variable in work partner selection. *Journal of Abnormal and Social Psychology, 53,* 96–99.

French, J. W. (1973). *Toward the establishment of noncognitive factors through literature search and interpretation.* Princeton, NJ: Educational Testing Service.

Freud, A. (1946). *The ego and the mechanisms of defense.* New York: International Universities Press.

Freud, S. (1893). Quelques considerations pour une étude comparative des paralysies motrices organiques et hystèriques. *Archives de Neurologie, 26,* 29–43.

Freud, S. (1900/1995). The interpretation of dreams. In J. Strachey (Ed.), *The standard edition of the complete psychological works of Sigmund Freud.* (Vols. IV & V). London: Hogarth Press.

Freud, S. (1922a). *Beyond the pleasure principle.* London: International Psychoanalytic Press.

Freud, S. (1922b). *Reflections* (A. A. Brill & A. B. Kuttner, Trans.). New York: Moffat Yard.

Freud, S. (1925a). Character and anal erotism. In S. Freud, *Collected papers* (Vol. 2). London: Institute for Psychoanalysis and Hogarth Press.

Freud, S. (1925b). The infantile genital organization of the libido. In S. Freud, *Collected papers* (Vol. 2). London: Institute for Psychoanalysis and Hogarth Press.

Freud, S. (1925c). Instincts and their vicissitudes. In S. Freud, *Collected papers* (Vol. 4). London: Institute for Psychoanalysis and Hogarth Press.

Freud, S. (1925d). On the transformation of instincts with especial reference to anal erotism. In S. Freud, *Collected papers* (Vol. 2). London: Institute for Psychoanalysis and Hogarth Press.

Freud, S. (1925e). Some character types met with in psychoanalysis work. In S. Freud, *Collected papers* (Vol. 4). London: Institute for Psychoanalysis and Hogarth Press.

Freud, S. (1927). *The ego and the id.* London: Institute for Psychoanalysis and Hogarth Press.

Freud, S. (1930). *Civilization and its discontents.* New York: Norton.

Freud, S. (1933). *New introductory lectures in psychoanalysis* (W. J. H. Sprott, Trans.). New York: Norton.

Freud, S. (1936). *The problem of anxiety.* New York: Norton.

Freud, S. (1938). Three contributions to the theory of sex. In Brill, A. A. (Ed.), *The basic writings of Sigmund Freud.* New York: Modern Library.

Freud, S. (1952). *Totem and taboo.* New York: Norton.

Freud, S. (1957). The history of the psychoanalytic movement. In J. Strachey (Ed.), *The standard edition of the complete psychological works* (Vol. 14). London: Hogarth Press.

Freud, S. (1960). The psychopathology of everyday life. In J. Strachey (Ed.), *The standard edition of the complete psychological works* (Vol. 6). London: Hogarth Press.

Frick, J. W., Guilford, J. P., Christensen, P. R., & Merrifield, P. R. (1959). A factor-analytic study of flexibility of thinking. *Educational Psychological Measurement, 19,* 469–496.

Fromm, E. (1941). *Escape from freedom.* New York: Holt, Rinehart & Winston.

Fromm, E. (1947). *Man for himself.* New York: Holt, Rinehart, & Winston.

Fromm, E. (1955). *The sane society.* New York: Holt, Rinehart, & Winston.

Fromm, E. (1956). *The art of loving.* New York: Harper.

Fromm, E., & Maccoby, M. (1970). *Social character in a Mexican village.* Englewood Cliffs, NJ: Prentice-Hall.

Fuerst, K., & Zubek, J. P. (1968). Effects of sensory and perceptual deprivation on a battery of open-ended cognitive tasks. *Canadian Journal of Psychology, 22,* 122–130.

Funder, D. C. (1983). The consistency controversy and the accuracy of personality judgements. *Journal of Personality, 51,* 346–359.

Funder, D. C. (1991). Global traits: A neo-Allportian approach to personality. *Psychological Science, 2,* 31–39.

Funk, S. C. (1992). Hardiness: A review of theory and research. *Health Psychology, 11,* 335–345.

Funk, S. C., & Houston, B. K. (1987). A critical analysis of the hardiness scale's validity and utility. *Journal of Personality and Social Psychology, 53,* 572–578.

Galambos, R. (1956). Suppression of auditory nerve activity by stimulation of efferent fibers to cochlea. *Journal of Neurophysiology, 19,* 424–431.

Galambos, R., Sheatz, G., & Vernier, V. G. (1956). Electro-physiological correlates of a conditioned response in cats. *Science, 123,* 376–377.

Ganellen, R. J., & Blaney, P. H. (1984). Hardiness and social support as moderators of the effects of life stress. *Journal of Personality and Social Psychology, 47,* 156–163.

Garlington, W. K., & Shimota, H. (1964). The change seeker index: A measure of the need for variable stimulus input. *Psychological Reports, 14,* 191–924.

Geen, R. G. (1984). Preferred stimulation levels in introverts and extraverts: Effects on arousal and performance. *Journal of Personality and Social Psychology, 46,* 1303–1312.

Gelbort, K. R., & Winer, J. L. (1985). Fear of success and fear of failure: A multitrait-multimethod validation study. *Journal of Personality and Social Psychology, 48,* 1009–1014.

Gelfand, D. M. (1962). The influence of self-esteem on rate of verbal conditioning and social matching behavior. *Journal of Existentialism, 65,* 259–265.

Gendlin, E. T. (1965–1966). Experiential explication and truth. *Journal of Existentialism, 6,* 131–146.

Gendlin, E. T. (1973). Experiential psychotherapy. In R. Corsini (Ed.), *Current psychotherapies.* Itasca, IL: Peacock.

Gendlin, E. T., & Tomlinson, T. M. (1967). The process conception and its measurement. In C. R. Rogers, E. T. Gendlin, D. J. Kiesler, & C. B. Truax (Eds.), *The therapeutic relationship and its impact: A study of psychotherapy with schizophrenics.* Madison: University of Wisconsin Press.

Gerard, H. B., & Rabbie, J. M. (1961). Fear and social comparison. *Journal of Abnormal and Social Psychology, 62,* 586–592.

Getzels, J. W., & Csikszentmihalyi, M. (1976). *The creative vision: A longitudinal study of problem finding in art.* New York: Wiley.

Gibbins, K. & Douglas, W. (1985). Voice recognition and self-deception: A reply to Sackheim & Gur. *Journal of Personality and Social Psychology, 48,* 1369–1372.

Gleser, G. C., & Ihilevich, D. (1969). An objective instrument for measuring defense mechanisms. *Journal of Consulting Clinical Psychology, 33,* 51–60.

Gleser, G. C., & Sacks, M. (1973). Ego defenses and reaction to stress: A validation study of the Defense Mechanisms Inventory. *Journal of Consulting Clinical Psychology, 40,* 181–187.

Glover, E. (1925). Notes on oral character formation. *International Journal of Psychoanalysis, 6,* 131–154.

Glover, E. (1926). Einige probleme der psychoanalytischen Characterologie. *Internationale Zeitschrift für Psychoanalyse, 12,* 326–333.

Glover, E. (1928). The etiology of alcoholism. *Proceedings of the Royal Society of Medicine, 21,* 1351–1356.

Gold, J. A., Ryckman, R. M., & Rodda, W. C. (1973). Differential responsiveness of dissonance manipulations by open and closed-minded subjects in a forced compliance situation. *Journal of Social Psychology, 90,* 73–83.

Goldberg, L. R., & Saucier, G. (1995). So what do you propose we use instead? A reply to Block. *Psychological Bulletin, 117,* 221–225.

Goldfried, M. R., & D'Zurilla, T. J. (1969). A behavioral-analytic model for assessing competence. In C. D. Spielberger (Ed.), *Current topics in clinical and community psychology* (pp. 151–196). New York: Academic Press.

Goldiamond, I. (1968). Moral behavior: A functional analysis. *Psychology Today, 70,* 31–34.

Goldiamond, I., & Dyrud, J. (1967). Some applications and implications and behavioral analysis for psychotherapy. In *Research in psychotherapy* (Vol. 3). Washington, DC: American Psychological Association.

Goldstein, A. (1973). Behavior therapy. In R. Corsini (Ed.), *Current psychotherapies.* Itasca, IL: Peacock.

Goldstein, K. (1963). *The organism.* Boston: Beacon Press.

Good, L. R., & Good, K. (1973). An objective measure of the motive to avoid appearing incompetent. *Psychological Reports, 32,* 1075–1078.

Gore, P. M., & Rotter, J. B. (1963). A personality correlate of social action. *Journal of Personality, 31,* 58–64.

Gorney, J. E., & Tobin, S. S. (1969). Experiencing the age: Patterns of reminiscence among the elderly.

Paper presented at the Eighth International Congress of Gerontology, Washington, DC.

Gough, H. G. (1957/1987). *Manual for the California Psychological Inventory.* Palo Alto, CA: Consulting Psychologists Press.

Grace, H. K. (1974). *The development of a child psychiatric treatment program.* New York: Schenkman.

Graff, R., & Bradshaw, H. (1970). Relationship of a measure of self-actualization to dormitory assistant effectiveness. *Journal of Counseling Psychology, 17,* 502–505.

Graham, W. K., & Balloun, J. (1973). An empirical test of Maslow's need hierarchy theory. *Journal of Human Psychology, 13,* 97–108.

Granberg, D., & Corrigan, G. (1972). Authoritarianism, dogmatism and orientations toward the Vietnam War. *Sociometry, 35*(3), 468–476.

Granick, S., & Scheflen, N. A. (1958). Approaches to reliability to projective tests with special reference to the Blacky Pictures Test. *Journal of Consulting Psychology, 22,* 137–141.

Granit, R. (1955). *Receptors and sensory perception.* New Haven, CT: Yale University Press.

Grant, C. H. (1969). Age differences in self-concept from early adulthood through old age. *Proceedings of the 77th Annual Convention of the American Psychological Association, 4,* 717–718.

Graves, T. D. (1961). *Time perspective and the deferred gratification pattern in a tri-ethnic community* (Research Report No. 5, Tri-Ethnic Research Project). Boulder: University of Colorado, Institute of Behavioral Science.

Gray, J. J. (1969). Effect of productivity on primary process thinking and creativity. *Proceedings of the 77th Annual Convention of the American Psychological Association, 4,* 157–158.

Graziano, W. G., Rahe, D. F., & Feldesman, A. B. (1985). Extraversion, social cognition, and the salience of aversiveness in social encounters. *Journal of Personality and Social Psychology, 49,* 971–980.

Green, B. L., & Kenrick, D. T. (1994). The attractiveness of gender-typed traits at different relationship levels: Androgynous characteristics may be desirable after all. *Personality and Social Psychology Bulletin, 20,* 244–253.

Greene, D., Sternberg, B., & Lepper, M. R. (1976). Overjustification in a token economy. *Journal of Personality and Social Psychology, 34,* 1219–1234.

Greever, K. B., Tseng, M. S., & Friedland, B. U. (1973). Development of the Social Interest Index. *Journal of Consulting and Clinical Psychology, 41,* 454–458.

Griffin, G. A., & Harlow, H. F. (1966). Effects of three months of total social deprivation on social adjustment and learning in the rhesus monkey. *Child Development, 37,* 533–547.

Grinker, R. R., & Spiegel, J. P. (1945). *Men under stress.* Philadelphia: Blakiston.

Groesbeck, B. L. (1958). Toward description of personality in terms of configurations of motives. In J. W. Atkinson (Ed.), *Motives in fantasy, action, and society.* Princeton, NJ: Van Nostrand.

Grossack, M., Armstrong, T., & Lussieu, G. (1966). Correlates of self-actualization. *Journal of Human Psychology, 37,* 87–95.

Guilford, J. P. (1959). *Personality.* New York: McGraw-Hill.

Guilford, J. P. (1967). *The nature of human intelligence.* New York: McGraw-Hill.

Guilford, J. P. (1975). Factors and factors of personality. *Psychological Bulletin, 82,* 802–814.

Guilford, J. P. (1977). Will the real factor of extroversion-introversion please stand up? A reply to Eysenck. *Psychological Bulletin, 84,* 412–416.

Guilford, J. P., & Zimmerman, W. S. (1956). Fourteen dimensions of temperament. *Psychological Monograph, 70*(10).

Guilford, J. P., Zimmerman, W. S., & Guilford, J. P. (1976). *The Guilford-Zimmerman temperament survey handbook: Twenty-five years of research and application.* San Diego, CA: Robert R. Knapp.

Guinan, J., & Foulds, M. (1970). Marathon group: Facilitator of personal growth? *Journal of Counseling Psychology, 17,* 145–149.

Gur, R. C., & Sackheim, H. A. (1979). Self-deception: A concept in search of a phenomenon. *Journal of Personality and Social Psychology, 37,* 147–169.

Gurin, P., Lao, R. C., & Beattie, M. (1969). Internal-external control in the motivational dynamics of Negro youth. *Journal of Social Issues, 14,* 29–53.

Haan, N., & Dey, D. (1974). A longitudinal study of change and sameness in personality development: Adolescence to later adulthood. *International Journal on Aging Human Development, 5,* 11–39.

Haber, R. N., & Alpert, R. (1958). The role of situation and picture cues in projective measurement of the achievement motive. In J. W. Atkinson (Ed.), *Motives in fantasy, action, and society.* Princeton, NJ: Van Nostrand.

Hall, C. S., & Lindzey, G. (1970). *Theories of personality.* New York: Wiley.

Hall, C. S., & Lindzey, G. (1985). *Introduction to theories of personality.* New York: Wiley.

Hall, C. S., & Van de Castle, R. L. (1965). An empirical investigation of the castration complex in dreams. *Journal of Personality, 33,* 20–29.

Hall, E. (1965). Ordinal position and success in engagement and marriage. *Journal of Individual Psychology, 21,* 154–158.

Hall, E., & Barger, B. (1964, May). Background data and expected activities of entering lower division students. *Mental Health Project Bulletin, 7.* Gainesville, FL: University of Florida.

Hall, J. A., & Taylor, M. C. (1985). Psychological androgyny and the masculinity × femininity interaction. *Journal of Personality and Social Psychology, 49,* 429–435.

Hall, W. B., & MacKinnon, D. W. (1969). Personality inventory correlates of creativity among architects. *Journal of Applied Psychology, 53,* 322–326.

Hanewitz, W. B. (1978). Police personality: A Jungian perspective. *Crime and Delinquency, 24,* 152–172.

Harlow, H. F. (1953). Mice, monkeys, men, and motives. *Psychological Review, 60,* 23–32.

Harlow, H. F. (1959). Learning and satiation of response in intrinsically motivated complex puzzle performance by monkeys. *Journal of Comparative and Physiological Psychology, 43,* 289–294.

Harlow, H. F., Harlow, M. K., Dodsworth, R. O., & Arling, G. L. (1966). Maternal behavior of rhesus monkeys deprived of mothering and peer associations in infancy. *Proceedings of the American Philosophical Society, 110,* 58–66.

Harlow, H. F., Harlow, M. K., & Meyer, D. R. (1950). Learning motivated by a manipulation drive. *Journal of Experimental Psychology, 40,* 228–234.

Harrington, D. M., & Andersen, S. M. (1981). Creativity, masculinity, femininity, and three models of psychological androgyny. *Journal of Personality and Social Psychology, 41,* 744–757.

Harrison, A. A. (1967). *Response competition and attitude change as a function of repeated stimulus exposure.* Unpublished doctoral dissertation, University of Michigan, Ann Arbor.

Harrison, N. W., & McLaughlin, R. J. (1969). Self-rating validation of the Eysenck Personality Inventory. *British Journal of Social and Clinical Psychology, 8,* 55–58.

Harter, S. (1983). Developmental perspectives on the self-system. In P. H. Mussen (Ed.). *Carmichael's manual of child psychology* (Vol. 4). New York: Wiley.

Hartmann, H., Kris, E., & Loewenstein, R. M. (1947). Comments on the formation of psychic structure. In A. Freud et al. (Eds.), *The psychoanalytic study of the child.* New York: International Universities Press.

Harvey, J. H., & Barnes, R. (1974). Perceived choice as a function of internal-external locus of control. *Journal of Personality, 42,* 437–452.

Havener, P. H., & Izard, C. E. (1962). Unrealistic self-enhancement in paranoid schizophrenics. *Journal of Consulting Psychology, 26,* 65–68.

Heaton, A. W., & Kruglanski, A. W. (1991). Person perception by introverts and extraverts under time pressure: Effects of need for closure. *Personality and Social Psychology Bulletin, 17,* 161–165.

Hebb, D. O. (1955). Drives and the C.N.S. (conceptual nervous system). *Psychological Review, 62,* 243–254.

Hegelson, V. S. (1994). The psychology of curiosity: Evidence and potential explanations. *Psychological Bulletin, 116,* 412–428.

Heilbrun, A. B., Jr. (1981). Gender differences in the functional linkage between androgyny, social cognition, and competence. *Journal of Personality and Social Psychology, 41,* 1106–1118.

Heilbrun, A. B., Jr. (1984). Sex-based models of androgyny: A further cognitive elaboration of competence differences. *Journal of Personality and Social Psychology, 46,* 216–229.

Helson, R. (1973a). Heroic and tender modes in women authors of fantasy. *Journal of Personality, 41,* 493–512.

Helson, R. (1973b). The heroic, the comic, and the tender: Patterns of literary fantasy and their authors. *Journal of Personality, 41,* 163–184.

Helson, R. (1977). The creative spectrum of authors of fantasy. *Journal of Personality, 45,* 310–326.

Helson, R. (1982). Critics and their texts: An approach to Jung's theory of cognition and personality. *Journal of Personality and Social Psychology, 42,* 409–418.

Helson, R. (1992). Women's difficult times and the rewriting of the life story. *Psychology of Women Quarterly, 16,* 331–347.

Helson, R. (1993). Comparing longitudinal studies of adult development: Toward a pardigm of tension between stability and change. In D. C. Funder, R. D. Parke, C. Tomlinson-Keasey, & K. Widaman (Eds.), *Studying lives through time: Personality and development* (pp. 93–119). Washington, DC: American Psychological Association.

Helson, R., & Crutchfield, R. S. (1970). Creative types in mathematics. *Journal of Personality, 38,* 177–197.

Helson, R., Mitchell, V., & Moane, G. (1984). Personality and patterns of adherence and nonadherence to the social clock. *Journal of Personality and Social Psychology, 46,* 1079–1096.

Hendrick, I. (1943). The discussion of the instinct to master. *Psychoanalysis Quarterly, 12,* 561–565.

Hernandez-Peon, R., Scherrer, H., & Jouvet, M. (1956). Modification of electric activity in the cochlear nucleus during attention in unanesthetized cats. *Science, 123,* 331–332.

Hernstein, R. J. (1977). The evolution of behaviorism. *American Psychologist, 32,* 593–603.

Hess, E. H. (1958). Attitude and pupil size. *Scientific American, 212,* 46–54.

Heyns, R. W., Veroff, J., & Atkinson, J. W. (1958). A scoring manual for the affiliation motive. In J. W. Atkinson (Ed.), *Motives in fantasy, action, and society.* Princeton, NJ: Van Nostrand.

Hibbard, S., Farmer, L., Wells, C., Difillipo, E., Barry, W., Korman, R., & Sloan, P. (1994). Validation of Cramer's Defense Mechanisms Manual for the TAT. *Journal of Personality Assessment, 63,* 197–210.

Higgins, E. T. (1987). Self-discrepancy: A theory relating self and affect. *Psychological Review, 94,* 319–340.

Hilgard, E. R. (1956). *Theories of learning* (2nd ed.). New York: Appleton-Century-Crofts.

Hill, C. A. (1991). Seeking emotional support: The influence of affiliation need and partner warmth. *Journal of Personality and Social Psychology, 60,* 112–121.

Hill, W. F. (1978). Effects of mere exposure on preference in nonhuman mammals. *Psychological Bulletin, 85,* 1177–1198.

Hinde, R. A., & Stevenson-Hinde, J. (Eds.). (1973). *Constraints on learning.* New York: Academic Press.

Hjelle, L. A., & Lomastro, J. (1971). Personality differences between high and low dogmatic groups of Catholic seminarians and religious sisters. *Journal for the Scientific Study of Religion, 10,* 49–50.

Hoffman, M. L. (1981a). Is altruism part of human nature? *Journal of Personality and Social Psychology, 40,* 121–137.

Hoffman, M. L. (1981b). Perspectives on the difference between understanding people and understanding things: The role of affect. In J. H. Flavell & L. Ross (Eds.), *Social cognitive development* (pp. 67–81). Cambridge, MA: Cambridge University Press.

Hogan, R., DeSoto, C. B., & Solano, C. (1977). Traits, tests and personality research. *American Psychologist, 32,* 255–264.

Holahan, C. J., & Moos, K. H. (1985). Life stress and health: Personality, coping and family support in stress resistance. *Journal of Personality and Social Psychology, 49,* 738–747.

Holden, K. B., & Rotter, J. B. (1962). A nonverbal measure of extinction in skill and chance situations. *Journal of Experimental Psychology, 63,* 519–520.

Holland, J. G. (1978). Behaviorism: Part of the problem or part of the solution? *Journal of Applied Behavior Analysis, 11,* 163–174.

Holland, J. M. (1968). Creativity in relation to socioeconomic status, academic achievement, and school: Personal and school adjustment in elementary school children. *Dissertation Abstracts, 29,* 147.

Hollander, E. P., & Willis, R. H. (1967). Some current issues in the psychology of conformity and nonconformity. *Psychological Bulletin, 68,* 62–76.

Holmes, D. S. (1968). Dimensions of projection. *Psychological Bulletin, 69,* 248–268.

Holmes, D. S. (1974). Investigations of repression: Differential recall of material experimentally or naturally associated with ego threat. *Psychological Bulletin, 81,* 632–653.

Holmes, D. S. (1979). Projection as a defense mechanism. *Psychological Bulletin, 86,* 225–241.

Holmes, D. S., & Jackson, T. H. (1975). Influence of locus of control on interpersonal attraction and affective reactions in situations involving reward and punishment. *Journal of Personality and Social Psychology, 31*(1), 132–136.

Holmes, D. S., & Shallow, J. R. (1969). Reduced recall after ego threat: Repression or response competition? *Journal of Personality and Social Psychology, 13,* 145–152.

Houston, B. K, & Holmes, D. S. (1974). Effect of avoidant thinking and reappraisal for coping with threat involving temporal uncertainty. *Journal of Personality and Social Psychology, 30,* 382–388.

Howarth, E. (1976). A psychometric investigation of Eysenck's personality inventory. *Journal of Personality Assessment, 40,* 173–185.

Howarth, E., & Browne, J. A. (1971). Investigation of personality factors in a Canadian context: I. Marker structure in personality questionnaire items. *Canadian Journal of Behavioral Science, 3,* 161–173.

Howes, D., & Solomon, R. L. (1950). A note on McGinnies' emotionality and perceptual defense. *Psychological Review, 57,* 229–234.

Howes, D., & Solomon, R. L. (1951). Visual duration threshold as a function of word probability. *Journal of Experimental Psychology, 41,* 401–410.

Hull, C. L. (1943). *Principles of behavior.* New York: Appleton-Century-Crofts.

Hull, C. L. (1945). The place of innate individual and species differences in a natural science theory of behavior. *Psychological Review, 52,* 55–60.

Hull, J. G., & Schwartz, R. M. (1987). *Physiological and attributional responses of hardy individuals to situational stress.* Unpublished manuscript, Dartmouth College at Hanover, N.H.

Hull, J. G., Van Trueren, R. R., & Virnelli, S. (1987). Hardiness and health: A critique and alternative approach. *Journal of Personality and Social Psychology, 53,* 518–530.

Hunt, H. F. (1975a). Behavior therapy for adults. In S. Arieti (Ed.), *American handbook of psychiatry.* New York: Basic Books.

Hunt, H. F. (1975b). Problems in the interpretation of "experimental neurosis." *Psychological Report, 15,* 27–35.

Hunt, H. F., & Dyrud, J. E. (1968). Commentary: Perspective in behavior therapy. *Research in Psychotherapy, 3,* 140–152.

Huntley, C. W. (1940). Judgments of self based upon records of expressive behavior. *Journal of Abnormal and Social Psychology, 35,* 398–427.

Hutt, L. D., & Anderson, J. P. (1967). The relationship between pupil size and recognition threshold. *Psychonomic Science, 9,* 477–478.

Hyman, H. H., & Sheatsley, P. B. (1954). "The authoritarian personality"—a methodological critique. In R. Christie & M. Jahoda (Eds.), *Studies in the scope and method of the authoritarian personality.* New York: Free Press.

Ickes, W., & Turner, M. (1983). On the social advantages of having an older, opposite-sex sibling: Birth order influences in mixed-sexed dyads. *Journal of Personality and Social Psychology, 45,* 210–222.

Ilardi, R., & May, W. (1968). A reliability study of Shostrom's Personal Orientation Inventory. *Journal of Human Psychology, 8,* 68–72.

Isaacson, G. S., & Landfield, A. W. (1965). Meaningfulness of personal vs. common constructs. *Journal of Individual Psychology, 21,* 160–166.

Iyzett, R. R. (1971). Authoritarianism and attitudes toward the Vietnam war as reflected in behavioral and self report measures. *Journal of Personality and Social Psychology, 17,* 145–148.

Jackson, D. N. (1974). *Personality Research Form Manual.* Goshen, NY: Research Psychologists Press.

Jackson, D. N., & Messick, S. (1958). Content and style in personality assessment. *Psychological Bulletin, 55,* 243–252.

Jackson, D. N. & Paunonen, S. V. (1980). Personality structure and assessment. In M. R. Rosenzweig & L. W. Porter (Eds.), *Annual Review of Psychology.* Palo Alto, CA: Annual Reviews.

Jackson, P. W., & Messick, S. (1965). The person, the product, and the response: Conceptual problems in the assessment of creativity. *Journal of Personality, 33,* 309–329.

Jacobi, L., & Cash, T. F. (1994). In pursuit of the perfect appearance: Discrepancies among self- and ideal-percepts of multiple physical attributes. *Journal of Applied Social Psychology, 24,* 379–396.

Jacoby, J. (1967). Open-mindedness and creativity. *Psychological Report, 20,* 822–823.

James, W. (1957). *Internal versus external control of reinforcements as a basic variable in learning theory.* Unpublished doctoral dissertation, Ohio State University, Columbus.

James, W., & Rotter, J. B. (1958). Partial and 100% reinforcement under chance and skill conditions. *Journal of Experimental Psychology, 55,* 397–403.

Janis, I. L., & Gilmore, J. B. (1965). The influence of incentive conditions on the success of role playing in modifying attitudes. *Journal of Personality and Social Psychology, 1,* 17–27.

Jasper, H. H. (1958). Reticular-cortical systems and theories of the integrative action of the brain. In H. F. Harlow & C. N. Woolsey (Eds.), *Biological and biochemical bases of behavior.* Madison: University of Wisconsin Press.

Jenkins, H. M. (1973). Effects of the stimulus-reinforcer relation on selected and unselected responses. In R. A. Hinde & J. Stevenson-Hinde (Eds.), *Constraints on learning.* New York: Academic Press.

Jensen, M. (1987). *Psychobiological factors in the prognosis and treatment of neoplastic disorders.* Unpublished doctoral dissertation, Yale University, New Haven, CT.

Johnson, J. H., Null, C., Butcher, J. N., & Johnson, K. N. (1984). Replicated item level factor analysis of the full MMPI. *Journal of Personality and Social Psychology, 49,* 105–114.

Johnson, J. T., & Boyd, K. R. (1995). Dispositional traits versus the content of experience: Actor/observer differences in judgements of the "authentic" self. *Personality and Social Psychology Bulletin, 21,* 375–383.

Johnson, P. B. (1981). Achievement motivation and success: Does the end justify the means? *Journal of Personality and Social Psychology, 40,* 374–375.

Jones, E. (1955). *The life and work of Sigmund Freud.* New York: Basic Books.

Jones, E. E., Brenner, K. J. & Knight, J. G. (1990).

When failure elevates self esteem. *Personality and Social Psychology Bulletin, 16,* 200–209.

Jones, H. E. (1960). Consistency and change in early maturity. *Vita Humana, 3,* 17–31.

Jung, C. G. (1933a). *Modern man in search of a soul.* New York: Harcourt Brace Jovanovich.

Jung, C. G. (1933b). *Psychological types.* New York: Harcourt Brace Jovanovich.

Jung, C. G. (1953a). The psychology of the unconscious. In H. Read, M. Fordham, & G. Adler (Eds.), *Collected works* (Vol. 7). Princeton, NJ: Princeton University Press.

Jung, C. G. (1953b). The relations between the ego and the unconscious. In H. Read, M. Fordham, & G. Adler (Eds.), *Collected works.* Princeton, NJ: Princeton University Press.

Jung, C. G. (1959a). The archetypes and the collective unconscious. In H. Read, M. Fordham, & G. Adler (Eds.), *Collected works* (Vol. 9). Princeton, NJ: Princeton University Press.

Jung, C. G. (1959b). Concerning the archetypes, with special reference to the anima concept. In H. Read, M. Fordham, & G. Adler (Eds.), *Collected works.* Princeton, NJ: Princeton University Press.

Jung, C. G. (1959c). The shadow. In L. Arion (Ed.), *Collected works* (Vol. 9, Part II). Princeton, NJ: Princeton University Press.

Jung, C. G. (1960a). On psychic energy. In H. Read, M. Fordham, & G. Adler (Eds.), *Collected works* (Vol. 8). Princeton, NJ: Princeton University Press.

Jung, C. G. (1960b). The stages of life. In H. Read, M. Fordham, & G. Adler (Eds.), *Collected works* (Vol. 8). Princeton, NJ: Princeton University Press.

Jung, C. G. (1960c). Synchronicity: An acausal connecting principle. In H. Read, M. Fordham, & G. Adler (Eds.), *Collected works* (Vol. 8). Princeton, NJ: Princeton University Press.

Jung, C. G. (1961). The theory of psychoanalysis. In H. Read, M. Fordham, & G. Adler (Eds.), *Collected works* (Vol. 4). Princeton, NJ: Princeton University Press.

Kagan, J. (1972). Motives and development. *Journal of Personality and Social Psychology, 22,* 51–66.

Kagan, J., & Moss, H. A. (1962). *Birth to maturity: A study in psychological development.* New York: Wiley.

Katkin, E. S. (1964). The Marlowe-Crowne Social Desirability Scale: Independent of psychopathology? *Psychological Report, 15,* 703–706.

Katz, D., Sarnoff, I., & McClintock, C. (1956). Ego defense and attitude change. *Human Relations, 9,* 27–45.

Katz, I. (1967). The socialization of academic motivation in minority group children. In D. Levine (Ed.), *Nebraska symposium on motivation.* Lincoln: University of Nebraska Press.

Keen, E. (1970). *Three faces of being: Toward an existential clinical psychology.* New York: Appleton-Century-Crofts.

Kelly, E. L. (1955). Consistency of the adult personality. *American Psychologist, 10,* 659–681.

Kelly, G. A. (1955). *The psychology of personal constructs* (Vol. 1). New York: Norton.

Kelly, G. A. (1962). Europe's matrix of decision. In M. R. Jones (Ed.), *Nebraska symposium on motivation.* Lincoln: University of Nebraska Press.

Keniston, K. (1966). *The uncommitted: Alienated youth in American society.* New York: Harcourt Brace Jovanovich.

Kernberg, O. F. (1976). *Object relations theory and clinical psychoanalysis.* New York: Jason Aronson.

Kierkegaard, S. (1954). *The sickness unto death.* New York: Doubleday.

Kiesler, C. A., & Pallak, M. S. (1976). Arousal properties of dissonance manipulations. *Psychological Bulletin. 83,* 1014–1025.

Kirsch, I. (1985). Self-efficacy and expectancy: Old wine with new labels. *Journal of Personality and Social Psychology, 49,* 824–830.

Kirscht, J. P., & Dillehay, R. C. (1967). *Dimensions of authoritarianism: A review of research and theory.* Lexington, KY: University of Kentucky Press.

Klavetter, R., & Mogar, R. (1967). Stability and internal consistency of a measure of self actualization. *Psychological Report, 21,* 422–424.

Kleck, R. E., & Wheaton, J. (1967). Dogmatism and responses to opinion-consistent and opinion-inconsistent information. *Journal of Personality and Social Psychology, 5,* 249–252.

Klein, E. B., & Gould, J. (1969). Alienation and identification in college women. *Journal of Personality, 37,* 468–480.

Klein, M. (1948). *Contributions to psychoanalysis.* London: Hogarth Press.

Klein, M. H., Mathieu, P. L., Gendlin, E. T., & Kiesler, D. J. (1969). *The Experiencing Scale: A research and training manual* (Vol. 1). Madison: Wisconsin Psychiatric Institute.

Kleitman, N. (1939). *Sleep and wakefulness.* Chicago: University of Chicago Press.

Kleitman, N., & Ramsaroop, A. (1948). Periodicity in body temperature and heart rate. *Endocrinology, 43,* 1–20.

Kline, P. (1968). Obsessional traits, obsessional symptoms and anal erotism. *British Journal of Medical Psychology, 41,* 299–305.

Klineberg, S. L. (1968). Future time perspective and the preference for delayed reward. *Journal of Personality and Social Psychology, 8,* 253–257.

Klinger, E. (1966). Fantasy need achievement as a motivational construct. *Psychological Bulletin, 66,* 291–308.

Knapp, R. J. (1965). Relationship of a measure of self actualization to neuroticism and extraversion. *Journal of Consulting Psychology, 29,* 168–172.

Knapp, R. J. (1976). Authoritarianism, alienation, and related variables: A correlational and factor-analytic study. *Psychological Bulletin, 83,* 194–212.

Kobasa, S. C. (1979). Stressful life events, personality, and health: An inquiry into hardiness. *Journal of Personality and Social Psychology, 37,* 1–11.

Kobasa, S. C. (1982). Commitment and coping in stress resistance among lawyers. *Journal of Personality and Social Psychology, 42,* 707–717.

Kobasa, S. C., & Maddi, S. R. (1977). Existential personality theory. In R. Corsini (Ed.), *Current personality theories.* Itasca, IL: Peacock.

Kobasa, S. C., Maddi, S. R., & Courington, S. (1981). Personality and constitution as mediators of the stress-illness relationship. *Journal of Personality and Social Psychology, 42,* 168–177.

Kobasa, S. C., Maddi, S. R., Donner, E., Merrick, W., & White, H. (1987). *The personality construct of hardiness.* Unpublished manuscript, University of Chicago.

Kobasa, S. C., Maddi, S. R., & Kahn, S. (1982). Hardiness and health: A prospective study. *Journal of Personality and Social Psychology, 42,* 168–177.

Kobasa, S. C., Maddi, S. R., and Puccetti, M. (1982) Personality and exercise as buffers in the stress-illness relationship. *Journal of Behavioral Medicine, 4,* 391–404.

Kobasa, S. C., Maddi, S. R., Puccetti, M. & Zola, M. (1986). Relative effectiveness of hardiness, exercise and social support as resources against illness. *Journal of Psychosomatic Research, 29,* 525–533.

Kobasa, S. C., & Puccetti, M. C. (1983). Personality and social resources in stress resistance. *Journal of Personality and Social Psychology, 45,* 839–850.

Koenig, F. (1969). Definitions of self and ordinal position of birth. *Journal of Social Psychology, 78,* 287–288.

Koestler, A. (1960). *The lotus and the robot.* London: Hutchinson.

Koestner, R., Weinberger, J., & McClelland, D. C. (1991). Task-intrinsic and social-extrinsic sources of arousal for motives assessed in fantasy and self-report. *Journal of Personality, 59,* 57–82.

Kohler, W. (1925). *The mentality of apes* (E. Winter, Trans.). New York: Harcourt Brace Jovanovich.

Kohut, H. (1971). *The analysis of the self.* New York: International Universities Press.

Kohut, H. (1977). *The restoration of the self.* New York: International Universities Press.

Konrad, K. W., & Bagshaw, M. (1970). Effect of novel stimuli on cats reared in a restricted environment. *Journal of Comparative and Physiological Psychology, 70,* 157–164.

Koutrelakos, J. (1968). Authoritarian person's perception of his relationship with his father. *Perceptual Motor Skills, 26,* 967–973.

Kramer, E. (1969). The Eysenck Personality Inventory and self-ratings of extraversion. *Journal of Projective Techniques and Personality Assessment, 33,* 59–62.

Krasner, L., & Ullmann, L. P. (Eds.). (1965). *Research in behavior modification.* New York: Holt, Rinehart & Winston.

Krauskopf, C. J. (1978). Comments on Endler and Magnusson's attempt to redefine personality. *Psychological Bulletin, 85,* 280–283.

Kris, E. (1952). *Psychoanalytic explorations in art.* New York: International Universities Press.

Kuhl, J., & Beckman, J. (eds.). (1985). *Action control: From cognition to behavior.* New York: Springer-Verlag.

Kuhlen, R. G. (1945). Age differences in personality during adult years. *Psychological Bulletin, 42,* 333–358.

Lamiell, J. T. (1981). Toward an idiothetic psychology of personality. *American Psychologist, 36,* 276–289.

Lamiell, J. T., Foss, N. A., Larsen, R. J., & Hempel, A. M. (1983). Studies in intuitive psychology from an idiothetic point of view: Implications for personality theory. *Journal of Personality, 51,* 438–467.

Lamiell, J. T., & Trierineiler, S. J. (1986). Interactive measurement, idiothetic inquiry, and the challenge to conventional "nomotheticism." *Journal of Personality, 54,* 460–477.

Landfield, A. W. (1977). The complaint: A confrontation of personal urgency and professional construction. In D. Bannister (Ed.), *Issues and approaches in psychological therapies.* New York: Wiley.

Lao, R. C. (1970). Internal-external control and competent and innovative behavior among Negro college students. *Journal of Personality and Social Psychology, 14,* 263–370.

Laursen, B., & Collins, W. A. (1994). Interpersonal conflict during adolescence. *Psychological Bulletin, 115,* 197–209.

Lauterbach, C. G. (1958). The Taylor A scale and clinical measures of anxiety. *Journal of Consulting Psychology, 22,* 314.

Lazarus, A. A. (1977). Has behavior therapy outlived its usefulness? *American Psychologist, 32,* 550–554.

Lazarus, R. S., Eriksen, C. W., & Fonda, C. P. (1951). Personality dynamics in auditory perceptual recognition, *Journal of Personality, 19,* 471–582.

Lee, D., & Ehrlich, H. J. (1971). Beliefs about self and others: A test of the dogmatism theory. *Psychological Review, 28,* 919–922.

Lefcourt, H. J. (1965). Risk-taking in Negro and white adults. *Journal of Personality and Social Psychology, 2,* 765–770.

Lefcourt, H. J. (1976). *Locus of control: Current trends in theory and research.* Hillsdale, NJ: Erlbaum.

Lefcourt, H. J., Hogg, E., Struthers, S., & Holmes, C. (1975). Causal attributions as a function of locus of control, initial confidence, and performance outcomes. *Journal of Personality and Social Psychology, 32,* 391–397.

Lefcourt, H. J., & Ladwig, G. W. (1965). The effect of reference group upon Negroes' task persistence in a biracial competitive game. *Journal of Personality and Social Psychology, 1,* 668–671.

Lefcourt, H. J., & Ladwig, G. W. (1966). Alienation in Negro and white reformatory inmates. *Journal of Social Psychology, 68,* 153–157.

Lehr, U., & Rudinger, G. (1969). Consistency and change of social participation in old age. *Human Development, 12,* 255–267.

Leith, G. O. M. (1972). The relationships between intelligence, personality, and creativity under two conditions of stress. *British Journal of Educational Psychologists, 42,* 240–247.

Leith, G. O. M. (1974). Individual differences in learning: Interactions of personality and teaching methods. *Association of Educational Psychologists 1974 Conference Proceedings,* London.

Leitner, L. M., & Cado, S. (1982). Personal constructs and homosexual stress. *Journal of Personality and Social Psychology, 43,* 869–872.

Lemann, G. F. J. (1952). Group characteristics as revealed in sociometric patterns and personality ratings. *Sociometry, 15,* 7–90.

LeMay, M., & Damm, V. (1968). The Personal Orientation Inventory as a measure of self actualization of underachievers. *Measurement and Evaluation in Guidance, 1,* 110–114.

Lepper, M. R., Greene, D., & Nisbett, R. E. (1973). Undermining children's intrinsic interest with extrinsic rewards: A test of the overjustification hypothesis. *Journal of Personality and Social Psychology, 28,* 129–137.

Lesnik-Oberstein, M., & Cohen, L. (1984). Cognitive style, sensation-seeking, and assortative mating. *Journal of Personality and Social Psychology, 46,* 112–117.

Lessac, M. S., & Solomon, R. L. (1969). Effects of early isolation on later adaptive behavior of beagles: A methodological demonstration. *Developmental Psychology, 1,* 14–25.

Leventhal, H., Jacobs, R. L., & Kudirka, J. (1964). Authoritarianism, ideology, and political candidate choice. *Journal of Abnormal and Social Psychology, 69,* 539–549.

LeVine, R. (1966). *Dreams and deeds: Achievement motivation in Nigeria.* Chicago: University of Chicago Press.

Levinson, D. (1977). The mid-life transition. *Psychiatry, 40,* 99–112.

Levinson, D. J., & Huffman, P. E. (1955). Traditional family ideology and its relation to personality. *Journal of Personality, 23,* 251–273.

Liebert, R. M., & Spiegler, M. D. (1982). *Personality: Strategies and issues* (4th ed.). Chicago: Dorsey Press.

Liem, G. R. (1973). Performance and satisfaction as affected by personal control over salient decisions. *Journal of Personality and Social Psychology, 31,* 232–240.

Lindzey, G., & Heineman, P. S. (1955). Thematic Apperception Test: A note on reliability and situational validity. *Journal of Projective Techniques, 19,* 36–42.

Linton, R. (1945). *The cultural background of personality.* New York: Appleton-Century-Crofts.

Litz, J. E. (1979). Life stresses and alcoholism in women. *Dissertation Abstracts International, 39,* 3525–3526.

Liverant, S., & Scodel, A. (1960). Internal and external control as determinants of decision-making under conditions of risk. *Psychological Report, 7,* 59–67.

Loevinger, J. (1994). Has psychology lost its conscience? *Journal of Personality Assessment, 62,* 2–8.

Loevinger, J., & Knoll, E. (1983). Personality: Stages, traits and the self. In M. R. Rozensweig & L. W. Porter (Eds.), *Annual Review of Psychology.* Palo Alto, CA: Annual Reviews.

Loewenstein, G. (1994). The psychology of curiosity: A review and reinterpretation. *Psychological Bulletin, 116,* 75–98.

Longstreth, L. E. (1970). Birth order and avoidance of dangerous activities. *Developmental Psychology 2,* 154.

Lowell, E. L. (1950). *A methodological study of projectively measured achievement motivation.* Unpublished master's thesis, Wesleyan University, Middleton, CT.

Lubinski, D., Tellegen, A., & Butcher, J. N. (1981). The relationship between androgyny and subjective indicators of emotional well-being. *Journal of Personality and Social Psychology, 40,* 722–730.

Lubinski, D., Tellegen, A., & Butcher, J. N. (1983). Masculinity, femininity, and androgyny viewed and assessed as distinct concepts. *Journal of Personality and Social Psychology, 44,* 428–439.

Lundin, R. W. (1974). *Personality: A behavioral analysis* (2nd ed.). New York: Macmillan.

Maas, H. S., & Kuypers, J. A. (1974). *From 30 to 70: A forty-year longitudinal study of adult life styles and personality.* San Francisco: Jossey-Bass.

Maccoby, M. (1976). *The gamesman.* New York: Simon & Schuster.

MacKinnon, D. W. (1965). Personality and the realization of creative potential. *American Psychologist, 20,* 273–281.

MacKinnon, D. W., & Dukes, W. (1962). Repression. In L. Postman (Ed.), *Psychology in the making.* New York: Knopf.

Maddi, S. R. (1961a). Affective tone during environmental regularity and change. *Journal of Abnormal and Social Psychology, 62,* 338–345.

Maddi, S. R. (1961b). Exploratory behavior and variation-seeking in man. In D. W. Fiske & S. R. Maddi (Eds.), *Functions of varied experience.* Homewood, IL: Dorsey Press.

Maddi, S. R. (1961c). Unexpectedness, affective tone, and behavior. In D. W. Fiske & S. R. Maddi (Eds.), *Functions of varied experience.* Homewood, IL: Dorsey Press.

Maddi, S. R. (1963). Humanistic psychology: Allport and Murray. In J. M. Wepman & R. W. Heine (Eds.), *Concepts of personality.* Chicago: Aldine.

Maddi, S. R. (1965). Motivational aspects of creativity. *Journal of Personality, 33,* 303–347.

Maddi, S. R. (1967). The existential neurosis. *Journal of Abnormal Psychology, 72,* 311–325.

Maddi, S. R. (1968a). Meaning, novelty, and affect: Comments on Zajonc's paper [Monograph]. *Journal of Personality and Social Psychology, 9*(2), 28–30.

Maddi, S. R. (1968b). *The seeking and avoiding of variety.* Unpublished manuscript, University of Chicago.

Maddi, S. R. (1970). The search for meaning. In M. Page (Ed.), *Nebraska symposium on motivation.* Lincoln: University of Nebraska Press.

Maddi, S. R. (1971). Novelty, meaning, and intrinsic motivation. In H. I. Day, D. E. Berlyne, & D. E. Hunt (Eds.), *Intrinsic motivation: A new direction in motivation.* Toronto: Holt, Rinehart & Winston.

Maddi, S. R. (1979). The uses of theorizing in personology. In E. Staub (Ed.), *Personality: Basic issues and current research.* Englewood Cliffs, NJ: Prentice-Hall.

Maddi, S. R. (1984). Personology for the 1980s. In R. A. Zucker, J. Aronoff, & A. I. Rabin (Eds.), *Personality and the prediction of behavior.* New York: Academic Press.

Maddi. S. R. (1986). Existential psychotherapy. In J. Garske & S. Lynn (Eds.), *Contemporary psychotherapy,* Columbus, OH: Merrill.

Maddi, S. R. (1987). Hardiness training at Illinois Bell Telephone. In J. P. Opatz (Ed.), *Health promotion evaluation.* Stephens Point, WI: National Wellness Institute.

Maddi, S. R. (1988). On the problem of accepting facticity and pursuing possibility. In S. B. Messer, L. A. Sass, & R. L. Woolfolk (Eds.). *Hermeneutics and psychological theory: Interpretive perspectives on personality, psychotherapy and psychopathology.* New Brunswick, NJ: Rutgers University Press.

Maddi, S. R. (1990). Issues and interventions in stress mastery. In H. S. Friedman (Ed.), *Personality and disease.* New York: Wiley.

Maddi, S. R. (1993). The continuing relevance of personality theorizing. In K.H. Craik, R. Hogan, & R. N. Wolfe (Eds.), *Fifty years of personality psychology* (pp. 85–101). New York: Plenum.

Maddi, S. R. (1994). The Hardiness Enhancing Lifestyle Program (HELP) for improving physical, mental, and social wellness. In C. Hopper (Ed.), *Wellness lecture series.* Oakland, CA: University of California/HealthNet.

Maddi, S. R., & Andrews, S. (1966). The need for variety in fantasy and self-description. *Journal of Personality, 34,* 610–625.

Maddi, S. R., & Berne, N. (1964). Novelty of productions and desire for novelty as active and passive forms of the need for variety. *Journal of Personality, 32,* 270–277.

Maddi, S. R., Charlens, A. M., Maddi, D., & Smith, A. (1962). Effects of monotony and novelty on imaginative productions. *Journal of Personality, 30,* 513–527.

Maddi, S. R., & Costa, P. T., Jr. (1972). *Humanism in personology: Allport, Maslow, Murray.* Chicago: Aldine-Atherton.

Maddi, S. R., & Hess, M. (1992). Hardiness and basketball performance. *International Journal of Sports Psychology, 23,* 360–368.

Maddi, S. R., Hoover, M., & Kobasa, S. C. (1979). *Alienation and exploratory behavior.* Unpublished manuscript, University of Chicago.

Maddi, S. R., Hoover, M., & Kobasa, S. C. (1982). Alienation and exploratory behavior. *Journal of Personality and Social Psychology, 42,* 884–890.

Maddi, S. R. & Khoshaba, D. M. (1994). Hardiness and mental health. *Journal of Personality Assessment, 63,* 265–274.

Maddi, S. R., & Kobasa, S. C. (1984). *The hardy executive: Health under stress.* Homewood, IL: Dow Jones-Irwin.

Maddi, S. R., Kobasa, S. C., & Hoover, M. (1979). An alienation test. *Journal of Humanistic Psychology, 19,* 73–76.

Maddi, S. R., & Propst, B. (1971). Activation theory and personality. In S. R. Maddi (Ed.), *Perspectives on personality: A comparative approach.* Boston: Little, Brown.

Maddi, S. R., Propst, B., & Feldinger, I. (1965). Three expressions of the need for variety. *Journal of Personality, 33,* 82–98.

Mahoney, J., & Hartnett, J. (1973). Self-actualization and self-ideal discrepancy. *Journal of Psychology, 85,* 37–42.

Mahler, M.S. (1963). Thoughts about development and individuation. In *The psychoanalytic study of the child* (Vol. 18, pp. 307–324). New York: International Universities Press.

Major, B., Carnevale, P. J. D., & Deaux, K. (1981). A different perspective on androgyny: Evaluations of masculine and feminine characteristics. *Journal of Personality and Social Psychology, 41,* 988–1001.

Mancuso, J. C. (1977). Current motivational models in the elaboration of personal construct theory. In A. W. Landfield (Ed.), *Nebraska symposium on motivation.* Lincoln: University of Nebraska Press.

Mandler, G., & Kessen, W. (1959). *The language of psychology.* New York: Wiley.

Marceil, J. C. (1977). Implicit dimensions of idiography and nomothesis. *American Psychologist, 32,* 1046–1055.

Marcia, J. E. (1966). Development and validation of ego-identity status. *Journal of Personality and Social Psychology, 3,* 551–558.

Markus, H., & Wurf, E. (1987). The dynamic self-concept: A social psychological perspective. In M. R. Rosenzweig & L. W. Porter (Eds.), *Annual Review of Psychology,* Palo Alto, CA: Annual Reviews.

Marsh, H. W., Antill, J. K., & Cunningham, J. D. (1987). Masculinity, femininity, and androgyny: Relations to self esteem and social desirability. *Journal of Personality, 55,* 661–686.

Marsh, H. W. & Richards, G. E. (1989). A test of bipolar and androgyny perspectives of masculinity and femininity: The effects of participation in an outward bound program. *Journal of Personality, 57,* 115–138.

Marshall, I. N. (1967). Extraversion and libido in Jung and Cattell. *Journal of Analytical Psychology, 12,* 115–136.

Martin, R. A., & Lefcourt, H. M. (1983). Sense of humor as a moderator of the relation between stressors and moods. *Journal of Personality and Social Psychology, 45,* 1313–1324.

Maslach, C., Stapp, J., & Santee, R. T. (1985). Individualization: Conceptual analysis and assessment. *Journal of Personality and Social Psychology, 49,* 729–738.

Masling, J., O'Neill, R., & Katkin, E. S. (1982). Autonomic arousal, interpersonal climate and orality. *Journal of Personality and Social Psychology, 42,* 529–534.

Masling, J., Weiss, L., & Rothschild, B. (1968). Relationships of oral imagery to yielding behavior and birth order. *Journal of Consulting and Clinical Psychology, 32,* 89–91.

Maslow, A. H. (1955). Deficiency motivation and growth motivation. In M. R. Jones (Ed.), *Nebraska symposium on motivation.* Lincoln: University of Nebraska Press.

Maslow, A. H. (1962). Some basic propositions of a growth and self-actualization psychology. In *Perceiving, behaving, becoming: A new focus for education.* Washington, DC: Yearbook of the Association for Supervision and Curriculum Development.

Maslow, A. H. (1967). A theory of metamotivation: The biological rooting of the value-life. *Journal of Human Psychology, 7,* 93–127.

Maslow, A. H. (1968). *Toward a psychology of being* (2nd Ed.). Princeton, NJ: Van Nostrand.

Masserman, J. H. (1943). *Behavior and neurosis: An experimental psychoanalytic approach to psychobiological principles.* Chicago: University of Chicago Press.

Matarazzo, J. D., & Saslow, G. (1960). Psychological

and related characteristics of smokers and non-smokers. *Psychological Bulletin, 57,* 493–513.

May, R. (1958). Contributions of existential psychotherapy. In R. May, E. Angel, & H. F. Ellenberger (Eds.), *Existence: A new dimension in psychiatry and psychology.* New York: Basic Books.

McAdams, D. P. (1982). Experiences of intimacy and power: Relationship between social motives and autobiographical memory. *Journal of Personality and Social Psychology, 42,* 292–302.

McAdams, D. P. (1985). *Power, intimacy, and the life story: Personological inquiries into identity.* Homewood, IL: Dorsey Press.

McAdams, D. P. (1992). The five-factor model in personality: A critical appraisal. *Journal of Personality, 60,* 329–361.

McAdams, D. P., & Bryant, F. B. (1987). Intimacy motivation and subjective mental health in a nationwide sample. *Journal of Personality, 55,* 395–414.

McAdams, D. P., & Constantian, C. A. (1983). Intimacy and affiliation motives in daily living: An experience sampling analysis. *Journal of Personality and Social Psychology, 45,* 851–861.

McAdams, D. P., Healy, S., & Krause, S. (1984). Social motives and patterns of friendship. *Journal of Personality and Social Psychology, 47,* 828–838.

McAdams, D. P., & Powers, J. (1981). Themes of intimacy in behavior and thought. *Journal of Personality and Social Psychology, 40,* 573–587.

McCarroll, J. E., Mitchell, K. M., Carpenter, R. J., & Anderson, J. P. (1967). Analysis of three stimulation-seeking scales. *Psychological Report, 21,* 853–856.

McClain, E. (1970). Further validation of the Personal Orientation Inventory: Assessment of the self-actualization of school counselors. *Journal of Consulting and Clinical Psychology, 35,* 21–22.

McCleary, R. A., & Lazarus, R. S. (1949). Autonomic discrimination without awareness. *Journal of Personality, 18,* 171–179.

McClelland, D. C. (1951). *Personality.* New York: Dryden Press.

McClelland, D. C. (1958). Risk taking in children with high and low need for achievement. In J. W. Atkinson (Ed.), *Motives in fantasy, action, and society.* Princeton, NJ: Van Nostrand.

McClelland, D. C. (1961). *The achieving society.* Princeton, NJ: Van Nostrand.

McClelland, D. C. (1971a). *Assessing human motivation.* New York: General Learning Press. (No. 4021V00).

McClelland, D. C. (1971b). *Motivational trends in society.* New York: General Learning Press (No. 4020V00).

McClelland, D. C. (1975). *Power: the inner experience.* New York: Irvington.

McClelland, D. C. (1978). Managing motivation to expand human freedom. *American Psychologist, 33,* 201–210.

McClelland, D. C. (1980). Motive dispositions: The merits of operant and respondent measures. *Review of Personality and Social Psychology, 1,* 10–41.

McClelland, D. C. (1981). Is personality consistent? In A. I. Rabin, J. Aronoff, A. M. Barclay, & R. A. Zucker (Eds.), *Further explorations in personality* (pp. 87–113). New York: Wiley.

McClelland, D. C. (1985). *Human motivation.* Glenview, IL: Scott, Foresman.

McClelland, D. C., Atkinson, M. W., & Clark, R. A. (1949). The projective expression of needs: III. The effect of ego-involvement success and failure on perception. *Journal of Psychology, 27,* 311–330.

McClelland, D. C., Atkinson, J. W., Clark, R. A., & Lowell, E. L. (1953). *The achievement motive.* New York: Appleton-Century-Crofts.

McClelland, D. C., Davis, W. N., Kalin, R., & Wanner, H. E. (1971). *Alcohol and human motivation.* New York: Free Press.

McClelland, D. C., & Franz, C. E. (1992). Motivational and other sources of work accomplishments in mid-life: A longitudinal study. *Journal of Personality, 60,* 679–708.

McClelland, D. C., Koestner, R., & Weinberger, J. (1989). How do self-attributed and implicit motives differ? *Psychological Review, 96,* 690–702.

McClelland, D. C., & Pilon, D. A. (1983). Sources of adult motives in patterns of parent behavior in early childhood. *Journal of Personality and Social Psychology, 44,* 564–574.

McClelland, D. C., Sturr, J. F., Knapp, R. H., & Wendt, H. W. (1958). Obligations to self and to society in the United States and Germany. *Journal of Abnormal and Social Psychology, 56,* 245–255.

McCrae, R. R. & Costa, P.T., Jr. (1988). Do parental influences matter? A reply to Halveson. *Journal of Personality, 56,* 445–449.

McCrae, R. R., & Costa, P. T., Jr. (1989). Reinterpreting the Myers-Briggs Type Indicator from the perspective of the Five-Factor Model of personality. *Journal of Personality, 57,* 17–40.

McCrae, R. R., & Costa, P. T., Jr. (1990). *Personality in adulthood.* New York: Guilford.

McCrae, R. R., & Costa, P. T., Jr. (1991). Adding

Liebe und Arbeit: The full Five-Factor Model and well-being. *Personality and Social Psychology Bulletin, 17*, 227–232.

McCrae, R. R., & Costa, P. T., Jr. (1994). The stability of personality: Observations and evaluations. *Current Directions in Psychological Science, 3*, 173–175.

McGinnies, E. (1949). Emotionality and perceptual defense. *Psychological Review, 56*, 244–251.

McGuire, W. J. (1984). Search for the self: Going beyond self-esteem and the reactive self. In R. A. Zucker, J. Aronoff, & R. I. Rabin (Eds.), *Personality and the prediction of behavior*. New York: Academic Press.

McGuire, W. J., McGuire, C. V., & Cheever, J. (1986). The self in society: Effects of social contexts on the sense of self. *British Journal of Social Psychology, 25*, 259–270.

McQuaid, J. (1967). A note on trends in answer to Cattell personality questionnaire by Scottish subjects. *British Journal of Psychology, 58*, 455–458.

Medin, D. L. (1972). Role of reinforcement in discrimination learning set in monkeys. *Psychological Bulletin, 77*, 305–318.

Medinnus, G. R., & Curtis, F. J. (1963). The relation between maternal self-acceptance and child acceptance. *Journal of Counseling Psychology, 27*, 542–544.

Megargee, E. I., & Parker, G. V. (1968). An exploration of the equivalence of Murrayan needs as assessed by the Adjective Check List, the TAT and Edwards Personal Preference Schedule. *Journal of Clinical Psychology, 24*, 47–51.

Mehlman, J. (1972). The "floating signifier": From Levi-Strauss to Lacan. *Yale French Studies, 48*, 10–37.

Mehrabian, A., & Ksionzky, S. (1970). Models for affiliative and conformity behavior. *Psychological Bulletin, 74*, 110–126.

Mehrabian, A., & Russell, J. A. (1973). A measure of arousal seeking tendency. *Environmental Behavior, 5*, 315–333.

Meichenbaum, D. (1976). Cognitive behavior and modification. In J. T. Spence, R. C. Carson, & J. W. Thibaut (Eds.), *Behavioral approaches to therapy*. Morristown, NJ: General Learning Press.

Melendy, M. R. (1901). *Maiden, wife, and mother: How to attain health, beauty, happiness*. Chicago: American Literary and Musical Association.

Melzack, R., & Wall, P. D. (1968). Gate control theory of pain. In A. Soulairac, J. Cahn, & J. Charpentier (Eds.), *Pain*. New York: Academic Press.

Mendelsohn, M. B., Linden, J., Gruen, G., & Curran, J. (1974). Heterosexual pairing and sibling configuration. *Journal of Individual Psychology, 30*, 202–210.

Mikol, B. (1960). The enjoyment of new musical systems. In M. Rokeach, *The open and closed mind*. New York: Basic Books.

Mikulincer, M., & Orbach, I. (1995). Attachment styles and repressive defensiveness: The accessibility and architecture of affective memories. *Journal of Personality and Social Psychology, 68*, 917–925.

Miller, N. E. (1959). Liberalization of basic S-R concepts: Extension to conflict behavior, motivation, and social learning. In S. Koch (Ed.), *Psychology: A study of science* (Vol. 2). New York: McGraw-Hill.

Miller, N. E., & Dollard, J. C. (1941). *Social learning and imitation*. New Haven, CT: Yale University Press.

Mischel, T. (1964). Personal constructs, rules and the logic of clinical activity. *Psychological Review, 71*, 180–192.

Mischel, W. (1958). Preference for delayed reinforcement: An experimental study of a cultural observation. *Journal of Abnormal and Social Psychology, 56*, 57–61.

Mischel, W. (1961). Delay of gratification, need for achievement, and acquiescence in another culture. *Journal of Abnormal and Social Psychology, 62*, 543–552.

Mischel, W. (1966). Theory and research on the antecedents of self-imposed delay of reward. In B. A. Maher (Ed.), *Progress in experimental personality research* (Vol. 3). New York: Academic Press.

Mischel, W. (1968). *Personality and assessment*. New York: Wiley.

Mischel, W. (1971). *Introduction to personality*. New York: Holt, Rinehart & Winston.

Mischel, W. (1973a). On the empirical dilemmas of psychodynamic approaches. *Journal of Abnormal Psychology, 82*, 335–344.

Mischel, W. (1973b). Toward a cognitive social learning reconceptualization of personality. *Psychological Review, 80*, 252–283.

Mischel, W. (1981). *Introduction to personality*. (3rd ed.). New York: Holt, Rinehart & Winston.

Mischel, W., & Ebbesen, E. (1970). Attention in delay of gratification. *Journal of Personality and Social Psychology, 16*, 329–337.

Mischel, W., Ebbesen, E. B., & Roskoff, Z. (1972). Cognitive and attentional mechanisms in delay of gratification. *Journal of Personality and Social Psychology, 21*, 204–218.

Mischel, W., & Shoda, Y. (1995). A cognitive-affective system theory of personality: Reconceptualizing situations, dispositions, dynamics, and invariance in personality structure. *Psychological Review, 102,* 246–268.

Mitchell, H. E. (1973, May). *Authoritarian punitiveness in simulated juror decision-making: The good guys didn't always wear white hats.* Paper presented at the Midwestern Psychological Association Convention.

Modell, A. H. (1975). A narcissistic defense against affects and the illusion of self-sufficiency. *International Journal of Psychoanalysis, 56*(3), 275–282.

Modell, A. H. (1976). The holding environment and the therapeutic action of psychoanalysis. *Journal of the American Psychological Association, 24*(2), 285–307.

Moll, L., & Kuypers, H. G. (1977). Premotor cortical ablations in monkeys: Contralateral changes in visually-guided reaching behavior. *Science, 198,* 317–319.

Moos, R. H. (1968). Situational analysis of a therapeutic community milieu. *Journal of Abnormal Psychology, 73,* 49–61.

Moos, R. H. (1969). Sources of variance in responses to questionnaires and in behavior. *Journal of Abnormal Psychology, 74,* 405–412.

Moos, R. H. (1970). Differential effects of psychiatric ward settings on patient change. *Journal of Nervous and Mental Disease, 5,* 316–321.

Morgan, C. D., & Murray, H. A. (1935). A method of investigating fantasies: The Thematic Apperception Test. *Archives of Neurological Psychiatry, 34,* 289–306.

Mosak, H. H. (1972). Life style assessment: A demonstration focussed on family constellation. *Journal of Individual Psychology, 28,* 232–237.

Mowrer, O. H. (1940). An experimental analogue of "regression" with incidental observations on "reaction formation." *Journal of Abnormal and Social Psychology, 35,* 56–87.

Mowrer, O. H. (1950). *Learning theory and personality dynamics.* New York: Ronald Press.

Munroe, R. (1955). *Schools of psychoanalytic thought.* New York: Holt, Rinehart & Winston.

Munsinger, H., & Kessen, W. (1964). Uncertainty, structure and preference. *Psychological Monograph, 78*(9).

Murray, H. A. (1938). *Explorations in personality: A clinical and experimental study of fifty men of college age.* New York: Oxford.

Murray, H. A. (1943). *Thematic Apperception Test.* Cambridge, MA: Harvard University Press.

Murray, H. A. (1954). Toward a classification of interaction. In T. Parsons & E. A. Shils (Eds.), *Toward a general theory of action.* Cambridge, MA: Harvard University Press.

Murray, H. A. (1959). Preparations for the scaffold of a comprehensive system. In S. Koch (Ed.), *Psychology: A study of a science* (Vol. 3). New York: McGraw-Hill.

Murray, H. A., & Kluckhohn, C. (1956). Outline of a conception of personality. In C. Kluckhohn, H. A. Murray, & D. M. Schneider (Eds.), *Personality in nature, society, and culture* (2nd ed.). New York: Knopf.

Murstein, B. I. (1956). The projection of hostility on the Rorschach and as a result of ego-threat. *Journal of Projective Techniques, 20,* 418–428.

Murstein, B. I. (1961). The relation of the Famous Sayings Test to the self- and ideal-self-adjustment. *Journal of Consulting Psychology, 25,* 368.

Myers, I. B. (1962). *Manual (1962), the Myers-Briggs type indicator.* Princeton, NJ: Educational Testing Service.

Naditch, M. P. (1975). Locus of control and drinking behavior in a sample of men in army basic training. *Journal of Consulting and Clinical Psychology, 43,* 96.

Nalven, F. B. (1967). Some perceptional decision-making correlates of repressive and intellectualizing defenses. *Journal of Clinical Psychology, 23,* 446–448.

Narayanan, L., Menon, S., & Levine, E. L. (1995). Personality structure: A culture-specific examination of the Five-Factor Model. *Journal of Personality Assessment, 64,* 51–62.

Natsoulas, T. (1965). Converging operations for perceptual defense. *Psychological Bulletin, 64,* 393–401.

Neugarten, B. L. (1964). A developmental view of adult personality. In J. E. Birren (Ed.), *Relations of development and aging.* Springfield, IL: Thomas.

Neugarten, B. L. (1979). Time, age and the life cycle. *American Journal of Psychiatry, 136,* 887–894.

Neugarten, B. L. (1980). Acting one's age: New rules for old. *Psychology Today, 13,* 66–80.

Neuman, G. G., & Salvatore, J. C. (1958). The Blacky Test and psychoanalytic theory: A factor-analytic approach to validity. *Journal of Projective Techniques, 22,* 427–431.

Nickel, T. W. (1974). The attribution of intention as a critical factor in the relationship between frustration and aggression. *Journal of Personality, 42,* 482–492.

Norman, W. T. (1963). Toward an adequate taxonomy of personality attributes: Replicated factor structure in peer nomination personality ratings. *Journal of Abnormal and Social Psychology, 66,* 574–583.

Novy, D. M., Frankiewicz, R. G., Francis, D. J., & Liberman, D. (1994). An investigation of the structural validity of Loevinger's model and measure of ego development. *Journal of Personality, 62,* 87–118.

Nowicki, S., & Roundtree, J. (1974). Correlates of locus of control in secondary age students. *Developmental Psychology, 10,* 33–37.

Nunnally, J. (1971). Visual attention to novel pictures. In H. I. Day, D. E. Berlyne, & D. S. Hunt (Eds.), *Intrinsic motivation: A new direction in education.* Toronto: Holt, Rinehart & Winston.

O'Connell, W. E. (1960). The adaptive function of wit and humor. *Journal of Abnormal and Social Psychology, 61,* 263–270.

Odell, M. (1959). *Personality correlates of independence and conformity.* Unpublished master's thesis. Ohio State University, Columbus.

Olds, J. (1975). Mapping the mind onto the brain. In F. G. Worden, J. P. Swazey, & G. Adelman (Eds.), *The neurosciences: Paths of discovery.* Cambridge, MA: Colonial Press.

O'Leary, A. (1985). Self-efficacy and health. *Behavior Research and Therapy, 23,* 437–451.

O'Leary, J. T., & Coben, L. A. (1958). The reticular core—1957. *Physiology Review, 38,* 243–276.

Oliveus, D. (1978). *Aggression in the schools.* New York: Halsted.

Orlofsky, J. L., Marcia, J. E., & Lesser, I. M. (1973). Ego identity status and the intimacy versus isolation crisis in young adulthood. *Journal of Personality and Social Psychology, 27,* 211–219.

Ornduff, S. R., Freedenfeld, R. N., Kelsey, R. M., & Critelli, J. W. (1994). Object relations of sexually abused female subjects: A TAT analysis. *Journal of Personality Assessment, 63,* 223–238.

Orr, E., & Westman, M. (1990). Hardiness as a stress moderator: A review. In M. Rosenbaum (Ed.), *Learned resourcefulness: On coping skills, self-control, and adaptive behavior* (pp. 64–94). New York: Springer-Verlag.

Osgood, C. (1962). Studies on the generality of affect meaning systems. *American Psychologist, 17,* 10–28.

Page, H. A., & Markowitz, G. (1955). The relationship of defensiveness to rating scale bias. *Journal of Psychology, 40,* 431–435.

Paloutzian, R. F. (1981). Purpose in life and value changes following conversion. *Journal of Personality and Social Psychology, 41,* 1153–1160.

Paunonen, S. V., & Jackson, D. N. (1986). Nomothetic and idiothetic measurement in personality. *Journal of Personality, 54,* 447–459.

Pavlov, I. P. (1927). *Conditioned reflexes.* Oxford, England: Oxford University Press.

Pawlicki, R. E., & Almquist, C. (1973). Authoritarianism, locus of control, and tolerance of ambiguity as reflected in membership and nonmembership in a women's liberation group. *Psychological Reports, 32,* 1331–1337.

Peabody, D. (1966). Authoritarianism scales and response bias. *Psychological Bulletin, 65,* 11–23.

Peabody, D. (1984). Personality dimensions through trait inferences. *Journal of Personality and Social Psychology, 46,* 384–403.

Pearson, P. H. (1969). Openness to experience as related to organismic valuing. *Journal of Personality, 37,* 481–496.

Pearson, P. H. (1974). Conceptualizing and measuring openness to experience in the context of psychotherapy. In D. A. Wexler & L. N. Rice (Eds.), *Innovations in client-centered therapy.* New York: Wiley.

Peck, R. F., & Havighurst, R. J. (1960). *The psychology of character development.* New York: Wiley.

Penn, N. (1964). Experience improvements on an analogue of repression paradigm. *Psychological Record, 14,* 185–196.

Peplau, L. A. (1976). Impact of fear of success and sex-role attitudes on women's competitive achievement. *Journal of Personality and Social Psychology, 34,* 561–568.

Perls, F. (1969a). *Ego, humor and aggression.* New York: Random House.

Perls, F. (1969b). *Gestalt therapy verbation.* Lafayette, CA: Real People Press.

Perls, F. (1969c). *In and out of the garbage pail.* Lafayette, CA: Real People Press.

Pervin, L. A. (1983). The stasis and flow of behavior: Toward a theory of goals. In M. M. Page (Ed.), *Personality: Current theory and research.* Lincoln: University of Nebraska Press.

Pervin, L. V. (1970). *Personality: Theory, assessment, and research.* New York: Wiley.

Peters, R. S. (1958). *The concept of motivation.* New York: Humanities Press.

Petersen, R. C., & Hergenhahn, B. R. (1968). Test of cognitive dissonance theory in an elementary school setting. *Psychological Report, 22,* 199–202.

Pettit, T. F. (1969). Anality and time. *Journal of Consulting and Clinical Psychology, 33,* 170–174.

Phares, E. J. (1957). Expectancy changes in skill and chance situations. *Journal of Abnormal and Social Psychology, 54,* 339–342.

Phares, E. J. (1962). Perceptual threshold decrements as a function of skill and chance expectancies. *Journal of Psychology, 53,* 399–407.

Phares, E. J. (1976). *Locus of control in personality.* Morristown, NJ: General Learning Press.

Phillips, W. S., & Greene, J. E. (1939). A preliminary study of the relationship of age, hobbies, and civil status to neuroticism among women teachers. *Journal of Educational Psychology, 30,* 440–444.

Piedmont, R. L. (1993). A longitudinal analysis of burnout in the health care setting: The role of personal dispositions. *Journal of Personality Assessment, 61,* 457–473.

Piedmont, R. L., McCrae, R. R., & Costa, P. T., Jr. (1992). An assessment of the Edwards Personal Preference Schedule from the perspective of the Five-Factor Model. *Journal of Personality Assessment, 60,* 67–78.

Pierce, J. W. (1959). *The educational motivation of superior students who do not achieve in high school.* Washington, DC: U.S. Department of Health, Education, and Welfare, Office of Education.

Pines, H. A., & Julian, J. W. (1972). Effects of task and social demands on locus of control differences in information processing. *Journal of Personality, 40,* 407–416.

Pishkin, V., & Thorne, F. C. (1973). A factorial study of existential state reactions. *Journal of Clinical Psychology, 29,* 392–402.

Plant, W. T., Telford, C. W., & Thomas, J. W. (1965). Some personality differences between dogmatic and non-dogmatic groups. *Journal of Social Psychology, 67,* 67–75.

Platt, J. J., & Eisenman, R. (1968). Internal-external control of reinforcement, time perspective, adjustment, and anxiety. *Journal of Genetic Psychology, 79,* 121–128.

Poe, C. A. (1969). Convergent and discriminant validation of measures of personal needs. *Journal of Educational Measurement, 6,* 103–107.

Pollak, J. M. (1979). Obsessive-compulsive personality: A review. *Psychological Bulletin, 86,* 225–241.

Porter, C. A., & Suedfeld, P. (1981). Integrative complexity in the correspondence of literary figures: Effects of personal and societal stress. *Journal of Personality and Social Psychology, 40,* 321–330.

Porter, N., Geis, F. L., Cooper, E., & Newman, E. (1985). Androgyny and leadership in mixed-sex groups. *Journal of Personality and Social Psychology, 49,* 808–823.

Postman, L., Bruner, J. S., & McGinnies, E. (1948). Personal value as selective factors in perception. *Journal of Abnormal and Social Psychology, 43,* 142–154.

Powell, F. A. (1962). Open- and closed-mindedness and the ability to differentiate source and message. *Journal of Abnormal and Social Psychology, 65,* 61–64.

Priel, B., Gonik, N., & Rabinowitz, B. (1993). Appraisals of childbirth experience and newborn characteristics: The role of hardiness and affect. *Journal of Personality, 61,* 300–315.

Procink, T. J., & Breem, L. J. (1974). Locus of control, study habits and attitudes, and college academic performance. *Journal of Personality and Social Psychology, 88,* 91–95.

Procink, T. J., & Breem, L. J. (1975). Defensive externality and its relation to academic performance. *Journal of Personality and Social Psychology, 31,* 549–556.

Pyron, B., & Kafer, J. (1967). Recall of nonsense and attitudinal rigidity. *Journal of Personality and Social Psychology, 5,* 463–466.

Qualls, P. J. (1983). The physiological measurement of imagery: An overview. *Imagination, Cognition and Personality, 2,* 89–101.

Rachman, S. (1973). The effects of psychological treatment. In H. Eysenck (Ed.), *Handbook of abnormal psychology.* New York: Basic Books.

Radloff, R. (1961). Opinion evaluation and affiliation. *Journal of Abnormal and Social Psychology, 62,* 578–585.

Rado, S. (1959). Obsessive behavior. In S. Arieti (Ed.), *American handbook of psychiatry* (Vol. 1). New York: Basic Books.

Rank, O. (1929). *The trauma of birth.* New York: Harcourt Brace Jovanovich.

Rank, O. (1945). *Will therapy and truth and reality.* New York: Knopf.

Rapaport, D. (1958). The theory of ego autonomy: A generalization. *Bulletin of Menninger Clinic, 22,* 13–25.

Rappaport, H., Enrich, K., & Wilson, A. (1985). Relation between ego identity and temporal perspective. *Journal of Personality and Social Psychology, 48,* 1609–1620.

Raskin, R., Novacek, J., & Hogan, R. (1991). Narcissism, self-esteem, and defensive self-enhancement. *Journal of Personality, 59,* 19–38.

Raskin, R., & Shaw, R. (1988). Narcissism and the use of personal pronouns. *Journal of Personality, 56,* 393–404.

Raven, B. H., & Fishbein, M. (1961). Acceptance of

punishment and change in belief. *Journal of Abnormal and Social Psychology, 63,* 411–416.

Razik, T. A. (1965). *Bibliography of creativity studies and related areas.* Buffalo: State University of New York at Buffalo.

Reich, W. (1931). Character formation and the phobias of childhood. *International Journal of Psychoanalysis, 12,* 219–230.

Reich, W. (1933). *Charakteranalyse.* Berlin, Germany: Selbstverlag des Verfassers.

Reimanis, G. (1966). Childhood experience memories and anomie in adults and college students. *Journal of Individual Psychology, 22,* 56–64.

Reimanis, G. (1974). Psychosocial development, anomie, and mood. *Journal of Personality and Social Psychology, 29,* 355–357.

Renken, B., Egeland, B., Marvinney, D., Mangelsdorf, S., & Stroufe, L. A. (1989). Early childhood antecedents of aggression and passive-withdrawal in early elementary school. *Journal of Personality, 57,* 257–282.

Restle, F., Andrews, M., & Rokeach, M. (1964). Differences between open- and closed-minded subjects on learning-set and oddity problems. *Journal of Abnormal and Social Psychology, 68,* 648–654.

Reuman, D. A. (1982). Ipsative behavioral variability and the quality of thematic apperceptive measurement of the achievement motive. *Journal of Personality and Social Psychology, 42,* 1098–1110.

Reuman, D. A., Alwin, D. F., & Veroff, J. (1984). Assessing the validity of the achievement motive in the presence of random measurement error. *Journal of Personality and Social Psychology, 47,* 1347–1362.

Rhine, R. J. (1967). Some problems in dissonance theory research on information selectivity. *Psychological Bulletin, 68,* 21–28.

Rhodewalt, F., & Zone, J. B. (1989) Appraisal of life change, depression, and illness in hardy and nonhardy women. *Journal of Personality and Social Psychology, 56,* 81–88.

Rice, L. N., & Wagstaff, A. K. (1967). Client voice quality and expressive style as indexes of productive psychotherapy. *Journal of Consulting Psychology, 31,* 557–563.

Richek, J. G., Mayo, C. D., & Pirgean, H. B. (1970). Dogmatism, religiosity, and mental health in college students. *Mental Health, 54,* 572–574.

Riesen, A. H. (1961). Stimulation as a requirement for growth and function in behavioral development. In D. W. Fiske & S. R. Maddi (Eds.), *Functions of varied experience.* Homewood, IL: Dorsey Press.

Roberts, B. W., & Donahue, E. M. (1994). One personality, multiple selves: Integrating personality and social roles. *Journal of Personality, 62,* 199–218.

Robinson, S. A. (1968). The development of a female form of the Blacky Pictures. *Journal of Projective Techniques and Personality Assessment, 32,* 74–80.

Robinson, S. A., & Hendrix, V. L. (1966). The Blacky Test and psychoanalytic theory: Another factor-analytic approach to validity. *Journal of Projective Techniques and Personality Assessment, 30,* 597–603.

Rogers, C. R. (1959). A theory of therapy, personality, and interpersonal relationships, as developed in the client-centered framework. In S. Koch (Ed.), *Psychology: A study of a science* (Vol. 3). New York: McGraw-Hill.

Rogers, C. R. (1961). *On becoming a person.* Boston: Houghton Mifflin.

Rogers, C. R. (1963). Actualizing tendency in relation to "motives" and to consciousness. In M. R. Jones (Ed.), *Nebraska symposium on motivation.* Lincoln, NE: University of Nebraska Press.

Rogers, C. R. (1977). *Carl Rogers on personal power: Inner strength and its revolutionary impact.* New York: Delacorte Press.

Rohrer, J. H., & Edmonson, M. S. (Eds.). (1960). *The eighth generation.* New York: Harper.

Rohrer, L. G., & Widiger, T. A. (1983). Personality structure and assessment. *Annual Review of Psychology, 34,* 431–463.

Rokeach, M. (1945). Studies in beauty: II. Some determiners of the perception of beauty in women. *Journal of Social Psychology, 22,* 155–169.

Rokeach, M. (1960). *The open and closed mind.* New York: Basic Books.

Rokeach, M., Swanson, T. S., & Denny, M. R. (1960). The role of past experience: A comparison between chess players and non-chess players. In M. Rokeach, *The open and closed mind.* New York: Basic Books.

Rorschach, T. (1921). *Psychodiagnostik.* Bern, Switzerland: Huber.

Rosen, B. C. (1961). Family structure and achievement motivation. *American Sociological Review, 26,* 574–585.

Rosenbaum, M. E., Horne, W. C., & Chalmers, D. K. (1962). Level of self-esteem and the learning of imitation and non-imitation. *Journal of Personality, 30,* 147–156.

Rosenberg, L. A. (1962). Idealization of self and social adjustment. *Journal of Consulting Psychology, 26,* 487.

Rosenberg, M. J. (1965). When dissonance fails: On eliminating evaluation apprehension from attitude measurement. *Journal of Personality and Social Psychology, 1,* 28–42.

Rosenberg, S. D., Blatt, S. J., Oxman, T. E., McHugo, G. J., & Ford, R. Q. (1994). Assessment of object relatedness through a lexical content analysis of the TAT. *Journal of Personality Assessment, 63,* 345–362.

Rosenman, S. (1955). Changes in the representations of self, others and interrelationship in therapy. *Journal of Counseling Psychology, 2,* 271–277.

Rosenow, C., & Whyte, A. H. (1931). The ordinal position of problem children. *American Journal of Orthopsychiatry, 1,* 430–444.

Rosenzweig, S. (1933). The recall of finished and unfinished tasks as affected by the purpose with which they were performed. *Psychological Bulletin, 30,* 698.

Rosenzweig, S. (1943). An experimental study of repression with special reference to need-persistive and ego-defensive reactions to frustrations. *Journal of Experimental Psychology, 32,* 64–74.

Rosenzweig, S., & Mason, G. (1934). An experimental study of memory in relation to the theory of repression. *British Journal of Psychology, 24,* 247–265.

Rotter, J. B. (1954). *Social learning and clinical psychology.* Englewood Cliffs, NJ: Prentice-Hall.

Rotter, J. B. (1964). *Clinical psychology* (2nd ed.). Englewood Cliffs, NJ: Prentice-Hall.

Rotter, J. B. (1966). Generalized expectancies for internal versus external control of reinforcement. *Psychological Monograph, 80*(609).

Rotter, J. B., Chance, J. E., & Phares, E. J. (Eds.). (1972). *Applications of a social learning theory of personality.* New York: Holt, Rinehart & Winston.

Rotter, J. B., Liverant, S., & Crowne, D. P. (1961). The growth and extinction of expectancies in chance controlled and skill tasks. *Journal of Personality, 52,* 161–177.

Rotter, J. B., Seeman, M., & Liverant, S. (1962). Internal versus external control of reinforcements: A major variable in behavior theory. In N. F. Washburne (Ed.), *Decisions, values, and groups* (Vol. 2, pp. 473–516). London: Pergamon Press.

Runyan, W. M. (1982). In defense of the case study method. *American Journal of Orthopsychiatry, 52,* 440–446.

Rutter, M. (1984). Continuities and discontinuities in socioemotional development. In R. N. Emde & R. J. Harmon (Eds.), *Continuities and discontinuities in development* (pp. 41–68). New York: Plenum.

Rybak, W. S., Sadnavitch, J. M., & Mason, B. J. (1968). Psychosocial changes in personality during foster grandparents program. *Journal of American Geriatrics Society, 16,* 956–959.

Ryckman, R. M., Rodda, W. C., & Sherman, M. F. (1972). Locus of control and expertise relevant as determinants of changes in opinion about student activism. *Journal of Social Psychology, 88,* 107–114.

Sackheim, H. A., & Gur, R. C. (1978). Self-deception, self-confrontation, and consciousness. In G. E. Schwartz & D. Shapiro (Eds.), *Consciousness and self-regulation: Advances in research* (Vol. 2). New York: Plenum.

Sackheim, H. A., & Gur, R. C. (1979). Self-deception, other-deception, and self-reported psychopathology. *Journal of Consulting and Clinical Psychology, 47,* 213–215.

Sackheim, H. A., & Gur, R. C. (1985). Voice recognition and the ontological status of self-deception. *Journal of Personality and Social Psychology, 48,* 1365–1368.

Sadave, S. W., & Forsyth, R. (1977). Person-environment interaction and college student drug use: A multivariate longitudinal study. *Genetic Psychology Monographs, 96,* 211–245.

Salas, R. G. (1967). Some characteristics of the Eysenck Personality Inventory (EPI) found under Australian conditions. *Australian Military Forces Research Report, 6.*

Sampson, E. E. (1962). Birth order, need achievement, and conformity. *Journal of Abnormal and Social Psychology, 64,* 155–159.

Sampson, E. E. (1965). The study of ordinal position: Antecedents and outcomes. In B. A. Maher (Ed.), *Progress in experimental personality research.* New York: Academic Press.

Samuels, I. (1959). Reticular mechanisms and behavior. *Psychological Bulletin, 56,* 1–25.

Sandvik, E., & Diener, E. (1993). Subjective well-being in self-report and performance. *Journal of Personality, 61,* 317–342.

Sanford, N. (Ed.). (1962). *The American College.* New York: Wiley.

Sarason, I. G., (1957a). The effect of anxiety and two kinds of failure on serial learning. *Journal of Personality, 25,* 383–392.

Sarason, I. G., (1957b). Effect of anxiety and two kinds of motivating instructions on verbal learning. *Journal of Abnormal and Social Psychology, 54,* 166–171.

Sarason, I. G. (1958). Interrelationships among individual differences variables, behavior in psychotherapy, and verbal conditioning. *Journal of Abnormal and Social Psychology, 56,* 339–344.

Sarnoff, I. (1951). Identification with the aggressor: Some personality correlates of anti-Semitism among Jews. *Journal of Personality, 20,* 199–218.

Sarnoff, I. (1960). Reaction formation and cynicism. *Journal of Personality, 28,* 129–143.

Sarnoff, I. (1962). *Personality: Dynamics and development.* New York: Wiley.

Sarnoff, I., & Corwin, S. M. (1959). Castration anxiety and the fear of death. *Journal of Personality, 27,* 374–385.

Sarnoff, I., & Katz, D. (1954). The motivational bases of attitude change. *Journal of Abnormal and Social Psychology, 49,* 115–124.

Sartre, J. P. (1956). *Being and nothingness.* New York: Philosophical Library.

Scarpetti, W. L. (1974). Autonomic concomitants of aggressive behavior in repressors and sensitizers: A social learning approach. *Journal of Personality and Social Psychology, 30,* 772–781.

Schachter, S. (1959). *The psychology of affiliation: Experimental studies of the sources of gregariousness.* Stanford, CA: Stanford University Press.

Schachter, S. (1963). Birth order, eminence, and higher education. *American Sociological Review, 28,* 757–767.

Schachter, S. (1964). Birth order and sociometric choice. *Journal of Abnormal and Social Psychology, 68,* 452–456.

Schaefer, C. E. (1969). The self-concept of creative adolescents. *Journal of Psychology, 72,* 233–242.

Schaeffer, D. L. (1968). Addenda to an annotated bibliography of the Blacky Test (1949–1967). *Journal of Projective Techniques and Personality Assessment, 32,* 55–555.

Schaller, M., Boyd, C., Yohannes, J., & O'Brien, M. (1995). The prejudiced personality revisited: Personal need for structure and formation of erroneous group stereotypes. *Journal of Personality and Social Psychology, 68,* 544–555.

Schooler, C. (1961). Birth order and schizophrenia. *Archives of Genetic Psychiatry, 4,* 91–97.

Schooler, C. (1964). Birth order and hospitalization for schizophrenia. *Journal of Abnormal and Social Psychology, 69,* 574–579.

Schubert, D. S. P. (1959a). Impulsivity and other personality characteristics of cigarette smokers. *American Psychologist, 14,* 354–355.

Schubert, D. S. P. (1959b). Personality implications of cigarette smoking among college students. *Journal of Consulting Psychology, 23,* 376.

Schulberg, H. (1961). Authoritarianism, tendency to agree, and interpersonal perception. *Journal of Abnormal and Social Psychology, 63,* 101–108.

Schultz, D. P. (1964). Spontaneous alternation behavior in humans: Implications for psychological research. *Psychological Bulletin, 62,* 394–400.

Schwartz, B. J. (1955). The measurement of castration anxiety over loss of love. *Journal of Personality, 24,* 204–219.

Schwartz, B. J. (1956). An empirical test of two Freudian hypotheses concerning castration anxiety. *Journal of Personality, 24,* 318–327.

Schwartz, D. W., & Carp, S. A. (1967). Field dependence in a geriatric population. *Perceptual and Motor Skills, 24,* 495–504.

Schwartz, M., & Gaines, L. (1974). Self-actualization and the human tendency for varied experience. *Journal of Personality Assessment, 38,* 423–427.

Sears, R. R. (1936). Experimental studies of projection: I. Attribution of traits. *Journal of Social Psychology, 7,* 151–163.

Sears, R. R. (1943). *Survey of objective studies of psychoanalytic concepts.* New York: Social Science Research Council.

Sears, R. R. (1944). Experimental analysis of psychoanalytic phenomena. In J. McV. Hunt (Ed.), *Personality and the behavior disorders* (Vol. 1). New York: Ronald Press.

Sears, R. R. (1950). Personality. In C. P. Stone & D. W. Taylor (Eds.), *Annual Review of Psychology.* Palo Alto, CA: Annual Reviews.

Sechrest, L. (1963). The psychology of personal constructs: George Kelly. In J. M. Wepman & R. W. Heine (Eds.), *Concepts of personality.* Chicago: Aldine.

Sechrest, L. (1968). Personal constructs and personal characteristics. *Journal of Individual Psychology, 24,* 162–166.

Sechrest, L. (1977). Personal constructs theory. In R. Corsini (Ed.), *Current personality theories.* Itasca, IL: Peacock.

Seeman, M. (1963). Alienation and social learning in a reformatory. *American Journal of Sociology, 69,* 270–284.

Seeman, M., & Evans, J. (1962). Alienation and learning in a hospital setting. *American Sociological Review, 27,* 772–782.

Segal, H. G., Westen, D., Lohr, N. E., & Silk, K. R. (1993). Clinical assessment of object relations and social cognition using stories told to the Picture Arrangement subtest of the WAIS-R. *Journal of Personality Assessment, 61,* 58–60.

Sells, S. B., Demaree, R. G., & Will, D. P. (1971). Dimensions of personality: II. Separate factor structures in Guilford and Cattell trait markers. *Multivariate Behavior Research, 6,* 136–165.

Sells, S. B., & Roff, M. (1963). Peer acceptance-rejection and birth order. *American Psychologist, 18,* 335.

Senniker, P., & Hendrick, C. (1983). Androgyny and helping behavior. *Journal of Personality and Social Psychology, 45,* 916–925.

Shapiro, K. J., & Alexander, I. E. (1969). Extraversion-introversion, affiliation, and anxiety. *Journal of Personality, 37,* 387–406.

Sharpe, D., & Viney, L. (1973). Weltanschauung and the Purpose of Life Test. *Journal of Clinical Psychology, 29,* 489–491.

Shaw, J. S. (1982). Psychological androgyny and stressful life events. *Journal of Personality and Social Psychology, 42,* 145–153.

Shaw, L., & Sichel, H. (1971). *Accident proneness.* New York: Pergamon Press.

Sheerer, E. (1949). Analysis of the relationship between acceptance of and respect for self and acceptance of and respect for others. *Journal of Consulting Psychology, 13,* 169–175.

Sheffield, F. D., & Roby, T. B. (1950). Reward value of a non-nutrient sweet taste. *Journal of Comparative and Physiological Psychology, 43,* 471–481.

Shepperd, J. A., & Kashani, J. H. (1991). The relationship of hardiness, gender, and stress to health outcomes in adolescents. *Journal of Personality, 59,* 747–768.

Sherman, S. J. (1973). Internal-external control and its relationship to attitude change under different social influence techniques. *Journal of Personality and Social Psychology, 23,* 23–29.

Shlien, J. M. (1962). The self-concept in relation to behavior: Theoretical and empirical research. *Religious Education* (Research Suppl.).

Shlien, J. M. (1963). Phenomenology and personality. In J. M. Wepman & R. W. Heine (Eds.), *Concepts of personality.* Chicago: Aldine.

Shlien, J. M. (1987). A countertheory of transference. *Person Centered Review, 2,* 15–49.

Shostrom, E. (1965). An inventory for the measurement of self actualization. *Educational and Psychological Measurement, 24,* 207–218.

Shostrom, E. (1966). *Manual for the Personal Orientation Inventory (POI): An inventory for the measurement of self actualization.* San Diego: Educational and Industrial Testing Service.

Shostrom, E., & Knapp, R. (1966). The relationship of a measure of self actualization (POI) to a measure of pathology (MMPI) and to therapeutic growth. *American Journal of Psychotherapy, 20,* 193–202.

Shweder, R. A. (1975). How relevant is an individual differences theory of personality? *Journal of Personality, 43,* 455–483.

Shweder, R. A. (1982). Fact & artifact in trait perception: The systematic distortion hypothesis. In B. A. Maher (Ed.), *Progress in experimental personality research* (Vol. 2). New York: Academic Press.

Sidis, B. (1908). An experimental study of sleep. *Journal of Abnormal and Social Psychology, 3,* 1–32, 63–96, 170–207.

Siegelman, M. (1968). Origins of extraversion-introversion. *Journal of Psychology, 69,* 85–91.

Silverman, I. (1964). Defense of dissonance theory: Reply to Chapanis & Chapanis. *Psychological Bulletin, 62,* 205–209.

Silverman, L. H. (1976). Psychoanalytic theory: The reports of my death are greatly exaggerated. *American Psychologist, 31,* 621–637.

Singer, J. L., & Kolligian, J., Jr. (1987). Personality: Developments in the study of private experience. *Annual Review of Psychology, 38,* 533–574.

Skinner, B. F. (1938). *The behavior of organisms: An experimental analysis.* New York: Appleton-Century-Crofts.

Skinner, B. F. (1950). Are theories of learning necessary? *Psychological Review, 57,* 193–216.

Skinner, B. F. (1953). *Science and human behavior.* New York: Macmillan.

Skinner, B. F. (1957). *Verbal behavior.* New York: Appleton-Century-Crofts.

Skinner, B. F. (1961). *Cumulative record.* New York: Appleton-Century-Crofts.

Skinner, B. F. (1971). *Beyond freedom and dignity.* New York: Knopf.

Skinner, B. F. (1974). *About behaviorism.* New York: Knopf.

Skinner, B. F., Howarth, E., & Browne, J. A. (1970). Note on the role of neuroticism and extroversion in the "nice personality" stereotype. *Psychological Report, 26,* 445–446.

Slade, L. A., & Rush, M. C. (1991). Achievement motivation and the dynamics of task difficulty choices. *Journal of Personality and Social Psychology, 60,* 165–172.

Sletto, R. F. (1934). Sibling position and juvenile delinquency. *American Journal of Sociology, 39,* 657–669.

Smart, R. G. (1963). Alcoholism, birth order, and family size. *Journal of Abnormal and Social Psychology, 66,* 17–23.

Smith, M. B. (1966). Explorations in competence: A study of Peace Corps teachers in Ghana. *American Psychologist, 21,* 555–566.

Smith, M. B. (1968). Competence and socialization. In J. A. Clausen (Ed.), *Socialization and society.* Boston: Little, Brown.

Snyder, M. (1987). *Public appearances/private realities.* New York: Freeman.

Soderstrom, D., & Wright, E. W. (1977). Religious

orientation and meaning in life. *Journal of Clinical Psychology, 33*(1), 65–68.

Solomon, R. L., & Howes, D. (1951). Word frequency, personal values, and visual duration thresholds. *Psychological Review, 58*, 256–270.

Sosis, R. H. (1974). Internal-external control and the perception of responsibility of another for an accident. *Journal of Personality and Social Psychology, 30*, 1031–1034.

Spangler, W. D. (1992). Validity of questionnaire and TAT measures of need for achievement: Two meta-analyses. *Psychological Bulletin, 112*, 140–154.

Spanos, N. P. (1978). Witchcraft in histories of psychiatry: A critical analysis and an alternative conceptualization. *Psychological Bulletin, 85*, 417–439.

Spence, K. W. (1948). The postulates and methods of "behaviorism." *Psychological Review, 55*, 67–78.

Spence, K. W., & Spence, J. T. (1966). Sex and anxiety differences in eyelid conditioning. *Psychological Bulletin, 65*, 137–142.

Spielberger, C. D. (1962). Role of awareness in verbal conditioning. In C. W. Eriksen (Ed.), *Behavior and awareness*. Durham, NC: Duke University Press.

Spranger, E. (1928). *Types of men* (W. Pigors, Trans.). Halle, Germany: Niemeyer.

Staffieri, J. R. (1970). Birth order and creativity. *Journal of Clinical Psychology, 26*, 65–66.

Staub, E. (1978). *Positive social behavior and morality: Vol. 1. Social and personal influences*. New York: Academic Press.

Stein, M. I. (1968). Creativity. In E. F. Borgatta & W. W. Lambert (Eds.), *Handbook of personality theory and research*. Chicago: Rand McNally.

Stephenson, W. (1950). The significance of Q-technique for the study of personality. In M. L. Reymert (Ed.), *Feeling and emotions: The Mooseheart symposium*. New York: McGraw-Hill.

Stephenson, W. (1953). *The study of behavior: Q-technique and its methodology*. Chicago: University of Chicago Press.

Stern, G. G. (1958). *Preliminary record: Activities index —College Characteristics Index*. Syracuse, NY: Syracuse University Psychological Research Center.

Stevenson, I. (1957). Is the human personality more plastic in infancy and childhood? *American Journal of Psychiatry, 14*, 152–161.

Stewart, R. A. C. (1968). Academic performance and components of self actualization. *Perceptual and Motor Skills, 26*, 918.

Stock, D. (1949). An investigation into the interrelations between self-concept and feelings directed toward persons and groups. *Journal of Consulting Psychology, 13*, 176–180.

Stokes, G. S., Mumford, M. D., & Owens, W. A. (1989). Life history prototypes in the study of human individuality. *Journal of Personality, 57*, 509–545.

Stotland, E., & Cottrell, N. B. (1961). Self-esteem, group interaction, and group influence on performance. *Journal of Personality, 29*, 273–284.

Strassberg, D. S. (1973). Relationships among locus of control, anxiety, and valued goal expectations. *Journal of Consulting and Clinical Psychology, 2*, 319.

Strauman, T. J., & Higgins, E. T. (1988). Self discrepancies as predictors of vulnerability to distinct syndromes of chronic emotional distress. *Journal of Personality, 56*, 685–708.

Strickland, B. R. (1965). The prediction of social action from a dimension of internal-external control. *Journal of Social Psychology, 66*, 353–358.

Strickland, B. R. (1978). Internal-external expectancies and health-related behaviors. *Journal of Consulting and Clinical Psychology, 46*(6), 1192–1211.

Strickland, B. R., & Jenkins, O. (1964). Simple motor performance under positive and negative approval motivations. *Perceptual and Motor Skills, 19*, 599–605.

Strong, E. K., Jr. (1943). *Vocational interests of men and women*. Stanford, CA: Stanford University Press.

Suinn, R. M. (1961). The relationship between self-acceptance and acceptance of others: A learning theory analysis. *Journal of Abnormal and Social Psychology, 63*, 37–42.

Sukemune, S., Haruki, Y., & Kashiwagi, K. (1977). Studies on social learning in Japan. *American Psychologist, 32*, 924–933.

Swann, W. B., Jr., & Read, S. J. (1981). Acquiring self-knowledge: The search for feedback that fits. *Journal of Personality and Social Psychology, 41*, 1119–1128.

Swanson, G. E. (1951). Some effects of member object-relationships on small groups. *Human Relations, 4*, 355–380.

Symonds, P. M. (1961). *From adolescent to adult*. New York: Columbia University Press.

Taft, R. (1967). Extraversion, neuroticism and expressive behavior: An application of Wallach's moderator effect to handwriting analysis. *Journal of Personality, 35*, 570–584.

Taulbee, E. S., & Stenmark, D. E. (1968). The Blacky Pictures Test: A comprehensive annotated and indexed bibliography (1949–1967). *Journal of Projective Techniques and Personality Assessment, 32*, 102–137.

Taylor, C. B., Bandura, A., Ewart, C. K., Miller, N. H., & DeBusk, R. F. (1985). Exercise testing to enhance wives' confidence in their husbands' cardiac capabilities soon after clinically uncomplicated acute myocardial infarction. *American Journal of Cardiology, 55,* 635–638.

Taylor, C. W. (1963). *Creativity: Progress and potential.* New York: McGraw-Hill.

Taylor, I. A., & Getzels, J. W. (1975). *Perspectives in creativity.* Chicago: Aldine.

Taylor, J. A. (1953). A personality scale of manifest anxiety. *Journal of Abnormal and Social Psychology, 48,* 285–290.

Taylor, S. E., & Brown, J. D. (1988). Illusion and well-being: A social psychological perspective on mental health. *Psychological Bulletin, 103,* 193–210.

Tedeschi, J. T., Smith, R. B., III, & Brown, R. C., Jr. (1974). A reinterpretation of research on aggression. *Psychological Bulletin, 81,* 540–562.

Terman, L. M., & Miles, G. C. (1936). *Sex and personality.* New York: McGraw-Hill.

Terman, L. M., & Oden, M. H. (1959). *The gifted group at mid-life.* Stanford, CA: Stanford University Press.

Tesch, S. A., & Whitbourne, S. K. (1982). Intimacy and identity status in young adults. *Journal of Personality and Social Psychology, 43,* 1041–1051.

Tesch, S. T., & Cameron, K. A. (1987). Openness to experience and development of adult identity. *Journal of Personality, 55,* 615–630.

Tetlock, P. E. (1984). Cognitive style and political belief systems in the British House of Commons. *Journal of Personality and Social Psychology, 46,* 365–375.

Thayer, R. E. (1967). Measurement of activation through self-report. *Psychological Reports, 20,* 663–678.

Thompson, J. K. (1990). *Body-image disturbance: Assessment and treatment.* Elmsford, NY: Pergamon Press.

Thompson, W. R., & Schaefer, T. (1961). Early environmental stimulation. In D. W. Fiske & S. R. Maddi (Eds.), *Functions of varied experience.* Homewood, IL: Dorsey Press.

Thorndike, E. L., & Lorge, I. (1944). *The teacher's word book of 30,000 words.* New York: Teachers College, Columbia University.

Thorne, A. (1989). Conditional patterns, transference, and the coherence of personality across time. In D. M. Buss & N. Cantor (Eds.), *Personality psychology: Recent trends and emerging directions* (pp. 150–159). New York: Springer-Verlag.

Thorne, F. C., & Pishkin, V. (1973). The Existential Study. *Journal of Clinical Psychology, 29,* 389–410.

Tillich, P. (1952). *The courage to be.* New Haven, CT: Yale University Press.

Tittler, B. (1974). A behavioral approach to the measurement of openness to experience. *Journal of Personality Assessment, 38,* 335–340.

Tobacyk, J. (1981). Personality differentiation, effectiveness of personality integration, and mood in female college students. *Journal of Personality and Social Psychology, 41,* 348–356.

Toder, N. L., & Marcia, J. E. (1973). Ego identity status and response to conformity pressure in college women. *Journal of Personality and Social Psychology, 26,* 287–294.

Tolman, E. C. (1948). Cognitive maps in rats and men. *Psychological Review, 55,* 189–208.

Toman, W. (1959). Family constellation as a character and marriage determinant. *International Journal of Psychoanalysis, 40,* 316–319.

Tompkins, S. S. (1979). Script theory: Differential magnifications of affects. In *Nebraska symposium on motivation.* Lincoln: University of Nebraska Press.

Trapp, E. P., & Kausler, P. H. (1958). Test anxiety level and goal-setting behavior. *Journal of Consulting Psychology, 22,* 31–34.

Tribich, D., & Messer, S. (1974). Psychoanalytic character type and status of authority as determiners of suggestibility. *Journal of Consulting and Clinical Psychology, 42,* 842–848.

Trope, Y. (1986). Self-enhancement and self-assessment in achievement behavior. In R. M. Sorrentino & E. T. Higgins (Eds.), *Handbook of motivation and cognition: Foundations of social behavior.* New York: Guilford.

Truax, C. B. (1957). The repression response to implied failure as a function of the hysteria-psychasthenia index. *Journal of Abnormal and Social Psychology, 55,* 188–193.

Tuddenham, R. D. (1959). Constancy of personality ratings over two decades. *Genetic Psychology Monograph, 60,* 3–29.

Tudor, T., & Holmes, D. (1973). Differential recall of successes and failures: Its relationship to defensiveness, achievement motivation, and anxiety. *Journal of Experimental Research in Personality, 7,* 208–224.

Tunnell, G. (1981). Sex role and cognitive schemata: Person perception in feminine and androgynous women. *Journal of Personality and Social Psychology, 40,* 1126–1136.

Turner, R. H., & Vanderlippe, R. H. (1958). Self-ideal congruence as an index of adjustment. *Journal of Abnormal and Social Psychology, 57,* 202–206.

Tversky, A., & Kahneman, D. (1974). Judgement under uncertainty: Heuristics and biases. *Science, 185,* 1124–1131.

Tyler, L. E. (1978). *Individuality: Human possibilities and personal choice in the psychosocial development of men and women.* San Francisco: Jossey-Bass.

Uleman, J. S. (1965). *A new TAT measure of the need for power.* Unpublished doctoral dissertation, Harvard University, Cambridge, MA.

Ullman, C. (1987). From sincerity to authenticity: Adolescents' views of the "true self." *Journal of Personality, 55,* 583–596.

Ulrich, R. E., & Azrin, N. H. (1962). Reflective fighting in response to aversive stimulation. *Journal of Experimental Analysis of Behavior, 5,* 511–520.

Ulrich, R. E., Dulaney, S., Kucera, T., & Colasacco, A. (1972). Side effects of aversive control. In R. M. Gilbert & J. D. Keehn (Eds.), *Schedule effects.* Toronto: University of Toronto Press.

Vacchiano, R. B. (1977). Dogmatism. In T. Blass (Ed.), *Personality variables in social behavior.* Hillsdale, NJ: Erlbaum.

Vacchiano, R. B., Strauss, P. S., & Schiffman, D. C. (1968). Personality correlates of dogmatism. *Journal of Consulting Psychology, 32,* 83–85.

van Ijzendoorn, M. H. (1995). Adult attachment representations, parental responsiveness, and infant attachment: A meta-analysis. *Psychological Bulletin, 117,* 387–403.

Veroff, J. S. (1958). A scoring manual for the power motive. In J. W. Atkinson (Ed.), *Motives in fantasy, action, and society.* Princeton, NJ: Van Nostrand.

Verplanck, W. S. (1954). Burrhus F. Skinner. In W. K. Estes et al. (Eds.), *Modern learning theory.* New York: Appleton-Century-Crofts.

Vidulich, R. N., & Kaiman, I. P. (1961). The effects of the information source status and dogmatism upon conformity behavior. *Journal of Abnormal and Social Psychology, 63,* 639–642.

Vitz, P. C. (1966). Affect as a function of stimulus variation. *Journal of Experimental Psychology, 68,* 176–183.

Volpe, J. (1969). *The practice of behavior therapy.* Elmsford, NY: Pergamon Press.

Vroom, V. H. (1959). Projection, negation, and self-concept. *Human Relations, 12,* 235–244.

Wallach, M. A., & Gahm, R. C. (1960). Personality functions of graphic construction and expansiveness. *Journal of Personality, 28,* 73–88.

Wankowski, J. A. (1973). *Temperament, motivation and academic achievement.* Birmingham, AL: University of Birmingham Educational Survey and Counseling Unit.

Warehime, R. G., & Foulds, M. L. (1973). Social desirability response sets and a measure of self-actualization. *Journal of Human Psychology, 13,* 89–95.

Warehime, R. G., Routh, D. K., & Foulds, M. L. (1974). Knowledge about self-actualization and the presentation of self as self-actualized. *Journal of Personality and Social Psychology, 30,* 155–162.

Warren, J. R. (1966). Birth order and social behavior. *Psychological Bulletin, 65,* 38–49.

Waskow, I. A., & Ginsberg, V. (1975). The form for rating degree of disturbance. In C. R. Rogers (Ed.), *The therapeutic relationship and its impact: A study of psychotherapy with schizophrenics.* Chicago: University of Chicago Press.

Waterman, C. K., Buebel, M. E., & Waterman, A. S. (1970). Relationship between resolution of the identity crisis and outcomes of previous psychosocial crises. *Proceedings of the 78th Annual Convention of the American Psychological Association, 5,* 467–468.

Waters, L. K. (1967). *Stability of Edwards PPS need scale scores and profiles over a seven-week period.* (USNAMI Report, 1019, 6 pp.)

Watson, J. B. (1924). *Behaviorism.* New York: Norton.

Watson, J. B. (1929). *Psychology from the standpoint of a behaviorist* (3rd ed.). Philadelphia: Lippincott.

Watts, A. W. (1957). *The way of Zen.* New York: Pantheon.

Weber, M. (1930). *The Protestant ethic and the spirit of capitalism* (T. Parsons, Trans.). New York: Scribner.

Weibe, D. J. (1991). Hardiness and stress moderation: A test of proposed mechanisms. *Journal of Personality and Social Psychology, 60,* 89–99.

Weibe, D. J., & McCallum, D. M. (1986). Health practice and hardiness as mediators in the stress-illness relationship. *Health Psychology, 5,* 425–438.

Weigel, R. G., & Frazier, J. E. (1968). The effects of "feeling" and "behavior" instructions on responses to the Edwards Personal Preference Schedule. *Journal of Educational Measurement, 5,* 337–338.

Weinberger, D. A., & Davidson, M. N. (1994). Repression, desirability impression management, and defensiveness. *Journal of Personality, 62,* 587–613.

Weinberger, D. A., Schwartz, G., & Davidson, R. (1979). Low-anxious, high-anxious and repressive coping styles: Psychometric patterns and behavioral and physiological responses to stress. *Journal of Abnormal Psychology, 88,* 369–380.

Welker, W. I. (1959). Escape, exploratory, and food seeking responses of rats in a novel situation. *Journal of Comparative and Physiological Psychology, 52,* 96–111.

Wells, W., & Goldstein, R. (1964). Sears' study of projection: Replications and critique. *Journal of Social Psychology, 64,* 169–179.

Welsh, G. S. (1956). Factor dimensions A and R. In

G. S. Welsh & W. G. Dahlstrom (Eds.), *Basic readings on the MMPI in psychology and medicine.* Minneapolis: University of Minnesota Press.

Wessman, A. E., & Ricks, D. F. (1966). *Mood and personality.* New York: Holt, Rinehart & Winston.

Westman, M. (1990). The relationship between stress and performance: The moderating effect of hardiness. *Human Performance, 3,* 141–155.

Wexler, D. (1974). Self actualization and cognitive processes. *Journal of Consulting and Clinical Psychology, 42,* 47–53.

Wherry, R. J., & Waters, L. K. (1968). Motivational constructs: A factor analysis of feelings. *Educational and Psychological Measurement, 28,* 1035–1046.

White, M. S. (1985). Ego development in adult women. *Journal of Personality, 53,* 561–574.

White, R. W. (1959). Motivation reconsidered: The concept of competence. *Psychological Review, 66,* 297–333.

White, R. W. (1960). Competence and the psychosexual stages of development. In M. R. Jones (Ed.), *Nebraska symposium on motivation.* Lincoln: University of Nebraska Press.

White, R. W. (1961). Competence and the psychosexual stages of development. In D. W. Fiske & S. R. Maddi (Eds.), *Functions of varied experience.* Homewood, IL: Dorsey Press.

White, R. W. (1963). Ego and reality in psychoanalytic theory. *Psychological Issues, 3,* 1–210.

Williams, R. L., Verble, J. S., Price, D. E., & Layne, B. H. (1995). Relationship of self-management to personality types and indices. *Journal of Personality Assessment, 64,* 494–506.

Willington, A. M., & Strickland, B. R. (1965). Need for approval and simple motor performance. *Perceptual and Motor Skills, 21,* 879–884.

Wilson, G. (1977). Introversion-extroversion. In T. Blass (Ed.), *Personality variables in social behavior.* Hillsdale, NJ: Erlbaum.

Wilson, G., & O'Leary, V. (1980). *Principles of behavior therapy.* Englewood Cliffs, NJ: Prentice-Hall.

Wink, P. (1992). Three types of narcissism in women from college to mid-life. *Journal of Personality, 60,* 7–30.

Winter, D. G. (1971). The need for power in college men. In D. C. McClelland, W. N. Davis, R. Kalin, & H. E. Wanner (Eds.), *Alcohol and human motivation.* New York: Free Press.

Winter, D. G. (1973). *The power motive.* New York: Free Press.

Witkin, H. A., Dyk, R. B., Faterson, H. F., Goodenough, D. R., & Karp, S. A. (1962). *Psychological differentiation.* New York: Wiley.

Witkin, H. A., Lewis, H. G., Hertzman, M., Machover, K., Meissner, P. B., & Wapner, S. (1954). *Personality through perception.* New York: Harper.

Woike, B. A. (1995). Most-memorable experiences: Evidence for a link between implicit and explicit motives and social cognitive processes in everyday life. *Journal of Personality and Social Psychology, 68,* 1081-1091.

Wolff, P. H. (1959). Observations on newborn infants. *Psychosomatic Medicine, 21,* 100–118.

Wolk, S., & DuCette, J. (1974). Intentional performance and incidental learning as a function of personality and task dimensions. *Journal of Personality and Social Psychology, 29,* 91–101.

Wolpe, J. (1958). *Psychotherapy by reciprocal inhibition.* Stanford, CA: Stanford University Press.

Wolpe, J. (1969). *The practice of behavior therapy.* New York: Pergamon Press.

Wolpe, J. (1978a). Cognition and causation in human behavior and its therapy. *American Psychologist, 33,* 437–446.

Wolpe, J. (1978b). Self-efficacy theory and psychotherapeutic change: A square peg in a round hole. In S. Rochman (Ed.), *Advances in behavior research and therapy* (Vol. 1). Oxford, England: Pergamon Press.

Wolters, B. J. (1976). The "Need for Variety" by Maddi et al. in connection with creativity. *Gedrag: Tijdschrift voor Psychologic, 4*(5–6), 307–324.

Worthen, R., & O'Connell, W. E. (1969). Social interest and humor. *International Journal of Social Psychiatry, 15,* 179–188.

Wright, B. P. (1940). *Selfishness, guilt feelings, and social distance.* Unpublished doctoral dissertation, State University of Iowa, Iowa City.

Wrightsman, L. S., Jr. (1960). Effects of waiting with others on changes in level of felt anxiety. *Journal of Abnormal and Social Psychology, 61,* 216–222.

Yalom, I. D. (1980). *Existential psychotherapy.* New York: Basic Books.

Yarrow, L. J. (1961). Maternal deprivation: Toward an empirical and conceptual reevaluation. *Psychological Bulletin, 58,* 459–490.

Yerkes, R. M., & Dodson, J. D. (1908). The relation of strength of stimulus to rapidity of habit formation. *Journal of Comparative and Neurological Psychology, 18,* 459–482.

Yufit, R. I. (1969). Variations of intimacy and isolation. *Journal of Projective Techniques and Personality Assessment, 33,* 49–58.

Zaccaria, J. S., & Weir, W. R. (1967). A comparison of alcoholics and selected samples of non-alcoholics in terms of a positive concept of mental health. *Journal of Social Psychology, 71,* 151–157.

Zagona, S. V., & Zurcher, L. A. (1964). Participation, interaction, and role behavior in groups selected from the extremes of the open-closed cognitive continuum. *Journal of Psychology, 58,* 225–264.

Zagona, S. V., & Zurcher, L. A. (1965). The relationship of verbal ability and other cognitive variables to the open-closed cognitive dimension. *Journal of Psychology, 60,* 213–219.

Zajonc, R. B. (1968). Attitudinal effects of mere exposure. *Journal of Personality and Social Psychology Monograph 9* (Suppl. 2).

Zeigarnik, B. (1927). Über das Behalten von erledigten und unreledigten Handlungen. *Psychologische Forschrift, 9,* 1–85.

Zeller, A. (1950). An experimental analogue of repression: II. The effect of individual failure and success on memory measured by relearning. *Journal of Experimental Psychology, 40,* 411–422.

Zeller, A. (1951). An experimental analogue of repression: III. The effect of induced failure and success on memory measured by relearning. *Journal of Experimental Psychology, 42,* 32–38.

Zucker, R. A., Manosevitz, M., & Langon, R. I. (1968). Birth order, anxiety, and affiliation during a crisis. *Journal of Personality and Social Psychology, 8,* 354–359.

Zuckerman, M., Kolin, E. A., Price, L., & Zoob, I. (1964). Development of a sensation-seeking scale. *Journal of Consulting Psychology, 28,* 477–482.

Zuckerman, M., Persky, H., Miller, L., & Levin, B. (1969). Contrasting effects of understimulation (sensory deprivation) and overstimulation (high stimulus variety). *Proceedings of the 77th Annual Convention of the American Psychological Association, 4,* 319–320.

Zuckerman, M., & Wheeler, L. (1975). To dispel fantasies about the fantasy-based measure of fear of success. *Psychological Bulletin, 82,* 932–946.

Zuroff, D. C. (1994). Depressive personality styles and the Five-Factor Model of personality. *Journal of Personality Assessment, 63,* 453–472.

INDEX